THE ENCYCLOPEDIA OF HEALTH AND THE HUMAN BODY

THE ENCYCLOPEDIA OF HEALTH AND THE HUMAN BODY

Edited by Gerald Newman

FRANKLIN WATTS   NEW YORK | LONDON | 1977

Library of Congress Cataloging in Publication Data

Main entry under title:

The Encyclopedia of health and the human body.

Includes index.
SUMMARY: Alphabetical entries give information on diseases, treatments, bodily parts and systems, anatomical structure, and physicians and scientists who have made contributions in these areas.
1. Medicine—Dictionaries, Juvenile. 2. Health—Dictionaries Juvenile. 3. Body, Human—Dictionaries, Juvenile. [1. Medicine—Dictionaries. 2. Health—Dictionaries. 3. Body, Human—Dictionaries] I. Newman, Gerald.
R125.E57   610'.3   77-71179
ISBN 0-531-01331-6

Library of Congress Catalog Card Number: 77-71179

Copyright © 1975, 1974, 1973, 1972, 1971, 1970, 1969, 1968, 1967, 1966, 1965, 1964, 1963 by Grolier Incorporated

Copyright © in Canada 1975, 1974 1973, 1972, 1971, 1970, 1969, 1968 by Grolier Limited

Copyright © 1967, 1966, 1965, 1964, 1963 by Grolier of Canada Limited

Copyright © Philippines 1975, 1974, 1973, 1972 by Grolier Incorporated

6   5   4   3   2   1

INTRODUCTION

The Encyclopedia of Health and the Human Body is not a medical text, but a reference book. For ease of research, it lists entries alphabetically and offers a clear, easy-to-understand explanation of diseases, treatments, bodily parts and systems, anatomical structure, and physicians and scientists who have made contributions in these areas.

In addition, the *Encyclopedia* offers information that may not directly deal with health and the human body, but is closely related to these areas.

Entries such as **Cell, Genetics,** and **Evolution** discuss other living organisms (plant and animal) as they relate to humans. Other entries cover information about the environment and the human's place in it.

Areas such as nutrition discuss human diet and its effect on health and vitality. Topics including psychiatry, mental illness, and intelligence are also incorporated to add insight into mental as well as physical well-being.

Biographical entries offer data on scientists such as Gregor Mendel, Charles Darwin and Anton van Leuwenhoek, whose work, while not specifically about humans, has had a profound impact on life itself and, as such, plays an important role in the understanding of human existence.

Some topics are discussed briefly, offering the reader concise information. Others are covered in detail for a broader understanding. Often, an entry is accompanied by detailed diagrams, illustrations and/or charts so the topic to be studied is more easily understood.

For those interested in further information, most entries are followed by "See also" listings for easy cross-referencing.

A

ABERRATION [ăb-ə-rā'shən], **OPTICAL,** failure of a lens or mirror to form an exact image of an object. It is a result of the natural laws of optics. Not all light rays entering a lens or mirror parallel to the principal axis focus at the same

The lens fails to form an exact image of an object because the light rays from the top and bottom focus at A while those from the selected intermediate points on the lens focus at B.

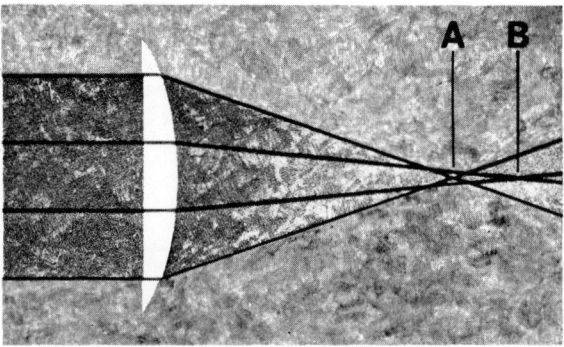

point; this phenomenon is spherical aberration. Coma and astigmatism are aberrations produced by rays entering at an angle to the principal axis. Curvature of field is the tendency of a flat object to be imaged as a curved surface. Distortion is a nonuniformity in the scale of the image, some portions being magnified or reduced more than others. Chromatic aberration is the failure of the various wave lengths of light to come to the same focus.

ABORTION, termination of pregnancy, regardless of cause, before the fetus is capable of living outside the mother's womb, or uterus. Two categories are spontaneous abortion and induced abortion. Most spontaneous abortions occur before the fourth month.

Spontaneous abortion, or miscarriage, is an early interruption of pregnancy through natural causes. It occurs in about one of every ten pregnancies. The majority of miscarriages are caused by faulty development of the conceptus due either to imperfections in the egg, the sperm cell, or the mechanism of implanting in the lining of the uterus. Other factors causing spontaneous abortions include abnormalities of the uterus, severe infections of the mother, such as pneumonia, and glandular disorders which include poor thyroid or ovarian function. It is extremely rare for emotional tension or external physical injury to cause spontaneous abortion.

The first sign of spontaneous abortion is vaginal bleeding, occasionally associated with abdominal cramps. Various types are: complete, incomplete, threatened and missed.

In a complete abortion, the entire product of conception is expelled by the uterus and bleeding may stop spontaneously. Occasionally, a woman may not realize she is pregnant, and an abortion is frequently mistaken for a late menstrual period. An incomplete abortion occurs when the fetus is passed, but a fragment of the tissue (placenta) that supplies nourishment to the fetus remains attached to the uterus, causing prolonged bleeding. The retained tissue is removed by an operation which requires dilatation of the opening or cervix of the womb and scraping or curetting its inner surface, an operation often referred to as a "D & C," meaning dilatation and curettage. A threatened abortion is also preceded by vaginal bleeding, but the fetus is not yet dead. Chances of fetal survival are poor, but may be increased with bed rest and hormone therapy. In a missed abortion the fetus dies but remains within the uterus.

Induced abortions occur following a deliberate attempt to terminate a pregnancy. Such abortions may be either legal or illegal. A legal abortion is performed by a physician for conditions approved by the laws of the state. A criminal or illegal abortion is performed for indications not recognized by law. The death, illness, and sterility caused by illegal abortions are difficult to estimate.

In the United States each of the 50 states has its own law regulating the grounds for legal abortion. Until the late 1960's all the laws were quite similar, permitting abortion only "to preserve the life of the mother." However, beginning in 1967, several states liberalized their previously very restrictive abortion laws and on Jan. 22, 1973, the U.S. Supreme Court ruled that no state may prevent a woman from having an abortion within the first six months of pregnancy. However, the Court further ruled that, in reference to abortions performed after the third month, individual states can introduce licensing requirements to maintain medical standards and that the state may refuse to permit abortions within the last ten weeks of pregnancy except where necessary to preserve the life or health of the mother. At the time of the ruling, the abortion laws of 46 states were overturned while only four states—New York, Hawaii, Alaska, and Washington—had statutes sufficiently liberal to meet the Court's criteria.

ABSCESS, an accumulation of pus in the tissues. An abscess represents the battleground on which the body defends itself against invasion by foreign elements, such as bacteria and irritating chemicals. When these substances enter the tissues, the blood vessels in the area expand, bringing large white blood cells to the site; these cells are

able to engulf foreign particles. The bacteria lie at the center of the abscess, surrounded by the defending white blood cells. The outcome of the battle is pus, consisting of dead white blood cells with their engulfed bacteria, dead tissues from the site of the abscess, and bacterial poisons. If the white blood cells succeed in destroying the invaders, the pus is absorbed and the abscess vanishes. If they fail, the bacteria escape into the surrounding tissue to produce new abscesses or into the blood stream to set up infections in distant organs.
See also BOILS.

ACCLIMATIZATION, process by which an organism adjusts to living in an environment normally unsuited to it. The term originally referred to adjustment to new climatic conditions, especially temperature. Temperature plays an important role in all plant and animal nutritive functions, as well as in reproductive habits. An organism migrating from its normal environment to one of different temperature must modify various functions and activities if it is to survive. Most species can become acclimatized to temperatures slightly above or below those to which they are accustomed. In some groups, including tropical orchids and many reptiles, adjustment to low temperatures is impossible. Heat and cold acclimatization by different races of man is an important factor in their distribution in arctic and tropical regions.

The present-day concept of acclimatization has been broadened to include adjustment to other factors also, such as altered pressure resulting from changes in altitude or depth of water, changes in the chemical environment, availability of food, and the presence or absence of enemies, particularly parasites and microorganisms. In man, as well as among many animals, acclimatization to life on high plateaus and mountains is possible through physiological adjustments that offset the decreased pressure and lower oxygen content of the atmosphere. On the other hand, the demands of a new environment may be too great for individuals to meet. The different composition of fresh and salt water generally prevents migration of fish from one to the other (eels and salmon are outstanding exceptions), and the chemical composition of soil limits many plants to certain areas. Acclimatization, which involves relatively rapid individual adjustments, should not be confused with adaptation nor with other biological changes that extend over long periods of time and occur through the interaction of natural or artificial selection and the genetic make-up of organisms.
See also ADAPTATION; EVOLUTION.

ACETYLCHOLINE [ăs-ə-tĭl-kō′lēn], compound found in nervous tissue. One theory of nervous activity associates the electric events occurring during the transmission of the nervous impulse with the secretion of acetylcholine by the nerve. According to this theory, the action of acetylcholine permits electrically charged atoms (ions) to flow through the membrane that covers the nerve fiber; this flow of ions constitutes the nervous impulse.

The clearest evidence of the action of acetylcholine has been found in three locations outside of the brain and spinal cord. In each of these places acetylcholine is secreted into a gap—either between one nerve and another (the synapse) or between nerve and muscle.

Ganglions. These are special relay points in the nervous system where one group of nerve fibers ends and another begins. Acetylcholine is secreted by the incoming fiber into the synapse and stimulates the outgoing cell to discharge.

Muscle-nerve junctions (myoneural junctions). These are the points where nerve ends in muscle. Acetylcholine secreted by the nerve causes the muscle to contract. Numerous poisons and drugs exert their action at this point. Curare, the poison used by South American Indians to tip their arrows, causes paralysis by opposing the action of acetylcholine at the myoneural junction.

Cholinergic fibers. Certain nerve pathways secrete acetylcholine at the point where they end upon the muscle in the walls of small arteries. These cholinergic, or parasympathetic fibers, are not under conscious control. When stimulated they lower the blood pressure, slow the heartbeat, and increase the flow of blood to the digestive organs. In contrast, an opposing set of pathways, the sympathetic, or adrenergic, liberate adrenalin at their endings and prepare the body for intense exertion by speeding the heartbeat, raising the blood pressure, and increasing the flow of blood to the muscles.
See also NERVOUS SYSTEM.

ACHILLES' TENDON. See TENDON.

ACHLORHYDRIA [ăk-lôr-hī′drē-ə], absence of hydrochloric acid in the stomach. In some persons achlorhydria may be congenital and persist throughout life; however, it does not interfere with digestion. The condition is always found in pernicious anemia and is frequently associated with sprue and tumors of the stomach. Achlorhydria often appears in older persons who are apparently normal in every other respect. When it occurs by itself, there may be no symptoms; however, in conjunction with other disorders, vomiting, lack of appetite, diarrhea, and constipation often occur. Hydrochloric acid is given to remedy the deficiency, together with appropriate therapy for the associated disorder.
See also DIGESTION.

ACHROMYCIN [ăk-rō-mī′sĭn], also called tetracycline, antibiotic drug produced by chemically modifying the antibiotic aureomycin (chlortetracycline). This modification reduces the nausea, vomiting, and diarrhea that are associated with the use of the latter drug. Achromycin is used to treat a large variety of bacterial diseases and is frequently effective against organisms that are resistant to other antibiotics, such as penicillin.
See also ANTIBIOTICS.

ACIDOSIS [ăs-ĭ-dō′sĭs], condition characterized by a decrease in the ability of the blood to neutralize acidic substances. This may develop as a result of increased production of acids by the body (as occurs in starvation and diabetes) or excessive loss of alkaline substances from the body (as occurs in severe diarrhea and kidney diseases). In mild acidosis no symptoms are present. As the condition becomes more severe, weakness, rapid breathing, abdominal pain, nausea, dehydration, vomiting, stupor, and coma develop. Acidosis is treated by administering fluids to relieve the dehydration and alkalis to restore the proper alkali-acid balance in the blood. The underlying disorder must also be treated.

See also BLOOD; KETOSIS; KIDNEY.

ACNE [ăk′nē] (Acne Vulgaris), common skin condition characterized by blackheads, infection, and excessive oiliness of the skin. Overactivity of the sebaceous, or oil-secreting, glands of the skin predisposes toward acne. This tendency may be inherited or may arise from the hormonal changes which occur in adolescence. The condition may be aggravated by overconsumption of fats and carbohydrates, poor personal hygiene, and indiscriminate use of cosmetics.

Acne begins with oversecretion of the sebaceous glands. The opening through which the secretion (sebum) flows onto the surface of the skin becomes filled with a mixture of sebum, dust, and dirt. The result is a blackhead. If the opening becomes completely blocked, the sebum backs up in the gland and forms a fluid-filled pocket, or cyst. If the cyst becomes infected, pus collects in the gland duct, and inflammation may extend under the skin, creating a large, firm, red nodule. Blackheads and infected ducts appear chiefly on the face and occasionally on the shoulders, back, and chest. Mild cases of acne disappear without leaving any traces, but the severe cases leave pitted scars on the skin.

Medicated lotions and ointments are applied to soften the oily plugs, enlarge the gland openings, and control superficial infection and excessive oiliness. Antibiotics and sulfonamides are used to control deep infections. A person suffering from acne is advised to wash his skin frequently with bland soap, take regular shampoos, and eliminate excess fatty foods, sweets, and iodine (in salt) from his diet.

ACROMEGALY [ăk-rō-mĕg′ə-lē], rare disease of adult life in which an enlargement of many portions of the body, including bones, liver, and heart occurs. Particularly noticeable are enlarged hands, feet, head, and nose, and a protruding lower jaw. The cause is usually a tumor of the pituitary gland, which results in excess production of growth hormone. As the tumor increases in size, headache, weakness, and loss of vision may occur. Complications may include diabetes, overactivity of the thyroid gland, and abnormal functioning of the sex glands. The progress of the disease may be halted by X-ray treatment or surgical removal of the tumor.

See also GIGANTISM; PITUITARY GLAND.

ACTH, in full, adrenocorticotrophic hormone, hormone secreted by the pituitary gland. It stimulates the cortex, or outer layer of the adrenal gland, to secrete the adrenal hormones. The adrenal hormones, which include hydrocortisone and related compounds, are important in regulating the volume and mineral composition of the body

REGULATION OF ACTH SECRETION

The secretion of ACTH by the pituitary gland is controlled by the brain and by adrenal hormones in the blood. (1) Emotional excitement, or other forms of stress stimulate the pituitary through the brain. (2) ACTH from the pituitary stimulates release of cortisone and other adrenal hormones by the outer layer, or cortex, of the adrenal gland. (3) Increased concentration of adrenal hormones in the blood inhibits further pituitary secretion of ACTH.

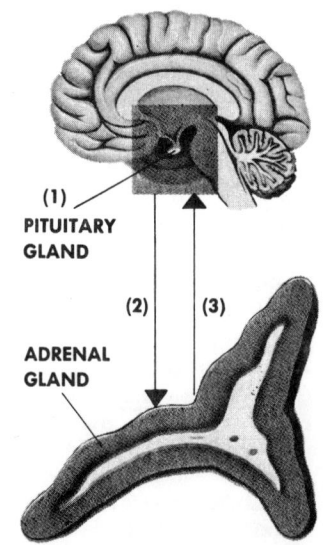

fluids and in the consumption of sugar and starches by the tissues. These hormones are particularly important in enabling the body to respond to stress. The body controls the secretion of adrenal hormones through the action of ACTH. The pituitary gland responds to a lowered blood level of adrenal hormones by secreting ACTH, which in turn stimulates the adrenal cortex to secrete more hormone.

Since the effect of ACTH is to increase the quantity of adrenal hormones in the blood, either ACTH or an adrenal hormone (such as cortisone) may be given in most conditions where an increased supply of adrenal hormones is necessary. ACTH, however does not relieve the symptoms of Addison's disease, a condition in which the adrenal cortex is diseased and is not capable of producing hormones in response to stimulation by ACTH. This provides a useful diagnostic test for Addison's disease: if the patient is given ACTH and there is a subsequent failure to detect the presence of increased adrenal hormone, disease of the adrenal cortex is indicated.

ACTH and cortisone have been used with varying degrees of success in rheumatoid arthritis, pituitary deficiency, allergies, skin diseases, gout and in numerous other conditions. The drugs must be used with caution, since undesirable side effects such as high blood pressure, nervous breakdown, diabetes, acne, and ulcers may develop.

See also ADDISON'S DISEASE; ADRENAL GLAND; PITUITARY GLAND.

ACTINOMYCETES [ăk-tĭ-nō-mī-sē′tēz], moldlike bacteria belonging to the order Actinomycetales and sometimes called ray fungi. The body, or mycelium, is composed of fine, branching filaments. Some actinomycetes reproduce by fragmentation; others reproduce like certain fungi, by means of external spores. Actinomycetes are important oxidizers of organic matter in soil, and the characteristic odor of rich soil is largely due to their musty smell. Several,

ACTINOMYCIN

especially of the genus *Streptomyces*, excrete antibiotic substances toxic to other bacteria. Important antibiotics such as streptomycin and the tetracyclines are produced commercially from cultures of selected species. Lumpy jaw, a disease of cattle that sometimes affects man, is caused by an actinomycete.

See also MICROBIOLOGY.

ACTINOMYCIN [ăk-tĭ-nō-mī′sĭn], antibiotic obtained from soil fungus. It kills various microbes or prevents their growth, but it is extremely toxic to humans. A variety of actinomycin has been reported to be beneficial in the treatment of certain types of cancer.

See also ANTIBIOTICS.

ACTINOMYCOSIS [ăk-tĭ-nō-mī-kō′sĭs], is a chronic, noncontagious disease caused by *Actinomycosis israeli*, a fungus closely related to true bacteria. *Actinomycosis bovis* causes a disease in cattle called lumpy jaw. In man, the disease is characterized by abscess formation and draining wounds. *A. israeli* is an anaerobic organism normally found in the mouth, but which cannot grow in healthy tissue. The disease occurs only when tissue has already been devitalized. The first phase of the disease is a painful, hard swelling of the jaw following a fracture or dental work. Today this form is rare because of improved dental care and antibiotics. Other forms of the disease are abscess formation in the lower lungs, liver, or, rarely, in the appendix. When sulfur granules are found in a draining wound, disease caused by *A. israeli* is considered likely. Surgical drainage and penicillin are used to treat such an infection. Since the advent of antibiotics, the number of actinomycotic infections has been greatly reduced.

ACUPUNCTURE, a method of medical treatment in which fine needles are inserted into the body at specified points and rotated. The practice was developed in China about 5,000 years ago and was refined into an intricate art. Its use was banned by the government of Chiang Kai-shek in the 1930's and 1940's in an effort to Westernize and modernize Chinese life. During China's Cultural Revolution of the 1960's, acupuncture was revived by Chairman Mao Tse-tung in an effort to provide more medical care. Though its use had quietly spread to Japan and Western Europe, acupuncture came into new prominence in the United States and elsewhere in the 1970's.

Treatment. A doctor trained in traditional Chinese medicine makes a diagnosis by feeling the patient's pulses (six on either wrist, each corresponding to a vital organ) and the warmth of the skin. Since, according to Taoist philosophy, illness is caused by an imbalance of two vital forces, *yin* and *yang*, the aim is to bring these back into equilibrium in whatever organ is causing the complaint. The acupuncturist decides on his method of treatment after taking into account the season, the time of day, the weather, and the patient's emotional state. He chooses one or more of the 365 main acupuncture points (some authorities count as many as 800) along 12 meridians through which flows *ch'i*, or the life force. The meridians do not parallel the nervous or circulatory systems as identified by Western medicine, and their existence has not been verified by Western scientists.

Very fine needles, usually of steel but occasionally of silver or gold, are inserted into the chosen points with the cooperation, frequently, of the patient, who will tell the doctor when he feels the expected sensation that indicates that the right depth has been reached. The doctor will then rotate the needles, or he may connect them to a small electrical apparatus that sends a current through them. The effect of the treatment will depend on the distance along the meridian from the affected organ, the angle of insertion of the needle, and the direction of rotation. The acupuncturist may also place a tiny pile of wormwood leaves on the skin or on the outer end of the needle and set it afire. This is known as moxibustion and is believed to have added therapeutic value.

Uses. Acupuncture is used in China to provide anesthesia for a variety of dental and surgical procedures, to treat chronic diseases of all kinds, and even for such conditions as sterility, paralysis, and deafness. It is basically used for the treatment of functional disorders in which there has been no destruction or degeneration of tissue. It is not ordinarily used for infectious diseases or trauma—wounds or injuries due to accidents.

Outside of China, it is used chiefly to relieve chronic pain and stiffness, though some operations have been performed under acupuncture anesthesia. Most Western practitioners do not pay much attention to the *yin/yang* theory and do not learn all the classic points; there is evidence that it is not necessary that the needles be inserted precisely on the points.

Theories. There is considerable disagreement as to how acupuncture works, and many investigators attribute its effects to hypnosis. However, physicians with experience in both hypnosis and acupuncture feel that, though there are undoubtedly elements of hypnosis in acupuncture, especially as it is used by some practitioners, this cannot be the sole explanation.

A number of neurophysiological theories have been proposed to explain the transmission and perception of pain, and in time no doubt one of these will also account for the success of acupuncture in curing or preventing pain. This will not, however, account for the variety of cures with which acupuncture is credited. Studies of the value of acupuncture in curing disease have as yet yielded little objective data.

ADAM'S APPLE, enlargement in the front of the neck produced by the bulging cartilage walls of the larynx, or voice box. Found in both sexes, it is more prominent in men.

ADDISON'S DISEASE, disease characterized by adrenal insufficiency resulting from underactivity of the outer layer, or cortex, of the adrenal gland. It was first described by the English physician Thomas Addison in 1855.

Addison's disease may be caused by tuberculosis of the adrenal gland or result from an unexplained wasting away of the gland. Typical symptoms include the following: weakness and fatigue; diffuse tanning of the skin, with the formation of dark patches on the knees, elbows, knuckles, and the inside of the mouth; multiple black freckles over the body; white patches on the skin; low blood pressure;

loss of appetite and weight; nausea, vomiting, diarrhea, and abdominal pain; and emotional instability. The symptoms result from the inadequate production of certain adrenal hormones (such as hydrocortisone) which are needed for the proper utilization of food and for the regulation of the composition of the body fluids. Salt is lost and the blood sugar tends to be low. Individuals with Addison's disease lack the capacity to adapt to conditions of stress; therefore infections, injury, or surgery may produce an "adrenal crisis," a state characterized by fever, nausea, vomiting, lowered blood pressure, and possibly shock. Treatment of Addison's disease consists of the administration of adrenal hormones, such as cortisone and related drugs.

See also ADRENAL GLAND.

ADENOIDS, an accumulation of specialized tissue, called lymphoid tissue, located at the back of the nasal passages. The adenoids, together with the tonsils, present a barrier to infections entering the body through the nose and mouth. Enlargement of this tissue occurs normally in childhood, possibly aiding the body in acquiring immunity to infections.

Chronic infections cause the adenoids to become abnormally large. This growth may block the nasal airway and cause mouth-breathing in children. Enlarged adenoids also cause chronic ear infections by blocking the Eustachian

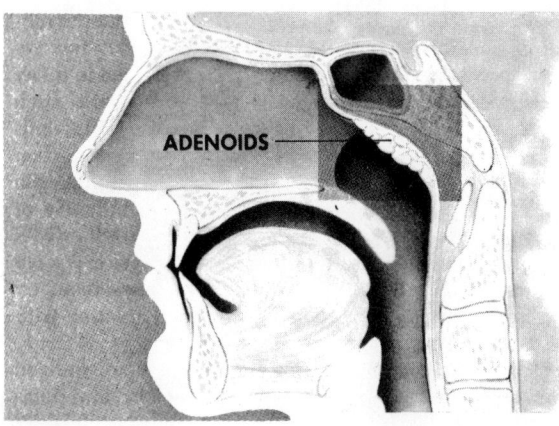

tubes, which lead from the ear to the nose. Removal of the adenoids, or adenoidectomy, cures the child, but complete removal is not possible and regrowth is frequent.

ADENOSINE TRIPHOSPHATE. See ATP.

ADHESIONS, thin bands of scar tissue formed within the body in response to inflammation or injury. These usually appear following abdominal surgery or peritonitis (an inflammation of the inner lining of the abdomen). They may also occur around the heart and lungs. Adhesions do not produce any discomfort. However, if the intestines become twisted around them or are pinched between an adhesion and another organ, the flow of food through the intestinal tract may be obstructed. When bodily functions are impaired by adhesions, surgery is necessary to cut the adhesive bands; however, it is always possible that they may grow back.

ADOLESCENCE is the period of life from the beginning of puberty to the attainment of adulthood. Popularly, this is often spoken of as the teen-age period, but strictly adolescence includes a greater length of time than is contained in the teen years. Although there are many individual differences, for girls adolescence begins at about age 12 and ends at about age 21; for boys the age range is from about 13 to about 22. Puberty is that period of life during which the reproductive organs and secondary sex characteristics mature. In the female, it is usually considered that puberty begins with the first menstrual period, but this is not a very dependable criterion. For the male, it is more difficult to fix a specific time as indicating the beginning of puberty, but such conditions as the need for occasional shaving, the deepening of the voice, and the rapid growth of the external sex organs may be noted. Adulthood is achieved when the individual is not only physically mature but has sufficient practical wisdom, emotional stability, and social adjustment so that he can take his place in adult society.

Physical Growth and Development

Some time between the last half of the eighth year and the middle of the eleventh year, girls begin growing rather rapidly and continue to do so for about two years. A similar growth period begins for boys somewhere between the tenth and the middle of the fourteenth year. From age 11 to 13 or 14 girls are usually taller than boys of their age. Following this period, males, on the average, again become taller than females. Between the ages of 10 and 15 years, girls, on the average, are heavier than boys, a fact to be understood in terms of their earlier sexual maturity. After the age of 15 boys are generally heavier than girls. During these years there are many bodily changes directly related to sex maturation.

The figures given are averages for large groups of adolescents, but there are marked individual differences. Many times such statistics cause unwarranted concern to the adolescent who feels that he or she is not "normal" because his or her pattern of development does not fit in with the averages. Actually, students of growth and development tend to minimize chronological age in presenting statistics on growth and to substitute emphasis on the fact that some individuals mature earlier than others. Children who mature relatively early go through a much more intense period of growth than do children who mature late in the adolescent period. Rather suddenly they become maturely developed. Then, oftentimes, the period of rapid growth comes to an end quite abruptly.

Children maturing relatively late in the adolescent period grow less rapidly but more evenly and continue growing over a longer period of time than do children who mature early. Late-maturing girls tend to grow up along with most boys of their own age rather than earlier. Eventually, late-maturing individuals are often larger than those of their age group who mature earlier.

Acne, a chronic skin eruption, is a normal phenomenon found to a greater or lesser extent in many adolescents. It is to be understood largely in terms of activity of the sebaceous glands (glands in the skin which secrete oil) and may

ADRENAL GLANDS

be affected by endocrine gland imbalance. However, indiscreet eating, especially of sweet and fatty foods, tends to accentuate the condition, as does lack of attention to cleanliness. Although normal, acne is often a source of great embarrassment to the adolescent. If thorough washing and wholesome diet do not materially reduce the condition, a physician may be asked to provide help. At any rate, the acne usually clears up by age 19 or 20.

Adolescents are often unnecessarily concerned and embarrassed by the normal changes that are taking place in their bodies. Adults can do much to prevent their worries by telling them in advance what to expect in the way of bodily development as they pass from childhood.

Physical and Mental Health

Before puberty the child is often physically below par but in adolescence he enters what can be a period of good health and vitality. However, he may go rather quickly from enthusiasm and vigor to tiredness and quiescence. A number of factors may impair the good health that is possible in adolescence.

Adolescents are often careless about their health, neglect sleep, and, in general, "burn the candle at both ends." Fads or self-imposed diets may result in malnutrition. The adolescent often dislikes to admit that he does not feel well, fails to report minor ailments to his parents, and thus does not get needed medical care.

Eye defects become fairly common during adolescence, in large measure because education involves so much reading. Defective eyesight is often accompanied by headaches and even digestive disturbances. The boy or girl may neglect school work without realizing that the basic problem is the need to relieve eye strain.

Broken romances, friction at home, unpopularity, and failing or poor school work often cause emotional upsets whose seriousness is not realized by adults. Problems in mental health need the same respect and attention as any other health problems.

In U.S. culture, the adolescent is faced with a long and often severe period of social adjustment. It is little wonder that some adolescents find it easier to withdraw from social situations than to face them. Such withdrawal is especially likely to occur if the young person is not in the best physical health or if he has been overprotected in childhood so that he does not know how to face life's problems. In fact, a major form of mental illness, schizophrenia, tends, in some cases, to develop in the late teens or early twenties. The adolescent who constantly refuses to face the problems of life and tends to withdraw from social contacts should be placed under the care of a physician. The services of a psychiatrist may be needed.

Intellectual Development

Adolescence is a period of intellectual as well as physical development. The child who has been somewhat indifferent to intellectual pursuits may show a distinct improvement as he gains experience and knowledge in many areas and as he realizes that he is preparing to enter the adult social and vocational world.

It is somewhat difficult to define intellectual ability but, in general, it involves the ability to learn, to profit from experience and deal with new situations quickly and successfully, to handle effectively those problems of life requiring abstract thinking. During the 20th century, psychologists have striven to develop tests that will measure intellectual ability. Popularly, but inaccurately, such tests are often spoken of as "I.Q. tests." Although the tests do not give perfect measures of intellectual ability, they are very helpful for practical purposes.

Tests of intellectual ability indicate that individuals ordinarily achieve their maximum scores during the late teen years or early twenties. That is, learning ability is potentially as great as it will be during the adult years of life, and adolescence can be a period of high achievement in education. Fortunately, high schools and colleges are developing special programs designed to challenge adolescent capacities, especially the capacities of individuals of superior intellectual ability.

A question often heard is: "Are girls smarter than boys?" The consensus of psychologists is that there are no true sex differences in general intellectual ability, although analyses of test scores often show that girls tend to excel in verbal items and boys tend to excel in mathematics and science. When adolescents and young adults are given equal opportunities, and when there is sufficient motivation, there seem to be no significant sex differences in either test scores or the ability to achieve success in life.

ADRENAL [ə-drē'nəl] **GLANDS,** paired, thumbnail-sized endocrine organs located above the kidneys. They are divided into a central portion (medulla) and an outer portion (cortex), each of which produces different hormones.

The medulla produces the hormones epinephrine and norepinephrine (adrenalin and noradrenalin). Epinephrine stimulates the production of sugar in the liver and its release into the blood stream; it also increases the production of body heat and expands the blood vessels in the muscles. Norepinephrine constricts blood vessels, with a consequent elevation of blood pressure. Nervous stimulation of the medulla causes the release of its hormones.

The adrenal cortex produces three kinds of hormones: mineralocorticoids, glucocorticoids, and androgens. The

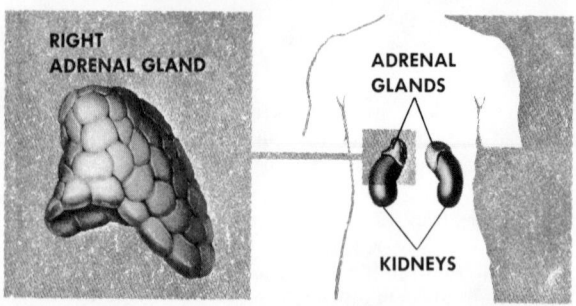

most important mineralocorticoid is aldosterone, which regulates the retention and excretion of body fluids. The glucocorticoids (such as hydrocortisone) promote the conversion of protein to sugar in the liver, stimulate protein breakdown in other tissues, and increase the levels of fat in the blood. The adrenal androgens have the same action

CONTROL OF THE SECRETION OF ADRENAL HORMONES

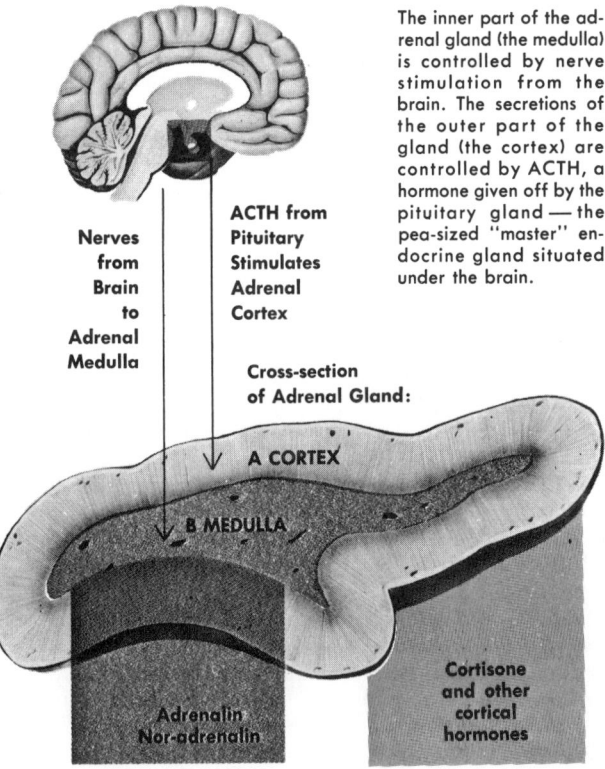

The inner part of the adrenal gland (the medulla) is controlled by nerve stimulation from the brain. The secretions of the outer part of the gland (the cortex) are controlled by ACTH, a hormone given off by the pituitary gland — the pea-sized "master" endocrine gland situated under the brain.

The hormones of the adrenal medulla help the body to respond to stress by stimulating the heart, increasing the blood flow to the muscles, raising the blood pressure, and increasing the concentration of energy-rich sugar in the blood.

The hormones of the adrenal cortex perform several vital functions: they regulate the mineral composition of the body fluids through their action on the kidneys and promote the conversion of proteins (from foods such as meat, eggs, milk) into sugar in the liver.

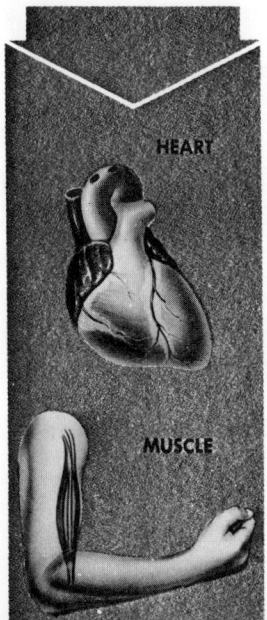

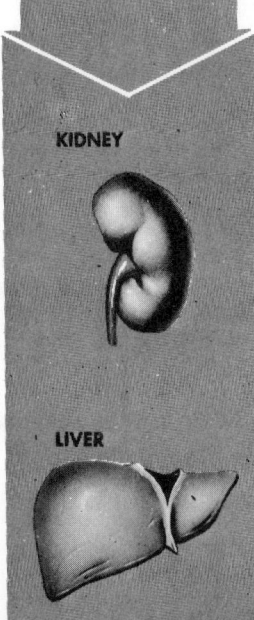

as the male sex hormone, testosterone, but ordinarily they are produced in small quantities and their effects are not great. In certain adrenal diseases, the androgens are overproduced and can cause masculinization in the female and premature sexual development in the immature male. Hormone production of the adrenal cortex is stimulated by the adrenocorticotrophic hormone (ACTH), produced by the anterior pituitary gland. However, aldosterone is not controlled by ACTH, but responds to changes in the mineral and water content of the blood.

Several diseases have been attributed to the over- or underproduction of adrenal hormones. Cushing's disease results from overproduction of certain adrenal hormones which produce masculinization, peculiar distribution of body fat, and signs of diabetes. Addison's disease is caused by a partial or complete loss of function of the adrenal cortex. Symptoms include muscular weakness, low resistance to infection, and a characteristic brownish pigmentation of the skin. This condition is readily corrected by administration of adrenal hormones.

See also ACTH; Cortisone; Cushing's Syndrome and Cushing's Disease; Testosterone.

ADRENALIN. See Epinephrine.

AGAMMAGLOBULINEMIA [ā-găm-ə-glŏb-ū-lĭn-ē'mē-ə], rare, inherited inability to produce gamma globulin, a part of the fluid portion of the blood that contains special substances (antibodies) needed by the body to fight bacterial and viral diseases. The condition is present at birth but does not become evident until about the third month of life, when the child succumbs to various infectious diseases. The condition is treated by giving monthly injections of gamma globulin prepared from the blood of healthy persons.

See also Gamma Globulin; Immunity.

AGRANULOCYTOSIS [ā-grăn-ū-lō-sī-tō'sĭs], disease in which there is a severe reduction in the number of certain white blood cells. The condition is usually caused by a sensitivity to drugs, such as aminopyrine and sulfonamides. The body's reaction to the drug may destroy granulocytes, a type of white blood cell vital for the defense of the body against bacterial infection. Heavy loss of granulocytes in the blood stream often leads to infection. The patient suffers from fever, chills, and sore throat, and has difficulty in swallowing. Ulcers may appear in the digestive tract, mouth, vagina, and skin. Agranulocytosis is treated by administering anti-infective drugs to stem the infection while the body replenishes its supply of granulocytes.

AIR POLLUTION, extraneous gases and small, suspended particles in the earth's atmosphere. These materials are mostly waste products given off by such sources as factory chimneys, automobile exhausts, and home furnaces. Some pollution is caused by natural phenomena, such as dust storms, forest fires, and volcanic eruptions. Atmospheric pollutants may range from innocuous odors to radioactive materials and highly reactive chemicals. Air pollution be-

AIR POLLUTION

comes a problem when these foreign materials reach a concentration great enough to cause adverse effects, ranging from reduced visibility to fatal illnesses. A common form of air pollution is the smog often seen in cities. Smog is a mixture of smoke and fog; it often contains noxious gases or other foreign materials in suspension.

Dilution by the Atmosphere. Air pollutants, whether the result of natural forces or of human activities, are diluted by the atmosphere. The amount of dilution depends upon the area of the pollution source, the volume of polluting material, the wind speed, and the amount of atmospheric turbulence.

Contaminants from a small source, such as a single chimney, are diluted rapidly if the volume of contaminating material is not too great. If the volume is increased, however, the effect of dilution is lessened. The dilution of contaminating material from large sources is proportionately slower at all stages. The smoke cloud from a group of factory chimneys, for example, may remain quite dense as long as the factories are in operation.

Moderate to strong winds have a ventilating effect that helps to reduce air pollution. Atmospheric turbulence, or the irregular movement of air, has a similar effect. The amount of turbulence is controlled both by wind velocity and by the temperature layers of the atmosphere. Normally, the temperature of air decreases with altitude and there is a certain amount of ventilation by upward movement as the underlying warm air rises and cools. Occasionally, however, atmospheric conditions cause a layer of air to become warmer with altitude. Within this layer, called a temperature inversion, there is almost no vertical movement. If the inversion occurs at a relatively low level, the underlying layer of cooler air forms a trap where polluting materials may become concentrated.

Influence of Topography. The concentration of pollutants may reach serious proportions when a temperature inversion intersects hills and mountains around a city. The surrounding topography forms a basin that restricts lateral movement of air, and the basin is effectively capped by the inversion layer. This situation is seen often in the area around Los Angeles, Calif., where the frequent occurrence of smog is a well-known problem.

Pollution Damage. The continuing growth of cities, the increase in motor vehicle use, and the greater industrial activity have combined to produce serious air pollution in many areas. The effects on human health and plant and animal life and the deterioration of property are difficult to assess. Reduced visibility, the soiling of buildings and of furniture in homes, and the discomfort of eye irritation and disagreeable odors are all easily recognized and associated with air pollution. The more subtle effects on health, however, are not so easily recognized. In order to determine what these effects may be and to learn more about the relationship between air pollution and the spread of diseases such as lung cancer, intensive studies are being undertaken by several organizations. Chief among these in the United States are the National Institute of Health, the U.S. Public Health Service, and various state health agencies.

There can be little doubt that the cost of air pollution is high and that it is increasing as urban areas expand. Because of the wide variety of pollution effects and the many possible sources, estimates of the cost are necessarily approximate. It is believed that at least 2 billion to 4 billion dollars' worth of damage is caused by pollution in the United States each year.

Major Air Pollution Incidents. Several major incidents of air pollution, resulting in human fatalities, have been recorded. Most notable are the incidents that occurred in the Meuse Valley in Belgium in 1930; in Donora, Pa., in 1948; and in London, England, in 1952.

The Meuse Valley and Donora incidents were similar in that both localities have considerable industrial activity, are densely populated, and are situated in valleys. In each case, light winds and fog had persisted for several days, and temperature inversions had formed below the tops of the surrounding mountains. The accumulation of air pollutants increased rapidly under these conditions, and the first illnesses attributed to the pollution were reported within the first two or three days. These illnesses were

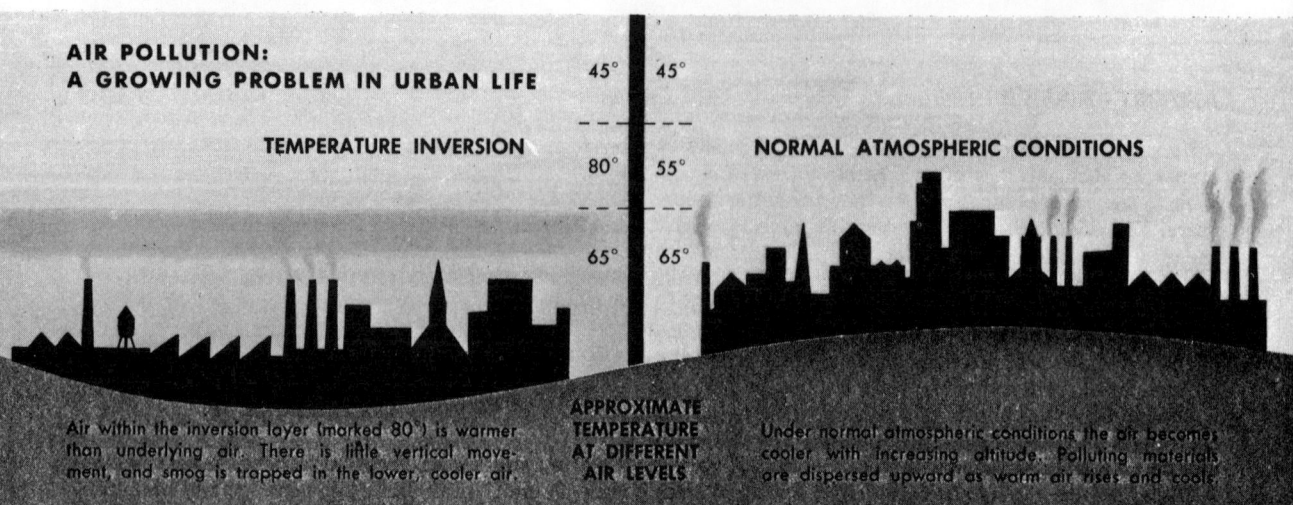

AIR POLLUTION: A GROWING PROBLEM IN URBAN LIFE

TEMPERATURE INVERSION — NORMAL ATMOSPHERIC CONDITIONS

APPROXIMATE TEMPERATURE AT DIFFERENT AIR LEVELS

Air within the inversion layer (marked 80°) is warmer than underlying air. There is little vertical movement, and smog is trapped in the lower, cooler air.

Under normal atmospheric conditions the air becomes cooler with increasing altitude. Polluting materials are dispersed upward as warm air rises and cools.

generally respiratory in nature. Burning of the eyes, nose, and throat, and coughing, shortness of breath, constriction and burning in the chest, and nausea and vomiting were typical symptoms. In the Meuse Valley, 60 people died; in Donora, 20 people. In both cases, thousands became ill.

In London during the first part of Dec., 1952, weather conditions were similar to those described above. It is known that there were about 4,000 more fatalities during December than is normal for that month. More recently, in Nov., 1966, New York City was the site of a major pollution crisis. Dense smog covered the city for 3 days, and 168 deaths were attributed to it.

Pollution Control. Since there is little that can be done to increase the atmosphere's capacity to disperse pollutants, the prevention of damage to health and property can be achieved only by effective control of polluting materials at their source. Such control is a complex and growing field of technology. In general, control measures fall into one or more of the following categories:

Dispersal. Tall chimneys are built so that contaminants may be released far enough above the ground to be dispersed and diluted by clean air. This method takes advantage of the natural ventilation of the atmosphere; it is particularly useful when the source area and amount of material released are not too large. When wind speeds are low or when temperature inversions occur, however, it is quite possible to overload the atmosphere.

Reducing the Production of Contaminants. In some industries it is possible to reduce or eliminate entirely the production of contaminants. Various techniques are used, most of which involve changing the materials used in a manufacturing process, using a different type of fuel, or simply making manufacturing and combustion methods more efficient.

Trapping Contaminants. Where manufacturing processes cannot be changed, it is often possible to install equipment to trap the pollutants before they reach the atmosphere. The design of such equipment depends upon the chemical and physical nature of the pollutants. Gases sometimes can be trapped by condensation, and both gases and liquids may be trapped by absorbing them in other materials. The trapped material may be made inoffensive by chemical reactions; in some cases, it may be burned. Small particles generally are trapped by filters or washed out by "scrubbers." Mechanical devices, such as centrifuges and electrostatic precipitators, are also available for removing particles.

Zoning Industrial Areas. In many cities industrial areas are zoned so that homes and offices may not be built close to sources of pollution. This method generally is used only when no completely reliable control devices are available or when the cost of such devices would be prohibitive compared to the cost of land.

Government Legislation. Because some areas are serious pollution sources, it has become necessary to enact legislation restricting the amount of material that can be emitted into the atmosphere. The scope of these laws varies. Some are strictly local ordinances controlling only the density of smoke emitted from chimneys. Others are more comprehensive.

ALBINISM [ăl′bə-nĭz-əm], a congenital condition in which there is complete or partial absence of pigmentation. Complete albinism frequently appears in several members of the same family. The hair is white and silky, the pupils of the eyes appear red and the irises pink, and the skin of the face has a pinkish hue. Albinos are unable to tolerate bright light, and the absence of protective pigmentation in the skin renders them especially sensitive to ultraviolet light; prolonged exposure to the sun may result in a serious burn.

ALCOHOLIC PSYCHOSES, mental disorders resulting from prolonged use of alcohol. Certain individuals are prone to a form of alcoholic psychosis called pathological intoxication. This transitory mental state represents a violent reaction to alcohol, different from ordinary drunkenness. Pathological intoxication may be considered a form of psychomotor epilepsy evoked by the alcohol.

Pathological intoxication occurs only in certain individuals. Prolonged excessive use of alcohol can result generally in more extended psychotic states. Delirium tremens, a state of weakness, tremors, and impaired interpersonal functioning, is often caused by the sudden withdrawal of alcohol from a habitually heavy drinker. Typical symptoms are terrifying visual hallucinations of small animals or men engaged in odd activities. A patient suffering from the psychosis called acute alcoholic hallucinosis complains of hearing threatening voices, often accusing him of homosexual practices.

Chronic use of alcohol may lead to nutritional and vitamin deficiencies, resulting in psychotic and debilitating states. Alcoholic paranoia is characterized by delusions of jealously and infidelity. Other nutritionally linked alcoholic psychoses are Korsakoff's psychosis, with memory defects, and alcoholic deterioration, in which brain and nerve functions are gradually impaired.

See also ALCOHOLISM; PSYCHOSIS.

ALCOHOLICS ANONYMOUS (A.A.), organization to promote recovery from alcoholism through self-help and the help of former alcoholics. Organized in 1934, Alcoholics Anonymous grew out of the efforts of two men, identified only as Bill W., and Dr. Bob S., to conquer their own drinking problems and to use their experiences for the benefit of others similarly distressed. In 1961 A.A.'s total membership was estimated at 300,000. Within the organization there are autonomous local groups; some hospital and prison groups; internationalists (seamen); and "loners," members not associated with local groups. Alcoholics Anonymous stresses a belief in spiritual values as the way toward cure. The only membership requirement is a desire to stop drinking, and the tradition of anonymity reassures potential members who might fear exposure. National headquarters are in New York City.

ALCOHOLISM, a dependence on alcoholic beverages that causes a deterioration in the physical and mental health of the individual and interferes with his economic and social life. The alcoholic is a compulsive drinker and although he may be aware of the destructive nature of his habit, he is unable to control it.

The addiction to alcohol begins gradually. The earliest sign is the tendency to drink to relieve tension. This is followed by drinking in private, "gulping" drinks, and frequent blackouts. The crucial phase appears when the alcoholic loses control of his drinking and begins to make excuses for his erratic behavior. He becomes aggressive, hoards drinks, neglects eating, and takes regular morning drinks. From this point he may slip into prolonged bouts and is well on the way to developing severer symptoms, such as tremors and impairment of thinking.

Although it was once thought that alcoholism was inherited or in some way caused by physical factors, most present-day psychiatrists emphasize psychological and social factors as causes of the disease. There is some evidence, however, that inherited deficiencies of body chemistry may also be involved.

Alcoholism and Family Life. According to many authorities, alcoholism has its origins in a disturbed family situation in which the mother is typically overprotective and indulgent. As a result the youngster makes excessive demands for emotional contact that are doomed to frustration, especially when he begins to function in the world outside of the home. The pattern persists into adult life. The alcoholic becomes disappointed in and enraged at persons who fail to accede to his demands. He expresses his anger in various ways that leave him with guilt feelings. The guilt leads to depression, and finally relief may be sought through alcohol.

This pattern of childhood experiences applies to other psychiatric disturbances as well and need not lead inevitably to alcoholism. The choice of alcohol as a means of relieving the tensions and frustrations may be influenced by an alcoholic father or by an environment in which social drinking is common. Alcoholism is much less likely to develop in a teetotal culture, such as that of the Quakers.

The Personality of the Alcoholic. The question is often raised whether there may not be certain characteristics that are shared in common by all alcoholics. Most studies have been unsuccessful in disclosing any consistent personality pattern. However, extensive research conducted at the State University of New York College of Medicine has revealed five characteristics that seem to be regularly present in alcoholics:

(1) Schizoid features. Beneath the usual façade of friendliness and sociability there is a deep-seated distrust and an emotional detachment from people. This is found to be associated with a self-centered attitude and immature thinking.

(2) Depression. This may not be apparent as such and may take the form of boredom or loneliness. It may be masked by joviality. Suicidal thoughts are frequent.

(3) Dependency. Like an infant, the alcoholic is demanding; he looks to others to fulfill his needs and feels that he has no control over what happens to him.

(4) Hostility. The alcoholic is frequently aggressive toward parents and others who have frustrated his demands.

(5) Sexual immaturity. Among men there are frequent doubts about one's masculinity. Homosexuality may be a feature.

Physiology and Pathology. Ethyl alcohol, the active ingredient in alcoholic beverages, produces exhilaration in small dosages (blood levels of 100–200 mg./cc.), depression and severe loss of muscular co-ordination with blood levels of 200–300 mg., and, frequently, interference with breathing, and death, if the blood level exceeds 500 mg.

Approximately one-fourth of all alcoholics develop medical problems, such as cirrhosis of the liver, pellagra (a nutritional deficiency), and gastritis. Disorders of the nervous system also are common. Since alcoholics invariably suffer from nutritional deficiencies, because of poor eating habits, there is considerable doubt as to how much of the observed tissue damage can be ascribed to the alcohol itself.

Treatment. Acute intoxication (drunkenness) usually does not require treatment, except when shock develops. In such cases immediate hospital care is necessary. Alcoholism itself presents a far more serious challenge. Three widely differing approaches are worthy of mention:

(1) Antabuse, a drug that makes alcoholic drinking unpleasant, if not impossible; even a small amount of alcohol produces vomiting and palpitations. Antabuse must be taken daily if it is to be effective.

(2) Alcoholics Anonymous, an organization in which former alcoholics actively help those fighting the addiction. They may, for example, intercept a backsliding member who has set off on a tour of the bars.

(3) Psychotherapy, which attempts to help the alcoholic discover the unconscious conflicts that drive him to drinking. This is the only approach that attempts to deal with the actual source of the problem. It may be applied on an individual or a group basis.

Alcoholism as a Social Problem. Estimates indicate that there are more than 4½ million alcoholics in the United States, which thus outranks all other countries by a substantial margin. Eighty-five percent of these are males, though the number of female alcoholics is on the increase. The severe social impact of this affliction results from its crippling effect on family life and upon the economic productivity of the individual.

Alcoholism is also a major problem in some European countries. In recognition of these facts the World Health Organization has set up committees to study the problem and to make recommendations for dealing with it.

See also ALCOHOLICS ANONYMOUS; ANTABUSE; DELIRIUM TREMENS.

ALKALOSIS [ăl-kə-lō'sĭs], condition caused by an excess of alkaline substances or a shortage of acidic substances in the body fluids. The commonest cause of alkalosis is excessive vomiting, which results in the loss of large quantities of stomach acids. Alkalosis also develops following diarrhea (in infants); from the overconsumption of alkaline substances, such as bicarbonate of soda; and from the overproduction of certain hormones by the adrenal gland, a condition known as aldosteronism. The symptoms found in alkalosis are those of the underlying disorder, plus muscular cramps, spasms, and convulsions. The condition is treated by administering medication to restore the acid-base balance and by correcting the underlying disorder. See also KIDNEY.

ALLERGY [ăl'ər-jē], abnormal response to certain substances, which may cause asthma, hay fever, and other allergic diseases. The body may react to the presence of certain materials (allergens), such as animal and plant products, by producing substances called antibodies. When the same material enters the body a second time, a reaction ensues between this substance and the antibodies. In the course of this reaction certain chemicals, such as histamine, are liberated into the tissues, where they produce the symptoms of allergy. They accomplish this by causing fluid to escape from the bloodstream into the tissues and by stimulating the contraction of certain types of muscle. When the reaction occurs in the skin, the escape of fluid and the contraction of the smooth muscles around the hair follicles produce the swellings seen in hives. When it occurs in the nose, collections of fluid in the mucous membranes cause the familiar symptoms of hay fever. An allergic reaction in the air passages (the bronchioles) produces asthma, and such a reaction in the intestines results in cramps and diarrhea.

Common Allergic Diseases

Allergy Produced by Airborne Allergens. Asthma and hay fever may be caused by airborne substances that are inhaled into the respiratory passages. Such substances include the wind-carried pollens of ragweeds, grasses, and trees; the seeds of molds that grow on grains; insect dust; the dandruff of dogs and horses; and house dust.

These irritants may affect the nose, causing sneezing, discharges, and blocking of the nasal passages. If the allergy is caused by seasonal allergens, such as pollen, molds, and insect dust, it is called hay fever. If the irritant is present throughout the year (dogs, house dust, feathers), the allergy is termed perennial allergic rhinitis. Allergic asthma is a more serious ailment; it develops when the air passages are sensitive to the air borne allergens. The allergic reaction causes a spasm of the muscles of the bronchioles and stimulates the production of thick mucus. The consequent narrowing and blocking of the air passages make breathing difficult. Although most cases of asthma are allergic in nature, some may be caused by infection or heart disease. In many instances the cause is unknown.

Allergy Produced by Skin Contact with Allergens. An allergic skin inflammation (contact dermatitis) can be caused by contact with a number of substances, including plants (poison ivy, poison oak, primrose, ragweed), dyes (used on fur and clothing), metals (mercury in antiseptics, nickel-containing jewelry), nail polish, penicillin, sulfa drugs, and plastics.

Allergy from Foods and Drugs. Almost any type of allergy can be produced by food. These types include asthma; skin conditions, such as hives and eczema; and gastrointestinal complaints involving cramps, stomach gas, nausea, vomiting, and diarrhea.

Drugs are also a frequent source of allergy. Some types of anemia (deficiency of red blood cells), leukopenia (deficiency of white blood cells), or thrombocytopenia (deficiency of blood platelets) may be caused by drug allergy. Injected drugs are more likely to produce an allergy than those taken by mouth. Aspirin, barbiturates, and sulfa drugs are common allergy-producing drugs given by mouth. Streptomycin, insulin, liver extracts, and various vaccines and serums are potential allergy-producing agents that are given by injection. Penicillin is one of the most important causes of drug allergy, whether injected or given by mouth. Serum sickness is an allergic reaction that occasionally follows the injection of penicillin or serum prepared from animals. This reaction usually develops several days after the injection and consists of hives, giant swellings, inflammation of the joints, and fever.

Allergy from Insect Stings. Allergic reactions from the stings of bees, wasps, and hornets are common. The oldest recorded case of this type is found in the hieroglyphic account on the tomb of King Menes of Egypt, which tells of his death from the sting of a hornet in 2641 B.C.

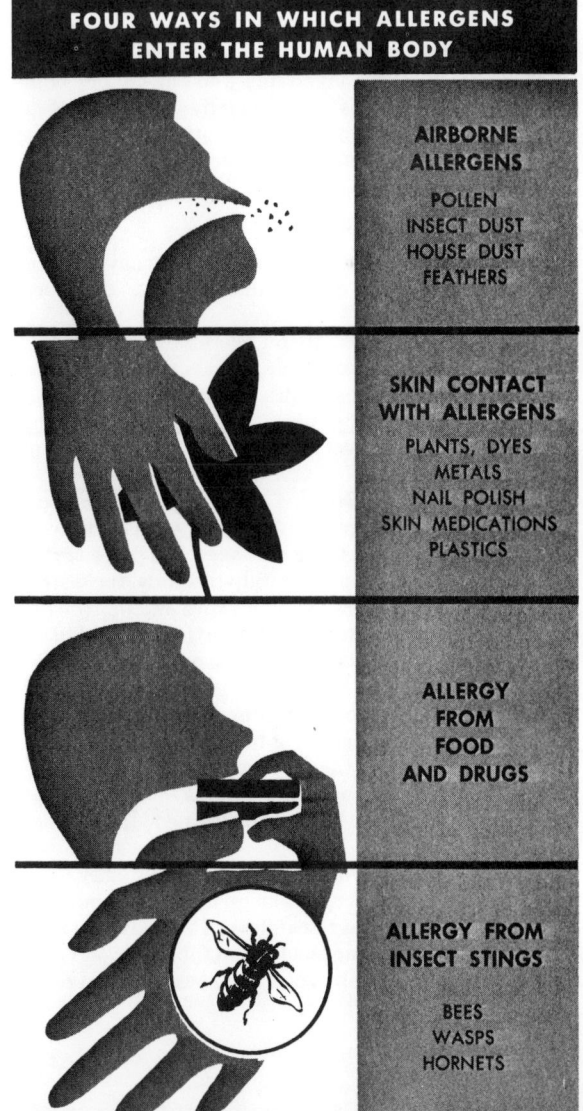

FOUR WAYS IN WHICH ALLERGENS ENTER THE HUMAN BODY

AIRBORNE ALLERGENS
POLLEN
INSECT DUST
HOUSE DUST
FEATHERS

SKIN CONTACT WITH ALLERGENS
PLANTS, DYES
METALS
NAIL POLISH
SKIN MEDICATIONS
PLASTICS

ALLERGY FROM FOOD AND DRUGS

ALLERGY FROM INSECT STINGS
BEES
WASPS
HORNETS

Detection and Treatment of Allergies

Once the physician has determined that a particular condition is allergic in nature, he seeks to identify the allergen. The tests used for this purpose are based upon the presence of antibodies in the tissues of the patient, which will react with the specific allergic substances. Most allergic conditions can be traced by introducing a quantity of the suspected substance into the skin, either by scratching the skin or by injection. If the body is allergic to the material, redness and swelling will develop within 15 to 20 minutes. A patch test can detect substances responsible for contact dermatitis. In this test the suspected material is applied to the skin. Redness and blistering will appear in 24 to 48 hours if the patient is allergic to the material. Systematic modification of the patient's diet may also enable the physician to isolate a particular allergy-producing food.

Once detected, the allergic agent should be eliminated. It may be necessary to give away a pet, to change one's cosmetic habits, or to modify the diet. Where it is not practical to avoid the offending substance, as in the case of allergies to pollen, molds, and dust, it is usually possible to provide relief by developing an immunity to the substance. This is achieved by injecting the patient with increasing dosages of the allergen over a period of time. Temporary relief from the allergic symptoms can frequently be obtained through the use of medications such as antihistamines, decongestants, and anti-itching compounds. In difficult cases, particularly in asthma, cortisone-related drugs will usually provide relief. These compounds are safe when their use is supervised by a physician.

Other Aspects of Allergy

Allergic phenomena are important in many medical problems aside from the familiar ailments described above.

Allergy and Infection. Almost every infection involves an allergic phase. For example, in tuberculosis, the tissues of the body produce antibodies to the tuberculosis bacteria. The reaction between the antibodies and the bacteria may be responsible for some of the symptoms of the disease.

Allergy and Tissue Grafts. The surgery of tissue or organ transplantation is severely limited because the body is able to "recognize" a tissue as foreign. If a patch of skin from another person is grafted onto the body, the system manufactures antibodies that react with and destroy the graft. The single exception to this rule is the case of identical twins, who are biochemically one person. In 1960 Sir Macfarlane Burnet and P. B. Medawar received the Nobel Prize in medicine for demonstrating that an animal could be "taught" to accept grafts of foreign tissues. This was achieved by injecting the foreign cells into the animal early in life. Later, the adult animal was found to accept grafts of the same tissue that it had "learned" to accept as its own.

Self-allergy (Autosensitization). The possibility of an individual becoming allergic to his own tissues has come to the attention of medical researchers. The body may suddenly treat its own tissue as a foreign substance and produce antibodies against it. The antibodies may then react with the tissue, producing further injury and disease. Experimental animals have been made allergic to their own kidneys, thyroid, pancreas, and brain, with resulting disease of these organs. There is strong evidence for the existence of self-allergy in man. In certain blood diseases, for example, it has been demonstrated that antibodies in the victim's blood destroy his own blood cells. In some types of thyroid disease, antithyroid antibodies are found, and there is some indication that certain kidney diseases and eye inflammations may be produced by similar mechanisms. It is also possible that some of the puzzling cases of asthma and eczema, in which external allergens cannot be found, may result from self-allergy.

Research in allergy is now directed at these basic problems and is supported by various governmental, private, and philanthropic agencies, including the National Institute of Allergy and Infectious Diseases, the Allergy Foundation of America, and the Asthmatic Children's Aid.
See also ANTIBODIES AND ANTIGENS; ASTHMA; HAY FEVER.

ALTITUDE SICKNESS, disorder caused by exposure to high altitudes. It is caused by breathing air with a lowered oxygen content, which leads to diminished oxygen in the blood. Man is affected by altitude sickness both when visiting or climbing in mountainous areas or in high flight in an unpressurized airplane cabin. Earliest symptoms appear at about 10,000 ft.

Lack of oxygen in the blood first affects mental function in much the same way as alcohol. Fine judgment is affected first, followed by disorders in speech, coordination, perception, and color vision. Physical symptoms are usually breathlessness, especially during exertion, and a feeling of lightheadedness. If exposure continues for several hours, headaches, weakness, and, in severe cases, prostration may occur. The most severe manifestation of altitude sickness is congestive heart failure. Considered a medical emergency, it is potentially fatal. Altitude sickness can be overcome by breathing into an oxygen-containing apparatus, or by exerting a minimum amount of energy, until the body becomes acclimatized to the high altitude.

AMBULANCE, vehicle to transport sick and injured persons safely and quickly to a place for medical care. Often called on in cases requiring emergency treatment, ambulances may be equipped with surgical instruments, oxygen equipment, stretchers, drugs, or incubators and are sometimes attended by a physician. Horse-drawn military vehicles, equipped to dress wounds, accompanied soldiers into the field during the Napoleonic Wars; they are considered to be the forerunners of modern ambulances. Some were used as field hospitals, and others transported wounded soldiers to hospitals.

AMEBA, one of the protozoans belonging to the order Sarcodina. These one-celled organisms are found in water, both fresh and salt and in damp soil. Some live in the digestive tracts of animals and a few are parasitic. The ameba, like higher animals, is able to move about, find food, grow, and reproduce. The main body of the cell is composed of granular protoplasm called endoplasm. Surrounding this is a thin layer of clear ectoplasm. The outside of the cell is covered by a thin membrane.

AMEBA (Amoeba proteus)

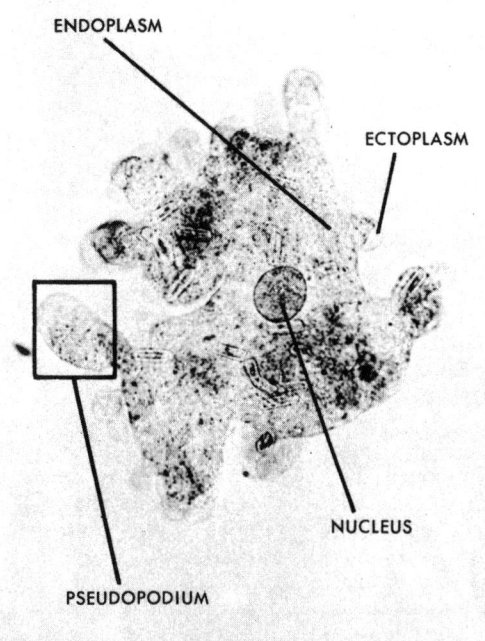

(BAUSCH & LOMB, INC., ROCHESTER)

The most striking characteristic of an ameba is its constantly changing shape. The name "ameba" derives from the Greek word *amoibe*, meaning "change." This may be seen when looking through a microscope at the species *Amoeba proteus*, a common pond ameba, which moves by pushing forth extensions of itself, known as pseudopods, then flowing into the extensions. It also obtains food by means of these pseudopods. Other protozoans or algae are surrounded and finally engulfed by the ameba. Digestion takes place in a food vacuole, a clear area which temporarily forms around the food. Any indigestable portions are left behind when the ameba moves on. Other clear, round areas, called contractile vacuoles, continually form and disappear as they regulate the amount of liquid in the ameba. The nucleus, a darker spot usually near the center, contains the essential life of the ameba. Amebas reproduce by dividing in half and the nucleus also splits in half. If an ameba is cut in two so that only one half contains the nucleus, that part lives, but the part without the nucleus, unable to reproduce itself, finally dies.

There are a great many species of amebas. One of the largest is *Pelomyxa carolinensis*, sometimes referred to as *Chaos chaos*, which can sometimes be seen with the naked eye. It contains several hundred nuclei and many contractile vacuoles. Another, *Amoeba verrucosa*, found in stagnant water, lacks the long pseudopods of *Amoeba proteus*, but it has many short, rounded pseudopods that give it a wrinkled or scalloped appearance.

Most amebas are harmless to man, but *Entamoeba histolytica* is able to dissolve the intestinal lining and is the cause of amebic dystentery.

AMEBIC DYSENTERY. See DYSENTERY.

AMERICAN CANCER SOCIETY, pioneer cancer-control organization in the United States, founded in 1913. It is a national, voluntary agency, composed of physicians and laymen, with divisions and chapters throughout the United States. The society's programs include research in cancer prevention, support of facilities for detection, diagnosis, and treatment of cancer, and professional and public education. Publications are *CA*, *Cancer, a Journal for the Physician,* and *Cancer News*.

AMERICAN COLLEGE OF SURGEONS, organization of North and South American surgeons, founded in 1913. The organization seeks to improve surgical treatment by supporting fellowships and conducting basic medical research. The official publication is *Surgery, Gynecology, and Obstetrics*.

AMERICAN HEART ASSOCIATION, organization founded in 1924 as a professional medical society and reorganized in 1948 as a national voluntary health agency. It has over 350 local chapters and associations throughout the United States. Its program includes public and professional education, community service, and medical research in cardiovascular diseases. The principal source of funds is the annual Heart Fund Campaign. The association publishes *Circulation*, a professional journal, and the popular periodical *American Heart*.

AMERICAN MEDICAL ASSOCIATION (AMA), national organization of physicians, founded in 1847 in Philadelphia under the leadership of Dr. Nathan S. Davis of New York. Its primary purpose was to insure that all licensed physicians were adequately trained and qualified. Medical faculties at that time were independent groups chartered by state legislatures to grant degrees. There were no entrance requirements and courses were of 10 to 20 weeks' duration, with the scantiest facilities. Today the AMA is composed of 70% of all U.S. doctors (teachers, specialists, general practitioners), and 90% of all doctors in private practice. Its organizational structure is a federation of state, county, and city medical societies, with officers elected directly from the local societies.

Among the AMA's activities are the continuing education of members through scientific meetings, periodic inspection of hospital and medical school facilities, support of basic research, and the introduction of new treatment. It publishes numerous scientific journals. The *Journal of the AMA*, first published in 1880, is read around the world. The AMA has gone from policing to advising American medicine and has been instrumental in raising the quality of medical practice in the United States.

See also NATIONAL MEDICAL ASSOCIATION.

AMERICAN PSYCHOLOGICAL ASSOCIATION, INC., major professional organization in the field of psychology in the United States, founded in 1892. It furthers its purpose—"to advance psychology as a science and as a

AMINO ACIDS

means of promoting human welfare"—by holding annual meetings, publishing 12 journals of psychology, and working toward improved standards for psychological research, training, and service. In an increasing number of states a certificate or license is required for the practice of psychology. Policies for certification are set by the association. The association is a source of information on the profession, on licensing requirements, and on universities having approved graduate courses. A central office is maintained in Washington, D.C.

AMINO [ăm'ə-nō, ə-mē'nō] **ACIDS,** nitrogen-containing acids that constitute the building blocks from which plant and animal tissues are made. The proteins found in all living things are composed of amino acids. The enormous variety of proteins that are found in plants and animals represents different combinations of about 25 basic amino acids.

The proteins found in foods, such as eggs, meat, and fish, are broken down into amino acids in the stomach and small intestine. The amino acids are absorbed into the blood stream: most of them enter the liver where they are converted into sugar or other substances which are burned as fuel by the body. Others pass from the blood into the cells of the body, where they are used to build tissue proteins. These proteins are in a constant state of change, much like a professional baseball team in which the positions are always filled but the individual players are constantly exchanged.

Amino acids provide the body with a number of hormones and enzymes. The amino acid tyrosine is changed into thyroxine, a hormone that regulates the pace of body activity. Tyrosine also becomes melanin, the pigment that produces tanning in the skin. Histidine becomes histamine, a substance released from injured tissues; it is important in allergic reactions. The amino acid phenylalanine is converted into adrenalin (epinephrine), a hormone, given off by the adrenal gland, which helps prepare the body for strenuous effort. This acid is also involved in phenylpyruvic oligophrenia, a rare condition found in some feeble-minded children.

Certain amino acids, if they are not supplied in the diet, can be manufactured in the body from other materials. An essential, or indispensable, amino acid is defined as one that cannot be made by the body in amounts adequate for normal growth or nutrition. Of the 25 amino acids found in proteins, 10 are considered indispensable for normal growth. The amino acid requirements of a growing animal are greater than those of the adult. Eight amino acids are considered sufficient for adult humans.
See also PROTEINS.

AMNESIA [ăm-nē'zhə], loss of memory. It may result from disease of, or injury to, the brain (organic amnesia) or may occur as a complication of certain personality disorders (psychogenic amnesia). Organic amnesia may appear during old age, or in cases of alcoholism, concussion, or stroke. In a chronic condition such as cerebral arteriosclerosis, which involves narrowing of the blood vessels of the brain, amnesia develops slowly, and memory of certain recent and remote events may be permanently lost. In cases of acute alcoholism and in cases of minor injury to the brain, amnesia is more likely to be temporary. Brain injury may produce distinctive types of amnesia. A boxer may be injured in the early rounds of a bout and continue fighting, unaware of the events following his injury (anterograde amnesia), or he may forget the events that immediately preceded it (retrograde amnesia).

Psychogenic amnesia is most often a symptom of a personality disorder, and appears most frequently in highly emotional persons of a hysterical type (see HYSTERIA). Painful memories may become dissociated, or detached, during periods of great nervous tension. Amnesia of this type, usually limited to specific memories, both appears and vanishes suddenly. In extreme cases the tendency of parts of the personality to become detached from consciousness may be so strong that the individual assumes a second personality: he changes identity and is unable to recall his name, address, family, and all other facts concerning his everyday self.

AMPUTATION [ăm-pyōō-tā'shən], surgical removal of a part of the body. If severe injuries damage extensively the blood supply of a limb, amputation may be performed to avoid gangrene. In cases of infection, amputation of a limb may be necessary if the release of poisonous substances from the infected limb into the body endangers the life of the patient.

Diseases involving poor circulation may also lead to amputation. In arteriosclerosis (hardening of the arteries), fatty deposits may collect in the arteries of the leg, obstructing the blood supply and reducing the vitality of the tissues. Amputation may be necessary if these tissues become infected and gangrenous. Amputation may be performed in certain types of cancer as a life-saving measure. Bone cancer, for example, may originate in an arm or leg and spread to other parts of the body. If the limb is amputated before the cancer has spread the life of the patient can be saved.

In all cases the surgeon must decide exactly how much of the limb is to be removed. In emergency situations, such as following accidents, the surgeon may perform a provisional amputation, removing whatever is required to save life. At a later date, when the patient is strong enough to tolerate more surgery, a definitive amputation can be undertaken. The surgeon will save that part of the limb which has a good blood supply and which will best permit the use of an artificial arm or leg.

Following surgery, great care is taken to avoid infection. Reamputation may be necessary if the bone in the stump becomes infected or if painful scars cannot be corrected by simpler surgery. The ends of severed nerves may become tender and require surgical treatment. Occasionally "phantom pain" develops; the patient feels sensation in the missing limb and may complain that his toes are cold or that his skin itches. These sensations usually subside in time. The stump must be exercised to develop muscular strength; it is usually wrapped tightly in an elastic bandage to facilitate the shrinking required for an artificial limb to fit properly.
See also PROSTHETICS.

AMYLOIDOSIS [ăm-ə-loid-ō'sĭs], condition characterized by the infiltration of the organs of the body with amyloid, a pale, waxy protein. In the uncomplicated form of amyloidosis, deposits of amyloid are found principally in the heart, voluntary muscles, tongue, blood vessels, intestinal walls, skin, lungs, and thyroid gland. More frequently the amyloid deposits occur together with chronic infectious diseases, such as tuberculosis, osteomyelitis (bone infection), and rheumatoid arthritis. In these cases amyloid is found in the spleen, liver, adrenal glands, kidneys, and heart. The presence of the amyloid deposits may interfere with the normal functioning of the affected organ. This is especially true when the heart and kidneys are involved.

ANALGESICS, a group of drugs which reduce or dull the perception of pain by their action on the lower brain centers. These agents do not, unless taken in excess, affect conscious central nervous functions, that is, they do not cause drowsiness or stupor. Quinine was the original analgesic, and a search by chemists for cheaper substitutes led to the development of aspirin, phenacetin, and aminopyrine, the major analgesic drugs. Analgesics are not addicting and as such must be distinguished from narcotic drugs, which also relieve pain by dulling its perception, but reduce conscious brain function, causing drowsiness.

Analgesic drugs are effective in alleviating pain of musculo-skeletal origin, such as sore muscles from exertion, bursitis, bruises, and arthritis. Aspirin, the most effective, least harmful, and least expensive analgesic, is a preferred treatment for the pain of arthritis. Given in large doses, under a physician's supervision, aspirin reduces the redness, heat, and swelling caused by rheumatic diseases. Analgesic drugs are also antipyretic, that is, they act to reduce fever.

See also ASPIRIN, NARCOTICS

ANAPHYLAXIS [ăn-ə-fə-lăk′sĭs], allergic phenomenon observed in laboratory animals, consisting of a severe reaction to foreign substances in the body. The animal is sensitized to the foreign material, for example, horse serum, by an injection. A second injection in about two weeks produces a violent reaction, which includes vomiting, diarrhea, and muscular collapse; it frequently results in death. The anaphylactic reaction probably results from the interaction of the foreign material with substances (antibodies) produced by the body and the consequent release of harmful substances into the blood.

A similar reaction, sometimes called allergic shock, occurs in man, and may follow the injection of penicillin. The symptoms produced are rapid heartbeat, fall in blood pressure, difficult breathing, outbreak of giant blisters on the skin, and swelling of the entire body.
See also ALLERGY.

ANEMIA [ə-nē′mē-ə], blood disorder in which the number of red blood cells or the quantity of hemoglobin (the oxygen-carrying chemical of the blood) which they carry, or both, are below normal levels.

Anemia may result from excessive bleeding, from destruction of the red blood cells, from a deficiency of substances needed for the production of red blood cells, from disorders of the blood-forming tissues, or from a combination of two or more of these factors. In all anemias the decrease in the oxygen-carrying capacity of the blood produces weakness, dizziness, and shortness of breath.

Anemia from Hemorrhage

This may arise from bleeding in any part of the body, usually from the gastrointestinal tract, the uterus, or the lungs. The body replaces the lost blood fluid within a few hours after the hemorrhage, but the hemoglobin and the red blood cells cannot be replaced as rapidly. The bone marrow, the site of red cell production, reacts by pouring out large quantities of young red blood cells (reticulocytes).

If the hemorrhage is not too severe, and if the body has enough iron with which to manufacture hemoglobin, then the bone marrow can restore the blood to normal over a period of weeks. If, however, the hemorrhage is severe or protracted, or if the iron supply is inadequate, then the bone marrow produces pale, hemoglobin-deficient red blood cells, a condition called hypochromic anemia.

Anemias from Blood Destruction

These are termed hemolytic anemias and may arise from defects of the red blood cells, which may be inherited or be produced by infection, poisoning, or blood transfusion.

Inherited hemolytic anemias appear in infancy and are usually characterized by the presence of bizarre and misshapen red cells that have considerably shorter life spans than normal red blood cells. Some of these inherited defects appear predominantly within specific racial and ethnic groups; sickle cell anemia, for example, in which crescent-shaped red cells are present, occurs mainly in Negroes. Occasionally, inherited hemolytic anemias involve red cells that appear normal but function abnormally.

Hemolytic anemias may be present in certain infectious diseases. Malaria is an outstanding example of hemolytic anemia resulting from infection. A type of hemolytic anemia is also found in cases of lead poisoning.

In blood transfusions, the possibility of producing a hemolytic anemia in the patient necessitates accurate blood typing, since anemia may occur if the blood of the donor contains cells that will react with the antibodies of the recipient. The Rh factor may be responsible for a hemolytic anemia of the newborn. In this case antibodies from the mother may enter the blood stream of the embryo and destroy its red blood cells.

A curious form of hemolytic anemia is an allergy of the body to its own blood cells. For reasons yet unknown, an individual may form antibodies that destroy his own blood cells.

Deficiency Anemias

These may develop if substances for the manufacture of red blood cells are lacking. This may result from a dietary deficiency, from a failure to properly absorb materials from the intestine, or from an excessive loss of iron through bleeding (as noted in anemia from hemorrhage).

Iron Deficiency. Infants frequently develop anemia toward the end of the first year of life as a result of rapid growth and a milk diet that provides little iron. Adolescent girls may become anemic as a consequence of rapid growth combined with menstrual blood loss, and perhaps from dietary fads.

ANESTHESIA

Deficiency of Vitamin B₁₂ and Folic Acid. Vitamin B₁₂ is found in liver, and folic acid is contained in spinach, peas, and certain other plants. Both substances are needed for the normal production of red blood cells. When they are not available, the production of red cells declines and those cells that are produced are much larger than normal. Anemias from dietary deficiencies of folic acid and vitamin B₁₂ are seldom encountered in the United States.

Anemia Through Failure to Absorb

In certain conditions vitamin B₁₂ may be present in the diet in adequate amounts but may not be absorbed from the intestine. Pernicious anemia is the consequence of a failure to absorb vitamin B₁₂ normally. The anemic individual lacks a certain factor, called the intrinsic factor that makes this absorption possible. The absence of the intrinsic factor is usually associated with a disturbance in the acid-secreting activity of the stomach. The disorder can be adequately treated by giving vitamin B₁₂ through injection.

Failure to absorb essential blood-producing substances is also encountered in sprue. In this condition the intestines are unable to absorb a variety of foods, including fats, proteins, and carbohydrates.

Anemia Through Underproduction

A serious anemia develops when the site of red-cell production, the bone marrow, fails to function normally. In such cases, nonfunctioning fat cells are found in the marrow. If the condition is severe almost all of the normal blood-forming cells may be absent, giving the marrow a completely fatty and yellowish appearance.

The condition may appear at birth. More frequently the anemia is produced by exposure to substances that injure the bone marrow, such as may be encountered in insecticides or various medications. Heavy dosages of radiation and certain drugs used in the treatment of cancer may also be lethal to the bone marrow.

The absence of functioning bone marrow results in an underproduction of red cells. Since the bone marrow also produces the white blood cells, there is a reduction in their numbers as well. The white blood cells are a principal bulwark against infections, and a decline in their concentration renders the body susceptible to disease. The blood platelets, which are important in the mechanism of blood clotting, are also in short supply and there is consequently a tendency to hemorrhage.

The treatment of these conditions is at present unsatisfactory. If an offending agent can be found it is, of course, eliminated. Frequently, however, further damage seems to develop even after the cause has been eliminated. Unsuccessful attempts have been made to stimulate marrow regrowth. Persons suffering from bone-marrow failure may be kept alive for many years through blood transfusions, living literally on the blood of other persons.

Blood-cell production may also be lowered by the replacement of bone marrow by other tissues. In a group of conditions known collectively as the lipoidoses, storage cells containing peculiar fatty substances accumulate in the marrow. Cancer cells may invade the bone and disrupt the normal blood-forming elements. In some conditions, the bone marrow is transformed into scar tissue. In leukemia an anemia develops as a result of the crowding out of marrow tissues by abnormal numbers of white blood cells. Treatment of these disorders is also unsatisfactory.

Other Forms of Anemia

Anemia may appear in cancer, in cases of serious infection, and in rheumatic disorders. In part, these anemias result from red-cell destruction, but interference with the production of red cells in the marrow and their emergence into the blood stream are also thought to be involved.

In view of the great number of potential causes, the diagnosis of anemia presents a considerable challenge. It is essential that the treatment be based upon an exact knowledge of the cause, since anemia is so frequently not a disease in itself, but a symptom of underlying disorder. *See also* BLOOD.

ANESTHESIA [ăn-ĭs-thē′zhə], loss of sensation. In ancient times anesthesia was produced by blows to the head or through the use of substances such as alcohol, opium, and hashish. Ether was first used as an anesthetic by the American physician Crawford W. Long in 1842, after he had observed that people who inhaled the drug at so-called ether parties became intoxicated and insensitive to pain. In 1846 the American physician William Morton gave the first successful public demonstration of the value of ether in surgery. Since then anesthesia has provided surgeons with the opportunity to develop delicate, precise operations lasting several hours, if necessary.

Anesthesia may be general or local. General anesthesia, which is usually used for major operations, involves a complete loss of consciousness and a relaxation of the muscles. In local anesthesia the patient is conscious and sensation is lost in a part of the body, such as a hand or an entire arm or leg.

General Anesthesia. Drugs that produce general anesthesia act upon the brain and higher parts of the nervous system. The higher brain centers, which regulate the thought processes are affected first, there is a depression of other parts of the brain as the anesthesia deepens. While receiving the anesthetic the patient passes through a characteristic sequence of behavior reflecting the degree of anesthesia. By observing this behavior the anesthetist is able to determine the stage of anesthesia and the amount of the anesthetic drug that the patient has absorbed.

In the first stage of anesthesia the patient is conscious but his sensitivity to pain is diminished. If the anesthetic compound is nonirritating there may be pleasant sensations of giddiness, floating, and freedom from care. In the second stage the patient loses consciousness and may shout and struggle violently. Nausea and vomiting may also appear. This stage may be shortened by skillful administration of anesthesia. The first two stages are called the induction period of anesthesia. Most surgical operations are performed in the third stage, in which the patient is unconscious and the muscles of the body are relaxed so that the surgeon is not bothered by movements of the patient.

During abdominal operations it is necessary to relax the muscles in the wall of the abdomen. Once an incision is made these muscles must be lax enough to permit the

ANESTHESIA

TYPES OF ANESTHESIA

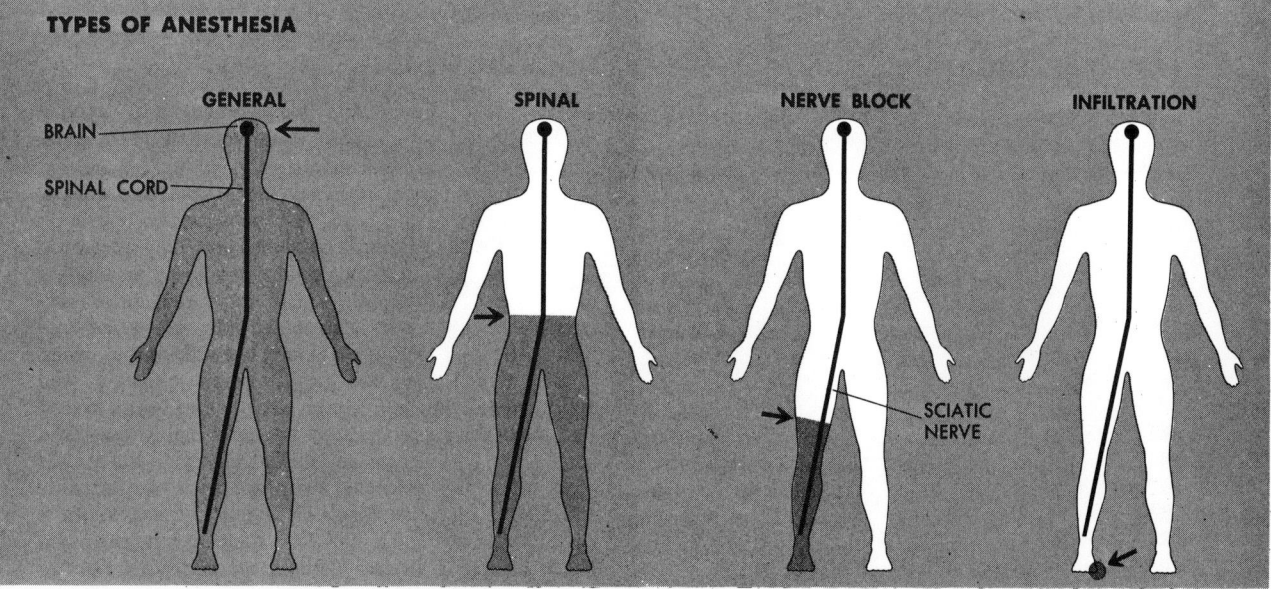

surgeon to stretch them away from the site of the operation. If the anesthetic does not permit enough relaxation, various muscle-paralyzing drugs can be used to supplement the anesthesia. One such drug is curare (q.v.).

Explosions are one of the hazards associated with certain anesthetic gases. Small electric sparks, like those that result from walking on a thick rug, may set off an explosion. This danger has been minimized by using special machines that do not permit the anesthetic gases to escape into the air. Additional safeguards are provided by grounding the apparatus used in the operating room and by requiring the operating-room personnel to wear leather-soled shoes, which conduct electricity.

Techniques of Applying General Anesthetics. General anesthesia is most frequently induced by having the patient inhale anesthetic gas into the lungs, where the gas is rapidly absorbed into the blood stream. Ether is the safest and most widely used of the inhalation anesthetics. It is easy to administer and provides adequate muscular relaxation. The disadvantages of ether include an unpleasant induction period, irritation of the breathing passages, and postoperative nausea and vomiting.

Chloroform, though once used extensively, is now considered too toxic for routine inhalation anesthesia. It is nonexplosive and easily administered but may produce abnormalities in the rhythm of the heartbeat.

Cyclopropane is an anesthetic gas that has a pleasant induction period, but it has the same limitations as chloroform and is expensive.

Nitrous oxide, or laughing gas, is the least toxic of all the general anesthetics. It has a pleasant induction period but does not provide the deep anesthesia needed for surgery.

Rectal anesthesia is performed by mixing various compounds in an enema to be absorbed through the lower part of the large intestine. It is rarely used because it is difficult to administer. Certain anesthetics may be introduced directly into the blood stream (intravenous anesthesia). This technique is fast-acting but does not provide the degree of anesthesia required for most operations. Sodium pentothal, one of the "truth drugs," is the best-known compound of this class. Intravenous anesthesia is frequently used in combination with inhalation anesthesia.

Local anesthesia is a loss of pain in an area of the body without loss of consciousness. It is ordinarily produced by applying drugs to a surface (topical anesthesia) or by injecting them into the nerves or soft tissues.

Surface tissues, such as the skin and the inner lining of the mouth, may be anesthetized by topical anesthetics. These substances are applied directly to the painful area and deaden the nerves in that region. They are used for minor surgical procedures and to alleviate pain arising from sunburns, abrasions, and other skin irritations.

In infiltration anesthesia, the anesthetic is injected into the soft tissues and anesthesia is produced as the drug infiltrates into the nerves. This procedure is often used to provide anesthesia while stitching a wound. The edges of the wound are injected with the anesthetic, which causes a loss of pain at the site of injection.

Anesthesia of an arm or leg may be obtained through the use of a nerve block, a technique in which the anesthetic is injected into the nerves leading to the limb. The injection can be made into the neck or back where the nerves leave the spinal cord.

Spinal anesthesia is a type of nerve block in which the anesthetic solution is injected into the spine. Sensation is lost in all parts of the body below the point of injection. A needle is inserted between two vertebrae in the patient's spine and the drug is injected into the fluid surrounding the spinal cord. This type of anesthesia permits the patient to be awake during the operation, and does not cause postoperative nausea and vomiting. Spinal anesthesia produces a complete muscular paralysis and therefore cannot be used in operations on parts of the body that lie above the abdomen, since this would paralyze the

chest muscles and the diaphragm, which are necessary for breathing. Spinal anesthesia may also cause dangerous lowering of the blood pressure in elderly persons and should not be used in diseases of the nervous system or in the presence of infection in the injection area. In rare cases permanent paralysis may result from this method of anesthesia. The risk is negligible, however.
See also COCAINE; NOVOCAINE; SURGERY.

ANEURYSM [ăn'yə-rĭz-əm], a bulge in a weakened area of the artery wall. There are several types whose names usually refer to their location, shape, or cause. An aortic aneurysm affects the largest artery, the aorta. A fusiform aneurysm is spindle shaped. Arteriosclerotic and traumatic aneurysms are named for the cause of the arterial wall weakness. An arteriovenous aneurysm denotes an abnormal communication between an artery and vein. In a dissecting aneurysm, a break occurs in the inner layer of the wall of a large artery and blood breaks into the middle layer, often causing considerable pain. If an aneurysm ruptures, there is serious hemorrhage, whose effect depends on the location and size. A ruptured aneurysm in the brain, for example, may cause a stroke. Treatment is always surgical. After removing the aneurysm, an arterial graft or synthetic tube is put in its place. A saccular aneurysm may be repaired by placing a silver clip across its base. Large aneurysms can be treated by placing a firm plastic substance around them to prevent further ballooning of the artery wall.

ANGINA PECTORIS. See HEART DISEASES.

ANGIONEUROTIC EDEMA [ăn-jē-ō-nōō-rŏt'ĭk ĭ-dē'mə], condition characterized by the appearance of swellings in any part of the body, usually on the skin of the hands, face, or feet. The swelling is caused by a collection of fluid in the tissues (edema). Swelling of the tissues of the throat may cause suffocation and swelling of the internal organs may give rise to symptoms characteristic of diseases of those organs. Angioneurotic edema can be inherited. In some cases allergies to specific substances are responsible.

The swelling remains for a few hours or days. When the condition is caused by an allergy, the disease may disappear spontaneously. Epinephrine (adrenalin) and antihistamines are used to control the severity of the attacks; in severe cases, cortisone derivatives may be necessary.

ANILINE [ăn'ə-lĭn], also called aminobenzene and phenylamine, an aromatic chemical compound. It is a colorless liquid having the formula $C_6H_5NH_2$. It is used extensively as a solvent and in the preparation of other organic compounds, dyes, rubber accelerators, photographic developers, and medicinals.

Aniline was originally obtained from indigo (Span. *anil*), from which it derives its name. Its current annual U.S. production of over 100,000,000 lb. results chiefly from the reduction of nitrobenzene with scrap iron and dilute acid.

Aniline darkens on standing; it is purified by steam distillation. It is toxic and is absorbed through the skin, producing a giddy feeling. The properties of aniline are those of an amine and of an aromatic compound: it is weakly basic, and is higher boiling and less reactive than the corresponding six-carbon aliphatic amine, hexylamine, $C_6H_{13}NH_2$. With sulfuric acid, aniline slowly forms sulfanilic acid, one of the sulfa drugs. Acetanilide, made from aniline and acetic acid, is used as a fever depressant and as a source of sulfanilamide. Substituted anilines—for example, dimethylaniline—are used to make many dyes, and explosives, such as tetryl. Melting point, $-6.2°$ C. ($20.8°$ F.); boiling point, $184.4°$ C. ($363.9°$ F.).
See also SULFA DRUGS.

ANOREXIA NERVOSA [ăn-ə-rĕk'sē-ə nĕr-vō'sə], uncommon neurotic disorder characterized by a persistent lack of appetite associated with disgust for food. It occurs mainly in sensitive, young, unmarried women. Frequently menstruation ceases, and constipation, falling of the hair, vomiting, and extreme emaciation may occur. There is often a previous history of overeating and concern about being overweight. Disturbed mother-daughter relationships and rivalry for parental favor with brothers or sisters are also frequent background factors. Treatment by psychotherapy is indicated.

ANOXIA [ăn-ŏk'sē-ə], decrease in the oxygen supply to the tissues of the body. Oxygen reaches the tissues through the blood stream, and anoxia may result from an interference with the oxygen supply at the point in the lungs where the oxygen enters the blood, from an inability of the blood to carry enough oxygen, from a slowing or obstruction of the blood flow, or from an inability of the tissues to utilize the oxygen they receive.

Inadequate oxygenation of the blood in the lungs may develop in lung diseases or from breathing oxygen-poor air at high altitudes. Decrease of the oxygen-carrying capacity of the blood may occur because of anemia resulting from extensive bleeding or because of an interference with the functioning of the hemoglobin, the oxygen-carrying chemical in the blood. The latter situation appears in carbon monoxide poisoning. Slowing of the blood flow may occur in shock or heart failure. Obstruction of the flow of blood through an artery may result from a blood clot, or thrombus, which produces a local anoxia limited to the tissues supplied by that artery. Characteristic anoxias appear in certain types of poisoning; for example, in cyanide poisoning the utilization of oxygen by the tissues is prevented.
See also ALTITUDE SICKNESS; ASPHYXIATION.

ANTABUSE [ăn'tə-būs], trade name for disulfiram (tetraethylthiuram disulfide), used to treat chronic alcoholism by reinforcing the patient's desire to stop drinking. During Antabuse therapy even one drink of liquor may cause rapid heartbeat, lowered blood pressure, fainting, nausea, vomiting, and possibly coma. Because Antabuse is excreted slowly from the body, the patient cannot drink alcohol for several days after each dose without risking disastrous effects.
See also ALCOHOLISM.

ANTACIDS [ănt-ăs'ĭdz], **GASTRIC,** substances used to neutralize hydrochloric acid in the stomach. Gastric antacids are of two types, systemic and local. Systemic antacids are absorbed into the blood stream, whereas local antacids remain confined to the gastrointestinal tract. The systemic antacids affect the alkali-acid balance of the blood and may, if taken in excessive quantities, cause the blood to become too alkaline, resulting in a serious condition known as alkalosis. Antacids are used principally in the treatment of hyperchlorhydria, a condition in which there is an overproduction of hydrochloric acid in the stomach, and in cases of peptic ulcer. Sodium bicarbonate is a popular systemic antacid; magnesium hydroxide (milk of magnesia) is a well-known local antacid.

See also DIGESTION.

ANTHRAX, highly infectious disease of domestic animals and, occasionally, of man. It is caused by the *Bacillus anthracis*, a hardy bacterium that is capable of surviving great changes in environmental conditions. The German physician and bacteriologist Robert Koch used this bacillus in 1877 to demonstrate conclusively, for the first time, that germs can cause disease.

Sheep, cattle, and other domestic animals usually get anthrax by grazing in pastures that are contaminated with the organism. The disease occurs throughout the world, but is most prevalent in Europe and in Asia—particularly in China, India, and Turkey. Most cases of human anthrax occur on the skin. Butchers and farmers who handle diseased animals may develop a single pustule on the arm, which swells rapidly, causing intense itching. Tannery workers who carry hides on their shoulders are often infected on the neck, where the leather rubs against the skin. The infection may spread rapidly from the skin to the blood stream. A frequently fatal form of anthrax (woolsorters' disease) damages the lungs; it is probably caused by inhaling infected dust. An intestinal variety is produced by consuming contaminated meat or milk. Antibiotic drugs, such as penicillin, are used to treat anthrax.

ANTIBIOTICS [ăn-tĭ-bī-ŏt'ĭks], chemical substances, produced by microorganisms, which have the capacity, in dilute solution, to inhibit the growth of or to kill other microorganisms.

History. The ability of various microorganisms, especially bacteria and fungi, to inhibit the growth of other microbes had been known since the latter part of the 19th century, and attempts were made to utilize the products of such microorganisms in the treatment of different infectious diseases, including tuberculosis. Although some success was achieved with substances prepared from certain bacteria and fungi, the results were not sufficiently impressive to justify great hopes for this type of therapy.

In 1928 the British bacteriologist Alexander Fleming demonstrated that cultures of a green mold, later identified as *Penicillium notatum*, produced a substance that inhibited the growth of staphylococci and certain other bacteria. Numerous attempts to isolate this substance in pure form failed, and more than 10 years elapsed before a group of British scientists, led by Howard W. Florey and Ernest Chain, succeeded in producing penicillin preparations that could be used in the treatment of disease. In 1939 René Dubos of the Rockefeller Institute for Medical Research isolated gramicidin and tyrocidine (together called tyrothricin) from certain soil bacteria. These substances were found to have remarkable antimicrobial properties that could be used to combat certain infectious diseases. In 1940 Selman Waksman and Harold Woodruff isolated actinomycin from a culture of moldlike organisms (*Actinomyces antibioticus*). Although this substance was active against various bacteria it was too toxic for medical use. Shortly afterward streptothricin and streptomycin were isolated from the same group of organisms. Streptomycin has since been widely used as a therapeutic agent.

The discovery of antibiotics has revolutionized medical practice by bringing within the scope of treatment an entire category of deadly illnesses. They have also found extensive use in veterinary medicine, in the treatment of certain plant diseases, in animal feeding, and in the preservation of various biological materials and foodstuffs.

The antibiotics consist of a great variety of complex organic chemicals, which include fats, starches, protein derivatives (polypeptides), and sulfur and iron compounds. On the basis of their elementary composition they have been grouped as follows:

1. Compounds containing carbon, hydrogen, and oxygen—for example, clavacin.
2. Compounds containing carbon, hydrogen, oxygen, and nitrogen—for example, streptomycin and actinomycin.
3. Compounds containing carbon, hydrogen, oxygen, nitrogen, and sulfur. These include the penicillins.
4. Compounds containing chlorine. These include chloramphenicol and chlortetracycline.

Production of Antibiotics. The most important groups of antibiotic-producing organisms are the bacteria, fungi, and actinomycetes (moldlike organisms). Some microbes are able to produce more than one antibiotic. The organism *Pseudomonas aeruginosa*, for example, produces pyocyanase, pyocyanin, pyolipic acid, and certain other compounds. The actinomycetes, *Streptomyces griseus*, produce not only the antibacterial substances streptomycin, mannosidostreptomycin, and grisein, but also the antifungal substances actidione and candicidin, and the antiprotozoan agent streptocin.

The first step in the production of an antibiotic is the selection of an antibiotic-producing microorganism. Following this a more potent strain of the organism is isolated from the original culture. The antibiotic-forming culture is then transferred through a series of stages from the test tube to small fermenting tanks, and finally to large vats. The final stage of growth usually lasts 2 to 6 days, when the concentration of antibiotic reaches a maximum. After the antibiotic has been isolated and purified, a registered standard is established by the Antibiotics Control Division of the Food and Drug Administration in Washington.

Some antibiotics are chemically modified in an attempt to yield substances with more desirable properties. Dihydrostreptomycin is prepared by adding hydrogen to streptomycin. Tetracycline is prepared from chlortetracycline by removing chlorine. Only a few antibiotics, notably penicillin and chloramphenicol, have been synthesized chemically.

Antibiotic Therapy. The principal action of antibiotics is to inhibit the growth of bacteria and fungi, although in some instances the antibiotic actually destroys the microorganisms.

ANTIBIOTICS

Upon continued contact with a given antibiotic, bacteria that were originally sensitive may become resistant to the drug. As a result of the constant use of penicillin, resistant strains of staphylococci have emerged; these strains have been responsible for many hospital infections. *Mycobacterium tuberculosis*, the causative agent of tuberculosis, may become resistant to streptomycin after repeated exposure to the drug.

An organism that has become resistant to one antibiotic, however, usually remains sensitive to other antibiotics. An exception to this is seen in cross-resistance, which develops among certain groups of antibiotics, such as the tetracyclines: an organism made resistant to chlortetracycline automatically becomes resistant to oxytetracycline. To overcome the development of resistance, two antibiotics may be combined. A combination of streptomycin and penicillin is used in the treatment of certain mixed infections. Sometimes an antibiotic is combined with a chemical compound, such as a sulfa drug or isoniazid.

Antibiotics are not equally effective against all microorganisms. The range of diseases for which an antibiotic is useful is termed its antimicrobial spectrum. Penicillin is effective in a wide variety of conditions, including syphilis, pneumonia, and gas gangrene. It is of little value in cholera, leprosy, and tuberculosis. Streptomycin is effective in the treatment of tuberculosis and urinary tract infections, but it is useless against fungus diseases. The tetracyclines are highly active against chancroid, typhus, and brucellosis. Some antibiotics, like actidione, candicidin, and nystatin, are active primarily against fungi. Certain microorganisms are apparently capable of producing substances that inhibit the multiplication of, or destroy, viruses; none of these substances, however, has found any practical application.

As a result of the introduction of antibiotics, many formerly dreaded diseases are seldom fatal today. Tuberculosis, which was formerly the greatest killer of humanity, is gradually coming under control. This has resulted in an increase of the average life expectancy. Unfortunately, antibiotics are usually ineffective against virus infections. A few diseases caused by rickettsialike organisms (the Chlamydozoaceae), which are not true viruses, have responded to antibiotic therapy.

Some progress has been made in the isolation of antibiotics effective against certain tumors. Unfortunately, these substances are highly toxic, and their effect is limited.

Many antibiotics cause allergic and other reactions. Allergic reactions to antibiotics, such as penicillin, may be fatal. In some patients, streptomycin may cause dizziness, loss of balance, or loss of hearing. This can usually be avoided by reducing the dosage of the drug or by combining streptomycin with certain chemical agents, such as isoniazid. The tetracyclines, taken by mouth, may occasionally cause nausea, diarrhea, overgrowth of fungi (*Candida*), and certain other undesirable reactions. These reactions can be largely overcome by switching to another antibiotic or by the use of antifungal agents.

The manufacture of antibiotics has increased from a small beginning in 1940 to a tremendous industry totalling hundreds of millions of dollars a year in sales in the United States alone. Penicillin is the leading antibiotic; the tetracyclines take second place; and streptomycin, dihy-

DEVELOPMENT OF DRUG-RESISTANT ORGANISMS (MUTANTS)

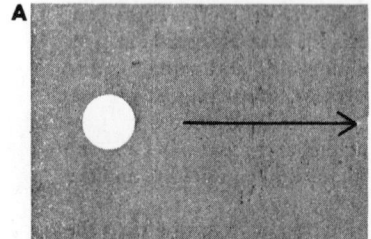
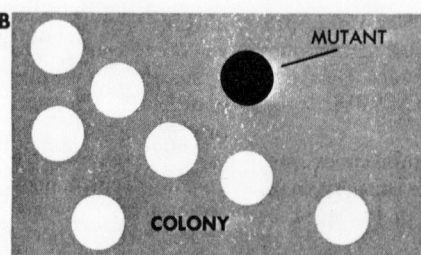

From a single bacterium (A) a colony of organisms develop (B). In the colony are "mutants," individuals that deviate from the others in many of their characteristics.

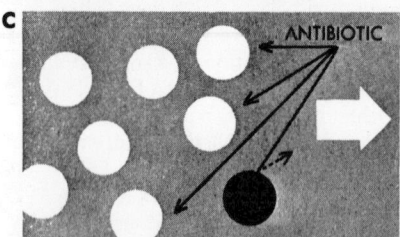
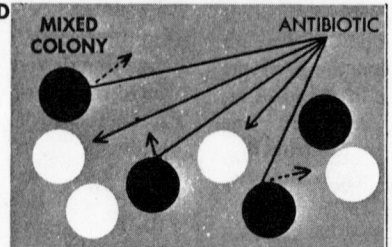
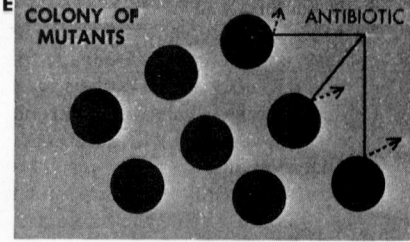

Mutants might not be able to reproduce effectively under ordinary circumstances. But if an antibiotic is introduced into the colony (C) and if the characteristics that distinguish the mutant from the other organisms also enable it to resist the action of the antibiotic, the mutant will reproduce more effectively than its companions (D). Eventually it will completely dominate the culture (E). The colony is now drug resistant. This process is believed to occur in the human body when an antibiotic, after being used extensively, loses its effectiveness.

drostreptomycin, chloramphenicol, oleandomycin, erythromycin, nystatin, griseofulvin, neomycin, and kanamycin follow. The importance of these drugs in modern medical practice is reflected in the estimate that nearly 50% of all prescriptions sold in drug stores throughout the United States are made up of antibiotics.

ANTIBODIES [ăn'tĭ-bŏd-ēz] **AND ANTIGENS** [ăn'tə-jənz], complex organic substances involved in immunity and allergy. The body responds to the presence of certain foreign materials (antigens) by producing special substances called antibodies, which can react with the foreign substance in characteristic ways. The antigens are usually proteins and polysaccharides (q.v.) that are part of, or products of, living organisms.

Each antigen may be considered a lock, and the antibody a key designed to fit it. An antibody that is produced as a response to an antigen of diphtheria bacteria will not be able to react with antigens contained in tuberculosis bacteria. This exclusiveness is not complete, for the key does not mesh quite perfectly with the lock, and the antibody may react with antigens that bear a close resemblance to the original. Thus it has been found that antibodies developed in response to chicken protein will react in varying degrees with the proteins of other birds.

The effect of the antibody-antigen reaction is to permit the body to deal with the foreign element. (A) The antibody may combine with antigens on the surface of the bacterial cells, causing the cells to clump together (agglutinate) so that scavenging white blood cells may consume them in convenient bundles. (B) If the antigen is a soluble material, the antibody may combine with it to form a precipitate. (C) Normal blood contains a substance, called complement, which is potentially lethal to bacteria. By combining with the bacterial antigen, antibodies enable complement to react with and dissolve the bacterial cells. This process is termed complement fixation, and forms the basis for certain blood tests used in the diagnosis of syphilis and other infectious diseases.

The body does not produce large numbers of antibodies upon first exposure to the antigen. Following a lapse of 10 days to several weeks, a second exposure to the antigen results in the mass production of antibodies. In immunization procedures this effect is utilized by giving multiple, or "booster," injections at specified intervals, as in the administration of antipolio vaccine.

Immunity, or the ability to resist disease, is directly linked to the presence of suitable antibodies in the blood, which can react with and neutralize the invading organisms. Natural immunity occurs when the body produces antibodies in response to the antigens of invading organisms. Artificial immunity can be achieved with special preparations of living or dead microorganisms (vaccines) which stimulate antibody production without causing disease. The built-in immunological response to foreign tissue requires the use of radiation and drugs to suppress the rejection mechanism which endangers permanent transplantation of organs and tissue. The symptoms of hay fever and many other allergic conditions result from vigorous and destructive antigen-antibody reactions. Blood typing for purposes of blood transfusion is made necessary by the possibility that antigen-antibody reactions may produce widespread agglutination of blood cells and result in the death of the patient. A similar situation exists with regard to the Rh factor, a potential antigen present in the blood of most, but not all, people; antibodies present in the blood of a mother who lacks this substance may kill or injure her developing child. Drugs, such as penicillin, may also act as antigens and the ensuing reaction may result in fever, skin rash, and, in some cases, death.

In 1969 American researchers reported that they had deciphered the chemical structure of a specific gamma globulin molecule—a protein antibody consisting of 1,320 amino acid units produced by victims of myeloma, a cancer

MECHANISMS OF ANTIGEN-ANTIBODY REACTIONS

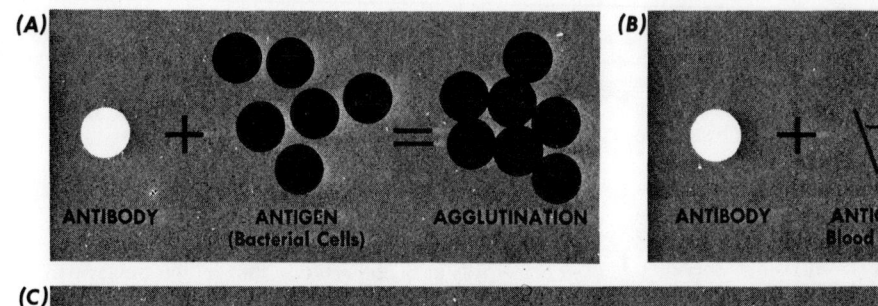
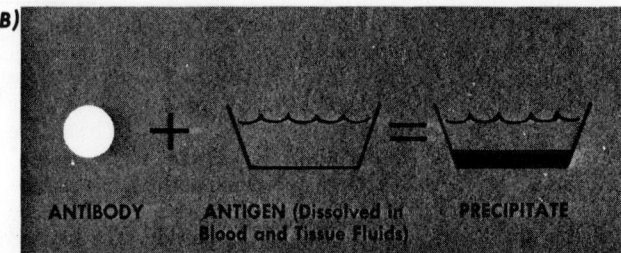
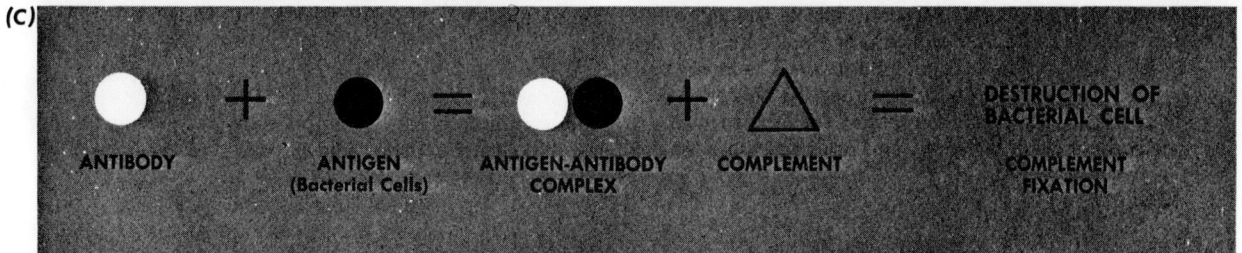

of the bone marrow. This represented progress towards complete understanding of the immunological process. See also ALLERGY; IMMUNITY.

ANTICOAGULANTS [ăn-tĭ-kō-ăg'yə-lənts], substances that inhibit blood clotting. Anticoagulant drugs may interfere with clotting by suppressing the formation of substances needed for clotting or by directly interfering with the action of clotting agents in the blood stream. Heparin and dicoumarol are the best-known anticoagulants. Heparin is normally present in the lungs, liver, muscles, and in other tissues. When used as a drug it acts directly upon the blood, but its anticoagulant effect lasts only a few hours. Dicumarol (bishydroxycoumarin) is an anticoagulant drug first extracted from spoiled sweet clover, which caused a hemorrhagic disease in clover-eating farm animals. Dicoumarol does not act on the blood itself, but inhibits the production of substances (including prothrombin) in the liver that are necessary for coagulation. It is, consequently, a slowly acting drug requiring from 24 to 72 hours to become effective. Heparin and dicoumarol are often used in combination.

Anticoagulants are used to prevent the formation of blood clots (thrombi) in the blood vessels of the legs, lungs, heart, and brain. These clots may obstruct the flow of blood to vital tissues. A clot in a vein of the leg may become dangerous if it breaks away and is carried along in the blood stream until it lodges in a vital artery of the lungs. In such cases anticoagulants are given to prevent further clots from developing. On occasion these drugs may so reduce the coagulability of the blood that fatal hemorrhages result. To avoid this complication, blood tests are done regularly to insure that the clotting power of the blood is maintained within safe limits.

ANTIGEN. See ANTIBODIES AND ANTIGENS.

ANTIHISTAMINES [ăn-tĭ-hĭs'tə-mēns], group of drugs that counteract the action of histamine, a compound, released from injured cells, that causes the blistering, itching, redness, and swelling seen in allergic diseases. The antihistamines are a diverse group of drugs that possess a chemical base similar to that of histamine. When histamine is released in the body it produces its effects by entering the cells of the various tissues. The antihistamines, being chemically similar, are able to take the place of histamine in the cell.

The drugs are particularly useful in treating allergic diseases, such as hives and contact dermatitis. They relieve itching and consequently help in cases of poison ivy and insect bites. In hay fever they effectively control sneezing, watering of the eyes, and running nose. Antihistamines have not proven effective in the treatment of severe asthma, but they provide some relief in mild cases. In serum sickness and drug reaction antihistamines help control fever and rash.

Antihistamines were at one time heralded as a cure for the common cold. Later investigations failed to substantiate such claims, but the drugs are of value in alleviating some of the cold symptoms. Certain of the antihistamines have proven effective in treating motion sickness and vertigo, but the drugs' action in these cases is not understood.

All antihistamines produce side effects, the most frequent of which is drowsiness. Dizziness, dis-co-ordination, blurred vision, nausea, and vomiting are less common side effects. In rare instances blood diseases have resulted from the use of antihistamines.
See also ALLERGY; HAY FEVER.

ANTISEPTICS [ăn-tĭ-sĕp'tĭks], drugs applied to the living tissues of men or animals to destroy or prevent the growth of disease-producing microorganisms.

History of Antiseptics. While it had been known for many centuries that certain substances could be applied to wounds to facilitate their recovery, physicians did not become fully aware of the possible role of contamination in causing disease until the early 19th century. The American physician Oliver Wendell Holmes advocated cleanliness as a means of controlling childbed fever (puerperal fever) in 1843, and shortly afterward the Hungarian physician Ignaz Semmelweis suggested that surgeons and midwives wash their hands and instruments in chlorinated lime prior to delivering children. Semmelweis' policy met with great resistance but succeeded in reducing the frequency of childbed fever in the General Hospital in Vienna. In 1867 the Scottish surgeon Joseph Lister laid the foundation of modern surgical techniques by using carbolic acid (phenol) to prevent infections after surgery.

The work of Louis Pasteur and Robert Koch established the relationship between germs and disease and explained the success of the techniques of Lister and Semmelweis. The full emergence of the germ theory of disease also inspired the search for more effective antiseptics. A great variety of antiseptics has since replaced the chlorine compounds and the carbolic acid used by the early workers in the field.

The most powerful antiseptic is iodine, which was first used in the treatment of wounds in 1839. In 1881 Koch suggested the use of bichloride of mercury as an antiseptic. For many years this compound replaced the early chlorine solutions and carbolic acid. Combinations of mercury with organic substances (Mercurochrome, Merthiolate), which are more effective and less irritating than bichloride of mercury, are now used in place of it. The essential oils, such as thymol and eucalyptol, were introduced at about the same time as bichloride of mercury. The essential oils are among the least irritating of all the antiseptics. In the 1880's silver compounds were also introduced as antiseptics and are still used extensively.

Newer Antiseptics. In the 20th century two new groups of antiseptics were discovered: the bis-phenols and the quaternary ammonium compounds. The bis-phenols are used principally as bacteriostatics: they inhibit the growth of, rather than destroy, microorganisms. Hexachlorophene, a well-known member of this group, is the active ingredient in many deodorant soaps. Hexachlorophene decreases body odor by preventing skin bacteria from converting the substances contained in sweat into odorous compounds. The quaternary ammonium compounds are nitrogen-containing substances that are powerful germ killers. Zephiran is probably the best known.

What Makes a Good Antiseptic? Antiseptics can be compared in terms of a number of properties that render them desirable or undesirable for certain uses. Certain antiseptics lose their effectiveness in the presence of blood, pus, and other organic substances, and consequently cannot be used in certain types of wounds. This is true of the mercurial antiseptics and the quaternary ammonium compounds. The latter are also adversely affected by soap.

In order to be effective an antiseptic must be "wet." The property of wetness refers to the ability of the antiseptic to flow into minute crevices. If the antiseptic does not penetrate, bacteria will breed in the minute pores of the tissues. Antiseptics dissolved in alcohol are generally wetter than those dissolved in water. The bis-phenols are highly penetrative when added to soap.

A good antiseptic should not injure the tissues. Most antiseptics will irritate tissue if they are used in sufficiently high concentrations. Some of the stronger antiseptics, such as iodine, must be used with caution and should not be allowed to remain in contact with the tissues for a long period. It is therefore advisable to wash away the iodine before covering the wound with a bandage. Iodine compounds (iodophors) that release iodine slowly when diluted with water are also available. These preparations are less irritating than the iodine tinctures. The essential oils are particularly valuable for their blandness and are safe for use on sensitive tissues.

Uses of Antiseptics. The choice of an antiseptic for a specific purpose depends upon the place where it is to be used (uninjured skin, abraded skin, or infected skin), the length of time it is to remain in contact with the tissue, the presence of organic substances such as pus, and the nature of the organisms against which it is to act. With regard to the last it must be kept in mind that antiseptics differ in their effectiveness against particular types of microorganisms. Not all of the antiseptics, for example, are effective against fungi. Iodine is the strongest antifungal antiseptic. The bis-phenols and the quaternary ammonium compounds are also fungicidal. Examples of antiseptics that are useful in particular circumstances are given in the following section.

Antiseptics for the Skin. *First Aid.* Iodine solutions, organic mercury compounds (Mercurochrome, Merthiolate, Metaphen), and alcohol are used to treat minor cuts, bruises, and scratches.

Surgery. Alcohol, and hexachlorophene contained in soap, are frequently used by surgeons to clean their hands before operations. Iodine in alcohol is widely used to prepare the skin of the patient for surgery.

Skin infections. The presence of large amounts of organic matter prevents the use of the mercurial compounds in cases of skin infection. The physician may select special antiseptics that are effective against particular bacteria or fungi. Iodine preparations, silver compounds, and dyes, such as gentian violet, may be used in these cases.

Antiseptics for the Mucous Membrane. The mucous membranes, which include the tissues lining the mouth, nose, and eyes, are more sensitive than the skin and require nonirritating antiseptics. Solutions of the essential oils in alcohol are excellent as mouthwashes, as are some of the bis-phenols (hexachlorophene). Silver nitrate is used as an antiseptic in the eyes. In many states silver nitrate solutions were routinely applied to the eyes of newborn children to prevent gonorrhea of the eyes; although it is still occasionally used in this way, silver nitrate has been largely supplanted by penicillin solutions.

The Choice of an Antiseptic. As can be seen from this discussion, no single antiseptic can be regarded as ideal for all situations. The selection should always be based upon a knowledge of what is needed and of the properties of the different antiseptics.

See also ANTIBIOTICS; BACTERIA; HYDROGEN PEROXIDE.

ANTITOXIN [ăn-tĭ-tŏk'sĭn], a preparation that neutralizes bacterial poisons (toxins). Antitoxins consist of antibodies (special substances produced by the body to fight disease) and are usually prepared by immunizing horses or other large animals. The blood from these animals is treated in order to concentrate the antibodies and to remove substances that could produce allergic reactions in sensitive individuals. Antitoxins are used in the treatment of diseases such as diphtheria, tetanus, and botulism.

See also TOXIN.

ANXIETY, in psychiatric usage, an emotional reaction of fear, in which there is usually no clear, visible source of danger. The concept of anxiety forms a central part of psychoanalytic theory. Neurosis is thought to be the outcome of subconscious attempts by the individual to master anxiety.

The victim of the anxiety reaction experiences great difficulty in sleeping and may suffer from severe attacks of rapid pulse, sweating, nausea, pain in the chest, and palpitations. Anxiety reactions often develop into phobic reactions in which the anxiety becomes attached to specific objects and situations (*see* PHOBIA). Tranquilizers are useful in controlling the physical symptoms of the anxiety reaction but psychotherapy is required to treat the deep-lying causes.

See also PSYCHOANALYSIS.

AORTA [ā-ôr'tə], the main artery of the body. Arising from the left ventricle of the heart, it arches back and de-

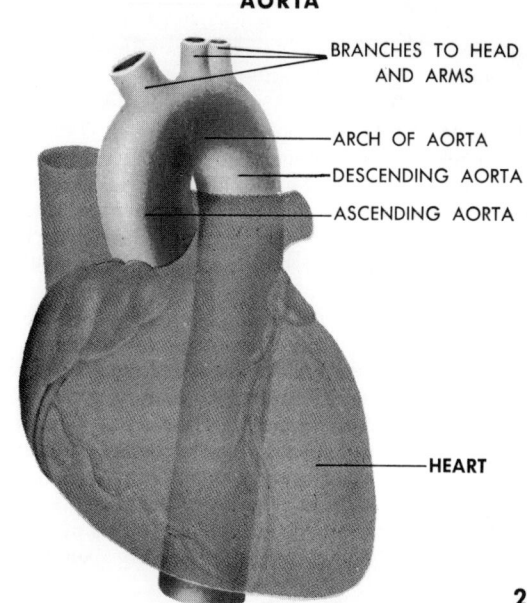

AORTA

scends in front of the spinal column. Along its course, the aorta branches to all parts of the body, ending in the lower abdomen where it divides into the two common iliac arteries.

See also ARTERY; BLOOD.

AORTITIS [ā-ôr-tī'tĭs], inflammation of the aorta, the great vessel which carries blood from the heart. The inflammation begins with swelling and infiltration of white cells containing destructive enzymes. Later, fibrosis or scar tissue develops. The two most common causes of inflammation in the aorta are syphilis and an inflammatory arthritis of the spine called ankylosing spondylitis. A relatively rare form of aortitis occurs in young women, usually of Asian or African origin. This type may affect the branches of the aorta, causing blindness, kidney failure, or loss of brain function, depending on the artery involved. A common feature of the diverse types of aortitis is thickening of the tiny vessels which supply the aorta. All three layers of the aorta—intima, media, adventitia—are usually involved in all types of aortitis.

Aortitis weakens the elasticity of the aorta, creating aneurysms, sacs or pouches which may rupture and cause fatal internal hemorrhage. Or, it may stretch the aorta where it joins the heart, causing a separation of the valves which normally prevent blood from backing up into the heart after it has been pumped into the aorta. This second consequence, called aortic insufficiency, can produce heart failure.

See also ANEURYSM.

APHASIA [ə-fā'zhə], disturbance of language functions resulting from injury to, or disease of, certain parts of the brain. The nature of the disturbance depends upon the exact region of the brain in which the disease or injury occurs. Three major types of aphasia are:

Expressive Aphasia: Inability to communicate thoughts through speech, writing, or gestures. The individual knows what he wishes to say, but finds difficulty in expressing his ideas.

Receptive Aphasia: Inability to recognize words pronounced by others (word deafness) or written (word blindness), although these words were familiar prior to the illness.

Amnestic or Nominal Aphasia: Difficulty in finding the right name for a familiar object.

These difficulties sometimes improve without treatment as the brain damage that caused them heals. Other cases require help through remedial training. True aphasia should be distinguished from the language problems that appear in the mentally retarded, and from physical disturbances of the tongue, the larynx, or other parts of the vocal apparatus.

APPENDICITIS [ə-pĕn-də-sī'tĭs], inflammation of the appendix, a small worm-shaped pouch that opens into the large intestine in the lower right portion of the abdomen. Although the appendix forms a large part of the digestive tract in rabbits and some rodents, it has no known function in man.

The bacteria-laden contents of the human appendix normally empty into the intestine. If the opening becomes narrowed or blocked by a fecalith (a stone made of hardened feces) this material may accumulate, exerting pressure against the walls of the appendix and squeezing off the blood supply. Eventually the trapped bacteria may attack the devitalized walls of the appendix, causing appendicitis.

Pain may be felt at first in the upper part of the abdomen and later shift to the lower right portion. Nausea and vomiting are frequent. Signs of appendicitis include spasm of the abdominal muscles over the appendix, and possibly fever and an increase in the number of white cells in the blood (leukocytosis). The attack may subside spontaneously or result in a rupture of the appendix, allowing bacteria to escape into the abdominal cavity. This may cause either a limited abscess or peritonitis, a general infection of the membrane that lines the abdominal cavity.

Appendicitis is treated by surgical removal of the appendix. If the appendix ruptures, both surgical treatment and antibiotics are required. Laxatives should be avoided in all cases of suspected appendicitis.

Repeated attacks of appendicitis may occasionally occur; but chronic appendicitis is believed to be rare, usually developing when the appendix is involved in a chronic disease of the bowel, such as tuberculosis.

APPENDIX, in anatomy, the vermiform appendix, a nonfunctioning part of the intestine in man. It is a twisted, wormlike tube, about 3 in. long, which ends blindly after arising from the cecum, a portion of the large intestine in the lower right part of the abdomen.

ARCUS SENILIS [är'kəs sĭ-nī'lĭs], white ring around the cornea of the eyes, seen most commonly in elderly persons. The opacity is caused by deposits of fatty substances. No disturbance in vision is produced and no treatment is required.

ARSENIC [är'sə-nĭk], a semimetallic chemical element, similar in chemical properties to phosphorus. Arsenic occurs naturally in the form of sulfides such as orpiment and realgar, which were known to the ancients, and as arsenopyrite, its most common mineral. It was isolated as an element by the alchemists, possibly as early as 1250.

Arsenic compounds such as Paris green (copper acetoarsenite) and sodium arsenite were formerly used as insecticides and weed killers, but have been replaced by organic compounds. The war gases adamsite and lewisite are compounds of arsenic. The less toxic compounds have some medical uses. The best known of these is arsphena-

PROPERTIES	
Symbol	As
Atomic Number	33
Atomic Weight	74.9216
Density (black crystalline form)	5.7 g./cc.
Valences	3, 5
Melting Point	814° C. (1,497° F.)
Sublimation Point	614° C. (1139° F.)

mine, also known as Salvarsan and 606, which, before the advent of antibiotics, was the only successful treatment for syphilis.

The uncombined element arsenic is not toxic, but its compounds are. Arsenic trioxide (As_2O_3), called white arsenic and frequently miscalled arsenic, is responsible for most arsenic poisoning. Traces of arsenic compounds in the tissues of persons suspected of death by such poisoning are detected by the Marsh test. The tissue is treated to convert any arsenic present into the gas arsine (AsH_3), which is led through a hot tube where it decomposes to metallic arsenic and is deposited as a black stain in a cold section of the tube.

ARTERIAL GRAFTING, technique in which a diseased or injured section of artery is replaced with tubing prepared from synthetic materials, or with a section of healthy artery taken from the patient's own body (autograft) or from another person (homograft). Arterial grafting is used to treat conditions in which the arterial passageway is narrowed or weakened, as in arteriosclerosis (hardening of the arteries), birth abnormalities, and injuries and infections of the major blood vessels.

See also ANEURYSM.

ARTERIES, HARDENING OF. See ARTERIOSCLEROSIS.

ARTERIOSCLEROSIS [är-tēr-ē-ō-sklə-rō′sĭs], disease of the arteries in which they lose their normal elasticity and become rigid and narrowed. This condition is popularly called hardening of the arteries. It is an ancient disease, evidence of it having been found in well-preserved fragments of arteries removed from Egyptian mummies.

Arteriosclerosis occurs primarily in later life, and because of the increase in life expectancy it is the most frequent cause of death in the United States and Canada. The disease is distributed in striking patterns that still puzzle researchers. Certain ethnic groups, such as Jews of eastern European derivation, seem especially prone to severe arteriosclerosis while Yemenite Jews are not particularly susceptible. Evidence indicates that arteriosclerosis is less of a problem in Japan than among Japanese living in Hawaii and southern California. Women in their reproductive period are much less prone to arteriosclerosis than are men. This advantage disappears after the menopause, an observation that has led to speculation about the possible role of sex hormones in this disease.

Three basic changes may occur in arteriosclerosis: (1) The arteries may lose their elasticity if the elastic fibers in the arterial wall degenerate. (2) They may become rigid if sufficient quantities of mineral salts are deposited within their walls. (3) The arterial openings may narrow as tissue builds up on the inner wall, thus obstructing the passageway.

The loss of elasticity of the arteries is a serious blow to the normal functioning of the circulatory system, and results in an increase in blood pressure. The destructive changes in the artery may so weaken it that it is liable to rupture, causing hemorrhage. If this happens in the brain, the result is a stroke. The weakening may also lead to the formation of pouchlike blow-outs, or aneurysms, in the walls of the large arteries. The deposits of tissue along the inner wall of the artery reduce the flow of blood. Since the tissues depend on the blood supply for their life, the reduction of the blood flow devitalizes them and renders them liable to injury.

The symptoms produced by the decrease in blood supply depend upon the particular part of the body affected. Arteriosclerosis of the arteries supplying the heart weakens the heart muscles and is a common cause of heart disease. Arteriosclerosis of the arteries of the brain may produce, in addition to hemorrhage, many of the changes observed in senility. Arteriosclerosis of the blood vessels of the legs causes numbness, tingling, and coldness in the feet, and painful spasms in the muscles of the legs when walking. Arteriosclerosis of the kidneys may lead to the formation of scar tissue in the kidneys and to high blood pressure. Patients with arteriosclerosis are liable also to thrombosis—the formation of blood clots in the vessels. If the clot is large enough to block the opening completely, the tissues dependent on the artery are deprived of their blood supply; when this occurs the previously described symptoms of tissue distress appear.

Causes of Arteriosclerosis. The causes of arteriosclerosis are not yet clearly understood. Much attention has been focused on the possible role of fatty substances (especially cholesterol) in the production of the disease. Increased interest in this factor was brought about by the discovery that animals fed egg yolk and other foods high in fat content develop a high blood-fat level and large fatty cushions on the inner surface of the artery wall. These cushions eventually obstruct the flow of blood. Similar cushions, high in fat content, are found in human arteries. The emphasis on blood fat as a possible cause of this disease has led to the substitution of the term "atherosclerosis" (literally, porridgelike hardening) for arteriosclerosis.

Many scientists believe that there are three factors that, singly or in combination, may cause arteriosclerosis —inflammation, mechanical injury, or fatty deposits. They point out that in many diseased arteries little fat is found. In addition it has been shown that arteries can manufacture their own fats and that consequently the fatty deposits need not be related to the quantity of fats in the blood. Although considerable research has been devoted to relating blood-fat levels and eating habits to the severity of the disease, the exact connection between the two is still disputed.

Those researchers who feel that more than one cause is at work in arteriosclerosis emphasize the patterns of the affected arteries. According to their view, arteriosclerosis involving arteries in a limited region is caused by inflammation. Arteriosclerosis that is distributed throughout the body but occurs particularly at certain locations, such as where arteries branch, is thought to arise from mechanical causes. That form of the disease which strikes arteries indiscriminately is regarded as arising from high blood-fat levels.

Prevention and Treatment. Arteriosclerosis cannot be cured, in the sense that the abnormal changes in the arteries cannot be reversed. Treatment is aimed at controlling the possible complications and preventing further damage to the arteries.

Patients who tend to develop blood clots in the arteries

are given drugs (specifically anticoagulants) to prevent the formation of further clots. Certain substances may also be given to dissolve those clots that have already formed. Surgical treatment is occasionally used. Sections of arteries that have developed blow-outs from weakening of the walls can be removed and replaced with synthetic tubing or arterial grafts. When patients are afflicted with arteriosclerosis of the extremities, cutting certain nerves that tend to constrict the arteries may increase the blood supply to the affected parts.

The commonest preventive measure consists of regulating the diet to reduce the amount of fat taken in. Certain drugs have been used which are claimed to decrease the amount of fat that enters the blood stream. Attempts are also being made to replace the solid (saturated) fats with liquid (unsaturated) fats, which are believed to be less harmful. Since it is known that high blood pressure accelerates the development of arteriosclerosis, persons with this condition are given drugs to lower the blood pressure. There is also some evidence that mental stress may contribute to arteriosclerosis; efforts to reduce tensions may therefore be helpful.

See also CHOLESTEROL; HEART DISEASES.

ARTERY, tube through which blood is pumped away from the heart. The largest artery in the body, the aorta, is about an inch in diameter and carries blood directly from the heart. Smaller arteries branch off from the aorta, and with each subsequent branching the arteries decrease in size. The arterial wall consists of three layers: an outer layer of elastic tissue, which predominates in the aorta and large arteries; a middle layer of muscle, which is relatively the thickest in the medium-sized and small arteries; and an inner layer of smooth, thin cells.

See also ARTERIOSCLEROSIS.

ARTHRITIS [är-thri'tis], term commonly applied to a group of diseases that affect primarily the joints, muscles, and ligaments. These disorders occur in every country and climate. It has been estimated that there are over 12 million arthritics in the United States and Canada. There are more than 60 conditions that can give rise to arthritis, which can be discussed conveniently under the following headings:

Connective-Tissue Diseases

These are a group of diseases that affect various organs and the connective or supporting, tissues of the body, such as the joints, skin, and internal organs.

Rheumatoid Arthritis. This is the most important of the connective-tissue diseases and the most severely crippling and disabling of all forms of arthritis. Although rheumatoid arthritis may strike in any age group, most cases appear in the age range 30–40; women are especially susceptible. The course of the illness is marked by periods of well-being alternating with periods of extreme distress. The cause is still unknown; many authorities feel that rheumatoid arthritis arises from alterations of the normal mechanism by which the body defends itself against disease. Physical injury, mental stress, and other factors may trigger the development of the illness.

Rheumatoid arthritis causes an inflammation of the joint lining (the synovial membrane). This inflamed tissue may extend and destroy the joint and its supporting structures, resulting in a "stiff" and deformed joint. One joint may be stiff and painful for weeks or months before other joints are attacked. Typically, the joints of the fingers, hands, and knees become swollen. The fingers acquire a sausage-shaped appearance as the joints closest to the palm of the hand become swollen. Nodules may appear immediately under the skin, around the elbows, wrists, fingers, and ankles. In addition to the joint symptoms, there is a marked wasting away of the muscles. The patient presents a generally emaciated appearance, fatigues easily, and frequently suffers from anemia.

The diagnosis of the condition is aided by the presence of a distinctive, large protein—"the rheumatoid factor"—in the blood of most patients suffering from the disease. Tests for rheumatoid arthritis, based on the presence of this substance, are not completely accurate since similar types of proteins may be present in other chronic diseases.

There is no cure for rheumatoid arthritis. However, most patients receive great benefit from an integrated program of physical therapy and medication. The most widely used drugs are salicylates (including aspirin) in adequate dosages, butazolidin, certain antimalarial compounds, adrenal hormones such as cortisone and related drugs, and injections of gold compounds.

Rheumatic Fever. This disorder is marked by fever and a distinctive "migratory" arthritis that travels from joint to joint. Although the exact cause is unknown, the disease is apparently linked in some way to a streptococcal infection of the throat that appears one to three weeks earlier. It is most common between the ages of six and nine years, but adults also may be affected. The disease was once quite prevalent, but its occurrence has been reduced considerably by the prompt treatment of throat infections with antibiotics and by improved public health measures.

Permanent joint damage does not occur. However, the tissues of the heart may become inflamed and scarred (particularly in the area of the mitral valve, which regulates the flow of blood on the left side of the heart).

Treatment includes bed rest, large doses of salicylates, and, in the more serious cases, cortisone and its derivatives. All patients are told to take an antibiotic or sulfa drug, under a physician's supervision, for some time after the attack in order to control future infections that might lead to a serious recurrence of the disease.

Other Connective-Tissue Diseases

Lupus Erythematosus Disseminatus. This is a serious connective-tissue disease that affects mainly young women. In addition to the joints and muscles, the kidneys and heart are frequently involved. Many patients develop a characteristic "butterfly patch" of reddened skin across the bridge of the nose and under the eyes.

Rheumatoid Spondylitis. This is a crippling disease of young men that results in the deposition of calcium in the soft tissues of the spine, resulting in the formation of a rigid, or "poker," spine.

Arthritis from "Wear and Tear": *Osteoarthritis.* This is arthritis produced by degeneration of the cartilage found at the joint surfaces and by overgrowth of bone at the margin of the joint. Some evidence of this process can be found in the joints of most adults. While osteoarthritis is commonly believed to result from aging and the normal process of wear and tear, research indicates that heredity, body chemistry, injury, and birth deformities also play a large part. Any joint may be involved; the hips, knees, and spine are affected most frequently.

Osteoarthritis does not generally cause the severe crippling deformities seen in rheumatoid arthritis, but some cases may be extremely painful and disabling, especially when the hips are involved.

Osteoarthritis is treated by resting the affected joint, by using physical therapy in the form of heat and muscle strengthening exercises, and analgesic drugs, and, in some cases, by injection of cortisone derivatives into the joint. In cases of severe hip involvement surgery can be of great benefit.

Arthritis from Disturbances in Body Chemistry: *Gout.* A fairly common arthritic disease, gout, contrary to the image of the gouty, upper-class figure of popular literature, occurs in all races, nationalities, and social levels. Gout rarely appears before the age of 30 in men or before the change of life in women. It is associated with an inherited defect in the body's ability to metabolize certain protein foods, called purines. The defect results in an increase in uric acid in the body. The relationship of this increase to gouty arthritis is obscure, since frequently a member of a gouty family will have a high uric acid level without ever developing the disease. In some cases, gout develops as a result of increased purine metabolism in certain blood diseases.

Attacks may be brought on by many factors, including emotional stress, surgery, infections, and the consumption of certain foods. Any joint may be involved, but the most common site is the great toe. The affected joint suddenly becomes red, hot, swollen and intensely painful. These symptoms gradually subside over a period of four to ten days. The pattern of the disease varies widely, but ordinarily the attacks are at first sporadic and gradually increase in frequency, until permanent damage to the joint results. In the more severe, untreated cases uric acid deposits, called tophi, appear in the tissues of the joints and other parts of the body, such as the ear. These deposits may become large enough to produce gross deformity and joint destruction. Deposits in the kidney can lead to serious kidney disease and the formation of urate kidney stones.

Gout is diagnosed by measuring the amount of uric acid in the blood and by x-ray examination of the joints. Tophi or joint fluid may also be examined for uric acid crystals.

Gout is one of the few rheumatic diseases that can be controlled effectively by present forms of therapy. Colchicine is used to relieve the attacks and, since gout is the only type of arthritis in which this drug is effective, it can be used as an aid in diagnosis. Butazolidin and cortisone derivatives are more effective in controlling the attacks. Certain drugs, such as probenecid, are used to diminish the uric acid deposits in the body by increasing the rate at which the acid is excreted through the kidney. However, these drugs are of no value in controlling the gouty attacks.

Diets aimed at reducing the intake of purines are generally not advocated, except for severe cases. All patients, however, are warned to avoid foods such as liver, kidneys, and anchovies, which are high in purines.

Ochronosis. This disorder is a rare, inherited disease that is marked by the absence of a specific chemical (ordinarily produced in the liver), which the body needs to process certain amino acids (q.v.). As a consequence of this deficiency, a dark pigment is deposited in the joint cartilage, resulting in a severe and progressive arthritis.

Arthritis from Infection. Invasion of the joints by infecting organisms can occur in gonorrhea, syphilis, tuberculosis, and in streptococcal and staphylococcal infections. Since the discovery of antibiotic drugs and other antibacterial agents, arthritis caused by bacterial infection has been effectively reduced. Staphylococcal infections of the joints (caused by the same bacteria that produce boils) are still difficult to control because of the resistance of many of these organisms to antibiotics. In some cases of joint infection surgical treatment is necessary. A joint that has been the site of an infection usually develops osteoarthritis later.

Rheumatism

Many conditions which mistakenly are said to be arthritis do not involve the joints, but affect the surrounding tissues, such as the bursa, tendons, and muscles. Although these diseases are extremely common they are not well understood, chiefly because of the difficulty in producing them experimentally.

Bursitis. The latter is an inflammation of the tissue spaces that are found around joints and tendons. It is common around the shoulder, elbow (tennis elbow), and wrist. The inflammation may result from physical injury or be associated with more serious arthritic diseases. The symptoms are usually pain, on movement, accompanied by tenderness, swelling, and redness over the affected area. Slings and splints are used to rest the affected part and drugs are administered to relieve pain and combat the inflammation. In some cases cortisone derivatives may be injected into the painful area. Bursitis usually responds well to treatment.

Fibrositis or Myositis. This condition is marked by pain, tenderness, and frequent spasm, in groups of muscles, particularly those around the shoulder and lower spine. The causes of the condition and the manner in which the symptoms are produced are not clear. In some cases the symptoms are associated with muscle spasms resulting from emotional tension. In other instances exposure, injury, or an underlying disease may be responsible. Treatment is directed at the primary cause, if this can be found. Analgesics, heat, liniments, and various physical therapy measures are of value.

General Considerations

Diet. Diets and various dietary supplements were extensively investigated some time ago. Although many claims have been and still are made, no diet has been shown to affect the course of any of the major arthritic diseases (apart from gout). Neither has it been proven that arthritics suffer from vitamin and mineral deficiencies.

Climate. Some, but not all, arthritics feel better after moving to a hot, dry climate. Since arthritis of all types is

ARTIFICIAL RESPIRATION

common in all climates, extraneous factors, such as relaxed living conditions and improved emotional health, undoubtedly play a large part in the benefits derived from such a move.

Although it is widely felt by laymen that the symptoms of arthritis fluctuate with weather changes, such responses are not general or consistent. The changes do not seem to be related to air pressure or temperature, but there is some evidence that the electrical activity of the air (ionization) may be a factor.

Spas and Hot Springs. It has not been demonstrated that the waters or mud from various sources have, in themselves, any effect on arthritis. The relaxed atmosphere, the use of warm pools and warm water or mud for heat, and the careful medical supervision, combine to provide excellent therapy.

Analgesics. The cheapest and most effective pain-relieving drug for the arthritic patient is aspirin or a related salicylate. Usually the products advertised as offering "amazing relief from arthritic pains" are aspirin or related compounds offered for sale under elaborate names at exorbitant prices.

Rehabilitation. The use of rehabilitation techniques and easily taught exercises can prevent or overcome much of the disability and deformation resulting from arthritis. It has been effectively demonstrated that good rehabilitation can return many arthritics to gainful employment.

ARTIFICIAL RESPIRATION, process of moving air into and out of the lungs of persons in whom the breathing mechanisms have failed. Drowning, carbon-monoxide poisoning, electric shock, and overdosages of sleeping drugs are some familiar situations which may cause breathing to stop. In such circumstances the immediate first-aid application of artificial respiration—to breathe for the victim until he is able to breathe for himself—may be a lifesaving measure. Although various techniques of chest and back pressure, and arm lifts, have been taught in the past, the oral (mouth-to-mouth or mouth-to-nose) method of artificial respiration is now considered the most practical for emergency use. This technique requires no equipment, can be used on an individual of any age, and enables the rescuer to check accurately the effectiveness of his efforts.

After the patient revives, he should be kept as quiet as possible and treated for shock. If he starts to shiver, cover him. A number of disturbances may follow the stopping of breathing, and therefore a doctor should always care for the patient during his recovery.

ASCARIASIS [ăs-kə-rī′ə-sĭs], infestation with the giant, intestinal roundworm, *Ascariasis lumbricoides*. Ascariasis is found throughout the world but is more common in warm, moist regions where sanitary conditions are poor. The eggs of the worm are swallowed in food that has been contaminated with the feces of infested persons. The eggs hatch in the small intestine and the larvae enter the blood stream by penetrating the intestinal wall. They travel through the body, eventually burrowing out of the lungs and proceeding up the windpipe to the throat. At this point they are swallowed and return to the intestine;

METHODS OF ARTIFICIAL RESPIRATION

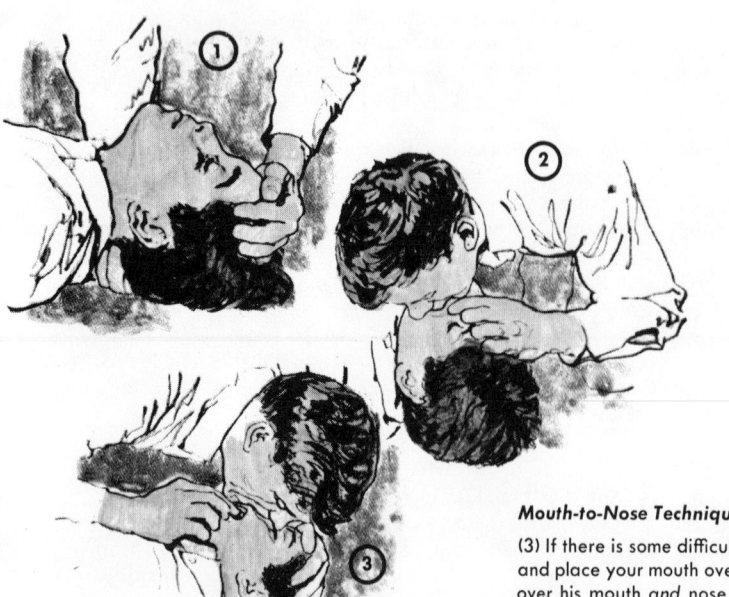

Mouth-to-Mouth Technique

(1) Clear the victim's mouth of foreign matter. Point the chin directly upward by lifting under the neck with one hand and tilting the head back with the other. Pull or push the jaw into a jutting position. These actions should clear the airway by moving the base of the tongue away from the back of the throat.

(2) Close the victim's nostrils with one hand. Open your mouth wide and place it tightly over the victim's mouth, forming as tight a seal as possible. After breathing into the victim, remove your mouth and listen for the return rush of air. For an adult, vigorous blowing at a rate of about 12 times a minute is required. For a child, gentle blowing at the rate of about 20 times a minute is called for.

Mouth-to-Nose Technique

(3) If there is some difficulty in getting air into the lungs, close the victim's mouth and place your mouth over his nose. With a small child, place your mouth tightly over his mouth *and* nose and blow shallow puffs of air at a rate of about 20 breaths per minute.

METHODS OF ARTIFICIAL RESPIRATION

Clearing Throat Obstructions

(1) If the victim's position is correct and air does not enter the lungs, something may be lodged in his throat. Quickly turn him on his side and slap him sharply between the shoulder blades. Return him to his back and continue artificial respiration.

(2) To clear the throat of a small child, suspend him briefly by the ankles and pat sharply between the shoulder blades.

(3) A larger child may be inverted over one arm and patted between the shoulder blades.

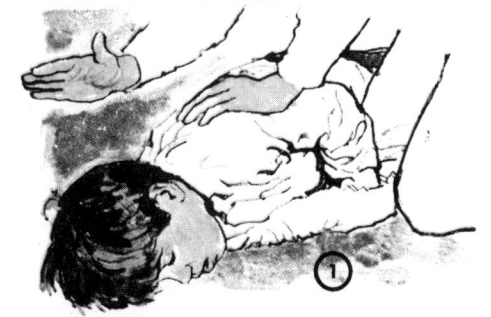

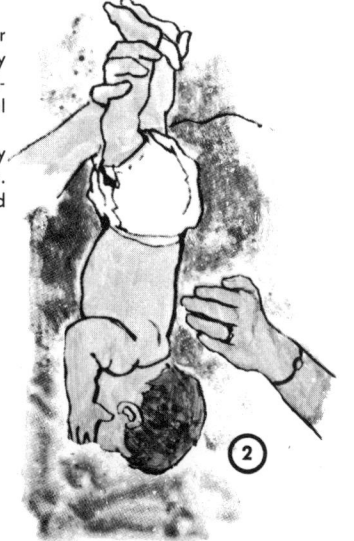

(ARTIST: MILLER POPE)

there they grow to adulthood. The female worm, which reaches 14 in. in length, deposits her eggs in the intestine. These eggs pass out of the body in the feces. They can survive for months in moist soil.

The symptoms of ascariasis are numerous and depend on the number and location of the worms. Infestations frequently go unnoticed. The larval invasions of the lungs may produce a pneumonialike illness. In the intestine the worms may cause vague abdominal discomfort, vomiting, diarrhea, appendicitis, and perforation of the intestine. The worms secrete poisons that can attack the nervous system, and, in cases of severe infestation, nervousness, convulsions, delirium, and coma may result. The condition can be cured by several excellent drugs; chief among these are the piperazine compounds.

ASCITES [ə-sī′-tēz], accumulation of large amounts of fluid in the abdomen. It occurs most frequently in certain types of heart, liver, and kidney ailments.
See also EDEMA.

ASPERGILLOSIS [ə-spûr-jə-lō′sĭs], fungus disease that may attack the skin, ear, nose, lungs, and other parts of the body. Infection of the lungs may occur among fur cleaners and certain agricultural workers who are exposed to the spores of the fungus.

ASPHYXIATION [ăs-fĭk-sē-ā′shən], disturbance of breathing in which there is a deficiency of oxygen and an excess of carbon dioxide in the body. Asphyxiation should be distinguished from anoxia, in which there is simply an oxygen deficit and the carbon dioxide concentration in the blood remains normal.

Obstruction of the airways (larynx, trachea and bronchi) may be a cause of asphyxiation. Obstruction may occur during diphtheria, when a membrane forms across the larynx; from other infections of the larynx; or from a foreign body lodged in an air tube. Certain lung diseases, such as pneumonia, may cause asphyxia by interfering with the normal exchange of oxygen and carbon dioxide between the air in the lungs and the circulating blood. Asphyxia may also result from disorders of the nerves and muscles used in breathing. Poliomyelitis may damage the nerves that supply the breathing muscles. Patients suffering from this disease may require an iron lung to breathe for them. Birth damage to the breathing center of the brain may produce asphyxia neonatorum (asphyxia of the newborn).

The symptoms of asphyxia include irregular breathing, bluish tinting of the skin (cyanosis) caused by lack of oxygen, stupor, convulsions, and various mental effects. The treatment of asphyxia depends upon the cause.
See also ANOXIA.

ASPIRIN (acetylsalicylic acid), introduced into medicine in 1899 by Hermann Dreser in Germany, is widely used for the relief of fever, headache, pain, and arthritic complaints. Aspirin acts to lower body temperature by resetting the central nervous system's temperature-regulating center. It increases heat loss by increasing sweating and blood flow. By acting as a mild depressant on the central nervous system, aspirin relieves low-intensity pain. Its use does not lead to tolerance or addiction. The strong antirheumatic activity of aspirin has made it the preferred treatment of rheumatic fever, rheumatoid arthritis, and osteoarthritis. Although it relieves arthritic symptoms, aspirin is ineffective against the disease itself. It is readily absorbed from the stomach and intestines, reaching peak activity after two hours. Aspirin enters all the tissues, even crossing the placenta to the fetus.

Used in moderation, aspirin has few adverse side effects, but in children especially it can cause very rapid breathing and alter the body's acid-base balance. It may cause stomach upset and, rarely, bleeding from an ulcer.

ASTHMA

In very high doses, it causes salicylate poisoning. Candy-flavored children's aspirin has fatally poisoned small children who swallowed many tablets. An individual who is allergic to aspirin may react badly even to small doses of the drug.
See also ANALGESICS; SALICYLIC ACID.

ASTHMA [ăz'mə], difficulty in breathing. Allergic, or bronchial, asthma is caused by an abnormal sensitivity to certain substances or irritations. It may result from an allergy to substances that are inhaled (such as pollen and dust), eaten (such as milk, wheat, and chocolate), or injected (such as drugs and insect stings), or which come in contact with the skin. The individual may also be sensitive to organisms that infect the respiratory system. Asthma may appear at any age. Often several members of the same family are affected.

During an asthmatic attack, the air passages become narrowed by spasms of the muscles that encircle them. The linings of these passages swell with fluid, and a thick mucous secretion collects, making it difficult for air to enter or leave the lungs. Air is trapped in the smaller passageways, causing the chest to expand. The patient gasps for breath, wheezes, and coughs up a thick sputum. He may sit upright or lean forward in an effort to breathe more fully. The attacks usually subside within a few hours, but in some cases they may persist for days or weeks (status asthmaticus).

After the first allergic reaction, further attacks may be brought on by nonallergic irritations, such as drafts, excessive humidity, chemical fumes, or emotional disturbances. The attacks can be relieved by administering drugs such as epinephrine, aminophylline, or cortisone derivatives. To prevent recurrences it is necessary to discover and eliminate the substances and conditions that provoke the attacks. In cases where the individual is sensitive to materials that cannot be easily avoided, such as dust or pollens, it may be helpful to desensitize the patient by injecting increasing dosages of these substances over a period of time.
See also ALLERGY; HAY FEVER.

ASTIGMATISM [ə-stĭg'mə-tĭz-əm], inability to focus clearly all portions of horizontal, diagonal, or vertical lines. It results in a blurring of the visual image, headache, eye pain, and fatigue. The condition is caused by a difference in the ability of various sections of the eye to refract, or bend, light. Most cases of astigmatism are inherited and develop during the course of growth. The visual disturbances do not increase after the eye is fully grown. Minor degrees of astigmatism require no correction, but in more severe cases eyeglasses may be needed. Contact lenses are highly effective in correcting astigmatism.

ATABRINE [ăt'ə-brēn] (technically known as quinacrine hydrochloride), a yellow dye used in the treatment of malaria. It was developed in Germany in 1932 and was widely used by the American armed forces during World War II, when the supplies of quinine were cut off by the Japanese invasion of the Southwest Pacific.

The drug effectively controls malarial attacks but, in most cases, does not cure the disease. It is more effective and less dangerous than quinine but is inferior in all respects to chloroquine, which has largely superseded it. Atabrine has also been used with varying degrees of success in tapeworm and pinworm infestations.
See also CHLOROQUINE; MALARIA; QUININE.

ATAXIA [ə-tăk'sē-ə], a disturbance of muscular co-ordination in which the patient cannot properly control the movements of various parts of the body, such as the arms and legs, or the muscles used in speaking. Muscular coordination is regulated by the portion of the brain called the cerebellum. Ataxia can be produced by injury to or disease of the cerebellum or spinal cord. This may occur in multiple sclerosis, brain tumors, infections, and congenital disorders. A well-known type of ataxia, marked by a staggering gait, occurs in the third stage of syphilis, many years following the original infection.
See also TABES DORSALIS.

ATELECTASIS. See LUNGS, COLLAPSE OF THE.

ATHLETE'S FOOT, popular name for dermatophytosis or tinea pedis, a fungus infection of the skin of the feet. It appears most frequently in male adults but can be acquired at any age by persons of either sex. Although the condition is commonly considered contagious, the fungi that cause it are often present on the feet of persons who do not display any symptoms. Many authorities feel that athlete's foot results from a change in the condition of the skin, perhaps induced by excessive sweating, which permits a rapid growth of normally present fungi. The skin between the toes becomes scaly and fissured. Blisters may appear on the soles along with hard plaques of thickened skin. Itching is frequent. In some cases bacteria may enter the deeper tissues through the fissures, producing a serious infection of the leg.

The symptoms usually appear in warm weather and abate during the winter. Numerous medications containing fungicides and absorbent powders are helpful in controlling the severity of the attacks. Griseofulvin, an antibiotic drug taken by mouth, has proven effective in many cases.

ATP or ADENOSINE TRIPHOSPHATE an energy-rich substance essential for many of the body's metabolic func-

The New York skyline as seen by the astigmatic eye.

Ben Ross

tions. It is composed of one molecule of adenine (a ringed structure), one molecule of d-ribose (a sugar), and three molecules of phosphoric acid (an inorganic acid). Formed in virtually all cells and all tissues of the body, ATP serves as a source of high energy which can be converted into mechanical work (muscular contraction), building blocks of growth and repair (structural synthesis), or heat (maintenance of body temperature).

Energy transfer from ATP is accomplished by the removal of one molecule of phosphoric acid. The resulting low energy compound, adenosine diphosphate, (ADP), can be reconverted into ATP by energy derived from the breakdown of foods, or from body tissue such as fat or sugar stored in the liver and muscles as glycogen. Once used, ATP is re-formed rapidly by means of a stored high-energy phosphate compound, creatine phosphate.

ATP can be considered the energy messenger of the body. It is present every time a muscle contracts, a sugar molecule enters a cell from the blood, or a nerve impulse is sent from the brain. All body cells maintain the proper concentration of salts, such as sodium, potassium, chloride, calcium, and phosphate, by the action of ATP at the cell surface membrane.
See also MUSCLE.

ATROPINE [ăt′rə-pēn], a drug that acts upon the brain and nervous system. Atropine and its sister drug scopolamine constitute the active agents of the belladonna plant (deadly nightshade). Atropine stimulates breathing and in high dosages causes restlessness, irritability, and hallucinations. While stimulating some parts of the brain it seems to depress others.

AUDITORY or ACOUSTIC NERVE, eighth cranial nerve. It arises from a portion of the base of the brain, called the pons, and divides into two parts in the ear. One part serves the sense of hearing; the other extends to the semicircular canals of the ear that help the body to maintain balance when standing and walking.
See also CRANIAL NERVES.

AUREOMYCIN [ô-rē-ō-mī′sĭn], antibiotic drug chemically related to terramycin and achromycin, and known technically as chlortetracycline. Aureomycin is effective in the treatment of a wide variety of diseases caused by bacteria, protozoa, and certain large viruses and viruslike organisms. The use of the drug may cause loss of appetite, nausea, vomiting, diarrhea, and fungus growths. Since the development of newer antibiotics, aureomycin is rarely used in human medicine; however, veterinarians use it in the treatment of animal infections and as a feed additive to stimulate the growth of cattle.
See also ANTIBIOTICS.

AUTISM [ô′tĭz-əm], the tendency to see the world in terms of one's own needs and wishes. An example of autistic thinking may be seen in the fantasies of children, who populate their world with imaginary creatures and objects. Autism in adults, when carried to extremes, becomes the type familiarly seen in mental illness. The mental patient who thinks he is Napoleon, and expects deference from others, is distorting reality in terms of his own desires. Autism in mental disease is most frequently associated with schizophrenia.
See also SCHIZOPHRENIA.

AUTOPSY [ô′tŏp-sē] **or POST-MORTEM,** the medical examination of a body after death. Normally, permission for an autopsy is granted by a surviving relative. However, in cases where a crime is suspected, an investigating authority (usually the coroner) can order an autopsy. In the course of the examination small samples of body tissue are removed to be studied under the microscope in order to determine the cause of death. This procedure is important in enabling the physician to confirm his diagnosis and in helping to understand the tissue changes produced by disease and injury.

B

BACILLUS [bə-sĭl′əs], term applied loosely to all rod-shaped bacteria and more specifically to the rod-shaped bacteria belonging to the genus *Bacillus*. Members of the genus *Bacillus* produce within the cell specialized reproductive bodies (spores) that can survive prolonged boiling and other unfavorable conditions. Anthrax, a serious disease of domestic animals and occasionally of man, is caused by *B. anthracis*. Another bacillus, *B. thuringensis*, which is poisonous to some insects, has been used for destroying insect pests. Some species produce antibiotic substances such as subtilin, gramicidin, bacitracin, and the polymyxins that have found a limited use in human and veterinary medicine.
See also BACTERIA.

BACKACHE. See LUMBAGO.

BACTERIA [băk-tēr′ē-ə], primitive microscopic organisms belonging to the lowest division of the plant kingdom. Bacteria are widely distributed in nature, beng found in soil, air, water, and on plants and animals. They exist in environments where few other life forms can maintain

BACTERIA

themselves, such as in hot springs where the temperature reaches 180° F., in the Antarctic Ocean, and in deep oceanic waters where they live under pressures of thousands of pounds per square inch.

These microorganisms play an extremely important role with respect to other living organisms and the cycle of organic processes on earth. They decompose and putrefy dead organisms, making the organic materials available for use by other living things; they are also responsible for many plant and animal diseases.

Bacteriologists recognize more than 100 separate classes of bacteria and classify them according to a variety of criteria, such as form and structure, nature of growth, site where found in nature, the different types of stains that are taken up by the organisms, the way in which they can be grown or prepared, the chemical variation they bring about, and the diseases that they cause.

When viewed under an ordinary microscope, bacteria generally do not show much detail. It is customary to stain them to make the specific cell structures visible. Two of these staining techniques are also used to classify bacteria: the Gram and the acid-fast stains.

The Gram stain divides bacteria into two general classes, Gram positive and Gram negative, which differ distinctly in terms of physiology and shape. For example, all of the bacteria which have a whiplike process (flagella) at one one end are Gram negative.

Acid-fast stains are of considerable importance in identifying the mycobacteria (the causative agent of tuberculosis) and other closely related forms. The presence of acid-fast staining organisms in the sputum of suspected cases is accepted as proof of tuberculosis.

The ability of bacteria to grow under various conditions also forms an important basis of classification. Aerobic bacteria are completely dependent upon oxygen for growth. Strict anaerobic bacteria cannot grow in the presence of even minute quantities of oxygen. Other bacteria are unaffected by the presence or absence of oxygen.

Bacteria can also be grouped in terms of their ability to grow in the absence of complex organic compounds and on the basis of their ability to use inorganic compounds, such as hydrogen sulfide, as food.

Reproduction of Bacteria

Most bacteria reproduce by binary fission, a process in which the organism splits into two new cells. The splitting occurs from every 20 minutes to every 24 hours. One can calculate that a bacterial cell that can split every 20 minutes could produce about 24,000,000,000,000,000,000,000,000 tons of cells (4,000 times the mass of the earth) after 48 hours of continuous growth. Actually, of course, this rapid rate of growth is maintained only for a short period while conditions are ideal. A colony of bacterial cells quickly limits its own growth by consuming the available food supply and by secreting waste products that hamper further growth.

Other forms of reproduction among bacteria include the formation of specialized reproductive bodies (such as spores), and processes that closely resemble the sexual reproduction seen in higher life forms.

For many years it was thought that bacteria inherited their traits from the parent organism by mechanisms that differed from those found in higher life forms. This has now been shown to be not true. The principles of genetics formulated by Gregor Mendel and Thomas Hunt Morgan have been demonstrated to apply to bacteria. In fact, many geneticists have turned to bacteria as a tool for studying the manner in which different traits are passed from parent to offspring. The advantages of studying bacteria are clear when one considers that one bacterial generation appears every 20 minutes as compared to one human generation every 20 or 30 years.

Bacteria and the Cycle of Life

Bacteria and Carbon Dioxide. Life on earth is maintained by the steady input of energy from the sun. Green plants utilize this energy to convert carbon dioxide from the air into organic compounds. These compounds furnish the energy for other forms of life, including man.

In order to maintain this cycle, the elements that go into making the organic compounds must be converted to carbon dioxide again. The larger part of this conversion is achieved through the action of microorganisms, which in this way play an essential role in maintaining the flow of organic materials through the cycle of life.

Bacteria and Nitrogen. All plant life is dependent upon nitrogen. It is estimated that the total nitrogen content of an acre of soil is about 150 lb., whereas the air that overlies each acre contains about 35,000 tons of nitrogen. Plant growth would exhaust the nitrogen content of the soil in a relatively short time were it not for the presence of soil bacteria that are capable of binding nitrogen from the atmosphere into organic compounds that can be readily utilized by plants. Soil bacteria require moisture and warmth for luxuriant growth. The farmer, who is often a good practical bacteriologist, can recognize suitable pastures on the basis of their ability to support bacteria.

In addition to carbon dioxide and nitrogen, other elements, such as sulfur and phosphorus, are kept in a process of cyclic exchange by bacteria.

The Biological Relationships of Bacteria

Bacteria often enter into the cycle of life and other biological phenomena by establishing characteristic living arrangements with other forms of life. Whereas most bacteria are found in soil and water, many establish themselves in special environments such as the bodies of living plants and animals. In such relationships, the bacteria are quite specific in their choice of plant or animal. They may be useful to the host organism (symbionts or mutualists), harmless (commensals), or harmful (pathogens).

An excellent example of bacteria that are useful to the host organism can be seen in cattle, sheep, and goats. These grazing animals are dependent upon plants as their chief source of food. Since the animals cannot digest the cellulose found in plants, they would perish were it not for the presence of cellulose-digesting bacteria in their intestinal tract. Louis Pasteur once commented on the importance of such animal-bacteria relationships by predicting that if young animals were raised in a strictly germfree environment they would not be able to survive.

Harmless (commensal) bacteria occur on plants and animals. The intestine, mouth, skin, and sexual organs of

BACTERIA

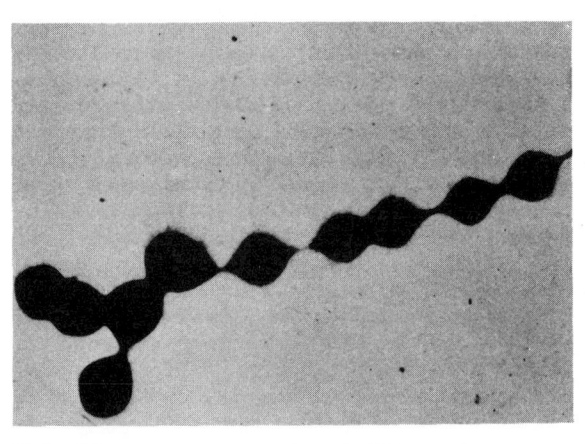

Chain of *Streptococcus pyogenes* bacteria. This organism is a common inhabitant of the throat but may invade other tissues, causing skin and eye infections or blood poisoning.

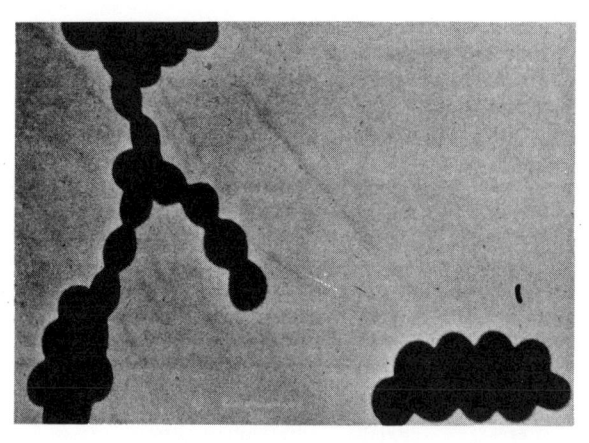

Grapelike clusters of *Staphylococcus* bacteria are normally present on the skin and may cause wound infections or boils.

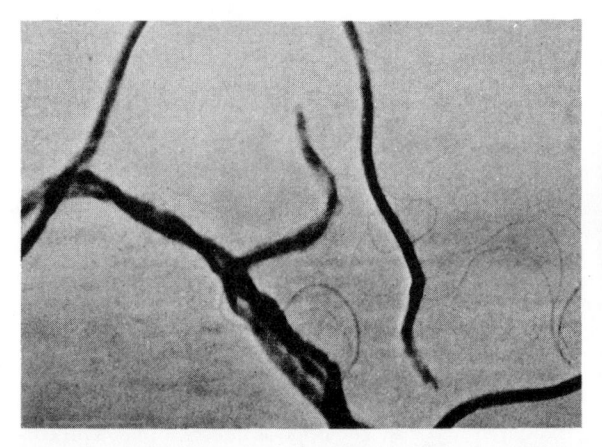

Treponema pallidum, the spiral, threadlike organism responsible for syphilis, may invade almost any tissue of the body.

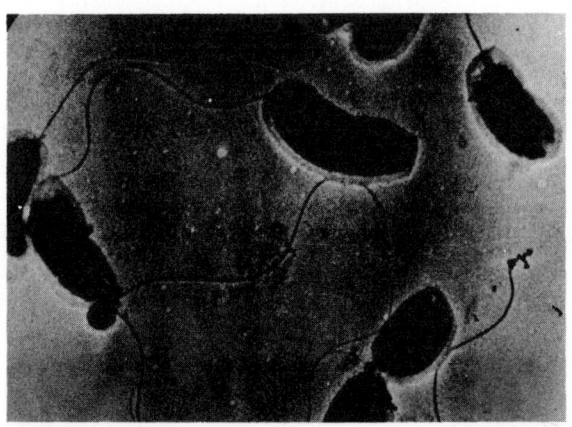

Vibrio comma (cholera bacteria), showing the whiplike process (flagellum) at one end. These organisms secrete a toxin that irritates the intestinal wall, causing a profuse diarrhea.

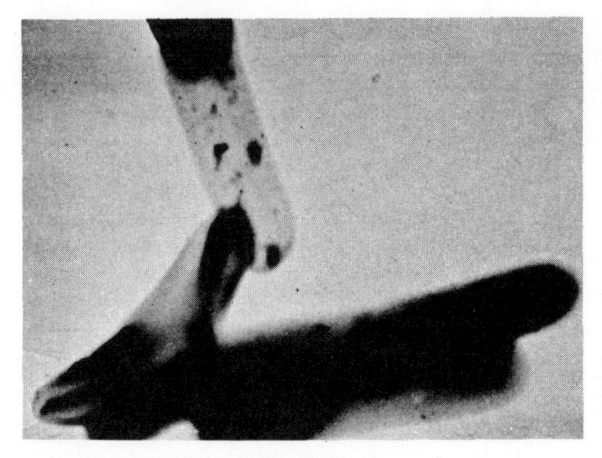

Clostridium tetani (tetanus bacteria). The large, dark spores at the ends of the cells may survive for long periods in soil. The spores can germinate in wounds where they may liberate the toxin that produces the symptoms of tetanus.

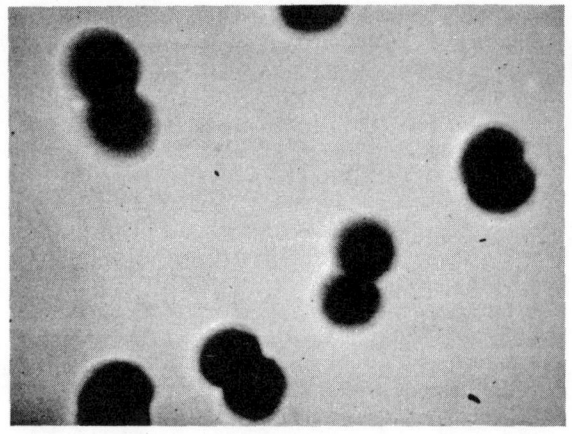

Various stages of division in gonorrhea bacteria. These organisms infect mankind only and are particularly troublesome because they do not stimulate the body to produce immunity.

Photos this page—Society of American Bacteriologists

man are habitats of a great variety of bacteria that are essentially harmless and, in some cases, beneficial.

Commercial Uses of Bacteria

Bacteria are important in the production of cheese, butter, yoghurt, sour cream, sauerkraut, pickles, and vinegar. They are used to process linen (see RETTING) and to soften animal hides. Certain antibiotic drugs are obtained from bacteria, and the important industrial solvents, acetone and butyl alcohol, are produced by bacterial fermentations.

Bacterial Diseases

To man, undoubtedly the most significant attribute of bacteria is their ability to cause disease. Few events in the history of mankind have been as devastating as the Black Death, or bubonic plague, which swept through Europe in the 14th century, killing approximately 25 million people. In the 19th and 20th centuries, physicians have identified a host of ailments as being caused by bacteria, including syphilis, typhoid fever, diphtheria, scarlet fever, and many others.

Exposure to pathogenic (disease-producing) bacteria does not guarantee that disease will result. This depends upon the particular bacteria involved, the number of organisms that enter the body, and the ability of the body to fight the infection (immunity). Some bacteria are everyday inhabitants of the skin and the intestinal tract. As long as they remain confined to these places they are harmless; however, should they gain entrance to other parts of the body they are capable of producing serious diseases. Thus, infections of the kidneys (pyelonephritis) or bladder (cystitis) are caused by bacteria that have escaped from the intestinal tract.

Bacteria are transmitted in a number of ways. Pneumonia bacteria are carried through the air on small droplets of moisture that result from sneezing and coughing. The victim inhales the contaminated material into his own lungs. Gonorrhea is spread by direct sexual contact and may also be passed from an infected mother to the eyes of her newborn child during the passage of the infant through the birth canal. The organisms that produce typhoid fever, dysentery, and cholera are found in the feces of persons suffering from the disease. The feces may be carried to food by insects or by food handlers. The bacteria that cause undulant fever (brucellosis) infect the udders of cows and find their way into milk. If the contaminated milk is not pasteurized it may spread the disease to human beings.

Bacteria may produce the symptoms of disease through the effects of bacterial poisons (toxins). These substances may be secreted by the bacteria (exotoxins) or be built into the structure of the bacterial cell (endotoxins). The endotoxins are liberated only upon the death of the cell.

Food poisoning results from the activity of bacteria that secrete exotoxins. The staphylococcus bacteria (which also produce boils) grow luxuriantly in creamed foods, producing tasteless exotoxins. In one to six hours following a meal of contaminated food, the poison produces nausea and vomiting. One of the most powerful poisons known to man is an exotoxin produced by the *Clostridium botulinum*. This bacteria grows only in the absence of air, and an excellent breeding place is provided by improperly canned foods, especially those canned at home.

Exotoxins are also secreted by the organisms which cause tetanus (lockjaw), diphtheria, and scarlet fever. The tetanus organisms, like the botulinum bacteria, do not grow well in the presence of air. They usually enter the body through deep puncture wounds, such as those inflicted by rusty nails. They thrive, free from the harmful effects of air, in the deep, narrow cavity created by the wound and secrete an exotoxin that produces the muscular spasms characteristic of lockjaw. These organisms are found in soils throughout the world. Diphtheria bacteria (*Corynebacterium diphtheria*) cause the formation of a membrane that may block the main air passageway to the lungs, resulting in suffocation. The bacteria also excrete a powerful exotoxin that frequently damages the heart and the nervous system. Scarlet fever is produced by streptococci that usually first attack the throat.

Endotoxins are released into the body upon disintegration of the bacterial cell. Toxins of this type are characteristic of the bacteria that infect the intestinal tract. The severe diarrhea and shock of cholera and dysentery are caused by endotoxins that irritate the intestine. Typhoid-fever bacteria (*Salmonella typhi*) release an endotoxin that causes an extremely high fever.

Bacteria are selective in the parts of the body that they choose to invade. The staphylococci infect the skin, producing boils and acne. The streptococci attack the throat. Tuberculosis and pneumonia are caused by organisms that settle in the lungs. Meningitis, an infection of the tissues surrounding the brain, is caused by various organisms, including the meningococcus, pneumococcus, streptococcus, and staphylococcus. In many cases bacteria enter the blood stream at the point of their first entrance into the body. This is most common in the case of the staphylococcus. The original infection may be a boil, from which point the bacteria invade the blood stream, producing bacteremia, or, as it is commonly known, blood poisoning. This may occur in many diseases, including tuberculosis, gonorrhea, and typhoid fever. Bacteremia is accompanied by high fever and chills. The bacteria may use the blood stream as a jumping-off point to enter other organs, such as the liver, spleen, or brain.

In earlier times little could be done to treat or prevent bacterial diseases. Today, diseases such as diphtheria, tetanus, and typhoid can be prevented by immunization, and many other bacterial diseases can be treated by antibiotic drugs. Most deaths from bacterial infections are now caused by organisms that have become resistant to the action of antibiotics.

See also MICROBIOLOGY.

BACTERIAL ENDOCARDITIS [ĕn-dō-kär-dī′tĭs], bacterial infection of the lining of the heart, particularly of the heart valves. Bacterial endocarditis usually appears in individuals who have previously had rheumatic or congenital heart disease. The bacteria, which may be any of a number of different kinds, settle on the scarred heart valves where they multiply, forming friable masses which may break off and travel through the blood stream, eventually lodging in, and obstructing small blood vessels, or giving rise to abscesses in various organs. The bacterial growths may deform the heart valves. The acute form of bacterial endocarditis may develop as a complication of pneumonia, gonorrhea, or other infectious conditions. In subacute cases the origin of the infection is not apparent.

Typically, weakness, fatigue, lack of appetite, joint pains and fever develop gradually over a period of weeks or months. Small painful nodules may appear on the pads of the fingers and toes and disappear within a few days. Small hemorrhagic spots may develop on the skin, in the eyes, or under the fingernails and toenails. The spleen may be slightly enlarged. Heart murmurs and anemia are usually present. If left untreated, acute bacterial endocarditis may be fatal within a few months.

Treatment is with antibiotic drugs and depends upon the proper identification of the infecting bacteria. Penicillin-resistant organisms may be responsible in some cases and require special selection of antibiotics.

BACTERIOPHAGES [băk-tēr'ē-ō-fāj-īz], viruses that infect bacteria. They consist of a core of deoxyribonucleic acid (one of the compounds that make up the heredity units of living cells) and an outer coat of protein. In many types the outer coat is organized into a head that contains the deoxyribonucleic acid and a tail that is used to fasten onto the bacteria. After the virus attaches itself to a bacterium, the nucleic acid enters the bacterial cell and the protein coat is left outside. Two kinds of infection may result:

(1) The virus may reproduce itself in the cell, eventually destroying the bacterium and liberating the virus.

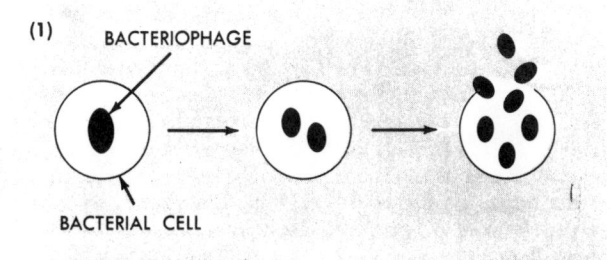

(2) The virus may become part of the genetic material of the bacterial cell and not reproduce, a condition called lysogeny. Some generations later the latent virus may change into the active form and reproduce as in (1).

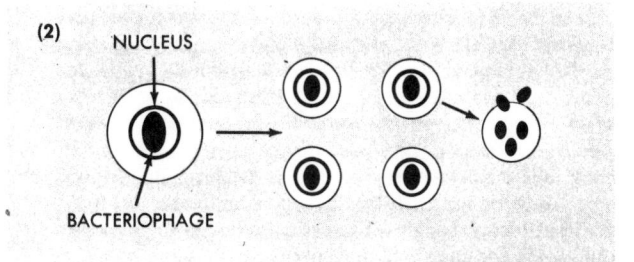

The bacteriophages may retain some of the genes from their host and pass them on by infecting other bacteria. This process is called transduction. The most detailed information on virus and cell interactions has come from bacteriophage studies.

See also BACTERIA; MICROBIOLOGY; VIRUSES.

BALDNESS, complete or partial loss of the hair of the scalp. It may develop as an inherited tendency, or be caused by disease or injury. The hair loss frequently follows distinctive patterns. In men over 20, the hairline may recede and a bald spot may appear at the top of the head. In baldness present from birth (congenital baldness), the hair loss is usually complete. Congenital baldness is frequently associated with other defects, such as abnormal or absent teeth, or an inability to sweat.

Causes of Baldness. Baldness may result from scarring of the skin by chemicals (acids or alkalis), overexposure to X rays, severe sunburn, or electric burns. It may follow certain skin diseases. Baldness from exposure to radiation was observed in many survivors of the atomic explosions in Japan. Certain bacterial, viral, and fungus diseases can also lead to scarring and baldness. These include syphilis, tuberculosis, and leprosy.

Baldness without scarring of the skin may follow or accompany high fevers and infections. Thallium, arsenic, and quinine can cause loss of hair. Improper functioning of the glands, as occurs occasionally in menstrual disorders, may be accompanied by baldness. In cases of baldness without scarring, the hair usually regrows once the underlying disturbance is corrected. Long-standing cases of dandruff may result in baldness. When substances (amino acids and proteins) necessary for growth of hair are absent from the diet, loss of hair may result. A deficiency or an excess of vitamin A can also cause baldness.

Treatment. Many cases of baldness—such as the congenital forms, those arising from scarring of the skin, or from an inherited tendency to lose the hair—cannot be treated successfully. Baldness that develops from certain infections, fevers, and glandular disorders can be treated by correcting the underlying disorder. Most cases of spotty baldness are temporary; the hair usually grows back within three to six months.

BALLISTOCARDIOGRAPH [bə-lĭs'tō-kär'dē-ə-grăf], device that records body movements that result from the beating of the heart. The contraction of the heart induces motion in the body in the same manner as the recoil of a rifle jolts the body of the rifleman. This motion is amplified and recorded by the ballistocardiograph. Although the fluctuations in the record of the ballistocardiograph seem to be clearly associated with the phases of the heartbeat, its usefulness in the diagnosis of heart disease has not yet been firmly established.

See also HEART.

BARBER'S ITCH, infection of the hairs of the bearded area of the face by bacteria or fungi. The infection may produce pus pimples, boils, or large boggy abscesses. In severe cases scarring of the face may result. Treatment consists of hot compresses, skin lotions, X rays, and internal medications.

BARBITURATES [bär-bĭch'ə-rĭts, bär-bĭ-tūr'ĭts], group of drugs used principally as sedatives and to induce sleep.

BARTHOLIN

The first barbiturate (Veronal, or barbital) was synthesized in 1903. Since then over 2,500 barbiturates have been prepared and clinically studied, and about 50 have been placed on the market.

The barbiturates produce their effects by depressing the activity of the brain and spinal cord. The individual drugs differ in the duration of their action. The effects of the longer-acting drugs, such as phenobarbital, may last for over six hours, while the action of the shorter-acting drugs, such as pentobarbital, may last for less than three hours. Comparatively small doses are used for sedation in cases of anxiety, nervousness, and hyperthyroidism. Larger doses are given to induce sleep. Patients who have difficulty in falling asleep are given short-acting barbiturates, while those who tend to wake repeatedly during the night may be given the longer-acting type. Barbiturates are often given before surgery, and are occasionally used to produce anesthesia. Psychiatrists have employed these drugs to produce a state of deep sedation and relaxation in which a variety of neurotic conditions can be diagnosed and treated (narcoanalysis).

Barbiturates tend to augment the action of certain pain-relieving drugs (analgesics), and are included in some commercial preparations for this purpose.

A serious addiction can develop from the unsupervised use of barbiturates. Acute barbiturate poisoning has occurred accidentally, but has more frequently resulted from attempts at suicide. As a consequence of the potential danger of their use, many states have passed laws forbidding the retail sale of barbiturates without a prescription.

BARTHOLIN [bär-tōō'lĭn], **THOMAS** (1616–1680), Danish physician, considered the greatest anatomist of his time. He was physician to the King of Denmark, and taught anatomy and mathematics at the University of Copenhagen. He is noted for research on the lymphatic system.

BARTON, CLARA (CLARISSA HARLOW) (1821–1912), founder of the American Red Cross. She began her career as a teacher and later went to Washington, D.C.; where she worked as a clerk in the Patent Office. When the Civil War began, she was impressed with the stories of the suffering, caused in part by the lack of medical supplies. She advertised in the Worcester *Spy* for provisions for the wounded and the response was immediate. Although she had no official capacity, she was able to obtain permission to transport supplies through the lines. For four years after the war, she was in charge of the search for missing men. During the Franco-Prussian War (1870–71) she assisted in setting up military hospitals and worked with the International Red Cross. In 1881 the American Red Cross was organized, and she served as its first president. From that time until 1904, when she resigned, she was active in Red Cross work in all parts of the world. Her works include *History of the Red Cross* (1882), *The Red Cross in Peace and War* (1898), and *A Story of the Red Cross* (1904).

BASAL METABOLIC RATE (BMR), measure of the over-all body-energy output at rest and in the fasting state. It is particularly useful in the diagnosis of thyroid disorders. Specifically, it is a measure of the heat given off per square meter of body surface per hour; it is determined by measuring the amount of oxygen consumed within a given period and is usually expressed as a percentage above or below the averate rate for the patient's age group and sex. A normal BMR is within about 15% of this average. When the thyroid gland is overactive (hyperthyroidism), the rate may be as much as 85% above normal; when the gland is underactive (as in myxedema), the rate may be as much as 40% below normal. Other conditions, however, also produce an abnormal BMR. For example, marked anxiety, leukemia, heart failure, and fever raise the rate; certain pituitary disorders, starvation, and Addison's disease lower it. The test requires great technical skill and considerable patient co-operation. It is falling into disuse, yielding to newer methods of detecting thyroid disturbances.

See also METABOLISM; RESPIRATION.

BATHS, MEDICINAL, form of therapy generally used to apply heat or cold to the body, or used for the specific effect of chemicals dissolved in the bath solution (medicated baths).

Hot and Cold Baths. Since mud retains heat well and distributes it evenly to the skin, mud baths have long been used to apply heat to the body. Paraffin baths were first used in France in the early part of the 20th century. They are especially effective for applying heat to the limbs. A hand or foot is plunged into a mixture of melted paraffin and mineral oil and quickly withdrawn, permitting a layer of congealed paraffin to form. This is repeated until the part is coated by a thick glove of paraffin. The paraffin glove is kept on for approximately 20 minutes, during which time the skin and deeper structures are uniformly heated. The whirlpool bath combines heat and gentle massage by using a stream of rapidly circulating, warm water. This technique was pioneered by the French in World War I and is particularly effective for cleansing wounds and burns and for softening scar tissue. The paraffin, mud, and whirlpool baths are used to treat arthritis and rheumatic disorders, and to relieve muscle spasm and pain. They cannot be used on persons who suffer from

Charles Phelps Cushing
Clara Barton, from a 19th-century engraving by John Sartain.

poor circulation or from impairment of skin sensation.

The sitz bath may be used to apply heat or cold to the body. In this technique the lower half of the body is immersed in water. A hot sitz bath may help relieve the pains of menstrual disorders or hemorrhoids. A cold sitz bath may increase the blood supply to the organs of the abdomen and benefit some forms of constipation and pelvic disturbances.

Medicated Baths. Of possible value in rheumatic conditions are salt or brine baths, which increase skin circulation and sweating. Bland baths, consisting of starch, borax, or boric acid solutions, are used in skin conditions to relieve itching and inflammation. Mustard baths irritate the skin, increasing the circulation in deeper tissues and relieving rheumatic pains and muscle spasms. Sulfur baths are mildly antiseptic and are used for some skin ailments. Carbon dioxide or gas baths were used for centuries at European spas, such as Bad Nauheim in Germany. The stimulant effect obtained from the liberation of minute bubbles of CO_2 on the skin is claimed to be of some value in the treatment of menstrual disorders, obesity, and insomnia.

BCG VACCINE, a vaccine of live but weakened tuberculosis bacteria, used to immunize against tuberculosis. BCG, which stands for Bacillus Calmette-Guérin may provide some protection for persons who have not been previously exposed to the infection. A principal disadvantage of the vaccine is that it interferes with the tuberculin test, which is used to detect the presence of active tuberculosis infection. The BCG vaccine has been widely used in the Soviet Union and among certain Indian tribes in the western United States.
See also TUBERCULOSIS.

BEADLE [bē′d′l], **GEORGE WELLS** (1903–), American geneticist educated at the University of Nebraska and Cornell University. He has taught at Stanford and Harvard universities, and at the California Institute of Technology. In 1958 he was awarded the Nobel Prize in physiology and medicine for experiments which showed that mutations of the breadmold, *Neurospora crassa*, have altered nutritional requirements, thereby demonstrating that specific enzymatic reactions are controlled by specific genes. In 1961 Beadle became Chancellor of the University of Chicago.

BEDBUG, small, wingless insect of the genus *Cimex*, having a flattened body and a characteristic unpleasant odor. *C. lectularius*, the common bedbug, lives in mattresses or the cracks of furniture, walls, and floors, and is a pest to man. They inflict painful bites, and may be the carriers of certain infectious diseases. Other species of bedbug parasitize small mammals and birds. Tularemia, a bacterial disease affecting rabbits, is known to be transmitted by bedbugs. Although they breed at the rate of two to four generations a year, and have been known to survive for more than a year without food, bedbugs may be easily controlled by thorough spraying of infested areas.

BEDLAM (ST. MARY OF BETHLEHEM HOSPITAL), the first institution for the mentally ill erected in England. Inmates are believed to have been accepted at the end of the 14th century. In the course of time this institution became notorious for its brutality toward the insane. Until around 1770 patients were kept in chains and irons, and visitors were permitted to obtain amusement from their antics. The term "bedlam" subsequently became associated with any scene of general disorder and confusion and as such has become part of the English language.

BEDSORES or DECUBITUS ULCERS, open sores caused by the breakdown of skin in areas on which pressure is exerted. Bedsores often occur in the elderly, or in paralyzed patients who must lie for long periods in the same position. They are caused by a combination of poor blood circulation and the further reduction of circulation produced by local pressure. Bedsores appear first where the body's weight is greatest in reclining—heels, buttocks, elbows, and shoulders. Once started, the ulcers usually become infected as a result of moisture from perspiration, decreased air circulation, and rough bed linens.

The best treatment for bedsores is prevention. Bedridden elderly or paralyzed patients should be frequently turned and regularly bathed. The skin should be kept dry by powder, gentle heat, and adequate ventilation. Cushioning the pressure points with lamb's wool cloth is a standard preventive measure. Once bedsores form, they may be treated by changing the position so that the sores do not touch the bed and by rigorous cleansing to remove bacteria. Applied heat will improve circulation and reduce moisture. Antiseptic powder should also be used.

BED-WETTING or ENURESIS, the involuntary passage of urine during sleep by individuals who are beyond the age when control should have been established. Some children may have voluntary control of urination after 18 months of age, but most achieve full control by the age of 4. Bed-wetting may persist from childhood or follow an interval of successful training. Physical causes are sometimes responsible, but the vast majority of cases result from emotional disturbances. Too early or too vigorous toilet training may produce frustration and guilt, and urination may become the focus of a power struggle between parent and child. Night control is often unsuccessful and the child uses bed-wetting to express his hostility toward his parents.

Enuresis that develops after control has been established is viewed as a return to an earlier mode of dealing with problems. This may be brought on by situations that threaten the security of the child, such as moving to a new home, the birth of a brother or sister, separation from the parents, or efforts to stop thumb-sucking.

Treatment is directed at establishing a secure parent-child relationship in which understanding replaces punishment. Encouraging urination prior to retiring and restricting the consumption of water may help. If bed-wetting persists and is accompanied by other symptoms a psychiatrist should be consulted.

BEHRING [bā′rĭng], **EMIL ADOLF VON** (1854–1917), German physician who received the Nobel Prize in 1901 for his pioneer work in immunology. Working with Shibasaburo Kitasato, he produced the first antitoxin to counteract diphtheria. He also developed an antitoxin against tetanus. In 1894 he became professor at Halle, and the following year was appointed director of the hygienic laboratory at Marburg, where he gained an international reputation for his contributions to immunology.

BEKHTEREV [byāкн'tyĭ-ryəf], **VLADIMIR MIKHAILOVICH** (1857–1927), Russian physiologist and neurologist. His work on reflexes was the basis for a theory of all human behavior which he called "reflexology." His system reduced all psychological processes to physiological terms through the use of the conditioned response. This point of view, supported by clinical and experimental research, brought him acknowledgment from American experimental psychologists of the behaviorist school. He founded an institute in St. Petersburg (1907) for psychophysiological research. His books include *General Principles of Human Reflexology* (1904) and *Objective Psychology* (1913).

BELL, SIR CHARLES (1774–1842), Scottish surgeon, anatomist, and physiologist, known for his work on the nervous system and his description of paralysis of the facial nerve (Bell's Palsy). He wrote a score of books including a famous treatise on the anatomy of the brain, which remains unrivaled for accuracy and elegance.

BELLADONNA [bĕl-ə-dŏn'ə], herbaceous plant, *Atropa belladonna*, native to the Old World from southern Europe to India. It is also appropriately called "deadly nightshade" for its bell-shaped flowers that ripen into highly poisonous purple berries. Belladonna is not widely grown as an ornamental plant, but is cultivated for the medicinal preparations made from its leaves and roots. Atropine, the most important belladonna derivative, is used to relieve pain and muscle spasm, and also in eye examinations, where it has the action of dilating the pupil.

BELL'S PALSY, a paralysis of one side of the face produced by swelling and degeneration of the nerve that supplies the muscles of the face. The cause is unknown. The paralysis develops suddenly, producing a flattening of the features on one side of the face. Speech becomes muffled, eating is hampered, and the patient is unable to whistle. The eye on the affected side waters excessively and cannot be closed. In some cases, taste sensation may be lost in parts of the tongue. There is no specific cure for Bell's Palsy, but most patients afflicted with the disorder eventually recover completely.

BENZEDRINE [bĕn'zə-drēn] **or AMPHETAMINE,** drug with potent stimulatory effects on both the central nervous system and the peripheral (sympathetic) nerve network. Because at one time it was marketed as an ingredient of nasal inhalants, available without prescription, it has been subjected to much abuse by thrill-seekers and drug addicts. Amphetamine and the related compounds dextro amphetamine (Dexedrine) and methamphetamine cause nervousness, alertness, a temporary sensation of elation, and a false sense of increased ability at such tasks as arithmetic, writing, and memorizing. By objective tests, the individual's performance is usually below his best while the drug's influence lasts. Physiologically, it increases pulse rate, blood pressure, and excitability.

It is used by physicians to treat coma resulting from an overdose of sedatives and in certain forms of epilepsy (narcolepsy). Amphetamine is also used to decrease appetite in weight-reduction programs. Appetite loss probably results from dulling the sense of taste and smell and by central brain action. Continued use of the drug may cause true addiction. A few doses can produce feelings of fatigue without the ability to sleep. After frequent repeated doses, severe weight loss, irritability, agitation, tremors, and hallucinations often occur.

Amphetamine addiction is a serious illness. Withdrawal of the drug has severe effects on the brain, cardiovascular system, and peripheral nerves. Its continued use must be considered as serious as narcotic addiction.

BERIBERI [bĕr'ē-bĕr'ē], disease caused by a deficiency of vitamin B_1 (thiamine). In the Orient beriberi usually arises from an inadequate diet. It was widespread in the Japanese navy in the late 19th century, until the Japanese physician Kanehiro Takaki substituted barley, which contains vitamin B_1, in place of polished rice, which had been the principal food in the sailors' diet. In Western countries the disease develops more frequently in circumstances requiring an increased amount of thiamine, such as in pregnancy, nursing, or fever. Chronic alcoholics frequently suffer from a severe thiamine deficiency.

Beriberi occurs in three major forms:

Dry beriberi. The symptoms involve chiefly the nervous system. Parts of the skin become insensitive and certain reflexes are lost. There is a rapid wasting away of the muscles, first of the legs and then of the arms. Eventually the mentality of the patient is affected.

Wet beriberi. The outstanding symptom is edema, a collection of fluid in the tissues, which resembles the type frequently seen in heart failure. The muscles waste away, but this is obscured by the generalized swelling of the body.

Fulminating beriberi. The heart is affected. Palpitations, rapid pulse, difficulty in breathing, and lowered blood pressure commonly occur. The patient may die suddenly without any warning symptoms.

The three forms of the disease are not always distinct; patients often display the symptoms characteristic of two or more types. Beriberi may also develop in infants, particularly in children suckled by mothers who suffer from the disease. Beriberi is treated by administration of large doses of vitamin B_1.

See also VITAMINS.

BERNARD [bĕr-nàr'], **CLAUDE** (1813–78), French physiologist, noted not only for specific discoveries, but also for generalizing concepts influential in physiology and medicine. Trained first in a Jesuit college and later at the Collège de France, he held positions in the Collège de France, the Sorbonne, and at the Museum of Natural History in Paris. He demonstrated the digestive actions of pancreatic fluid, the function of the liver in storing blood sugar and releasing it again to the blood by what he called internal secretion, and the vasomotor functions of the nervous system. His views that no matter what the guiding principles of vital processes may be, these processes must be investigated and described in physicochemical terms in the laboratory, were influential in establishing physiology as an experimental laboratory science.

BERTILLON [bûr′tĭ-lŏn, bər-tĭl′yən] **MEASUREMENTS**, system of measurements devised in 1882 by a French physician, Alphonse Bertillon, for the purpose of identifying criminals. The system is divided into three parts: (1) precise measurement of bodily dimensions; (2) observation of characteristic bodily movements, physical behavior patterns, and mental and moral qualities; and (3) observation of peculiarities of the body surface, such as moles, scars, tattoo marks, missing limbs, and deformities. Most police departments have discarded the system as a means of absolute identification in favor of fingerprinting, a technique perfected during the 1890's. Nevertheless, Bertillon's methods are still used by investigators as the best scheme for providing a minutely accurate verbal description of a person.

BERYLLIOSIS [bə-rĭl-ē-ō′sĭs], or beryllium poisoning, results from inhalation of, or contact with, fumes or dusts of beryllium salts and alloys. Workers involved in the casting of beryllium alloys and in the extraction of beryllium from its ores may be exposed. Contact with beryllium may cause irritation of the eyes and skin. Of more concern, however, is damage to the lungs caused by inhalation of beryllium dust. Coughing and shortness of breath are frequent symptoms. The victim may suffer from lack of appetite, weakness, and weight loss. In severe cases, bed rest and oxygen therapy are necessary. Striking benefit has been achieved in some cases by the use of ACTH and cortisone and its derivatives.

BEST, CHARLES HERBERT (1899–   ), Canadian physiologist, best known for his work with Sir Frederick Banting in the latter's Nobel Prize-winning discovery of insulin. In 1941 he was appointed Head of the Banting and Best Department of Medical Research at the University of Toronto. With N. B. Taylor he wrote the widely used medical text, *The Physiological Basis of Medical Practice* (1937).

BIBLIOTHERAPY, therapeutic aid in treatment of illness, through the use of books. Hospitalized persons often resort to reading as an escape from boredom or to forget their ailments. This is a simple type of bibliotherapy, which may even take the form of storytelling for children. Bibliotherapy for emotionally disturbed or mentally ill persons consists of organized reading programs, planned by librarians and psychiatrists, followed by a discussion of the books read, and applications by the patients of ideas found in those books.

BICEPS [bī′sĕps], any muscle having two heads or origins, especially the biceps brachii, located on the front of the upper arm, and the biceps femoris, found on the rear and side of the thigh. The principal action of these muscles is to flex the limb with which they are associated.

BILE, a greenish-yellow fluid secreted by the liver. It is stored in the gall bladder and released into the small intestine. Bile is essential for the absorption of fats and certain vitamins. The ancients gave bile an exalted position in medicine. A major theory used to explain nearly all types of disease was based on the changing color of bile in the gall bladder. They believed that bile was able to poison specific organs of the body.

Bile is composed of a mixture of chemicals of which only one, bile salts, has an important function. The others are waste products. The bile salts are secreted by the liver and remain for some time in the gall bladder. There they are concentrated by the removal of water. Then they enter the small intestine, where they join with various fats (lipids) and make them soluble, to be digested and absorbed by the body. Bile salts function in the intestine to dissolve greases and allow their removal with water. The most common disease involving bile is the blockage of its secretion by the formation of gallstones, which are solidified bile. They may cause pain, fever, and jaundice, an accumulation in the blood of one of the bile chemicals, bilirubin.

See also GALL BLADDER; JAUNDICE; LIVER.

BINET [bē-nā′], **ALFRED** (1857–1911), French psychologist, author of the first standard measure of intelligence. His work embraced personality study, research with gifted and mentally deficient children, and investigation of the reasoning and thinking processes of children and adults. In 1905 the French government asked him to devise a method of detecting children incapable of school learning. Collaborating with Théodore Simon, he produced the Binet-Simon Test of Intelligence, which consisted of tests arranged in age levels from three to twelve. A score called "mental age" was earned according to how many test levels a child passed. A revision of this test, the Stanford Revision of the Binet-Simon Scale, achieved wide use in the United States.

See also INTELLIGENCE; INTELLIGENCE QUOTIENT.

BIOCHEMISTRY [bī-ō-kĕm′ĭs-trē], the study of the chemistry of living organisms. This study seeks to understand the chemical properties of the substances found in biological materials, the chemical changes which take place in living organisms, and the role which these substances and chemical changes play in living things. The importance of biochemistry springs from the fact that all manifestations of life, such as growth, movement, responses to changes in environment, reproduction, disease, and even the behavior of higher organisms, have a material, that is, chemical, basis and are accompanied by chemical processes. By studying the chemical basis the biochemist helps to elucidate many of the great problems of biology and its applied branches, the medical and agricultural sciences.

History. The development of biochemistry has been linked to the history of chemistry. In the 1770's and 1780's the discovery of oxygen and the discovery of the chemical nature of carbon dioxide and water led to the understanding that respiration in living organisms is, chemically speaking, a combustion. The idea that the substances contained in living organisms could only be produced by living things was shattered in 1828, when the German chemist Friedrich Wöhler demonstrated that urea could be synthesized in the laboratory. Prior to this time it was

BIOCHEMISTRY

widely thought that many chemical activities in living cells were inseparably linked to the intact living structures and that "vital" forces, not accessible to chemical analysis, were behind these activities. In 1897 the German bacteriologist Hans Büchner discovered that the fermentative power of yeast could be extracted from living cells and brought into solution. The 19th-century French physiologist, Claude Bernard advanced the view that chemical substances in living cells obey the same laws as they do in the test tube. It is now universally accepted that this view is correct. It has formed the foundation of modern biology and has encouraged biochemists to tackle the most complex problems, such as the chemical basis of brain function and the mechanism by which chemical substances transmit inherited characteristics.

Emergence of Biochemistry as a Separate Discipline. There are two major reasons why biochemistry branched off from chemistry as an independent subject. The first is connected with the subject matter and the kind of questions scientists ask when they design experiments; while chemistry establishes the chemical properties of substances, biochemistry poses the further question of what role the substances play in the life of the cell. The second reason arises from the need for special techniques. Biochemistry uses most of the tools of chemistry, but in addition it has developed techniques adapted to the special peculiarities of biological materials. Many biological substances are relatively unstable. Proteins, for example, are partially destroyed ("denatured") by exposure to temperatures above 140° F. and by strong acid or alkali. Moreover, the quantities in which biochemical substances are available may be minute, and it is often of great importance to know exactly their amounts. Biochemists have therefore developed microanalytical procedures of many kinds; fractionation techniques (chromatography, electrophoresis, and ultracentrifugation), which separate substances having similar chemical properties; methods for handling cells and tissues after removal from the organism so as to preserve their biochemical properties; centrifugation techniques which separate the various cell components, such as nuclei and mitochondria, without damaging them; and last but not least the use of isotopic tracers.

Constituents of Living Things. Quantitatively, the principal substances found in, and characteristic of, biological materials are the proteins, carbohydrates, fatlike substances (lipids), and nucleic acids. In addition there is a host of other substances occurring in smaller, often minute, quantities but of decisive importance nevertheless to the functioning of the organism. To these belong the porphyrin pigments (found in green plants as chlorophyll), the steroids, and a variety of different substances which play a special role in the structure of the enzymes, which catalyze, or promote, chemical reactions. All of these substances occur in every type of living organism. Plants possess additional groups of substances, the most important of which are the lignins, a characteristic component of wood.

Apart from these organic substances, all cells and tissues contain inorganic salts, consisting chiefly of potassium, sodium, calcium, magnesium, chloride, phosphate, and bicarbonate. Iron, manganese, copper, zinc, cobalt, molybdenum, selenium, iodine, and sulfate occur in smaller quantities.

The proteins are the chief organic material of most animal tissues. Muscle, skin, connective tissue, and hair all contain distinctive proteins.

Carbohydrates, such as sugars and starches, serve mainly as an energy source for living tissues. In plants, carbohydrates in the form of cellulose provide much of the structural skeleton of the cells. Many invertebrates form another structural carbohydrate derivative, chitin, which is found in the shells of crabs and the outer coating of insects. Higher animals also use carbohydrate derivatives as building materials, especially in cartilage (chondroitin sulfate) and in mucus (mucopolysaccharides). Lipids serve either as structural material or provide energy by undergoing combustion. Nucleic acids are the carriers of genetic information and control the synthesis of proteins.

Enzymology. What distinguishes above all the chemistry of living organisms from that of lifeless substances is the presence in the living cells of special substances called enzymes. The enzymes promote and direct chemical reactions in a highly specific and unique manner. Each enzyme as a rule catalyzes one reaction or one type of reaction. This means that, in the long sequences of reactions which occur during the breakdown of foodstuffs and the synthesis of cell constituents, a series of many enzymes is required. The substance which the enzyme causes to react is called the "substrate." It is true that the chemist also makes use of catalysts in the laboratory and in industrial processes, but his catalysts are much less specific and often require either high temperatures or other conditions which are incompatible with life, such as high concentrations, strong alkalinity, or strong acidity. Because of the key position of the enzymes much biochemical research is concerned with the study of their structure and the mechanism of their action.

All enzymes are proteins. Some contain a nonprotein component which often is the reactive part, or "prosthetic group," of the enzyme molecule. In some instances the prosthetic group is one of the B-vitamins (which accounts for the physiological importance of these vitamins); in others it is a heavy metal, such as iron, copper, or zinc. The prosthetic group alone usually has no appreciable catalytic properties. These properties depend on the protein molecule to which the prosthetic group is attached. Those enzymes which possess no nonprotein component owe their characteristic properties largely to an "active center." This is the site which combines with, and acts upon, the substrates; it is distinguished by a specific spatial arrangement of the amino acids which make up the enzyme.

Energy Production in the Cell. The cell obtains its energy either from oxygen-consuming reactions, in which foodstuffs are converted into carbon dioxide and water, or from fermentations, which do not use oxygen and which convert sugars to smaller molecules, such as lactic acid, ethanol, butyric acid, butanol, acetic acid, and other products, including carbon dioxide. The energy obtained from these reactions is used for various kinds of work, such as mechanical work, or movement, in muscle; osmotic work (moving substances from solutions of lower to solutions of higher concentration) in secreting glands or in the intestine when it absorbs digested food; generating electricity in nervous tissue; or performing chemical syntheses in glands or in growing cells.

Chemical Synthesis in the Cell. Other chemical reactions are those leading to the synthesis of enzymes, hormones, tissue proteins, and other cell constituents. One of the most important reactions of living organisms is the synthesis of starch in green plants. Using the energy of light, plants form starch from carbon dioxide and water, a process known as photosynthesis. The balance of this reaction is

$$6CO_2 + 6H_2O \xrightarrow{light} C_6H_{12}O_6 \text{ (glucose)} + 6O_2$$

In certain pigmented bacteria a similar photosynthesis takes place with the production of water instead of gaseous oxygen. The primary photosynthetic process is the same in plants and bacteria:

$$6CO_2 + 6H_2O \xrightarrow{light} C_6H_{12}O_6 + 12O$$

In plants, however, the oxygen atoms form molecular oxygen:

$$12O \longrightarrow 6O_2$$

Whereas in bacteria they combine with hydrogen to form water:

$$12O + 12H_2 \text{ (or } 24H) \longrightarrow 12H_2O$$

Hormones. Many tissues in animals, especially the endocrine glands and cells, produce hormones, substances which in small quantities influence the function of other tissues. Examples are insulin, produced by the islet cells of the pancreas, the thyroid hormones, the sex hormones, epinephrine (adrenalin), and a variety of hormones produced by the pituitary gland, located on the undersurface of the brain. Plants produce hormones which influence cell division and cell elongation. They control the formation of plant tissues, flower and fruit formation, and many other activities. Hormones are an important link in the mechanisms which regulate cell activities, and co-ordinate them in such a way that the organism functions as an integrated whole. How hormones exert their action is not fully known. Some directly affect the activity of enzymes, either stimulating or inhibiting them. Several hormones are proteins, such as insulin. Others are polypeptides (those produced by the pituitary gland), steroids (sex hormones and adrenal cortex hormones), or derivatives of amino acids (thyroid hormone, epinephrine, and some plant hormones). Because of their powerful action, hormones are of great medical and agricultural interest.

The Special Biochemistry of Cells and Tissues. The basic chemical constituents and reactions described here are common to most types of cells and tissues, but the specialized cells of the higher organisms all have particular biochemical features which are related to their function. Thus the liver produces bile, and as the main chemical laboratory of the animal body, it synthesizes many substances, such as steroids, fats, purines, and pyrimidines. The distinctive feature of muscle tissue is its ability to convert chemical energy into movement. The kidney and other glands select substances from the blood and secrete them. The wall of the gastrointestinal tract manufactures, and secretes, digestive enzymes and mucus, and absorbs the digested food. All these processes are accompanied by special chemical reactions. This is also true of the activities of the brain. Thought and emotions, and therefore behavior, depend on chemical activities in the higher centers of the brain. The nature of these activities and the questions of how they can be artificially influenced are of the greatest interest, and successful beginnings have been made in the study of brain biochemistry and its relation to brain function. A number of substances, such as lysergic acid and reserpine, are known to modify the function of the higher brain centers. The elucidation of the mechanism of their action promises to throw light on the problem of the material basis of brain function.

Biochemical Genetics. An important area of biochemical research concerns the mechanism of transmission of hereditary, or genetic, information. It is now known that the deoxynucleic acids (DNA) carry this information, and that they are the main constitutents of the hereditary units, the genes. DNA contains four different nitrogenous bases—adenine, guanine, thymine, and cytosine—which are linked to special sugar phosphates, deoxyribosephosphate. The latter in turn are linked together to form the skeleton of large molecules. The four nitrogenous bases attached to this skeleton form the letters, as it were, of the language, or code, of genetical information. The sequence in which the units are arranged in the long-chain molecule determines the nature of the information. This is analogous to the sequence of the letters of the alphabet in a meaningful sentence, or to the transcription of such a sentence to the Morse Code; while the alphabet uses 26 physical shapes, the "language" of the genes employs four different chemical substances as elementary units. The primary information contained in the DNA molecules concerns the synthesis of protein molecules. In other words the DNA of genes controls protein synthesis, including the synthesis of all enzymes. The enzymes in turn control all other chemical processes, and as chemical events form the basis of all manifestations of life, the genes may be said to control the course of life through their role in enzyme manufacture.

Practical Applications of Biochemistry. Biochemical knowledge bears on many problems of medicine, veterinary science, agriculture, forestry, and a variety of industries. Medical and veterinary biochemistry assists in the diagnosis of disease by providing information on the chemical composition of the body fluids, such as blood and urine. It aids in the assessment of the effectiveness of treatment and can throw light on the nature of diseases. Agricultural biochemistry studies problems connected with pest control, plant diseases, weed control, fertilizers, soil fertility, and the composition of food rations for farm animals. Foremost among the industries which make use of biochemical knowledge are the pharmaceutical industries; the fermentation industries, including the manufacture of beer, wine, and antibiotics; and many branches of the food industries, including milling, baking, and the storing, preserving, and packing of food. Other industries which present biochemical problems are those dealing with the utilization of biological materials, such as wool, hides, tobacco, plant fibers, and natural dyes. The preparation of enzymes from biological materials for use in

BIOLOGICAL CLOCKS

medicine and in industry is now also an industrial process.

This brief survey should make clear that biochemical thought has gradually penetrated all branches of pure and applied biology. Biologists are becoming more and more biochemically oriented. This is a natural historical development. Early biologists observed, dissected, and described living organisms, as seen with the naked eye.

From the macroscopic scale biologists proceeded to the microscopic one when suitable instruments became available, but still remained mainly descriptive. With the advent of biochemistry the dissection, as it were, of the structure of living matter became finer and reached the molecular, that is, the chemical level. Biologists now "dissect" living organisms with the tools of chemistry and physics. These are tools which provide much more than a description of life. They analyze its nature, and help man to understand how the machinery of living cells works.

BIOLOGICAL CLOCKS, the means by which living things can time the major rhythmic periods in their physical environment, even in the absence of all the obvious external cues. Biological clocks play many useful roles for living creatures. They are widespread, perhaps everywhere present, among plants, animals, and micro-organisms.

The unicellular alga, *Gonyaulax*, luminesces only at night; leaves of bean seedlings droop at night and rise by day; cockroaches, mice, and rats forage actively at night and hide by day; fiddler crabs are dark during the day and pale at night; and man himself has a daily rhythm of wakefulness and sleep. Even when such usually varying factors as light, temperature, and humidity, which normally signal the onset of day are held constant, the organisms' rhythmic behavior continues much as before.

Man also has many other 24-hour rhythms. These include nervous and endocrine activities, liver and kidney functions, blood composition, and body temperature. Disruption of this complex of rhythms when man moves rapidly to a new time zone results in the well-known "jet-syndrome." The readjustment requires several days.

Periods of activity of fiddler crabs are timed to their uncovering by ebbing tides. Removed from their tidal habitat they continue to time their activity by a tidal clock, running about 50 minutes later each day. A comparable tidal clock operates also for a shore-inhabiting diatom.

Biological clocks also play other roles. Employing them enables animals to navigate using the sun and moon as geographic references. These clocks measure the changing lengths of day and night to inform organisms of the time of year.

The useful, clock-timed rhythmic patterns are usually modifiable. The onset of such rhythmic activity can be adjusted to different times of day by altering the times that lights are turned on and off. Animals can be trained to seek food at specific times of day and crabs or mussels will gradually readjust their tidal activity patterns when translocated to a different beach. This may be compared to resetting the hands or alarm while the clock continues running uninterruptedly.

Theory. Biological clocks are remarkable for their continuing timing precision and dependability in spite of experimental attempts through temperature changes and metabolic inhibitors to slow or speed them. Their nature remains unknown. There are two likely theories. An "endogenous" school postulates that living systems contain inherited, physico-chemical clocks, able independently to time the environmental periods. An "exogenous" school, recognizing that living systems are sensitive to very weak physical fields such as the earth's electromagnetic field, postulates that the clocks comprise a continuing response to these environmental rhythms.

BIOLOGICAL WARFARE, also referred to as germ warfare or bacteriological warfare, is the deliberate employment by the military of living organisms, toxic biological products, or chemical plant-growth regulators to produce death or casualties through disease in man, animals, or crops. The term also includes any defensive measures taken against such action. Biological attacks are primarily directed against man and his food supply, although transport animals and nonedible plants may also serve as targets. The modern agents used to spread epidemic disease are pathogenic organisms or their biological products, known as toxins. Plant hormones or growth regulators, such as those employed in weed control, do not fall into these categories but are usually grouped with them because of their similar tactical uses in warfare.

In ancient conflicts, attempts were made to induce disease among the enemy by exposing him to the bodies of cholera and plague victims and by poisoning the sources of his water supply. In the New World, traders and military units sometimes distributed smallpox-contaminated blankets among the warlike Indian tribes. Early in World War I, the Germans infected horses with glanders disease, thus striking at Allied cavalry and draft animals. In World War II, allegations were made, but never substantiated, that Japanese troops used biological agents against the Chinese.

In Mar., 1952, during the Korean War, the Chinese Communists charged that the United Nations forces, and particularly those of the United States, were disseminating disease-producing agents in North Korea. This accusation was unequivocally denied by representatives of both the United States and the United Nations. During the late 1960's, U.S. forces in Vietnam employed defoliants, usually by spraying from planes, to clear heavily forested areas believed to conceal enemy troop and supply installations. Defoliants also were used to strip away leaves and brush along communication routes to protect U.S. convoys.

Biological warfare has had no major impact on military campaigns in the 20th century. It remains a potential weapon, and certain nations with adequate scientific facilities continue to experiment with biological weapons. Such agents could be employed in warfare to affect enemy troop movement and deployment and to lower civilian efficiency and productivity in enemy countries. By attempting to control nature for military ends, however, biological warfare threatens to permanently unbalance ecological forces presently in equilibrium.

BIOLOGY [bī-ŏl′ə-jē] is the science that deals with life: plant, animal, and human. As used today, the term refers to a unified group of life sciences dealing with development, growth, metabolism, response, reproduction, evolution, and interrelations of all living things. The term "biology" (Gr. *bios,* "life"; *logos,* "discourse") was coined by the German biologist Gottfried Treviranus (1776–1837) and given widespread usage by the French biologist Lamarck (1744–1829). Long before the term existed, however, man had been acquiring biological knowledge, urged on by insatiable curiosity about himself and the living world of which he was a part, as well as by a need for practical information about edible and poisonous plants, and dangerous and useful animals. In this sense biology is quite old, and includes knowledge gained in primitive hunting and fishing and from ancient practices in agriculture and medicine. Before such knowledge could become a science, it had to be organized, subjected to the criteria of the scientific method, and reduced to fundamental generalizations, or laws. In this sense, biology is a young science whose major development has been within the last 300 years.

Biology, like other sciences, originated from a twofold urge: to understand nature and to make use of nature. The former has as its aim the discovery of fundamental truths; basic research accomplishes this objective. The latter, the practical aspects, are the province of applied research which turns the fundamental knowledge acquired in biology to man's use, as in agriculture, medicine, and industrial biology. Basic and applied research merge into one another so imperceptibly that it is often impossible to tell where one ends and the other begins. In the same way, a biologist may be a "basic-research" man, studying whatever his curiosity may lead him to; an "applied-research" man with a specific practical objective to guide him in his investigations; or, as is most often the case, a combination of the two. Thus an entomologist may study the respiratory system of insects, in order to understand how they breathe, and at the same time experiment with an insecticide, to see how it kills insects by interfering with their respiratory mechanism.

Organization of Biological Knowledge

As man developed an understanding of the fundamental laws of the living world, the various biological sciences that began as separate fields of knowledge became welded into the unified science of biology, based on principles and concepts that hold true for all forms of life from sea urchins to man, from seaweeds to sequoias. Today there are at least 100,000 professional biologists (50,000 in the United States alone) who devote some or all their time to finding out what life is and how it functions. Because of the tremendous scope of the subject, individual biologists must concentrate on a small area within the field. Such specialization has led to the division of biology into many subsciences, organized along two main paths: one group of biosciences emphasizes the kind of life under investigation; the other group, the aspect of life being studied.

The Life Sciences. Based on the kind of life studied, the biosciences can be arranged in three smaller groups: those that deal with plants, those concerned with animal life, and those that study plants and animals sharing the same environment. The first group includes botany and its allied fields. "Botany" is the traditional term for general plant biology, applied today mainly to the study of higher plants: the herbs, shrubs, and trees that make up the spermatophytes, or seed plants. Botanists often specialize further, especially in areas related to forestry and agriculture; they may carry on research with trees (dendrology); with garden or crop plants (horticulture); or with an even smaller group of cultivated plants such as fruit trees (pomology). The study of the lower plants, or thallophytes, comprises several additional plant sciences. Algology concerns itself with algae. It is a field of increasing importance, since these aquatic plants are being investigated as a source of food for space travelers. Bacteriology is the study of colorless microscopic plants, the bacteria, knowledge of which is basic to studies of human and animal disease. Mycology is the study of mushrooms and other fungi, including the molds. The latter have recently become important as a source of antibiotics.

The second group of biosciences includes zoology and its allied fields. "Zoology" is the traditional term for general animal biology, comparable to the word "botany," as used for plant life. A zoologist today usually confines his attention to one segment of the animal world, often to a single phylum or class of animals. Protozoology is the study of unicellular animals, or protozoa. This bioscience provides us with information as to how single-celled life can exist, and what the most primitive forms of animal life may have been. Entomology, the study of insects, is a large field, engaging the attention of many researchers because of the tremendous number of insects and their economic importance to man. A number of zoological sciences deal with individual classes of vertebrates: ichthyology is the study of fishes; herpetology, the study of amphibians and reptiles; ornithology, the study of bird life; and mammalogy, the study of mammals.

A third group of biosciences, some of very recent origin, deals with both plants and animals in a specific environment or with common living habits. Microbiology is the study of microorganisms such as bacteria, molds, protozoa, and small invertebrate animals. Parasitology is the study of organisms that live as parasites in or on other organisms. Like bacteriology, parasitology is closely allied to veterinary and medical research. Limnology is the study of fresh-water organisms (chiefly algae, invertebrates, and fish) and their aquatic environment. Oceanography and marine biology are comparable fields, dealing with ocean plants and animals, and with factors of the marine environment. These studies are growing in importance as man depends more and more upon the sea for his food. Certain biosciences do not fit into this artificial organization; among them is virology, the study of viruses, which are living things without the cellular organization of higher forms of life.

There are many biosciences that deal with structure, function, development, inheritance, and interrelations of organisms. One of the oldest biosciences is anatomy. It deals with the gross structure of organisms and organs, most of which are visible to the unaided eye. Histology is concerned with the minute structure of tissues and their cell components. Cytology penetrates even further into the secrets of life by concentrating on the structure of the cell. Histology and cytology depend upon the microscope as a tool, and hence had to wait for its invention before investigations in this field could be made. In each of these biosciences the investigator usually specializes further by studying a particular kind of organism; thus there is plant anatomy, animal anatomy, and human anatomy.

BIOLOGISTS AT WORK

Biology, the science of living organisms, is divided into two main branches—zoology, the study of animals, and botany, the study of plants. Within each of these branches are many specialized areas of study relating to particular aspects of the development, structure, vital processes, and living habits of animals and plants.

Right, biologists measure a previously marked horseshoe crab to chart its rate of growth. (NAT. MESSIK—CARNEGIE INSTITUTION BIOLOGICAL STATION)
Below, a hospital technician examines a slide specimen through a microscope to aid a diagnosis. (ESTHER BUBLEY)

A guinea pig being examined during the course of research in a pathology laboratory. The laboratory room is kept sterile to prevent the experimental subjects from becoming infected with organisms other than those being studied. (THE UPJOHN COMPANY)

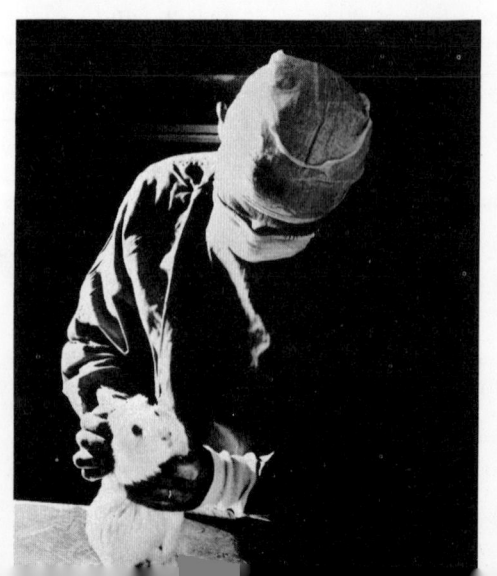

A pharmaceutical researcher observes and records data on a culture of bacteria. (USDA)

A technician examines a sample of antibiotic solution during a stage in its preparation. Sterile gloves, mask, and garments protect the worker and prevent contamination of the drug product. (CHARLES PFIZER CO., INC.)

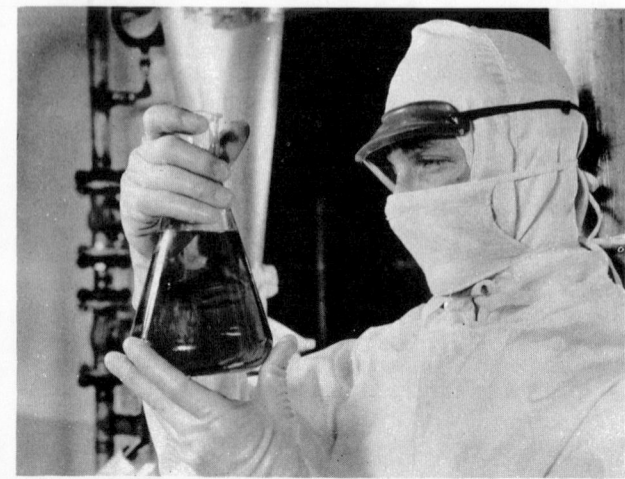

The functional aspects of life and the resulting activities performed by organisms make up the broad field of physiology. Here, too, there is specialization into plant physiology, animal physiology, and human physiology. Embryology is the study of the early development of the young organism, until it leaves the egg covering, or its mother's body.

Genetics deals with the structures and mechanisms governing the inheritance of traits. Human heredity and the breeding of new varieties of cultivated plants and domesticated animals are some of the practical areas into which genetics leads the biologist. The bioscience taxonomy is responsible for an orderly inventory of the entire living world; it deals with the classification of all species of plants and animals.

Ecology is a rapidly growing bioscience concerned with interrelations of organisms with each other and with their environment. Practical applications of ecology are numerous: conservation makes use of ecological research in wise use of our resources, and wildlife management improves our control of useful native species, especially game animals.

Other fields include endocrinology, the study of the endocrine glands and hormones, and pathology, the study of disease structures.

Biology holds an intermediate position between the physical sciences of chemistry, physics, and geology, and the social sciences. There are biosciences that overlap these areas. Much has been learned of the nature of life through biochemistry, the study of the chemical phenomena, such as digestion, respiration, and hormone production, which are basic to living activities. Similarly, through biophysics many physical phenomena associated with protoplasm and its functions have been explained. Paleontology and paleobotany, study animal and plant fossils and are subjects closely related to geology.

On another frontier of biology, many phases of human social relations have their roots in biological phenomena. Psychology deals with the mind and mental activities; these, in turn, are closely related to the anatomy and physiology of the nervous system. The physical basis of anthropology has roots in paleontology as well as in many aspects of human anatomy and physiology. In like fashion, many phases of sociology, such as population problems, are basically problems in human ecology.

Methods of Biological Research

Accurate and objective observation is the foundation of biology, as of all the other sciences. As long as observations were based on the unaided human senses, only gross anatomy and externally obvious functions could be studied. A milestone in the development of modern biology was the invention of the compound microscope, in about 1600. The invention of the electron microscope, in 1931, opened up new horizons at the ultramicroscopic levels of life. Many other biological tools have influenced the development of special fields in biology, among which are the microtome, with which extremely thin slices of tissues can be prepared for study; the calorimeter, which measures the energy content of foods; the electrocardiograph, which measures and records electric changes in the heartbeat; and the electroencephalograph, an instrument for detecting and recording brain waves. The use of radioisotopes as tracers in studying the movement of elements and compounds through plants and animals has added much to our fundamental physiological data.

Two approaches are used in biological study. One, which can be called field biology, studies living organisms in their natural environment. The present-day status of field biology has been attained through accurate observation, systematic organization of data, and conclusions based on interpretations of the data. Botany, mycology, ichthyology, herpetology, ornithology, mammalogy, and ecology are sciences which have achieved high status. A masterful example of the field approach was the worldwide collection of data by Charles Darwin while on the *Beagle*.

In the second approach, biologists study living organisms and their activities under controlled laboratory conditions. The experimental method has led to an increasing body of data relevant to physiology, genetics, and psychology. The combination of field study and laboratory experiment has given modern biology a comprehension of the fundamental laws that govern all life.

History of Biology

The story of biology can be briefly summarized in four stages: the primitive period, the classical period, the Renaissance, and the modern era.

The primitive period of biology was characterized by uncritical accumulation of information, mainly derived from the practical necessities of obtaining food, materials for clothing and shelter, substances to cure ailments, and necessary information about the human body. During this period, the haphazard accumulation of knowledge was not recorded, nor were the scientific method and its associated intellectual activities a part of the procedure in learning about life.

The classical period of biology began with the Greeks and continued with the Romans. It was marked by great curiosity about natural phenomena for their own sake and by an ability to organize biological knowledge and record it. The period began with the contributions of Hippocrates (c.460–377 B.C.), who is called the Father of Medicine. The most significant biological contributions, however, were made by Aristotle (384–322 B.C.), a philosopher and scientist who excelled in making careful observations and remarkably correct interpretations of what he saw. Three of his surviving works cover such broad topics as the nature of life, the natural history of animals, and the structure of animals. His pupil Theophrastus (c.372–c.287 B.C.) carried on pioneer studies of the nature of plants; his works are the most complete biological treatises to reach us from the classical period. After a lapse of several centuries, the Greek physician Galen (c.130–c.200 A.D.) began to study human anatomy and carried out the first physiological experiments on animals. After Galen a biological darkness enveloped all Europe, continuing for a thousand years. Biology in 1300 A.D. was little different from that of the Romans and Greeks.

The Renaissance in biology took place during the 14th to 16th centuries. It was part of a general revival of all learning. Curiosity about the structure of living things was rekindled by artists such as Leonardo da Vinci (1452–

1519) and Michelangelo (1475–1564), who made accurate studies in plant, animal, and human anatomy. In the 16th century, what might be called the first biology textbooks appeared, written by the German botanists Otto Brunfels (1489–1534) and Leonhard Fuchs (1501–66), and by the Swiss naturalist Konrad von Gesner (1516–65). Andreas Vesalius (1514–64) was a Belgian anatomist who published a voluminous text entitled *On the Structure of the Human Body*, significant in that its observations were based on direct study of human anatomy. A milestone in the developing science of physiology was the discovery of circulation of the blood by the English physician William Harvey (1578–1657). By the end of the Renaissance, anatomy, physiology, botany, and zoology were well established.

The introduction of the microscope at the beginning of the 17th century marked the start of modern biological investigation. A foundation of modern biology is the cell theory, the concept that the cell is the basic unit of structure and function. Chief among those who established this concept were the Englishman Robert Hooke (1635–1703), who discovered the cellular nature of cork and to whom we owe the term "cell"; and the team of botanist Matthias Schleiden (1804–81) and zoologist Theodor Schwann (1810–82). Anton van Leeuwenhoek (1632–1723) explored the invisible world of unicellular organisms, founding the sciences of protozoology and microbiology.

A fundamental concept of biology is that all life comes only from living things. The spontaneous origin of life from nonliving matter was experimentally disproved by Francesco Redi (c.1626–97) and by later experiments of Lazzaro Spallanzani (1729–99). Taxonomy had become a specialized science by the end of the Renaissance with the work of Andrea Cesalpino (1519–1603), and was continued with the studies of the Englishman John Ray (1627–1705). However, the systematic classification of all kinds of living plants and animals reached a climax in the brilliant work of the Swedish botanist Carolus Linnaeus (1707–78); he established the system of nomenclature in which all living things are arranged by genera and species.

The concept which has become the greatest unifying idea in biology is evolution: the descent of existing species from pre-existing ones by gradual changes and adaptations, rather than by special creation of each species in its present form. A hint of this concept appeared in the works of the ancient Greeks, and traces appeared in the writings of various biologists of the 17th and 18th centuries. In the early 19th century, Jean Baptiste Lamarck (1744–1829), outlined the so-called use and disuse theory of evolution, by which he tried to show that physical characteristics acquired during the life of an individual could be passed on to its offspring. Although experiments have since failed to uphold the theory and the facts of genetics give it no support, it became very popular and served to focus attention on the subject of organic evolution. Lamarck should be remembered as the first to publicize the term "biology" and to champion the new science as a comprehensive study of all organisms. But the outstanding contributor to the concept of evolution was Charles Darwin (1809–82), who proposed natural selection as an explanation of the mechanism by which evolutionary changes take place.

During the 19th century, fundamentals of many of the biosciences were crystallized. Louis Pasteur (1822–95) laid the foundations of modern bacteriology; Claude Bernard (1813–78) and Johannes Müller (1801–58) established experimental and comparative physiology; Karl von Baer (1792–1876) founded comparative embryology; Gregor Mendel (1822–84) initiated the study of genetics with his classic experiments on plants; and Hugo de Vries (1848–1935) formulated the mutation theory.

During the 20th century, many of the ideas of the past centuries were consolidated and refined, and new concepts have been added. The most significant of these were in genetics. The concept of the gene as the carrier of inherited traits was largely due to the American biologist Thomas Hunt Morgan (1866–1945), whose contributions in this field won him the Nobel Prize. H. J. Muller (1890–1967), also a Nobel Prize winner, was the first to show that mutations could be artificially induced by radiation. Two American biologists, George Beadle (1903–   ) and Edward Tatum (1909–   ), studying the relation between genes and metabolism, formulated the generalization that each biochemical reaction in an organism is controlled by a particular enzyme, which in turn is activated by a particular gene. In endocrinology, our knowledge of hormones was increased by the work of the British physiologist E. H. Starling (1866–1927). Ecology came into existence at the time of the German biologist Ernst Haeckel (1834–1919), who stated that an organism was the product of the interaction of its environment with heredity factors. Ecology was put on a modern basis by the American botanists H. C. Cowles (1869–1939) and F. E. Clements (1874–1945), and the American zoologist V. E. Shelford (1877–   ). Today, the generalization that all organisms living in a given area are closely interdependent with each other and with the environment is as unifying a biological concept as that of evolution.

See also:

ECOLOGY   LIFE
EVOLUTION   MEDICINE
GENETICS

BIOLOGY, MOLECULAR, had its origin in genetics and biochemistry and is often referred to as modern biology. Classical or descriptive biology is concerned with whole organisms or even species of plants and animals and their interrelationships. Molecular biology is particularly concerned with biological structure at the level of the molecule. Such a molecule is often large and complex and because of its structure is capable of storing information. Cells are able to retrieve this stored molecular information and convert it into meaningful biological functions, such as cell division, growth, or respiration.

Early biochemical genetic studies related genes to enzymes, those special proteins which serve as biological catalysts. For example, sugar may be converted in the cell to a variety of products, yielding in the process both energy and the carbon chain of the thousands of small molecules which make up living cells. Each of these small steps requires the presence of an enzyme. Each enzyme has a unique structure (sequence of amino acids) which reflects the unique structure of the genetic material which is DNA (deoxyribonucleic acid).

Nucleic Acids. DNA is probably the best known of all molecules in which information may be stored. This giant molecule directs the chemistry of all living things and is the one component of cells that must be transmitted to the new generation to maintain continuity. In it is encoded all the information necessary to produce, in an acceptable environment, a whole organism (even man), in all its complexity. DNA is, in a sense, a simple molecule which contains only four repeating chemical subunits. These subunits (bases) are arranged as two coiled molecular chains. It is the sequence of bases in each chain that provides a means of storage of genetic information. Molecular biologists have been investigating the transcription of this sequence into a similar sequence in RNA (ribonucleic acid), another giant molecule. It is this sequence that is in turn translated from RNA molecules into proteins that serve as structural components as well as for metabolic functions of cells.

DNA has the characteristics of a primary hereditary tape stored in the nucleus and chromosomes of the individual cells so that it might be protected as well as distributed in an orderly fashion to daughter cells. However, mistakes do occur in the replication of DNA and these lead to the heritable changes known as mutations.

RNA serves as a messenger molecule linking DNA and protein. It is (except for slight differences in the building blocks) a molecular mirror-image of one of the strands of DNA. It then has a sequence of bases reflecting the sequence of bases in DNA.

Genetic Code. In the language of the gene, each three bases of RNA translates into a single word which corresponds to one of the amino acid building blocks of proteins. The cell is able to "read" one word at a time along the chain and put together words (amino acids) into paragraphs (proteins) or even chapters (combinations of proteins). It is apparent that the sequence and combination of simple subunits is the means by which living organisms may store useful biological information. There are only four subunit bases in DNA, which will give 64 possible combinations (4x4x4) of three bases (codons). The genetic code then contains a corresponding number of words. There are only about 20 different amino acid subunits in proteins so all the possible words are not used. In fact, certain sets of bases are used as genetic punctuation. They serve to identify the beginning and end of genetic sentences, paragraphs and perhaps even chapters.

The replication of DNA in the test tube has long been the dream of molecular biologists and they have been successful in reproducing the DNA of one of the simpler viruses. Perhaps far more important than this achievement was the discovery that the cell is able to edit its own DNA to eliminate mistakes (mutations). It accomplishes this by cutting out one of the DNA strands and synthesizing a new strand to fill the gap. Thus, even when mutations occur they may be eliminated by genetic editing before the mistake is passed along to the next generation.

Living systems are far more complex than their simple components. Molecular biologists are increasingly concerned with the assembly and function of the subunits as the organism proceeds through the various developmental phases characteristic of each life cycle. Such studies include the complexities of memory and behavior as well as the many subtle responses of organisms to their environment, both physical and chemical.

See also BIOCHEMISTRY; CELL; GENETICS; NUCLEIC ACIDS.

BIOMEDICAL ENGINEERING, or simply bioengineering, is a field in which applications engineers, doctors, and biological researchers co-operate in the development of instruments and procedures necessary to treat the problems of living systems. There is no clear-cut discipline nor combination of disciplines which can be called biomedical engineering. Rather, the men and women working in this broad field are those who investigate problems whose solutions require the application of knowledge and techniques from both engineering and biology or medicine.

Great progress has been made in the field of biomedical engineering in the development of the artificial heart and kidney. Artificial kidneys have been used successfully to keep scores of otherwise hopeless patients alive for prolonged periods of time. Only a very limited success has been achieved with the use of the artificial heart but the device is being constantly refined in the light of ongoing research. Other life-saving biomedical instruments include a leg-implanted heart by-pass pump and electronic pacemakers now worn by more than 40,000 Americans to regulate their heartbeats.

Bioinstrumentation, however, is a very diversified field. Biomedical engineers have developed sensors for implantation deep under the skin for the purpose of recording the pulse, heartbeat, changes in blood chemistry, temperature, and muscular strain of animals and man. Telemetry equipment includes transmitters which can be totally implanted within an animal to relay information to en-

Machines like this blood synthesizer, and mechanical parts to replace no longer serviceable living parts, attest the genius of the biomedical engineer. (UPI)

BIONICS

cephalograms and other recording devices. Large backpacks and collars developed by bioengineers are used for tagging wild elk on the Wyoming ranges and similar telemetric devices permit satellite tracking of fish, turtles, waterfowl, and terrestrial animals. Lasers are being used almost routinely in eye operations to weld detached retinas, and laser canes are being developed to guide the blind. New prosthetics provide amputees with a broad range of sensory impulses and control impossible to achieve with traditional devices. Instruments employing infrared radiation and ultrasound for various diagnostic purposes are becoming standard medical equipment.

While burgeoning health-care needs have stimulated the development of a variety of biomedical instruments, America's space effort is credited for the recent expansion of the field. Bioengineers were called on to develop smaller and more sophisticated sensing and recording equipment for alerting earth-bound doctors to any critical changes in an astronaut's body chemistry. Many instruments developed for space activities are becoming commonplace in the nation's hospitals and research laboratories.

Under development are completely automatic screening centers for use by hospitals and large organizations such as the military service. These so-called multiphasic screening centers are designed to perform a battery of tests on patients, ranging from blood tests to cardiograms and urinalysis. Results of the tests will then be fed into computers to aid physician teams in the diagnosis of illness.

BIONICS, the study of phenomena found in living organisms and the application of the underlying biological principles to the design of engineering systems. Man has long tried to utilize abilities found in the animal world for his own purposes. Early human attempts to fly with birdlike wings strapped to the arms can be considered a crude effort at acquiring those abilities.

Today, the study of living systems, and the construction of analogues to be applied to nonliving systems, extends into many areas. For example, it is known that the eye of a frog transmits only signals of immediate interest—movements that signify food or danger. Studies of the screening mechanism of the frog's eye have been aimed at the construction of more selective radar systems. Similarly, studies of the meaning of variations in the pitch of the "voice" of the porpoise have been aimed at the development of new sonar systems. Another area under investigation is electrochemiluminescence, the generation of light by passing an electric current through organic compounds. Fireflies, squid, shrimp, and certain protozoa and bacteria are capable of bioluminescence. Attempts to reproduce the process experimentally have been inefficient because inordinate amounts of electricity are required to create only a small amount of light. By studying bioluminescence in living organisms researchers hope to design an efficient, heat-free lighting system.

Biomedical engineering, the development of instruments and procedures to treat the problems of living systems, is related to bionics. Study of the human organism itself has led to the design of improved prosthetic devices to replace or assist the function of various parts of the body.

BIOPHYSICS, the physics of living organisms. The term biophysics is applied to two separate activities. First, biophysicists study the biological systems and events that generate physical responses, for example, the structures and biochemical reactions that produce muscle action. Second, they study the physical processes that give rise to biological phenomena, for example, the absorption of light by the eye, a physical process that eventually produces vision. A more appropriate designation for the science might be physical biology, since it yields new insights into biology but no new insights into physics.

The major areas of research included under biophysics tend to be those that involve physical events. For example, biophysicists investigate the processes of vision and hearing, photobiology, and radiation and temperature effects on biological systems. Biophysicists also develop physical methods for examining biological and biochemical phenomena.

Biophysical Research. Some examples of the insights provided by the field into various biophysical processes follow:

Vision. Light energy is absorbed by the eye's retinal cells and converted into an electric signal. This signal is in turn transmitted to nerve cells, which relay the information to higher centers of the brain where the signal is interpreted as a visible event. Studies by biophysicists reveal that the light energy received by the eye is fairly directly utilized in twisting a certain molecule (related to the vitamin A molecule). This twisting motion then releases other molecules to activate the chemical reactions which initiate the nerve-stimulation processes.

Radiobiology. High-energy radiation, such as X-rays or the radiation released by nuclear reactions, may dislodge electrons from target molecules. Since these are the outermost electrons in the individual molecules, they are the ones primarily involved in forming chemical bonds. Thus, radiation can produce bond-breakage in target molecules. If, for example, the radiation target were the chromosome of a cell, chromosome cleavage might result, leading to the death of the cell. If chromosome-breakage were only partial, however, the alteration could instead produce malfunctioning or even cancerous cells.

Photobiology. A focus of attention in the area of photobiology is the process of photosynthesis, that is, the production of biochemical energy by plants upon absorption of visible light. Study of the various spectral colors that release energy in photosynthesis (as measured by the oxygen liberated by plant leaves) reveals that the most effective light for producing oxygen is light of certain red and blue wavelengths. Since the green pigment chlorophyll absorbs light of the appropriate wavelengths it was concluded that chlorophyll was the main agent of photosynthesis in plants. Chlorophyll, however, does not absorb green light (thus appearing green to the eye). Therefore it was surprising that light of this wavelength nevertheless produces oxygen fairly efficiently. It was therefore concluded that another kind of molecule was also active in the photosynthetic process. Carotenoids (the pigments that give leaves their autumn colors) absorb green light, and later work demonstrated that they transfer this light energy to chlorophyll. Therefore, it was determined that all spectral colors work to produce useful energy in the photosynthetic process.

Muscle Action. X-ray diffraction analysis of muscle tissue has determined the arrangement of the molecules that compose muscle. It was found that the active structures in muscle are two forms of long thin rods or fibers known as actin and myosin, that slide past each other to produce a shortened muscle, the muscle therefore exerting its pull as it shortens. Biophysicists have not yet conclusively determined what produces the sliding motion of the rods but it is believed that slender arms reach out from one kind of rod and attach firmly to the other, thereby forming a bridge between the two. During muscle action, energy is released in a chemical reaction which twists the end of the attached arm to produce the sliding motion of the rods.

Biophysical Techniques. *Ultracentrifugation.* High-speed centrifuges can be used to determine the rate at which small particles, such as viruses or even proteins, move in a high-gravity field. Once the rate of motion is known an estimate of the overall size of the molecules or organisms can be obtained.

Electron Microscopy. Electrons can be induced to flow along paths similar to those traveled by light rays but of much shorter wavelength so that very small objects can be detected under a suitably equipped electron microscope. For example, the structure of the nucleic acids and proteins that constitute the basic biological materials of heredity and activity, respectively, can be discerned under the electron microscope.

However, the standard electron microscope does not render an image of the interior of an intact cell. A more recent development in this field, the scanning electron microscope, permits the examination of the rays scattered by the surface of cell structures just as light rays are scattered from objects in bright sunlight. Using the scanning electron microscope, biophysicists can now examine cell interiors by breaking the cells open immediately before placing them in the microscope.

Future Research. The study of cell membranes is an important new area of biophysical research. Advances in electron microscopy and electronics have permitted a more detailed examination of the structure and activities of these membranes in various cellular processes. The central role played by electric signals and switches in nervous-system activities makes the study of nerve structures and the brain a most intriguing area of research for present and future biophysicists. Biologists have learned so much about the molecules active in ordinary cell processes that it is now possible to ask detailed questions about the molecular bases of learning, memory, sensory detection, and image-storage. Knowledge gained from such research may ultimately lead to a more precise understanding of the relation between the physical entity—the brain—and the psychological entity—the mind. *See also* BIOLOGY.

BIOPSY [bō′ŏp-sē], the removal of tissue from the living body for microscopic examination in the laboratory. Such examination assists in the accurate diagnosis of disease, especially in the diagnosis of cancer. A commonly used technique is the needle biopsy, which may be performed in the physician's office. In this procedure a hollow needle is inserted into the tissues and suction is applied. Biopsies may also be performed during the course of operations when a small section of tissue can be removed easily with the scalpel.

BIRTH CONTROL, purposeful attempts to prevent the birth of children. In the absence of all birth control efforts, sexual activities on the part of married couples will often result in the birth of a child every one or two years. Ordinarily, men and women who use birth control methods do not do so to prevent all births, but rather to limit the number of their offspring and to space their children so as to allow a convenient interval between births. In this sense, "birth control" has come to be called "family planning" or "planned parenthood."

Generally speaking, births are controlled in three ways—through continence, or refraining from the sex act; through contraception, or the prevention of pregnancy in spite of the sex act; and through abortion, or the termination of pregnancy before the baby is ready to be born. In the past few have objected to birth control in principle, least of all when continence was the method employed. However, abortion has been widely objected to by those who regard it as immoral.

History of the Movement. Thomas Malthus (1766–1834), an English economist, professor, and Anglican minister, in *An Essay on the Principle of Population* (1798), tried to prove that populations have a natural tendency to grow faster than their food supplies, thus insuring that a large portion of mankind will always live in misery. Although Malthus advocated "prudent restraint" (continence) as the acceptable method of combating excessive population growth, his followers, called the Neo-Malthusians (notably Francis Place in England and Robert Dale Owen in the United States), advocated contraception. Those opposed to their views succeeded in passing laws (such as the so-called Comstock Law, passed in the United States in 1873) banning the sale and use of contraceptive devices as well as the distribution of information about them.

Two famous women advocates of birth control came into conflict with these laws and both were arrested and tried. In England, Annie Besant (the Bradlaugh-Besant Trial, 1877) was acquitted of a charge of distributing obscene literature. In America, Margaret Sanger served 30 days in a New York prison in 1917 and was in almost continual trouble with the law until 1929. Mrs. Sanger founded the National Birth Control League, whose work is now carried on by the Planned Parenthood Federation. She opened a birth control clinic, the first in the United States, in Brooklyn on Oct. 16, 1916.

In Great Britain and the United States the birth control movement focused so intently on contraception that the term "birth control" is often taken to apply exclusively to contraceptive practices. Contraception, involving so-called "artificial" means of preventing births, has been a controversial subject in these and other countries, and opposition to birth control has become almost synonymous with opposition to contraception. Nevertheless, the use of contraceptives has spread widely in Europe and North America, and opposition to their use has greatly decreased.

The position of the Roman Catholic Church on the issue of contraception was clearly enunciated by Pope Pius XI in his 1930 encyclical on marriage (*Casti Connubii*) which proclaimed that deliberate frustration of the "natural power to generate life is an offense against the law of God and Nature." However, in 1951 Pope Pius XII publicly approved regulation of births by the rhythm method (which consists of abstinence during the period of the month when a woman is most likely to become pregnant) and recognized the pertinence of social and economic motives. In July, 1968, Pope Paul VI, in his encyclical on human life (*Humanae Vitae*), not only condemned sterilization and abortion but reiterated the Catholic teaching that rhythm is the only acceptable method of contraception. However, the increasing awareness of the alarming rate of growth of the world's population and of the demand for the widespread use of contraception by Catholic families continues to generate a great deal of discussion within the Church.

Methods of Birth Control. In the 1960's two effective methods—the "pill" and the intra-uterine device (IUD)—were added to the catalog of medically-approved means of birth control. The pill, which is taken daily for 20-21 days of the menstrual cycle, is composed of two types of female sex hormones, estrogens and progestins. The first comprehensive study (1966) on its use by American women showed that it had gained rapid acceptance and was being employed by 15% of all married women in the United States under the age of 45. In 1968 it was estimated that over 20% of the aforementioned group were using the pill and that it was being taken by 17–19 million women worldwide. IUDs, such as the Lippes Loop and the Margulies Coil, among over 50 types manufactured, have not gained as wide popularity, but by 1968 it was estimated that they were being used by 1–2 million women in the United States and worldwide by 5–6 million.

Induced abortion was at one time illegal in most countries because of moral and religious considerations and because of the high risks frequently involved, particularly when abortions are self-induced or performed by those with inadequate or no training. Nevertheless, abortion has long been practiced throughout the world and may in fact be the most frequently utilized method of birth control. Abortion is legal in a number of countries, notably Japan, Scandinavia, most of the communist countries, and Britain. When performed early in the pregnancy and under adequate medical conditions and supervision, the risk attending abortion has been found to be as low as or lower than the risk involved in childbirth.

In the United States, termination of pregnancy by abortion had been almost entirely prohibited by law in every state, but by 1970, 17 states had liberalized their abortion laws. Four states—Alaska, Hawaii, New York, and Washington—removed virtually all legal restrictions on abortions when performed early by licensed physicians, leaving the final decision to the patients and their doctors.

Sterilization by vasectomy in the male and by tubal ligation (tubectomy) in the female is an increasingly used method of contraception. Vasectomy is a relatively simple surgical procedure which can be performed in a doctor's office or even in field "camps" in developing countries. Tubal ligation, though safe and relatively easy, is regarded as a hospital procedure, since it usually involves opening the abdominal cavity. These procedures introduce a mechanical obstruction to the passage of sperm and ova in the male and female, respectively, thereby producing sterility without any accompanying change in sexual desire or function. Fertility can sometimes be restored after either operation. At present, however, the sterility is generally regarded as permanent, and these procedures are therefore recommended primarily for those who desire no additional children. Sterilization, predominantly by vasectomy, has been one of the principal methods of contraception advocated by several countries in their national family-planning programs.

The search for better birth-control methods continues. For the female, studies focus on improved IUD's, better low-dose daily pills, a once-a-month pill, a post-coital pill, pills and injections causing early abortion, long-acting injections and under-the-skin implants, and methods of immunization against pregnancy. For the male, research is largely focused on ways of suppressing the production of or interfering with the reproductive capability of the sperm. The possibility of controlling the sex of a child, so that parents might choose the sex as well as the number of their offspring, is also being investigated.

Population Control. Concern in developing nations over the economic and social effects of the unprecedented rates of population growth (of from 2% to 4% per year) that followed rapid declines in their death rates has led many of them to institute national family-planning programs. In 1955 India became the first country to launch a government-sponsored birth-control program. By 1970 about 35 countries were promoting such activities. Several countries, particularly Sweden, have for some years helped support birth-control activities abroad, and since 1965 the United States has increased its governmental support of research in contraception and of family-planning activities, both domestically and abroad. In 1967 a United Nations Fund for Population Activities was established to assist governments with their population programs.

Government-supported family-planning programs appear to have helped decrease the birth rates in Japan, Taiwan, South Korea, Singapore, and Hong Kong. How much effect such efforts have had elsewhere is questionable, but quick results should not be expected, since most of these programs are relatively new and their implementation in developing countries is slow and difficult. *See also* ABORTION; VASECTOMY.

BIRTHMARKS, or nevi, are skin blemishes which are usually present at birth or appear shortly afterward. Most birthmarks appear within a few weeks of birth and are usually caused by an overproduction of one or more parts of the skin. Birthmarks of this type include freckles, moles, and the blood-vessel birthmarks, such as port-wine stains, strawberry marks, and the cavernous hemangioma.

Freckles contain an excess of normal skin pigmentation. Common moles are overgrowths of normal skin tissue which may be flat or raised, brown or skin-colored. Port-wine stains are large, dull-red or flat-purplish discolorations. Raised strawberry marks are bright-red or purple growths. Cavernous hemangiomata are large, baggy round or flat deep masses. Some birthmarks consist of areas which lack certain skin structures. These include the nevus apigmentosus, caused by a lack of pigment, and the nevus anemicus, a pale spot devoid of blood vessels.

Birthmarks are usually treated for cosmetic reasons; if they are located in areas subject to irritation, they can be removed by dry ice, liquid nitrogen, acids, surgery, X ray, or radium. In rare instances a birthmark can become cancerous.

BLACK, JOSEPH (1728–99), Scottish chemist, physicist, and physician who made important contributions in both chemistry and physics. He was born in Bordeaux, France, where his Scottish father, a native of Belfast, had a wine business. Joseph received his medical diploma from the University of Edinburgh, and there he became a celebrated lecturer, attracting students from Europe and the American Colonies. He was among the first scientists to accept the new chemistry of Lavoisier, and he clarified the nature of many chemical compounds. For instance, while trying to find a remedy for gout, he heated magnesium carbonate and discovered carbon dioxide, which he called "fixed air." His theories laid the foundation for quantitative analysis. In 1761 he pointed out the difference between temperature and quantity of heat, developed the ideas of specific and latent heats, and then experimentally determined the latent heat of fusion of ice, the latent heat of vaporization of water, and the specific heat of several other substances. Thus his work began the clarification of the controversial field of heat. His manuscripts were published posthumously in 1803 as *Lectures on the Elements of Chemistry, Delivered in the University of Edinburgh*.

BLACK DEATH, name given to the plague (q.v.) that swept over Europe in several waves in the middle and late 14th century. The first and most famous onslaught occurred in 1348–50, but severe recurrences took place in 1358–60, in 1373–75, and sporadically from 1380 to 1400. No exact figures as to mortality are possible, but according to the most recent estimates the European population in the early 15th century had been reduced by 40% from what it had been in 1346.

Historians have traditionally regarded the Black Death as a major factor in the breakup of the medieval world, and some historians have even dated the beginning of modern times from 1348. According to this view, the Black Death engendered a great shortage of labor and radically changed the European economy. Competition for workers increased. In order to keep their surviving peasants from leaving the land, feudal lords were forced to lower rents and to commute heavy payments in labor and in kind to payments in money; the last vestiges of serfdom and of manorial organization were thus swept away. The lords also tried to keep the peasants attached to the land by legislation, thus provoking peasant uprisings, such as the English Peasants' Revolt of 1381. Wages in the towns rose rapidly, though the efforts to control them also led to considerable social unrest. The calamities also bred a mass psychological depression and a morbid concern with death. These led in turn to dissatisfaction with the established church and were factors in the spread of heresies. Thus, on every level, intellectual as well as economic, the Black Death undermined medieval systems and prepared the way for the modern world.

Many of these changes, however, can no longer be considered the direct results of the Black Death. The decline of serfdom, for example, and the breakup of the manor were processes that in most areas of Europe had begun long before 1348. Moreover, the Black Death was only one aspect of a general European crisis, particularly pronounced over the century 1350–1450. This crisis was caused not only by the plague, but also by the period's many wars, frequent crop failures, famines, and perhaps by resultant malnutrition, which paved the way for plague.

BLACK WIDOW SPIDER, a poisonous spider, *Latrodectus mactans*, found in cool, dry, dark places from southern Canada through South America and in the West Indies. It is most common in the southern United States. The velvety black female, seldom more than one-half inch long, is easily identified by a red or yellow hourglass marking on the underside of the abdomen. The male is much smaller and harmless. In fact, he is frequently eaten by the female after mating. The insects trapped in the female's shapeless, crisscross web, include many crop pests. As a menace to human life, the black widow is overrated. Its venom, though highly poisonous, is injected in such small amounts

Alfred Renfro—National Audubon Society
An hourglass-shaped marking is clearly visible on the abdomen of this female Black Widow Spider.

BLADDER

that it is rarely fatal. Pain, weakness, and fever do result, however, and immediate medical attention is advisable.

BLADDER, URINARY, a muscular membranous sac, located in the lower portion of the abdominal cavity. It collects and stores the urine coming from the kidneys. Two tubes, the ureters—one from each kidney—carry urine to the bladder. As the amount of urine in the bladder increases, the bladder distends, and nerves located in the walls of the bladder transmit an awareness of this condition to the brain. A desire to void results. The urine is passed out of the body through a narrow tube, the urethra, the opening of which is in the bottom of the bladder.
See also EXCRETORY SYSTEM.

BLASTOMYCOSIS [blăs-tō-mī-kō'sĭs], also known as Gilchrist's disease or North American blastomycosis, a fungus disease, apparently limited to the North American continent, which affects the skin and internal organs. On the skin, blastomycosis appears as a reddish pimple that enlarges to form a crust and eventually a craterlike ulcer. The disease frequently attacks the lungs first, and may involve the bones, nervous system, liver, spleen, and kidneys. The skin types are treated with X rays. Stilbamidine and related drugs have been used successfully as internal medication.

BLINDNESS can be produced by a defect in the visual apparatus at any point from the cornea (the transparent membrane which covers the front of the eye) to the hind portion of the brain, which receives the sight impulses and converts them into images. In cases where the retina, the optic nerve, or the visual portion of the brain is destroyed, the blindness is complete and incurable. In most other cases a partial cure is possible. The commonest causes of blindness are congenital disorders, diseases of old age, infections, and injury.

The cornea is susceptible to infections which may lead to scarring and darkening. Gonorrhea neonatorum, a gonorrheal infection of the cornea in the newborn, was previously a common cause of blindness in children, but is now relatively rare in the United States because of laws requiring antibiotics to be routinely applied to the eyes of the newborn. Trachoma, an infection prevalent in the Middle East, also attacks the cornea, producing opacification. The commonest cause of corneal blindness is injury. Fortunately, vision can be restored in many cases of corneal scarring by transplanting corneas obtained from deceased persons.

Cataract is a term given to a darkening of the normally transparent lens of the eye. Most cases appear in older persons, and are often associated with other diseases such as arteriosclerosis (hardening of the arteries) and diabetes. Blindness produced by cataract can be treated by surgical removal of the lens. This operation restores sight, but leaves the individual with certain restrictions in his vision, so that he may not be able to see objects which lie too far to his right or left.

Glaucoma also occurs in older persons, and results from interference in the normal mechanism whereby fluid drains from the eye. The damming-up of fluid causes pressure on the optic nerve, leading to a degeneration of this structure, and to blindness if left untreated.

Uveitis is an inflammation of the pigmented layer of the eye, which may be caused by allergy or infection. This condition can in turn lead to opacification of the cornea, cataract, degeneration of the optic nerve, or glaucoma.

The retina, the light-sensitive layer in the rear of the eyeball, may become detached following injury to the eye or head. In some cases detachment occurs without apparent cause. Surgical treatment is possible for this condition. Blindness resulting from destructive changes in the retina may also occur in diseases such as diabetes, high blood pressure, and arteriosclerosis. Although tumors of the eye are relatively rare, the two commonest eye tumors involve the retina. These may be retinoblastomas, which usually appear in children under three, or malignant melanomas, which usually occur in older people.

Degeneration of the optic nerve and blindness may result from glaucoma, pressure of tumors on the nerve, or from diseases of the nervous system. Brain hemorrhages and tumors may cause blindness when they occur in the visual areas of the brain.

The ability of modern medicine to prevent many infectious types of blindness has been clearly demonstrated in the Western countries, where trachoma, gonorrhea, and syphilis have been largely eliminated as causes of blindness. Paradoxically, medical progress has also resulted in an increase in certain types of blindness. This develops from the fact that blindness resulting from such disorders as diabetes, cataracts, and glaucoma increases in older age groups; as the life span is extended the size of these age groups, and therefore the number of elderly blind persons, increases.

Incidence of Blindness. According to the best estimates, there are 12 million blind persons in the world. It is difficult to know how accurate this figure is since information

The hands of a blind person model clay into the shape of a head. For the blind the sense of touch is a main source of learning of the outside world. (THE LIGHTHOUSE)

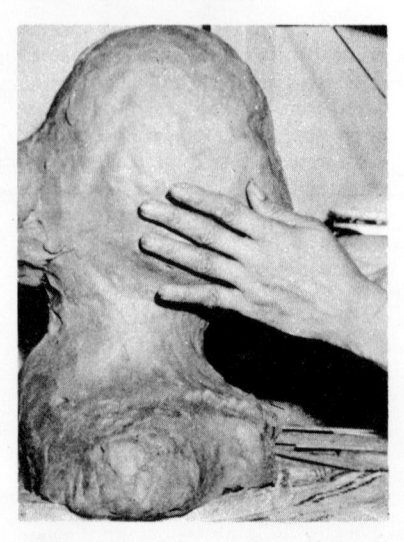

is lacking from many underdeveloped countries and the definition of blindness varies.

In the United States, the blind population is estimated as 1.98 per 1,000 of the general population. On a state-by-state basis, the number of blind persons per 1,000 varies considerably, ranging from 3.42 in one Southern state to 1.40 in a state with a generally higher living standard. It is estimated that about 10% are under 21 and that at least 50% are over the age of 65.

Canada reports a blind population of about 23,500, and England and Wales list 100,000 as registered blind persons. On the continent of Europe the blind populations vary, being lower in the Scandinavian countries (Denmark, 6,000) and somewhat higher in the countries bordering on the Mediterranean (France, 40,000; Italy, 44,000; Spain, 23,000).

A much higher incidence is found in other parts of the world, such as the Middle and Far East and certain parts of Africa. It is estimated that there are at least 2,000,000 blind persons in India and 100,000 in the Philippine Islands.

Education. The first school for the blind in the world was established in Paris in 1784 by Valentin Haüy, who also had the first books for the blind printed in an embossed system which he invented. In America three schools were established almost simultaneously in the early 1830's, in Boston, New York, and Philadelphia. Today there are residential schools for blind children in 41 states; nearly half of the country's blind children receive their education in such schools. About 53% of the blind children are educated with sighted children in regular public or private school systems, with the co-operation of a resource room teacher, or under the supervision of an itinerant teacher available at regular or needed intervals. Some adaptations of educational methods and devices are necessary, such as the use of Braille and "talking books," special mathematical apparatus, and embossed maps. Since 1879 the federal government has made an annual appropriation to the American Printing House for the Blind in Louisville, Ky., for the provision of books and tangible apparatus for the use of blind school children. The material is allocated according to a quota system based on pupil enrollment in the various schools and classes.

After finishing high school many blind students go on to college, where they pursue courses under the same conditions as sighted students. Many volunteer groups assist in transcribing into Braille or onto sound records the textbooks needed by these students. Especially noteworthy work has been done in this respect by Recording for the Blind, Inc., in New York, an agency which has member units in various parts of the country.

Blind persons can read by touch by means of the Braille system, or in the case of a very few who became blind in later life, by means of the Moon type, which slightly resembles the Roman alphabet. In addition to systems involving touch, another reading medium for the blind has been developed: the talking books. These are long-playing phonograph records or magnetic tapes, on which are recorded classic and contemporary literature, books, and periodicals, as well as textbooks. Since their introduction in 1934, talking books have become the main medium of reading for a vast majority of blind readers in the United States. Braille, however, is the only system which may be written as well as read by the blind. Therefore, no other reading medium can replace Braille, especially in the education of the young blind.

Library Service. Books and reading play an important part in the life of a blind person. Braille and talking books, however, are very expensive to produce and it would be impossible for the average library to build up a representative collection. The federal government, therefore, provides an annual appropriation for the manufacture of Braille and talking books for general and recreational reading. This appropriation is administered by the Library

The development of acute senses of touch and hearing enables many blind people to become successful piano tuners. (OAK HILL SCHOOL)

This blind man earns his living in industry as a fabricator of aluminum products. (TEXAS STATE COMMISSION FOR THE BLIND)

BLINDNESS

of Congress, which in turn has selected 31 libraries located in various parts of the country to serve as regional distributing centers. The books are circulated by mail, postage free, under an amendment to the U.S. postal laws. In addition, more than 100 Braille and about 20 recorded magazines are available to the blind reader.

Rehabilitation. The rehabilitation of the adult blind has been greatly stimulated by various federal legislative measures. The services established through such legislation are usually administered by divisions of the respective state governments under state plans which must be approved by the federal government. Local voluntary agencies supplement these services, sometimes through contractual arrangements with the state or federal government.

Occupational opportunities for blind persons were immensely increased by the passage in 1943 and in 1954 of amendments to the Vocational Rehabilitation Act of 1920. Under this program which is supervised by the Office of Vocational Rehabilitation of the U.S. Department of Health, Education, and Welfare, the federal government allocates, on a formula basis, funds which have been provided by Congress, to be added to state-appropriated funds, for vocational rehabilitation of physically handicapped persons, including the blind. About 5,000 blind persons are trained each year and placed in jobs through these programs.

The Vocational Rehabilitation Act of 1954 also expanded the opportunities first provided by the Randolph-Sheppard Act of 1936. This authorized the operation of vending stands in federal and other buildings by blind persons, and has provided employment for almost 2,000 blind men and women. Federal funds are available for a major part of the necessary expenditures for the acquisition of vending stands and other equipment, to be controlled by the state agency for the blind.

Blind persons have become active in the professions, in business, industry, agriculture, and many other fields, in competition with sighted workers. But there are still many who for various reasons cannot compete successfully in the open labor market. Such persons find employment in sheltered workshops or in industrial homework programs. Today 4,000 blind persons are earning a fair living wage in these sheltered industries. A market for blind-made products is provided by the Wagner-O'Day Act of 1938, which requires that federal departments under certain conditions purchase brooms, mops, and some 40 other approved articles from workshops for the blind at a fair market price. A number of states have enacted similar legislation, making it mandatory that state departments purchase certain articles from workshops for the blind located within the state.

Special Privileges. Other federal legislation has afforded certain privileges to the blind. A blind person may claim an exemption of $750 on his federal income tax over and above all other exemptions. If a joint return is filed, a husband, whether blind or sighted, can also claim this exemption for a wife who is blind, even though she has no income. Some state governments have also enacted legislation giving blind persons certain exemptions on state tax payments. And some states exempt blind persons from paying certain property taxes and fees for dog licenses and fishing licenses.

According to an amendment to the Interstate Commerce Act passed in 1927, railroads are permitted, at their discretion, to carry a blind person and his guide for one full fare. And this privilege has been extended to a number of interstate bus lines.

Financial Aid. Because so many blind persons are too old, or otherwise unable to work, at least one-half of the blind population of the United States receives direct financial aid under a federal-state co-operative arrangement supervised by the Social Security Administration. According to law only those blind persons who are in need

A woman stitching the seam of a bag. Needlework is one of the crafts at which the blind can excel.

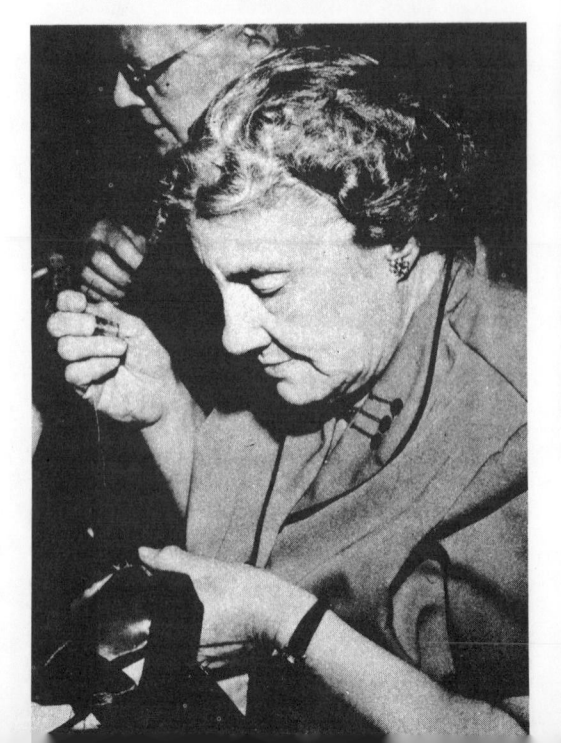

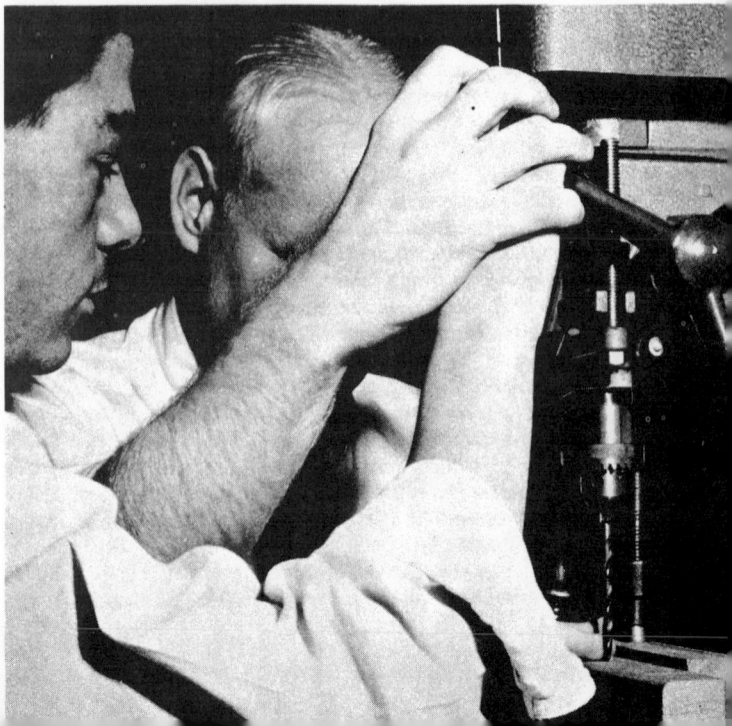

A trainee learning to operate a drill press. Vocational training enables the blind to become productive members of society.

can receive this aid, and the amount of money they get is determined on the basis of a budget made up for them. However, in determining the needs of a blind person, the state agency is directed to disregard the first $85.00 per month of the person's earned income, if he has any. This clause is considered an encouragement to partial employment if such can be found.

The law provides that the federal government pay four-fifths of the first $30.00 of the monthly grant, and from 50% to 65% of the balance, depending upon the state's per capita income. In October, 1960, the average monthly payment for the entire country was $72.98, although the actual grant varied considerably, depending upon the needs of the person, and upon the financial resources of the state.

An increasing number of blind persons who, before losing their sight in middle life, were already fully insured under social security now benefit from the disability-insurance program established by the 1956 amendment to the Social Security Act. If such individuals can prove their eligibility, they may begin to draw social security payments at the age at which the disability was established.

Mobility. Aside from the problem of reading, the greatest difficulty confronting a blind person is that of getting about by himself independent of sighted friends or his family. A special technique for using a long cane was developed by the U.S. Army for its blinded service personnel. This technique, with certain modifications, is now taught in a number of centers throughout the country. Many blind persons use a white cane which, by virtue of legislation in 49 states, gives them the right of way in traffic.

Dog guides are another means selected by blind men and women for independent travel. The first schools for training dog guides were established in Germany during World War I to aid in the rehabilitation of blinded veterans. The Seeing Eye Inc., the first training school in the United States, was opened in 1929. Today there are about a dozen schools scattered throughout the states, some offering a nation-wide program, others limiting their service to blind persons within a specific state or several nearby states. It is estimated, however, that less than 5% of the blind population can make proper use of a dog guide. The blind person must be of at least average intelligence, must not be too old or too young, and must be strong enough to undergo the rigorous training with the dog which is required by the training schools.

National and International Services. In the United States, services for the blind are based on a system of co-operation between public agencies, both federal and state, and voluntary agencies, both national and local. *The Directory of Agencies Serving Blind Persons* lists about 700 agencies and associations active in the field. The need and effectiveness of government participation in this field of social welfare have been amply demonstrated over a number of years. The need for central national voluntary agencies is equally apparent.

The American Foundation for the Blind, established in 1921 and located in New York City, is a national voluntary agency created by action of other agencies serving blind persons, and by their friends, to promote higher standards of service throughout the United States on behalf of all blind and deaf-blind persons. It serves as a clearing house for all information relating to blindness and works closely with other agencies—federal, state, and local. Among its activities are research, consultation and field services, publication of professional literature, special library service, scholarships and fellowships, institutes and workshops, exhibits and public education.

The National Society for the Prevention of Blindness in New York City is a national voluntary agency which carries on a program to study causes of blindness; to advocate measures leading to their elimination; and to serve as a clearing house and stimulating agency for professional groups, directly and indirectly responsible for saving sight. Among its activities are institutes, courses and meetings, consultation services, exhibits, and public education.

The American Foundation for Overseas Blind, Inc., furnishes practical and financial aid to blind persons outside the United States. The World Council for the Welfare of the Blind, established in 1951, provides an international forum for discussion of mutual problems for some 50 member countries in various parts of the world. The need for international co-operation is generally recognized, and through conventions and conferences, principles and policies are formulated for future action.

BLIND SPOT, specific area of the light-receptive portion of the eye, or retina, at which the optic nerve enters the eye. It is not supplied with light receptors and is thus insensitive to light. The term "blind spot" also describes the area in perceived vision which corresponds to this retinal area.

BLOCH, KONRAD EMIL (1912–), American biochemist, born in Neisse, Germany. Educated in Germany and America, he became Higgins Professor of Biochemistry at Harvard in 1954. In 1964 Bloch shared the Nobel Prize in physiology and medicine with Feodor Lynen for investigations of the biosynthesis of cholesterol and of fatty acids.

BLOOD [blŭd]. In the early development of life the waters of the ocean surrounded the primitive cell and provided it with oxygen and carried away its waste products. As life evolved into more complex land-dwelling forms the liquid environment of the cells was transferred to a closed circulatory system. Evidence for this origin of the blood system can be observed today in the close similarity between the composition of sea water and blood.

Blood is composed of cells and fluid (plasma). The red blood cells carry oxygen to the tissues; the white blood cells help combat infection. The platelets aid in the process of blood clotting.

The plasma, or fluid portion of the blood, contains over 90% water. In the plasma are proteins, minerals, organic substances such as cholesterol, fats, sugar (glucose), amino acids, and a number of enzymes and hormones.

Functions of the Blood

Respiration. The red blood cells carry oxygen from the lungs to the tissues and carbon dioxide from the tissues to the lungs.

Nutrition. Food in the form of sugar (glucose), fats, and amino acids reaches the tissues via the blood plasma.

Excretion. The waste products of cell activity, such as

BLOOD COMPONENTS AND THEIR FUNCTIONS

RED BLOOD CELLS
(Erythrocytes)

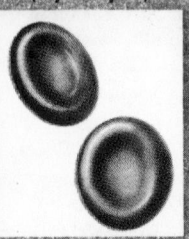

These disc-shaped cells are manufactured in the marrow cavities of the ribs, the flat bones of the skull, and the vertebrae of the spinal column.

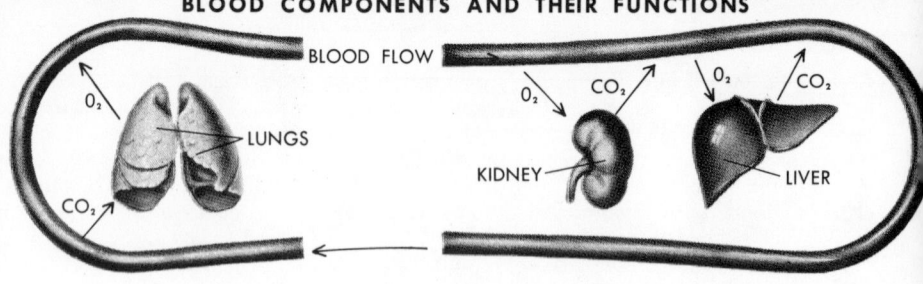

THE RED BLOOD CELL AND OXYGEN-CARBON DIOXIDE EXCHANGE

The red color of the cells derives from the presence of hemoglobin, the oxygen-carrying pigment of the blood. In the lungs the red blood cells surrender carbon dioxide and take up oxygen. In the tissues the reaction is reversed as the blood cells exchange oxygen for carbon dioxide (CO_2).

WHITE BLOOD CELLS
(Leukocytes)

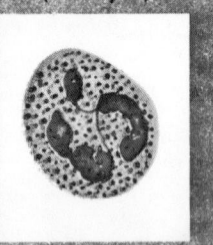

Normally there are from 5,000 to 9,000 of these cells in every cubic millimeter of blood.

THE WHITE BLOOD CELL IN DISEASE

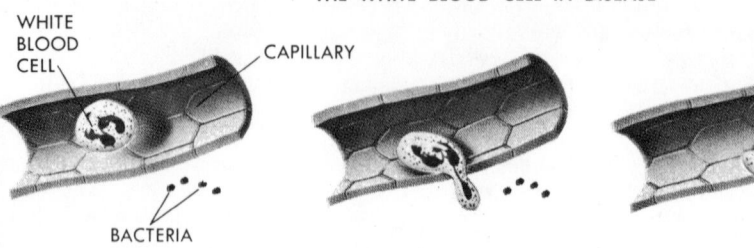

The white blood cell is a major element in inflammation, the body's response to foreign substances in the tissues. The blood vessels in the affected region expand, bringing large numbers of leukocytes to the blood. Drawn by chemical forces (chemotaxis), the white cells squeeze through the intact walls of the blood vessels (diapedesis) to encounter, engulf, and destroy the invaders. The latter process is known as *phagocytosis*.

PLASMA PROTEINS

ALBUMINS

Albumins are manufactured in the liver. They comprise the largest fraction of the plasma proteins.

ALBUMIN AND FLUID EXCHANGE

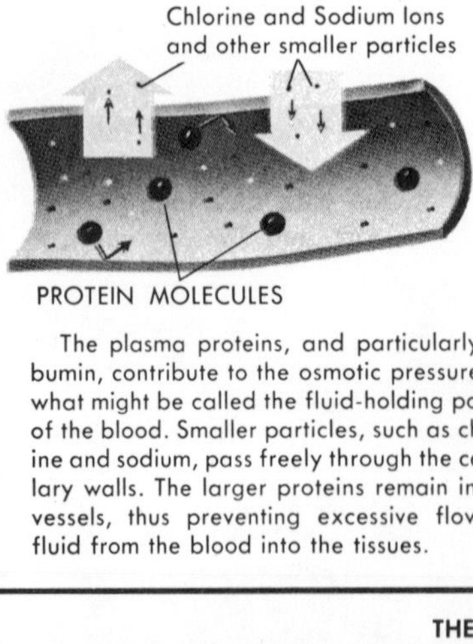

The plasma proteins, and particularly albumin, contribute to the osmotic pressure, or what might be called the fluid-holding power of the blood. Smaller particles, such as chlorine and sodium, pass freely through the capillary walls. The larger proteins remain in the vessels, thus preventing excessive flow of fluid from the blood into the tissues.

ANTIBODY REACTION

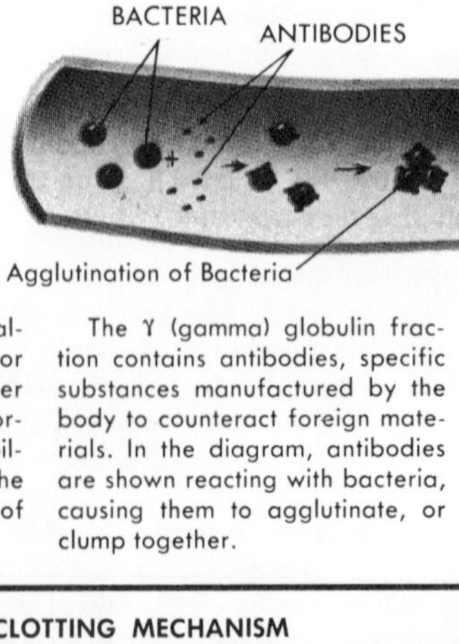

The γ (gamma) globulin fraction contains antibodies, specific substances manufactured by the body to counteract foreign materials. In the diagram, antibodies are shown reacting with bacteria, causing them to agglutinate, or clump together.

GLOBULINS

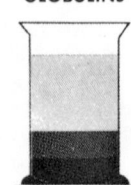

Globulins are grouped into several distinct fractions. Shown here are α (alpha) and β (beta) globulins.

PLATELETS

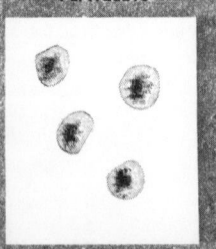

The platelets are not cells and are usually described as fragments of protoplasm. They are important in blood clotting.

THE CLOTTING MECHANISM

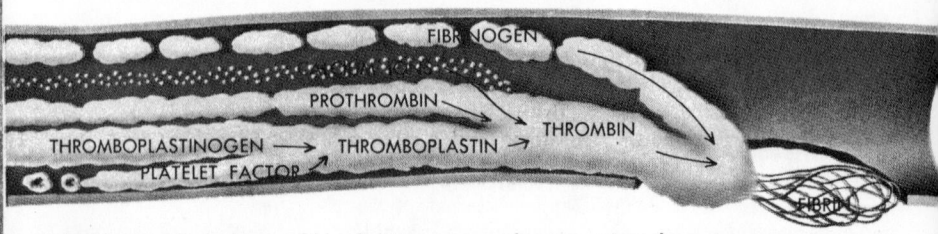

A highly simplified scheme of blood clotting groups the process into three stages:

1. Formation of Thromboplastin

Following injury, ruptured blood platelets give off the platelet factor which reacts with substances normally present in the blood to produce thromboplastin.

2. Formation of Thrombin

In the presence of calcium and other substances, thromboplastin reacts with prothrombin to produce thrombin.

3. Formation of Fibrin

Thrombin promotes the conversion of the blood protein fibrinogen into fibrin, the matrix of the clot.

BLOOD

urea, uric acid, and creatine, are carried from the tissues by the blood stream.

Regulation of Body Temperature. The blood stores heat and distributes it. When the body is chilled, the blood shifts from the skin to the deeper organs of the body to conserve heat. When the temperature rises, more blood enters the vessels of the skin, permitting heat to be lost.

Water Balance. There is a continual exchange of water between the blood stream and the tissue spaces. The large protein molecules contained in the blood are particularly important in preventing excess fluid from leaving the blood stream. When, in certain conditions, such as in some liver and kidney diseases, the blood protein concentration is reduced, this control is lost and large quantities of water collect in the tissues producing swellings (edema) in the legs, ankles, and other parts of the body.

Protection Against Infection. The white blood cells are capable of devouring disease-producing organisms. In addition, the blood fluid contains other substances, including antibodies, which may dissolve or agglutinate germs.

Regulation of Body Activity. The blood carries the hormones secreted by the thyroid, pituitary, adrenal, and other endocrine glands. These substances are important in determining the rate at which the body burns food, the mineral composition of the body fluids, the rate of the reproductive cycle, and other important bodily functions.

Circulation of the Blood

In the human body blood is contained within many tubelike structures, the arteries and the veins, which compose the vascular system. The blood is forced to flow continuously to all parts of the body by the powerful pumping action of the heart. The continuous circular motion of the blood flow was conclusively demonstrated by William Harvey in 1628. Prior to that time popular belief held that the blood was in continuous motion, but in a to-and-fro pattern. It was not until after many experiments with animals, and numerous human dissections, that Harvey formulated his theory of the circulation of the blood. His observations have withstood the test of time and are the basis of our present knowledge of the circulation.

The heart is composed mainly of muscle and is about five inches long, four inches in breadth, and weighs a little over half a pound. The two ventricles, right and left, are the powerful pumping portions of the heart, and beat synchronously. The ventricles are rapidly filled with blood by contraction of the atria or auricles. Blood flows to the heart through the veins of the body, enters the right atrium and is forced into the right ventricle.

Flow of Blood in the Heart. From the right ventricle blood is pumped into the pulmonary arteries, through the lungs, and is returned to the left atrium by the pulmonary veins. The circuit of blood through the lungs and the right side of the heart is known as the lesser, or pulmonary, circulation.

In the systemic, or greater circulation, blood is forced from the left atrium to the left ventricle and then into the aorta, the major artery leaving the heart. It is distributed from there to the rest of the arterial system. The flow of blood continues from the arteries to the smallest blood vessels, the capillaries, and back to the heart via the veins.

PULMONARY AND SYSTEMIC CIRCULATION

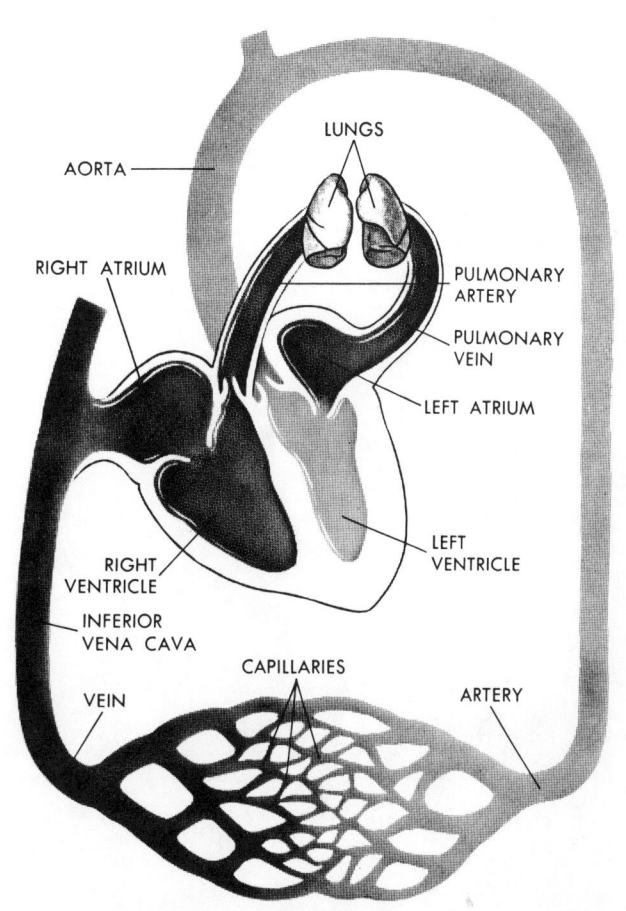

Circulation Time. A clinical test has been devised to measure the speed of circulation. A substance is injected into a vein in the arm and is carried by the blood stream to the taste buds of the tongue, where it produces a bitter sensation. Normally it takes from 10 to 16 seconds for blood to flow from the arm to the right side of the heart, through the lungs, back to the left side of the heart, through the aorta and to the tongue. The time required for a complete circulation of blood from a vein to the same vein is about 25 seconds. The circulation time is prolonged in heart failure.

Arterial System. The arteries are distributed to various parts of the body like branches of a tree, the trunk being the aorta, the first branches being the major arteries, and the smallest twigs being similar to the arterioles which precede the minute capillaries. All arteries have muscular tissue that allows the vessel to contract or dilate as bodily needs change. The amount of blood flowing to certain organs remains fairly constant under normal circumstances. The brain usually receives about one-sixth of the heart's output of blood; the liver and the kidneys receive about one-fifth of the cardiac output. The rest of the blood supplies the skin, muscles, intestines, and other organs.

Each contraction of the heart, called systole, is followed

arteries to the capillaries have the additional purpose of regulating the amount of blood flowing through the capillary area of the organs that they supply.

As the aorta fills, the elasticity of the vessel allows it to expand and become distended. While the heart relaxes, the walls of the aorta contract and maintain the flow of blood to distant parts of the body. The recurring cycle of a sudden entrance of blood into the aorta during cardiac contraction and its more gradual release by the aorta during relaxation results in a steady flow of blood in the arterial system. The wave of blood resulting from the contraction of the heart is called the pulse and may easily be felt at the wrist, foot, temple, or any other accessible artery.

Blood Pressure. The standard blood pressure apparatus is called a sphygmomanometer and is used to measure the force which blood exerts on the walls of the arteries. The instrument consists of a dial, or column of mercury, connected to a hollow rubber cuff. The cuff is wrapped around the upper arm and a stethoscope is placed over a large artery below the cuff. The cuff is inflated with air until the artery is squeezed shut. The air is then slowly released until a tapping sound can be heard, which is caused by a spurt of blood being forced through the artery by the contraction of the heart. The reading at this point indicates the blood pressure during the phase of heart contraction (systolic pressure). The cuff is further deflated until the sounds disappear, indicating that blood is flowing in a smooth stream through the artery. The reading at this time represents the blood pressure during the phase of heart relaxation (diastolic pressure).

There is a tendency for arterial pressure to increase with age. The blood pressure in late infancy is about 80 millimeters of mercury systolic and 55 mm. diastolic. These numbers are usually written 80/55. At ten years of age the normal pressure is about 100/70, and at fifteen the pressure is about 113/75. The normal values for young adults are about 120/80.

With advancing age, the aorta and other arteries gradually lose their elasticity and the systolic pressure may rise in the entire arterial system. This occurs because the vessels cannot expand to absorb the impact created by each cardiac contraction. In addition to arteriosclerosis, or "hardening of the arteries," there are many other causes for abnormal elevation of the blood pressure. In most cases, however, the cause is not known.

Many healthy persons have systolic blood pressure in the range of 95-110 mm. mercury. These readings are regarded by some physicians as "low blood pressure," but they are not commonly associated with any symptoms or abnormalities and require no treatment. Low blood pressure levels are also found in cases of Addison's disease. Systolic blood pressures of less than 80 mm. mercury are usually associated with a circulatory disorder commonly known as shock.

Some of the branches of the circulatory system are interconnected. These connections are important whenever a main arterial blood supply is shut off, either by thrombosis, embolism, injury, surgical operations, or narrowing of the arteries. No harm results if the blood flow through the interconnected, or collateral system, is sufficient to adequately nourish the tissues previously supplied by the

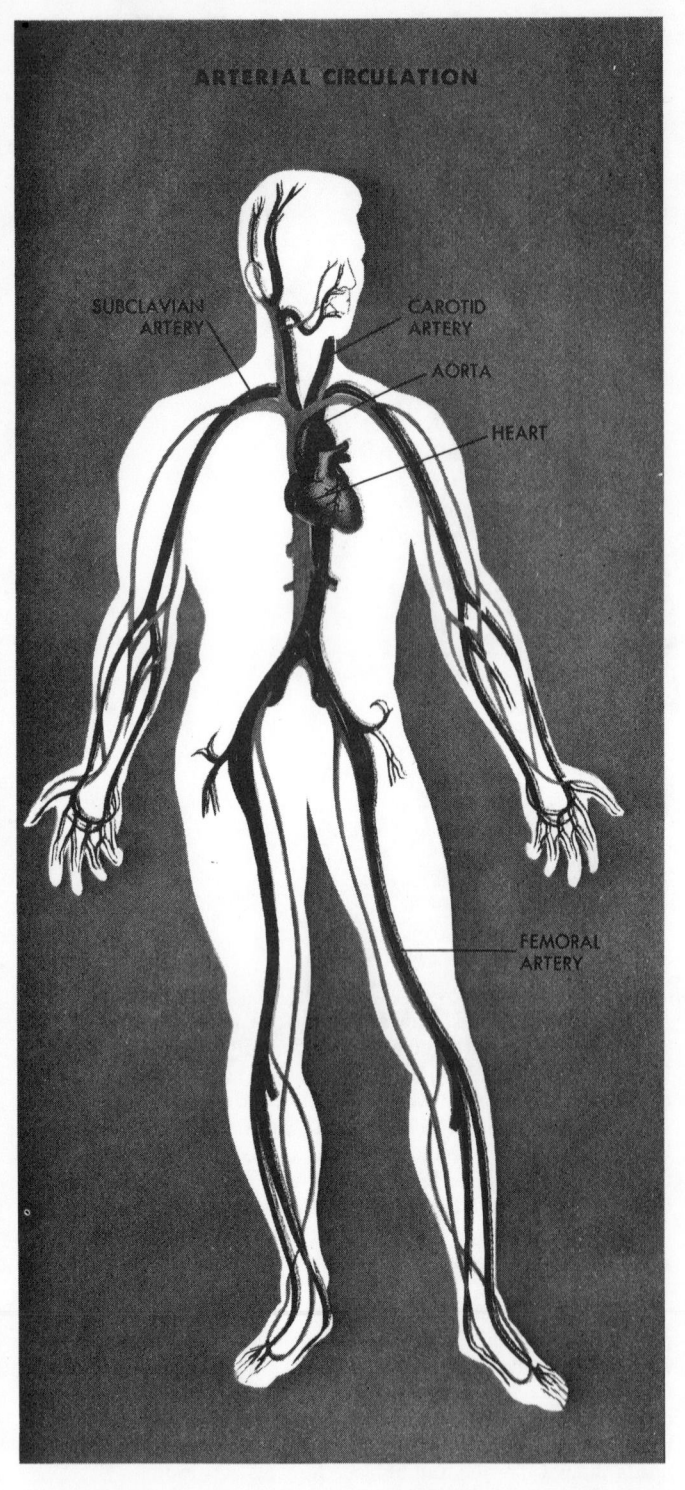

by a period of relaxation, called diastole. In the normal heart this cycle is repeated 60 to 90 times per minute. Each contraction forces blood from the heart. The major function of the large arteries is to serve as elastic receptacles to permit a steady flow of blood to distant parts of the body. The small arteries and arterioles leading from the obstructed vessel. If, however, the collateral system is absent or inadequate, the cells once nourished by the obstructed artery will die. The death of tissue secondary to arterial obstruction is called an infarction. The seriousness of the infarction depends upon the area involved. Infarction of a portion of the spleen is not significant because of the nonessential nature of this organ, whereas a small infarction of the heart muscle (myocardial infarction or heart attack) may lead to death.

The Arterioles

Microscopic cross section of arteriole

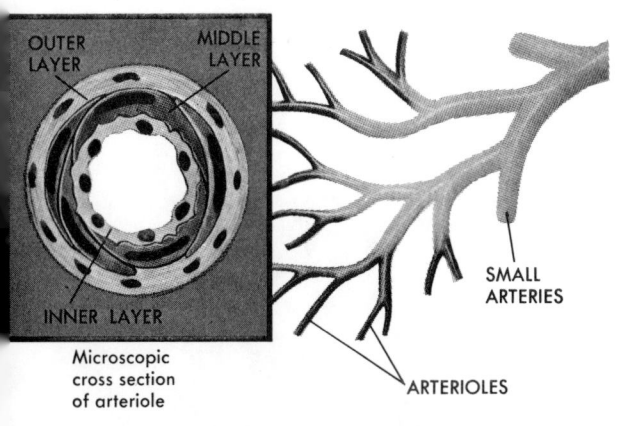

The arterioles are the smallest branches of the arterial system. Many factors acting together serve to regulate blood flow through these small vessels. Emotional factors play a role, as can be seen in the blush of embarrassment. During blushing, the arterioles expand (vasodilation), bringing more blood to the face and neck, and causing an increase in the normal red coloration of the skin. This is a reflex mechanism which is carried over nerve pathways. Hormones also affect the blood flow in the arterioles. In sudden emergencies, adrenalin is released into the blood stream by the adrenal gland. This hormone causes arterioles in the skin to close down, or vasoconstrict, so that blood is shunted to other areas of the body where the need is greater.

The arterioles are particularly important in regulating the blood pressure: by expanding, they offer less resistance to the flow of blood and lower the blood pressure; by contracting, they increase resistance to blood flow, thus raising the pressure.

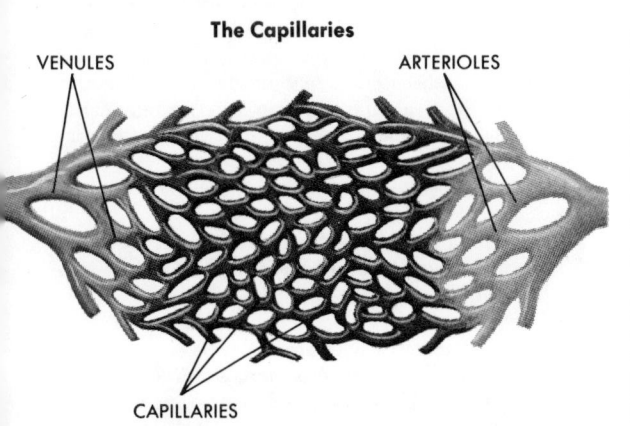

The Capillaries

Capillaries are located between the arterioles and the beginning of the venous system. The capillary system consists of numerous microscopic vessels, wide enough to allow the passage of only one or two blood cells. It is the function of these vessels to provide the living cells of the body with nourishment and oxygen in exchange for waste products. The capillaries present an enormous surface area for the exchange of vital substances between the blood and the body tissues. It has been estimated that if all the capillaries of the body were flattened out they would form a sheet over 12 mi. long and a foot wide, and yet so thin that it could be rolled into a cylinder of about the thickness of a lead pencil.

The thin walls of the capillaries permit fluid, salts, and even red and white blood cells to pass through them into the tissue spaces. Normally, the blood pressure is higher at the arterial end of the capillary than at the venous end. The sum total of forces acting on the blood tends to force fluid out of the capillary at the arterial end, and return fluid to the capillary at the venous end. This fluid bathes the cells of the body and exchanges nutrients with them. The amount of fluid which leaves the capillary is usually balanced by the amount which returns. Under abnormal circumstances more fluid may leave the capillaries than is returned. This results in an abnormal amount of fluid in the tissue spaces (edema). According to one theory, in heart failure, edema is produced because the heart is unable to pump the amount of blood that it normally does, and blood accumulates in the veins, elevating the pressure. The increased pressure is transmitted to the venous end of the capillaries where the pressure also rises. This sequence of events decreases the amount of fluid which can return to the capillaries and results in edema. Severe injury may also cause loss of fluid and, occasionally, blood into the tissue spaces from direct disruption of the capillary wall.

The pulmonary circulation is composed mainly of capillaries. The function of the pulmonary circulation is to expose venous blood to air in the lungs, allowing it to exchange its carbon dioxide for oxygen. This exchange of gas must occur in the few seconds that blood remains in the pulmonary capillaries. These capillaries are so numerous that they expose the blood to 100 sq. ft. of surface in the short time that the blood is in the lungs.

Venous System

In the arterial system, blood flows because of the pulsing action of the heart, but little of this pressure is transmitted to the veins. The systemic veins usually parallel the arteries and convey blood back to the heart. Veins originate at the capillaries as tiny vessels and join together in vessels of increasing caliber before entering the right atrium of the heart. Unlike the arteries, veins have thin walls and little muscular tissue. Blood flow through the veins depends upon many factors. In the upright position, gravity aids return of blood from the region of the head but works to retard its return from the legs. The greater portion of veins in the body are enclosed within muscles, and the contraction of these muscles squeezes the vein walls and causes blood to flow. In order to prevent the forces of gravity from overcoming the muscular pumping action, most veins have valves along their course

BLOOD

which allow blood to flow in the direction of the heart. These valves close when blood tends to flow in the opposite direction. The valves are small outpouchings from the inner wall of the vein with the free or unattached end directed toward the heart. As blood flows toward the heart, the valves lie flat against the vein surface, but if blood begins to flow in the wrong direction, the valve falls away from the vein wall and prevents the backflow.

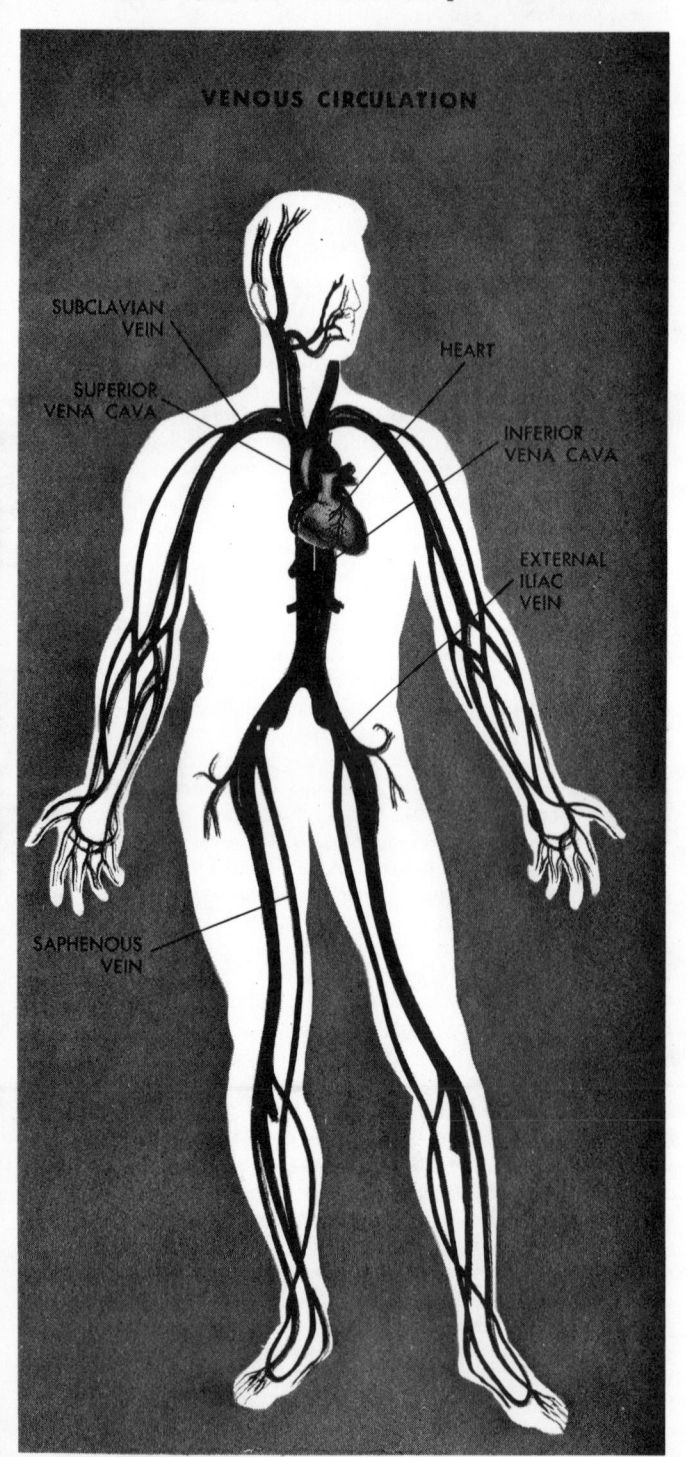

VENOUS CIRCULATION

Portal Circulation

A special division of the circulatory system is the portal circulation, which consists only of veins. The blood collected from the stomach, intestines, spleen, and pancreas all flows into one large vein, the portal vein. This

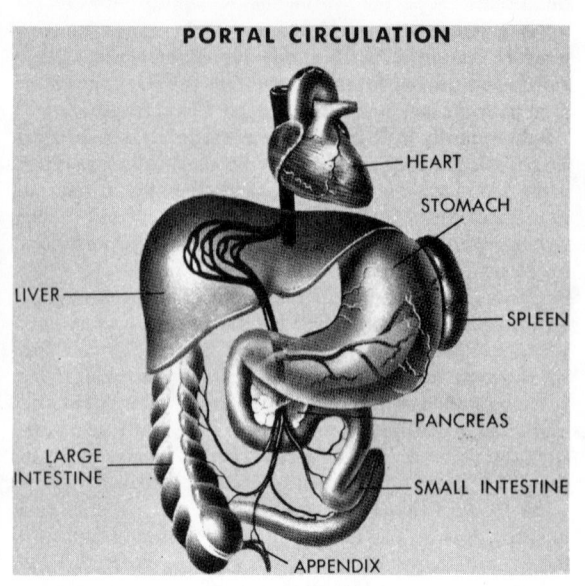

PORTAL CIRCULATION

vessel carries food products from the intestines to the liver. The blood then leaves the liver via the hepatic veins, which empty into the inferior vena cava just before the latter enters the right atrium of the heart.

Blood Clotting

The ability of the blood to clot is important in preventing excessive loss of blood when blood vessels are ruptured. The process of clotting consists of a complex series of chemical reactions which culminates in the conversion of a fluid substance (fibrinogen) into a mass of thin fibrin threads which forms the core of the clot.

The exact sequence of events in the formation of the blood clot is still unknown. A great number of substances have been shown to be involved in the clotting reaction. Some of these are normally present in the blood in inactive form and are changed to an active state during clotting (prothrombin → thrombin). Other substances are liberated into the blood during the course of the reaction. These include the platelet factor, which enters the blood stream when the platelets disintegrate, and thromboplastin, which is liberated from injured tissues. Still other materials such as calcium are normally present in the blood and contribute to the clotting process without changing their form.

The clotting reaction may be considered to proceed in three stages:

(1) The formation of thromboplastin.

(2) The formation of thrombin. Thromboplastin + prothrombin = thrombin.

(3) The formation of fibrin, the matrix of the clot: Thrombin + fibrinogen = fibrin.

The process begins when blood comes into contact with injured tissue, such as the damaged inner lining of a blood vessel. It is believed that the blood platelets give off a substance called the platelet factor, which, in combination with other substances normally present in the blood, leads to the formation of thromboplastin. One of these substances has been named the antihemophilic factor (AHF), since its absence is associated with hemophilia, an inherited disorder of the clotting mechanism.

The second stage of clotting is the formation of thrombin from the prothrombin normally found in the blood. This reaction is promoted by thromboplastin, calcium, and other substances.

Thrombin in turn activates the third and final clotting reaction, the conversion of fibrinogen into fibrin.

Blood Clotting as a Cause of Disease

The normal and helpful tendency of the blood to clot may be undesirable and even lethal under certain circumstances. A clot forming in an injured vein or artery is called a thrombus. The clot, or a portion of it, may be carried away in the blood stream (as an embolus) to lodge in a distant portion of the body. If the clot completely blocks the opening of an artery it will cause the death of those tissues which depend upon that artery for their blood supply. A thrombus in a vein of the leg may become detached and be carried to a blood vessel of the lung; this may be fatal. A clot or embolus in an artery of the brain may cause a stroke. Thrombosis may develop after surgery, in certain heart ailments, and in cases of chronic confining diseases. Important factors in thrombosis are damage to the lining of the blood vessel wall and sluggishness of the blood flow.

Blood Diseases

The blood diseases may generally be considered to involve either an excess or a deficiency of the materials normally found in the blood.

Anemia. A reduction of the number of red blood cells or of the quantity of hemoglobin in the blood is termed anemia. Anemia may be caused by bleeding, by destruction of the blood within the body (hemolysis), by disruption of red blood cell production in the bone marrow, by inadequate iron in the diet, or by an inability to properly absorb vitamin B_{12} from the intestine. In some instances two or more of these factors may be present simultaneously.

Whatever the cause, severe anemia will result in pallor, palpitation, fatigue, and shortness of breath. Particular forms of anemia will produce characteristic disturbances. Anemias resulting from blood destruction (hemolytic anemias) may cause yellowish discoloration of the skin and eyes (jaundice) and enlargement of the spleen. Pernicious anemia, which results from inadequate absorption of vitamin B_{12}, causes soreness of the tongue, difficulty in walking, and mental disturbances.

Polycythemia. This condition involves an excess of red blood cells and may arise without apparent cause. In other cases it develops when the bone marrow overproduces red blood cells as a response to a chronic oxygen deficiency. This may occur in certain lung and heart disorders. In polycythemia, the concentration of red cells makes the blood thick and sluggish, decreasing the circulation in outlying parts of the body, and resulting in headaches, dizziness, sweats, numbness of the extremities, and itching. The face becomes excessively ruddy or bluish in color, owing to the presence of large amounts of nonoxygen containing hemoglobin in the small vessels of the skin.

Disorders of the White Blood Cells. Leukopenia (too few white cells), a harmless decrease in the number of white blood cells, may follow recovery from infection or be associated with disorders of the spleen. A more serious decrease in white-cell concentration is seen in bone marrow disturbances. In these disorders, leukopenia occurs along with a decrease in the quantity of all of the formed elements of the blood (red cells and platelets). A serious blood disorder, agranulocytosis, occurs as a reaction to certain drugs and involves a decline in the numbers of a particular type of white cell, the granulocytes. The condition often disappears once the offending drug is removed, but it may be fatal.

The white blood cells are formidable bacteria-fighters, and a large decrease in their ranks will usually predispose the body to infection. In cases of agranulocytosis, fever, blood stream infections, and ulcerations of the mouth, rectum, and vagina are common.

Leukocytosis (high white-cell count) is commonly seen in bacterial infections and in leukemia. In the latter condition there is an overproduction of various types of white cells in the bone marrow. The normal blood-producing tissues of the bone marrow are replaced by white-cell-manufacturing tissue. This results in an underproduction of red blood cells and platelets. Many of the symptoms of leukemia result from anemia, infection, and bleeding.

Disorders of Blood Clotting— The Hemorrhagic Diseases

In these diseases, factors involved in the long chain of the clotting reaction are either missing from birth or become deficient in later life as a consequence of disease or a deficiency of vitamin K. In the absence of a normal clotting mechanism the patient may bleed spontaneously from the gums and other parts of the body. Often he bruises easily and loses large amounts of blood from minor cuts.

The congenital clotting disorders include the hemophilias, in which clotting substances are absent from the blood. Disruptions of the clotting mechanism may develop in later life, as in certain complications of pregnancy and in some cancers, in which a clot-dissolving enzyme appears in the blood and fibrinogen concentration is reduced. In certain liver diseases bleeding tendencies develop as the manufacture of prothrombin, a necessary clotting element, declines.

Platelet Deficiencies. Since the blood platelets are intimately associated with the control of hemorrhage, decline in their numbers results in a tendency towards easy bruising and bleeding from various parts of the body. Platelet deficiencies may appear suddenly following infections or the ingestion of certain drugs. Leukemia, disorders of the spleen, and bone marrow disturbances may also result in platelet decline.

Blood Transfusions and Blood Groups

The ancient Romans drank blood to regain youth and vitality. The idea that blood possessed life-giving properties persisted into later times; in 1492 Pope Innocent VIII was given blood to drink as a therapeutic measure. Following William Harvey's discovery of the circulation of the

BLOOD

blood in 1616, numerous experiments on transfusion were initiated. About 50 years later a patient in France was successfully transfused with sheep blood; however a later transfusion proved fatal, and in 1678 the French parliament passed a law prohibiting further blood transfusions.

Subsequently little progress was made in the field until the pathologist Karl Landsteiner discovered the existence of the blood groups in 1900. Landsteiner found that, in some cases, the blood cells of one person would clump together when they were mixed with the fluid portion of the blood (the serum) obtained from another. In other instances this reaction did not occur. The clumping, or agglutination, was explained by the presence of certain substances (antibodies) in the blood serum. The fact that this reaction did not always take place was accounted for by the existence of different combinations of antigens and antibodies in different persons; these combinations constituted the different blood groups. The knowledge of blood groups has made transfusions medically feasible.

The Blood Groups. The blood cells may contain two antigens, A or B. The blood serum may contain two antibodies, Anti-A (which can react with the antigen A) or Anti-B (which can react with the antigen B).

Each of the four blood groups contains a particular combination of these four factors.

Group O: Cells contain no antigen; serum contains Anti-A and Anti-B.
Group A: Cells contain A; serum contains Anti-B.
Group B: Cells contain B; serum contains Anti-A.
Group AB: Cells contain A and B; serum contains no antibodies. The antibody-antigen composition of the major blood groups is shown below.

Group A can be illustrated by placing the antigens and antibodies within this scheme:

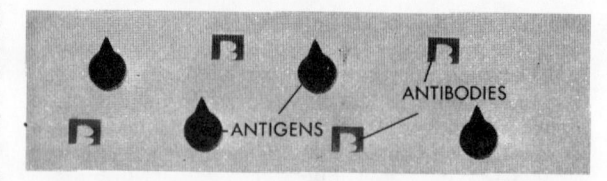

If group A blood is mixed with group B blood, the cells of group A will be agglutinated by the serum of group B and vice versa:

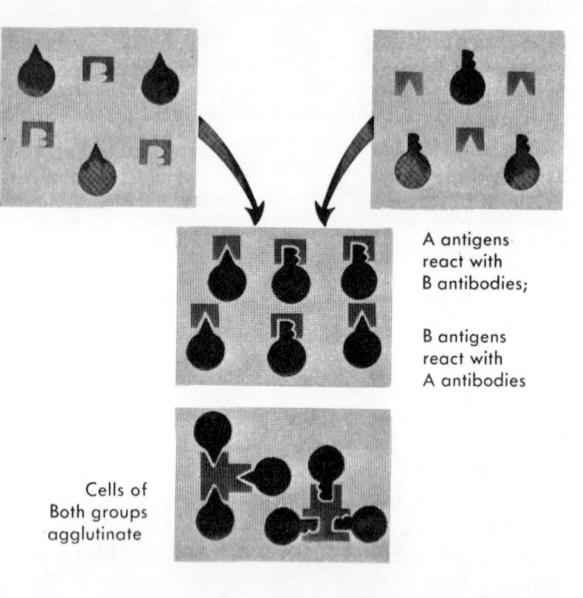

A antigens react with B antibodies;

B antigens react with A antibodies

Cells of Both groups agglutinate

If group A blood is transfused into a group B patient, a severe reaction develops which may include severe back pain, chills, and rapid pulse. Kidney failure may develop and the outcome may be fatal. Owing to this possibility, samples of blood taken from patients and donors are tested prior to blood transfusion.

The terms "universal recipient" and "universal donor" are sometimes mentioned in discussions of blood groups. "Universal recipient" refers to a patient with type AB blood, whose serum contains no antibodies which could agglutinate the blood of the donor. Although the cells of the AB patient should be agglutinated by the serum of donors of the other groups (since these cells contain A and B antigens), this usually does not occur. The term "universal recipient" is, however, misleading since under certain circumstances agglutination may result. This is particularly true in the case of children.

"Universal donor" describes an individual possessing type O blood, the cells of which contain no antigens. As in the case of "universal recipient," the term may be misleading, since occasionally agglutination will occur using the blood of a universal donor. To avoid mishaps it is advised that the blood of the donor should always match the blood of the patient.

BLOOD GROUP	CELL CONTAINS ANTIGEN	SERUM CONTAINS ANTIBODY
O	—	∩ ∩
A	●	∩
B	●	∩
AB	●	■

The groups may be pictured as a rectangle, representing the fluid portion of the blood, within which are circles representing the blood cells:

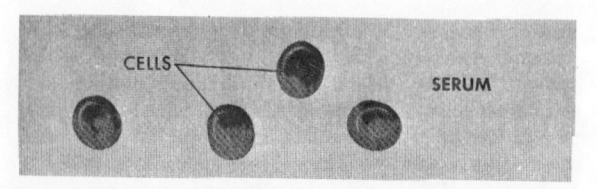

Other Blood Factors

In 1927 Landsteiner, working with Levine, discovered two new substances present in blood, which they designated M and N. They found that everyone carried either or both of these antigens and that they were independent of the regular blood groups. Later, numerous additional factors were discovered.

The Rh Factor. The Rh factor was named after the Rhesus monkey. By injecting Rhesus monkey blood into rabbits and guinea pigs Landsteiner and his associate Wiener produced a serum which contained a factor that agglutinated the blood cells of 85% of the white population. This factor turned out to be quite complicated, involving eight or more different types of blood.

The Rh factor is responsible for erythroblastosis fetalis, a disease of newborn children. If the mother is Rh negative and the father is Rh positive, the developing child may be Rh positive. During pregnancy the mother may produce antibodies against the blood cells of the fetus. In subsequent pregnancies in which the embryo is Rh positive, the antibodies in the blood of the mother may enter the circulation of the embryo and destroy its red blood cells. The child may be born with a severe anemia. Children born with this condition can be treated after birth by replacing their blood with Rh negative blood.

Applied Knowledge of Blood Groups

The knowledge that blood groups are inherited according to specific patterns has been applied in certain areas of legal medicine, such as disputed paternity and the accidental interchange of newborn infants. While blood tests can prove that a particular person is *not* the parent of a child, they cannot prove with certainty that the individual is the parent.

Some scientists have attempted to use blood groups to trace the ancestry of particular groups of people as a clue to historical migrations. For example, evidence obtained from archeological studies indicated that in earlier times the Vikings had established a settlement at the town of Pembroke, in Wales. Blood tests of the local population yielded 33% A group, a percentage higher than that found in other areas of Great Britain and comparable to those obtained in present day Norway.

Another application of blood group studies concerns the relationship between blood groups and disease. A higher percentage of stomach cancer, pernicious anemia, and diabetes, has been found in group A individuals than in other groups. Gastric and duodenal ulcers are more prevalent in group O persons. These studies promise to contribute much to our understanding of susceptibility to disease.

With the discovery of many additional blood groups other than the basic types used for purposes of blood transfusion, it may be possible eventually to identify every person in terms of his unique combination of blood factors, as is presently done with fingerprints. The FBI realizes the usefulness of blood groups in criminal work and their serological unit runs thousands of blood analyses each year for purposes of identification.

BLOOD BANK, collection of various blood preparations, usually stored in a hospital laboratory, to meet medical emergencies. The fluid portion of the blood, the plasma, keeps almost indefinitely when frozen; however, the red cells tend to disintegrate with age. Whole blood, containing the plasma and the red cells, can be stored for several weeks if it is kept at a temperature of 4° C. to 7° C. Chemicals can be added to preserve the red cells and to prevent clotting. Blood banks often exchange supplies in order to have different types of blood available. Dr. Charles Drew, an American black, headed the first Red Cross blood bank, and was a pioneer in the field.

BLOOD COUNT, a laboratory procedure in which the concentrations of red cells, white cells, and platelets (disc-shaped cells that lack nuclei) are determined. The concentration of hemoglobin, the oxygen-carrying chemical of the blood, is also ascertained in the blood count.

The concentration of cells and platelets is determined by diluting a measured amount of blood and placing it in a counting chamber marked with horizontal and vertical grid lines, much like the latitude and longitude lines on a map. The number of cells that appear in the squares formed by the grid lines are counted, and from this count an estimate can be made of the average density of cells in the blood. The amount of hemoglobin is determined by measuring the redness of solutions that contain a known quantity of broken-down red blood cells.

The blood count is an important guide to health and disease. Blood diseases that involve anemia (lack of hemoglobin or red cells), leukocytosis (too many white cells), and thrombopenia (too few platelets), are diagnosed through the use of blood-counting techniques.

BLOOD COUNT

Drops of diluted blood are deposited on a specially ruled glass surface. Red cells are counted in the areas marked R, and white cells in the areas marked W. The grid for red cells is tighter because of the higher concentration of these cells in normal blood.

COUNTING CHAMBER

An enlargement of a red cell counting chamber (left). Red cells are represented by black dots; white cells by circles.

BLOODLETTING, or phlebotomy, is the technique of withdrawing blood from the body to treat disease. Bloodletting has been in use for centuries, having been practiced by the ancient Greeks, Hindus, and Hebrews. The physicians of the Middle Ages, who often used leeches to draw blood, thought that bloodletting permitted harmful substances to be drawn from one organ to another. There was heated discussion in medical circles concerning the proper number of bleedings and the amount of blood to be withdrawn with respect to the age of the patient, the season, and the locality. Bloodletting is little used today, but is of value in certain conditions. In congestive heart failure the removal of quantities of blood may help the heart by reducing its work-load. Bloodletting is the standard treatment in cases of polycythemia vera, a disease involving overproduction of red blood cells.

BLOOD POISONING. The invasion, or "poisoning," of the blood by bacteria is termed a bacteremia; when the organisms produce the symptoms of disease, the condition is termed a septicemia. Among the most frequent causes of bacteremia are the staphylococcus, the organism that commonly produces boils, and the streptococcus, which is often responsible for sore throats. The bacteria that cause pneumonia, typhoid fever, meningitis, and gas gangrene may also cause bacteremia and septicemia.

The germs may enter the blood stream from the point of their first entry which may be the skin, wounds, boils, sore throat, teeth (following an extraction), or lungs. Ordinarily, bacteria in the blood are destroyed by the white blood cells; however, when the body is weakened or the bacterial invasion is overwhelming, the organisms flourish and the infection may spread through the blood stream to other organs. This is most common in the case of the staphylococcus but also occurs in the other forms of bacteremia. The presence of bacteria in the blood and their poisonous secretions produce a rapid pulse, fever, and chills. The condition may be fatal if not treated. Antibiotics are employed to destroy the infecting organisms.

BLUE BABY, term used to describe a newborn infant whose skin color is bluish-gray owing to the presence of large amounts of nonoxygen-containing blood in the circulation. These infants suffer from congenital heart defects which permit quantities of blood to pass from the veins to the arterial circulation without entering the lungs and taking up oxygen. Infections or injury occurring during pregnancy and hereditary factors have been suspected as possible causes of these defects. There is considerable evidence that German measles infection of the mother early in pregnancy can be responsible. While formerly most blue babies died in infancy or childhood, many are now successfully treated by surgery.
See also HEART DISEASE.

BLUMENBACH [blōō'mən-bäkH], **JOHANN FRIEDRICH** (1752–1840), German anatomist, influential as a teacher and investigator of comparative anatomy, and a pioneer in comparative anthropology. He was educated in Jena and Göttingen and was professor of medicine and anatomy at the University of Göttingen from 1776 to 1835. He made the first major successful attempt to compare skeletal and other physical characteristics of men of different races. His classification of man into five races (Caucasian, Mongolian, Ethiopian, American, and Malay) of a single species, became the basis for later studies of racial traits. He also studied the differences between men and other mammals, especially the apes.

BMR. See BASAL METABOLIC RATE.

BODY TYPES, categories of human physique based on major anatomical characteristics, and usually developed within theories relating body structure to personality. Relationships between body type and certain personality characteristics may reflect common underlying causal factors: for example, the thyroid gland can affect physique and temperament. It is important to note that certain personality characteristics might include behavior—such as overeating—that would in turn affect physique, and that certain physiques may lead to the success of certain ways of behaving.

Most research on relationships between body build and personality has focused on the theories of a German, Ernst Kretschmer, and an American, W. H. Sheldon. The latter developed three descriptive categories for body build: endomorph, ectomorph, and mesomorph. The endomorph, to give an approximate description, is round and soft, with prominent abdomen, short limbs, small hands and feet, and smooth skin. The ectomorph is thin and long-limbed, with narrow shoulders, long neck, slight muscular development, and thin skin. The mesomorph has strong skeletal structure, well-developed musculature, and thick skin. These descriptions are of extremes which are rarely found; the body builds of most individuals are mixtures of components. A person's physique can be rated to show how much he tends to resemble one of the three categories. Sheldon reported relationships between patterns of body build and patterns of temperament. Persons who rated high in endomorphy tended to rate high in viscerotonia—a term covering such traits as relaxation in posture, preference for physical comfort, sociability, complacency, and tolerance. Persons who tended toward ectomorphy were found to tend toward cerebrotonia—a temperament marked by restraint in posture, secretiveness, desire for privacy, inhibitions, and preference for intellectual activity. Persons who rated high in mesomorphy tended, according to Sheldon, toward somatotonia—a personality description including such traits as boldness, aggressiveness, and liking for exercise, adventure, and risk.

Evidence has been found for the relationships between body build and personality described by Sheldon. The nature and extent of the relationships, however, have not been precisely determined.

BOERHAAVE [bōōr'hä-və], **HERMANN** (1668–1738), Dutch physician, considered the greatest medical teacher of his time. He introduced clinical teaching at Leiden and contributed to the knowledge of physiology and digestion. An area of the University of Leiden is named in his honor.

BOGOMOLETS [bŏ-gŏ-mô'lĭts], **ALEKSANDR ALEKSANDROVICH** (1881–1946), Russian physiologist and pathologist, known for his preparation of antireticular cytotoxic serum (ACS), supposed to prolong life. He was educated at Kiev Gymnasium and Odessa University. He held positions in Saratov, Moscow, and Kiev. In 1930 he was elected president of the All-Ukrainian Academy of Sciences. ACS, claimed to be promising for the treatment of chronic diseases of old age, is said to have been used successfully in promoting wound-healing in Russian soldiers in World War II.

BOILS, or furuncles, infections just beneath the skin which start when bacteria, usually staphylococci, invade a hair follicle or sweat gland. As the germs multiply and produce toxins, the body responds by sending millions of white cells to help wall off the infection. Initially, a small tender red lump appears which enlarges, forming a central cavity containing white cells, bacteria, dead tissue, and serum. Often this material forms a hard core which is extruded with the pus when the boil "points" (comes to a head) and drains.

Boils are very painful because of the pressure they produce when enlarging, but the pain is greatly relieved when they drain. They are not considered serious infections unless they occur in the nose, upper face, or lip. Infection may spread from these areas in sinuses within the brain. Boils occuring in the ear canal are particularly painful and difficult to treat. Hot, wet salt compresses help the body localize the infection. Surgical drainage may be necessary, resulting in a smaller scar as well as faster healing than if the boil is allowed to rupture and drain spontaneously. Antibiotics are occasionally necessary as well. Lack of good skin hygiene, severe illness, diabetes, and various skin diseases, such as, eczema, all may foster the development of a boil.

See also ABSCESS; INFLAMMATION; STY.

BONE, the hard, white tissue that forms the skeleton, or framework, of bony fishes and land vertebrates. About 45% of the total weight of bone consists of mineral substances, mainly calcium salts. Water constitutes about 25% of bone weight, and the remainder is composed of organic material, chiefly a network of protein fibers called collagen. Because of its combination of materials, bone is extremely hard; but it also has elastic properties due to the arrangement of mineral crystals within the collagen network.

The Development of Bone. The supporting structures of the fetus are composed of cartilage (gristle) and membranous tissue. During pre-birth development, the cartilage and membranous tissue is gradually replaced by the components of bone. Osteoblasts, or bone-building cells, are largely responsible for this process. Even at birth, and in the higher vertebrates for many years after, total replacement of cartilage by bone tissue is not complete. In man, the skull of a newborn individual contains non-bony intervals of membranous tissue, called fontanels, which are not replaced by bone until about the middle of the second year. The ribs do not become completely bony until the mid-twenties. In addition to the gradual replacement of supporting structures by bony tissue, bone is constantly rebuilt throughout life, because of normal growth, or to repair diseased tissue (as in fractures).

The Structure of Bone. A thin, fibrous layer of cells, called the periosteum, covers each bone. Within this layer are the osteoblasts, or bone-building cells. The mineral components of bone, within their protein network, are deposited in thin layers beneath the periosteum. Bone tissue is porous due to a system of channels, called Haversian canals, which provide pathways for blood vessels and nerves to travel to the interior of the bone. In flat bones, such as those of the skull, the interior is spongy. In the long bones of the body (the arm and leg bones), the interior of the bone is a roughly circular cavity filled with marrow, a soft, fatty substance. The red marrow of the vertebrae, ribs, sternum, and skull are sites of blood cell production. *See illustration on page 66.*

The Function of Bone. In addition to its obvious use of providing the basic shape and framework of the body, bone serves other necessary functions. Muscles, which are attached to bones, permit the bones to function as levers for the body. Bones act also as protective devices for bodily organs, as in the case of the skull protecting the all-important brain. Further, bony tissue is a storage depot for minerals which are not immediately needed by the body, and certain highly specialized bones of the middle ear aid in the maintenance of equilibrium.

Historical Importance of Bone. Of all bodily tissues, bone is the most impervious to the ravages of time. Through fossil remains of the skeletons of ancient creatures, man has been able to piece together a history of life on earth that would not have been possible by other means. Bone has also been useful to man in the crafting of tools and ornaments, and is today used in the manufacture of such diverse products as fertilizer, china, and gelatin.

See also EMBRYOLOGY; FRACTURES; HUMAN ANATOMY; OSTEOMYELITIS; OSTEOPOROSIS; PAGET'S DISEASE; SKELETAL SYSTEM.

BONE GRAFTS, sections of bone used to repair injured or diseased bone. The grafts may be taken from the patient's ribs, shinbone (tibia), or pelvis, or from bone banks (collections of bones obtained from cadavers).

Bone grafts are placed in the gaps in diseased or injured bones, and serve as a framework into which bone cells from the patient can grow and build a new structure of healthy bone tissue. To stimulate the growth of new bone, small bone grafts in the form of chips are placed into unhealed or poorly united fractures, and into the cavities that are left after the removal of bone tumors. Large pieces of bone from the patient's ribs are used to patch defects of the skull and forehead. Plastic surgeons use bone from the patient's pelvis to reconstruct noses and faces. Bone grafting today also saves limbs that were previously amputated because of extensive injury resulting from automobile and industrial accidents.

See also SURGERY: *Orthopedic Surgery.*

BONE STRUCTURE

THE STRUCTURE OF BONE

Bone is composed of mineral salts deposited among a network of organic fibers. Its hardness and flexibility (derived respectively from the mineral and organic components) make bone an ideal structural material. Despite its rocklike solidity, bone is not lifeless. It exchanges minerals with the blood and continually destroys and rebuilds itself, changing its internal architecture to accommodate the shifting stresses placed upon it.

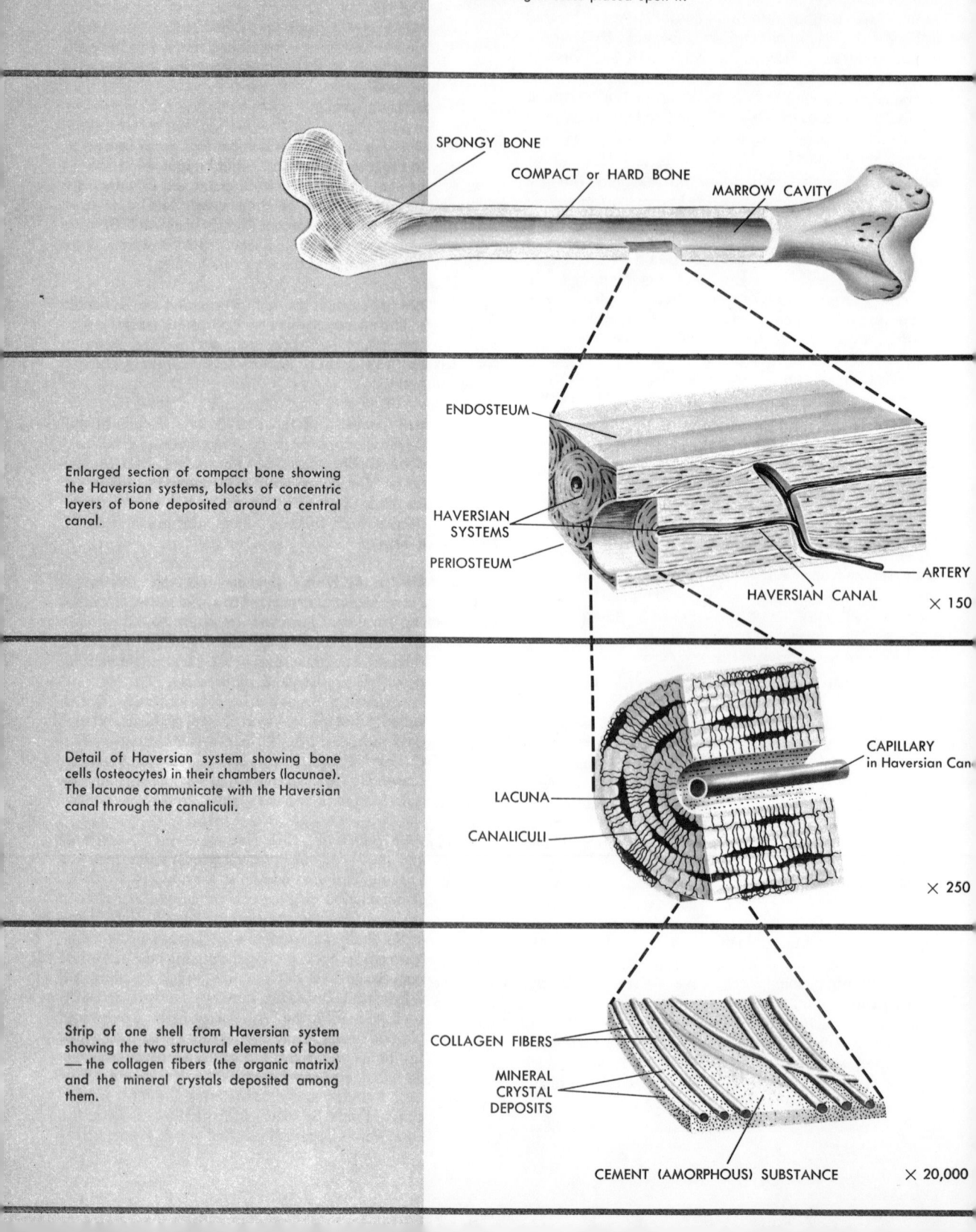

SPONGY BONE
COMPACT or HARD BONE
MARROW CAVITY

Enlarged section of compact bone showing the Haversian systems, blocks of concentric layers of bone deposited around a central canal.

ENDOSTEUM
HAVERSIAN SYSTEMS
PERIOSTEUM
ARTERY
HAVERSIAN CANAL
× 150

Detail of Haversian system showing bone cells (osteocytes) in their chambers (lacunae). The lacunae communicate with the Haversian canal through the canaliculi.

CAPILLARY in Haversian Canal
LACUNA
CANALICULI
× 250

Strip of one shell from Haversian system showing the two structural elements of bone — the collagen fibers (the organic matrix) and the mineral crystals deposited among them.

COLLAGEN FIBERS
MINERAL CRYSTAL DEPOSITS
CEMENT (AMORPHOUS) SUBSTANCE
× 20,000

BORDET [bôr-dĕ′], **JULES JEAN BAPTISTE VINCENT** (1870–1961). Belgian bacteriologist who received the Nobel Prize in 1919 for his studies in immunity. Along with Octave Gengou, he discovered the organism responsible for whooping cough and described the complement fixation reaction which is used in the diagnosis of syphilis and numerous other infectious diseases.

BORIC ACID, H_3BO_3, white, crystalline boron compound formerly in wide use as an antiseptic, eyewash, and skin ointment. At one time boric acid was considered nonpoisonous and was used to preserve food. It was used by the medical profession in the form of ointments and solutions until its poisonous properties were discovered. Large doses have resulted in death and, since the compound is excreted slowly, small doses over a period of time may lead to the accumulation of dangerous amounts in the body. Boric acid should therefore be used with caution and should not be applied to large areas of the body surface. The compound is still employed as a dusting powder for some skin irritations and as an eyewash.

In industry, boric acid is used in electroplating and welding; in the manufacture of leather, cosmetics, and electric capacitors; and as a raw material for the manufacture of other boron compounds.

BOTULISM [bŏch′ə-lĭz-əm], disease caused by the consumption of food which has been contaminated with the common soil bacillus *Clostridium botulinum*. Since this organism cannot survive in the presence of oxygen, it finds an excellent breeding place in canned foods which have not been properly sterilized. The major source of botulism in the United States is from the products of home canning. The botulism poison is perhaps the deadliest known, and approximately two-thirds of those afflicted die. It has been estimated that a few ounces of this substance would be sufficient to poison millions of persons. The first symptoms, nausea and vomiting, usually appear within six hours after eating the contaminated food. Later headache, dizziness, weakness, and double vision develop. There may be muscular incoordination and difficulty in chewing and swallowing. Death results from paralysis of the muscles used in breathing. An antitoxin is available but usually does not help when given after symptoms have developed. To prevent botulism, foods that appear spoiled should be discarded and home-canned products should be boiled for at least 10 minutes before being eaten.

BOVET [bō-vā′], **DANIEL** (1907–   ), Swiss-born pharmacologist who received the Nobel Prize in 1957 for his development of antihistamines and for his synthesis of muscle-relaxing drugs that are used in surgery. While at the Pasteur Institute from 1929 to 1947 he and his colleagues synthesized many of the sulfa compounds used in the treatment of infectious diseases. In 1947 he became head of the department of pharmacology at the Italian Health Institute in Rome.

BOWDITCH [bou′dĭch], **HENRY PICKERING** (1840–1911), foremost American physiologist of his day. Professor of physiology at Harvard and later dean of the Harvard Medical School, he established the first physiological laboratory in America and was a founder of the American Physiological Society. His many investigations included studies of muscle and nerve function and research on the growth rates of children.

BRADYCARDIA [brăd-ĭ-kär′dē-ə], heartbeat rate of less than 60 per minute. A slowing of the heart beat may occur, following certain infectious diseases, in malnutrition, jaundice, heart disorders, and in normal persons such as athletes and young adults. Ordinarily no symptoms are presented.
See also HEART.

BRAIN [brān]. The brain of almost every animal is a piece of its living tissue near the front or head end of its body and is usually collected into a compact mass, although occasionally it is found distributed as a chain of small masses. Generally whitish in color, the brain is invariably connected by many strands (nerves) with the sense organs and with the muscles of the body. When cut across, the exposed surface of the brain often shows a mixture of patches of gray and white tissue.

Under the microscope brain tissue at first seems little differentiated, but after treatment with various selective stains it shows an extremely rich structure. Scattered throughout the gray patches are great numbers of nerve cells (in the human brain about 10 billion) each branching out into many ramifying threads, the dendrons and the axons. The branches seem to be intermingled in a network of bewildering complexity. Some of the nerve cells have one especially long and thick branch, the axon, which may travel quite a distance (many feet in the larger animals) before ending either at another nerve cell or at a muscle. The brain thus forms an extremely rich network between the sense organs and the muscles.

All nerve cells are extremely sensitive, and share one kind of special behavior: when a nerve cell is disturbed by an appropriate stimulus, it "fires" by producing an electric wave (the nervous impulse), which then travels over all of its branches. This may be likened to a flame traveling over a network of trails of gunpowder, the flame at each point igniting the next. The impulses are usually set up by the activities of the world around (light, sound, heat, touch) which impinge on the sense organs, since the sense organs contain nerve cells in which the impulses originate. These impulses are conducted over various parts of the nervous network, cell firing off cell in the process. If the stimulation leads to action, the final impulses arrive at the muscles, which they cause to contract.

Chemically, the substance of the brain is mostly protein, like the rest of the body, but with an unusually large amount of special fatty substances (lecithin, for example) which act to insulate one nerve from another, stopping any single impulse from spreading over the whole brain.

The energy for these nervous activities comes largely from the burning of glucose (a simple sugar) by oxygen. The physical and chemical processes used by the brain in the course of its work do not differ in any essential way from those used by other tissues of the body.

Brain Function

The description just given does not suggest what is the main function of the brain and of what use it is to the organism. To answer this, one must go back to the basic facts of evolution. The rough-and-tumble of existence and natural selection (a mechanism of evolution whereby those organisms and particular qualities of an organism, best adapted for survival, are selected and perpetuated), ensure that forms will develop that are extremely resistant to the destructive forces around them. This earth, after about 5 billion years, has produced its well-adapted forms. Among these are the higher animal organisms, such as the mammals, whose power of resistance can be properly appreciated only when we remember that they have survived the ice ages and are, in fact, older than the Alps. In general, the forms produced by evolution tend to achieve their resistance in one of two ways: by developing simple physical hardness (as the tortoise protects itself by an inert but almost unbreakable shell) or by developing complex mobility (as a fly avoids being caught or as a fencer avoids being wounded). The development of complex mobility is the function of the brain: to produce the right action at the right time, so that the threats from the world around will cause no serious harm to the organism. All of the brain's functions can thus be seen as a complex form of homeostasis, or maintenance of internal balance by an organism. This word ("homeostasis") was coined by physiologist Walter Cannon, in 1929, to represent the fact that the body's internal mechanisms, especially the autonomic (involuntary or vegetative) nervous system, always react to disturbance so that the effects of the disturbance are eventually neutralized. The same neutralization, however, is just as essential in the wide-ranging activities of the free living animal. The threat of drying up, for example, leads the organism to drink water, to search for water, or (in man) to build pipelines to bring water. In all cases the end is the same: the brain's activity is so related to the threatening disturbance that the disturbance hardly hurts the organism at all. The organism survives, and the brain, which has read the threat and produced an appropriate action, proves its value to the organism.

When the threat is simple (such as that of drying up) and the cure simple (such as "go toward the smell of water and then drink") a simple brain is adequate. But evolution has shown that there is advantage in being able to deal with more complex threats. "Complex" means here that the threat has many components and what the best reply to each component is depends on the direction of the other components. Thus "red" coming to the eye may at one time be a light at a traffic crossing, at another time part of a meal with red meat and white potatoes, and at a third time a poisonous red berry in green foliage. What the reaction should be to "red" depends, therefore, on what other stimuli are coming in from other sense organs. It becomes necessary for the brain to receive information from many different sources at once, and to act, using the muscles, in a way depending on complex comparisons between the various partial pieces of information. From this arises the necessity for the brain itself: a central station operating so that the pattern of action sent to all the muscles can depend on an interweaving of what information has come from all the sense organs.

Not only may the correct response to a stimulus depend on what is happening at other places being stimulated, it may also depend on what has happened to the organism in the past. The more highly evolved brains have developed methods by which what happened in the past is preserved in some physical trace, ready to exert its effect on a later process. When this happens, the psychologist says that the organism is showing the effects of memory. Although there is as yet very little known about what form these traces take, there can be little doubt that they are in the form of some physical, that is material, change, possibly in molecular structures in the brain. Discovery of their nature is one of the outstanding problems of brain function awaiting solution.

When a threat recurs there is a clear advantage, once a suitable form of response has been found, in retaining the form of the response so that it can be reproduced at once on future occasions. Living organisms do show this retention. How it is done depends markedly on the duration between the first presentation of a threat and the last. Sometimes the duration is very great, such as the threat of winter's cold, which has recurred annually for millions of years. When the recurrence is over many generations, natural selection tends to develop a uniform reaction which is inherited and transmitted by the genes, so that the young animal produces the correct response on its first encounter. Such a response is called a reflex. The brain of the higher organism contains many such reflexes, each an appropriate reaction to some threat.

Other threats, however, while recurring over a period of time, do not last long enough for natural selection to be able to develop the appropriate response. It is then advantageous if the individual can find a response and retain it over his own lifetime. The higher organisms have all developed special mechanisms by which the individual can find and retain, for his own lifetime, any response that is adaptive for him individually. The mechanisms responsible are those of "learning." The general mechanism is provided by heredity, but the details come from the world around. Thus, it is a characteristic of the species that the kitten can learn, but the details of what the kitten learns— of how to catch mice and of how mice behave—come ultimately from the mice themselves.

To summarize, then, the brain may be characterized biologically as that part of the organism which protects it by receiving information in complex patterns and by recoding these patterns into suitable patterns of action that show in the muscles. Its purpose is to keep constant those variables on which the organism's life depends. It recodes the patterns in the right way, rather than in a random or chaotic way, either because evolution has formed the right nervous mechanisms in it (for those disturbances that recur over the centuries), or because evolution has formed in it the neuronic mechanisms for learning, and actual experience has provided the brain with the details.

Artificial Brains

The whole subject of "brain in general," however, cannot be adequately understood today unless one also considers the artificial, man-made forms of the brain; for the development of the modern, general-purpose electronic computer has thrown a flood of light on what is implied by "brainlike activity."

The point is that the general-purpose computer is a completely willing slave. It will carry out any process that it is told to do, but it must be told what to do in terms that do not require previous knowledge or explanation. The terms must also be totally devoid of ambiguity. Thus the command "be clever" is useless; one must decide what "being clever" means; one must break the instruction down to commands of the most basic and practical type. The attempt to define what one really means by a machine "being clever" has forced much intensive thinking. As a result, we now have an understanding of what is meant by brainlike activity that far surpasses what was known in, say, 1935.

Feedback. One of the discoveries made was the importance, in brainlike activity, of "feedback." Feedback is said to be present if two systems, A and B, are so acting that A has an action on B, and B at the same time has an action on A, so that the chain of cause and effect goes back and forth between the two. A simple example is provided by the heater of a room and the controlling thermostat: the thermostat controls the heater, and the heater acts, through the air of the room, on the thermostat. Another example occurs when one holds a telescope to look at a distant object: movements of one's hands shift the position of the image in the field of vision; but at the same time (if one wishes to keep the image central) the movement of the image causes one to make readjusting movements with one's hands. A continuous double action is produced: the movements of the hands affect what is seen, and what is seen determines the movements made by the hands. There is feedback between position of image and movement of hands.

The recognition of the importance of feedback, and its practical use in such "clever" devices as the automatic pilot and the self-aiming antiaircraft gun, made obsolete the dogma that no machine could correct its own errors. The automatic pilot does this incessantly. Some physiologists had earlier attempted to use the concept of feedback to describe biological phenomena, but the concept is a difficult one that needs a properly developed logic and mathematics if arguments about it are not to break down in confusion. About 1935 certain engineering problems made it necessary to develop an adequate mathematical description of feedback. Today the understanding derived from those early (and subsequent) investigations is of the greatest assistance in making clear what is meant by brainlike activity.

Information Theory. A second development that has thrown a great light on brain function is that of information theory. During World War II, two noted American mathematicians, Claude Shannon and Norbert Wiener, found that "information" could be measured. (In this special sense, information corresponds to the freedom of choice that one has in selecting, from all the possibilities, a message for transmission.) Today there exists an extensive body of knowledge about how information can be received, transformed, lost, recovered, and stored. This knowledge is relevant to brainlike behavior, for we now realize that many of the brain processes that once seemed most mysterious are in fact just those processes that are today well understood in information theory. It is, for instance, an expression of a deep and exact truth to say that the fundamental homeostatic processes in the brain are identical with those that remove noise from a communication system.

Briefly, just as noise is that which tends to corrupt a telephone message and drive it away from its proper form, similarly, when the disturbances of the world threaten to drive a living organism away from its own proper form, brain activity helps to oppose the threats so that the form is maintained. What is important about this identification is that it makes us aware that both natural and artificial (mechanical) brains have a fundamental limitation: any system that is to achieve appropriate selection (to a degree better than chance) can do so only as a consequence of information received.

Information theory has made us realize that all the "remarkable" properties of the brain fall into one of two categories. First, there are processes that were considered unique simply because the living brain was the only known example of a system both highly dynamic (active) and really complicated. The other processes are those that show evidence of intense selection, and they are the ones usually thought of as being peculiarly brainlike. Selection was shown dramatically, in 1846, when J. C. Adams and U. J. Leverrier said to their fellow astronomer, J. C. Galle, "Aim your telescope at the point P in the sky and you will there see a new planet." Here, out of all the points in the sky they selected the particular one, and the planet Neptune was discovered. But selection is also shown just as clearly (though less dramatically) when a person leaves home and, after traveling for hundreds of miles, eventually returns to exactly the same house. Again, the ordinary intelligence test shows in detail how a good score is inseparably connected with the ability to select a small set of (correct) answers from the great range of what is possible.

When a brain, either natural or artificial, is regarded from this point of view, its selective power is limited by the amount of information that has come to it previously. Here one may easily make a gross error by overestimating the amount of information that must be given ("programmed" into) a computer before it can solve a problem, or by underestimating the amount of information held by the brain of the higher organism after it has been shaped by two billion years of evolution (together with all the experiences of youth, and perhaps by the training of school). When the magnitude of the difference between these two quantities of information (programmed and previously stored) is appreciated, we see that as far as the biological activities of the higher organisms are concerned (those, for example, by which they get their food and avoid their enemies), what goes on in the living brain is not essentially different from what goes on in the artificial brainlike mechanisms that can be made today. It can be said that the brain is understood, in the sense that any of its functions can be reproduced mechanically, its function of being "intelligent" not excepted.

See also NERVOUS SYSTEM.

BREASTS, milk-producing organs or mammary glands of the adult female. They are also present in rudimentary form in children and adult males, but reach their full de-

BREATHING

velopment only in the mature female. Located on the lower half of the chest, the breasts are rounded projections, composed of fat and glandular tissue. In the center of each breast is an elevated area of pigmented tissue called the nipple. This is surrounded by a flat, circular area of pinkish skin, the areola. The areola contains oil glands that lubricate the nipple, especially during nursing. The bulk of the breast in a woman who is neither pregnant nor nursing consists of fat. The glandular tissue, which produces and secretes milk in a nursing mother, forms 15 or 20 lobes arranged radially about the nipple, within the breast. Each lobe is connected by its own duct to a minute opening at the surface of the nipple. The glands are present at birth in the female, but do not show any real development until the onset of puberty. Between the ages of 11 and 14 years, hormones secreted by the ovaries and pituitary gland cause the development of fat and glandular tissue in the breast. Further growth of breast tissue takes place during pregnancy, when the ducts send out more branches. During the last half of pregnancy, the ends of these branches become rounded sacs lined with milk-producing cells. Lactation, the phenomenon of milk-production, is controlled by hormones secreted by the ovaries, pituitary gland, and placenta. As the milk is secreted, it passes into the ducts leading to the nipples. When an infant nurses, nerve endings in the nipple are stimulated, resulting in the secretion of a hormone by the pituitary gland. This hormone causes musclelike cells surrounding the milk-filled sacs to contract. Milk then passes out of the duct openings on the nipple. After lactation ceases, the breasts return to about the same size they were before pregnancy.

In the male, the breast is represented mainly by the nipple and areola. Certain abnormal conditions occur, however, in which fatty deposits form within the male breast. The resulting enlargement, known as gynecomastia, is thought to be due to hormonal irregularities. Other breast abnormalities found in males and in females include amastia, a rare condition of absence of the breasts; polymastia, the presence of more than two breasts; and polythelia, the presence of more than two breasts, represented only by rudimentary nipples.

BREATHING. See Respiration.

BROCKEN [brŏk′ən] **SPECTER,** an optical phenomenon in which an observer sees his shadow projected upon a cloud in apparently gigantic proportions. In some cases faintly colored rings surround the image. The name comes from Brocken Mountain in Saxony, Germany, where the phenomenon is often seen. Brocken specters have been observed from many high places and from aircraft. Strong sunlight from a low angle is needed to throw the observer's shadow onto a cloud or fog bank. Recent research has attributed the apparent size of the Brocken specter to psychological, as well as physical, causes. It is believed that the observer may subconsciously associate far-off objects, seen through thin clouds or fog, with his relatively nearby shadow seen on the same clouds.

BROMIDES [brō′mīdz], salts of hydrobromic acid, HBr, found in underground deposits and in sea water. The bromide ion, which exists in sea water to the extent of 67 parts per million, is oxidized in a commercial process to produce the element bromine. Bromides are obtained by the action of hydrobromic acid on metals or metal oxides or in some cases by direct reaction of metals or their hydroxides with bromine. Lithium, sodium, potassium, and ammonium bromides are used as sedatives and are of some value in treating nervous disorders. Sodium and potassium bromides are used in photography for the preparation of silver bromide emulsions.

BRONCHI [brŏng′kī], tubes that carry air from the windpipe, or trachea, to the lungs. The two largest bronchi branch from the trachea, one going to each lung. In the lung they subdivide into successively smaller tubes until they reach the alveolar sacs, the small pockets in the lung where respiration occurs. The walls of the larger bronchi contain muscle tissue and cartilage rings, open at the rear, which serve to keep the passageway open. In the small bronchi (bronchioles) the cartilage disappears and the relative thickness of the muscular coat increases. In asthmatic attacks, spasms of these muscles narrow the bronchioles.
See also Respiration.

BRONCHIECTASIS [brŏng-kē-ĕk′tə-sĭs], a disease of the air passages (the bronchi), marked by weakening and stretching of the walls of the small bronchi. Bronchiectasis may be caused by a tumor or foreign body obstructing the air passages, or it may develop following pneumonia, tuberculosis, or other infections. In some cases it may appear without any obvious predisposing cause. The weakening of the bronchial walls permits small saclike pouches to form which become filled with bacteria-laden secretions. The chief symptom is a severe cough, frequently with large amounts of sputum. Bronchiectasis is one of the most common causes of a bloody cough. The patient may suffer from repeated attacks of pneumonia and fever. The condition may become progressively worse with each succeeding bout of pneumonia. The administration of antibiotics is often helpful. In severe cases it is necessary to surgically remove the affected portion of the lung.

BRONCHITIS [brŏng-kī′tĭs], inflammation of lining of the air passages (the bronchi). Acute bronchitis may be caused by bacteria, viral, or fungus infections; by irritants, such as smoke, dust, tobacco, or chemicals; or by certain parasitic infections in which the life cycle of the parasite involves a migration through the lungs.

Long-standing lung diseases are frequently associated with chronic bronchitis. In congestive heart failure infection of the bronchioles and chronic bronchitis results from accumulation of fluid in the bronchial wall. All types of bronchitis may be aggravated by allergies.

Changes Occurring in Bronchitis. The bronchial tubes normally possess certain mechanisms which displace the mucous secretion of the bronchial linings toward the throat and mouth. These include a wavelike motion of the bronchial tube (peristalsis), and the propelling action of the fine hairs (cilia) which project from the bronchial cells into the passageway. The cough reflex also operates to remove bronchial secretion. In bronchitis these actions are

BRONCHIAL TREE

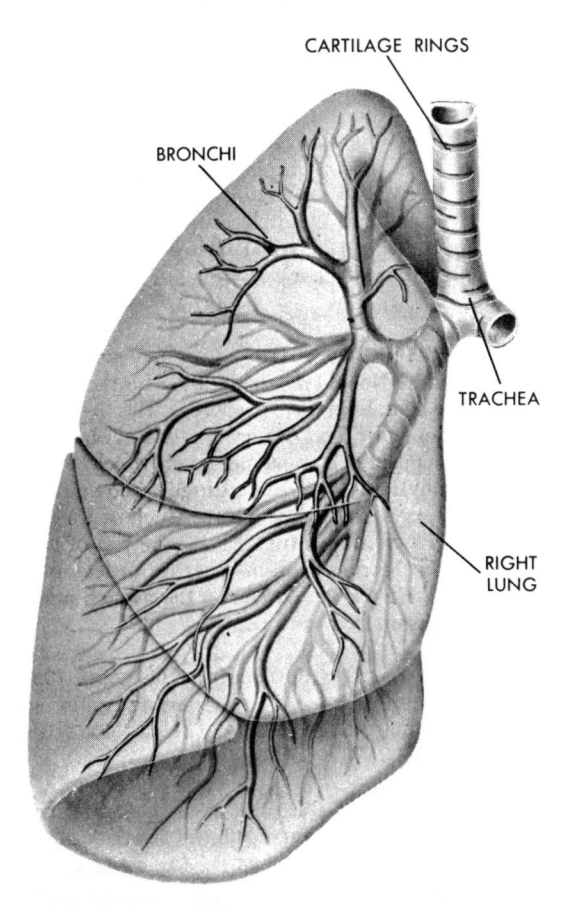

impaired, permitting mucus to collect in the air passages. The mucous accumulation and the swelling of the bronchial lining tend to narrow the air passageway, and may make breathing difficult.

Acute bronchitis, developing from infections of the upper breathing passages, is usually accompanied by chills, headache, and fever. The cough is at first dry, but later abundant sputum is coughed up. There may be a sensation of rawness in the front of the chest. Chronic bronchitis may produce no symptoms. However, in severer cases, the patient may cough up mucus and suffer from shortness of breath.

Various characteristic wheezes may be produced by the passage of air through the narrowed bronchial passages and the mucus accumulations in the bronchi. Pneumonia may develop as a complication of bronchitis.

Treatment. Infections of the bronchi may be treated with antibiotics and other drugs. Physical and chemical irritants should be eliminated. Steam inhalations help to relieve cough. In chronic bronchitis repeated respiratory infections gradually worsen the condition, and it is sometimes recommended that the patient live in a warm, dry climate.

BRONCHOSCOPE [brŏng'kə-skōp], straight, hollow metal tube containing a small light at one end, used to inspect the bronchi (the air passageways). The instrument is passed through the mouth into the windpipe. By viewing through the tube, the physician can frequently detect the presence of tumors, infections, foreign bodies, or plugs of mucus obstructing the airways. By introducing surgical instruments into the bronchoscope, obstructions and small tumors can often be removed, and samples of tissue can be obtained for microscopic examination. The bronchoscope is of particular value in enabling the surgeon to locate the precise area of disease prior to certain types of lung surgery.

BRUCE, SIR DAVID (1855–1931), British military physician who made important investigations into the causes of certain infectious diseases. In 1887 while stationed on the island of Malta in the Mediterranean he identified the microorganism responsible for Malta fever (brucellosis). Later he discovered the manner in which certain tropical diseases (African Sleeping Sickness and Nagana) were transmitted by tsetse flies. In 1908 he was knighted.

BRUCELLOSIS [broō-sə-lō'sĭs], also known as Malta fever, undulant fever, and Mediterranean fever, a bacterial disease produced by three closely related organisms of the *Brucella* group. These bacteria produce infections of varying severity in goats, cattle, hogs, and man. In animals, particularly in cattle, brucellosis causes spontaneous abortions. The infections tend to localize in the udders and contaminate the milk. Humans may contract the disease by drinking the contaminated milk or by direct contact with infected animals. Brucellosis appears more frequently in farmers, livestock producers, meat-packing plant employees, veterinarians, and others whose occupations bring them into frequent contact with animals.

In man, the incubation period is from 5 to 21 days. The disease may strike suddenly or develop gradually over a period of weeks. Weakness is almost always present. The slightest physical exertion may cause extreme exhaustion. Chills, backache, and headache are frequent symptoms. The patient may suffer from profuse sweating and aching joints. A distinctive sign of brucellosis is a fever which fluctuates over long periods of time. There is a persistent lack of appetite with a resulting loss of weight. In women, the menstrual cycle may be disrupted. The patient may become irritable, depressed, and may suffer from tremors of the finger and tongue and from visual disturbances.

Complications may involve the valves of the heart, the joints, the nervous system and the testicles.

With adequate bed rest and antibiotic therapy, most patients recover within three to six months.

Brucellosis can be prevented by identifying infected animals and by pasteurizing milk.

BUERGER'S [bûr'gərz] **DISEASE,** also known as thromboangiitis obliterans, is a circulatory disease of unknown cause which gradually closes off arteries and veins in the arms and legs. It chiefly affects men under 45. Most patients are smokers and display aggravated symptoms when smoking. The disease usually affects one or both legs and is marked by pain on walking, and, in severe cases, by ulcers and gangrene. There is no specific medication, but the patient should avoid all tobacco, extreme cold, and ill-fitting shoes. Home surgery practiced on the feet or the use of harsh chemicals may result in injury, ulceration, and eventually amputation of an extremity.

BUNION (HALLUX VALGUS), deformity of the great toe in which the toe points outward instead of straight ahead. Usually the bone is enlarged at the point where the toe meets the forefoot, and the surrounding skin is toughened and calloused. Narrow, pointed, and short shoes are the chief causes of the bunion. Frequently a bursa, or fluid-filled sac, is formed at the joint as a result of constant friction in the shoe. Mild cases can be treated through the use of proper shoes and devices that reposition the toe. In extreme deformity surgical treatment is necessary.
See also FOOT.

BURNET, SIR FRANK MACFARLANE (1899–), Australian microbiologist and immunologist. He was educated at Melbourne University, and in 1926 went on a fellowship to the Lister Institute in London. He later returned to Australia and became professor of experimental medicine at Melbourne University. A recipient of many honors for his researches in the fields of antibody formation and cellular immunity, he has lectured extensively in the United States and in England. In 1960 he shared the Nobel Prize in medicine, with Peter Brian Medawar, for their studies in immunological responses.

BURNS, wounds produced by the action of heat, caustic chemicals, or electricity. The seriousness of a burn depends upon the degree of injury to the skin and the extent of the body surface involved. A first-degree burn causes reddening of the skin; a second-degree burn causes reddening and blistering; a third-degree burn destroys the skin. Burns may be fatal if they involve large areas of the body surface.

The greatest danger to the severely burned patient results from the loss of body fluid through the damaged skin. If enough fluid is lost the circulatory system cannot function normally and the patient goes into shock. Burned patients may also develop anemia, fever, and nutritional deficiencies.

Treatment of Burns. Minor Burns. Apply ointment, cover with a light bandage. Do not break blisters.

Chemical Burns. Douse with water immediately to wash away the chemical. This is especially important in chemical burns of the eye. Bathe the open eye with running water for several minutes.

Severe Burns. Immediate hospitalization is essential. Do not attempt to clean the wound or to remove the clothes over the burn. If the victim cannot be moved without touching the wound, it should be covered lightly with sterile gauze or clean towels. At the hospital, the patient is given antibiotics to prevent infection and transfusions of blood or blood substitutes to replace the lost fluids. First- and second-degree burns usually heal without scarring. Third-degree burns result in scars, which may be treated by plastic surgery.

Prevention. Most fatal burns are suffered by children and elderly persons, and can be prevented by keeping caustic chemicals out of reach of children, by not allowing children to play in the kitchen without supervision, and by using nonflammable materials at home or work.
See also FIRST AID.

BUTENANDT [bōō′tə-nänt], **ADOLF FRIEDRICH JOHANNES (1903–),** German biochemist best known for his studies on hormones. In 1929 he prepared the female hormone estrone and he later isolated the male hormone androsterone and a second female hormone, progesterone. He was named co-winner of the Nobel Prize in 1939, along with Leopold Ruzicka, but he was unable to receive the award because of the Nazi ban on acceptance. After 1936 he directed the Max Planck Institute for Biochemistry.

C

CAFFEINE, naturally occurring chemical of the xanthine family, used in high doses to stimulate the nervous system. Found in plants widely distributed throughout the world—the coffee bean, tea leaf, cocoa bean and kola nut—caffeine is best known as a component of coffee, tea, and cola drinks. Its earliest use as a beverage is lost in the past but it was popular enough to give rise to legends, perhaps due to its stimulating properties. As a stimulant, caffeine has a powerful effect on the central nervous system. Its main action is on conscious mental functions. Intellectual effort becomes more sustained and there is better association of ideas. Motor activity increases and reaction time to stimuli decreases. A typist, for example, might work faster with fewer errors. Caffeine reduces muscle fatigue and increases the capacity for work. Because of the energy consumed, however, fatigue and mild depression may occur as its effect wears off. Caffeine causes faster heartbeat, slightly increased blood pressure, and a greater production of gastric acid. Sleeplessness may result from its use, as well as stomach irritation and diarrhea. It also stimulates the production of urine. Combined with aspirin, caffeine is often used in headache and pain-relieving mixtures.
See also STIMULANTS.

CALCIUM [kăl′sē-əm], an element and a metal of the alkaline earth group. It is the fifth most common element in the earth's crust, of which it makes up 3.63%. It occurs most commonly as calcium carbonate, or limestone,

$CaCO_3$. The skeletons of many creatures, from microorganisms through corals to clams and oysters, are essentially limestone. The limestone deposits of the world are probably built up of the skeletons of sea organisms. The shells of birds' eggs are calcium carbonate. The bony skeletons of vertebrates, including man, are calcium phosphate. Calcium makes up 2% of the human body.

CALCULI [kăl′kyə-lī], in medicine, a term for the stones that are sometimes found in the gall bladder, urinary bladder, and kidneys, and occasionally in the pancreas and the salivary and prostate glands. The stones usually consist of a central core of organic material, such as cast-off cells or bacteria, around which minerals have been deposited.
See also KIDNEY.

CALLUS [kăl′əs], thickening of the upper layer of the skin, usually produced by friction and pressure, as on the hands and feet. The term also refers to the new growth of incompletely solidified bone tissue that appears at the site of a fracture during the process of healing.

CAMPHOR, crystalline, highly odorous substance obtained from the wood and bark of the camphor tree. It is used on the skin as a mild antiseptic and irritant. Although no evidence for its effectiveness has been demonstrated, it is still widely used as a respiratory and circulatory stimulant. It is also used in photographic film, in the manufacture of plastics, and as a moth repellent. Probably because of its strong odor, camphor is popularly believed to have the power to ward off disease. It was once common to see children wearing camphor bags around their necks to prevent colds and other illnesses.

CANCER, an abnormal and uncontrolled growth of the cells that make up living things.

Cancer was recognized by the Egyptians as early as 1500 B.C. In modern times the death rate from this disease has steadily increased: in 1900 cancer ranked 7th as a cause of death in the United States; in 1925 it was 4th and in 1955 it was the 2d-greatest killer, after diseases of the heart and blood vessels. The extended life span and the increase in total population are two major factors responsible for this increase. The American Cancer Society estimates that, according to present rates, one out of every four persons will eventually have cancer.

The Nature of Cancer

All plants, animals, and man are composed of cells, the microscopic units of life. For reasons not yet fully understood, certain cells may suddenly undergo abnormal changes and begin to reproduce at an unusual rate. This is cancer—uncontrolled, irregular cell growth.

Instead of dividing in two as is normal, the cancerous cell may split to form three, four, or more new cells. The cells become irregular in size and shape. They tend to lose their distinctive characteristics and approach more primitive, embryonic cell types. They do not stop multiplying. The nucleus, or inner center of the cell, shows the most dramatic signs of abnormality, appearing larger than normal, and distorted in shape. Masses of these abnormal cells eventually form a lump or swelling which is called a tumor.

Benign and Malignant Tumors. There are two main groups of tumors, benign and malignant. Benign tumors are made up of cells which tend to differ only slightly from normal cells and tissues. They are usually sharply separated from the tissue of origin by a well-defined border or capsule. Benign tumors do not generally endanger life, since the abnormal cells do not invade other areas. Examples of this kind of tumor are warts and moles. Usually, benign tumors are named by attaching the suffix -oma to the name of the cell from which the tumor arises. Benign tumors of the bone are called osteomas, and benign tumors originating from fibrous tissue are termed fibromas.

If a growth penetrates and spreads, it is a malignant tumor, since it may cause death if it is not removed or destroyed. The abnormal cells may enter the blood stream or lymph channels to be carried to other parts of the body where they establish colonies called metastases.

Malignant tumors arising from muscle, bone, tendons, cartilage, fat, vessels, lymphoid and connective tissue are called sarcomas. If a malignant tumor arises from the epithelial cells, which line the organs of the body, it is termed a carcinoma.

Cancer in Plants and Animals. Cancer is often thought of as a human disease but is actually widespread in most forms of plant and animal life. Tumors have been found in insects, fish, amphibians, reptiles, birds, and mammals and in fungi, ferns, carrots, spruce, willow, and sugar beets.

Over 200 different kinds of cancer are recognized in man, including cancer of the lungs, intestinal tract, stomach, female breast, prostate gland, uterus, urinary organs, brain, bone, endocrine glands, pancreas, skin, ovary, testes, liver, and in blood-forming tissues, leading to leukemia and the lymphomas.

What Causes Cancer?

Why do some individuals get cancer, while others do not? Unlike other diseases of man, many of which are known to be caused by a specific bacteria or virus (such as tuberculosis or polio), an inborn metabolic defect (diabetes), or anatomical deterioration (heart disease), cancer appears to be a disease that may result from not one, but many factors. Different types of cancer may be caused by different combinations of conditions. A cancer cell is a cell which has become altered and has escaped normal growth regulation. But does the change originate within a single cell, or are certain cells affected by alterations in the tissues around them, or perhaps by changes in the chemistry of the body?

Cancer research has yielded evidence showing that all of these possibilities may be important in the final development of cancer. Some forms of cancer are known to be caused by viruses, which can penetrate single cells and change the cell's heredity, chemistry, and fate. Other cancers may result from an abnormality of the body's hormone balance. Cancer may be caused by exposure to certain chemicals like azo dyes, polycyclic hydrocarbons, heavy metals, tobacco tars, or X rays, solar radiation, or ionizing radiation. Certain forms appear to have some hereditary basis.

CANCER

SOME REPRESENTATIVE EXAMPLES OF THE GEOGRAPHIC DISTRIBUTION OF CANCER

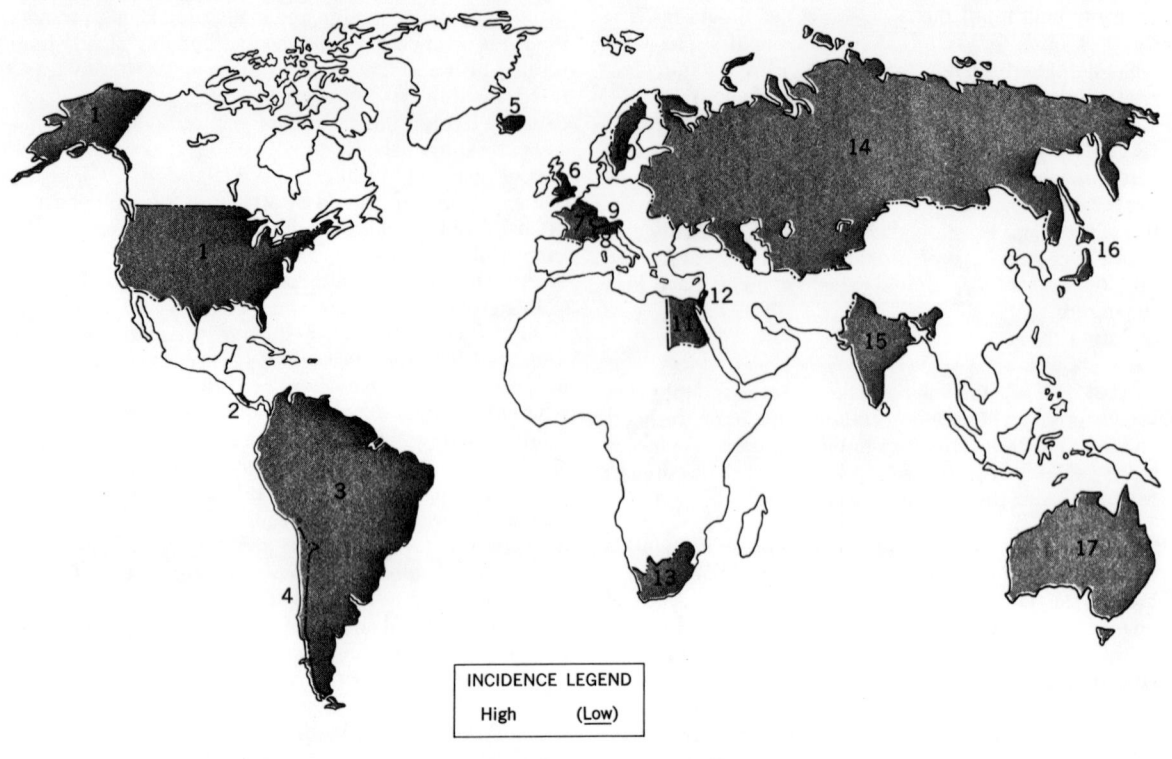

INCIDENCE LEGEND
High   (Low)

1. U.S.A. .... Prostate, Colon, Breast, Lung (Stomach)
2. COSTA RICA .... Stomach
3. SOUTH AMERICA .. Cervix
4. CHILE .... Stomach
5. ICELAND .... Stomach (Lung)
6. ENGLAND .... Lung, Breast
7. FRANCE .... Esophagus
8. NORTHERN ITALY .. Stomach
9. SWITZERLAND ..... Esophagus
10. SWEDEN .... Hypopharynx
11. EGYPT .... Bladder
12. ISRAEL .... (Cervix)
13. SOUTH AFRICA .... Liver
14. U.S.S.R. .... Stomach
15. INDIA .... Cervix, Oral Cavity
16. JAPAN .... Stomach (Colon) (Lung) (Breast) (Prostate)
17. AUSTRALIA .... Skin

Information compiled by Dr. Ernest L. Wynder, Section of Epidemiology, Division of Preventive Medicine, Sloane-Kettering Institute, N. Y.

Study of the frequency of cancer throughout the world may lead to an understanding of the factors which contribute to its development. A high occurrence of cancer in one country suggests that some feature of the surroundings or living habits of the people may be associated with a particular type of cancer.

Cancer and Viruses. Viruses have been proved to cause various forms of cancer in chickens, rabbits, frogs, mice, hamsters, deer, and monkeys. Laboratory evidence suggests, but does not prove, that human leukemia (cancer of the blood) and also certain human solid cancers may be caused by viruses.

Cancer and Hormones. Hormones, the chemical substances secreted by the endocrine glands (the thyroid, pituitary, adrenal, ovary, and testes), appear to play a role in the causation of some cancers. Although the endocrine glands themselves may occasionally become cancerous, malignancy appears more frequently in organs which are stimulated by hormones, the so-called "target organs," such as the female breast and uterus, and the male prostate gland. According to one theory, an over-production of hormones by one of the endocrine glands results in excessive stimulation of the cells of the target organs. Hormones could accumulate in the target organ, causing overactivity of the cells and then cancer.

Another intriguing fact is the chemical similarity between certain hormones and a group of cancer-causing chemicals (the polycyclic hydrocarbons). It is possible that a deviation in hormone synthesis or metabolism could lead to the formation of a carcinogen (a cancer-causing substance) instead of the natural hormone.

Chemical and Physical Agents. It is known that chemical and physical agents play an important part in causing many human cancers. The first cancers in man ascribed to a chemical substance were cancers of the scrotum which frequently appeared in young chimney sweeps, in England. In 1775 the British physician Pott postulated that coal tar was the carcinogenic substance in soot which caused these cancers to develop. Since then, skin and lung cancers in animals have been proved to be caused

CANCER

by coal tar derivatives and cancers of the bladder have been related to exposure to aromatic amines (such as aniline).

Radiation. Ultraviolet radiation such as that found in sunlight can cause skin cancer. There is a higher incidence of skin cancer in individuals engaged in occupations requiring constant exposure to the sun than in those employed indoors. Skin cancer has also been experimentally induced in mice and rats by exposing them to ultraviolet irradiation.

Leukemia, lymphosarcoma (cancer of the lymph glands), and skin cancer can result from exposure to high-energy radiation. An increased frequency of these diseases in people exposed to radiation has been noted repeatedly during the past 40 years. The Japanese atomic bomb survivors represent the most important single series of cases. The incidence of leukemia in this group was clearly related to the distance from the explosion. Scientists lack the necessary information at present to determine what dosages of radiation might be "safe." It appears probable that age at ex-

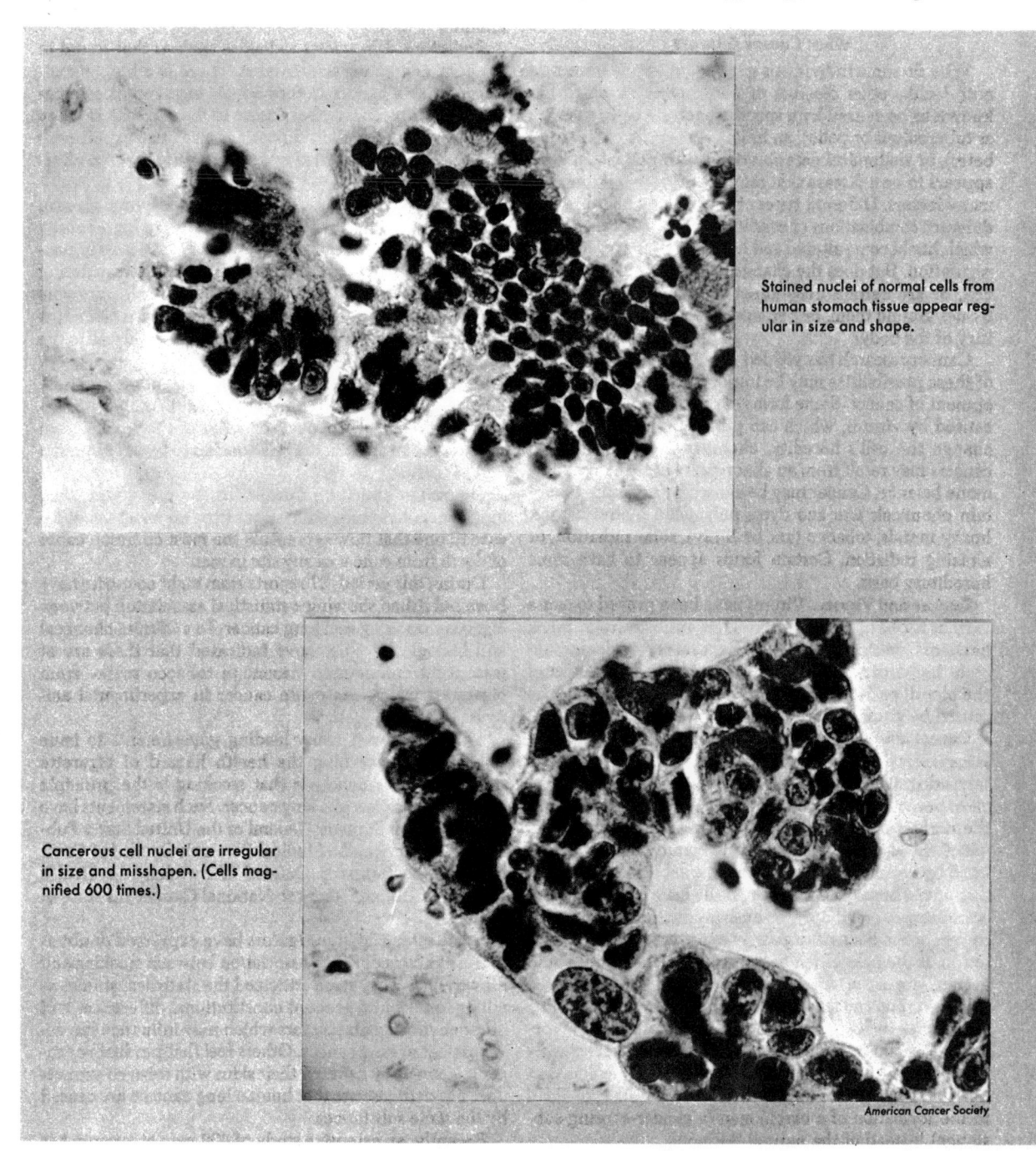

Stained nuclei of normal cells from human stomach tissue appear regular in size and shape.

Cancerous cell nuclei are irregular in size and misshapen. (Cells magnified 600 times.)

American Cancer Society

CANCER

posure, sex, and anatomic distribution of the radiation are important variables in the relationship between radiation and cancer.

Cigarettes and Lung Cancer. In the past generation, lung cancer has changed in status from an uncommon disease to one that now represents the most common cause of death from cancer of any site in men.

During this period, 27 reports from eight countries have been published showing a statistical association between cigarette smoking and lung cancer. In addition, chemical and biological studies have indicated that there are at least eight compounds present in tobacco smoke from cigarettes which can cause cancer in experimental animals.

This has moved many leading governments to issue statements concerning the health hazard of cigarette smoking and to conclude that smoking is the principle cause of the increase in lung cancer. Such statements have come from the Surgeon General of the United States Public Health Service, the Medical Research Council of Great Britain, The Research Council of Sweden, the Health Council of Holland, and the National Cancer Institute of Canada.

Some scientific investigators have expressed doubt as to the significance of the association between smoking and lung cancer. They have criticized the statistical studies as failing to take into account constitutional differences and other environmental factors which may influence the development of lung cancer. Others feel that producing cancer in animals by painting their skins with tobacco extracts does not demonstrate that human lung cancers are caused by the same substances.

Recently, an extensive study of 402 men at autopsy has given added weight to the correlation between cigarette smoking and lung cancer. The report, based on microscopic examination of 19,797 lung sections, showed that changes in the air passageways (the tracheo-bronchial tree) varied dramatically with the amount of cigarettes smoked. (The pathologists were not told of the type of case or smoking history during the reading of the slides.)

The smallest number of changes were found in those who never smoked or smoked only occasionally. With the increase in amount of cigarettes smoked, there was a progressive increase in the number of abnormal changes present. The greatest number of changes were present in those who smoked two or more packs of cigarettes per day.

Research on lung cancer is currently in progress to improve methods for early diagnosis and treatment, to investigate personality factors which may govern acquiring the cigarette smoking habit, to identify other factors in the environment such as air pollution which some investigators believe is a contributing cause, and to develop a so-called "safe" cigarette, one which is free of cancer-causing (carcinogenic) agents.

Heredity and Cancer. Biologically speaking, all human traits are determined at the moment of conception when the genes (the units of inheritance) of the two parents unite. However, the actual traits which emerge in later life depend on the way in which the genes interact with each other. Of equal importance are the prevailing conditions inside and around the embryo during the course of development.

Large, mixed populations may be expected to contain many genes which could affect the tendency to develop or to resist cancer. In order to demonstrate the presence of such genes it is necessary to mate close relatives (to inbreed). In experimental animals, at least 20 generations of brother-sister matings are required before a strain is considered genetically "pure" with respect to a single trait. Such laboratory inbreeding studies have produced many strains of mice which differ markedly in their tendencies to develop cancers. These studies have clearly demonstrated that under certain conditions a hereditary basis for cancer exists. The importance of inheritance in certain human cancers has been fairly well established—there is, for example, a higher incidence of retinoblastoma (cancer of the eyes) in Bantu than in white babies.

Immunity to Cancer

Does a human being possess natural defense mechanisms against cancer? Knowledge of this subject is at present imprecise and often speculative, but there is reason to believe that the patient is not completely defenseless in the face of the growing cancer. Some cancers have been found to grow slowly in certain individuals; however, when removed from the body and placed in a test tube, they grow wildly. This suggests that the growth of the cancer was restrained while it was in the patient's body.

The rare, but documented, phenomenon of spontaneous cure of cancer in man provides another reason for believing that some immunity might exist. Over 100 cases have been reported in which the body subdued the tumor without treatment.

Some cancers develop extremely slowly and often escape detection during the life of the patient. Cancer of the prostate, for example, has been found to be at least 4 to 10 times more frequent at autopsy than was apparent from clinical evidence of the disease. Cancer metastases (thyroid and breast cancer are good examples) may lie dormant for years and even decades before they undergo a period of rapid growth and produce the symptoms of disease.

All these facts, and more, indicate an active reaction by the patient to the cancer. This has important implications for the prevention, detection, and treatment of cancer. Practical efforts designed to increase or stimulate the defense mechanisms of the body against cancer are still in their earliest stages. Some scientists have attempted to remove tumors, grind them up, and reintroduce them into patients in an effort to stimulate the production of defensive substances (antibodies) against the person's own cancer. Others have attempted to inject human cancer cells into horses and cows and collect the serum with the hope that antibodies against human cancer have been formed by the animal. These antisera have been given to patients dying of cancer.

The results of these experiments are as yet inconclusive. But this is a continuing area of cancer research.

Chemotherapy

In 1955, the Cancer Chemotherapy National Service

Center was established to press the search for effective anticancer drugs. The Center, located on the grounds of the National Institutes of Health in Bethesda, Md., is sponsored by the National Cancer Institute, American Cancer Society, Damon Runyon Memorial Fund for Cancer Research, Veterans Administration, Atomic Energy Commission, and the Food and Drug Administration.

The Center co-ordinates the procurement and screening of chemicals, and the prompt, adequate clinical trial of promising agents in the treatment of human cancer. Approximately 40,000 chemicals are tested in this way every year. A chemical is first tested for activity against mice tumors. In addition, tests for activity are conducted against human cancer cells grown in the laboratory. These primary tests eliminate all but a few hundred compounds as candidates for further animal testing. Secondary tests involve spontaneous animal tumors, tumors known to be resistant to other drugs, and human tumors transplanted into animals.

Fewer than two out of 1,000 chemicals entering the screening program are deemed worthy of clinical trials in human patients. Clinical trials are performed on patients in 175 hospitals. Today, about 20 chemicals are in general clinical use. They are classified in terms of their action and include: alkylating agents, antimetabolites, hormones and steroid compounds, antibiotics and natural products, and miscellaneous.

Alkylating Agents. The exact mechanisms by which these chemicals produce their effects are not known. An example of an effective alkylating agent used against certain cancers is nitrogen mustard. During World War II it was found that mustard gas depresses white blood cell counts in human beings. This led to tests of nitrogen mustard, a related compound, against leukemia, a form of cancer characterized by overproduction of white blood cells. Although it is an extremely toxic substance nitrogen mustard is widely used clinically against lymphosarcoma and other forms of cancer. Other effective alkylating agents include chlorambucil, TEM (triethylenemelamine), TEPA (N, N′, N″-triethylene phosphoramide), and THIOTEPA (N, N′, N″-triethylene thiophosphoramide). The latter compound appears promising in the treatment of solid cancers, and excellent results have been reported for this drug in the treatment of breast cancer, in combination with surgery. The drug cytoxan, containing both nitrogen mustard and phosphoramide groups, also has proved effective against certain cancers, although the problem of toxicity remains.

Antimetabolites are compounds with structures closely related to substances normally used by cells for metabolism and growth. As a consequence of their similarity to biological substances, they are able to enter into the chemical activities of the cell and sabotage its functioning.

Examples of antimetabolite activity can be seen in the substances aminopterin and amethopterin. These compounds interfere with the vitamin, folic acid, which plays a role in the manufacture of blood cells. Aminopterin has proved to be an effective anticancer agent, providing temporary improvement in children with leukemia. Methotrexate (amethopterin) is less toxic than aminopterin, and has proved effective against choriocarcinoma, a rare cancer developing in connection with pregnancy, and against liver cancer, as well as leukemia. Other effective antimetabolites include 6-mercaptopurine, 8-azauracil, 8-azaguanine, and 5-fluorouracil.

Alteration of the body's hormone balance by using estrogens (female sex hormones) to treat cancers of the prostate, and androgens (male sex hormones) to treat cancers originating from the breast, is a useful procedure, although side effects involving the secondary sexual characteristics are common.

Success with antibiotics against bacterial diseases has prompted an unprecedented search for substances of this type which possess anticancer activity. Some good results have been reported for mitomycin C and actinomycin D, although these compounds are highly toxic.

Two main problems plague the field of cancer chemotherapy: drug resistance and drug toxicity. A large number of excellent anticancer drugs have become available for clinical use, but after continued use these compounds cease to have any beneficial effect. This resistance is poorly understood and is the subject of active research. Combinations of drugs which differ in their action are being tried in an effort to increase the effectiveness of treatment. Sequential therapy, the use of one drug after another, is also being used on the theory that when the cancer cells become resistant to the first drug, the second will attack them.

Bone marrow damage is one of the major toxic actions of the clinically useful chemotherapeutic agents. A study involving 200 tests of drugs has indicated that bone marrow cells are more sensitive to damage than certain human cancer cells, a pointed illustration of the problem of drug toxicity.

Value of Early Detection

The greatest hope at present for controlling cancer lies in early detection. Cancers of the skin are readily diagnosed, but it is difficult to detect internal cancers since in their early stages they generally do not produce pain or any definite symptoms.

For years, scientists and doctors have been looking for a simple and sure means of detecting cancers before they have grown to a size when they can be felt or have made themselves known by interfering with body function. One method has been found for detecting cancer of the cervix, the neck of the uterus. This technique is so effective that the death rate for cancer of the cervix has been cut roughly in half in about a generation. It is believed that cervical cancer as a cause of death can be virtually eliminated if women avail themselves of present techniques for early detection. The method is a cytologic examination method, called the "Pap" smear (after its originator, Dr. George N. Papanicolaou). Its usefulness is based on the fact that some cancers shed cells when they are beginning to grow. The shed cells can be found in tissue fluids or can be removed from the surface of the tissue, smeared onto a glass slide (hence the term, smear) and examined under a microscope, where the cancerous cells can be readily recognized by a trained eye.

This cell examination technique has been expanded and now sample cells from stomach washings, sputum and

CAPILLARIES

other body fluids, can be examined for detection of cancer of the lung, stomach, breast, and occasionally other organs.

Unusual substances in the blood and urine of cancer patients can often be detected and many scientists are actively engaged in research aimed at using this information to develop simple diagnostic tests. The urine, blood, and tissues of some cancer patients definitely exhibit chemical differences not found in healthy individuals. But where these chemicals are produced and how this information can be used in cancer detection is not yet understood.

Since early detection and prompt treatment are the best protection against death from cancer, it is important that all adults have a thorough physical checkup once a year, regardless of whether any symptoms are present. This should include a proctoscopic examination for detection of cancer of the colon and rectum and, for women, a pelvic examination, including a "Pap" smear. Between checkups, the American Cancer Society recommends that individuals be alert to "Cancer's Seven Danger Signals." These are:

1) Unusual bleeding or discharge.
2) A lump or thickening in the breast or elsewhere.
3) A sore that does not heal.
4) Change in bowel or bladder habits.
5) Hoarseness or cough.
6) Indigestion or difficulty in swallowing.
7) Change in a wart or mole.

If a signal lasts longer than two weeks, it is essential that a doctor be consulted.

Once cancer is detected, there are two basic methods of cure available: complete removal of the cancerous tissue by surgery; or the destruction by radiation from X rays, radium, or radioisotopes. Which method is more effective depends upon the location, size, and type of growth, and how far it has progressed. Combinations of surgery with radiation, or surgery with chemotherapy also have proved useful.

In spite of substantial progress, cancer remains one of the most baffling, complicated, and devastating diseases confronting science, medicine, and the public. A gigantic effort will be required now and in the future to bring this growing problem under control.

See also TUMOR.

CAPILLARIES [kăp'ə-lĕr-ēz], extremely small blood vessels, found in most tissues, and connecting arteries with veins. The capillaries are the point of interaction between the blood and the body tissues. Oxygen and nutritive materials reach the tissues by passing from the blood through the capillary wall. The waste products formed by tissue activity pass into the capillaries to be carried away by the blood stream.

See also BLOOD.

CARBOHYDRATES [kär-bō-hī'drāts], group of organic compounds that constitute an important source of energy for

FORMS AND USES OF CARBOHYDRATES

Carbohydrates are the primary foods produced by plants. Owing to their wide availability and versatility, carbohydrates have become basic materials for many industries.

FORMS OF CARBOHYDRATES	CARBOHYDRATES IN FOOD	INDUSTRIAL USES
STARCH	(1) Starches occur in grains and tubers (such as potatoes) in great quantity. The body converts starches into various sugar forms.	CLOTH PRODUCTION; GLUE AND BINDERS; LAUNDRY
SUGAR	(2) Sugar occurs in quantity in sugar beets and sugar cane. Simple sugars can be used almost directly by the body for energy.	CANDIES; CURING; FLAVORING
CELLULOSE	(3) Cellulose has no nutritional value for humans. The primary industrial sources of cellulose are wood and cotton.	CELLOPHANE; RAYON; PAPER

plants and animals. These compounds contain carbon, hydrogen, and oxygen and range from simple sugars, which contain a few carbon atoms, to complex substances (polysaccharides) which are large groups of simple sugars joined together to form giant units, such as starch.

Plants possess the unique property of being able to use the energy of sunlight to manufacture carbohydrates from carbon dioxide and water (photosynthesis). The plant uses the carbohydrate cellulose as a framework to provide support and rigidity. Other carbohydrates, such as starches and sugars, are used as food. The energy of sunlight trapped in carbohydrates is eventually made available to animals in the form of sugars and starches contained in beets, wheat, corn, potatoes, and other plants. In the human body, starches are broken down into sugar in the intestines and are stored in the liver and other tissues as the carbohydrate glycogen, which supplies the energy for muscular activity and many other bodily functions. The body converts excess carbohydrate into fat.

Starch and cellulose are industrially important carbohydrates, serving as raw materials for the manufacture of rayon, cotton cloth, glue, paper, and certain explosives. Cellulose in the form of cotton (one of the purest forms of cellulose found in nature) and wood are used to manufacture cellophane films, rayon and paper products.

Carbohydrates have long provided man with a large variety of alcoholic beverages. The fermentation of the starch contained in various plants forms the basis for the manufacture of rye, vodka, scotch, and other liquors. Wines are prepared from the fermentation of the sugars contained in grape juices.

CARBON CYCLE, in biology, continuous movement of atmospheric carbon first into plant, then into animal tissues, from which the carbon is released back into the atmosphere. Plants utilize carbon in the form of carbon dioxide from the air. During photosynthesis, carbon dioxide becomes part of the molecules of glucose, a simple sugar, and is further transformed within the plant into complex sugars, fats, and proteins. These are the sources of the plant's own nourishment. The plants containing the carbon compounds are eaten by animals, who incorporate the carbon into their body tissues. During animal respiration, carbon obtained directly from the air and from the ingestion of plants is returned to the atmosphere as carbon dioxide. A third part of the carbon cycle is seen in the mechanism of decay; carbon is released back into the atmosphere by the action of fermentation-producing bacteria on the tissues of dead plants and animals.

See also PHOTOSYNTHESIS; RESPIRATION.

CARBON MONOXIDE, CO, colorless, tasteless, odorless, poisonous gas. It is a product of the incomplete combustion of certain hydrocarbons. It is obtained commercially by the reduction of carbon dioxide with coke or by the action of steam on coke. Carbon monoxide is used in the synthesis of many organic compounds, and is the principal reducing agent in the blast furnace and in the Mond process for the recovery of nickel.

Carbon Monoxide Poisoning. Carbon monoxide is present in automobile exhaust fumes; if allowed to accumulate in an enclosure, it may be fatal. Carbon monoxide has a tremendous affinity for hemoglobin, which carries oxygen in the blood stream. Oxygen is therefore displaced by CO and the victim suffers from lack of oxygen. Headache is usually the first symptom and the skin may turn a cherry red. Depending on the concentration of inspired CO, symptoms may progress to muscular weakness and impairment of judgment, to unconsciousness and death. The victim should be immediately brought into the fresh air and be given artificial respiration, preferably with an inhalator and pure oxygen, if he is not breathing.

CARBUNCLE. *See* BOILS.

CARCINOID SYNDROME [kär′sə-noid sĭn′drōm], a disease caused by a cancerous tumor of glandular tissue. The tumor usually develops from the intestines and secretes serotonin, a substance that acts upon the muscles in the walls of the bronchi, intestines, and blood vessels. The most striking symptom of the disease is a rapid change in skin color—ranging from violet to red to white—that is caused by the action of serotonin upon the blood vessels of the skin. Other symptoms are cramps, blue pallor of the skin (cyanosis), asthma, fainting spells, and diarrhea. The heart and liver are frequently involved. The only effective treatment is early removal of the tumor.

See also SEROTONIN.

CARREL [kə-rĕl′], **ALEXIS** (1873–1944), physician and physiologist, best known for his work in transplanting organs and keeping tissues and organs alive outside the

THE CARBON CYCLE

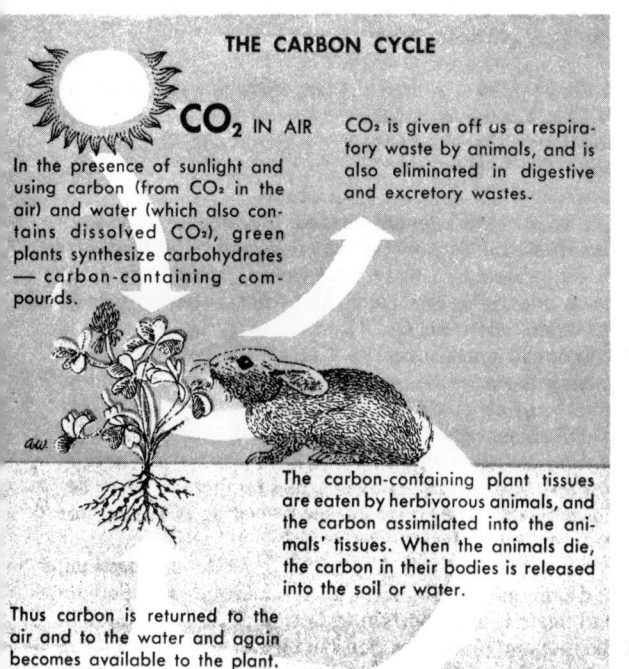

CO_2 IN AIR

CO_2 is given off as a respiratory waste by animals, and is also eliminated in digestive and excretory wastes.

In the presence of sunlight and using carbon (from CO_2 in the air) and water (which also contains dissolved CO_2), green plants synthesize carbohydrates — carbon-containing compounds.

The carbon-containing plant tissues are eaten by herbivorous animals, and the carbon assimilated into the animals' tissues. When the animals die, the carbon in their bodies is released into the soil or water.

Thus carbon is returned to the air and to the water and again becomes available to the plant.

WATER CO_2 DISSOLVED IN WATER

body. He was educated in France and later went to the Rockefeller Institute in the United States, where he developed a method for suturing blood vessels. This technique enabled him to successfully transplant a kidney from one animal to another. In 1912 he received the Nobel Prize for this work. With Charles A. Lindbergh he developed a perfusion pump for keeping organs alive outside of the body. He returned to France in 1939 and in Aug., 1944, was arrested for wartime collaboration with the Germans; however, because of ill health, he was never brought to trial.

CARTILAGE [kär′tə-lĭj], a type of hard, flexible connective tissue, lacking blood vessels and nerves, composed of living cells imbedded in a solid substance.

There are three types of cartilage: hyaline, elastic, and fibrous cartilage. Hyaline cartilage is glassy in appearance owing to large amounts of solid material between the cells. It is found in the nose, larynx, and joint surfaces. Elastic cartilage is yellowish and contains elastic fibers. It composes the cartilage of the external ear and inner portions of the hearing mechanism. Fibrous cartilage contains tough, nonelastic fibers and is found in the vertebral column and in some tendons.

CASTOR OIL, a yellowish or colorless thick oil obtained from the seeds of a tropical herb (*Ricinus communis*) which is grown chiefly in India. Taken by mouth, castor oil irritates the intestinal lining, stimulating bowel activity and relieving constipation. It is also used as a skin softener and as a lubricant in aircraft engines.

CASTS, URINARY, consist of protein substances, blood cells, fatty materials, or hemoglobin, which have been molded by the tubules of the kidney. Their presence is usually an indication of kidney disease. Occasionally small numbers of casts are present in the urine of healthy persons.

CATALEPSY [kăt′ə-lĕp-sē], a state of muscular rigidity and fixation of posture associated with a lack of response to stimulation, often extending to a complete loss of contact with the world. Cataleptic states are seen most frequently in catatonic schizophrenia; a waxy flexibility (cerea flexibilitas) develops in which the patient tends to remain in whatever posture he is placed for long periods of time. Local catalepsies of the eyelids and limbs can be induced during hypnosis.
See also SCHIZOPHRENIA.

CATAPLEXY [kăt′ə-plĕk-sē], sudden loss of muscle tone causing the victim to sink limply to the ground. He is unable to move or speak, though fully conscious. The attack is usually precipitated by strong emotion such as laughter. It lasts less than a minute, and is followed by a rapid return to normal. Considered a form of epilepsy by some, cataplexy is more likely related to narcolepsy (a disturbance of sleep), but restricted to the centers concerned with movement and posture.
See also NARCOLEPSY.

CATARACT [kăt′ə-răkt], an opacification of the transparent lens of the eye. Most cataracts appear in elderly persons; it has been estimated that 90% of all individuals over the age of 70 have some degree of cataract. Less commonly, cataracts are present at birth or develop as complications of other ailment (such as diabetes). They may also result from occupational activities, such as glass-blowing, and arc-welding, which involve frequent exposure to powerful lights.

The darkening of the lens blurs the visual image. Cataracts in the center of the lens interfere with vision to a greater extent than those lying at the edges. As the condition progresses frequent changes of glasses may be needed to maintain good vision.

While it is not possible to halt the development of the cataract, good vision can be restored by surgical removal of the lens. With corrective glasses, vision following surgery compares favorably with that which existed prior to the cataract formation.

CATATONIA [kăt-ə-tō′nē-ə], an abnormal type of behavior seen in some persons suffering from schizophrenia. The catatonic person is usually in a trancelike stupor, but may occasionally be violent and dangerous. Typically, the catatonic is mute and motionless. He may spend the entire day standing in one position or sitting on the edge of the table. Although the patient seems unaware of the world about him he may actually be alert and thinking actively.
See also SCHIZOPHRENIA.

CATHETER [kăth′ə-tər], a hollow tubelike instrument used to empty the contents of the hollow organs of the body, such as the urinary bladder (when urinary flow is obstructed), or to fill these cavities with different foods, medications and dyes, or to obtain samples of the organ contents for diagnostic studies. Among the various types of catheters are those which can be inserted into a vein and passed along to the heart and those which can be moved through the bladder up into the kidneys.

CAT SCRATCH DISEASE, infectious disease, possibly caused by a virus, which is acquired from a cat's scratch or occasionally from splinters and thorns. A sore appears at the site of the scratch and is followed by headache, fever, and rash. Swelling appears in the lymph glands around the infected region. These glands may eventually develop abscesses.

CAUTERIZATION, the destruction of tissue by the application of a hot iron, an electric current, or strong acids. The technique is used to treat bleeding areas in the nose, to remove warts and small growths, and to treat various lesions of the cervix (the neck of the uterus). A disadvantage of cauterization in the treatment of small tumors is that the destruction of tissue makes it impossible to examine the growth microscopically to determine if it is cancerous.

CAVITY, DENTAL, a process of decay which may successively penetrate the various structures of the tooth, eventually resulting in its death and loss. Current theory holds that bacteria cause decay, either by producing acids which dissolve the mineral components of the tooth, or by directly attacking its organic tissue. According to the first concept, sugars and starches contribute to decay by providing food for acid-producing bacteria.

In the earliest stage of decay, bacteria accumulate on the surface of the tooth. The bacteria slowly penetrate the enamel until they reach the softer inner portion of the tooth (the dentine). The dentine decays rapidly, enlarging the cavity in a mushroomlike fashion beneath the enamel, which eventually collapses as the underlying dentine is destroyed. The cavity may then enter the pulp, or "life-line" of the tooth which contains blood vessels, nerves, and connective tissues. The pulp becomes inflamed, engorged, and painful, and may die if the inflammation obstructs the narrow entrance through which blood vessels pass into the root of the tooth. Abscesses may develop in the supporting tissues around the tooth.

While pain may be felt at any time after decay penetrates the enamel, the excruciating, throbbing pain characteristic of severe toothache occurs when the inflamed and engorged pulp compresses the nerves within it. Cavities are best treated by removing the decay-producing bacteria before they have penetrated the pulp and by replacing the destroyed tooth substance with gold, silver, porcelain, or some other hard, durable material.

CELIAC [sē'lē-ăk] **DISEASE,** a disease of young children in which food cannot be normally absorbed through the intestine. In this condition a large part of the food-absorbing surface of the small intestine is flattened and does not function properly. As a result the child is undernourished and fails to grow. The abdomen is swollen and the arms and legs are thin. Diarrhea is frequently present with large amounts of pale, greasy feces being passed. Since there is some evidence that the disorder may be caused by a sensitivity to wheat proteins, children with celiac disease are usually placed on a wheat-free diet.

CELL, the basic structural and functional unit of all higher forms of life. A single cell may constitute the entire body of a plant, as in certain algae, or of an animal, as in the ameba and other protozoans. In such cases all life functions, such as reproduction, metabolism, and response to stimuli are performed by and within the single cell.

In multicellular plants and animals, on the other hand, there are many different kinds of cells, each of which performs a special function. A high degree of specialization is found, for example, in the human nervous system, where there are certain cells that receive only one of the varied surface sensations, such as touch, heat, cold, pressure, or pain.

The specialization of function of large masses of cells is quite obvious. In complex organisms cells with like structure and function are arranged in groups or layers to form tissues. Various tissues that perform related functions are in turn grouped together to form an organ. The leaf, for example, is a plant organ composed of several kinds of tissue, all of which contribute, as part of their function, to the process of photosynthesis. In higher animals, the groups of cells that constitute the different tissues of the kidneys perform the function of excretion.

Cells are remarkable for their diversity of function as reflected both by their range of size and variation of form. A common-sized spherical bacterium seen through a microscope appears as a tiny dot and is approximately one micron wide (about 1/25,000 in.). At the opposite extreme is a very large cell, the yolk of the ostrich egg, with a diameter of about 8 cm. (slightly more than 3 in.). The contrast between the almost perfectly spherical outline of a fat cell and the grotesque star shapes of certain mammalian nerve cells gives but a hint of the enormous variation in the form of cells.

The Discovery of the Cell

In the light of the present vast body of knowledge on the structure and function of cells, it is remarkable to note that until 1665 the cell was unknown; and it was not until over a century later that the cell was first described as the basic structural unit of all living matter. Because most cells are invisible to the unaided eye, their discovery was not possible until the very important invention of the compound microscope in 1590 by the Dutch spectacle makers Jans and Zacharias Janssen. The discoverer of the cell was the English scientist Robert Hooke, who was responsible for significant advances in many areas of science and technology. In 1665 Hooke observed with a microscope that cork and other plant materials contained many partitions separating cavities. These hollow chambers he called "cells." Hooke, however, was unaware of the vital nature of the material within the cell walls of most living material. Shortly thereafter Anton van Leeuwenhoek discovered and described spermatozoa, some protozoa, and bacteria.

The Cell Theory

In 1824, just a little over a century after the death of Leeuwenhoek, the French biologist René Dutrochet announced that both plants and animals were composed of cells. He further stated that all organic tissues are in reality cellular tissue with various modifications. Although no single person can be credited with the announcement of the cell theory, perhaps the greatest recognition of the importance of the cell came after the papers presented in 1838 and 1839 by two German biologists, Matthias J. Schleiden and Theodor Schwann. The cell theory then included the earlier finding that all organic tissues were composed of cells, but in addition it included the theory that the cells are the basic functional units of all living matter and that cells divide to form other cells. Rudolph Virchow's great contribution in 1858 was in his emphasizing that all cells come from preexisting cells, although this idea was discernible in earlier writings. The understanding of cell structure and behavior became of utmost importance to the field of embryology and later to genetics. The cell theory had become a great unifying concept to all phases of biology, because it was the basis for man's subsequent understanding of the structure, function, continuity, and evolution of living matter. In essence, the cell theory became a theory of life.

Many important discoveries rapidly followed in the latter half of the 19th century. Biologists put much of their effort into observing and describing the contents of the cell, with special attention to the nucleus. Attention was also focused on the nature of the division of cells and the discovery that chromosomes were equally proportioned to each daughter cell during cell division. This discovery later helped to confirm that the genes, which are responsible for the transmission of characteristics from one generation to the next, are located on the chromosomes.

From the beginning of the 20th century, cellular investigations tended to follow two divergent paths: some biologists continued their elucidation of cell structure, whereas some physiologists and biochemists studied the physiological activity of cells and cell components. As biologists observed smaller and smaller components within the cell, they found the need for better microscopes to see these components in greater detail. The light microscope was simply not good enough for such observations. In 1934 an electron microscope was constructed and in the 1940's it became generally available for biological studies. This type of microscope is a large, complex piece of equipment based on a principle quite different from that of the common light microscopes. The electron microscope can reveal detailed structures in objects which appear as tiny dots under a light microscope. It is therefore one of the most important tools available for the study of the cell and its minute components.

Cell Structure

In spite of the many different kinds of cells that have been identified, each having its own particular form and special structures that enable it to perform functions different from those of other cells, there are certain features common to all cells. Protoplasm, which the eminent English biologist Thomas Henry Huxley called "the physical basis of life," comprises the total substance of all plant and animal cells. The actual chemical composition of protoplasm may vary in different species, and in different cells within the same organism, but certain components, such as oxygen, carbon, hydrogen, nitrogen, and small quantities of other elements, are found in all protoplasm. In the plant cell, the protoplasm is contained within a rigid cell wall composed of cellulose, a woody carbon-hydrogen-oxygen compound. The protoplasm of the animal cell is surrounded by a flexible membrane which accounts, in part, for the variety of shapes that animal cells assume. A roughly rectangular form is typical of plant cells.

The cell membrane permits certain substances to move in and out of the cell. The concentration of these substances in the cell depends largely on the concentration of the same substances in the area surrounding the cell. In this case, the movement of certain substances is from the area of their higher concentration to the area of their lower concentration. But the cell also engages in the "active transport" of substances through its membrane. Active transport requires chemical energy and can move substances from areas of lower concentration to those of higher concentration. The precise nature of this movement of substances in and out of cells is not well understood and is the object of ongoing study by scientists.

Cytoplasm. The cytoplasm is all the protoplasm of the cell except the nucleus. Under slight magnification the cytoplasm appears as a translucent, granular, and fairly homogeneous substance. When viewed through an electron microscope, however, various complex structures can be seen, each of which plays an important role in synthesizing chemical compounds necessary for the life and activity of the cell. Some of the important cytoplasmic components are the *mitochondria*, spherical structures which are the main sites of energy production for the cell. They are found in those places in the cell where energy is needed. The *lysosomes* are spherical bodies containing digestive enzymes. Lysosomes break down fats, proteins, and other large molecules into smaller compounds which can then be acted upon by other enzymes of the cell. The *Golgi bodies*, which occur in both plant and animal cells, are stacks of membrane-bound sacs. They are the primary sites for packaging substances for transport outside the cell, and have been implicated in the synthesis of certain carbohydrates. The *endoplasmic reticulum* is an extensive network of tiny interconnected canals extending throughout the cytoplasm. It may serve to separate different groups of chemical reactions. Much of the endoplasmic reticulum is lined with tiny particles called *ribosomes*. The ribosomes are the main sites for the synthesis of enzymes and other proteins. Indeed, the number of ribosomes in a cell reflects the extent of protein manufacture by that cell. The *centrosome* is a small, round structure near the cell nucleus. It is usually indistinct, but when a cell is about to divide, small dots—the centrioles—become clearly visible within the centrosome. During cell division, the centrioles act as part of the apparatus that divides the nuclear components.

Clear, watery areas called vacuoles are also found in the cytoplasm of living cells. They most commonly occur in plant cells and in some one-celled animals. A vacuole consists of an outer, semipermeable membrane (a membrane through which only certain substances are able to pass) and an inner, viscous fluid called, in plant vacuoles, the cell sap. The size of vacuoles varies considerably; in some plant cells they may occupy most of the cell volume, or they may be so small as to be barely visible under great magnification. In single-celled animals the vacuoles are generally not permanent structures; within but a few seconds a vacuole may appear, grow, and then disappear entirely. In both plant and animal cells, vacuoles function primarily as storage areas for materials to be used or excreted by the cell. They may also function in regulating the pressure between intra- and extracellular fluids.

The plastids are rounded structures within the cytoplasm of most plant and some animal cells. When they contain the green pigment chlorophyll, as in all green plants and in the peculiar one-celled animal *Euglena*, they are called chloroplasts. These cell components play a vital role in the manufacture of "chemical fuels" during the process of photosynthesis.

The Nucleus. Generally located somewhere near the center of the cell, and surrounded by the cytoplasm, the nucleus, as befits its importance, is the largest structure within the cell. The nucleus not only controls the metabolic activities of the cell, but also carries within it all

A TYPICAL ANIMAL CELL

Cells are microscopic units common to all forms of life except the viruses, which stand between the living and the nonliving. All cells can produce energy and manufacture proteins. Animal cells produce energy from food and can apply this energy to special purposes, such as chemical manufacture (gland cells), mechanical movement (muscle cells), conduction (nerve cells), excretion (kidney cells), or for a host of other essential activities.

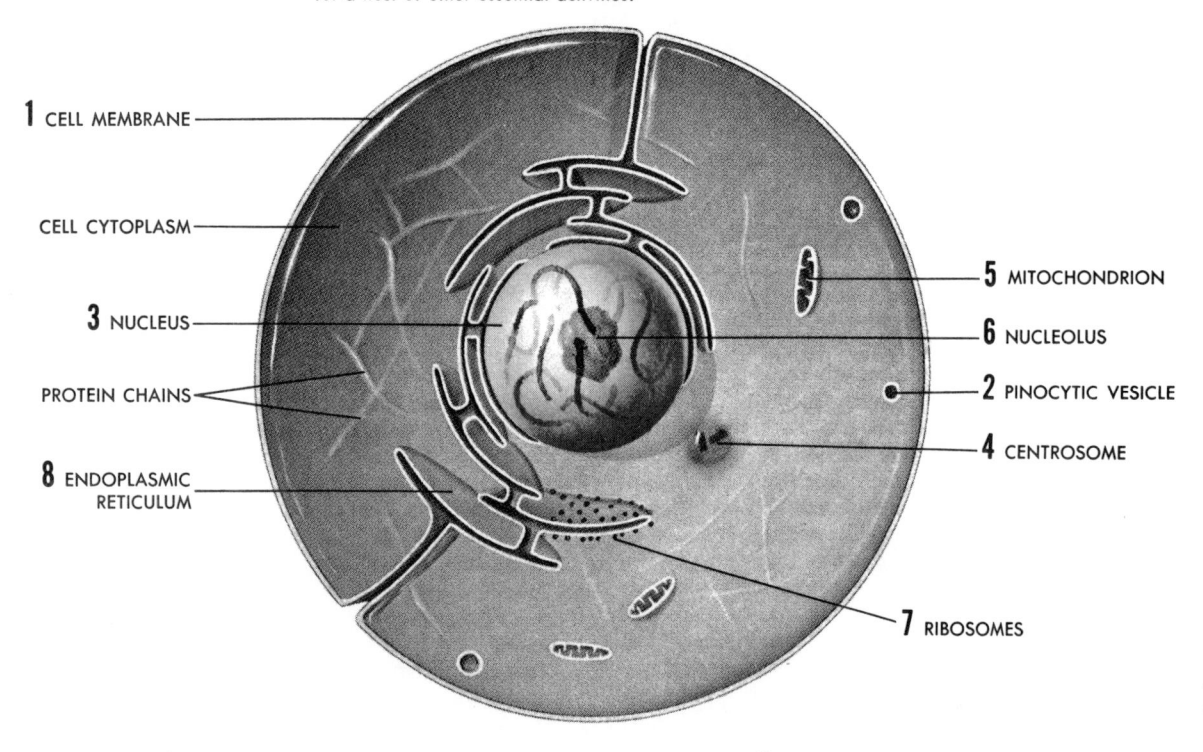

1 CELL MEMBRANE
CELL CYTOPLASM
3 NUCLEUS
PROTEIN CHAINS
8 ENDOPLASMIC RETICULUM
5 MITOCHONDRION
6 NUCLEOLUS
2 PINOCYTIC VESICLE
4 CENTROSOME
7 RIBOSOMES

1 THE CELL MEMBRANE

This structure maintains the chemical integrity of the cell by virtue of its ability to exclude certain substances from entering the cell while admitting others.

2 PINOCYTIC VESICLE

The cell also takes in food by means of infoldings in the cell membrane. The membrane enfolds particles, forming a sac which finally pinches off (as a vacuole) and migrates into the cell.

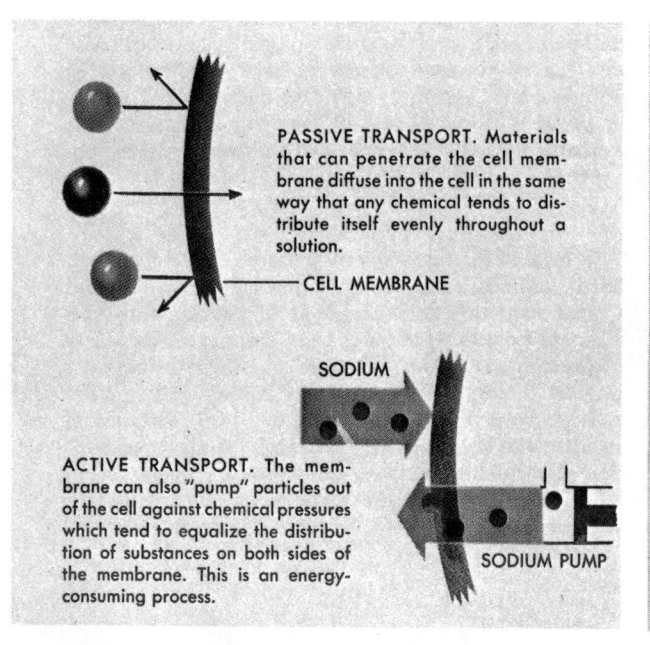

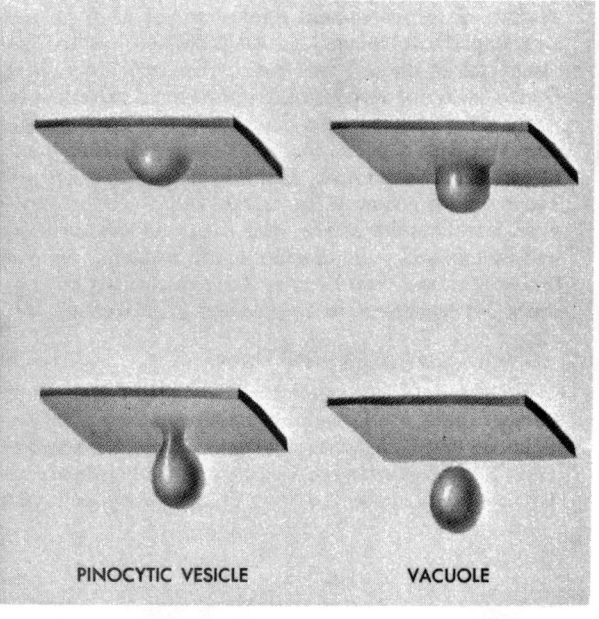

PASSIVE TRANSPORT. Materials that can penetrate the cell membrane diffuse into the cell in the same way that any chemical tends to distribute itself evenly throughout a solution.

CELL MEMBRANE

SODIUM

ACTIVE TRANSPORT. The membrane can also "pump" particles out of the cell against chemical pressures which tend to equalize the distribution of substances on both sides of the membrane. This is an energy-consuming process.

SODIUM PUMP

PINOCYTIC VESICLE   VACUOLE

83

3 THE NUCLEUS

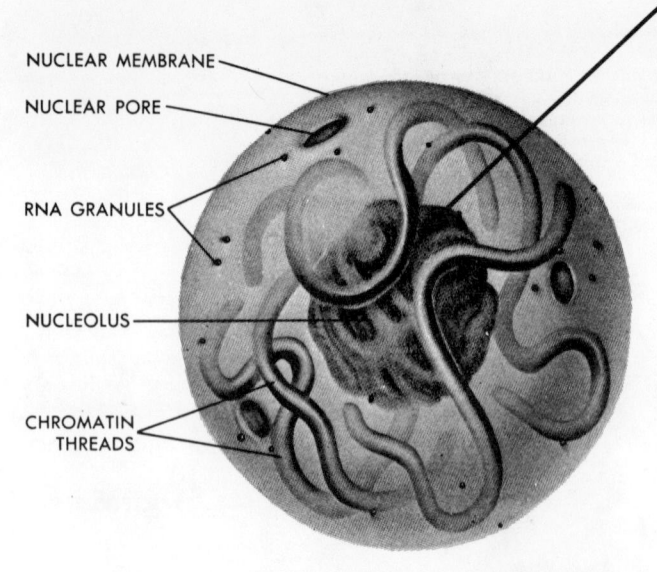

NUCLEAR MEMBRANE
NUCLEAR PORE
RNA GRANULES
NUCLEOLUS
CHROMATIN THREADS

This largest and most important part of the cell contains within its chromatin filaments the inheritance of the species. This is in the form of nucleic acids, complex substances which contain coded instructions enabling the cell to manufacture the specific proteins that distinguish one species from another. The code is "written" into the nucleic acid in the ordering of the component parts of its long, spiral molecule. The master pattern is found in the deoxyribonucleic acid (DNA) of the chromatin filaments.

4 CENTROSOME.
This structure near the nucleus is important in cell reproduction. When this process occurs, the two cylindrical bodies (centrioles) contained in the centrosome separate and form between them a spindle, or frame, which guides the division of material in the cell nucleus.

5 MITOCHONDRIA

These are the "powerhouses" of the cell. Here energy-rich foods are processed through a complex series of chemical reactions. The resulting energy is trapped in the chemical adenosine triphosphate (ATP) and in this form can be made available for energy-consuming cell activities.

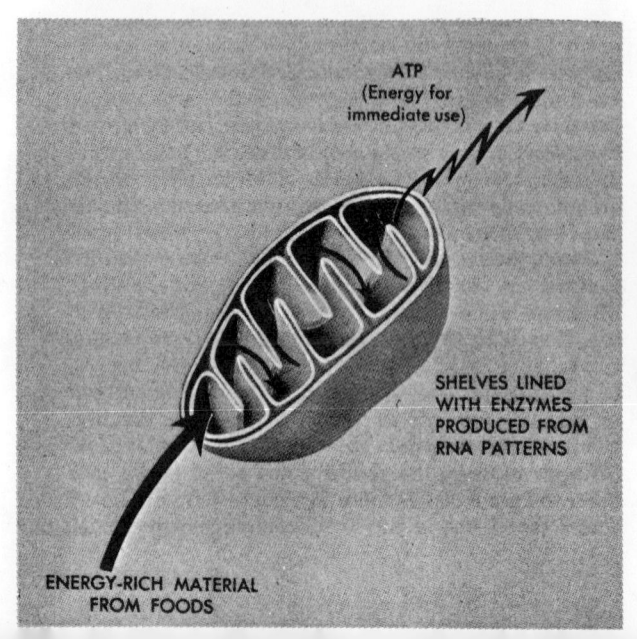

ATP (Energy for immediate use)
SHELVES LINED WITH ENZYMES PRODUCED FROM RNA PATTERNS
ENERGY-RICH MATERIAL FROM FOODS

6 THE NUCLEOLUS.
Here "messenger" nucleic acids (RNA) are produced from the DNA pattern.

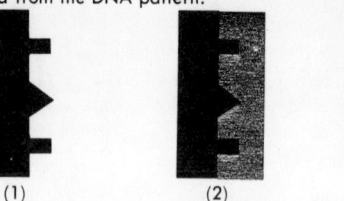

(1) (2) (3)

(1) Schematic fragment of DNA molecule.
(2) RNA is fashioned on DNA mold.
(3) RNA peels off DNA mold.

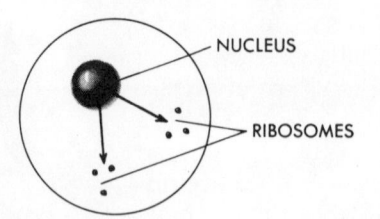

NUCLEUS
RIBOSOMES

THE RNA MOLECULE carries the coded message for enzyme manufacture from the nucleus to the ribosome.

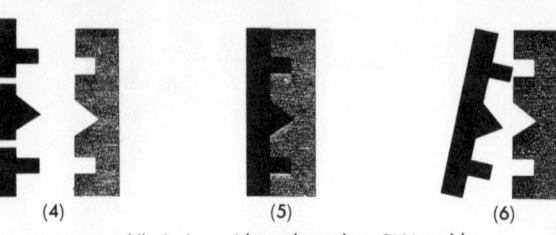

(4) (5) (6)

(4) Amino acids are brought to RNA mold.
(5) Amino acids link to form protein chain.
(6) Completed protein leaves RNA mold.

7 IN THE RIBOSOME
the RNA molds are used to manufacture the proteins needed by the cell. Many of these proteins are enzymes, chemical agents which promote particular reactions. Some enzymes are used to produce energy in the mitochondria.

8 ENDOPLASMIC RETICULUM

The ribosomes described above are distributed along the *endoplasmic reticulum*, an extensive network of channels formed by foldings of the cell membranes.

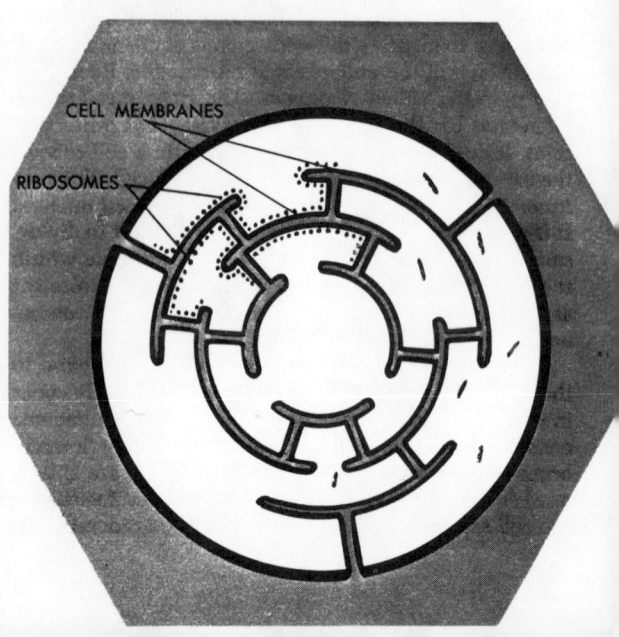

CELL MEMBRANES
RIBOSOMES

the genetic information about the cell which it passes on to the "daughter cells," the two new cells formed during cell division. The nucleus has a membrane enclosing its components—filaments of chromatin and smaller, rounded bodies called nucleoli. These nuclear components are suspended in the so-called nuclear sap or karyolymph. Both the nucleoli and chromatin material are composed of vastly complex organic compounds called nucleic acids. The nucleoli are a center for the manufacture of ribonucleic acid (RNA), which regulates protein manufacture within the cell. The manufacture of RNA is controlled by what can perhaps be called the ultimate nuclear component—deoxyribonucleic acid (DNA). The chromatin filaments are composed largely of DNA and are the sole repository and manufacturing center for this all-important compound. When the cell is about to divide, the chromatin filaments condense into paired, tightly coiled, rodlike bodies called chromosomes. Each somatic, or body, cell of an organism generally has the same number of chromosomes—a number which is characteristic for that particular species of plant or animal. The chromosomes contain all the information necessary to generate and maintain the characteristics of the entire cell. Since the chromosomes duplicate themselves exactly during cell division, each of the two resulting daughter cells is the same as the parent and is, in turn, capable of passing on the identical characteristics to its own daughter cells. The secrets of this amazing process are gradually being unveiled through intensive study of the DNA molecule.

Deoxyribonucleic Acid (DNA). DNA, which was first isolated in 1869 by the Swiss pathologist Friedrich Miescher, is now known from the work of James D. Watson, Francis H. C. Crick, and others, to be composed of two parallel chains of nucleotides. A nucleotide consists of a phosphate, a complex sugar (deoxyribose), and one of four nitrogen-containing bases (adenine, thymine, guanine, and cytosine). The repeated sugar-phosphate linkages make up the chains which spiral about each other to form a double helix. The nucleotides are linked across the chains in two specific arrangements of the bases—adenine with thymine, and guanine with cytosine. The DNA molecule, then, is a long, twisted, double coil consisting of many nucleotides. The actual coding of the genetic information is determined by the sequence of the nucleotide pairs within the DNA molecule. The information thus coded consists of "instructions" as to the precise nature of the protein molecules the cell must synthesize. The DNA molecules, therefore, comprise a most important part of the genetic material of the cells.

All DNA molecules are not the same; the particular arrangement and combination of the bases make it possible to have billions of different molecules, each of which is still called a DNA molecule. Indeed, the enormous variation in appearance and physiological make-up found among members of even the same species is attributable to the tremendous variation of molecular structure of DNA. The sequence of nucleotide pairs within the DNA molecule is capable of almost infinite variation, and hence, an almost infinite number of codings of genetic information is possible. In addition, to further increase the genetic variability between members of the same species, DNA molecules which may be linked together on the same chromosome do not necessarily have to remain together for more than one generation. The chromosomes, while lined up two-by-two before the meiotic divisions, can exchange genetic material in various sized groups of DNA molecules. This exchange phenomenon, called genetic crossing over, creates new arrangements of DNA molecules and thus new diversity in morphological and physiological characteristics. To further increase the possibility of genetic variation, spontaneous changes can occur in the genetic material—a phenomenon called mutation. The nature of the change in the gene which produces a change in a characteristic is not completely understood, but it is known to involve changes in the DNA, or DNA arrangements. Mutation is a spontaneous and inheritable change in the genetic material and for any particular gene is highly unlikely to occur. But since cells contain thousands of genes, the chance that a gene mutation will occur somewhere in the cell is not so improbable. The likelihood of mutations can be increased in a cell or organism by a variety of environmental effects, the best known of which is irradiation.

Cell Study

The study of the cell in its various aspects, including structure, function, division, and disease, is called cytology. Cytological investigations into the innermost activities of cells have provided only partial answers to such fundamental questions as how do multicellular organisms, which contain many different kinds of highly specialized cells, arise from the union of two tiny cells; how do cells utilize energy in their metabolic processes; how does information concerning regulation of various bodily functions pass from cell to cell, particularly in the vastly complex human nervous system; what makes some cells become cancerous when others remain normal; and what are the structural and biochemical changes that occur in a cell before and after a cell becomes diseased. Intensive studies have provided a fairly good understanding of the process by which the cell makes proteins. Such studies have also revealed that the manufacture of specific proteins in brain tissue may be important for determining specific memories.

Cytologists have developed a sophisticated technology to enable them to study the biochemistry and minute components of the cell. The electron microscope mentioned earlier is one of the tools of their trade. Another tool is the ultracentrifuge, whose incredibly rapid rotation literally whirls the cell apart, enabling biochemists to isolate and examine specific structures within the cell. Biochemists employ other highly sophisticated analytic techniques to detect and assay the minute amounts of complex chemical substances responsible for physiological function at the subcellular level. At these basic levels of structure, physiological (functional) and morphological (structural) phenomena become much the same.

Other important cytological tools include the tiny recording electrode—an extremely thin needle which is inserted through the membrane of a single cell to study the electronic potential of the cell membrane. Further, a micropipette, with an opening of about one micron, is used to inject or withdraw substances from a single cell. Using microtechniques of this kind cytologists have transferred nuclei and cytoplasm between different cell types and then observed the functioning of the transformed cells. This work has led to a better understanding of the protein relationships of species and of the arrangement of genes on human chromosomes.

Since the cell is the basic functional unit of living matter, answers to questions about cells will afford answer to questions about masses of similar cells (tissues), and groups of tissues of similar function (organs), and complex groups of organs and tissues (organisms). Thus cytology and its related studies are leading us rapidly to an understanding of the very basic properties of living matter. This understanding will provide not only practical applications for alleviating medical problems of human beings, but will also eventually provide a more basic understanding of life itself.

See also:

BIOCHEMISTRY	GENETICS
CHROMOSOME	HISTOLOGY
EGG	LIFE
EMBRYOLOGY	METABOLISM
EVOLUTION	NUCLEIC ACIDS
FERTILIZATION	TISSUE
GENE	

CENTER OF GRAVITY, point, usually within a body, at which the total weight of the body effectively acts. If a body is to be balanced on a knife edge, the center of gravity (CG) must be directly over the knife edge. Any object resting on its base is in a stable position only if the vertical line through the CG passes through the base. The higher the CG, the less stable is the body. The body is then more easily tilted until it topples over, which occurs when its CG is no longer over its base.

CEREBRAL ARTERIOSCLEROSIS, hardening of the arteries of the brain which usually appears in elderly persons. Narrowing of the arterial opening and loss of elasticity of the arterial wall reduces the blood supply to the brain, causing physical and mental symptoms, such as headache, dizziness, decreased ability to concentrate, irritability, and impairment of memory. The memory for recent events is affected first, but as the condition progresses even well-known names and dates are forgotten. The patient becomes confused and helpless, possibly developing delusions and hallucinations. An artery in the brain may rupture, causing hemorrhage (stroke), followed by coma, paralysis, and death. The symptoms of cerebral arteriosclerosis may be temporarily relieved by medication but the condition cannot be cured.

See also ARTERIOSCLEROSIS.

CEREBRAL EMBOLISM. See STROKE.

CEREBRAL HEMORRHAGE. See STROKE.

CEREBRAL PALSY [sĕr'ə-brəl pôl'zē], a group of conditions in which abnormal functioning of certain areas of the brain causes paralysis, muscular weakness, disturbances, and convulsions. Cerebral palsy may result from brain damage occurring during the period of development in the womb or it may develop later in life, following injury or disease. Older persons may acquire cerebral palsy from brain hemorrhage resulting from hardening of the arteries (arteriosclerosis) or from high blood pressure. The vast majority of cases appear in children: it has been estimated that 1 out of every 176 children born alive is afflicted with cerebral palsy.

Causes

The causes of cerebral palsy are not clearly understood. It is known that the brain damage is closely linked to the factors responsible for premature birth, spontaneous abortion, birth defects, and stillbirths. These factors include improper positioning of the fetus in the womb, disruption of the placenta (the structure through which the child receives its food from the mother), interference with the circulation in the umbilical cord, anemia, infection, and hemorrhage. A particularly important element in the production of the brain damage may be anoxia—a lack of oxygen. Since the brain is most sensitive to an oxygen deficiency, disturbance in brain function is likely to result if the oxygen supply of the developing embryo is poor or if breathing is abnormally delayed in the newborn child.

The nature of the cerebral palsy depends upon when, during the course of development, the damage occurs and where the damage is located in the brain. Damage occurring during the first few months of pregnancy may interfere with the development of the nervous system and produce more profound disturbances than injury which appears after the brain is fully formed. Since areas of the brain differ in their function, the disturbances will be determined to a great extent by the location of the injury.

Types of Cerebral Palsy

Spastic. Over 40% of cerebral palsy patients show some spasticity, a tendency of the muscles to contract too vigorously in an explosive, or jerky manner. The large muscles of the body which maintain body posture against the force of gravity are typically involved. As a result of this spasticity the cerebral palsy child tends to assume distinctive postures, such as the "scissors gait," in which the legs are drawn together and are rotated inwardly at the hip joint. The calf muscles contract, pulling up the heel so that the child walks on the outer edge of the foot and toes.

Spasticity of the arms may cause them to be held in against the body with the elbows flexed, the forearm twisted so that the palms point down, and the wrists and fingers flexed.

Athetoid. This refers to the uncontrollable writhing, irregular, wormlike movements seen in some types of cerebral palsy. The movements are usually reduced while at rest, but increase when the individual attempts to walk or perform some other voluntary act. He cannot organize and co-ordinate his movements and thus has a constantly changing and unpredictable posture and a lurching and stumbling gait. The muscles involved in chewing and speaking are typically affected.

Other disturbances appearing in cerebral palsy include a loss of balance, extreme extension of the back and trunk muscles producing an arched back, and tremors which appear during voluntary movement.

In addition to the physical disturbances, the brain damage may also cause difficulties of vision and hearing, convulsions, and mental defects.

Treatment

Treatment is adapted to the specific type of disability. Physical therapy is used to stretch tightened muscles, to achieve muscular relaxation, to increase strength, and to improve gait. Occupational therapy is used to occupy the individual and to provide opportunity for achievement and self-expression. Speech therapy is an important aspect of treatment. While the use of drugs in cerebral palsy has been somewhat disappointing, muscle relaxants and stimulants have proved useful in some cases. It is important for the psychological health of the child that the family becomes reconciled and adjusted to the fact of a long-term disability.

With proper training approximately 20% of patients with cerebral palsy can become self-sufficient. Another 20% can work successfully in special workshops. The remaining 60% need some type of total or partial care within the home, an institution, colony, or village.

CEREBRAL THROMBOSIS. *See* STROKE.

CEREBRUM. *See* BRAIN; NERVOUS SYSTEM.

CHAGAS' [chä'gäs] **DISEASE or SOUTH AMERICAN TRYPANOSOMIASIS** is caused by infection with a parasite (*Trypanosoma Cruzi*) which is transmitted by a number of insects, including the assassin bug and bedbugs. The disease is found in Central and South America, and, rarely, in the southern United States. The parasite usually enters the body through the eyes or skin and frequently affects the heart, causing heart failure and death. Treatment is usually ineffective. To prevent Chagas' disease it is necessary to destroy infected domestic animals which may harbor the parasite, as well as insects which transmit it.

CHALAZION [kə-lā'zē-ən], a painless enlargement of one of the glands of the eyelids, which may follow an inflammation of the gland or blockage of its opening. The chalazion may eventually break open or gradually disappear. It may be removed surgically.

CHARCOT, JEAN MARTIN (1825–93), French physician, considered the greatest neurologist of his time. He made important contributions to the study of spinal cord changes in poliomyelitis, syphilis, and other nervous disorders. He established the world-famous neurological clinics at La Salpêtrière, in Paris. A joint deformity seen in certain cases of syphilis and diabetes is named after him (Charcot's Joint).

CHARCOT'S JOINT, a painless, deformed joint which is usually seen in middle-aged men suffering from certain neurologic disorders. The knees and spinal column are usually involved; the joint surfaces are destroyed and bone is deposited around the joint margins. The deformity appears to be caused by a loss of deep sensation in the joints, as may occur in diabetes, or in advanced syphilis. Further destruction of the joint may be prevented by crutches, braces, or surgery to lock the joint.

CHEMICAL SENSE. The chemical senses include the senses of taste and smell. Usually distinguished from these is common chemical sense. Concentrated forms of many substances bring about a stinging sensation or pain in the mouth or nasal passages. Ammonia produces the effect on nasal tissue, and strong acids are painful to mouth tissues. *See also* SENSATION; SMELL, SENSE OF; TASTE, SENSE OF.

CHEMICAL WARFARE, the use of chemical energy, as distinguished from physical and explosive energy, in military operations. Substances employed are chemical agents, and the chemical reactions occur when the agent is released to atmospheric conditions of pressure and temperature. Agents reacting directly on human organisms are toxic or irritants. These are the poison gases, though they may be employed also to make equipment unusable and areas uninhabitable. Smokes are used to suffocate enemy troops and animals, to conceal troop movements, and to signal. Incendiaries are agents that burn.

Fire was an early chemical weapon, and it produced noxious and asphyxiating gases and smoke. In the Peloponnesian War, 431–04 B.C., burning pitch and sulfur created suffocating gases. A proposal made in 1855 during the Crimean War to burn sulfur as a means of overcoming the defenders of Sevastopol was disallowed by the British government, which believed the practice an uncivilized means of waging war. For the same reason, the U.S. government in 1862 declined to permit the use of poison gas chlorine in artillery shells. A proposal offered at The Hague International Peace Conference (1899) proposed that governments abstain from diffusing by projectiles asphyxiating or deleterious gases because this was an inhuman method of warfare.

Modern chemical warfare dates from Apr. 22, 1915, when the German army opened a chlorine attack against the Allies near Ypres in an effort to break the World War I stalemate on the Western Front. The gas, allowed to escape from cylinders and to drift downwind across the Allied lines, achieved complete surprise and opened a breach in the Allied defenses, but the Germans were surprised also and lacked the forces to decisively exploit the opportunity. The Allies quickly developed primitive respirators, then gas masks, designed to filter the air and cleanse it of chemical agents before it was breathed. In July, 1917, the Germans used mustard gas on the battlefield and caused severe and slow-healing burns on the skin and along the respiratory tract. In World War I, mustard gas, chlorine, and chlorine-phosgene mixtures were the greatest casualty-producing poison gases.

All the major powers developed sophisticated gases and methods of delivery after World War I. Poison gases were not employed in World War II, mainly because all the large nations were equipped to retaliate instantly against the initiator.

Military gases are classified in a variety of ways. By their physiological effects, the casualty-producing gases are divided into the following classes. (1) Choking gases, or lung irritants, such as chlorine and phosgene; (2) vesicants, or blister gases, such as mustard gas and lewisite;

(3) nerve gases, sometime called blood gases, that cause systemic poisoning. The fourth group are harassing gases that have a severe effect but incapacitate only up to 24 hours. These are sternutators (vomiting or sneeze gases) and tear gases, or lachrymators, the latter having been used in Vietnam.

The chemical warfare employed in World War II, Korea, and Vietnam made much use of the nontoxic agents in smokes and incendiaries. Incendiaries were used in artillery and mortar shells, airplane bombs, grenades, and flamethrowers. Metal incendiaries—a mixture of magnesium, powdered aluminum and zinc, and iron oxides—were used in great measure by the Germans bombing Britain early in World War II and by the Americans against Japan later in the war. Oil incendiaries have a base of gasoline, which is mixed with heavier oils or with an aluminum soap-thickener, the latter known as napalm.

CHEMOTHERAPY, the use of chemical or biological agents of precise composition to rid the body of harmful organisms without ill effects on the body itself. The term was introduced by Paul Ehrlich, a German pharmacologist, whose dream was to find specific compounds which would kill specific infections caused by bacteria, parasites, or other unknown agents, without harming the body. The first highly successful chemotherapeutic agents were the sulfa drugs, introduced in 1933. Isolation of penicillin in 1942, followed by other antibiotics, has made possible the cure of many once-fatal infections, such as syphilis, pneumonia, meningitis, and tuberculosis. Because all living things change, many bacterial strains have developed complete resistance to the antibiotics which once destroyed them. Staphylococcal infections and meningococcal meningitis are examples of this selective evolution and of the continuous need for new agents. Chemotherapy of viral infections and cancer is still in an early stage.

CHICKENPOX or VARICELLA, a highly contagious disease caused by a virus and characterized by small blisters on the skin. Few children avoid it and adults who escaped the illness in childhood may be infected at any age. Epidemics occur in winter and spring every three to four years.

The incubation period is usually 15 days, but ranges from 10 to 20. Typically, each "pock" starts as a small red spot, soon becoming an itchy dewdrop blister surrounded by redness. Successive crops of lesions appear on different parts of the body, more on the trunk than on arms, legs, or face. Blisters may also occur on the scalp and in the mouth. Various stages of eruption are seen simultaneously in the same body areas. Unless infected by scratching, the blisters turn to scabs and fall off, normally leaving no scars.

Chickenpox is usually mild, lasting one to two weeks; quarantine is rarely necessary. There may be high fever, headache, and loss of appetite, especially in older children and adults. Complications may involve the lungs, brain, kidneys, and skin, but are usually mild. Although there is no specific cure, antihistamines taken by mouth, and skin lotions and ointments, help control itching. Fever and headache may also require treatment. Fingernails should be kept short and clean to prevent the spread of infection; the face especially should not be scratched, for infected blisters may leave scars.

Chickenpox may be more severe and complications more likely in newborn babies whose mothers have not had the disease, in children receiving steroids (as for asthma), and in adults.

In 1953 Dr. Thomas H. Weller first grew the chickenpox virus in tissue culture. It was later discovered that the same virus causes either chickenpox or shingles (herpes zoster), apparently a quite different disease.

CHIGGERS [chĭg′ərz], also called harvest mites, redbugs, small mites that, when in their larval stage, attack men. Chiggers of different species are found throughout the world. The parasite attaches itself to the skin and secretes a saliva that dissolves tissue, producing a small, red, inflamed spot that itches intensely. Hundreds of these red-orange insects may appear on the body. Medicated ointments (benzyl benzoate) are used in treatment. Chigger bites can be avoided by dusting clothing with DDT and by wearing tightly-woven clothing in infested areas.

CHILBLAIN [chĭl′blān] **or PERNIO** [pĕr′nē-ō], a red, burning, itchy swelling which usually appears on the back of the fingers, hands, or feet, and results from prolonged or repeated exposure to mild cold. It appears frequently in persons who suffer from cold limbs and extremities. The swelling may form large blisters, or blebs, which may eventually ulcerate. The lesions tend to recur in cool weather and heal in the summer.
See also FROSTBITE.

CHILDBIRTH occurs about 280 days after the last menstrual period, unless the child is delivered prematurely. At the end of pregnancy the baby lies in the uterus (womb), floating in a watery liquid (the amniotic fluid) that maintains a constant body temperature for the child and protects it against injury. The child is connected to the mother by the umbilical cord, which extends from the infant's navel to the placenta, a pancake-shaped slab of tissue that lies along the inner wall of the uterus. In this cord are blood vessels that supply the infant with its food and oxygen.

Labor. The first stage of labor begins with the contractions of the muscles in the walls of the uterus. These contractions, which cause the pains felt in childbirth, come at first at 20-minute intervals and last for 30 to 60 seconds. The first stage ends when the lower portion of the uterus, the cervix, is fully opened. This may take an average of 13 hours with the first baby and 8 hours with subsequent children.

When the child enters the vagina, or birth canal, the second stage of labor begins. This is the most painful period of childbirth and may require anesthesia. Many types are available, including anesthetic gases that are inhaled and anesthetic fluids that are injected into the spinal canal. Many women require no anesthesia, thus undergoing what is known as natural childbirth.

The passage through the birth canal may last from 20 minutes to an hour. As the contractions of the uterus increase in frequency the mother is encouraged to aid in the descent of the child by tightening her abdominal muscles and "bearing down."

Complications. Various complications may develop when the child passes through the narrow opening of the pelvis. The largest part of the baby to be delivered is the head. At birth the skull bones are not yet fused together so that ordinarily the head can undergo elongation in the course of delivery without damage to the child. If the child is too large for the pelvic opening, delivery may have to be accomplished by Caesarean section. This involves making an incision in the abdomen, opening the uterus, and removing the child and the afterbirth (the placenta and the amniotic membrane that enclosed the child). The term Caesarean section, though probably derived from the Latin word *caedere* ("to cut"), is popularly thought to be named after Julius Caesar, who was said to be so large at birth that a normal delivery was impossible.

Other obstetrical complications may require Caesarean section: If the afterbirth lies below the child (placenta previa), or if the child lies crosswise in the uterus (transverse presentation), a normal delivery may not be possible.

The infant usually emerges head first (vertex delivery). In approximately one out of 30 births, however, the baby presents the buttocks or the feet first. This is a breech delivery and, with proper management, is no more dangerous to the mother and child than a head-first delivery.

Although the child normally faces the mother's spine, it may face the abdomen. Nine out of 10 such babies gradually turn around until they face the spine. Occasionally the physician may resort to the use of forceps to help turn the infant into the proper position. The forceps consist of a pair of rounded, thin metal blades with long handles, which are placed carefully around the baby's head to turn it. In well-trained hands, a forceps delivery does not injure the child.

In many deliveries a small incision (an episiotomy) is made at the opening of the vagina to allow delivery of the baby without undue stretching, and consequent permanent damage, to the tissues of the mother.

After the child is delivered, the umbilical cord is tied and cut. The child, now free from the mother, breathes and cries spontaneously. The uterus continues to contract and usually expels the afterbirth a few minutes later.

Newborn babies weigh about 7½ lb. Premature infants weigh less than full-term babies.

Convalescence. Formerly the mother was kept in bed for several weeks following childbirth. Today she is allowed up in the first day or two and resumes full activity in four to six weeks. Great care is taken to prevent excessive postdelivery bleeding and infection. The uterus returns to normal size in about six weeks. At about the same time menstrual periods resume, although a mother who is nursing may not resume menstrual periods until the baby is weaned.

In modern times there has been an increasing tendency for women to deliver their babies in hospitals or maternity homes. Under these circumstances they can be made more comfortable than at home and there is much greater safety for both mother and child.

See also EMBRYOLOGY; GYNECOLOGY; PEDIATRICS; PREGNANCY.

CHILDBIRTH FEVER. *See* PUERPERAL FEVER.

CHILD DEVELOPMENT is the growth of children in all aspects—physical, psychological, and social—from birth to maturity. The period of development is ordinarily divided into a preadolescent and an adolescent phase, marked off by the onset of puberty. Adolescence is treated in a separate article, and the present discussion deals only with changes during the years before puberty.

At birth, an infant can eat, eliminate, cry, and sleep—but he can do little else. A child of three is fairly agile, shows a considerable amount of self-control, and has developed to a respectable degree the ability to talk and to understand, which makes him uniquely human. By the time he is 12 he is capable of athletic accomplishments requiring intricate physical co-ordination, and his intellectual and other capacities are more like those of an adult than of an infant. Attitudes, desires, and beliefs that will affect him all the rest of his life have already been formed. These changes, and the principles that govern them, are of interest to parents, teachers, psychologists, pediatricians, and other professional and nonprofessional groups. Understanding children and the way they grow is important in its own right, but the study of child development is also significant for understanding the behavior of adults, whose characteristics are largely formed in childhood.

The Normal Course of Development

A great deal of research has been aimed toward charting the normal course of human growth. Children are observed at different ages, changes in behavior are noted, and when enough research has been done, it is possible to describe the typical characteristics of new-born infants, two-year-olds, or children of any other age. In reading such accounts, including those to follow, it is important to keep in mind that they represent averages and nothing more. Descriptions of typical behavior help people know what to expect of children in a general way, and they are essential for determination of lawful behavior sequences, but this does not mean that every child must conform precisely to the behavior pattern of other children his age.

Behavior of the Newborn. All the basic sensory capacities of man are present when an infant is born, but these function in a rather poorly organized way. The newborn infant (neonate) can see, hear, taste, smell, and respond to touch, but he has little ability to arrange sensations into coherent patterns and to attach meaning to the things that happen around him. He must learn before he can tell what an event signifies. The subjective experience of the neonate cannot be known directly, but a classic statement from William James' *Principles of Psychology* is probably very close to the truth: "The baby, assailed by eyes, ears, nose, skin, and entrails at once, feels it all as one great blooming, buzzing confusion."

He is capable of a considerable variety of reflex actions. If the palms of his hands are touched, the fingers will close in a surprisingly strong grasp. If he is held with his feet just touching a surface he will make prancing movements with his legs that are not unlike the movements involved in walking later on. If his cheek is touched when he is hungry he will turn his head, and if a nipple is present his lips will close about it and he will begin to suck. He may choke and sputter a bit at first, but he will soon be able to manage the rather complex cycle of acts required to suck, swallow, and breathe in a smoothly co-ordinated way. And, as any parent knows, he can cry. The average newborn infant cries 113 minutes per 24-hour day, though babies differ widely in this respect as in others. Some cry less than an hour a day; others cry more than four hours out of the 24.

Conditioned responses can be established at this time. If a signal, such as a buzzer, is repeatedly followed by presentation of a bottle from which the infant takes food, he will soon begin to make sucking movements with his mouth whenever he hears the buzzer, even though he is not given any milk. In a primitive way, he has learned to expect the bottle to appear after the buzzer sounds, and this is just one experimental example of an important kind of learning that continues to take place from birth on. The conditioned responses, however, are difficult to establish and do not last very long. There is no reason to suppose that learning just after birth has any extraordinary effect on later behavior, and there is evidence to suggest that most of the learning of specific responses that takes place at this time is very feeble indeed. Certain early deprivations, including severe denial of maternal attention, can have harmful and probably permanent effects on intelligence, personality, and social behavior; but these effects evidently appear only if the damaging conditions are extreme and endure into infancy and early childhood.

The First 18 Months. Perhaps the most striking changes that occur during the first year and a half of life are those having to do with the ability to move about and inspect the world. From a squirming infant the child is transformed into an active, self-directed person, poking, searching, exploring, "into everything." After one month the infant can lift his chin, before another month has passed he can lift his chest from a supporting surface and assume the pose so popular in photographs of nude babies. By the age of four months he can sit if someone supports his back, and two or three months later he can sit alone. In still another month he can stand with help, and at nine months he can pull himself to a standing position by the bars of a playpen. In his crib he may have been rocking back and forth on hands and knees and occasionally flopping forward. These movements are integrated, usually at about ten months, into actual creeping. By 11 months he can walk if someone holds onto his upraised hands, and shortly thereafter, near his first birthday or a little later, he takes his first steps alone. Nobody has to teach him to do this, and the common phrase "learning to walk" is a rather misleading term for what actually goes on. The nervous system matures, the ankles straighten, the muscles grow and become better co-ordinated. These changes come to pass no matter what parents may do, though opportunity and encouragement have an influence on the child's rate of progress.

The ability to manipulate objects develops in much the same way. The earliest attempts to grasp things are jerky, lurching movements not only of the arms, but of the shoulders and trunk as well. The hands are ordinarily fisted at birth but tend to remain open after the infant is around 16 weeks old. He is then able to manage a crude palming of objects, but the thumb and fingers are basically nonfunctional. At six months a baby can not only grasp an object, but he can voluntarily let it go; this reflects his growing control over movements that before were little more than automatic reflexes. By the time he is a year old his actions have been refined to the point where he can rather daintily pick up a pellet with his thumb and forefinger.

If at the same time he has become able to walk, he will begin to explore the world about him with tireless energy and curiosity. He looks at, listens to, feels, shakes, bangs, lifts, pokes into, pulls at, and chews everything he can. As far as possible, dangerous and breakable objects should be kept out of his reach at this time. Parents can teach him to avoid unmovable dangerous objects, such as electric outlets, by saying "No," and following with a slap on the hand or elsewhere; but household life is simplest if the number of forbidden objects and situations are reduced to a minumum.

All the while the infant's motor skills are growing, his awareness of the world, and especially of other people, develops at a prodigious rate. At one month he begins a wavering, cross-eyed inspection of the faces hovering above him. These faces often smile at him, and at six or seven weeks of age he rather crookedly smiles back. Up to the age of six months he may smile at any face that appears, but after a half year he becomes more discriminating, and the face of a stranger often brings forth a howl of distress. If an infant is exposed to various other people during this time, and if the other people are reasonably calm and composed, the fears will generally subside. By one year most babies are quite sociable with adults, playing peek-a-boo and pat-a-cake until the patience of the older person has been exhausted. The one-year-old also shows a strong interest in others his own age. He may babble enthusiastically when he sees another baby and perhaps hand him a toy, though he will usually want this returned along with anything else that captures his interest. His sense of the difference between his own and others' possessions is largely unformed, and while he may play contentedly alongside another child for rather long periods of time, cries of outrage will occasionally arise from the playpen as toys are snatched back and forth.

For all these difficulties, the child has changed tremendously in the first year and a half. Never again will so much progress be made in so short a time. He can walk and he can, probably, talk a little. His language development has advanced to the point where a few of his needs can be communicated and some of the desires of others can be understood. In a poorly differentiated way he is aware of himself as distinct from other people, and he is on his way to becoming an autonomous, but socially conscious, person.

The Toddler (Age 1½ to 2½). A child between the ages of one and a half and two and a half does not toddle for long. He much prefers to run, and as soon as his muscular co-ordination and balance permit, that is what he will do. Walking is much too slow. He loves wheeled vehicles and drags or pushes them through the house with no concern whatever for the condition of walls and furniture. He prefers activities calling for use of large muscles—bouncing on a bed until he is taken off, climbing on a chair and getting down again—though he is also capable of such

CHILD DEVELOPMENT

STAGES OF DEVELOPMENT

No child exactly fits any arbitrary pattern of physical and social growth, but children pass through stages of maturing and learning. The photographs here show typical behavior through 5 stages described in the article.

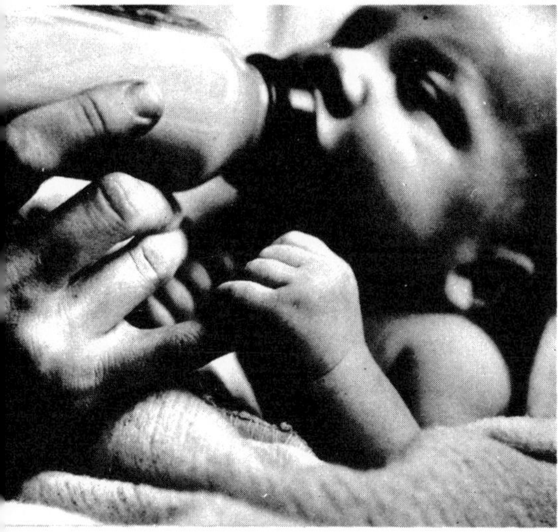

FIRST STAGE: The infant, helpless except for his reflex actions. (ESTHER BUBLEY)

SECOND STAGE: The crawling-walking period (6 mos.—1½). (TED SPIEGEL—RAPHO GUILLUMETTE)

THIRD STAGE: The more sociable toddler (1½—2½). (ESTHER BUBLEY)

FOURTH STAGE: The preschool years (2½—5), marked by increasing dexterity, imagination, and independence. (KEN HEYMAN)

FIFTH STAGE: The early school years (6—12), during which ideas multiply, physical skills are developed, and interests outside the home increase. (KEN HEYMAN)

small-muscle accomplishments as the construction of a sizable block tower. His attention span is short and he is easily distracted.

In his play, he is more sociable than before, taking evident pleasure in the company of another child, but he seldom works co-operatively with his playmate in any joint endeavor. That will come later. The beginning of dramatic play can often be seen in a two-year-old. Instead of biting or banging a toy telephone, he pretends he is talking to someone. He may put a doll to bed; he may solemnly inform his mother that he is going to work and then say "Bye-bye" as he leaves the kitchen. The scenes he enacts are simple and quickly performed. They will later be elaborated, improvised, organized, and other children will be involved in "playing house" or "cowboys and Indians," but even the earliest ventures at dramatic play involve important advances in maturation and learning. To "pretend" usually requires taking the role of another person, and out of this experience grows the capacity for looking at things from different vantage points.

The child begins to be able to perceive himself from the point of view of other people, and this is a crucial factor in the development of a sense of personal identity.

The sense of autonomy grows. More and more, the child comes to think of himself as a distinct human being, with desires, capacities, and limitations of his own. His desires are urgent, his capacities are only partly developed, his limitations are many, and he is often in trouble. This stage of development has been called the "Terrible Two's"—and for excellent reason. Temper tantrums are at their peak, especially before meals and at bedtime, and children in Western society usually go through a period of negativism when they are about two and a half, countering practically any suggestion parents might make with a vigorous "No!" Punishment of these tendencies seldom has any beneficial effect, except possibly to offer the parent some release; and it is generally agreed that if parents can firmly continue to put the child into bed or do whatever else is necessary without becoming unnecessarily involved in a battle of wills, the tantrums and unrealistic objections of the child will gradually diminish. He will learn that there are better ways to satisfy his needs.

There are other difficulties during this year. Sooner or later children have to be toilet trained, and if this is badly done certain problems may arise. Bowel training can often be established when a child is about a year and a half old —whenever he can signal that he "has to go." Muscle control for bladder training is not generally achieved until the child is two or older, and it is still another year before most children can stay dry at night. Alertness and patient effort are required to get a child trained. Attempting training too early or punishing failure too severely may attach more emotional importance to elimination than this simple body function deserves.

During this time children are strong in motility but weak in judgment. As they test the limits of the world, certain restrictions have to be set on their behavior. Discipline is probably necessary to their own security and is surely essential to the comfort of others around them. The beginnings of self-control can be seen in a two-year-old as he says "Hot!" and stays away from a stove, or pats the head of a baby sister very gently as his parents have taught him to do. But such control, and the eventual emergence of a conscience, comes slowly. Meanwhile, controls must be imposed by parents and others outside.

The Preschool Years (2½ to 5). Rapid changes in behavior continue during the next three years. At two the child uses a kiddy-car with vigor and determination but little ability to control his direction, at three he can pedal a tricycle, and by the time he is five he may be riding a bicycle with only a little wobbling. Two-year-olds are continually falling down, three-year-olds are much more sure-footed, four-year-olds can skip, though somewhat clumsily. At five, the highly complex co-ordinations required for skipping have matured. From banging kettles and scattering blocks, the child progresses to the point where he can play with rather complicated mechanical toys; and at five he may be using his father's tools to build boats and airplanes. Crude as these may seem, he is very proud of his creations and will play with his own airplane or some other barely identifiable thing for hours, leaving its expensive manufactured counterpart in the box.

The ability to think, to form concepts, and to solve problems by using ideas instead of acts develops along with other skills. If a pair of two-year-olds get into a dispute over a doll, they will tug at it until one wins and the other cries. Three-year-olds are more willing to share, and if arguments arise, these are often settled by appeals to a nearby adult. By five, fewer of the arguments are over things. They often deal with such social concerns as fairness and rules for play ("I shot you and you won't stay dead!"). Some arguments between five-year-olds may be

CHILD DEVELOPMENT

THE GROWTH OF UNDERSTANDING

Children's growth in skills and deepening understanding of the world about them are reflected in their drawings. There is great variation owing to individual personality, but development occurs in discernible stages. Scribbles are replaced by object symbols, which are refined as awareness of details increases.

Elaborate scribble (preschool).

Rudimentary human object (3—5 years).

directly concerned with the validity of ideas ("There is *too* an Easter bunny!"), and the difficulties are commonly dealt with on a verbal plane. This is not to say that physical assaults abruptly cease, only that the ability to use ideas has developed enough to permit many problems to be solved by words rather than blows. Number concepts expand. Three-year-olds have little sense of number, but four-year-olds can distinguish between one thing, two, and lots of things. At five, most children can count ten objects, know their age, and can manage some simple addition. Changes in the ability to think and plan are manifest in the drawings children make. The beginnings of representative drawing typically appear around three, but a child of that age often draws first and decides afterwards what he has made. At five he can draw a recognizable man, and it is clear as he works that he is setting out to portray something he has previously thought about. He is executing a plan.

The ability to think and imagine has in it obvious potential for dealing with human and physical problems. Now the child can wait a while for something he wants and fill in the delay with reasonably clear ideas about what is going to happen later on. Not only can he anticipate the future, he can also mull over the past and, in some measure, profit from his experience. But like so many of man's abilities, imagination can lead to trouble. Two-year-olds are more afraid of the novel and sudden than anything else. They are terrified by loud noises and strange situations. These fears have greatly diminished by five, and children of that age tend instead to fear imaginary objects or vague threats of danger. They are worried about ghosts and animals in the bedroom; they anxiously wonder what it is like to die. With further maturation, the fearful child will be more able to distinguish fantasy from reality, but now he has difficulty keeping them apart. If his fears are excessive, professional help may have to be obtained at a child guidance clinic or similar facility, but many irrational fears are "outgrown" as fact and fancy become distinct, and spooks and goblins are put in their place.

With the growth of ability to imagine how he looks to others, the child develops a new social awareness. At two he wants his way, at three he mainly wants to please, at four he wants to be noticed. He shows off, he plays the clown, he indulges in childish word-play. He calls a playmate a silly name and is convulsed with laughter at his own wit. Sibling rivalry is most severe if a new baby arrives when the older child is around three or four years of age. He is old enough then to have some awareness of his position in the family, he wants attention very badly, and the newcomer may constitute a real threat to his security. Bringing the older child into preparations for the arrival of the brother or sister, and helping him feel that the baby is his too, can help somewhat. But it is danger-

Objects become more coherent (early school).

Studio for Young Artists, Annapolis
The child develops a better understanding of the world around him.

93

ously easy to overdo the preparation in a gushy sentimental way, and no parent should be surprised if, in spite of his efforts, the older child starts to suck his thumb again or tries to hurt the baby. There is no substitute for seeing to it that the older child actually does not lose his place in the family, though his role must change; that he still gets the attention he needs, though he may not be able to have all the attention he wants; and that his basic security is truly unimpaired.

In any case, the preschool child is beginning to sever some of the ties with his parents and is no longer as completely dependent on them as is the toddler. Other people—playmates, perhaps a kindergarten teacher—assume progressively greater importance in his life. With his new sense of who he is, and the growing awareness of what he can do, the five-year-old may be arrogant and domineering at times; but in playing with other children he generally works with them rather than against them, and he is rarely content just to play beside them in the parallel activity of his earlier years. Roles are exaggerated in his dramatic play, and adults have been known to receive some sobering insights into their own characteristics as they listen to five-year-old "parents" arguing with each other and screeching at the children.

There are problems during the preschool years, as at any other age, but children of three, four, and five are more delightful than otherwise. They are not nearly such a care as they were before. They do not have to be watched all the time, though they still need some supervision. In general they like to conform, can be surprisingly dependable, are fairly sure of themselves, and normally tend to trust other people. By this time, they have a tolerably clear idea of who they are and where they stand in the world. Some basic character structures have been established, and though changes will continue throughout life, the distinct core of personality is already formed.

The Early School Years (6 to 12). Between the ages of six and 12, children slow down a bit in their growth. The rapid physical changes of the earlier years have levelled off somewhat, and the growth spurt of adolescence has not yet begun. Still, motor skills continue to improve as the muscles of the body come under increasingly refined control. At six, children are inclined to wriggle and sprawl, especially at table, and their abundant energy is worked off elsewhere in rather aimless running, jumping, and chasing. A six-year-old can care for himself in a reasonably thorough way, but there are flaws in his competence. He can bathe himself, but he usually needs some encouragement to wash his ears and neck; he can dress himself, but his sweater may be put on backwards. At nine, all these actions are more nearly automatic, and the small muscle movements involved are far better co-ordinated. New abilities are expressed through a growing interest in activities requiring fine dexterity, such as playing marbles and catching a ball. By 12, boys particularly are concerned with attaining excellence in performing certain physical feats. They may spend hours learning to juggle or making jump shots in basketball. The sudden growth of adolescence may later introduce the appearance of gangling awkwardness; but even before puberty, motor skills of a highly refined sort can be quite fully developed, and feats that would defy an adult can often be performed with consummate grace by a 12-year-old.

Ideas multiply and are more and more clearly differentiated during the school years. Children then are greedily concerned with finding out about the world they live in, with what is and what is not, with ideas of the most far-reaching kind. Their information comes from every possible source: personal observation, teachers, books, parents, and more and more from other children. It is the task of each generation of second graders to tell the less sophisticated beginners about Santa Claus. Facts and myths about sex and reproduction are spread among the children—with typical confusion over the difference between birth and elimination. After six, memories are fairly continuous, rather than isolated and episodic. With more coherent awareness of the past comes a constantly improving ability to plan ahead. Elementary school children become progressively more able to think in abstract terms. Six-year-olds are inclined to think in a concrete or purely functional way. A chair is to sit on; milk is to drink. At that time, they are mostly concerned with the differentiation of ideas, and are able to recognize differences between objects in a fairly clear way. By the time they are eight, they can note and verbalize similarities between such objects as wood and glass, and at 12 they are capable of defining such abstract terms as loyalty and courage.

In school, in their games, and in the other activities that children carry on together, they truly become members of society at large—the society outside the home. Aside from the information and attitudes they incorporate at school, this is probably the most important thing that happens to them during the school years. At six, most children are still somewhat babyish and like to be held now and then. They typically think their parents know everything that matters. At nine, they are somewhat embarrassed by displays of affection, and they are likely to recognize their parents' limitations. Other adults, and particularly their own age group, "the gang," have assumed greater importance as sources of essential knowledge. At 12, most children are ostentatiously disdainful of childish ways and may scorn their parents in a fierce effort to be independent. In the search for autonomy, they may exchange dependence on parents for the tyranny of other children, who decide what will be worn, what will be done, which children will be outcasts and which heroes. But growing away from the family and forming intimate attachments to other children constitute an important, perhaps a necessary, step on the road to self-direction and personal integrity.

Some of the most dangerous threats of this time lie in the standards of conduct maintained by the groups with which the child becomes affiliated. If the group happens to be a delinquent gang, where acceptance and status can only be gained by stealing, fighting, and defying adult authority, the new member is likely to adopt those standards as his own. It is difficult for adults to remember the desperation of a child's need to be accepted by other children, but parents should be aware that children will sometimes do outrageous things to gain that acceptance. Here, as throughout childhood, some restraints may be necessary. Children of 12 are not ready for complete self-determination, and cries of "All the other kids are doing it" sometimes have to be met with every bit of conviction the parents can muster. Still, children have to be given some freedom to make their own decisions—even wrong decisions—if they are ever to learn to get along on their own. This is the eternal dilemma of growing up. Every child must learn to satisfy his needs and become an individual within the limits set by his society. Every parent must restrict his child yet still let him go—and to do this the parent must use all the good judgment, love, and common sense at his command.

Principles of Development

Observations of behavior during childhood have led to the formulation of certain principles that summarize the general character of growth, suggest causes that determine change, and carry some implications for putting knowledge about child development to use in rearing and educating children.

Differentiation and Integration. The direction of behavior change is, first, from mass activity to specific activity. Specific functions are then integrated into larger behavior patterns. The earliest attempts to throw a ball, for example, involve movements of the entire body. The child thrusts energetically with both arms, his face is contorted with effort, he may jump clear of the ground, though this movement is irrelevant to propelling the ball. Later, only the muscles needed for throwing are used, superfluous movements have dropped out, and the action is performed much more smoothly and effectively than before. At the same time the child may have been learning to swing a bat with his arms and shoulders, instead of moving trunk and limbs stiffly together in a cumbersome effort to hit the ball. Still later these two specific skills are integrated with others, such as running and catching, in the complex activity of playing ball.

Not only motor behavior but also perceptual tendencies and ideas change in accordance with principles of differentiation and integration. Out of the "blooming, buzzing confusion" of infancy, shapes, colors, sounds, images, ideas, and meanings are distinguished one from another. Horses and cows look much alike to a two-year-old; later he can tell them apart. When he is older still he can connect his ideas of these and other things, of himself and other people, into a coherent frame of reference for his own role in the world.

Maturation and Learning. Two processes are involved in all behavior change: physical maturation of the muscles, neural tracts, glands, and other body structures; and the learning of information and skills through experience. In any given accomplishment both processes are inextricably involved. If a child obtains a score of 130 on an intelligence test, he does so because his brain has matured to a certain level and because he has had certain opportunities and experiences in his life. One process or the other, however, may be predominant in determining behavior change. If most children walk at a given age despite severe environmental restriction and lack of experience, it is reasonable to attribute this change principally to maturation. If a child in a wretched home environment develops emotional conflicts and an inclination to avoid other people, one may legitimately assume that learning has been primarily involved.

Developmental Readiness. It is inefficient and sometimes harmful to begin training in any activity before children have matured enough to respond to the experience. It is senseless to try to teach a baby to walk when he is six months old. Insisting on performance of which a child is maturationally incapable can only lead to distress and disappointment on the part of everyone involved. On the other hand, the principle of developmental readiness offers no excuse for parental negligence, as in the case of a rude and insolent nine-year-old whose parents explained that he was not yet ready to learn manners. Nor does it exclude the problems that arise when educational measures are delayed too long. The principle amounts merely to a statement that changes in behavior are most efficiently and painlessly fostered if training procedures are paced to coincide with periods of optimal developmental readiness. As such, the principle is very important for parents, educators, and others to comprehend, but it is difficult to apply. Judicious pacing, to challenge a child without placing impossible demands upon him, requires a good deal of knowledge about the norms of child development and a fine sensitivity to the differences in capability that individual children show.

See also:
ADOLESCENCE
PEDIATRICS
SLEEPWALKING

CHILDREN'S DISEASES. See PEDIATRICS.

CHINESE TRADITIONAL MEDICINE, that form of medicine practiced by Chinese physicians prior to the advent of Western-type medicine. The earliest known records of Chinese medicine are *The Herbal*, and the *Nei Ching*, or *Classic of Internal Medicine*. *The Herbal*, shrouded in mysticism, is a three-volume work said to have been written in the 27th century B.C.; the style of writing, however, places it more accurately in the 1st century B.C. This book classifies over 300 drugs and has been constantly revised. The table of contents lists many unusual items such as tiger bones and bat's dung, and also includes some drugs used in modern medicine, such as chaulmoogra oil and ephedrine. The *Nei Ching*, although thought to have originated in the 26th century B.C., was probably written about 1000 B.C. There have been no major changes in traditional Chinese medicine since this book was written. The *Nei Ching* is still venerated by many Chinese physicians.

According to the *Nei Ching*, there were two major forces controlling the state of the body: Yang and Yin. These two forces represented complete opposites such as life and death, or light and dark, and existed in a complicated state of flux; perfect harmony means health, disharmony brings disease. These two vital forces were thought to be contained in 12 main ducts coursing through the body. The ducts were usually imbedded deeply in the muscles, but rose to the surface at 365 distinct sites. Depending on the disease, the physician directed his therapy to one or more of these locations.

Two ancient forms of therapy, still in use today, were

acupuncture and moxa, or moxibustion, both used to correct the imbalance of Yang and Yin. In acupuncture long needles were driven into the body, either manually or with a mallet. The number of needles, sites used, duration and depth of penetration, as well as the direction in which the needle was rotated, all depended on the nature and severity of the illness. Moxa, the ignition of small cones of combustible material placed on the skin, was of actual value only as a counterirritant.

Because of the belief in the sacredness of the human body, cadaver dissection was prohibited; this led to a fanciful concept of the anatomy and physiology of the human body.

The most important part of the patient's examination was the taking of the pulse, which was thought to be in direct communication with various internal organs; hence diseases could be diagnosed without further investigation. The *Nei Ching* listed many rules for this, including the time of day the pulse was to be taken, the effect of seasonal changes, and the position of the stars.

Surgical procedures were virtually unknown, yet the ancient Chinese physicians discovered a form of smallpox vaccination as far back as the 11th century A.D.

At the present time, many hospitals on the Chinese continent are divided into two units, the modern and the traditional, with patients assigned alternately to each division. This practice insures the preservation of Chinese traditional medicine in spite of modernization.

CHIROPODY. See PODIATRY OR CHIROPODY.

CHIROPRACTIC [kī-rə-prăk'tĭk], the principle and method of drugless healing originated by Daniel D. Palmer in 1895. Chiropractic theory holds that dysfunction is caused by the inhibition of nerve impulses flowing to the different parts of the body; this inhibition also causes the body to be less resistant to infection. According to the theory, treatment by manual manipulation, particularly of the spinal vertebrae, allows nerve impulses to flow normally and restores good health. Educational and licensing requirements for chiropractors vary widely. There are 19 schools accredited by the National Chiropractic Association and the International Chiropractors Association. Chiropractors are licensed in most states.

CHLORAL HYDRATE, also called chloral, organic chemical used in medicine to produce sleep and sedation and in veterinary medicine as an anesthetic and anticonvulsive drug. Commercially, it is used in the manufacture of the insecticide DDT. When given in ordinary dosages, chloral hydrate produces a deep long-lasting sleep which is usually free of harmful aftereffects. The drug may irritate the stomach and large dosages may interfere with breathing, especially if it is combined with alcohol (as in "knockout drops" or in the "mickey finn").

CHLOROFORM [klôr'ə-fôrm], a compound of carbon, hydrogen, and chlorine, used as an anesthetic, liniment, cleansing agent, solvent for fats and oils, and as an antifreeze in carbon tetrachloride fire extinguishers. Chloroform was widely used as an anesthetic after Queen Victoria of England allowed it to be administered to her during childbirth in 1853. Although it is far less safe than ether, it is still occasionally used as an anesthetic.

CHLOROQUINE [klôr'ə-kwīn], also called SN-7618, Aralen, or Resochin, an antimalarial drug which is more potent and less toxic than quinine. Chloroquine is effective in stopping attacks of vivax malaria, the most common form, and suppresses and often cures the less common falciparum malaria. It is also used to treat amebic infections of the liver.
See also MALARIA.

CHLORPROPAMIDE [klôr-prō'pə-mīd], a drug which when taken by mouth as a one-, two-, or three-a-day pill, eliminates the need for insulin injections in some diabetics and decreases the insulin requirements of others. It is often effective in patients with mild diabetes that has originated in adulthood but is not of value in those who have had the disease since childhood.
See also DIABETES MELLITUS.

CHOLANGITIS [kŏl-ăn-jī'tĭs], an inflammation of the ducts which carry the bile fluid from the liver to the gall bladder and the small intestine. Cholangitis usually results from obstruction of the ducts by stones, tumors, or by constricting bands of fibrous tissue and is characterized by chills, fever, and jaundice (yellowish tinting of the skin and eyes). Infection is sometimes present and may spread to the liver and blood stream. Treatment consists of surgical relief of the obstruction in conjunction with the use of antibiotic drugs.

CHOLECYSTECTOMY. See GALL BLADDER.

CHOLERA [kŏl'ər-ə] acute infection of the gastrointestinal tract caused by a small, comma-shaped bacterium, *Vibrio comma*. Cholera is both endemic and epidemic in Southeast Asia, particularly India and Pakistan. Although the bacteria occurs worldwide, the last epidemic in the United States was in 1866. The disease is spread by contamination of water supplies with infected human feces. Cholera is perpetuated by crowding and poor sanitation. There are no known animal hosts.

Swallowed cholera bacteria multiply in the large intestine and produce a toxin which acts on the intestinal cells that normally resorb salt. The patient begins to have severe diarrhea about 12 to 48 hours after he has swallowed contaminated fluid. Vomiting without nausea and severe muscle cramps follow. The extreme loss of fluid from the system results in saline and potassium deficiency, leading to circulatory collapse, shock, and death.

The disease lasts from 2 to 7 days and can be controlled if adequate amounts of fluid and salt—12 to 24 liters a day—are given intravenously. In remote areas, the mortality rate is about 60%. The antibiotic tetracycline, taken by mouth, rids the stool of vibrio's, thereby shortening the duration of illness and reducing the chance of infecting others. Vaccination is required for travel to and from endemic areas, countries where cholera is always present, but there is no proof that it works. Careful hygiene provides the only sure protection against cholera. Only when proper sanitary facilities and practices are available throughout the world will cholera be completely controlled.

CHOLESTEROL [kə-lĕs′tə-rōl], an organic compound, chemically related to vitamin D and the sex hormones, and found in all tissues of the human body, particularly in the brain and spinal cord. Cholesterol is important as one of the substances which are deposited in the wall of large arteries, and lead to atherosclerosis, a form of hardening of the arteries.

In the human body, cholesterol is manufactured principally in the liver. The main sources of cholesterol in the diet are egg yolk, meats, milk products, and animal fats. Cholesterol is found in the blood in a free, or uncombined state, and also in combination with fats and proteins. In individuals suffering from atherosclerosis, a form of hardening of the arteries, the quantity of this cholesterol-fat-protein combination which is deposited in the walls of large arteries is frequently increased, and there is some evidence to indicate that excessive consumption of foods with a high cholesterol content may contribute to the development of this disease.

Although its exact function in the body is not yet understood, it is known that cholesterol can be converted into a number of hormones and into a substance which acts similarly to vitamin D in preventing rickets. Cholesterol is also converted into the bile acids which are the principal constituents of the bile fluid. Free cholesterol in the bile may be deposited in the gall bladder in the form of gallstones. Cholesterol is prepared commercially from the spinal cord of cattle and is used in skin lotions and as an emulsifying agent for various pharmaceuticals.

CHOLINE [kō′lēn, kŏl′ēn], a nitrogen-containing organic compound widely distributed in the human body and in foods such as meats, eggs, and cereals. It is chemically related to acetylcholine, an important compound of the nervous system, and to muscarine, a poison found in some mushrooms. In the body, choline prevents the accumulation of fat in the liver. Although it is sometimes included in vitamin capsules, its effectiveness in preventing fatty degeneration of the liver when used this way is uncertain. Choline has also been used in the treatment of certain liver diseases.

CHORDOTOMY [kôr-dŏt′ə-mē], an operation in which groups of pain-carrying fibers in the spinal cord are severed. Chordotomy is usually reserved for incurable, intensely painful diseases, such as cancer.

CHOREA [kô-rē′ə], also called Sydenham's chorea, or St. Vitus' dance, is a disorder of the brain which causes brief, purposeless muscular movements. The disease was called chorea (in Greek: "dancing") because of the similarity of these movements to those seen in hysterical dancing mania. The cause is unknown. Chorea is most common in girls between the ages of 5 and 15. Most cases in children are associated with rheumatic fever. Chorea has occurred in pregnant women and may also develop as a complication of infections, such as scarlet fever, pneumonia, and measles.

The disease begins gradually with fragmentary movements of the lips, tongue, cheeks, and eyes. The movements become more exaggerated and eventually involve the arms, legs, and the entire body. Irritability, restlessness, and emotional instability may precede or accompany the movements. The symptoms may gradually subside in six to eight weeks, although in some cases vestiges of the disorder may linger on and become chronic.

There is no specific treatment. In severe cases bed rest and sedation are necessary. Tranquilizing drugs are sometimes used to control symptoms.

See also RHEUMATIC FEVER.

CHOROIDITIS [kôr-oid-ī′tĭs], an inflammation of the eye, involving the choroid, a layer of tissue, richly supplied with blood vessels, which envelops most of the eyeball. It is believed that in most cases the inflammation is produced by infection. The condition produces a painless blurring of vision and in some cases vision may be permanently impaired. Cortisone and related drugs are helpful; the underlying infection is treated if it can be identified.

CHROMOSOME [krō′mə-sōm], name for certain of the

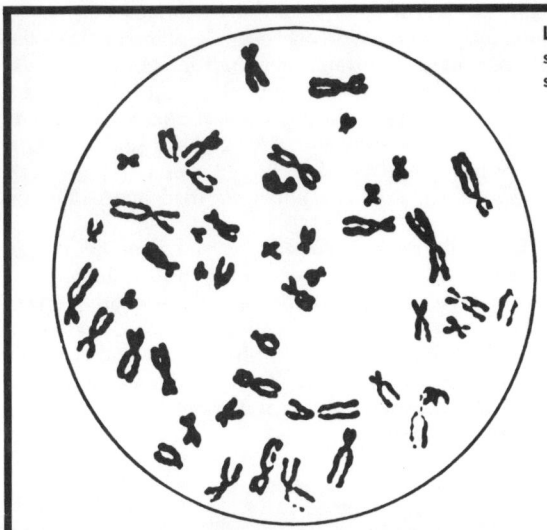

Left, chromosomes as seen under a microscope. *Below*, chromosomes from the same cell arranged in pairs—a karyotype of the cell. The two X chromosomes show that this is a cell from a female. (NATIONAL FOUNDATION—MARCH OF DIMES)

small, generally oblong bodies found in the nucleus of plant and animal cells. Incorporated in the chromosomes are genes, the units of inheritance, which determine the characteristics of an organism. Chromosomes are found in pairs. The number of chromosomes in a cell is constant for any particular species. Man has 23 pairs of chromosomes, or a total of 46 in each cell.
See also GENE; GENETICS.

CIRRHOSIS [sĭ-rō'sĭs] **OF THE LIVER,** a group of disorders in which the cells of the liver degenerate and are replaced by scar tissue. The most common form is Laennec's, or portal, cirrhosis, which is frequently associated with alcoholism. It is believed that a nutritional deficiency may also be responsible. Scarring leads to the obstruction of the flow of blood through the liver. The blood which would normally return to the heart through the liver seeks other routes and swells and weakens the veins of the gullet (the esophagus), the stomach, the abdominal wall, and other areas.

Many patients with this form of cirrhosis do not display any symptoms. The disease advances slowly, causing at first loss of appetite, nausea, vomiting, and loss of weight. In many cases the first sign is bloody vomiting. The legs may be swollen and a mild jaundice (yellowish tinting of the skin and eyes) is sometimes seen. Slight fever may be present for weeks or months. In the advanced stages the patient becomes weak and the abdomen swells with fluid. A serious complication is hemorrhaging from large, weakened veins (varices) in the esophagus. Coma may occur.

A less frequent variety of cirrhosis appears following poisoning from carbon tetrachloride or phosphorus, or following a virus infection of the liver (hepatitis). This disease, called post-necrotic, or toxic cirrhosis, appears in all age groups. In many cases the original damage to the liver is not detected and the condition may go unnoticed for many years. Abdominal pain and jaundice are common. Cirrhosis of the liver may also be caused by obstruction of the tubes which drain the liver secretions (the bile ducts) or by inflammation of the liver.

Treatment. The treatment of the different forms of cirrhosis is similar. A diet rich in vitamins and proteins and carbohydrates is important. If the abdomen is swollen with fluid, salt intake is restricted and medications (diuretics) are given to stimulate kidney action. In some cases fluid may be removed from the abdomen by introducing a large-bore needle into the abdominal cavity. Surgery may be necessary to treat hemorrhages from the large veins.
See also LIVER.

CLEFT PALATE, a congenital deformity in which openings in the palate (the roof of the mouth), join the cavities of the mouth and nose. Cleft palate results from the failure of the embryonic parts of the palate to fuse normally during the course of development. The cleft may lie only in the soft rear section of the palate or in the front bony portion as well (the hard palate). The deformity is often associated with cleft lip (harelip) and occasionally with a malformation of the bony ridge which contains the sockets of the upper teeth (cleft alveolar process).

The openings in the roof of the mouth may permit foods or liquids to enter the nose during the act of swallowing and it may be difficult to breathe through the nose while eating. Speech defects are usually present. The condition can be corrected by surgery and it is recommended that this be done in infancy, preferably before the child begins to speak.

CLUBFOOT, congenital deformity of the bones and joints of the foot and ankle which appears in approximately 1 out of 1,000 births. Boys are more often affected than girls. One or both feet may be involved. In the most frequent type, the toes are pointed down and the foot is twisted in at the ankle. The deformity can usually be corrected early in childhood by using plaster casts and splints to bring the foot into a normal position. In older children, surgical treatment may be necessary.

COCAINE [kō-kān'], an organic nitrogen-containing chemical obtained from the leaves of certain South American trees. For centuries leaves containing this substance have been chewed by South American Indians to increase endurance by stimulating the brain. Sir Arthur Conan-Doyle represented his famous fictional detective Sherlock Holmes as taking cocaine for the same purpose. Cocaine is addictive and its use is subject to narcotics regulations. The drug was once extensively used to produce limited, or local, anesthesia, but it has been largely replaced by less toxic compounds.

COCCIDIOIDOMYCOSIS [kŏk-sĭd-ē-oi-dō-mī-kō'sĭs], a fungus disease found principally in the southwestern United States. The fungi are carried by dust and when inhaled may produce a lung infection which resembles tuberculosis. The patient suffers from lack of appetite, fever, headache, backache, chills, cough, and chest pain. In one form of the disease, known as "the bumps" or "San Joaquin fever," the skin is involved. Most cases recover without difficulty; however, the disease may be fatal if the infection spreads to the central nervous system and other tissues. Dust-control measures may help reduce the number of cases in areas where coccidioidomycosis is prevalent.

COCCUS [kŏk'əs], general term for spherical, microscopic organisms, particularly bacteria. In various species, the individual spherical cells may occur in different characteristic groupings. An arrangement in pairs is termed a diplococcus. A chain of cocci resembling a string of beads is referred to as streptococcus, whereas an irregular cluster is called a staphylococcus. The names of some bacterial groups have been based on these terms.
See also BACTERIA; STAPHYLOCOCCUS; STREPTOCOCCUS.

CODEINE [kō'dēn], a narcotic derived from opium. Codeine is used to relieve pain and to induce sleep, but it is considerably less potent than morphine, another opium derivative to which it is chemically related. Codeine is particularly effective in controlling cough and is widely used in cough preparations for this purpose. Extensive use of the drug may result in addiction.
See also NARCOTICS.

COD-LIVER OIL, a mixture of oils obtained from fresh

codfish livers. These oils are rich in vitamins A and D and are used as a dietary supplement to prevent night blindness, rickets, osteomalacia (adult rickets), and other disorders which may result from vitamin A and D deficiency.
See also VITAMINS.

COLD, COMMON, an inflammation of the tissues lining the nose and throat, resulting in coughing, nasal discharges and congestion, sneezing, sore throat, and, frequently, fever. The common cold is the most frequent and perhaps the most baffling illness of man. At various times several different bacteria have been proposed as the responsible agent, and today, after years of intensive investigation, it can only be stated that the common cold is probably produced by one or more viruses.

Although it is commonly believed that drafts and chills predispose to developing a cold, studies have failed to confirm this. Evidence indicates that colds are probably contracted in crowded places. Children are more susceptible than adults and develop colds of greater severity. The average cold lasts for seven days. Treatment is limited to relief of symptoms and consists of bed rest, antipyretics, nasal decongestants, and cough preparations.

Some anticold vaccines have been claimed effective; however, tests have demonstrated that virtually any harmless drug given as a cold preventive will be as much as 50% effective, indicating a possible psychological action.

COLD SORES, also called fever blisters, are caused by a virus infection and may appear in clusters anywhere on the body, most commonly on the face, lips and mouth. The blisters are filled with a clear fluid and are surrounded by an area of reddened tissue. They usually heal and disappear within a few weeks. Cold sores on the eyes may leave scars which interfere with vision.

COLIC [kŏl′ĭk], pain produced by cramps of fluctuating intensity. Colic is not a disease in itself but is rather a symptom of a disturbance in one of the hollow organs of the body, such as the intestine, gall bladder, or urinary tract. The pain results from overactivity of the muscles in the walls of these organs. This may be caused by a mechanical obstruction, such as a stone, in the cavity of the organ, or by irritation of the muscle from inflammation, nervous imbalance, or biochemical abnormalities. The location of the pain, associated symptoms, and treatment are determined by the organ involved. In infants the term is used to describe bouts of crying which are thought to be caused by hunger, overfeeding, or swallowing of air.

COLITIS [kō-lī′tĭs], inflammation of the large intestine. The inflammation may be produced by infections, as in amebic and bacillary dysentery, or by the ingestion of chemicals, such as arsenic and mercury; often, the cause of the inflammation is unknown.

An important form of colitis is nonspecific ulcerative colitis. The cause is unknown, although various theories have attributed the condition to allergy, infection and nervous tension. Young adults are usually affected. The disease destroys sections of the intestinal wall, which are then replaced with scar tissue. Characteristic symptoms include pain, fever, and bloody diarrhea. Death may result from perforation of the intestinal wall and a subsequent infection of the abdominal cavity (peritonitis). Other complications include anemia, arthritis, and loss of weight. Children with ulcerative colitis are often retarded in growth.

Adrenal hormones, psychotherapy, diets, and vitamins help to relieve, but do not cure, the condition. In cases where ordinary medical measures prove inadequate, the diseased section of the intestine may be removed surgically.
See also DYSENTERY.

COLLAGEN [kŏl′ə-jĕn] **DISEASES,** also called connective tissues diseases, are a group of ailments characterized by inflammation of the connective, or supporting, tissues of the body, which are found beneath the skin and around the blood vessels and major organs. Each of the diseases presents a distinct pattern of symptoms: polyarteritis nodosa involves the walls of the arteries and may produce a wide variety of apparently unrelated symptoms, such as abdominal pains, headache, muscle soreness, or high-blood pressure; lupus erythematosus involves the joints, skin, kidneys, and other major organs. One of the most common collagen diseases, rheumatoid arthritis, is a major cause of joint disease.

COLON [kō′lən], a portion of the mammalian digestive tract arising at the end of the small intestine and terminating at the rectum. Muscle fibers in the walls of the colon cause rhythmic contractions, called peristalsis, which move undigested food residues through its length. During this passage, water is removed from the mass and it is formed into feces, the waste products of digestion, which leave the body via the rectum and anus.
See also COLITIS; DIGESTION.

COLOR BLINDNESS. See COLOR VISION; EYE.

COLOR VISION. The light-sensitive portion of the human eye responds in different ways to different wavelengths of light. When the light is relatively bright and is presented in the center of the visual field, the shorter wavelengths are perceived as violets and blues, and the longer wave lengths as oranges and reds.

About 6,000,000 microscopic elements, known as cones, are contained in the delicate membrane lining the interior of the eye. These cones are necessary for the perception of colors. The membrane in which they are contained is the retina, which also contains a very large number of elements (rods) responsible for black-and-white vision.

Much may be learned about the cones from a simple, standard experiment which the reader may perform for himself. A small circle of brightly colored paper is held in the right hand, the arm being horizontal and stretched out to the right. The left eye should be closed. The arm, still straight and horizontal, is now gradually moved toward the front while the right eye is gazing at a point straight ahead. The observer will first see the paper, out of the corner of the eye, as a gray disc. However, as the paper continues toward the direct line of sight, at some point it will be seen rather abruptly in its true color. If the arm movement is continued to the left of the center position, there will be a point where the disc will again become gray. If papers of different colors are used, and if the observations are carefully made, it will be found that different colors are first perceived at different distances from the center of the visual field, which is defined as the point at which the right eye is looking.

The above experiment brings out two basic relations between the perception of color and the cones. First, the cones are concentrated near the center of the retina with very few on the outer edges; thus objects are seen as colored only when they are in the center of the visual field. Secondly, the fact that only some colors are perceived at some of the points in the middle of the visual field must mean that all cones are not equally sensitive to all colors. This, in turn, supports the widely held theory that normal color vision involves more than one type of cone.

The varieties of color blindness also suggest that there is more than one type of cone in the retina. The most common kind of color blindness is a confusion of red and green, but even this single type of color blindness actually involves either an abnormally weak response to red light or an abnormally weak response to green light. Which weakness is present may be discovered by testing sensitivity to red and green separately. It will be found that some people are insensitive to green and others to red. There are rarer kinds of color blindness, but these can also be attributed, in most cases, to cone deficiencies.

Total color blindness is extremely rare. When it does occur it is found about equally in men and women. Partial color blindness is more prevalent, being found in about 8% of the males in the world but only rarely in females. Deficiency in color vision may be a handicap in some occupations and in the armed forces. Tests such as the chart devised by a Japanese scientist named Ishihara are used to detect color blindness.
See also EYE.

COMA [kō′mə], a serious state of profound unconsciousness, in which the patient does not respond to stimulation. In deep coma there is no reaction at all and even the reflexes are absent. In light coma the patient may move or moan when strongly stimulated. The coma may appear suddenly, as in cases of brain hemorrhage, or develop gradually through stages of drowsiness and stupor, as in diabetic coma. A coma may last for long periods; if so, the patient may be kept alive by nourishment administered through the veins. The most common causes of coma are brain injury, stroke, alcoholism, overdose of sleeping pills (barbiturate poisoning), carbon monoxide poisoning, diabetes, epilepsy, heart failure, and severe general infections.

COMBAT FATIGUE, also known as combat neurosis, combat exhaustion, or shell shock, is a form of nervous breakdown that appears under the stress of battle. Although common misconception has it that it is usually the passive, timid, and emotionally immature personality who succumbs, even normally strong personalities may also collapse under the strain of prolonged combat.

The breakdown is ordinarily preceded by certain danger signals, such as a lack of appetite, insomnia, irritability, and a lack of interest in maintaining one's equipment. If, at this point, the soldier is not given an opportunity for rest and recuperation, he is likely to "freeze" in the next combat situation, developing amnesia, extreme anxiety, sweating, and palpitations. In severe cases, he may pass into a stupor in which he loses contact with reality or he may impulsively flee from the battlefield.

A chronic form of combat neurosis develops gradually over a period of time and is characterized by a limited emotional response and a reliving of combat experiences in the form of nightmares, anxiety, and convulsions.

Most cases of combat fatigue respond quickly to rest and relaxation.

COMPENSATION, one of several so-called defense mechanisms, is defined by behavior that is aimed (usually) at indirect or partial achievement of a goal when direct achievement is frustrated or leads to anxiety. For example, the boy who is unable to make the school basketball team may achieve partial satisfaction from being official scorekeeper. Much of the play and fantasy of children and daydreaming by adults may be considered compensatory in nature, when goals that are unattainable in reality are achieved in imagination. In addition, behavior designed to correct or "make up for" a real or imagined deficiency may be considered compensatory. The deaf person who learns to read lips and the blind person who learns to depend on other senses for knowledge of the environment provide examples of constructive compensatory behavior.

Some forms of compensation are less constructive, and may be indicative of major adjustment difficulties. Examples might be the father whose feelings of inferiority (imaginary or real) are compensated for by harsh disciplining of his children or the unmarried woman who spends her life "babying" cats and dogs instead of caring for children.
See also MENTAL HEALTH.

CONCUSSION [kən-kŭsh′ən], widespread temporary paralysis of brain function, apparently caused by a massive electrical discharge of brain cells, following a blow to the head, such as might be suffered by a prize fighter. Concussion sets in immediately after injury and varies in severity from confusion to brief unconsciousness. Mental function may be disturbed for several hours following the blow and a temporary amnesia for events immediately preceding or following the injury may develop. Recovery is usually complete within a few days.

CONJUNCTIVITIS [kən-jŭngk-tə-vī′-tĭs], inflammation of the outer covering of the eye, which may be caused by infection, allergy, or irritation from foreign bodies, extreme light, dust, wind, or snow. Conjunctivitis is the commonest eye disorder and may occur in epidemics ("pink eye") when infection is responsible. It is frequently seen in measles and a number of other infectious diseases. The symptoms consist of sensitivity to light, tearing, itching, and the sensation of having sand or other foreign particles in the eye. The eyes are red and watery and the lids are swollen. Conjunctivitis may exist in a chronic form, disappearing for a while, only to return again. An allergic conjunctivitis (vernal conjunctivitis) affects young men principally. It usually appears in the spring and lasts through the summer.

Dark glasses may be worn to protect against strong light, and cold compresses and eye drops are applied to relieve the inflammation. Locally applied antibiotics are used in cases of bacterial infection. Solutions of cortisone and related drugs are used in the allergic cases.

CONSCIENCE [kŏn'shəns], the internal sense of right and wrong with respect to moral or ethical conduct. It is revealed both in self-control (resistance to temptation) and in self-censure (guilt). To many psychologists conscience is not a specific faculty but is a designation for various learned ways of guiding, or reacting to, one's own ethical behavior.
See also SUPEREGO.

CONSCIOUSNESS, like "experience" and "awareness," is a word which cannot be adequately defined in terms of more elementary concepts. In daily language consciousness is used to denote those kinds of experiences which almost anyone can privately verify. Public knowledge about consciousness can only be inferred from behavior. When an organism is able to react to its environment and to take past events and future possibilities into account, it fulfills a necessary condition for being considered "conscious." It is generally considered that consciousness is a characteristic found in the animal kingdom, and that it coincides with a functional state in which instincts, or drives, are carried out to the advantage of the organism.

The following examples outline the progressive increase of consciousness in the animal kingdom. By attributing a subjective life to an animal we are employing *empathy*, which becomes quite speculative for animals low on the evolutionary scale. The drives of insects, for example, appear to have no overall goals, such as avoiding pain or finding pleasure. Action follows immediately upon stimulus, or impulse, even if this leads to the destruction of the organism. The attraction to light will lure a moth to a flame where, not feeling pain, the moth will burn. There cannot be consciousness in such an action. Behavior at this level consists of reflex, tropism, and instinctual action.

In vertebrates the beginnings of sensory awareness are apparent. Sensory experience becomes indirect because of the possibility of perceiving space and time. This results in virtual imagination and striving for overall goals, rather than merely carrying out individual instincts. Starlings with the "cat-danger" figure held in memory will postpone the pleasure of eating insects on a freshly mown lawn when a cat is present, thus avoiding danger. They may mob the animal and by acting as a group chase him away, thereby consciously removing danger. In man, awareness of the impressions made upon one's senses and awareness of one's actions is constantly present, except during periods of sleep and central nervous system malfunction.

Another meaning of consciousness is the awareness of one's awareness, of one existence and mental states. This is a reflexive state in which indirect experience can be related to something else. One might say, "I experience that my head aches." In this sense consciousness can be perfected only through that extension of the human brain known as language. Only language gives man the ability to objectify the experiences of pleasure and pain of which he is aware. Through mental acts, he may suppress his experience, and thought can then be his guide to action. Man has thereby surpassed the animal stage of evolution in which experiences themselves can be determinants of action. This in turn is an improvement upon the lower animals, whose instinctual drives determine all action.
See also SUBCONSCIOUS AND UNCONSCIOUS.

CONSTIPATION, a disorder of elimination which may be caused by obstruction of the bowel or by interference with the normal muscular movements of the bowel wall. Within approximately 12 hours after food is eaten digestion is complete and the undigested residue enters the bowel (the large intestine). During the next few days the contractions of the muscles of the intestinal wall propel this residue into the rectum.

Constipation occurs when the movement of this material through the bowel is delayed. Tumors of the intestine, or fibrous bands of tissue which pinch the intestine, may produce constipation by narrowing the passage through which waste materials pass.

The presence of stones in the urinary passages, inflammation of the gall bladder, back injuries, or a variety of other conditions may cause constipation by interfering with the normal nervous stimulation which maintains the muscular activity of the intestinal wall. Excessive use of laxatives may also disrupt normal muscle function. Emotional tension may induce a spasm of the intestinal muscles, resulting in constipation. In some cases constipation may be a symptom of diseases of the endocrine glands or of the nervous system.

Treatment of constipation is directed at the underlying cause when this can be determined. Often simple measures, such as the establishment of regular habits and the consumption of fruit juices, are helpful. Laxatives are sometimes necessary and, in difficult cases, suppositories or enemas may be used.
See also LAXATIVES.

CONSUMPTION (DISEASE). *See* TUBERCULOSIS.

CONTACT DERMATITIS. *See* DERMATITIS.

CONTACT LENSES, type of corrective lenses which are fitted close to the outer surface of the eye. Contact lenses were first made in Europe in the middle of the 19th century and were designed to protect the cornea, the transparent covering of the front of the eye, from diseases of the lid. These early lenses were made of glass, shattered easily, were uncomfortable to wear, took as long as a year to be fitted properly, and presented a bulging, goldfishlike appearance to the observer. It was not until light, shatterproof and malleable plastics were developed that contact lenses actually became feasible.

Today contact lenses are made of thin transparent

CORNEA

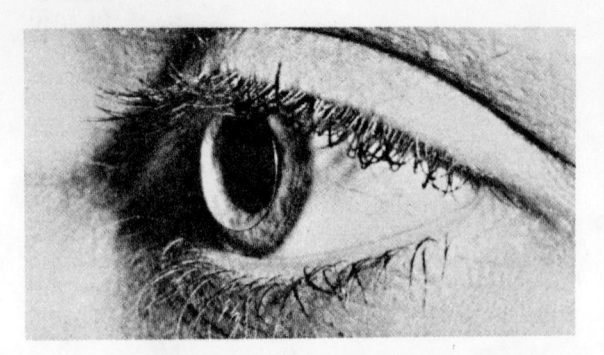

Close-up of a contact lens floating on the natural tear layer of the eye. Normally not visible, the lens has been made to stand out by the use of special lighting. (NATIONAL EYE RESEARCH FOUNDATION)

layers of plastic and consist basically of two types: the sclera-contact lens which fits over the entire visible portion of the eye but rests only upon the sclera (the white of the eye) and is held in place by the eyelids—this lens requires a chemical solution to fill the area between the eye and the lens; the second type is the corneal contact lens which merely covers the pupil and the surrounding colored portion of the eye (the iris) and rides upon the wearer's natural tear film. To properly prepare scleral lenses a plaster cast of the front of the eyeball must be made under local anesthesia. Corneal contact lenses are simpler to fit, are practically invisible to the observer, give the best visual results, and can be worn for as long as 18 hours at a time. Approximately 90% of the contact lenses worn today are of this type.

Contact lenses are particularly effective for obtaining proper vision in certain eye disorders, such as astigmatism, and severe scarring of the cornea. The lenses actually function as part of the eye and as a result they can never become steamed or streaked. Since they move with the eye, they provide a wide and normal distortion-free field of vision, which is not possible with ordinary glasses. For these reasons they are a great boon to athletes, sportsmen, and surgeons.

Persons suffering from certain disorders of the cornea may not be able to wear contact lenses. Some patience and persistence are necessary to overcome the initial discomfort of wearing the lenses. Given the proper degree of determination, however, it is safe to say that almost 95% of the population can comfortably and safely wear contact lenses.

CORNEA [kôr′nē-ə], the tough, thin, transparent outer layer of the front of the eyeball, continuous with the opaque white of the eye, or sclera. It covers about one-sixth of the eyeball and is steeply curved and shaped like a watch glass, thicker at the edges than at the center. The cells of its outermost layer are very flat, forming a smooth, lustrous surface.

CORNEAL TRANSPLANT, a cornea (the transparent covering of the front of the eyeball), usually obtained from a deceased individual, and used to replace the diseased or deformed cornea of a blind, or partially blind, person. The problem of procuring enough corneas to meet the demand has been solved in some countries by laws that permit the removal of eyes from unclaimed cadavers, to be used as needed. To insure a favorable outcome the corneas must be removed and transplanted with the least possible delay. Today approximately 75% of all corneal transplants are successful, with the result that sight can be restored to individuals who have been blind for many years, or even from birth.

CORNEAL ULCER, a patch of destroyed cornea which may result from injury or infection. Most commonly the ulcers are caused by infection produced by foreign bodies penetrating the cornea. The ulcer causes pain, tearing, increased winking of the eyes, interference with vision, and sensitivity to strong light. If left untreated the infection may spread and result in loss of the eye.

CORNS are overgrowths of the horny upper layers of the skin, caused by intermittent friction and pressure which usually result from tight, or ill-fitting shoes. In some cases, corns develop over abnormal bony projections. The corn is shaped like an inverted cone, with the point pressing into the tissues. Soft corns are found between the toes and are usually macerated by sweat. Treatment consists of paring or applying chemicals, such as salicylic acid, which dissolve the horny overgrowth. The corn usually returns unless the mechanical irritation is eliminated.

CORONARY ARTERY DISEASE. *See* HEART DISEASES.

COR PULMONALE [kôr pŭl-mō-nā′lē], type of heart disease which occurs as a complication of certain chronic lung diseases, principally chronic bronchitis, bronchial asthma, and emphysema. In these conditions narrowing and closing of the small arteries of the lung may produce a strain on the right ventricle of the heart which pumps blood through the lungs. As a result the right ventricle becomes enlarged, but the heart may continue to function efficiently for many years before it begins to fail. Extreme care must be taken to avoid colds or other respiratory infections as they may precipitate heart failure.
See also HEART DISEASES.

CORROSIVE SUBLIMATE or MERCURIC CHLORIDE, $HgCl_2$, a deadly poisonous, heavy, white powder. If taken internally, it will produce burning in the throat; abdominal cramps; vomiting; weak, rapid pulse; convulsions; and coma. The antidote is sodium formaldehyde sulfoxylate. Mercuric chloride is used in medicine in dilute solution of about 1:1000 as an antiseptic, in the treatment of syphilis, and as an insecticide. It is produced by heating mercuric sulfate, $HgSO_4$, and sodium chloride, $NaCl$.

CORTISONE [kôr′tə-zōn] **AND CORTICOSTEROIDS** [kôr-tĭ-kō-stĕr′oidz]. The term "corticosteroids" is applied to the hormones secreted by the outer layer of the small glands which sit astride the kidneys (the adrenal glands). These hormones are generally grouped into three categories: (1) those which help regulate the mineral content of the body fluids; (2) those which are involved in the energy-producing activities of the body; and (3) those which help regulate male and female sexual characteristics (such as the distribution of body hair).

The corticosteroids often overlap these categories and exhibit the characteristics of one or more groups. An example of this can be seen in the case of cortisone, which acts upon the mineral content of the body fluids and increases the rate at which the body converts protein into sugar. Cortisone, along with other corticosteroids, also has the important property of reducing inflammation and combating allergic reactions.

The corticosteroids are given in conditions such as Addison's disease, in which the adrenal glands fail to manufacture adequate amounts of these substances. The antiinflammatory and antiallergic actions of the corticosteroids are used in the treatment of rheumatic fever, rheumatoid arthritis, ulcerative colitis, severe asthma, gout, eye inflammations, itching, and many related conditions in which allergic and inflammatory reactions are prominent. Temporary improvement in some cases of leukemia, anemia, and certain bone tumors has also been obtained from the use of these substances.

The corticosteroids must be used with caution as many undesirable side effects may appear, including excessive accumulation of fluid in the tissues (edema), peptic ulcers, mental changes, and impairment of the body's ability to heal. Under no circumstances should these compounds be used without close medical supervision.

See also ACTH; ADRENAL GLANDS.

COSMETIC SURGERY. See PLASTIC SURGERY.

COUGH, a reflex involving the forcible expulsion of air from the lungs. The cough is set off by stimulation of sensitive portions of the air passages, and serves to remove irritating substances and excessive secretions from the lungs. In coughing, air is first taken into the lungs, after which the muscular fold which lies across the airway at the base of the throat (the glottis) is closed, while lung air is forced against it. The glottis is then opened suddenly, causing air to be propelled from the lungs at great speed. According to some estimates, during a cough the air may be expelled from the windpipe at velocities approaching the speed of sound.

Coughs may be caused by infections (pneumonia, tuberculosis, whooping cough), tumors, smog, smoke, dust, allergies, and by foreign bodies in the air passages. They may be classified as productive (sputum is coughed up), unproductive (no sputum appears), tight (scanty sputum), loose (abundant sputum), or insufficient (the cough is not vigorous enough to expel the sputum). Medications may help relieve cough by depressing nerve activity, by soothing inflammation, or by stimulating the flow of mucous secretions. Further treatment is directed at the underlying cause.

COURNAND [koor-näN'], **ANDRÉ FRÉDÉRIC** (1895–   ), American physician and physiologist. Born in Paris, he was educated at the Sorbonne and the University of Paris where he received his M.D. degree in 1930. He went to America that same year and became professor of medicine at Columbia University. He is best known for his work in studying the activity of the heart by means of a flexible tube passed into the heart through a blood vessel in the arm. He shared the Nobel Prize for this work with Drs. Dickinson Richards and Werner Forssman in 1956.

COWPOX, a virus disease of cattle which assumed medical importance in 1798 when Edward Jenner demonstrated that humans could be protected against smallpox by deliberately being given cowpox. Cowpox infection in man resembles that produced by smallpox vaccination, consisting of a red sore at the site of infection and possibly a slight fever. A scab later forms and separates.

COXSACKIE [kook-säk'ē] **VIRUS INFECTIONS,** diseases caused by a group of viruses, the first strains of which were discovered in children in the town of Coxsackie, N.Y., in 1948. Similar viruses were later identified in New England and in other parts of the world. The infections most frequently involve children and tend to occur in the late summer and fall.

The viruses are divided into two groups: group A viruses may cause herpangina, a form of sore throat with mouth sores; group B viruses are known to cause pleurodynia (Bornholm disease), which is characterized by severe chest and abdominal pains. Group B viruses also cause heart disease (myocarditis) in newborn infants. Both groups may cause meningitis, which is often confused with nonparalytic polio.

See also VIRUSES.

CRANIAL CAPACITY, a measurement of the internal capacity, or brain volume, of the skull. It is ascertained by filling the cranium with such materials as mustard seed or lead shot, and then measuring the volume of the seed or shot in a calibrated container. It is useful in distinguishing and comparing paleontological and archeological specimens. During the Pleistocene geological epoch, there was a trend toward larger brain size in the genus *Homo*—from a range of 435 to 700 cc. in the Lower Pleistocene (*Homo africanus*), to 1300 to 1700 cc. in the Upper Pleistocene (*Homo sapiens*). The relationship of brain volume to mental capacity is not clear. The range in modern man's cranial volume is great, from about 900 to 1,700 cc., averaging about 1,450 cc., or two to three times as large as the apes (gorilla, averaging 500 cc.; chimpanzee, averaging 400 cc.). Brain size in man does not necessarily correlate with intelligence. Cranial capacities of the living are obtained through external measurement of the braincase and the use of various formulas.

CRANIAL NERVES, nerves arising directly from the brain of vertebrate organisms that communicate mainly with structures in the head and neck. The cranial nerves are unique in this respect, as all other nerves leaving the brain pass through the spinal cord. The cranial nerves consist of fibers that carry sensation, fibers that control muscles, or both types mixed. Twelve cranial nerves are found in all vertebrates with the exception of fishes and amphibians, in which the XIth and XIIth are absent. The cranial nerves and their associated functions are:

I Olfactory. Sensation of smell.
II Optic. Sensation of vision.
III Oculomotor. Controls muscles which move the eyelids, eyeball, and contracts the pupil.
IV Trochlear. Controls muscles which rotate the eyeball.
V Trigeminal. Carries sensation from the skin of the face and controls the tongue muscles and muscles used in chewing.
VI Abducens. Controls muscles which move the eyeball.
VII Facial. Carries sensation of taste and controls muscles involved in expressive movements of the face, chewing, and movement of the neck.
VIII Auditory or Acoustic. Carries the sensation of hearing and sensations from the semicircular canals of the ear which are important in maintaining equilibrium.
IX Glossopharyngeal. Carries sensations of taste and touch.
X Vagus. Runs into the chest and abdomen, sending fibers to the heart, stomach, and lungs. Important in the automatic nervous control of digestion and circulation.
XI Accessory or Spinal Accessory. Controls the muscles of the neck.
XII Hypoglossal. Controls the muscles of the tongue

CREATINE [krē′ə-tēn], a nitrogen-containing organic substance found primarily in muscle tissue where it stores energy and later releases it when needed for muscular contraction. Creatine acquires energy by combining with a phosphate unit and releases energy by surrendering the phosphate unit to the principal energy-exchanging substance in muscle, ATP. Creatine is probably changed in the body into creatinine, a chemically related substance which is excreted in the urine at a constant daily rate for each individual. The amount of creatinine excretion is considered to be related to the muscular development of the individual, being greatest in athletic males and lowest in women.
See also ATP or ADENOSINE TRIPHOSPHATE; MUSCLE.

CRETINISM [krē′tən-ĭz-əm], disorder of development caused by a total or partial deficiency of thyroid hormone during infancy and early childhood. The thyroid gland, which is situated in the front of the neck alongside the windpipe, requires iodine in order to manufacture the thyroid hormone which helps regulate body activity. In certain parts of the world where iodine is lacking in the diet, cretinism is widespread as a result of the lack of iodine at critical periods during the growth of the embryo (endemic cretinism). In other cases cretinism arises from a failure of the thyroid gland to develop or from an inherited abnormality of the gland.

Children suffering from this disorder are typically dwarfed and mentally retarded. The head is large, the abdomen protrudes, and the arms and legs are short.

If recognized early and properly treated with thyroid extract, the cretin may develop in an almost normal fashion. The abnormalities usually cannot be corrected in older children and adults. Endemic cretinism can be prevented by the use of iodized salt in iodine-deficient areas.

CROUP [kroōp], term given to a group of symptoms which include difficulty in breathing, spasm of the larynx (the region between the root of the tongue and the windpipe), hoarseness, and cough. The condition occurs most frequently in young children and is serious in infants under the age of three when the larynx, windpipe, and the air passages of the lungs are involved simultaneously.

Croup may be caused by the presence of a foreign body in the air passages, by infections (hemophilus influenza, diphtheria, streptococcus, staphylococcus) or by a spasm of the larynx which sometimes appears in children suffering from rickets.

In these conditions the space between the vocal cords is narrowed and the child becomes pale, anxious, and restless as breathing becomes more difficult. The presence of edema or swelling or patches of membrane covering the larynx may cause a high-pitched sound to be heard on inhaling.

Steam inhalations and warm drinks may provide some relief. If a steam inhalation apparatus is not available, running the hot water tap in the shower may be used in an emergency. Other treatment includes the use of antitoxin (in diphtheria cases) and antibiotics. In severe cases an immediate tracheotomy may be necessary. This procedure consists of opening the windpipe through an incision in the throat so that air can reach the lungs. Croup can be prevented by immunizing against diphtheria and by obtaining medical treatment for sore throat and upper respiratory infections.
See also DIPHTHERIA.

CRUVEILHIER [krü-vĕ-yā′], **JEAN** (1791–1873), French physician noted for his books on pathological anatomy. Among his published works the best known are *Anatomie pathologique du corps humain* and *Traité d'anatomie pathologique générale* (4 vols.). In honor of his description of ulcers of the stomach, the French still call this ailment "la maladie de Cruveilhier."

CRYPTOCOCCOSIS [krĭp-tō-kŏ-kō′sĭs], also called torulosis, a fungus infection which is found throughout the world. The disease may involve any part of the body, but usually attacks the brain and its linings (the meninges). It is frequently fatal, but prospects for recovery have been greatly improved since the introduction of the drug amphotericin B.

CULTURE, in biology, a population of living cells or organisms grown under artificial conditions. Specimens of various microorganisms, such as bacteria, yeasts, molds, and protozoans, are put into a nutritive solution where they can thrive and reproduce. The nutritive environment is called the medium. Bacteria, mold and yeast cultures are used in the production of cheese, vinegar, antibiotics, vaccines, and commercial solvents. Pathogenic bacteria, which cause disease, can often be identified by growing them on a special medium.

A pure culture contains only one kind of organism.

Such cultures are usually produced by allowing a single organism or cell to reproduce asexually in an otherwise sterile medium. A tissue culture contains offspring cells from one part of an animal or plant. For example, cells may be taken from a kidney or from a tumor and encouraged to grow and reproduce. Liquid nutrients or a preparation of blood to which nutrients have been added provide the medium. Tissue cultures are particularly valuable in the study of many different diseases.

CURARE [kyōō-rä'rē], drug which relaxes skeletal (voluntary) muscles and which was used as an arrowtip poison by South American Indians. The major sources of curare, found by Amazon basin witch doctors, were species of two plants of the region, Strychnos and Chondrodendron. In 1940 sufficient amounts of these crude sources were brought to the United States to permit precise chemical identification of their active products. It was quickly used by the medical profession, first to prevent muscle spasm in psychiatric electroshock therapy and, two years later, to induce muscle relaxation in surgical procedures as an addition to general anasthesia. A closely related drug, succinylcholine, is used for the same purpose.

The main action of curare is to prevent the transmission of nerve impulses to muscle fibers. It is not absorbed through unbroken skin and is ineffective orally except in huge doses. When injected into a vein its effect is rapid. Small muscles in the fingers, toes, eyes, and ears are reached before muscles in the limbs, neck, and trunk. As a poison, curare paralyzes the chest muscles and finally the diaphragm, causing death by asphyxiation. Because the duration of the drug's effect is brief, life can be saved by artificial respiration, with complete recovery. Throughout the stage of muscular paralysis, there is no lapse of consciousness, loss of memory, or disturbance of the senses.
See also ACETYLCHOLINE.

CURETTAGE [kyōōr-ə-täzh'], surgical technique in which the walls of a cavity are scraped with a spoon-shaped instrument (a curette). The term most commonly refers to the scraping of the walls of the uterus. This may be done to obtain samples of tissue to aid in the diagnosis and treatment of menstrual disorders and tumors of the womb. Curettage is also used to interrupt pregnancy.

CUSHING, HARVEY (1869–1939), American brain surgeon. After receiving his M.D. degree from Harvard in 1895 he went to Johns Hopkins and was closely associated with that institution until he returned to Harvard in 1911. A pioneer in neurological surgery, he introduced many new techniques and operations into the field. He described tumors of the pituitary gland and their relation to the development of sexual characteristics. In recognition of his classic work in this area, a disorder of the pituitary gland is called Cushing's disease.

CUSHING'S SYNDROME and CUSHING'S DISEASE, related disorders that are characterized by an excessive secretion of cortisonelike hormones from the adrenal gland. Cushing's disease, which is less common than Cushing's syndrome, results from a tumor of the pituitary gland. The excessive secretions from this gland stimulate the adrenal glands to produce unusually large quantities of hormone. Cushing's syndrome may result from an unusually large adrenal gland or from a tumor of the outer layer (cortex) of the gland.

In both cases the oversecretion of the adrenal hormones causes a disturbance in the utilization of carbohydrates and proteins by the body. The patients typically show a "moon face," deposits of fat over the neck and collar bones, muscle weakness, acne, high blood pressure, and, occasionally, mental disturbances. In women the hormonal imbalance may produce deepening of the voice and changes in the distribution of body hair.

Cushing's disease may be treated by X-ray therapy of the pituitary gland. Cushing's syndrome may be treated by surgical removal of the adrenal glands or the adrenal tumor.
See also ADRENAL GLANDS; PITUITARY GLAND.

CUTANEOUS [kū-tā'nē-əs] **SENSE,** also called dermal sense or skin sense. Some small points on the skin are especially sensitive to painful stimuli, others to cold, others to warmth, and still others to pressure. These are generally considered to be the four primary skin experiences. There are specialized structures in the skin underlying pressure and pain points, but such structures have not been identified for warmth or cold points. If the skin is stimulated by cold, warmth, or pressure for a short time, the individual will experience sensory adaptation; for instance, the still hot bath water seems tepid after the first few minutes of immersion.
See also SENSATION.

CYANIDES [sī'ə-nīdz], compounds containing the cyanide group, which consists of a carbon atom attached to a nitrogen atom. They occur naturally in small quantities in plants, as in oil of bitter almonds, and are prepared commercially from ammonia or cyanamide. Cyanides form complexes used to concentrate gold and silver ores. Sodium cyanide, NaCN, or potassium cyanide, yield hydrocianic acid, HCN, a colorless gas, when exposed to moisture or acids. These gases are used for fumigating buildings.

Both acid and its organic salts are rapidly fatal because they interfere with enzymes which enable the body to utilize oxygen. Symptoms of poisoning include giddiness, headache, rapid breathing, blueing of the skin, and the odor of bitter almonds. Professional treatment must be administered immediately.

CYANOSIS [sī-ə-nō'sis], bluish tinting of the skin that appears in persons suffering from an oxygen deficiency. The normal pink color of the skin is produced by the presence in the blood of bright red oxygen-rich hemoglobin. Hemoglobin without oxygen is darker in color. Consequently, in conditions where the oxygen content of the blood is low the skin color is changed. Cyanosis is seen in heart and lung conditions, such as heart failure and pneumonia and in congenital heart conditions in which the blood bypasses the lungs. Certain drugs may also chemically alter hemoglobin, changing its color and thus producing a cyanosis.

CYBERNETICS [sī-bər-nĕt′ĭks], science of control and communication in machines and living organisms. Cybernetics is used in the guidance of a missile from its launching pad; in the study of a wage-price spiral in economics; and in the study of the physiological system that controls hand movements to grasp an object.

In any of these systems the function of the control is to direct the elements to accomplish a purpose. The need for control is most essential when this action is carried out in the presence of a changing environment and disturbing influences. The feedback theory, which is used in most control systems, is important together with the communications problems involved in feeding back information about the status of the system's variables; clearly the control over a variable can be no better than the information which is available about that variable.

Although the theory of feedback control systems was applied to the operation of machinery for many years, the earliest recognition that it might be applied to the study of living systems was in 1943. Then Arturo Rosenblueth, Norbert Wiener, and Julian Bigelow observed that most animal activity can be viewed as a feedback system. A part of the central nervous system directs a certain muscular activity, and sensory nerves feed back into the central nervous system information on the progress of the activity. This point of view was explored in a series of meetings beginning in 1944 which brought engineers, mathematicians, physiologists, and neurologists together to share their respective backgrounds in the hope of gaining new insight into the nature of animal systems. Out of this series of meetings, the inter-disciplinary science of cybernetics grew. Norbert Wiener gave it the name "cybernetics" in 1947, after the Greek word meaning "steersman."

Although the popular connotation of the term has come to mean the study of animal systems, the originators intended the science of cybernetics to cover social sciences and psychology as well. It is clear that closed feedback loops exist in economics; for example the wage increases that tend to increase product prices, which in turn tend to increase the cost-of-living index that brings wages up still farther in union contracts with escalator clauses. However, the possible applications of cybernetics in the social sciences are not well developed.

The application of cybernetics requires a complete understanding of the properties and behavior of the system under study. Both the major disciplines upon which cybernetics is based—the theories of feedback control and of communications—depend heavily on the basic mathematical tools of operational calculus and statistics.

CYCLOPROPANE [sī-klō-prō′pān], colorless gas with a sweet odor, prepared from trimethylene glycol. It is the most potent of the anesthetic gases used in surgery. Cyclopropane provides a wide margin of safety during anesthesia and does not irritate the lungs. It is, however, highly explosive and must be used with caution. Its most serious drawback as an anesthetic is its tendency to cause irregularities in the heartbeat.
See also ANESTHESIA.

CYST [sĭst], **SEBACEOUS**, also called wen, a round or oval swelling often occurring on the scalp and the skin of the ear, face, and back. Cysts are caused by blocking of the openings of the oil (sebaceous) glands of the skin, resulting in the accumulation of the oily gland secretion within the gland. They are usually painless, unless they become inflamed. They may be surgically removed.

CYSTIC FIBROSIS [fī-brō′sĭs], an inherited disorder involving malfunction of the duct-possessing exocrine glands of the body, such as the sweat and salivary glands, but primarily of the pancreas gland and the glands lining air passages (the bronchi). The disease occurs in approximately one out of every 1,500 live births and appears principally in members of the Caucasian race.

In cystic fibrosis the ducts which empty the secretions of the pancreas become blocked. In the absence of these secretions food, especially fats, cannot be properly digested. This may result in malnutrition, even though the individual eats heartily.

In most cases chronic lung disease (emphysema) results from obstruction of the bronchi by thick secretions. At first the child may cough without producing sputum; later severe difficulty in breathing may follow development of lung infection. There may be frequent and progressively worse cycles of such infection. In some cases the liver may be involved. The sweat glands tend to secrete abnormal quantities of salt and, in hot weather, massive salt loss may lead to collapse and death.

The greatest danger to the patient lies in the lung involvement. Intensive treatment with antibiotics is used to prevent progressive and chronic pneumonia. Care should also be taken to provide the individual with a proper diet. Pancreatic enzymes can be given with meals to supply the missing digestive enzymes.

CYSTITIS [sĭs-tī′tĭs], inflammation of the urinary bladder. The principal causes of cystitis are an enlarged prostate gland, infections which have spread from the kidney, urethra, or other structures, or incomplete emptying of the bladder with subsequent infection of the retained urine. The latter may be seen in cystocele (a downward sagging of the bladder occurring in women), in tumors of the bladder, and in diseases which interfere with the nerves leading to the bladder. Chronic cystitis may result from infection following prolonged obstruction of the flow of urine. The symptoms of cystitis include frequent and painful urination; pus is often found in the urine. Treatment depends upon the underlying cause.

CYSTOCELE, protrusion of the urinary bladder into the vagina. This may occur as a complication of childbirth and is accompanied by a sense of pressure in the pelvis with fatigue developing after standing or walking. Backache is a frequent complaint. Frequency of urination with a burning sensation is present in some cases. In severe cases surgery is necessary to repair the rupture.

CYSTOSCOPY [sĭs-tŏs′kə-pē], visual examination of the urinary bladder with the cystoscope, a tubular instrument with a light-giving attachment which is passed through the urinary tract into the bladder. The technique aids in the diagnosis of inflammations, tumors, and other disorders of the bladder and makes possible certain operations on the urinary tract.

CYTOCHROMES [sī'tə-krōms], pigments widely distributed in plant and animal tissues. Cytochromes consist of a combination of a protein, with heme, an organic iron compound. They are very important in enabling air-breathing plants and animals to utilize atmospheric oxygen.

CYTOPLASM. See CELL.

D

DALE, SIR HENRY HALLET (1875–1968), English physiologist and pharmacologist who shared the Nobel Prize with Otto Loewi in 1936 for his investigations on the role of acetylcholine in the transmission of nerve impulses. His other contributions include studies of the action of histamine and of extracts of the pituitary gland on the body. Dale was director of the National Institute for Medical Research from 1928 to 1942 and was Fullerian Professor of Chemistry and Director of Laboratories at the Royal Institution from 1943 until his retirement in 1946. He was knighted in 1932 and was president of the Royal Society from 1940 to 1945.

DANDRUFF, greasy, yellowish-whitish scales which appear principally on the scalp, but may also occur on almost any part of the body. The scalp becomes itchy and covered with fine, dry scales. At a later stage the scales may become greasy and more adherent. Infection may follow severe scratching; severe dandruff can lead to baldness. Dry, red, scaly patches may also appear on the eyebrows. If the eyelashes are involved they may fall out. Treatment of scalp dandruff consists of frequent shampooing with medicated soaps or detergents containing sulfur or tar compounds, plus the application of lotions or creams containing sulfur, selenium, mercury, or antiseptics.

DARWIN [där'wĭn], **CHARLES ROBERT** (1809–82), English naturalist, popularly associated with the theory of evolution, of which he is frequently assumed to have been the sole discoverer. In actuality Darwin's principal contribution to biology was his development of the theory of natural selection as the mechanism of organic change. This theory, presented in his great work, *The Origin of Species* (1859), was the most massive documentation and demonstration of the arguments for evolution to appear after the modern birth of the theory in the 18th century.

Darwin had cautiously avoided direct reference to man in *The Origin of Species*, but 12 years later, in *Descent of Man* (1871), he published a study of human evolution. An occasional defect of this work is the failure to distinguish satisfactorily between biological inheritance and cultural influences upon the behavior of human beings. This proved to be a common failing of Darwin's early adherents, and can be attributed to the fact that the more sophisticated branches of anthropology were as yet undeveloped.

National Portrait Gallery, London
Charles Darwin, as painted by John Collier.

Although today far more is known about the inner mechanisms of the cell and about genetics than was known in Darwin's time, the essential features of natural selection are still a keystone of modern biology. Darwin's place in the history of thought remains secure even though more sophisticated generations will recognize that other workers, including his own grandfather, Erasmus Darwin, played an important, if anonymous, role in the scientific victory which made Charles Darwin's name familiar throughout the entire civilized world.
See also EVOLUTION.

DEAFNESS. Strictly defined, deafness means the lack or total loss of hearing in one or both ears. In common usage the term describes a hearing loss which is sufficiently se-

DEAFNESS

vere to prevent perception of sounds and voices of average intensity.

Normally sound waves are gathered by the outer ear and conducted to the eardrum, which sets in motion the ossicles, the three delicately balanced bones of the middle ear, which transmit sound to the cochlea of the inner ear. The cochlea, a spiral structure resembling a snail's shell, is the actual organ of hearing which sends nerve impulses along the auditory nerve to the brain.

Conduction deafness occurs when disorders of the ear canal, eardrum, middle ear, or eustachian tube interfere with the transmission of sound to the inner ear. Perceptive, or nerve, deafness is caused by damage to the cochlea or auditory nerve. This is generally more severe and more difficult to treat than conduction deafness.

Conduction deafness may be present from birth, resulting from improper development of the structures of the external and middle ear. Some of these defects can be corrected by surgery. A common and easily treated hearing impairment is caused by obstruction of the ear canal with earwax or a foreign body.

Bacterial infection of the middle ear frequently causes conduction deafness. The infection may originate in the adenoids or sinuses and reach the middle ear through the eustachian tube, which runs from the middle ear to the rear of the nose. This tube maintains equal air pressure on both sides of the eardrum.

Acute infections can usually be successfully treated with antibiotics or sulfa drugs. Occasionally surgical removal of the adenoids may be necessary. This may also be done in cases where the adenoids are not infected, but where they block the eustachian tubes, causing abnormal pressures in the middle ear and impaired hearing. Damage to the ossicles and eardrums, resulting from chronic infection or injury, can often be repaired surgically by building a new eardrum from skin grafts or by reconstructing substitutes for the ossicles.

Otosclerosis is a frequent cause of conductive hearing loss in adults, particularly in young women. In this condition abnormal bony deposits restrict the motion of the stapes (the third ossicle). The cause is not known, but the condition often appears in several members of the same family. Surgical treatment of otosclerosis is generally successful.

The outlook for conductive hearing impairments, such as those discussed above, is considered good. In addition to medical and surgical treatment, hearing aids offer an effective means for restoring hearing.

Perceptive deafness is sometimes present from birth, resulting from damage to the inner ear in infants whose blood is incompatible with that of the mother (Rh positive child, Rh negative mother—*see* BLOOD). Infection of the mother with German measles during the first three months of pregnancy may cause inner ear deafness in the child. There is also the possibility that the child of a syphilitic mother may acquire the disease in the womb and be born deaf. Perceptive deafness may be acquired at any age by injury to, or disease of, the inner ear. It may also result from automobile accidents causing head injuries with fractures of the cochlea or from exposure to loud sounds and noise, such as are encountered in industry. Infections such as meningitis and mumps may involve the inner ear. Occasionally cochlear damage may be caused by drugs, especially the antibiotic dihydrostreptomycin. Perceptive hearing loss in older persons is seen in Ménière's disease, a disorder which affects the balancing mechanism of the body (the vestibular apparatus of the ear), causing severe attacks of dizziness (vertigo). The increase in the life span has also made a major problem of presbycusis—the gradual loss of hearing, presumably caused by a decrease in the blood supply to the inner ear.

Inner ear deafness can often be helped by hearing aids, although they are not as effective for this purpose as they are in conductive deafness. Speech and lip reading training are of particular value to this group.

Much perceptive deafness can be prevented by the use of seat belts in automobiles to avoid head injuries, by regular hearing tests in industries to avoid overexposure to loud noises, and by improved public hygiene and vaccines to avoid inner ear infections.

The Social Aspect of Deafness

The number of deaf and hard of hearing has never been accurately ascertained. It is generally estimated that there are approximately 160,000 deaf persons in the United States. It is known that 21,583 deaf children were enrolled in schools and classes for the deaf throughout the United States in 1960. It has been said that the total number of persons with impaired hearing in the United States probably approaches 3,000,000. The World Federation of the Deaf, with headquarters in Rome, estimates that the ratio of deaf persons to the general population throughout the world is 1 to 1,000 and points out that the incidence of deafness is considerably greater in underdeveloped countries.

In earlier periods, the deaf were considered uneducable. In the 16th century a Milanese philosopher, Giro-

PARTS OF THE EAR

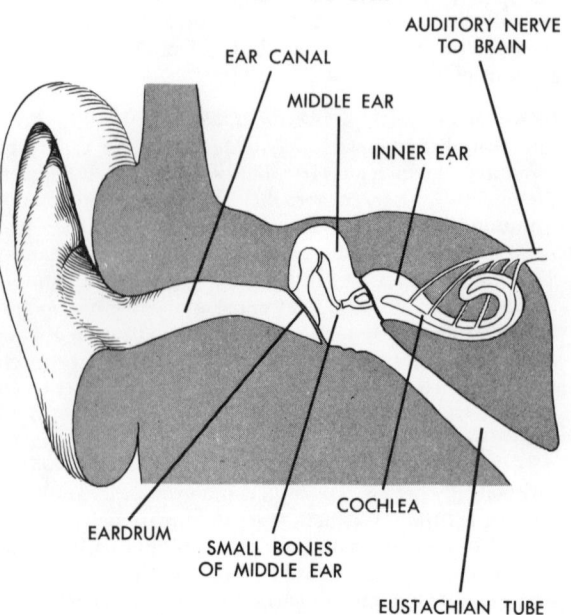

lamo Cardano, or Jerome Cardan, had given some thought to the deaf and wrote that they should be able "to hear by reading and speak by writing." Some of Cardano's theories were resurrected in 1760 and schools for the deaf were established in France, Germany, England, and, later, in other countries. Several scholars attempted to devise a manual alphabet for the deaf, but it remained for the Abbé de l'Épée, founder of a school for the deaf in Paris, to devise a lasting sign language. His system of signs, with variations, is still used by the deaf in the United States and other parts of the world. It is their chief means of communication among themselves.

In 1815 Thomas Hopkins Gallaudet, a New England clergyman, went to France to study methods of teaching the deaf. He returned with a deaf teacher from the Paris school, and they established a school in Hartford, Conn., in 1817. The first permanent school for the deaf in America, it is now known as the American School for the Deaf and is located in West Hartford. Today there are state supported schools for the deaf in all the states except Nevada, and there are numerous private and denominational schools. There are schools and classes for deaf children within the public school system in many cities. In 1864 a college for the deaf was established in Washington, D.C., by the federal government; it is now called Gallaudet College. A fully accredited liberal arts college, it is the only one for the deaf in the world.

From the beginning, efforts were made to teach the deaf to speak and to read the lips. Some wonderful results have been achieved in oral training, but the great majority of the deaf do not acquire a complete mastery of speech or lip reading. Many are able to make only slight progress orally. For this reason it is the opinion of most educators of the deaf, and of the deaf themselves, that oral communication should not be the sole means of instruction. The most successful schools employ a combination of speech, writing, the manual alphabet, and the sign language, fitting the method to the needs of each individual. These are the schools the deaf have found most adequate in providing a well-rounded education.

In their social and recreational activities the deaf tend to gather together because of their more or less common educational background, their common interests, and their ability to communicate freely and fluently among themselves in the sign language. There are social clubs of the deaf in most cities. These organized groups not only provide an avenue for social contacts but also engage in activities to promote the general well-being of the deaf. In addition to the local organizations, there are state associations of the deaf, united into a federation, known as the National Association of the Deaf. In other leading countries of the world the deaf are similarly organized and all together these national associations form the World Federation of the Deaf.

The deaf are found in different social and economic strata in about the same proportions as other citizens. They deny that they are handicapped, and they have rejected efforts on the part of legislators and philanthropists to secure special income tax exemptions for them. They are substantial citizens, many of them owning their own homes, rearing normal families, and driving their own automobiles. In compensating for their hearing handicap, they develop unusual alertness and reliance on vision, and as a result they are widely recognized as being among the safest of all drivers of automobiles.

Still, the deaf are unable to make the fullest use of the usual public and social services because service personnel are unable to communicate effectively with them and are unfamiliar with their needs and capabilities. A deaf person in court is frequently at a disadvantage because the courts do not provide interpreters. The English language is difficult for many of the deaf, especially those with limited education. Finding written communication inadequate and being limited in oral skills, the deaf person feels that his handicap is due more to difficulty in communication than to deafness itself.

DEATH, the cessation of life. Biologically speaking, the death of some organisms is necessary for the life of other organisms. Animals destroy and eat plants or other ani-

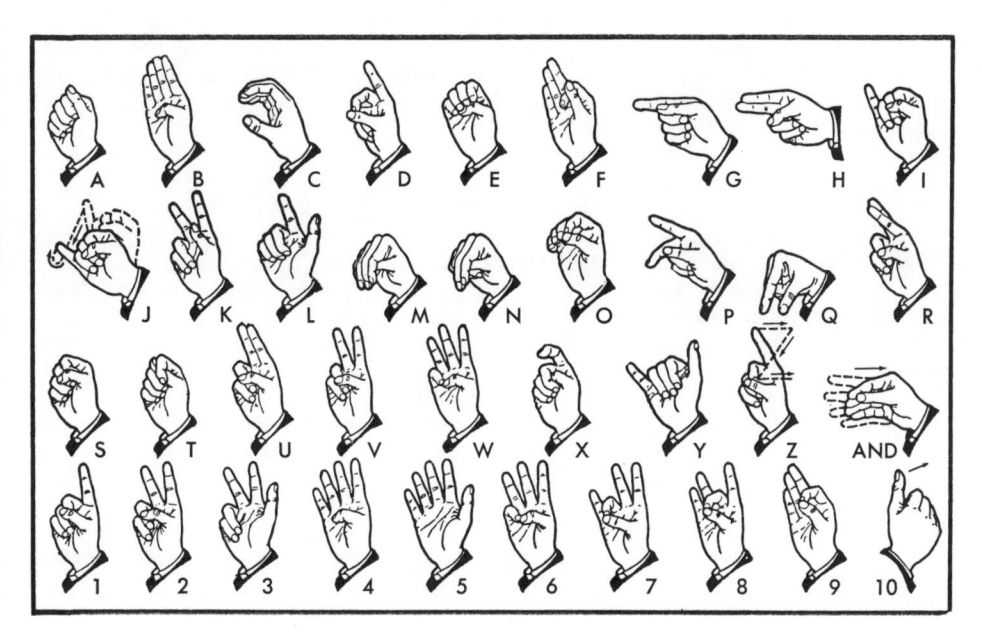

THE SINGLE HAND MANUAL ALPHABET
The manual alphabet has undergone little change since perfected by Charles Michel Abbé de l'Épée (1712-89).

mals; and dead plants and animals supply much of the nitrogen, through bacterial action, that sustains the life of other plants.

Among human beings death occurs when the heart stops beating. The cells of the body do not all die at the same time. Hair cells may live for hours after death, whereas some of the brain cells die almost immediately.

Not only do individual organisms die, but entire species, genera, and even larger groups also die; that is, they become extinct. The most famous instance of this was the complete extinction of the dinosaurs.

Death of all life on planet earth is virtually a scientific certainty, as a direct result of currently accepted laws and theories of physics and astronomy. Total death on earth will probably occur in a few billion years.

Death, in Law. The death of a person imposes several legal duties on a number of people in connection with certification requirements. These duties are prescribed by statute and usually require the funeral director or person in charge of interment to complete those parts of the death certificate which call for personal information about the deceased and to file, within the prescribed period, the death certificate with the local registrar of the district where the death occurred. The attending physician or a public medical officer completes the medical certification on the causes of death. Death certificates are important as a source of mortality statistics and are used to determine the incidence of specific diseases as causes of death, to measure the need for health and medical services, and to evaluate progress in the control of diseases.

Generally, the death of a person may be proved by any competent evidence. If a person has been absent from his home or his usual place of residence and has been unaccounted for, usually for over a period of seven years, a presumption of death arises. This presumption may be rebutted if there are circumstances to show, for example, that the testator had good reasons to remain in hiding and was likely to have done so. On the other hand, the death of a person may be established, although he has been absent less than seven years, if the circumstances strongly indicate that death must have occurred earlier.

A problem arises when two or more persons are killed in a common disaster under circumstances which make it impossible to determine the order in which they died. In the Roman law, the younger was deemed to have survived the older and between coeval persons of different sex, the male was presumed to have survived. These principles are still followed in civil law jurisdictions and have been incorporated into statutes in England and some of the states of the United States, and in all the provinces of Canada except Quebec (the Quebec rule is based on Roman or Civil Law). In Canada, in the case of life insurance, the beneficiary is deemed to have survived the common disaster. In most American jurisdictions, however, there is no presumption as to who died first in a common disaster. Hence if there is no evidence indicating survivorship, the assumption is that they died at the same time. This may be altered by will.

In many states statutes also provide that one sentenced to life imprisonment shall be considered "civilly dead." Normally this results in the loss of his civil rights and may serve as a basis for the dissolution of his marriage.

DEATH RATE, the number of deaths occurring in a community during a calendar year, divided by the average number of people living in that community within the year. A death rate for a specific group in the population is obtained when the number of deaths and the number of people are specified in the same way. A death rate may also be computed for a specific age group if the number of deaths and the number of people relate to that age group. Lastly, death rates may be computed for separate causes of death when the numbers are so specified.

Death rates are high for the first year of life, drop to a minimum about age 10, increase slowly to about age 45, and then increase rapidly to the end of life. Death rates are higher for males than for females, for single persons than for married ones, and highest for the widowed and divorced. Laborers have a higher death rate than semi-skilled workers, and managerial and professional people have the lowest death rate.

See also LIFE, EXPECTATION OF.

DECAY, the breakdown of dead plant and animal bodies into basic inorganic materials, such as carbon dioxide, water, and nitrates. Through their metabolic processes, living organisms constantly remove from their environment great quantities of carbon and nitrogen, which become part of their bodies. If decay did not take place, the vast number of dead organisms would not only retain essential supplies of carbon and nitrogen, but would also cover the earth's surface, leaving no room for living organisms. Decay, by removing the remains of life, is an expeditious method for dismantling the elaborate framework of life and making vital elements available for re-use by the living. Many plants and animals contribute to decay, but of these the bacteria are by far the most important since they possess enzymes capable of reducing complex organic molecules into simpler ones. Decay involves two main processes: the first, which is also termed fermentation, is the breakdown of organic compounds to form water and carbon dioxide. The second, known also as putrefaction, is the breakdown of proteins into water, carbon dioxide, sulfur compounds, ammonia, and eventually into nitrates. From some viewpoints, decay is often costly and injurious. The decay of food materials and other organic products can be prevented by eliminating the agents of decay through sterilization, toxic chemicals, and irradiation.

See also BACTERIA; CARBON CYCLE; NITROGEN CYCLE.

DECOMPOSITION. *See* DECAY.

DECOMPRESSION SICKNESS, also known as caisson disease, diver's paralysis, and the "bends," is a condition produced by a rapid reduction in atmospheric pressure. Individuals who work under increased air pressure, such as deep-sea divers, skin divers, and caisson workers, may develop decompression sickness if they return to normal pressure too quickly. In rapid ascents to high altitude in unpressurized aircraft, a similar situation occurs because of the quick change from normal to subnormal pressures.

Under normal conditions the blood contains oxygen, carbon dioxide, and nitrogen. If the pressure of the surrounding air is increased, more of these gases enter the blood stream. Should the air pressure suddenly return to normal, the extra gas dissolved in the blood escapes in the form of bubbles. The oxygen and carbon dioxide are quickly absorbed, but the nitrogen bubbles float through the blood, becoming lodged in, and obstructing, small blood vessels. Nitrogen bubbles also appear in fatty tissues since nitrogen is easily dissolved in fat.

The most common symptom is the "bends," severe pains in the joints and muscles causing contortion of the body. The most serious damage usually occurs in the nervous system, which is particularly susceptible because of its high fat content. The nervous symptoms include paralysis, double vision, loss of equilibrium ("the staggers"), convulsions, and coma. A disturbance in breathing, known as the "chokes," is seen frequently. The patient is unable to take a deep breath and complains of cough and constriction of the chest. Milder symptoms of decompression sickness include rash, itching, and unusual fatigue. Permanent paralysis and death may result in serious cases. The single effective treatment is to place the patient quickly in a compressed air chamber at the pressure under which he was working, and then to gradually adjust to normal pressure.

DEHYDRATION, excessive loss of body fluid. A common cause of dehydration is severe perspiration. Dehydration also appears in conditions which lead to excessive vomiting, diarrhea, and urination. These include diabetes, dysentery, and certain kidney diseases. The deficiency of water in the body produces a scant, highly concentrated urine and changes in the skin and blood.

DELIRIUM [dĭ-lĭr'ē-əm]. Once a synonym for insanity, the term now describes a form of mental disturbance characterized by varying degrees of bewilderment, restlessness, confusion, hallucinations, and illusions. The symptoms fluctuate in intensity and may be more marked at night than during the day. There is always an alteration in the state of consciousness, ranging from mild confusion to deep stupor. The patient is usually incoherent and may suffer from delusions of persecution. Delirium is most commonly associated with high fever and infectious diseases and with diseases that seriously impair bodily functions. It is sometimes seen in extremely agitated mental patients. Treatment is directed at the underlying cause; sedatives are given to relieve the symptoms.

DELIRIUM TREMENS [trē'mənz], a serious mental disturbance that usually develops in chronic alcoholics during, or following, a drinking bout. The delirium appears suddenly, often with frightening visual hallucinations, such as grotesque animals, which leave the patient in panic. All intellectual functions are affected, resulting in confusion concerning time, place, and identity. A characteristic tremor appears in the muscles of the face, tongue, and fingers. The victim is feverish and loses body water. The condition usually passes in a few days, but it may be fatal. If heavy drinking is continued the disturbance recurs, possibly resulting in a fully developed psychosis.
See also ALCOHOLISM.

DELTOID MUSCLE, the most prominent muscle of the shoulder. It is thick and triangular and covers the front, side, and rear portions of the shoulder joint. The deltoid muscle arises from the collar bone and shoulder blade and inserts into the humerus, the long bone of the upper arm. When the deltoid contracts, the arm is raised to the side.

DEMENTIA [dĭ-měn'shə], a deterioration of intellectual faculties resulting from brain damage produced by disease, injury, or changes accompanying old age. The afflicted person suffers from a loss of memory, restriction of interests, difficulty in grasping and retaining new ideas, and confusion as to his identity and whereabouts.
See also SENILITY.

DEMEROL [děm'ə-rōl] or **MEPERIDINE** [mě-pěr'ĭ-dēn], a synthetic pain-relieving (analgesic) drug which shares some of the actions of morphine and atropine. Demerol has been used as a substitute for morphine in the relief of pain in heart and lung conditions, in arthritis, migraine, burns, and cancer. It is somewhat less likely than morphine to cause side effects, such as stupefaction, interference with breathing, and constipation. The drug can be habit-forming and may lead to addiction.

DENGUE [děng'gē] **FEVER or BREAKBONE FEVER,** virus disease found most often in subtropical and tropical countries. The disease is transmitted to humans by the Aedes mosquito. Five to eight days after infection, fever, headache, and pronounced muscle soreness may appear. Pain behind the eyes and extreme weakness are common symptoms. In some cases a skin rash may develop. There is no specific treatment, but almost all cases recover completely within four to six weeks. Although some deaths have been reported in large-scale epidemics in Australia and Greece, there is some doubt as to whether the infection itself can be lethal. Spraying of mosquito breeding areas with DDT is effective in controlling the spread of dengue fever. A vaccine against the disease is available.

DENTAL ASSOCIATION, AMERICAN (ADA), founded in 1859 to improve public health through furtherance of the art and science of dentistry. The association sponsors extensive research programs; evaluates drugs, materials, and instruments for use by the profession and public; accredits educational institutions; and offers professional guidance on public aspects of dentistry. Membership is about 100,000, representing five out of every six practicing dentists in the nation. Headquarters are in Chicago.

DENTISTRY, the science which deals with diseases of the teeth and mouth. The dentist defines his area of responsibility as extending within the mouth from the inner border of the lips to the entrance of the throat. Most often he deals with disorders of the teeth and gums.

The Teeth. The most common disorder of the teeth is decay (cavities) which may affect both children and adults, but is particularly severe in the 3 to 21 age group. If untreated, decay may cause excruciating toothache and, eventually, loss of the affected tooth. A common mechanical tooth problem is malocclusion, or improper contact between the teeth of the upper and lower jaw during chewing. This may result from loss of teeth; from

DENTISTRY

distrubances of normal alignment caused by such habits as thumb sucking (extending beyond the ages of three or four); from improper placement of the tongue when swallowing; or from injuries, such as jaw fractures. In some cases inherited abnormalities of the jaws or teeth are responsible. The poor alignment of the teeth may cause the opposing teeth to strike each other with excessive force. In severe cases the resultant pounding may inflame the soft pulp of the tooth, causing pain, death of the tooth, and abscess formation.

Disorder of the Gums. Pyorrhea, the second most common mouth disorder, is an inflammation of gums which may result in bleeding, swelling, recession of the soft tissue, and destruction of the underlying bone. The bone destruction causes loosening and, eventually, loss of the teeth. Abscesses may occur between the roots of the teeth and the surrounding bone and gums. Pyorrhea may occur at any age, but its more severe manifestations are usually found in persons over 25. The main cause of pyorrhea is the deposition of plaque on the tooth surfaces adjacent to the gums. Plaque is primarily composed of carbohydrates (dextrans) from decomposing food in which bacterial colonies rapidly develop and flourish. Such bacterial colonies are responsible for both tooth decay and inflamed gums. Mineralized plaque, that is, plaque that contains calcium-phosphate salt deposits from the saliva, can also irritate the gums, while trauma from malocclusion may contribute to loosening of the teeth. A severe and rapid form of pyorrhea with associated tooth loss sometimes occurs due to unknown causes.

Miscellaneous Disorders. The dentist also treats a variety of mouth inflammations and ulcerations, which may be caused by bacterial, fungus, or viral infection, by skin diseases which produce mouth lesions, by vitamin deficiencies, or by injury, irritation, or allergy.

Diagnosis and Treatment

The dentist uses X rays to locate areas of decay in the teeth, abscesses, and tumors within the jaw bones, and to determine the extent of bone loss around the teeth. X rays also detect teeth which have not emerged from the jaw (impacted teeth). X rays of a child's mouth may reveal the presence of permanent adult teeth, enabling the dentist to determine whether they are so positioned as to develop normally.

The alignment of the teeth can be carefully studied by means of plaster reproductions of the mouth, obtained by pouring plaster of Paris into impressions of the mouth. The dentist frequently uses such reproductions to plan surgery of the jaw or to study approaches for reshaping and covering the teeth to provide proper occlusion and appearance.

Tooth-cutting instruments are used to prepare cavities for fillings and to reshape teeth so that they may be covered with porcelain, plastic, or gold, or with combinations of these materials. The greatest mechanical advance in dentistry in recent decades has been the development of cutting instruments which rotate at speeds of up to 500,000 rpm, as compared to 7,000 rpm for the earlier models. These high-speed instruments almost completely eliminate the uncomfortable vibrations of the slow-speed drills. They are also easier to control and substantially reduce the time needed to complete an operation.

Repairing and Replacing Teeth. Root canal therapy, or endodontia, may save a tooth with an infected or decayed pulp. The diseased pulp is removed from the tooth, creating a canal which is then sterilized, enlarged, and finally filled with gutta-percha or silver points.

Damaged or decayed teeth may be repaired by tooth coverings, or crowns, prepared from porcelain, plastic, gold, or combinations of those materials. In deteriorated mouths the teeth may be reconstructed so that they bite properly, avoiding further bone damage from malocclusion. This is known as occluso-rehabilitation.

Lost teeth are replaced by artificial teeth made of plastic, porcelain, or gold. Permanent, or fixed, dentures are cemented to the neighboring teeth. Removable bridges are attached to the remaining teeth with clasps and various friction devices. Full dentures are used when all the teeth are missing. They are held in place principally by the closeness of fit between the denture and the contours of the mouth. A layer of saliva fills the narrow gap between the denture and the soft tissues of the mouth. This fluid holds the denture to the tissues in much the same way as a thin film of water holds two glass plates together.

Improperly aligned teeth are corrected through the use of a number of springlike devices which first move the teeth and then hold them in a proper position until the bone has permanently re-formed around the roots.

Tooth extraction is necessary when the damage or disease is too serious to permit saving the tooth. The patient may be put to sleep under general anesthesia or an anesthetic solution may be injected around the tooth.

Research

A significant amount of research in dentistry is directed toward the prevention of dental disease, that is, caries and pyorrhea. Since it is recognized that dental plaque containing bacterial colonies is the primary cause of dental disease, experiments are being conducted with the enzyme dextranase, which breaks down those carbohydrates (dextrans) harboring the bacteria. It is hoped that such an enzyme will prove safe for use by humans (in toothpaste, for example). Another approach to disease prevention has been the development of plastic sealants which mechanically protect pits and fissures in the tooth that can not easily be reached by brushing. This technique is effective in reducing decay at the applied sites for at least one year. Implants, both endosteal (into the bone) and periosteal (straddling the bone), have been used in recent years to replace lost teeth, with mixed results. The best results have been obtained with implants made of inert metals, such as the cobalt-chromium alloy vitallium, and with plastic implants, but more research is needed before a meaningful evaluation of these experimental procedures can be made.

Specialties in Dentistry

Oral Surgery. The oral surgeon specializes in difficult tooth extractions (such as impacted wisdom teeth), tumor surgery, plastic surgery, and treatment of jaw fractures. This specialty requires postgraduate training at a university dental school and also hospital residency.

A NORMAL TOOTH

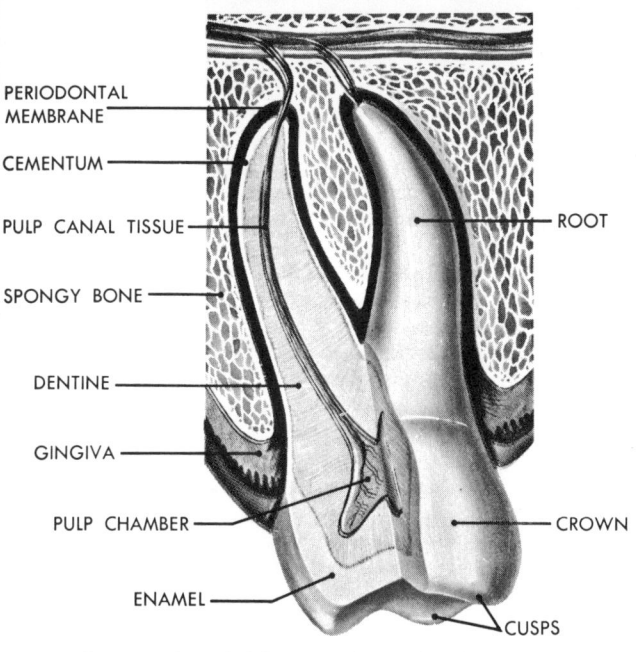

- PERIODONTAL MEMBRANE
- CEMENTUM
- PULP CANAL TISSUE
- SPONGY BONE
- DENTINE
- GINGIVA
- PULP CHAMBER
- ENAMEL
- ROOT
- CROWN
- CUSPS

Cutaway view of right upper first molar showing the principal structures of the normal tooth.

THE USE OF X RAYS IN DENTISTRY

IMPACTED TEETH

Impacted wisdom tooth as seen in X-ray photograph.

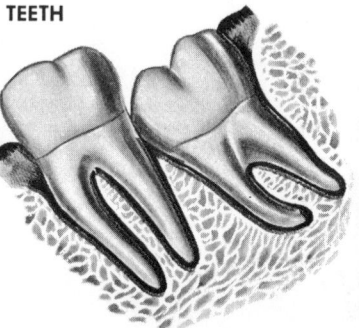

Impaction as it would appear if the surrounding tissues were cut away. The adjacent second molar prevents the tooth from emerging.

CAVITIES

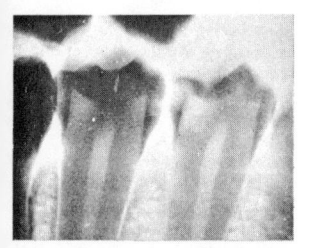

Cavities as they appear on the X-ray plate. The area of the cavity is less resistant to the passage of X-rays and therefore appears different from the surrounding healthy portion of the tooth.

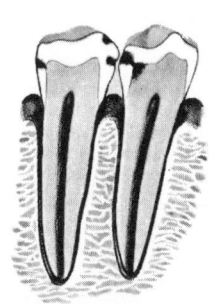

Multiple Cavities. The decay between the teeth can usually be seen only with the aid of X rays.

HOW A CAVITY DEVELOPS

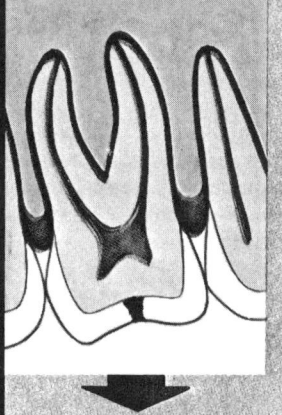

A cavity is a process of decay which if left untreated may successively penetrate the various structures of the tooth. Here in the earliest stage the cavity involves only the enamel and has not reached the softer dentine. At this point the cavity can be filled.

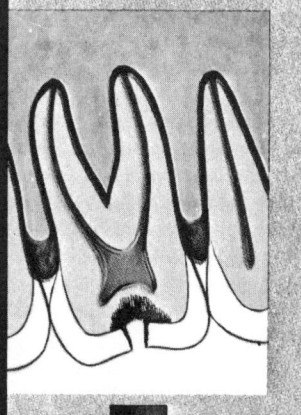

The cavity mushrooms out when it reaches the dentine. This may be treated by filling or by crowning.

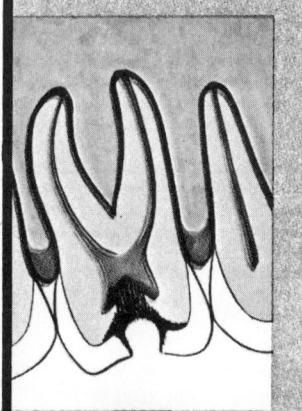

Decay has reached the pulp chamber. Root canal therapy is now necessary.

The inflammation may destroy the pulp of the tooth by obstructing its blood supply. The tooth may now require extraction, or may possibly be preserved by root canal therapy.

HOW CAVITIES ARE REPAIRED

FILLING

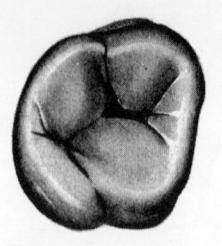

Cavity as it appears on the surface of the tooth.

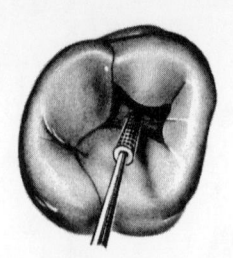

All decay is removed and cavity is prepared for filling.

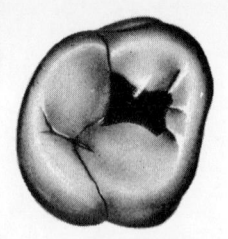

Filling in place. An ideal filling reproduces the original contours of the tooth.

CROWNING
THIS MAY BE DONE FOR EXTENSIVE CAVITIES OR FOR FRACTURED TEETH.

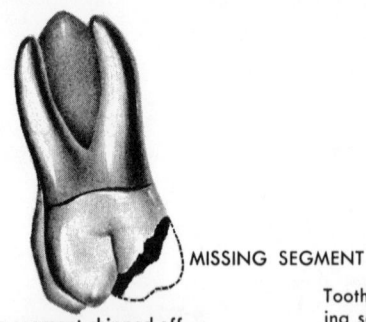

Tooth with a segment chipped off. — MISSING SEGMENT

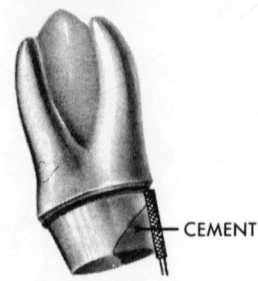

Tooth is shaped for crown. The missing segment of the tooth is replaced with dental cement. — CEMENT

Full gold crown is fitted over tooth. — GOLD CROWN

ROOT CANAL THERAPY

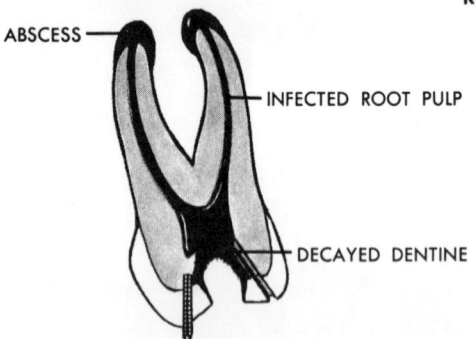

ABSCESS
INFECTED ROOT PULP
DECAYED DENTINE

(1) An opening is made into the pulp chamber of the decayed tooth.

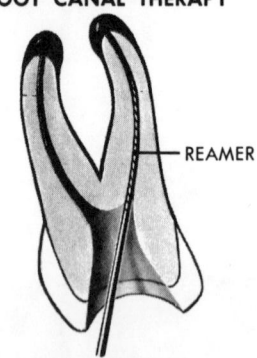

REAMER

(2) Pulp chamber is cleaned. A reamer is shown removing the soft tissues from the root canal.

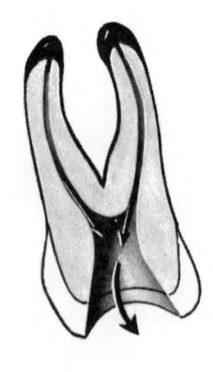

(3) After pulp chamber is cleared, the abscess is allowed to drain.

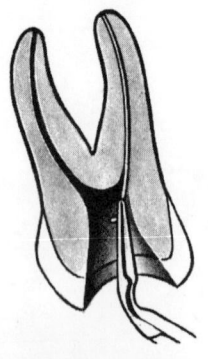

(4) Gutta-percha points or silver wires are placed in the root canal.

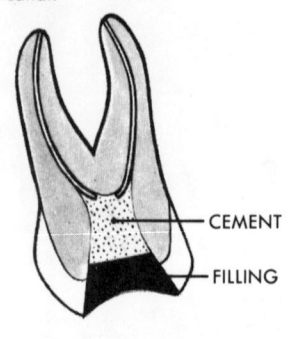

CEMENT
FILLING

(5) When points are in place, remaining parts of pulp chamber are filled.

Illustrated on these pages are some common dental problems. The treatments indicated have been chosen for purposes of illustration, and represent only a few of the many possible methods of dealing with these disorders.

Alfred Carin, D.D.S.
Artist: Leonard Dank

SOME PROBLEMS THAT MAY FOLLOW TOOTH EXTRACTION

IN ADULTS

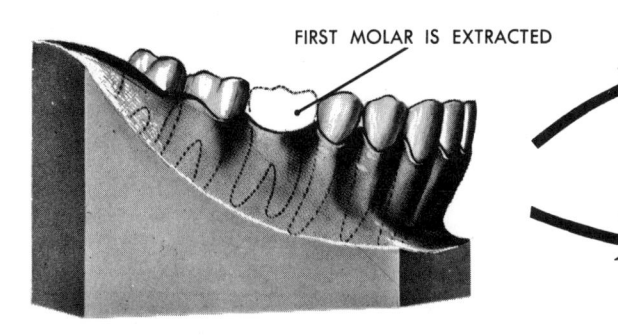

FIRST MOLAR IS EXTRACTED

Mouth following extraction of first molar.

Adjacent teeth, deprived of support of the missing teeth, may drift out of position.

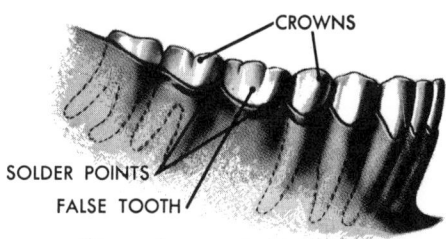

CROWNS
SOLDER POINTS
FALSE TOOTH

This can be prevented by bridging across the space with a false tooth attached to two crowned neighboring teeth.

IN CHILDREN

PERMANENT TEETH — WHITE
DECIDUOUS TEETH — PINK
BONE
DEVELOPING PERMANENT SECOND BICUSPID
GUM LINE
SIX-YEAR FIRST MOLAR
SECOND DECIDUOUS MOLAR MISSING

(1) LOSS OF A DECIDUOUS, OR MILK TOOTH MAY CAUSE

(2) THIS MAY BE PREVENTED BY

Drifting of adjacent teeth. This may prevent normal eruption of underlying teeth.

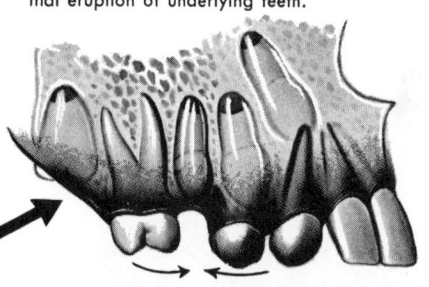

ADJACENT TEETH DRIFT

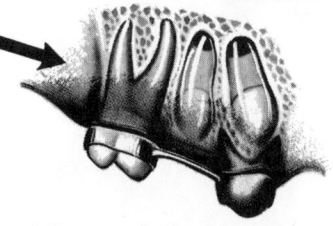

A "space maintainer" to prevent movement of adjacent teeth.

TO REPLACE MISSING TEETH—THE REMOVABLE DENTURE

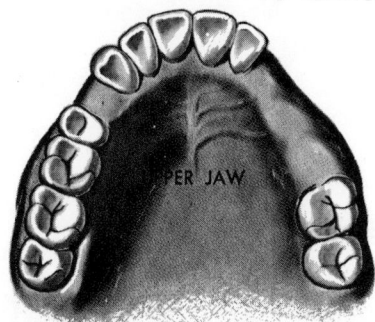

UPPER JAW

View of upper jaw showing missing teeth.

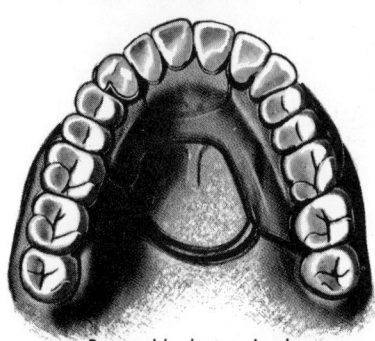

Removable denture in place.

DISEASE OF THE SUPPORTING STRUCTURES OF THE TEETH

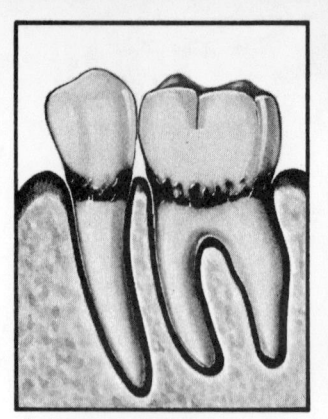

Tartar, or calculus, accumulates above and below the gum line.

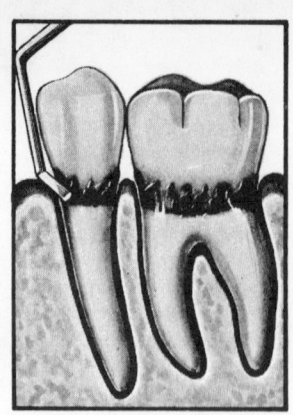

This should be removed by scaling.

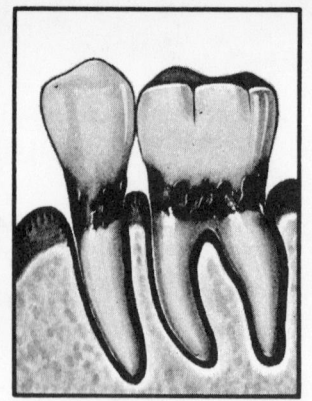

If tartar is not removed, gums become inflamed and eventually recede. This is accompanied by loss of underlying bone.

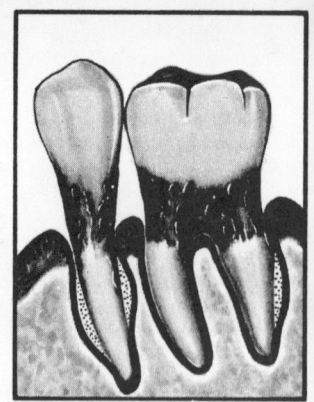

If still not treated, teeth loosen as more supporting gum and bone are lost. Abscesses may form and teeth may be lost.

ABNORMAL POSITIONING OF THE TEETH — MALOCCLUSION

A NORMAL OCCLUSION

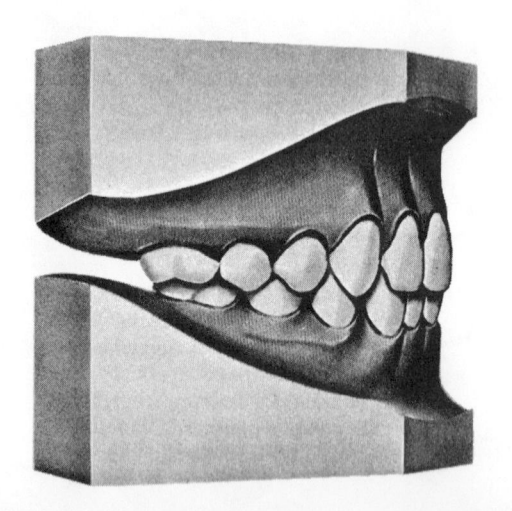

A variety of congenital, acquired, and inherited factors may result in abnormal positioning of the teeth. This may interfere with normal function and appearance. Problems of this nature are treated by the orthodontist.

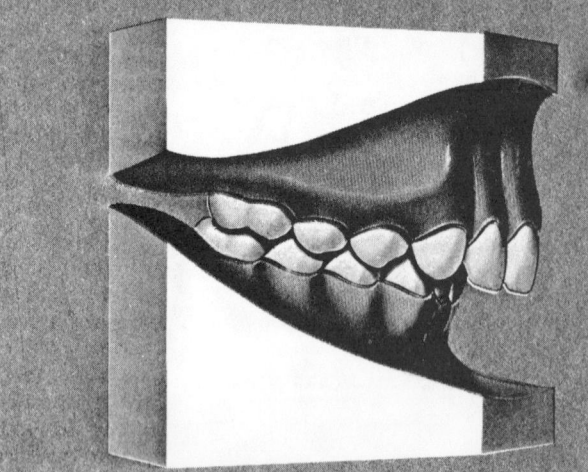

SOME CASES OF MALOCCLUSION

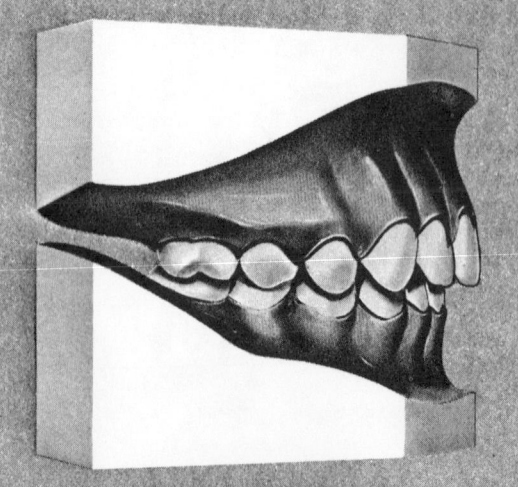

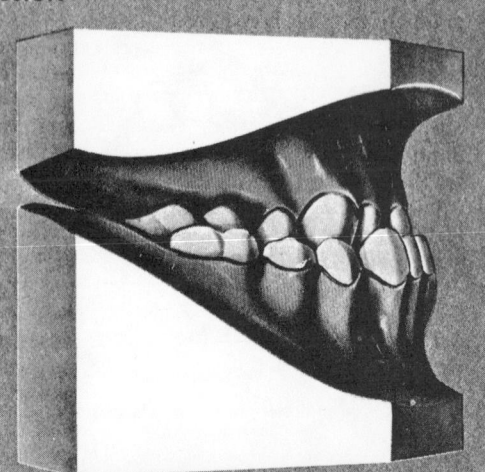

Orthodontia deals with the realignment of the teeth to correct faulty occlusion and unsightly appearance. The orthodontist may receive his training in postgraduate work or by working with a board-qualified orthodontist.

Periodontia. The periodontist treats the gums, bone, and related structures which surround the teeth. Postgraduate training is required.

Prosthodontia deals with the replacement of missing teeth with dentures and the reconstruction of existing teeth. The prosthodontist usually receives his training in hospitals, clinics, or in the offices of experienced prosthodontists. Some dental schools offer postgraduate courses leading to board qualification.

Endodontists (see Root Canal Therapy above) may be trained in postgraduate courses or by working with experienced endodontists.

The History of Dentistry

Dental problems have afflicted men since prehistoric times, when the coarse food of the cave dwellers wore their teeth down to the gums. Probably the first attempts at treatment took place in ancient Egypt, where medications were applied to the teeth. In the 5th century B.C. the Greek physician Hippocrates, known as the "Father of Medicine," gave clear descriptions of dental diseases and accurately described the anatomy of the mouth. Hippocrates also discussed treatment, such as the wiring of the teeth together to splint jaw fracture. Techniques of wiring loose teeth and constructing bridges were developed by the Phoenicians at about the same time. In ancient Rome bridgework was used to replace teeth by attaching the missing tooth to the adjacent teeth.

In the Middle Ages dentistry was practiced by barbers and "tooth-drawers," as well as by physicians. The first book devoted exclusively to dentistry, *Zene Arzney*, was published in Germany in 1530. In the late 16th century dentistry began to become distinct from general medicine. Methods were developed for drilling decayed teeth and filling them with soft gold leaf. Pierre Fauchard, the "Father of Dentistry," stimulated the development of professional literature on dentistry with his *Le Chirurgien Dentiste ou Traité des Dents* (Dental Surgery, or a Treatise on the Teeth) in 1728.

The outstanding figure in American dentistry was Greene V. Black (1836–1915), best remembered for his *Anatomy of the Human Teeth,* and *Operative Dentistry.* He introduced the first scientific cavity preparation and numerous other contributions which constitute the basis of modern scientific dentistry. Black is credited with having transformed dentistry from a trade to its present professional status, grounded in the basic sciences of pathology, bacteriology, surgery, and pharmacology.

See also CAVITY, DENTAL; FLUORIDATION; TEETH.

DENTITION [děn-tĭsh'ən], an anatomical term for the arrangement, kind, and number of teeth. All classes of vertebrate animals have teeth, except the birds, and the members of each vertebrate family have a characteristic dentition which is closely associated with their adaptations for life. For example herbivorous, or plant-eating mammals have teeth that are quite different from those of carnivorous, or flesh-eating, mammals. Omnivorous mammals, which eat both plants and flesh, have teeth suited to their varied diet. This difference in dentition is used as a basis for classifying mammals.

A simple tooth, like that of a shark, is flattened and pointed, and especially useful for cutting. Such teeth are similar to the scales of the shark and are arranged in renewable rows. In other fishes and in amphibians, teeth may also be numerous and located on the palate as well as emerging from the jaws.

Reptiles and mammals have teeth arranged along the edge of the jaws. The teeth of reptiles are typically conical and undifferentiated, while those of mammals take several forms—sharp-edged incisors for cutting, pointed canine teeth for tearing and stabbing, and more flattened premolars and molars for grinding. Highly modified teeth are characteristic of certain mammalian groups. Members of the cat, dog, and bear families have carnassial teeth along the side of the jaw, which are especially useful for cutting. The tusks of elephants actually are modified incisor teeth, and these huge beasts also have very large molars for grinding. Some whales have undifferentiated peglike teeth, while others have none, and many anteaters lack functional teeth entirely.

The dentition of a mammal is often expressed in a so-called dental formula indicating the number and kind of tooth in each half jaw. In man the formula $\frac{2 \cdot 1 \cdot 2 \cdot 3}{2 \cdot 1 \cdot 2 \cdot 3}$ means that there are 2 incisors, 1 canine tooth, 2 premolars, and 3 molars in each half upper and lower jaw.

DEOXYRIBONUCLEIC ACID (DNA). *See* NUCLEIC ACIDS.

DEPRESSION, in psychiatric usage, describes a feeling of despondency which may range from simple unhappiness to complete despair. It may be seen as a common reaction to misfortune, in association with physical illness, or bodily changes, or as part of a fully-developed psychotic condition.

Depression following the death of a close friend or relative normally disappears with time. Distressing personal relationships or occupational problems often cause a severe depression, which may include loss of appetite, loss of interest in usual activities, and insomnia. In some cases, physical and mental activity is impaired and the individual may contemplate suicide. In children and adolescents depression may arise as a reaction to an intolerable family situation. It is frequently seen in children living in institutions, and in those separated from their parents.

Change-of-life in both men and women may bring on depression as a reaction to the prospect of vanishing youth. In older persons failing health, the death of close friends and relatives, and financial dependence on their children may bring on depression. Physical illness is a common cause of depression, especially among active persons who cannot tolerate limitations of activity—as, for example, in the case of an energetic businessman who becomes partially disabled following a heart attack.

Depression is a characteristic feature of a mental disorder called manic-depressive psychosis. In this condi-

DERMATITIS

tion the individual alternates between moods of great elation (mania) and profound depression. In general, depression which does not arise from an obvious cause, such as death of a loved one, and which persists for more than a few days, should be referred for psychiatric care.

DERMATITIS [dûr-mə-tī′tĭs], an inflammation of the skin, which may be caused by allergies, by various physical and chemical irritants, by drugs, or which may appear as a complication of other diseases.

Allergic (contact) dermatitis follows skin contact with materials to which the individual is sensitive. From 7 to 24 days after the first exposure the skin becomes red, swollen, blistered, and itchy. The offending substances may be found in plants (such as poison ivy), in cosmetics, fabrics, plastics, skin ointments, or in compounds used for industrial purposes. A dermatitis may also follow the consumption of certain drugs, resulting in redness, blistering, and hives.

Radiation dermatitis follows exposure to large doses of high-energy radiation. A marked reddening and swelling of the skin may appear soon after exposure, and years later dry skin, dark and light spots on the skin, loss of hair, ulcerations, thinning of the skin, and skin cancers may develop.

Strong chemicals may irritate the skin, producing an inflammation with peeling, redness, fissures, ulcerations, scales, or blisters. A generalized scaling or redness of the skin, called exfoliative dermatitis, may appear as a complication of certain diseases, or in drug reactions. A dermatitis may result from an allergy to sunlight or from overexposure (sunburn).

The various forms of dermatitis are usually treated by ointments, creams, and antibacterial solutions. Avoidance of the source of irritation is important. In cases of allergic dermatitis, the skin is systematically exposed to samples of suspected substances to determine the allergy-producing agent.

DERMATOMYOSITIS [dûr-mə-tō-mī-ō-sī′tĭs], a disease of unknown origin involving the inflammation and degeneration of the muscles of the limbs and trunk. There may be a rash and other skin changes, as well as swelling of the face and eyes, weakness, loss of appetite, and a low-grade fever. The disease is frequently fatal. Cortisone and related drugs have been used in treatment with some success.
See also COLLAGEN DISEASES.

DEVIATED SEPTUM, an abnormal displacement of the bone and cartilage partition which divides the nasal cavity into two halves. The deviation may result from abnormal development of the septum or from a hard blow to the nose. A deviated septum may obstruct one of the nasal passages, possibly interfering with breathing, speech, and smell and taste sensations. Habitual mouth breathing may result from the obstruction. The condition can be corrected surgically.
See also NOSE.

DEXEDRINE (DEXTROROTATORY AMPHETAMINE). See BENZEDRINE OR AMPHETAMINE.

DEXTRAN [dĕk′străn], gummy polysaccharide of high-molecular weight produced by certain bacteria, especially *Leuconostoc mesenteroides,* from sucrose (table sugar). The accumulation of dextran in the pipes and machinery used in sugar refineries is a serious nuisance in the sugar industry. Dextran has been found to be useful as a partial substitute for blood plasma in transfusions and has been produced industrially for this purpose.
See also PLASMA EXPANDERS; POLYSACCHARIDES.

DIABETES INSIPIDUS [dī-ə-bē′tĭs, -tēz ĭn-sĭp′ĭ-dəs], a disease characterized by the excretion of large quantities of dilute urine. The disorder is usually caused by the failure of the pituitary gland to secrete vasopressin, a hormone which helps regulate the excretion of urine. Most cases result from disease or injury to the pituitary gland or adjacent regions of the brain. A less common inherited form of the disease appears chiefly in men. The loss of large amounts of water produces excessive thirst. The disorder cannot be cured but can usually be controlled by the regular administration of vasopressin.

DIABETES MELLITUS, a disease characterized by a complete or partial inability of the body to burn sugar as a fuel.

Diabetes is prevalent throughout the world. In the United States alone, it is estimated that two million persons are afflicted. Jews appear to be particularly susceptible; however, no ethnic group is exempt. Although it occurs in all age groups, most diabetics are obese, or slightly obese, middle-aged women. The tendency to diabetes may be inherited and in such cases the disease may be brought on by obesity, infection, emotional shock, surgery, pregnancy, or the onset of change-of-life. Diabetic women often bear abnormally large children some years before they develop the disease.

What Causes Diabetes?

The key to diabetes is thought to be the improper functioning of the pancreas, a long gland that is found in the rear of the abdomen behind the stomach. The diabetic pancreas may not produce enough insulin, a hormone that is essential to the utilization of carbohydrates as a food by the human body. The abnormality of the pancreas is not one that can always be seen with the naked eye or even with a microscope, since diabetics may occasionally have a pancreas that appears perfectly normal whereas scarring and injury may be observed in the glands of normal persons.

Carbohydrates are composed of sugar units, which are bound into larger units called starches. The body breaks down the starches into sugar, or glucose, which is then absorbed into the blood stream. In order to be used for energy the sugar must be taken up by the cell. It is believed by some investigators that insulin facilitates the passage of sugar into the cell. If it is imagined that sugar passes over a drawbridge from the blood to the cell, then insulin can be conceived of as a gatekeeper who keeps the bridge lowered. If the pancreas does not produce enough insulin sugar piles up in the blood. When the blood sugar reaches a certain level it spills over into the urine.

Under certain circumstances, which are not yet well

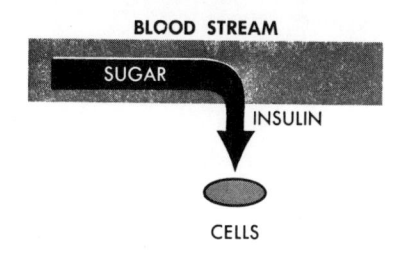

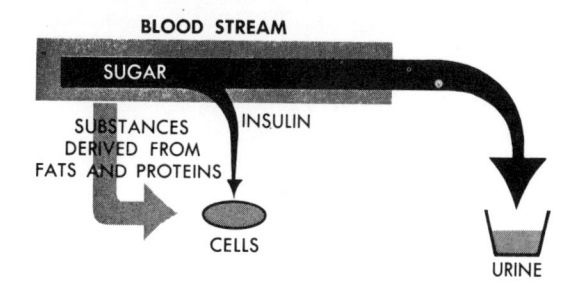

NORMAL METABOLISM

Carbohydrates are broken down into sugar in the process of digestion. The sugar enters the blood stream and must be carried to the cells in order to be utilized for energy. It is believed that insulin aids in the absorption of sugar by the cells.

METABOLISM IN DIABETES

In diabetes the insulin supply is deficient and not enough sugar can be utilized by the cells. Consequently, sugar accumulates in the blood and spills over into the urine. The body then draws upon fats and proteins as sources of energy.

understood, diabetes may develop even if the pancreas produces normal amounts of insulin. In these cases there is apparently a *relative* deficiency of insulin.

Because it is unable to utilize sugar as a source of energy, the body then draws upon protein and fat as energy sources. This results in a gradual wasting away of muscular tissue, which becomes evident as a loss of weight. The use of fats for fuel is potentially even more dangerous, for these are broken down into substances called ketone bodies, which upset the acidity-alkalinity balance of the body. The result is a condition called acidosis, which may terminate in a coma. This coma is characterized by a fruity aroma of the breath, which is produced by the presence of acetone, one of the ketone bodies. Diabetic coma is distinct from the shock which develops when the patient takes too much insulin. In the latter case too much sugar enters the cells too quickly, resulting in a serious shortage of glucose in the blood.

The Symptoms

The diabetic may appear well and may be completely unaware of his condition until a routine examination of his blood or urine reveals an abnormally high concentration of sugar. In other cases the condition progresses until symptoms appear. These include: excessive urination, thirst, dryness of the mouth, weakness, loss of weight, and itching of the genital areas. Less frequent symptoms are excessive hunger and disturbances in vision.

Prior to the discovery of insulin many diabetics could not be treated properly. Today, although diabetes can be controlled, it presents many medical problems. Diabetics are susceptible to cataracts, arteriosclerosis (hardening of the arteries), and heart disease. Arteriosclerosis is especially common in older diabetics. The arteries of the legs are a favorite site. These become clogged with fatty deposits that interfere with the flow of blood. As a result, the tissues of the leg are starved and become vulnerable to infection and gangrene. For this reason diabetics must maintain scrupulous care of their feet, avoiding ill-fitting shoes, harsh chemicals, and home surgery. In diabetics of long standing the kidneys and nervous system may be affected and blindness may be produced by hemorrhages in the eyes. Diabetic women can conceive and bear children but they require close medical supervision throughout pregnancy, as they are prone to miscarriage and stillbirth and other complications. With proper care and attention diabetics can lead normal lives.

Diet is an essential aspect of treatment. It should be well-balanced, provide enough calories to maintain ideal weight, and restrict carbohydrates. Many older patients can be controlled on diet alone. Others require insulin or other drugs to lower the blood sugar. Caution must be observed to avoid insulin shock which may result from too little food, as well as from too much insulin. Drugs that can be taken by mouth, such as chlorpropamide, tolbutamide, and phenethylbiguanide (DBI), are also available. *See also* CARBOHYDRATES; INSULIN; PANCREAS.

DIAPER RASH, redness, maceration, and erosion of the skin of the diaper area in infants. It usually results from injury to the skin caused by the ammonia in the urine. Frequently infection follows the injury. Treatment consists of frequent diaper changes, the application of soothing antiseptic pastes, and washing with mild soap and water. Rubber or plastic diapers should be avoided during an attack of the rash.

DIAPHRAGM [dī″ə-frăm], in anatomy, a thin disc of muscle that extends in a horizontal plane across the trunk of the body, separating the chest from the abdomen. The

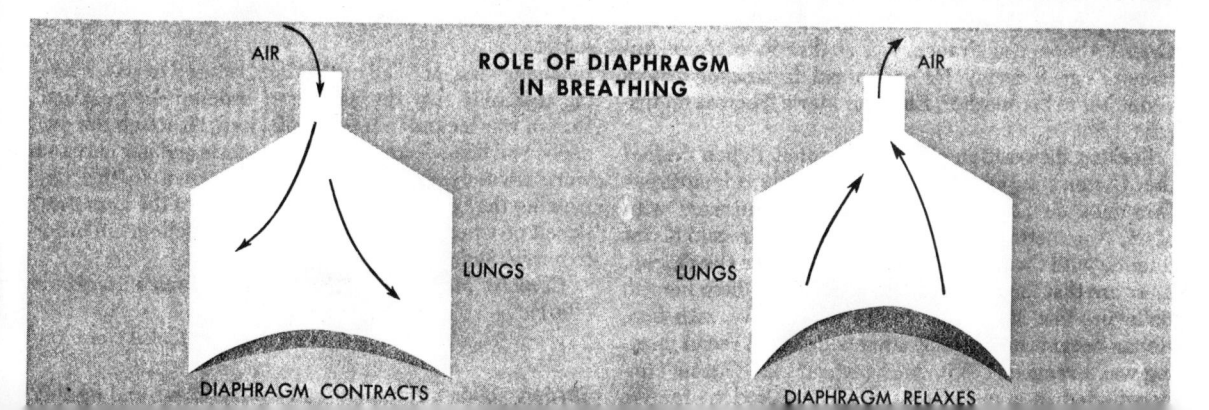

ROLE OF DIAPHRAGM IN BREATHING

DIARRHEA

heart and lungs rest upon the diaphragm, and the liver, stomach, spleen, and kidneys lie immediately below it. The diaphragm is important in the rhythmic action of breathing. While relaxed the diaphragm is dome-shaped and rises into the chest; as it contracts the dome flattens. The change in shape alters the size of the chest cavity, alternately drawing in and expelling air. Hiccups are caused by intermittent spasms of the diaphragm.

See also RESPIRATION.

DIARRHEA [dĭ-ə-rē′ə], disorder of elimination in which there is usually an increased number of loose bowel movements. Diarrhea is a symptom of an underlying disorder and may be caused by infections of the gastrointestinal tract, allergic reactions to food, emotional upsets, tumors, vitamin deficiencies, or a great variety of other conditions. In severe diarrhea excessive loss of water, vitamins, and minerals may produce serious disturbances, including anemia, vitamin deficiencies, loss of weight, and an upset in the acidity-alkalinity balance of the body. Treatment consists of removing the underlying cause and replacing the lost materials.

DIATHERMY, a form of physical therapy in which a high-frequency electric current is used to warm the tissues deep below the surface of the skin. The warmth soothes pain and muscle spasm, increases blood circulation, and hastens healing, and is therefore useful for chronic infections, fractures, sprains, and dislocations. Inflammations of the joints and muscles respond especially well to diathermy.

The types of diathermy apparatus include (1) the conventional, or long-wave, unit which is now almost obsolete. This device generates 500 thousand to 3 million cycles per second (cps) and requires electrodes to be placed directly on the skin; (2) short-wave diathermy units, which generate 10 million to 100 million cps, through a thickly insulated wire cable which is coiled over the body part to be treated without touching the skin; (3) microwave diathermy, which uses frequencies

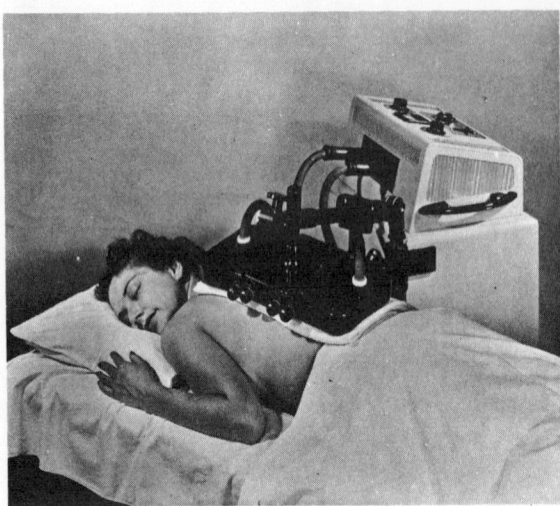

The Burdick Corp.
Short-wave diathermy machine used to heat large areas.

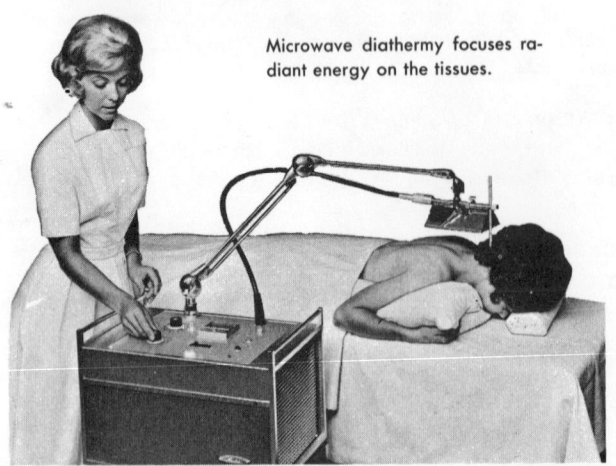

Microwave diathermy focuses radiant energy on the tissues.

The Burdick Corp.

DIATHERMY

APPLICATIONS OF SHORT-WAVE DIATHERMY

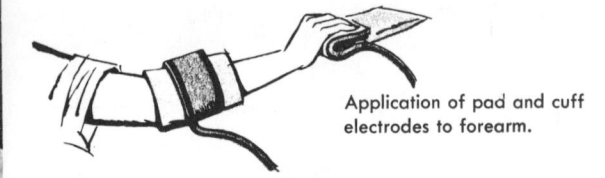

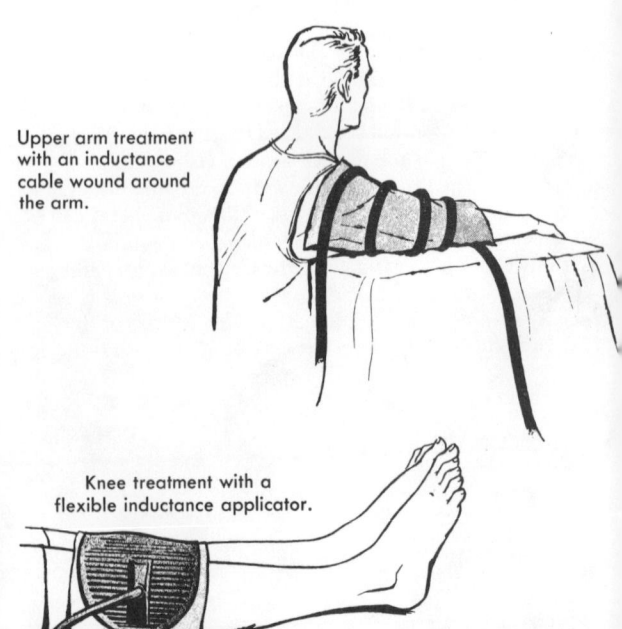

Application of pad and cuff electrodes to forearm.

Upper arm treatment with an inductance cable wound around the arm.

Knee treatment with a flexible inductance applicator.

of about 3,000 million cps. In this technique no electrodes or cables are used. Instead a beam of energy is directed at the tissues.

The average diathermy treatment lasts about 20 minutes and may be given from twice daily to twice weekly, depending on the type and severity of the illness. For especially stubborn chronic infections diathermy may be used to warm the entire body and thus induce artificial fever. For this purpose the patient lies in an aluminum cabinet which prevents heat from escaping.

Since diathermy increases blood flow, it may not be used in conditions where there is a tendency to bleed easily or in the pelvic area during menstruation. It should also be avoided in cases of acute infections and malignant growths, which are aggravated by excess heat.

DICUMAROL [dī-koo'mə-rôl], also known as bishydroxycoumarin, a drug used to prevent the formation of blood clots in veins and arteries. Dicumarol was first isolated from spoiled sweet clover hay, which was found to be responsible for excessive and sometimes fatal bleeding in cattle. The drug decreases the clotting power of the blood by inhibiting the formation of an essential clotting agent (prothrombin) in the liver. Dicumarol is used in certain types of heart disease and to prevent clotting in blood vessels throughout the body.
See also ANTICOAGULANTS.

DIETETIC FOODS. There are six principal types of dietetic foods: low-calorie, or reducing; low-sodium, or salt-free; sugar-restricted (principally for diabetics); foods for persons with specific allergies; vegetarian, and so-called health foods, featuring coarse or stone-ground grains, blackstrap molasses, and similar products.

Most important are the low-calorie foods. Canned, water-packed fruits with non-nutritive sweetening are the most popular. Other widely distributed reducing foods include dietetic, sugar-free carbonated beverages; low-calorie salad dressings; sugar-free preserves; sugar- and salt-free baking mixes and frostings; and noncaloric sweeteners available in tablet, crystal, powdered, and liquid form. Some artificial sweeteners are made from saccharin; others are of the cyclamate types which do not leave a bitter aftertaste.

Also available on the market are breads, toast, and breadsticks made from gluten, soy, artichoke, and rice flour; low-sodium cheeses; vegetarian brown gravy; soy and low-sodium milk; and salt substitutes.

DIGESTION, the process by which food is changed from a complex to a simple form so that it can be absorbed and utilized by the body. Foods consist principally of carbohydrates (starches and sugars), proteins (in meats, eggs, and fish), and fats (cream, animal fat, butter, and vegetable fat). During the course of digestion each of these foods is broken down into its constituents: carbohydrates are changed into simple sugars, proteins are broken down into their component amino acids, and fats are changed into fatty acids and glycerol. These changes occur during the passage of food through the digestive tract, a hollow tube which extends from the mouth to the anus. Food is moved along the tract by muscular action while chemicals (enzymes) poured into the tube break down the food substances into successively finer form, until they can be taken into the blood and lymph streams.

Digestion begins in the mouth, where the teeth grind and tear the food, reducing it to a semisolid mass. Three pairs of salivary glands located under the jaw (submaxillary), under the tongue (sublingual), and next to the ear (parotid), continually pour out a watery secretion which bathes the teeth and moistens the mouth and throat. The presence of food in the mouth stimulates these glands to secrete an enzyme (salivary amylase), which breaks down complex starches into simpler units.

Food leaves the mouth and enters the stomach via a long passageway, the gullet, or esophagus. In the stomach, proteins are broken down into simpler forms (proteoses and peptones) by the enzyme pepsin. The stomach juice also contains hydrochloric acid, which maintains the proper acid level necessary for the action of pepsin. The muscles of the stomach wall facilitate the action of the enzymes by churning the food and stomach juices into a thoroughly mixed liquid, called chyme. Certain stomach cells secrete mucus, which coats the lining of the stomach, thereby preventing it from being digested by its own enzymes. The stomach of infants secretes the enzyme rennin, which curdles milk, keeping it in the stomach longer and permitting pepsin to digest it more thoroughly.

When the pressure in the stomach becomes sufficiently great, a muscular valve (the pyloric sphincter) situated in the lower portion of the stomach is pushed open, allowing some liquid chyme to pass into the small intestine. The pyloric sphincter is one of many valves found along the digestive tract. These include a valve in the esophagus (the esophageal sphincter), and one in the small intestine (ileo-cecal valve). These structures prevent material from being regurgitated and from being passed too rapidly forward along the digestive tract.

The small intestine is the most active site of digestion. Large quantities of enzyme-containing digestive juices enter the small intestine from the pancreas and from glands in the intestinal lining. The intestinal juices are alkaline in contrast to the acidic stomach contents, so that the hydrochloric acid from the stomach is neutralized in the small intestine. The final stage of protein breakdown is achieved here as the intestinal enzymes break down the peptones and proteoses to simple amino acids. Large fat globules are broken up into smaller particles by the bile salts and are changed into fatty acids by another pancreatic enzyme—lipase.

The food has now been broken down into its basic components: carbohydrates into simple sugars, proteins into amino acids, and fats into fatty acids and glycerol. In these forms food is absorbed into the blood stream, primarily from the midportion of the small intestine. While sugars and amino acids are absorbed directly into the blood stream from the intestine, most fat enters the lymph vessels and reaches the blood stream at the point where the large lymph channel, the thoracic duct, empties into a large vein in the lower part of the neck.

In the large intestine fluid is absorbed from the undigested residue which leaves the small intestine. Rhythmic muscular contractions of the intestinal wall propel this waste to the rectum, from where it is excreted.

THE CHEMISTRY OF DIGESTION

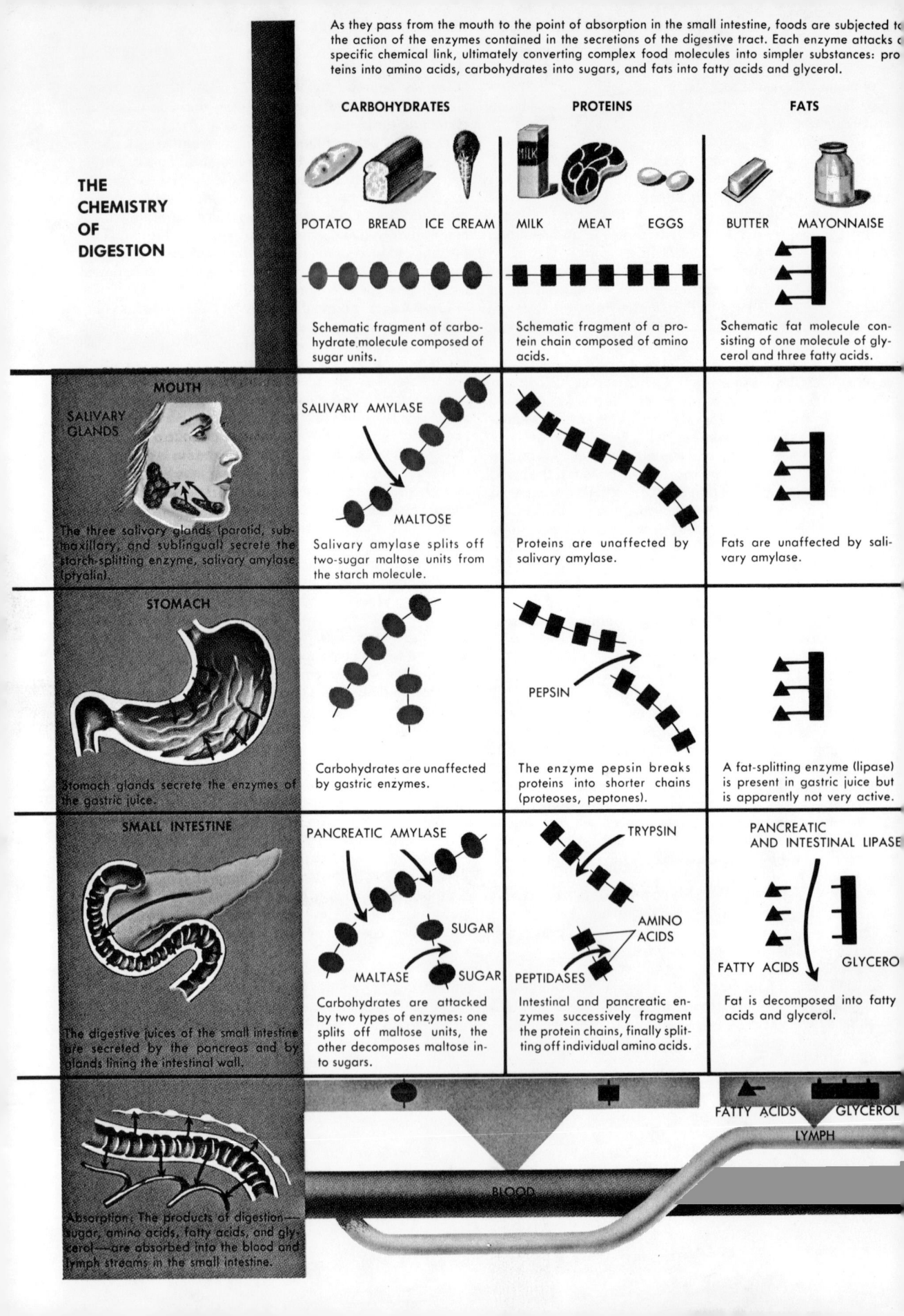

As they pass from the mouth to the point of absorption in the small intestine, foods are subjected to the action of the enzymes contained in the secretions of the digestive tract. Each enzyme attacks a specific chemical link, ultimately converting complex food molecules into simpler substances: proteins into amino acids, carbohydrates into sugars, and fats into fatty acids and glycerol.

CARBOHYDRATES
POTATO   BREAD   ICE CREAM

Schematic fragment of carbohydrate molecule composed of sugar units.

PROTEINS
MILK   MEAT   EGGS

Schematic fragment of a protein chain composed of amino acids.

FATS
BUTTER   MAYONNAISE

Schematic fat molecule consisting of one molecule of glycerol and three fatty acids.

MOUTH
SALIVARY GLANDS

The three salivary glands (parotid, submaxillary, and sublingual) secrete the starch-splitting enzyme, salivary amylase (ptyalin).

SALIVARY AMYLASE → **MALTOSE**
Salivary amylase splits off two-sugar maltose units from the starch molecule.

Proteins are unaffected by salivary amylase.

Fats are unaffected by salivary amylase.

STOMACH

Stomach glands secrete the enzymes of the gastric juice.

Carbohydrates are unaffected by gastric enzymes.

PEPSIN
The enzyme pepsin breaks proteins into shorter chains (proteoses, peptones).

A fat-splitting enzyme (lipase) is present in gastric juice but is apparently not very active.

SMALL INTESTINE

The digestive juices of the small intestine are secreted by the pancreas and by glands lining the intestinal wall.

PANCREATIC AMYLASE → **MALTASE** → **SUGAR**
Carbohydrates are attacked by two types of enzymes: one splits off maltose units, the other decomposes maltose into sugars.

TRYPSIN, **PEPTIDASES** → **AMINO ACIDS**
Intestinal and pancreatic enzymes successively fragment the protein chains, finally splitting off individual amino acids.

PANCREATIC AND INTESTINAL LIPASE → **FATTY ACIDS**, **GLYCEROL**
Fat is decomposed into fatty acids and glycerol.

Absorption: The products of digestion—sugar, amino acids, fatty acids, and glycerol—are absorbed into the blood and lymph streams in the small intestine.

BLOOD   LYMPH

THE MOVEMENT OF FOOD THROUGH THE DIGESTIVE TRACT

Food is propelled through the digestive tract by contractions of the smooth muscles which line the walls of the digestive organs. These contractions also mechanically grind the food and mix it with the digestive juices.

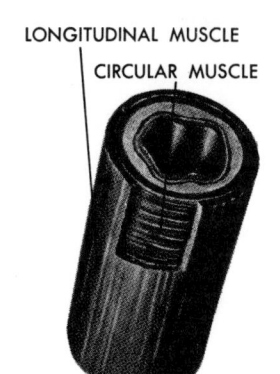

LONGITUDINAL MUSCLE
CIRCULAR MUSCLE

Section of esophagus showing characteristic musculature of digestive tract: an inner layer of circular muscle and an outer layer of longitudinal muscle.

THE SPHINCTERS are muscular rings that maintain a one-way flow of digestion by closing off segments of the digestive tract so that food masses can be mixed without spilling back into other sections of the tract.

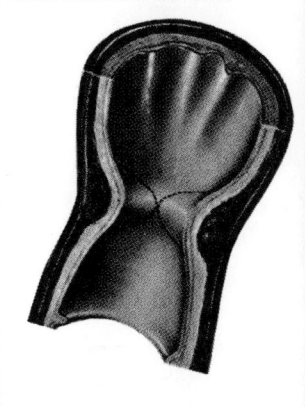

THE LARGE INTESTINE. The large intestine undergoes peristaltic waves similar to those of the small intestine.

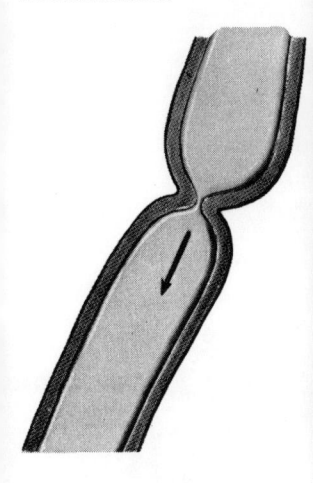

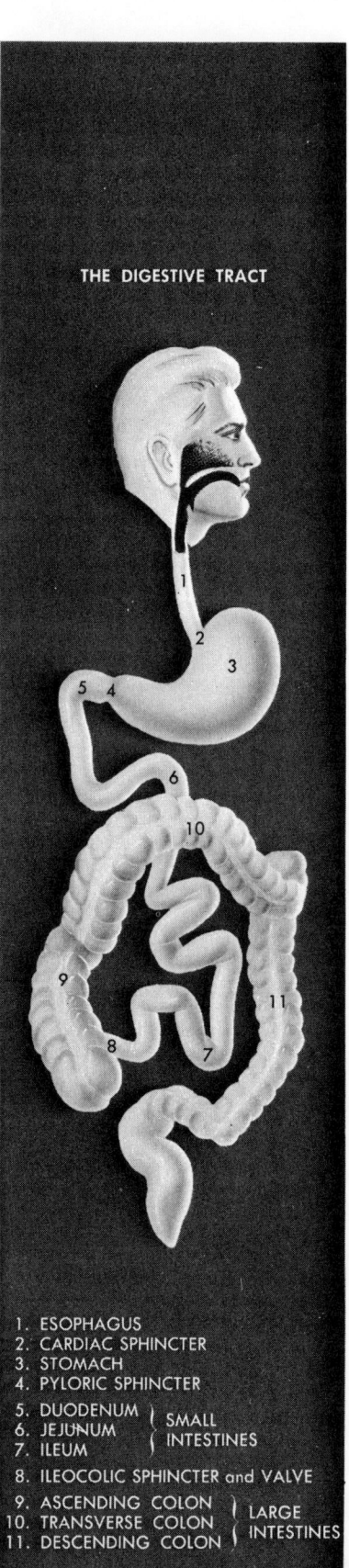

THE DIGESTIVE TRACT

1. ESOPHAGUS
2. CARDIAC SPHINCTER
3. STOMACH
4. PYLORIC SPHINCTER
5. DUODENUM ⎫
6. JEJUNUM   ⎬ SMALL INTESTINES
7. ILEUM   ⎭
8. ILEOCOLIC SPHINCTER and VALVE
9. ASCENDING COLON ⎫
10. TRANSVERSE COLON ⎬ LARGE INTESTINES
11. DESCENDING COLON ⎭

THE ESOPHAGUS. Food is carried to the stomach by wave-like (peristaltic) contractions.

FOOD MASS

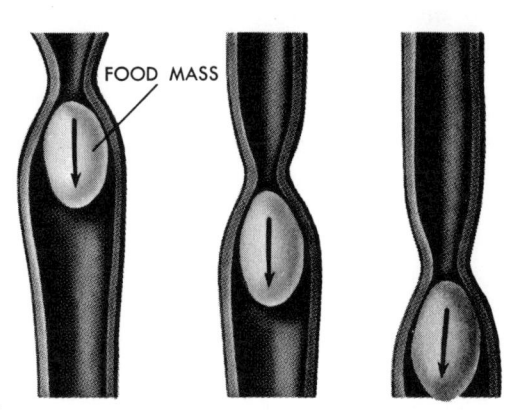

Peristaltic wave moves along esophagus.

THE STOMACH. Peristaltic waves sweep toward the pylorus, mixing and grinding the stomach contents. Two or more such waves may grip the stomach simultaneously.

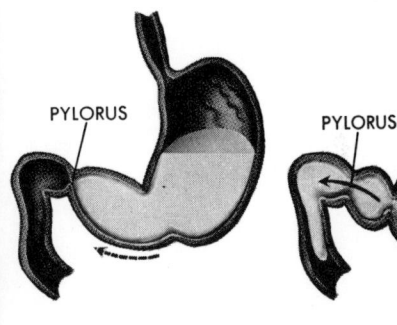

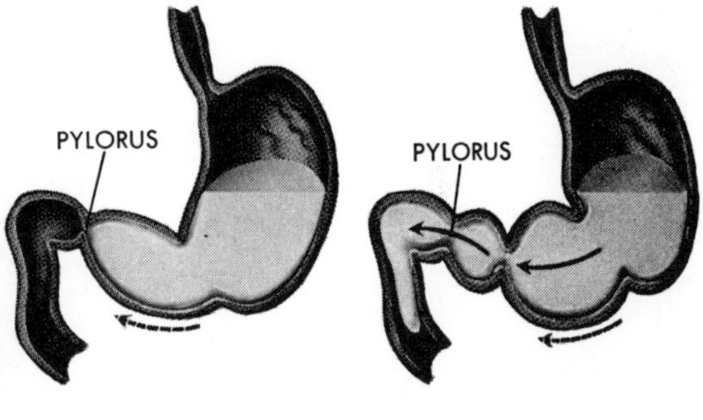

PYLORUS

PYLORUS

(A) Peristaltic wave begins moving toward pylorus.

(B) Second wave begins on heels of first.

The small intestine undergoes two basic types of movement: (1) a rhythmic contraction of intestinal segments and (2) peristaltic contractions.

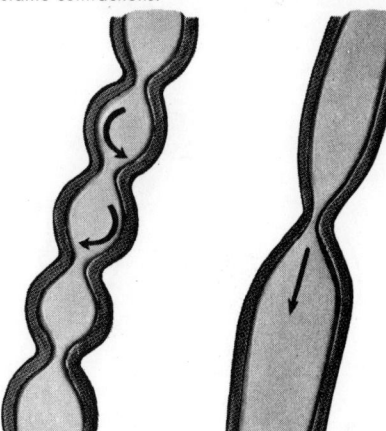

(1) Segmental contractions

(2) Peristaltic waves

THE CONTROL OF THE DIGESTIVE SECRETIONS

STIMULATION BEFORE EATING

The secretions of the digestive glands are controlled by nerve impulses and hormones. Stimulation first begins at the sight, smell, or taste of food, which through reflex action generates nerve impulses to the salivary glands, stomach, and pancreas.

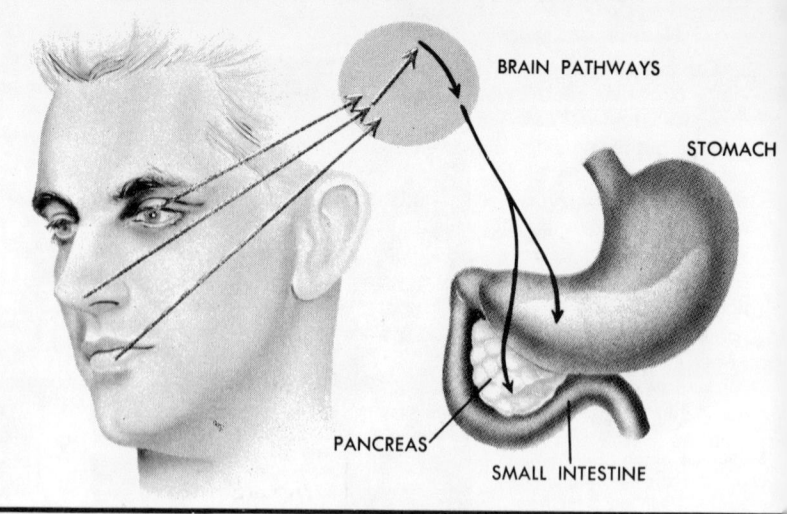

FOOD IN THE STOMACH

Food in the stomach stimulates the release of GASTRIN, which travels to the stomach glands via the blood stream and induces the secretion of gastric juice. Nerve mechanisms are apparently important in this process.

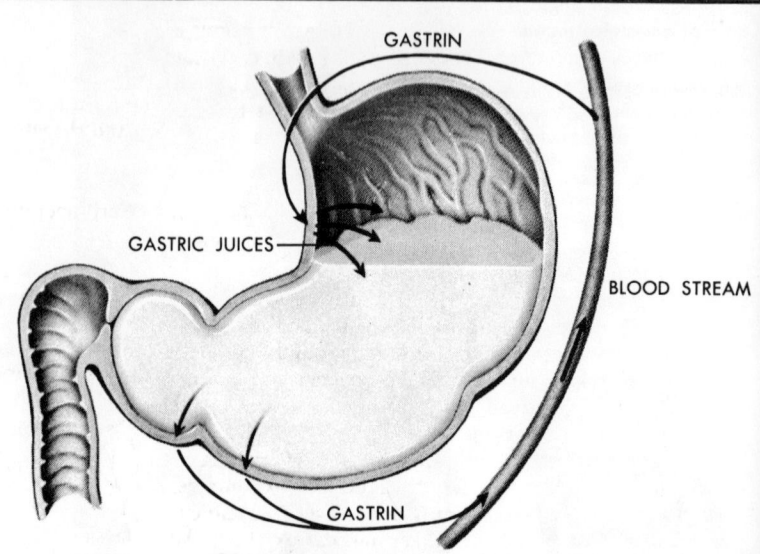

FOOD IN THE INTESTINE

(A) STIMULATION. In the intestine certain foods increase gastric secretion, probably by the action of a chemical which is liberated from the intestine and travels to the stomach. Two pancreas-stimulating substances, SECRETIN and PANCREOZYMIN, are known to be released from the intestine by the action of foods and gastric juice.

(B) INHIBITION. Fats in the intestine stimulate the release of intestinal hormone enterogastrone, which inhibits gastric secretion.

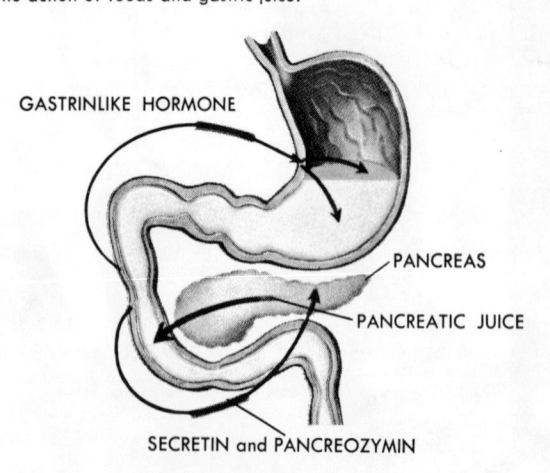

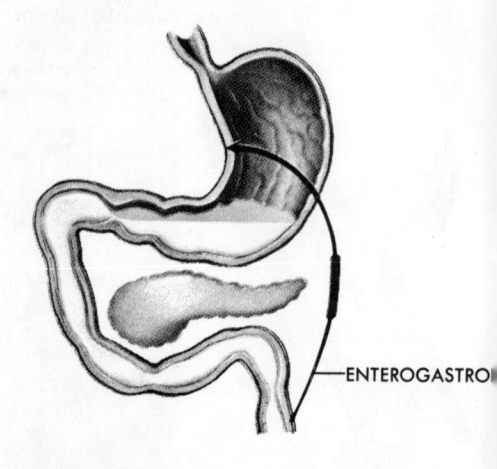

Nervous and Hormonal Control of Digestion

The digestive apparatus is richly supplied with nerves which control the activity of the muscles and glands of the digestive organs. These nerves are not under conscious control, but form part of the vast automatic, or autonomic nervous system, which has its centers of control in the more primitive parts of the brain. The system is divided into two parts: one division stimulates digestive function, while the other inhibits digestion and prepares the body for vigorous exertion. These effects result from the action of the two basic types of nerves found in the autonomic nervous system, the cholinergic and the adrenergic. The cholinergic fibers stimulate the flow of digestive juices and increase muscular activity in the digestive organs. The adrenergic fibers are activated by strong emotions such as fear and anger. They mobilize the body's resources for intense exertion by inhibiting digestion and by shunting blood from the skin and abdominal organs to the muscles of the arms, legs, and brain.

The secretions of the digestive tract are also regulated by hormones given off by the small intestine. Various foods stimulate the intestine to secrete hormones which travel through the blood stream to act upon the stomach, pancreas, liver, and on the intestinal lining itself.

Digestive Disorders

Digestive disturbances may be brought about by abnormal changes in the digestive organs, by diseases in other organs which result in poor digestive functioning, or by emotional problems which produce digestive symptoms in the absence of actual disease of the digestive organs. For example lack of appetite (anorexia) may result from an inflamed stomach lining (gastritis), from a common cold, or from a psychic disorder—such as anorexia nervosa, which appears in young women.

Disease of the organs of digestion may be present from birth, as in cystic fibrosis, in which the obstruction of certain ducts in the pancreas prevents essential fat and protein digesting enzymes from reaching the intestine. Other conditions arise later in life, such as gallstones which may block the normal flow of bile, causing severe abdominal pains and jaundice. Intestinal parasites which rob the body of nutrients are common in some tropical regions. Bacterial toxins are responsible for the violent digestive upsets associated with certain types of food poisoning.

Symptoms of digestive disorders may be produced by disease of the heart, lungs, kidneys, or other organs. A heart attack may be mistaken for an upset stomach, pneumonia may be responsible for abdominal pains, inflammation of the fallopian tubes which carry the egg from the ovary to the womb may result in pains which mimic acute appendicitis.

Emotional distress may produce peptic ulcers, and possibly ulcerations of the colon (ulcerative colitis). Chronic constipation, belching, and heartburn may also be produced by emotional difficulties.

The frequently misleading nature of abdominal pains and digestive difficulties makes the problem of diagnosis particularly difficult.

See also INTESTINE; LIVER; PANCREAS; STOMACH.

DIGESTIVE SYSTEM. *See* DIGESTION; HUMAN ANATOMY.

DIGITALIS [dĭj-ə-tăl′ĭs], name given to a group of chemically related drugs obtained from the dried leaves of certain flowering plants (*Digitalis purpurea* and *D. lanata*). Digitalis was mentioned in the writings of Welsh physicians as early as 1250 and for some time it was indiscriminately used to treat a wide variety of unrelated disorders. It is now recognized that the therapeutic benefits of digitalis can be traced to its action on the heart. It is used today to treat heart failure and certain irregularities of the heartbeat.

DIPHOSPHOPYRIDINE NUCLEOTIDE [dī-fŏs-fō-pĭr′ə-dēn nū′klē-ə-tīd], also known as DPN, a complex substance found in muscle, blood cells, and the retina of the eye. DPN acts in conjunction with numerous enzymes to process foods (amino acids, fats, glucose) in the body. It is found in particularly high concentrations in yeast, where it is essential for the fermentation of sugar into alcohol.

DIPHTHERIA [dĭf-thēr′ē-ə], an infectious disease caused by the diphtheria bacillus. The bacilli are sprayed from the throat of a patient or carrier of the disease to land in the throat, windpipe, or other exposed surface of a victim (usually a susceptible child). Although they tend to grow only where they have entered the body, the bacteria secrete a poison which damages the heart and nervous system.

The symptoms of diphtheria depend on where the bacillus has attacked. The most dreaded form of the disease affects the larynx (the voicebox) and the windpipe below it, both small enough to be blocked by the diphtheritic membrane which develops in response to the infection. The child may strangle unless an opening is made in its windpipe (tracheotomy).

Other major forms of diphtheria affect the tonsils and the nose. Tonsillar diphtheria causes a severe sore throat, in which the diphtheritic membrane is clearly visible. In nasal diphtheria there is less danger of obstruction to breathing, but more danger of toxin flooding the body, causing heart damage and paralysis. In rare cases the diphtheria bacillus may invade exposed areas outside the respiratory passages, such as the eye, the ear, or injured skin.

The principal means of treatment is an antitoxin which can counteract the effect of the poison given off by the diphtheria bacillus. The antitoxin cannot reverse the damage done to tissues which have been exposed to the toxin. Consequently it must be given immediately after the diagnosis is made, as even a few hours' delay may be fatal. Other treatment consists of bed rest and a humidity tent or steam room to help relieve the obstruction to breathing.

Immunization is the only known means of controlling the disease. Two or three injections of diphtheria toxoid are given at one-month intervals, usually starting at the age of three months. Booster doses are given afterward. Immunization has been so successful that it has actually increased the peril to each patient for diphtheria is now so rare that it may go unrecognized at first, resulting in a dangerous delay in treatment.

DIPLOCOCCUS [dĭp-lō-kŏk′əs], designation for spherical

DISEASE

bacteria which occur in pairs, and particularly for a genus of such bacteria (*Neisseria*). This genus includes organisms which cause pneumonia, gonorrhea, and epidemic meningitis. A variety of diplococci are normally present in the upper respiratory tract.
See also BACTERIA.

DISEASE, condition of impaired health resulting from a disturbance in the structure or function of the body.

The History of Ideas Concerning Disease

Ancient man believed that disease was caused by a supernatural being or through magic practiced by another person. Treatment was administered by medicine men who achieved their results largely through the power of suggestion.

Some clear thinking concerning the origin of disease was introduced by Hippocrates, the ancient Greek physician, who is known as the "Father of Medicine," and whose oath is still sworn to by modern physicians. Hippocrates denied that diseases were punishments of the gods, but believed that they were caused by food, occupation, and climate. The physicians of this time held that there were four "humors": blood, phlegm, yellow bile, and black bile. All diseases were thought to be caused by a disturbance of the delicate balance of these humours.

It was not until the 19th century that the role of microorganisms as a cause of disease was firmly established. The German physician Robert Koch conclusively demonstrated that anthrax, a disease of animals and men, was caused by the *Bacillus anthracis*. Following Koch's proof of the germ theory of disease, a large number of micro-organisms were shown to be disease-producing agents. In recent years much attention has been focused on understanding the causes of noninfectious diseases, such as diabetes, gout, and arteriosclerosis. Advances in the knowledge of physiology and biochemistry have brought with them a greater understanding of those diseases which are unrelated to infection, but which are caused by disturbances in the normal functioning of the body.

The Types of Diseases

Diseases may be classified into the following major categories: infectious, allergic, congenital, deficiency, hereditary, metabolic, neoplastic, toxic, and psychosomatic and mental.

Infectious Diseases. One of the largest disease categories is the infectious group. This includes diseases caused by viruses, rickettsia, bacteria, fungi, protozoa, and worms.

The viruses are the smallest of the infectious organisms and are further distinguished by the fact that they can multiply only within living cells. Important virus diseases are the common cold, poliomyelitis, chickenpox, smallpox, and mumps. Many but not all of the virus infections are followed by long-lasting immunity.

The rickettsia are larger than viruses, but are smaller than bacteria. They share some of the characteristics of both groups. The rickettsia are almost always transmitted to man by ticks, fleas, mites, and lice. The rickettsial diseases produce fever and skin rashes and include typhus, Rocky Mountain spotted fever, Tsutsugamushi disease, and Q Fever. Like viruses, rickettsia frequently produce a long-lasting immunity after infection.

Bacteria cause disease directly by multiplying in a part of the body, or indirectly by causing an allergic reaction, or by giving off poisonous substances. Some of the diseases caused directly by bacteria are: pneumonia, caused by the pneumococcus; sore throat, caused by the streptococcus; meningitis, an infection of the central nervous system caused by the meningococcus; whooping cough, caused by the hemophilus pertussis; and tuberculosis, caused by the tubercle bacillus. Lockjaw (tetanus), diphtheria, and various types of food poisoning are caused by poisonous substances given off by bacteria.

Fungi produce skin diseases such as athlete's foot, and generalized infections of the body such as actinomycosis, blastomycosis, and histoplasmosis.

Protozoa are single-celled, primitive animals which are responsible for malaria and amebic dysentery, among other disorders.

Infestations by parasitic worms, such as ascaris, pinworm, tapeworm, and hookworm are common in warm climates where sanitary facilities are poor. The ascaris, or giant intestinal roundworm, may reach an adult length of about 14 in. in the human digestive tract.

Allergic Diseases. These diseases are caused by the interaction of antigens, foreign substances, usually proteins, with antibodies, substances produced by the body to combat antigens. The symptoms of allergic disease appear to be caused by the release of histamine, or a histaminelike substance, at the site of the allergic reaction. These chemicals cause fluid to be released into the tissues, resulting in the swellings which characterize allergic diseases. Diseases included in the allergic category are hay fever, asthma, drug reactions, and skin inflammation resulting from contact with allergic materials (contact dermatitis).

Congenital Defects. These include clubfoot, dwarfism, cleft palate, hare lip, and certain forms of heart disease. The defects result from disturbances in development while the fetus is in the womb. For the most part the causes of congenital defects are unknown, but some are inherited through the parents. The only other known causes are the occurrence of German measles in the mother during the first three months of pregnancy and exposure of the pregnant woman to high doses of X-ray treatments or to drugs.

Deficiency Diseases. The absence of certain food substances from the diet, or the failure to properly absorb them from the intestinal tract may interfere with normal body function and cause disease. Scurvy, once the plague of sailors, develops from lack of vitamin C; pellagra, a disease of the skin, gastrointestinal tract, and nervous system, results from the absence of niacin. Other vitamin deficiency diseases are rickets and beriberi. A failure to absorb vitamin B_{12} is found in pernicious anemia. In the intestinal disorder sprue there is interference with the absorption of many necessary food substances.

Hereditary Diseases. These diseases are transmitted by defective hereditary units, or genes. A classical example is hemophilia, a tendency to bleed excessively. The gene is carried by women, but the disease appears only in men. In some diseases, such as diabetes mellitus, a tendency to develop the disease may be inherited, but the disorder may not actually appear unless some stress is present.

Metabolic Diseases. This group includes those illnesses which are caused by defects in the body's ability to carry out the normal chemical activities involved in the production of energy and the building-up of body tissue. These defects may be inherited as in the case of phenylketonuria, a disease resulting in a particular form of mental deficiency. An example of a possibly nonhereditary metabolic disease is atherosclerosis, a form of hardening of the arteries in which substances deposited along the walls of arteries narrow the opening and interfere with circulation.

Neoplastic Disease. This includes cancer—a wild, uncontrolled growth of the cells of the body. Cancer may arise in any part of the body and can cause a variety of symptoms, depending upon location and type of cancer.

Toxic Diseases. This category includes those diseases which result from the consumption of, or exposure to, toxic agents, such as carbon tetrachloride, benzene, carbon monoxide, arsenic, lead, and barbiturates. Overdoses of certain vitamins may also be toxic.

Psychosomatic and Mental Diseases

Psychosomatic Diseases. In recent years it has been realized that many bodily ailments, such as peptic ulcer, high blood pressure, and asthma, may be caused or influenced by emotional disorders. A dramatic example of the ability of the mind to interfere with bodily function appears in hysteria, which may cause blindness or paralysis in the absence of any organic injury or disease. The number of diseases placed within the psychosomatic group is steadily expanding.

Mental Disease. The two broad classifications of mental disease are the psychoses and the neuroses. The psychotic individual is usually regarded as having lost contact with reality. The neurotic is aware of reality, but is the victim of powerful unconscious drives which distort his behavior. Little is known of the causes of mental diseases and a long-standing controversy in the field concerns the extent to which these diseases are of physical or mental origin.

In conclusion, it is frequently not possible to place a disease within a single classification. For example, since some metabolic diseases are inherited they could be grouped in the hereditary category. The causes of other diseases, such as rheumatoid arthritis, are not completely understood, making categorization even more difficult. One can expect that, as the knowledge of diseases and their causes becomes more extensive, the classification of diseases will change considerably.

See also MEDICINE.

DISINFECTANTS, agents which kill disease-producing organisms. Most disinfectants are chemicals, such as acids, alkalis, halogens, heavy metals, formaldehyde, alcohols, phenols, dyes, and soaps. Less commonly, ultraviolet radiation and solutions of silver and copper are used as disinfectants. Disinfectants are used to destroy harmful micro-organisms found in food and water and on household surfaces and utensils. Unlike antiseptics, disinfectants can generally not be safely applied to living tissues.

See also ANTISEPTICS.

DISSOCIATION, in psychology, the breakdown of a complex conscious mental process into simpler components, which continue to function autonomously but which can only become conscious singly. After a severe accident, a person may enter a dreamlike state in which he perceives everything around him but in which everything seems unreal. In this state, his perception has become dissociated from his emotions, and only the former remains conscious. Similar cleavages in the psyche may also occur during illness with high fever, and in hypnosis, or trance.

Most often, dissociation is seen in emotional disorders where the splitting off of parts of consciousness may lead to a dual personality. In such cases the patient may be in a so-called fugue state, during which his awareness is narrowed and his memory impaired. The patient may lead a totally different life, and if he regains knowledge of his former life, he may forget everything he experienced during the fugue. Stevenson's *Dr. Jekyll and Mr. Hyde* is an example of alternating fugue states, resulting in a multiple personality.

DIURETICS [dī-yōō-rĕt'ĭks], compounds which reduce the amount of fluid in the body by increasing the volume of urine flow. Normally the human body consists of 45% to 70% water, which is contained in the cells, in the tissue spaces between the cells, and in the blood. In certain conditions, such as congestive heart failure, nephrosis, cirrhosis, and premenstrual edema, the fluid balance is upset and fluid accumulates in the tissue spaces, a condition known as edema. In congestive heart failure, for example, the heart does not pump enough blood, and fluid which would normally be changed into urine accumulates in the tissue spaces and the blood. This may first be noticed as a swelling in the ankles. Edema was recognized by the ancient Greeks; the Romans treated the condition by inserting a tube through the skin to drain fluid from the abdomen. In modern therapy diuretics are used to relieve edema.

Diuretics differ in the manner in which they promote urine flow. The most frequently used diuretics act directly upon the kidney (thiazides, acetazoleamide, organic mercurials, xanthines). Others may alter the acidity-alkalinity balance of the blood (ammonium or calcium chloride), or increase the fluid-holding power of the blood by raising its osmotic pressure (acacia, albumin). These drugs may occasionally cause side effects, such as skin rashes, nausea, vomiting, weakness, dizziness, muscle cramps, and acute pancreatitis. Diuretics are generally of no value when urine is not produced because of inadequate kidney function or when urine is retained in the bladder.

DIVERTICULOSIS [dī-vər-tĭk-yə-lō'sĭs], the presence of pouches in the walls of the gastrointestinal tract. They occur most commonly in the lower portion of the large bowel. Diverticula are more common in older persons and may be associated with chronic constipation, obesity, and the tissue degeneration that occurs with age. Usually symptoms are not present unless the pouch becomes infected, with resultant abdominal pain, tenderness, and fever.

DRAMAMINE [drăm'ə-mēn], trade name for dimenhy-

drinate, an antihistaminic drug used to treat and prevent sea, air, and car sickness. It is also used to treat certain ailments of the ear and brain which cause dizziness and loss of balance. Drowsiness is a common side effect of dramamine.
See also ANTIHISTAMINES.

DREAMS, a series of images, thoughts, or emotions occurring in the mind during sleep or daydreaming. Dreams have aroused interest and reverence since the beginnings of mankind—examples of prophetic dreams and dream explanations are found throughout the Bible. In many primitive societies the dream state is considered a sojourn of the soul outside the body during sleep.

For the individual, fantasy and dreams may be considered irrational symbolic ways of dealing with reality, comparable to the use of myth and legend by societies. Sigmund Freud published *The Interpretation of Dreams* in 1900. This study of the nature of dreams shows them to be expressions of unconscious processes, such as suppressed wishes or unresolved problems.

Dream research has acquired a physiological aspect through the discovery of periods of Rapid Eye Movement (REM) during sleep. It is during REM periods that occur the vividly detailed, unrealistic, and "hallucinatory" dreams remembered after awakening. Although rapid eye movements are the most obvious indicator of such REM periods during sleep, other changes have also been documented, such as changes in the brain-wave patterns and increases in respiratory and cardiovascular activity.

Four to five REM periods normally occur each night, lasting approximately 20 min. each. These REM periods are separated by Non Rapid Eye Movement (NREM) periods, lasting approximately 90 min. NREM periods produce realistic, though vague, dreams, which are difficult to recall upon awakening. Deprivation of REM sleep, by awakening the subject every time he shows signs of REM, leads to increasingly disturbed mental life. The significance of this observation for determining the causes of mental disease is under extensive study.
See also SLEEP.

DREW, CHARLES RICHARD (1904–50), U.S. Negro medical researcher. Born in Washington, D.C., he graduated from McGill University Medical College. Drew did pioneer research in methods of collecting and storing blood plasma. He established a blood bank for the British government during World War II, and was then appointed director of the first U.S. Red Cross blood bank. After the war he served as chief surgeon of Howard University Medical School, and did research on fluid balances in surgery.

DROPSY. See EDEMA.

DROWNING, death from suffocation caused by water in the lungs. Ordinarily, an individual cannot be revived after five minutes of submersion in water, but in some cases life may be restored even after 15 minutes under water.
See ARTIFICIAL RESPIRATION.

DRUG ADDICTION, a term used in drug abuse discussions, is frequently confused with psychological dependence (or habituation) and physical dependence. These expressions are often erroneously interchanged, causing semantic confusion. The World Health Organization (WHO) has recommended that these terms be replaced by a single generic expression, "drug dependence," which is itself qualified by designating the particular drug under discussion—for example, "drug dependence of the barbiturate type." Common usage and many laws employ all of these terms and they should be understood in the following context:

Psychological dependence is a state of drug abuse which exists when the user feels that the effects of the drug are necessary to maintain a sense of well-being. There is an emotional or mental adaptation to the effects of the drug, since continued usage appears to satisfy some emotional or personality needs of the individual. The user may experience a degree of psychological involvement ranging from desire to craving to compulsion. An accepted synonym for this particular state is habituation.

Physical dependence is a physiological adaptation in which the drug is required to prevent the onset of a withdrawal or an abstinence syndrome. Abstinence syndromes vary depending upon the particular drug dependency. When a heroin addict is intoxicated, he is sedated, but in withdrawal, a state of excitation predominates. The intoxicated amphetamine user is agitated and excitable, but in withdrawal, a state of depression and exhaustion prevails, and the individual often lapses into deep sleep for long periods. It is probable that physical dependence occurs, at least to a certain degree, after a single dose of an opiate or barbiturate. The aftereffect of this initial drug experience may be a slight aggravation of the underlying anxieties which led to the use of the drug originally and the beginning of the withdrawal phase. The cycle of chronic and repetitive use may thus have been triggered in the susceptible user. The absence of physical dependence, such as noted with most hallucinogens or psychedelics, for example, LSD, does not prove that such drugs are innocuous.

The exact cause or mechanism of the abstinence syndrome is unknown. The reaction to the sudden deprivation of a drug which causes physical dependence depends, to a large degree, upon the dosage level and frequency of use of the particular drug. The withdrawal symptoms disappear as the body readjusts over a period of time or if the drug is reintroduced.

Tolerance is a potentially serious medical and pharmacological problem, in which increasing quantities of the drug must be taken in order to obtain the same effect. This becomes especially dangerous when dealing with narcotics, amphetamines, and the sedative-hypnotic group of drugs, such as the barbiturates and alcohol. The various effects of a particular drug are not necessarily affected by this phenomenon at the same rate. For example, insomnia persists in the amphetamine user as do the constricted pupils of the opiate user, regardless of changes in dosage or frequency of administration. Tolerance is most often associated with drugs causing physical dependence.

Addiction is properly defined as a state of periodic or chronic intoxication produced by the repeated consumption of a drug. Associated with this state is a compulsive and overwhelming involvement on the part of the addict with the procurement and use of the drug. Addiction to the specific drug involves psychological dependence, tolerance, and usually, physical dependence. Physical dependence may be present without "addiction," in this generally accepted sense, as evidenced by the newborn child of a heroin addict. Clearly, there is no psychological involvement on the part of the infant.

Types of Addiction

In general, the commonly abused drugs fit into four major categories: *narcotics, central nervous system stimulants, psychedelics,* and the *sedative-hypnotic group.* In a broad sense "drug abuse" is defined as the self-administration of a drug in a manner that deviates from approved social patterns. In reality, this may involve any drug, but we are here referring to the abuse of drugs that are taken for the purpose of producing changes in mood and behavior, and which are obtained illicitly (not forgetting the other major problem of legal drug abuse). Implicit in this concept is the consideration that society's acceptance of various drugs changes from time to time and from culture to culture—for example, the practice of opium smoking was accepted in China until quite recently.

Narcotics. This group includes opiates derived from the opium poppy, such as morphine, or chemically related derivatives, such as heroin or methadone. They are best characterized as effective analgesics (actually, there is an altered reaction to pain, since the pain itself may be perceived), and profound central nervous system depressants. The frequently described euphoria associated with narcotics may be due to the relief of pain, tension, and anxiety in those with low thresholds. The terms "addiction" and "addict" most commonly refer to the problem of opiate dependence, which is now considered a medical illness rather than a form of criminality. Criminal activity results from the need to obtain a supply of the drug rather than from the effects of the drug itself.

The majority of the effects of opiate addiction, excluding so-called overdose and respiratory depression, are not directly related to the drug action. Most complications or untoward medical effects such as serum hepatitis, skin infections, blood poisoning, anemia, tetanus, and malnutrition are related to the manner in which the illicit drug is used and the kind of life the addict lives.

Recognition of the chronic narcotic addict by means of his pin-point pupils and scars or pigmentation over the veins is usually not difficult. The major medical problems due to the action of the opiates are related to overdosage and to abstinence symptoms. The nonfatal overdose can be diagnosed promptly in the suspected user if widespread fluid accumulation in the lungs is accompanied by stupor, small pupils, and either a normal or slowed breathing rate. The overdose produces profound central nervous system depression, including respiratory center depression, leading to the paradox of fluid accumulation in the lungs without the usual increase in rate of respiration. Since the effects are reversible, the use of specific antinarcotic chemicals and prompt supportive treatment, including positive pressure oxygen and maintenance of the blood pressure, may be life-saving.

In the United States most of the illicit narcotics use involves heroin, the most potent of the opiates. If the narcotic addict cannot obtain his drug, he displays the abstinence syndrome. The intensity of withdrawal increases with the degree of physical dependence, symptoms usually starting 8 to 12 hours after the last "fix" and peaking at 36 to 72 hours. Symptoms include any or all of the following: nervousness, anxiety, sleeplessness, yawning, tearing, profuse perspiration, muscle cramps and twitching, vomiting and diarrhea, rapid heart beat and breathing rate. Administering methadone, itself a synthetic narcotic, or certain tranquilizers for three to five days eases the withdrawal symptoms, and there is no objection to the use of sedatives.

Whereas the initial medical withdrawal from narcotics is relatively easy, the prospects for long-term success are not good. In addition to the effects of tolerance and overwhelming drug dependence, the high percentage of failure of rehabilitation efforts may result from the considerable reinforcement of the habit due to the following factors: (1) heroin suppresses all disturbing sources of the user's anxiety (those related to pain, sexuality, and expressions of aggression)—a total satiation of drive; (2) acceptance into the fraternity of other addicts; and (3) conditioning, an eventual state whereby even after long-term withdrawal, there is an intense craving for the drug in situations where the drug is known to be available. Occasionally, an addict's mere presence in a familiar neighborhood has been said to precipitate a modified abstinence syndrome.

Concerning long-term therapy, it is generally agreed that there is no universally acceptable program nor any single effective method for the rehabilitation of all narcotic addicts. Arrest and incarceration have taken addicts "off the street" but have not acted as deterrents to increased drug addiction. The United States Public Health Service hospitals at Lexington, Ky., and Fort Worth, Tex., established for the treatment of narcotic addicts, likewise have a high readmission rate. Self-help communities run by ex-addicts and following the Synanon-Daytop model have been developed while the chemotherapeutic approach, most notably using methadone in high doses to block the euphoric effects of heroin, is being expanded.

Central Nervous System Stimulants. The abuse of amphetamines, the major representative of this category, is a major health hazard due to the rapid increase in their use and the drugs' inherent biological dangers. The amphetamines are powerful central nervous system stimulants and with moderate dosages, an increase in work performance, alertness, agitation, sleeplessness, diminished fatigue, and loss of appetite are usually observed. With chronic and increasing use, the following adverse effects often occur: irritability, insomnia, aggression, bizarre and sometimes inappropriate repetitive actions, and, eventually, panic, confusion, and paranoid psychosis. Other medical problems include effects related to unsterile intravenous usage, as noted with heroin addiction. The use of the stimulant to augment energy and produce euphoria is often intermittently counteracted by the use of barbiturates to allay agitation and insomnia—the "yo-yo" phenomenon or the "ups and downs" syndrome. There is a rapid onset of tolerance and considerable psychological dependence on the part of the user.

Although a characteristic withdrawal syndrome does

not develop when amphetamines are suddenly stopped (thus there is no true physical dependence) there is a reaction phase of exhaustion, sleep, and depression (the "crash"). Because of the sometimes overwhelming psychological dependence they produce, amphetamines are considered addicting. In some areas, young persons are told that heroin eases the crash, and the increasing use of heroin in the schools and suburbs may, in part, reflect and parallel the "speed," or amphetamine, epidemic. In addition, in order to augment the opiate euphoria, intravenous amphetamines are now frequently being used together, with heroin substituting for the older cocaine-heroin combination (colloquially known as the "speedball").

Psychedelics. Because of its potency and widespread availability, LSD is by far the most important hallucinogen, Marihuana, the object of a greater notoriety, is a minor medical or pharmacological drug. The psychedelics are potentially capable of producing psychological dependence in the user, but there is no evidence that they cause physical dependence or addiction. LSD, and probably the other psychedelics, act almost entirely on the higher central nervous system centers. Apparently they permit a bombardment of sensory stimuli, which are unaffected by the usual selective filtering-out processes that function in the brain. A short-lived tolerance occurs with LSD whereby a loss of hallucinogenic effect is noted after a few doses are taken within a short period. After a few days, the psychedelic effects are again evident. A cross-tolerance to other psychedelics such as mescaline also occurs.

Sedative-Hypnotic Group. The model is the barbiturates, the "downs" or "goof-balls," but the group includes among others, alcohol. Each has a potential for abuse, and chronic use results in tolerance and psychological and physical dependence. Taken in combination, there may be a greater reaction than when each is used alone, and each, especially on withdrawal, can cause convulsions, coma, and death.

The initial feeling of tranquility, elation, and well-being, which low doses of barbiturates provide, soon gives way in the chronic, excessive user to irritability, impairment of mental ability, reduced motor co-ordination, confusion, lack of concern, time distortion, inappropriate mood shifts, and general emotional instability. He simultaneously experiences a decreased inhibition of basic drives with the resultant exaggeration of basic conflicts. This state differs from that of the opiate addict, who usually experiences a total satiation of drives.

Despite tolerance, the lethal dose for the addict does not differ greatly from that for the non-addict. The innocent cocktail party thus may prove lethal for the barbiturate addict. Withdrawal from barbiturate addiction is serious, often deadly, clearly more difficult to handle than heroin withdrawal, and should be treated only in a general hospital setting. The withdrawal mimics the delirium tremens of alcohol, and similar brain-wave abnormalities are noted. This is really a "general depressant withdrawal" syndrome.

Symptoms of withdrawal, resembling those of intoxication and starting in about 12 hours, include restlessness, anxiety, fine tremors, abdominal cramps, nausea and vomiting, and low standing blood pressure. After 24 hours, coarse tremors and hyperactive reflexes begin and the addict literally pleads for the drug. Convulsions and coma follow within a few days if therapy is not initiated. Actually, withdrawal should be a gradual, tapering process, lasting several weeks.

See also BARBITURATES; HEROIN; LSD; MARIHUANA; NARCOTICS; NARCOTICS TRAFFIC; OPIUM; PSYCHOPHARMACOLOGY.

DRUGS, substances used in the treatment of disease. Drug therapy is one of the oldest forms of medical treatment. The Ebers Papyrus, an ancient Egyptian medical treatise, contains recipes and prescriptions for the treatment of diseases of the eyes, skin, and internal organs. In China and India "herbals," or collections of herb remedies, were compiled hundreds of years before the birth of Christ. Primitive tribes used quinine for malaria, ipecac for dysentery, and rauwolfia for a host of ailments.

Until the 20th century drugs were obtained primarily from plants. Beginning about 1900 drugs from animal sources became available. These included the hormones, such as epinephrine (adrenalin), insulin, and the male and female sex hormones. The development of organic chemistry made possible the synthesis of pure compounds to replace the crude mixtures prepared by brewing or steeping plants.

Many drugs can now be synthesized more cheaply than they can be isolated from plants and animals. In some cases new and better compounds can be synthesized.

Types of Drugs

While there is no completely satisfactory or logical method of classifying drugs, most can be grouped on the basis of their general effects on the body, or by their medical use.

Drugs used to combat infections and infestations caused by bacteria, viruses, protozoa, or worms, are known as "antiparasitic" drugs. The antibiotics are included in this group.

Drugs Which Depress the Central Nervous System. A large category includes those drugs which depress the activity of the brain and spinal cord. Some of these drugs produce a loss of sensation and consciousness and are used for general anesthesia (ether). The narcotics (opium, morphine) are important pain-relievers. Sedatives and hypnotics produce calm and sleep, respectively. The most important sedatives are the barbiturates, which are found in many sleeping potions. The "anticonvulsants" reduce or prevent the epileptic seizures seen in epilepsy. Aspirin and related compounds are termed "antipyretic analgesics," because they have the dual action of relieving pain and reducing fever. A comparatively new group of drugs are the tranquilizers, which calm anxiety and dull emotional responses without producing drowsiness.

Drugs Which Act upon the Automatic (Autonomic) Nervous System. A large group of drugs act on certain portions of the nervous system (the autonomic nervous system) that control automatic, involuntary functions such as the rate of heartbeat, blood pressure, intestinal movements, and the size of the pupils. These autonomic drugs include epinephrine, a substance normally present in the body, which helps to prepare the body for muscular exertion by increasing the blood pressure and heart rates and by stimulating the release of sugar into the blood stream. Other autonomic drugs, such as methacholine, lower the blood pressure and stimulate the movement of the digestive tract and the flow of digestive juices.

Other classifications of drugs include those which help prevent clotting of the blood (anticoagulants) and those which stimulate kidney action (diuretics). The term "digitalis" describes a group of drugs obtained from digitalis and related species. These drugs strengthen the force of the heartbeat and are useful in treating certain types of heart disease. Hormones, such as insulin and thyroxin, may be used as drugs to meet the deficiencies which may arise from the malfunctioning of the pancreas and thyroid glands. Cortisone and hydrocortisone are hormones which are used to treat a large number of diseases involving inflammatory responses.

The Administration of Drugs

The method of giving a drug is often determined by the manner in which the body acts upon it. Many commonly used substances are readily absorbed from the stomach or intestine, and so can be taken by mouth. Examples of such drugs are aspirin, the sulfonamides, and the barbiturates. Certain drugs, however, cannot be readily absorbed from the gastrointestinal tract and so must be injected under the skin, or into muscles or veins. The hormone insulin must be injected, since it is not absorbed well from the gastrointestinal tract and it is destroyed by digestive enzymes.

Disposition in the Body. After entering the body, some drugs remain in the blood stream. Others may leave the circulatory system to penetrate the tissue fluids. Still others may gain access to particular regions, such as the brain or eye. The action of the drug will be influenced by its ability to penetrate to the target area and the manner in which the body acts upon it. The chemical activity of the body may rapidly change the drug to an inactive form. Also of importance is the rate at which the substance is removed from the body. In the case of potentially harmful drugs their rapid removal from the body may make possible their use.

Drug Action. Knowledge of the exact mechanism by which drugs produce their effects is as yet quite hazy. While it is known, for example, that when insulin is given to the diabetic the blood sugar will be lowered, the manner in which insulin achieves this effect is not clear. Similarly the ability of ether to produce stimulation in small doses and loss of sensation and consciousness and ultimately death, with increasing dosages, is familiar but poorly understood. The question remains as to exactly what changes ether causes in the cells of the brain and spinal cord.

Drug Toxicity. Since drugs are by definition chemicals that alter body function, it is clear that excess doses of any drug may produce harmful effects. The difference between the dose of a drug producing a desired effect (the therapeutic dose), and that producing a toxic effect (toxic dose), is sometimes referred to as the margin of safety. This margin varies, both for different drugs and for different individuals given the same drug. In some cases the margin is so narrow that undesired actions ("side effects") will appear. In addition to toxicity there is the possibility of an allergic sensitivity even to small doses of the substance which are quite harmless for the nonallergic subject. A well-known example is penicillin, which is normally not toxic for man at the doses needed to kill susceptible bacteria. In rare cases, however, a patient may experience a violent allergic reaction even to minute doses of penicillin.

Drug Resistance. In the decades since antimicrobials were introduced, it has become increasingly clear that many bacteria develop resistance to their effect. Among the most serious problems are infections caused by staphylococci and the Enterobacteriaceae. This group includes *Escherichia coli*, the colon bacillus; *Salmonella*, which causes many ills, including typhoid; and *Shigella*, a dysentery bacillus. The staphylococci are resistant to most antibiotics, including penicillin G, the tetracyclines, chloramphenicol, streptomycin, and erythromycin. The basis of staphylococcic resistance is small, extrachromosomal elements called plasmids—minute pieces of DNA which allow the bacteria to make proteins able to interfere with antibiotic action.

The concept of antibiotic resistance originated in Japan in 1959 with the discovery of *Shigella* bacteria, able to resist six antibiotics. Some bacteria also contain a transfer factor, a small piece of DNA called an episome, which is not attached to the chromosome and not essential to the cell. When such a bacterium mates with another, it transfers this factor to the new cell, enabling it, too, to make antibiotic-resistant proteins. With the use of antibiotics in animal feeds, more and more bacteria have developed resistance factors. If a bacterium has both resistance and transfer factors, it can infect other, unrelated bacteria. Because these bacteria mate in the intestines, they are known as enteric bacteria. Enteric bacteria resistant to six or more antibiotics have been found in Japan, the United States, Britain, and Africa.

See also ANTIBIOTICS; SALMONELLA; STAPHYLOCOCCUS.

DUNN, LESLIE CLARENCE (1893–   ), American geneticist. He received a B.A. from Dartmouth, a D.Sc. from Harvard. After holding positions elsewhere, in 1928 he became professor of zoology at Columbia University. His most influential contributions have concerned studies of lethal mutations in mice which permitted investigation of the effects of genes in early stages of development. Among his many published works are *Heredity and Evolution in Human Populations* (1959), and *Heredity, Race, and Society* (1946), co-authored by Theodosius Dobzhansky.

DWARF, abnormally small human being. The term "dwarf" is frequently used to mean a person of small stature born in a racial group of normal size. "Pygmy" refers to a member of a racial group in which average height is unusually small. Dwarfs are mentioned in the records of ancient Egypt, Greece, and Rome. Mark Antony is said to have had a dwarf named Sisyphus, 24 in. tall. Many European rulers of more recent times, including Charles IX of France and Peter the Great of Russia, kept dwarfs at their courts. Midgets at the court

DWARFISM

Charles S. Stratton, known as General Tom Thumb.

of Spain appear in paintings by Velázquez. In England, Henrietta Maria, wife of King Charles I, had two famous dwarfs: Richard Gibson was, appropriately enough, "court miniature painter"; Sir Jeffrey Hudson was a courtier who figured in two duels and the Civil War.

Probably the best known dwarf in history was General Tom Thumb (Charles Sherwood Stratton), an American circus performer whose fame was promoted by P. T. Barnum. At maturity he was about 3 ft., 4 in. tall.

In Teutonic mythology dwarfs were diminutive, ugly, clever, malevolent creatures who grew from the maggots in the body of the giant Ymir. Inhabitants of large isolated rocks and dark subterranean caverns, dwarfs were unable to bear sunlight. They were guardians of mines and metals and skillful craftsmen of weapons and ornaments. Four dwarfs—Austri, Vestri, Nordri, and Sudri—upheld the sky. The most famous dwarfs in European folk tales were the seven dwarfs in the story of Snow White.
See also DWARFISM; ELF; PYGMY.

DWARFISM, abnormally small stature which is most commonly caused by disease of the bones or glands. Dwarfism resulting from a deficiency of the growth hormone of the pituitary gland produces a well-proportioned dwarf usually with no signs of mental deficiency or impaired sexual development. In cretinism, caused by the absence of thyroid hormone in infancy and childhood, a deformed and mentally-retarded dwarf results, with pronounced skeletal deformity. In achondroplasia, a congenital disease involving abnormal bone development, the arms and legs are short in relation to the length of the body. These individuals display a typical facial expression which is formed by the high broad forehead, the flattened nose bridge, and the prominent lower jaw. The arms and legs are often bowed. Mental and sexual development are usually normal. In rickets, a nutritional disorder caused by a deficiency of vitamin D, bone growth is interfered with, producing dwarfism with marked bowing of the legs. In inherited, or genetic, dwarfism, body proportion and sexual development are normal. Dwarfism may also result from abnormal functioning of the gonads or from malnutrition.

Tendencies to dwarfism resulting from glandular disorders can be halted in some cases by administering glandular extracts. Rickets can be treated and prevented by giving vitamin D.

DYSENTERY [dĭs′ən-tĕr-ē] is a painful inflammation of the large intestine; it is usually accompanied by severe diarrhea. The principal types are amebic dysentery and bacillary dysentery.

Amebic Dysentery is caused by the ameba *Endamoeba histolytica*. This single-celled organism is found throughout the world, but is more common in the tropics. In the United States approximately 12 million people are estimated to be infected. In areas of the world having poor sanitation the organism may be present in half of the population.

The parasite has two forms. Outside of the body it exists as a cyst, consisting of several amebae contained within a protective wall, which enables them to resist drying and freezing. The cysts are swallowed with contaminated food. In the intestine the wall of the cyst is shed and the liberated organisms burrow into the intestinal wall. In the lower portion of the intestine, new cysts form and pass out into the feces. Infection spreads through the contaminated feces, which may pollute drinking water or be carried to food by insects or human hands. In some localities infection is spread by the practice of using human waste to fertilize crops.

The majority of persons infected with *E. histolytica* manifest no symptoms or discomfort. They are called carriers because, although not apparently ill, they may transmit the disease to others through their infected feces. Some cases may have mild indigestion and a slight fever. In severe cases diarrhea, developing over a three-to-four day period, is the most common symptom. Weakness, nausea, vomiting, and abdominal cramps are usually present. The attacks may disappear and recur at variable intervals. In rare instances the ameba may be carried by the blood stream to the liver, causing an abscess of that organ.

Severe untreated cases may be fatal. However, amebic dysentery can be treated readily through the use of various medications, including diodoquine, oxytetracycline, and carbarsone. The prevention of infection can be accomplished by sanitary disposal of human waste, control of food and water supplies, and the detection and treatment of carriers.

Bacillary Dysentery is caused by infection with bacteria of the genus *Shigella*. The most dangerous varieties of these organisms are found in the Orient. Epidemics are likely to occur where conditions are crowded and unsanitary, and for this reason the disease has played an important role in military history. The Greek historian Herodotus ascribed the defeat of the Persian armies in 480 B.C. to such an epidemic.

The infection is spread through infected feces, as in

amebic dysentery. Although some persons may act as carriers, bacillary dysentery differs from the amebic form in that most cases develop rapidly and display symptoms consisting of violent, often bloody, diarrhea, fever, chills, abdominal cramps, nausea, and vomiting. Five or more bowel movements an hour are not uncommon during the first day, and severe dehydration may result.

In treating bacillary dysentery fluids must be administered to replace those that are lost. In severe cases solutions containing sodium and potassium are introduced through the veins. Treatment with antibiotic drugs, such as the tetracyclines, helps relieve the symptoms in two or three days, and usually results in complete recovery within a week. In milder infections symptoms may be limited to one or two days of mild diarrhea.

Bacillary dysentery is not ordinarily fatal. The death rate in epidemics, however, may run as high as 30% if the victims are undernourished or are otherwise in poor physical condition. The preventive techniques used in amebic dysentery also apply to the bacillary form.

E

EAR, the organ of hearing and balance. The ear translates air-borne sound waves first into mechanical vibrations and then into electrical impulses which are conducted to the brain. The human ear can hear sounds ranging in loudness from a fleeting whisper to the roar of a subway train and can detect frequencies extending from the lower register of the bass fiddle to the upper notes of the trumpet. The familiar characteristics of heard sound are derived from the physical features of the sound wave. The intensity of the wave roughly corresponds to the loudness of the sound. The frequency is heard as pitch and the complexity lends timbre. How the ear faithfully transforms sound into nerve impulses and how the brain perceives tonal patterns and other complexities is not yet completely understood, but much has been learned.

The Three Parts of the Ear

The visible part of the ear is the least important from the point of view of hearing. Together with the external ear canal it comprises the external ear.

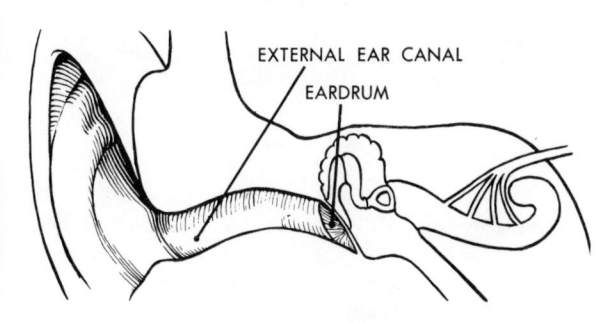

The middle ear begins at the eardrum which is linked to the ossicles, three delicate bones which are often picturesquely described as the hammer (malleus), anvil (incus), and stirrup (stapes). Actually, of the three, the stapes is aptly named, while the malleus looks more like a club, and the incus is nondescript.

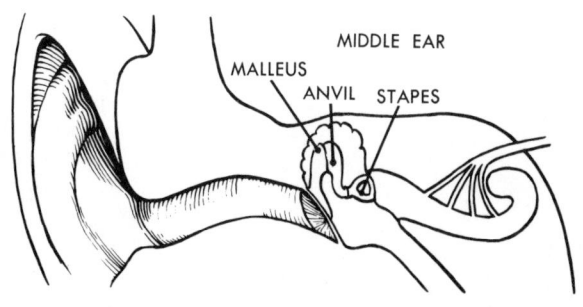

Sound vibrations are transmitted by the lever system of the ossicles to the oval window. The mechanical arrangement is such that the vibrations are conducted from the eardrum to an area approximately $\frac{1}{13}$ its size at the oval window. Correspondingly the pressure at the stirrup is about 17 times greater than that at the drum.

It should also be noted that the middle ear joins the inner ear at two points, the oval window and the round window. The inner ear can be described as a fluid-filled chamber enclosed in bone.

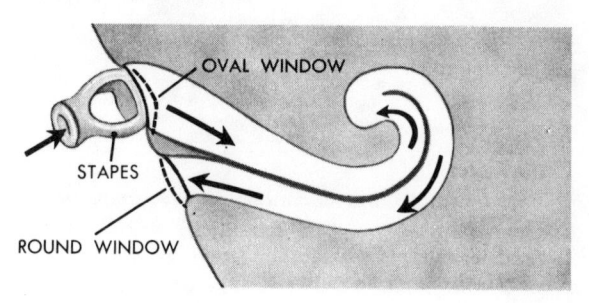

The advantage of the round window becomes apparent from this diagram. As the stirrup moves in, the round window is pushed out. Without this flexible second window, it would be difficult to transmit energy to the fluid of the inner ear, since fluids are compressed with great difficulty and the surrounding bone is inelastic.

THE EAR—HEARING

We do not hear sound directly. What we actually experience are nerve impulses in the brain. The diagram follows the path of two musical notes through the ear and into the brain. In the "translation" from physical sound to nerve impulse the hearing apparatus attempts to preserve the physical properties of the sound wave which cause us ultimately to experience sound as loud or soft, or as high or low in pitch. Part of this process is detailed in the "portraits of sound," presented with each of the stages, showing how the pitch of two notes is distinguished at each point along the hearing pathway.

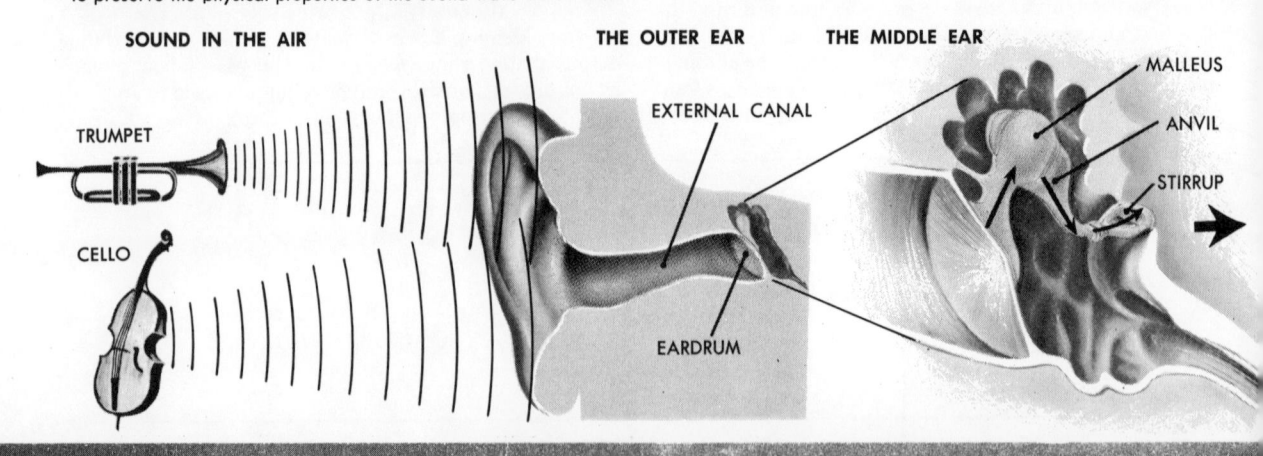

SOUND IN THE AIR

In the atmosphere sound consists of vibrations of air. A snapshot of the sound moving in the air would show alternate regions of highly packed and loosely spaced molecules. The high-pitched note would show more waves per unit of time than the low-pitched note.

THE OUTER EAR

The funnel-shaped outer ear directs the sound waves to the eardrum. At this point the pitch of the two sounds is translated into vibrations of the eardrum. The vibration frequency is higher for the high-pitched sound and lower for the low-pitched sound.

THE MIDDLE EAR

The movements of the eardrum are transmitted through the small bones of the middle ear (hammer, anvil, and stirrup). Here the two notes are distinguished by the frequency of vibrations in the bones.

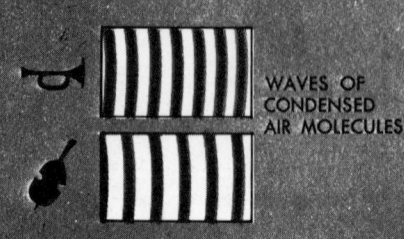

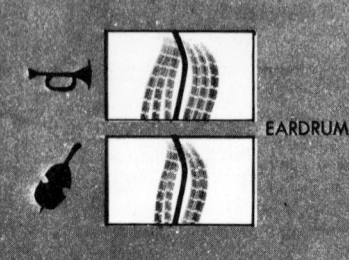

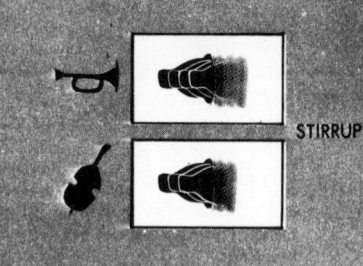

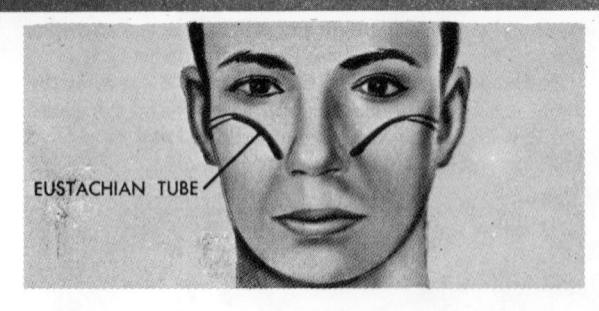

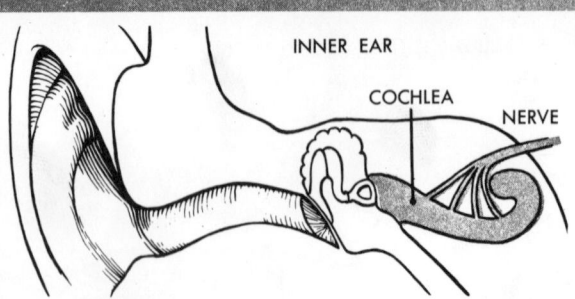

The Eustachian Tubes—Balancing Air Pressure on the Eardrum

The unpleasant "stopped" sensation in the ears, experienced when rapidly ascending from one height to another, results from an outward bulging of the eardrum caused by inequality in air pressure. The condition is remedied by opening the mouth; this permits air to flow through the eustachian tube to the middle ear, equalizing the air pressure on either side of the eardrum.

The Inner Ear—Vibrations Into Nerve Impulses

The sound-sensing part of the inner ear is the cochlea, a spiral structure which resembles a snail's shell. If the cochlea is examined in cross section it can be seen to be composed of a number of canals, which extend throughout its length. Each canal is subdivided into three parts. The smallest contains the organ of corti, which is actually the organ of hearing.

The hair cells of the organ of corti are thought to be the sensing elements which convert mechanical movement into nerve impulses. One of the basic problems in the study of hearing concerns how the organ of corti detects sounds of different frequency so that we are aware of differences in pitch.

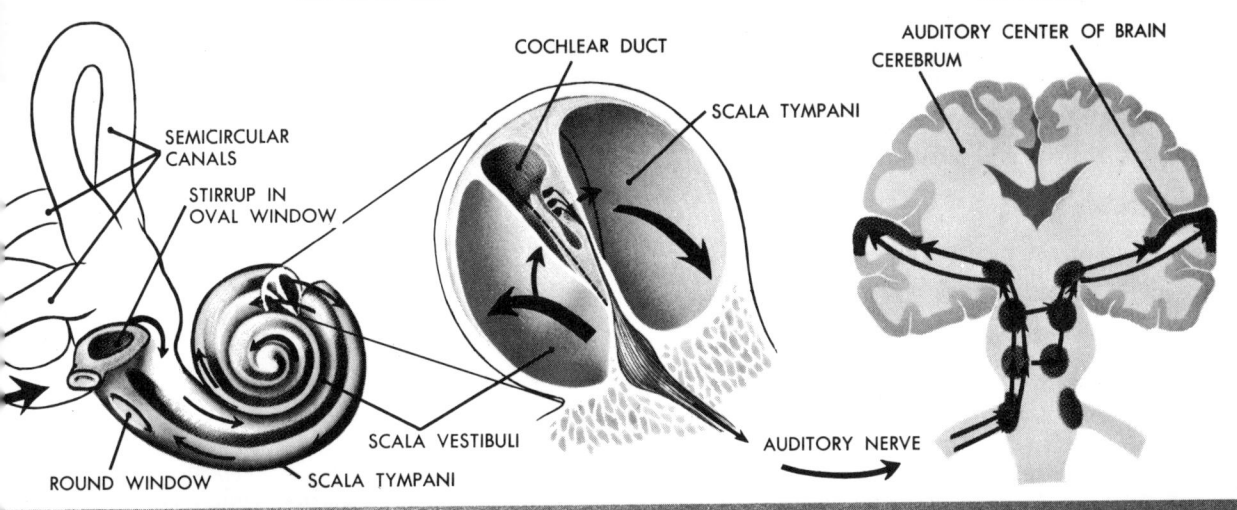

THE INNER EAR

Labels: SEMICIRCULAR CANALS, STIRRUP IN OVAL WINDOW, COCHLEAR DUCT, SCALA TYMPANI, SCALA VESTIBULI, SCALA TYMPANI, ROUND WINDOW, AUDITORY NERVE

THE BRAIN

Labels: AUDITORY CENTER OF BRAIN, CEREBRUM

The stirrup vibrates against the oval window, setting up waves in the fluid of the spiral cochlea. The arrows indicate the path of these waves. They originate at the oval window and then travel through the inner channel (scala vestibuli), reaching the outer chamber (scala tympani) by way of the middle section (the cochlear duct). They may also curve around the tip of the spiral. The waves terminate at the round window. Differences of pitch are preserved in the frequency of the waves.

The fluid waves of the inner chamber of the cochlea are transmitted to the middle chamber, or cochlear duct. Here the waves generate tension on hair cells, thus exciting a nerve impulse that travels from the ear in the auditory nerve. At this point pitch discrimination is no longer a question of how often stimulation occurs (frequency), but rather where in the cochlea the nerve impulses arise (with exceptions: see text). The higher the pitch of the sound the more toward the base of the cochlea the stimulation occurs.

The sound travels toward the brain, now coded in the electrochemical language of the nervous system. Sounds of specific pitch apparently travel in specific fibers. As seen in the diagram, impulses from one ear cross over to reach both halves of the brain. The nerve message ultimately reaches the auditory portion of the cerebral cortex where the pitch is recognized by virtue of which brain cells are stimulated, as the pitch of the piano depends upon which key is struck.

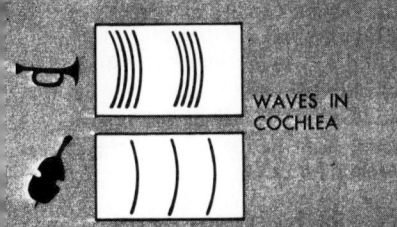

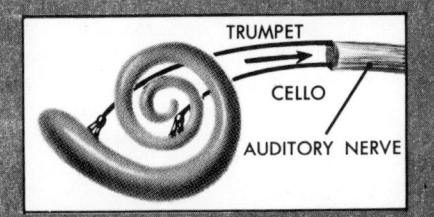

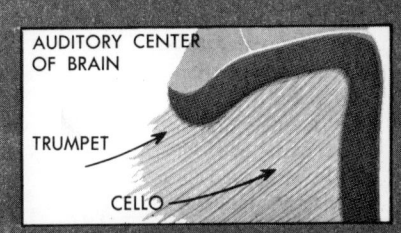

WAVES IN COCHLEA

TRUMPET / CELLO / AUDITORY NERVE

AUDITORY CENTER OF BRAIN / TRUMPET / CELLO

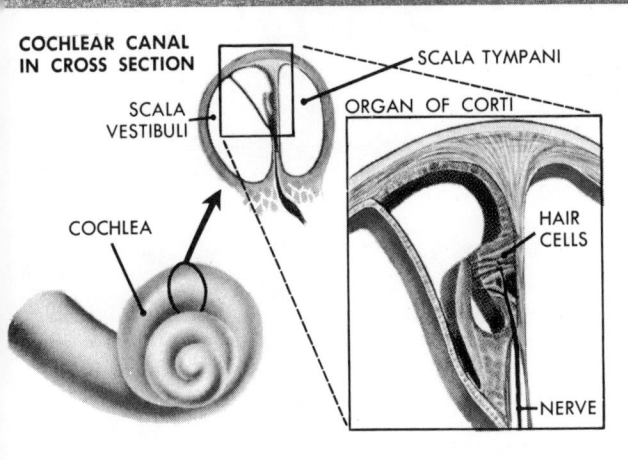

COCHLEAR CANAL IN CROSS SECTION — SCALA TYMPANI, SCALA VESTIBULI, ORGAN OF CORTI, COCHLEA, HAIR CELLS, NERVE

The "Resonance," "Telephone," and Other Theories of Pitch Perception

In 1863 the German physicist Helmholtz suggested that the cochlea might contain a special structure for each frequency of sound. Helmholtz proposed that a specific element of the cochlea resonated at a definite frequency in much the same way as a drinking glass vibrates to a particular note of a vigorous tenor—in effect, a different-sized glass for each note. This became known as the "resonance" theory. Some time later a "telephone" theory was advanced which placed the responsibility for frequency analysis with the brain. According to this view a sound impulse of say 15,000 cycles per second would be converted into a nerve message consisting of 15,000 impulses per second. The message would reach the brain which would in some way become aware of the difference between this and other frequencies.

The two theories have now been merged into the modern concept of frequency analysis. It has been demonstrated that one theory describes hearing at low frequencies and the other at high frequencies. In one case the brain "recognizes" pitch on the basis of a time factor—the interval between impulses (frequency); in the other case by a space factor—the specific part of the nerve which carries the impulse. At low frequencies the entire cochlea vibrates and pitch is analyzed on the basis of the frequency of impulses traveling in the nerve (the telephone theory). These impulses travel in fibers which are

EAR

randomly distributed in the nerve. At higher frequencies a specific part of the cochlea resonates with a specific frequency—similar to the Helmholtzian notion, but not quite the same, since the entire cochlea is fused and vibrates as a unit, but with greater vigor at the point of resonance. The fibers, carrying impulses from a specific part of the cochlea, travel in a particular section of the nerve, so that the brain can "recognize" a frequency by the particular fibers that carry it.

The Perception of Loudness. Loudness is thought to be indicated by the total number of fibers discharging and the rate at which they discharge. The matter is not quite clear since, as observed above, the rate of fiber discharge is also supposed to indicate low-frequency sounds.

Binaural Hearing and the Localization of Sound. Sounds are heard as originating from a point in space. This localization is accomplished by the difference in time interval required for the sound to reach each ear (for lower frequencies) and by difference in intensity (for higher frequencies). "Stereophonic" sound is obtained by detecting these differences as picked up by two or more separated microphones and playing them back through separate speakers.

Hearing Tests—Audiometry

The measurement of hearing is known as audiometry. A standard procedure consists of presenting a series of pure tones (a single frequency) to the subject. In this way the sensitivity of the ear can be mapped out over the entire frequency range.

Two ingenious techniques have been devised for use with children and with those who cannot understand instructions. In the galvanic skin response (GSR) method the subject is exposed to a mild electric shock whenever he hears a tone. After a series of such shocks, presentation of an audible tone will cause an automatic reaction which lowers the electrical resistance of the skin. The operator can then test each tone by presenting successively louder impulses and noting at what level of loudness the resistance of the skin changes. In the electroencephalograph test, electrodes placed on the skull detect changes in the brain waves which occur in response to sound.

The Social-Adequacy Index (SAI) is a measure of the individual's ability to understand conversational speech. This is determined by presenting a spoken group of words at uniform intensities; the subject's ability to correctly repeat the words provides his social-adequacy index.

Bone Conduction. Sound can reach the inner ear by means of vibrations transmitted directly through the skull. This by-passing of the middle ear is useful in testing hearing in individuals suffering from middle-ear damage. A vibrator is applied to the skull for this purpose.

The Ear and Balance—the Semicircular Canals

The inner ear contains, in addition to the cochlea, a group of structures which are concerned with body balance. These structures are the three semicircular canals and the vestibule.

The sensitive elements of the canal are cone-shaped structures (cristae) found in the large open ends of the canals—the ampullae. When the head is rotated or moved in a vertical plane the fluid contained in the canals lags behind the motion of the body, deflecting the sensory structures and informing the brain of the motion. The stimulation depends upon the drag, or inertia, of the fluid against the cristae and consequently occurs only when motion begins or ceases. If the individual spins in a continuous motion, stimulation ceases after the initial accel-

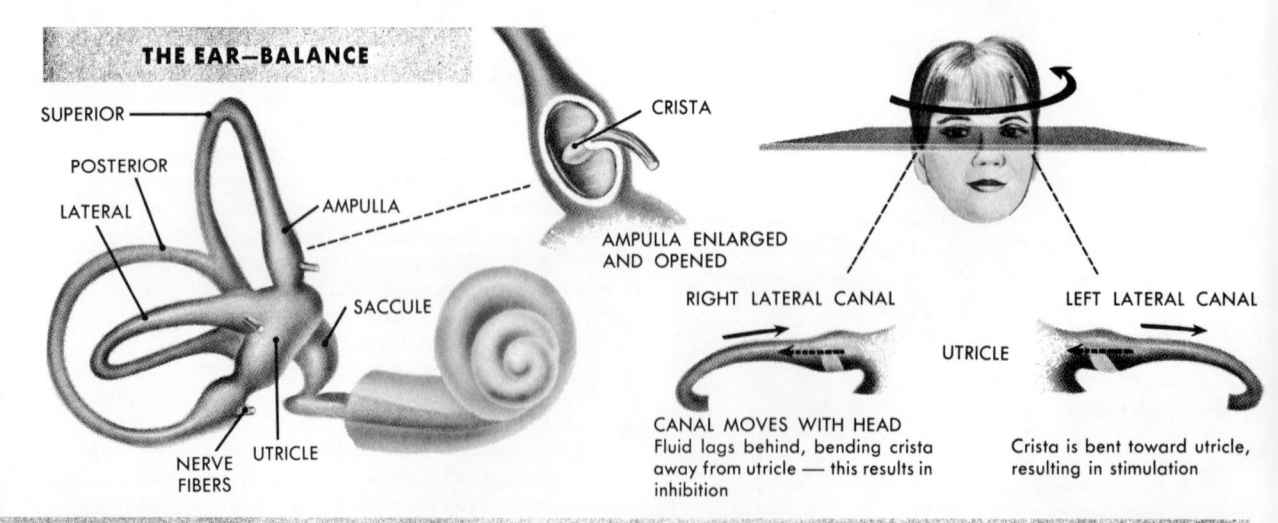

THE EAR—BALANCE

SUPERIOR
POSTERIOR
LATERAL
AMPULLA
SACCULE
NERVE FIBERS
UTRICLE

CRISTA
AMPULLA ENLARGED AND OPENED

RIGHT LATERAL CANAL
UTRICLE
CANAL MOVES WITH HEAD
Fluid lags behind, bending crista away from utricle — this results in inhibition

LEFT LATERAL CANAL
Crista is bent toward utricle, resulting in stimulation

THE SEMICIRCULAR CANALS are an important source of information concerning body movement. The three canals lie at approximately right angles to each other in the inner ear. The sensory receptors (cristae) are found in the openings (ampullae) at one end of the canal. When bent by movements of fluid within the canal, the cristae generate nerve impulses that are conducted to the brain via the vestibular nerve.

The canals are maximally activated by rotation in their own plane. When this occurs, the fluid lags behind in the canals, bending the cristae which move with the head — as a cyclist is bent by the wind when he pedals vigorously. Stimulation occurs only when the cristae are bent toward the utricle. Thus the right to left rotation above stimulates the left canal and inhibits the right canal.

eration and the brain receives no information as to the state of body motion. This accounts for the confusion experienced when one whirls around rapidly. Ballet dancers avoid such confusion during pirouettes by alternately increasing and decreasing their motions, stimulating the cristae with each acceleration and deceleration.

In contrast to the sensory elements of the ampullae, which detect rotary motion, other receptors (in the utricle) are stimulated principally by changes in the position of the head and by straight-line movements. These are known as "gravity" receptors.

The nerve impulses from the semicircular canals are co-ordinated with messages from the eyes and the body muscles to maintain the normal upright position.
See also DEAFNESS; MOTION SICKNESS.

ECHO VIRUSES, or enteric cytopathogenic human orphan viruses, a group of viruses which infect the human gastrointestinal tract. These organisms were discovered before their association with the diseases they produce was known, hence the expression "orphan." The Echo viruses primarily affect young children during the summer, producing "summer grippe," a respiratory disease with fever, "summer diarrhea," and various disorders involving fever and rashes. Some of the viruses attack the lining of the nervous system (the meninges) causing an ailment which may be mistaken for nonparalytic poliomyelitis. There is no specific treatment for Echo virus infections, but most patients recover spontaneously.
See also VIRUSES.

ECLAMPSIA [ek-lămp′sē-ə], convulsions and coma which may develop in late pregnancy in association with a group of disorders known as the toxemias of pregnancy. The cause of eclampsia is not known. It is immediately preceded by a rapid increase in blood pressure, swelling of the body (resulting from the retention of fluid), abdominal and stomach pains, headache, visual disturbances, and decreased output of urine. The disorder rarely appears before the sixth month of pregnancy and seems to occur more frequently in first pregnancies, in diabetic women, in women who suffered from high blood pressure before pregnancy, and in twin pregnancies.

Treatment includes terminating the pregnancy and the use of sedatives and drugs to lower the blood pressure and to stimulate kidney activity (diuretics).
See also PREGNANCY.

ECZEMA [ĕk′sə-mə, ĕg′zə-mə, ĕg-zē′mə], a group of skin diseases characterized by redness, swelling, blisters, and scaling, in the severe forms, and thickening and roughening of the skin in the chronic forms. In both forms of eczema there is extreme itching. The condition may be caused by allergies, dandruff, infection, or poor circulation. Many other skin diseases, at some time in their development, display the characteristics of eczema.

In eczema, the skin frequently becomes infected as a result of the injuries inflicted by violent scratching. The severe eczemas are treated by removing the cause (in the case of allergies) or by treating the underlying condition. Wet compresses, medicated lotions, antihistamines, and drugs similar to cortisone are used. The chronic eczemas are treated similarly but instead of lotions and compresses, radiation and medicated creams are employed.

EDEMA [ĭ-dē′mə], also called dropsy, a swelling of a portion of the body caused by excessive accumulation of fluid in the tissue spaces. Edema results from changes in the circulatory system that interfere with the normal exchange of fluids between the blood and the body tissues. A lowered concentration of proteins in the blood permits fluid to escape into the tissue spaces. Edema of this variety occurs in various kidney diseases, in which protein is lost through the urine; in malnutrition; and in cirrhosis of the liver.

Mechanical interference with the circulation of the blood produces increased blood pressure in the veins, and stasis, or slowing of the blood flow. The increased pressure in the veins forces fluid into the tissue spaces. This type of edema may result from heart failure, varicose veins, thrombophlebitis, and tumors that press upon the veins.

Allergic edema, or hives, and the swelling around insect bites is caused by the release of histamine from injured tissues. This substance makes the walls of the capillaries more porous and permits fluids to pass into the tissues. The treatment of edema is aimed at removing the underlying cause.

EGG. The egg, or ovum, is the reproductive cell of female animals. It is derived from oogonia, the dividing germ cells of the ovary. The cells produced by the final division of the oogonia, the oocytes, grow and develop to form the mature egg. After completion of this maturation process the egg is extruded from the ovary and is carried to a position where it may be fertilized by the male reproductive cell, the sperm.

The oocyte undergoes great chemical and physical changes before it becomes an egg, the most apparent of which is its change in size. In all species the mature egg is very large compared to other cells of the body. The largest eggs are found among the birds and reptiles. The oocyte of the frog, an amphibian, enlarges to 27,000 times its original size before it becomes a mature egg. Most of the egg's growth is the result of accumulation of yolk required to nourish the embryo during its initial period of development.

The process by which oocytes become mature eggs, or ova, is called gametogenesis. The resulting matured cells are called gametes. In addition to the profound change in size of the maturing oocyte, equally prominent alterations take place in the nucleus during maturation. The nucleus of an oogonium contains the same number of chromosome pairs (chromosomes are the bearers of genetic information) as all other body cells. If this oogonium merely enlarged to become the mature oocyte, then, when it was fertilized by a sperm, the resulting fertilized egg, or zygote, would have twice the number of chromosome pairs characteristic for the species. In order that the zygote have the correct number of chromosome pairs, the oogonium undergoes what is known as two meiotic divisions, with the result that the nucleus of the mature egg contains one member of each former chromosome pair—a

THE EGGS OF DIFFERENT ANIMALS

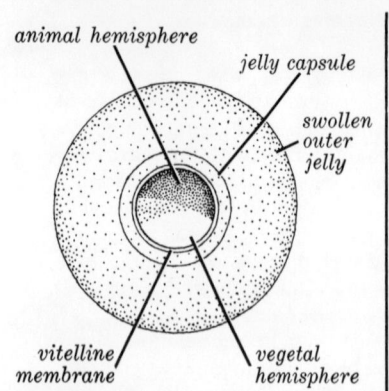

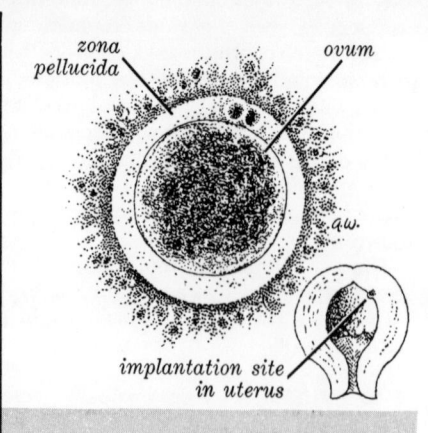

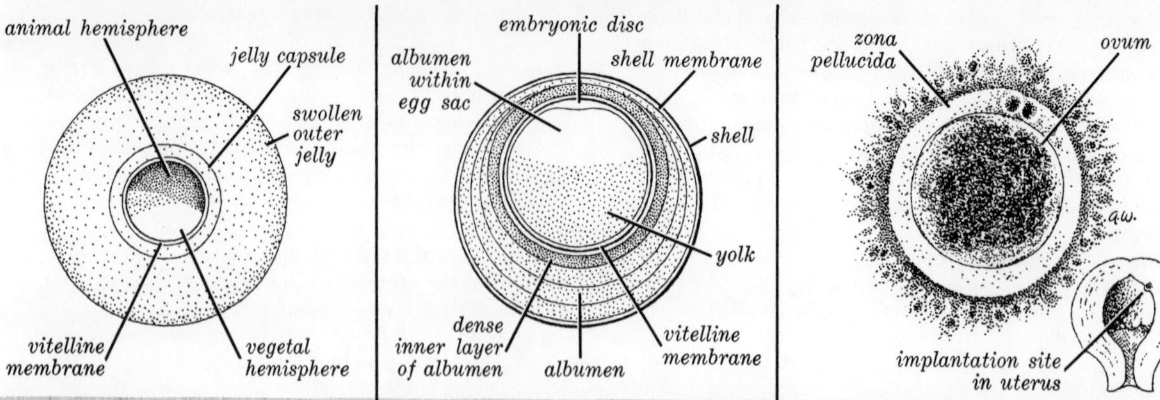

AMPHIBIAN EGG

The spherical center of the amphibian egg is roughly divided into two hemispheres: the darker animal hemisphere, in which the embryo develops; and the lighter vegetal hemisphere, which supplies nutrients to the developing embryo. The vitelline membrane and the layers of jelly protect the embryo and prevent it from becoming desiccated.

REPTILE EGG

The embryo of a reptile begins to develop on the egg's periphery at the embryonic disc. It is nourished by yolk and albumen and is surrounded by a protective membrane. Outside the vitelline membrane are additional nutrient albumen layers. The entire egg is surrounded by a shell. Because the shell prevents desiccation, the eggs of reptiles can develop on land.

MAMMALIAN EGG

The egg, or ovum, of a mammal remains inside the female's body and develops there after fertilization. The ovum is surrounded by a glassy membrane, the zona pellucida. The ovum contains virtually no nutrient material: the fertilized egg implants on the wall of the uterus, and the placenta, formed jointly by embryo and uterus, nourishes the developing embryo.

"haploid" number of chromosomes. This is just one-half the original number. The developing sperm cell also undergoes meiotic divisions. Thus, when the sperm and egg (each contains in its nucleus one member of each pair of chromosomes) unite, the zygote has the proper number of chromosomes.

Most eggs are spherical in shape but may have enclosing membranes and outer coverings that give them a different form. Mammalian eggs are nearly spherical and are covered by membranous layers. The eggs of birds and reptiles are also spherical and are covered by protective membranes; they also have, as an additional protective feature, an exterior shell. External shells and other egg coverings are characteristically present in species in which the development of the young occurs outside the mother's body—in worms, insects, crustaceans, spiders, and lower vertebrates.

The number of eggs produced at one time, the size of the egg, and the nature of the egg's protective covering are all determined by the environment in which the egg is fertilized and in which it subsequently develops as an embryo. Nature has provided well for the continuation of species. Lower animals usually produce many thousands of eggs, since the eggs are not only sought after by other animals for food, but the conditions under which the young animals develop (outside the mother's body) also claim many victims. Higher animal groups produce fewer eggs, but those eggs are better protected, Mammals produce the least number of eggs of any animal group—usually only one or two at a time. Mammalian young, however, are so well protected in their early developmental stages that those few eggs actually have a better chance of becoming adult individuals than does any one of the 3 or 4 million eggs produced annually by, for example, a codfish. *See also* EMBRYOLOGY; FERTILIZATION.

EHRLICH [ār'lĭκH], **PAUL** (1854–1915), German bacteriologist and immunologist, who pioneered in the development of chemicals in the treatment of infectious diseases. In 1908 he shared the Nobel Prize with Élie Metchnikoff for studies on the mechanism of immunity. In 1909 Ehrlich and his coworkers succeeded in finding a potent antisyphilitic agent called salvarsan, or arsphenamine, or popularly, "606," since it was the 606th compound tested by Ehrlich and his group. Ehrlich's other contributions included the development of staining techniques for use in the laboratory and the introduction of various laboratory tests and blood-counting techniques.

ELECTRIC SHOCK may occur when the body becomes part of a conducting electric circuit. The consequences depend upon the wetness of the skin, the nature of the ground material, and the characteristics of the electric current. Skin resistance to current flow is lowered by sweating or wet clothing. If the individual is in contact with a good conductor, such as a radiator, or a water bath, he might be killed by a current which would otherwise be tolerated. Alternating currents are generally more dangerous than direct currents, particularly low-frequency currents. The shock may cause momentary or prolonged loss of consciousness, convulsions, and burns, where the current enters or leaves the body. Death may result from heart failure or paralysis of respiration. Electric-shock victims should be given immediate artificial respiration.

ELECTROCARDIOGRAM [ĭ-lĕk-trō-kär′dē-ə-grăm] **(ECG)**, a record of the electric activity of the heart. Minute voltages from the auricles and ventricles of the heart are transmitted to a recording instrument (an electrocardiograph) by means of metal electrodes placed on the arms, legs, and chest. The electrocardiograph amplifies these voltages which then activate a stylus to write upon a moving paper strip.

The electric events in the chambers of the heart are reflected in characteristic fluctuations or "waves" of the ECG. Certain changes in these waves have been associated with various heart conditions and other disorders.

The ECG is extremely important in the diagnosis of coronary thrombosis, enlargement of the heart, and irregularities of the heart beat (arrhythmias). Great care is required in the interpretation of the ECG, as it has been found that many persons with severe heart conditions exhibit a normal ECG and conversely many normal persons present abnormal patterns.

ELECTROENCEPHALOGRAPH [ĭ-lĕk-trō-ĕn-sĕf′ə-lə-grăf], instrument used to record the electrical activity of the brain. Electrodes placed over the scalp detect electrical impulses from the brain (the so-called "brain waves"), which are then amplified and recorded as a continuous line on a moving paper strip.

The electroencephalograph has been used to diagnose brain tumors, epilepsy, and other types of brain disease. Neurophysiologists have made extensive use of the instrument in research. It has been found, for example, that certain regular fluctuations called alpha waves appear during light sleep and disappear in the waking state. Other distinct patterns of the electroencephalogram have been identified and have been associated with various mental states and activities.

ELEPHANTIASIS [ĕl-ə-fən-tī′-ə-sĭs] or **ELEPHANT DISEASE**, a term often used to describe any thickening of the skin and underlying tissues. It is most commonly caused by infection with certain tropical parasites, the filarial worms. The parasites enter the body when an infected mosquito bites into the skin. Following this male and female worms mature in the tissues where they eventually mate and release thousands of microscopic offspring into the blood stream.

Frequently the infection produces no symptoms. In a certain percentage of long-standing cases, the lymphatic vessels (the channels through which tissue fluids normally pass) in the legs, scrotum, arms, and breasts become obstructed. In such instances fluid backs up in these areas, resulting in a massive swelling. The legs may become so unwieldy as to make walking impossible. Over a period of time fibrous tissue grows in the swollen parts rendering them thick and hard.

Elephantiasis may also develop following operations in which the lymphatic vessels are disrupted. Elephantiasis of the arm occasionally appears after cancer surgery of the breast.

Elephantiasis resulting from worm infestation may be treated with hetrazan, a drug that destroys the worms. Tight bandages are applied to control the swelling, but surgical treatment may be necessary in advanced cases. *See also* FILARIASIS.

EMBOLISM, PULMONARY. *See* PULMONARY EMBOLISM.

EMBOLUS [ĕm′bə-ləs], a clot or other obstruction which is carried along in the blood stream until it becomes lodged in a blood vessel too narrow to permit its passage. Most emboli arise from blood clots, or thrombi, which form in veins or on the heart wall. Postoperative patients may develop clots in the veins of the legs and, later, emboli. A heart attack may damage the inner lining of the heart, with subsequent formation of clots, and possibly, emboli. When newly formed the clots are fragile and fragments are likely to break loose and become emboli. In decompression sickness a sudden change from high to low atmospheric pressure results in the release of nitrogen bubble emboli into the blood stream. In other cases emboli may be composed of fat, tumor cells, or atherosclerotic plaques which break loose from diseased arteries.

The symptoms resulting from the embolus depend roughly upon its size and the location of the vessel in which it lodges. Emboli which plug arteries supplying the heart and lungs are extremely dangerous. Emboli in the brain may cause a stroke.
See also THROMBOSIS.

EMBRYOLOGY is the study of the development of the individual from the egg. This study has long been of interest to man and knowledge of animal development reaches back into antiquity. The Greek philosopher Aristotle made some acute observations on chick development, and also posed questions about the nature of development that still remain valid in the 20th century. He raised the question as to whether the parts of the animal are all represented in the egg at an early stage, and reach their full development consecutively, at later times; or alternatively, whether the fact that the appearance of one organ follows that of another implies a causal relationship between these events. Aristotle expressed his preference for the latter alternative.

Embryology enjoyed its next real burst of progress during or after the Renaissance. In 1600 Hieronymus Fabricius published two embryological treatises, on the chick and on the human fetus, both based on direct observation and splendidly illustrated. Fabricius' knowledge of the valves in the veins was an important influence in directing the thought of his pupil, William Harvey, toward his later discovery of the circulation of the blood. Harvey may also have gained from Fabricius some interest in development, and himself published in 1651 a large book *On the Generation of Animals*. Harvey, like Aristotle, posed the possibility of two types of development, and felt that at least in some animals development is a sequence of actions ensuing one upon another. Harvey also made an important contribution to embryology by demonstrating that the part of the hen's egg that forms the embryo is the "cicatricula" (now called the blastodisc), the white spot of what we would call cytoplasm that surmounts the yolk. Fabricius had erroneously considered the chalazae (the thick white spirals of albumen so conspicuous when a raw hen's egg is opened into a glass dish) to be the rudiment of the embryo. Development could not be studied until it was known what actually develops.

Although the whole hen's egg is very large because of its content of yolk and albumen (which provide water and nourishment for the developing embryo), the embryo itself is very small in its early stages; and the embryos of other eggs popular for study because of their accessibility (those of frogs, fishes, or insects) are also small. True understanding of developmental processes, therefore, necessitates the use of the microscope.

One influential embryological concept developed by those who began to study the egg microscopically in the 17th century was called *evolutio* in Latin, the language in which biological treatises were then written. In English this concept is referred to as preformation. It implies that all parts of the adult are present in the egg in miniature, and that they simply unfold as the parts of a bud unfold to form a flower. This concept was eventually supplanted by another. In the mid-18th century, Casper Friedrich Wolff examined the chick blastodisc more carefully and saw that no organ rudiments are present in it before incubation and that the disc appears homogeneous. His concept of development as proceeding from the homogeneous to the heterogeneous, with new organs appearing in their turn, was called epigenesis; its similarity to that of Aristotle is apparent. Wolff saw that the intestine and the nerve tube of the chick form by the folding of layers. In 1817 Christian Pander described the early development of the chick in terms of foldings of three layers, an outer, a middle, and an inner one, later called the germ layers (ectoderm, mesoderm, and endoderm). Karl Ernst von Baer (who also discovered the mammalian egg, found that these layers are present in many vertebrates, forming the same organs in each. He wrote a careful and comprehensive treatise that established embryology as an independent science.

After the publication of Darwin's *Origin of Species* (1859), Ernst Heinrich Haeckel, in a long series of popular books, postulated similarities between stages in the individual development of members of one species and adult stages in the evolutionary development of its ancestors. This idea had been held by some before the days of von Baer, and von Baer pointed out its fallacy, emphasizing that embryos of one species might resemble the embryos but never the adults of another species. Nonetheless, Haeckel's concept, persuasively presented, became influential, and its emphasis on events in adult evolution as causative of changes in the individual embryo delayed an experimental analysis of causal relationships within individual development. Finally, at the end of the 19th century, embryology became, like the rest of biology, an experimental science.

Experimental embryology has shown that if parts of some eggs, for instance those of snails or earthworms, are isolated from the whole at an early stage, they develop only what they would have formed if they had remained in place in the intact egg. This is not precisely comparable to preformation since organs are not actually present in miniature in the part, but it does imply that precursors of what an isolated part will form are contained within it, and develop without influence from other parts of the egg (a process known as independent differentiation). In other eggs, for instance those of frogs, what one part forms is determined by its relationships with other parts (a concept called dependent differentiation). One organ forms after another (as Aristotle had postulated) because of the presence of the other; differentiation is progressive. The controlling effect of one embryonic part upon another is called induction, and in 1935 Hans Spemann received a Nobel Prize for its discovery, which experimentally validated the concept of epigenesis.

Actually, no egg develops solely by dependent or solely by independent differentiation. The principal aim of experimental embryology has been to ascertain to what degree the development of various parts of different eggs is independent or dependent; the time at which their development becomes independent; and the nature of the factors bringing about their change. The genes, or hereditary factors, contained in the nucleus of the fertilized egg are the ultimate factors that determine how development occurs, but the methods by which they express themselves in development are not yet completely worked out and are under active investigation. What is clear is that when embryos of closely related groups resemble each other, they do so because they have inherited similar genes. The demonstration that deoxyribonucleic acid (DNA) carries genetic information that is transmitted to ribonucleic acid (RNA), and expressed in the formation of specific proteins, is of great significance, since proteins are important factors in producing differences in cells. (See NUCLEIC ACIDS.)

The role of nucleic acids in development is studied in many different ways. Chemical studies have determined the kind and size of nucleic acid molecules present at particular phases in development and have shown some of the changes that nucleic acids undergo. Transplantation of nuclei from older cells to enucleated eggs, that is, eggs from which the original nuclei have been removed, have proved that all the nuclei contain all the genes. These experiments imply that factors must be operative to activate or repress certain genes during certain phases of differentiation. Control mechanisms for genetic production of enzymes have been demonstrated for bacteria. Presumably comparable but more complicated control mechanisms, influenced by cytoplasmic factors, are at play while progressive differentiation occurs during the development of many-celled animals. But the solution to the problem of how molecular change is expressed in visible change of biological structure is not yet in sight. Nor is there yet an answer to the problem of what agencies regulate all the manifold and separate complicated processes of development into an orderly and organized whole.

Embryological Development

The sequence of events observed in development is best described in several successive phases, as follows:

Gametogenesis. Each animal develops from a special cell, the female germ cell, or egg. In most species, the egg undergoes development only after fusion with a male germ cell, or spermatozoon. The male and female germ cells are known as gametes, and their formation by the body is called gametogenesis.

Oogenesis is the formation of the egg by the female reproductive organ, the ovary. An egg, no matter how large, is a single cell. Little if anything is yet known of the development of the principal feature which distinguishes the egg from other cells, namely, its capacity to form a whole new individual. It is known, however, that during the production of the egg by the ovary, a nutritive material, yolk, is added to the cell to provide food and energy for the developing embryo. The amount of yolk in the egg varies greatly according to the species. Eggs of mammals, which are about ¼ mm. in diameter, contain little yolk. Those of frogs are yolkier and larger; they may measure over 1 mm. in diameter. Birds' eggs are the largest of all cells. What is commonly called the yolk of a breakfast egg represents one cell with its included yolk; the albumen and shell are accessory coats added by the oviduct and uterus after the egg has left the ovary. Many egg cells also contain pigment or other special inclusions. (See CELL.)

Spermatogenesis is the production of the spermatozoon by the male reproductive organ, or testis. The egg usually develops only after fusion with the spermatozoon. This latter cell is even more visibly modified, in comparison with other body cells, than is the egg. During the course of its development in the testis, the spermatozoon loses most of its cytoplasm and becomes an elaborate structure consisting principally of head and tail. It is usually extremely small. The head consists almost exclusively of the nucleus, but has at the front a special region called the acrosome that is important as the agent that perforates the egg—to permit the nucleus of the spermatozoon to enter the egg. A small middle piece connecting head and tail consists principally of mitochondria. The tail is a long filament that the electron microscope has shown to be made of 11 contractile fibers, 2 central and 9 peripheral ones. The egg has no means of movement. The spermatozoon, which is highly motile, proceeds toward it by means of vigorous lashing of its tail. Since many spermatozoa may not locate eggs to fertilize, the number of spermatozoa formed is usually far larger than the number of eggs, reaching into the millions. Some fishes, however, such as herring or cod, also produce millions of eggs each per year.

The development of the cytoplasmic structure of the gametes is not the only function of gametogenesis. Changes also take place within the nucleus. The nucleus of each body cell in most many-celled animals contains a double set of chromosomes. Provision must be made to ensure that this number does not continually redouble each time two gametes fuse. Accordingly, during gametogenesis, two special nuclear divisions occur, the maturation divisions, or meiotic divisions. These reduce the chromosome number of the gametic nucleus to half, so that each gamete is haploid. When the male and female gametes and their nuclei fuse, the diploid number characteristic of the species is restored. (See MEIOSIS.)

Fertilization. The fusion of the egg and spermatozoon is called fertilization. The process has a double significance. It furnishes to the new individual the paternal chromosomes along with their genes, and thus is of vital importance in determining the individual's inherited traits. Further, it activates the egg to begin its development. Most eggs do not develop unless activated by the spermatozoon. Eggs of a few species may develop without being fertilized; such development is termed parthenogenesis, and is characteristic of aphids, bees and even occurs in some races of turkeys. Eggs of some species that do not ordinarily develop parthenogenetically may do so after experimental treatment; frogs and, according to some authors, rabbits, are included among these.

Many organisms shed their eggs and spermatozoa into the water in which they live, and fertilization is external. In others, the spermatozoa are introduced into the reproductive tract of the female. There is a very high degree of specificity in fertilization, and usually the spermatozoa unite only with eggs of their own species. The mechanism that ensures this is sometimes described as analogous to that in which antibodies combine with antigens. (See ANTIBODIES AND ANTIGENS.)

The fertilized egg of each species contains genes different from those of the eggs of other species, and, accordingly, development differs in each species. It is not possible, therefore, to provide a description that fits all developing animals. Some generalizations, however, may be made, but to most of them there are exceptions.

Cleavage. Since the egg cell and the spermatozoon fuse at fertilization, the resulting structure, the zygote, which will form the new individual, is a single cell. The first visible event of embryonic development is cleavage, the repeated mitotic division of the fertilized egg. As a result of these divisions, the single-celled egg becomes many-celled. The position of the cleavage planes and the specific pattern of cleavage differ in different organisms. The size of the egg and the amount of yolk it contains are among the many factors that influence cleavage types. In relatively yolkless eggs, such as those of the frog, the whole egg cleaves. In the very yolky egg of the chick, only the blastodisc cleaves.

There is no particular moment that can be designated as the time that cleavage ends; some cells (those that line the intestine in man, for example) continue to divide throughout life. In some species in which the whole egg cleaves, after a number of cells are present they produce a fluid internally, and what was formerly a solid mass of cells becomes a hollow sphere, the blastula. The blastula stage is much more conspicuous and recognizable in some forms than in others. No hollow blastula is formed in such eggs as the hen's, where cleavage involves only part of the egg. The emphasis on the blastula as a stage, found in most textbooks, is misplaced, and is simply a reminiscence of generalizations made by Haeckel that might better be forgotten. More important events occur in development than the occasional formation of a hollow sphere.

Gastrulation. Major rearrangements, called, in the aggregate, gastrulation, soon take place. Gastrulation is the process whereby cells migrate to take up their positions in the germ layers (ectoderm and endoderm in two-layered organisms such as polyps and jellyfishes; ectoderm, mesoderm, and endoderm in three-layered organisms). These are the layers mentioned earlier in this article as having been discovered by von Baer to be relatively similar among the vertebrates. Other investigators demonstrated their existence in other many-celled animals.

It has been stated above that the precise pattern of cleavage varies among various animals; the same is true of the pattern of cell movements in gastrulation. These movements, however, always involve migration of cells into the interior of the embryo to form mesoderm and endoderm; the cells remaining on the outside are the ectoderm. In species where the blastula is a hollow sphere, one side of it may push in to form the endoderm. (Since the endoderm forms the digestive system, this is the origin of the term gastrula, which means "little stomach" in Latin.) Sometimes, as in the frog, cells roll in from the outside to the inside, over a distinct lip, to form the mesoderm and endoderm. But in many embryos, including those of the chick and the mammal, individual cells may drop inward from the surface to take up their places in the middle and inner layers. The immediate factors responsible for the co-ordination of these movements into an orderly pattern are being studied but are largely unknown at present.

Differentiation. Wolff's concept of epigenesis as a mode of development, the production of heterogeneity from homogeneity, and von Baer's interpretation of the formation of the germ layers as a step in the embryo's attainment of heterogeneity, have been mentioned above in this article. Before gastrulation, all the cells of an embryo, barring differences in pigment and yolk or other cell inclusions, are not very different from one another. During gastrulation, as they assort themselves into layers, the cells still resemble each other. But after the completion of gastrulation, drastic alterations become apparent both within the cells themselves and in cell arrangements. These are the result of differentiation: the parts of the embryo, cells and cell aggregates, have become different from what they were, and also different from one another. Differentiation is the most essential feature of epigenesis, of homogeneity becoming heterogeneity.

Differentiation occurs at every level of the body: cell, tissue, organ, and organism as a whole. At each of these levels it involves a functional and structural specialization of the part concerned for its adult role. Cell differentiation may be expressed by the appearance of particular visible structures within cells, such as muscle striations, or by the production of chemical substances, such as enzymes, involved in cell function. Differentiation at the tissue level most often involves the grouping together of cells of like structure and function; at the organ level, differentiation involves grouping of cells of various types and from various tissues to form a special part that plays a vital function in the body mechanism. The brain as an organ, for example, contains not only nerve cells but also glia cells (a special type of connective tissue). It is enveloped in particular kinds of covering membranes (dura, pia, and arachnoid), and it contains a large number of blood vessels essential to its function. The orderly joining together of the parts to form the whole organ is part of the process called organogenesis.

One way in which these processes are investigated is by chemically dissociating embryonic cells and then combining them in tissue culture with dissociated cells of embryos of other ages or other species. Similarly, dissociated cells of different tissues or organs can be combined in order to observe their properties of self-assorting or self-assembly.

But each body organ has a shape of its own, characteristic of the species. The whole body, too, attains its own particular shape. The development of such changes of size and shape is sometimes called morphogenesis; but since all embryonic development entails changes in size and shape, this term is probably superfluous except as descriptive of all embryonic development. Sometimes attempts are made to contrast growth, or increase in size, with differentiation, but growth is really one component process in differentiation, and inseparable from it.

During normal embryonic development, the ectoderm usually forms the skin, the sense organs, and the nervous system. The endoderm forms the digestive system, that is, the alimentary canal and the glands associated with it, such as the liver and pancreas in vertebrates. In some organisms, including the vertebrates, the endoderm also forms the respiratory organs—gills or lungs. The mesoderm forms heart, blood vessels, skeleton, muscle, and excretory and reproductive organs and their ducts, and connective tissue.

The specific mechanisms of organ formation are highly varied among different organisms, but they often involve the folding of layers or the pinching off of parts of layers. Wolff, as we have said, first became aware of the epigenetic nature of development when he observed the folding of layers to form the nerve tube and the intestine of the chick. Such tubular organs are not the only ones to form by folding; some parts that are solid in the adult body also form as hollow structures. The vertebrate liver, for example, is at first a hollow outgrowth of the intestinal canal; the tube representing its original connection to the intestine remains as the bile duct. The vertebrate eye is at first a hollow outgrowth of a hollow brain vesicle. The vertebrate lens and the vertebrate inner ear develop from patches of ectoderm that drop in below the surface to form hollow vesicles that only later change shape. Comparable organs are not necessarily formed, however, in the same manner in all organisms, even closely related ones. In many fishes the nerve cord first sinks below the surface as a solid keel and does not form by folding as it does in the chick, frog, and mammal. And many other organs, in vertebrates and invertebrates, form as solid rather than hollow ingrowths or outgrowths.

In vertebrates, and in some invertebrates also, some organs are induced to differentiate by contact with neighboring parts; this is referred to above as dependent differentiation. In the newt, for example, the mesoderm and notochord that turn in during gastrulation induce the overlying ectoderm to form the nerve tube, which would not have formed in the absence of contact with the mesoderm and notochord layer. In some vertebrates, the retina of the eye, an outgrowth from the brain, induces the ectoderm of the head to differentiate the lens of the eye. Many investigators have tried to isolate and identify the specific substances that might be transmitted from an inducing part to the responding part in order to initiate the differentiation of the latter. Thus far they have not met with success. If substances are transmitted, and if they are macromolecules, they may or may not be the same for all organ systems; if they do exist, they almost certainly act as genetic control factors.

More frequently in invertebrates than in vertebrates, organs form as a result not of induction but of independent differentiation, as mentioned above. In snail development, for instance, cells isolated from the rest of the embryo form what they would have formed normally even if isolated from the embryo at very early cleavage stages. In other invertebrates, their relative position along the axis from top to bottom of the egg determines the fate of the parts. In sea urchin eggs, for instance, the lowermost part of the egg turns in to form the endodermal gut, and the cells above them along the axis form mesoderm. If the lowermost cells are removed at early cleavage stages, the cells that normally would have formed mesoderm, now at the bottom, form the gut. Each organ, and each organism, develops in its own way, and the fact that organisms differ in their development is responsible for their diversity as adults. And this diversity is the most striking attribute of the various members of the animal kingdom.

See also CELL; EGG; FERTILIZATION; GENETICS; NUCLEIC ACIDS; REPRODUCTION.

EMETIC [ĭ-mĕt'ĭk], drug which produces vomiting. Emetics generally cause vomiting by stimulating the vomiting center of the brain, or by irritating the gastrointestinal tract. In the past, the principal use of these drugs was to induce vomiting to empty the stomach in cases of poisoning by foods or drugs. The use of the stomach pump has now rendered emetics obsolete for this purpose. They are used in some cases of severe asthma to help loosen plugs of mucus in the air passages. They are also used in certain cases of rapid heartbeat and in breathing difficulties in infants involving the upper airways (croup). The latter uses are based upon the stimulation of the vagus nerve which occurs during the act of vomiting: this nerve sends fibers to the heart and the upper air passages.

Among the principal emetics are apomorphine, which acts upon the vomiting center, and ipecac, copper sulfate, and mustard, which act in the stomach. Emetics should not be administered to pregnant women, or to persons suffering from high-blood pressure, or lung tuberculosis.

EMOTION usually refers to mental states or processes accompanied by marked bodily reactions, which occur in anticipation or realization of frustration or satisfaction of needs. Such states also are termed "affects," since they typically are accompanied by feelings of pleasantness or unpleasantness. They were called "passions" by early Greek writers. In Latin, emotion originally meant an inner turbulence, as in a storm cloud, which discharged its forces outward. Today, the Latin terminology is accepted. Emotion, for man, connotes an inner turbulence with outward expression.

Theories. At this time all theories of emotion take one of three forms. Theory I may be stated as follows: emotion is an indivisible mind-body reaction. Many authors disagree, and their proposals take two general forms. Theory II, the most frequently encountered, may be stated thus: emotion is a mental event which depends upon other bodily events. Less prevalent is Theory III: emotion is a bodily event which may produce mental events.

EMPHYSEMA [ĕm-fə-sē'mə], **PULMONARY,** distension of the terminal air sacs (alveoli) of the lungs. A common form of emphysema (the obstructive type) is that which develops in conjunction with bronchitis. The condition results from partial obstruction of the small air passages in the lungs (the bronchioles). Air enters the alveoli more easily than it can leave them, causing the lungs to become distended with trapped air. In severe cases there is a serious interference with oxygen absorption and carbon dioxide elimination by the lungs. The disturbance in oxygen supply to the tissues often results in changes in the blood, such as an increased number of oxygen-carrying red blood cells (polycythemia) and increased blood volume. The patient may suffer from coughing, wheezing, and shortness of breath. Eventually heart failure may occur. Infections of the breathing passages are especially dangerous to the patient since they can bring on heart failure or further interfere with breathing. Treatment includes the use of antibiotics to combat infection and drugs to dilate the air passages, and to promote the coughing up of sputum. Breathing exercises and cortisone derivatives may help.

ENCEPHALITIS [ĕn-sĕf-ə-lī'tĭs], an inflammation of the brain which may be caused by bacteria, fungi, or parasites, but more commonly results from a virus infection. Most types of virus encephalitis are contagious and can cause epidemics. Although the manner in which the viruses are spread is not known in all cases, ticks, mosquitoes, and other animals are the transmitting agents for many of the infections.

Many different viruses may cause encephalitis. The names of the various virus forms of encephalitis are frequently associated with the sites at which epidemics occurred. These include: Japanese B encephalitis, St. Louis encephalitis, Australian X disease, Russian spring-summer disease, Venezuelan equine encephalitis, Eastern equine encephalitis, and Western equine encephalitis. The equine forms affect horses and various other animals, and can be transmitted to humans, producing infections of varying severity. Other forms of encephalitis may appear during or after infectious diseases such as measles, mumps, and chickenpox, or following vaccination against smallpox or rabies.

The different viruses produce diverse symptoms which include headache, fever, drowsiness, gastrointestinal disturbances, double vision, coma, tremors, convulsions, and paralyses. The infections may be fatal, although some viruses produce only mild disturbances.

There is no specific treatment for these disorders. In the case of the insect-borne viruses, spread of the disease can be controlled by screening doors and windows and attempting to eliminate the insect carrier. Vaccines have been developed which protect animals from the equine forms of encephalitis, but these have not proven practical for humans.

ENDERS [ĕn'dərz], **JOHN FRANKLIN** (1897–   ), American bacteriologist and immunologist. After receiving his

ENDOCRINE GLANDS

Ph.D. from Harvard University he remained there to teach, becoming a full professor at the Children's Hospital, Harvard Medical School, in 1956. In 1954, together with Thomas Weller and Frederick Robbins, he was awarded the Nobel Prize for medicine and physiology for his work on the cultivation of the poliomyelitis virus.

ENDOCRINE [ĕn′dō-krĭn] **GLANDS,** ductless glands which pour their secretions directly into the blood stream. The first scientific study of the endocrine glands was made by Berthold in 1849 when he observed that the henlike changes in body build and behavior which occurred in castrated cocks could be reversed by transplanting healthy testes into the operated animal. This effect resulted from the secretion of hormones from the transplanted tissues into the blood stream of the cock.

The endocrine system includes the pituitary gland, the thyroid, the adrenals, the ovaries, the testes, the parathyroids, the pancreas, and, in pregnancy, the placenta (the afterbirth). While the structural features of these glands are different, they are all alike in having a large number of secretory cells, a well-developed blood supply, and no ducts.

The endocrine secretions, the hormones, are often aptly described as "chemical messengers," since by their action they enable one part of the body to regulate the activity of another part. Hormones help control the pace of body activity, the rate of growth, the reproductive cycles, and the physical characteristics which distinguish men from women. The hormones are not usually stored to any great extent in the glands or the tissues and they must consequently be continuously produced. The exact mechanism of their action is not known, but it has been established that hormones alter the rate of metabolic reactions rather than initiate them. Some hormones are believed to affect enzyme reactions, while others are thought to act upon the surface of the cell, or combine with substances within the cell. Hormones are generally effective in minute amounts. Comparatively small fluctuations in the supply of these substances can spell the difference between a normal individual and a dwarfed, deformed, or mentally retarded person.

The Regulation of Endocrine Activity

The control of endocrine output is crucial for the normal functioning of the body. The activity of the endocrine glands is governed by the direct action of the nervous system or by the concentration of hormones and certain other substances in the blood stream.

The key region in the central nervous system involved in the control of endocrine function is the hypothalamus, a structure located at the base of the brain. Nerve pathways connect the hypothalamus with the posterior pituitary and the inner part, or medulla, of the adrenal glands. The hypothalamus also controls the activity of the anterior pituitary. This latter control is particularly important since the anterior pituitary is an influential gland, which secretes hormones which in turn stimulate the activity of the ovary, testis, thyroid, and adrenal cortex. Through its control of the anterior pituitary, the hypothalamus assumes the position of the power behind the throne in endocrine affairs. Some of the endocrine glands, such as the parathyroids and the pancreas, do not seem to be influenced by the central nervous system or by anterior pituitary secretions. Their secretions are regulated instead by the blood concentration of calcium and glucose respectively.

The Pituitary or Master Gland. The pituitary gland is a small oval structure which is attached to the base of the brain by a slender stalk. It consists of two lobes: the anterior, or adenohypophysis, and the posterior, or neurohypophysis. This gland is aptly described as the master gland of the endocrine system because of the great number of functions regulated by its hormones. In addition to secreting hormones which stimulate the thyroid, adrenals, and other endocrine glands, the pituitary releases hormones which control growth, regulate the secretion of milk, and stimulate contractions of the uterus.

The rate of pituitary secretion is controlled by what has been called a feedback mechanism. A pituitary hormone, for example, stimulates the thyroid gland to secrete thyroid hormone into the blood stream. The thyroid hormone in turn inhibits the secretion of the thyroid-stimulating hormone by the pituitary. As the blood concentration of the thyroid hormone decreases, pituitary secretion increases, and so on. Evidence suggests that this feedback regulation is effected through the hypothalamus rather than directly on the pituitary itself.

The Adrenal Glands. These glands are a pair of pyramidal structures seated on the upper pole of each kidney. They are made up of two distinct parts, an inner medulla and an outer cortex. The medulla is linked by nerve fibers to the central nervous system. The medulla secretes the hormone epinephrine (adrenalin) which shunts blood from the skin to the muscles, stimulates heart action, and induces the release of sugar into the blood, thereby preparing the body for intense physical exertion. The adrenal cortex is a vital structure which exerts an important influence upon the energy-producing activities of the body, the mineral composition of the body fluid, and the sexual characteristics which distinguish men and women.

The Thyroid Gland. The thyroid gland is an H-shaped gland which straddles the trachea, or windpipe. The thyroid hormone, thyroxine, controls the pace at which various organs burn oxygen and produce energy.

The Sex Glands. The gonads, or sex glands (testis and ovary), secrete hormones which regulate reproductive functions. The chief hormone of the testis, testosterone, brings about the development of the sexual characteristics of the male, in addition to exerting important effects on body activity. The ovary secretes hormones which regulate a variety of functions in the female reproductive tract and produce the distinctive female body characteristics.

The Placenta—The Master Gland of Pregnancy. The placenta, the disclike structure through which food substances pass from the blood of the mother to the circulation of the fetus, is thought to be the major endocrine gland of pregnancy. The placenta secretes hormones which are indispensable for the maintenance of pregnancy.

The Parathyroid Glands. The parathyroid glands are pairs of small oval structures situated closely behind the thyroid. The parathyroid secretion regulates the calcium balance in the skeleton and the body fluids. A decrease in the blood calcium concentration stimulates the secretion of parathyroid hormone.

THE HORMONES
CHEMICAL ACTION AT A DISTANCE

Long-distance communication in the body can be achieved in two ways: (1) through the nervous system and (2) by chemical secretions carried in the blood. The second method is effected through hormones secreted by the endocrine glands.

PITUITARY GLAND

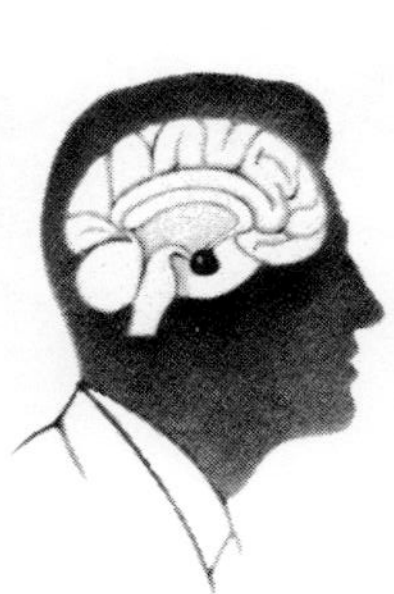

ANTERIOR PITUITARY HORMONES

(1) GROWTH HORMONE (STH) stimulates general growth.

(2) THYROID-STIMULATING HORMONE (TSH) stimulates the thyroid gland.

(3) ADRENOCORTICOTROPIC HORMONE (ACTH) stimulates the outer layer (cortex) of the adrenal gland.

(4) FOLLICLE-STIMULATING HORMONE (FSH) induces ripening of ovarian follicles (in females) and sperm production (in males).

(5) LUTEINIZING HORMONE (LH) stimulates ovulation (in females) and gonads (in males).

(6) PROLACTIN, OR LUTEOTROPHIC HORMONE (LTH), stimulates lactation.

POSTERIOR PITUITARY HORMONES

OXYTOCIN stimulates contractions of smooth muscle of uterus and breast.

ANTIDIURETIC HORMONE (ADH) regulates volume of urine.

ADRENALS

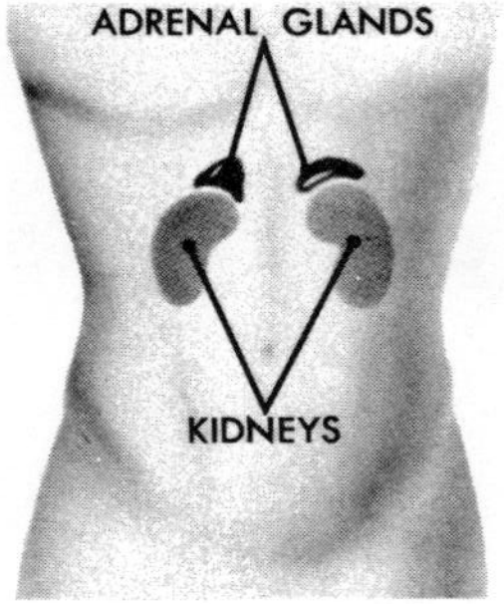

ADRENAL HORMONES

OUTER LAYER (cortex)
GLUCOCORTICOIDS promote conversion of protein into sugar, aid in transport of fat from storage sites to liver, and increase resistance to stress. MINERALOCORTICOIDS act on kidneys to regulate mineral composition of body fluids, increase sodium concentration, and decrease potassium concentration of body fluids. The action of the ANDROGENIC CORTICOIDS is similar to that of male sex hormones.

INNER LAYER (medulla)
ADRENALIN stimulates heart beat, inhibits gastrointestinal activity, promotes release of sugar from liver into blood, and increases blood flow to skeletal muscles. NORADRENALINE acts to constrict blood vessels throughout the body.

THYROID GLAND

THYROID HORMONES regulate metabolism and oxygen consumption of body cells and contribute to growth and development.

PARATHYROID GLANDS

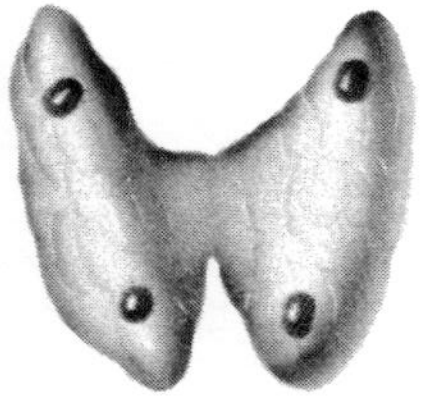

PARATHORMONE regulates calcium concentration of blood.

PANCREAS

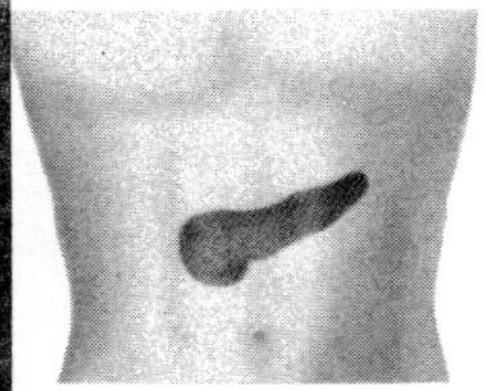

PANCREATIC HORMONES

The endocrine cells of the pancreas are contained in groups known as the Islets of Langerhans. The α cells secrete the hormone glucagon, which raises blood sugar. The β cells secrete the hormone insulin, which lowers blood sugar.

GONADS

OVARIAN HORMONES

ESTROGENS: important in regulation of menstrual cycle, stimulate uterus, and maintain female physical characteristics.

RELAXIN relaxes pelvic ligaments during pregnancy.

TESTICULAR HORMONES

ANDROGENS stimulate growth of muscle, kidneys, bone, and other tissues and influence sexual behavior.

PLACENTA

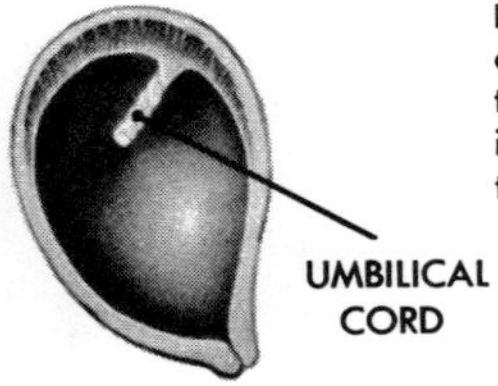

During pregnancy the placenta (the afterbirth) links the circulation of the mother and child. The placenta secretes the hormone progesterone, which maintains pregnancy and prevents eggs from ripening in the ovary. Progesterone is also produced by the corpus luteum of the ovary during the normal menstrual cycle.

SOME IMPORTANT ACTIVITIES REGULATED BY HORMONES

ENERGY PRODUCTION

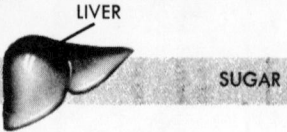

PROTEIN → LIVER → SUGAR → BLOOD STREAM → OXYGEN / SUGAR → CELLS

Adrenal corticosteroids promote conversion of proteins to sugar in the liver.

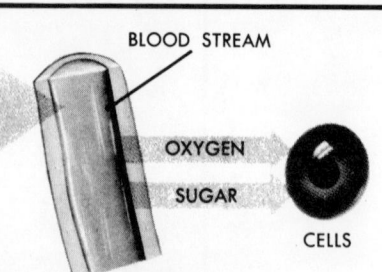

Thyroid hormone promotes utilization of oxygen by cells.

Insulin enables the cells of the body to burn sugar as fuel.

BODY CHEMISTRY

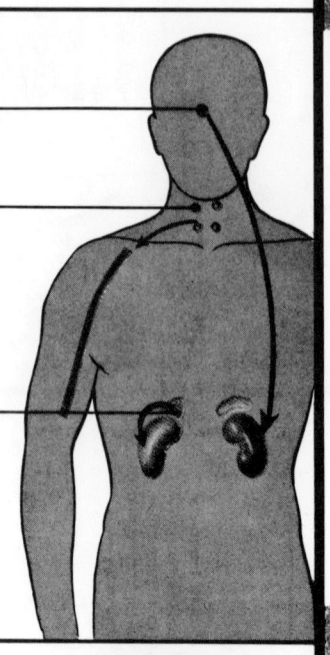

Antidiuretic hormone of the pituitary gland prevents an excessive loss of water from the body in urine.

Parathyroid hormone regulates calcium concentration of blood.

Adrenal mineralocorticoids prevent an excessive loss of sodium from the body in urine.

GROWTH

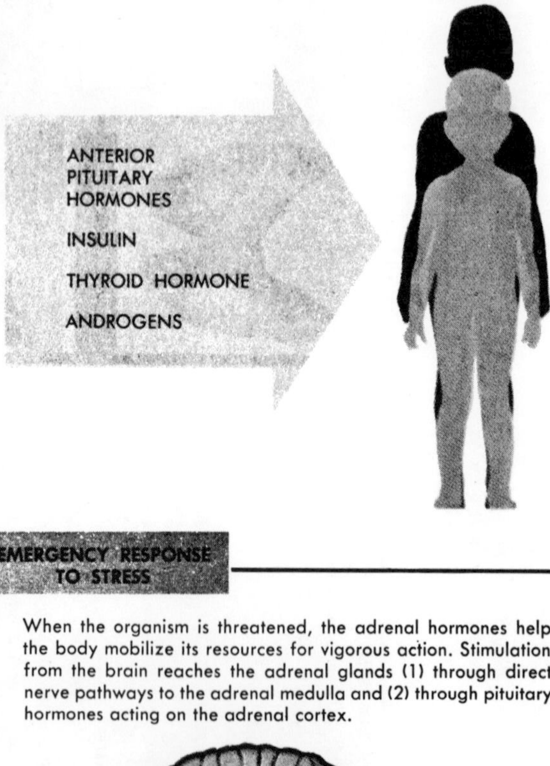

ANTERIOR PITUITARY HORMONES

INSULIN

THYROID HORMONE

ANDROGENS

MENSTRUATION

(1) Follicle-stimulating hormone (FSH) from pituitary stimulates development of egg-containing follicle in ovary.

(2) Egg ruptures from the follicle and leaves the ovary. The follicle remains behind to become the "yellow body," or corpus luteum. This occurs under the influence of the luteinizing hormone (LH) of the pituitary gland.

(3) Progesterone from the corpus luteum inhibits secretion of LH and FSH from the pituitary gland.

(4) Estrogen and progesterone from the ovary prime the lining of the uterus for the implantation of the egg. If the egg is not fertilized, the built-up uterine lining is discarded with the menstrual flow.

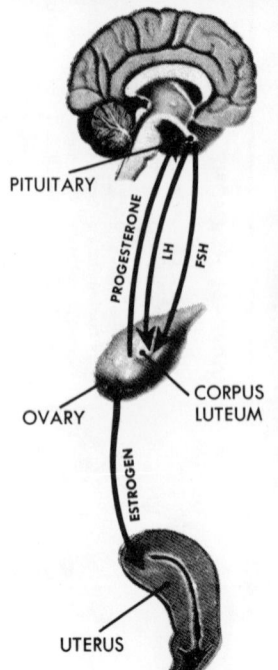

PITUITARY — PROGESTERONE / LH / FSH — OVARY — CORPUS LUTEUM — ESTROGEN — UTERUS

EMERGENCY RESPONSE TO STRESS

When the organism is threatened, the adrenal hormones help the body mobilize its resources for vigorous action. Stimulation from the brain reaches the adrenal glands (1) through direct nerve pathways to the adrenal medulla and (2) through pituitary hormones acting on the adrenal cortex.

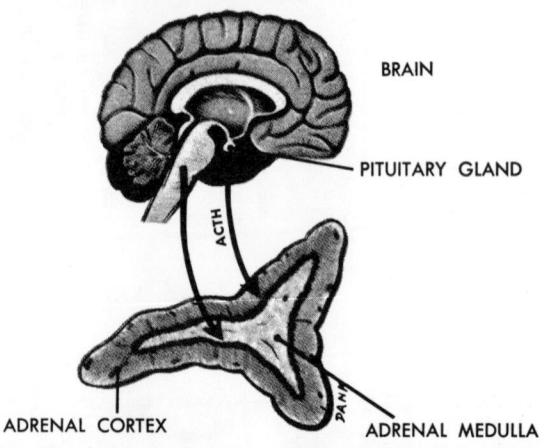

BRAIN

PITUITARY GLAND

ACTH

ADRENAL CORTEX — ADRENAL MEDULLA

Adrenal cortical hormones stimulate release of sugar from the liver and promote muscular efficiency.

Adrenalin and noradrenaline raise the blood pressure, stimulate heart action, and increase the blood flow to the skeletal muscles.

The Pancreas. The pancreas is a dual-nature gland, in that some of its secretions pass through ducts into the small intestine, while others enter the blood stream directly. The endocrine cells of the pancreas are contained in groups of cells called the Islets of Langerhans. Two different types of cells are present in the islets: α cells which probably secrete glucagon and β cells which are the source of insulin. These substances apparently work in opposite directions: Glucagon raises the blood sugar while insulin lowers it.

The Endocrine Diseases

An imbalance of hormone supply usually leads to disease. The variety of hormones and their effects is paralleled by the diversity of endocrine diseases.

The Pituitary: *Overactivity.* An excess of growth hormone during childhood may produce giants nine ft. tall. If the hormone is in oversupply after adolescence, acromegaly results, an enlargement of the hands, feet, jaw, and other body parts. An overproduction of the hormones which stimulate the outer layer (the cortex) of the adrenal glands causes Cushing's disease, which involves a distinctive type of obesity, a round face, high blood pressure, and altered sexual characteristics.

Underactivity. An undersupply of the growth hormone results in dwarfism. Pituitary dwarfs are usually well-proportioned and are not mentally retarded.

The Adrenals: *Overactivity.* Excessive secretion of male sex hormones from the cortex causes deepening of the voice and growth of a beard in women and precocious sexual maturity in boys.

Underactivity. A wasting away of the adrenal cortex causes Addison's disease, characterized by muscular weakness, loss of weight, low blood pressure, and excess pigmentation of various parts of the body.

The Thyroid: *Overactivity,* or hyperthyroidism, is marked by excessive energy, nervousness, tremors, loss of weight, rapid heart beat, and occasionally, protruding eyeballs.

Underactivity in the prenatal period or in infancy causes cretinism, a disorder marked by stunted growth, retarded mentality, and underdevelopment of the sexual organs and the sexual characteristics. In adults undersupply of the thyroid hormone results in myxedema, characterized by puffiness of the face, dry skin and hair, diminished vigor, and slow pulse.

Goiter is a swelling of the thyroid gland which may be accompanied by either an excess of or underproduction of thyroid hormone. A common form of goiter results from a dietary deficiency of iodine, the essential constituent of the thyroid hormone. Such goiters are seen in regions where the iodine content of the water or soil is low, as in mountain villages in the Alps and the Himalayas, and in certain parts of North America near the Great Lakes. In these regions the disease is controlled by adding small quantities of iodine to the diet.

Pancreas. Diabetes, a major endocrine disease, results from inadequate supply of the pancreatic hormone—insulin. Diabetes is characterized by high blood sugar, excessive urination, and sugar in the urine. The ability of the body to burn starchy foods as a fuel is seriously impaired. The disease can be controlled, but not cured, by administering insulin.

Other endocrine diseases include disorders of the parathyroid and the sex glands. The endocrine disorders are usually treated either by supplying the missing hormone (in the case of underproduction) or by surgically removing some glandular tissue (in the case of overproduction). The isolation and commercial preparation of hormones have made possible the treatment of serious illnesses that had defied treatment.

ENEMA [ĕn'ə-mə], the introduction of fluid into the rectum for the purpose of cleansing the bowel or administering sedatives, anesthetics, or other medications. Drugs may be given with retention enemas: The fluid is injected slowly and permitted to remain for several hours. Enemas of barium salts are used for X-ray examination of the gastrointestinal tract. Since barium is opaque to X rays the barium-filled intestines appear sharply outlined on the X-ray photograph. Ice-water enemas have been used to reduce fever rapidly.

ENZYMES [ĕn'zīmz], protein substances which make possible most of the chemical reactions occurring in living organisms. All living systems, from the lowest to the highest, carry out several thousand different chemical reactions which form the basis of activities such as digestion, the contraction of muscle, the beating of the heart, the secretion of urine, the processes of seeing, hearing, smelling, and thinking, and the coagulation of blood. Apart from a few exceptions, none of these reactions would take place in living things were it not for the presence of enzymes which catalyze, or speed up, these reactions. In virtually all cases the enzyme also initiates the reaction.

The Nature of Enzymatic Reactions. A simple chemical reaction can be described as the conversion of molecule A to molecule B. A few molecules of the enzyme which catalyzes this reaction would be sufficient to convert billions of molecule A to molecule B. Barring wear and tear, the enzyme could proceed indefinitely, converting more and more A into B.

An outstanding feature of the reaction is that only one thing happens: A is changed into B. In organic chemistry it is extremely rare for a reaction to have only one outcome. Usually a percentage of molecules react in some other way than that desired. In enzyme-catalyzed reactions, however, there are no side reactions of any kind.

In addition to there being only one product of the reaction, there is only one enzyme which will catalyze the reaction. This specificity derives from the fact that the enzyme and the molecule it acts upon (the substrate) have a lock and key relationship. The substrate fits perfectly into the contours of the enzyme protein and by virtue of this fit the substrate molecule becomes unstable and readily susceptible to chemical change.

The specificity of enzymes for their substrates can be very sharp. For example, certain types of molecules have two forms which are mirror images of one another. In all other respects these forms are indistinguishable chemically, yet the enzymes unerringly select the right form to act upon. Another type of specificity is based upon the size of the molecule. Enzymes will accurately distinguish three-carbon molecules from four-carbon molecules. These specificities result from the perfect fit of substrate molecules to the enzyme. They are of great biological importance because they insure that only one type of molecule and no other, regardless of how similar it might be, will undergo a given chemical change. In the laboratory of the living cell, where thousands of reactions go on at all times, the specificity of enzyme action is the safeguard against potentially dangerous reactions.

What Does the Enzyme Do to the Substrate? When the substrate molecule is seized in the chemical embrace of the enzyme it is subjected to considerable strain, which induces a high degree of chemical reactivity. The substrate molecule can be changed in a number of ways. The particular change will be determined by the area of the enzyme molecule to which the substrate becomes attached and by the distribution of electric charges over the enzyme as a whole. The part of the enzyme molecule which links with the substrate is known as the active group. The distribution of electric charges concerns the charges (positive or negative) carried by some of the amino acids which make up the enzyme molecule.

The Enzyme Team. Enzymes usually work in teams and in many parts of the cell enzymes are attached to one another like the tiles of a mosaic. Such an arrangement makes it possible for reactions to follow one another in a definite order with a minimum of lost motion. The mitochondrion of animal cells and the chloroplast of plant cells are essentially mosaics of this type. Within the mitochondrial enzyme mosaic, glucose is burned to CO_2 and water; the released chemical energy is converted into a form more useful to the cell. Within the chloroplast, light energy is changed into the chemical energy of sugar. Similarly, all energy conversions in living systems are brought about by specialized enzyme teams.

The Prosthetic Group. Many enzymes require an additional molecule, called the prosthetic group, in order to act. The prosthetic group may be a metal atom (iron, copper, zinc, molybdenum) or a complex organic molecule. Many, if not all, of the vitamins are building stones of these prosthetic groups. Consequently, if our diet is deficient in a particular vitamin, certain enzymes which contain this vitamin as part of their prosthetic group cannot function. If these enzymes do not function then certain reactions essential for life cannot go on.

The quantity of vitamins needed is minute compared to the amount of food required. The tremendous potency of small amounts of vitamins results from the extraordinary efficiency of the enzymes which they activate. The need for extremely minute, or "trace," elements of certain metals, such as copper and cobalt, is also related to the role of these metals as parts of the prosthetic groups of enzymes.

Enzymes, Poisons, and Drugs. Certain poisons and drugs are effective in minute amounts because they interfere with the action of enzymes. Some bacteria, such as the organism which produces gas gangrene in putrefying wounds, are exceedingly dangerous because of an enzyme which they release into the body. These enzymes are known as toxins and are lethal in extremely small concentrations—a few molecules are sufficient to wreak havoc in sensitive areas of the body. Drugs such as curare, and poisons such as cyanide, specifically suppress the action of certain enzymes.

Enzymes and Bacteria. Antibiotics are drugs which are able to suppress the growth of disease-producing microorganisms without harming human cells or tissues. The antibiotics paralyze the microorganism by combining with and immobilizing some key enzyme in the organism which is essential for its growth. If that particular enzyme is not present or plays a minor role in human cells, then the growth of the microorganism can be halted without damaging the body. The best antibiotics are obviously those which are potent inhibitors of enzymes, which are both unique to, and important to, the disease organisms.

The Manufacture of Enzymes. The cells of the living organism must manufacture the enzymes needed to bring about vital chemical reactions. The knowledge of enzyme manufacture is inherited by each cell and this inheritance is represented in the cell as the particular ordering of molecules which make up a substance called deoxyribose nucleic acid—the master enzyme-maker of the cell. When a particular enzyme is synthesized under the direction of deoxyribose nucleic acid, each of the enzyme molecules produced is exactly the same. The process of synthesis never slips up and all molecules are identical down to the last detail. If the molecule of deoxyribose nucleic acid, which carries the blueprint for the synthesis of an enzyme, is damaged by radiation, the blueprint could be altered, resulting in production of a modified version of that particular enzyme. Changes of this type could result in a "mutant," an organism which departs from the norm of the wild type.

In 1969 two research teams working independently synthesized ribonuclease, an enzyme 124 amino-acid units long, which serves to break down ribonucleic acid in the cell. This final step in establishing the structure of the molecule perhaps opened the way for artificial synthesis of other enzymes. With mounting evidence of the effectiveness of enzymes in treating such diverse ailments as blood clots, tooth decay, and certain forms of leukemia, enzyme synthesis assumes even greater significance.
See also BIOCHEMISTRY.

EPHEDRINE [ĭ-fĕd'rĭn], drug similar in action to the adrenal hormone epinephrine (adrenalin). Like adrenalin, ephedrine dilates the breathing passages, increases heart output, raises the blood pressure, and constricts blood vessels; it also dilates the pupil of the eye. Used in Chinese medicine for over 5,000 years (as the herb mahuang), ephedrine was first investigated by Western researchers in the 20th century upon the advice of a Chinese druggist. The drug has been used principally in the treatment of asthma and hay fever and other allergic disorders. Ephedrine is also used to maintain the blood pressure during spinal anesthesia and in ophthalmologic practice as a pupil dilator.

EPIDEMICS [ĕp-ə-dĕm'ĭks] **AND EPIDEMIOLOGY** [ĕp-ə-dē-mĭ-ŏl'ə-jĭ]. An epidemic is an unusual occurrence of a disease, which affects many persons. Throughout history epidemics have been among the most dreaded of natural calamities. In the 14th century the Black Death, believed to have been bubonic plague, killed over 20,000,000 people. Smallpox epidemics took an enormous toll before the English physician Jenner developed the technique of vaccination. The great influenza epidemic of the early part of

EPIDEMICS

Immigrants to Singapore are examined by port health officers for infectious diseases before being permitted to debark.
Jean Manevy—World Health Organization

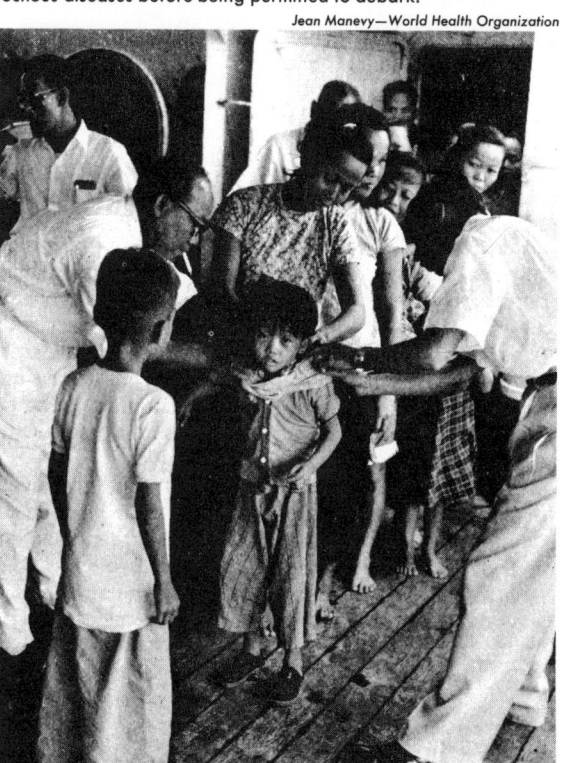

The effective use of DDT spray against mosquitoes is explained to Libyan school children during an antimalaria campaign.
Roche Medical Image

Bread samples, to be tested for bacteria, are removed by health officers from the public market at Zavia, Libya.
Roche Medical Image

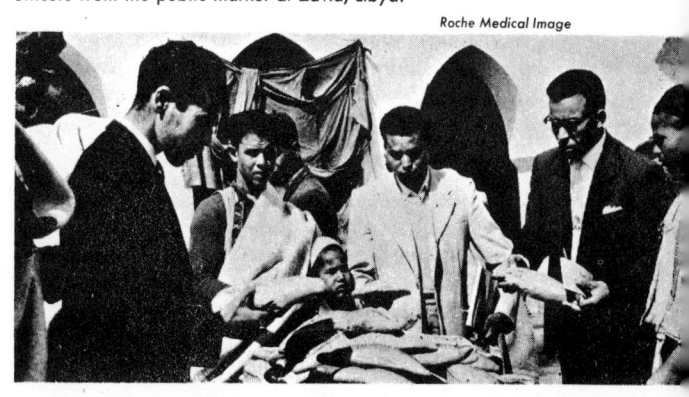

the 20th century took an estimated 21,000,000 lives.

While the term "epidemic" originally referred to these massive outbreaks of infectious diseases, it is now also applied to noninfectious conditions. Thus the prevalence of coronary heart disease, lung cancer, and automobile accidents in the United States is said to be of epidemic proportions.

Unlike the practitioner of clinical medicine who deals with an individual patient, the epidemiologist concerns himself with an entire community which is afflicted with an epidemic disease. His responsibility is to identify the disease and to find out how it began and how it is spread.

Investigation of Epidemics in the Field. When many cases of a similar illness appear in a community an epidemiologist must first identify the disease. This may be accomplished by studying the disease in individual patients. Often laboratory procedures are necessary. For example, culturing virus from stool specimens taken from patients is the best way of diagnosing epidemics of certain infections of the nervous system.

The sequence in which the epidemic develops may be a vital clue to its origin and manner of transmission. If most cases appear at the same time, a single common source, such as a contaminated food or water supply, might be suspected. If cases of an infectious illness appeared at different times, the epidemiologist might look for a chain of infection among patients. In the case of an infectious disease, such as smallpox, he would seek information about patient contacts with persons or places which could have been the original source of infection. When dealing with diseases such as typhoid or infectious hepatitis, which are transmitted chiefly through the gastrointestinal tract, he would also investigate food or water sources which the victims used in common, food handlers who might carry the agent, contamination of the water supply by sewage, and possible contamination of the food by flies. In the case of an insect-transmitted disease, such as yellow fever or malaria, the search would be directed to finding the type of mosquito known to carry the infectious organism.

The epidemiologist is also vitally concerned with those persons who do not contract the illness. He asks: "What common factor is shared by those who remain free of the illness as contrasted to those who succumb?" He may employ statistical techniques to determine whether the differences he finds result merely from chance variation or whether they are significant. An early example of the value of such studies was provided by John Snow, an Englishman, who in 1855 fixed the responsibility for a large cholera epidemic in London upon the water supply. Snow was able to do this by observing the very low cholera rate among groups of people who lived in the center of an epidemic area, but used a different water source.

Endemic Diseases. A disease is said to be endemic in a community if it is constantly present within the community but without causing more than a few persons to become seriously ill. A case in point is poliomyelitis, which is endemic in many areas, especially in the tropics and in underdeveloped countries. The virus circulates constantly, and is so widespread that infants are infected while still protected by the temporary immunity with which they are born. As a result, almost all children in such areas have their first infections and become immune without showing signs of illness. When living standards and hygiene improve, more children escape early infections and first encounter the polioviruses at ages when they are more likely to develop paralytic poliomyelitis. Nowadays it is possible to confer immunity on all susceptible persons by means of vaccination.

Prevention. Community health departments check food, water, and milk supplies to detect and eliminate potential disease-producing organisms. In many localities the chemical pollution of air and water is regularly investigated. An important responsibility of health departments is the maintenance of vaccination programs in non-epidemic periods to turn susceptible persons into immune persons and thus to prevent outbreaks from occurring.

EPIGLOTTIS [ĕp-ə-glŏt′ĭs], a thin, leaf-shaped structure, composed of cartilage, which projects upward behind the root of the tongue in reptiles and mammals. The epiglottis prevents the entrance of food into the larynx, or "voice box," either by diverting it to either side, or by folding back over the entrance to the larynx.

EPILEPSY [ĕp′ə-lĕp-sē], a disorder of the nervous system characterized by sudden, temporary disturbances of brain function. Although epilepsy was recognized as a medical disorder as far back as the time of the ancient Greeks (who called it the "sacred disease"), it has continued to inspire dread in uninformed persons who consider the epileptic to be "possessed of the devil." In many primitive societies the epileptic was regarded as being gifted with supernatural powers.

Today epilepsy is considered to be a symptom of an underlying disease of the brain which may be caused by a tumor, infection, or injury. In some cases there is no evident disturbance and the patient is said to have "idiopathic" epilepsy. Epilepsy of this type often appears in several members of the same family. The epileptic attacks result from abnormal, uncontrolled electrical activity of the brain cells. The massive electrical discharges occurring during the attack can be recorded by the electroencephalograph, which is used to detect electrical "brain waves." This instrument is often valuable in diagnosing epilepsy.

Types of Attacks. The most familiar seizure is the *grand mal* ("great illness"). The attack is usually preceded by a warning or "aura" which may consist of hallucinatory sounds, smells, or flashes of light. The limbs stiffen briefly, after which the body jerks violently. The patient may cry or scream just before losing consciousness. During the convulsion he may foam at the mouth, bite his tongue, or, occasionally, urinate, as the bladder sphincter muscle is relaxed.

In *petit mal* (literally, "little illness"), there is usually a momentary loss of consciousness, often called "faints" or "spells." The patient sits motionless as though dazed or in a trance. He stops whatever activity he is engaged in and later resumes his work without mishap.

Psychomotor epilepsy is marked by confusion and anxiety, without loss of consciousness. The patient may perform automatic movements such as chewing and smacking the lips. The attack lasts for 1 to 2 minutes. Afterward the patient has no recollection that he has had an attack.

There is no definite evidence that the epileptic attacks produce any damaging physical effects on the organism, beyond the injuries resulting from falls that occur during seizures. Such disorders as psychosis or feeblemindedness may coexist with epilepsy, but are not caused by it.

Treatment. A number of drugs are available to control epileptic attacks; the commonest are phenobarbital, dilantin, and tridione. Patients must take medication daily, as the seizures will generally reappear if treatment is discontinued. Approximately half of all epileptic patients can be maintained completely free of seizures, while another 30% can be substantially improved. Surgery may be effective in certain cases, such as in epilepsy caused by a tumor pressing on the brain.

The frequency of epilepsy makes it a medical and social problem. It is estimated that there are between one and two million epileptics in the United States. Because of its dramatic and frequently unpredictable nature, epilepsy has often posed serious social handicaps for its victims. Epileptic children have been educated in special classes or schools and many industries will not employ epileptics, feeling that the risks of accidents are too great. The patient, aware of being a "special case," develops many psychological problems. Actually, except in cases where seizures cannot be medically controlled, most epileptics are able to lead a normal existence. Because of the importance of heredity in some types of epilepsy, marriage is still forbidden to epileptics in many states. Many authorities, however, are no longer in agreement with this policy.

EPINEPHRINE [ĕp-ə-nĕf′rĭn], also called adrenalin, is a hormone secreted by the inner portion, or medulla, of the adrenal gland. Epinephrine helps to mobilize the resources of the body for strenuous or emergency activity. It accomplishes this by shunting blood from the skin and digestive tract to the muscles of the arms, legs, and trunk, by increasing heart action and blood pressure, by widening the air passages, and by raising the sugar level of the blood.

Epinephrine is used in medicine in certain heart emergencies. It is also used in cases of bronchial asthma to relax spasms of the bronchi (the air passages) and in certain allergic conditions such as hives and severe, shocklike, serum sickness. The ability of epinephrine to constrict small blood vessels has made it useful in controlling superficial hemorrhages from the skin. For this reason the drug is frequently incorporated in anesthetic solutions. The narrowing of the blood vessels slows the rate of absorption of the anesthetic and thus prolongs its action.
See also ADRENAL GLANDS; ENDOCRINE GLANDS.

ERASISTRATUS [ĕr-ə-sĭs′trə-təs] (c.3d century B.C.), Greek physician, anatomist, and pioneer physiologist who was one of the renowned medical teachers at the Alexandria Museum in Egypt. He traced the veins and arteries to the

heart and regarded the blood as a nourishing substance. He also devised a catheter, a tubelike instrument to be introduced into body cavities, and was an early opponent of bloodletting as a therapeutic procedure.
See also MEDICINE.

ESTROGENS [ĕs′trə-jənz], the name applied to a group of compounds which stimulate the growth of the uterus and the development of the female body characteristics, and regulate the menstrual cycle. Estrogens are manufactured in the ovaries of mammals. They are widely distributed in animal and plant tissues and have been isolated from human and animal urine, from petroleum, peat, and from plants, such as the pussy willow. Synthetic estrogens have also been made.

In the human body, estrogens appear to be manufactured from cholesterol. They are deactivated by the liver. Estrogens are used to treat menopausal disturbances, certain vaginal inflammations, menstrual disorders, and cases of engorgement of the breasts following pregnancy. They have also been used with some success in the treatment of cancer of the prostate and breast.
See also ENDOCRINE GLANDS.

ETHER [ē′thər] **or DIETHYL ETHER,** an anesthetic compound first prepared in 1540, but not used in medicine until the middle of the 19th century.

Ether is prepared by heating together concentrated sulfuric acid and ethyl alcohol. It is a colorless liquid which evaporates readily and becomes highly flammable when mixed with air or oxygen.

When used as an anesthetic, ether first increases the heartbeat and breathing rates. This effect is reversed as the patient passes into a deeper anesthesia. When properly used, ether relaxes the abdominal muscles sufficiently so that the surgeon may stretch them away from the site of the operation.

Ether is a comparatively safe anesthetic, but should not be used on patients suffering from diabetes and kidney diseases. Other disadvantages associated with its use are post-operative nausea and vomiting and a tendency to stimulate mucous secretions which block the air passages.
See also ANESTHESIA.

ETHOLOGY, biological study of animal behavior in its natural state. For the ethologist, all animal behavior must be analyzed not only in regard to its cause, but also for its function in furthering survival. The mechanistic views held by science around the turn of the century favored other psychological theories, notably behaviorism, which explains an animal's action on the basis of its response to a stimulus. Experimentalists are looking for "how" the animal behaves, but the ethologist first asks "why." In the last few decades, especially through the work of K. Z. Lorenz and Niko Tinbergen in Europe, the naturalistic observation of behavior has come to supplement the laboratory study of behavior which has burgeoned in the United States.

The ethologist likes to make a dossier of all the animal's behavior, called an ethogram. The units of behavior in this catalogue are subsequently analyzed, especially stereotyped behaviors that could have an instinctive background. In such behavior sequences it is possible to find motor actions that seem automated because they always proceed in the same manner—the so-called fixed action pattern (FAP). They are brought about by a "sign stimulus," or releaser. It is hypothesized that a drive makes the animal look for the specific stimulus situation needed for such actions. The predictable defensive behavior of the male European robin, when it sees another male robin while patrolling its territory, may serve as an example. The releaser for the robin's threatening actions is the orange-colored breast of the intruder, since it has been shown that a stuffed robin without the orange breast is not attacked, and a tuft of orange feathers is attacked by the irate territory-owner.

Another typical animal behavior pattern revealed by ethological studies is imprinting. Imprinting is the rapid establishment of social preferences in the young animal, which will remain in force for life without continuous reinforcement. Lorenz imprinted himself on young geese by being present at their hatching. They followed him as their mother, and when they were mature they even tried to mate with him. This type of instantaneous learning differs both from instinctual activities and from other types of learning, such as conditioning.

By careful description of the objective behavior of organisms, ethologists have revived interest in the instinctual basis of behavior and the processes by which learned and unlearned behavior merge imperceptibly. The study of ethograms provides insight into innate behavior patterns that determine social behavior, such as the phenomenon of imprinting, and the releasers and fixed action patterns which are components of complex behavior. The concept of drive, the purposiveness of many behavioral activities and their meaning for the survival of the species, have become legitimate concerns for the comparative psychologist. Laboratory research based on ethological findings has very much increased. Such research is an important supplement to the experimental findings of studies based on stimulus-response and learning theories which held the dominant position. Consequently, many new insights into the motivational aspects of animal behavior are now available for possible application in testing theories of human behavior, such as the drive theory of psychoanalysis, which hitherto could not be substantiated.
See also AGGRESSION; PSYCHOLOGY.

EUNUCH [ū′nək], a castrated man. The custom of castrating men was particularly widespread in the Near East, but it was also known in Greece, Rome, India, and China. Eunuchs were employed as guards, especially of the women's quarters, or harems. They also held much more important posts such as counselors to nobles and rulers, and frequently became great ministers of state in Persia, China, and the Byzantine Empire. Some men were made eunuchs as punishment for sexual crimes, but others chose this role. Eunuchism was deliberately sought by the Galli, priests of Near Eastern fertility goddesses such as the Ephesian Diana, Astarte, or Ishtar, and Cybele.

EUNUCHOIDISM [ū′nək-oid-ĭz-əm], a glandular disturbance marked by the development of female physical characteristics in men. Eunuchoidism is caused by improper functioning of the testicles, resulting in an inadequate

EVOLUTION

production of the hormones that are necessary to maintain normal masculine characteristics. If the disturbance arises prior to puberty the sex organs remain small, the skin is soft, the voice is high-pitched, and the body fat is distributed in the feminine pattern. When eunuchoidism develops after puberty the changes are less dramatic, the main effects being a feminine fat distribution, decrease in the growth of the beard, and a weakening of sexual drives. Treatment consists of administering male hormones to correct the deficiency.

See also ENDOCRINE GLANDS.

EVOLUTION [ĕv-ə-lōō'shən], the natural process through which organisms have acquired their characteristic structure and function. The term is derived from the Lat. *evolvere*, "to unroll or unfold," and refers to the orderly development of species from pre-existing ones.

The past few centuries have witnessed a thorough inventory of the million or more species of plants and animals living today, as well as of the thousands of extinct species. Many biologists have studied in detail the structures, functions, habits, and distribution of these organisms. The result has been an accurate picture of the amazing variety and complexity of life. But at the same time it has spurred curiosity as to how this has all come into existence. How can the many similarities and differences among plants and animals be explained? How do new species come into being? What happens to ancestral species? Biologists believe that the evolutionary concept gives the most adequate answer to these questions. Evolution is the logical application to life of the truth that change is inevitable and universal.

EXCRETORY [ĕks'krə-tôr-ē] **SYSTEM**, name for the various structures that collectively serve to remove metabolic waste from the animal body. The simplest excretory apparatus probably is the contractile vacuole, found in many one-celled animals. This spherical, fluid-filled cavity is believed to gather waste from the cell, then discharges its contents into the surrounding water. Flatworms have an excretory system consisting of a network of flame cells. Wastes are collected in tubules of this network and leave the body through surface openings. Earthworms and other segmented worms have a pair of excretory organs, the nephridia, in all but the first and last few of their body segments. The nephridia collect nitrogenous wastes from both the fluid of the body cavity (the coelom) and from the blood stream; filter out any useful proteins which are reabsorbed by the body; then transfer the urine to tube-shaped bladders where it is temporarily stored before being excreted at openings along the body surface.

In reptiles, birds, and mammals the excretory function is performed primarily by the kidneys. The kidneys collect metabolic wastes from the blood stream; filter out and reabsorb any useful material such as sugars, sodium, and calcium; and concentrate the resulting nitrogenous fluid by reabsorbing large amounts of water. The fluid waste then passes from the kidneys to the bladder by ducts (one from each kidney) known as ureters, and from the bladder through a single duct, the urethra.

Although the kidneys are the most important excretory organs of higher organisms, some excretory function is performed by other parts of the body. Carbon dioxide and water are eliminated during the respiratory process; the wastes of heavy metals and water are voided with the feces; and (especially in man) the sweat glands of the skin serve to eliminate water, salts, and traces of carbon dioxide and nitrogenous wastes.

See also KIDNEY; PERSPIRATION; RESPIRATION.

EXOPHTHALMOS [ĕk-sŏf-thăl'məs], protrusion of the eyeball which may result from inflammations, fluid swellings, or tumors developing behind the eyeball and pushing it forward. Overactivity of the thyroid gland (hyperthyroidism) is a common cause. Some cases of congenital enlargement of the eyeball may simulate exophthalmos.

EXPECTORANT [ĕk-spĕk'tər-ənt], drug or agent which aids in the removal of secretions from the breathing passages. The expectorants may accomplish this by stimulating the flow of secretions, thus making the sputum thinner. They are most frequently used to relieve inflammations of the respiratory tract. Among the expectorant drugs are ammonium chloride, ipecac, and ammonium carbonate. Steam and carbon dioxide inhalations are also excellent expectorant agents.

EYE, the organ of vision. The eye is a sphere approximately one inch in diameter. It consists essentially of a transparent front portion which bends, transmits, and focuses light onto a light-sensitive layer in the rear (the

THE OUTER LAYERS OF THE EYE

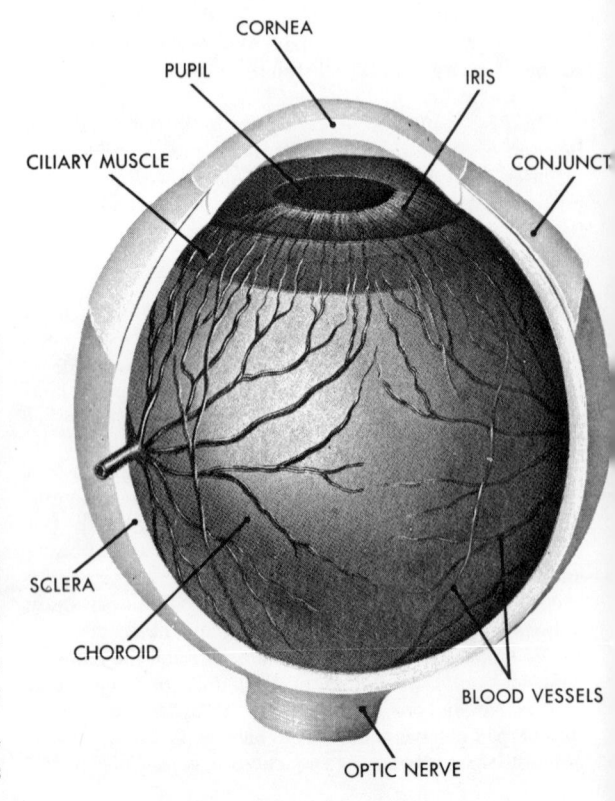

CORNEA
PUPIL
IRIS
CILIARY MUSCLE
CONJUNCT
SCLERA
CHOROID
BLOOD VESSELS
OPTIC NERVE

retina). The optic nerve conducts impulses from the retina to the visual portion of the brain where the work of perception is completed.

The Structure of the Eye

The Outer Layers. The outermost layer, or fibrous tunic, forms the sclera, or "white of the eye." It is opaque throughout its extent, save for a circular transparent section in front (the cornea).

Underneath the fibrous tunic is the choroid, a dark-brown layer, richly supplied with blood vessels. In the back of the eye, this pigmented tissue acts like the layer of black paint inside a camera, which absorbs excess light and prevents internal reflections.

The Iris and Pupil. The iris, or colored part of the eye, is a circular curtain with a hole in its middle (the pupil). Blue eyes receive their color from two layers of pigmented cells in the rear of the iris. In brown eyes the front layers of the iris are also pigmented. The pupil acts as a light-adjusting mechanism, opening wide under conditions of low illumination, and contracting in bright daylight.

The Lens and the Ciliary Muscle. The lens lies directly behind the iris. The surrounding ciliary muscle helps to focus light on the retina by adjusting the shape of the lens.

The Retina. The retina is the light-sensitive membrane in the rear of the eye which corresponds to the film of a camera. It consists basically of three layers of cells: the rods and cones; an intermediate layer of conducting bipolar cells; and the ganglion cells, which conduct nerve impulses along the retina to the optic nerve. From the viewpoint of the approaching light ray, the retina is upside down, since light must pass through the upper layers to reach the light-sensitive rods and cones in the lower layer.

Knowledge of the anatomy of the retina provides interesting insights into the mechanism of vision. If the retina is compared to the film in the camera, the analogy can be extended to note that the quality of the picture obtained depends upon the grain—the number of individual light-sensitive points in the film. The finer the grain, the more detailed the image. The grain of the retina is supplied by approximately 126 million separate light-sensitive elements called rods and cones (about 120 million rods and 6 million cones). This excellent grain is lost, however, since the optic nerve which conducts visual impulses to the brain contains only about one million individual fibers. A further limiting factor is the number of cells (bipolar and ganglion) which link the rods and cones to the optic nerve fibers. In the periphery of the retina many rods must share a single ganglion cell, while in the center, where vision is sharper, more ganglion cells are available.

From the Eye to the Brain

Visual impulses travel from the optic nerve to the occipital portion of the brain.

Prior to reaching the visual cortex half of the fibers cross at the optic chiasma and travel to the opposite side of the brain.

Thus the images are fragmented so that the left side of both visual fields travels to the right side of the brain and the right portion of the fields reaches the left half of the brain.

FROM THE EYE TO THE BRAIN

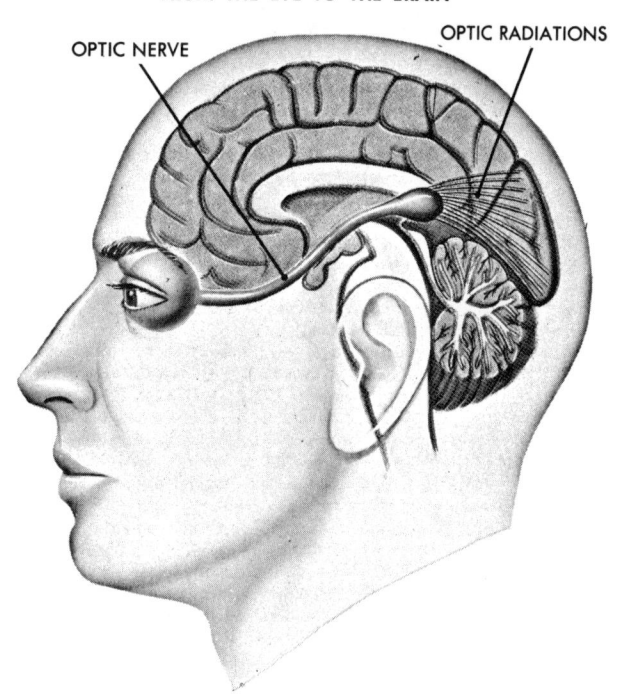

The Mechanisms of Vision

Directing the Eyes to the Object. The eye is fixed on its target by contractions of the ocular muscles which move the eyeballs.

Focusing is accomplished by the ciliary muscle which alters the shape of the lens.

The Double Function of the Retina—Day and Night Vision. If a person suddenly passes from the sunlit outdoors into a dark room he finds that while at first he can see nothing, objects gradually become visible over a period of time. If this process of "dark adaptation" is plotted on a graph, a distinct rapid increase in sensitivity is noticeable.

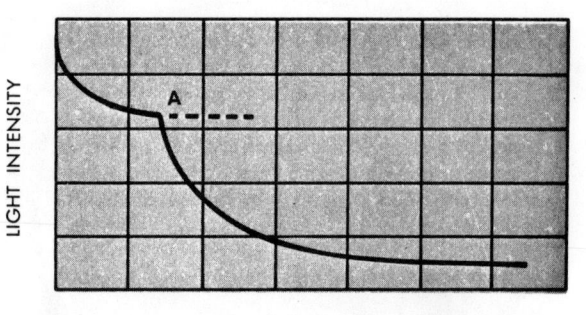

At the point of sudden inflection, the rods, which function more effectively in poor illumination, take over function from the cones, which are active principally under daylight conditions. The rods and the cones differ in other important respects: (1) the rods are found chiefly in the periphery of the retina; (2) rod vision is not as

THE EYE AND VISION

RIGHT EYE **RIGHT OPTIC NERVE**

THE VISUAL PATHWAY
Vision, which provides the most precise information about the world, is the most complex of the senses. During the passage from the eye to the brain the image is transformed from light waves to nerve impulses, and undergoes a series of distortions. Somehow the brain compensates for these alterations to yield the detailed images of everyday experience. Some idea of the complexity of the visual pathway is given here. The image in the optic nerve may not appear as it is drawn here — exactly what occurs in the optic nerve and brain during vision is still a mystery.

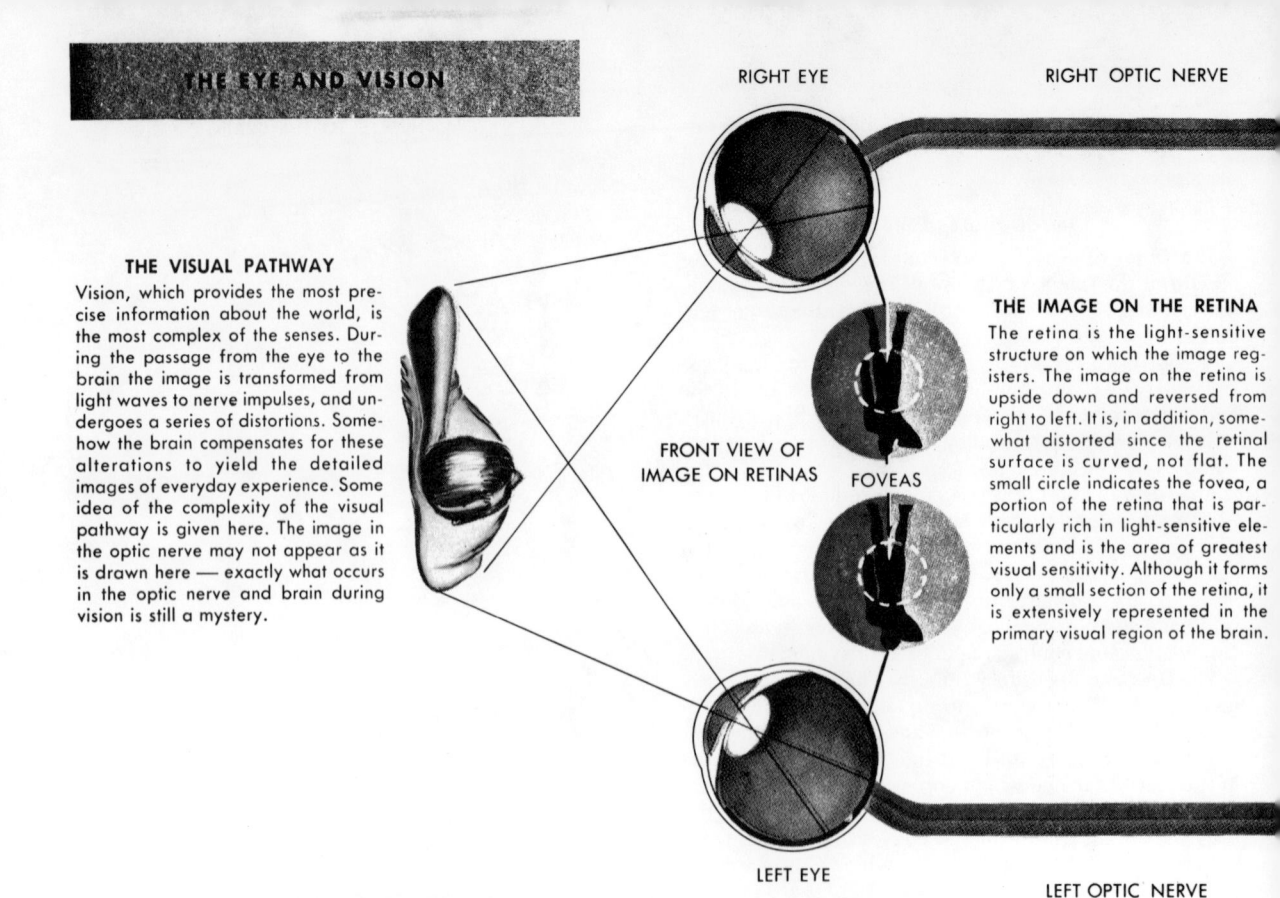

FRONT VIEW OF IMAGE ON RETINAS

FOVEAS

THE IMAGE ON THE RETINA
The retina is the light-sensitive structure on which the image registers. The image on the retina is upside down and reversed from right to left. It is, in addition, somewhat distorted since the retinal surface is curved, not flat. The small circle indicates the fovea, a portion of the retina that is particularly rich in light-sensitive elements and is the area of greatest visual sensitivity. Although it forms only a small section of the retina, it is extensively represented in the primary visual region of the brain.

LEFT EYE **LEFT OPTIC NERVE**

SOME DETAILS OF EYE STRUCTURE

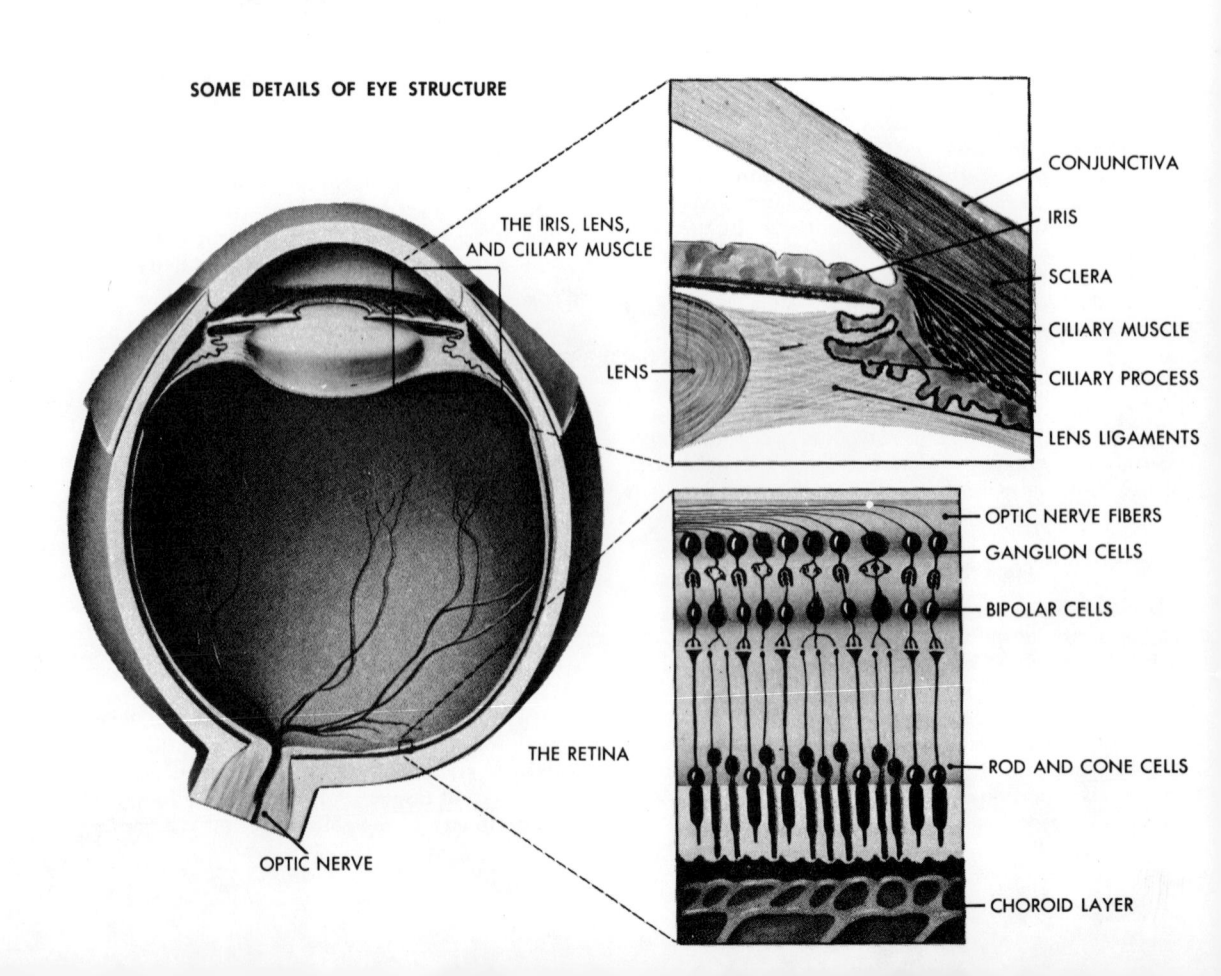

THE IRIS, LENS, AND CILIARY MUSCLE

- CONJUNCTIVA
- IRIS
- SCLERA
- CILIARY MUSCLE
- CILIARY PROCESS
- LENS LIGAMENTS

LENS

- OPTIC NERVE FIBERS
- GANGLION CELLS
- BIPOLAR CELLS
- ROD AND CONE CELLS
- CHOROID LAYER

THE RETINA

OPTIC NERVE

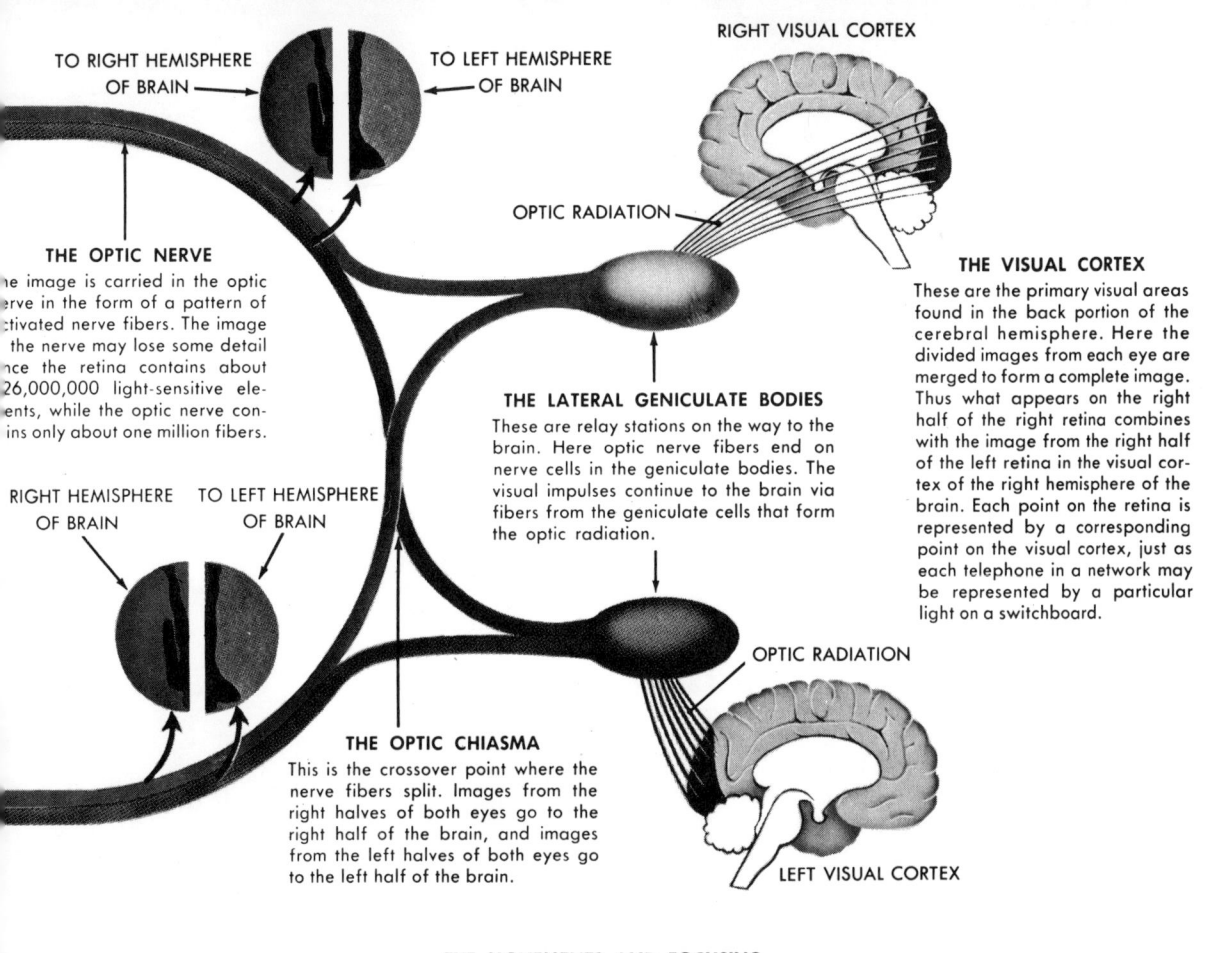

TO RIGHT HEMISPHERE OF BRAIN

TO LEFT HEMISPHERE OF BRAIN

RIGHT VISUAL CORTEX

OPTIC RADIATION

THE OPTIC NERVE
The image is carried in the optic nerve in the form of a pattern of activated nerve fibers. The image in the nerve may lose some detail since the retina contains about 126,000,000 light-sensitive elements, while the optic nerve contains only about one million fibers.

THE VISUAL CORTEX
These are the primary visual areas found in the back portion of the cerebral hemisphere. Here the divided images from each eye are merged to form a complete image. Thus what appears on the right half of the right retina combines with the image from the right half of the left retina in the visual cortex of the right hemisphere of the brain. Each point on the retina is represented by a corresponding point on the visual cortex, just as each telephone in a network may be represented by a particular light on a switchboard.

RIGHT HEMISPHERE OF BRAIN

TO LEFT HEMISPHERE OF BRAIN

THE LATERAL GENICULATE BODIES
These are relay stations on the way to the brain. Here optic nerve fibers end on nerve cells in the geniculate bodies. The visual impulses continue to the brain via fibers from the geniculate cells that form the optic radiation.

OPTIC RADIATION

THE OPTIC CHIASMA
This is the crossover point where the nerve fibers split. Images from the right halves of both eyes go to the right half of the brain, and images from the left halves of both eyes go to the left half of the brain.

LEFT VISUAL CORTEX

EYE MOVEMENTS AND FOCUSING

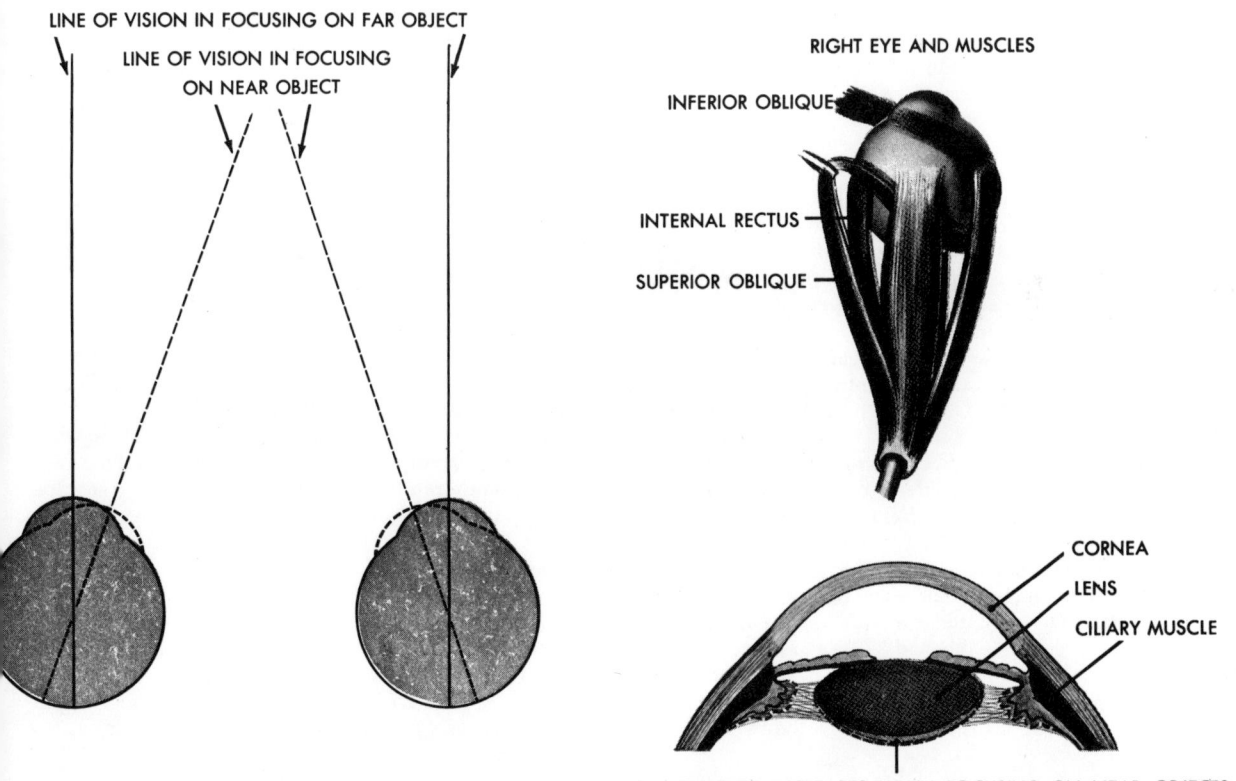

LINE OF VISION IN FOCUSING ON FAR OBJECT

LINE OF VISION IN FOCUSING ON NEAR OBJECT

RIGHT EYE AND MUSCLES

INFERIOR OBLIQUE

INTERNAL RECTUS

SUPERIOR OBLIQUE

CORNEA

LENS

CILIARY MUSCLE

LENS CURVATURE INCREASES WHEN FOCUSING ON NEAR OBJECTS

EYE BANK

clear as cone vision (that is, side vision is not as sharp as central vision); and (3) rods do not participate in seeing color. The cones are found in greatest concentration in a small patch of the retina called the fovea. Cone vision is sharper, since, as we noted before, the cone section of the retina is more densely supplied with the ganglion cells which generate impulses to the optic nerve. For this reason, when the eye fixes on an object it focuses the image on the fovea for clearest perception. Another difference between the two types of light receptors is their sensitivity to different "kinds" of light. The cones are more sensitive to red, while the rods are more sensitive to blue and green.

The difference in sensitivity becomes evident during dark adaption when function shifts from the cones to the rods. This is known as the Purkinje shift, and accounts for the changes in colors observed when the eye becomes dark-adapted. Among the color changes associated with the shift is the well-known phenomenon in which red flowers appear black at twilight, while blue flowers appear gray or white. Purkinje shift night blindness occurs when the rods do not function properly.

How Light Stimulates the Retina. The remarkable sensitivity of the retina may best be appreciated by considering that the light given off by a single candle would be visible at a distance of one mile, if the intervening air were perfectly transparent. Light acts upon the rods of the retina by bleaching the pigment visual purple, or rhodopsin, which is derived from vitamin A. It is probable that photosensitive pigments are also present in the cones.

Binocular Vision. If one reflects upon the matter it becomes evident that each eye sees a different image.

In some unknown manner these images are fused in the brain to yield a single image. Although it has been suggested that binocular vision gives depth to the image, this cannot exclusively account for three-dimensional perception, since the third dimension does not vanish if the world is seen through one eye. Other factors have been cited as playing a role in depth perception. These include knowledge of the world acquired through experience, such as the actual size of objects seen at a distance, the apparent change of color of distant objects, and the role of interposition of objects. Physiological factors, such as the differences in muscle sensation developing from focusing on near as opposed to far objects, have also been invoked in explanation of depth perception.

Other Problems in Vision. The eye and the brain manage to see objects as they really are despite great variations in the position and the lighting conditions in which the objects appear. Consider the example of a piece of white paper, which is seen as white when under bright light and when in shadow, although the total quantity of light reaching the eye differs greatly under the two conditions. This is called "brightness constancy" and has been explained as resulting from the constant "ratio" of reflected light between the object and its surroundings. Other "constancies," that is the tendency to see objects in a particular way under a wide variety of conditions, remain largely unexplained. These include "size constancy" (a 6-ft. man appears 6-ft. tall whether seen at a distance of 4 ft. or 40 ft., even though the size of the image on the retina differs greatly in the two cases); and "shape constancy" (a table-top is seen as rectangular from all points of view, although its image on the retina is not always rectangular).

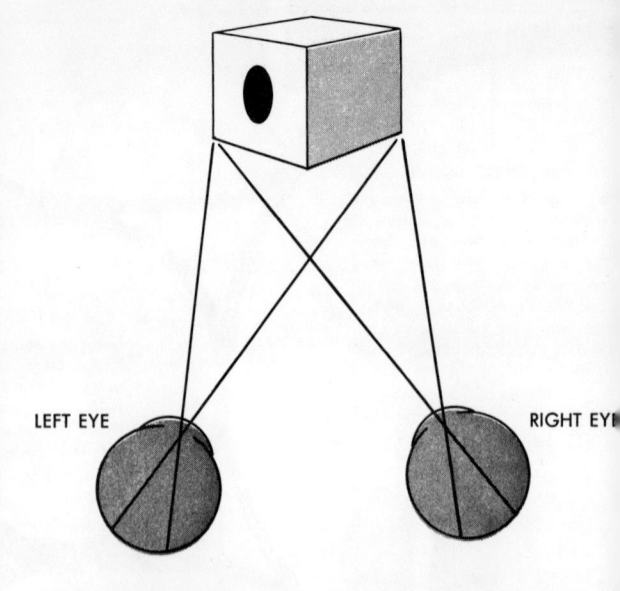

See also BLINDNESS; CATARACT; COLOR VISION; GLAUCOMA; NIGHT BLINDNESS.

EYE BANK. *See* CORNEAL TRANSPLANT.

EYEGLASSES. Although used in China prior to the 13th century, it is not known whether eyeglasses were worn at that time to improve vision or to bring good fortune. Beginning in the 13th century in Europe eyeglasses were worn as an aid to vision. The early lenses were convex and helped older people to see close objects. Concave lenses for the nearsighted probably did not appear until the 16th century. Prismatic lenses, used in cases of cross-eyedness, were developed in the 1850's. Cylindrical, or toric, lenses for the correction of astigmatism did not come into common use until around 1900.

Benjamin Franklin invented the first bifocal lens, which consisted of the top half of one pair of lenses and the lower half of another in the same frame. In this way the upper lens can be used for distance vision and the lower for reading and close work. Trifocal lenses, which incorporate three different lenses, are also available. Eyeglasses can be made to include different principles of correction in the same lens: the lens may be concave to correct nearsightedness, toric, to correct astigmatism, and prismatic, to correct the tendency to cross-eyedness.

See also ASTIGMATISM; CONTACT LENSES; FARSIGHTEDNESS; NEARSIGHTEDNESS.

F

FAINTING or SYNCOPE, impairment of consciousness, accompanied by muscle weakness and an inability to stand upright. It is a condition of abrupt onset and brief duration. At the beginning of a fainting attack, the person has a sensation of giddiness. He has spots before his eyes, his vision dims, and his ears ring. His face becomes ashen and he may feel nauseated. The depth and duration of unconsciousness varies. Sometimes the person can hear the voices around him and see blurred images. In other cases there is a total inability to respond. The pulse is thin, blood pressure low, and breathing almost imperceptible. Upon regaining consciousness, if he arises too soon, another faint may occur. Often headaches, drowsiness, and mental confusion follow an attack.

The most common cause of fainting is a reflex action which opens the blood vessels in the trunk and legs. Blood collects in these dilated vessels, and the supply to the brain becomes insufficient. Pain, anxiety, excessive hunger, or a sudden shock can trigger this reflex. More serious forms of fainting are caused by changes in the heart and pulse rate, in blood pressure, or with bleeding and severe anemia. Fainting is effectively treated by lying flat with the head below the level of the rest of the body and the feet elevated.

FAITH HEALING, the practice of curing physical and spiritual ills or alleviating suffering by the supposed use of supernatural force or the exorcism of evil spirits. Medicine men, shamans, witch doctors, saints, priests, and faith cultists, both in primitive and advanced societies have, on occasion, effected such cures. Psychosomatic medicine today recognizes faith as a factor in certain types of cures. The effectiveness of these "miracle cures" is accounted for psychologically by the state of mind developed in the subject through the power of suggestion.

FARSIGHTEDNESS or hypermetropia, common eye condition in which the eye cannot focus properly. In normal vision the image of the object is focused upon the retina, the light-sensitive surface in the back of the eye. In farsightedness the image of a distant object is focused behind the retina. The farsighted person can bring distant objects into clear focus by contracting the ciliary muscle which controls the curvature of the crystalline lens of the eye. The changed lens curvature projects the image on the retina. Although the young farsighted individual can see clearly by making this correction in lens shape, the ciliary muscle becomes overworked in the process, often causing headache and eye fatigue. The strain is even greater when looking at near objects since the ciliary muscle normally contracts in order to focus nearby objects; in the farsighted eye the muscle must produce a much greater contraction; consequently, farsighted persons experience more symptoms when doing close work.

At about the age of 40 the crystalline lens begins to harden and the ciliary muscle cannot change the lens curvature as easily as before. By the age of 60 or so the lens shape cannot be altered by muscle contractions and the farsighted person sees distant objects as blurred.

Eyeglasses correct the condition by focusing the image on, instead of behind, the retina. The need for glasses usually increases with age: the farsighted child may need them only when close work is being done. Older persons may require glasses to make the corrections which were earlier accomplished by muscular contraction.

See also Eye; Nearsightedness.

FATIGUE, MUSCLE. *See* Muscle.

FATS AND OILS. Edible fats and oils make up one of the three principal classes of food products, the others being carbohydrates and proteins. Fats are usually solid or semisolid at room temperatures and are obtained from the fatty tissues of hogs, sheep, and cattle by rendering. In dry rendering, the fatty tissue is heated to 225° F. to 250° F. and stirred in open or closed vessels. The fat melts, and is strained from the solid residue. In wet rendering, the tissues are put in pressure cookers, and the fat floats to the surface, where it is drawn off after about five hours.

Edible oils are liquid and are vegetable in origin, coming largely from seeds of corn and from cottonseed, soybeans, peanuts, and olives. The seeds are usually cleaned and hulled; the meats are separated from the hulls by screening, are ground or flaked to a small size, and are cooked before final processing. Continuous screw presses reduce oil content of the seed to about 5%. All but ¼% is then recovered by extraction with hexane. Refined oil can be chilled to crystallize solid materials, then filtered and deodorized. The process is called winterizing. Hydrogenation is an industrial process that increases the hydrogen atoms in the molecules of oil and makes them solid at ordinary temperature.

Nonedible fats and oils include castor oil, the purgative and lubricant; chaulmoogra oil, long used for treating leprosy; and neat's foot oil for preserving leather. Nonedible oils are frequently converted to edible fats by hydrogenation.

The substances described are known as fixed oils to distinguish them from another group called essential oils, which are odorous, highly volatile, and frequently have

FATTY ACIDS

to be removed from edible oils to make the latter palatable. Grease is a name applied to petroleum oils that have a stiffening substance added for use where flow-resistant lubricants are needed.

FATTY ACIDS, organic compounds with the formula RCOOH where R represents a hydrocarbon radical and COOH the carboxyl group. The lower members such as acetic and propionic acid, which are found in fruit esters and essential oils, were originally not included under the term but now are. The higher members, like palmitic, stearic, and oleic acids, occur in vegetable oils and animal fats as esters of glycerine. Some fatty acids are saturated, that is, they have no double bonds; others, like linoleic acid, are unsaturated and their oils, called drying oils, react with atmospheric oxygen to produce hard films. In the presence of alkalies, acids, or enzymes, water acts on fats and oils to break them down into glycerin and fatty acids. Potassium and sodium salts of these acids make soap. Important uses are in the manufacture of paints, cosmetics, soaps, detergents, plastics, and resins.

FERTILITY. See STERILITY.

FERTILIZATION, a process characteristic of multicellular plants and animals during which the male and female germ cells are united. Fertilization may occur either externally or internally, depending on the species. In lower plants and animals it occurs in the external aqueous medium in which the organisms live. In the higher forms it occurs within the female tissues. Although the actual mechanism of fertilization varies in different species, the major features are the same. In animals, after the sperm and eggs have been introduced into the same medium, the sperm move toward the eggs. The paths of the sperm are random, and contact with an egg thus depends on chance. The chance that a meeting will occur, however, is greatly enhanced by the extremely large number of sperm released at one time. When a meeting occurs, the sperm usually stick to the egg. Chemicals from the sperm called lysins dissolve the external egg membranes in a small area so that the sperm can penetrate. If the external membranes are thick, as in the case in the eggs of fishes and insects, there is generally a special opening into the interior of the egg called a micropyle through which the sperm may pass.

Sudden changes occur in the egg when a sperm begins to penetrate the egg membrane. These changes begin at the point of sperm penetration and spread over the surface of the egg. In many species there is an immediate elevation on the surface of the egg. Shortly thereafter, the membrane becomes greatly reinforced and effectively prohibits further entry of sperm. In the sea urchin this blocking mechanism is completed within one minute after sperm penetration. The reinforced surface membrane is called the fertilization membrane. Thus, usually only one sperm is able to enter the cytoplasm of the egg. If more than one sperm happen to penetrate the egg—a condition known as polyspermy—the embryo usually develops abnormally, or only one sperm actually functions within the cytoplasm.

The penetration of the sperm also stimulates the egg to complete its meiotic divisions (cell divisions during which the number of chromosomes in the nucleus of the reproductive cell is halved) if it has not already done so. The haploid nuclei (the nuclei of cells that have undergone meiotic divisions) of the egg and sperm are at this stage called pronuclei. The pronucleus of the sperm enlarges and moves through the egg cytoplasm toward the female pronucleus. During the migration, the egg cytoplasm undergoes changes in preparation for the first mitotic division (normal cell division producing two identical cells) of the newly formed organism. The pronuclei unite to form a diploid nucleus (a cell nucleus containing the number of chromosomes characteristic for the species). After fusion of the pronuclei the cell is called a zygote. The zygote then undergoes successive divisions as a developing embryo.

The details of fertilization in plants differ from those in animals in the events which precede and follow the fusion of the pronuclei. In flowering plants, for example, the sperm nuclei are discharged into the embryo sac where fertilization takes place. After fusion of the pronuclei, changes take place in the surrounding parts of the flower—some structures that are no longer of use wither away; other structures which will be important to the developing embryo are stimulated to grow. As in animals, the zygote then begins a series of cell divisions.
See also CHROMOSOME; EGG; EMBRYOLOGY.

FEVER, an abnormal elevation of body temperature which usually develops in response to invasion of the body by microorganisms.

In health the average body temperature, which is usually given as 98.6° F., is maintained by an accurate balance between heat production and heat loss. Heat production is increased by exercise, shivering, and contraction of the muscles. The digestion of food and certain types of glandular activity also contribute to heating the body. Heat is lost by sweating, by vaporization of water from the lungs, and by radiation of heat from the surface of the body.

The body temperature is controlled by the heat regulating center of the brain which is located in a part of the brain called the hypothalamus. Infections bring about a disturbance in this center, resulting in increased heat production, diminished heat loss, and raised body temperature. The elevation of temperature is accompanied by an increase in the pace of activity of the tissues, including a greater production of white blood cells and special substances (antibodies) which combat the infection. A subnormal temperature in a patient with a severe infection is a serious sign, as it indicates that the body is not responding properly in its own defense. No attempt should be made to reduce body temperature unless it becomes excessive, in which case sponging, or immersion in tepid water is indicated. When the fever breaks, the patient perspires heavily so that heat loss exceeds heat production and the temperature returns to normal. Fever can develop without infection as in cases of heat stroke in which there is a disturbance of the heat-regulating mechanism, in injury to the brain which damages the heat-regulating center, or following the injection of foreign proteins into the body.

Fever Patterns. The pattern of temperature fluctuations can be of value in diagnosis. In lobar pneumonia and scarlet fever there is an abrupt temperature rise and fall; in typhoid fever the temperature rises and subsides gradually over a period of days.

Certain descriptive terms are applied to temperature fluctuations. When the temperature reaches its maximum height and remains at that level it is described as "continued"; this is seen in typhoid and typhus fevers. A "remittent" temperature is an elevated temperature which fluctuates. Such a pattern is seen in tuberculosis. An "intermittent" temperature returns to normal or below normal in a 24-hour period, a characteristic feature of malaria. In brucellosis, or undulant fever, there is a prolonged remittent fever of several weeks' duration, interrupted by periods of normal temperature. In lice-borne and tick-borne relapsing fevers the clinical diagnosis is based on bouts of fever lasting several days and separated by fever-free intervals, during which the patient's condition improves. There may be three or more such relapses. A notable example of a disease in which the temperature is alternately elevated and normal is Hodgkin's disease, a disorder involving the lymph nodes.

Changes in Body Function in Fever. In fever there is a marked decrease in urine output. The pulse is rapid and the skin is hot and dry, owing to the suppression of glandular secretions. The activity of the body cells is increased so that more than the normal number of calories is consumed. The body may consume its own tissues (which consist of protein) in an attempt to meet the abnormal energy demands if the diet does not contain large amounts of energy-supplying carbohydrates.

FEVER THERAPY, treatment of disease through elevation of body temperature. Fever produces certain physiological changes in the body, such as an increase in the number of bacteria-fighting white blood cells, which enhance the ability of the patient to fight infection.

This technique has been used for centuries by the Chinese, Japanese, and American Indians, who employed steam baths (made by throwing water over heated stones), heated sand, and hot springs to raise the body temperature. Many of these techniques are still in use. Fever has been induced in syphilitic patients by injecting them with living malarial germs. Similar use has been made of typhoid vaccine. These methods have been supplanted by the use of antibiotic drugs in treating syphilis. Other procedures for inducing fever utilize cabinet electric-light baths, and high-frequency electric currents.

FIBIGER [fē'bē-gər], **JOHANNES ANDREAS** (1867–1928), Danish pathologist who was awarded the Nobel Prize in 1926 for his research on cancer. He was the first to attempt to produce cancer experimentally (1913) and claimed to have caused cancer in the fore-stomach of rats by infesting them with the worm *Gongylonema neoplasticum* (then called *Spiroptera*). He served as director of the Institute of Pathological Anatomy of Copenhagen, Denmark, and as chairman of the International Union for Cancer Research.

FIBRIN [fī'brĭn] **AND FIBRINOGEN** [fī-brĭn'ə-jən], substances involved in the clotting of blood. Fibrinogen is a protein which is produced in the liver and is normally present in circulating blood. During clotting the soluble fibrinogen is converted into fine threads of fibrin which form the matrix of the blood clot. In the rare congenital blood disease, afibrinogenemia, bleeding tendencies result from absence of fibrinogen. Fibrinolysis, or the dissolution of the fibrin threads, occurs normally to some extent but may cause hemorrhages when excessive amounts of fibrin-dissolving enzymes are present in the blood. This sometimes occurs in cases of cancer of the prostate and in certain abnormalities of pregnancy.

See also BLOOD.

FIBROMA [fī-brō'mə], a noncancerous tumor of fibrous tissue which may develop spontaneously anywhere in the body but is most common in the skin and subcutaneous tissue. Unlike cancerous tumors, fibromas are separated from the surrounding tissue by a capsule and do not tend to spread to other parts of the body. The tumors may be excised, but tend to recur if not removed completely. Rarely, fibromas may become cancerous and invade other parts of the body.

See also TUMOR.

FIBROSITIS [fī-brō-sī'tĭs], a rheumatic condition involving stiffness, pain, and swelling of the soft tissues, most commonly affecting the neck, shoulders, and back. The cause of the condition is unknown, although it has been associated with chilling, dampness, and sudden changes in temperature. Psychological factors are also suspected. Stiffness in the involved part usually increases after rest and can be relieved by activity. Specific painful, "trigger" points can sometimes be located. The general health is unaffected. The condition does not become worse with time and patients are rarely incapacitated. Treatment consists of heat and exercise.

FIBULA. *See* SKELETAL SYSTEM.

FILARIASIS [fĭl-ə-rī'ə-sĭs], infection by one or more species of threadlike roundworms. Infection begins when the worm larvae are deposited in the skin by infected insects. They mature in the human body where they produce pain, swelling, and other disturbances.

Wuchereria bancrofti is the most important filarial parasite. It is carried by several varieties of mosquitoes. The organisms tend to collect in the lymph glands and in the lymphatic vessels which conduct fluid from the body tissues. The worms may produce an inflammatory reaction with fever, chills, headache, vomiting, and localized areas of redness and swelling on the arms and legs. The filaria may obstruct the lymph vessels, causing massive swelling of the arms, legs, or other parts of the body, a condition known as elephantiasis.

Loa loa (African eye worm) is limited to west and central Africa. The adult worms migrate throughout the body. The worms may pass immediately under the skin of the face and the covering of the eye (the conjunctiva), causing considerable pain, irritation, swelling and congestion. Characteristic swellings (calabar), sometimes approaching the size of a hen's egg, are seen in the skin,

FINLAY

particularly on the wrists and arms. The worm is carried by the mango fly.

Onchocerca volvulus is found in Africa and certain parts of Central and South America. The worms frequently invade the eye and sometimes cause blindness.

Filarial infestations can often be diagnosed by examining the peripheral blood or urine for the presence of the small microfilarias, the prelarval form of the worms. A remarkable feature of some of the infections is that the microfilarias appear in the peripheral blood only at night.

The microfilarias may be destroyed by the drug diethylcarbamazine (Hetrazan). Surgery is often required to relieve the swellings seen in elephantiasis and to remove adult worms from the eye or worm-infested nodules from under the skin.

See also ELEPHANTIASIS; ONCHOCERCIASIS.

FINLAY [fēn-lī'], **CARLOS JUAN** (1833–1915), Cuban physician, of Scottish and French ancestry. Finlay studied medicine in the United States, Cuba, and France. While engaging in general practice in Havana, he sought to determine the cause and to trace the spread of yellow fever, long endemic in Cuba. A paper he wrote in 1881 pointed to the mosquito as the carrier of the disease. Finlay's hypothesis contributed to the spectacular work of Walter Reed and colleagues two decades later. Although Finlay at the time received insufficient credit, he later won many Cuban and foreign decorations and other honors.

FINSEN, NIELS RYBERG (1860–1904), Danish physician who was awarded the Nobel Prize in 1904 for his use of concentrated light rays in the treatment of tuberculosis of the skin (lupus vulgaris). He investigated the action of ultraviolet light on the skin and observed particularly its bactericidal effect. The Finsen lamp, which used a carbon arc as a light source, is the forerunner of the modern ultraviolet, or "sun," lamp.

FIRST AID refers to the immediate, temporary care of limited extent given to the victim of an accident or sudden illness before the arrival of a physician. Immediate action is required only (1) when there is severe bleeding (hemorrhage); (2) when breathing has stopped for any reason; (3) when poison has been swallowed; and (4) when irritating chemicals come in contact with the skin or get in the eyes. Should any of these situations confront one who has had even elementary first-aid training, he may be able to save a life.

In first aid the words "signs" and "symptoms" are frequently used. Signs refer to what can be seen either with respect to the body or at the accident scene. Symptoms refer to the feelings of the victim. For example, in shock, signs are perspiration, dilated eyes, shallow and irregular breathing, weakness or absence of pulse, and so on. Symptoms are feelings of weakness, nausea, dizziness, and the like.

Remedial First-Aid Action

Control of Bleeding: *Hemorrhage.* When a large artery or vein is severed, a person can bleed to death in a minute or so. In cases of severe bleeding, always be con-

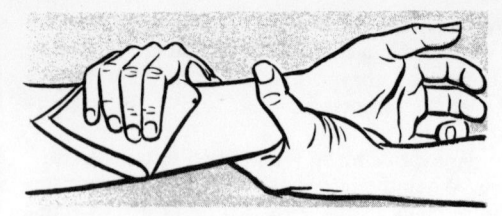

Clean cloth applied to wound with direct pressure controls bleeding.

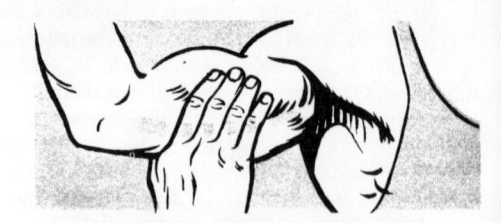

Finger pressure on brachial artery will reduce bleeding of arm wound below pressure point.

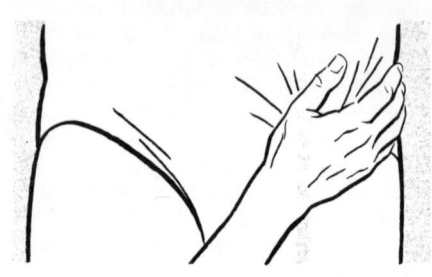

Pressure on femoral artery crossing groin lessens bleeding of leg wound.

A tourniquet should be used as a last resort *only if all other methods to stop profuse bleeding have failed.* Application: Tourniquet strip is tied. Stick is twisted, and secured to halt bleeding.

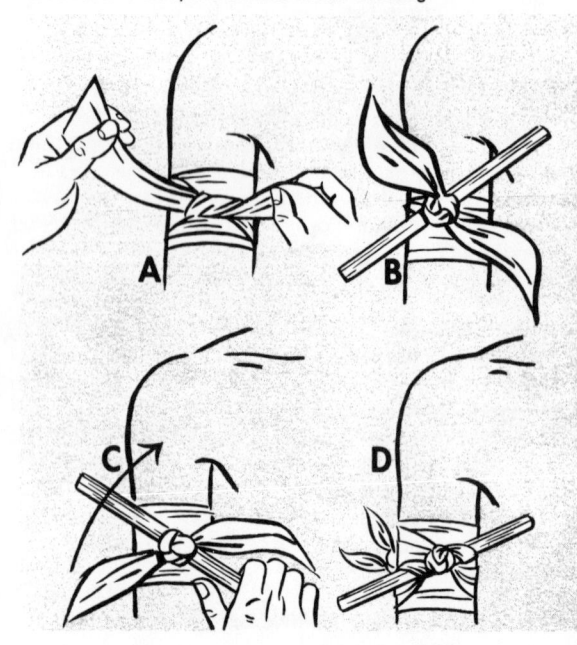

cerned first with applying pressure *directly* over the bleeding part, preferably with a clean cloth but, if necessary, with the bare hand. If the cloth held on the part becomes saturated with blood, do not remove it, but place another on top of it. Removal of the saturated cloth will disturb the normal clotting processes. At two places on each side of the body large arteries lie close to the surface along one of the long bones. There are instances when pressure on the supplying blood vessel combined with direct pressure on the part may be helpful in controlling profuse bleeding. For example, pressure on the artery in the area about midway between the armpit and the elbow will sometimes reduce the flow of blood into the part below. If pressure is exerted on the artery where it crosses the groin, the flow of blood should be lessened in the part below that point.

Tourniquet. The tourniquet is mentioned principally to discourage its use. Its application usually causes tissue injury, and many times it is applied needlessly. Its function is to shut off the *entire* blood supply to the area immediately adjacent to the point where it is applied. Use of the tourniquet is justified only when all other attempts to control life-threatening bleeding fail, or where there is partial or complete severance of an arm or leg.

If it is decided to use a tourniquet, it should be placed close above the wound, toward the heart, but not at the wound edge. There should be normal uninjured skin between the tourniquet and the wound. If the wound is near a joint, the tourniquet should be applied at the nearest practical point above the joint. Make sure that the tourniquet is applied tightly enough to stop bleeding. If improperly applied, it is likely to increase venous bleeding.

Improvised tourniquets should be made of flat material about 2 in. wide. Avoid using ropes, wires, or sash cords, since they will cut into and damage the underlying tissues and blood vessels. To apply an improvised tourniquet: (1) wrap the material tightly twice around the limb, if possible, and tie a half knot; (2) place a short stout stick or similar article on the half knot and tie a full knot; (3) twist the stick to tighten the tourniquet until the flow of blood ceases; (4) secure the stick in place with the loose ends of the tourniquet or another strip of cloth.

Once a tourniquet is applied, the victim should be taken as soon as possible to a physician. Only a physician who is prepared to control hemorrhage and replace lost blood volume should release it. Experience has shown that a properly applied tourniquet can be left in place 1 or 2 hours without causing undue damage. However, a note should be attached to the victim, giving the location and the hour of application of the tourniquet if the first-aider does not accompany him to the hospital or physician's office.

Wounds in Which Bleeding is Not Severe. The best source of information concerning home care for minor cuts and scratches is your family physician. Lacking such advice, the following procedure is recommended: (1) wash the hands thoroughly with clean water and soap; (2) cleanse the wound thoroughly, using plain soap and boiled water cooled to room temperature or clean running tapwater and soap; (3) use a sterile or, at least, a clean piece of cloth to apply the soap and water; (4) apply a dry sterile dressing or a dressing made from clean cloth and bandage it snugly into place; (5) be sure to tell the victim to see his doctor promptly, especially if soreness develops.

Stoppage of Breathing. A person may cease to breathe as a result of disease or accident. If breathing stops as a result of disease, body conditions may not permit life, and artificial respiration efforts are of questionable value. On the other hand, if breathing has been suspended due to accidental causes, it is often possible to revive the person if artificial respiration can be given in time.

The causes of asphyxiation may be divided into four categories.
1. Complete shutting off of air (drowning, choking, strangling).
2. Insufficient supply of oxygen in the air (in abandoned ice boxes, empty silos, vats, wells, and cisterns).
3. Displacement of oxygen from the circulating blood (carbon monoxide poisoning, certain combinations of gases).
4. Paralysis or depression of the breathing center (electric shock, sleeping drugs).

Because nonmedical people are usually not equipped to distinguish between suspension of breathing as a result of disease and that resulting from accident, it is best to apply some form of artificial respiration in all cases until the condition can be identified by a physician.

An open airway from the lungs to the mouth must be maintained if any form of artificial respiration is to be successful. Thus, it is important to free the throat if it is blocked by foreign matter and to be able to keep the mouth clear at all times. If the person is discovered quickly and artificial respiration started, his muscles usually retain sufficient tone, so that opening an airway is not a major problem. Alternately increasing and decreasing the size of the chest will move air in and out of the victim if there is no obstruction. If air is not quickly moved in and out of the lungs and the person revived, the throat begins to close from an internal source. When muscle tone is lost, the base of the tongue, which weighs approximately a quarter of a pound, relaxes against the windpipe and shuts off entry and exit of air. Since the tongue is attached to the lower jaw, when the first-aider tilts the head of the victim backward and stretches the neck muscles as tightly as possible, a small opening is created that permits passage of air. In addition when the rescuer lifts the lower jaw upward the air passage will usually open completely.

Once a passage for air has been guaranteed, any action that alternately increases and decreases the size of the chest cage will revive the person if body conditions permit life. This increase and decrease may be accomplished by blowing directly into the lungs through the mouth or nose or by alternately compressing and expanding the chest. The oral or mouth-to-nose technique of artificial respiration is now considered to be the most practical for emergency use (*see* ARTIFICIAL RESPIRATION).

Ingestion of Poisons. Poisonous substances—household cleaners, disinfectants, medicine, and many other things—are taken accidentally by hundreds of people. In all instances diluting the poison by having the victim drink

FIRST AID

large amounts of plain water or milk is the first step. Generally, the antidote for the poison is on the label of the container and should be administered if it is available. Diluting the poison will usually be sufficient until medical advice can be obtained. If there is a delay, it may be wise to induce vomiting, except when the victim is known to have taken an acid, an alkali, or a petroleum product such as kerosene. In these cases vomiting should not be provoked. If an acid has been taken, it should be diluted and a weak alkali given to counteract the acid. If an alkali has been taken, giving a weak acid is indicated. If a petroleum product has been taken, it should be diluted only. It is more dangerous to take a chance on fumes entering the lungs than it is to allow the poison to pass through the digestive tract and be absorbed into the blood stream.

Rescuer may roll shock victim off exposed live wire with a dry stick.

In cases where the poison is unknown and no directions are available, a universal antidote is recommended. Made up of magnesium oxide, activated charcoal, and tannic acid, it is available commercially in most parts of the country. It can also be improvised by using one part milk of magnesia, two parts crumbled burned toast, and one part strong tea measured in terms of volume rather than weight (see POISONS).

Many chemicals are dangerous even if they only come in contact with a body surface, especially with the eyes. The part affected by an irritating substance should be washed thoroughly with large amounts of "running water." Putting salve, ointment, or other medications on the skin or in the eye is not recommended as a first-aid measure: (1) because it will obstruct the physician's view of the damaged areas, and (2) the presence of medication makes the physician's cleansing of the area more painful than it would otherwise be.

Shock. Nearly all accidental injuries are accompanied to some degree by a condition called shock. This reaction to injury should not be confused with electric shock or the temporary shock of simple fainting or with neurogenic shock, previously called shell shock. If the injury involves loss of blood, the circulatory system sets up an automatic, self-regulating action that tries to keep the blood in the deeper parts of the body near the vital organs. The skin often becomes cold, wet, and clammy.

First aid to deal with shock and prevention of shock are the same. The most important single first-aid measure is to keep the patient in a lying-down position and thus help the flow of blood to the brain. Unless there are head or chest injuries, the victim may be placed with his head somewhat lower than his feet.

In treating shock, the over-all objective is to prevent a large loss of body heat. Good judgment and observation should dictate whether or not external heat should be applied to the body surface. The victim should not be warmed to the extent of sweating.

If there must be a long interval between the onset of shock and medical care and if the patient is conscious, it may be beneficial to give him a mixture of common baking soda and table salt, one-half level teaspoon of each in a quart of water. This mixture may be administered in small sips at 15-minute intervals. All handling of the victim should be as gentle as possible; rough handling will add to shock.

First-Aid Supportive Action (Protection)

Injuries to Bones, Muscles, and Joints: *Fractures*. A fracture is a break in the continuity of the bone. If there is no wound associated with the break, it is called a simple fracture. If there is a wound associated with the break, it is called a compound fracture. In all fractures the broken bone ends, as well as the adjacent joints, must be kept immobile. If materials are available and if the first-aider is skillful, he may wish to splint the injured limb. The best splints are made of rigid materials, such as wood of varying thicknesses. Magazines, newspapers, and even pillows may be used as temporary substitutes. In almost every instance the broken bone ends can be kept from moving by the hands alone, and if ambulance service and a physician are near at hand, it is usually best to use only the hands.

Signs: Odd position of limb; distortion.

Symptoms: Pain on movement of part.

Dislocation. Dislocations are difficult to identify because they often resemble simple fractures. Normally the same supportive care is given, with the part being kept as quiet as possible until the arrival of the physician. Do not attempt to reduce dislocations, except possibly of the lower jaw and the first joint of the fingers and toes.

Signs and symptoms: Similar to those in fractures.

Sprains. The word "sprain" should be associated with the word "joint" since sprains occur at joints, most frequently at the ankle and at the wrist. As many of the same symptoms are present, sprains are often mistaken for fractures. Hence, sprains should be treated like fractures until properly identified. The part should be kept as quiet as possible. No serious damage will result if this is done.

Signs: The joint is greatly enlarged and sometimes discolored.

Symptoms: Pain if the joint is moved.

Strains. Strains occur when muscles are overstretched. Although uncomfortable, they usually are not serious. Application of heat and bed rest will generally be sufficient.

Signs: Usually not evident.

Symptoms: Soreness and discomfort when the muscle area is touched or when movement is attempted.

Burns

Thermal Burns. When the skin comes in contact with heat, either moist or dry, the skin reddens, becomes blistered, or is charred, depending upon the degree of heat and the length of the contact. The severity of the burn is judged by the degree or damage to the tissues and by the extent of the burn. A burn is said to be of limited extent when less than 10% of the body surface is involved; when there is 10% or more involvement, the burn is referred to as extensive. Those with extensive burns need hospitalization as soon as possible.

The most essential job for the first-aider is to reduce pain and the possibility of infection. Cover the part as quickly as possible with layers of clean, dry, lint-free material to exclude air and protect the burned area from contamination. If there are blisters, wrap the part so that you do not break them. If the part such as a finger, arm, or leg, is merely reddened, quick relief can be given by letting cold running water cover the burned area. First-aiders should not apply ointments, salves, butter, or lard to burned areas. Such coverings may not only be absorbed into the subcutaneous tissues but they also invariably interfere with the physician's examination of the burned area and his choice of treatment.

Signs: Reddening, blistering, and charring of the skin.

Symptoms: Intense pain, nausea, fear.

Other Conditions Associated with Heat: *Sunburn* is caused by exposure to ultraviolet rays. The small blood vessels in the skin dilate, and the skin becomes red. Prolonged exposure to the rays of the sun may even cause blisters to appear.

Commercial preparations of varying degrees of efficacy are available to protect the skin from the effects of ultraviolet rays. Some are highly effective but may cause allergic reactions. The best first-aid practice is to prevent overexposure. Long initial sunbathing periods especially should be shunned, and length of exposure gradually increased.

Heat Exhaustion, although more prevalent in hot weather and among the aged, the obese, and those with systemic diseases, can affect anyone working under conditions that cause profuse perspiration and loss of body fluids and certain minerals. Persons working for long periods in poorly ventilated areas should increase the intake of water. Taking extra salt occasionally may be helpful. A well-balanced diet also helps prevent heat exhaustion. A person suffering heat exhaustion should have a period of bed rest.

Signs: Profuse perspiration; pale, damp skin; nearly normal body temperature; rarely unconsciousness.

Symptoms: Unusual fatigue; occasionally headache and nausea.

Heatstroke. Elderly people are more prone than others to develop heatstroke, a condition which may be caused by overexposure to the sun. The body temperature may rise as high as 109° F. Medical attention should be given as soon as possible. While awaiting the arrival of the physician or the ambulance, bring the patient indoors, provide bed rest, and sponge the body freely with alcohol or lukewarm water to reduce the temperature. If a thermometer is not at hand, the only guide may be the pulse rate. A rate below 110 per minute usually means a temperature the body can tolerate.

Signs: Dry skin, rapid pulse, temperature well above normal.

Symptoms: Headache, dizziness, nausea, unconsciousness in severe cases.

Cold Injuries. Heat affects the skin surface and so does cold. Parts of the body distant from the heart—the nose, ears, fingers, and toes—are most frequently affected by what is known as frostbite. Formerly it was believed best to warm frostbitten and frozen parts slowly. It is now known that they should be warmed quickly as long as they do not come in direct contact with heat.

As the victim himself usually is not aware of the onset of frostbite, companions should note the color of one another's ears and noses. If any of these parts have become grayish-white, warming should start as soon as possible, even with warm scarves and clothing. If possible, the frostbitten part should be immersed frequently at short intervals in water not exceeding 90° F. to 100° F. If the victim's entire body is affected, bring him into a warm room and wrap him in warm blankets. If he has stopped breathing, give artificial respiration. If water is available, immerse him in a tub of warm (78° F. to 82° F.) water; then dry the body thoroughly. When he reacts, give him a hot drink.

Transportation

Transporting accident victims is a difficult task and may be harmful if done improperly. Safe transportation of an injured person calls for good group co-operation and understanding of the problem involved and the parts of the body affected. The objectives are to avoid disturbing the victim and to prevent the injured parts from twisting or bending. Therefore, if a person "must" be moved and no help is available, pull him by the ankles or at the armpits but do not try to lift him. When assistance is available, it is best to use a cot or a litter.

Bandages and Dressings

A dressing is a sterile or clean piece of cloth that is placed directly over the wound. A bandage is a piece of cloth or other material used to hold a dressing in place. Bandage compresses combine the benefits of both in that a large gauze pad is affixed to strips of cloth which may be used to encircle the part in opposite directions. A sterile compress of this type can be applied as snugly or as loosely as one desires. The chief danger in bandaging injuries is making the bandage too tight and thus interfering with the circulation of the blood in the part.

First-aiders should not have to learn intricate bandaging skills. It is sufficient for them to know how to cover a dressing so that it will stay in place until medical aid can be reached. It is necessary to know how to do a circular turn, how to anchor the bandage, and how to tie it off when completed.

FIRST AID

If the body surface to be covered is tapered, such as a forearm, a closed spiral turn is used.

If the part tapers sharply, the turn will have to be an open spiral. In this, gaps will appear, but as long as it holds the dressing in place it is satisfactory.

If the body part to be covered is angular, a figure-of-eight turn—two loops crossing each other in opposite directions—should be used. Knees, elbows, shoulders, and the like can best be covered by this type of turn.

If an irregular surface—fingers, toes, or head—must be covered, a recurrent turn is first used; that is, the bandage goes back and forth over the ovoid surface and is held in place by a circular turn.

Anchoring bandage: (A) Strip end is angled so that (B) top flap can be turned down over first winding and (C) secured by second.

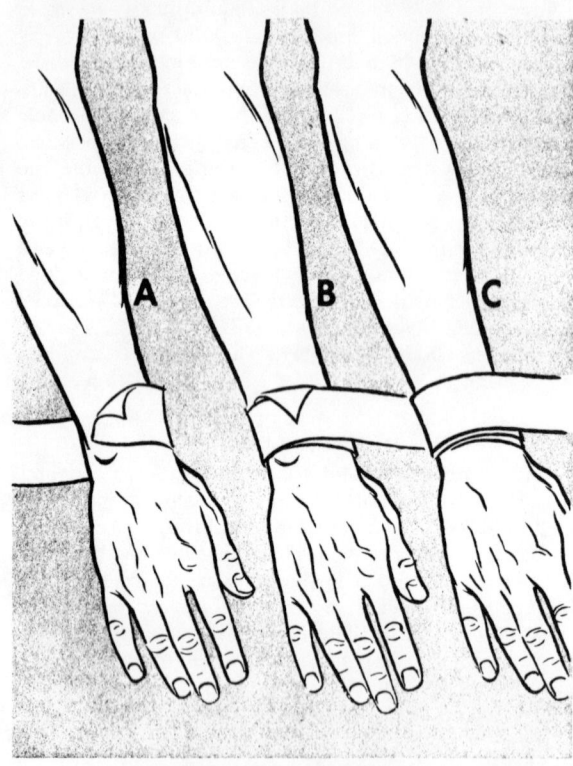

Common Emergencies

There are many kinds of heart attacks, but the two most common are congestive heart failure and coronary thrombosis. In heart failure, the signs are shortness of breath, occasional bluish color of the lips and fingernails, and swelling of the ankles. The symptoms are chest pain and extreme fright. In coronary thrombosis, the signs are quite often negligible, but because the symptoms are indigestion and nausea, the illness is often mistaken by friends and first-aiders for simple indigestion and upset stomach.

In all cases where heart attack is suspected, reassuring the victim with encouraging words is probably of primary importance. Second in importance is to allow him to select the position he finds most comfortable—lying on his back or propped up at any comfortable angle that gives some relief. Except for these two services, the first-aider's main responsibility is to see that the victim gets medical attention. If he is taken to the hospital by ambulance or other vehicle, the driver should be instructed to drive SLOWLY.

Apoplexy (Stroke). Apoplexy is usually brought about by a blood clot or hemorrhage involving a vessel of the brain. The victims are often those suffering high blood pressure. The signs of apoplexy are paralysis on one side of the body and possibly unconsciousness and heavy breathing. Again, this disorder calls for prompt medical attention. While awaiting the arrival of the physician, keep the victim as quiet as possible and lying down, face up or face down. If mucus tends to collect in the mouth, put him slightly on his side and turn his head completely to the side to allow the fluids to drain out.

Simple Fainting. Simple fainting is a reaction of the nervous system that results in a temporary lack of sufficient blood supply to the brain. It can be caused by injury, by the sight of injury, or by lack of sufficient concentration of oxygen in a room.

Recovery can be effected by bending the victim over or laying him down so that his head is lower than his heart. From time to time many kinds of medication have been recommended. It may help to give aromatic spirits of ammonia and the like or to hold smelling salts under the victim's nose at the onset of fainting.

If recovery of consciousness is not prompt, medical attention is needed because the underlying cause of the unconsciousness is more serious than simple fainting.

Epileptic Seizures. In epilepsy episodes of unconsciousness may appear for only a moment or they may be of long duration and be accompanied by convulsions involving the entire body. Epileptics who recognize the symptoms that precede an attack usually seek a quiet place and lie down with something between their teeth to prevent injury to the tongue. If a victim is found during an epileptic seizure, his convulsive motions should not be restricted. Try to keep him from injuring himself and, if possible, gently place something—a book cover or a spoon handle wrapped with clean cloth—between the teeth. When the convulsive motions have ceased, loosen the clothing about his neck and allow him to lie flat with his head turned to one side to prevent aspiration of food and other stomach contents that may have been regurgitated and are in the mouth. Allow him to rest undisturbed during the deep sleep that follows a seizure.

Unconsciousness—Cause Unknown. Unconsciousness is associated with many injuries and illnesses, but when its cause is unknown, the only classifications a first-aider can make are: (1) cases requiring artificial respiration and (2) cases where breathing is adequate. The accident scene nearly always provides a good clue to the cause of unconsciousness. If it does not, the first-aider, in the presence of reliable witnesses, should search the victim for a statement concerning specific diseases that may be the cause, such as diabetes, heart disease, or others.

If breathing is not adequate, start artificial respiration immediately and have someone notify a physician or police officer.

Foreign Body in the Eye. Injuries to the eye include

FIRST AID

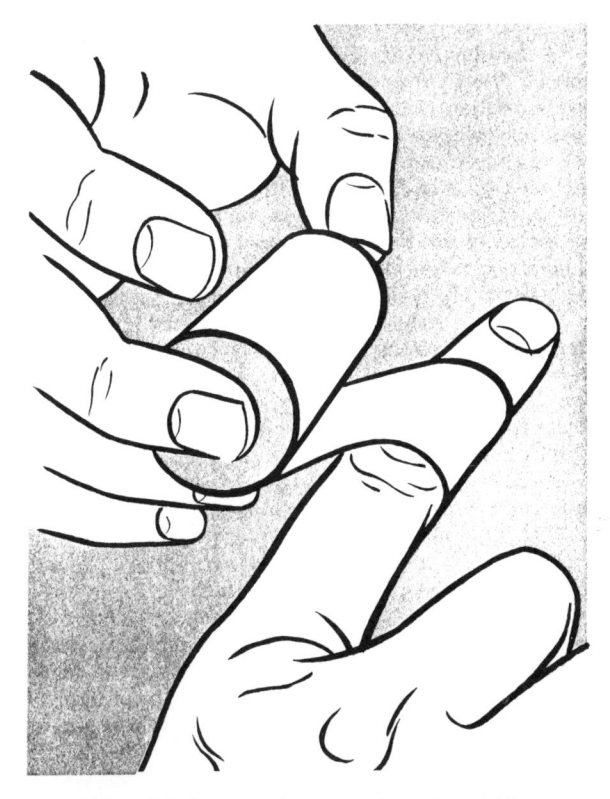

Circular turn of the bandage, layer upon layer, is useful for wrapping body parts of uniform width, as finger, neck, or head.

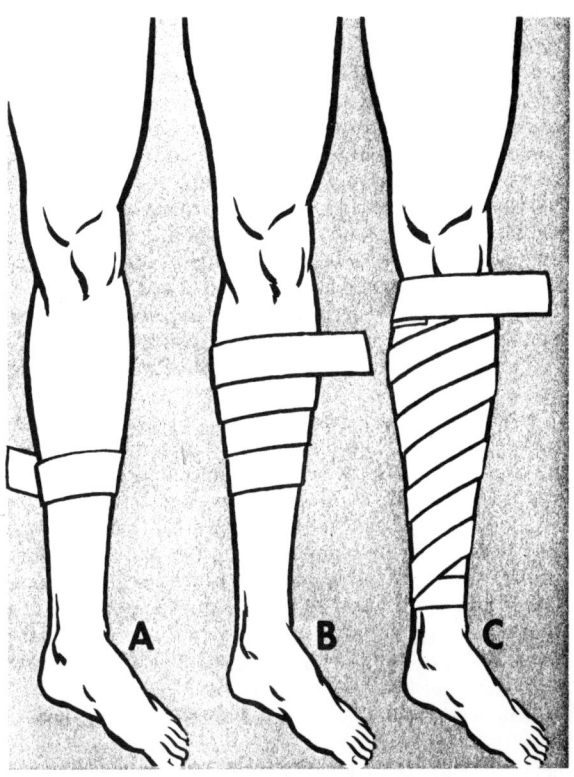

(A) Anchoring spiral turn on the calf. (B) Closed spiral, strips overlapping. (C) Open spiral, more oblique, no overlap.

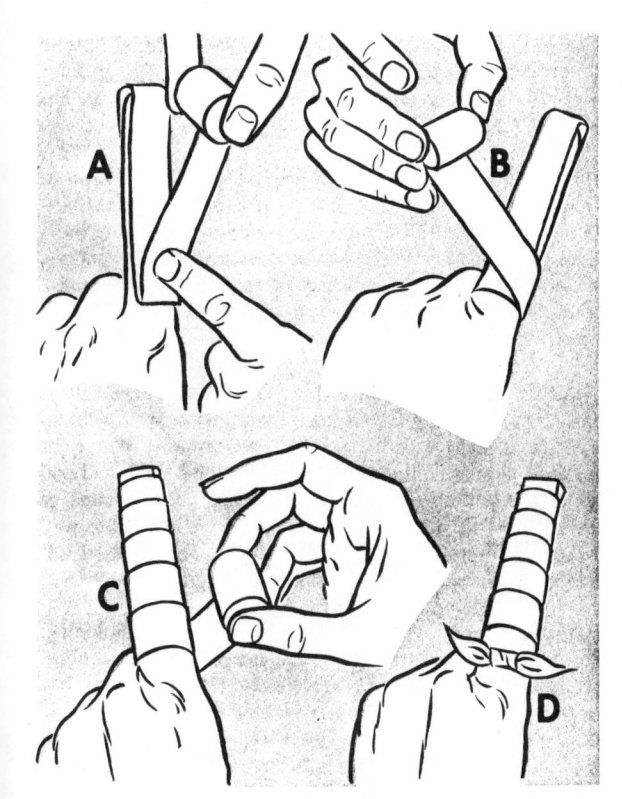

(A) Recurrent turn on opposite side of finger. (B) Circular turn holds bandage and (C) continues along finger. (D) Finished bandage.

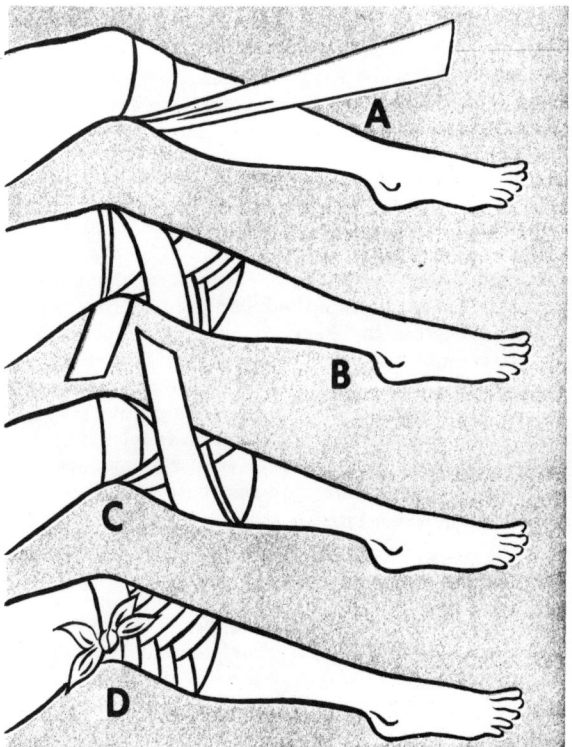

Figure-of-eight turn, useful for a joint or whole limb. Spiral turns, one up and one down, cross each other and then are secured.

damage to the soft tissue around the eye, scratching of the eye surface, and puncturing of the eyeball. No matter what the injury to the eyes may be, first-aid care should be held to a minimum. If the soft tissue about the eye is damaged place a fairly tight bandage over the eye and the affected area after giving normal first-aid care for wounds. When the eye itself is involved, cover it with moist cotton held in place with a bandage until medical assistance can be obtained.

Occasionally small foreign bodies become lodged on the inner surface of the upper lid. These may be removed by pulling the upper lid outward and downward over the lower lid so that the small object will be picked up on the outer surface of the lower lid.

Foreign Body in the Throat or Air Passage. If a foreign body lodges in the throat or air passage, violent choking and spasm will likely occur. These reactions alone often eliminate the object, but in other cases it must be removed by a bronchoscope or operation.

Let the victim first attempt to cough up the object. Do not probe with the fingers down the throat because you may force the object deeper. If breathing ceases, give artificial respiration and have someone get medical assistance quickly.

Foreign Body in the Food Passage. Most foreign objects that have been swallowed pass harmlessly along and are excreted. However, some objects require extraction either by special instruments or by operation. Medical care, therefore, should be obtained as soon as possible. Remain calm and do not excite the victim. Do not give him a cathartic nor, in general, any food. If the victim is an infant or small child and feeding is necessary do not give cereal or other bulky foods.

Suggested First-Aid Supplies

1-in. gauze roller bandage	Cleansing agent—rubbing alcohol, plain soap
2-in. gauze roller bandage	
3-in. × 3-in. gauze pads	Eye dropper
Plain gauze, ½ sq. yd.	Hot-water bottle
Absorbent cotton—½-oz. box	Flashlight

American National Red Cross

FISCHER, HANS (1881–1945), German organic chemist noted for his synthesis of the blood pigment, hemin. He received degrees in chemistry and in medicine, and taught chemistry at the universities of Innsbruck and Munich. His work on the structure and synthesis of hemin also explained the nature of the pigments in the bile. The chemical structure of hemin is related to that of chlorophyll, the green pigment of plants, and he worked out the relation between these substances. He received the Nobel Prize in 1930 for his work.

FLAT FEET. See FOOT.

FLEA, name for the more than 200 species of small, wingless insects, of world-wide distribution, that constitute the order Siphonaptera. Almost all fleas are parasites at some stage of their life cycle, and some species feed on the blood of mammals and birds. Their narrow, laterally compressed bodies and absence of wings enable them to move easily through fur or feathers. The body bears many small, rearward-projecting bristles; unusually long legs give fleas their jumping prowess; the mouth parts are of the piercing-sucking type. Fleas leave their hosts to lay their eggs in dirt, debris, or the nests of birds. Flea larvae are small, white, legless, and armed with a pair of hooks on the last segment of the body. The pupa is protected by a silken cocoon. Some species, such as the human flea, *Pulex irritans,* and the dog flea, *Ctenocephalides canis,* are merely annoying; others are carriers of disease. Bubonic plague and marine typhus are transmitted to humans by the Indian rat flea, *Xenopsylla cheopis.* The chigoe flea, *Tunga penetrans,* is a parasite that burrows into the skin, usually between the toes or under the toenails, and causes a painful sore.

FLEMING, SIR ALEXANDER (1881–1955), Scottish bacteriologist who shared the Nobel Prize in physiology and medicine with Ernest Boris Chain and Howard Walter Florey in 1945 for his discovery of penicillin. Fleming's first significant discovery was lysozyme, a bacteria-destroying enzyme which is normally present in body fluids, such as tears and saliva. In 1928, while working in St. Mary's Hospital in London, he neglected to cover some culture dishes containing staphylococci bacteria. An airborne mold grew in the culture and inhibited the growth of the surrounding bacteria. Fleming subsequently determined that the mold secreted a substance (penicillin) which interfered with bacterial reproduction. He attempted to use this substance as a dressing for infected wounds, but the results were discouraging, owing to the low potency of the natural material. Fleming's description of the antibiotic effect of penicillin would have remained buried in the literature were it not for the efforts of Florey and Chain in refining and developing penicillin for practical medical use.
See also ANTIBIOTICS.

FLEXNER, SIMON (1863–1946), American physician well known for his investigations of infectious diseases. He served for many years as director of the Rockefeller Institute for Medical Research in New York. Among his numerous contributions were studies of diphtheria toxin, isolation of one of the organisms responsible for bacillary dysentery (Flexner's bacillus), and investigations on the transmission of poliomyelitis in monkeys.

FLU. See INFLUENZA.

FLUKE or TREMATODA are flattened, leaflike worms which are found as parasites on or within certain land and water animals. Flukes which infest humans have complex life cycles, during which time they infect two, three, or even four different types of animals. It has been estimated that there are approximately 148,000,000 cases of human fluke infestation throughout the world, principally in the Orient.

The most important infection is produced by blood flukes, which are contracted by working in or drinking water which has been contaminated by larva-infested snails. The worms attack the bladder, intestine, and liver (*see* SCHISTOSOMIASIS).

Other flukes also infect snails and enter the human body through the digestive tract. The parasites then mature in the intestine, liver, or lung. In the intestine, flukes may produce inflammations and ulcers with bleeding, severe diarrhea, nausea, and vomiting. Severe cases may be fatal. Liver fluke is contracted by eating contaminated raw, pickled, or smoked fish. The worms produce a chronic disease with symptoms varying from indigestion and stomach pain to diarrhea, enlarged liver, and swollen abdomen. Lung fluke may be acquired by eating contaminated uncooked crabs or crayfish. The patients may suffer from cough with bloody sputum, chest pains, fever, and shortness of breath.

A number of drugs are available for treating these conditions, but results are frequently unsatisfactory.

FLUORIDATION [flōōr-ə-dā'shən], the addition of specific amounts of fluorine to drinking water for the purpose of preventing tooth decay. The earliest relationship noted between fluorine and dental health was mottling of the tooth enamel. This was strongly suggested in 1931 when it was demonstrated that the water in five localities, where mottling was present, contained fluorine in amounts ranging from 2.0 to 13.7 parts per million. Later studies proved that mottling of the enamel could be halted by lowering the fluorine content of the drinking water.

The role of fluorine in cavity-prevention first became evident when a new low-fluorine water supply was introduced in Bauxite, Ark. Children born after the water supply was installed showed a much higher incidence of cavities than those who were raised while the old water was still used. Following this, the U.S. Public Health Service undertook large-scale studies which indicated that a 50% to 66% reduction of cavities could be safely achieved by adding 1 part per million of fluorine to the drinking water.

Vigorous opposition to the fluoridation of public water supplies has been forthcoming from various groups, which contend that the safety of fluoridation is still in doubt, that it imposes unprecedented mass medication on the population, and that its efficiency in preventing caries is questionable. Both the American Dental Association and the American Medical Association have endorsed fluoridation. The U.S. Public Health Service reported that in recent years many American communities, with a total population ranging into the tens of millions, were using fluoridated water. In nonfluoridated areas many dentists use repeated applications of a 2% solution of sodium fluoride to the teeth to reduce caries: evidence indicates that this may help to reduce cavities by as much as 40%.

FLUOROSCOPE, specially prepared screen that glows when exposed to X rays. A sheet of glass or other material that is transparent to X rays is coated with a substance, such as barium platinocyanide, that fluoresces (emits visible light) at a brightness proportional to the concentration of X-ray radiation upon it. By using such a screen, a physician, for example, can observe directly bones, foreign objects, or other details revealed in a body by the X rays. The fluoroscope has been supplanted almost entirely by the use of photographic film, except where rapid changes are being studied.
See also FLUORESCENCE; X RAYS.

FLUOROSCOPY. See X RAYS, DIAGNOSTIC.

FLY, name commonly given to many small, flying insects, but correctly applied only to members of certain families in the order Diptera, the true flies, characterized by a single pair of transparent forewings. The hindwings of flies are represented by a pair of knobby structures, the halteres, which function as balancing organs. Of the several thousand species of true flies, many are merely pests, but others pose a serious health threat as disease vectors. They have achieved this dubious distinction through their scavenging habits which enable them to pick up and transmit many disease-causing microorganisms. On the credit side of the ledger, some flies are useful as pollinators of crops; others destroy harmful insects.

FOOD, any substance other than water that can be taken into the body of an organism for its maintenance, growth, and reproduction or to provide energy for other activities. Thus defined, it includes not only the familiar organic materials which form the bulk of human foodstuffs, but oxygen (carbon dioxide in the case of plants), inorganic salts, and traces of various elements which are ingested or absorbed by living things. In ordinary English usage, however, "food" has a more restricted meaning, and may exclude spices, beverages consumed for nonnutritive purposes, or even nutritious substances in liquid form. Here, food will be discussed in its relation to human culture and history. For chemical and physiological aspects of food, see the list of related articles at the end of this entry.

For hundreds of millions of years, plant and animal organisms have been competing for nutritive materials in the waters and on the land surfaces of the earth. Even though nutritive materials can be used over and over again, thanks to the use of the sun's energy by green plants, this competition for foodstuffs explains their relative scarcity. Another reason is that each species tends to expand its numbers toward the limits of its food supply. Man has been no exception to this, and as he has increased his ability to extract foods from the environment, his numbers have risen correspondingly. Until the last few centuries, a large part of human labor and intelligence went into the task of obtaining a food supply, leaving little time and energy for other activities. Usually the population of a given animal species comes into balance with the food resources of a rather limited area, or *niche*, as it is called in ecology. Man, with his high intelligence and ability to use tools and fire, has not confined himself to one region or environment, but has spread in the course of the last million years into all the major land environments of the planet, and has learned to exploit part of the aquatic environment as well. In each of these different environments he has had to develop a food supply, and he has been able to do so without fundamental biological changes, thanks to his developing culture. All major increases in the human population of any region beyond the tiny numbers able to subsist by simple wild-food gathering have required technological advances. Human history could be written in terms of foods and the techniques used to secure them, though, of course, this would be to focus on only one of many aspects. For

FOOD

PHASE 1 (Several Million Years Ago)

The sketchy evidence available indicates that our ancestors ate what food came to hand — fruit, buds, grubs — just as they found it.

PHASE 2 (About One Million Years Ago)

Meat — obtained by scavenging and perhaps hunting — was added to the diet. Stones may have been used to cut up carcasses, and sticks may have been used to dig for vegetable foods.

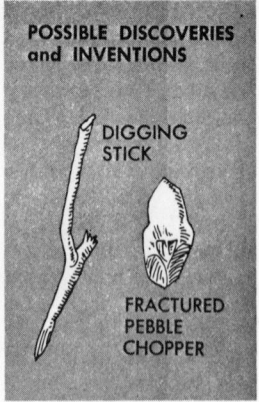

POSSIBLE DISCOVERIES and INVENTIONS

DIGGING STICK

FRACTURED PEBBLE CHOPPER

---

mankind, food is a many-layered topic, extending beyond nutrition to values, ritual, and social relationships—even to the level of what has been called the fine art of cookery.

Man is a mammal, and therefore lives in infancy on a special food secreted by the mother, milk. He is also a primate, an order of mammals which embraces tree shrews, lemurs, tarsiers, monkeys, and apes, in addition to man. As is the case with most primates, man's teeth and digestive system are adapted to a remarkably diversified diet consisting of fruits, berries, seeds, shoots, buds, stalks, leaves, roots, tubers, birds' eggs, insects and larvae, and the flesh of mammals, birds, reptiles, fishes, and many kinds of mollusks and other shellfish. Under natural conditions most primates are vegetarians, consuming animal foods only incidentally. Several million years ago our own primate ancestors were probably also chiefly vegetarian. Yet the primate's capacity to live on a highly varied diet, including meat, is of the utmost importance in explaining how the human body developed. Man's evolution has probably depended in part on dietary shifts related to environmental changes and migration into new regions. Modern mankind lives mainly on vegetable foods derived from grass seeds, legumes (peas and beans, for example), roots, and tubers. Most of man's foods are cooked and otherwise prepared in ways employed by no other animal.

Primate omnivorousness (ability to subsist on a very variegated diet) was not the only factor involved in the development of man. Others were the ability to manipulate tools and weapons, not only for hunting but also for butchering, for grubbing out wild plants, and to carry food burdens gathered from a wide area back to a central lair, where food could be chopped up at leisure. Out of this last habit the important human trait of sharing food among immediate family members may have arisen. Other primates are disinclined to share food. The fact that some carnivores share food suggests that it may have been big game hunting or regular stealing of carrion which initiated this important social change among the ancestors of man.

Phases in the History of Food-getting

Several phases in the history of man's food-getting can be described, though not all peoples or all world areas passed through all of them.

Phase 1. Several million years ago, during the Miocene Era, our ancestors lived on the same foods as modern monkeys and apes. This required no tools and little foresight or ingenuity.

Phase 2. At an indeterminate date, but perhaps on the order of 1 million years ago, certain man-apes called Australopithecines already adapted for bipedal, upright walking, were eating flesh and marrow of big game animals, which they were either hunting regularly or perhaps only stealing from the kills of lions or other predators. The onset of meat eating did not eliminate the gathering of wild plant foods, but it is possible that some very simple tools, such as digging sticks and fractured pebbles, were being used in the quest for vegetable food, as well as to help cut up the carcasses of wild animals. Food-sharing may well date from this epoch.

Phase 3: Hunting and Gathering. During the next 200,000 years, known to archeology as the Lower Paleolithic (the early part of the Old Stone Age), two specialized food-getting patterns were established, one much better known than the other. These were big-game hunting and systematic food-gathering. The animals hunted included bison, wild cattle, wild horses, antelope, deer, members of the elephant family, and rhinoceroses. Spears, clubs, and techniques such as stampeding, running down, and perhaps the fire-drive were used. Fire is known from a cave occupied about 250,000 B.C. by Peking Man, who presumably used it for cooking and heat. Man spread into different and cooler regions as his hunting became more skillful; between 100,000 and 50,000 years ago he managed to penetrate regions with severe winter climates; some archeologists consider this period to form the Middle Paleolithic. Not all the regions into which man expanded had great herds of wild game. In some areas, gathering plants and other wild foods (snails and other mollusks) was more important than big-game hunting. The gathering process had been gradually improved by the use of tools, and was probably carried on mostly by women and children. Both big-game hunting and wild-food gathering imposed a wandering existence, though within recognized territories or ranges. Cooking was apparently limited to broiling, roasting, and baking

FOOD

PHASE 3 Hunting and Gathering, Early Old Stone Age

Men learned to use fire for cooking as well as for comfort. They developed rudimentary weapons with which they successfully hunted such big-game animals as wild horses, bison, and elephants.

DISCOVERIES and INVENTIONS
FIRE
KNOBBED CLUB
STONE-POINTED SPEAR

PHASE 4 Improved Hunting and Food Collecting (c. 50,000 B.C.-c. 12,000 B.C.)

Seals, fish, and other marine life increased the quantity and variety of edibles. Weapons were improved. Baskets made systematic food gathering possible. Stones were used to grind seeds.

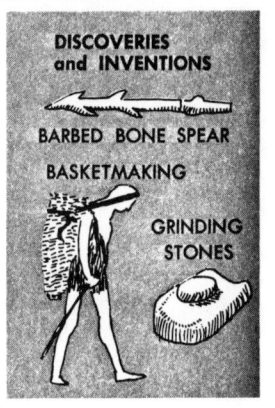

DISCOVERIES and INVENTIONS
BARBED BONE SPEAR
BASKETMAKING
GRINDING STONES

in hot ashes; there were no cooking vessels of pottery. Boiling with hot stones and the "earth oven" (a pit in which foods were cooked by hot stones) had probably not yet been invented.

Phase 4: Improved Hunting and Food-collecting. In the Upper Paleolithic, extending from about 50,000 to 12,000 B.C., big-game hunting continued with greater efficiency owing to the invention of projectile weapons such as the spear thrower, and perhaps also the bow and arrow. Fishing and sealing were made easier by the inventions of multibarbed spears and harpoons. Food-gathering methods were becoming still more efficient, and the term "food-collecting" is sometimes used to mark this change. More and more, the foods collected consisted of smaller seeds, nuts, and roots and tubers, many of which require special preparation before they can be eaten. Such preparation included grinding (milling), pounding, or mashing, with the resultant meal capable of being cooked as an unleavened bread. Hard seeds could also be made more edible by parching or popping. More effective harvesting required devices such as seed-beaters and containers such as bark, wood, or basketry trays. Fish and other aquatic foods also were becoming more important, a tendency that became even more noticeable in the succeeding Mesolithic Period.

More attention was paid to the harder-to-get foods in the environment, not only because in some regions big-game herds were diminishing (perhaps because man was becoming too efficient as a hunter), but also because the total population was steadily increasing, and people were being forced to move into regions where it was much harder to find enough to eat. During the Lower Paleolithic, man had probably been aware of the edibility of fish and shellfish, but was rarely placed in environmental situations where survival depended on finding efficient ways of living off such resources.

The Mesolithic was a widespread cultural phase in the Old and New Worlds which began at the end of the last glacial episode of the Pleistocene. This phase lasted a few thousand years in some regions until it was succeeded by the Neolithic, a period marked by the appearance of agriculture and animal husbandry. But in areas that agriculture or livestock raising did not reach, a Mesolithic way of life persisted until modern times, as in aboriginal Australia, the Kalahari Desert of South Africa, the southernmost part of South America, and in much of western and northern North America. In some of these areas big-game hunting continued, but in others it was the seed-collecting, shellfish-gathering, and fishing aspects of the Mesolithic that survived. The food economy of the California Indians and those of the Great Basin was until a few generations ago an excellent sample of Mesolithic subsistence. Even where agriculture and livestock raising were established, big-game hunting, fishing, and wild-plant gathering did not entirely vanish.

Phase 5: The Food-producing Revolution. The Neolithic, or food-producing revolution, beginning around 7000 B.C. or earlier, saw the emergence of agriculture and animal husbandry, or livestock raising. These innovations were in fact long-drawn-out processes of development and not sudden inventions. They meant that man could depend increasingly upon harvests from controllable and predictable sources, produced in fixed localities, and that up to a point, greater expenditure of human labor could produce greater amounts of food within a given area. Of course, many hazards and uncertainties remained. Nevertheless, people could settle down in permanent communities instead of moving about from one camp site to another. Another result of the food-producing revolution was a major expansion in the world's human population.

Food production was not a uniform procedure, however. The plants and animals that could be domesticated varied tremendously, as did the kinds of environment in which they could thrive. Many hundreds of plants were brought under cultivation, but only two dozen or so animal species turned out to be worth domesticating. Though the dog, probably the first domestic animal, was not primarily kept for food, dog flesh is eaten by various peoples. The most important domestic animals are hoofed animals, such as goats, sheep, cattle, donkeys, horses, camels, reindeer, and llamas; the first seven of these provide both flesh and milk, and the last six transportation as well as meat. Only the pig among major domestic animals is ordinarily neither milked nor used for transport or work. Among birds, only ducks, geese, chickens, and turkeys have much economic importance. No reptiles or amphibians have become regular domestic animals, but several fish species are raised in ponds and provide significant amounts of food

FOOD

for man in Southeast Asia and Indonesia. Among invertebrates, domestic animals include honeybees, silkworms (not used for food), and some types of oysters which are regularly "planted" and harvested in shallow waters.

The most important plant domesticates are of three main types: (1) grasses yielding small, hard seeds, such as wheat, barley, oats, millets, rice, and corn; (2) plants with starchy roots, tubers, or rootstocks such as the potato, sweet potato, yam, taro and manioc; and (3) legumes, such as peas, lentils, gram or chick-peas, and beans. The staple vegetable foods of the world's peoples consist mainly of some of these, plus oilseeds like rape or sesame, the peanut, banana or plantain, and squashes, melons, and cucumbers. Cultivated fruits, vines, berries, nuts, leafy vegetables, and the like, although of great nutritional importance, provide only a small portion of the food supply of mankind as a whole.

Brewing beer, an invention of Neolithic or possibly early metal-age agriculturalists, is another way of utilizing cereals. Fruits, berries, honey, and even milk can be made into alcoholic beverages, too, usually called wine. That prepared from honey is mead, and from milk—usually mare's milk, as in Central Asia—kumiss. A few types of naturally fermented fruit or berry juices may have been in wide use even before the development of agriculture.

Agriculture did not at first require many new tools. The digging stick of earlier times could also be used for planting and weeding. The adze, a stone-bladed implement like a mattock, developed in the Mesolithic for such purposes as woodcutting and chopping out dugout canoes, was also usable in agriculture. Clearing of land for crops was probably done much as it is in some primitive farming areas of the world today: by a combination of wood and brush cutting and burning known as "slash and burn." No really new tools were needed for food preparation, at least at first. The same kinds of milling and food-pounding stones used during the Mesolithic for wild seeds were used for cultivated grains. Bread could be baked in simple ovens or even ashes, but lengthy boiling of beans, of mushes and gruels, stewing, and brewing required not only watertight but also fireproof containers. Baskets could be made watertight, and liquids stored or carried in gourds, but Neolithic cookery led to the invention of pottery. This did not appear automatically wherever agriculture emerged or

PHASE 5 The Food-producing Revolution (From c.7000 B.C.)

At widely different times, in widely different places, men began to settle down. Plants were brought under cultivation. Domesticated animals and poultry provided meat, milk, and eggs. Food processing began with butter, cheese, beer, and wine. Food preservation was accomplished by drying, smoking, or salt curing. Tools and pottery were improved aesthetically as well as practically.

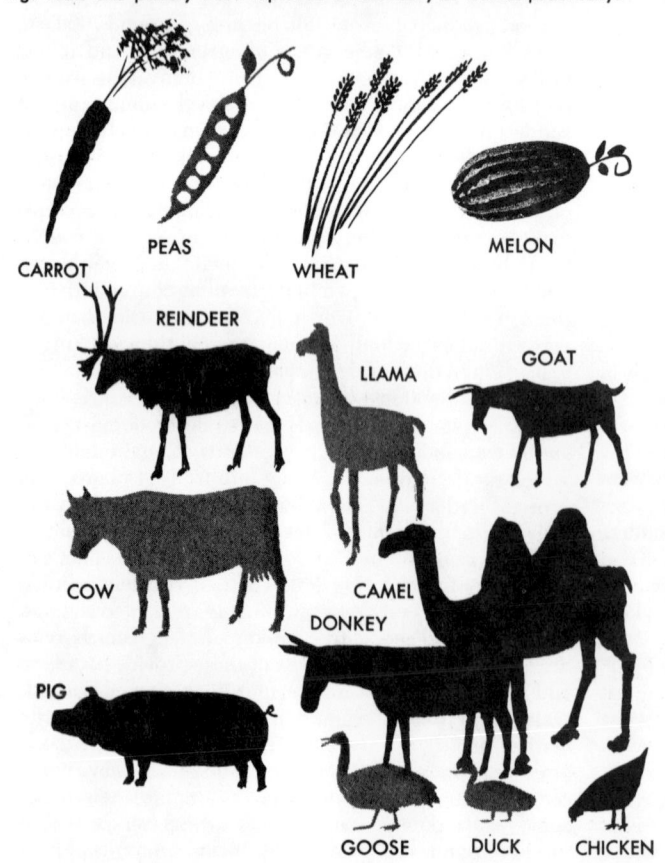

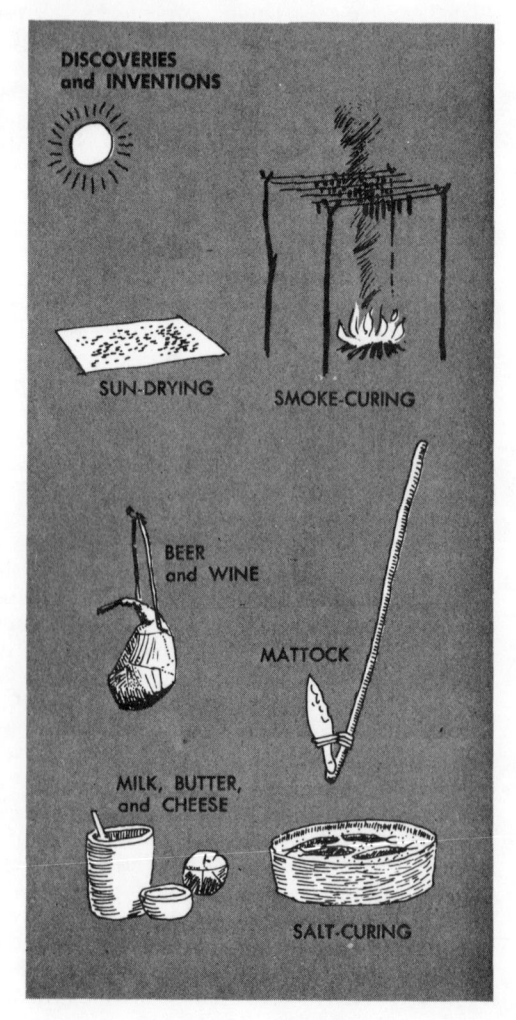

CARROT · PEAS · WHEAT · MELON
REINDEER · LLAMA · GOAT
COW · CAMEL · DONKEY
PIG · GOOSE · DUCK · CHICKEN

DISCOVERIES and INVENTIONS

SUN-DRYING · SMOKE-CURING · BEER and WINE · MATTOCK · MILK, BUTTER, and CHEESE · SALT-CURING

PHASE 6 Improvements in Production and Distribution

This phase was marked more by improvements in methods than by new or different foods, although olives and olive oil gained great importance and pepper and spices were used as preservatives. Animals were used for plowing and transport. Levees and canals controlled water supplies and made irrigation possible. Metal was used for tools, such as sickles.

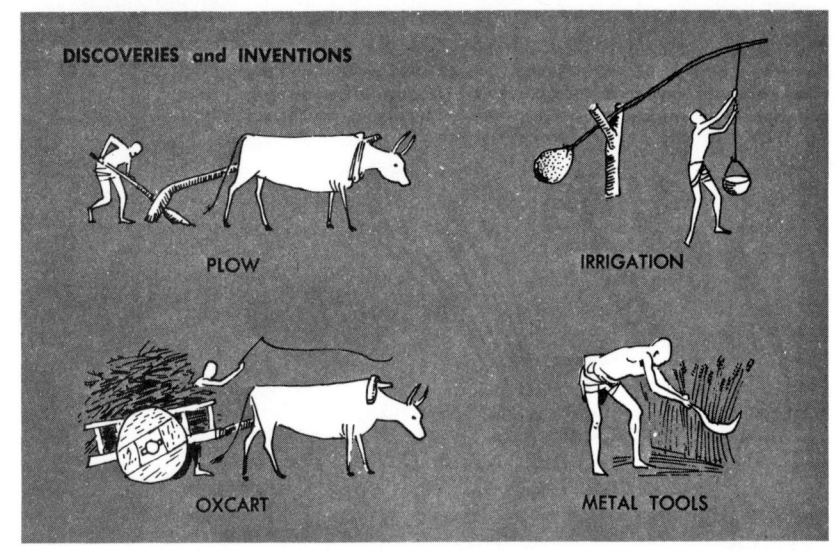

DISCOVERIES and INVENTIONS

PLOW

IRRIGATION

OXCART

METAL TOOLS

OLIVES

spread, but it certainly tended to accompany it. On the other hand, breakable pots were inconvenient for nomads, whether hunters and gatherers or pastoralists.

Experimentation with plant cultivation and animal breeding covered several thousand years, nor were such efforts limited to a few favored regions like the famous Middle Eastern Fertile Crescent. In most areas with suitable resources, such attempts at domestication probably occurred. Exceptions—lands suitable for agriculture or livestock raising, but whose inhabitants did not practice either until recent times—include the Pacific coast of North America, the Canadian Prairies, the southern grasslands of South America, and parts of South Africa and Australia. Significantly, in none of these areas has modern man found any wild plant or animal worth trying to domesticate which the native inhabitants overlooked.

Many early domesticated plants were species of what we now regard as weeds, quick-growing annuals that flourish on recently disturbed or cleared soil. Many were abandoned as crop plants when other species were found to be more productive or more palatable. It is no accident that most of the highly successful staple food crops produce seeds or roots that are easy to store for long periods in dry places. Regular food storage is characteristic of most, though not all, agricultural peoples. Meat and other animal food products can also be dried or otherwise preserved, as by salting, smoking, or packing in fat. Some of these techniques were probably developed in the Mesolithic or even in the Upper Paleolithic, others during the course of the Neolithic.

Taking milk from other mammals is in all likelihood a by-product of keeping flocks or herds as a handy source of meat and hides. It could well have started as a way of meeting emergency feeding needs of livestock sucklings or human infants whose mothers had died or could not provide enough milk for their offspring. She-goats may have been the first regularly milked, with cows, she-asses, mares, female camels, and female reindeer following in about that order. Other dairy products, such as curds, clabber, butter, cheese, and kumiss, would have come later, and their use reflects the difficulty of storing liquid whole milk. Dairying arose only in the Old World, and even there did not spread to all peoples who kept cattle or other stock. It was virtually unknown until the last century in the Far East, Southeast Asia, and Indonesia. In the Americas, the only domestic animals that might possibly have been milked were the llama and alpaca in the Andean area of South America; but they were not milked, nor are they now.

Phase 6: Improvements in Producing and Distributing Food. The early metal ages (Bronze Age, early Iron Age) saw the rise and spread of civilization, which rested on the food-producing economy achieved in the preceding Neolithic. Few really new domesticated plants or animals stem from this period, which began in the Middle East about 3000 B.C. What was important from the food standpoint was a great improvement in food-processing and food-producing technology and in facilities for food transport. A major innovation was the plow, with the ox as power. Other applications of nonhuman animal power to the food economy were for grain threshing, lifting water for irrigation, turning grain mills, and transport—by pack animal and eventually by oxcart. An outstanding feature of most of the early metal-age civilizations was the development of elaborate irrigation systems, which greatly increased food production in suitably situated river valleys, for the first time permitting a significant fraction of the population to engage in nonagricultural work.

One result of this was to greatly expand trade relations, based partly on mining and handicrafts, but also on certain food commodities. The expanded trade intensified contacts between peoples, speeding the interchange, not only of ideas, tools, and luxuries, but of crop plants, spices, and animals. Much valuable crossbreeding between local varieties of domesticated species thus took place. The restricted food patterns of formerly isolated populations began to be enriched by borrowings from other cultures. Two foodstuffs—olive oil and grape wine—played an enor-

FOOD

mously important role in the trade of the Mediterranean from late Bronze Age times onward. Trade in tropical spices tied remote Indonesia, via India and Ceylon, to the Middle East and Mediterranean worlds in classical (Greco-Roman) times. A similar trade, in which highly prized spices and other foodstuffs were involved, linked China with Southeast Asia and Indonesia. On a less extensive scale, trade in foods between tropical lowlands and interior highlands in Middle America (Southern Mexico and Guatemala) seems to have played an important role in the elaboration of civilizing contacts there, starting 2,000 or more years ago. Africa south of the Sahara was deeply affected in terms of its food supply by the spread there of various crops from India and of the humped breeds of Indian cattle. Honey from northern Russian forests was shipped south by river, along with Baltic amber and furs, to markets in the Middle East. An important element in the trans-Saharan trade, which was starting about the same time, was common salt.

The spread of city life during the early metal ages also was marked by the professionalization or commercialization of many food-processing and food-preparing operations which in earlier times had been home or family activities. Fishing and the collecting of other aquatic foods, the milling of grains and the baking of bread, and brewing and winemaking became businesses practiced by specialists. Taverns and eating houses, where meals could be had by paying for them, appeared in some ancient cities.

Not long before the onset of the next period, distillation to make beverages with higher alcoholic content, such as whiskies, brandies, and rum, was developed. It can be regarded as one of the first industrial-chemical food-refining processes.

Phase 7: The Spread of Foods over the World. The next food era, considering the subject from a world perspective, began about 1450–1500 A.D., and was characterized by a world-wide interchange of food resources and techniques, based on the new ocean routes pioneered by the Portuguese and Spanish to Africa, Southern Asia, and the Americas. The East Indian spice trade was a major factor in this epoch of exploration and discovery. The Portuguese found valuable sources of pepper in West Africa, even before rounding Africa and crossing to India. Though the gold of Mexico and Peru and the silks and porcelains of East Asia were more spectacular than foodstuffs, the European overseas expansion of the 15th and 16th cen-

PHASE 7 The Spread of Varieties of Food Throughout the World

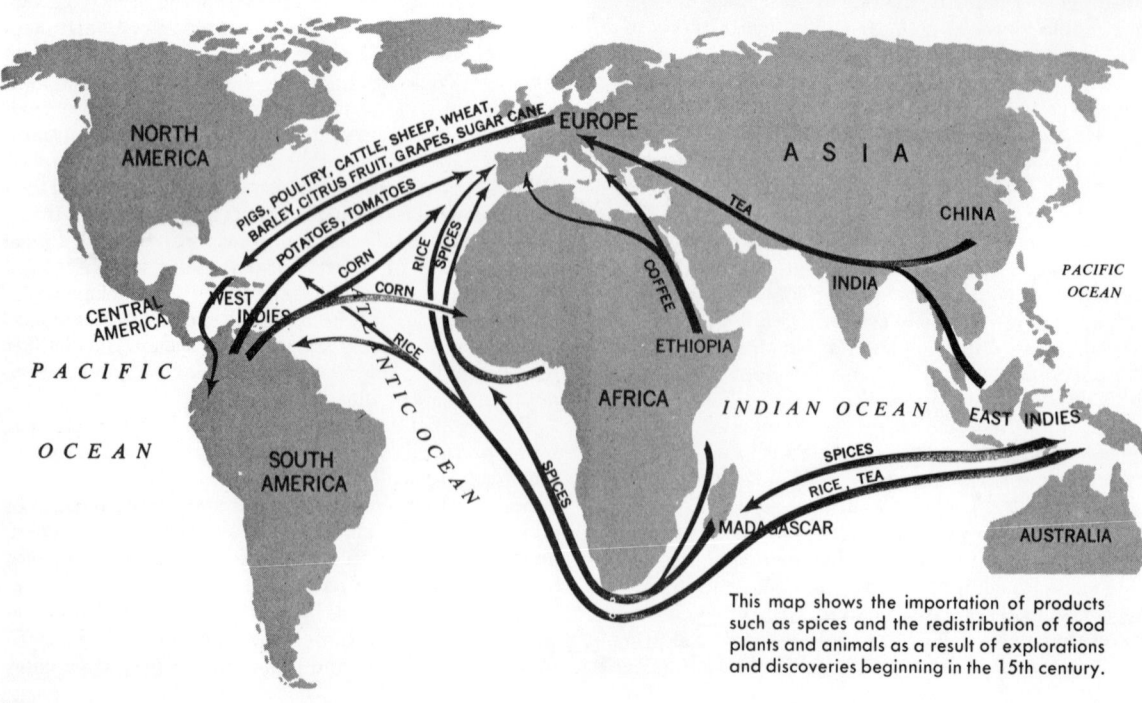

DISCOVERIES and INVENTIONS
The establishment of sea routes during the 15th century between West and East, with the incidental discovery of the Americas, was encouraged by the highly profitable spice trade. Foods and techniques were exchanged on a world-wide basis.

This map shows the importation of products such as spices and the redistribution of food plants and animals as a result of explorations and discoveries beginning in the 15th century.

turies vastly changed the food patterns of much of the world. Sugar cane, rice, and the banana were brought to the New World by the Spanish and Portuguese, who also introduced such Old World crops as wheat, barley, citrus fruits, wine grapes, and many vegetables to the New World areas they visited. They also brought pigs, chickens, horses, cattle, goats, sheep, and donkeys to regions where these domestic animals had not been previously known. From the Americas the Portuguese took corn to tropical Africa, where it spread with amazing rapidity, and to Southeast Asia. Other American food plants followed: New World beans and squashes, tomatoes, peanuts, pineapples, potatoes, and many more. It is now difficult even for botanists to be sure which direction some of these food plants traveled during this period.

In the 17th and 18th centuries Europeans began to consume formerly "exotic" foods in increasing volume. These included tea from Southeast Asia; coffee, originally from Ethiopia, but spread to other areas of Africa by the Arabs and other Muslims, who were forbidden by religion to drink alcoholic beverages; and the Mexican-Guatemalan cocoa, or chocolate. There was also an immense and growing demand for cane sugar, leading to a spread of the plantation system on which its production was based. Rum, made from sugar cane, also became an important trade commodity in the Atlantic area. Corn and potatoes had harder going in gaining acceptance as foods in Europe, and even in the 20th century many Europeans still think of corn as an animal fodder. The potato, however, after encountering great opposition, was finally not only accepted but became the staple food of millions in Ireland and in Central and Northeastern Europe.

By the 18th century A.D. the main outlines of the world's present food pattern had been established as a result of the great era of intercontinental exploration and colonization and the trade relations then created.

Phase 8: Food Since the Industrial and Scientific Revolutions. The latest phase in the history of man's food supply began only about 200 years ago (1750–60) and has been one aspect of the industrial (and scientific) revolution. One of the first results of the new attitudes was the deliberate effort to improve livestock breeds and promote certain food crops (such as turnips) in Great Britain. The British blockade of Napoleonic Europe stimulated the

PHASE 8 The Industrial and Scientific Revolutions (1750 A.D.–Present)

Through selective breeding and hybridization, existing strains of livestock and plants have been improved and new strains have been developed. Modern inventions make more — and better — food available to ever-increasing numbers of people in all parts of the world.

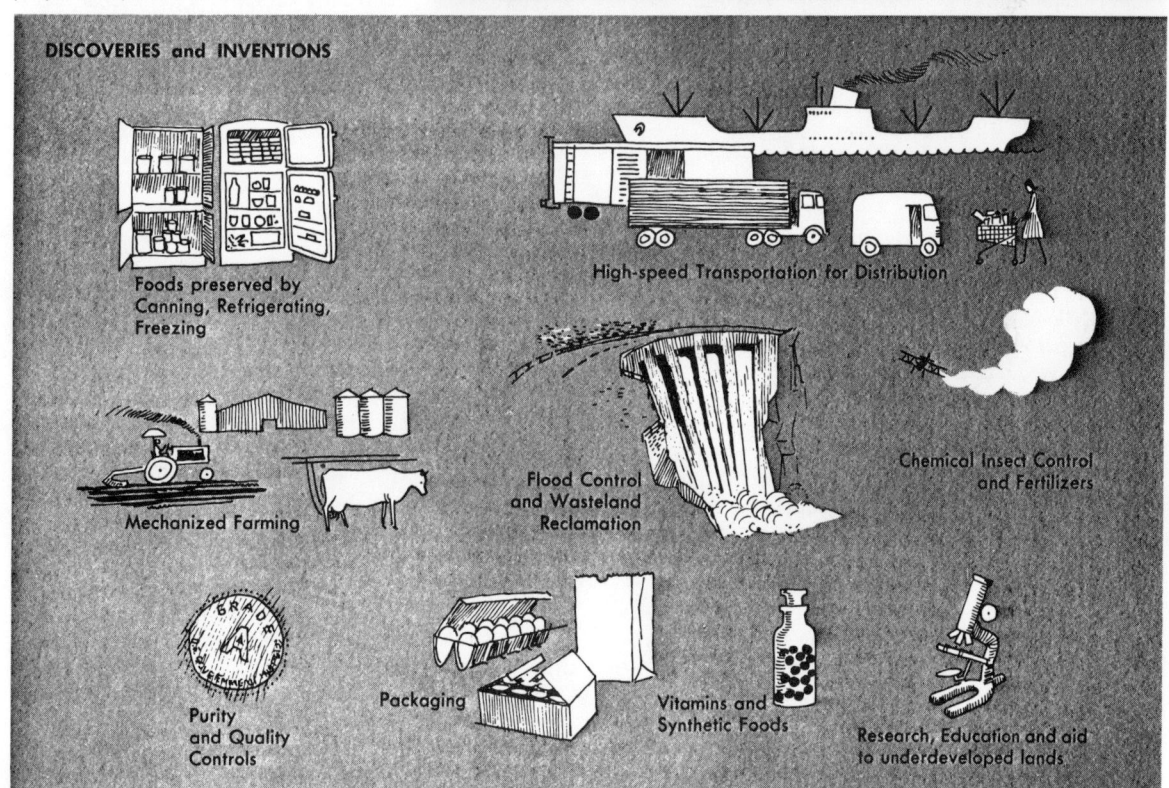

DISCOVERIES and INVENTIONS

Foods preserved by Canning, Refrigerating, Freezing

High-speed Transportation for Distribution

Mechanized Farming

Flood Control and Wasteland Reclamation

Chemical Insect Control and Fertilizers

Purity and Quality Controls

Packaging

Vitamins and Synthetic Foods

Research, Education and aid to underdeveloped lands

173

development of extracting sugar from beets, beginning in 1801. Great progress was under way in sciences having a bearing on food industries. Studies of plant respiration and nutrition paved the way for later discoveries in applied biology, chemical fertilization, and soil science. Louis Pasteur demonstrated the role of microorganisms in fermentation and food spoilage, starting with wines, beer, and milk, in the 1860's. Toward the beginning of the 19th century, even without this knowledge, Nicolas Appert, a French chef, had started food canning, which has been an important factor in the modern food revolution. A science of nutrition emerged by the end of the 19th century, though some of its key findings, such as those relating to the role of vitamins, were to come in the early decades of the 20th century.

Population growth in urban industrial regions during the 19th century was accompanied by marked changes in food production and distribution. In the United States and Great Britain and somewhat more slowly in the industrial countries of continental Europe, staple foods came to be shipped and processed in bulk by commercial enterprises. Foodstuffs that had formerly been processed in the home or at most in small local shops began to issue more and more from food factories and packing houses. At first the commercially handled items were such things as wines, sauces, fancy teas, spices, candies, and biscuits. But a century and a half later, in the United States at least, all foods except fresh vegetables and some fruits were reaching the consumer in commercially packaged form or had been processed in the plants or stored in the cold-storage warehouses of great industrial food firms.

More rapid and dependable transport by railroad and by fast sailing ships and, later, steamships carried ever-increasing quantities of foodstuffs to markets in industrial areas from sometimes distant food-producing regions. Early in the 19th century natural ice was being used in some cities for cold storage. Mechanical refrigeration superseded this, and by the late 1870's, frozen meat was shipped from the United States to Great Britain in refrigerated ships. A few years later regular shipments of frozen meats were being made from Australia, and cold storage of dairy products was becoming common. After the U.S. Civil War, meat packing, centralized in a few cities, began to replace local slaughtering. Centralized grain milling was part of a pattern of industrialization of food processing which involved railroads, river and lake transport, and the building of elevators to facilitate grain handling. Barbed-wire fencing and improved windmills changed livestock herding methods. By the end of the 19th century producers in countries like the United States, Canada, Australia, Argentina, and Russia were supplying much of the grain, and some were also supplying much of the beef and mutton, consumed by the heavily industrialized zones of western Europe.

During the 19th century many governments organized ministries or departments of agriculture and agencies concerned with fisheries. Colleges and universities began to provide courses and research facilities to study the problems of agriculture, animal husbandry, and food technology. Systematic studies of weather and climate have also had an impact on man's food supply and on plans for expansion of it. Economists, agronomists, and other experts, in and outside of government, devoted their careers to food-supply questions. Though there had been sporadic study and writing on such topics in the past, and in ancient China even a Bureau of Agriculture, the attention devoted to food production in the 19th and 20th centuries by scientists, engineers, and government administrators has been without precedent. Also for the first time in history, international efforts to combat famines and malnutrition have been made by both private and governmental agencies.

Food Customs and Taboos

For human beings, foods fulfill more than physiological needs. Food consumption is often the focus of religious rituals and other social interactions, reinforcing group solidarity. Just as eating together may emphasize the closeness of those who join to break bread, not eating with people from other groups may serve to emphasize social distinctions, as in the caste system of India. Foods are the object of complex beliefs and values in most cultures. Most such ideas are prescientific in origin and without nutritional foundation. Among such traditions are customary mealtimes and the notion that certain kinds of foods are suitable for certain meals but not others. Foods are frequently offered as sacrifices to the supernatural. Cannibalism usually has a strong ritual aspect, and few known peoples who eat human flesh ever do so in a casual fashion, as if it were an ordinary food. Such group beliefs about foods, however, are not the explanation for individual food preferences and idiosyncrasies, which are more likely related to individual personality factors or to actual food allergies. Food notions are sometimes held tenaciously, even when it can be shown that customary food practices may lower or destroy important food values. Thus prolonged cooking of fruits and vegetables is common, even though it may eliminate many vitamins.

Food taboos are rules against eating certain foods, against taking any food for certain periods of time, against mixing certain foods, and so on. Familiar instances are the Jewish and Muslim prohibition on pork, the Jewish rule against mixing milk and meat dishes, and the special ways in which even acceptable meat animals must be butchered in order to be kosher. Most Europeans and Americans have a taboo on eating dog flesh, though there is no explicit religious rule against it. In fasts some or all food is given up for a specified time or until some desired result is obtained. Fasting varies from abstention from meat on Fridays among Roman Catholics, to the longer abstentions of Lent among many Christians, the daytime ban on food or drink among Muslims in the month of Ramadan, and the fasts undertaken by individuals or groups to fulfill vows or produce a political or other effect, as in hunger strikes. Several religions impose a vegetarian diet on their followers—notably Buddhism, Jainism, orthodox Hinduism (at least among members of the highest castes) and, among Christians, Seventh-day Adventists and some others.

Eating in most or all human groups involves some form of food etiquette, or manners, which may prescribe the order of serving food, when to start eating, what to say when one finishes, or whether to talk at all while at meals, whether men and women should eat together, and the proper way of handling food, with or without eating utensils. About half of mankind eat with their fingers and not with knives, forks, and spoons, or with chopsticks; yet food-handling etiquette may be meticulously prescribed even when only the fingers are used. In some cultures food is served in small bits, chopped in the kitchen into bite-size pieces suitable for chopsticks, as in China. In other cultures, the diner may be expected to do a considerable amount of food cutting at the table. Foods are served on leaves or sea shells, in their own skins, pods, or husks, wrapped in leaves or thin breads, or as liquids, pastes, powders, at room temperature, hot, cold, or even frozen. In the cultures where cooking is a fine art, much attention may be lavished on modes of serving or presenting food, including purely visual effects. About half the world's peoples eat their meals while sitting on the floor or ground, from mats or cloths, or from very low trays. Dining tables are found among European or Europeanized peoples, and among the Chinese.

Food Supply and Technology

Most of mankind has suffered at one time or another from food scarcity, and in some parts of the world people are chronically undernourished or endure frequent famines. While starvation when it occurs is fairly obvious, food deficiencies resulting from insufficient protein, vitamin, or mineral intake may not be recognized as such by the victims of this deprivation.

Until the 19th century, little could be done to alleviate the effects of famines. Relief supplies could not be moved very rapidly in the days before railroads or steamships, and national and international agencies had not yet been organized to distribute food on a large scale. Chronic malnutrition was not universally recognized as a problem by the medical profession. Scurvy was the first major food-deficiency disease to be treated or prevented, through the use of citrus fruits or juice in the 18th century, but the discovery of its cause—insufficient Vitamin C—was delayed for over a century.

In the 19th century another deficiency disease, rickets, now known to be due to Vitamin-D deprivation, was treated or prevented by administering cod-liver oil. Beriberi and pellagra were later also found to be connected with food deficiencies. Still later, kwashiorkor, a widespread condition in infants with insufficient protein intake, was recognized. In fact, protein deficiency is probably the single most serious human dietary problem, particularly in the less developed tropical countries. Unfortunately, it has been much more difficult and costly to overcome massive protein deficiencies in large populations than insufficiencies in vitamins or trace minerals, and other essential elements such as iodine.

Increasing Man's Food Supply. Until recent times, the problem of enlarging and expanding man's food supply mostly entailed putting more land under cultivation, and in the case of lands already cultivated, of improving the productivity of crops through better seed, more efficient tools, fertilizers, and comparable improvements in handling, storage, processing, packing, and distribution. Similar improvements could be made in animal husbandry, or in fisheries. The basic environmental resources on which all food production rests—air, soil, water, and sunlight—were generally looked upon as inexhaustible or endlessly renewable through natural processes. The fragility of the world's ecosystems was not yet perceived.

Although a few countries were already becoming overcrowded, it was assumed that man could go on expanding his numbers practically indefinitely in the vast, thinly populated "new" continents of the Americas and Australia. It was not, in fact, until 1798 that anyone set forth a more pessimistic hypothesis in unambiguous terms. The English economist Thomas R. Malthus, in his *Essay on the Principle of Population,* proposed that there were limits to man's expansion on the planet. Foreseeing war, famine, misery, and disease as the ultimate controls, he could only advise continence or self-control of man's reproductive instincts. Birth-control methods, which already existed, he regarded with dismay. He was opposed by various more optimistic thinkers, including the English writer William Godwin, who had confidence that science and technology would always find a way out of the Malthusian dilemma.

Actually, the world situation in Malthus' time was still far from critical. In 1800 there were less than one billion people on the planet. The world's population passed two billion early in the 20th century, three billion in the 1960's, and by 1970 had reached approximately 3.5 billion. Expert estimates tend to agree that by the year 2000 it will have reached, if not exceeded, 6 billion. Little more land suitable for cultivation remains, unless desalinization, that is the removal of salt from ocean or other salty waters, can be employed to permit the irrigation of existing desert or near-desert lands. A few more areas may be reclaimed by expanding irrigation, or by creating farmlands from coastal marshes or lowlands, as in the Netherlands, but these efforts are not likely to change the prospects substantially. Nor is the dream of being able to extract greatly increased amounts of food from the oceans very likely of fulfillment. Most experts are not very optimistic about the prospect of vast new harvests from the sea, whether of fish and other animal species not yet being exploited, or of the small plants (chiefly algae) on which fish and other sea animals subsist. Virtually no experts see much hope for circumventing future food shortages by improvements in animal husbandry. While meat, dairy products, and eggs are of great nutritional value, they are already a luxury for the vast majority of mankind. In the future we shall probably be able to afford relatively less, not more, of animal food products, which, acre for acre, are inherently less efficient than foods on which animals too must depend.

Technological Advances. To be sure, the outlook for progress in meeting the world food problem is not entirely hopeless. We have seen remarkable improvements in certain staple crops, such as rice, wheat, and maize, as a result of both genetic research and advances in the technology of tillage, fertilizers, pesticides, and weedkillers. The age-old scourge of farming, unforeseen storms and droughts, and other adverse weather conditions, has been mitigated by great improvements in weather prediction. Efforts, still mostly experimental, suggest that man can hope to control some weather phenomena, such as local rain or hailstorms, and minimize the destructiveness of others, such as hurricanes. Worldwide "remote sensing of the environment" should also provide data on world farm

FOOD POISONING

crop prospects, far more accurate than the present piecemeal collection of statistics.

Pesticides, weedkillers, chemical fertilizers, and soil conditioners are steadily reducing risks for farmers, and more efficient controls over both plant and animal diseases also continue to flow from laboratories and testing stations. However, many of these improvements have undesirable side-effects, which may, even in the fairly short run, upset delicate environmental balances. Chemical pest and weedkillers, along with residues of chemical fertilizers, run off into streams and lakes and eventually reach the sea, where they combine with industrial and other pollutants. What may benefit farmers may destroy fisheries. At the food processing level, the effectiveness of some products may be enhanced by improved treatment and additives. Unfortunately, some of these technological improvements have great disadvantages, either to the consumer directly—as in the furor in the late 1960's over cyclamate sweeteners—or because along with masses of other trash they contaminate the environment, as has been the case with disposable or non-returnable containers.

On the other hand, faced with the increasing costs of meat, dairy, and other animal food products, we may have to depend on the ingenuity of food technologists for synthetic substitutes for such products. Some have already appeared on the market, though the impetus for their creation has come mainly from consumers with religious or other objections to animal foods. The first major substitution of this kind was oleomargine or margarine, a vegetable product designed to replace butter. Synthetic substitutes for coffee, cream, and whipped cream, and approximations of bacon, all from vegetable sources, are now available. Producers of animal food may resent these synthetics, but the hard economic facts suggest that their role in man's diet will steadily increase. It should be noted that even some vegetable foods may eventually become so expensive that substitutes made from cheaper sources may enter the market. Artificially flavored and colored "fruit-juice" substitutes have been available for many years, and orange-juice like products are sold in powdered form.

Environmental Perspective. All of the above problems came into much sharper focus around 1970 with a great growth of popular interest in ecology. Many of the technological improvements that had led to increased food production were seen to be double-edged, with polluting side-effects on the environment, or deleterious effects on living organisms in the food-chain.

Equally serious have been the problems of the less developed countries. After World War II, much was expected of planned economic development, guided by foreign experts and international agencies. Some spectacular advances were achieved in public health care—for example, in malaria control or in the realm of plant breeding. But many of the hopes of the development planners were undermined by political instability, ideological conflicts, and regional warfare. Unbridled urban growth and excessive expenditures for armaments have been some of the unexpected checks on rational planning to achieve modernization.

While a few of the underdeveloped countries have achieved an economic "takeoff" into modernization, most have not. Countries such as India and Pakistan do not offer great promise of overcoming the Malthusian dilemma in this century. Mainland China, which is likely to have a billion people by 1985 and over two billion by 2000, is faced with a particularly ominous problem. China has not had a favorable record of meeting the food requirements of all its people over the past several centuries, and it is unreasonable to suppose that by 2000 A.D. the Chinese administrators, planners, and technologists can cope with a population in a single country which will approximately equal the 1930 world population.

The immense difficulties that are likely to confront even the most advanced countries in the next three decades—from avoiding disastrous international war to the maintenance of internal order and salvaging what remains of the environment—suggest that the food supply question will become a paramount problem for mankind. Until recently, the experts most concerned with food concentrated their attention on agriculture, animal husbandry, and fisheries, and the technical means to improve them. The present and presumably future prospects would seem to link this set of problems inextricably to those of demography, sociopolitical structures, and all the other factors which shape our environment, thus immeasurably complicating the search for solutions.

FOOD POISONING most commonly results from contamination of food by bacteria or by toxic bacterial secretions. The term also includes disorders produced by consuming naturally poisonous substances and chemical poisons. Food poisoning should be distinguished from "ptomaine poisoning," which refers to the condition supposedly caused by consuming ptomaines, substances produced by the putrefaction of proteins. It is no longer believed likely that these substances can in themselves produce food poisoning.

Food poisoning resulting from consumption of food containing living bacteria is most commonly caused by organisms of the genus *Salmonella*, which includes the bacteria responsible for typhoid fever. An acute intestinal upset occurs from 6 to 48 hours after eating food that has been heavily contaminated. Fever, headache, abdominal pains, nausea, vomiting, and diarrhea appear suddenly and usually persist for a few days.

Toxins given off by bacteria may contaminate food and produce severe and sometimes fatal poisoning. One of the deadliest poisons known is manufactured by the *Clostridium botulinum*, a bacillus that cannot grow in the presence of air and which consequently thrives in home-canned foods which have been inadequately sterilized. The toxin can be completely destroyed by cooking the contaminated food at 80° C. for 10 minutes. Within 12 to 36 hours after the meal there is a sudden onset of dizziness and double vision. Other symptoms include difficulty in breathing, talking, and swallowing. More than half the victims die, usually within three to six days. A specific antitoxin is available against the botulinum poison, but if it is to be effective it must be given before advanced symptoms appear.

The commonest type of food poisoning in the United States is that which results from eating food contaminated with the toxin of the staphylococcus bacteria. Inadequately refrigerated, perishable foods, such as chicken salad, potato salad, and cream-filled pastries may be responsible. Nausea, vomiting, retching, abdominal cramps and diarrhea occur within one to six hours after eating. Large amounts of fluid may be lost through the vomiting and diarrhea and, in rare cases, shock may result.

Other Types of Food Poisoning. Shellfish or mussel poisoning may occur because of toxic materials which form part of the shellfish diet. Certain types of poisonous mushrooms cause severe watery diarrhea, abdominal pain, vomiting, jaundice, convulsions, and in some cases, death. See also BOTULISM; POISONING.

FOOT, in human anatomy, mechanically intricate structure, composed of 26 small bones which are bound together by capsules, ligaments, tendons, and muscles into a strong, flexible organ of locomotion.

The bones of the foot bear the entire weight of the body, which is transmitted to them through the talus, or ankle, bone. The talus distributes this weight to the heel bone (calcaneus) and to the bones of the arches in front. The longitudinal arch runs from the heel to the heads of the long, slender metatarsal bones which form the ball of the foot. Muscles and bands of strong, fibrous tissue run from the heel bone to the metatarsal heads, being drawn across the arch like the string of a bow; the resiliency of these tissues gives the arch its spring. The metatarsal arch runs crossways across the foot, being formed by the metatarsal heads.

The long arch is depressed in flatfoot, a common condition often characterized by pain and fatigue following long periods of walking or standing. The height of the arch is extremely variable; in some feet it is normally depressed, while in others it is markedly high. Contrary to popular belief, a congenitally low-arched foot is usually strong and does not require treatment.

Most of the muscles which move the bones of the foot originate in the leg and send tendons alongside the ankle to insert in the foot. The largest and strongest of these muscles is the gastrocnemius-soleus group in the calf, which attach to the heel by means of the Achilles' tendon (the heel cord). These muscles raise the heel off the ground during walking and are responsible for the spring in the gait. Other muscles originating in the leg include those which bend and straighten the toes. The tendons of these muscles help to stabilize and support the ankle joint.

The foot receives its nourishment from two main arteries: the dorsalis pedis on the top of the foot and the posterior tibial, which runs behind the inside prominence of the ankle bone. The pulsation of these arteries can be felt by the fingers in the same way as the wrist pulse, and is used to test the adequacy of circulation in the foot.

DISORDERS OF THE FEET

FOOT DISORDERS CAUSED BY IMPROPER FOOTGEAR, HARD WALKING SURFACES, AND STRAIN TO THE MECHANICAL STRUCTURES OF THE FOOT.

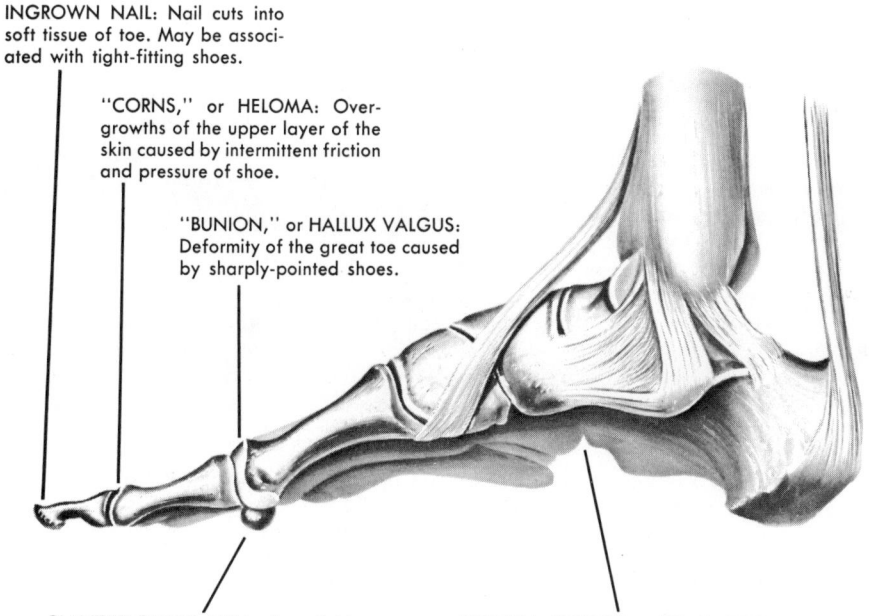

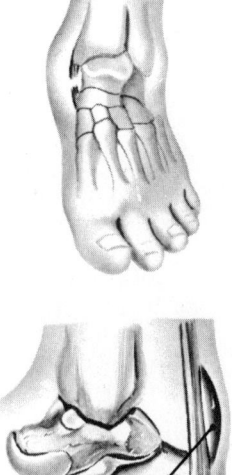

INGROWN NAIL: Nail cuts into soft tissue of toe. May be associated with tight-fitting shoes.

"CORNS," or HELOMA: Overgrowths of the upper layer of the skin caused by intermittent friction and pressure of shoe.

"BUNION," or HALLUX VALGUS: Deformity of the great toe caused by sharply-pointed shoes.

ANKLE SPRAIN: Caused by strong lateral twist, often occurs when walking on rocky, uneven surfaces.

PLANTAR CALLUS: Thickening of skin on ball of foot may be caused by long hours of walking on hard surfaces in thin-soled shoes.

"FALLEN ARCHES" or "FLAT FEET": Depression of the long arch of the foot may be caused by excessive strain on a congenitally weak foot.

ACHILLES BURSITIS: Friction of the shoe against the heel tendon causes the development of a fluid-filled sac (bursa) at the point of irritation.

FOOT

FOOT DISORDERS ASSOCIATED WITH DISEASES OCCURRING ELSEWHERE IN THE BODY.

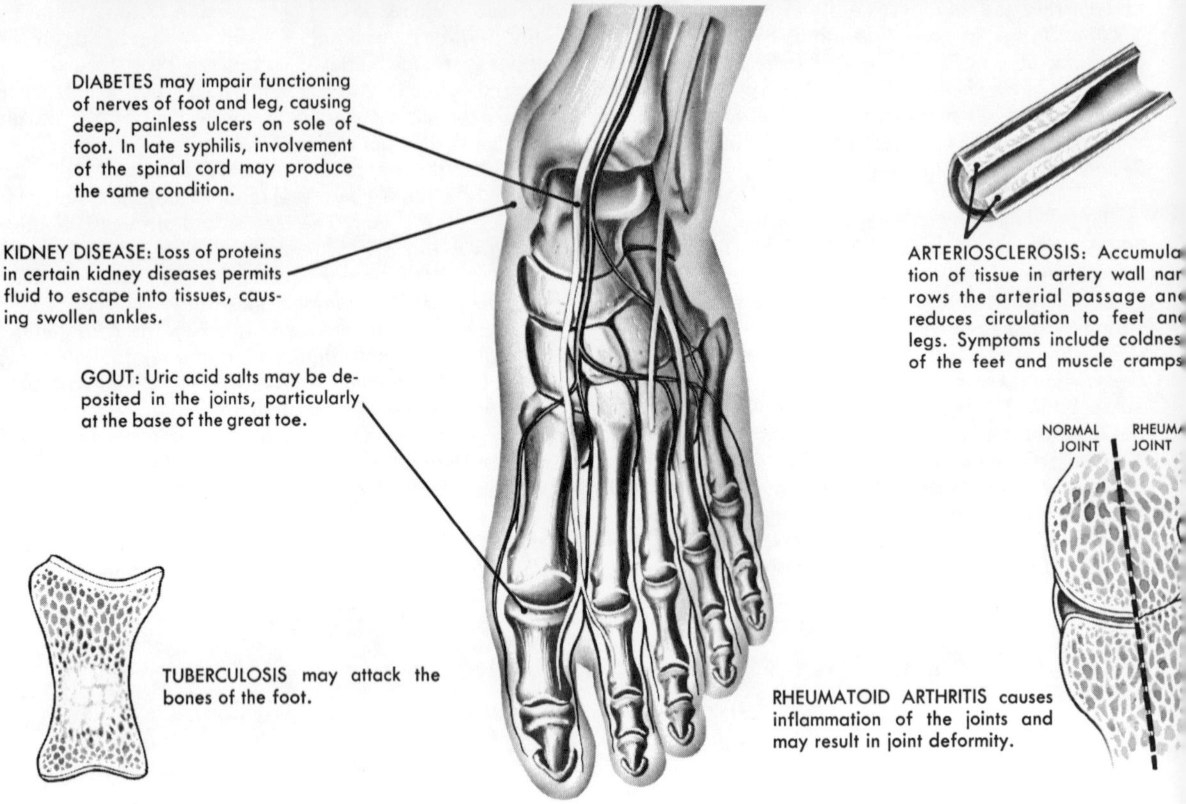

DIABETES may impair functioning of nerves of foot and leg, causing deep, painless ulcers on sole of foot. In late syphilis, involvement of the spinal cord may produce the same condition.

KIDNEY DISEASE: Loss of proteins in certain kidney diseases permits fluid to escape into tissues, causing swollen ankles.

GOUT: Uric acid salts may be deposited in the joints, particularly at the base of the great toe.

ARTERIOSCLEROSIS: Accumulation of tissue in artery wall narrows the arterial passage and reduces circulation to feet and legs. Symptoms include coldness of the feet and muscle cramps.

NORMAL JOINT RHEUMA JOINT

TUBERCULOSIS may attack the bones of the foot.

RHEUMATOID ARTHRITIS causes inflammation of the joints and may result in joint deformity.

Foot Disorders

The hard pavements and the constricting shoes of civilized living are responsible for the common foot complaints, such as corns, calluses, and bunions. Corns and calluses are the product of intermittent friction and pressure which stimulate the skin to thicken its outside horny layer. Shoes which are tight and pointed may bend the great toe, producing the deformity of the great toe joint, the bunion. Athlete's foot is caused by infection with certain fungi which produce itching and fissuring of the skin.

A number of disorders which affect other parts of the body also manifest themselves in the foot. Gout frequently attacks the first toe joint and the ankle. Infectious arthritis, such as that resulting from gonorrhea, may also attack the ankle joint. Diseases of the nervous system may damage the nerve supply to the feet so that the individual sustains constant damage to the skin of the foot without being aware of it. This occasionally develops in diabetes and in late syphilis and may result in deep, penetrating ulcers on the sole of the foot. Poliomyelitis may leave permanent muscle weakness, resulting in a characteristic limp and foot deformity.

A common and serious manifestation of a general bodily disease in the foot is impairment of the blood supply. Arteriosclerosis, or hardening of the arteries, often affects the arteries of the legs, reducing the blood supply to the foot and devitalizing its tissues. Individuals with advanced arteriosclerosis of the extremities are unable to resist infection effectively and comparatively minor injuries of the foot may lead to infection, gangrene, and eventually, amputation. This is especially true in diabetics, who for this reason should avoid home foot surgery, ill-fitting shoes, and the application of heat or harsh chemicals (iodine, for example) to the feet.

FORCEPS, tonglike instruments used for grasping and pulling objects. Examples include hemostatic forceps used during surgery to grasp and close severed blood vessels, dental forceps for extracting teeth, and splinter forceps for removing splinters. Obstetrical forceps are occasionally used in childbirth to grasp and pull the baby's head.

FOURNEAU [foor-nō'], **ERNEST FRANÇOIS AUGUSTE** (1872–1949), French physician, chemist, and pharmacologist. Chief of staff at the Pasteur Institute in Paris, Fourneau became well known for his investigations leading to the introduction of anesthetics (stovaine, 1903) and for drugs used in the treatment of tropical diseases, especially African sleeping sickness. His principal work on the chemical synthesis of drugs, *Organic Medicaments and Their Preparations* (1925), was translated into several languages.

FRACTURES, disruptions of bone structure which most commonly result from accidents in which excessive stresses are applied to bones. The nature of the fracture depends upon the strength, direction, and location of the force applied to the bone, the condition of the bone, and the age of the patient. Every fracture damages the soft tissues of the body, producing injuries which may range from slight bruising to severe crushing and tearing. Such damage is especially serious when it involves nerves or major blood vessels.

Types. When the skin over a fracture remains unbroken, it is spoken of as a closed (or simple) fracture. If there is communication with the outside, or, as in the case of the skull, with one of the air-containing cavities of the nose or ear, the fracture is called an open (or compound) fracture. The opening may be produced by some object penetrating the skin from without, or by a sharp portion of the broken bone penetrating the skin from within. The presence of bleeding and tissue damage at the fracture site provides an ideal medium for the growth of bacteria. Every open fracture is contaminated to some degree, and should the patient's resistance be inadequate, or treatment delayed too long, a serious infection may develop. Persistent infection may prevent the fracture from healing.

When a force that normally could be well tolerated causes a bone to break, it does so because some process has reduced the strength of the bone. The bone may be weakened because of abnormal development, as in "brittle bone disease" (osteogenesis imperfecta); nutritional inadequacy, such as scurvy caused by lack of vitamin C; hormonal disturbances (such as hyperparathyroidism, where there is oversecretion of the parathyroid hormone); or in senile osteoporosis (a generalized decrease in the amount of bone substance). Tumors may also weaken the bone and cause pathologic fractures. These may have arisen in the bone (primary tumors) or, more commonly, spread to the bone from elsewhere in the body.

Diagnosis. Fractures alter the form of the affected part, preventing normal function and permitting motion where normally there is none. Bleeding from the broken blood vessels of the bone and surrounding tissue produces early and marked swelling. Pressure or movement at the fracture site stimulates the nerve endings causing pain. The grating together of broken bone ends—crepitus—is proof of a fracture, but is a sign which should not be deliberately sought. In certain fractures in which the bone ends may be jammed together there will be little bleeding, moderate swelling, and no abnormal motion. The examination of an injured person suspected of having a fracture is not considered complete until good quality X rays are taken to confirm or rule out the presence of a break in the bone.

Treatment. Treatment begins with first-aid splinting. Splinting serves to prevent further bleeding, to relieve the pain, and to minimize further damage to adjacent soft tissues. All fractures should be splinted as soon as possible after they have occurred. Almost any rigid object can be used in an emergency to splint a part of the body.

Medical treatment of a fracture aims to bring the two segments of the broken bone back into their normal alignment. This is usually spoken of as reduction and is best done as soon as possible, before too much swelling has occurred. Adequate anesthesia is essential to reduce the voluntary and involuntary muscle contractions which interfere with the surgeon's attempts to set the bone. Manipulation of the fracture is carried out carefully and deliberately to achieve reduction with the least additional injury to the tissues. After manipulation, further X rays are taken and if the position is satisfactory, it is maintained, usually by the application of a plaster cast to the injured limb. In certain cases, however, a plaster cast alone is not adequate and must be supplemented by other means. In some instances weights are used to maintain a constant pull on the limb so as to keep the bone fragments properly aligned: this is termed traction.

In still other situations, surgery is necessary. The bones are reduced under direct vision, and the position is maintained by plates, nails, screws, or other devices made of special nonreactive metal.

Although the physician brings the bone fragments back into a normal position, the body itself joins the two ends in a firm union. The specialized tissue which forms for this purpose is called callus. The external callus is produced by the bone-forming cells of the covering layer of bone; the internal callus is produced by the cells which line the marrow cavity. A collar of callus composed of some fibrous tissue, some cartilage, and some newly formed bone, grows from each end of the broken bone. The collars get larger and thicker and finally meet. This is the first stage in the healing process of the fracture. The callus eventually is converted completely into new bone, and usually at that time the splinter, or cast, or other external support of the fracture can be removed. The final stage in the healing process consists of a reconstitution of the shaft of the bone, and a remodeling process which removes that portion of the callus which is no longer needed for strength.

Abnormally prolonged callus formation with a delayed conversion of callus to mature bone is usually referred to as a slow, or delayed, union. This term implies that if the treatment is continued the fracture will eventually heal. In some cases, where optimum conditions for healing are not present, the bone ends become united by fibrous tissue, which will not be converted to bone, no matter how long the fracture is immobilized. This is referred to as nonunion, and requires special treatment, such as bone grafting.

Treatment cannot be considered complete until the patient has regained as nearly normal function of the injured part as can be expected from the type and severity of the injury. As soon as the degree of healing will permit the removal of whatever type of fixation has been applied, the patient is carefully instructed in the way in which to start using the injured limb again, to regain normal function of the muscles and joints. In some cases specific physical therapy may be helpful, but in the majority of instances functional restoration is best secured by active exercises, under the supervision of the doctor.

FREEMAN, WALTER (1895–   ), American neurologist and neurosurgeon best known for his work in introducing prefrontal lobotomy into the United States. In this procedure a portion of the cerebrum is detached from the lower brain to treat certain mental disorders. Freeman's

best-known works are *Neuropathology* (1933) and *Psychosurgery* (with J. W. Watts, 1942).
See also LOBOTOMY.

FREUD, SIGMUND (1856–1939), Austrian physician widely known as the founder of psychoanalysis. Freud entered the medical school of the University of Vienna in 1873 with the intention of preparing himself for a career in science. In medical school he studied with the eminent physiologist Ernst von Brücke, from whom he learned to regard the living person as a dynamic system to which the

Sigmund Freud, founder of psychoanalysis.

The Bettmann Archive

laws of chemistry and physics apply. During his eight years in medical school and for several years following graduation, Freud engaged in original research on the nervous system. His investigations were well thought of and he was rapidly making a name for himself in science. Anti-Semitism in Austrian universities and the practical necessity of supporting a family, however, led Freud to choose private practice over an academic career.

In spite of a heavy practice which occupied his days, Freud was a prodigious writer. His complete psychological writings are published in an English edition of 24 volumes. Among his best-known books, in addition to *The Interpretation of Dreams*, are *The Psychopathology of Everyday Life* (1901), which explains the unconscious significance of forgetting, mistakes, and accidents; *Three Essays on the Theory of Sexuality* (1905), which traces the development of the sex impulse and its aberrations; *Jokes and Their Relation to the Unconscious* (1905); *Introductory Lectures on Psychoanalysis* (1916–17); *Beyond the Pleasure Principle* (1920), which postulates the existence in man of a death instinct as well as a life instinct; *The Future of an Illusion* (1927), which is a psychoanalytic study of religion; *Civilization and Its Discontents* (1930), in which he examines the reasons for modern man's unhappiness, and *New Introductory Lectures on Psychoanalysis* (1933). His style of writing is lively and lucid and reflects his highly developed sense of humor and his broad knowledge of literature. He was awarded the Goethe Prize in 1930.

In 1923 the first signs of cancer in his upper jaw and palate were detected and during the rest of his life Freud suffered from the progressive ravages of the disease, for which he underwent 33 operations. Although he was preoccupied by the thought of death, he continued to write and to see patients to the very end of his life.
See also PSYCHOANALYSIS; PSYCHOTHERAPY.

FRÖHLICH'S [frō′lĭ-кнs] **SYNDROME,** rare glandular disorder characterized by obesity, with fat deposits in the upper arms, legs, back, and chest, and by small sex organs. Although seen in adolescents of both sexes, it is more common in boys. The disease is caused by a tumor or inflammation of the pituitary gland, which lies on the undersurface of the brain, or of the adjacent region of the brain, the hypothalamus. Disturbances also appear in other endocrine glands, particularly in the sex glands. When a tumor is responsible, the condition can be treated by X-ray therapy or surgery. Hormones are given to correct the deficiencies in hormone production.
See also ENDOCRINE GLANDS.

FUNK, CASIMIR (1884–1967), naturalized Polish-American biochemist who pioneered in the study of vitamins. He isolated a substance from rice polishings which effectively prevented beriberi. He named this substance "vitamine." It is now known as vitamin B_1, or thiamine. Following this discovery, Funk was invited to English, American, and Polish research institutes and universities. From 1928 to 1935 he owned a private pharmaceutical firm near Paris, which he gave up to become research consultant of the U.S. Vitamin Corporation of New York.

G

GALEN [gā′lən], Lat. name Claudius Galenus (c.150–c.200), "the prince of physicians," revered as the supreme medical authority until the 16th century. Born in Pergamum in Asia Minor and educated at Pergamum, Smyrna, and Alexandria, he served as personal physician to three Roman Emperors. He wrote more than 500 books, including a dictionary of five volumes. Galen made extensive anatomical and physiological investigations, and although his contributions were significant, his authority was such that his erroneous concepts stifled medical progress for centuries.

GALL [gäl], **FRANZ JOSEPH** (1758–1828), German physician, pioneer in brain studies and founder of the pseudoscience of phrenology. Gall correctly pointed out that gray matter is the active part of the brain in which nerve impulses originate, while white matter is connecting material. He also believed that specific areas of the brain control specific body movements. Modern neurologists can now map the brain and pinpoint the part which controls finger movements, for example, thus proving Gall's idea correct. Gall felt that the shape of the brain, and thus the shape of the skull, had to do with mental capacity, emotional qualities, and character. By touching the skull, he believed, one could deduce the relative amount of the characteristic located directly underneath. This was the beginning of the pseudoscience of phrenology, in which a man's character may be analyzed by feeling the bumps on his head. While his views were not accepted by the medical profession, they gained wide favor with the general public. After his death, Gall's disciples exaggerated his "science" to almost total nonsense. As a result, the stigma of quack in now attached to Gall, and his valuable work tends to be forgotten.

GALL BLADDER AND GALLSTONES. The gall bladder is a pear-shaped sac attached to the under-surface of the liver. Its function is to store bile—the greenish-yellow liver secretion which contains both waste products and substances important in the digestion and absorption of fats. The gall bladder receives bile from the liver and discharges it into the small intestine via the common duct.

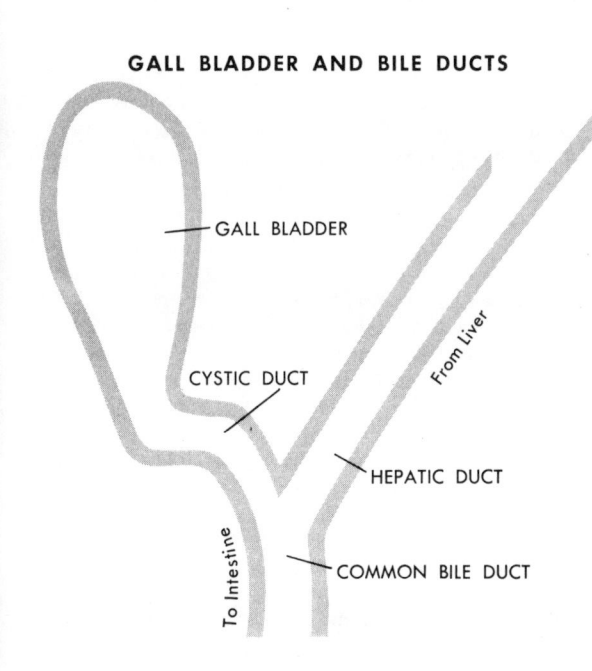

GALL BLADDER AND BILE DUCTS

Gallstones, or biliary calculi, are concretions, consisting principally of cholesterol, calcium, and bile salts, which are formed in the gall bladder. The number and size vary from one large stone completely filling the gall bladder to hundreds of stones no larger than small pebbles. The stones result from the precipitation of cholesterol and other components of the bile fluid while the bile is stored in the gall bladder. Factors which are thought to contribute to the formation of the stones include a sluggishness of bile flow from the gall bladder, a relative increase in the cholesterol content in the bladder, excessive bile pigment formation and inflammation and infection of the bladder. In some cases gallstones taken from patients who have previously had typhoid fever have been shown to contain live typhoid germs.

Gallstones may develop in pregnancy as a consequence of the slowing of bile flow and an increased cholesterol content in the blood. It has been estimated that approximately 20% to 30% of women over 40 who have borne children have gallstones. Diabetics and obese persons also develop gallstones more frequently than others. There has been speculation that a diet rich in cholesterol may predispose to gallstone formation. The comparative rarity of gallstones among Orientals supports this view.

Many individuals with gallstones have no symptoms. When symptoms do appear they vary with the location of the stone. Stones in the gall bladder may produce dull sensations of discomfort, especially after eating fried foods. Attacks are apt to follow a heavy meal. Stones lodged in any of the ducts which conduct the bile from the liver and gall bladder to the intestine may cause biliary colic—attacks of severe pain in the right upper quarter of the abdomen. The pain radiates to below the right shoulder blade. Stones lodged in the cystic duct cause the bladder to become distended and sometimes infected. Stones lodged in the common duct, through which bile enters the intestine, often cause jaundice, a yellowish tinting of the skin and eyes resulting from the presence of excess bile pigments in the blood.

Diagnosis of gallstones may be made through X rays; calcium-containing stones appear as opaque ring-shaped areas in regular X-ray plates; noncalcium-containing stones appear as negative shadows on X-ray plates made after the patient is given a dye which concentrates in the gall bladder. Patients suffering from gallstones are advised to avoid fatty or fried foods, pork, and gas-producing foods. Surgical removal of the gall bladder (cholecystectomy) may be necessary in many cases. This operation leaves intact the duct which conducts bile from the liver to the intestine.

GAMMA GLOBULIN [găm'ə glŏb'yə-lĭn], a group of proteins, in the blood plasma, that includes most of the antibodies used by the body to fight bacterial and viral diseases. Gamma globulin extracted from the blood of any donor may be used to prevent or modify the course of measles, hepatitis, and poliomyelitis. To protect against chicken pox, German measles, or mumps, gamma globulin from convalescent donors is used, since their blood contains the necessary high concentration of antibodies for their specific disease. An injection of gamma globulin provides protection for about four weeks.

Individuals suffering from agammaglobulinemia, a rare

GANGRENE

congenital deficiency of gamma globulin, are subject to frequent infections and require periodic injections of gamma globulin for protection.
See also ANTIBODIES AND ANTIGENS; IMMUNITY.

GANGRENE [găng′grēn], death of body tissue caused by inadequate blood supply. The most common and well-known type of gangrene is associated with arteriosclerosis obliterans. This type of arteriosclerosis is seen most frequently in elderly people (especially diabetics) and causes gangrene by a slow and gradual obliteration of the blood supply. Substances are deposited in the arterial walls, causing the opening to narrow until the blood flow is insufficient to supply the needs of the tissues. The legs are usually affected; the area involved may include a large portion of the foot or be limited to the toes. Tissue death of this type is called "dry gangrene," because the skin becomes dry as parchment. The term "wet gangrene" is usually used when a gangrenous portion of the body becomes infected.

Gangrene may also be caused by other conditions that decrease blood supply. Mechanical obstruction to blood flow may be the result of freezing or an arterial embolus. An embolus is a blood clot that forms in one portion of the circulatory system and is carried away by the blood stream until it becomes wedged in an artery in another part of the body. An embolus may obstruct an artery in a limb, causing sudden severe pain, coldness, paralysis, and absence of pulse. The tissues of the affected portion eventually die.

Gangrene may occur in the intestinal tract when a portion of the bowel loses its blood supply either from infection, embolus, or by twisting upon itself—a condition known as a volvulus.

The term "gas gangrene" is applied to an infection caused by bacteria of the Clostridium group. These organisms grow only in the absence of air and produce bubbles of gas that distend the tissues. They may contaminate wounds and frequently produce infections following criminal abortions. Gas gangrene is almost always fatal if not treated.

GASTRECTOMY [găs-trĕk′tə-mē], operation involving the complete or partial (subtotal) removal of the stomach. After a section of the stomach is removed the remaining portion is connected with the small bowel. The majority of partial gastrectomies are performed for ulcers which have resisted medical therapy or which have been complicated by hemorrhages, obstruction, or perforation. Most total gastrectomies are performed in cases of stomach cancer. In most instances the body adjusts well to partial gastrectomy. When the stomach is completely removed, malnutrition, digestive disturbances, and anemia may result.
See also DIGESTION.

GASTRIC JUICE, secretions given off by the stomach glands during the process of digestion. The principal constituents are hydrochloric acid and the enzyme pepsin, which breaks down the proteins found in meat, eggs, milk, and other foods into simpler substances.
See also DIGESTION.

GASTRIC ULCER. See ULCERS.

GASTROENTERITIS, illness of the gastrointestinal tract. In the United States it is primarily an acute illness characterized by watery diarrhea, abdominal cramps, nausea, and vomiting. Dietary indiscretions, excess alcohol, and psychological stress can cause these symptoms, but many cases are caused by viruses. The most important are the entero viruses, which produce an illness that begins with loss of appetite and nausea. Vomiting occurs on the first day and is followed by abdominal pain and diarrhea. Some individuals have mild headache and fever up to 101° F. The illness lasts 3 to 4 days. Viral gastroenteritis occurs mostly in the summer and fall, but one form occurs in the winter.

Gastroenteritis caused by bacteria or protozoa can usually be distinguished from the viral forms. Staphylococcal food poisoning occurs 1 to 6 hours after eating contaminated food. Vomiting and retching are most severe, without diarrhea. An outbreak of salmonella gastroenteritis, often associated with fever and a raised white blood-cell count, is sometimes confused with a viral illness. There is no specific treatment for viral gastroenteritis, except replacement of fluids. Bacterial forms must be treated with an appropriate antibacterial agent.

GASTROINTESTINAL INTUBATION, a procedure in which a tube is passed either through the nose or mouth into the stomach or small bowel. The tubes are constructed of a flexible material so that they may be passed easily and exist in a variety of sizes and shapes in order to accomplish specific functions, such as removal of stomach or bowel contents in cases of poisoning, to obtain material for analysis, or to relieve distention. Occasionally patients are fed through tubes.

GASTROINTESTINAL ("GI") SERIES, an X-ray examination of the digestive tract. The structures of the tract are made visible by administering a suspension of barium sulfate in water. This material blocks passage of the X rays, so that the stomach and intestines appear opaque on X-ray film. A series of X-ray exposures may be made as the barium sulfate passes along the digestive tract. A barium enema is used to investigate the lower parts of the digestive tract.

GENE [jēn]. Gregor Johann Mendel, an Austrian monk, first described the gene in his investigations on peas in 1865, although the term "gene" was not used until 1909. Genes are the fundamental units of heredity. They are located along the chromosomes in the cells of living it serves as much in routine policing of rural areas as in particular chromosome. Through the genes of the sperm and egg the potentialities for growth and development are transmitted to new organisms. Genes permit certain enzymes to be formed, and the enzymes in turn permit specific chemical reactions to take place which ultimately determine specific patterns of growth and development. Genes can also reproduce themselves. These unique characteristics make the genes important objects of study in investigations on the nature of living material.

The great majority of present evidence indicates that genes are composed of deoxyribonucleic acid (DNA), although some protein must also be present in order for the genes to function. Approximately 1 time in 100,000 a gene, through a change in its chemical structure, will produce a new hereditary trait. Such a spontaneous change is called a mutation. Genes mutate more often under irradiation or in the presence of certain chemicals.

GENETICS [jə-nĕt′ĭks], the science of heredity. The primary concern of genetics is the transmission of hereditary units from generation to generation and the expression of these hereditary units during the development of the organism. The fact that heredity exists has been known for hundreds of years. The rules by which heredity operates were first discovered and published by the Austrian monk Gregor Mendel in 1866. Unfortunately, the scientists of that time failed to appreciate the extraordinary significance of Mendel's lucid experiments, and it was not until 1900 that Mendel's laws were rediscovered independently by Karl Correns, Hugo De Vries, and Erich Tschermak. Six years later the English biologist William Bateson coined the word "genetics" (from Greek, "to generate").

Early Genetic Investigations

The early genetic investigations were carried out not for their own sake but to serve as confirmatory evidence for the theory of evolution. The major weakness of Charles Darwin's concept of the origin of species was his ignorance of the rules of heredity, which were unknown when his great treatise was published in 1859. It it not surprising that two of the early American geneticists, William E. Castle and Thomas Hunt Morgan, were embryologists intent on demonstrating the truths of evolution as reconstructed during the development of an organism.

There was also an early burst of activity in human genetics. Interest in eugenics (the science that deals with the improvement of human heredity) was widespread and it, like evolution, lacked the essential knowledge of the principles of heredity. The first demonstration of a human trait that behaved according to the Mendelian rules was provided in 1903 by William C. Farabee and William E. Castle, who showed that albinism in three generations of a Negro family behaved as a Mendelian recessive. A much more significant paper by Archibald Garrod appeared in 1908 but was generally neglected. He suggested that four human metabolic disorders—albinism, alkaptonuria, cystinuria, and pentosuria—were genetic and were present at birth. The baby was assumed either to lack an enzyme necessary for normal metabolism, or the enzyme was present and blocked in its activities. Since then many more diseases have been found to result from genetic inborn errors of metabolism. Years later, the Nobel Prize winners George Beadle and Joshua Lederberg utilized Garrod's concept in demonstrating the direct control of enzymes and metabolism by specific genetic units (genes) in the mold *Neurospora* and in bacteria.

Mendel's studies with peas grown in a monastery garden established the first principles of genetics, but peas were not the best organisms for genetic research. Studies on poultry, mice, and man confirmed the essential truths of Mendel's laws, but these subjects were also not the ideal material for the explosive growth of genetic research that was to come. The creature that was to revolutionize biology was introduced by Professor William Ernest Castle to the genetics laboratory. He utilized some very small flies, now known as *Drosophila melanogaster*, raising them first on grapes and then on bananas. A paper by Castle and several of his students brought *Drosophila* to the attention of Professor Thomas Hunt Morgan at Columbia University. Morgan and his students could not have possibly imagined the fame that this then insignificant insect would bring to them. For it was through *Drosophila* that the structure of genetics was established.

The first of Morgan's classic papers, which appeared in 1910, was entitled, "Sex Limited Inheritance in *Drosophila*." The behavior of many traits in plants and animals according to Mendel's rules had been reported, but this time the trait involved was linked (not limited as Morgan stated) to the determination of the sex of the particular fruit fly. The new trait was white eye color as contrasted with the usual red eye color. It had been shown previously that in other insects sex was determined by the presence of specific chromosomes, the easily observable bodies in each cell nucleus which contain the hereditary units, or genes. The first miracle of *Drosophila* was that all of its genes were contained on only four pairs of chromosomes. One of the four pairs carries genes that affect the usual wing and eye colors and in addition determine the sex of the developing fly. This pair of chromosomes determines sex by altering the balance of the genetic make-up of the animal. Nature's device for doing this is remarkable for its simplicity. During evolution the pair of sex chromosomes has become visibly different with respect to the size of each of the two members of the chromosome pair. One member is long and contains genes of the usual kinds and is called the X chromosome. Its partner, if it is proper to call it a partner, is very short and does not have anything corresponding to the genes in the part of the X chromosome which extends beyond it. Thus, much of the X chromosome has no possible gene mates for most of its length. The short, genetically deficient chromosome is known as the Y chromosome.

The female fruit fly, *Drosophila*, has two X chromosomes. In each cell of the male there is only one X and one nonmatching Y chromosome with relatively few functions. It is the balance of two X chromosomes against the other three pairs of chromosomes which causes development of the egg to proceed toward femaleness. If there is only one X chromosome, and the very different Y chromosome, balanced against the other three pairs of chromosomes, it is easy to see that the chemical interactions would be somewhat different, and in this case the egg develops into a male.

Genes located on the X chromosome, such as Morgan's gene for white eyes, will have no mate in males because of the lack of anything on the Y chromosome to mate with. Consequently, the ratios of red- to white-eyed offspring will be different depending upon whether the father or the mother has the white eyes. Thus, the development of both sex and eye color is dependent upon whether the embryo has two X chromosomes or only one X, and whether each X chromosome has a gene for white or

GENETICS

for red eye color upon it. The correlation between the determination of the sex and the color of the eye of the fly is predictable, and this association is termed sex-linkage.

Many other genes at other loci on the X chromosome were soon found. They resulted from new mutations, that is, chemical changes of the material along the X chromosome so that eyes, wings, bristles, or other parts of the body were different from the "wild" type flies. These changes were hereditary and appeared in the offspring in the predictable Mendelian ratios.

One of the truly amazing discoveries of science was made in the early years of genetics. It was found that the two X chromosomes, as well as the other three pairs, called autosomes (any chromosome other than a sex chromosome), not only came into physical contact with each other, but the chromosome pairing was precise, each gene pairing with its similar partner all up and down the length of the chromosome. Each pair of chromosomes is coiled about itself during the gene pairing, and at a few points along the length there may be sufficient torsion produced so that both chromosomes break and the four broken ends will then rejoin. If they rejoin in the same order as before breaking, no genetic change will be observed. However, if the two chromosomes swap partners, the new genetic order which results may be observable. This partner-swapping is known as crossing over. It is detectable when different mutant genes, such as those for white eye and miniature wings, enter the cross together on the same X chromosome and come out separately, the white eye gene on one X chromosome and the gene for miniature wings on the other X chromosome. Sometimes the two X chromosomes will not cross over between the genes for white eye and miniature wings, and the resulting chromosomes will be like the parental chromosomes and called noncrossovers.

It should be clear from the above discussion that the genes for white eye color and miniature wings are associated, or linked, with each other because they are found to be located on the X chromosome. This last fact means that both white eye and miniature wings are also sex-linked as well as being linked with each other. (Sex-linked means that the gene for the particular trait is located on the sex chromosome.)

The Principles of Genetics

At the end of the first decade of *Drosophila* genetics, or about 1920, the major principles of transmission of the hereditary units had been well established. The four general principles are listed below.

The Principle of Segregation. In the offspring of a hybrid individual there is a separation and redistribution of all the unit characters which were in the hybrid. (A hybrid individual is one that differs in one or more heritable characters from its two parent organisms.) When two different varieties of a particular gene pair are present in a hybrid, each maintains its chemical and physical identity and segregates out cleanly without contamination in subsequent generations.

The Principle of Independent Assortment. When two pairs of genes are studied simultaneously, it is found that the two pairs segregate, or assort, completely independ-

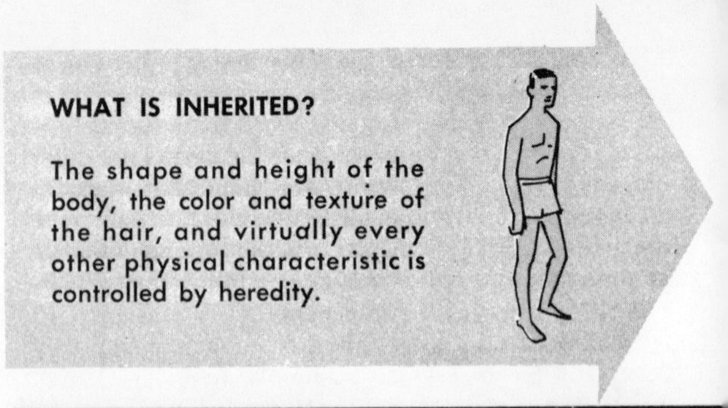

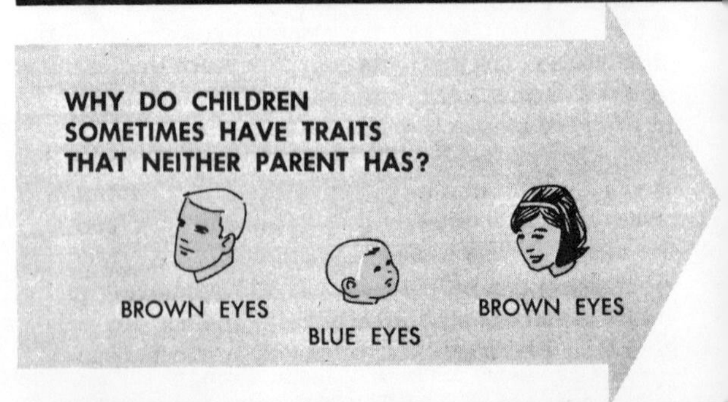

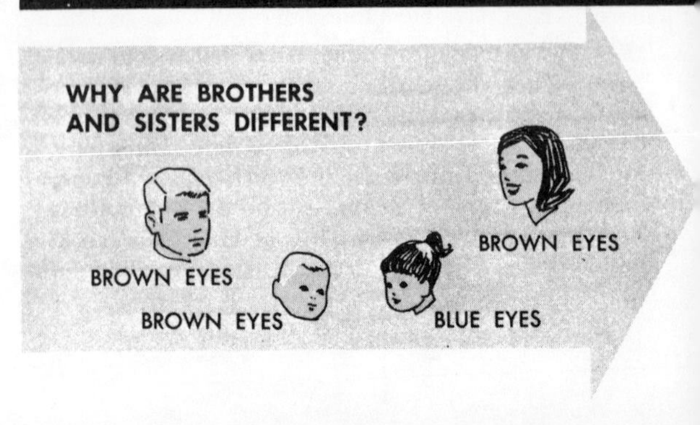

WHAT IS INHERITED?

The shape and height of the body, the color and texture of the hair, and virtually every other physical characteristic is controlled by heredity.

WHAT DOES EACH PARENT CONTRIBUTE?

The child receives half of his hereditary potential from each parent.

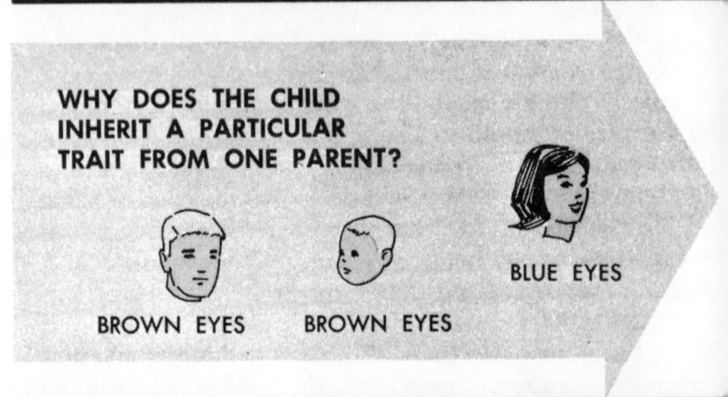

WHY DOES THE CHILD INHERIT A PARTICULAR TRAIT FROM ONE PARENT?

BROWN EYES   BROWN EYES   BLUE EYES

WHY DO CHILDREN SOMETIMES HAVE TRAITS THAT NEITHER PARENT HAS?

BROWN EYES   BLUE EYES   BROWN EYES

WHY ARE BROTHERS AND SISTERS DIFFERENT?

BROWN EYES   BROWN EYES   BLUE EYES   BROWN EYES

SOME FACTS ABOUT HEREDITY

INHERITANCE IS TRANSMITTED BY GENES

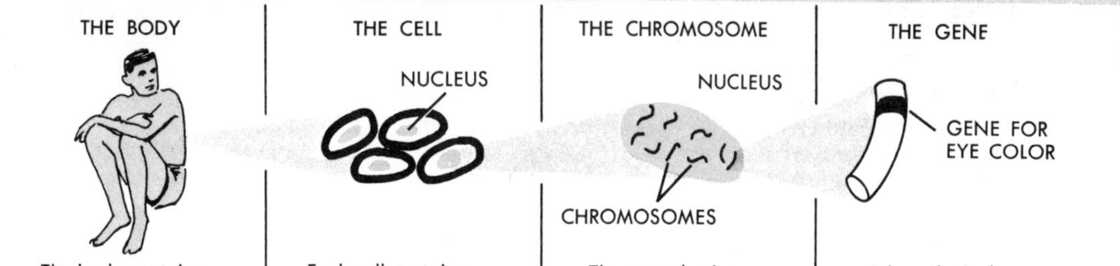

THE BODY — The body contains billions of cells which are organized into tissues and organs.

THE CELL — Each cell contains a central structure (the nucleus), which controls reproduction.

THE CHROMOSOME — The reproductive material is contained in the chromosomes.

THE GENE — A hypothetical chromosome showing the gene which controls eye color.

THE CHILD RECEIVES TWO COMPLETE SETS OF CHROMOSOMES.

The heredity contribution is wrapped in specialized reproductive cells called gametes.

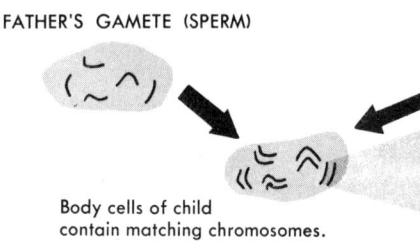

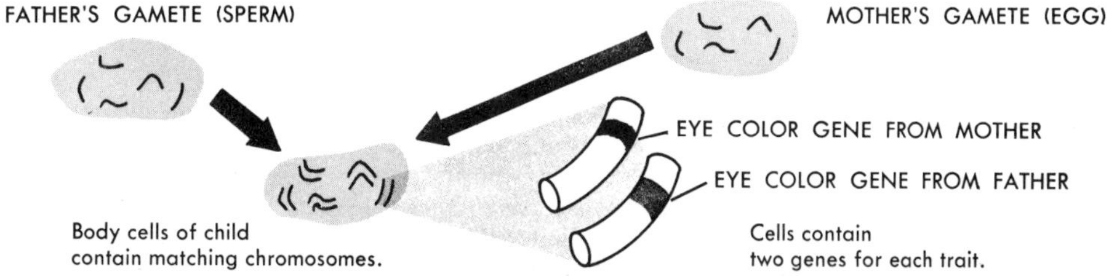

FATHER'S GAMETE (SPERM) — MOTHER'S GAMETE (EGG)

Body cells of child contain matching chromosomes.

EYE COLOR GENE FROM MOTHER
EYE COLOR GENE FROM FATHER

Cells contain two genes for each trait.

GENES MAY BE DOMINANT OR RECESSIVE

Father's gamete contains brown-eye gene.

Mother's gamete contains blue-eye gene.

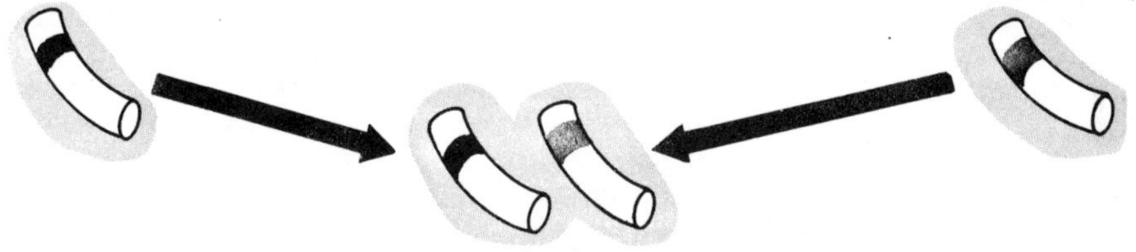

Cells of child contain both genes: Brown-eye gene is dominant—therefore child has brown eyes. Blue-eye gene is recessive.

RECESSIVE GENES CAN BE EXPRESSED.

FATHER — BROWN EYES — GAMETE

MOTHER — BROWN EYES — GAMETE

Here, the cells of both parents contain a dominant brown-eye gene and a recessive blue-eye gene. The blue-eye gene may appear in the gametes of both parents.

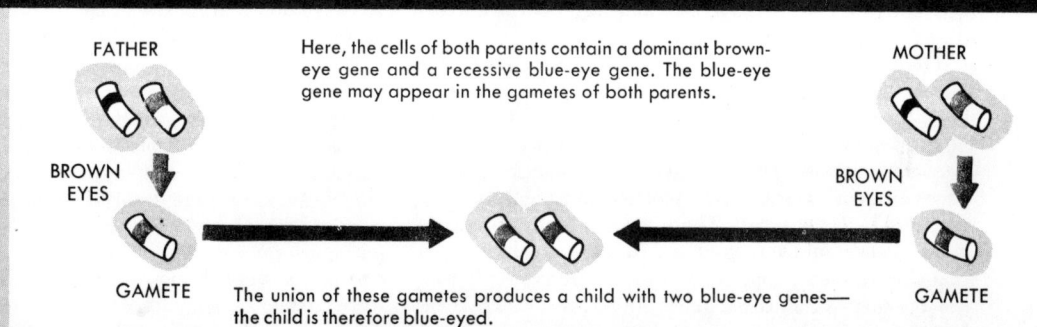

The union of these gametes produces a child with two blue-eye genes—the child is therefore blue-eyed.

EACH CHILD RECEIVES A UNIQUE COMBINATION OF GENES FROM THE PARENTS.

FATHER'S GAMETES — MOTHER'S GAMETES

Both parents produce many different kinds of gametes from their chromosomes, just as any two hands drawn from a deck of cards are different.

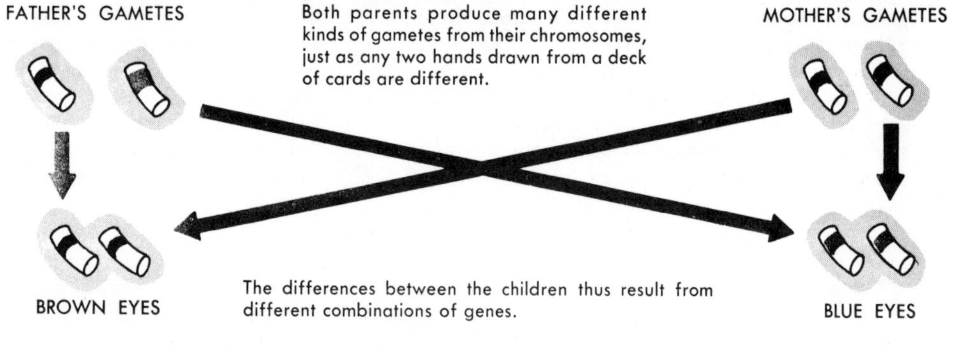

BROWN EYES — BLUE EYES

The differences between the children thus result from different combinations of genes.

GENETICS

ently of each other, if the two pairs of genes are not on the same pair of chromosomes.

The Principle of Linkage. If two pairs of genes are located on the same pair of chromosomes, they remain linked to each other during subsequent generations except when chromosomal crossing over separates them. The physical location of two pairs of genes on one pair of chromosomes prevents their independent assortment, as would be expected according to the second principle of independent assortment.

The Principle of the Linear Order of the Genes. The genes are arranged on the chromosomes in a linear order. The distances between the genes can be determined from the amount of crossing over which occurs between them.

The first two principles of heredity were discovered by Mendel and the second two by Morgan and his students. In order to study genetics at all there must be differences between the organisms that are to be crossed. Mendel crossed tall with dwarf peas. No matter how he did it, "tall" pollen with "dwarf" egg cells, or vice versa, the mixed, or hybrid, offspring of the first generation were all tall. The dwarf character had disappeared in the first filial generation (F_1). Plants of this generation were self-fertilized and produced plants of the second filial generation (F_2). Mendel counted 787 tall plants and 277 dwarfs, a ratio of 3 to 1. This second generation 3 to 1 ratio is the most famous of all genetic ratios, but there are also many other important Mendelian ratios. The fact that the dwarf plants reappeared in pure, unaltered form in the second generation proves that the gene for the dwarf trait passed through the first generation plants without being changed. The genes are independent units. The dwarf gene was "recessive" to the tall gene in the first generation hybrid. In the second generation one-fourth of the plants had both genes of the dwarf type and so had no alternative but to be dwarf in stature. The "tall" gene was completely efficient in the first generation hybrid, producing by itself enough growth substance to give a normal tall plant, and therefore was considered to be "dominant" to the partner dwarf gene in the hybrid.

The fact that crossing over between genes on the same pair of chromosomes occurs prevents their being inseparably linked. The greater the distance between two genes on a chromosome, the more often they will cross over and become separate. This permits the distances between genes on a chromosome to be plotted, and a chromosome map can be constructed. There are hundreds of pairs of genes known in Drosophila and since it is also known that there are only four pairs of chromosomes, only four linkage maps of all these genes should result. This was found to be the case. Corn has 10 pairs of chromosomes and 10 linkage groups. Man has 23 pairs of chromosomes, but because of the widespread lack of support for human genetics, hardly anything is known about the human linkage groups.

The principles of genetics apply to all forms of life. They are so remarkably simple and straightforward that any high school student can confirm them with ease. The student can raise Drosophila in his home, confirm the crossover percentages obtained by Morgan, and construct a map of the locations of the genes which will agree with those published in the textbooks of genetics.

Salivary Gland Chromosomes

Geneticists used to dream of an organism as useful genetically as Drosophila but which also possessed large chromosomes that could be studied easily under the microscope. In 1933 such desired giant chromosomes were found, and miraculously enough they were discovered in the species where they were most wanted—in Drosophila melanogaster. The important cells containing the giant chromosomes are in the maggots of Drosophila, not in the adults. The giant chromosomes are in the cells of the salivary glands and are from 100 to 200 times longer and from 1,000 to 2,000 times greater in volume than the salivary gland chromosomes of the adult flies. The extraordinary phenomenon of the salivary chromosomes results from the continuous longitudinal division of the chromosomes without the usual separation, and without cell division. They continue to grow and divide but remain in place instead of being pulled away from each other. This process of chromosome enlargement without cell division is called endomitosis. The second miracle of Drosophila had occurred.

Geneticists worked day and night utilizing the giant salivary gland chromosomes to test genetic theories. It was possible to locate the position of each gene on the salivary chromosomes because of their striking banded structure. A direct comparison could then be made between the positions of the genes of the chromosome map constructed from crossing over data, and their positions as determined by microscopic observation of the giant chromosomes. The linear order of the genes is identical for both methods, a convincing proof of the principle of linear order of the genes.

The discovery of the salivary chromosomes permitted numerous exciting advances, one of which was the study of the precise genetic differences between the chromosomes of different species of Drosophila. Some Drosophila species can be crossed, and the salivary chromosomes of the hybrid larvae are a tangled and disorderly mass of chromosomes instead of the neatly paired chromosomes found in a fly of either of the parent species. The American geneticist Theodosius Dobzhansky, and others, have made a band-by-band analysis of the differences in the chromosomes in the hybrids from D. pseudoobscura crossed with D. persimilis. It was found that some bands (or genes) present in the chromosomes of one of the parent species were absent in the other parent. Most obvious were the rearrangements of large segments of the chromosomes. A block of genes located on the first chromosome in one parent would be found attached to a different pair of chromosomes in the other parent. When genes are moved from their normal position on one pair of chromosomes to another pair of chromosomes a translocation has occurred. If a block of genes is broken out of a chromosome, inverted 180° and replaced, the changed order of these genes is known as an inversion. A set of genes may be repeated in tandem on the chromosome and is then referred to as a duplication. Study of these chromosomal aberrations which varied from one species to the next provided great insight into incipient speciation and information as to how evolution proceeds through the ages.

Evolution and Speciation

The cycle is now complete. Genetics was at first of interest because it might contribute something to the theory of evolution. Today, evolution is a major subdivision of genetics. This shift resulted from the understanding that evolution is fundamentally the genetic change which occurs as a result of mutation, with natural selection determining which genes of one generation will survive through the subsequent generation. Natural selection is inefficient and its genetic screening is very coarse-meshed, but it is the most important factor in the survival or extinction of a species. The survival of a species depends upon its successful adaptation to the available environments encountered over millions of years. The phrase "survival of the fittest" merely means that those individuals who become the ancestors of the most descendants are reproductively the fittest. The fitness has no necessary relationship to athletic ability or intelligence. One of the evolutionary "fittest" of the animals is the oyster; not much can be said for its intelligence.

Large genetic changes may have occurred in the formation of some species, but generally evolution has depended upon change at the level of the gene. Some plant species have resulted from polyploidy, the duplication in the cell of complete sets of chromosomes. Inversions and translocations have also played their part in speciation. However, the fundamental genetic changes have been the appearance of gene mutations which permitted the organism to adapt itself to the environment more successfully than its ancestors. The new gene mutations with selective advantages work with the rest of the genes in the organism in order to produce their beneficial effects and cannot be considered separately from them. However, the new mutant must gradually replace its less desirable partner in the population. Mathematical models for this dynamic process of substitution of the more advantageous mutant for the established, less effective gene have been constructed. The mathematical description of speciation has been primarily the product of Professor Sewall Wright and Sir Ronald Fisher.

Evolution is always progressive in that, by definition, it implies genetic change, even though the genetic changes may result in extinction of the species. Successful evolution depends upon three aspects of population dynamics.

1. Gene mutations should occur at moderate rates. Very high rates would result in an array of freaks.
2. Moderate inbreeding is necessary to fix the successful genotype (the genetic constitution of an organism). Too much inbreeding would reduce the necessary genetic variability which is needed to prevent extinction when the environment changes.
3. There must be moderate natural selection. Too severe selection would eliminate genetic variability when the environment changes.

Thus, the species depends upon moderation in the many factors that produce it if it is to survive.

Practical Genetics

It is probably true that domestic plants and animals have been improved more by the breeder during the last 50 years than in the previous 5,000 years. The superabundance of agricultural products in the United States is due in good measure to genetically improved strains. The continuing failures to meet agricultural quotas in the Soviet Union are certainly due in part to the rejection of Mendelian genetics on political grounds. Genetic improvements have resulted in better yielding strains with genetic resistance to diseases, economy in nutrition, and specialized strains for cold and dry climates. The desired strains can be obtained most effectively by the utilization of the Mendelian principles of genetics. It is somewhat difficult to apply the Mendelian rules to economic traits, such as milk production or yield of oats, because many pairs of genes are involved with these physiological characteristics. The more pairs of genes involved, the more complicated the genetic ratios become. Nonetheless, the Mendelian principles still hold and rapid genetic progress can be made.

One of the most brilliant accomplishments of practical genetics has been the development of hybrid corn. This was not an accidental discovery but the result of theoretical genetic considerations. A number of strains of maize were inbred for several generations. These inbred strains were inferior products, but a few of them, which were selected for combining ability, gave extremely uniform, vigorous, high yielding hybrids when crossed. The valuable hybrid vigor which resulted from the crosses of the inbred strains depended upon the masking of deleterious genes (which are unavoidably present in all strains) by advantageous genes in the strains with which they are crossed. It is also likely that some pairs of genes give beneficial reactions called "over-dominance" when the partner genes (alleles) are slightly different chemically. During the decade from 1930 to 1940, corn yields in the United States were raised from 22 bushels an acre to 33 or more bushels an acre in areas where hybrid corn had been introduced. This agricultural revolution paid millions of dollars of profits to the farmer for no extra work. Similar exploitation of the principle of hybrid vigor (heterosis) has been successful with hogs, chickens, and many other useful species of plants and animals. Further gains are to be expected.

Counseling in human genetics is a very practical application of the Mendelian rules. Parents who have produced a child with a gross mental or physical defect are always upset by this misfortune and wish to know what the chances are of a repetition of the calamity at each subsequent pregnancy. Any trait that behaves as a simple, clear-cut Mendelian recessive can be expected to affect one-quarter of the offspring subsequent to the affected child. It is also possible to predict with reasonable accuracy the expectation of a repetition of a trait with complicated genetic and environmental causes in the same way insurance companies determine life insurance premiums. The risk of repetition of a complicated genetic trait is called an empiric risk, which means that it is the average expectation of a repetition of the trait subsequent to an affected child. The risk figure for harelip and cleft palate is in the neighborhood of 5% to 10% among babies born subsequent to the affected child. The risk figure is higher if one or both of the parents, as well as a child, have been affected. It is not necessary to settle upon a precise percentage as the parents will usually be concerned only with the general magnitude of the possible risk.

One of the most exciting scientific breakthroughs has been the development of human cytogenetics. If human cells are grown in tissue culture and then treated with colchicine (a plant alkaloid), each member of the 23 pairs of chromosomes becomes distinct. By the use of this new technique it was shown that the common type of mental retardation known as Mongolism is due to the presence of an extra member of the 21st pair of chromosomes in each cell of the affected child. The presence of an extra or third member of a particular pair of chromosomes is well known in laboratory organisms and it is no surprise to find a trisomic, as it is called, in man. In fact, since the classic example of Mongolism, several different anomalies in man have been found to be due to the trisomic condition for other specific chromosome pairs. The third member of a particular pair of chromosomes results most frequently from what is known as nondisjunction. In the formation of the egg (or sperm) each pair of chromosomes in the cell of the ovary (or testis) must separate so that the egg or sperm will have only one member of each pair of chromosomes. This process of reducing the chromosomes from pairs to single members is called meiosis. The fertilization of the egg by the sperm then restores the usual cell picture of two members of each of the 23 pairs of chromosomes. If meiosis is faulty, in that the egg fails to lose one member of each pair of chromosomes, and one chromosome gets left in the egg, we have nondisjunction. When the chromosome that is left behind is of the 21st pair, the entrance of the sperm will bring the total chromosomes of this pair up to three, and Mongolism results.

The practical advances in plant and animal genetics have raised the standard of living very significantly, but the practical side of human genetics (eugenics) has been grossly neglected. Adequate support for applied human genetics will not come about until it becomes a universally accepted fact that the Mendelian laws apply to man as well as to corn. The eugenic approach depends upon the willingness of the present generation to make sacrifices in personal desires in order to benefit future generations.

Biochemical Genetics

The earliest genetic investigations were devoted to the study of such edible subjects as peas, poultry, rabbits, and larger mammals. Some work was done on insects, and by coincidence *Drosophila* turned out to be superb genetic material. However, it was many years before geneticists really selected organisms for experimentation solely because of their advantages for research in theoretical genetics. It was discovered that microorganisms were the best genetic material, partly because of their rapid reproduction. A mold, Neurospora, and certain bacteria and viruses, all multiply at such amazingly rapid rates and are simple enough in structure so that the path between the gene and the trait it influences is short. Use of such microorganisms has permitted examination of the way in which the gene regulates the most fundamental growth processes. The work of George Wells Beadle, Edward Tatum, Joshua Lederberg, and others brought about the final union between biochemistry and genetics.

Mutations can be readily produced by exposing bacteria and the mold *Neurospora* to X rays. In the bacterium *Escherichia coli* mutations were obtained, each of which prevented the synthesis of important constituents of protoplasm, such as various amino acids. One mutant gene was observed to block the synthesis of thiamin, another methionine, and another biotin. Still another mutant gene results in the inability to ferment lactose, and resistance to virus infection by the bacterium was similarly provided by the usual process of gene mutation. It has been possible to work out the linkage relationships of these genes and others in the bacterium *E. coli*.

An interesting example of biochemical genetics may be observed in *Neurospora*. All living things require the amino acid tryptophan as a part of their protoplasm. *Neurospora* can live on a medium which does not include this amino acid because the mold can produce it from other compounds which are present in the medium on which it is grown. It does this through the action of a particular enzyme which it produces. This enzyme is capable of combining the amino acid serine with indole to produce tryptophan. The enzyme is tryptophan synthetase and can be extracted from *Neurospora*. A mutant form of *Neurospora* was found which cannot synthesize tryptophan. Consequently, tryptophan must be added to the food if the mutant mold is to grow. The mutant gene has somehow altered the enzyme so that it cannot function.

Many traits in molds and man have been found to depend upon the rather direct effects of genes on enzymes. Once the precise way by which the genes control enzymes is discovered, a great deal more will be known about the essential qualities of life itself.

The Nature of the Gene

Study of microorganisms has focused attention on the nature of the gene and has contributed much of the information about the finer details of the structure of the gene. Some strains of bacterial viruses have been utilized for this work. Mutants in the T4 strain of virus (one of a group of viruses that attack bacteria) are easily isolated, and their recombinations can be detected, even in extremely low frequency, by a selective technique. When two mutants are crossed, one expects that some "wild" type organisms will be obtained as a result of the recombination of the genetic material after crossing over has taken place. The reciprocal recombinant, containing both mutational alternations, also occurs. The results of crosses involving a group of mutants can be plotted on a diagram where each mutant is represented by a point, thus giving a chromosome map. Virus T4, which parasitizes *E. coli*, has been mapped and behaves as a single chromosome.

The rapid reproduction of the virus and the techniques available allow the study of extremely short map distances and, in fact, even the subdivision of the gene itself. Indeed, it is now feasible to "resolve" the detailed structure of the gene down to the molecular level.

The genes are thought to be arranged in precise linear

order on the chromosome, but they should not be thought of as beads on a string because there is no insulation between any two neighboring genes. The differentiation along the chromosome results from the variation of the atoms in a continuing giant chemical molecule which makes up the core of the chromosome. The essential genetic material is deoxyribonucleic acid (DNA) which extends from one end of the chromosome to the other. The variations in the structure of the DNA molecule provide the opportunity for the differences observed from one species to the next. If the configuration at one point is altered by irradiation, or some other mutant-producing agent, the organism will be different from its ancestors because of the chemical (structural) change.

It is fortunate that a well-established hypothesis is available as to the structure of the all-important DNA molecule. This is known as the Watson-Crick model, named for the biochemists who proposed the configuration in 1953. The DNA molecule consists of repeating units of smaller molecules called nucleotides, each of which contains phosphate and deoxyribose (a 5-carbon sugar), plus one of four bases—adenine, thymine, guanine, and cytosine. The phosphate and deoxyribose are linked in two chains which are coiled around a common axis to form a double helix. The two chains are joined together by hydrogen bonds connecting the nucleotide bases. (See NUCLEIC ACIDS). The distance from the axis of the helix to the phosphorus atoms (of the phosphates) on the outside is ten angstrom units. The unique feature of the molecule depends upon the arrangement of the bases. These are arranged perpendicular to the axis and are joined together by the hydrogen in specific pairs. Adenine always pairs with thymine, and guanine pairs with cytosine. The order of the bases within a pair varies, but the pairing must be that just given.

The linearity of the DNA structure, which can be visualized as a double spiral staircase, and the nondetermined sequence of bases fit the genetic requirements for a molecule that determines hereditary characteristics, since the genetic information can be contained in the sequence of bases which forms a linear code. It has been determined that a specific sequence of three nucleotide bases in the DNA molecule encodes for each of the approximately 20 amino acids which form the chief components of proteins. Perhaps, then, a mutation represents a mistake in the duplication of the order of the bases.

The isolation of a single gene, the one that directs the metabolism of sugar in the bacterium *E. coli*, was achieved in 1969, and in 1970 scientists accomplished the first complete chemical synthesis of a gene. This gene, 77 nucleotide pairs long, specifies the synthesis of alanine transfer RNA in yeast.

New Mutations

There is more than ample evidence that the genetic material which is transmitted from generation to generation is DNA. It is true that heredity also functions through the transmission of cytoplasmic particles (called kappa particles) in paramecia and plastids in plants. Cytoplasmic, or maternal, inheritance is intriguing but does not give promise of being of great importance in explaining the grand scale of evolutionary change.

The building blocks of evolution are the genes. New combinations of genes can produce infinite variation, but changes or mutations in the genes are the ultimate source of new variations. The specific chemical to be changed is therefore some part of a DNA molecule. In the late 1800's the German biologist August Weismann pointed out that heredity is transmitted through the germ plasm, which is well insulated against trivial environmental fluctuations. Biologists were generally unsuccessful in demonstrating the production of mutations by environmental agents, but this was due to poor techniques and not to the failure of mutations to appear. This impasse was removed by the American geneticist Hermann Muller, who devised a brilliant breeding plan for *Drosophila* which demonstrated the linear relationship between the number of mutations produced and the amount of irradiation used on the flies. This clever proof that mutations were produced by an environmental agent such as X rays earned the 1946 Nobel Prize in physiology for Professor Muller. Since that time other ionizing irradiations, various chemicals, and even heat shocks have proved to be mutagenic agents.

Muller's discovery was not only of the greatest theoretical importance, but also of immense practical importance. With irradiation, new strains of Penicillium were obtained which gave much greater yields of penicillin and thus cut the cost of the drug many-fold. Other examples of useful mutations are produced almost daily. However, the great majority of mutations which deviate from the "wild" type are harmful to the organism and are eliminated by natural selection. The rare mutation that proves to be of greater adaptive value than the "wild" type gene will spread throughout the population and will itself then become the "wild" type.

Genetic Engineering

Eugenics is the application of our knowledge of human genetics to social affairs. Numerous other terms such as euthenics and environmental engineering have been employed to indicate a manipulation of the environment in order to permit more advantageous expression of the genetic makeup, or genotype. Genetic engineering is the application of basic principles of molecular and cellular biology to the prevention of disease. Genetic engineering includes not only the manipulation of the genotype by technical means but also the replacement of proteins, vitamins, enzymes, and other substances which are abnormal in quality or quantity because of the person's heredity. Genetic counseling would often be undertaken before genetic engineering techniques were initiated.

A few of the specific therapies employed at present to correct genetic defects include the transfusion of the hemophiliac with normal blood plasma, the administration of insulin to the diabetic, and the withholding of phenylalanine-containing foods from the baby with phenylketonuria. Other techniques involve enzyme replacement in the treatment of cystic fibrosis and transfusions of Rh-immune globulin to prevent erythroblastosis—a disease which results in red-blood cell destruction—in children of high-risk mothers. The development of amniocentesis, a technique for sampling human amniotic fluid (the fluid that surrounds the fetus), permits the detection of gross chromosomal abnormalities and enzyme deficiencies as well as viral infections of the embryo in the uterus.

Speculative developments in genetic engineering include genetic surgery and clonal reproduction. Genetic surgery would involve the introduction of "normal" chromosome material in order to replace or neutralize the deleterious gene. Genetic surgery is not possible in man at present. Clonal reproduction could become a practical technique within a few years. This technique involves the propagation of cells from an individual in such a manner as to produce numerous other genetically identical persons. Fortunately, society still has time to decide if, and in what circumstances, this technique should be used.

Speculation as to how genetic engineering will develop is highly exciting but rather uncertain because the direction and results of future research defy prediction.

See also CELL; CHROMOSOME; EVOLUTION; GENE; LIFE; MUTATION.

GENIUS, an individual with extraordinary creative talent in some area of intellectual or artistic ability. Geniuses are difficult to define statistically or in terms of psychological tests. In general they are individuals who with respect to any esteemed ability fall, when ranked according to some order of merit, among the topmost minute per cent of the population—perhaps 1 in 10,000. Persons with intelligence quotients over 140 have sometimes been classified as near genius, but this is a misappropriation of the ordinary use of the term "genius." Even an I.Q. of 160 does not proclaim a genius; the classification depends on what factors go with the superior intellectual ability.

See also INTELLIGENCE.

GERM, a primitive cell from which an adult living individual develops. The term has become popularly associated with microorganisms, particularly bacteria, and is commonly used as a synonym for "microorganism." See BACTERIA; GERM THEORY; MICROBIOLOGY.

GERMAN MEASLES, also called rubella, is a contagious disease of childhood which is characterized by a skin rash and by swelling of the lymph nodes. Although the illness usually has little effect on the health of the patient, it may cause severe damage to the unborn child when it occurs in pregnant women.

The illness begins approximately three weeks after exposure, with moderate fever and possibly mild sore throat, sneezing, and coughing. On the same day a rash may appear on the face and neck, later spreading to the trunk and extremities. The rash may resemble that of measles or scarlet fever. It usually disappears within three days. A common sign of German measles is tenderness and swelling of the lymph glands behind the ear and in the back of the neck. The disease tends to be more severe in adults than in children. Complications may involve the joints or brain, but are not frequent.

If a woman contracts German measles in the first three months of pregnancy, there is a great risk of her baby being born with one or more serious abnormalities. It is generally agreed that a pregnant woman should be protected from exposure to the illness. A German measles vaccine was licensed for use in the United States in 1969 and a large-scale vaccination program was undertaken with school-age children. The vaccine was not routinely administered to women of child-bearing age but it was hoped that the mass immunization of children would greatly reduce the risk of any pregnant woman contracting the disease. The effectiveness of the ongoing vaccination program was being evaluated in the early 1970's.

GERMICIDE [jûr′mə-sīd], agent that kills bacteria. The term commonly refers to chemical agents. Certain germicides, such as phenol, act to destroy the structural organization of the bacterial cell. Others, such as merthiolate, interfere with metabolism of bacteria. Germicides are used principally to disinfect sickrooms and to sterilize surgical instruments.

See also ANTISEPTICS.

GERM THEORY, the theory that certain diseases are caused by specific microbes. The theory was suggested long before the discovery of bacteria, but did not receive general acceptance until 200 years after the discovery of these microorganisms. In the early part of the 19th century convincing evidence was offered that certain plant diseases, such as the potato blight, were caused by fungi.

In 1876 Robert Koch demonstrated that the disease called anthrax is caused by a specific bacterium, *Bacillus anthracis*. Koch established a set of criteria for assigning a specific organism as the cause of a specific disease. Known as Koch's postulates, these state that (1) the suspected organism must always be found in natural cases of the disease; (2) the organism must be isolated in pure culture; (3) when introduced into a susceptible animal, the organism must produce the typical disease symptoms; (4) the presence of the organism must be demonstrated in the diseased tissues of the artificially inoculated animal by growing a pure culture of the organism from these tissues.

The germ theory of disease is generally accepted in the scientific world today.

See also MICROBIOLOGY.

GESTATION [jĕs-tā′shən], the period of pregnancy, or carrying of the young in the uterus, in mammals. Gestation is usually reckoned from the date of conception, or insemination of the egg, to the date of birth of the young. In the Virginia opossum, a marsupial, or pouched mammal, gestation lasts only about 12 days, and the partially

Ass, 12 mo.	Giraffe, 14 mo.
°Bat, 2 to 6 mo.	Guinea Pig, 68 days
°Bear, 6 to 9 mo.	Hamster, 16 days
Beaver, 4 mo.	Horse, 11 mo.
Camel, 13 mo.	Lion, 108 days
Cat, 60 days	Man, 280 days
Chimpanzee, 8 mo.	Monkey, Rhesus, 164 days
Cow, 285 days	Mouse, domestic 19 to 21 days
°Deer, 203 to 215 days	Pig, domestic, 113 days
Dog, 62 days	Raccoon, 63 days
Elephant, Indian, 20 to 23 mo.	Rat, domestic, 21 to 22 days
	Reindeer, 8 mo.
Fisher, 11 to 12 mo.	Sheep, 5 mo.
°Fox, 50 to 60 days	°Whale, about 1 yr.

° Depending on species.

developed young spend the remainder of a 70-day period of development within the female's pouch. In other mammals, such as those of the weasel family, the embryo may develop partially and then cease development for some months, resulting in an extremely long gestation period. The Indian elephant has one of the longest gestation periods, about 22 months.

GIGANTISM [jī-găn'tĭz-əm], abnormal growth of the skeleton caused by disorders of the endocrine glands. Undersecretion of the sex hormones may cause gigantism. This results from continued growth of the skeleton beyond the point at which the sex hormones normally halt bone growth. Pituitary gigantism is usually caused by a tumor of the pituitary gland in the skull (the "master" endocrine gland). In this condition excess secretion of growth hormone enlarges the soft tissues as well as the skeleton, producing changes similar to those seen in acromegaly, a closely related pituitary disorder.
See also ACROMEGALY; PITUITARY GLAND.

GLANDERS, contagious disease affecting horses, mules, and donkeys, caused by small, rod-shaped bacteria of the species *Pseudomonas mallei*. The disease is spread by contact with water or food contaminated by infected animals. At first, nodules appear, which turn into weeping sores, or ulcers. If the nose, mouth, and lower breathing passages are affected primarily, the term "glanders" is used. If the ulcers are in the skin, the term "farcy" is used. By the time ulcers or nasal discharge appears, the disease will be fatal if not treated. Men rarely contract glanders while caring for affected animals, but if they do, they may die quickly from overwhelming infection. Animal sanitation, cleaner livestock housing, and antibiotics have all but eliminated this once-common disease. In Southeast Asia, related bacteria, *Pseudomonas pseudomallei*, cause melioidosis in animals and man.
See also Melioidosis.

GLANDS. See ENDOCRINE GLANDS.

GLANDULAR FEVER. See INFECTIOUS MONONUCLEOSIS.

GLAUCOMA [glô-kō'mə], eye disorder in which there is an increase in the fluid pressure within the eye, leading to a progressive loss of vision and eventual blindness. The increased pressure results from obstruction of the channels through which fluid normally leaves the eye. The more common type of glaucoma (chronic simple glaucoma) usually affects both eyes and is found in 2% of the population over the age of 40. In this type there is a slow steady loss of vision. The patient may see halos around lights and suffers from mild headaches.

An acute form of glaucoma may be limited to one eye (narrow angle glaucoma). In the early stages vision is misty, colored halos appear around lights, and vague headaches develop about the eyes. The attacks may subside only to recur weeks or months later. Eventually a full-blown attack develops with severe throbbing, radiating eye pain and headaches, often associated with nausea and vomiting. The eye tears and becomes inflamed and sensitive to light. There is a temporary loss of vision. Successive attacks result in permanent damage to the optic nerve, finally causing blindness.

Glaucoma is treated with drugs such as acetazolamide, which inhibit the secretion of eye fluid, and with miotics, drugs which constrict the pupil, thus widening the channel through which fluid drains. In some cases surgery is necessary to relieve the fluid tension.

If properly treated, glaucoma does not lead to blindness. Because of the insidious nature of chronic simple glaucoma it has been suggested that persons over the age of 40 should have regular eye examinations.

GLOBULINS [glŏb'yə-lĭns], class of proteins found throughout the plant and animal kingdoms. Many of the enzymes which carry out cell functions in man are globulins. The blood globulins have been separated into three groups—gamma, beta, and alpha. Gamma globulins are the antibodies made by the body to resist infection and remove foreign materials from the blood. Larger antibodies, called macroglobulins, are found in the beta globulin group. The alpha globulin fraction contains both macroglobulins and ceruloplasmin, the transport protein for copper. Inherited cellular deficiencies can cause the absence of one or another type of globulin. In aggammaglobulinemia, the absence of antibodies is suspected when there are repeated infections, without development of the usual immunity. This deficiency can be corrected by administering gamma globulins prepared from another person's blood.
See also GAMMA GLOBULIN.

GLOMERULONEPHRITIS [glŏ-měr-ū-lō-nĭ-frī'tĭs], term used to describe certain kidney inflammations which affect primarily children and young adults. *Acute glomerulonephritis*, seen most frequently between the ages of three and seven, most often follows infection of the nose, throat, or tonsils, with streptococcus bacteria. The bacteria do not actually invade the kidneys but appear to stimulate the body to produce substances which attack the kidneys. The patient usually suffers from swelling and puffiness of the face, high blood pressure, headache, and a decrease in urine production. Heart failure is frequent, and collections of fluid in the lungs may cause difficulty in breathing. Blood and protein are usually found in the urine. Complete recovery is the rule although in some cases chronic glomerulonephritis results.

Chronic glomerulonephritis appears most frequently without known previous infection. The condition develops gradually, usually first becoming evident when the patient develops fluid swellings (edema) in the face or ankles, recurrent headaches, or difficulty in breathing. It may first be detected by a routine urine examination which reveals protein in the urine. Weakness and loss of weight are commonly present. The course of the disease is extremely variable; the patient may experience remissions and severe attacks over a period of years or die within a few weeks of first noticing symptoms. High blood pressure may cause distressing headaches and, late in the disease, severe anemia, heart disorders, and visual disturbances may appear.

There is no specific treatment for these conditions. Bed rest is advised in acute glomerulonephritis and during active periods of chronic glomerulonephritis. Salt consumption may be restricted when high blood pressure, edema, or decreased urine output are present.

GLOSSITIS [glŏ-sī'tĭs], inflammation of the tongue which may cause redness, pain, swelling, and ulceration. Glossitis may result from the use of antibiotics, from vitamin deficiencies, infections such as syphilis and tuberculosis, anemia (pernicious), or from injury or irritation to the tongue. In long-standing cases the surface of the tongue may be smooth, owing to atrophy of the papillae, the conelike structures which normally project from the tongue surface. The condition disappears when the underlying cause is treated.

GLUCOSE [glōō'kōs], also called dextrose, grape sugar, corn sugar, or blood sugar, is a simple sugar (a monosaccharide) which is found widely distributed in nature, both in the free form and as a component of more complex substances such as cellulose, starch, and glycogen.

Glucose is the principal source of energy of all living organisms. In the human body it is stored in the liver as glycogen, a substance composed of thousands of glucose units. Under the influence of certain hormones glycogen breaks down and releases glucose into the blood stream. Another hormone, insulin, promotes the absorption of glucose by the body cells where it is burned (oxidized) to provide energy for bodily activity. A deficiency of insulin, such as occurs in diabetes, permits sugar to pile up in the blood and eventually to spill over into the urine.

Solutions of glucose are used in medicine in the treatment of dehydration, for supplying nutrition through the veins when food cannot be taken through the digestive tract, and with insulin in the treatment of diabetic coma. Glucose is commercially produced from corn and potato starch and is important as a constituent of candies, creams, chewing gum, and cakes.

See also CARBOHYDRATES.

GLUCOSE TOLERANCE TEST, test of the ability of the body to use sugar. The test is used in the diagnosis of diabetes mellitus. The patient is given 100 g. of glucose by mouth, and hourly determinations of blood sugar are made for three hours. Normally, blood sugar levels are not unduly elevated at one hour and return to fasting levels in two hours. In diabetes the blood sugar level remains elevated for an abnormal period. The ability of the body to utilize sugar is also disturbed in certain glandular disorders.

See also DIABETES MELLITUS.

GLYCOGEN [glī'kə-jən], also called animal starch, the chief form in which energy-rich carbohydrate (sugar and starches) is stored in the body. Glycogen is found principally in liver and muscle, but also in bone, blood, skin, and other tissues.

Glycogen is manufactured in the body from the sugar, glucose. In emergencies and during periods of vigorous muscular activity, hormones induce the breakdown of liver glycogen into sugar, which is released into the blood stream where it can be readily taken up by the body cells and be used as a source of energy. In the muscles, glycogen is decomposed into lactic acid to supply the energy for contraction. The liver converts some of this lactic acid back into glycogen.

The supply of liver glycogen declines sharply in starvation and in certain diseases, such as diabetes. Muscle glycogen may also decrease in these conditions, but in particular declines after prolonged physical exercise.

Commercially, glycogen is prepared from animal tissues and is used in the lacquer and varnish industries as a plasticizer.

See also METABOLISM.

GOITER [goi'tər], abnormal enlargement of the thyroid gland, which usually appears as a swelling, or protrusion, in the front of the throat.

Goiters which are found in 10% or more of the population of a given area are termed "endemic." These may be seen in certain parts of the world, such as in the Alps and Himalayas, where there is a low concentration of iodine (which is an essential ingredient of the thyroid hormone) in the soil and water. When endemic goiter is mild it is usually limited to females. Ordinarily, the only manifestation of the condition is an enlargement of the thyroid. In severely affected regions the children may suffer from cretinism—a deficiency of thyroid hormone during infancy and childhood, resulting in retarded physical and mental development. Endemic goiter can be prevented by adding iodine to salt or other food in endemic areas.

In some cases thyroid enlargement cannot be related to a dietary deficiency of iodine. Such goiters occur principally in adolesent females; the cause is unknown. It has been suggested that excessive intake of certain foods, especially those of the cabbage family, which are known to inhibit the manufacture of thyroid hormone, may be responsible in some cases. Symptoms, other than gradual thyroid enlargement, are usually not present. If the goiter becomes sufficiently large, pressure on the gullet or windpipe may cause difficulty in swallowing or breathing, and may require surgical treatment.

Toxic goiters cause excess production of thyroid hormone. These are most frequent in young adults, particularly females. The cause is unknown, although theories have been advanced concerning the possible overstimulation of the thyroid by the pituitary gland, the master endocrine gland which secretes hormones that stimulate the thyroid and other glands.

Most of the symptoms of toxic goiter result from the oversecretion of thyroid hormone. The patient may suffer from weakness, loss of weight, excessive sweating, and tremors of the fingers. The heart rate is increased and irregular heart action is common. Bulging eyeballs may be the principal symptom in some cases.

Treatment varies and may include the use of antithyroid drugs, or radioactive iodine. The effectiveness of the latter is based upon its tendency to concentrate in the thyroid gland where the radioactive emissions can reach the thyroid cells. Treatment with iodine in the early stages of the disease usually decreases goiter size. Partial removal of the thyroid gland is called for in some cases.

See also CRETINISM; MYXEDEMA; THYROID-BLOCKING DRUGS; THYROID GLAND.

GOLDBERGER, JOSEPH (1874–1929), American physician best known for his discovery of a dietary cure for pellagra, a serious vitamin deficiency disease which attacks the skin, digestive tract, and nervous system. While with the U.S. Public Health Service Goldberger was impressed by the fact that physicians and nurses exposed to pellagra (then generally considered an infectious disease) never contracted it. Goldberger and his wife demonstrated that pellagra was not contagious, by failing to develop the disease after eating bits of pellagrous skin and infecting themselves with blood from pellagrous patients. He then proved that pellagra could be induced by manipulating the diet. Convicts in a Mississippi prison acquired pellagra after being placed on a diet deficient in lean meat, milk, and fresh vegetables. Goldberger finally showed that pellagra could be prevented by eating liver and yeast.

GONADOTROPINS [gō-năd-ō-trō′pĭnz], hormones which stimulate the sex glands, or gonads. These substances are secreted by the pituitary gland in the skull and stimulate the production of sperm in the male and activate and maintain the menstrual cycle in the female. In certain diseases of the pituitary, gonadotropin secretion declines and abnormalities in sexual function appear. Gonadotropins manufactured by the placenta (the afterbirth and "master gland of pregnancy") appear in the urine of pregnant women where their presence forms the basis of various pregnancy tests. These hormones have been used to treat certain cases of undescended testicles in men. They have also been given to men in whom the male sexual characteristics have failed to appear owing to impaired testicular function.
See also ENDOCRINE GLANDS; PITUITARY GLAND.

GONORRHEA [gŏn-ə-rē′ə], venereal disease caused by the bacterium *Neisseria gonorrhoeae*. Gonorrhea is almost always transmitted by sexual contact and is the most common of the venereal diseases. It is estimated that approximately 1,000,000 cases occur every year in the United States alone, most of them in adolescents and young adults.

The organism usually enters the body through the genital tract, although in some cases it may enter through the eye or rectum. After an incubation period of at least 3–5 days, men note increasing pain on urination and pus issuing from the urethra. If untreated, the infection may spread to the male reproductive organs, causing pain, fever, retention of urine, swelling of the testicles, and possibly eventual sterility or narrowing and obstruction of the urinary tract. In women the early inflammation of the urethra may not be painful enough to command attention and the vaginal discharge may be ignored. The infection may eventually spread to the fallopian tubes which conduct the egg from the ovary to the womb. Inflammation of the tubes (salpingitis) may cause intense abdominal pain, similar to that of appendicitis, and may lead to sterility. Untreated gonorrhea may also spread by way of the blood stream to attack the heart valves and various joints, such as the knee or ankle, in some cases causing a permanent loss of joint movement. Other complications include inflammation of tendon sheaths, especially those around the wrists and ankles, and infection of the eyes (conjunctivitis).

Gonorrhea may be contracted by infants born of infected mothers. The eyes of the newborn may become infected with the gonococcal bacteria while it passes through the birth canal. The prompt administration of silver nitrate or antibiotic drops into the eyes of all newborn infants reliably prevents the development of such gonorrheal infection and possible future blindness.

Gonorrhea is successfully treated with penicillin. Although some strains of *N. gonorrhoeae* have become less sensitive to penicillin, none is resistant. Other antibiotics such as tetracycline are also effective against these bacteria.

A single attack of gonorrhea does not produce immunity and recurrences are common. Control and prevention of the disease is made particularly difficult by the fact that it may present no symptoms in women, who thereby unknowingly act as carriers.

GOUT. *See* ARTHRITIS.

GRANULOMA [grăn-yə-lō′mə], tumorlike nodules which develop in response to infection or irritation. In the granuloma are found reticuloendothelial cells which have migrated from other parts of the body and newly grown connective tissue and blood vessels (capillary buds). The growth may result from infections such as tuberculosis, leprosy, or syphilis, from the presence of foreign bodies in the tissue, or from certain diseases of unknown cause. Some granulomas may be treated by X rays or surgery. In other cases treatment is directed at the underlying infectious disease.

GROWTH, increase in total size of a plant or animal, in the mass of a group of single-celled plants or animals (*See* CELL), or the increase in numbers of a population of complex organisms.

Growth in Animals

The ultimate size an individual animal can attain is fixed within narrow bounds by hereditary restrictions. The rate at which an animal grows, however, or how much of its genetic potential is realized, is determined by a host of environmental factors. Nutrients, in sufficient amount and of proper quality, are needed to provide the raw material from which new protoplasm is formed. Fats, proteins, and carbohydrates are taken into the animal body. In order to process these into the protoplasm needed for growth, vitamins and minerals are necessary in the complex chemical factory of the cell, helping to make the chemical reactions move along swiftly. Especially important to growth are vitamins A and D. Minute quantities of these vitamins allow growth to progress at a normal rate, while their lack prohibits growth.

Chemical substances known as hormones also have a great effect on an animal's growth. Hormones are produced by ductless glands, called endocrine glands, located in several places within the body. In man, the most important gland affecting growth is the pituitary. The pituitary produces a secretion called growth hormone. Undersecretion of this substance in the young produces a dwarf,

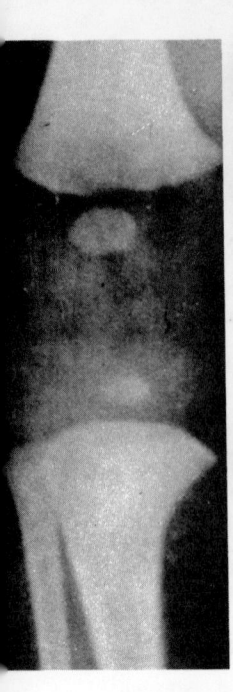

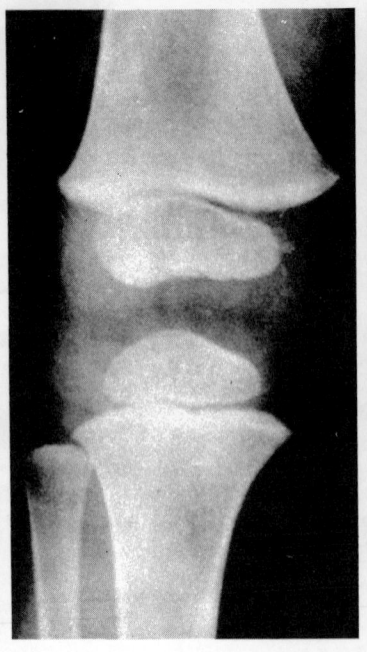

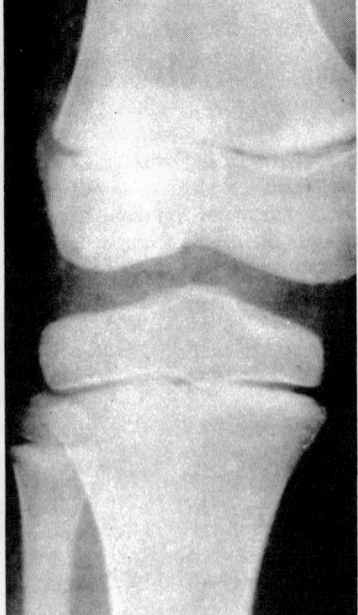

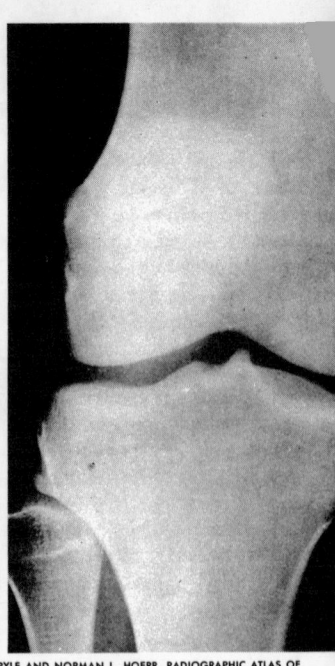

Bone growth in the human leg is not completed until about the 25th year of life. In the first photograph, an X ray of the knee region of a newborn male, the uppermost bone is the femur (thigh bone). The oval structure immediately beneath it is a bony nodule at the center of a cartilaginous mass (epiphysis) at the end of the femur. The lower bones are the fibula (smaller calf bone, to the left) and the tibia (shin bone). The oval structure above the tibia is a bony nodule in its epiphysis. At the age two years (second photo) bone growth in the epiphyses is pronounced. By eight years of age (third photo) the cartilaginous parts of the epiphyses have been almost completely replaced by bone. At 18 years of age (fourth photo) the epiphyses have become united with the femur and tibia.

(S. IDELL PYLE AND NORMAN L. HOERR, RADIOGRAPHIC ATLAS OF SKELETAL DEVELOPMENT OF THE KNEE)

oversecretion produces gigantism. In an adult, an oversecretion of growth hormone causes bones to increase in diameter. The forehead, nose, and lower jaw become greatly enlarged, and the skin of the face becomes thick and coarse. This condition is known as acromegaly.

Another factor affecting growth is climate. The seasons of the year, for example, appear to influence the growth of children. Youngsters tend to grow faster in the spring than during the rest of the year. However, weight gain is greatest on the average, in the fall.

Rate of Growth in Man. In general, growth in man can be roughly divided into five distinct intervals. The period of greatest growth occurs before birth, the prenatal state, when, in nine months, a single fertilized egg reproduces and differentiates to become a viable human being. In the infantile stage, from birth to 10 months, the newborn's growth is extremely rapid. From 10 months to four or five years, the child grows rapidly, but at a diminishing rate of speed. The rate of growth is sustained at a fairly low level during the juvenile years. The end of the juvenile period is marked by puberty, with the development of the sex organs and the start of the adolescent period.

During this time, starting at about 10½ in girls and a year later in boys, the child begins to change into an adult. By 16½ in girls and 17¾ in boys, the human being has attained almost full adult stature. Over the years, the average age at which youngsters attain puberty has steadily declined.

An example of the dynamic quality of animal growth may be seen in such apparently lifeless material as bone. In the developing embryo, a long bone in the arm or leg, for example, is first made of cartilage. As the cartilage becomes calcified and blood vessels enter the material, cells called osteoblasts begin producing bone. Changing conditions require changes in the shape of the forming bone, and other cells, called osteoclasts, selectively destroy the new bone. Following the growth of cartilage in the ends of the bone, the new bone continues growing in length. As the period of growth comes to an end, the cartilage plates are completely replaced by bone, making further growth in length impossible.

Relative Growth. When an animal grows, it may change not only in size, but in shape. This may be because different body parts grow at different rates, because body tissues grow in various ways, or because new parts, such as horns, are added. Comparison of an infant with an adult human being makes it obvious that the parts of the body have grown at differing rates. The head, for example, grows much more slowly than do the legs and arms. Such differential patterns of growth are not universal in the animal kingdom. Many fishes maintain the same relative growth rate among the various body parts. Young and old fish may differ only in size.

While growth in size is achieved through the multiplication and sometimes the enlargement of cells, the rates at which these cellular activities take place vary with the tissues involved. Adults have many more skin and blood cells than do infants. There is also a lifelong turnover of these cells as the old ones wear out and must be replaced. Specialized structures of the body have distinctly different patterns of growth. The tiny heart of an infant contains the same number of cells that it will have as an adult. As the individual cells increase in size, so does the whole organ. The newborn infant is also endowed with all the nerve cells it will ever have. With increasing body size, the individual cells become larger, and the interconnections between cells grow longer and more complex.

Size Limits. If single cells can increase in size, why are there no giant single-celled animals—the giant ameba of science fiction fame? A cell must obtain nutrients and oxygen through its membrane. When a cell grows, however, the membrane's area increases at a different rate than the cell volume. While the membrane grows as the square of the cell's diameter, the volume increases as its cube. In other words, as the diameter doubles, the surface increases four times, and the volume increases by eight. As the cell's mass increases it must divide to reinstate the necessary surface-to-volume relationship.

A similar mathematical relationship governs the absolute size of multicellular animals, and even controls the relative growth rates of their parts. An animal's weight increases as the cube of its linear size, but its strength increases only as the square of its linear size. Thus, with increasing size, the muscles of an animal become relatively larger, while the internal organs, for example, become relatively smaller.

For instance, small, light birds are able to walk on extremely thin legs, while an elephant needs legs like massive columns. If a bird grew to the size of an elephant, and its legs grew in proportion, the legs would be so thin that they would collapse under the weight. Another favorite animal of science fiction stories is a horse-sized insect. Such giants are impossible for at least two reasons. First, with increasing size the insect's external skeleton would be too fragile to support the creature. The second restriction on insect size is imposed by their way of breathing. A complex of branching tubes carries air from openings in the body wall to the individual cells. The air in these tubes cannot be readily replenished, if the insect is much more than an inch in diameter. Insects that need a great deal of oxygen, such as the swift darning needle, are usually quite slender. All the cells are thus quite close to the surface.

Minimum size of animals, notably birds and mammals, with their high metabolic rate, is also affected by the surface-volume relationship. The relatively enormous surface areas of hummingbirds and shrews make it imperative that these creatures consume great quantities of food to make up for the heat lost. The shrew spends almost all its time eating. Nighttime finds the hummingbird in a state similar to hibernation to avoid starvation.

See also ADOLESCENCE; CHILD DEVELOPMENT; ENDOCRINE GLANDS; NUTRITION; VITAMINS.

GUINEA WORM, tropical round worm, *Dracunculus medinensis*, which enters the human body through drinking water contaminated with infected crustaceans (cyclops). About one year after mating the pregnant females, each three or more feet long, migrate to the skin, where they discharge living larvae through ruptured blisters. When the blisters appear the patient may experience nausea, diarrhea, vomiting, and giddiness. The parasites may be removed surgically or be wound out, a few inches each day, on a stick or spool. There are an estimated 48,000,000 cases of Guinea worm infestation, principally in India and the Middle East.

GYNECOLOGY [gī-nə-kŏl′ə-jē, jī-nə-kŏl′ə-jē], the medical specialty which deals with diseases of the female, particularly of the female reproductive organs. These diseases include tumors, infections, and complications of childbirth. The structures which may be involved are the ovaries, which contain the egg, or ovum, the fallopian tubes, which conduct the egg from the ovary to the uterus, the uterus, or womb, itself, and the vagina and labia.

The Ovary. The ovary may be the site of 20 types of benign (noncancerous) tumors, and 29 types of malignant, or cancerous, tumors. A common ovarian condition is a follicular cyst, consisting of a sac which contains an egg and some fluid. Normally one sac of this type ruptures each month, releasing an egg which passes down the fallopian tubes to the uterus. A cyst develops when, instead of rupturing, the sac grows, producing an enlarged, cystic ovary. Fortunately, the fluid is often reabsorbed and the condition usually does not require surgery. The ovary may be removed in cases of extensive tumors or cysts. In such cases, the remaining normal ovary is able to assume the function of the missing organ.

The Fallopian Tubes. Gonorrhea may spread to the fallopian tubes, causing a serious infection. Although penicillin and other antibiotics are effective in halting the infection, the disease usually leaves the patient with partially, or completely, blocked fallopian tubes, resulting in sterility.

Occasionally, a tube will be partly blocked off, and the egg will be caught part of the way down on its descent. If pregnancy occurs the developing embryo remains in the tube, eventually rupturing it and causing bleeding into the abdomen. In such cases immediate surgery is necessary to save the woman's life.

The Uterus. Cancer of the uterus usually occurs at either the cervix (the neck of the uterus), or in the uterine lining. In either site, cancers may be present for many years without causing symptoms, but may be discovered by means of a microscopic examination of vaginal fluid (Papanicolaou smear). The cancer may be removed surgically or be treated by radiation.

Noncancerous tumors of the uterus are much more common. They are usually of the type called fibroids and may grow on the outer wall of the uterus, within the wall, or into the uterine lining. The latter type may cause heavy menstrual flow, and may have to be removed.

Another condition involving excess growth of tissue occurs when the lining of the uterus extends into the muscle wall which surrounds the uterus, causing painful and heavy periods (adenomyosis). The uterine lining may also grow through the fallopian tubes into the abdominal cavity and may continue to grow on the tube or ovary, or even the intestines (endometriosis).

Infections of the uterus usually affect the cervix and may be caused by *Monilia* (a yeast) or *Trichomonas* (a protozoan). Gonorrheal infection of the cervix can persist for some time; frequently the bacteria pass through the body of the uterus without infecting it, to reach the fallopian tubes, as mentioned above.

The supporting structures of the uterus may be weakened during childbirth, and, with the passage of time, the uterus may slip down to protrude through the vaginal opening. This is called a prolapse and frequently requires removal of the protruding uterus (vaginal hysterectomy).

The Vagina. The vagina is a tubular structure of mucous membrane. Around it is a layer of thicker tissue which supports the bladder in front and keeps the rectum in place in the back. During childbirth, especially with a large baby, these supporting tissues may be stretched and weakened. As a woman becomes older, the tissues relax more and the bladder or rectum may protrude through the vagina (cystocele or rectocele, respectively). Temporary relief may be obtained by inserting an irregularly shaped ring of hard rubber or plastic (a pessary) Permanent correction requires surgery.

Infections of the vagina by fungi, bacteria, or protozoa may produce an annoying yellowish or whitish discharge (leukorrhea). These infections may also affect the labia, or outer lips. The "chancre," or hard ulcer of syphilis, usually appears on the labia.

Congenital Disorders of the Reproductive Organs

One well-known congenital abnormality is retroversion, or tipping, of the uterus. In one out of six women the uterus is not up forward against the bladder, but is turned backward and leans more against the rectum. Although it has been speculated that this situation may cause backache or sterility, there is seldom, if ever, any connection between retroversion and these conditions.

See also PREGNANCY; REPRODUCTION.

H

HAHNEMANN [hä′nə-män], **CHRISTIAN FRIEDRICH SAMUEL** (1755–1843), German physician known as the founder of homeopathic medicine. Born at Meissen, Germany, he studied at several German universities before taking his M.D. at Erlangen in 1779. After spending many years wandering from place to place, supporting his wife and daughters partly by medical practice, but largely by translating books (he read nine languages), he announced to the world the "rational" system of medicine called homeopathy. During the period from 1812 to 1821, while a lecturer in medicine at the University of Leipzig, he gained many disciples and a wide reputation. He believed that treatment was more important than a knowledge of the cause of disease and that the best treatment was a minute dose of a drug which in large doses would induce the symptoms of the disease. He regarded most chronic diseases to be forms of psora (the itch).

When Hahnemann was 80 and widowed, he was sought out by an "emancipated" Frenchwoman of 35 who became his patient and then his wife. They went to Paris, and with her support he became a fashionable practitioner. He died there, a millionaire, at the age of 88. His ideas, which became especially popular in the United States, were almost all disproven later by the new scientific medicine which established itself early in the 20th century.

See also HOMEOPATHY.

HAIR, the typical outgrowth of the epidermis, or outer layer of skin, characteristic of mammals. Hair develops from an in-pocketing of the epidermis, resulting in a follicle, or pit, from which the hair grows. Straight hair is usually round in cross section, while curly hair is somewhat flattened. Pigments give hair its color; white or gray hair is due to lack of pigment or the presence of air within the hair structure. Associated with the hair follicle are oil glands which keep the hair supple and moist. There are also tiny muscles which serve to erect the hair, enabling some animals to appear larger than they really are.

Hair may become modified into horn, as in the rhinoceros; into scales, as in the armadillo; into spines, as in the porcupine; or into the vibrissae, or whiskers, of the cat. Even such specialized marine mammals as the whales and manatees possess a few lip bristles or other body hairs at some time in their lives.

HALLUCINATIONS [hə-lōō-sə-nā′shənz] are errors of perception in which the individual sees, hears, feels, smells, or tastes objects which are not present. Although hallucinations occur principally in persons suffering from mental illness, relatively normal persons may experience them under certain circumstances.

The most common hallucinations are voices and sounds heard by mental patients (*see* SCHIZOPHRENIA). Visual hallucinations are frequently seen in alcoholics suffering from delirium tremens. Hallucinatory smells and tastes, which are comparatively rare, are seen in certain brain diseases. Children with schizophrenia often report voices and objects residing within their own bodies. A special type of hallucination occurs in normal persons in the twilight state between waking and sleeping.

HAND, organ of touch and grasping, characteristic of most primates. It consists of the wrist, or carpus; the palm, or metacarpus; and the digits, or fingers. In certain species the action of the thumb is such that it can be apposed to the fingers, thus allowing for great dexterity and strength of grip. The muscles that move the digits are in the forearm and are connected to them by means of strong tendons. Extensor muscles cause the fingers and thumb to extend; flexor muscles cause them to curl, or flex.

HANDICAPPED, REHABILITATION OF THE, term designating either the services required by the handicapped person to enable him to make the fullest use of his physical, mental, and vocational capabilities or the processes aiding the individual in utilizing existing services to effect his maximum functioning, or both. In rehabilitation the individual's ability rather than his disability is emphasized.

It is estimated that there are more than 16 million persons in the civilian noninstitutional population of the United States who are partially or totally limited in their major activity because of chronic conditions. The major disabilities of the handicapped are loss of vision and hearing, mental illness, cardiac disease, mental retardation, and orthopedic impairments. These conditions result from hereditary defects, congenital abnormalities, chronic diseases, accidents, and war injuries.

The increase in the number of handicapped is due to a variety of factors. General improvement in medical services and in the standard of living results in increased expectation of life for the handicapped. A decrease in infant mortality results in an increase in the number of handicapped reaching maturity. Increased industrialization and greater use of automobiles cause more accidents resulting in a greater number of individuals with permanent disabilities, and modern wars disable large numbers of civilian and military personnel.

Rehabilitation has four aspects: medical, social, educational, and vocational. Governmental and voluntary agencies must provide services in each of these areas if rehabilitation is to be accomplished. In recent years emphasis has been placed on the provision of all services needed by the handicapped in one agency such as a rehabilitation center. Rehabilitation is a world-wide movement in which many organizations and professions participate. In 1950 the United Nations established a coordinated program for the rehabilitation of the physically handicapped which is carried out in co-operation with the World Health Organization (WHO), the International Labor Organization (ILO), and the United Nations Children's Fund (UNICEF), and international voluntary organizations.

The International Society for the Rehabilitation of the Disabled, founded in 1922 as the International Society for the Welfare of Cripples, is a federation of voluntary organizations in 53 countries which provide services for the disabled. The society holds a triennial world congress and regional and technical meetings throughout the world.

Medical Services. Medical restoration of the handicapped individual, which aims to eliminate the disability or reduce it to the greatest degree possible, utilizes the medical specialties of orthopedics, neurology, pediatrics, and physical medicine. Paramedical services such as physical, occupational, and speech therapy must also be provided in an integrated plan co-ordinated with the educational, social, and vocational phases of rehabilitation.

Vocational Aspects. In 1955 the ILO adopted a recommendation (No. 99) emphasizing that rehabilitation should be available to all disabled persons regardless of the origin and nature of the disability, if the individual has reasonable prospects of securing and retaining suitable employment. When an adult becomes handicapped, special vocational guidance is frequently needed to enable him to discover and develop previously unrecognized skills.

Vocational training for both youths and adults may be provided in a sheltered work setting in programs such as that of the Goodwill Industries in America and Canada. These are designed to provide training and experience that will enable the handicapped to make the transition from inactivity and dependence to employment and regular work and provide work opportunities to those handicapped who probably will never enter ordinary employment.

Sheltered workshops offer training for those not regularly employed as well as for the handicapped unable to enter competitive employment. Those in transition from "bed to job" need the opportunity to improve their work

REHABILITATING THE HANDICAPPED

Rehabilitation programs seek to help handicapped persons overcome their physical difficulties and lead lives useful to themselves and society.

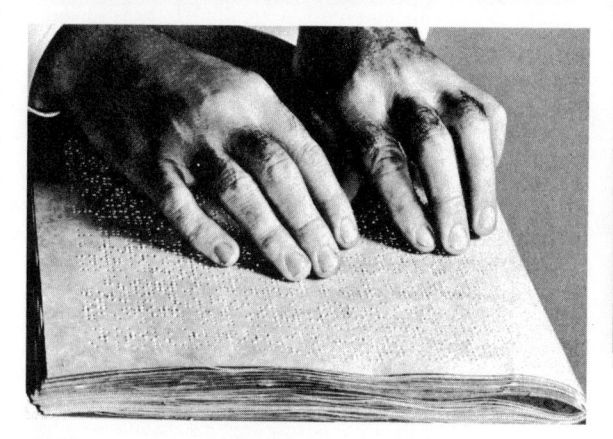

The blind can read through Braille. (THE NEW YORK ASSN. FOR THE BLIND)

The man at the left, though crippled as a result of an accident, works alongside other full-time employees in an electronics factory. (KESSLER INSTITUTE FOR REHABILITATION)

skills and to prepare to enter or return to regular employment. Many handicapped persons for whom work opportunities do not exist must continue working in a sheltered facility.

Employment of the handicapped is relatively easier in areas of low unemployment; high unemployment means fewer work opportunities for the handicapped. In such circumstances increased emphasis is placed on sheltered work opportunities. Special attention must be given to the homebound to provide not only self-care and recreational activities, but also employment opportunities. Many homebound disabled persons are partially or entirely self-supporting through handicraft, industrial, or service work done at home for organizations and industries.

Social Services. Where the community does provide some or all of the specialized extensive social services required by a handicapped person, he must know how to avail himself of them. Social services available to the handicapped should include psychological and social counseling for the individual and his family. Therapeutic recreation services stressing active participation are needed by the handicapped to enable them to make creative and effective use of their leisure. Rehabilitation must extend beyond physical reclamation to facilitate full social and emotional growth. The achievement of the highest potential for physical function is only part of the process of rehabilitation. The leadership in the neglected field of recreation programs is being provided by the organization known as Comeback, Inc.

The effectiveness of all rehabilitation services depends upon public understanding of the problems encountered by the handicapped. The ability of the handicapped to participate in the social and economic life of the community is largely determined by the attitudes of their employers, their families, and all who have contact with them.

HARDENING OF THE ARTERIES. *See* ARTERIOSCLEROSIS.

HARELIP or CLEFT LIP, a common congenital defect in which there is a fissure in either one or both sides of the upper lip next to the mid-line, usually just beneath the center of the nostril. The deformity may range from a slight notch to a wide open cleft involving the complete width of the lip. The condition results from a failure of the embryonic parts of the face to fuse during the course of development. It is frequently associated with cleft palate, a fissure in the roof of the mouth which joins the cavities of the mouth and nose. Infants with harelip may become undernourished since the passage of air through the cleft lip interferes with proper sucking action. Feeding by medicine dropper or stomach tube may be necessary. The condition can be corrected by surgery, which should be done in early infancy.

HARVEST MITE or RED BUG, common names applied to the parasitic larvae of mites of the family, Trombiculidae. The larvae, which are also known as chiggers, are about 1/120 in. long. They are often red in color and are distinguished from the nonparasitic nymphs and adults by the possession of three pairs of legs; nymphs and adults have four pairs. The larvae attach to the skin of mammalian hosts and produce the familiar chigger bite, the effects of which are apparent long after the larva has dropped off. The principal North American red bug is *Trombicula alfreddugesi*. Related Oriental species act as a vector for the organism that causes scrub typhus.

HARVEY, WILLIAM (1578–1657), English physician who discovered the circulation of the blood. He was educated at Cambridge and later at Padua (M.D.,1602). He first developed his idea concerning circulation in lectures given at the Royal College of Physicians. At this time it was believed that blood was manufactured in the liver from food, that from there it entered the heart, finally to pass into the vessels of the body. After careful experimentation and observation on dogs, pigs, fishes, and other animals, Harvey published his slim volume on circulation, *Exercitatio anatomica de motu cordis et sanguinis in animalibus*, in Germany in 1628. In this work, considered the greatest medical treatise of all time, Harvey detailed the flow of blood from the right side of the heart through the lungs, into the left side of the heart, then through the arteries into the veins, and finally back into the right side of the heart. This argument required Harvey to take a bold deductive leap from the arteries into the veins, since the

The Bettmann Archive
English physician William Harvey published his brilliant treatise on blood circulation in 1628.

minute blood vessels (the capillaries), which carry blood from the arteries to the veins, could not actually be seen until the microscope had been perfected. Harvey's correct description of circulation abounded in radical departures from the firmly established ideas of Aristotle, Galen, and other scientific notables. He demonstrated that blood was not freshly produced in large quantities, but rather circulated continuously. He showed that the heart was a muscular pump which propelled blood through the body, and that the pulse coincided with the heartbeat.
See also BLOOD.

HAÜY [*à-wē'*]**, VALENTIN** (1745–1822), French pioneer in educating the blind. In 1784 he founded the world's

first school for the blind in Paris. The success of this venture proved the feasibility of educating the blind and led to the establishment of similar schools in other countries. Haüy also produced the first books for the blind, printed in an embossed type resembling large Roman letters.
See also BLINDNESS.

HAVERHILL FEVER, also known as streptobacillary fever, is an acute bacterial disease usually transmitted by rat bites. After an incubation period of one to five days, the illness begins abruptly with chills, fever, headache, and severe back pain and joint pains. A rash appears within 48 hours. The fever then drops but returns within five days when one or more joints become swollen, red, and painful. Penicillin and streptomycin have been used effectively in treating the condition.
See also RAT-BITE FEVER.

HAY FEVER is not caused by hay and does not involve a fever. Known medically as allergic rhinitis, it is a common acute allergic disorder, affecting chiefly the eyes and upper breathing passages, and is caused by a sensitivity to air-borne pollens or molds.

Pollen is the male fertilizing element in flowering trees, plants, and grasses. It is a fine powder which is transferred to the female cell (the ovum) for the purpose of fertilization. Among the air-borne pollens which cause hay fever are the tree pollens from elm, maple, oak, and birch, which are found in the spring; grasses, such as timothy, redtop, and bluegrass, which are present in the summer; and weeds, such as ragweed, tumbleweed, and sage, which are active in the fall. Molds, or fungi, which grow in warm weather on grasses, cereal grains, hay, leather, food, clothing, and soil, also give rise to air-borne spores which may cause hay fever. The season and duration of the episodes vary with the responsible agent found in different localities.

The condition usually appears in persons under the age of 40, often appearing in several members of the same family. The symptoms consist of sneezing and itching of the eyes, nose, and throat. The hay fever victim may appear to have a heavy cold: the eyes water and appear swollen, the nasal passages are clogged, and the nose runs profusely. Asthma may develop in severe cases.

Some cases of hay fever subside spontaneously over a period of years while others become worse, eventually developing into asthma. Antihistamines are effective in suppressing the symptoms in mild cases. Cortisone and related drugs are effective in severe cases but may cause undesirable side effects.

The preferred treatment is desensitization. Skin tests are performed to identify the pollen or mold to which the patient is allergic. The patient is then injected with successively larger dosages of this material until he has developed an immunity. The injections may be repeated every year or may be given throughout the year (perennial therapy). Many persons obtain relief by migrating to pollen-free areas during the hay fever season.
See also ALLERGY.

HEAD, SIR HENRY (1861–1940), English neurologist known for his studies on language defects (aphasia) and sensation. Among his numerous contributions to neurology were a description of the role of the vagus nerve in breathing, studies on the effects of injuries to peripheral nerves, investigations on pain (referred pain), and a classic two-volume work on aphasia, *Aphasia and Kindred Disorders of Speech* (1926).

HEADACHE may be caused by pain arising from tissues on the surface of the head or from structures within the skull. Outside of the skull pain may be produced by such structures as the arteries of the scalp and face, the muscles of the scalp and upper neck, the orbital contents, the linings of the nasal cavities, the external and middle ears, and the teeth. Pain-sensitive structures within the skull include the sinuses, the major arteries at the base of the brain, and the nerves which carry fibers from the brain to the head. The brain is insensitive to pain.

Pain may be produced by the following mechanisms: (a) through dilatation and distention of arteries; (b) by traction on major vessels or nerves within the skull, producing compression or stretching; (c) by inflammation of any of the structures of the head, particularly of the blood vessels; (d) through sustained contraction of the skeletal muscles of the scalp and neck; and (e) by spread of pain from diseases of the eye, ear, nose, paranasal sinuses, and teeth.

Emotional illness may produce pain as part of a major psychological disorder. How and where such pain is "felt" remains unknown. This is often termed "psychogenic" headache.

Tension headache is probably the commonest type. It is thought to result from sustained contraction of the muscles of the scalp and neck. Such headaches occur in relation to constant or periodic emotional conflicts of which the patient is usually partly aware. They are usually located in the back of the skull or neck but in some cases may extend in a band around the entire head. The discomfort develops gradually and is frequently described as an aching, pressing, or tightness; however, it may simulate any type of pain. Frequency, duration, and severity are variable, but once the headache begins, it usually persists for hours or even days. Muscle contraction headache may be a secondary reaction to any other type of headache or disorder of the neck, including migraine, high blood pressure, lesions within the skull or intraspinal tumors. In many instances such patients also have symptoms of anxiety and tension.

Migraine Headache. "Migraine," from the Greek *hemicrania*, means "half of the head." The term describes the characteristic tendency of this disorder to be limited to one side of the head. Migraine headache is a symptom complex, consisting of periodic, recurrent, unilateral headaches, often associated with nausea and vomiting, and preceded by a variety of prodromal, or "warning," symptoms, including visual, sensory, motor, and psychological. Frequently there is a history of similar headaches in the parents or other members of the patient's family. Although headache is the most prominent feature of migraine, the syndrome may manifest itself in a widespread derangement of body function.

Migraine is more frequent in women than in men. Although it may occur in all social and economic groups, it is more prevalent in urban areas among active housewives, executives, and professionals. A majority of patients with migraine note the onset between 15 and 35 years of age; but frequently the condition begins in childhood, and occasionally it does not appear until later in life.

Situations associated with emotional stress long have been recognized as capable of precipitating an attack of migraine. The personality structure of a number of patients with migraine indicates they are meticulous, perfectionistic, compulsive, and have an unusual capacity for making a success of any endeavor; nevertheless, not all patients with migraine follow this personality profile.

Migraine headache may take a number of clinical forms. In classical migraine the warnings, or prodroma, are usually well defined and may be visual, sensory, or motor. The more common type of migraine seen, probably representing 80% of the patients, is called ordinary migraine. In distinction to the classical migraine, the prodroma are not sharply defined and may involve the psyche and the gastrointestinal system. Ordinary migraine may affect both sides of the head.

The pain frequently is longer than that of classical migraine, and the headache usually manifests itself in a wide disorganization of bodily functions, including nausea, vomiting, fatigue, chills, fluid swelling in various parts of the body, and excessive urination.

Another group of migraine headaches is called the "cluster" migraine headache. In this group there is a cyclical type of vascular headache of an intense and increasing pain, which is frequently localized to the orbit and temple, and is of short duration—minutes to an hour. Usually it is associated with profuse watering and congestion of the eyes and running of the nose, or rhinorrhea. Such bouts of headache may last for six to eight weeks and may not recur for months or years.

In rare instances migraine may be associated with persistent neurological phenomena, such as paralysis of the eye muscles or of an extremity.

Although the complete mechanism of migraine is unknown, present evidence indicates that excessive dilatation of an artery or set of arteries, particularly in the branches of the extracranial circulation, plus the presence of a pain-sensitizing substance at the site of these vessels, is responsible for the pain in migraine.

Other Causes. Less common causes include tumors, infections, chemical agents, eye disorders, and diseases of the muscles of the scalp and neck. Headaches often follow minor or severe head injuries. In many cases the headache may be localized to the site of a scalp or skull injury and probably results from stimulation of injured nerve endings in the contused scalp. In a few instances the headache is due to direct injury to pain-sensitive structures within the skull. However, in the majority of cases of chronic posttraumatic headache, the mechanism of the production of head pains is probably similar to that which is present in patients with tension headaches.

Headache may also occur in relation to major emotional illnesses, including hysterical conversion, depression, schizophrenia, and involutional and toxic psychosis. This type of headache cannot be distinguished from a tension headache, migraine, or any other type of headache on the basis of description alone.

Treatment of the patient with headache includes the removal of all causative factors. This may require surgery, chemotherapy for infection, removal of any allergic factors, correction of a systemic disturbance, or psychotherapy in cases where the symptoms are related to excessive emotional stress and personality maladjustment.

The common nonnarcotic analgesics are valuable in relieving the symptoms in the majority of patients with headache. In more intense and severe pain, frequently it is necessary to use codeine sulfate or demerol for relief. In patients with headaches of the migraine type, the use of ergotamine tartrate is indicated.

In treatment of patients with tension headaches and some psychogenic headaches, tranquilizers and sedative drugs are of some value. Psychotherapy is the best prophylactic treatment for the patient with migraine and tension headache.

HEAD DEFORMATION, artificial modification of the human skull during early stages of growth, performed for enhancement of ethnic concepts of beauty or status, or occurring as the result of traditional practices. Applied pressure inhibits growth in one direction, with a compensatory growth in another, thus modifying the shape of the cranium. Methods range from simple bindings of cloth and cord, boards, cotton pads, clay balls, and stones, to elaborate combinations thereof. Some forms of head deformation are unintentional results of certain customs, such as carrying babies on cradleboards or wearing heavy headdresses and coiffures.

Little is known of the physiological effects of head deformation. Apparently, it neither changes the weight or volume of the cranium, nor has a noticeable effect on intelligence. Resultant types include *simple occipital* (flattening of the back plane of the skull), *fronto-occipital* (elongation of both front and back, either vertically or horizontally), *circular* or *annular* (producing a knoblike projection at the top), and less common miscellaneous varieties. The practice of head deformation has been found on all continents, with highest frequency in the Americas. It occurred mainly in prehistoric and early historic times.

HEALTH, EDUCATION, AND WELFARE, UNITED STATES DEPARTMENT OF, principal U.S. government agency for promotion of general welfare in the fields of health, education, social service, and social insurance. In addition to its own programs, the department also administers many grants-in-aid and provides advisory services to state and local programs.

Organization and Functions. The department consists of an office of the secretary and six main operating units. These are the Public Health Service, Office of Education, Social Security Adimination, Food and Drug Administration, Social and Rehabilitation Service, and St. Elizabeth's Hospital. Outside Washington, D.C., there are nine regional offices.

The Public Health Service, dating from 1798, is under the direction of the U.S. surgeon general. Reorganized in 1968, it is made up of the Health Services and Mental Health Administration, the Consumer Protection and Environmental Health Service, and the National Institutes of Health. Major functions include improvements of physical and mental health services; support of research and training in the medical and related sciences; protection of the public against health hazards; and administration of health manpower programs.

The Food and Drug Administration, whose origins go back to 1906, is primarily a regulatory agency. It is concerned with the purity and standardization of food, drugs, and cosmetics, the regulation of caustic poisons, and the promotion of truthful and informative labeling of these consumer products.

The Social and Rehabilitation Service was established in Aug., 1967, by merging the department's Welfare Administration, Vocational Rehabilitation Administration, Administration on Aging, and Mental Retardation Division of the Public Health Service. The employees of this agency are involved in a wide variety of welfare activities. These include assistance to individuals and families in need, welfare, medical, and health services for children, mothers, and the aging; and administration of the Medicaid program.

St. Elizabeth's Hospital, founded in 1855 for care of the mentally ill, is located in the capital, and is administered by the department.

HEALTH, MENTAL. See MENTAL HEALTH.

HEARING. See EAR.

HEARING AID, miniaturized amplifier specifically designed to aid persons who have difficulty in hearing. The unit consists of a small microphone attached to a battery-powered amplifier, which sends a signal to a tiny earplug. The hearing aid will amplify the sounds a person finds hardest to hear, while avoiding confusion from unnecessary sounds. An important feature is economy in power requirements. The battery must be small with a long life.

Transistors have made possible extremely small, compact hearing aids that can be built into eyeglass frames or a small earplug. Batteries that are as small as an aspirin tablet have been designed.

HEART. The heart first appears in animal life as a means of driving circulatory fluid into deep and inaccessible tissues. The most primitive forms of life lack a true circulatory system; each cell is bathed by the waters of its habitat which supply it with nutrients and carry away wastes. In more complex animals a rudimentary heart is needed to propel this fluid into remote parts of the organism. In the closed circulatory system of humans the heart keeps the blood in constant motion, enabling a comparatively small volume of fluid to supply the body cells with food and oxygen and to remove waste products.

The human heart is a hollow muscular organ about the size of a closed fist. It beats continuously during life, propelling blood through the arteries and veins. The heart is actually a double pump: the right portion pumps blood to the lungs where it takes up oxygen; the left portion sends this oxygen-rich blood through the arteries to nourish the tissues of the body. Each portion consists of two chambers: a thin-walled atrium and a thickly muscled ventricle.

This diagram presents in schematic form the path of blood through the heart. (1) Blood from the veins passes into the inferior and the superior vena cava, leading into the upper chamber of the right heart, the right atrium. (2) From the right atrium the blood enters the right ventricle which pumps it to the lungs by way of the pulmonary artery. (3) After absorbing oxygen in the lungs, blood re-enters the heart at the left chamber, the left atrium. (4) Blood passes from the left atrium into the left ventricle to be propelled into the aorta, the largest artery of the body.

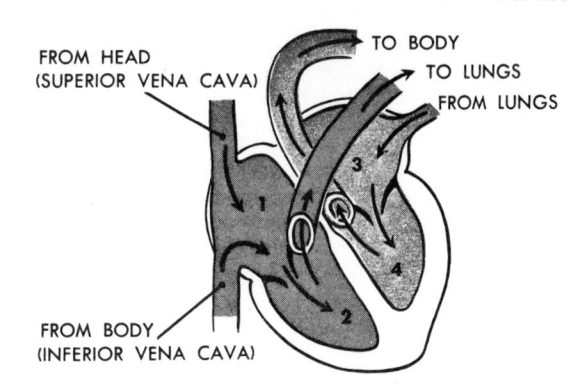

How Is the Heart Excited? The heart is a self-stimulating organ. It beats regularly and automatically, relying upon a network of special tissue which originates and conducts an electrochemical impulse that stimulates contraction of the heart muscle. The "pacemaker" or key point in this system is the *sinoauricular* (SA) *node* which lies along the upper right border of the right atrium. This structure generates exciting impulses (between 60 and 90 per minute) which spread along the walls of both the right and left atria.

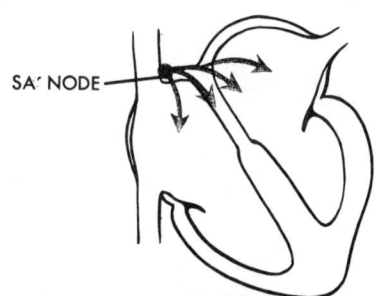

When the impulse reaches the wall which separates the left and right atria (the interatrial septum) it excites another bundle of specialized tissue, the *atrioventricular* (AV) *node*. This second wave of excitation passes from the AV node down the *bundle of His* and branches off along the walls of both ventricles. By means of this rapidly conducting system the impulse reaches all parts of the ventricle almost simultaneously, making possible a powerful and highly synchronized contraction.

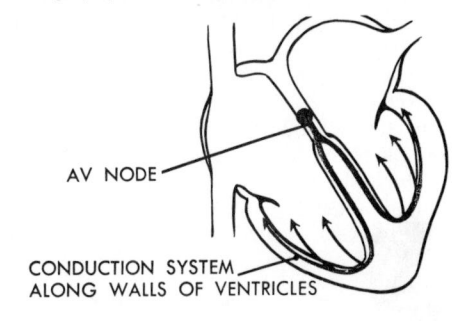

HEART

The Cycle of the Heartbeat. From the above description of the excitation of the heart it can be seen that there are two phases of contraction in the cycle of the heartbeat: contraction of both atria followed by contraction of both ventricles.

The period of ventricular contraction is called *systole*. The period of ventricular relaxation is called *diastole*.

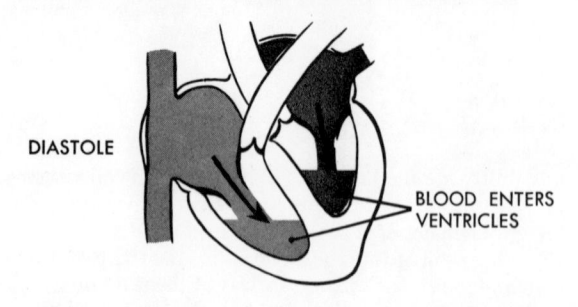

Diastole. During diastole blood passes from the atria into the ventricles. The valves at the pulmonary artery and the aorta are closed, permitting blood to accumulate in the ventricles.

Systole. This is the period of massive contraction of the ventricles. In the presystole phase the atria contract, helping to drive blood into the ventricles. Although at one time great stress was placed on the role of atrial contraction in filling the ventricles, it is now thought that this is comparatively unimportant—filling of the ventricles occurs chiefly while the ventricles are resting and results from differences in the pressure of blood in the atria and ventricles.

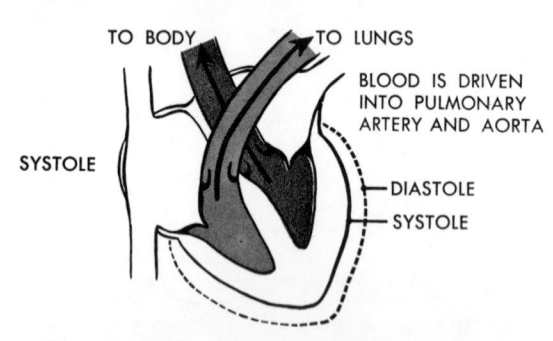

As the ventricles contract, the valves between the atria and ventricles are forced shut, while those which open into the pulmonary artery and aorta are forced open. Blood is thus driven into the lungs and through the body. At the same time the atria fill with blood. As the ventricles relax, blood again enters and the cycle repeats.

The Heart Sounds. Two sounds are generally recognizable during the heart cycle. The first is relatively long in duration and low in pitch and occurs at the beginning of ventricular systole. The sound is produced by the closing of the AV valves, by the rush of blood from the ventricles, and by the contraction of the ventricular muscle. The second sound, somewhat higher pitched than the first, occurs at the end of systole. The sound results from vibrations set up in the walls of the aorta and pulmonary artery by closure of the arterial (semilunar) valves. A faint third sound is occasionally heard in normal hearts. This has been attributed to the vibration of the ventricular walls, movements of the AV valves, and other factors; but no explanation is considered generally acceptable. A fourth heart sound, resulting from contraction of the atria, has also been described.

The Regulation of the Heartbeat. The heartbeat is under three types of control: (1) the automatic control of the heart's own "pacemaker," which has already been described; (2) nervous reflex control which prevents the blood pressure from rising too high or falling too low; and (3) nervous regulation which enables the heart to respond to varying states of body activity.

The Heart Reflexes. These operate on a feedback principle, similar to that of the common thermostat. When the blood pressure rises excessively, pressure receptors in the carotid artery (which supplies the brain) are highly stimulated, sending impulses to centers in the lower brain, which in turn relay inhibiting nerve messages to the heart. These slow the heartbeat, helping to lower the blood pressure and thus reducing the stimulation of the carotid receptors. Conversely, when the blood pressure drops below a certain point, the pressure receptors stimulate a cardiac-accelerating center in the brain which increases the heart rate and helps to raise the blood pressure. These mechanisms are known as the *carotid sinus reflex* and serve to control the blood supply to the brain. Similar receptors are found in the aorta and possibly in other arteries.

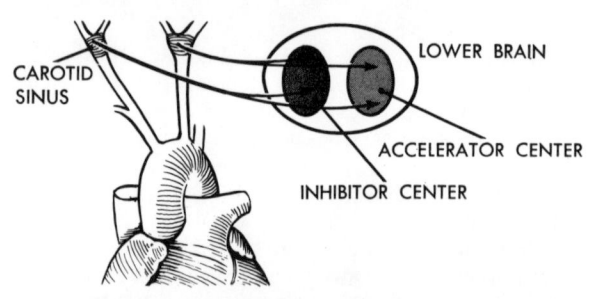

Nervous Regulation of the Heartbeat. The reflex mechanism described above acts upon the heart through two sets of nerves: the heart-inhibiting nerves travel directly from centers in the lower brain to the heart; heart-stimulating nerves travel from the brain to the heart by way of the spinal cord and nerve centers adjacent to it.

Through these same nerves various changes in body

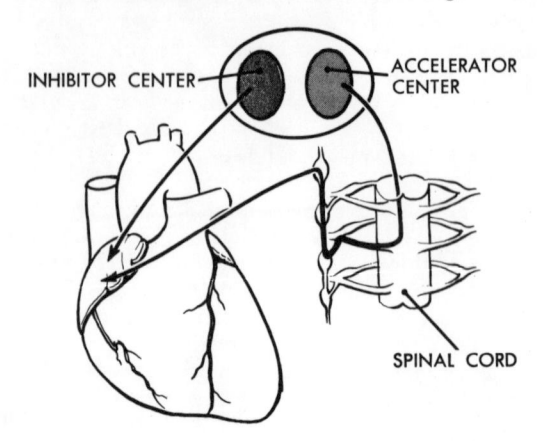

conditions cause the heart to increase or decrease its beat. Exercise, excitement, and emotional stress increase the heartbeat by stimulating the accelerator pathways. During sleep the heartbeat is diminished. Even in the absence of abnormal stress a constant stream of impulses flows through these nerves, maintaining a delicate balance in stimulation to the heart. This organ is thus always poised between its own automatic control and two conflicting sets of nerve impulses.

Cardiac Reserve—the Emergency Capacity of the Heart. The basic task of the heart is to supply the oxygen needs of the body. In strenuous exercise these needs rise sharply, and the heart is called upon to increase its total delivery of oxygen-rich blood to the tissues. The difference between the maximum output of the heart and its normal output at rest is described as the cardiac reserve. The increased output is largely achieved by increasing the heartbeat, which may rise to a maximum of 210 beats per minute, and by increasing the force of the contraction so as to pump more blood with each stroke. In the trained athlete the force of the heartbeat is normally greater; this permits a normally slower pulse of 50 to 60 beats per minute. Consequently the cardiac reserve of the athlete is greater than that of the untrained individual since each increase in pulse rate delivers a correspondingly larger volume of blood. In certain heart diseases the contraction is weakened, and the heart must pump faster to supply the necessary volume of blood to the tissues.

HEARTBURN, a burning sensation which originates in the upper abdomen and travels upward behind the breastbone. The condition is initiated by a backflow of juice from the stomach into the gullet (esophagus). It is not known whether the pain is caused by the acid itself or by a muscular spasm of the esophagus. Heartburn usually occurs after a large meal or when lying down after eating. The pain usually appears suddenly and lasts several minutes, until the acid drains from the esophagus or is neutralized.

HEART DISEASES may be divided into two groups: the organic and the functional. The organic diseases involve damage to the heart tissues. In the functional diseases the tissues are not directly injured, but conditions outside the heart, such as anxiety, nervousness, anemia, and diseases of the thyroid gland, gall bladder, or lungs, cause abnormal changes in the heartbeat. Both types of heart disease may cause similar symptoms, including shortness of breath, palpitation, and chest pain. The functional disorders are not serious and can usually be corrected. While the organic disturbances present a graver problem they can often be successfully treated; most persons so afflicted may look forward to a long and useful life.

The Organic Heart Diseases

Coronary Disease. This is a form of arteriosclerosis, or hardening of the arteries, which affects the blood vessels that supply the heart muscles. It is the commonest heart ailment, and although formerly considered a disease of middle and old age, it is now being diagnosed in men in their thirties and occasionally even in younger men. It seldom occurs in women before the change of life.

In coronary disease the arteries of the heart gradually become thickened and irregular as fatty deposits build up along the inner lining of the arterial wall. The opening is narrowed, reducing the blood flow. Fortunately, small branches of the narrowed artery dilate and join with branches of neighboring arteries to carry the blood which can no longer pass through the main channel. This "collateral" circulation may be able to supply the heart muscle with enough blood for all activities. For this reason coronary disease of considerable severity may develop without producing any symptoms. In most cases, however, the disease causes angina pectoris—pain, pressure, or discomfort beneath the breastbone, following exertion or excitement. This usually subsides promptly if the patient rests or places a nitroglycerin tablet beneath his tongue. The pain of angina pectoris may be felt in other areas of the chest, in the arms (usually the left), or even in the upper abdomen. It may therefore be confused with arthritis, neuritis, stomach ulcer, hernia of the diaphragm, gall bladder disease, and especially with nervous states which cause spasm of the esophagus, stomach, or bowel. An important distinction between coronary disease and these other conditions is that only heart pain appears with exertion.

The electrocardiograph, an instrument which records the electrical activity of the heart, is often of value in diagnosing coronary disease. Although the electrical record may be normal, even in cases when the pain is severe enough to prevent the patient from walking, specific exercise frequently produces characteristic changes. An ingenious diagnostic technique consists of introducing an opaque substance into the coronary arteries by way of a tube (catheter) passed into the aorta, the largest artery of the body. X rays can then be taken, enabling the physician to see if the arteries are narrowed or occluded.

Acute Heart Attacks in Coronary Disease. At times a clot, or thrombus, develops in a sclerosed artery and completely obstructs the flow of blood. The section of heart muscle normally supplied by that artery decays. This is commonly called a heart attack, or, in medical terminology, coronary thrombosis (a coronary clot) and myocardial infarction (indicating obstruction of blood flow to the heart muscle).

The severity of the symptoms seen in coronary thrombosis varies greatly. Frequently a routine electrocardiogram (ECG) reveals that a heart attack occurred sometime in the past in persons who have apparently been perfectly well. Usually, however, intense chest pain develops. Profuse perspiration and vomiting are common. The circulation may fail, resulting in a marked fall in blood pressure (shock) or heart failure (see below). Typical changes in the ECG develop shortly after the attack.

In some cases heart attacks appear without thrombosis. The damage is caused by inadequate blood flow in the diseased artery. These attacks may occur at rest or following exertion, excitement, sudden hemorrhage from the stomach, operations, or acute infections.

Treatment of Acute Heart Attacks. The vast majority of patients recover from heart attacks, and nine out of ten return to work. The period of bed rest or chair confinement is much shorter than it was formerly, and many patients are able to do light work within two or three months. Recovery from a second attack is often as good as that from the first.

HEART DISEASES

HEART DISEASES AND HEART DEFECTS

CONGENITAL HEART DEFECTS

DEFECTS IN THE WALLS THAT SEPARATE THE CHAMBERS OF THE HEART

Openings in the walls that divide the heart into chambers may result in abnormal short-circuiting of the flow of blood. Shown here are openings in the membrane which separates the atria of the heart. Usually in these cases the flow of blood is from the left to the right side of the heart. However, in some instances it may be reversed. When a right-to-left flow does occur, oxygen-poor blood bypasses the lungs and passes into the general circulation, thus depriving the tissues of a normal oxygen supply.

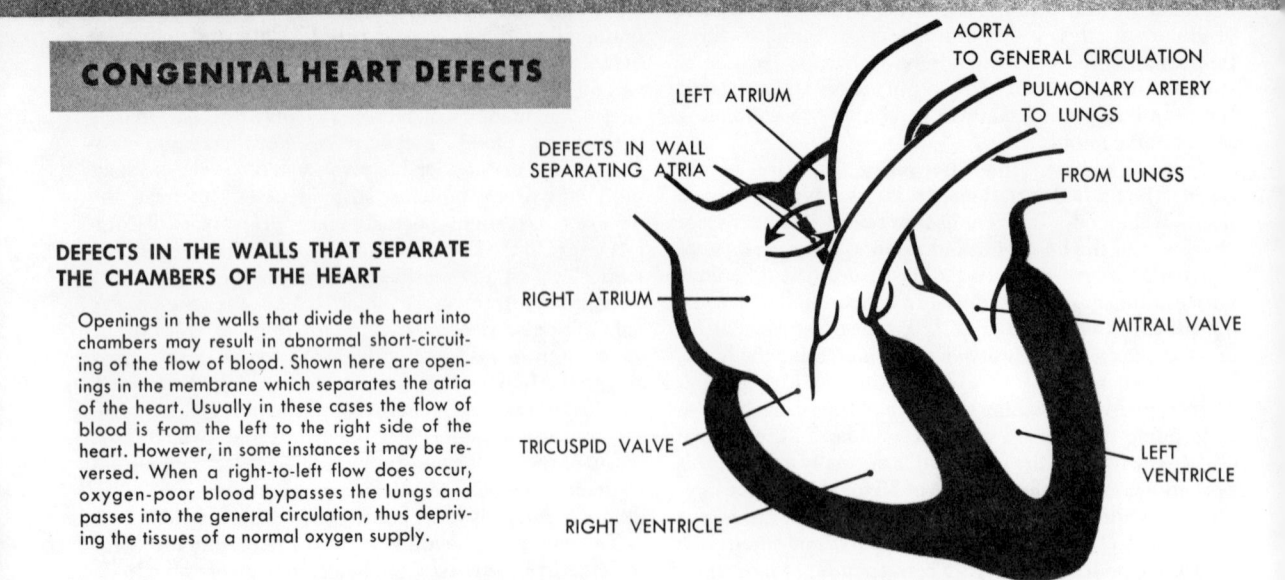

Labels: AORTA TO GENERAL CIRCULATION; PULMONARY ARTERY TO LUNGS; LEFT ATRIUM; DEFECTS IN WALL SEPARATING ATRIA; FROM LUNGS; RIGHT ATRIUM; MITRAL VALVE; TRICUSPID VALVE; LEFT VENTRICLE; RIGHT VENTRICLE

CORONARY ARTERY DISEASE

(1) Fatty deposits build up in inner wall of coronary arteries, reducing blood flow to heart muscle.

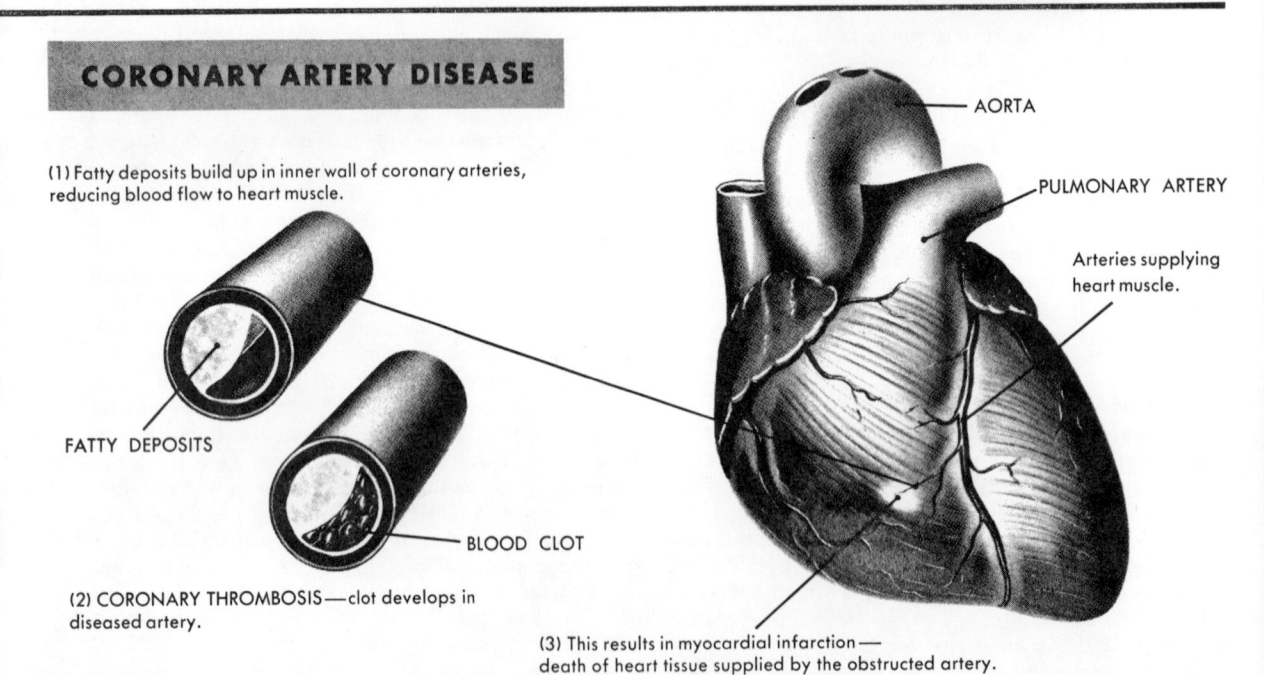

FATTY DEPOSITS

(2) CORONARY THROMBOSIS—clot develops in diseased artery.

BLOOD CLOT

(3) This results in myocardial infarction—death of heart tissue supplied by the obstructed artery.

Labels: AORTA; PULMONARY ARTERY; Arteries supplying heart muscle.

In many cases further attacks can be prevented by the use of drugs (anticoagulants) which inhibit the tendency of the blood to clot. These drugs are given to persons who continue to experience frequent angina pains after a heart attack, or who have had more than one attack within one or two years. This treatment is not without danger since the lowered coagulability of the blood may cause bleeding almost anywhere in the body. To avoid this possibility, tests of the clotting power of the blood are performed regularly.

Prevention of Coronary Disease. Prevention of coronary disease has been hampered by lack of definite knowledge as to its cause. Various theories have suggested that a predisposition to the disease is inherited, that it develops from sedentary habits and insufficient exercise, that it is caused by a sensitivity to tobacco, or that it results from the frustration, anxiety, and repression of modern life.

By far the greatest attention has been focused on the diet as a cause of coronary disease, particularly the intake of foods such as butter, cream, milk, eggs, and red meats,

HEART DISEASES

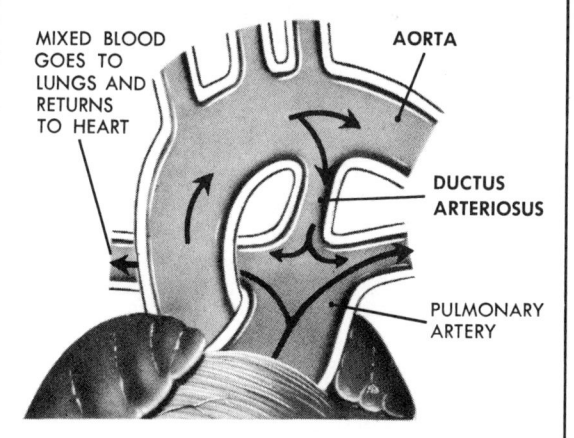

PATENT DUCTUS ARTERIOSUS
The defect here involves the failure of the ductus arteriosus, a connection between the pulmonary artery and the aorta, to close after birth. In most cases some blood flows from the aorta back into the pulmonary artery, repeating a circuit through the lungs. Symptoms depend upon a number of factors, such as the amount of regurgitation, the resistance to blood flow in the lungs, and the presence or absence of other defects.

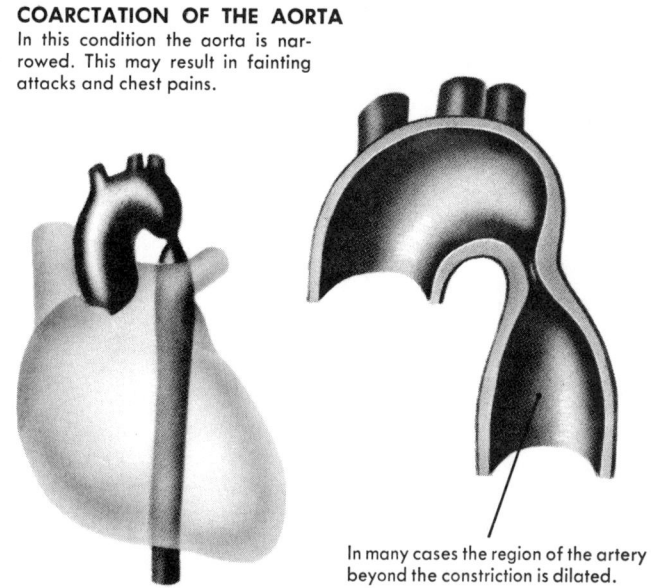

COARCTATION OF THE AORTA
In this condition the aorta is narrowed. This may result in fainting attacks and chest pains.

In many cases the region of the artery beyond the constriction is dilated.

RHEUMATIC HEART DISEASE

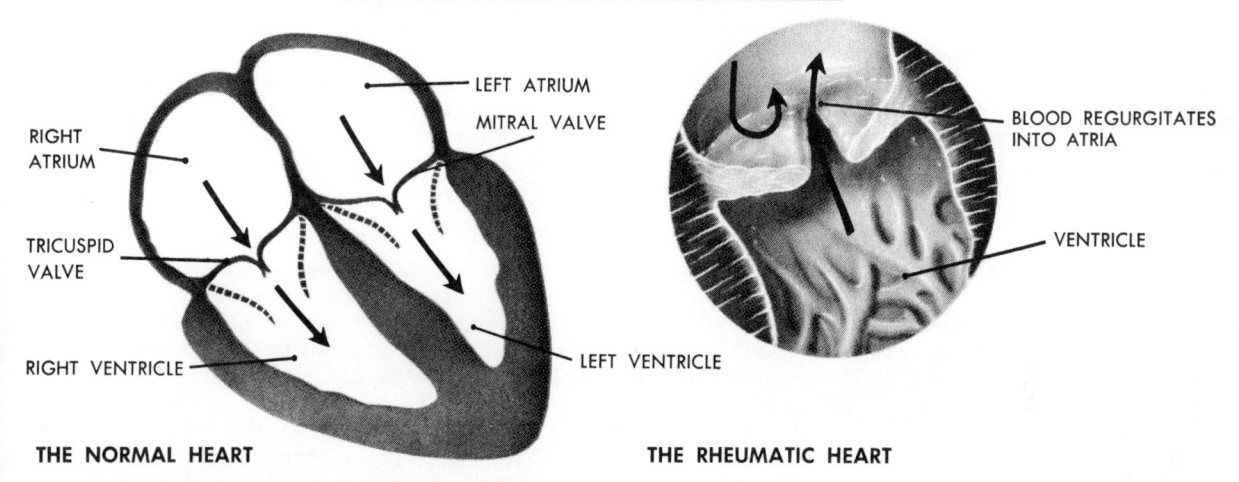

THE NORMAL HEART
In the normal heart the valves between the atria and ventricles open to permit blood to flow through and close firmly when the ventricles contract, thus preventing backflow of blood into the atria.

THE RHEUMATIC HEART
In the rheumatic heart the valve openings are narrowed and the deformed valves may not close completely, permitting blood to flow back into the atria. This produces the heart *murmurs*, which may serve as a diagnostic clue to the disease.

which contain cholesterol and other fatty substances. These materials are deposited in the arteries and are frequently present in the blood in elevated amounts in patients with coronary disease. In diabetes there is a high blood cholesterol and an increased susceptibility to arteriosclerosis. Communities which subsist on low-fat diets, such as in southern China, have a low incidence of the disease. For these reasons some physicians believe that large amounts of fat in the diet may cause arteriosclerosis, and have severely restricted the diet of patients with coronary disease. Some have even advocated a change in the dietary habits of the general population to prevent the disease. Other physicians do not believe that high-fat diets cause the disease, citing as evidence numerous individuals with coronary disease who have a low blood-cholesterol level. They also note that the body can manufacture its own cholesterol even if fats are not present in the diet.

Despite this controversy many physicians advise patients with coronary disease to restrict the amount of fat in their diets, but not to eliminate all fats. Several drugs

HEART DISEASES

are now available which lower the blood cholesterol, but their effect on the body generally is not yet known.

Most persons with this condition lead fairly normal lives, particularly if they avoid undue anxiety and exertion and keep their weight down.

Rheumatic Fever. Rheumatic fever may deform the heart valves, leading to enlargement of the heart and heart failure. It occurs primarily in children as a peculiar reaction to infection with certain strains of streptococcus bacteria, which usually attack the nose or throat. The frequency of rheumatic fever in the United States has declined considerably owing to improved diet and living conditions and the use of penicillin to treat streptococcus infections.

In most cases there are joint pains and a slight fever. The child may not appear ill, but is listless, irritable, and somewhat pale. He may complain of "growing" pains in the legs and may have nosebleeds. The disease may develop rapidly in some children, producing high fever and pain which migrates from one joint to another. In severe cases heart failure occurs.

More than half the children with rheumatic fever make a complete recovery without any heart valve damage. Some develop rheumatic heart disease, with a heart murmur, in a year or two. The heart may continue to function well and remain normal in size until old age, or it may become steadily larger and eventually fail. The outlook depends on which valves are involved (mitral, aortic, or both) and whether the valve has become narrowed (stenosis) or is unable to close (causing regurgitation). An exact diagnosis is essential, as surgical treatment is highly successful for mitral stenosis and satisfactory for aortic stenosis. Operations for mitral and aortic regurgitation are less effective. To prevent new attacks, persons who have had rheumatic fever should be given regular doses of antibiotics for an indefinite period.

Congenital Heart Disease. Each year a considerable number of babies are born with defects of the heart or large blood vessels (aorta and pulmonary artery). Some of these anomalies may cause blood to bypass the lungs so that it does not take up oxygen (as in "blue" babies). Before the recent advances in heart surgery many children with heart defects died soon after birth or in early childhood. While some anomalies permit the child to develop somewhat normally, a majority of these individuals become ill by the age of 40.

The first surgical cure of a congenital heart defect was accomplished in 1938 when an opening between the aorta and the pulmonary artery was closed. This operation involved structures outside the heart, but since then many more serious defects within the heart have been corrected by "open heart" surgery. In this procedure the circulation bypasses the heart: the major blood vessels are connected to a "heart-lung" machine—an apparatus which assumes the heart's function of pumping the blood and the lung's function of exposing the blood to oxygen. To facilitate his task the surgeon may halt the beating of the heart by injecting a drug into the heart muscle. Although many common heart anomalies can be corrected by such surgery, some still resist treatment.

Other Organic Heart Conditions. Heart disease may be caused by infection. In syphilis the aorta and the aortic valve may be attacked 10 or more years after the original infection. Diphtheria may cause acute inflammation of the heart muscle (myocarditis) which may be serious or even fatal but probably does not result in chronic heart disease. Virus diseases may also cause acute myocarditis and possibly permanent damage. It is possible that unexplained enlarged hearts and severe heart failure seen in some patients may have originated with a virus infection.

Heart Failure. Heart failure is not a disease in itself but is rather a common end point of all organic heart diseases. It usually occurs when some type of heart disease has existed for a considerable period and particularly when the heart has become enlarged to compensate for disease or to work against increased blood pressure. This is effective up to a point, but further enlargement reduces the efficiency of the heart, which may fail when it is strained by emotional upset, unusual effort, infections, or overactivity of the thyroid gland.

Heart failure frequently develops gradually. The patient becomes aware of shortness of breath, at first only when climbing stairs or later even at rest. He may begin to cough and think he has caught cold. He may feel increasing weakness and observe some swelling about the ankles. Less commonly, heart failure appears suddenly: the patient feels suffocated and begins to wheeze and perspire profusely. This may be confused with an asthmatic attack.

The severity of congestive failure is influenced by the amount of salt (sodium chloride) in the diet. As the heart output declines, kidney function also decreases and less salt is excreted in the urine. Sodium is important in the fluid balance of the body, and when sodium is retained it holds fluid in the tissues. This first becomes evident as a gain in weight and later as swelling about the ankles.

Treatment of congestive failure is usually effective. The patient's activity is restricted, and he is given digitalis to increase the efficiency of the heart, and diuretics (drugs which increase the flow of urine, thus ridding the body of salt and water).

Functional Heart Disorders

A number of conditions, including nervousness, anemia, and thyroid disturbances, can cause the heartbeat to become irregular, rapid, or slow. This may cause severe discomfort, felt as pounding in the chest, faintness or dizziness, and choking and shortness of breath. These alterations in the heartbeat (arrhythmias) also occur frequently in persons with organic heart disease.

The commonest type of irregularity is premature beat, or extrasystole, in which there is an extra beat of the heart inserted between the normal beats. Extrasystole is not significant, and frequently the individual is unaware of it. If they are annoying, premature beats can often be prevented by giving quinidine several times a day.

More disturbing are episodes in which the heart suddenly begins to beat rapidly; the rhythm may be regular (atrial tachycardia, or flutter) or irregular (atrial fibrillation). Usually these attacks last for a few minutes to an hour or two, during which time it is extremely important for the patient to remain as calm as possible.

Many normal persons have a slow heartbeat (bradycardia) of 40–50 beats per minute. At times the rate may fall even lower, causing fainting. Persons with organic heart disease sometimes develop heart block, in which the heart rate may be under 30. The heart may at times stop beating completely. An ingenious technique of maintaining the heartbeat electronically has been developed for these individuals (*see* MEDICAL ELECTRONICS).

HEART-LUNG MACHINE, a device which duplicates the heart's function of pumping blood and the lung's function of exchanging the carbon dioxide of the blood for oxygen. Heart-lung machines differ principally in the method by which they expose the blood to oxygen. Methods currently popular are bubbling oxygen through a column of blood; running blood over screens in an atmosphere of oxygen; or dipping the lower portion of a series of vertical discs in a trough of blood (as the discs spin, red cells are drawn up on the discs and exposed to oxygen). The machines pump 5 quarts of blood a minute. They remove any bubbles or clots before returning the blood to the body and maintain the blood at the proper temperature. The blood is kept completely sterile throughout the cycle. Through the use of this machine the patient's blood can be diverted around the heart and lungs, making it possible to perform open-heart surgery, to repair congenital heart defects and disease-damaged valves, and to operate on blood vessels which have been weakened by disease or injury. The device has also proven useful in cancer therapy; individual cancer-ridden organs can be isolated from the blood stream so that drugs can be administered to the cancerous tissue in doses which would ordinarily be toxic if allowed to flow through the general circulation.

HEART TRANSPLANT. *See* ORGAN TRANSPLANTS.

HEAT CRAMP, HEAT EXHAUSTION, AND HEAT STROKE, disorders which may result from strenuous activity in hot environments.

Heat cramps are painful muscle contractions which follow heavy loss of body salts through perspiration. Usually the blood pressure and body temperature remain normal. The administration of sodium chloride (ordinary table salt) by mouth or injection brings about rapid recovery.

Heat exhaustion develops most frequently in individuals freshly exposed to arduous activity in hot climates. The circulation to the skin increases in order to facilitate cooling of the blood and to support the increased activity of the sweat glands. The circulatory system, which has not adapted to the warmer climate, cannot supply the additional skin circulation while simultaneously maintaining adequate blood flow to the brain and muscles. This results in palpitation, fatigue, dizziness, nausea, vomiting, headache, and slightly raised body temperature. Salt deficiency and excess loss of water contribute to the condition. The victim is unconscious and perspires freely. The blood pressure is low. Treatment consists of rest and the administration of mildly salted water. In older persons heart failure may occur because of previously existing disease of the heart or blood vessels.

Heat stroke is an extremely serious condition involving a breakdown of the heat-regulating mechanisms of the body. The sweat glands cease to function, and the body temperature rises to 105° F or higher. The early symptoms are mental confusion, staggering gait, and headache. Later the patient collapses. The skin is hot, and, unlike in heat exhaustion, it is *dry*.

The body temperature must be lowered as rapidly as possible to prevent brain damage. An effective means is to immerse the patient in an ice bath or cold water until the temperature is reduced to 102° F or lower. Cooling sprays and fans may help. The arms and legs should be massaged to stimulate sluggish circulation while the patient is being cooled. *Heat stroke is considered a true medical emergency: untreated cases are invariably fatal.*

Heat stroke is not likely to occur if the sweat glands are permitted occasional rest, such as in air-conditioned apartments or in desert areas where the nights are cool.

HEEL SPUR, a bony growth which develops at the point where the layer of fibrous tissue found on the sole of the foot (the plantar fascia) inserts into the heel bone. The spur apparently develops from an abnormal tension exerted by the plantar fascia on the heel bone. The spur is likely to be painful during the early stages of formation and painless once fully formed. Arch supports which correct the mechanical dysfunction of the foot are usually effective in relieving discomfort.

HEMATOMA [*hē-mə-tō′mə, hĕm-ə-tō′mə*], tumorlike swelling resulting from the escape of blood from a ruptured blood vessel into the tissues. Hematomas are usually produced by direct injury, such as a hammer blow to the nail. Blood may seep between cleavages in the tissues and extend some distance from the site of the injury, producing black-and-blue marks. Pain may result from tension on surrounding tissues. The blood is absorbed spontaneously within a few weeks. A subdural hematoma is a collection of blood on the surface of the brain caused by head injury. This may be fatal. In some cases an apparently trivial head injury results in a hematoma some time later. If the hematoma persists and enlarges, the patient experiences headache, drowsiness, vomiting, mental changes, and paralysis. Treatment is surgical.

HEMOGLOBIN [*hē′mə-glō-bĭn*], the coloring matter which constitutes the bulk of the red blood cells. The principal function of hemoglobin is to carry oxygen from the lungs to the tissues. Hemoglobin is a combination of heme, an iron-containing complex, with globin, a protein. Oxygen combines with the iron of hemoglobin to form the bright-red oxyhemoglobin of arterial blood. In the minute blood vessels of the tissues, oxyhemoglobin releases oxygen, forming the dark-red hemoglobin of venous blood. Part of the carbon dioxide produced in the tissues as a waste product combines with the globin portion of the hemoglobin, while the remainder is carried in the blood plasma. In the lungs the hemoglobin molecule releases the carbon dioxide and is free to combine again with oxygen. Hemoglobin also helps to regulate the acidity-alkalinity balance of the blood.

The red blood cells have a normal life span of approximately 100–120 days, and when they are decomposed the heme and globin portions of hemoglobin are separated. The iron is detached from the heme and with the globin is used to synthesize new hemoglobin. The remaining part of the heme molecule is eventually changed into the bile pigment bilirubin, which is secreted by the liver in the bile fluid into the gall bladder and the small intestine. In certain forms of anemia involving an excessive destruction of red blood cells, the overproduction of the bile pigment results in jaundice, a yellowish tinting of the skin and eyes.

In some forms of poisoning, the hemoglobin of the blood is altered in such a way that it loses its oxygen-carrying capacity, resulting in oxygen starvation of the tissues. Carbon monoxide, which is found in coal gas and in the exhaust vapors from automobiles, can enter into a firm combination with hemoglobin, which prevents hemoglobin from uniting with oxygen. Certain drugs and chemicals when taken internally can change hemoglobin into methemoglobin, a form in which the electrical charges on the iron of the hemoglobin molecule are altered so that it can no longer combine with oxygen. At one time diapers freshly stamped with aniline ink caused poisoning of this type in infants.

In anemia the hemoglobin content of the blood is inadequate to meet the oxygen demands of the tissues. This may result from excessive destruction of red blood cells, inadequate dietary intake of iron, underproduction of hemoglobin or red blood cells, or excessive loss of blood, as in hemorrhage.

Hemoglobins are found in all higher animals and in many lower invertebrate animals. While the heme is the same, in most of these globin varies from species to species and even in the same individual. The hemoglobin F (fetal) found in human embryos disappears within a few months after birth and is replaced by the adult form, called hemoglobin A.

HEMOLYTIC STREPTOCOCCI [hē-mə-lĭt′ĭk strĕp-tə-kŏk′sī], bacteria which cause several serious illnesses in man, the type depending on the invasion site and the patient's reaction. "Strep" throat, scarlet fever, puerperal fever, glomerulonephritis, and lymphangitis are caused by these organisms. Of the 12 known streptococcal strains, group A hemolytic streptococci are of greatest interest because they produce rheumatic fever and glomerulonephritis kidney inflammation). One of the group A strain, called beta streptococcus, is identified by its ability to destroy red blood cells in sheep-blood culture. Beta streptococci produce an enzyme which destroys blood fibrin, allowing the bacteria to spread through tissue, and also produces the toxin responsible for scarlet fever rash. Streptococci enter the body through the nose and mouth, invading the throat, specially the tonsils. Most such infections last less than a week, but any beta hemolytic infection should be treated.

HEMOPHILIA [hē-mə-fĭl′ē-ə], an inherited disorder of the blood-clotting mechanism, marked by excessive bleeding following minor injury or by spontaneous bleeding from the digestive tract, skin, muscles, or other parts of the body. At least three different types of hemophilia are now recognized, each lacking a different essential clotting protein in the blood.

The deficiency of two of these proteins is inherited according to a sex-linked recessive pattern: females may carry and pass on the gene (the hereditary unit) but do not have the disease; males with the gene have hemophilia. The inheritance of the gene associated with the third protein is apparently not sex-linked, and therefore both males and females can be affected. Because of the sex-linkage in most cases of hemophilia, the disease is almost exclusively limited to males.

Tooth extractions, minor cuts and bruises, and other ordinary trivial injuries may cause severe blood loss in hemophiliacs. By far the most common symptom is bleeding into the joints. This produces a severely painful and disabling arthritis. Hemophilia is treated by transfusions of fresh blood (containing the missing coagulation protein), which are given when the individual is bleeding. The coagulability of the blood cannot be maintained continuously, since the effect of each transfusion lasts for only a short period, and massive amounts of blood would be required during the lifetime of the individual.

It is estimated that the number of hemophiliacs in the world is increasing. Modern methods of treatment have vastly increased the life span of hemophiliacs, who may now marry and transmit the disease to their own children.

HEMORRHAGE [hĕm′ər-ĭj], the escape of blood from the circulatory system. Hemorrhage is most frequently caused by injury to or disease of the walls of blood vessels. Knife and gunshot wounds often involve large arteries and veins. Stomach ulcers may produce hemorrhage by eroding large arteries. Certain infectious diseases, such as syphilis, may cause a weakening and bulging (aneurysm) of the arterial wall, which may eventually rupture. Aneurysms also develop in arteriosclerosis, or hardening of the arteries. In many instances the arterial walls may be weak from birth and rupture under stress later in life.

Hemorrhage may be an early sign of cancer. This is particularly true in cancer of the stomach, intestines, lungs, and kidneys. The bleeding may come from neighboring blood vessels which have been eroded by the tumor or from rupture of fragile, newly formed vessels which have grown with the cancer.

Hemorrhagic diseases result from alterations in the composition of the blood which interfere with the ability of the blood to clot. In hemophilia, a blood disease which has plagued some royal houses, the deficiency is inherited. In pregnancy the blood may be deficient in fibrinogen, a substance which is needed to form the threadlike matrix of the clot. These diseases are characterized by slow bleeding from many parts of the body, such as the gums and skin. Hemorrhages resulting from reduced coagulability of the blood may also be produced by overdoses of certain drugs (anticoagulants) which are used to treat blood clots in the veins and arteries.

Loss of large amounts of blood has serious consequences. The patient goes into hemorrhagic shock (see Shock), a condition in which the circulatory system is unable to function because of a shortage of fluid. The skin is cold and clammy, the pulse is rapid and weak, and the blood pressure is low. The condition is fatal if not properly treated.

In cases of violent hemorrhage the first aim of treatment is to halt the bleeding. Where the vessels are accessible, direct pressure over the point is effective. Internal bleeding is more difficult to treat and may require surgery. After the bleeding has been controlled it is essential to replace the lost blood with transfusions of blood or a blood substitute.

Treatment of the hemorrhagic diseases is aimed at restoring the clotting power of the blood.
See also Blood; First Aid.

HEMORRHOIDS [hĕm'ə-roidz], a mass of enlarged veins in the anus, or the lower part of the rectum. Internal hemorrhoids may be caused by increased back pressure in the veins of the rectum generated by excess straining at the stool. It is suspected that obstruction of the blood flow in the veins during pregnancy may be responsible for many internal hemorrhoids. Following defecation, the hemorrhoids may protrude through the anus and frequently can be felt. The principal symptoms are bleeding, pain, and soreness associated with defecation. Severe bleeding may result in anemia. External hemorrhoids are found outside the muscular sphincter which is situated at the termination of the rectum. The cause is not known. They rarely produce symptoms unless a blood clot (thrombus) forms within the veins, resulting in severe localized pain and tenderness.

Treatment includes local application of heat, shrinking by steroid drugs, or surgery. External hemorrhoids usually do not require treatment unless blood clots develop. Mineral oil or other stool softening agents are given by mouth, and suppositories may be used to soften the stool and reduce irritation. In some cases internal hemorrhoids can be treated by injecting sclerosing, or hardening, solutions into them.

HEPARIN [hĕp'ə-rĭn], a compound that inhibits clotting of the blood. Heparin is found in the liver, muscles, lungs, spleen, and other tissues. Although its role in the body is not clear, evidence suggests that heparin may help to prevent the clotting of blood circulating in small vessels. Heparin is used in the treatment and prevention of blood clots in arteries and veins.
See also Anticoagulants.

HEPATITIS [hĕp-ə-tī'tĭs], inflammation of the liver, which may be caused by infection with bacteria or viruses, by various agents that are poisonous to the liver, or by parasites, such as liver flukes. Although hepatitis has been recognized as a disease for centuries throughout the world, its history in the United States was obscure until 1952, when it became one of the nationally reportable diseases. Since then the disease has become well recognized and seems to ebb and flow in cycles of 6 or 7 years. The highest incidence is in the 5 to 20 age group.

Infectious Hepatitis. Special virus strains have been isolated and proved to be responsible for a form of hepatitis now designated as infectious or viral hepatitis or acute catarrhal or infectious jaundice. There are at least two types: (1) infectious hepatitis caused by virus A and (2) infectious (serum) hepatitis caused by virus B. These viruses are similar in many respects, and the clinical symptoms and features of the two forms of infection are not easily distinguishable. However, the incubation period, the route and manner of dissemination, and the specific immunity conferred by each virus are different.

Infectious hepatitis caused by virus A has a relatively short period of incubation—20 to 40 days. The virus is usually transmitted through contaminated food or water or through close personal contact with individuals harboring the virus.

Infectious (serum) hepatitis caused by virus B has a relatively long incubation period—60 to 160 days or longer. This virus is found only in the blood and is transmitted through transfusion of blood or injection of materials containing human blood serum or plasma. Inadequately sterilized syringes, needles, or other surgical tools may transfer the virus. Some individuals may carry the virus indefinitely and yet have no record of hepatitis and show no evidence of liver disease. The increase in the frequency and severity of infectious hepatitis has been blamed on the growing use of injected medicines and the administration of blood, plasma, serum, and many nutritive and therapeutic fluids directly into the blood or into the muscles or the tissues underlying the skin.

The Course of Infectious Hepatitis. Following the incubation period, the early symptoms appear. These may include fever, joint pains, and enlarged lymph glands. Loss of appetite, general weakness and fatigue, chilliness, nausea, vomiting, and itching are common complaints. The liver becomes tender, and the liver and spleen may be enlarged. This stage of the disease lasts, on the average, for one week, following which jaundice (a yellowish tinting of the skin) sets in. The jaundice deepens, reaching a maximum in about one week, and then gradually subsides. With proper care the patient usually recovers. During the period of recovery the patient may be weak for some time; excessive activity may result in a relapse. Relapses may occasionally lead to chronic hepatitis and eventually to scarring of the liver (cirrhosis).

Toxic Hepatitis. Among the many agents that may damage the liver are alcohol, phosphorus, arsenic, carbon tetrachloride, chloroform, and poisonous mushrooms. The severity of the hepatitis varies with the state of the liver, heart, and circulatory system; the general health of the patient; and the concentration of the toxic agent. Shock, anemia, and previous liver disease render this organ more vulnerable to damage. Hepatitis may appear within a few hours after exposure to large amounts of the toxic substance or may develop more gradually following repeated exposures to smaller quantities of the material.

Acute Yellow Atrophy of the Liver. This is a severe form of hepatitis, which may be caused either by infection or by toxic materials. There is a rapid reduction in the size of the liver, with extensive destruction of liver cells and marked interference with function. Jaundice develops quickly, and the patient becomes confused and sleepy and finally goes into a coma. The patient usually dies from failure of liver function.
See also Liver.

HEREDITY, the transmission of physical and physiological characters from parent organisms to their offspring. These characters, as well as instincts and even certain psychological traits, are passed from generation to generation in the physical form of genes—the units of inheritance which are ranged along the chromosomes. Genetics is the science which describes the mechanics by which hereditary characters are transmitted.
See also Chromosome; Gene; Genetics.

HERMAPHRODITE [hûr-măf'rə-dīt], an animal in which

HERNIA

functional male and female reproductive organs are simultaneously present. Such an animal (earthworms, leeches, and most flatworms are examples) is said to be monoecious, in contrast to dioecious animals, in which the male and female reproductive organs are in separate individuals, and in further contrast to protandrous animals, in which male and female sex cells are produced alternately by the same gonad, or reproductive organ. The hagfishes and certain oysters fall into this last-mentioned category.

The term hermaphrodite is also applied to abnormal individuals of dioecious species in which both male and female gonads are present. In such cases, however, only one type of gonad is functional: in other words the individual is truly either male or female, and the presence of the opposite type of nonfunctional gonad is the result of abnormal development.

True hermaphrodites, contrary to what might be expected, do not reproduce without contact with another member of their species. Generally two hermaphroditic individuals come together and exchange male sex cells, a procedure called cross-fertilization.

See also REPRODUCTION; SEX.

HERNIA [hûr′nē-ə], the protrusion of tissue through an abnormal opening in the wall of the cavity which normally contains it. Hernias may develop as a consequence of a congenital defect in the wall or from weakness caused by injury. If the protruding organ can be pushed back into the cavity from which it protrudes, the hernia is *reducible*. If inflammation or scarring prevent replacement, the hernia is *irreducible* (or incarcerated).

Most hernias appear in the abdominal cavity. One of the most common involves a protrusion of the viscera into the inguinal canal, which normally leads from the abdominal cavity to the scrotum. In congenital indirect inguinal hernia a sac of tissue in this canal fails to close normally during the course of development, leaving an open channel through which a portion of the intestines can slip into the scrotal sac. In the direct type, herniation occurs through a weakened part of the lower abdominal wall just above the groin (known anatomically as Hesselbach's triangle). The direct hernia breaks into the inguinal canal but usually does not penetrate into the scrotum and rarely becomes irreducible.

Umbilical hernias may result from congenital defects in the abdominal wall, at or near the umbilicus, and usually appear in infancy or in late adult life. One form of umbilical hernia appears at birth as a complete absence of the abdominal wall at the umbilicus. Immediate surgical correction is necessary to prevent a fatal infection of the abdominal cavity. Herniation of abdominal contents may also occur at the site of a scar resulting from an operation. Hernias may appear intermittently, becoming evident only when the pressure within the abdomen is increased by straining at the stool, by lifting heavy objects, or by coughing.

In diaphragmatic hernias, abdominal organs project through the diaphragm, the muscular disc which separates the abdomen from the chest cavity. Chest organs rarely enter the abdomen because the pressure within the abdomen usually exceeds that of the chest cavity. Most diaphragmatic hernias occur where the gullet (the esophagus) pierces the diaphragm, permitting part of the stomach to pass up into the chest. Congenital absence of a large portion of the diaphragm usually results in a congenital diaphragmatic hernia which, if large, causes shortness of breath, rapid heartbeat, and constipation. Diaphragmatic hernias developing later in life may cause symptoms similar to those seen in peptic ulcer or heart disease.

Protruding intestines may be so squeezed or pinched that the intestinal channel is narrowed or completely blocked, preventing the normal passage of food and waste products along the intestinal tract. In some instances the pressure at the hernia may be sufficient to close the blood vessels of the intestinal wall, leading to gangrene of that section of the intestine (strangulation). Strangulated and obstructed hernias require immediate surgery.

In many types of hernia, surgery is the only adequate treatment. In some cases external supports (trusses) may hold the herniated tissue in place. Mild diaphragmatic hernias may sometimes be controlled by following bland diets, eating small meals, and avoiding the recumbent position after meals.

HEROIN [hĕr′ō-ĭn], a narcotic derived from morphine. Heroin is several times more potent than morphine as a pain reliever, but is also more depressing to the nervous system. Its principal danger lies in its exceptional ability to produce an intense feeling of well-being which leads to a particularly serious addiction. The importation, manufacture, and sale of heroin are prohibited in the United States by the Harrison Narcotic Act. However, it is still legally available in some countries.

See also DRUG ADDICTION; NARCOTICS.

HEROPHILUS [hĭ-rŏf′ə-ləs] **OF CHALCEDON** (fl.300 B.C.), Alexandrian surgeon known as the "father of anatomy." He is said to have been the first to dissect human and animal bodies. He studied the anatomy of the brain and spinal cord and was the first to distinguish nerves from blood vessels. He described the anatomy of the spleen, the liver, and the genital organs. As a clinician, Herophilus introduced the practice of counting the pulse rate with a water clock and of analyzing its distinct components, systole and diastole.

HERPES ZOSTER. *See* SHINGLES.

HICCUP, reflex contraction of the diaphragm. The contraction draws air into the lungs suddenly, closing the glottis (entrance to the windpipe) and causing a "hic" sound. Hiccups are normal, especially in children, and usually go away in a few minutes without treatment. They are most often caused by a rapid distention of the stomach with food, liquid, or air. Severe hiccups which do not go away can be a sign of disease of the organs—heart, lungs, stomach, gall bladder, or spleen—lying on either side of the diaphram, which cause its irritation.

The simple treatment of hiccups includes concentrating on something else, swallowing water repeatedly while holding a deep breath, or breathing into an airtight bag to increase the carbon dioxide in the lungs and blood. More complex treatment of hiccups in severely ill persons involves sedatives, breathing masks with tanks of carbon dioxide and, rarely, cutting the nerve to the diaphragm. Hiccups do not occur during sleep.

HIPPOCRATES [hĭ-pŏk′rə-tēz] (c.460–c.377 B.C.), Greek physician known as "the father of medicine." Hippocrates lived during the Golden Age of Greece and was a contemporary of Pericles, Socrates, Plato, Aristophanes, and other famous figures.

He left a large number of writings, which have been collected and incorporated in the Hippocratic Corpus, a collection of medical treatises, some written by himself, others by his colleagues, pupils, and later disciples. From these writings we form our estimate of Hippocrates and understand why he has been called the father of medicine. Three reasons are clear.

First, he separated medicine from the priests who claimed to be in direct association with the gods who sent disease. At that time epilepsy was called the "sacred disease" since it was supposedly caused by divine displeasure. Hippocrates taught that no disease was sacred and that disease resulted from natural causes.

Secondly, Hippocrates set a high moral standard for the practice of medicine, as stated in the Hippocratic oath and in numerous other places in his writings. He never ceased to stress that a good physician must love his fellow man.

A third outstanding characteristic of Hippocrates was his professional skill. His descriptions of disease are so accurate that we can make a diagnosis today, two thousand years later, by reading the case history. His descriptions of pulmonary tuberculosis, puerperal septicemia, epilepsy, tetanus, and malaria, with a few minor alterations, could be incorporated in a textbook of medicine.

His method of diagnosis still has a modern ring. First, he took the history, paying special attention to hereditary diseases in the family, the patient's occupation, where he lived, and where he had traveled; next, he inspected the patient and in certain cases practiced percussion (thumping) and auscultation (listening). Then he examined the excreta.

Hippocrates was a skilled surgeon as well as a physician. He understood the treatment of fractures, devised methods of traction in fractures, and understood the complications of skull fractures. The memory of Hippocrates is regularly invoked today in the Hippocratic oath, which is sworn to by modern physicians upon graduation from medical school.

See also HIPPOCRATIC OATH.

HIPPOCRATIC [hĭp-ə-krăt′ĭk] **OATH,** an oath based upon the ethical precepts of the ancient Greek physician Hippocrates. A modified version of the oath is administered upon graduation to the students of most medical schools.

HIRSUTISM [hûr′soōt-ĭz-əm], an unusual growth of hair, such as on the face, upper lip, and trunk in women. In most instances the cause is unknown. However, in certain disorders of the adrenal and pituitary glands, abnormal hair growth appears in conjunction with a masculinization of the body features, deepening of the voice, and loss of normal sex drives. Females born with abnormally developed reproductive organs (pseudohermaphrodites) may also display abnormal patterns of hair growth. Treatment is directed at the underlying disorder, when this is known. In other cases the local removal of hair by electrolysis, shaving, or depilatory creams is the only treatment.

HISTAMINE [hĭs′tə-mēn], an organic nitrogen-containing compound which is widely distributed in the body, particularly in the cells of the lungs, liver, and digestive tract. Although its function in the body is unknown, there is abundant evidence that histamine released from the cells is involved in allergic diseases such as asthma and hay fever. It is also suspected that histamine may play a role in the normal regulation of the stomach secretions.

Histamine in Allergy. The symptoms seen in allergic diseases are believed to result from the release of histamine, following contact with substances called allergens. The reaction of the allergens with specific proteins (antibodies) produced by the body is thought to cause the release of histamine from the cells. Histamine dilates the minute blood vessels in the tissues and increases their permeability, permitting fluid to escape from the blood stream into the spaces between the cells, causing tissue swelling. In hay fever the swelling of tissues in the nose and eyes leads to stuffy, running nose; sneezing; and itching and redness of the eyes. Allergic skin reactions may cause reddening, swelling, itching, and the formation of blisters.

A severe allergic reaction (anaphylactic shock) occasionally follows the injection of substances such as penicillin or horse serum (which is used in immunization). In these reactions skin eruptions, asthma, and shock develop suddenly, apparently resulting from the release of histamine or histaminelike substances in the tissues.

Histamine and the Stomach Glands. When injected into the body, histamine powerfully stimulates the secretion of acid by the gastric glands. This property of histamine is used clinically to test the ability of the stomach to secrete free acid.

Histamine and Headache. Certain types of headache can be produced by injecting histamine into experimental subjects. These experiments suggest that histamine may be involved in the production of some types of headache.

Antihistamines. A number of substances have been developed which seem to prevent histamine from exerting its characteristic effects. These antihistamines have proved useful in relieving the symptoms of hay fever and some other allergic reactions; however, they may cause drowsiness and other side effects.

See also ALLERGY; ANTIHISTAMINES; HISTIDINE.

HISTOPLASMOSIS [hĭs-tō-plăz-mō′sĭs], disease caused by infection with a soil fungus, *Histoplasma capsulatum.* Histoplasmosis is found throughout the world, but particularly in the Mississippi and Ohio River areas of the United States. According to some estimates, from 25 to 30 million Americans have had some form of the disease. The fungus spores are usually inhaled, producing a lung infection which is most often mild and goes unnoticed. In a few severe cases the lung invasion results in fever, coughing, sweating, and loss of weight. The disease may spread to other parts of the body.

HIVES [hīvz] **or URTICARIA** [ûr-tə-kâr′ĭə], skin eruption characterized by the temporary appearance of reddish swellings of various sizes accompanied by itching. Allergies to foods, such as fruits, nuts, or seafood, may cause hives immediately or several hours after eating. Hives from medications may develop quickly or appear within a week or so as part of a general allergic reaction involving fever, swollen lymph glands, and joint and abdominal pains. Other causes of hives include infections of the teeth, tonsils, or sinuses, worm infestations, and insect bites. Stress and emotional factors are important in chronic urticaria. In many chronic cases a cause cannot be determined.

The swellings, or wheals, usually disappear in 6 to 24 hours, but may be replaced by new swellings in the same or different areas. The wheals are filled with fluid which has escaped from the blood stream through minute blood vessels in the skin. This is thought to result in most cases from an allergic reaction involving the release of histamine or histaminelike substances from the tissues and a subsequent dilatation and increased permeability of the capillaries of the skin.

Drugs, such as antihistamines, epinephrine, and cortisone derivatives, are used to relieve the acute attack. Therapy is often ineffective; the responsible factor should be identified, and if possible, avoided.

HODGKIN'S DISEASE, disease of unknown origin characterized by enlargement of the lymph glands. Many authorities consider it to be a form of cancer while others argue that an infection is responsible. It attacks males more frequently than females and may appear at any age; young adults are often affected. The lymph glands of the neck are usually involved first, undergoing a painless enlargement. Later the lymph glands under the arms, in the groin, and in the chest and abdomen enlarge. General symptoms include loss of appetite and weight, fatigue, night sweats, intermittent fever, and anemia. Enlargement of the lymph nodes in the chest with pressure on the surrounding tissues may produce cough, difficulty in breathing, and chest pain. Expansion of the lymph nodes which lie on the rear wall of the abdomen may compress the contents of the abdomen, displacing one or both kidneys. Other manifestations of the disease may be found in the lungs, bones, nervous system, and skin. The spleen and liver are often enlarged. In some patients itching may be the major complaint. A curious unexplained phenomenon in Hodgkin's disease is the appearance of pain in the involved areas following consumption of alcohol.

X-ray therapy is the preferred treatment and may relieve symptoms for weeks, months, or years. Nitrogen mustard has also proved useful. Although these and other methods of treatment may temporarily improve the patient's condition, they do not cure the disease. Despite this some patients with Hodgkin's disease may survive for as long as 20 years.

HOMEOPATHY [hō-mē-ŏp′ə-thē], system of medical therapy developed by Samuel Hahnemann, German physician, about 1800. Hahnemann believed that stimulating the body's resistance to disease was all-important, and that illness should be treated according to its symptoms. Assuming that like cures like, he thought that a drug which could produce disease symptoms in a healthy person would cure a sick person with similar symptoms.

According to homeopathy, the smaller the dose of a drug, the greater its curative powers. Although this was incorrect, it led to a more scientific use of drugs in a time when a prescription might contain 96 ingredients. Hahnemann tested individual drugs for their effect on normal, healthy people,* and used this experience in selecting drugs for his patients—a novel notion at the time.

Homeopathy was a revolutionary concept in medicine in an era when bleeding was the accepted treatment for most illnesses. Rarely practiced today, homeopathy recognized the importance of the body's resistance to disease. It presaged concepts of immunity and of stimulating resistance to infection with vaccination. The great value of homeopathy was that it counteracted the harmful, almost barbaric remedies of the early 19th century.

HOMEOSTASIS [hō-mē-ə-stā′sĭs], or steady-state regulation, the tendency of all living organisms to maintain their internal composition and state with relative constancy and within limits appropriate for continued functioning. Homeostatic regulation enables an organism to perpetuate itself under varying environmental stresses. In 1939, Walter B. Cannon of Harvard University set forth this concept in his classic work, *The Wisdom of the Body.* The term was coined initially to describe steady-state regulations in animals, but later assumed usage in many other fields. The concept is also employed in ecology for predatory-prey relationships and succession in plant and animal communities. In embryology it applies to maturation of the individual, development of cells, tissues, organs, and systems. In genetics homeostasis applies to the action of genes and to the genetics of population growth and survival.

Steady-state regulation may be applied to all physiological processes. Homeostasis is recognized in the control of blood-sugar levels, the menstrual cycle, blood formation, acid-base relationships, reflex activity, regulation of blood pressure, and body fluid balance.

HOOKWORM, infestation with the intestinal roundworm *Ancylostoma duodenale,* which is found in Europe, North Africa, and the Far East, or *Necator americanus,* which inhabits primarily tropical regions. Heavily infested areas are found in parts of the southern United States and in other localities where sanitary conditions are poor and where soil conditions are suitable for the development of the larvae.

The larvae develop in moist soil, where they may survive for several weeks after being deposited. In hookworm regions, most heavy infestations occur in children who walk barefooted. The larvae penetrate the skin, sometimes causing an eruption called "ground itch." After entering a blood vessel and being carried to the lungs, the organisms migrate up the windpipe to the throat where they are swallowed and carried into the digestive tract. The parasites cut into and lodge on the walls of the upper small intestine from which they obtain blood for food. The organisms reach their adult length of about ½ in. in the intestines. The eggs hatch in the feces or soil and the cycle resumes if the larvae-infested feces are deposited in moist soil.

Light infestations in well-nourished adults may produce no symptoms. In other cases larvae passing through the lungs may produce bronchitis. There may be abdominal discomfort, nausea, or diarrhea. Severe anemia may result from loss of blood since the worms secrete an anticoagulant substance which inhibits blood from clotting at the site of the worm attachment, permitting continuous hemorrhage. In heavy infestations this may cause weakness, pallor, fluid swellings (edema), and heart failure. In children physical and mental development may be retarded.

Antihookworm drugs, such as tetrachlorethylene are highly effective in reducing the number of worms in the intestine. Iron in the form of ferrous sulfate, or its equivalent, is given in large amounts to correct the anemia. Hookworm can be prevented by the sanitary disposal of human excreta and by wearing shoes.

HOPKINS, SIR FREDERICK GOWLAND (1861–1947), British biochemist who shared the Nobel Prize in 1929 with Christian Eijkman, for the "discovery of the growth-stimulating vitamins." A pioneer investigator in nutritional chemistry, Hopkins raised rats on artificial diets, demonstrating that fats, proteins, and carbohydrates alone were not adequate to produce normal growth and health, and that other substances, later known as vitamins, were needed to supplement the diet. Hopkins also studied the amino acids, the basic building blocks of proteins, and investigated the chemistry of muscular contractions.

HORMONES. *See* ENDOCRINE GLANDS.

HOSPITAL. The earliest hospitals date back to the ancient pre-Christian empires of India, Persia, Egypt, Greece, and Rome. Treatment of the ill was often closely associated with religious practice. In Egypt medical instruction and treatment were given by priests, while in Rome and Greece the ill gathered in temples where they would spend the night in the hope of receiving a divine cure.

Charity hospitals appeared, first in Rome, and later in other parts of Europe in the Middle Ages, under the influence of Christianity. Hospitals became well established, both in the monasteries of Europe and in the Muslim empire of the East. The latter were highly developed as in the hospital founded at Cairo in 1283, which had separate sections for women and for patients with fever and eye diseases.

Hospital development received its greatest stimulus in modern times from discoveries concerning the nature of infection. The success of the Scottish surgeon Joseph Lister in reducing postoperative infection through the use of the antiseptic phenol (carbolic acid) opened the era of aseptic surgery and helped establish the hospital as a place where the bacteria-free conditions necessary for surgery could best be achieved.

The development of the X ray, of elaborate medical apparatus, and of complex laboratory procedures for examining blood, urine, and spinal fluid has given the modern hospital a strategic role as the site of intensive diagnostic and therapeutic procedures and team medical practice, which represent the best combined capacities of modern medicine.

The Modern Hospital

Medical Services. The medical services of the modern general hospital are departmentalized into sections which treat specific categories of illness.

The medical section is subdivided into specialties which treat diseases of the blood (hematology); diseases of the heart and circulatory system (cardiovascular); diseases of the nervous system (neurology); diseases of the endocrine glands, such as the thyroid and adrenal glands (endocrinology); diseases of body chemistry (metabolism); diseases of the digestive tract (gastrointestinal); and diseases of the lungs (pulmonary); among others.

The surgical section includes subspecialties for general surgery, and for surgery of the brain and nervous system, the heart, the eyes, ears, nose, and throat (EENT), blood vessels, and other specific structures. The obstetrical section, which handles childbirth, is sometimes included here.

Separate sections are also established for psychiatry, neurology, and dermatology.

The hospital provides unexcelled laboratory facilities for diagnosis. Specimens of sputum, pus, blood, and scrapings from various tissues are sent to the bacteriology laboratory to identify suspected disease-producing microorganisms. The accurate identification of a specific organism may enable the physician to select exactly the right antibiotic. Blood and urine samples are sent to the chemistry section to detect abnormal concentrations of substances which may be clues to disease. Samples of tissue from tumors are sent to the pathology section, which has the important responsibility of distinguishing cancerous from noncancerous tissue. Recordings of the electrical activity of the heart and brain are made by the electrocardiograph and electroencephalograph sections, respectively.

The radiography unit takes X rays to detect fractures and the presence of tumors. Often a special portable X-ray apparatus is available, which can be brought to the bed of a patient. The radiotherapy unit makes use of apparatus which generates radiation for purposes of treatment, such as in cases of cancer.

The physical medicine section utilizes an assortment of specialized devices, such as diathermy units, whirlpool baths, ultraviolet lamps, and high-frequency (ultrasonic) sound generators. The occupational therapy unit provides an opportunity for patients to engage in productive and creative handcrafts, while exercising various body parts.

The outpatient department treats patients who have been released from the hospital and who require follow-up care or checkups, and those who do not require hospitalization but who need the special diagnostic or therapeutic services of the hospital.

A fairly recent development in hospital care is the social service department, which deals with the personal problems of the patient with respect to his family and relatives and his economic situation. This is part of the emerging concept of environmental medicine, which places emphasis on the patient as an individual with both medical and social problems.

Wards and Private and Semiprivate Accommodations. Many voluntary hospitals (those which are supported largely by charitable contributions) offer types of accom-

HOUSEFLY

modations which differ in terms of cost, physical surroundings, personal services, and privileges (for example, visiting hours). Private accommodations have one bed to a room, and the patient is attended by his own physician. Semiprivate rooms have two or more beds. Here, too, the patient uses his own physician. Wards have four or more beds, and medical care is usually administered by the hospital staff.

The Hospital as an Educational Institution

Some hospitals are associated with medical schools and provide clinical instruction during the various phases of undergraduate medical training. The medical house staff of the average hospital consists of interns and residents receiving postgraduate training.

Interns. Interns serve for one or two years after graduation from medical school. This period of service is generally regarded as a postgraduate requirement for appointment to a residency, for advancement to specialty training, or for private practice.

Residents are graduate interns who seek further educational opportunities leading to a career in a specialized field of medicine. The period of training varies from one to five years, and upon graduation the resident is eligible for certification by the various specialty boards.

The Visiting and Resident Staff. The staff of the hospital includes, in addition to the physicians in training (the residents and the interns), the attending physicians, who have completed their training and who serve on a full-time basis in the hospital, and the working staff, composed of physicians who maintain private practices or have other duties.

Clinical responsibility is vested in the visiting and attending staff in accordance with the rank conferred on them by the board of trustees of the hospital. The supreme authority in each of the specialties is known as the "chief" or "director" of the division. In university hospitals he is the professor on whom the conduct of the service and the teaching associated with it depend.

Nursing Service

Ward nurses are responsible for the execution of medical orders and the administration of medication. They also assist the medical staff in the diagnosis and treatment of patients. In modern hospital practice, nurses are restricted to professional nursing duties and have been largely relieved of the clerical and housekeeping tasks which formerly consumed much of their time.

Special Hospitals

Special hospitals treat particular categories of patients who may require treatment which is unobtainable in a general hospital or who need special techniques of isolation and restraint.

The first hospital used exclusively for the mentally ill was built in Virginia in 1773. Since then the trend has continued toward specialized treatment of psychiatric patients in mental hospitals.

Patients requiring long-term hospitalization for certain conditions may be sent to a hospital specializing in chronic diseases. This may be a wing of a general hospital or a separate unit.

Although special hospitals for tubercular patients are still maintained, it is expected that as the number of beds needed for this purpose declines, tuberculosis sanitariums will be supplanted by special wards in general hospitals.

Less well-known special hospitals include those which treat exclusively diseases of the eyes and ears, tumors, joint diseases, or other restricted categories of disease.

HOUSEFLY, an ubiquitous two-winged insect, *Musca domestica*, of the order Diptera, family Muscidae, found in all inhabited regions of the world and second only to the mosquito in its harmful relations to man. The housefly has a grayish or black body covered with short stiff bristles. The mouth parts form a two-lobed proboscis suspended from a conical projection, the rostrum, on the lower part of the head. In the proboscis are two channels, one for intake of liquids, the other for the ejection of saliva. Flies eat by lapping up liquid food, or by liquefying solid food with saliva before taking it into the proboscis; houseflies do not bite. They have a phenomenal birth rate; the females lay eggs every two weeks and may produce as many as 20 broods a season. Within a few months, the offspring of a single fly may number into the millions.

Housefly eggs are laid in refuse, filth, manure, and similar organic residues; for this reason houseflies are potential carriers of the microorganisms found in such surroundings. The housefly has been identified as a carrier of many disease-producing organisms including those that cause cholera, dysentery, and typhoid fever. The threat of these diseases has been much reduced, especially in slums and other overpopulated urban areas, by increased emphasis on sanitation and the elimination of the breeding places of houseflies. Flies still remain a problem in rural dairy and cattle regions where they lay their eggs in manure. Insecticides, however, offer a means of control.
See also FLY.

HUNCHBACK or KYPHOSIS, a curvature of the spine in which the back is rounded. The deformity involves that part of the spine located between the waist and the neck and may result from poor posture, arthritis of the spine, spinal tuberculosis, bone disease, or injury. Kyphosis developing in adult life is called adult round back and may be associated with pain, weakness of the back, and fatigue.

HUNTER, JOHN (1728–93), Scottish surgeon who made many important contributions to the techniques of surgery and the knowledge of anatomy and pathology. A student of the venereal diseases, he acquired a syphilitic chancre when he inoculated himself with what he erroneously thought was gonorrhea. He introduced a technique for ligating, or tying off a diseased artery some distance from the lesion, a procedure known as Hunter's operation. He also classified the teeth and described the descent of the testicles and the structure of the placenta.

HYALURONIDASE [hī-ə-loo-rŏn'ī-dās], an enzyme which breaks down hyaluronic acid, a substance found in human connective tissue. Hyaluronic acid forms a gel which impedes the passage of fluids between the cells. Hyaluronidase, by decomposing hyaluronic acid, renders the intercellular substances more liquid, promoting the movement and absorption of fluids through the tissues. Hyaluronidase is used principally to aid in the introduction of liquids directly into the tissues. It may be added to solutions which are to be passed into the body through a needle in the thigh or other soft tissues, or it may be mixed with local anesthetics to promote quick absorption following injection. It has also been injected to reduce swellings resulting from collections of blood in the tissues. Hyaluronidase is nontoxic, but cannot be used in infected areas where it might spread the infection.

HYDROCEPHALUS, condition in which there is an increased amount of fluid within and around the cavities (ventricles) of the brain. Ordinarily the brain floats in the cerebrospinal fluid which is produced within the ventricles. This fluid is absorbed by the blood vessels contained in the tissues encasing the brain (the meninges). Obstruction of the flow of fluid from the point where it is produced to the point where it is absorbed results in hydrocephalus. This may develop from a congenital malformation of the brain or from tumors, infections, or hemorrhages. A "nonobstructive" type of hydrocephalus, resulting from interference with fluid absorption at the meninges, sometimes follows inflammation of the meninges. In infants, hydrocephalus results in enlargement of the head. The scalp is thin and shiny and the scalp veins are congested. Mental development is retarded and blindness and difficulty in walking may appear. When the condition develops later in life, the symptoms are headache, vomiting, slow heartbeat, and stupor.

Treatment is surgical. Whenever possible the obstruction is attacked directly. However, in the congenital cases this is usually not possible and a number of ingenious operations have been devised to divert the fluid from the ventricles by means of plastic tubes, introduced into sites such as the ureter, chest, abdominal cavity, or the blood stream where the cerebrospinal fluid can be excreted or absorbed. While formerly most victims of congenital hydrocephalus did not develop into normal adults, improved surgical techniques offer promise of better results.

HYDRONEPHROSIS [hī-drō-nĭ-frō'sĭs], dilatation of parts of the kidney by damned-up urine. This may result from obstruction of some portion of the urinary tract, caused by pressure on the tract from tumors, an enlarged prostate gland, congenital abnormalities, adhesions, or a pregnant womb, or by the presence of stones within the tract. An important cause of congenital hydronephrosis is an aberrant artery lying across the ureter (the tube which carries urine from the kidney to the bladder). In hydronephrosis the kidney may contain several quarts of fluid and the kidney tissue may atrophy from the internal pressure. Mild hydronephrosis may present no symptoms. In advanced cases the kidney is enlarged, painful, and tender. Infection may occur, resulting in fever and pus in the urine. When the obstruction is intermittent, there may be attacks of pain with increased kidney size and a lessening of urinary flow, followed by excessive urination when the attack subsides. Severe hydronephrosis may result in kidney failure and death if both kidneys are involved. Frequently, the fluid can be drained by passing a catheter (a tubelike instrument) through the urinary tract into the kidney. In many cases surgery is necessary to remove an obstruction.
See also KIDNEY.

HYDROPHOBIA. See RABIES.

HYPERACIDITY [hī-pər-ə-sĭd'ə-tē], increased rate of acid production by the glands of the stomach. The only disease in which hyperacidity is definitely known to play a role is duodenal ulcer. It has not yet been determined whether the excessive secretion in these cases is responsible for, or is caused by, the ulcer. The "indigestion" which sometimes follows stimulation of the stomach by rich and highly seasoned foods has sometimes been attributed to hyperacidity. Although these foods do cause a temporary increase in the secretion of acid, it has not been shown that acid production is excessive or that the symptoms result from this secretion. It has been argued, however, that because antacids are occasionally helpful in relieving such distress, the possible role of oversecretion of acid in these cases should not be overlooked.
See also DIGESTION.

HYPERGLYCEMIA [hī-pər-glī-sē'mē-ə], abnormally high concentration of sugar in the blood. Hyperglycemia does not produce symptoms unless sugar spills into the urine. Important causes of the condition are diabetes, acromegaly, hyperthyroidism, diseases of the adrenal glands, and the administration of cortisone and related drugs.
See also DIABETES MELLITUS.

HYPERHIDROSIS [hī-pər-hī-drō'sĭs], excessive sweating, which may involve the entire body or be limited to particular areas such as the palms, feet, or underarm regions. The general type may appear in fevers and endocrine disorders, in obese persons, and during the change-of-life. The local form may be seen in highly sensitive, anxious persons. In a form of hyperhidrosis called bromidrosis the sweat has a foul odor, resulting from the consumption of aromatic compounds, such as garlic, or from the bacterial decomposition of the sweat. Treatment of hyperhidrosis and bromidrosis consists in the application of astringents, antiperspirants, and deodorants. When the feet are involved the shoes and stockings should be changed twice daily.

HYPERINSULINISM [hī-pər-ĭn'sə-lĭn-ĭz-əm], overproduction of the hormone insulin, which may be caused by an insulin-producing tumor of the pancreas gland. Since insulin promotes the passage of sugar from the blood into the tissues, hyperinsulinism results in a lowering of the blood sugar concentration. In these cases prolonged fasting or vigorous exercise may drastically lower the blood sugar causing sweating, trembling, weakness, hunger, headaches, and other symptoms, which are quickly relieved by the administration of sugar. Surgical removal of the tumor cures the condition, unless the growth is cancerous.
See also DIABETES MELLITUS; INSULIN; PANCREAS.

HYPERTENSION, or high blood pressure, is defined as the repeated elevation of the systolic or diastolic blood pressure above that considered normal for persons of a similar ethnic and environmental background. Hypertension is itself not a specific disease, but a manifestation of any one of several distinctly different disorders, such as kidney disease, hormonal imbalance, and disorders of the central nervous system.

In the measurement of blood pressure, two determinations are made: systolic pressure, which is the peak pressure reached during the heart's contraction, and diastolic pressure, the lowest pressure present when the heart is resting and filling. Medically the most significant form of hypertension is a persistent elevation of diastolic pressure, thought to be due to an increased resistance of the small muscular arteries, called arterioles, in relatively distant parts of the circulation.

Although the precise cause of hypertension is usually unknown (essential hypertension), the type of damage to the blood vessels is similar in all cases. Such damage to the blood vessels supplying the kidney may lead to a worsening of the hypertension. Likewise, heart failure is a frequent complication of hypertension because of the increasing stress placed on the heart by the damaged arterioles. Several drugs are effective in lowering blood pressure and in maintaining it in a normal range. These agents are more effective if the hypertension is detected and treated early.

See also BLOOD: *Blood pressure*.

HYPERTHYROIDISM [hī-pər-thī′roid-ĭz-əm], condition marked by excessive secretion of thyroid hormones. The cause of the disease is not known. It occurs most frequently in middle-aged women, often in members of the same family. The condition is marked by excitability, rapid pulse, weight loss, warm skin, elevation of the basal metabolic rate, diarrhea, and, occasionally, protruding eyeballs (exophthalmos). Heart involvement is common and in certain cases heart failure occurs. Treatment consists of the administration of radioactive iodine, drugs which suppress the formation of thyroid hormone, or surgery.
See also THYROID-BLOCKING DRUGS; THYROID GLAND.

HYPERVENTILATION SYNDROME, condition caused by overbreathing, usually resulting from emotional stress and anxiety in persons suffering from psychoneurotic disorders. The patient is usually not aware that he is overbreathing; over a period of time the concentration of carbon dioxide in the blood is altered, leading to the characteristic symptoms which include dizziness, breathlessness, and numbness and tingling sensations in the fingers, toes, and lips. If overbreathing continues, the patient may lose consciousness or develop convulsions. The attack can be halted by having the patient breathe in and out of a paper bag to elevate the carbon dioxide level of the blood. Further treatment consists of psychotherapy.

HYPNOSIS [hĭp-nō′sĭs], a psychological state of altered attention and awareness in which the individual is unusually receptive and responsive to suggestions.

Theories of hypnosis are numerous, but no single theory is generally accepted as completely explaining all aspects of hypnosis. One of the oldest theories regards hypnosis to be a form of sleep. This concept originated in 1784 and was further developed by the Russian physiologist Ivan Pavlov, who is known for his work on conditioned reflexes. Pavlov noted that the repetition of certain stimulations induced sleep in experimental animals. Before the animal lapsed into sleep, however, it passed through a drowsy state which Pavlov identified as a hypnotic trance. This theory is contradicted by evidence which indicates that the hypnotized person is not asleep: the knee reflex, which is absent in sleep, is present in the hypnotic state, and recordings of brain waves show the typical patterns of the waking state.

The Hypnotic State. Perhaps the most outstanding characteristic of the hypnotic state is the suggestibility of the subject. He readily accepts and responds to ideas offered by the hypnotist. He may even carry out suggestions offered to him while in hypnosis after he emerges from hypnosis. This is known as posthypnotic suggestion.

The hypnotized person may be in a light, medium, or deep trance. In the light trance the eyes are closed, breathing becomes slower, the facial muscles are fixed, and the subject is able to carry out simple posthypnotic suggestions. In the medium trance there is a partial amnesia, and simple hallucinations can be induced. The deep trance, or somnambulistic state, is characterized by the subject's ability to maintain the trance with the eyes open; a total amnesia; control over physiological functions, such as the pulse rate and blood pressure; and the ability to anesthetize a part of the body. There is also a *plenary* or *stuporous* trance in which the subject remains absolutely quiet and responds only to suggestions of the hypnotist. This state is achieved in only a small number of subjects and requires considerable effort to produce.

Contrary to popular belief, there is no possibility of the subject not awakening as a result of an accident to the hypnotist. It is also not true that a hypnotized subject is under the will or power of the hypnotist. As has already been noted, hypnosis is a co-operative venture between the subject and the hypnotist: no control can be exercised without the subject's implied or actual consent.

Applications. Hypnosis is used in dentistry, obstetrics, and in surgery to achieve anesthesia. Psychiatrists occasionally use hypnosis to enable the patient to recall early painful experiences he might otherwise not recall.

Hypnosis has also been used to overcome undesirable habits, such as excessive smoking, overeating, and nail biting. A valuable adjunct to this treatment is autohypnosis: the subject is taught to induce a trance by himself. This technique reinforces the suggestions of the doctor and reduces the number of office visits required.

HYPNOTICS [hĭp-nŏt′ĭks], drugs which induce sleep. They depress the activity of the brain, producing sedation when given in small dosages and sleep when given in larger amounts. A hypnotic should ideally induce sleep quickly and reliably without upsetting the stomach or causing a preliminary period of excitation. It should act over a sufficiently long period and in addition should not be toxic or addicting. Although a number of excellent hypnotics are available, none fully meets all of these criteria.

HYPOCHONDRIASIS [hī-pō-kŏn-drī′ə-sĭs], a term describing persons who are unusually preoccupied with their physical health, dwelling on symptoms that most persons would ignore. At times, fatigue, slight palpitations, or other minor variations in body activity may provoke an attack of anxiety. Hypochondriasis may be seen in senile persons, in those suffering from brain damage, or in certain forms of neurosis and psychosis.

HYPOGLYCEMIA [hī-pō-glī-sē′mē-ə], abnormally low con-

centration of sugar in the blood. Hypoglycemia is most common in diabetic patients who have taken an excess of insulin, a hormone which stimulates the absorption of sugar from the blood by the cells of the body. It may also develop in cases of tumors of the pancreas (the gland which secretes insulin) and in diseases affecting other glands of the body. The low blood sugar level causes weakness, tremors, hunger, cold sweats, dizziness, and headache. The individual may appear wild, confused, or lapse into a coma. Occasionally such persons are arrested for drunkenness. The condition is quickly corrected by giving sugar by mouth or injection.
See also DIABETES MELLITUS.

HYPOGONADISM [hī-pō-gō'năd-ĭz-əm], partial or complete lack of functioning of the gonads, or sex glands. The condition appears primarily in the male, resulting from disturbances within the testes or from disorders of the pituitary gland in the skull. In the latter case the pituitary fails to secrete the hormone which normally stimulates the gonads (pituitary gonadotrophic hormone).

Disturbances within the testes most often result from abnormal development, although in some cases exposure to radiation may be responsible. In these disorders inadequate secretion of male hormones before puberty may produce eunuchoidism, a condition characterized by a juvenile high-pitched voice, female fat distribution, sparse beard, poor muscular development, large breasts, small genitalia, and absent or reduced sexual drive. Hypogonadism occurring after puberty may cause comparatively few changes. In some testicular lesions male hormone production is normal, but sperm production is impaired, resulting in sterility. This may also be caused by failure of both testes to descend before puberty.

Pituitary hypogonadism may result from pituitary tumors, inflammations, or from other causes. The nature of the condition depends upon whether there is an undersecretion of only the gonad-stimulating hormone of the pituitary, or whether other pituitary hormones are affected as well. In "pituitary dwarfism," which results from underactivity of the pituitary in childhood, the growth hormone of the pituitary is also in short supply. In cases where the pituitary gonadotrophic hormone alone is involved the characteristic features are small testes and lack of development of the secondary sex characteristics. In most cases, sperm production is deficient.

The hormone deficiencies found in hypogonadism are effectively treated with male hormone preparations. Various forms of therapy including hormones and vitamins have been used to treat the infertility associated with hypogonadism; however, these treatments have generally proved unsatisfactory.

HYSTERECTOMY [hĭs-tə-rĕk'tə-mē], surgical removal of the uterus, or womb, which may be necessary in cases of tumors of the uterus and the cervix (the neck of the uterus), in rupture of the uterus during prolonged childbirth, or in cases of chronic excessive bleeding.

In a total hysterectomy the uterus and the cervix are removed; in a subtotal hysterectomy the cervix is retained. In cases of cancer it may be necessary to perform a radical panhysterectomy. This involves removing the uterus, the ovaries, the fallopian tubes which connect the ovaries, and the lymph glands which surround the uterus.

The operation may be performed through incisions in the back of the vagina or through an incision in the abdomen. The ligaments which hold the uterus in place are cut, the blood vessels and fallopian tubes are clamped and severed, following which the uterus is extracted. Although childbearing is no longer possible after hysterectomy, normal sexual activity is not interfered with.

HYSTERIA, in psychiatry, an emotional illness which mimics physical illness without organic disease. The word is derived from the Greek *hystera*, meaning "uterus," because Hippocrates believed hysterical symptoms occurred only in women. People suffering from hysteria were also believed to be possessed by the devil. Good descriptions of the consequences of such beliefs are given in Aldous Huxley's *The Devils of Loudon* (1952) and Arthur Miller's *The Crucible* (1953). It is now known that hysteric manifestations can occur in both sexes, at all ages; but more often among people with little education, especially in those in early adulthood or during periods of great stress, such as war.

Hysterical symptoms are preceded by an anxiety-producing situation, and serve as a solution to underlying psychic conflict concerning sexual roles, job frustrations, or family relationships. After physical symptoms appear, the hysteric is typically calm and tranquil, a state called *la belle indifférence* ("beautiful indifference").
See also AMNESIA; EPILEPSY; NEUROSIS.

I

ICHTHYOSIS [ĭk-thē-ō'sĭs], popularly called fish skin, is a skin disease characterized by excessively dry and scaly skin. It most commonly affects the legs, but in severe cases virtually the entire body surface may be involved. Ichthyosis usually appears in several members of the same family, developing shortly after birth. The scaliness and dryness are worse during the winter months and improve and sometimes completely disappear, in hot, humid weather. The annoyance and unsightliness of ichthyosis can be greatly relieved by the application of greasy oils and creams to the skin. A hot, soapless bath with coarse salt added greatly increases the effectiveness of this treatment.

IMMERSION FOOT AND TRENCH FOOT, circulatory disturbances which arise from prolonged exposure to below-freezing cold and dampness. Trench foot was seen frequently during World War I. In World War II sailors

IMMORTALITY

and airmen adrift for days in the ocean acquired a similar disturbance which was labeled "immersion foot." Exhaustion, malnutrition, chilling of the body, and immobility contribute to the effect produced by the prolonged cold. The blood vessels and nerves of the leg are affected, resulting in numbness, redness, swelling, and later, burning and throbbing pain. In severe cases gangrene appears, and amputation may be necessary. Recurring burning and tingling sensations, excessive sweating, and sensitivity to cold may be present for several years following recovery.

IMMORTALITY [ĭm-ôr-tăl'ə-tē], continued existence after death. The belief in immortality has been widely held among primitive peoples, as is shown by such customs as the putting of food and weapons in graves. Belief in immortality, however, does not always involve the idea that life beyond the grave is a better life. In this connection the words of Achilles in the *Odyssey* indicate the ancient Greek view of life after death: "I would sooner be a hireling servant of the most penurious man alive than ruler over all the kingdoms of the dead."

Immortality in the sense of a *better* life and an eternal one has been maintained on philosophical as well as religious grounds. Plato in the *Phaedo* advances the view that at death the soul, being set free from the body, which is concerned with imperfect and transient things, goes to be at one with eternal goodness, eternal beauty, and the other Platonic "forms," which are at once perfect and beyond the reach of change, and to which the soul is akin. Immanuel Kant, in his *Critique of Practical Reason*, maintains that we have an obligation to be perfect, and hence, according to his principle that "ought" implies "can," it must be possible for us to be perfect. But this is clearly impossible within the limits of the present life, and therefore there must be a future one involving the possibility of continued improvement.

Not all religions, however, lay stress on personal immortality. Hinduism does not, and the Buddhist goal of nirvana has been interpreted as release from the burden of existence. Nor is there much detailed positive teaching on immortality within the Old Testament.

For the Christian, immortality is bound up with Christ's victory over death at the Resurrection (I Cor. 15:12ff.). Basically, Christian belief in immortality follows from Christian belief in God. If God is what Christianity maintains Him to be, the God of love revealed in Jesus Christ, it is hard to imagine Him allowing the love which His children have for one another to be finally defeated by death. The doctrine of the resurrection of the body and St. Paul's conception of a spiritual body indicate that in some sense, however undefined, Christianity envisages a continuance of what we now know as the best elements of bodily life. In this way the Christian view differs from some of the Greek views of immortality, according to which the body was a tomb to be escaped from at death.

A good deal of traditional teaching on Hell would be classified as mythology by theologians such as Rudolf Bultmann. But central to Christian teaching remains the thought that we must give an account of our lives to God, together with the other thought that in any such future judgment we can put our trust, not in our own achievements, but in Christ.

The Christian hope is that no longer "seeing through a glass darkly" (I Cor. 13:12), we shall be able to enter into fuller and richer personal relations with God and with each other than are possible in this life.

IMMUNITY [ĭ-mū'nə-tē], the ability to resist infectious diseases. In nature, disease does not strike indiscriminately. Germs that attack animals leave plants unaffected, and, conversely, animals do not suffer from plant diseases. The susceptibility of organisms varies enormously. The rat is many times more resistant to bacterial poisons than the guinea pig, and the chicken does not succumb to anthrax, a disease of cattle.

The above are examples of native, or inborn, immunity to disease. This immunity depends, in part, upon the suitability of the host organism for the infecting germ. Thus, although the chicken is ordinarily immune to anthrax, it can be made a comfortable habitat for the anthrax bacteria by lowering its body temperature. Of great importance in native immunity are certain large white blood cells (phagocytes), which are able to migrate to sites of bacterial invasion, to engulf, digest, and remove intruding organisms.

If native resistance to disease is insufficient, an infection develops. The invading organism multiplies in the body and the process culminates in death unless the existing defenses win out or new substances are brought into play.

Antibodies. Certain tissues of the body respond to the presence of foreign elements by producing special proteins called antibodies, which react with and neutralize specific infecting bacteria. The antibodies produced in response to one kind of infection usually have no effect on another kind. The body continues to produce these substances for some time after the disease has passed.

In many instances the body can produce antibodies rapidly if a new infection should arise, even though the production of antibodies has declined. The body's ability to produce antibodies explains why a single attack of measles is usually sufficient to provide lifelong immunity from the disease. This process, in which immunity develops following exposure to the disease, is termed natural-acquired immunity.

Vaccines and Active Immunity. It is not necessary to rely upon accidental exposure to a disease to produce an immunity. Through the use of specially prepared suspensions of dead or weakened germs, the body may be induced to produce antibodies without actually contracting the illness. These preparations retain their ability to stimulate antibody production, although they are unable to cause infection. Such preparations are termed vaccines and provide immunity against smallpox, yellow fever, poliomyelitis, and other diseases. An immunity produced in this fashion is termed an artificial-active immunity.

Antitoxins and Passive Immunity. Under certain circumstances the body may not be able to produce antibodies rapidly enough to fight disease. In lockjaw (tetanus), for example, the infecting bacteria give off a deadly poison, which is responsible for the symptoms of the disease. For this purpose injections of tetanus antitoxin are given. The antitoxin is a preparation that contains specific antibodies to neutralize a specific bacterial poison. The temporary immunity produced by this process is termed

IMMUNITY

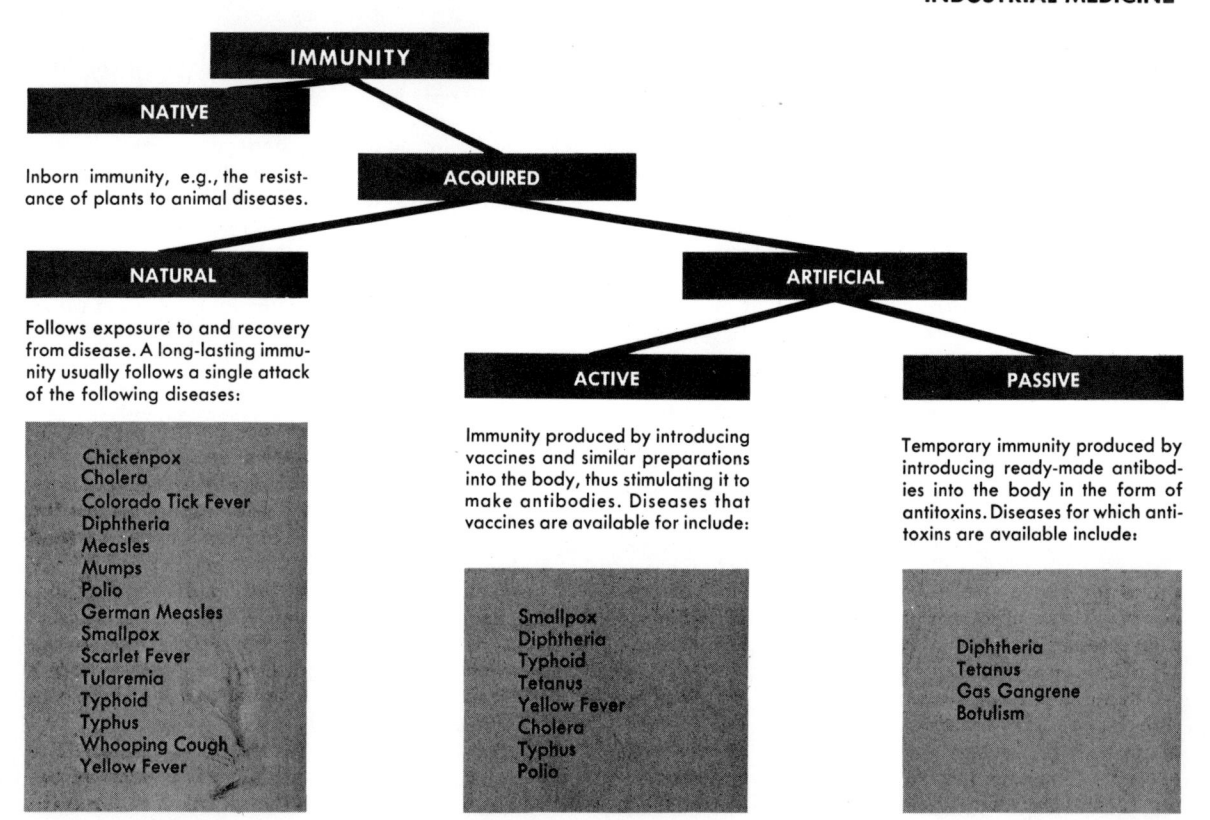

NATIVE
Inborn immunity, e.g., the resistance of plants to animal diseases.

ACQUIRED

NATURAL
Follows exposure to and recovery from disease. A long-lasting immunity usually follows a single attack of the following diseases:

- Chickenpox
- Cholera
- Colorado Tick Fever
- Diphtheria
- Measles
- Mumps
- Polio
- German Measles
- Smallpox
- Scarlet Fever
- Tularemia
- Typhoid
- Typhus
- Whooping Cough
- Yellow Fever

ARTIFICIAL

ACTIVE
Immunity produced by introducing vaccines and similar preparations into the body, thus stimulating it to make antibodies. Diseases that vaccines are available for include:

- Smallpox
- Diphtheria
- Typhoid
- Tetanus
- Yellow Fever
- Cholera
- Typhus
- Polio

PASSIVE
Temporary immunity produced by introducing ready-made antibodies into the body in the form of antitoxins. Diseases for which antitoxins are available include:

- Diphtheria
- Tetanus
- Gas Gangrene
- Botulism

"passive," since the body does not actively produce its own antibodies. Passive immunity against poliomyelitis and measles is provided by injections of gamma globulin, a fraction of blood that contains many antibodies.

Another type of passive immunity is given by a mother to her unborn child through the circulation of blood (and antibodies) across the membrane that connects the blood supply of the mother and child. After birth the child continues to receive antibodies from the mother through nursing. These substances protect the child against infectious diseases until it is able to produce an adequate supply of its own antibodies.

There is a growing awareness that not all acquired resistance, natural or artificial, can be explained on the basis of antibody production. An increase in the effectiveness of the bacteria-engulfing white blood cells could contribute to immunity. In tuberculosis and undulant fever (brucellosis), the white blood cells are destroyed by the bacteria that they have engulfed. After exposure to the disease, however, the white blood cells of certain animals are not so easily destroyed.

All of the above mechanisms have been observed in man and other mammals. Our knowledge of resistance in the lower animals is extremely limited. In plants there does not appear to be antibody production; however, there is native immunity to disease, and various strains of useful plants that show greater resistance have been selected for cultivation.

See also ANTIBODIES AND ANTIGENS; ANTITOXIN; TOXIN; VACCINATION; VACCINES.

IMPETIGO [ĭm-pə-tī′gō], a common, rapidly spreading, contagious skin infection which primarily affects children. Although previously attributed to uncleanliness, it is caused by bacteria, usually streptococci or staphylococci. The first sign may be a small itchy blister just inside the nose. Dirty fingers carry the germs to nearby parts of the face, scalp, and hands, where secondary infections soon begin. The tiny blisters are followed by open weeping areas, which are soon covered by golden-brown scales. Occasionally there are constitutional symptoms, such as fever, chills, and malaise. Rarely, impetigo is followed by nephritis, a severe kidney ailment.

Treatment is simple, beginning with a good wash and followed by regular cleansing. Antibiotic ointments may not be necessary in mild cases, but when they are used, the infection clears quickly. Pigment changes in the skin may occur, and impetigo occasionally leaves scars. Cleanliness and avoiding contact with infected persons, their garments, and utensils are the best means of prevention. Newborn babies are especially susceptible and epidemics may occur in nurseries or institutions housing large numbers of children in less than adequate surroundings.

INDUSTRIAL MEDICINE, also known as occupational medicine, is that branch of medical practice which deals with the medical care of workers. This specialty has developed rapidly in the United States in the 20th century under the impetus of state laws which provide compensation for injuries and diseases acquired on the job and as a result of the interest of employers in the health of their employees.

From the early part of this century until about 1928 occupational medicine was really a surgical specialty which treated principally physical injuries, such as abrasions, lacerations, burns, contusions, fractures, and foreign bodies in the eye or other portions of the body. Although injuries still constitute a large category of practice, this specialty has been extended to include job-related or occupational diseases and preventive medicine as well.

The Occupational Diseases. Occupational diseases usually develop gradually over a period of time and may result from contact with or the inhalation of infectious agents, chemicals, dusts, and gases, or from exposure to ionizing radiations and certain physical agents. An example of an infectious occupational disease is anthrax, also called woolsorter's disease. This potentially fatal bacterial disease may be contracted by persons who handle infected animal hides. The principal lesion, called malignant pustule, appears in the skin, often accompanied by fever, nausea, joint pains, and headache.

Inhalation of carbon tetrachloride, a chemical widely used in fire extinguishers and as a solvent, may cause severe liver and kidney damage.

Foundry workers and others who are exposed to dust containing free crystalline silicon dioxide may develop silicosis, a disease of the lungs, which may become complicated with tuberculosis.

One of the most common toxic gases in industry is carbon monoxide (CO), which occurs in significant concentrations in garages, refuse plants, coal mines, and refineries. Carbon monoxide combines with the hemoglobin of the blood, preventing this red pigment from carrying oxygen to the tissues.

Decompression sickness, also known as "the bends," or "diver's paralysis," appears in deep-sea divers, caisson workers, and others who undergo rapid changes in atmospheric pressure. The disease results from the formation of bubbles of nitrogen in various body tissues and may be fatal. Other types of diseases caused by physical agents are heat exhaustion, heat cramps, heat stroke, frostbite, and occupational deafness.

A more recent type of occupational disease is that which follows exposure to ionizing radiation. Atomic power plant employees, workers in nuclear-powered submarines, and employees of research laboratories may be affected. Physicians, dentists, and nurses may develop radiation sickness from cumulative small exposures to X rays used for diagnosis and treatment. In the past, employees engaged in painting watch dials with radium became ill as a result of their practice of tipping the radium-containing brush to their tongues. Today, through medical control and the monitoring of exposures by health physicists the hazards from ionizing radiation have been virtually eliminated.

Industrial Hygiene. Industrial hygiene is the subdivision of occupational medicine which seeks to prevent and control the occupational exposures such as those described above. Industrial hygienists collect dust to determine the concentration of the particles, their size, and chemical composition. They check noise levels, the adequacy of exhaust systems, the presence and quantity of toxic gases, vapors, fumes, dusts, or the type and quantity of radiation. An organization known as the American Conference of Governmental Industrial Hygienists periodically adopts "safe" limits of the concentrations of about 170 gases and vapors and about 55 dusts to which workers can be exposed.

Health Maintenance. This term describes a broader concept of industrial medicine which includes an evaluation of the physical capacities of the individual with respect to a particular job, periodic medical examinations, and education of the workers in the areas of personal and mental hygiene and safety. In larger industries, preplacement examinations are done to determine if the applicant is physically able to do the job for which he is being hired. For example, an individual with poor depth perception would not be hired as a crane operator. In order to be adequate to the task, the examining physician must familiarize himself with actual work situations and their physical demands. After the employee is hired, periodic examinations are performed, their frequency depending upon the industry and its unique hazards. Persons exposed to lead may be examined every three to six months, while truck and other vehicle operators might be examined every six to twelve months.

See also PREVENTIVE MEDICINE.

INFECTIOUS MONONUCLEOSIS [mŏ-nō-nū-klē-ō′sĭs], a disease of unknown cause which is characterized by swelling of the lymph nodes, and the presence of large numbers of abnormal white cells in the blood. Although it is suspected that a virus is responsible, this has not yet been proven. The disease may occur in localized epidemics. Individuals in the 10–35 age group (commonly medical students, nurses, and college students) are most frequently affected. The symptoms are highly variable and may simulate a large number of ailments. Typically, a young adult develops a feeling of illness, attended by fever and swelling of the lymph nodes, particularly those in the neck. The spleen is enlarged and there may be sore throat, swollen and painful gums, swollen eyelids, headache, and cough. There is an early decrease in the number of white cells in the blood, followed by an increase, accounted for largely by the presence of abnormal cells. The blood also contains a substance which agglutinates sheep cells; this is often an aid in diagnosis. Skin eruptions, and liver and nervous system involvement may appear. Most patients recover within three to six weeks without aftereffects; however, in rare instances death may occur from nervous system involvement or from rupture of the spleen. There is no specific treatment for the condition.

INFERIORITY COMPLEX, term used by the psychiatrist Alfred Adler for a repressed system of desires and memories associated with concern about real or imagined inferiority of a person's physical, social, or psychological characteristics. The inferiority complex must be distinguished from inferiority feelings, which are conscious self-judgments. The complex, by definition, means that the feelings of inferiority have been repressed so that the individual is no longer conscious of them. The complex is created because the individual's real or imagined difficulties make him unable to cope effectively with the world around him. Distorted or neurotic behavior is the usual outcome, frequently taking the form of defensive or aggressive acts.

These acts are presumed to be unconsciously determined.

INFERTILITY. *See* STERILITY.

INFLAMMATION, a response of the body to local irritation caused by invading microorganisms, chemical or physical irritants, or substance to which the body is allergic. The principal signs of inflammation are redness, heat, swelling, and pain. Redness develops as the local blood vessels widen, becoming filled with more blood. The increase in circulation of warm blood raises the regional temperature. Damage to the cells releases substances (*see* HISTAMINE) which alter the permeability of the blood vessels, permitting fluid to escape into and swell the tissues. Pain and tenderness develop from the pressure of this fluid upon the fine nerve endings in the tissues. An important part of the inflammatory response is the migration of white blood cells to the involved area. These cells penetrate the walls of the blood vessels and enter the tissues where they engulf and destroy bacteria. Other familiar effects of inflammation are fever, increase in the white blood cell count, swollen lymph glands, and increased heartbeat rate.

Many of these changes may be considered as defensive measures instituted by the body against the inflammatory agents. The increased blood flow brings with it added nutrients and bacteria-fighting elements (white blood cells and antibodies). The fluid which escapes from the blood into the tissues dilutes the toxic products found at the site of the inflammation. The raised local and general temperature (fever) increases the pace of cellular activity.

The course of the inflammation depends principally upon the cause. In the case of certain bacterial infections, the white blood cells may effectively halt the spread of the organisms, or result in a collection of pus in the tissues (an abscess). The pus consists of remnants of dead white blood cells with the bacteria which they have ingested. If the inflammatory reaction fails, the bacteria may enter the blood stream and set up infections in other parts of the body. This is commonly known as "blood poisoning," and may be fatal. Antiseptics and antibiotics are used to treat bacterial inflammations.

Inflammation caused by chemical or physical irritation usually subsides when the irritation is removed. Soothing ointments and lotions may hasten the process.

Allergic inflammation often is characterized by the formation of large fluid-filled wheals in the skin. The principal phenomenon appears to be the release of histamine from the cells and the escape of fluid into the tissues, following the reaction of the allergy-inducing material with special substances (antibodies) contained in the tissues of the allergic individual. This type of inflammation can frequently be relieved by the use of antihistamines or cortisone and related drugs.

Inflammation is also a prominent feature of a number of generalized diseases of the connective tissues of the body (for example, rheumatoid arthritis, periarteritis nodosa). Although the exact cause of the inflammation in these conditions in unknown, cortisone and other corticosteroids are often effective in providing relief.

INFLUENZA [ĭn-floo-ĕn′zə], an infectious disease caused by a virus of the influenza group. Influenza epidemics have been known since ancient times: an extensive world-wide outbreak occurred in 1918–19, resulting in the death of an estimated 20,000,000 people.

Modern knowledge of influenza began with isolation of the virus in 1933. There are three distinct influenza virus types, A, B, and C. Influenza A occurs in epidemic cycles every 2–4 years. The pandemic of Asian flu in 1957 was caused by a variant of the A virus. The 1968 epidemic of the so-called "Hong Kong Flu" was a new A virus. The outlook was relatively mild compared with those of 1957 and 1967. Influenza B epidemics occur every 4–6 years. Influenza C rarely produces disease. The continued struggle with recurring epidemics reflects the ability of the virus to change, thus partially eluding the efforts of science to prepare fully effective long-term vaccines. The virus probably enters the body through inhalation of droplets discharged from the mouth or nose of infected persons. After an incubation period of one or two days, the illness appears suddenly with chills, fever, pain behind the eyes, headache, lassitude, prostration, and severe muscular pains. There may also be coughing, congestion of the eyes, sneezing, or bleeding from the nose. A fairly high fever usually persists for two or three days and the patient ordinarily recovers within a week, but fatigue, depression, and a tendency to perspire easily may persist for 1–2 weeks. The influenza infection is ordinarily not fatal itself; however, death may occur from complications, particularly bacterial pneumonia. Aged persons and those in a generally poor state of health are particularly susceptible to pneumonia following an influenza attack. Most of the fatalities of the 1918–19 outbreak resulted from pneumonia and empyema (another lung complication). Influenza attacks in recent years have also been complicated by staphylococcal lung infections, but the use of antibiotics has decreased deaths from such infections.

Influenza vaccines can prevent illness in about 70% of those immunized. The virus which makes up the vaccine is grown in chick embryos and then inactivated by formalin. Recent use of virus banks, with yearly updating of the pooled virus strains, has greatly increased protection, but immunity lasts only 3–6 months. In the Soviet Union, attenuated live virus is placed within the nose to provide immunity, but the reliability of this method is not yet fully established. People suffering from heart disease, chronic lung problems, and diabetes should be immunized each winter, except for those allergic to egg, who should not receive the vaccine.

There are no drugs that can cure influenza, but amantadine hydrochloride is sometimes used, along with time-honored bed rest, to relieve symptoms. Amantadine does not kill the virus or prevent other individuals from becoming infected and is not given to children.

INHERITANCE OF ACQUIRED CHARACTERISTICS, a theory of evolution, now in disrepute with scientists, set forth in 1809 by the French biologist Jean Baptiste de Lamarck. Lamarck believed that through use, an organism develops part of its body, while an unused part becomes weak, and these changes are then passed on to the offspring. According to Lamarck, the ancestors of today's water birds had unwebbed feet and spread their toes as they swam. The swimming caused extra blood to flow to the feet. Combined blood flow and stretching, in this example, caused the formation of webbed feet, which were passed on to the birds' offspring.

Today scientists know that an individual's basic characteristics are carried in its genetic material. Only the genes of the sex cells are passed from parent to offspring, and these genes are unaffected by changes in the rest of the body. One of the last of the Lamarckians was Trofim Lysenko, a Russian biologist, whose work has been discredited.

See also HEREDITY.

INOCULATION, in microbiology, the introduction of a few living organisms into an environment prepared for their cultivation. Bacteriologists inoculate sterile growth media with bacterial cells to obtain cultures of the organisms for study. Inoculation is also used in the process of vaccination against certain diseases. A few potentially disease-producing microorganisms are introduced into the body to produce a limited infection. This exposure stimulates the production of special substances (antibodies) which enable the body to resist future invasions by similar organisms.

See also IMMUNITY; MICROBIOLOGY; VACCINATION.

INOSITOL [ĭn-ō'sĭ-tŏl], a substance found widely distributed in plant and animal tissues. Inositol has been demonstrated to be a necessary element in the diet of chickens, turkeys, pigs, rats, and certain microorganisms. In rats, absence of inositol in the diet results in failure to grow and loss of hair. Experimental studies have indicated that inositol is necessary for the growth of certain human cells in tissue culture (including cancer cells); however, it has not been proven that it is an essential ingredient in the human diet. Inositol plays some role in fat metabolism, but its exact function is not clear.

INSECT BITES may result in inflammation at the site of the bite, or vomiting, headaches, fever, convulsions, and other symptoms of general body involvement. In many instances infectious diseases are transmitted by the bite.

Insects bite or sting humans to obtain food (usually blood), in self-defense, or to lay eggs. As they feed on humans, ticks introduce a poison which causes paralysis, and possibly death, through involvement of the heart and the muscles used in breathing. Chigger larvae attach to the skin and secrete a saliva which digests the tissues, which are then sucked up as food. A red itching eruption results. Mosquitoes and flies of various species bite humans to draw blood, and in the process may infect man with diseases such as malaria, sleeping sickness, yellow fever, and dengue fever. When disturbed, bees and wasps attack humans, usually producing a painful, swollen puncture wound. In some allergic individuals a fatal reaction may follow the sting. Certain mites cause a reddening, swelling, and itching of the skin (scabies) when they burrow under the skin to lay eggs.

Centipedes, scorpions, and spiders procure food by injecting venom into their victims, and under certain circumstances may attack humans. The bites of the small centipede cause only local inflammation, but the large tropical forms may produce in addition fever, vomiting, and headache. The venom of the scorpion attacks the nervous system, causing vomiting, nausea, dizziness, rapid breathing, and weakened pulse. The sting may occasionally be fatal to small children. Bites of the black widow spider may cause dizziness, nausea, profuse perspiration, and fever. Painful spasms of the abdominal muscles may simulate abdominal disease. As in the case of the scorpion, spider bites may be fatal to small children.

Insects may produce illness in humans through means other than biting. Blister beetles and the Spanish fly secrete a substance which on contact with the skin causes blister formation. Certain caterpillars have hollow, venom-containing hairs, which may produce a painful skin inflammation. Occasionally, windblown caterpillar hairs may cause a severe irritation of the eye. Some flies may lay eggs in open wounds where the maggots can thrive on the exposed tissue.

INSOMNIA, sleeplessness, the inability to sleep. Some individuals, especially as they grow older, may need very little sleep, but sleeplessness may lead to complaints, especially among the elderly and the mentally diseased. Causes of insomia vary, but research has led to generally applicable explanations of the condition in healthy people who claim to sleep very little. Such people produce normal brain wave patterns during sleep, but are subject to unusually vivid, realistic dream images, which they may mistake for wakeful thought and thus maintain that they slept very little.

Children may fear falling asleep after a nightmare. Most persons occasionally experience difficulty in falling asleep because of legitimate concern over business, school, health, or personal affairs. When this condition occurs regularly, the subject may resort to sleeping pills. If he becomes dependent on them he has established an undesirable drug habit. A brisk walk or television before bed time is more advisable. Physical illness, especially when it is accompanied by pain or discomfort, causes insomnia. Often insomnia is the first sign of a depression, neurosis, or other mental disorder.

See also DRUG ADDICTION; NEUROSIS; SLEEP.

INSULIN [ĭn'sə-lĭn], a pancreatic hormone which is essential for the utilization of sugar by the body. Carbohydrates (sugars and starches) are broken down in the digestive tract to simple sugars (monosaccharides) such as glucose. When the glucose content of the blood increases after a meal, the normal pancreas responds by secreting more insulin into the blood. It is believed that insulin promotes the passage of sugar from the blood into the cells. In the cells, the sugar is stored as the starch glycogen, to be burned later as fuel for cellular activities. There is also evidence that insulin plays a role in the production of fats and proteins.

Insulin and Diabetes. Diabetes is characterized by an apparently diminished or absent insulin production. The passage of sugar into the cells is blocked, blood sugar rises (hyperglycemia), and eventually the excess sugar in the blood "spills over" into the urine where its presence serves as an indication of the disease. Prior to the discovery of insulin, diabetes could not always be satisfactorily treated and was usually fatal. In 1922 a group of Canadian scientists, led by F. G. Banting and J. J. R. Macleod, succeeded in extracting insulin from beef pancreas and used it to treat diabetic patients. Their achievement, for which they received the Nobel Prize in 1923, revolutionized the treatment of diabetes.

The Chemistry of Insulin. In 1958 Frederick Sanger in England received the Nobel Prize for determining the chemical structure of insulin. Sanger discovered that insulin is composed of two chains of amino acids (the basic building blocks of proteins), one containing 21, the other containing 30 amino-acid molecules. The two chains are linked by two bridges of sulfur atoms. The insulins of oxen, sheep, hogs, and humans differ slightly in their amino-acid composition, but have the same basic action.

The Clinical Use of Insulin. Since insulin is destroyed by the digestive juices, it cannot be given by mouth, but must be injected into the body. The amount of insulin needed by the diabetic patient must be carefully established. An overdose of insulin may lower the blood sugar excessively (hypoglycemia), resulting in hunger, headache, weakness, excessive perspiration, visual disturbances, and, later, bizarre behavior, coma, and possibly death, unless the blood glucose level is restored by giving the patient fruit juice, candy, or some other sugar-rich food. The same condition may be caused by an insulin-producing tumor of the pancreas.

Overdoses of insulin were once used as a form of shock treatment in certain mental disorders, but this technique has now been largely abandoned in favor of electrical forms of shock therapy.

Types of Insulin. The clinically used insulin preparations are derived from the pancreas of hogs or beef. The preparations (including regular insulin, crystalline insulin, globin insulin, and protamine zinc insulin) differ in the time and duration of their action. The longer-acting forms, such as protamine zinc insulin and globin insulin, may be slowly absorbed from the site of the injection over a period of a day or more. Regular or crystalline insulin acts more rapidly and for a shorter period.

A number of antidiabetic drugs which can be taken by mouth have been introduced. It is believed that some of these drugs (Orinase and Diabinase) function principally by stimulating some residual insulin-producing ability of the pancreas. They are most effective in treating the milder forms of diabetes.

See also DIABETES MELLITUS; ENDOCRINE GLANDS; PANCREAS.

INTELLIGENCE [ĭn-tĕl′ə-jəns], has been defined in many different ways, and writers on the topic are still in wide disagreement. Originally, the term was used synonymously with "intellect," which was defined as the "faculty or capacity of knowing." Present-day concepts of intelligence are broader, concerned more with adaptive human behavior, and sometimes cover so-called nonintellective factors of intelligence. Most definitions of intelligence emphasize certain capacities as basic to general intelligence. The three most often mentioned are the ability to learn, the ability to educe relations (abstract reasoning ability), and the ability to profit from experience. A fourth capacity is frequently added, the ability to envisage and solve problems. If one examines the instruments by which intelligence is appraised—namely, the tests used to measure it—one finds that not only these but other abilities as well are tapped. The current view is that general intelligence involves not only learning, adapting, reasoning, and problem solving, but also a variety of capacities which in one way or another enable the individual to cope effectively with his environment.

INTELLIGENCE QUOTIENT (IQ). Intelligence quotients are a range of numbers employed by psychologists and educators to define relative mental ability as measured by standard tests of intelligence. IQ's are arrived at by comparing a person's score with the average score of individuals of the same age. In the case of children IQ's may be computed by dividing the subject's mental age (MA) score by his chronological age (CA). The result is multiplied by 100 to eliminate a decimal point. The formula, then, is $IQ = \frac{MA}{CA} \times 100$. If an individual gets a mental age score of 12 on a test and his chronological age is 10, his IQ is 120.

One of the important questions concerning the IQ is whether it remains constant, that is, whether it continues unchanged over the years. There is considerable difference of opinion on this point. Results of studies depend upon the age at which a child is first tested, his co-operativeness at the time, the length of the interval between successive testings, and the nature of the test used. If one considers 5 to 10 points an allowable variation, then the IQ may be said to be relatively constant for most ages. It is surprisingly constant in the case of retested adults and fairly constant in the case of children aged 6 to 16, provided that the retest interval is not much more than two to three years. On the other hand, IQ's obtained from infants and very young children (under 5) often show shifts of as much as 20 points or more. This does not invalidate all IQ's obtained at these early ages but does imply the need for using supplementary criteria when the intelligence of very young children is evaluated. Again, IQ's obtained on emotionally and mentally disturbed individuals cannot always be taken at face value. For these reasons, psychologists are generally loathe to reveal IQ's to other than qualified professional persons.

INTERTRIGO [ĭn-tər-trī′gō], an inflammation caused by repeated friction between two opposing skin surfaces, such as in the groin, between the buttocks, under the arms, beneath the breasts, and between the toes and fingers. The inflammation is aggravated by heat and retention of sweat in the area (especially in obese patients). Treatment consists of separating the parts with cotton pads and applying soothing powders.

INTESTINAL OBSTRUCTION or ILEUS, an interference with the normal flow of the intestinal contents, which may be caused by mechanical obstruction of the intestine, or by disturbance of the intestinal blood or nerve supply. Mechanical obstruction is most common and may result from tumors, hernias, or from scar tissue and adhesions pinching or narrowing the intestinal opening. Certain abdominal infections may irritate the intestinal nerves, halting the normal movements which propel material through the in-

INTESTINE

testine. A clot in the large blood vessels which supply the intestine may also halt intestinal movements.

In acute mechanical obstructions the patient usually experiences intermittent cramplike abdominal pains. Large quantities of fluid may be lost through vomiting, leading to dehydration, loss of chloride and potassium, and disturbances in the acidity-alkalinity balance of the blood. The abdomen becomes distended as fluid and gas collect in the bowel above the obstruction. Chronic cases are usually caused by slow-growing tumors and are characterized by constipation which grows progressively worse. Treatment is directed at replacing the lost fluid (in acute cases) and salts, relieving the distension, and removing the obstruction. In cases of mechanical "strangulation" of the bowel, when the blood supply is pinched shut, immediate surgery is necessary to prevent gangrene.

See also INTESTINE.

INTESTINE [ĭn-tĕs′tĭn], the largest portion of the digestive tract, consisting of a tube some 26 ft. in length, which extends from the stomach to the anus.

The *small intestine* is a convoluted tube about 21 ft. long. The final stages of digestion are completed here as fats, proteins, and carbohydrates are broken down into simpler substances which are absorbed into the body. The intestinal wall is composed of several coats: an overlying serous coat beneath which are layers of muscle and connective tissue. The inner coat is a mucous layer which contains glands and numerous fingerlike projections, called villi. These constitute the absorbing surface of the intestine; amino acids (from proteins) and sugars (from carbohydrates) enter the blood vessels of the villi, while fats pass into the lymphatic tubes of the villi. The intestinal glands secrete a rich variety of digestive enzymes plus numerous hormones which regulate the secretions of the stomach, pancreas, and the intestine itself. The muscles of the intestinal wall rhythmically contract, mixing the intestinal contents and propelling food toward the large intestine.

The small intestine enters the *large intestine* at the *ileocecal valve*, a ring-like muscular structure which prevents the contents of the large intestine from regurgitating back into the small intestine. The principal function of the large intestine is to absorb water and salts from the food residues and to move this material by muscular action to the rectum, from which it is excreted.

Bacteria in the Intestine. The intestine is normally inhabited by a variety of bacteria, some of which perform useful functions, and others which are potentially dangerous. Certain intestinal bacteria synthesize vitamin K, a substance needed for normal blood clotting. Occasionally bacteria escape from the intestine and reach other parts of the body, such as the kidneys, where they cause serious infection. Because the intestine harbors bacteria which putrefy proteins, and produce poisonous by-products, the Russian bacteriologist Metchnikoff considered the large intestine to be the body's greatest enemy. It has since been demonstrated that most of these intestinal poisons are not absorbed into the body. The alleged value of bacteria-rich sour milk products, such as yoghurt, is based upon Metchnikoff's writings, which attributed the health and longevity of yoghurt-consuming Bulgarian peasants to a replacement of the normal colon bacteria by the nonpoisonous yoghurt bacteria (Bacillus acidophilus).

See also:
APPENDICITIS
CELIAC DISEASE
COLITIS
CONSTIPATION
DIARRHEA
DIGESTION
DYSENTERY
INTESTINAL OBSTRUCTION
INTUSSUSCEPTION
REGIONAL ENTERITIS
SPRUE
ULCERS

INTRAVENOUS FEEDING, the introduction of a solution containing food substances (sugar, salt, vitamins, and amino acids) into a vein. This method of nourishment is used when food cannot be taken by mouth, as in the case of patients who are in a coma, or in certain diseases in which food cannot be retained, properly digested, or absorbed. Intravenous feeding is frequently used before and after operations.

INTUSSUSCEPTION [ĭn-təs-sə-sĕp′shən], condition in which one segment of intestine is telescoped into another. Intussusception occurs most commonly in infants. The folding of the intestine compresses the blood vessels of the intestinal wall, causing swelling, ulceration, and eventually gangrene. At first the infant becomes irritable and cries frequently. Later, nausea and vomiting develop, followed by weakness, pallor, and prostration. The stools may contain mucus or blood, and the abdomen may eventually become distended. The condition is often fatal unless promptly corrected by surgery.

IODINE [ī′ə-dīn], chemical element of the halogen group. It is a blackish-gray solid with a metallic luster. When heated, a violet vapor forms before the melting point is reached. Its name comes from the Greek word for "violet."

The human body contains 0.00004% iodine, most of which is concentrated in the thyroid gland. The gland manufactures the iodine-containing hormones thyroxine and tri-iodothyronine.

The thyroid hormones govern the rate of metabolism of the human body. When produced in excess (hyperthyroidism) they cause tenseness and nervousness; insufficient quantities (hypothyroidism) bring about a dullness and a listlessness. Basal metabolism, the measurement of the rate at which a person consumes oxygen when at rest, gives information as to the level of thyroid activity. Nowadays, the same purpose is accomplished more easily by measuring the level of protein-bound iodine (PBI) in the blood stream. A deficiency of iodine in the diet usually causes the thyroid gland to become enlarged, forming a neck bulge called a goiter. Goiter is common where the soil is deficient in iodine.

IODINE TINCTURE, a solution of iodine (about 2%) and sodium iodide (2%–2.5%) in a mixture of alcohol and water (44%–50% ethyl alcohol). Frequently used as a first-aid treatment for minor cuts and scratches, it is one of the most effective antiseptics, being active against a wide variety of bacteria and fungi. Its disadvantages lie in its tendency to sting and to stain the skin.

IRON LUNG, also known as a mechanical respirator, an apparatus used in cases of paralysis of the respiratory muscles to enable the patient to breathe. In normal respiration the chest muscles and the diaphragm (a muscular disc which separates the chest and abdominal cavities) draw in air by expanding the chest volume. The iron lung expands the chest by suction. The lung consists of a large hollow metal cylinder attached to an electric bellows. The cylinder completely encloses the patient's body, leaving only the head projecting. The bellows draws air from the cylinder, lowering the air pressure around the lungs, thus causing them to expand. To produce artificial exhalation, the bellows compresses the air in the cylinder, thus squeezing air out of the lungs.

The iron lung may be needed in some cases of poliomyelitis in which the virus damages the nerve cells which control the breathing muscles. In such cases the victim may die of suffocation unless mechanical respiration is provided. The respirator is also used in certain other diseases of the central nervous system and in cases of paralysis produced by poisoning.

IRRITANTS, drugs which produce inflammation of the skin and mucous membranes. The body's response to irritation causes an increase in the local circulation and a feeling of warmth. The irritants vary as to the degree of inflammation produced. The milder irritants, called rubefacients, cause increased circulation with reddening. The harsher irritants, or vesicants, produce blisters. Frequently irritants are applied to the skin as *counterirritants* to relieve disturbances of deeper structures. They may accomplish this by increasing the circulation to the part, as the blood supply to the skin is increased, or by irritating nerve endings, thus sending nerve impulses to the spinal cord to block or alter the painful impulses emanating from the diseased tissues.

The mustard plaster, which contains powdered black mustard, spread on a backing material, is a popular irritant preparation used for rheumatic conditions, neuralgia, and arthritis. Less widely used irritants are chloroform, camphor, eucalyptol, turpentine, and methyl salicylate. Various commercial liniments, designed to relieve muscular and joint soreness, include these substances as their active ingredients. A more effective irritant and counter-irritant action can be obtained with hot packs, heat lamps, or diathermy, and for this reason many of the irritant drugs have fallen into disuse.

ISONIAZID [ī-sə-nī′ə-zĭd], chemically isonicotinic acid hydrazide, one of the most effective drugs available for treatment of tuberculosis. Streptomycin, its predecessor in tuberculosis therapy, is more toxic and must be injected. Isoniazid can easily be taken by mouth. The tubercle bacillus rapidly develops resistance to the drug. When it is combined with para-aminosalicylic acid, alone or with streptomycin, drug-resistance is delayed. There is considerable variation in susceptibility to Isoniazid's toxicity. Toxic complications are due to Isoniazid's interference with the body's use of Vitamin B_6. Lack of this vitamin leads to neuritis, convulsions, and anemia. By giving Vitamin B_6 along with Isoniazid, this toxicity is eliminated. For some reason that is not well understood, these complications rarely occur in children.
See also TUBERCULOSIS.

J

JAUNDICE [jŏn′dĭs], known also as icterus, is a condition in which bile pigments accumulate in the blood and other body fluids, tinting the skin and the whites of the eyeballs a greenish yellow.

The bile pigments are produced from hemoglobin, the oxygen-carrying red pigment of red blood cells. The bile pigments are manufactured in the cells of the reticuloendothelial system, which are distributed in various parts of the body, including the liver and the spleen. The liver removes the bile pigments from the blood and excretes them with the bile into the bile passages and gall bladder, from where they are discharged into the intestine.

Jaundice may develop if the bile ducts are obstructed (obstructive jaundice), if the liver cells cannot properly excrete bile pigments (hepatogenous jaundice), or if red blood cells are destroyed in abnormally large numbers, causing an overproduction of the bile pigments (hemolytic jaundice). Although one of these factors may originally be responsible for the jaundice, all may eventually appear as the condition progresses.

Obstructive Jaundice. Obstructive jaundice may be caused by a stone or tumor in the common bile duct which carries the bile from the liver and gall bladder to the intestine, or by a severe inflammation which narrows or occludes the ducts. Regardless of the nature of the obstruction, the bile backs up in the ducts and regurgitates into the blood stream. The stagnation of the bile in the minute bile ducts may lead to the formation of plugs or concretions of thickened bile in various parts of the liver. Although the kidney attempts to eliminate large amounts of bile in the urine, abundant amounts of bile pigments accumulate in the blood, imparting a yellowish color to the tissues. A distinctive feature of obstructive jaundice is a clay-coloring of the feces, which results from the failure of bile pigments to reach the intestine and give the characteristic yellowish-brown color to the stools.

A different variety of obstructive jaundice appears as a consequence of drug reactions in sensitive persons. The walls of the minute passages within the liver swell, producing what is known as intrahepatic (literally, "within the liver") obstructive jaundice. This type of jaundice usually disappears after the use of the offending drug is discontinued.

Hepatogenous Jaundice. This results from injury to liver cells, which may be produced by infection with viruses, bacteria, protozoa, liver flukes, or by chemicals such as chloroform, carbon tetrachloride, alcohol, phosphorus, and certain heavy metals, such as bismuth, arsenic, antimony, and lead. Not infrequently, persons in the dry-cleaning business develop jaundice after they have repeatedly used certain cleaning solutions containing carbon tetrachloride. Alcoholics usually develop jaundice following liver injury caused by the alcohol and the impurities in the liquor.

Hemolytic Jaundice. This may occur in certain forms of anemia in which there is excessive destruction of red blood cells, and subsequent overproduction of bile pigment from the hemoglobin released from the destroyed cells.

A special, but common type of hemolytic jaundice called icterus neonatorum (jaundice of the newborn) occurs in babies during the first week after birth. This results from the destruction of the oversupply of red blood cells which help sustain the infant's oxygen needs before its lungs begin functioning. After birth, these excess cells are no longer needed and are gradually broken down. The large amounts of hemoglobin released during this process are converted into bile pigment, producing high blood concentrations of these pigments and coloring the tissues. This form of jaundice is normal and requires no treatment. If the jaundice persists, however, other more serious causes may be responsible.

See also HEPATITIS; LIVER.

JENNER, EDWARD (1749–1823), English physician who discovered vaccination, a means of preventing smallpox. A country physician, Jenner observed that persons who had been exposed to the cattle disease cowpox did not contract smallpox. In 1796 he vaccinated a small country boy and afterward tried to infect him with smallpox. The child resisted the infection. In 1798 Jenner published his results in a small book entitled *An Inquiry into the Causes and Effects of the Variolae Vaccinae*. Within a few years the technique of vaccination spread throughout the world and succeeded in virtually eliminating smallpox wherever it was introduced. Parliament expressed the gratitude of the nation by voting Jenner £10,000 in 1802, and £20,000 in 1807.

See also SMALLPOX OR VARIOLA.

K

KARRER [kär′ər], **PAUL** (1889–1971), Swiss chemist. He earned his Ph.D. degree at the University of Zurich in 1911 and became professor of chemistry there. Jointly with Walter N. Haworth, he was awarded the 1937 Nobel Prize in chemistry for his work on carotenoids, flavins, and vitamins A and B.

KEEN, WILLIAM WILLIAMS (1837–1932), American surgeon who contributed to the development of the surgery of the nervous system. He was the first American to successfully remove a brain tumor and was coauthor of an important treatise on nerve injuries. He taught at the Jefferson Medical College in Philadelphia.

KENDALL, EDWARD CALVIN (1886–   ), American biochemist and physiologist who shared the Nobel Prize with Philip Hench and Tadeus Reichstein in 1950, for his research on cortisone and other adrenal hormones. Kendall's earliest contribution to hormone research was isolation of the thyroid hormone thyroxin. From 1921 to 1951 he was professor of physiological chemistry at the Mayo Foundation in Rochester, Minn.

KENDREW, JOHN COWDERY (1917–   ), English biochemist who successfully determined the spatial arrangement of the atoms in myoglobin—the body substance which delivers oxygen to the muscles. For this work, using X-ray crystallography, Kendrew shared the 1962 Nobel Prize for chemistry with his coworker, Max F. Perutz.

KENNY, ELIZABETH (1886–1952), Australian nurse known for her technique of treating poliomyelitis. In World War I, she served as a nurse in the Australian army. After her return to Australia, she devoted herself to the study and treatment of poliomyelitis, which she believed was being wrongly treated by the medical profession.

She developed a system of therapy based upon the maintenance of a bright mental outlook, continued effort to move apparently paralyzed muscles, continuous hot packs to the affected muscles, and the abandonment of all splints. None of these principles, except the last, were in conflict with those of qualified orthopedic surgeons. The regular orthopedic surgeons still maintained that, while immobilization of paralyzed limbs had often been carried to extremes, in many cases it was necessary to avoid contractures and serious deformities. In 1940 she went to the United States where she remained for 10 years, helping to popularize her method of treatment. The city of Minneapolis opened a treatment center, the Elizabeth Kenny Institute, in 1942 and several other cities followed suit.

Some of Sister Kenny's anatomical and physiological concepts were erroneous, and often her procedures of treating with warm packs were too elaborate, extensive, and time-consuming. Yet, on the whole, her influence was beneficial. She drew attention to poliomyelitis as a national problem. To quote H. J. Seddon, "Her vigor was such that she wakened up orthopedic surgeons and physiotherapists the world over. Had she been content to talk about treatment without embarking on speculation about pathology, and had she been a little kindlier and more tolerant, she might now be regarded as the Florence Nightingale of orthopedics, or at any rate of that part of it concerned with poliomyelitis."

KERATITIS [kĕr-ə-tī′tĭs], an inflammation of the cornea, the transparent outer covering of the front of the eye. Such inflammations may result from injury, allergy, or infection. The symptoms consist of pain, an extreme sensitivity to light, and tearing. Antibiotics are used in the infectious cases and steroids are used to quiet the inflammations.

KETOSIS [kē-tō′sĭs], disturbance of body chemistry produced by the excessive utilization of fat as a source of energy. When fat is burned as a fuel by the body certain substances called ketone bodies (acetoacetic acid, β-hydroxybutyric acid, and acetone) are produced. An excess of these substances (ketosis) disturbs the acidity-alkalinity balance of the body resulting in acidosis, a condition marked by weakness, dehydration, and coma. Fat is utilized in this way when carbohydrates (sugar and starches) are not available as foods. This occurs in starvation and in diabetes. In diabetes the sugar is found in the blood but cannot be taken up by the cells to be used as food. In diabetics, ketosis and subsequent coma may result from infections, vomiting, or from failure to take insulin injections.
See also DIABETES MELLITUS.

KIDNEY. The kidneys lie against the body wall close to the spine, one on each side. Their primary function is to cleanse the blood of chemical wastes and harmful substances and to regulate the acid-base balance of the body. Since the blood constantly exchanges materials with other body fluids, the kidneys, through their direct action on the blood, indirectly control the composition of these fluids.

The Production of Urine. The raw material for urine production is blood plasma. Normally about one-fifth of the blood pumped from the heart flows directly to the kidneys. There the blood enters vessels of successively smaller size until it enters a group of vessels called the glomerulus. Water, with dissolved salts and organic compounds, filters through the blood vessels of the glomerulus to enter the tubule. The glomerulus and the tubule together constitute the nephron, the functioning unit of the kidneys, of which there are about 1 million in each kidney. Fluid is driven into the nephron by the force of the blood pressure. Consequently, when the blood pressure is too low, as in shock, the pressure in the kidneys becomes inadequate and urine production ceases. Apparently, under certain circumstances, the kidneys are able to secrete a substance (renin) which indirectly raises the blood pressure. The kidneys are evidently also involved in less well understood mechanisms concerned with blood pressure regulation, and may be responsible for certain forms of high blood pressure.

The filtering membranes of the glomerulus ordinarily permit only smaller molecules and ions to pass into the tubule. Larger particles, such as proteins and blood cells, are held back to be swept out into the general blood circulation. In certain kidney diseases, such as nephrosis, a failure in the normal filtering process permits significant amounts of protein to enter the tubule and appear in the urine. The filtered fluid, or filtrate, which will eventually become the urine, runs a gantlet of cells which line the long convoluted tube through which fluid must pass on its way through the kidney. In the course of this passage, the cells of the tubule absorb water and other substances from the filtrate and secrete certain substances into it.

Absorption in the Nephron. Nature has devised an apparently roundabout method of producing urine. To begin with, as observed above, fluid filters from the blood into the nephron. If, however, all of this fluid were to be eliminated as urine, the body would soon be depleted of its vital liquids: this is evident when one considers that in one-half hour an amount of fluid equal to the entire blood volume of the body passes into the kidney tubules. To prevent such an excessive fluid loss, the cells of the tubules reclaim 99% of the water from the filtrate as it passes along the nephron. The rate of water reabsorption is accelerated by a hormone (the antidiuretic hormone ADH) secreted by the pituitary gland in the skull. In a rare disease, called diabetes insipidus, a failure of the pituitary gland to secrete enough ADH may interfere with water reabsorption, permitting abnormal quantities of fluid to escape in the urine.

The reabsorption of sodium and potassium from the fluid is regulated by certain hormones (adrenocorticosteroids) secreted by the outer layer, or cortex, of the adrenal glands which sit astride the kidneys. In Addison's disease, which affects the adrenal glands, a deficiency of these hormones causes a dangerous loss of sodium and chlorine in the urine.

Secretion in the Tubules. The cells of the nephrons take up certain substances from the blood and secrete them into the tubule fluid. These materials include foreign substances, such as dyes and penicillin, potassium ions (which are absorbed from the tubules as well), and various products of body activity.

The Flow of Urine Out of the Tubule. Urine passes from the tubule into a collecting duct which joins with other collecting ducts into larger and larger branches, finally passing into the pelvis of the kidney from where it enters the ureter, which in turn conducts it to the bladder. The urine is stored in the bladder until it is voided from the body through the urethra.

THE KIDNEY

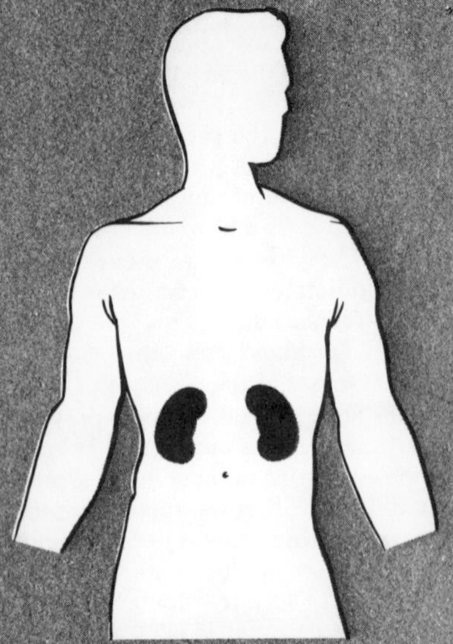

EXTERNAL VIEW AND CROSS SECTION OF RIGHT KIDNEY

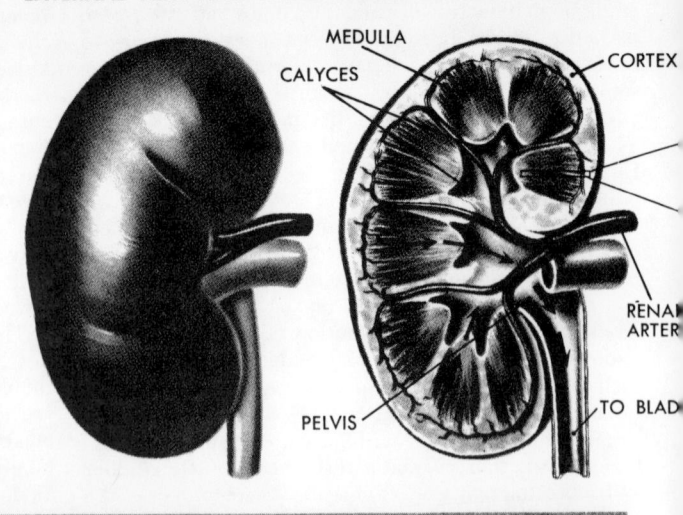

MEDULLA
CORTEX
CALYCES
RENAL ARTERY
PELVIS
TO BLADDER

The kidney excretes wastes and regulates the chemical balance of the body fluids. Its activities are essential to life and fortunately the body is provided with an excess of kidney tissue such that if one kidney fails the remaining organ can fully assume the functions of both.

CROSS SECTION OF KIDNEY (above, right). Blood enters through the renal artery. The flow of urine is indicated by the arrows. Urine production begins with the filtering of blood in the outer layers (cortex) of the kidney. The urine passes through one of the microscopic nephrons (the kidney unit shown in panels at the right) and ultimately flows out through the pelvis and ureter, to be collected in the bladder.

FILTRATION, REABSORPTION, AND SECRETION IN THE NEPHRON

FILTRATION

Blood, driven by pressure from the heart, filters through the glomerular membrane. As can be seen in the inset, the cells and large protein molecules of the blood do not normally pass into the urine. Thus the urine at this point (called the *glomerular filtrate*) consists of blood minus cells and proteins.

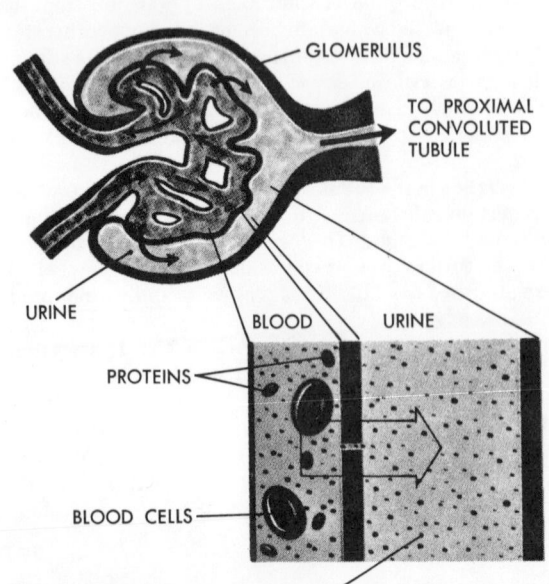

GLOMERULUS
TO PROXIMAL CONVOLUTED TUBULE
URINE
BLOOD
URINE
PROTEINS
BLOOD CELLS

SODIUM, CHLORINE, PHOSPHATE IONS, UREA MOLECULES, AND OTHER SMALLER PARTICLES

REABSORPTION

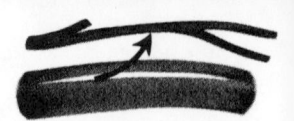

If all of the fluid filtered through the glomerulus were to escape in the urine the body would be rapidly dehydrated. Most of this fluid is reclaimed from the urine as it passes through the tubes of the nephron.

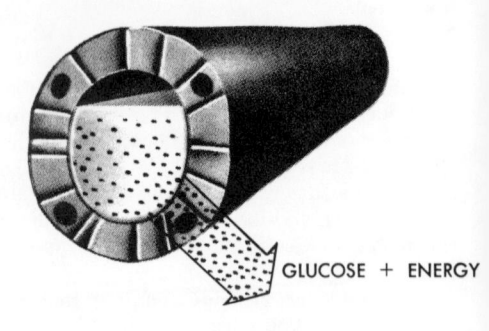

GLUCOSE + ENERGY

Active Reabsorption

In active reabsorption substances such as glucose and sodium are removed from the urine against electrochemical pressure. This is an energy-consuming process which may be compared to pumping water uphill against gravitational pressure.

Artist: Leonard Dank

THE KIDNEY UNIT — THE NEPHRON

1. GLOMERULUS
2. PROXIMAL CONVOLUTED TUBULE
3. HENLE'S LOOP
4. DISTAL CONVOLUTED TUBULE
5. COLLECTING TUBULE

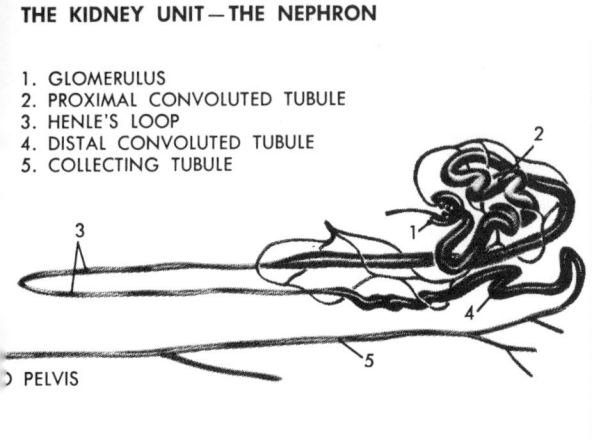

PELVIS

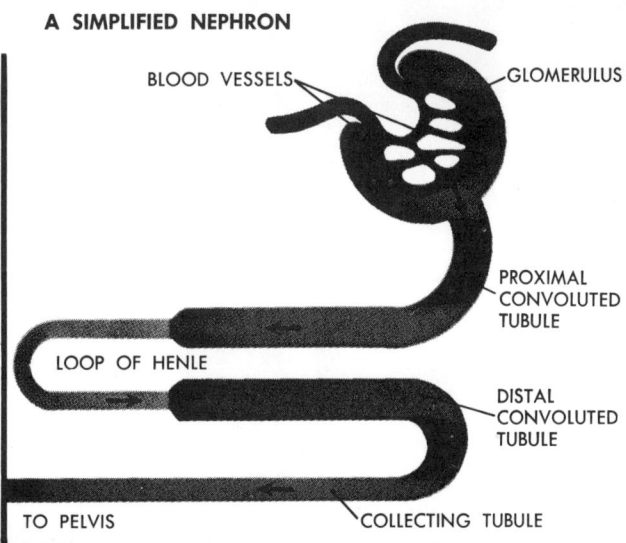

This enlargement of the kidney cross section shows a nephron — the basic urine-producing structure of the kidney. The activity of the entire kidney is the activity of the nephron multiplied 1,000,000 times (the approximate number of nephrons in each kidney).

A SIMPLIFIED NEPHRON

BLOOD VESSELS
GLOMERULUS
PROXIMAL CONVOLUTED TUBULE
LOOP OF HENLE
DISTAL CONVOLUTED TUBULE
TO PELVIS
COLLECTING TUBULE

The nephron is shown here in schematic form to illustrate the relation of its parts. Blood enters the vessels of the glomerulus on the left and some filters through the glomerular membranes, initiating urine production. As this filtrate passes through the convoluted tubules, material is removed (reabsorption) and added (secretion). Thus urine production involves three basic steps — *filtration, reabsorption, and secretion.*

Passive Reabsorption

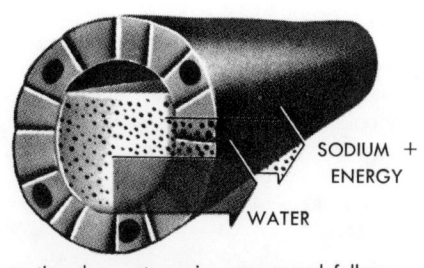

SODIUM + ENERGY
WATER

Passive reabsorption does not require energy and follows the principle that material flows from areas of higher to areas of lower concentration. In the first stage sodium passes out of the urine through active reabsorption. Water then passively follows sodium out of the tubule to balance the chemical pressure across the tubule wall.

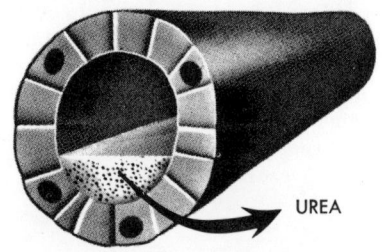

UREA

As water leaves the tubule the total fluid volume declines, thus raising the urea concentration. Urea now passively flows out of the tubule (region of higher concentration) to the surrounding tissue fluid (region of lower concentration).

SECRETION

The third basic activity of the nephron is the secretion of substances into the urine. These may be taken from the blood (for example, foreign substances such as penicillin) or be produced in the cells of the kidney tubule (hydrogen ions and ammonia).

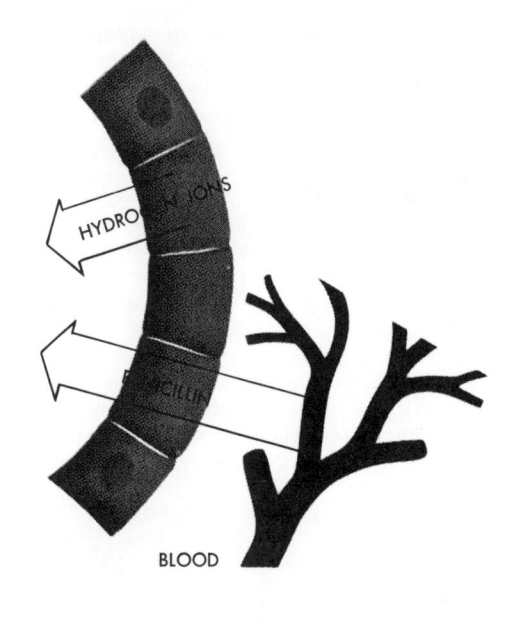

HYDROGEN IONS
PENICILLIN
BLOOD

THE KIDNEY AND WATER BALANCE

The kidney adjusts the volume of urine output according to the fluid intake of the body. As more water is consumed the blood and other body fluids become diluted. This is presumed to result in the swelling of specialized cells (osmoreceptors) in the brain, giving rise to impulses which inhibit the secretion of antidiuretic hormone (ADH) by the pituitary gland. The hormone acts upon the tubules of the nephron rendering them more permeable to water. As ADH secretion diminishes the distal tubule and collecting duct become less permeable, permitting more water to escape in the urine. The reverse effects occur when the body is deprived of water.

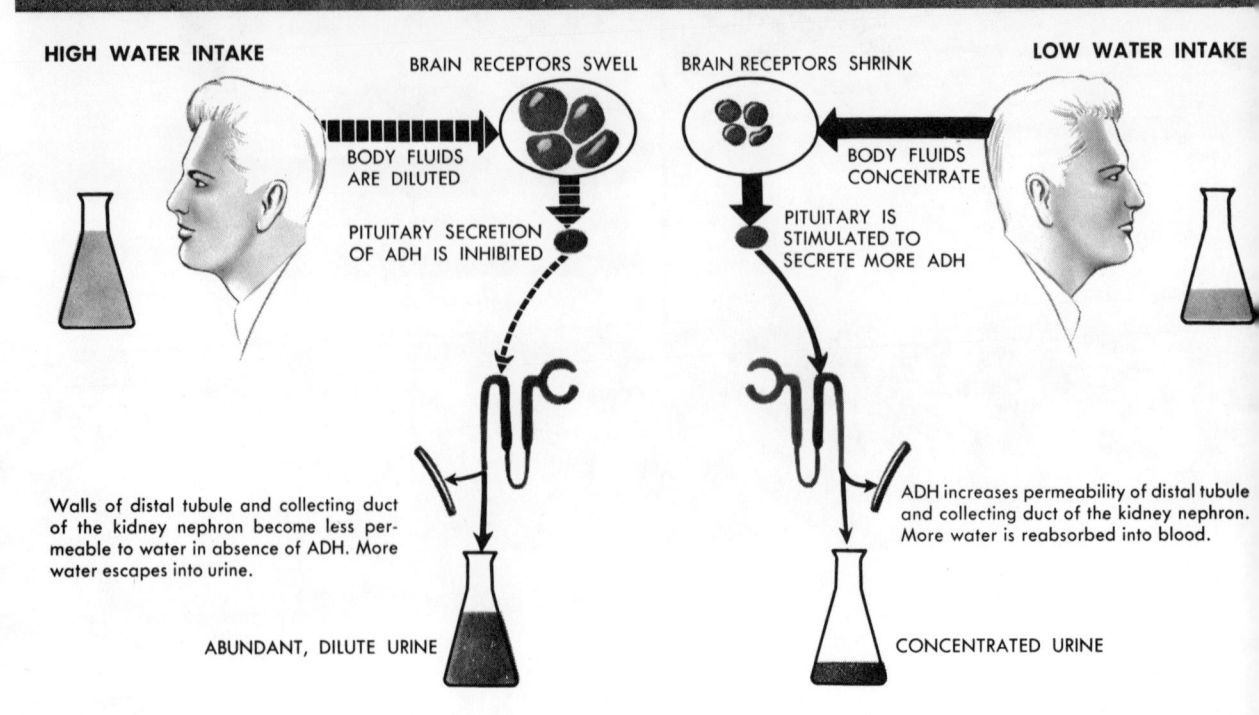

HIGH WATER INTAKE — BRAIN RECEPTORS SWELL — BODY FLUIDS ARE DILUTED — PITUITARY SECRETION OF ADH IS INHIBITED

Walls of distal tubule and collecting duct of the kidney nephron become less permeable to water in absence of ADH. More water escapes into urine.

ABUNDANT, DILUTE URINE

LOW WATER INTAKE — BRAIN RECEPTORS SHRINK — BODY FLUIDS CONCENTRATE — PITUITARY IS STIMULATED TO SECRETE MORE ADH

ADH increases permeability of distal tubule and collecting duct of the kidney nephron. More water is reabsorbed into blood.

CONCENTRATED URINE

How Much Kidney Do We Need? The kidney is a vital organ and fortunately the body is supplied with far more kidney tissue than it normally needs. If one kidney is damaged or removed, its function is taken over fully by the remaining kidney, which enlarges. There are cases on record in which one identical twin has saved the life of the other by donating one of his healthy kidneys to replace the nonfunctioning kidneys of the other twin. Unfortunately, kidney transplantation is severely hampered in the case of any but identical twins by the tendency of the body to develop an immunity against, and to eventually destroy, the transplant.

See also GLOMERULONEPHRITIS; KIDNEY, ARTIFICIAL; KIDNEY TRANSPLANT; NEPHROSIS; URINE.

KIDNEY, ARTIFICIAL, mechanical apparatus which substitutes for kidney function by removing diffusible substances from the blood. Used in animal research in 1913, the artificial kidney's practicality for man was demonstrated by W. J. Kolff in Holland in 1947. Recent improvements have not changed its basic principles. The patient's blood is pumped through cellophane tubing, while a solution, chemically similar to blood, washes the outside of the tube. The process is known as hemodialysis. The high concentration of various substances in the blood causes them to diffuse through the cellophane, improving the patient's condition. Hemodialysis removes toxic substances built up when the kidneys fail to function in uremia. It also removes high concentrations of poisonous drugs or chemicals, or an excess of water or salt.

There are several major problems requiring expert care in hemodialysis. Infection must be prevented and the blood returned undamaged and unclotted to the patient. The artificial kidney has been used successfully in patients with temporary kidney failure and in others who are awaiting kidney transplantation. Aided by frequent hemodialysis, some patients without kidneys have been maintained in good health for several years.

See also KIDNEY.

KIDNEY STONE. See CALCULI.

KIDNEY TRANSPLANT, a healthy kidney taken from one person and placed in the body of another. Ordinarily kidney transplants are permanently successful only when the donor of the kidney is an identical twin. In other cases the body of the recipient develops special substances, called antibodies, which react with and destroy the transplant. This unfavorable reaction is similar to the mechanism by which the body defends itself against infection and may actually be regarded as the development of an immunity on the part of the body to the foreign kidney tissue. Experiments have been undertaken to prevent such an immunity from developing. These have employed near-fatal doses of radiation to inhibit the formation of anti-kidney antibodies by the tissues.

KINESTHETIC [kĭn-ĭs-thĕt′ĭk] **SENSE,** sense that provides awareness of the relative position and movement of parts of the body, sometimes divided into muscle sense, tendon sense, and joint sense. The muscles, tendons, and joints are supplied with specialized nerve endings, which are stimulated by posture and movement. The endings near the joint surfaces are the most important, although the other endings make some contribution. A movement of less than one degree of rotation can be kinesthetically perceived. See also SENSATION.

KITASATO [kē-tä-zä-tō], **SHIBASABURO** (1852–1931), Japanese bacteriologist. While at Koch Institute in Berlin, Kitasato grew the tetanus bacillus in pure culture, and, with Emil von Behring, produced serums (antitoxins) which counteracted the effects of the poisons given off by tetanus and diphtheria bacteria. He established a laboratory in Tokyo where he discovered the bacillus that causes plague.

KLEBS [klāps], **EDWIN** (1834–1913), German bacteriologist known for his study of the diphtheria bacillus (called the Klebs-Löffler bacillus). He also made experimental studies on the transmission of syphilis to apes. He taught at Prague, Zurich, and several other European universities and at Rush Medical College in the United States.

KNOCK-KNEES, a deformity of the lower extremities in which both knees come together while the legs and feet go outward or laterally. It is commonly associated with flat feet. Occasionally, knock-knees result from abnormal growth or fractures. The condition gradually disappears in most children. Mild cases may be treated by raising the inner border of the heels. Corrective braces worn at night are sometimes necessary. Severe cases require surgical correction by osteotomy, an operation in which the bones are cut and realigned.

KOCH [kôKH], **ROBERT** (1843–1910), German bacteriologist, winner of the 1905 Nobel Prize in medicine and physiology for his discovery of the tubercle bacillus, the cause of tuberculosis. Koch's first significant work was to determine the life cycle of the anthrax bacillus, during a local epidemic in cattle. Next, he established the first system of culturing bacteria outside a living animal, devising three rules for identifying the infectious cause of a disease. These are, identification of the agent in the diseased animal, innoculation of healthy animals with the purified organisms, and reidentification of the organism by finding identical characteristics in the serially infected animals. Called Koch's postulates, these rules are the foundation of modern microbiology.

Koch developed two all-important laboratory techniques, the use of analine dyes to stain bacteria for easier identification, and the use of gelatin and agar to support bacterial growth in the laboratory. He also discovered the cholera bacillus, showed that bubonic plague is transmitted by a louse which infests rats, and that sleeping sickness is transmitted by the tsetse fly. These studies introduced the idea of interrupting the life cycle of a disease-producing organism by destroying its insect carriers. Thus, for example, mosquito control can eliminate malaria. Such indirect methods are much more effective than treatment of the infection after it occurs. They stand with the development of vaccines as man's most successful achievements in the prevention of disease.
See also GERM THEORY.

KOCHER [kôKH′ər], **EMIL THEODOR** (1841–1917), Swiss surgeon who was awarded the Nobel Prize in 1909 for his work on the pathology and surgery of the thyroid gland. Professor of surgery at Bern, he taught many of the finest surgeons of Europe and America and devised operations for excising the tongue, hip joint, rectum, and ankle joint, and for amputation of the breast.

KORSAKOFF'S PSYCHOSIS, also called amnestic confabulatory syndrome, a severe mental disturbance seen mainly in chronic alcoholics. The disorder is characterized by degeneration of nervous tissue, extensive loss of memory, and a tendency to fabricate stories to fill in the gaps of memory. The individual may be confused as to his identity and his surroundings. There may be pain and tenderness in the legs and a loss of normal reflexes. The actual cause of the condition may be a deficiency of the B-complex vitamins, particularly thiamine (vitamin B_1). This view is supported by the appearance of the psychosis in nonalcoholics and the frequent occurrence of vitamin deficiencies among chronic alcoholics. The condition sometimes improves with treatment. A complete cure is rare.

KREBS [krĕps], **SIR HANS ADOLF** (1900–   ), British biochemist who shared the Nobel Prize with Fritz Lipmann in 1953 for the discovery of the citric acid, or "Krebs," cycle, a chain of chemical reactions in mammalian cells by which food substances are burned with oxygen to yield energy. Krebs was born and educated in Germany but, being a Jew, was forced to leave when the Nazis came to power. Since 1933 he has held research and teaching positions at various British universities, including Oxford and Cambridge.

KREBS CYCLE, also known as the citric acid cycle, or the tricarboxylic acid cycle, is a series of chemical reactions occurring in the tissues of man and other mammals, by which oxygen from the lungs is used to burn food substances yielding energy, carbon dioxide, and water. Fats, proteins, and carbohydrates, after being broken down into fatty acids, amino acids, and simple sugars in the course of digestion, are further changed in the body into still simpler substances which enter the Krebs cycle in the mitochondria, the highly specialized metabolic units of the individual cells. In the cycle these substances are oxidized, generating energy which is bound in the form of high energy bonds to ATP, the chemical energy broker of the cell. ATP releases this energy when it is needed for muscu-

lar contraction, tissue synthesis, and other biological activities.
See also METABOLISM.

KROGH [krôg], **AUGUST** (1874–1949), Danish physiologist who received the Nobel Prize in 1920 for his investigations of circulation in the capillaries—the microscopic blood vessels found in most tissues of the body. Krogh discovered that the capillaries open and close in response to changes in tissue activity. Krogh's earlier studies dealt with the physiology of respiration. His publications include *The Respiratory Exchange in Animals and Man* (1916) and *The Anatomy and Physiology of Capillaries* (1922; rev. ed., 1928).

KWASHIORKOR [kwäsh-ē-ôr'kôr], disorder of infants and young children which is caused by a deficiency of protein in the diet. It is seen most frequently in underdeveloped parts of the world, particularly in the tropics and subtropics. The principal symptoms are retarded growth, irritability, listlessness, and fluid swellings of the feet, legs, or entire body. There may be skin disturbances, loss of pigment in the skin and hair, and wasting away of the muscles. The liver is often enlarged and infiltrated with fat. The condition is often complicated by other nutritional deficiencies or by parasitic disorders, such as malaria. Unless recognized early, and corrected by adding protein foods such as milk to the diet, kwashiorkor may be fatal in approximately 80% of the cases.

L

LACTIC ACID, $CH_3CHOHCOOH$, a sirupy organic acid, found in sour milk, and in a different form in blood and muscular tissues, particularly after heavy exercise. All forms are soluble in water, alcohol, and ether. Lactic acid is made commercially by the fermentation of sugars, such as glucose, sucrose, or lactose.

LACTOSE [lăk'tōs], a sugar composed of the simple sugars (monosaccharides) glucose and galactose. Because of its presence in the milk of mammals, it is also called milk sugar. Lactose is used primarily in the preparation of modified milk and other foods for children and convalescents. It is also used in the pharmaceutical and baking industries. The presence of lactose in the diet helps maintain the intestinal bacteria, *Lactobacillus acidophilus*, which are important for calcium absorption. These organisms convert lactose to lactic acid. The latter increases the acidity of the intestine, permitting more calcium to dissolve in the intestinal fluids.

LANCISI [län-chē'zē], **GIOVANNI MARIA** (1654–1720), Italian physician who made important studies on the epidemiology of malaria, cattle plague, and influenza. He was one of the first to recognize the possibility that malaria might be transmitted to man by mosquitoes. He was physician to Pope Innocent XI, Pope Innocent XII, and Pope Clement XI.

LANGENBECK [läng'ən-běk], **BERNHARD RUDOLPH KONRAD VON** (1810–87), German surgeon who pioneered in the development of plastic surgery. He modified the ancient Indian technique of plastic nose reconstruction and developed an operation for cleft palate. He also made significant contributions to orthopedic surgery. He founded the *Archiv für klinische Chirurgie* in 1861.

LAPAROTOMY [lăp-ə-rŏt'ə-mē], an operation in which an incision is made into the abdominal wall, or flank. Laparotomies are performed in cases of abdominal disorders to correct abnormalities, to remove organs, to halt bleeding, or to obtain samples of tissue to aid in diagnosis.

LARVA MIGRANS [lär'və mī'grănz], or "creeping eruption," a skin condition in which the larvae of worms (primarily *Ancylostoma braziliense*) or flies (the botfly, *Gastrophilus intestinalis*) burrow under the skin. The *A. braziliense* infections are usually contracted by skin contact with contaminated soil. Botfly infestations occur when fly eggs are deposited on human skin. The larvae penetrate the skin and as they migrate, usually at the rate of ½ to 1 in. per day, cause intense itching and an elevated red, snakelike lesion. Treatment consists of spraying the lesions with a freezing compound (ethyl chloride). Fly larvae are usually removed surgically.

LARYNGITIS [lăr-ən-jī'tĭs], inflammation of the larynx, or "voice box." Most cases of adult laryngitis are associated with the common cold, excessive use of the voice, or with irritation from tobacco or chemical fumes. The larynx becomes red and swollen, causing hoarseness, sore throat, and occasionally loss of voice. Treatment consists of rest, avoidance of speaking, and steam inhalations. Other forms of laryngitis occur in conjunction with infectious diseases such as tuberculosis, syphilis, measles, and influenza. Croup (q.v.), or acute obstructive laryngitis, may block the breathing passages and is particularly dangerous in small children.

LARYNX [lăr'ĭngks]. The larynx, or voice box, is a part of the respiratory system—situated between the root of the tongue and the trachea, or windpipe—which regulates the passage of air through the trachea (to the lungs) and aids in the production of sound. The larynx is a hollow, tapering structure, composed of paired and single cartilages which are connected by ligaments and moved by attached muscles. The largest cartilage of the larynx, the thyroid cartilage, forms the frontal portion and part of the sides of the larynx. In adult males, the thyroid cartilage may be large enough to form a prominence in the neck—the Adam's apple. The inner surface of the larynx is covered by a mucous membrane. Extending inward from the side walls of the laryngeal cavities are two sets of paired folds—the upper folds, or false vocal folds, and the lower, or true vocal folds (the vocal "cords").

The passage of air through the glottis (the slitlike opening between the true vocal folds), and the production of sound by the true vocal folds is regulated by the movement of the various laryngeal cartilages. The pitch of the sound is modulated by the vocalis muscle, which tenses the vocal folds.

LAUGHTER in man is a complex reflex of the muscles of respiration, face, and throat. It usually involves a series of involuntary spasmodic contractions of abdominal muscles, accompanied by contractions of cheek muscles (the smile) and semiarticulate sounds. The response may undergo modification in that facial expressions or vocalizations are altered or absent, hence the expressions "silent laughter," or "sardonic laughter." The essential characteristic of laughter, therefore, seems to be the serial abdominal contractions with expirations of air from the lungs. With minimal contraction of the vocal muscles the result is the familiar "ha-ha-ha"; marked contraction produces the "he-he-he."

Laughter has been regarded by most authors as peculiar to man, but this is debatable. The essence of laughter may be observed in many other species, and much has been written of the laughing crow, gull, hyena, and jackass. Moreover, most and possibly all of the monkeys and apes exhibit the fundamental characteristics of laughter.

The neurophysiology of laughter has received little study beyond the human clinic. There it has been learned that involuntary laughter may be produced by mild anesthetics such as nitrous oxide (laughing gas) or may be the result of various forms of accident or disease in the brain. One of these neurological disorders (pseudobulbar palsy) is even known as "laughing sickness." A person with this disorder may laugh but feel sad, or he may cry but feel happy. The most common form of psychosis, schizophrenia, often includes involuntary mirthless laughter.

LAXATIVES, or cathartics, are drugs which promote defecation. Most laxatives accomplish this by increasing the muscular activity of the intestines by irritating the intestinal tract, by increasing the bulk within it, or by lubricating the tract, thus facilitating the passages of feces. Although they are among the most widely used drugs, many authorities agree that laxatives are frequently misused by the general public.

Among the irritant laxatives are senna, cascara, phenolphthalein, and castor oil. Senna may cause cramps. It acts within six hours. Both cascara and senna irritate the large intestine. Castor oil is broken down in the intestine into the irritant ricinoleic acid, which produces a laxative effect by irritating the small intestine. It acts within two to six hours. Phenolphthalein, which is used in many gum and candy laxatives, irritates both the large and small bowel.

Bulk laxatives include bran, psyllium seed, and agar. Bran supplies indigestible roughage. Psyllium seeds swell in the bowel into an indigestible mass. They are taken with fruit juices or mixed with foods. Agar passes through the tract without being digested and adds bulk to the intestines by absorbing water.

Mineral oil, or liquid petrolatum, is a well-known laxative which lubricates the intestinal tract and softens its contents. Serious objections to its use have been raised on the grounds that elderly habitual users may repeatedly inhale small amounts into the lungs, eventually causing a dangerous lipid pneumonia.

A newer group of lubricant laxatives are the "wetting" agents, such as dioctyl sodium sulfosuccinate (Doxinate, Colace) and Poloxalkol (Polykol), which increase the wetting efficiency of the intestinal fluid, thus keeping the stool soft.

The saline laxatives, such as magnesium sulfate (epsom salts), magnesium hydroxide (milk of magnesia), and effervescent sodium phosphate, produce both a bulk and moistening effect by holding large quantities of fluid in the intestine. Epsom salts may cause magnesium poisoning if given to individuals suffering from impaired kidney function.

Laxatives are used in treating cases of stubborn constipation in the elderly and the bedridden, in certain types of poisoning to remove harmful substances from the bowels, in some patients with heart disorders to prevent straining at the stool, and in conjunction with other drugs in the treatment of intestinal parasites. They are also used to cleanse the bowel in preparation for X-ray studies of the digestive tract. Laxatives should never be used in individuals with undiagnosed abdominal pain. The indiscriminate, habitual use of laxatives may lead to serious organic disturbances.

LEAD POISONING, also known as plumbism, usually develops gradually from repeated exposure to lead over an extended period. Workers engaged in lead mining, smelting, or refining, or in the manufacture of lead wire, bullets, storage batteries, or other lead-containing products, have been affected. Household poisoning has resulted from drinking water carried through lead pipes; lead-based paints have caused poisoning in infants chewing on their cribs.

The symptoms of lead poisoning are highly variable. The patient may become moody and irritable. The face and lips may be pale, and a black line (the so-called "lead line") may appear in the margin of the gums. The red blood cells acquire a characteristic "stippling," which may be seen under the microscope. An outstanding symptom is "lead colic," which consists of severe, excruciating abdominal cramps, resulting from spasm of the bowel muscles. In advanced cases lead palsy may appear, usually involving weakness of the forearm muscles, causing "wristdrop." In young children, the brain is frequently involved, causing headache, vomiting, irritability, convulsions, and coma. This is called lead encephalopathy and is often fatal.

Calcium salts have been used to control the severe symptoms, such as lead colic. EDTA (ethylenediamine tetra-acetic acid) is used to safely remove lead from the tissues.

See also POISONING.

LECITHIN [lĕs'ə-thĭn] or **PHOSPHATIDYL CHOLINE** [fŏs'fă-tĭd-əl kō'lēn], one of a class of compounds known as phospholipids (phosphorus-fat compounds) which are found in high concentration in nervous tissue, liver, pancreas, heart, and in egg yolk and soybeans. Lecithin is present in normal blood and is believed to be one of the lipotropic substances which may prevent the accumulation of fats in the liver. In medicine it has been used in the treatment of chronic skin disorders and in controlling excess cholesterol in the blood (hypercholesterolemia). Lecithin is used in the manufacture of margarine, chocolate, and in pharmaceuticals and cosmetics. It is obtained commercially as a by-product in the manufacture of soybean oil or by organic synthesis.

LEECH, annelid in the class Hirudinea. Like earthworms, nercides (clam worms), and others in the phylum Annelida, leeches have segmented bodies. Numerous rings can be seen on the surface of the body, although some of these rings are not true segments, but just folds of skin. Nearly all leeches will suck the blood of vertebrate animals if they have the chance, but most species also eat snails, small crustaceans, and insect larvae. After a meal of blood, a leech can go for months without eating at all. Ordinarily, the wound made by a leech is not painful. It may continue to bleed for some time because the saliva of leeches contains a substance called hirudin, which prevents blood clotting. Leeches can be made to release their hold by sprinkling them with a little salt.

LEEUWENHOEK or **LEUWENHOEK** [lā'vən-hōok], **ANTON VAN** (1632–1723), self-taught Dutch microscopist. A shoe merchant, born at Delft, he was an amateur grinder of lenses and a maker of microscopes, through which he discovered and accurately described the protozoa in 1674 and the bacteria in 1676. For his contributions to the science of bacteriology and protozoology, he has been called the father of microbiology.

LEISHMAN [lēsh'mən], **SIR WILLIAM BOOG** (1865–1926), Scottish physician known for his discovery of the organisms which cause the infectious disease kala-azar. A genus of disease-causing protozoa, the *Leishmania*, is named in his honor.

LEISHMANIASIS [lēsh-mən-ī'ə-sĭs] refers to a number of conditions caused by infection with microscopic one-celled tissue parasites (protozoa) of the genus *Leishmania*. These organisms are transmitted to humans by bloodsucking sandflies (phlebotomus) which have previously bitten other infected humans or warm-blooded animals, such as dogs or rodents.

The entire body may be involved in kala-azar, or visceral leishmaniasis, which is caused by the *L. donovani* and is found in parts of Asia, Africa, and South America. The infection causes enlargement of the liver and spleen, anemia, and a low-grade irregular fever. Chills, sweats, dizziness, and headaches are frequent. Complications may include bronchitis and pneumonia. Kala-azar is often fatal if untreated.

The *L. tropica*, which is identical in appearance to *L. donovani*, causes a relatively mild skin condition called oriental sore; Baghdad, or Aleppo, boil; or cutaneous leishmaniasis. This is most often seen in the Mediterranean region, in southwest Asia, and in Africa. The disease begins as a red sore, commonly on exposed surfaces such as the face, ears, neck, backs of the hands, and forearms. The sore gradually spreads and may heal after a year or more, leaving a disfiguring scar. Many Baghdad mothers deliberately infect their babies on some covered part of the body to produce immunity and avoid subsequent infection and scarring of the face.

Between the extremes of kala-azar and oriental sore are a number of leishmanial infections which vary in the extent to which they invade the body tissues. A number of leishmanial disorders involving the skin, mucous membranes, and viscera are seen in the Western Hemisphere from southern Mexico to Argentina. *L. braziliensis* produces one or more skin lesions and eventually involves the mucous membranes of the mouth, nose, and pharynx, causing serious and extensive destruction. Death may occur from infection of the ulcerations.

Kala-azar and other leishmanial infections are treated with antimony compounds and stilbamidine and related drugs. Leishmaniasis can be prevented by eliminating the sandfly which carries the disease and by treating humans and dogs who harbor the infectious organisms. Rubbish and vegetation which serve as breeding places for the flies should be sprayed with DDT. Ordinary screens and sleeping nets are not effective against sandflies, but may offer some protection if sprayed with DDT.

LEPROSY [lĕp'rə-sē] or **HANSEN'S DISEASE** is a chronic infectious disease which involves primarily the skin and the peripheral nerves. Although leprosy is primarily a tropical disease, it has occurred as far north as Norway and Iceland. Most cases are found in a broad zone girdling the earth about 25° north and south of the equator. In the United States leprosy is found in southern Louisiana and in Texas along the coast of the Gulf of Mexico. It is estimated that there are 3.5 to 12 million cases of leprosy throughout the world.

The leprosy bacterium was first described by the Norwegian physician G. Armauer Hansen in 1874. It is similar in its structure and many of its characteristics to the organism which causes tuberculosis. The bacteria are believed to be transmitted from person to person by direct contact. The disease is not easily spread, however, as scarcely more than 5% of persons married to an individual suffering from leprosy will contract the disease. The average period of incubation is five years or more. Many unsuccessful attempts have been made to relate the likelihood of acquiring leprosy to climate, race, inheritance, or other factors.

The disturbances seen in leprosy are extremely variable: the skin is usually affected early while nerve damage appears later. Many of the more disabling phenomena result from nerve damage rather than infection. The ulcers of the feet and the atrophies and contractures of the fingers are caused by damage resulting from spread of the infection along the nerves of the extremities. Facial disfigurement is seen only in advanced stages, especially when the infection is untreated. The skin lesions vary from simple spots to thick infiltrations and nodule formation. The severity of the infections depends upon the type of leprosy: the most severe cases are caused by the lepromatous form which progresses steadily and involves infiltration of the skin, producing nodular lesions. The milder tuberculoid form usually improves spontaneously. In many instances, tuberculoid leprosy would be an unimportant skin condition were it not for the associated nerve involvement.

Leprosy is rarely fatal in itself. Death, when it occurs, usually results from complications, or a concurrent illness. The most serious complications are involvement of the nose and throat (which frequently accompanies the advanced disease), trophic ulcerations of the feet with secondary infection, osteomyelitis (bone infection), and lesions of the inner structures of the eye, leading to blindness.

Treatment. Since 1941 a group of drugs, called sulfones, have been widely used in the treatment of leprosy. These drugs are highly effective in the milder types and, although they do not cure the lepromatous types, serious complications are usually prevented. Treatment failures are observed in approximately 5% of the cases, apparently resulting from the development of drug-resistance by the leprosy bacteria.

Leprosy is being treated today with large-scale outpatient treatment programs.

LEPTOSPIROSES [lĕp-tō-spī-rō′sēs], a group of diseases caused by strains of corkscrew-shaped microorganisms of the genus *Leptospira*. These organisms are harbored in the bodies of wild rodents or domestic animals, which contaminate the water of fields and swamps with their germ-laden urine. In various parts of the world the diseases are named with respect to the type of exposure leading to infection: for example, cane-field fever, mud fever, swamp fever, and swineherd's disease. The organisms are thought to enter through small breaks in the skin, or by penetrating intact mucous membranes, particularly of the nose and eye.

The severity of the infections varies greatly, ranging from scarcely noticeable disorders to a mild grippe-like disease to rapidly fatal attacks. Usually there is an incubation period of 7–10 days followed by fever, vomiting, headache, intense reddening of the eyes, severe muscle pains, or small hemorrhages into the skin or the mucous membranes. Jaundice, a yellowish tinting of the skin and eyes, may be seen but is most often associated with *L. icterohemorrhagiae* infections (Weil's Disease). The central nervous system may be involved, particularly the meninges (the tissues which envelop the brain and spinal cord)..

Antibiotics have been used in treatment but, though effective in some cases, are often disappointing. Preventive measures have been directed at eliminating rats and other animal carriers. Wearing gloves and other protective clothing may help prevent the organisms from entering the body.

LEUKEMIA [loō-kē′mē-ə], serious blood disorder involving abnormalities of the white blood cells, the leucocytes. The cause of leukemia is not known. One theory traces the disease to the emergence of a single abnormal white blood cell which is able to reproduce itself vigorously and to infiltrate organs and tissues. How such a cell originates is a mystery. Possible inciting factors are believed to be exposure to radiation or to certain chemicals (particularly benzol derivatives), viruses, or genetic influences.

The Types of Leukemia. Several types of leukemia are recognized which differ in terms of the duration of the disease and the specific type of white blood cell affected. *Acute* leukemias are usually fatal within a period ranging from a few weeks to one or two years. Patients with *chronic*, or long-term, leukemias, may survive for up to ten years. The outlook also varies with the cell type. The duration of chronic lymphocytic leukemia (involving the lymphocytes—white cells having a single nucleus surrounded by clear extranuclear material) is from five to ten years whereas that for chronic granulocytic leukemia (involving the granulocytes—white cells having a lobed nucleus and granulated extranuclear material) is three to five years. Other white cell types may also be involved in distinct varieties of leukemia. In some cases the leukemia is described as "aleukemic," referring to the fact that the white cell population is low or normal, as distinct from the massive white cell counts seen in most cases.

Symptoms and Signs. In chronic leukemia the patient may appear to be in good health at the time his condition is detected by discovery of a high white blood cell count or an enlarged lymph gland. Acute leukemia may strike rapidly, producing weakness, fever, signs of infection, and other symptoms within a short period of time.

The changes seen in leukemia result from invasion of the tissues by the rapidly multiplying white blood cells. The lymph nodes, spleen, and liver are usually enlarged. Almost any organ may be affected, and nervous, abdominal, and skin disturbances are not unusual.

Of particular significance is the presence of large numbers of young immature white cells in the bone marrow, displacing the normal blood-forming tissues. This leads to the three most important signs and symptoms of leukemia—anemia (lack of red blood cells), tendency to bleed (caused by lack of blood platelets), and infection (resulting from a decrease in the numbers of mature bacteria-fighting white blood cells).

Treatment. The treatment of leukemia is generally unsatisfactory and the disease is invariably fatal. Treatment may temporarily relieve the symptoms and prolong the course of the disease, but no cure has been found.

Nonspecific therapy for leukemia is directed at the symptoms and includes antibiotics for the infection, blood transfusions for the anemia, and platelet transfusions to correct the bleeding tendencies.

Specific treatment is directed at the leukemic cells. X rays can reduce enlarged organs and lower the white cell count. A number of drugs are available, but their usefulness is limited in that most attack normal as well as abnormal cells. A notable characteristic of leukemia drug therapy is that these compounds are usually effective only in a specific type of leukemia. Drugs which interfere with cell chemistry (antimetabolites and corticosteroids) have been used in the acute leukemias. Unlike normal cells, certain types of leukemia cells are incapable of synthesizing the amino acid asparagine, which is essential to their growth. Thus, by using the enzyme asparaginase to break down this amino acid, the growth of leukemic cells can be checked, at least temporarily, without damage to the normal cells. The selectivity of asparaginase is a valuable asset and it has proved effective in inducing remissions in cases of acute leukemia.

Bone marrow transplantation is a type of leukemia therapy in which the leukemic bone marrow of the patient is destroyed by exposing the entire body to large doses of radiation. Following this, grafts of bone marrow taken from suitable donors are infused into the patient's bone cavities. This method is thought to offer promise.

LEUKOCYTOSIS [loo-ko-sĭ-tō'sĭs], increase of white blood cells in the circulating blood above normal. Leukocytosis occurs when the white cell count is greater than 11,000 cells per cubic millimeter of blood. Almost any type of foreign stimulus can cause leukocytosis, which is also called neutrophilia. The most common causes are infections of bacterial, viral, or parasitic origin.

Many disorders other than infections also cause leukocytosis. A partial list of these disorders includes toxic metabolic states, such as gout and uremia or kidney failure; chemical poisoning; acute bleeding; tissue destruction from surgery or heart attacks; and tumors of many types. Even strenuous exercise may cause leukocytosis. Leukemia is suspected when no cause can be found for persistent leukocytosis, and there are large numbers of abnormally immature forms of leukocytes. Often a study of bone marrow cells helps determine the cause.

LEUKOPENIA [loo-ko-pē'nē-ə], reduction below normal of the white cells in the circulating blood. Less than 5,000 white cells per cubic millimeter as determined by the blood count is considered leukopenia. Usually the reduction is due to an absence of the granulocytes, or neutrophilic polymorphonuclear leukocytes. A reduction in lymphocytes, called lymphopenia, can also be responsible. Specific types of infection, some bacterial, some viral, and some parasitic, are characteristically associated with leukopenia. Any overwhelming infection, to which the body cannot respond adequately, leads to leukopenia. Dietary and nutritional deficiencies, poisoning or toxic drug reactions, and disorders of the liver or spleen which destroy leukocytes also cause leukopenia. It is usually of critical importance to study the precursor cells of the bone marrow for clues to the cause of leukopenia.

In rare instances, leukemia begins with leukopenia, and leukocytosis, an excess of white cells, appears only at a late stage of the illness. A person with leukopenia from any cause is highly susceptible to infection.

LEUKOPLAKIA [loo-ko-plā'kē-ə], whitish, thickened plaques of mucous membranes, usually seen in the inside of the mouth or on the tongue; it may also appear in the genital area. Leukoplakia develops in response to irritation such as may be caused by tobacco, poorly fitting dentures, or sharp, irregular teeth. The patches may become cancerous and should be checked regularly. The condition often improves when the irritation is removed.

LEUKORRHEA [loo-kə-rē'ə], whitish discharge from the female genital tract. This may be seen normally during pregnancy and prior to menstruation. Leukorrhea may be caused by infections and inflammations of the genital tract and by tumors of the womb.

LICHEN PLANUS [plā'nəs], a skin disorder characterized by flat-topped, violet-colored, pinhead-sized raised spots seen most frequently on the front of the wrists and above the ankles. Although the cause is unknown, many authorities suspect that emotional or nervous factors may be involved. Though in rare cases lichen planus rapidly spreads over the trunk and extremities, more frequently it develops slowly and is limited in extent. The face is usually spared, but the inside of the mouth and the genitalia may be affected. The eruption usually persists for several months; recurrences are frequent. Arsenic, bismuth, and mercury compounds given by mouth have long been the standard treatment for lichen planus. More recently, tranquilizers and hormones of the cortisone group have also proven helpful. X rays are used in some cases.

LIFE. What is life? In his search for an answer to this age-old query, man has used all the varied approaches made possible by his powers of observation, reasoning, and insight. Philosophers, poets, prophets, artists, and writers have attempted to interpret life and its meaning. Today thousands of biologists and scientists in related fields are pursuing the elusive reality we call life. Scientific problems, however, have a way of eluding final solution, a feature fascinating to scientists but frustrating to the layman eager for a quick and simple answer.

The External Characteristics of Life

A great philosopher has said that it takes a very unusual mind to undertake an analysis of the obvious. Life is all around us; we deal daily with living activities; we ourselves are living organisms. We all know what life is, and can easily, among the higher organisms, tell the difference between an oak tree and the stones which lie at its base, or between a man and the automobile he drives. But as we proceed lower in the scale of life, it is sometimes difficult to separate decisively the living from the nonliving. A case in point is the virus, considered a nonliving chemical substance by some biologists, a primitive living organism by others. But let us, returning to life in general, begin with the obvious. The most constant feature of every kind of life is its ability to do things. The ability to do things in turn involves a number of correlated activities: self-maintenance, movement, growth and differentiation, self-duplication through reproduction, and adjustment to the environment through response and adaptability.

Self-Maintenance. A major difference between a living organism and a nonliving object is the ability of the organism to select and take in substances from the environment, incorporate them into its body matter (protoplasm), and utilize them by special energy transformations (metabolism). All this is done in such a way that the physical appearance of the organism and the special pattern of living remains practically unchanged during the process. We see examples of this process of self-maintenance taking place constantly, all about us. Every organism requires food, carries on respiration, eliminates wastes, and utilizes nutrients; yet the organism maintains its constant form in spite of this ceaseless internal energy transformation, in a changing and often hostile environment. This maintenance of an internally balanced energy-transforming system is known as homeostasis. It is one of the unique characteristics of life.

Movement. Movement is characteristic of all living organisms but is more obvious in animals than in plants. Within the cells of all organisms there is protoplasmic movement, and even in such relatively immobile organisms as plants, movement includes such phenomena as the twining of tendrils and phototropic responses of leaves. In this characteristic, the distinction between living and nonliving is not as clear-cut as in the previously discussed feature of self-maintenance. Nonliving objects, however, move when acted on by external force, such as gravity which causes rocks to move down a mountain slope. In living things the energy for movement comes from internal forces, and is directed and controlled from within.

Growth and Differentiation. If the criterion of growth is simply increase in volume or size, then both living and nonliving objects can grow. A stalactite in a cavern becomes thicker and longer, but such growth is addition of material from the outside; in a living organism growth occurs through an increase in the number of microscopic units (cells) of which the organism is composed. Such growth is caused by addition of new material within the organism, as a result of transformation of one kind of material (food) into another (protoplasm). Most organisms begin life as a single cell: the fertilized egg. By cell division this increases to many cells which differentiate and develop into specialized tissues. A seed weighing a fraction of an ounce not only grows into a plant of much greater size (a tree weighing several tons, for example), but also becomes a more complex object with parts not present in the seed. In the nonliving world, no parallel to such growth exists—for example, no pebble ever becomes more than a pebble; nor is a boulder, regardless of its size, ever anything more complex than a boulder.

Reproduction. Another obvious characteristic which distinguishes living from nonliving things is the ability to produce new "things" like themselves. Many different types of asexual and sexual reproduction exist in the living world, all designed to produce nearly exact copies of the parent. Comparable creation of new nonliving things does not take place. The reproductive capabilities of an organism are enormous, as can be seen in the periodic insect plagues or the multiplication of bacteria during an epidemic.

Response. A living thing is an organized and self-regulating system; when conditions disrupt this organization, death of the organism takes place. The maintenance of this organized living system requires a special type of activity, or response, by which the organism modifies its internal and external adjustments to changing conditions inside and outside the cell. In simple organisms this response may be a direct avoidance of an irritating object or attraction to a food fragment. Responses of higher animals are more complex, often requiring co-operation of a locomotor system and co-ordinating system. When the response involves a highly integrated central nervous system, intricate behavior patterns result. Nonliving objects exhibit what is often inaccurately called a response, as when exfoliation of a rock occurs as a result of temperature change. Such a physical change, however, is not an adaptation to an environmental change, bringing about a result useful to the rock itself.

The Physical Basis of Life

We have enumerated some of the ways in which living organisms, in comparison with nonliving things, are unique in their ability to do things. To discover how the organism is able to carry on these activities, we must delve into the minute structure of organisms.

Life is always associated with the material substance called protoplasm. This substance occurs in highly organized units known as cells. Some organisms, such as certain algae, bacteria, and protozoa, consist of only a single cell. The great majority of organisms, however, are multicellular, with bodies made up of millions or even billions of cells. In all cases the cell is the basic unit of life.

There is no such thing as a typical cell, although most cells are organized into a system of interrelated parts which includes a cell membrane, a nucleus, and cytoplasm. The cell membrane is the outer boundary of the cell, and through it all substances must enter and leave the cell. It is the physical boundary between the living material and the environment. The nucleus plays a key role in the self-maintenance and growth of the cell. Recently the molecular explanation of the directing power of the nucleus was discovered. The nucleus contains a master-protein, deoxyribonucleic acid (DNA). DNA, in turn, is responsible for the formation of ribonucleic acid (RNA), found in abundance in the cytoplasm and essential for its biochemical activities. DNA has been likened to the architect, RNA to the contractor, in the construction of the cell. The same DNA is the control (gene) for transmitting instructions from one generation of cells to the next, thus perpetuating an established pattern of form and function. In the cytoplasm the actual work of the cell takes place; this involves biosynthesis of the protein macromolecules essential for protoplasm formation, and the energy transformations essential for life.

The Energy Relations of Life

The capacity to transform and utilize energy is an essential requirement for maintaining the constancy of the cell organization. Life is energy. Living cells exhibit two types of energy transformation: autotrophic and heterotrophic. An autotrophic organism is one that is able to manufacture its own food—by transforming solar energy into the chemical-bond energy of fuel foods, of which the simplest is glucose. This transformation takes place only in cells containing chloroplasts; autotrophic energy transformations take place only in green plants, through the process of photosynthesis. A heterotrophic organism relies on transforming the chemical-bond energy of foods into

LIFE

life energy by respiration; all animals are heterotrophic, as are plants without chlorophyll, such as the fungi.

LIFE, EXPECTATION OF, average predicted life-span for a large population. When viewed in the perspective of history, the increase in life expectancy in the 20th century must be considered a major achievement of man. With few exceptions, life expectancy throughout the world increased by 20 years between 1900 and 1960. In the United States in 1968 a newborn baby could expect to live to the age of 70. It is estimated that in Greece at about 1000 B.C. the life-span was less than 20 years. In Rome at the time of Christ, it was 23 years, and in Europe during the Middle Ages, 30 years. It was 35 years in the United States in 1776, 30–40 years in Europe during the Napoleonic era, and 40 years in the United States in 1850.

An important part of life-expectancy statistics is the infant mortality rate. A small change in infant mortality has a large effect on life-expectancy figures. One baby saved from dying at birth has the same effect on expectancy averages as prolonging the life of seven adults from age 60 to age 70.

Progress in medical science has been a primary factor in increased life expectancy, largely by the elimination of infections which tend to kill children. For example, between 1945 and 1965, deaths due to whooping cough, polio, influenza, tuberculosis, and acute rheumatic fever were reduced to 10–20% of their earlier level. Most of these changes can be traced directly to the introduction of either a specific vaccine to prevent the disease or a specific form of therapy to cure it. The Salk and Sabin vaccines for polio and the use of streptomycin and isoniazid for tuberculosis are examples.

The major cause of death today in the United States is arteriosclerosis, or hardening of the arteries, which causes one-half of all deaths either by heart or kidney failure or strokes. The second most common cause of death is cancer in all its forms, which causes one death in six. The rate of death from arteriosclerosis and cancer actually increased slightly over the same 20-year period which saw such a remarkable decrease in deaths by infection. Until more is understood about these major causes of death, it is unlikely that the rapid increase in life expectancy seen since 1900 will continue.

LIPOMA [lī-pō'mə], a slow-growing tumor of fat tissue. Lipomas usually appear on the shoulders, back, neck, or the upper parts of the arms and legs. In rare cases they may appear in the pelvis, kidney, bone, and spinal cord. They are painless and may grow to fairly large size, sometimes causing symptoms by pressing on surrounding nerves. They may be removed surgically but tend to recur unless completely excised.

LIPOTROPIC [lĭp-ō-trŏp'ĭk] **FACTORS,** substances which prevent or reverse the abnormal accumulation of fat in the liver. These chemicals are thought to play a role in the transport of fats from the liver to the tissues. They include lecithin, choline (which forms a portion of the lecithin molecule), and methionine, an amino acid which helps the body to manufacture choline. Some substances, such as inositol, which are chemically unrelated to choline and lecithin, are apparently lipotropic under certain conditions. Although lipotropic factors have been used to treat fatty livers, their effectiveness in this respect remains in doubt.

LISTER, JOSEPH, BARON (1827–1912), English surgeon who pioneered in the use of antiseptics in surgery. Having heard of Pasteur's theories of putrefaction and fermentation as resulting from the activities of microorganisms, Lister attempted to apply this knowledge to wound healing by using carbolic acid in surgery. He used a spray of carbolic acid to form an antiseptic mist over the patient and dressed the wounds with acid-soaked compresses. Through these techniques, Lister was successful in significantly reducing cases of postoperative infections in his surgical wards in Glasgow.

LITHOTOMY [lĭ-thŏt'ə-mē], an operation to remove stones from the urinary bladder. Lithotomy was one of the first surgical procedures carried out hundreds of years before the advent of anesthesia. A variation of this operation is still performed today to remove large stones; smaller stones can be removed by passing instruments through the urinary tract into the bladder.

LIVER, the largest gland of the body, which, in consideration of its many functions, may be regarded as the most versatile of all the organs. The liver is essential for the processing of food for use by the body: It excretes waste products in the bile; it stores sugar, fat, vitamins, copper, and iron; it produces substances which are necessary for blood clotting; it manufactures substances needed to absorb fats and fat-soluble vitamins from the intestine; and it inactivates certain sex hormones, thus helping to maintain the hormonal balance of the body. It is not surprising therefore that the liver is essential to life and that diseases which impair its function are serious and sometimes fatal.

The liver weighs about 5 lb. (approximately one-thirtieth of the body weight) and lies under the diaphragm on the right side of the abdomen. It consists of two quite different types of cells, the parenchymal cells and the Kupffer cells. The parenchymal cells are the glandular, or secreting cells. The Kupffer cells, although located in the liver, are similar to cells found in the spleen and bone marrow, all being part of the diffuse reticuloendothelial system. These cells contribute to the body's resistance against disease by virtue of their ability to engulf bacteria and foreign particles.

The Liver and Food Metabolism. The three principal food substances, carbohydrates (in starchy foods and sugars), proteins (meats and fish), and fats, are broken down in the course of digestion to simple sugars, amino acids, and fatty acids, respectively. These compounds reach the liver via the blood stream to be stored or changed into potential energy-yielding substances.

Carbohydrates. Sugar is stored in the liver in the form of glycogen, a complex carbohydrate substance composed of thousands of individual sugar units. Liver glycogen can be reconverted into sugar which is released into the blood; from there it can be absorbed by the body tissues. The two-way transfer of blood sugar into liver glycogen and

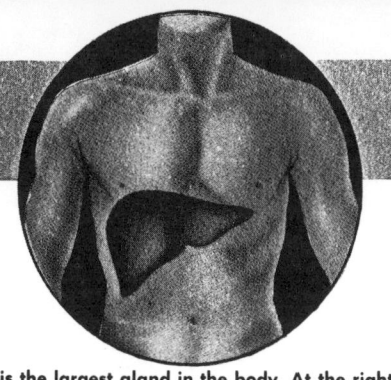

THE LIVER

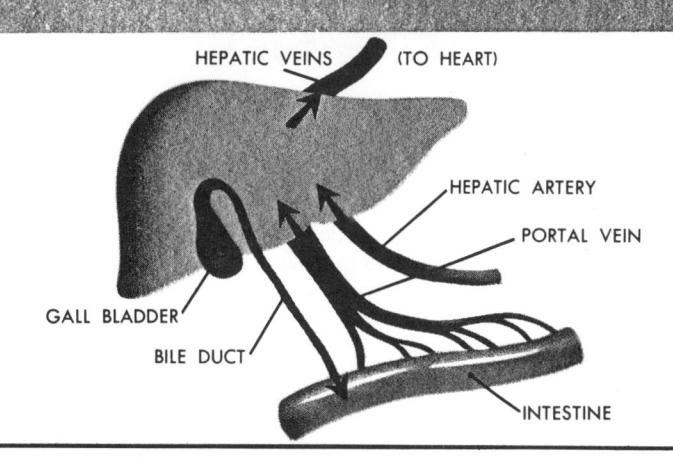

The liver is the largest gland in the body. At the right is shown a schematic view of the circulation to the organ. Blood enters through two vessels: the *hepatic artery* brings oxygen-rich blood from the heart; the *portal vein* brings blood carrying fats, sugar, and other products of digestion from the digestive tract. Blood leaving the liver is distributed through the body by way of the hepatic veins. Bile, produced by the liver, reaches the intestines through the bile ducts and is useful in the digestion and absorption of fats.

HEPATIC VEINS (TO HEART)
HEPATIC ARTERY
PORTAL VEIN
GALL BLADDER
BILE DUCT
INTESTINE

A liver section showing blood flow from the hepatic artery and portal vein to hepatic veins.

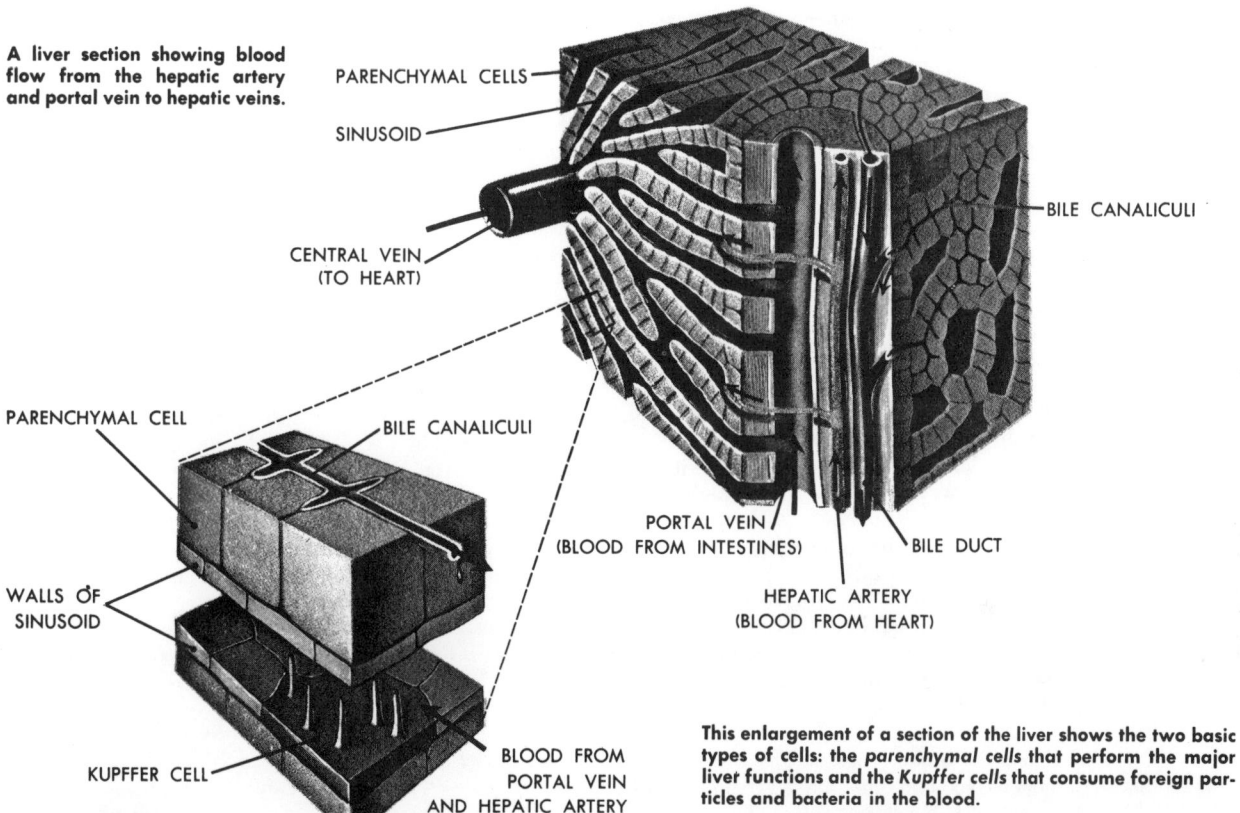

PARENCHYMAL CELLS
SINUSOID
CENTRAL VEIN (TO HEART)
BILE CANALICULI
PARENCHYMAL CELL
BILE CANALICULI
PORTAL VEIN (BLOOD FROM INTESTINES)
BILE DUCT
HEPATIC ARTERY (BLOOD FROM HEART)
WALLS OF SINUSOID
KUPFFER CELL
BLOOD FROM PORTAL VEIN AND HEPATIC ARTERY

This enlargement of a section of the liver shows the two basic types of cells: the *parenchymal cells* that perform the major liver functions and the *Kupffer cells* that consume foreign particles and bacteria in the blood.

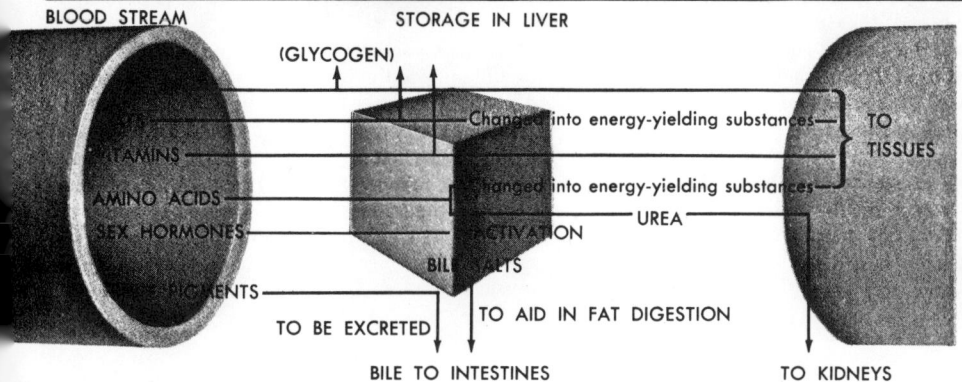

BLOOD STREAM | STORAGE IN LIVER
(GLYCOGEN)
Changed into energy-yielding substances — TO TISSUES
VITAMINS
AMINO ACIDS
SEX HORMONES
Changed into energy-yielding substances
UREA
ACTIVATION
BILE SALTS
PIGMENTS
TO BE EXCRETED
TO AID IN FAT DIGESTION
BILE TO INTESTINES
TO KIDNEYS

The parenchymal liver cell processes sugar, fats, and amino acids brought by the portal vein from the intestines. Some of this material is stored in the liver cell (fat, glycogen), some is used to manufacture blood proteins, some is carried to the tissues to be used as a source of energy, and some is excreted by the kidney (urea). Bile pigments, derived from broken-down red blood cells, are excreted through the bile into the intestines.

liver glycogen into blood sugar is regulated by hormones secreted by the adrenal glands and the pancreas (insulin). When the diet does not contain enough carbohydrates, the liver manufactures sugar from proteins and other substances.

Amino Acids. The liver breaks off the nitrogen-containing amino group from some of the amino acids which pass through it, manufacturing urea, which is excreted in the urine. The remaining portion of the amino-acid molecule may be used for energy.

Fats. There is evidence that fats are changed in the liver to a form which enables them to be used more easily for energy purposes. In this process potentially dangerous substances called "ketone bodies" are formed. In diabetes, for example, the body has difficulty in burning carbohydrates and may rely too heavily upon fats as an energy source, resulting in the production of excessive amounts of ketone bodies, which may upset the acid-base balance of the body.

Liver Secretions and Excretions—Bile. The normal human adult produces one-half to one quart of bile a day. This greenish-yellow fluid contains both waste substances, such as the bile pigments, and liver secretions, such as the bile salts and the bile acids.

The bile pigments are manufactured from products formed by the breakdown of hemoglobin, the red, oxygen-carrying pigment of red blood cells. They are produced by the cells of the reticuloendothelial system which include the Kupffer cells of the liver. The bile pigments pass into the intestine with the bile fluid and give the human excreta its characteristic brownish coloring. If bile is prevented from entering the intestine by severe liver damage, or by blocking of the bile ducts, the bile pigments accumulate in the blood. This eventually produces "jaundice," a yellowish tinting of the skin and eyes, and other serious bodily disturbances.

The bile salts, which are manufactured in the liver and secreted in the bile, are essential for the proper digestion and absorption of fats. They help to break large fat globules into smaller particles and enhance the action of certain fat-digesting enzymes. They are also important for the absorption of fat-soluble vitamins, such as vitamin K, which is essential for normal blood clotting. Individuals suffering from liver disease or from obstruction of the bile passages may develop bleeding tendencies as a consequence of their inability to absorb vitamin K from the intestine.

The Liver and the Blood Proteins. The liver manufactures a number of blood proteins, among them substances which are important in blood coagulation. The significance of one such protein, prothrombin, in blood coagulation was demonstrated in the case of the cattle which bled to death after they had eaten spoiled sweet clover hay. It was determined that the spoiled hay contained dicumarol, a substance which interferes with the manufacture of prothrombin by the liver.

Another important blood-clotting protein manufactured in the liver is fibrinogen, from which the fibrin threads which form the matrix of the clot are formed.

The Liver as a Storehouse. In addition to serving as a depot for the storage of sugar (as glycogen), the liver also stores essential metals, such as iron and copper and many vitamins including vitamins A, D, and vitamin B_{12}. The livers of cod and halibut are the richest sources of vitamins A and D, and their oils are given to children to prevent rickets, which develops from a vitamin D deficiency. Liver extract containing vitamin B_{12} (which is essential for the manufacture of red blood cells) is given to treat pernicious anemia.

See also HEPATITIS; JAUNDICE; METABOLISM.

LOBECTOMY [lō-bĕk'tə-mē], removal of a lobe of an organ. The term is almost always applied to the excision of a lobe of the lung. Lobectomy is performed to remove infected tissue and cysts and to prevent recurrent bleeding in bronchiectasis, a disorder involving chronic dilatation of the breathing passages (bronchi) of the lung. Lobectomy for inflammatory lung diseases such as tuberculosis and lung abscess may result in permanent cure.

LOBOTOMY [lō-bŏt'ə-mē], also called prefrontal lobotomy, or leucotomy, is a surgical method of treating certain mental disorders, which was introduced by the Portuguese physician Egas Moniz in 1936. The operation severs some of the connections between the frontal lobes of the cerebrum (the highest part of the brain) and the thalamus (a nerve relay station which lies below the cerebrum).

A great variety of techniques has been used to perform lobotomies. The early procedures consisted of introducing a cutting instrument through holes drilled in the skull. Other methods involve shaving off portions of the upper brain layer, approaching the brain through the eye cavity (transorbital leucotomy), injecting hot water or alcohol into the brain, or focusing ultrasonic beams on the thalamus.

The Effects of Lobotomy. Immediately after the operation the patient may be severely confused for a few days. Subsequently he may lose normal social habits and may soil himself, eat voraciously, and become noisy and unruly. In a few months these reactions subside and the effects of the operation can be assessed.

In some as yet unknown way, the quality of the patient's emotional experience is apparently altered, so that, although certain severe symptoms may persist, they no longer disturb the patient. A similar effect is observed in some cases in the patient's reaction to pain—the pain is still felt but ceases to be annoying. The intelligence of the patient is also subtly affected. He loses some capacity for higher thinking and cannot easily apply past experience to the solution of present problems. In considering the effects of lobotomy it should be kept in mind that the operation is performed on the most poorly understood part of the brain—the so-called "silent" areas of the cerebral cortex.

In the most successful cases, the patient is able to return to a useful life outside the hospital, and may even assume positions of responsibility though he may lose a certain degree of creativity. A less fortunate outcome is the "frontal-lobe personality," marked by selfishness, quick temper, inability to exercise good judgment, and often, mania.

The Present State of Psychosurgery. After many years of performing operations and modifying the original techniques, most physicians have concluded that the small number of good results does not justify the use of surgery in most cases of functional mental disorders. At present lobotomies are generally limited to patients with severe anxiety, incapacitating schizophrenic processes that do not respond to other forms of treatment, and to patients suffering from intractable pain, especially in the region of the head and neck.

LOEWI [lō'vē], **OTTO** (1873–1961), German pharmacologist who shared the Nobel Prize with Sir Henry Hallet Dale in 1936 for "their discoveries relating to the chemical transmission of nerve impulses." Loewi demonstrated that electrical stimulation of certain nerves caused a substance to be released (later identified as acetylcholine) that affected the transmission of the nerve impulse. Loewi's later work dealt with other aspects of nerve function and with diabetes and adrenalin. From 1940 he was research professor of pharmacology in the College of Medicine at New York University.

LÖFFLER [lûf'lər], **FRIEDRICH AUGUST JOHANNES** (1852–1915), German bacteriologist known for his numerous contributions to this science, including the discovery of the bacteria which cause glanders and the discovery of a filterable virus as the cause of foot-and-mouth disease. With Edwin Klebs, he gave the first full description of the diphtheria bacillus (the Klebs-Löffler bacillus).

LONG, CRAWFORD WILLIAMSON (1815–78), American physician thought to have been the first to use ether for surgical anesthesia. The possibilities of ether anesthesia first occurred to Long after he had observed its effects upon some friends who had sniffed it out of curiosity at a party. Beginning in 1842 Long used ether a number of times in his surgical practice at Jefferson, Georgia, but did not publish his results until 1849. The dentist W. T. G. Morton first received credit for the discovery, since his own work with ether was published in 1846.
See also ANESTHESIA.

LORDOSIS [lôr-dō'sĭs], also known as hollow back, is an exaggeration of the normal forward curve of the lower spine. It may be caused by muscular contractures, paralysis, diseases of the spine, poor posture, or obesity. The abdomen protrudes, and the patient suffers from generalized fatigue. Treatment depends upon the cause.

LOUSE, common name for many species of small, flat-bodied, wingless insects that lead exclusively parasitic lives. The biting, or chewing, lice of order Mallophaga are mostly external parasites of birds, although a few species parasitize mammals. Their mouth parts are modified for chewing and they feed on bits of feathers, hair, or skin. They are transmitted from one host to another by contact. Occasionally these lice may be picked up by man as a result of handling infested animals, but they do not remain on the human body. Common species are the body louse, *Menacanthus stramineus*, and the shaft louse, *Menopon gallinae*, both parasites of chickens.

The sucking lice, of order Anoplura, have mouth parts modified into protrusible needlelike structures that pierce the host organism's skin and suck its blood. Sucking lice are external parasites of mammals. Included in the order is *Pediculus humanus*, the human body louse, which infests hair and clothing. It is spread by promiscuous use of combs, brushes, and headgear. Other related species are spread by contact with infested clothing or bedding. Adult human body lice transmit typhus fever, European relapsing fever, and trench fever (which reached epidemic proportions among soldiers during World War I). Louse infestations appear through unhygienic living conditions, especially when there is little opportunity for thorough bathing. Infestations are controlled by dusting affected individuals with DDT and by fumigating or sterilizing their clothing.

LSD or LYSERGIC ACID DIETHYLAMIDE, an alkaloid made by a simple chemical modification of lysergic acid, which is obtained from the fungus *Claviceps purpurea*. Lysergic acid itself is not a hallucinogen (which produces mood changes and hallucinations of space, time, and vision) but its diethylamide derivative (LSD) is. LSD is the most potent hallucinogen known, being active in dosages of 100 to 200 micrograms. One to 3 hours after ingestion LSD produces profound effects. Colors are enormously vivid and a variety of intense hallucinations may occur, some pleasant and some unpleasant. Typically, the individual seems to lose his normal identification as "I" and to fuse with inanimate aspects of his environment. This sense of ego destruction and distortion of the body image may induce a severe panic reaction. Often the hallucinatory content is erotic and frequently religious figures and images are seen. The experience characteristically lasts 4 to 12 hours but may be far more prolonged.

LSD has potential medical use in treating severe alcoholism, childhood schizophrenia, psychoneurosis, sexual deviancy, and in aiding terminal patients with severe pain.

When LSD is taken under nonmedical supervision, many claims are made for it including the capacity to augment esthetic sensitivity, increase insight, enhance creativity, and increase the individual's capacity to love. None of these claims is substantiated; indeed, what evidence is available indicates that these claims are spurious.

The dangers of LSD taken under promiscuous or illicit circumstances are enormous. It can produce psychosis, acting out of antisocial impulses, acting out of homosexual impulses, inadvertent or intentional suicide attempts, uncontrolled aggression (including attempts at homicide), epileptic seizures, and overwhelming panic. Equally important, LSD can unequivocally produce such long-term effects as chronic psychosis, extended panic reactions, and recurrence of hallucinations as long as one year after their appearance even if no additional LSD is taken in the interim. Chronic use of LSD often is associated with complete withdrawal from society into a passive and self-centered cocoon. Additionally, recent studies suggest that LSD can produce genetic damage, raising the specter of an adverse hereditary effect.
See also DRUG ADDICTION; DRUGS; MARIHUANA; PSYCHOPHARMACOLOGY.

LUMBAGO [lŭm-bā'gō], a nonspecific term describing aching pain in the lower back. Probably the commonest cause of such pain is injury to, or strain of, the muscle and

ligaments of the back. The pain may be confined to one area or be distributed across the entire back. Radiating pain may be present if the large nerves emerging from the spinal cord are irritated. The muscles of the back may be in spasm. Back pain may also be caused by irregularities in the bony structure of the lower spine as in spondylolisthesis, a condition in which the 5th lumbar vertebra is displaced forward, causing severe or slight pain which may radiate down the legs. Other causes of lumbago include arthritis of the spine and abdominal diseases. In the latter case the source of pain is in the abdomen, but the pain is felt in the back.
See also SCIATICA.

LUNGS, the organs of respiration located one on each side of the chest cavity. The lungs are composed mainly of spongy elastic tissue. They appear pinkish white in infants, but assume a grayish tint in adults.

Air enters the lungs through the trachea, or windpipe, a tubular passageway which is stiffened by semicircular rings of cartilage. The trachea leads into the two principal bronchi, the air passages in the lungs. The bronchi in turn branch into smaller and smaller units, finally ending in the terminal bronchioles. All of the bronchi and bronchioles up to this point are termed "non-respiratory" since they merely serve as air passageways and are not directly involved in breathing. The terminal bronchioles lead into the "respiratory bronchioles," which have saclike alveoli on their walls. The actual exchange of gases between the air in the lungs and the blood stream takes place in these alveoli and in others on smaller branches of the airways. The segment of tissue which begins with the respiratory bronchiole and ends with the alveoli is the elastic or bellowslike portion of the lung which distends when air is inhaled and contracts when it is exhaled.

The alveoli are so designed that only two delicate membranes separate the air from the blood, permitting the greatest possible diffusion of oxygen and carbon dioxide between the two. It has been estimated that there are approximately 725 million alveoli in the lungs.

The Pulmonary Circulation. The circulation to the lungs is unique in that blood is brought to the lungs not simply to nourish the lung tissue but to take up oxygen and to release carbon dioxide. The pulmonary artery leaves the right side of the heart, and unlike other arteries throughout the body, carries unoxygenated blood. Similarly, the pulmonary veins, which leave the lungs to enter the left side of the heart, reverse the normal pattern by carrying oxygen-rich blood. The blood carried by the pulmonary artery goes mainly to the alveoli, the active respiratory portion of the lung where gaseous exchange occurs. The lung also has a more typical circulation which supplies the walls of the bronchi. These blood vessels are the bronchial arteries, which carry oxygen-rich blood, and the bronchial veins, which return oxygen-poor blood to the heart.

Lung Diseases. Lung diseases are particularly serious since they may interfere with the body's oxygen supply, without which life is impossible. This may occur at birth if the child is born with hyaline membrane disease, in which a proteinlike substance lines the alveoli, preventing oxygen from reaching the blood. Air may be blocked by the presence of foreign bodies or by the accumulation of abnormal secretions in the bronchi, resulting from infection, or in some cases, from an allergic reaction. In certain heart diseases, and in some disorders of the pulmonary circulation, fluid may collect in the alveoli, preventing normal respiration.

The lung can be collapsed by pressures around it. If the pleural space, which separates the lung from the ribs, is filled with air, the lung cannot expand. This is called pneumothorax and results from an abnormal opening between the rib cage and the pleural space, or from a punctured lung.

Lung disturbances also appear in a large variety of infectious diseases.
See also PNEUMONIA; RESPIRATION; TUBERCULOSIS.

LUNGS, COLLAPSE OF THE, also known as atelectasis. The lungs are inflated by negative pressure created when the chest expands. As the lungs fill, the elastic tissue in their walls stretches. Partial collapse occurs passively with each exhaled breath. But if the air pressure between the lungs and chest wall is equalized by injury or chest surgery, the lungs collapse completely and immediately. Collapse is most often caused by obstruction of the air passages by thick mucus, an inhaled foreign body such as a peanut, a blood clot, or a tumor. Atelectasis is common in severe asthma attacks or after surgery when the patient does not breathe deeply or cough well. It may be aggravated by heavy sedation or anesthesia. In both instances mucus plugs cause the obstruction. Premature infants with lung disease may have their illness complicated by lung collapse. The symptoms are related to the underlying cause, the size of the airway obstructed and the area of lung involved. Shortness of breath and difficult breathing alert the physician. Diagnosis is confirmed by chest X-ray. Treatment consists of removing the obstruction and providing positive pressure to inflate the collapsed lungs.
See also LUNGS.

LUPUS ERYTHEMATOSUS [loō'pəs ĕr-ĭ-thĕm-ə-tō'səs], an inflammatory disease of the connective, or supporting, tissues of the body, which occurs principally in young women. The disease may vary in severity from minor involvement of a patch of skin to a serious generalized illness. Although the cause is not known, it has been established that changes in protein metabolism occur in the disease. According to one theory, it is caused by a self-allergy in which the patient develops substances (antibodies) that react with his own tissues. The condition develops gradually, usually first involving the skin and joints. Patients may give a false positive blood test for syphilis several years before signs or symptoms become evident. Frequently the skin is sensitive to sunlight; exposure may precipitate a flare-up of symptoms. The lymph nodes throughout the body are enlarged and the joints may become painful. Muscle tenderness may accompany the arthritic pains.

The course of the disease is marked by periods of wellbeing, followed by relapses which may involve successive organ systems, such as the kidneys, heart, lungs, gastrointestinal tract, nervous system, and the liver and spleen.

This involvement may appear as pleurisy, convulsions, lack of appetite, severe abdominal pain, diarrhea, heart murmurs, and rapid heartbeat. Fever, anemia, and leukopenia (decrease in the white blood cell count) may be present. In some cases kidney failure may cause death within a few weeks or months. The mental symptoms may include anxiety, memory loss, hallucinations, and feelings of persecution. Because of the wide variety of symptoms, and the irregular course of the disease, lupus erythematosus is often difficult to detect. Diagnosis is aided by the "L.E." cell phenomenon: a protein substance in the blood of a patient suffering from lupus erythematosus causes white blood cells to change into a characteristic "L.E." cell.

Antimalarial drugs, such as atabrine and chloroquine, are used to treat the milder forms. Severer cases usually respond to cortisone and related drugs.

LUPUS VULGARIS [vŭl-găr'ĭs], form of tuberculosis of the skin which usually appears on the nose, face, or ears. The disease is marked by tiny soft masses which, if untreated, destroy the involved skin and immediate underlying tissues. The antituberculous drugs, isoniazid, para-aminosalicylic acid, and streptomycin are effective in treating lupus vulgaris.

LURIA, SALVADOR (1912–), U.S. biologist who shared the 1969 Nobel Prize in physiology or medicine with Max Delbrück and Alfred Hershey. Luria's work contributed to an understanding of the development of bacterial resistance to infection by phages (viruses). Using phage-resistant bacterial variants, Luria analyzed the phenomenon of variation, later developing a fluctuation test that clarified the spontaneous character of the bacterial mutations. Luria then analyzed spontaneous mutations in the growth phase of the phage—work that formed the basis for the study of mutagenesis.

LYMPH. See LYMPHATIC SYSTEM.

LYMPHADENITIS [lĭm-făd-ĭ-nī-tĭs], enlargement of lymph nodes. Bacteria and viruses may produce inflammation and enlargement of the nodes. Lymphadenitis may also be caused by malignant cells. Acute lymphadenitis may be accompanied by swelling, heat, and reddening of the overlying skin. The tender glands may fuse with one another. Enlarged lymph nodes may be hard or soft.

Streptococcal sore throat produces enlarged nodes in the neck, while infection of the fingers results in an enlarged node at the elbow. Many acute infections are accompanied by general lymphadenitis. Measles, german measles, mumps, and chicken pox all show lymph node enlargement. Toxoplasmosis, a parasitic disease, has a phase of generalized lymphadenitis, and infectious mononucleosis is characterized by generalized lymphadenitis, with striking enlargement of the neck nodes. The most common chronic infections producing lymphadenitis are tuberculosis and syphilis, with enlargement primarily in the neck and groin, respectively. A number of malignant diseases, such as Hodgkin's disease and various cancers, can produce either local or general lymphadenopathy.

LYMPHANGITIS [lĭm-făn-jī'tĭs], an inflammation of the lymphatic vessels. The usual cause is infection with streptococcus bacteria which may penetrate small skin wounds. The vessels become infected as these bacteria are carried through the lymphatic channels to the lymph glands. The inflamed lymph channels appear as long red streaks under the skin. Chills, fever, rapid pulse, and an increase in the number of white blood cells develop as the body reacts to the infection. Prompt treatment with antibiotics is necessary to prevent the bacteria from spreading to other parts of the body.

LYMPHATIC [lĭm-făt'ĭk] **SYSTEM,** an extensive network of vessels conducting fluid from the body tissues to the blood stream. The tissue fluid which bathes the cells is the link between the closed blood system and the cells of the body. This lymphatic fluid is composed of nutrients, water, and minerals which have escaped from the minute blood vessels in the tissue, the capillaries. Though much of this fluid, containing waste products of cell activity, returns directly to the blood stream, a portion is carried away through the lymphatic system. The lymph vessels begin as small closed tubes in the tissues and drain through the lymph glands, or nodes, eventually converging into major vessels which empty into large veins in the chest.

Lymph vessels are found principally in the skin, subcutaneous tissue, muscle, and the linings of various organs and cavities, and are absent from nervous tissue and bone marrow. An important function of the system is to return fluids and proteins from the tissue spaces to the blood. The lymph system also serves to redistribute fluid from one part of the body to another. The lymph vessels in the intestine are important in the absorption of fat. The lymph nodes are an effective bulwark against bacterial infection: special bacteria-consuming cells found in the nodes remove invading organisms from the lymph fluid before it enters the blood. Frequently, swelling and inflammation of the lymph glands or vessels are an early sign of infection.

Obstruction of the lymph vessels may cause an accumulation of fluid in the tissues, resulting in a massive swelling in the part drained by those vessels. This is occasionally seen in filariasis, an infestation in which small worms may block the lymph channels, leading to a grotesque enlargement of an arm, leg, or other part of the body. A similar involvement of the arm may occur following radical surgery for breast cancer with removal of the underarm lymph glands.

LYMPHOGRANULOMA VENEREUM [lĭm-fō-grăn-yə-lō'mə və-nēr'ē-əm], an infectious venereal disease caused by a viruslike microorganism. From three to twenty days after infection, a small ulcer may develop in the genital region. Often this initial lesion is overlooked or absent, and the first sign of the disease is swelling of the lymph glands in the groin (buboes). The overlying skin becomes reddened, an abscess forms, and pus drains through openings in the skin. The organism may spread through the body causing fever, joint pain, and headache. The disease may result in disfiguring, swelling, and scarring of the external genitalia. Treatment is with sulfonamide drugs and antibiotics.

LYMPHOSARCOMA [lĭm-fō-sär-kō'mə], a highly fatal disease involving overproduction of certain white blood cells in the lymph glands, spleen, and the lymphoid tissue of other organs. Of unknown cause, the disease is seen in middle-aged persons, affecting men more often than women. The symptoms are often highly variable, depending upon which lymphatic tissues are affected. Loss of appetite and weight, fever, fatigue, and anemia are common. The glands of the neck, underarms, or groin are often the first to enlarge. Later, swelling of the lymphatic tissue in particular areas may produce symptoms in the digestive tract, lungs, nervous system, or in virtually any part of the body. Treatment includes X-ray irradiation and drugs such as nitrogen mustard, triethylene melamine, and adrenal steroids.

LYNEN [lu'nən], **FEODOR** (1911–), German biochemist who shared the 1964 Nobel Prize in physiology and medicine with the American biochemist Konrad Bloch for research into the mechanisms and regulation of cholesterol and fatty acid metabolism, work that is basic to an understanding of the role of cholesterol in heart disease.

M

MADUROMYCOSIS [mă-dū-rō-mī-kō'sĭs], also known as madura foot, a fungus infection seen most frequently in the tropics, particularly among farm workers. Although many different fungi may cause the disease, the clinical pattern is usually the same. The organisms penetrate the tissues following injury to the foot, or in rare cases, other parts of the body. Over a period of time the organisms multiply, attacking the soft tissues, and even the bones. The foot becomes swollen, and fluid containing yellow, brown, or black granules drains through openings in the skin. Treatment with antibiotics is usually ineffective and amputation of the part may be necessary to prevent the spread of the infection and to spare the patient's life.

MAGENDIE [mȧ-zhăN-dē'], **FRANÇOIS** (1783–1855), French physiologist who made important contributions to knowledge of the nervous system, the function of the heart, the chemistry of the blood, and the action of various drugs. He is best remembered for the law named in his honor which states that the spinal nerves are divided into two divisions, or roots, one carrying sensations to the spinal cord (posterior root), the other carrying impulses away from the spinal cord to move the muscles (anterior root).

MALABSORPTION SYNDROMES, a group of diseases in which interference with the absorption of nutrients from the digestive tract results in deficiencies of vitamins, minerals, or other food substances. Malabsorption may be caused by disease of the small intestine, through which absorption occurs, or by inadequate concentration of the pancreatic and liver secretions which digest food in the intestine.

The most common intestinal diseases causing malabsorption are "sprue" in adults and celiac disease in infants. Although the causes of these diseases are not known, they are probably related. This is suggested by the fact that they are both often improved when the patient is given a diet free of the protein gluten, which is found in wheat and rye. It has been suggested that these conditions are caused by an abnormal sensitivity to this protein.

Pancreatic diseases causing malabsorption are chronic pancreatitis, in which the gland is partially destroyed by inflammation, and cystic fibrosis, in which the ducts of the gland are blocked, preventing the secretions from entering the bowel.

Malabsorption of fats occurs in diseases of the liver or bile tracts which interfere with the production or excretion of bile, a substance essential for the normal digestion and absorption of fats.

See also CYSTIC FIBROSIS; DIGESTION; INTESTINE; LIVER; PANCREAS; SPRUE.

MALARIA [mə-lâr'ē-ə], a disease caused by infection with microscopic, single-celled organisms of the genus *Plasmodium*. The impact of malaria on human life is probably without parallel: prior to the introduction of global malaria control in the 1940's, it caused an estimated 3 million deaths a year. The Ceylon malaria epidemic of 1934–35 paralyzed agriculture and public transportation and caused 100,000 deaths. It has been said that malaria imposes a hidden 5% tax on rubber, cocoa, minerals, and other raw materials exported from malarial areas because of the loss of human efficiency attributable to the disease.

The ancient Greek physician Hippocrates distinguished the different types of malarial fever in the 5th century B.C., and in the same century a town was reportedly freed of malaria by draining a swamp in the vicinity. Although some ancients felt that an invisible parasite was responsible, the disease was generally believed to be caused by bad air emanating from stagnant waters. The malarial parasite was first described in 1880, and in 1898 the British physician Ronald Ross discovered that bird malaria is transmitted by the bites of mosquitoes of the genus *Anopheles*. Shortly afterward it was confirmed that human malaria is transmitted by the same insect.

The Malarial Parasite

Man can be infected with four species of *Plasmodium*, which differ in the form of clinical malaria which they produce. Of these, the most lethal is *P. falciparum* which is found in tropical and subtropical countries.

When an infected mosquito bites a human, the threadlike infective forms of the plasmodium are injected with the insect's saliva. These enter the liver where they develop over a period of five to seven days into a new form called the schizont, which ruptures into many smaller units (merozoites) which are released independently into the blood stream. There they attach themselves to a red blood cell and develop afresh into new schizonts. These blood schizonts may rupture in batches every 48 hours in the tertian malarias, and every 72 hours in quartan malaria. The rupturing is accompanied by the periodic fever which is characteristic of malaria. The majority of the newly liberated merozoites seek out red blood cells to continue the cycle, but a few develop into male or female sexual forms known as gametocytes. These are inactive until swallowed by a mosquito which attacks an infected human for a blood meal. Fertilization takes place in the mosquito's body, and eventually the embryonic parasites make their way to the insect's salivary glands, ready to infect a new human victim. In simple infections, malarial attacks occur every 48 or 72 hours. Daily attacks, or other variations, may develop in mixed infections of vivax and quartan malaria.

The typical attack (of vivax, quartan, or ovale malaria) begins with chills lasting up to two hours. During this time the patient feels intolerably cold, and shivers violently, although his temperature continues to rise. This is followed by a "hot stage" during which the patient throws off the bed clothes and experiences intense thirst. The temperature usually reaches a maximum of 102° F. to 105° F., but may go even higher, in which case cold sponging is necessary. After about four hours, the sweating stage develops and the temperature drops. In early malaria this may leave the patient exhausted, but later in the disease he may be little the worse for wear.

Since each parasite destroys its host red blood cell, anemia develops. The spleen and liver, which are involved in the disposal of red blood cells, become enlarged. Indeed spleen enlargement is so typical in malarial infection that the spleen size is used throughout the world as a quick, reliable means of assessing the local intensity of malaria.

The clinical picture seen in falciparum malaria, the deadliest form, is somewhat different from that described above. The blood cells containing the young parasites stick in the minute blood vessels of the tissues (the capillaries) and the developing forms appear in the general circulation only in severe infections. Mild attacks are easy to treat and are not particularly disabling. Although the infection may persist for months without causing fever, the patient's physical and mental well-being are gradually weakened and any stress may bring on a serious attack.

Dangerous complications may develop if the capillaries become blocked with parasite-infested red blood cells. Obstruction of the blood vessels in the brain may cause the highly fatal complication of cerebral malaria. If the lungs or intestines are involved, respiratory complications or malarial dysentery result. Another frequently fatal complication is blackwater fever, caused by one or more sudden massive breakdowns of red blood cells. The altered hemoglobin from the destroyed red cells appears in the urine, giving it a characteristic black appearance. The long-held suspicion that improper use of quinine may precipitate blackwater fever has been confirmed by the observed decline in the frequency of this condition since other drugs have replaced quinine in malaria treatment.

Treatment and Prevention of Malaria

The classical drug for the treatment of malaria was quinine, which, according to one popular story, was introduced to Europe in 1640 by the Countess of Cinchon who brought back with her the bitter quinine-containing bark by which she had been cured of a fever in Peru (named cinchona bark in her honor). Quinine is now used only for cerebral malaria, having been replaced by chloroquine, amodiaquine, pamaquin, and other drugs.

The Mosquito. Many species of *Anopheles* mosquito can transmit malaria, but differ in their efficiency. In each malarial area there is usually one principal transmitting species (or vector) and one or more less important species.

The mosquitoes may differ in the type of water used for breeding: stagnant or running, fresh or brackish, shaded or sunlit. Many species bite cattle in preference to man. A few bite man specifically.

In order to transmit malaria a mosquito must take at least two human bites at an interval of not less than 12 days (one to become infected and the second to transmit the infection). Consequently, the efficiency of a species as a transmitter of malaria depends upon its inclination to bite humans and its length of life. A short-lived, cattle-biting species is an inefficient transmitter, whereas a long-lived, man-biting species is an ideal vector. Most malaria-carrying species are inefficient and can successfully transmit the disease only when the mosquito population is large. There is a lull during winter and in the dry seasons.

The outstanding example of an efficient malaria-transmitting mosquito is *A. gambiae*, of tropical Africa. In this region no cold weather intervenes to interrupt the parasite's cycle in the mosquito. The malaria is therefore stable and continues at maximum intensity throughout the year, year in and year out, but never causes epidemics. Because of the development of mass immunity under these circumstances, *P. vivax* may actually be eliminated, while *P. falciparum*, with its multitude of strains, flourishes. Children in this area suffer from malaria, but by the age of three those surviving have developed a resistance and although infections continue to occur, the individual usually suffers only a mild fever for from one to seven days annually.

Malaria Control and Eradication. Following the discovery of the mosquito transmission of malaria, the work of Gorgas in the Panama Canal Zone and of Watson in Malaya demonstrated that malaria could be controlled by

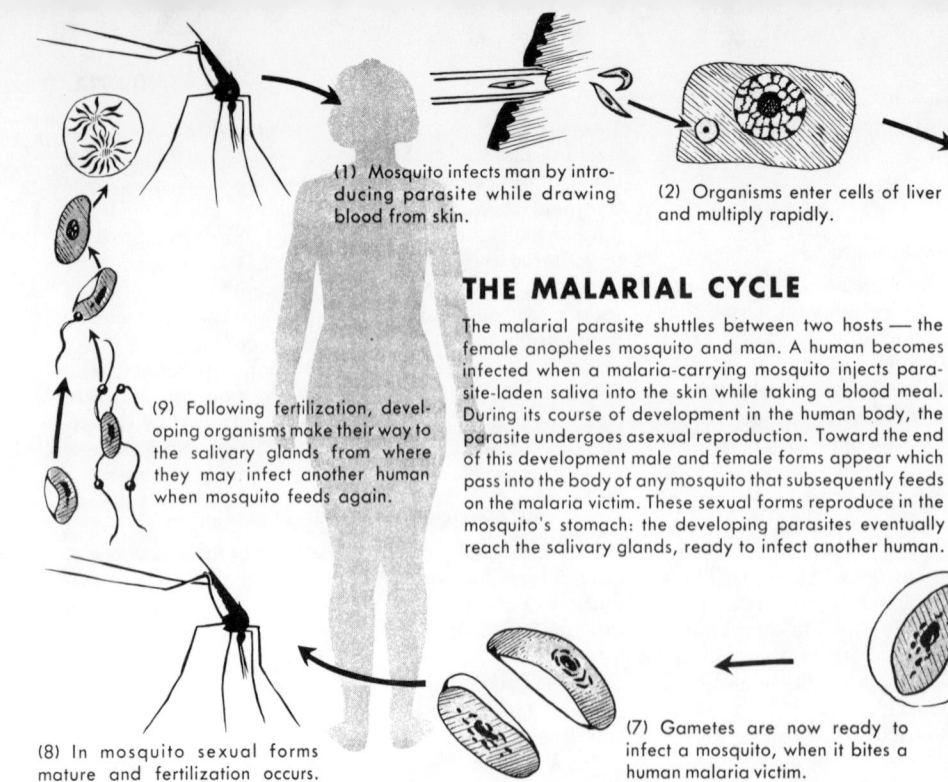

(1) Mosquito infects man by introducing parasite while drawing blood from skin.

(2) Organisms enter cells of liver and multiply rapidly.

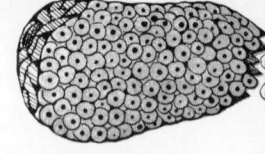

(3) Liver cell, engorged with thousands of parasites, ruptures releasing organisms into blood.

(4) Organisms develop in the red blood cells.

(5) Red cell ruptures, releasing organisms into blood, where they may infect new red blood cells.

(6) Some parasites develop into male and female sexual forms (gametocytes).

(7) Gametes are now ready to infect a mosquito, when it bites a human malaria victim.

(8) In mosquito sexual forms mature and fertilization occurs.

(9) Following fertilization, developing organisms make their way to the salivary glands from where they may infect another human when mosquito feeds again.

THE MALARIAL CYCLE

The malarial parasite shuttles between two hosts — the female anopheles mosquito and man. A human becomes infected when a malaria-carrying mosquito injects parasite-laden saliva into the skin while taking a blood meal. During its course of development in the human body, the parasite undergoes asexual reproduction. Toward the end of this development male and female forms appear which pass into the body of any mosquito that subsequently feeds on the malaria victim. These sexual forms reproduce in the mosquito's stomach: the developing parasites eventually reach the salivary glands, ready to infect another human.

THE MOSQUITO

The malarial parasite is carried by numerous species of *Anopheles* mosquito. The particular carrier (or vector) differs in various parts of the world. In each case it is the female of the species that carries and transmits malaria.

THE PARASITE

The malarial parasite is a microscopic, single-celled animal of the genus *Plasmodium*. Four species of the parasite affect man.

THE LIFE HISTORY OF THE ANOPHELES

Eggs: Female deposits eggs on surface of pond or stream. Up to 300 eggs may be laid at one time.

Larval Stage: In about 48 hours first larval stage emerges. Three succeeding larval stages appear, each marked by moulting of the skin.

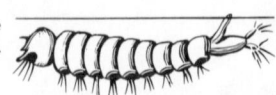

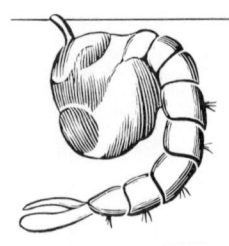

Pupal Stage follows last larval stage and may last 24-48 hours. During this time the adult organs of the mosquito develop.

Adult: The adult emerges from pupal case. Females are fertilized as soon as they can fly.

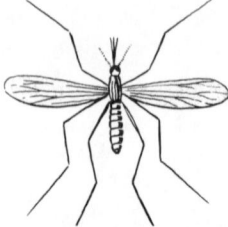

Adult as a malaria-carrier: Females seek blood meal within 12 to 24 hours after emergence from the pupal case. If the individual bitten has malaria, then the female mosquito acquires the infection and, after a period of 12 days, may transmit malaria to its human victims.

PLASMODIUM FALCIPARUM
This organism is largely confined to the tropics and subtropics. It causes the deadliest form of malaria.

PLASMODIUM VIVAX
Predominant form of malarial parasite found in the temperate zones; causes a chronic illness which is less severe than that caused by *P. Falciparum*.

PLASMODIUM OVALE
Occurs principally in tropical Africa and produces malaria similar to that of *P. Vivax*.

PLASMODIUM MALARIAE
This is a comparatively uncommon type of the malaria parasite with a patchy distribution in rural areas. It causes a mild, chronic form of malaria.

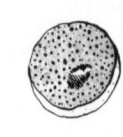

Artist: Leonard Dank

preventing the mosquitoes from breeding. This could be brilliantly successful if sufficient skilled supervision of drainage, oiling of dangerous water, and other tasks were continuously available. Breeding control actually succeeded in eliminating the potent *A. gambiae* from Brazil in the 1930's. Its costs, however, prohibit its use on a country-wide scale in the tropics.

Global control of malaria first became feasible with the discovery of the chlorinated hydrocarbon insecticides in the 1940's. These compounds, which include DDT, can be sprayed on a wall, rendering it lethal for some months to any mosquito that alights upon it. For this reason these compounds are known as residual insecticides. The mosquitoes normally feed at night in dwelling places and, after biting, feeling heavy and lethargic, they rest on a wall before leaving the room. Campaigns using residual insecticides are directed against the adult mosquitoes; only the inside walls of human dwellings are sprayed. After several years of spraying in malarial areas many malaria-carrying mosquitoes have developed resistance to the insecticides. The spraying campaign may nevertheless be successful if it can break the malaria cycle for three years. In that time infections of *P. vivax* and *P. falciparum* die out and mosquitoes can no longer acquire and transmit the infection. The mosquitoes survive, but the malaria is eradicated. Once this has been achieved epidemics can be prevented by finding and promptly treating persons with malaria before they can infect mosquitoes. To be permanently eradicated anywhere, malaria must be eliminated throughout the globe, otherwise it may be reintroduced to malaria-free areas by apparently healthy carriers.

Some countries have already eradicated malaria. In others, where the transmitting mosquitoes are inefficient and susceptible to residual insecticides, the odds are against the disease, and it is dying out. In tropical Africa the efficiency and other qualities of *A. gambiae* make the task of malaria eradication so difficult that it is questionable if spraying campaigns alone will ever break the transmission cycle all over the continent.

MALPRACTICE, term generally used to describe negligent treatment by a doctor or dentist resulting in injury to a patient. Unless he undertakes by contract to guarantee a cure, a doctor is not liable for failure to cure or for causing further illness or injury, unless he has been negligent. He is legally negligent only if he has failed to use the degree of knowledge and skill ordinarily exercised by members of the profession at the time of the treatment. What customary care and skill require in a given situation must be shown (except in the plainest cases) by the expert testimony of a member of the profession. This means, in effect, that a doctor can be held liable for malpractice only if another doctor testifies against him. Under the older cases this testimony had to come from a doctor practicing in the same locality as the defendant since the test of care was localized in place as well as time. The difficulty of obtaining such testimony is notorious and has made malpractice suits among the hardest for a plaintiff to win. Many recent cases have dropped the locality requirement.

MAMMARY GLAND. See BREASTS.

MANGE [mānj], term describing a group of contagious skin diseases that affect cattle, hogs, horses, dogs and cats, and man. The different kinds of mange are caused by minute parasitic animals called mites, which either burrow beneath the host animal's skin (producing the conditions known specifically as mange), or live on the surface of the host's skin around the base of the hairs (producing the conditions known as scabies). A specific mange or scabies organism attacks each different animal species. The mange organisms live beneath the host's skin and produce symptoms of intense itching, raised, reddened areas, and scabbing. The scabies organisms produce these symptoms and also cause hair loss by destruction of the hair follicles.

Large domestic animals with mange or scabies are immediately isolated to prevent contagion and are treated by dipping in vats containing insecticidal solutions. Smaller animals like dogs and cats are treated by local applications of insecticides.

MANIC-DEPRESSIVE [măn'ĭk-dĭ-prĕs'ĭv] **PSYCHOSIS,** a psychotic disorder characterized by moods of extreme elation or depression, or an alternation of both. Its most common age of onset is between the ages of 25 and 35. Females are more susceptible than males. There is a strong tendency for the condition to appear in several members of the same family.

Depression is the most common mood. In the mild forms the individual is fatigued, lacks confidence, and withdraws from society. As the depression progresses, physical symptoms appear. The patient loses weight and cannot sleep. Vague pains arise in the chest or stomach, and he may feel that these physical complaints are the cause of his mental distress. In the severe stage the depression advances into a stupor in which the patient does not speak or move.

The manic form usually begins as an acceleration of all normal activities. The patient is buoyant and happy. His ideas move rapidly. He is playful and full of grand schemes that he quickly abandons. He may squander his money and write large checks for both friends and strangers.

The patient usually recovers from the moods of depression and mania, only to fall ill again at a later date. In the cyclic form of the psychosis the manic and depressive states follow one another.
See also PSYCHOSIS.

MANSON [măn'sən], **SIR PATRICK** (1844–1922), British physician known as the "father of tropical medicine." His most significant discovery was that of the role of mosquitoes in producing filariasis (a worm infestation) in man. He later became convinced that malaria was transmitted in the same way and is said to have produced malaria in his son by mosquito bite. Final proof of the transmission of malaria by mosquito was obtained by a colleague, Ronald Ross. Manson's *Tropical Diseases* was a standard text of its time. He was instrumental in founding the London School of Tropical Medicine.

MARIE [mȧ-rē'], **PIERRE** (1853–1940), French neurologist known for his descriptions of nervous diseases. His name is associated with several conditions, including

MARIHUANA

Marie's syndrome (acromegaly), Charcot-Marie-Tooth disease (a disorder causing atrophy of the legs and arms), and Marie's ataxia (an inherited brain disorder).

MARIHUANA, [măr-ə-wä′nə], drug obtained from dried and crumpled parts of the ubiquitous hemp plant *Cannabis sativa* (or *Cannabis indica*). Smoked or otherwise consumed worldwide by an estimated 200,000,000 persons for pleasure, escape, or relaxation, marihuana is known by a variety of names such as kif (Morocco), dagga (South Africa), and bhang (India). Colloquially, in the United States, marihuana is called pot, grass, weed, or Mary Jane.

The main active principle of cannabis is tetrahydrocannabinol. The potency of its various forms ranges from a weak drink consumed in India to the highly potent hashish. The latter consists of pure cannabis resin.

Marihuana is not a narcotic and is not addicting. One can use mild cannabis preparations such as marihuana in small amounts for years without physical or mental deterioration. Marihuana serves to diminish inhibitions and acts as an euphoriant. Only infrequently does it produce actual hallucinations. More potent preparations of cannabis such as hashish can induce psychedelic experiences identical to those observed after ingestion of potent hallucinogens such as LSD.

Some who smoke marihuana feel no effects; others feel relaxed and sociable, tend to giggle a great deal, and have a profound loss of the sense of time. Characteristically, those under the influence of marihuana show incoordination and impaired ability to perform skilled acts. Still others experience a wide range of emotions including feelings of persecution, fear, megalomania, elation, love, and anger. Although marihuana is not addicting, it may be habituating. The individual may become psychologically rather than physically dependent on the drug.

Those who urge the legalization of marihuana maintain the drug is entirely safe. The available data suggest this is not so. Marihuana occasionally produces acute panic reactions or even transient psychoses. Furthermore, a person driving under the influence of marihuana is a danger to himself and others. If smoked heavily and chronically, its use has been clearly associated with mental breakdown. In many persons who smoke chronically, the drug reinforces passivity and reduces goal-directed, constructive activity. The chronic use of pure resin (hashish) has been associated both with mental deterioration and criminality.

There is no established medical use for marihuana or any other cannabis preparation. In the United States its use is a crime and the laws governing marihuana are similar to those regulating heroin. Many authorities now urge that the laws be modified to mitigate the penalties relating to conviction on marihuana possession charges.
See also Drug Addiction; Drugs.

MASSAGE [mə-säzh′], the application of mechanical force to the body by movements of the hands. The masseur strokes, compresses, kneads, and pounds the tissues, promoting circulation and muscle tone. The technique is used to reduce swellings, to soften scars and adhesions, to relieve muscle stiffness and fatigue, and to help prevent wasting of muscles in some diseases of the nervous system. Massage cannot increase muscle strength or remove collections of fat from the tissues. Therapeutic massage should be given under medical supervision by trained masseurs, since the wrong technique may aggravate instead of improve the condition being treated.

MASTECTOMY [măs′těc-tə-mē], amputation of the breast. This is usually performed in cases of cancer, but may also be done for noncancerous diseases of the breast. *Simple mastectomy* involves removal of the breast alone. In *radical mastectomy*, the breast is removed together with the adjacent chest muscles and the lymph glands under the arm on the same side. This operation is more extensive than simple mastectomy and a skin graft may be necessary to close the wound.

Super-radical mastectomy involves removal of the same structures as in radical mastectomy, and, in addition, excision of lymph glands in the root of the neck and inside the chest. This operation is carried out in selected cases. Certain physicians do not perform the radical or super-radical operations, preferring to do a simple mastectomy followed by radiation therapy to the lymph glands. Mastectomy of any type often creates psychological problems associated with the loss of the normal body contour. This can be corrected with modern prosthetic devices which leave no visible indications of the operation.

MASTITIS [măs-tī′tĭs], inflammation of the breast. This may occur in pregnancy or especially during nursing. Bacteria may enter through cracks and fissures in the breast. The infected area quickly becomes hot, red, and painful. Chills and fever may occur. Treatment consists of antibiotics, rest, and the application of heat. If an abscess forms, it must be lanced to permit pus to drain. A chronic abscess, which drains through openings in the skin, may develop if drainage is not complete. Mastitis may be prevented by careful breast hygiene.

MASTOIDITIS [măs-toid-ī′tĭs], infection of the lining of the air cells in the mastoid portion of the temporal bone of the skull. The infection usually spreads to the mastoid from the middle ear. Mastoiditis may cause pain, swelling, fever, bone destruction, and abscess formation. Treatment consists of antibiotics, and incision in the eardrum to permit pus to drain. The infection may recur and become chronic, possibly interfering with hearing.

A mastoidectomy, or surgical removal of the infected bone, is usually necessary when persistent infection causes progressive hearing loss, and threatens to spread to other parts of the body. If the infection is extensive the eardrum and adjacent ear structures may have to be removed. The effectiveness of antibiotics in treating ear infections has considerably reduced the need for mastoidectomy.

MAYO [mā′ō], family of outstanding American physicians, founders of the Mayo Clinic in Rochester, Minn. WILLIAM WORRALL MAYO (1819–1911) was born in a small town near Manchester, England. His ancestors included physicians, but his father, a sea captain, instilled in him a love of travel and adventure. An interest in medicine led Mayo to the famous Manchester Infirmary, but he did not stay long enough to receive a license to practice.

In 1845 he went to the United States. He worked first at Bellevue Hospital in New York City, then in Buffalo, N.Y., finally establishing himself as a tailor in Lafayette, Ind. A year later he entered Indiana Medical College, obtaining his degree in 1850. Following several moves he chose Rochester, Minn. as his home.

WILLIAM JAMES MAYO (1861–1939) and CHARLES HORACE MAYO (1865–1939), while still very young, began to work in their father's office, attending at the bedside with him and even aiding at surgery or with autopsies when necessary. William graduated in 1883 from the University of Michigan and Charles from the Chicago Medical College in 1888. The brothers joined their father in formal practice, taking over the care of patients in St. Mary's Hospital, Rochester, in 1899. From the brothers' co-operative practice evolved the Mayo Clinic in 1905. Dr. Will was a specialist in abdominal surgery, Dr. Charlie specialized in treatment of goiter and in neurosurgery. Several operations and some surgical instruments, which the Mayo brothers designed, bear their name. In 1915 the brothers gave $1,500,000 to the University of Minnesota to establish the Mayo Foundation, for research and training. Charles Mayo's son, CHARLES WILLIAM MAYO (1898–1968), also a surgeon, carried on the family's tradition of excellence and innovation in medical practice.

MAYO CLINIC, world-famous medical center in Rochester, Minn. The first clinic hospital, St. Mary's, was built in 1889 by the Sisters of St. Francis and was originally staffed by Dr. William Worrall Mayo and his sons, Drs. William James and Charles Horace Mayo. The clinic affiliated with the graduate medical school of the University of Minnesota in 1915 and became a nonprofit charitable association in 1919. Diagnoses are made at the clinic and treatment is given at one of the independent Rochester hospitals by clinic physicians.

MEASLES [mē′zəlz] **or RUBEOLA** [roō-bē′ə-lə], a highly contagious virus disease, characterized by a blotchy reddish-brown eruption of the skin. It is a common and sometimes serious disease of childhood, occurring in epidemic form every two to three years. Measles is particularly severe in adults. Measles should not be confused with German measles (rubella), a milder infection with somewhat similar symptoms. German measles are particularly likely to damage unborn babies.

About 10 days after exposure, the illness starts like a severe common cold. The temperature rises quickly to 102° F.–104° F. The main complaints are headache, cough, sneezing, and a running nose. The eyes are red, tender, and painful when exposed to strong light. Within a few days, a rash appears behind the ears or on the forehead, and takes several more days to spread to the legs.

The rash at first consists of small red spots, which gradually enlarge and merge, giving the blotchy appearance characteristic of measles. At its height, the eruption covers the entire body, but is much denser in the upper part.

Measles is not limited to the skin. All internal surfaces are likely to be affected, including the membranes covering the lids and eyes and the lining of the throat and windpipe. This causes the typical eye inflammation and cough. Lesions in the mouth appear a few days before the skin rash and resemble grains of salt sprinkled on a red background. Sometimes patches of intestinal tissue become inflamed, possibly causing symptoms similar to those seen in appendicitis.

When the rash is fully developed, the fever drops suddenly, the nose stops running, the eyes stop tearing, and the cough eases. Within less than 12 hours, if all goes well, the patient will apparently have recovered.

The most important complications of measles are bacterial infection, inflammation of the brain (encephalitis), and pneumonia. Bacterial infection is suspected if the temperature rises after having fallen, or if the ear becomes painful. Encephalitis is usually first recognized by a recurrence of the fever, excessive sleepiness, or stupor. Pneumonia is marked by rapid breathing and cough.

A vaccine which offers lifelong protection against measles was first released in the United States in 1963. Most babies are vaccinated against measles between 9–18 months of age. Because measles can disable and kill, vaccination by the age of one year for all babies is urged.

For the unvaccinated child or adult who has been infected, treatment is directed at preventing complications and relieving discomfort. Medications to relieve coughing, nasal congestion, or itching, are often given. Antibiotics are prescribed when there is a complicating bacterial infection. It is often possible to prevent or lessen an attack of measles in an unvaccinated individual who has been exposed to the infection by injecting gamma globulin, germ-fighting proteins extracted from the blood.
See also GERMAN MEASLES.

MEDICAL ELECTRONICS. One of the most promising and rapidly developing areas of medical research is the application of revolutionary electronic developments to the treatment and diagnosis of human disease. The comparatively familiar X-ray tube, ultraviolet lamp, diathermy unit, electrocardiograph (which measures electrical activity in the heart), and electroencephalogram (which records electrical "brain waves") are being joined by more sophisticated devices, such as pill-sized radio transmitters which broadcast while journeying through the digestive tract, "pacemakers" which prod the heart into beating properly, and complex electronic brains which "remember" thousands of case histories and compare them against any case submitted. The list of new devices includes an electrical apparatus that lulls the brain to sleep with rhythmic electrical pulses; an instrument which produces almost instant, electrically induced anesthesia; devices that send ultra-high-frequency sound impulses through the body to obtain pictures of soft tissues which are invisible to X rays; and similar sound generators that enable neurosurgeons to operate on parts of the brain without opening the skull. These remarkable developments have been made possible largely by the introduction of solid-state conductors (semiconductors) and by the development of electronic "thinking" techniques which often parallel those of the human mind.

Computers and Diagnosis

The application of computers to medical diagnosis may make possible for the first time the pooling of all existing medical data and its use in individual cases, where the

MEDICINE

physician is presently limited by his own knowledge and experience. A data-processing system is envisaged which would contain all of the information now stored in textbooks, hospital records, government statistics, and in the files of individual physicians. The device would be automatically kept up to date and would yield at any time a summary of all that is known about a particular medical subject. The machine might also automatically translate its knowledge into several languages.

Electronics and the Heart

The broad range and potential value of electronics in medicine may be seen in the various devices which have been developed to diagnose and treat heart disease.

The earliest electronic device used in diagnosing heart disorders was the electrocardiograph, which recorded the electrical currents associated with the activity of the heart. More recently, a miniature electrocardiograph has been perfected which can be carried about by the patient to record heart activity continuously for several hours. In this way it is presumed that brief periods of abnormal heart actions are more likely to be detected than in the half-minute or so of heart activity which is ordinarily recorded by the standard office instrument. Another refinement is the development of electronic apparatus which can automatically analyze large groups of electrocardiographic data.

Electrocardiographic information can also be automatically recorded by electronic monitoring systems, along with data on the blood pressure, body temperature, respiration rate, and other physiological activities. In some of these monitoring systems, information on the functioning of from 1 to 12 patients can be continuously presented to a ward nurse in a hospital. In other systems, alarms may be triggered when a vital index, such as pulse rate, slips above or below a significant figure.

A different electronic approach to heart diagnosis consists of recording heart sounds and then playing them back while filtering out extraneous noises and amplifying diagnostically relevant sounds to detect heart murmurs. An ingenious diagnostic device, developed in Japan, uses the Doppler effect, the physical principle which makes the pitch of an approaching train whistle sound higher and that of a retreating whistle sound lower than it actually is. Ultrahigh-frequency sound waves are bounced off the chambers and valves of the heart. The changes in pitch of the returned waves, when correlated with electrocardiographic data and heart sounds, give information on the movement of the parts of the heart which could not be obtained in other ways.

Heart Substitutes. The "pacemaker" is in effect a replacement for the SA node, the small group of specialized heart muscle cells that initiate the rhythmic beat of the normal heart. This is accomplished by generating electrical pulses at regular intervals and conducting these pulses to an appropriate place in, or on, the heart where they can stimulate the heartbeat. The pulse may be generated by apparatus carried on the clothing and can be conducted to the heart by a special tube which is passed to the heart through a vein in the arm. Devices of this type have been used in cases of "Adams-Stokes attacks," a type of fainting spell caused by a sudden slowing or stopping of the heartbeat. In this condition the pacemaker stimulates the heartbeat, thus maintaining blood circulation. The instrument does not cure the disease but serves to keep the patient functioning until the heart resumes its usual beating, and is analogous to the use of a crutch while waiting for a broken leg to heal.

A more ambitious medical electronic project is the replacement of a diseased heart with an artificial pump. In designing such an instrument a number of difficulties have to be taken into consideration. The artificial heart must be connected to at least seven major blood vessels and will have to be anchored in place without injuring adjacent tissues. Blood must be pumped through the device without destroying the blood cells or chemically altering the composition of the blood. A way will also have to be found of adjusting the output of the artificial heart to the changing needs of the body.

If the problems involved in the construction of an artificial heart can be solved, it may not be unreasonable to look forward to the replacement of other organs as well.
See also DIATHERMY; ELECTROCARDIOGRAM; ELECTROENCEPHALOGRAPH; PROSTHETICS.

MEDICINE [mĕd'ə-sĭn]. In earliest times primitive man had no real concept of disease. He considered illness and death to be forms of punishment wished upon him by supernatural forces. Later, but before the first known civilization, primitive man evolved theories and learned certain facts that formed the basis of medicine. Eating certain foods caused stomach-aches which were believed to be caused by some evil spirit or god. After many stomach-aches from the same foods, the realization came that the evil spirit resided in those foods, and they were to be avoided. From bitter experience, knowledge was amassed about the ill effects of poisonous fruits and berries, dead and decayed animal matter, poison ivy, and other materials. It was natural to extend these ideas of supernatural causes to other areas of disease such as earache, sore throat, and appendicitis. As a means of ridding the body of these evil spirits, man brewed and drank foul tasting concoctions in the belief that if they were unpleasant, the spirit would flee. Some of these mixtures acted as purgatives, some induced vomiting, and others were actually of value against the basic disease. Gradually a class of men, known as medicine men, capitalized on these religious-superstitious beliefs. They claimed skill in the art of healing and "drove out" evil spirits by dances and incantations. Many of the present traditional folk remedies are based on superstition and magical phenomena, forming a link to the supernatural disease theories of earliest times.

Over the centuries a large number of gods were named, almost one for each disease. With this highly mystical and supernatural attitude toward illness, healing of the sick became more and more a function of the religious leaders. The ancient practice of trephining, a type of surgery that was practiced in prehistoric times, is thought to have been performed by priests and religious leaders. This procedure involved cutting a portion of bone from the skull, leaving a hole from the scalp to the outside of the brain. The operation, performed with a flint scraper, probably to let out "evil spirits," was used in diseases such as epilepsy, migraine, or insanity. The fact that people survived these operations is evidenced by the well-healed bone edges found in skulls from the Neolithic Period. Until recent times trephining was still performed by primitive peoples in some parts of the world.

Early Egyptian, Chinese, Greek, and Roman Medicine

Knowledge of early medicine is limited by inadequate and poorly preserved records. One of the earliest known medical documents is the "Ebers Papyrus," written in Egypt about 1500 B.C. From the many prescriptions and remedies listed in this work, it is evident that treatment was based mainly on magical concepts. The Egyptians' knowledge of anatomy was limited because of their theological concepts. They believed that after death the body must be kept whole until the resurrection, or the spirit and body would not be able to reunite. Any desecration of the body, even by worms, would prevent this union, and hence the elaborate method of preserving the body known as mummification was developed.

Imhotep, an Egyptian politician and architect, was one of the earliest physicians known to history. He lived about 2900 B.C. and designed the Step Pyramid which may still be seen along the Nile. Although nothing is known of him as a physician, he was accorded the status of the god of medicine and was worshiped for many centuries. This same period also gave birth to the beginnings of medicine in a completely different culture—China. The Chinese treated disease by burning small cones of combustible material on the skin (moxibustion) and by inserting long metal needles into the body to correct imbalances of humors, or vapors (acupuncture). They described the taking of the pulse long before the Greeks, and knew how to immunize against smallpox as far back as the 11th century A.D.

Among the ancient Greeks Aesculapius was worshiped as a god and was said to have performed many miracles of healing. He introduced "temple healing"; the ill came to the temples, and departed miraculously cured of illness. Failures were never recorded, but many shrines and monuments were erected by those cured.

A completely different type of medicine was introduced by Hippocrates, who lived around 400 B.C. and is often called the "Father of Medicine." His "Oath of Hippocrates" is still respected by modern physicians as a code of professional ethics. Although he did not understand the true nature of disease, he made the first attempt to apply a combination of reasoning and observation to medicine. Hippocrates denied that disease was punishment sent by the gods but claimed that it was caused by external factors such as the sun, the cold, or winds. An excellent observer, he accurately described many diseases known to modern medicine. By a careful study of the natural course of illnesses he was able to predict the eventual outcome of various diseases. During Hippocrates' era a popular concept held that the human body was composed of four "humors"—blood, phlegm, black bile, and yellow bile—and that the body had four qualities—hot, cold, dry, and moist. Disease occurred when the proper balance of these factors was disturbed.

The Romans, who harbored little regard for Greek physicians, were suspicious of those who migrated to Rome to practice their profession. Before the appearance of the Greek physicians, Rome had no doctors; everyone acted as his own physician. The Romans added little to the diagnosis and therapy of disease because of their distaste for the practice of medicine. They did, however, make some important contributions to public health. They constructed excellent systems of sanitation, sewage, and water supply, and did much toward advancing the health of the populace in general.

It was not until Julius Caesar gave them the full rights of Roman citizenship in 46 B.C. that reputable Greek physicians became attracted to Rome. Of these, the greatest was Galen (c.2d century), a physician whose thoughts and teachings prevailed for many centuries. He was a great anatomist, but because of the general reluctance to dismember the human body, his studies were on apes and pigs. Galen transferred his findings to man without being aware that the muscles and bones of different species are not identical. A voluminous and dogmatic author, he was, unfortunately, not always correct. Because of his standing and the respect accorded to him, his teachings of both truths and myths were accepted without challenge.

As Greek medicine faded, the Arabian school grew strong, preserving much of the Greek teachings and adding some good observations of its own. The era of Arabian medicine lasted from the 7th to the 13th century. During the Middle Ages, medicine was almost exclusively practiced by the priests of the Christian church, who ascribed to patron saints the power of causing or curing many diseases. About the 9th century A.D. the first organized medical school was established at Salerno, Italy; it survived until closed by Napoleon in 1811. With the introduction of formal instruction in medicine, examinations were held to determine the competence of physicians, degrees were granted, and the title of "Doctor" was accorded to those who graduated from medical school.

The Medieval Period and the Renaissance

Advances in medicine waned during the medieval period. Religion lost much of its hold over medicine, although prayers and incantations were still widely used to treat illness. During this period the plague, or the Black Death, decimated Europe in the 14th century. Millions of people died from this disease, which was caused by the bacteria *Pasteurella pestis*, and transmitted from rats to man by the bite of the flea. The illness frequently ran its entire course within 24 hours and terminated in death. The cause was unknown and the people were advised to flee far and rapidly from a stricken area, causing further spread of the disease. The epidemic gradually abated although it sprang up sporadically for the next three centuries.

The Renaissance of the 15th and 16th centuries brought not only a cultural revival, but also stimulated great strides in medicine. The renowned anatomist Andreas Vesalius reformed the concepts of anatomy and brought to the profession an understanding of the human body that has needed but little improvement. In France Ambroise Paré, the great surgeon of the Renaissance, began his career as a barber surgeon, cutting hair and performing operations. Despite his ignorance of Latin, the international language of science, his skill and accurate observations won him a place in medical history. Well versed in the treatment of

MEDICINE

wounds, his knowledge and judgment revolutionized and advanced the field of surgery. He denounced the popular method of treating wounds with boiling oil and preferred soothing ointments. He is now recognized as the father of modern surgery.

Surgeons did not formally divorce their specialty from barbers until 1540, when King Henry VIII of England issued a royal decree separating the two professions. According to the decree, surgeons should no longer be barbers, and barbers should restrict surgery to dentistry. Internal medicine lagged behind surgery during this period. Vesalius and Paré had no counterparts in the field of medicine, and advances were slow and limited. Concepts of experimentation to find the true nature of disease had not become established during the Renaissance era.

Paracelsus, a physician who attempted to introduce new concepts into medicine, added many new drugs for the treatment of disease. Many of his ideas, however, appear now to be nonsensical, for example, his view that the human body was composed of three elements—sulfur, mercury, and salt. During this period other physicians were still making use of concoctions of worms, believing in witches, and regarding "humors" and stars as the regulators of bodily health.

In the early 17th century William Harvey wrote his classic book on the circulation of the blood, entitled *De motu cordis*. In it, Harvey described the movement of blood with the heart as the main pump (this was formerly attributed to the liver) and showed that there is a circular flow of blood from the arteries to the veins. Later workers, using the newly discovered microscope, found the small capillaries which are the actual link between the arteries and veins.

Anton van Leeuwenhoek, an early microscopist, was the first to describe bacteria and protozoa, although the significance of these observations was not to be realized for many years. In general, this era saw the return of medicine to the careful observations and case histories of Hippocrates.

Medicine in the New World

During this period of intense medical activity in Europe, the pilgrims began their journeys to the New World. Sickness and disease plagued early America during its slow beginning. The settlers themselves fared poorly on arrival to this continent. The voyage was long (about three months), many were sick from scurvy (resulting from a lack of vitamin C) during the trip, and many died before reaching land. It was not until a century later that Dr. James Lind popularized the use of citrus fruits to prevent scurvy. The settlers' diseases spread rapidly and severely among the Indians. One of these diseases, measles, although mild to Europeans, caused high mortality rates in the Indian population. It is thought that the Indians' opposition to the colonists would have been much greater had their tribes not been decimated by these illnesses.

Before the establishment of hospitals, patients who required special care not available in their own home, were treated in the physicians home. Special homes were established in the 18th century for the care of chronically ill or medically untreatable patients.

Infectious diseases were rapidly brought to America by the constant influx of new migrants. Among these diseases were whooping cough, influenza, yellow fever, diphtheria, and scarlet fever. Early American medicine was marked by its practicality; theorizers were not a part of the life at that time. Few young colonists returned to England to study medicine. The great majority who wished to become physicians became apprentices to practicing doctors, lived in the doctor's house, rolled pills, mixed remedies, read his books, and learned their medicine at the patient's bedside under the doctor's guidance.

The first American medical school was established in Philadelphia in 1765, a department of a college that is now the University of Pennsylvania. Medicine during the Revolution was severely handicapped by an almost complete lack of surgical instruments and lack of food, clothing, and medication. The ancient practice of bleeding, or puncturing a vein to allow blood to run out, begun among primitive people and repopularized during Galen's time, was still in use during this period. Bleeding first originated as a form of ritualism to appease spirits and gods, a miniature type of human sacrifice. Eighteenth-century physicians believed, however, that bleeding let "impurities" out of the body to improve health or cure disease. It has been said that George Washington's death from a severe throat infection was hastened by the bleeding performed by his physician.

Homeopathy

In the 18th century two schools of medical treatment arose. One system advocated extremely large doses of drugs and is said to have killed more persons than the French Revolution and the Napoleonic Wars combined. The other system, called homeopathy, advocated extremely small amounts of highly diluted drugs. This school held that a drug which caused certain symptoms to appear in a healthy person could be used to treat those same symptoms occurring in disease. The low dosages were to prevent the drug from acting on the nondiseased portions of the body. Homeopathy had many proponents. It was of value not only in helping to cut down on the massive overdoses given by the proponents of the first group, but also aided in the understanding of drug effects, since all drugs were first tried in healthy persons and the actions were carefully recorded.

Obstetrical forceps came into use during this century, and doctors began to assist in childbirth, a fact which horrified many physicians and was deplored by all midwives.

Advances in the 18th and 19th Centuries

Smallpox was prevalent at this time and attempts were made to prevent serious infections. Centuries before, the Chinese had discovered that a minor infection, produced by blowing dried crust from smallpox lesions into the noses of healthy children, protected against catching the disease in its full-blown form. Physicians in England gave this same protection by making a cut on the arm of a healthy person, and applying fluid obtained from a smallpox blister to the cut. A mild infection ensued, providing the person with immunity to the disease. This technique was not without its dangers, however, as serious infection and scarring sometimes resulted. The highly successful type of vaccination practiced today (using cowpox virus) was introduced by the English country-doctor Edward Jenner after he had been told by a dairymaid that an attack of cowpox protected against smallpox. We now know that the mild cowpox infection is caused by a virus similar to that which causes smallpox. Around the same time the drug digitalis was introduced for the treatment of heart failure. Country people of England used the leaves of the foxglove plant, brewed as a tea, for the treatment of edema, or dropsy. William Withering, a country practitioner, found that when dropsy was associated with heart disease, it could be cured by careful administration of the foxglove preparation. The active ingredient of this preparation has been found to be digitalis, and is now widely used in the treatment of the failing heart.

Percussion, the art of tapping the chest or abdomen with fingers of both hands, now used routinely by physicians, was introduced to medicine in the 18th century. Percussion was commonly used by innkeepers to ascertain the amount of wine remaining in a wooden cask. A physician, Leopold Auenbrugger, having worked in a wine cellar as a youth, applied this method to the human chest with gratifying results. Early in the next century the stethoscope was invented by the French physician René Laënnec. When confronted with a female patient he felt he could not employ the customary method of examining the chest—that of direct listening by placing his ear upon the chest wall. Instead, he rolled up a paper and discovered that he could hear well with one end on the chest and the other to his ear. Laënnec's paper tube has since been elaborated into the stethoscope, a trademark of the medical profession.

During the 19th century the fields of surgery and medicine achieved equal standing. The understanding of disease was placed on a firm base by thorough and intensive experimental investigation. The functions of nerves were discovered; the entire field of pathology, a study of disease by use of the microscope, was developed; and other new branches of medicine arose. Louis Pasteur discovered that spoilage of milk and wine was due to contamination with tiny organisms (bacteria), and suggested that heating would prevent this fermentation, a process now known as pasteurization. He was also the first to successfully treat victims of rabies. Following his pioneering studies the entire group of bacterial diseases was accurately studied and categorized.

While great advances were being made in Europe, American medicine began to flourish. Medical schools sprang up. Advances in surgery were numerous. The major American contribution to medicine came with the introduction of anesthesia. Prior to this discovery, operations were performed with either no pain-relieving medication, with alcohol intoxication, or sometimes with special drug mixtures which at best only partially reduced pain. A major assessment of the skill of the surgeon was in his speed of operation: the "best" surgeons performed amputations of limbs in less than one minute. More complex procedures were considered impossible because of the limitations imposed by the amount of pain the patient could withstand. Ether was the first anesthetic agent to be used, and after a painless operation was performed on a Boston patient in 1846, the value of the gas became firmly established in medicine.

Even though the severe pain associated with operations was conquered, many patients still died from infection. The typical surgeon of the era operated wearing a frock coat with suture material hanging through a buttonhole, and wiped his hands on his coat or an apron, if he happened to wear one. There was no concept of sterility, and doctors interrupted their cadaver dissections to deliver babies without having washed their hands. Not until 1847, when the Hungarian physician Ignaz Semmelweis insisted on thorough cleansing of the hands, did the mortality associated with childbirth due to puerperal fever decrease dramatically.

The real concept of cleanliness in the prevention of infections was introduced in 1865 by a Scottish surgeon, Joseph Lister. He studied Pasteur's work on fermentation caused by bacteria and devised a method of achieving a bacteria-free atmosphere. Prior to an operation, the surgeon's hands, instruments, and bandages were soaked in carbolic acid (phenol), a germ-killing substance. This same acid was sprayed around the operating room during the actual surgical procedure. Striking results were soon noticed, and the amount of wound infections declined abruptly as the system became widely accepted. These two major discoveries, anesthesia and sterility, or asepsis, allowed the surgeon to perform operations on parts of the body previously forbidden because of limitations in time and the danger of infection.

Florence Nightingale had already introduced female nurses into hospitals for the care of the sick. Special surgical techniques meant further special training, and the necessity for the separation of doctors into surgeons and medical physicians became evident. Surgery further divided itself into several other specialties. Surgeons performing operations on the female reproductive organs became known as gynecologists. Surgeons who performed operations on the brain and nervous system developed the field of neurosurgery, while those operating on the kidneys and urinary tract founded the field of urology. The treatment of broken, diseased, and deformed bones required further special skills, thus the surgical specialty of orthopedics grew.

Along with the expansion of surgery, the field of internal medicine also began to branch out. Neurology, the study of diseases of the brain and nervous system, became a separate specialty of medicine, as did cardiology, the study of diseases of the heart and blood vessels. The branch of medicine that requires special knowledge of blood cells is hematology. This field deals with the diagnosis and treatment of disorders such as anemia, leukemia, and bleeding tendencies. A comparatively new field of specialization is gastroenterology, which deals with those diseases that affect the stomach, the intestinal tract, the rectum, liver, and gallbladder. Pediatrics deals with the care of children and is a specialty distinct from medicine and surgery. Specialists in general internal medicine have a knowledge of all the various subspecialties but do not usually perform the intricate and precise tests used by the subspecialty groups. Many of these subspecialty groups require a complete training in the specialty of general internal medicine before the physician begins his subspecialty program. The backbone of medicine is still the general practitioner, who, in many areas, assumes com-

MEIOSIS

plete care of the patient, delivers babies, and performs surgery.

Some of the most impressive changes in medical thought have occurred in the field of psychiatry. It was not until the end of the 18th century that a French physician, Philippe Pinel, was the first to champion the cause of releasing mentally ill patients from chains and dungeons. Although this was a great advancement, it was not until a century later that Sigmund Freud revolutionized the field of psychopathology with his development of the system of psychoanalysis. Psychiatry is now well established as a separate portion of medicine. There is much research being performed in this field especially aimed toward uncovering a chemical basis for mental illness.

20th-Century Medicine

Approaching the 20th century, many new achievements appeared. The medical use of the X ray was discovered in 1895 by Wilhelm Konrad Roentgen. The early attempts to take X rays of the head required over an hour's exposure. Subsequent developments now permit such X rays to be taken in fractions of a second. This diagnostic aid has contributed much to the understanding and treatment of many diseases, notably tuberculosis. With the aid of the X ray, tuberculosis can be detected at an early stage, and treatment instituted. Recent development of potent medications has made this disease easier to control. Because of these new drugs, the treatment method of strict bed rest is no longer required in most cases.

The discovery of insulin by the physicians F. G. Banting and C. H. Best in 1922 opened a new world to diabetics, who formerly had been doomed to an early death by their disease. Insulin, now readily available, permits diabetics to live a relatively normal and full life. The more recent introduction of blood-sugar-lowering compounds that can be taken orally has, in certain selected patients, eliminated the necessity for insulin injections.

By far the greatest boon to mankind has been the introduction of drugs capable of destroying bacteria within the human body. These substances are called antibiotics, and, in the late 1940's were known as "miracle drugs." Until the third decade of the 20th century doctors still sat long hours watching their patients with pneumonia or other severe infections, waiting for the "crisis," or the time the fever reached its peak, and were usually powerless to control the outcome.

Surgery has now advanced to the extent that operations may last for hours at a time. Arteries and veins from one patient may be used in another, and arteries, veins, and even parts of the heart may be replaced by plastic or woven materials. A diseased organ, such as the kidney, may be replaced by a healthy one from a suitable donor (an identical twin).

Medical Education

The training of doctors in modern times is a long and arduous task. Up to the last century, Europe was still the center of medical education, and the most prominent American physicians had studied a few years abroad before practicing in this country. College was not always a fixed prerequisite for medical school; indeed the only requirement was an apprenticeship with a practicing physician. The training of modern doctors is now fairly well established, and most are college graduates before entering medical training. Medical school is an additional four years of intensive training, but some current programs offer a combined college and medical school course to be completed in a total of six years. All physicians must serve an internship of one year in clinical training after medical school graduation. During this time the physician comes into direct contact with patients, and assumes many medical responsibilities. After interning, the doctor may begin practice as a general practitioner, or take additional training in a medical specialty. If the doctor intends to specialize, he becomes a resident physician at an approved training hospital where he sees mainly cases in his specialty and gains both practical and theoretical knowledge in diagnosis and treatment. Time spent in residency training varies with the specialty field. Because of the need for manual training, the surgical specialties require the longest residency period—from four to five years for the urologist, general surgeon, and orthopedic surgeon, and from five to six years for the thoracic (chest) surgeon and neurosurgeon. Obstetrics and gynecology is a combined training program that requires three years of residency. Those physicians specializing in internal medicine have a minimum of three years in training after internship; any subspecialty of medicine, such as hematology, gastroenterology, cardiology, or endocrinology, requires an additional one or two years of residency. The X-ray doctor, or radiologist, and the pediatrician have training periods of two to three years. The pathologist, who studies the actual diseased tissues, performs autopsies to ascertain the exact cause of death, and conducts most of the laboratory tests, has a period of residency training lasting three to four years.

In this modern era when more and more is being learned about each disease, many illnesses previously thought to be one disease are now discovered to consist of many separate components, and new methods of diagnosis and therapy are being constantly developed. No physician can know all there is about all diseases. This is the reason for the long list of specialties and the years required in training. The specialty groups are not meant to supplant the general practitioner of medicine but to supplement him. The great burden of responsibility falls upon the shoulders of the general practitioner and the various specialty groups are available to lend their knowledge and experience to his for the welfare of the patient.

See also:

DISEASE	PSYCHIATRY
GYNECOLOGY	PUBLIC HEALTH
INDUSTRIAL MEDICINE	SURGERY
PEDIATRICS	TROPICAL MEDICINE
PREVENTIVE MEDICINE	

MEIOSIS [mī-ō′sĭs], a process that occurs during the maturation of germ cells whereby the chromosomes in the nucleus of each developing egg or sperm are reduced from the number characteristic for the species (the diploid number) to one-half (the haploid number). This process is necessary because when fertilization (of the egg by the sperm) occurs, the resulting fertilized cell, the zygote, will then have a correct (diploid) number of chromosomes.

Meiosis is contrasted with normal cell division, or mitosis, which takes place in all body cells except the germ cells. During mitosis, the nuclear material, including the chromosomes, is divided evenly among the two new daughter cells, each of which then has the same number of chromosomes as the parent cell.

MELANCHOLIA [měl-ən-kō'lē-ə], in psychiatry, a term describing mental disorders in which depression is the major symptom. These include neurotic depression, the depressive phase of manic-depressive psychosis, and involutional melancholia. The last condition occurs primarily in women in the age group 40 to 60. Affected persons are usually orderly, conscientious individuals who are basically insecure and have a highly developed sense of duty and responsibility. With the decline in physical vigor which accompanies aging and particularly with the changes in sexual functioning, these persons (who are often repressed sexually) may feel that life has passed them by. They withdraw from the world, narrowing their interests and activities and developing hypochondria, insomnia, loss of appetite, and a haunting fear of death. Characteristically, they awaken before dawn and lie in bed in the morning, unable to arise because of fatigue. The patient may attempt suicide.

Because of the association of melancholia with the menopause, hormone therapy was tried, but has proved unsuccessful. Electric shock therapy, alone or in combination with psychotherapy to reorient the patient's attitudes toward aging, has been helpful in many cases. Several antidepressive drugs have also been of value.

MELANIN [měl'ə-nĭn], a dark pigment found in the skin, hair, and eyes of many animals. In the skin of mammals melanin granules are deposited in the lower layer of the epidermis. The amount of melanin present determines the color of the skin. In lower vertebrates (fishes, amphibians, reptiles) melanin is deposited in special pigment cells, called melanophores, that are located in the dermis. In many lower vertebrates the distribution of melanin granules (and other pigments) in the dermal cells is variable, producing, for example, the color changes observed in the chameleon. In the eye, melanin is deposited in the iris: the amount of melanin present determines eye color—brown eyes contain considerably more melanin than blue eyes.

Some individuals are born without melanin or any other pigment in their tissues: their hair and skin are almost white and their eyes appear red from the underlying blood vessels. Such individuals are called albinos.
See also ALBINISM.

MELANOMA [měl-ə-nō'mə], tumor which contains melanin, the dark pigment found in the skin, hair, and eyes. The common mole is an innocuous type of melanoma which may become cancerous, and for this reason is sometimes surgically removed if it is located in an area subject to irritation. Cancerous melanomas are seen in adults. The most dangerous types appear on the skin of the face and feet. The tumor begins as a tiny, apparently harmless spot, which rapidly enlarges into a dark, ulcerating, bleeding mass. The cancer quickly spreads to other parts of the body. Early diagnosis and surgery are essential to save the patient's life.

MELANOSIS [měl-ə-nō'sĭs], excess deposition of melanin, the normal pigment of the skin, hair, and eyes, in the tissues. The pigmentation may be diffuse or localized (as in freckles). Melanosis may be a clue to the presence of a number of disorders, including Addison's disease and arsenic poisoning. Common causes of increased skin pigmentation are pregnancy (pigmentation of the breasts) and chronic irritations, such as pressure from clothing or excessive scratching of the skin.

MELIOIDOSIS [mě lē-oi-dō' sĭs], disease of man and animals, caused by *Pseudomonas pseudomallei*, a bacterium found in soil and water throughout many of the rice-growing areas of Southeast Asia. Man acquires the illness when the organism enters through broken skin or by inhalation. The acute form of melioidosis begins as pneumonia or blood poisoning. The more common chronic form of the disease usually appears as a chronic form of pneumonia or draining abscess. Because the bacteria can strike several body organs, melioidosis imitates many diseases, such as tuberculosis, cholera, plague, typhus, and even smallpox. Chloramphenicol, the drug of choice for treatment, has lowered the death rate to 30% in the chronic form, but 90% of persons with acute melioidosis still die. Melioidosis is now seen in the United States, because some military personnel who have served in Southeast Asia return home with symptoms of the disease.

MEMORY involves the reappearance or reinstatement of some previously learned behavior. Thus we may remember how to roller skate, remember a poem that we have learned or a movie we have seen, or recall that we went to the store. It was at one time widely held that memory was a special mental faculty which could be improved through exercise, as a muscle might be. This view is not held by modern psychologists, to whom memory is not a thing but rather a relation between stimuli and responses.

The reinstatement of a learned response depends on many things, among which are the following:

(1) The response must have been learned in the first place. Many times when we say that we have forgotten something, the truth is more nearly that it was never adequately learned. Many studies have shown that overlearning—continued study beyond the point of mastery—greatly improves retention.

(2) The time elapsing between the original learning and retention tests is important. Hermann Ebbinghaus showed that learned material is forgotten rapidly at first and then more slowly as the time since learning increases. The shape of this forgetting curve, obtained when results of experiments are graphed, has been repeatedly verified.

(3) The kind of activity within the retention interval is perhaps the most important variable in memory. For example, if a person sleeps in the interval between learning and testing he is likely to remember more than if he is awake. This is not because of the beneficial properties of sleep but rather because of the lack of opportunity to

MENDEL

learn additional responses that might be confusing or interfering. This tendency of later learning to interfere with earlier learning is called retroactive inhibition. It is greatest when the interpolated activity is similar to but not identical with the learned behavior. Thus, if a student has learned to speak French, forgetting is likely to be more rapid if he subsequently learns Spanish than if he later learns Hindu because of the differing degrees of similarity to the original learning. Bicycle riding shows great retention over many years, probably because few things are subsequently learned that are similar to the riding behavior.

(4) Forgetting may be motivated. As Freud has pointed out, events that are associated with painful or disturbing circumstances are likely to be forgotten. Thus, we may forget a dental appointment or an embarrassing experience because remembering reinstates painful stimuli, which are often avoided.

MENDEL [měn'dəl], **GREGOR JOHANN** (1822–84), Austrian monk and naturalist who discovered the laws of heredity.

In 1856, in the monastery garden at Brünn, he began the breeding experiments on the garden pea which were to lead to the formulation of his laws. He crossed different varieties of the pea, studying in the resulting hybrids the appearance of pairs of traits that were distinctly different from one another (for example, red and white flower color, tallness and shortness of the plants). He performed his first experiments using plant stocks that he knew would breed true (the offspring would have the same appearance as the parent plants). He took great care in making the cross-pollinations so that he was certain to have the particular crosses he wished to study.

Mendel recorded separately the various traits observed in the hybrids, and kept separate records of the progeny of the various generations. He found that in each cross one of the two contrasting types of traits that he was studying always appeared in the first hybrid generation. The dominant trait, tall, for instance, always appeared in a cross between tall and short plants. When members of the first hybrid generation were interbred the two types of traits reappeared in the ratio 3 (dominant—for example, tall) to 1 (recessive—for example, short). He concluded that the hybrids form seeds that carry factors determining one or the other of the two types. This is the principle of segregation, the first Mendelian law. When he studied two or more different traits in the same cross (for instance, tallness and shortness of the plants, and yellow and green seed color) he found that the various pairs of characters segregated independently of one another, and could appear in all possible combinations. This is the principle of independent assortment, the second Mendelian law. From this he concluded that each trait is governed by a separate factor, and that the various factors do not affect each other when carried together. He reported the results of his experiments to the Naturforschenden Verein in Brünn on Mar. 8, 1865, and published them in the transactions of this society in 1866. Their true significance was not, however, appreciated at the time, and his work was neglected until 1900 when it was rediscovered, independently, by Hugo de Vries, Erich Tschermak von Seysenegg, and Karl Erich Correns. Mendel's discoveries were found to be applicable to all living organisms, and became the foundation of the modern study of heredity.
See also GENETICS.

MÉNIÈRE'S [măn-nyârz'] **DISEASE,** a poorly understood, progressive disorder of the inner ear, or labyrinth, characterized by severe vertigo, ringing in the ears, and deafness of varying degree. Although called a disease, it is actually a syndrome, or collection of complaints and physical findings, with several different causes. It may arise from spreading middle ear infection. It is sometimes associated with injury to or disease of the arteries which supply the labyrinth, such as arteriosclerosis. Allergy and the toxic effect of certain drugs may also precipitate the condition, and it is a rare early manifestation of brain tumor. In spite of this long list of possible causes, there is no demonstrable cause in most patients. The most frightening and distressing symptom is vertigo, which causes patients to lose their spatial orientation. This is accompanied by severe nausea and vomiting. Relief comes only when lying very still with eyes closed and the head securely propped between pillows. Although hearing loss varies in degree, it is slowly progressive. Attacks may last from minutes to days, with varying intervals between attacks. Medication is often quickly effective in relieving symptoms. Surgical destruction of the nerve supplying the inner ear is done occasionally.

MENINGIOMA [mə-nĭn-jē-ō'mə], a tumor of the meninges, the membranes which envelop the brain. Meningiomas are usually not cancerous. Symptoms arise from pressure on adjacent brain tissue or from increased tension within the skull. Headaches, convulsions, and disturbances in behavior or in sight or smell may occur, depending upon the area of the brain involved. Treatment is surgical.

MENINGITIS [měn-ĭn-jī'tĭs], inflammation of the meninges, the membranes which envelop the brain and spinal cord. While most cases are caused by bacteria or viruses, fungi or parasites may also be responsible.

Bacterial meningitis may be caused by a number of different bacteria, including those responsible for tuberculosis, pneumonia, and ordinary boils. The infection usually reaches the meninges from other parts of the body by way of the blood stream or from infections of the ear, sinuses, or face which spread directly to the meninges. The patient suffers from fever, weakness, and stupor or coma. Increased pressure within the skull produces headache, nausea, vomiting, and convulsions. Muscular spasms cause stiffness of the neck and back. In infants the "soft spot" of the head may bulge.

Meningitis caused by the meningococcus is often characterized by a hemorrhagic rash caused by ruptured blood vessels (spotted fever).

Meningitis from virus infection may be a complication of diseases such as mumps, poliomyelitis, measles, and chicken pox. In addition, two large groups of viruses, the "ECHO" and the "Coxsackie" viruses, may cause meningitis. Fever, headache, and neck stiffness are seen in all forms of viral meningitis; but the course of the disease varies with the specific infection.

Although the outlook for bacteria-caused meningitis has improved considerably since the introduction of antibiotics, many cases are still dangerous. This is particularly true in cases caused by tuberculosis and pneumonia (pneumococcus) bacteria and in cases involving children under the age of two. Viral meningitis is generally less severe than the bacterial form, but there is no specific treatment.

MENNINGER [měn'ĭng-ər], **KARL AUGUSTUS** (1893–), American psychiatrist well known for his association with the Menninger Foundation of Topeka, Kans. Menninger established a psychiatric clinic with his father and brother. This eventually became the Menninger Foundation, a nonprofit center for education, research, and treatment in the field of mental disease. The foundation, which employs 650 persons, has a budget of $5,000,-000 and is the core of a unique affiliation of federal, state, and community mental health agencies. Under Menninger's guidance, Kansas reorganized and modernized its mental hospitals, a program later emulated by other states.

MENOPAUSE [měn'ə-pôz], period of gradual decline in the activity of the female reproductive organs, usually occurring between the ages of 42 and 52 years (average 47.5 years). During this time menstruation becomes irregular and finally ceases. Fertility declines, and it has been estimated that about 99 out of every 100 women are infertile one year after menstruation has ceased completely. The tissues of the breasts, womb, and vagina shrink and lose their elasticity, and the skin becomes thin and dry. Body activity generally declines, so that the menopausal woman burns fewer calories and tends to gain weight on a diet which formerly was not fattening. Disturbances in the nervous control of the blood vessels may cause hot flushes and sweating. Depression, heightened irritability, and other emotional responses are often seen at this time. The head hair thins, but this does not usually become evident until about the age of 60. In rare cases, there is an excessive growth of body hair (hirsutism) during the menopause. The extent of these symptoms varies greatly from woman to woman, and in some cases virtually no changes may be seen.

An "artificial menopause," with many of the above changes, may occur in younger women following surgical removal of the ovaries in certain diseases.

Female hormones may help relieve the hot flushes which are often disturbing. Hormones in the form of creams are applied locally to the vagina to restore the tissues to their earlier condition.

See also MENSTRUATION.

MENSTRUATION [měn-strōō-ā'shən], cyclic activity of the female reproductive organs associated with female fertility. The principal events underlying menstruation occur in three parts of the body: (1) the pituitary gland, which lies on the underside of the brain; (2) the ovaries, which contain the eggs; and (3) the uterus.

The pituitary gland initiates the cycle by secreting a hormone (follicle-stimulating hormone, FSH) which stimulates one of the egg-containing follicles in the ovary to mature. As the follicle ripens under this influence, the ovaries step up their production of the female sex hormone, estrogen. The latter stimulates growth in the cells lining the uterus. Around the 14th day of the cycle the egg ruptures from its follicle and is expelled from the ovary. The egg then travels down the fallopian tube and finally reaches the uterus. Shortly before the egg leaves the ovary, the pituitary gland begins to secrete a "luteinizing" hormone. This stimulates the ruptured follicle, which has been left behind in the ovary, to become the corpus luteum (literally, "yellow body"). The corpus luteum secretes progesterone, a hormone which continues the stimulation of the uterine lining and prevents further eggs from maturing in the ovaries. The final stage of menstruation is apparently triggered by the interaction of progesterone with the pituitary gland. When the blood concentration of progesterone reaches a certain level it inhibits further secretion of the luteinizing hormone by the pituitary gland. This results in degeneration of the corpus luteum and a sudden fall in the progesterone content of the blood. As the progesterone is withdrawn, the lining of the uterus is sloughed off as the menstrual flow, carrying the egg with it. If, however, the egg is fertilized before this time, the corpus luteum does not degenerate but continues to secrete progesterone for a period. This inhibits menstruation and prevents new eggs from ripening in the ovaries. In this way progesterone maintains pregnancy.

Characteristics of the Menstrual Cycle

The menarche, or beginning of menstruation, ordinarily occurs around the age of 13 or 14 in the temperate zones and about 9 or 10 in the tropics. In some families there may be an inherited tendency to an especially early or late menarche.

The average menstrual cycle ranges from 26 to 30 days. The menstrual flow usually lasts for four days. Prior to the flow various signs appear, such as swelling of the breasts, congestion of the reproductive organs, and irritability and nervousness ("pre-menstrual tension"). The normal blood loss is small and is not significant.

Menstrual Regularity. Though the great majority of women have regular menstrual cycles, the regularity may be upset by stress, anxiety, fever, colds, or other factors which act through the pituitary gland—which, as we have seen earlier, exercises an important control over menstruation. This regulation can be extremely precise: cases have been noted in which a dive into a cold pool started or halted menstruation. Climate may also affect the cycle: women raised in temperate climates may note an increase in the frequency of the menstrual cycle if they move to the tropics.

Menstruation and Pregnancy. The earliest sign of pregnancy appears in the pattern of changes in the basal body temperature. Normally, the temperature drops sharply when the follicle ruptures (ovulation) and then rises about a degree higher than the pre-ovulatory temperature. Pregnancy is likely if the temperature is maintained at this elevated level, meaning that a new ovulation is not taking place.

Menstruation has been known to occur during the first few months of pregnancy and in rare cases has continued throughout pregnancy.

Menstrual Disorders. These include absence of menstruation (amenorrhea), scanty menstruation (oligomenorrhea), excessive bleeding (menorrhagia), or painful

MENTAL DEFICIENCY

menstruation (dysmenorrhea). These disorders may be caused by tumors or abnormalities of the reproductive organs, or by pelvic infections or hormonal imbalances. Most cases of primary dysmenorrhea (appearing with the first menstruation) are caused by emotional stress.

See also MENOPAUSE; PITUITARY GLAND; PREGNANCY.

MENTAL DEFICIENCY, also called mental retardation, feeble-mindedness, or amentia, may be inherited or be caused by abnormal development, or by disease or injury in prenatal life or in infancy.

In the inherited types numerous abnormalities, including skin lesions, epilepsy, tumors, and stunted bone growth, accompany the mental defect. Some cases involve disorders of body chemistry in which specific substances (for example, amino acids) cannot be normally processed.

Noninherited forms of mental deficiency can be caused by injury or disease before birth (syphilis, German measles), by birth injury (cerebral palsy), or by disturbances appearing in infancy (encephalitis, lead poisoning, head injury).

Familiar types of mental deficiency include:

Idiopathic, also called physiological mental deficiency. This includes the vast majority of defectives. In these cases no specific cause of the deficiency can be identified.

Mongolism, which occurs approximately once in every 5,000 births and receives its name from the presence of certain features of the Mongolian race, such as slanted eyes and a fold over the inner corner of the eye. Mongolism has been shown to result from a developmental abnormality which results in the presence of an extra chromosome (one of the structures which transmit inheritance) in the cells of the child.

Cretinism, a form of mental deficiency caused by undersecretion of thyroid hormone. This may be inherited or result from a deficiency of iodine in the diet. The latter type, called endemic cretinism, is seen in certain areas such as the Alps, where the iodine content of the soil is low. The typical cretin has a low, wrinkled forehead, puffy eyes, wide and flattened nose, thick lips, and a large protruding tongue. Early diagnosis and treatment with thyroid hormone can produce much improvement in these cases.

Microcephaly, an inherited disorder marked by an undersized brain. The face is of normal size, but the forehead tapers markedly, giving a characteristic "pinhead" appearance.

Phenylpyruvic oligophrenia, an inherited disorder of body chemistry in which the body lacks a key chemical needed to process phenylalanine (one of the amino acids found in protein foods). Treatment of infants with low phenylalanine diets has been tried in this disorder.

Cerebral palsy, which results from brain injury at birth. Mental deficiency of varying degree is present in 50%–60% of these cases.

The Extent of Retardation. Mental defectives are generally classified in three groups, based upon performance on IQ tests. The *severely retarded* (idiots: 0–19 IQ) remain below the mental age of three and are entirely dependent on others for their needs. The mental age of the *moderately retarded* group (imbeciles: 20–49 IQ) is between three and seven years and while they too are largely dependent on others, they can be trained to a limited extent. The largest group (75%) of mental defectives are the *mildly retarded* (morons: 50–69 IQ) whose mental age extends beyond the eight-year-old level. These individuals can participate in elementary academic activities and can be gainfully employed in certain lines of work.

Social and Educational Problems of the Mentally Retarded. The early attitude of hopelessness which characterized the approach to the mentally retarded has been replaced by a feeling that much can be done for them. Efforts are now made to keep the defective child in as normal a setting as possible (preferably the home), and to develop his maximum potential. To this end, some communities have established special classes for the retarded, and some "sheltered" workshops have been made available in which the retarded person can develop vocational skills in a noncompetitive atmosphere. The emotional problems of the retarded child and his family have also received attention from the psychologist, psychiatrist, and social worker—indeed, the field has virtually become a psychiatric subspecialty.

MENTAL ILLNESS may be caused by changes in the structure or chemical function of the brain, or by psychological stress. The interrelation between the physical and psychic components that are believed to cause particular mental disorders, such as schizophrenia, is the subject of considerable debate and controversy.

Organic Mental Illness

Mental disturbances of organic, or physical, origin may result from infection, injury, poisoning, or other assaults on the structural and chemical integrity of the brain. Chemical poisoning caused by substances such as lead, mercury, carbon disulfide, or carbon monoxide may produce mental symptoms. Alcohol may cause a variety of mental disorders, ranging from the temporary derangement of pathological intoxication, seen in persons especially sensitive to alcohol, to Korsakoff's psychosis, which is marked by memory loss and degeneration of nervous tissue. Injury to the head may produce concussion, coma, and possibly long-lasting mental impairment resulting from brain damage. A decrease in the brain's blood supply, commonly seen in elderly persons with "hardening of the arteries" (arterio- or atherosclerosis), is thought to lead to changes in brain substance and a gradual loss of mental alertness. In certain disorders of the endocrine glands, personality changes may be observed. Deficiencies of certain vitamins of the B complex group (niacin and thiamine) frequently cause mental disturbance. Syphilis may cause insidious personality changes some 20 to 30 years after the original infection. The list of organic bases of disturbed mental function is rounded out by tumors, and diseases of the nervous system such as multiple sclerosis. Organic illnesses are regarded as acute, if they are reversible, and chronic, if they persist.

Functional, or Psychogenic, Illness

In contrast to the above group, functional mental illnesses are believed to be caused by psychological factors. The fact that no known structural or physiological changes are associated with these illnesses does not necessarily mean that such changes may not be present. The division of mental disorders into organic and functional groups may merely reflect present ignorance of the detailed chemical and physiological functioning of the brain. This possibility has been emphasized by the ability of certain chemicals (for example, LSD) to create psychoticlike reactions in normal persons, and by the effectiveness of some drugs (for example, tranquilizers) in relieving some of the severe symptoms of functional disorders.

The functional disorders include psychoneuroses, psychotic reactions, psychosomatic disorders, and character disorders. To various degrees, these are all assumed to result from disturbances in interpersonal relations, and to have anxiety as an important component. The psychotic disorders, which include schizophrenic and manic-depressive psychoses, frequently require hospitalization. The individual loses contact with reality and is unable to function effectively at work, in school, or with his family and friends. In psychoneurotic disturbances the person can function better, but is troubled by rigid patterns of behavior, such as unreasonable fears (phobias) or obsessions, which he is powerless to control. The personality, or character, disorders are a varied group, and include schizoid personality types, who are withdrawn and emotionally detached, and cyclothymic types, who alternate between states of elation and sadness.

Treatment of Mental Disorders

The principal therapeutic tool of the psychiatrist is psychotherapy, which may be supplemented by tranquilizing drugs, shock therapies, and, less often, psychosurgery. Psychotherapy basically involves talking about one's problems and experiences with a specially trained person. This type of treatment is usually reserved for neurotics, persons with character disorders, and certain types of psychotic patients. Hospitalization is indicated when it becomes necessary to help a patient get relief from the many stresses of daily living, as well as in the rarer cases where there is need to protect the patient from harming himself or others.

It should be emphasized that many mentally ill people are able to function without being treated. In support of this are reports which indicate that the incidence of mental illness is much higher than one would be led to believe on the basis of mental hospital admissions and the number of patients being treated by private practitioners. Many persons who might objectively be considered to be neurotic and to function at a level somewhat less than their full potential do not consider themselves sick and usually do not come to the attention of a psychiatrist unless some great personal or general stress intervenes.

Unfortunately many people still regard mental illness as a stigma and often block efforts to give prompt treatment to themselves or to members of their family. Many individuals who would not hesitate to seek prompt medical attention for a physical ailment, procrastinate until mental symptoms become so severe that help is often too late to be most effective.

An encouraging development, however, is the increasing tendency to regard the psychotic person not as a criminal, but as a victim of illness. Hospital planners are designing smaller buildings that will offer more privacy and avoid the depressing atmosphere of many currently used hospitals. There is also greater flexibility in allowing week-end passes and home visits; the time of hospitalization has been shortened and after-care programs are being established to help the patient when he returns home. Another innovation is the day hospital, where patients are treated during the day but are given the opportunity to live with their families at night. The oft-mentioned belief that "once you go to a state hospital, it is for life," is adequately refuted by the increasing number of discharges.
See also NEUROSIS; PSYCHIATRY; PSYCHOANALYSIS; PSYCHOTHERAPY.

MENTALLY RETARDED, THE, persons classified as having lower than average intelligence. In terms of tests of intellectual ability, their intelligence quotients are below 70. They may be classed, in descending order of IQ's, as educable mentally retarded, trainable mentally retarded, and custodial mentally retarded, or as morons, imbeciles, and idiots. *See* INTELLIGENCE; INTELLIGENCE QUOTIENT(IQ); MENTAL DEFICIENCY.

MERCUROCHROME [mər-kūr′ə-krōm], also known as merbromin, an antiseptic mercury-containing organic compound. It is a dye which stains human tissues a deep red, but which penetrates skin poorly. Probably because of its staining properties, mercurochrome is popularly considered to be an effective antibacterial agent. Actually, it is a comparatively weak antiseptic; it does not destroy bacteria but inhibits their growth. Its activity is greatly reduced by the presence of organic materials, such as pus. Mercurochrome has been used chiefly to disinfect the skin and mucous membranes.
See also ANTISEPTICS.

MESCAL, one of several popular names for a small, bluish-green cactus, *Lophophora williamsii*, in the cactus family, Cactaceae, native to southwestern United States and Mexico. Also known as peyote or peyotl, the plant consists of a low-growing cluster of coarsely ribbed, globular stems. Each stem, or joint, is covered with rounded protrusions (tubercles) and except in seedlings, the plants have no spines. The rounded parts, called mescal buttons, have long been used by various Indian tribes in the preparation of a beverage drunk during religious ceremonies. The beverage contains mescaline, a plant alkaloid, which produces hallucinations when ingested.
See also MESCALINE.

MESCALINE [měs′kə-lēn], an alkaloid drug obtained from the peyote (also known as peyotl or mescal), a cactus plant found in Mexico and the southwestern United States. Mescaline has been of interest to psychiatrists and pharmacologists as a tool for the experimental investigation of schizophrenia. It produces vivid hallucinations, consisting usually of brightly colored lights, animals, and geometric patterns. In sufficient doses it produces disturbances of thought and perception which appear to resemble those seen in schizophrenia. The peyote plant has been used for generations by the Indians of the southwestern United States as part of their religious rituals. Most authorities agree that it causes no harmful effects or addiction.

METABOLISM

METABOLISM [mə-tăb′ə-lĭz-əm], a term broadly describing all the chemical reactions occurring in living tissues, particularly those reactions involved in the production of energy, the synthesis of tissue, and the formation and excretion of waste products.

Energy Production. An organism requires energy to move muscles, to conduct impulses along nerve fibers, to manufacture tissue, and to sustain all of the activities of life. In measuring energy output, physiologists use the expression "basal metabolism." This designates the amount of energy given off by a person who is awake and lying quietly in a state approaching complete relaxation.

Energy production varies greatly from person to person. A heavier person produces more energy than a lighter person. For two individuals of the same weight the taller and leaner (with more surface area) will produce more energy than the shorter and stouter. Men produce more energy than women, and in certain diseases the basal metabolism may be increased (hyperthyroidism), or depressed (hypothyroidism). Powerful emotions may temporarily raise the metabolic output, an effect which accounts for the noticeable warming of movie theaters during love scenes and suspenseful moments. Individuals engaged in manual occupations (such as carpentry) produce considerably more energy than sedentary workers (clerks, typists). Scholars and thinkers may be surprised to learn that an hour of their arduous mental exertion can be sustained by the calories contained in one-half of a salted peanut.

The Manufacturing Aspects of Metabolism. The body is constantly destroying its tissues, a process sometimes described as *catabolism*. Consequently, the manufacture of new tissue, *anabolism*, is a vital part of metabolism. The body must also constantly synthesize hormones and other chemicals which enter into various tissue reactions.

The Raw Material of Metabolism. The two major features of metabolism—energy production and tissue and chemical manufacture—are made possible by food. Energy is supplied by fats (approx. 9 cal. per gram in cream, butter, and animal fats); carbohydrates (4 cal. per gram in sugar and starch); and proteins (approx. 4 cal. per gram in meat, fish, eggs, and milk). Tissues and body chemicals are built from proteins, carbohydrates, fats, and minerals. Vitamins and minerals are used in conjunction with enzymes to initiate and speed up tissue reactions.

How Energy Is Produced from Food

The body has often been compared to a combustion engine: the engine burns gasoline for energy, and the body burns food. The parallel is roughly acceptable, but should not obscure the essential differences. Gasoline releases its energy by exploding in the combustion chamber of the engine. Obviously the body cannot tolerate internal explosions of this type, and so it releases food energy through a series of chemical steps, small packets of energy being released at specific steps. A further distinction between body and engine is that the body can burn its own tissues for energy if other fuel is not available.

The three basic energy-producing foods (fats, carbohydrates, proteins) are absorbed through the wall of the small intestine after they have been broken down into simpler substances in the process of digestion. Fats become fatty acids and glycerol; proteins become amino acids; sugars and starches become simple sugar. In these forms, food substances enter the blood stream; most enter the liver to begin the chain of energy-liberating reactions. Products of these reactions leave the liver and travel through the blood to the cells of the body where they are stored, or used immediately for energy production. Although the basic energy-yielding foods are chemically quite different, their derivatives intermingle in a complex network of reactions during the course of metabolism.

Anabolism, the Manufacturing End of Metabolism

The relationship between body intake of protein and its transformation into new proteins might be compared to the situation of a builder who constructs his houses from bricks obtained from the wreckage of old buildings. The houses, in this case, are proteins; the bricks are the amino acids from which they are built. The body consumes proteins, reduces them to amino acids in the course of digestion, transports the acids through the blood, and takes them into the cells to build new proteins. The analogy fails at one crucial point: the bricks, that is, the amino acids, are not all the same. To meet the demands for specific amino acids, the body has two mechanisms at its disposal: it can manufacture certain amino acids from raw materials available in the body, or it can convert certain amino acids into others. The conversion is effected through shifting the amino portion of the molecule (NH_2) among the acids—a process known as transamination. The nutritional needs for amino acids can be understood in reference to the body's ability to manufacture them from raw materials. Those acids that cannot be synthesized in the body must be supplied in the diet; these are called *essential* amino acids, in distinction to the nonessential amino acids which can be manufactured in the body. (See NUTRITION; PROTEINS.)

How Amino Acids Are Linked to Form Proteins. In replenishing its tissues the body must link amino acids in a precise sequence to form specific proteins. The choice of the acids, and the length and pattern of the chain, determine the difference between the proteins of hair and muscle, of heart and brain, and of man and lower animals. Long a mystery, the details of this exact duplication, unerringly performed by each cell of the body, are now becoming clear. The instructions for protein manufacture are inherited by each cell in the form of the nucleic acids. These long-chain molecules contain specific arrangements of their component parts which correspond to the order of amino acids in the protein chain. The nucleic acids are, in effect, patterns upon which proteins are built. In the nucleus of the cell are found the *deoxyribose* nucleic acids (deoxyribose refers to the type of sugar incorporated in the molecule), the master template of the cell. From this master template working templates of *ribose* nucleic acids are made (here the sugar is ribose). Evidence indicates that another type of ribonucleic acid (called "transfer RNA" or "t-RNA") carries the amino acids to the RNA templates. The amino acids are then linked in the proper sequence and the finished protein is peeled off. It has been estimated that a protein, consisting of about 150 amino acids, can be made in this way in approximately 1.5 minutes. (See NUCLEIC ACIDS.)

HOW THE BODY "BURNS" FOOD TO PRODUCE ENERGY

The body obtains its energy from the chemical energy of foods, just as an automobile runs on the energy contained in the chemical bonds of gasoline. Unlike an engine, however, the body releases this energy in small packets during a complex series of chemical reactions.

THE PRINCIPAL ENERGY-RICH FOODS ARE FATS AND CARBOHYDRATES

IN THE SMALL INTESTINE

Fats and carbohydrates are broken down into simpler substances that can be absorbed into the body.

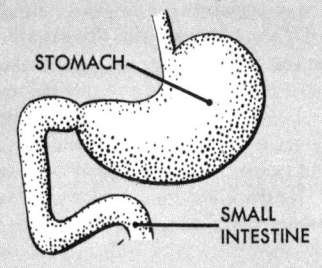

BUTTER — SALAD OIL

Fats are composed of fatty acids linked to a molecule of glycerol.

FATTY ACIDS — GLYCEROL

Fats are broken down into their constituents: fatty acids and glycerol.

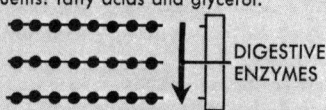

DIGESTIVE ENZYMES

POTATOES — BREAD

Carbohydrates are composed of simple sugar molecules linked in chains.

SUGAR MOLECULES

Carbohydrates are broken down into their constituent sugars.

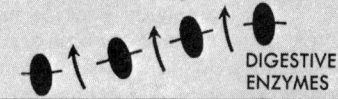

DIGESTIVE ENZYMES

IN THE LIVER

Sugar is stored as the starch glycogen, to be released as needed into the blood. Fatty acids are decomposed into simpler forms.

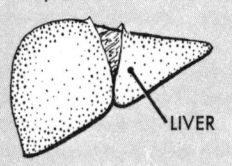

Two-carbon fragments are peeled off the fatty acid molecule. Some energy is produced in the process.

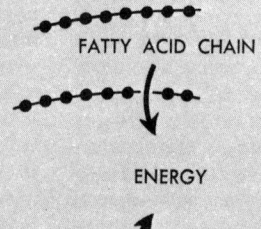

FATTY ACID CHAIN

ENERGY

Thousands of sugar molecules are joined to form glycogen and are stored in this form in the liver. Glycogen is decomposed when sugar is needed by the body.

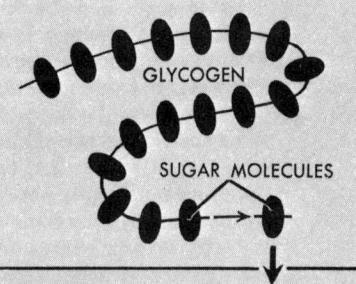

GLYCOGEN

SUGAR MOLECULES

IN THE CELLS

Sugar and products of fat breakdown travel from the liver to body cells.

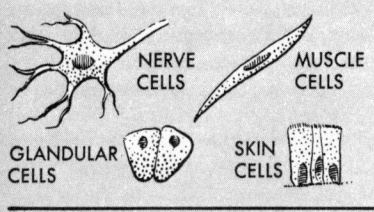

NERVE CELLS, MUSCLE CELLS, GLANDULAR CELLS, SKIN CELLS

Fat derivatives are eventually changed into Acetyl-CoA.

In the cells each sugar molecule is decomposed into two pyruvate molecules. Some energy is released during this process.

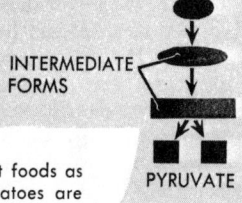

INTERMEDIATE FORMS

PYRUVATE

It is interesting to note that foods as diverse as butter and potatoes are changed into the same chemical form before being burned by the cells.

Pyruvate is changed into Acetyl-CoA.

In the "energy mill" of the Krebs cycle Acetyl-CoA, the common product of fat and carbohydrate metabolism, is processed to yield energy. The energy is released in small steps in a series of over thirty separate reactions, as contrasted to the single violent reaction that would result if the material were burned directly with oxygen. The smaller gears illustrate the chain of respiratory enzyme reactions which are driven by energy-rich electrons given off in the cycle. As these electrons pass along the chain of enzymes, they generate energy which is locked into the chemical bonds of ATP (Adenosine Triphosphate). In this form it can be used by the cell to promote energy-consuming reactions.

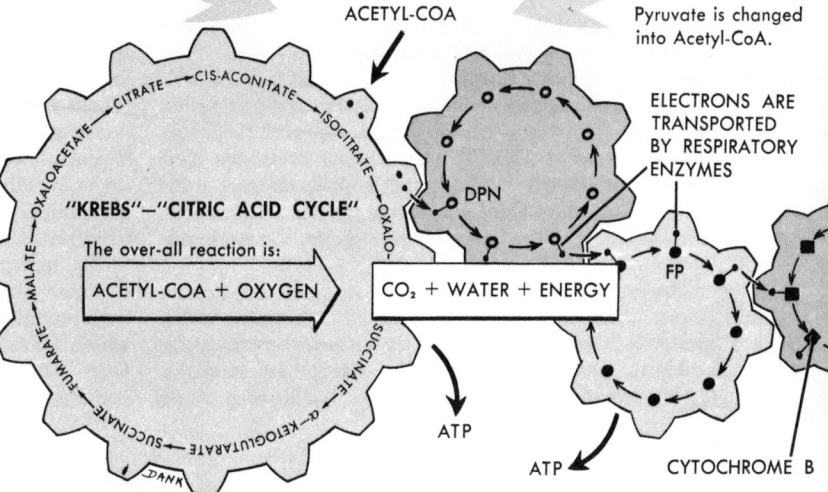

ACETYL-COA

"KREBS"—"CITRIC ACID CYCLE"

OXALOACETATE — CITRATE — CIS-ACONITATE — ISOCITRATE — OXALO- — α-KETOGLUTARATE — SUCCINATE — FUMARATE — MALATE

The over-all reaction is:

ACETYL-COA + OXYGEN → CO_2 + WATER + ENERGY

ATP

ELECTRONS ARE TRANSPORTED BY RESPIRATORY ENZYMES

DPN

FP

ATP

CYTOCHROME B

Amino Acids and the Production of Some Hormones and Essential Chemicals. In addition to serving as a source of energy and making possible tissue synthesis, amino acids are converted into a number of essential substances. The amino acid glycine makes possible the manufacture of the hemoglobin of red blood cells. The amino acid tyrosine is converted into thyroxine, the hormone of the thyroid gland, and into epinephrine (adrenalin) and norepinephrine, adrenal hormones, which play an important role in the functioning of the nervous system. Histidine is converted into histamine, the substance released from injured cells which causes the familiar blistering seen in allergic reactions.

Fat Manufacture, Transport, and Storage. A gentle pinch of the abdomen will confirm for many of us the well-known fact that the body stores fat as a reserve energy supply. The alternate form of energy storage is the starch glycogen, which is manufactured principally from glucose, and is stored in the liver and in other tissues throughout the body. Fat is stored in collections called depots, and offers some advantage over glycogen storage in that, unit for unit, fat yields more energy. It has been suggested that highly mobile animals rely on fat as a major form of storage for reasons of compactness and weight-saving.

Any person who has dieted is all too aware of the fact that carbohydrates can be, and regularly are, converted to fat. The site of this production is the liver.

When the energy supply is abundant, fat is produced. The fat manufactured in the liver is transported to the fat depots in the tissues. Although the mechanism of this transport is not yet clear, it is known that a nitrogen-containing compound, choline (and certain related compounds, such as lecithin), is essential for this transport. In the absence of these *lipotropic* substances, the liver may become fatty.

The fat stored in the tissues is not stagnant, but undergoes continual change. Fatty acids enter from the blood and leave going to the liver and tissues to be broken down and burned as energy. If carbohydrates are not available (as in starvation), or cannot be used by the cells (as in diabetes), excess amounts of fats are processed by the liver, resulting in the presence of fat derivatives, called *ketone bodies*, in the blood. Large amounts of these substances may cause a serious imbalance in the acid-base balance of the blood.

The Metabolic Diseases

A metabolic disease occurs when a vital link in the chain of reactions is severed. In many cases this is caused by an inherited absence of the enzyme necessary for the reaction. The block results in the piling up of substance "A" in the equation (A → B). The possible consequences are that "A" may act as a poison in high concentrations (as in the case of the ketone bodies), that the body may suffer from the absence of "B" since the reaction can no longer proceed to its necessary conclusion, or that both may happen.

Disorders of Carbohydrate Metabolism. The major disorder in this category is diabetes, a partial or complete inability to burn sugar as a fuel. This is associated with an inadequate supply of insulin, the pancreatic hormone that apparently promotes the passage of sugar from the blood into the tissues. In diabetes, blood sugar accumulates and eventually spills over into the urine.

Disorders of Fat Metabolism. Atherosclerosis, a form of hardening of the arteries, involves the deposition of a fatty substance (cholesterol) in the walls of arteries. The deposits steadily narrow, and often obstruct, the arterial passageway, depriving the tissues of their blood supply. Atherosclerosis of the coronary arteries is a common cause of heart disease.

Disorders of Protein Metabolism. Two disorders of protein metabolism are alkaptonuria and phenylpyruvic oligophrenia, both involving an inability to metabolize certain amino acids (tyrosine and phenylalanine in alkaptonuria, and phenylalanine in phenylpyruvic oligophrenia). In alkaptonuria, arthritis frequently develops as pigment is deposited in the joints, but the life span is evidently not affected. Phenylpyruvic oligophrenia is more serious: the victims are mentally retarded and are susceptible to infections.

See also NUCLEIC ACIDS; NUTRITION; PROTEIN; VITAMINS.

MICROBIOLOGY [mī-krō-bī-ŏl′ə-jē], the study of microorganisms, such as bacteria, viruses, yeasts, molds, protozoa, and primitive algae, and the application of the knowledge derived from this study to the fields of medicine, agriculture, and industry. Of all forms of life, microorganisms are the smallest and simplest. In many cases their bodies consist of single cells. The largest are barely visible to the naked eye, and the smallest (the viruses) can be visualized only with the electron microscope.

Microorganisms play a vital role in the economy of nature as agents that decompose organic matter and make inorganic materials, such as nitrogen compounds, available for use by plants and animals. Their activities are also of great direct importance to man. Microorganisms cause diseases of man, animals, and plants, but they also serve useful purposes in baking, brewing, industrial fermentations, and in the production of antibiotics. In addition, microbiology has contributed enormously to the development of modern biological science, in the fields of biochemistry, biophysics, and genetics.

The Development of Microbiology. The discovery of microorganisms was made during the last quarter of the 17th century by an amateur Dutch microscopist, Anton van Leeuwenhoek. With exquisitely polished homemade lenses he studied a great variety of natural materials, such as pond water, vinegar, and blood. He observed protozoa (microscopic animals) in mixtures of pepper and water, and bacteria in scrapings of human teeth. Leeuwenhoek's discovery of the microscopic "animalcules," as he called them, raised the question of their origin. Many scientists, as well as most laymen, believed that certain organisms could be generated spontaneously from nonliving materials—that frogs could arise from raindrops and maggots from the carcasses of dead horses. This theory of "spontaneous generation" was put to a rigid test during the 18th and 19th centuries, and the problem was finally resolved by Louis Pasteur who, in 1864, demonstrated that microorganisms arise from living "germs" rather than from nonliving matter (*see* GERM THEORY). From his studies Pasteur concluded that there exists a great variety of microorganisms, each capable of reproducing its own kind. According to his theory, the different fermentations and diseases are caused by different types of microorganisms.

The theory that particular germs cause particular diseases was proven by the German physician Robert Koch in 1876. He demonstrated that the disease called anthrax is caused by a specific organism, the *Bacillus anthracis*. In establishing the relation between an organism and a disease, Koch applied a series of critical conditions that have become known as "Koch's Postulates." These conditions may be summarized as follows: (1) wherever the disease is found, the germ must be found; (2) the germs must be grown in isolation from all other germs; (3) when the germ is introduced into a healthy, susceptible animal, it must produce the disease; and (4) it must be possible to grow the germ from the diseased tissues of this animal.

Variations of Koch's postulates have been used to establish the organisms responsible for the spoilage of foods, the production of industrial solvents and antibiotics, and other processes.

Microbiological Methods. Certain types of equipment and specialized techniques were essential for the development of microbiology. The microscope was from the very beginning the principal tool, and special techniques for staining, or coloring, certain structures in microorganisms were developed to aid in microscopy. During the first half of the 20th century the microscope was perfected almost to its theoretical limit, and a more powerful instrument became necessary to see the submicroscopic structures of microorganisms and to study the viruses. The electron microscope, which uses a beam of electrons instead of light, became such a tool.

Microbiological research requires the use of "pure" cultures, collections of living organisms which are the progeny of a single cell. These cultures are usually grown on special preparations containing the materials needed for the growth of microorganisms. The preparation is sterilized by placing it in an autoclave, a type of pressure cooker. All living organisms in the culture medium are destroyed in the autoclave by steam under pressure. When the preparation is taken from the autoclave, it is allowed to solidify in a flat plate (petri dish) or test tube. The microorganisms to be studied are diluted in a sterile fluid and spread across the surface of the medium. The preparation is placed in a chamber to incubate at the proper temperature. Some time later the surface can be seen to be studded with small spots, each of which represents a colony of millions of microorganisms that descended from one of the organisms originally introduced into the medium.

Microbiology of Disease. Many diseases of plants and animals are caused by microorganisms. Fungi are responsible for some of the most devastating diseases of plants. Among the better known fungal plant parasites are the rusts, the smuts, and the powdery mildews. Bacteria also cause a variety of plant diseases, such as wilts, soft rots, fire blights, leaf spots, and crown galls. The control of plant diseases is achieved by the use of sprays, the breeding of resistant varieties of plants, and, in some cases, by the destruction of disease-carrying insects or of intermediate hosts that are necessary in the life cycle of the parasite.

Human and animal diseases may result either from consuming poisonous materials produced by microorganisms outside the body or by the growth of the microorganisms as parasites within the body. In the first category is food poisoning and in the second category are a multitude of infectious diseases caused by protozoa, fungi, and bacteria. Protozoan diseases include malaria, African sleeping sickness, amoebic dysentery, and leishmaniasis (kala-azar). Fungus infections are responsible for blastomycosis, coccidioidal granuloma (known as San Joaquin Valley fever in California), and for a number of chronic skin infections such as ringworm and athlete's foot. Parasitic bacteria cause a great variety of human and animal diseases, including tuberculosis, pneumonia, scarlet fever, diphtheria, meningitis, tularemia, brucellosis, plague, cholera, typhoid fever, dysentery, gonorrhea and syphilis.

MICROCEPHALY [mī-krō-sĕf′ə-lə], a medical term describing an uncommon type of mental deficiency in which the brain is small and underdeveloped. These individuals are short in stature and present a characteristic appearance, resulting from the fact that the face is of normal size, but the skull is unusually small. The IQ falls in the severely retarded range of less than 40. Microcephaly may appear in several members of the same family.

MILK OF MAGNESIA, also known as magnesia magma, a smooth, creamy suspension of magnesium hydroxide (approximately 8%) in water. It is used chiefly to reduce stomach acidity and occasionally as a laxative. Its laxative action is based upon its ability to retain water in the intestinal tract, but it is comparatively less effective in this respect than magnesium sulfate (epsom salt).

MINOT [mī′nət], **GEORGE RICHARDS** (1885–1950), American physician who shared the Nobel Prize with William Murphy and George Whipple in 1934 for work on the treatment of pernicious anemia with liver extract. Following Whipple's demonstration that red blood cell regeneration could be stimulated in anemic dogs by feeding large quantities of raw liver, Murphy and Minot successfully applied the same technique to patients suffering from pernicious anemia. Later work has shown that the liver contains the vital blood-building factor Vitamin B_{12}.

MITOSIS [mī-tō′sĭs], duplication of cells in which the nuclear genetic material is equally divided between two daughter cells. In all animals, from the simplest to the most complex, and in all plants, except for bacteria and blue-green algae, mitosis is the usual method of cell division. In single-celled organisms, mitosis results in reproduction of the organism. In more complex plants and animals, mitosis provides the cells necessary for growth or for the replacement of parts.

The process of mitosis is essentially simple. During their formation within the nucleus, the chromosomes, which are the carriers of genetic information, duplicate themselves and migrate to opposite sides of the cell, to form part of the nucleus of the new cell. Although mitosis is a continuous process, it is usually divided into several distinct stages for the sake of clarity. These are called

MITOSIS

Mitosis, or direct cell division, is the process by which growth takes place in living organisms. It occurs at regular intervals depending on type of cell, species, age of organism, and such external factors as temperature and pressure.

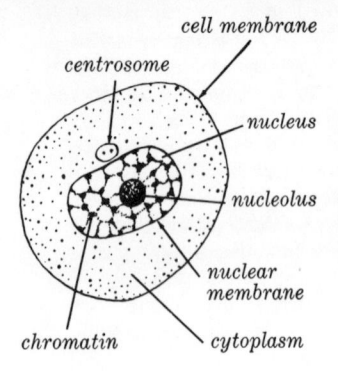

INTERPHASE. A cell not undergoing mitosis is said to be "resting," or in interphase. The cell nucleus, surrounded by its membrane, can be seen. Within it the genetic material forms a mass of chromatin. The nucleolus, which makes substances needed for synthesis of cell proteins, is also visible. The centrosome, containing two centrioles, functions in nuclear division during mitosis.

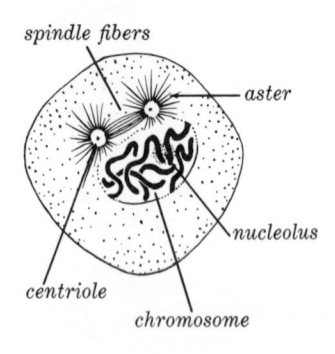

PROPHASE. During this first stage of mitosis the centrioles move toward opposite sides of the nucleus and around each appears an aster composed of short, radiating fibers. Between the asters the longer spindle fibers appear. At the same time the chromatin organizes into distinct chromosomes. Finally the nuclear membrane and nucleolus disappear.

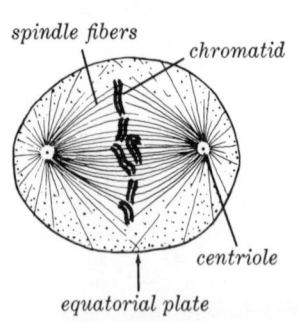

METAPHASE. During this second stage of mitosis the chromosomes separate into their two component halves, or chromatids. The chromatid pairs line up along the center of the cell on the equatorial plate. Each chromatid becomes connected to a spindle fiber which will later "pull" it toward the centriole on its respective side.

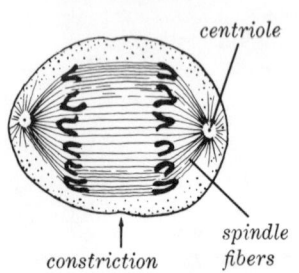

ANAPHASE. During this third stage of mitosis the chromosome halves move toward their respective poles (the centrioles), one complete set of "daughter" chromosomes moving toward each pole. Near the end of the anaphase a constriction appears at the upper and lower edges of the cell along the equatorial plate.

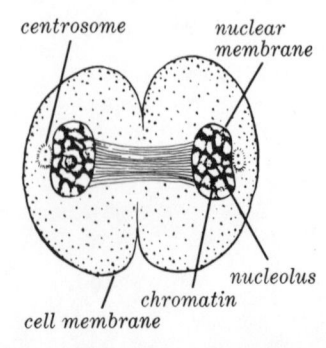

TELOPHASE. During this final stage of mitosis the two groups of chromosomes gather at their respective poles, then revert to their chromatin appearance. A nuclear membrane forms about each group and a nucleolus appears in each. As the spindle fibers disappear the centrioles divide in two. Finally a cell membrane forms along the equatorial plate and the two new cells enter the interphase.

prophase, metaphase, anaphase, and telophase. Cells not in the process of mitosis are in interphase.

Prophase. The centrosome, located near the nucleus of the cell, is composed of two centrioles. Each centriole moves to opposite sides of the nucleus. Filaments known as spindle fibers connect the two, while short fibers radiating from each centriole form asters. At the same time, the initially diffuse nuclear material begins to condense, forming distinct chromosomes. Each chromosome has already duplicated and consists of two chromatids lying parallel to each other and connected at one point, the centromere. Near the end of prophase, as the nuclear membrane disappears, the chromosomes become associated with the spindle fibers.

Metaphase. During metaphase, the chromosomes line up in an equatorial plate through the center of the cell, midway between the two asters. Each chromosome is connected to the spindle fibers.

Anaphase. The two halves of each chromosome separate from one another. Half of each chromosome then moves to the centriole closest to it.

Telophase. As the groups of chromosomes complete their movement, they become less distinct. A nuclear membrane forms around the two new groups of chromosomes, the spindle disappears, and each centriole divides into two, to become a new centrosome. As a cell membrane develops between the two newly formed nuclei, there results two daughter cells, and mitosis is complete.

The nucleus of each daughter cell reverts to the interphase formation, preparatory to the next cell division. See also CELL; MEIOSIS.

MONGOLISM. See MENTAL DEFICIENCY.

MORGAGNI [mōr-gä′nyē], **GIOVANNI BATTISTA** (1682–1771), Italian physician considered the founder of pathological anatomy. Professor of anatomy at Padua, Morgagni is best remembered for his classic *De sedibus et causis morborum per anatomen indagatis* (On the Seat and Causes of Diseases Investigated by Anatomy), 1761, in which he made numerous original and penetrating studies of diseased tissue in cases of heart ailments, tuberculosis, syphilis, pneumonia, cirrhosis of the liver, and other diseases.

MORNING SICKNESS, a medical term designating the nausea and vomiting seen in early pregnancy. Morning sickness usually appears a few weeks after conception and disappears spontaneously at the end of the third month of pregnancy. The cause is not known. The severity of morning sickness varies greatly. Mild cases are so frequent that it is sometimes regarded as a diagnostic clue of early pregnancy. In a small percentage of cases it is extremely severe (hyperemesis gravidarum): the patient vomits all food consumed and suffers from anxiety, restlessness, emaciation, and dehydration. Treatment in the mild cases consists of sedation and drugs which inhibit vomiting. Hospitalization is necessary in severe cases. See also PREGNANCY.

MORPHINE [môr′fēn], the principal active ingredient of opium, the dried juice of the oriental white poppy plant.

Morphine acts principally on the central nervous system—it relieves pain and induces sleep. It also slows breathing, and may cause constipation, nausea, or vomiting. In recognition of its unrivaled ability to control pain, morphine has been called "God's own medicine." Morphine tends to produce addiction, and for this reason it is used only in cases where other pain-relieving agents fail. Codeine, apomorphine, heroin, and several other narcotics are chemical modifications of morphine.

See also CODEINE; DRUG ADDICTION; HEROIN; NARCOTICS; OPIUM.

MORTON, WILLIAM THOMAS GREEN (1819–68), American dentist who pioneered in the development of ether anesthesia. Morton, searching for a pain-killer to use in his practice, first used nitrous oxide ("laughing gas"), and then abandoned it to experiment with ether. He obtained permission to use ether on a surgical patient at the Massachusetts General Hospital on Oct. 16, 1846. The results of this successful demonstration were published by the surgeon H. J. Bigelow, and the use of ether anesthesia spread rapidly throughout the world. Later a controversy developed about Morton and Dr. Crawford W. Long of Georgia as to who first used ether for anesthesia. Long had used ether in his practice from 1842, but did not publish his results until 1849.

See also ANESTHESIA.

MOSQUITO [məs-kē′tō], common name for over 1,500 species of small, delicate insects that constitute the family Culicidae, in the order Diptera, the true flies. The family is of considerable importance because the blood-sucking females of certain species transmit disease. Mosquitoes occur throughout most of the world, and are common in moist habitats—swamps, marshes, and pond margins, for example. They are characterized by their small size (most are less than ½ in. long); slender, usually humped bodies; a single pair of narrow, transparent forewings, the edges of which are fringed with scales; and highly specialized mouth parts. In adult male mosquitoes the mouth parts form a relatively short beak used to suck plant juices. In adult females the proboscis is a long, slender beak with which the female pierces, or "bites," the skin of warm-blooded animals (chiefly birds and mammals), and then sucks in the blood, at the same time injecting saliva into the wound. It is through this last-mentioned process that female mosquitoes transmit disease; any parasite in the female's saliva passes into the "bitten" host.

Mosquitoes breed during the warm months of the year. The eggs are laid—singly or in tight groups called rafts—on the surface of quiet ponds, on stagnant water, or in barrels, cans, and similar water-filled containers. The larval mosquitoes, known as "wrigglers," feed on algae and organic debris. In many species the larvae breathe by means of a snorkel-like siphon at the posterior end of the body. The larvae transform into rather active pupae, known as "tumblers," which also breathe at the water's surface. The pupal stage lasts for but a short time; soon the adults emerge.

Among the important genera of mosquitoes are *Anopheles*, some species of which transmit the protozoan organism (*Plasmodium*) that causes malaria; *Aedes*, species of which transmit the virus that causes human yellow fever; and *Culex*, one species of which is the annoying common house mosquito and another of which is the carrier of the parasitic nematode (roundworm) that causes filariasis (elephantiasis and related diseases). Disease-carrying mosquitoes are more common in moist semitropical and tropical regions and it is especially in such areas that extensive experimentation has been done to find methods of mosquito control. Among control methods now in use are the elimination of natural breeding areas by drainage; treatment of water surfaces with oils and insecticides; and the use of repellents applied to the body.

See also ELEPHANTIASIS OR ELEPHANT DISEASE; FILARIASIS; MALARIA; YELLOW FEVER.

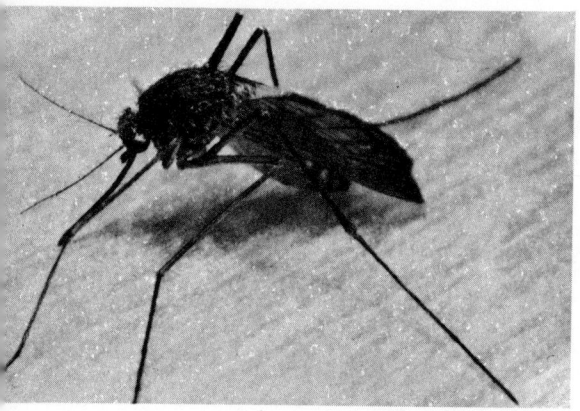

Dr. Alexander B. Klots
The common house mosquito, *Culex*. The female (*shown*) has a long, beaklike proboscis with which she pierces the skin of mammals.

MOTION SICKNESS, also known as air sickness, sea sickness, and car sickness, is caused by repeated side-to-side or up-and-down motions. The principal symptoms are headache, dizziness, sweating, nausea, vomiting, pallor, cold sweats, and depression. At times there may be a fall in the blood pressure, accompanied by a slow or fast pulse rate. The exact mechanism which produces motion sickness is not well understood, although it is apparently a disorder of balance caused by an upset in the normal cues by which the body maintains the upright position. These cues come principally from two sources: (1) from the semicircular canals of the ear and (2) from perpendicular and horizontal lines in the surroundings as perceived by the eye. In motion sickness the constant movement affects the fluid within the ear canals and causes normally perpendicular lines to appear at an odd angle.

That visual cues are important in motion sickness is indicated by the fact that fixing the eye on a single point helps considerably. Reducing head movements by placing the head firmly against the back of the seat is also of value in alleviating motion sickness. Psychological factors are also thought to be important. The condition is rarely dangerous, except in cases where it is prolonged and accompanied by excessive vomiting. Intravenous feeding is sometimes necessary. Many individuals may gradually adjust to the motion after an initial period of discomfort. Children seem less prone to develop motion sickness than adults.

MULLER

A number of drugs are available which help to prevent and relieve the symptoms of motion sickness. These include dramamine, bonamine, and marezine.

MULLER [mŭl'ər], **HERMANN JOSEPH** (1890–1967), American geneticist who won the 1946 Nobel Prize in physiology and medicine for demonstrating that mutations can be produced by X-radiation.

MÜLLER [mül'ər], **JOHANNES PETER** (1801–58), German physiologist and anatomist, noted as a teacher and as an investigator. He studied at Bonn and Berlin, and became professor first at Bonn, later at Berlin. Müller's most important work was concerned with the physiology of the senses and the nervous system. He was responsible for the law of specific nerve energies which states that when a sensory nerve is stimulated, the sensation depends not on the kind of stimulus but on the sense organ: a blow on the optic nerve, for example, causes a sensation of light.

MULTIPLE PERSONALITY, a condition in which an individual leads distinct and separate existences. Each personality may have a different name, different memories, and radically different attitudes toward life. Frequently the familiar everyday, or primary, personality is aware of the secondary personality, but the reverse does not hold true. A classic example of multiple personality is that described in Robert Louis Stevenson's *Dr. Jekyll and Mr. Hyde*. The multiple personality is thought to be an extreme expression of the tendency to repress and detach unacceptable aspects of oneself from conscious awareness.
See also HYSTERIA.

MULTIPLE SCLEROSIS [sklĭ-rō'sĭs], a disease of the human nervous system which affects persons between the ages of 10 and 50. Multiple sclerosis attacks the white matter of the brain and spinal cord. The fatty coverings, or myelin sheaths, of the nerve fibers are destroyed in scattered patches and replaced by scars or hard plaques. The myelin apparently insulates the nerve fibers, and its loss interferes with nerve conduction. There are several other diseases which affect the white matter of the brain in a comparable manner. Although the symptoms seen in these disorders are different, it is suspected that the underlying cause may be the same as in multiple sclerosis.

The symptoms, which include partial paralysis, double vision, or poor balance, may appear without apparent cause, remain for a few days or weeks, and then gradually abate and disappear. Typically, similar or other symptoms return after an indefinite period, often in greater severity. After 5 to 10 years of intermittent symptoms, partial paralysis, poor co-ordination, or other disturbances may persist indefinitely. Following this there may be slow, steady worsening of the condition and eventually permanent invalidism.

The absence of any sure means of diagnosis in the early phases of multiple sclerosis makes it impossible to predict the outcome of individual cases. There is evidence that some individuals have one or more attacks and then lead a normal life free of other symptoms. On the other hand, a few cases, possibly less than 1%, are very severe and may be fatal within weeks or months. Many methods of treatment have been tried; some relieve certain symptoms, but none has been found which arrests the disease.

The cause of multiple sclerosis is not known. Various theories have proposed bacteria, viruses, or specific poisons, such as lead or cyanide, as the cause. The theory which seems to most adequately explain the disease is that of hypersensitivity. According to this concept, for some as yet unknown reason the victim develops a sensitivity to certain proteins found in the myelin sheaths of his nerve fibers. These proteins stimulate the body to produce substances, called antibodies, which cause a destructive reaction when they come into contact with the myelin of the brain and spinal cord.

Other evidence indicates that geographical area and heredity are in some way involved in multiple sclerosis. The disease is significantly more frequent in northern latitudes, such as Canada, Scotland, and Scandinavia, than in the southern parts of the United States, France, and Italy. It is also found more often in family groups than one would expect on the basis of chance. The significance of these findings is as yet unknown.
See also NERVOUS SYSTEM.

MUMPS, also known as epidemic parotitis, is a virus disease which occurs chiefly in children. It is one of the oldest recognized diseases of man, having been accurately described in the 5th century B.C. by the Greek physician Hippocrates. Infections occur more frequently during the winter and early spring months, tending to reach epidemic proportions every seven to eight years. The virus is probably spread through direct contact and through airborne droplets of infected saliva. It has also been demonstrated that mumps virus appears in human urine.

The virus usually attacks the salivary glands, in particular the parotid glands adjacent to the ear, producing swelling, pain, and fever within 8 to 21 days after exposure. The nervous system and testicles are often involved, and, less commonly, the ovaries, pancreas, thyroid, and breasts. Deafness may occur. In many cases infection apparently occurs without causing any observable symptoms. The swellings subside in 7 to 10 days.

There is no specific medication against the mumps virus. Blood extracts (gamma globulin) prepared from the blood of persons convalescing from mumps may be of value in preventing involvement of the testicles (orchitis). This is based on the presence of antivirus substances (antibodies) in the blood of those who have been exposed. Hormones, such as cortisone, have also been used to prevent and treat orchitis, but their value is uncertain.

Long-lasting immunity usually follows exposure to mumps. Recently, a one-shot mumps vaccine has become available. It appears to offer the same immunity to mumps virus infection as an actual attack of the illness.
See also ORCHITIS.

MURPHY, JOHN BENJAMIN (1857–1916), American surgeon known for his many contributions to orthopedic and abdominal surgery. Considered the greatest teacher of surgery of his time, Murphy invented a device for speeding surgery of the intestine (Murphy's button) and developed an operation on the hip, called Murphy's operation.

MURPHY, WILLIAM PARRY (1892–   ), American physician who shared the Nobel Prize with G. R. Minot and G. H. Whipple in 1934 for the successful use of liver extract in the treatment of pernicious anemia. Murphy received his medical degree at Harvard, and later served at Peter Bent Brigham Hospital in Boston. From 1948 he taught at Harvard Medical School. He is author of *Anemia in Practice—Pernicious Anemia* (1939).

MUSCLE, specialized tissue which converts chemical energy into mechanical work. Muscles are instruments of action; the brain and nervous system command and muscles obey, moving arms and legs, forming the sounds of speech, and controlling the flow of blood. The muscles of the arms, legs, and trunk, which lend shape to the body, are skeletal muscles under the conscious control of the brain. The heart is composed of a specialized type of muscle which is under the unconscious control of the nervous system. A third type of muscle (smooth muscle) opens and closes blood vessels in response to body needs, as when an awareness of danger puts the body on an emergency footing—the nervous system automatically and unconsciously directs blood from the skin to the muscles by constricting the blood vessels of the skin and dilating those of the muscles. Smooth muscle is also found in the digestive tract where it propels food and waste products along the intestinal pathway. Of these three distinct types of muscle, *skeletal* (or voluntary), *cardiac*, and *smooth*, much more is known about the first and, consequently, the following discussion will apply to skeletal muscle only.

The Nervous System and the Voluntary Muscles

In certain physiology texts one finds a curious picture of an oddly shaped figure lying in the cerebrum, the highest part of the brain. The little man has an oversized head, large eyes and lips, massive hands with an enormous thumb, a puny trunk, and large feet. He does not represent a physiologist's fancy gone astray, but rather an attempt to depict the amount of brain tissue devoted to the control of muscles in particular parts of the body. The large lips indicate that a comparatively large number of brain cells direct the movements of the lip muscles. A correspondence is thus evident between the size of the body parts of the little man (called a homunculus) and the fineness of control over certain muscles. The skilled movements of the hands are reflected in the oversized hands of the homunculus.

The brain directs muscle movement by means of nerve pathways descending down the spinal cord. Nerve fibers from the cord end in specialized structures which come close to, but do not quite touch, the individual fibers of the muscle. This meeting place of the nerve-muscle system is the *myoneural* junction (literally, "nerve-muscle" junction). Nerve impulses stimulate the muscle fibers to contract by secreting a chemical (acetylcholine) into this junction. The observed muscle contraction represents the simultaneous contraction of thousands of individual muscle fibers.

The flowing, practiced movements of everyday life do not lead one to suspect the true nature of muscle contraction, which actually consists of a series of small spasms. The individual muscle fibers cannot adjust the strength of their contraction to the task at hand; each fiber must contract fully, or not at all. The successive overlapping contractions of many fibers produce the controlled steady movements involved in raising a cup to the lips, walking, or writing. In the large muscles of the trunk which maintain posture, groups of muscle fibers are constantly discharging to maintain an even tension. This type of contraction does not involve shortening of the muscle and is known as *isometric* contraction in distinction to the *isotonic* contractions mentioned above in which the muscle is able to shorten and produce movement. The two types of contraction differ in terms of the net outcome: isotonic contraction produces work; isometric contraction produces heat. This becomes evident in considering what happens when a man attempts to lift a weight. If he successfully raises the object from the floor he performs work (according to the physicist's definition: work = load × distance). If the weight is too heavy he tugs valiantly and, although he may grunt and sweat from the effort, the physicist tells us that his work output is zero (since he does not move the weight, distance = 0, work = 0). His muscles contract, but do not shorten, so that the energy is expended as heat. A certain amount of heat is also generated in isotonic contractions, a consequence of the fact that muscle is not a completely efficient machine. Although this heat represents wasted energy, it is significant in keeping the body temperature within proper limits. Indeed, shivering is an involuntary increase in muscular activity as a response to lowered body temperature.

Exercise and Muscle Strength and Endurance

What happens when a puny youth becomes transformed into a muscular Adonis? Can the increased size of the muscle be attributed to an increase in the number of muscle fibers? This is not the case: muscle fibers cannot be manufactured—the growth of the muscle results from an increase in the size of individual muscle cells.

The type of exercise is important. It can readily be seen that different forms of athletics produce different physiques, not only because of the particular muscle groups exercised, but also because of the nature of the exercise. Repeated movements of below maximum strength increase the blood supply, and therefore the endurance, of the muscle, but not the size. Muscle size can be increased by *maximum* contractions—even one maximum contraction a day will produce significant muscle growth. The practical consequences: to look good at the beach, lift the heavy weight a few times; to be tireless in performance, lift the lighter weight many times.

Fatigue, Stiffness, and Soreness

A working muscle consumes energy and generates waste materials. The blood sustains this activity by bringing energy-rich substances to the muscle and by carrying away the acid products of muscle metabolism (lactic acid and carbon dioxide). Muscle fatigue occurs when the blood supply fails to keep pace with muscle activity, resulting in a deficit of energy-producing materials and an accumulation of waste products. In extreme fatigue the muscle knots and fails to regain its original length, a state known as *contracture*.

A SKELETAL MUSCLE—THE BRACHIALIS OF THE ARM

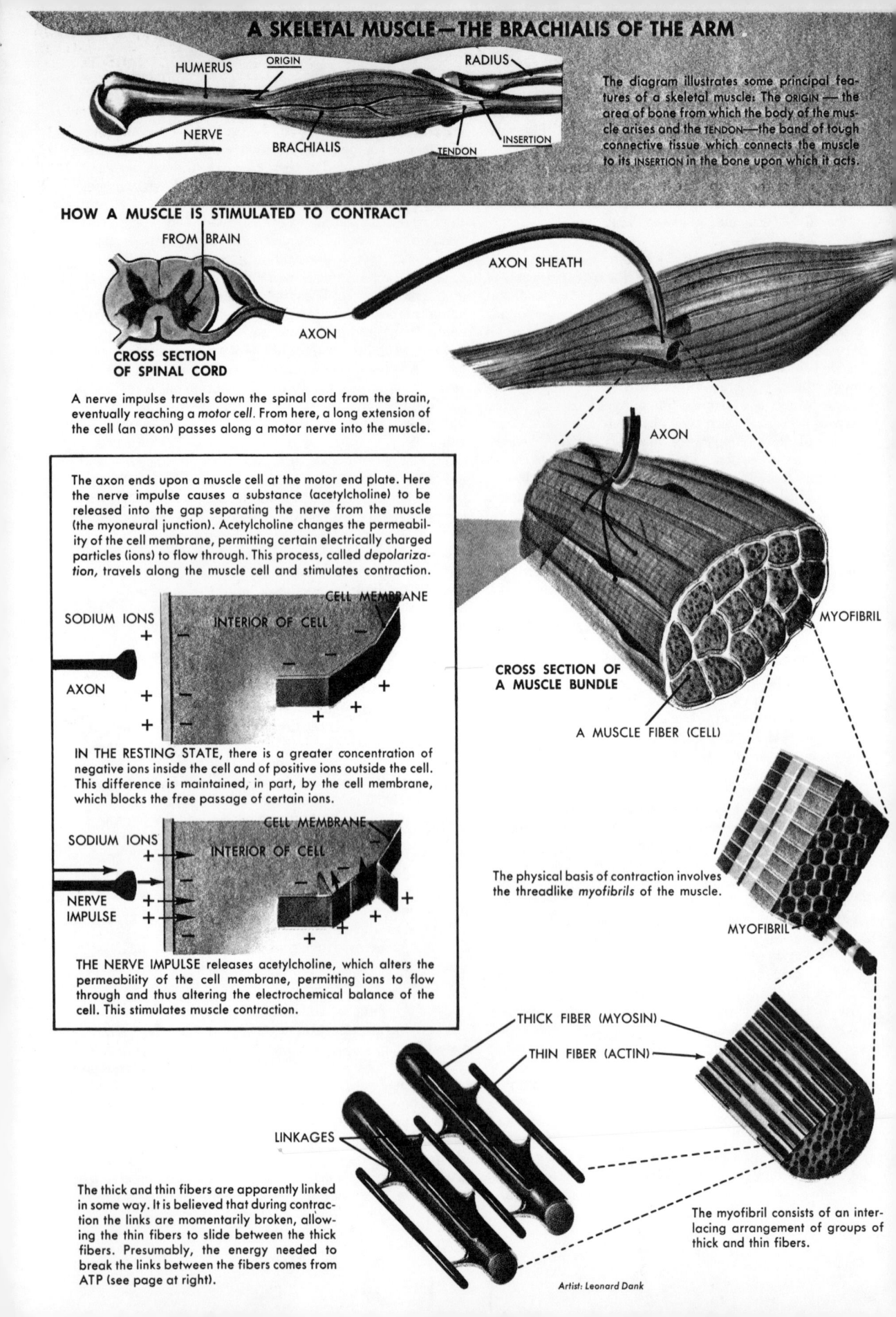

The diagram illustrates some principal features of a skeletal muscle: The ORIGIN — the area of bone from which the body of the muscle arises and the TENDON — the band of tough connective tissue which connects the muscle to its INSERTION in the bone upon which it acts.

HOW A MUSCLE IS STIMULATED TO CONTRACT

A nerve impulse travels down the spinal cord from the brain, eventually reaching a *motor cell*. From here, a long extension of the cell (an axon) passes along a motor nerve into the muscle.

The axon ends upon a muscle cell at the motor end plate. Here the nerve impulse causes a substance (acetylcholine) to be released into the gap separating the nerve from the muscle (the myoneural junction). Acetylcholine changes the permeability of the cell membrane, permitting certain electrically charged particles (ions) to flow through. This process, called *depolarization*, travels along the muscle cell and stimulates contraction.

IN THE RESTING STATE, there is a greater concentration of negative ions inside the cell and of positive ions outside the cell. This difference is maintained, in part, by the cell membrane, which blocks the free passage of certain ions.

THE NERVE IMPULSE releases acetylcholine, which alters the permeability of the cell membrane, permitting ions to flow through and thus altering the electrochemical balance of the cell. This stimulates muscle contraction.

The physical basis of contraction involves the threadlike *myofibrils* of the muscle.

The thick and thin fibers are apparently linked in some way. It is believed that during contraction the links are momentarily broken, allowing the thin fibers to slide between the thick fibers. Presumably, the energy needed to break the links between the fibers comes from ATP (see page at right).

The myofibril consists of an interlacing arrangement of groups of thick and thin fibers.

Artist: Leonard Dank

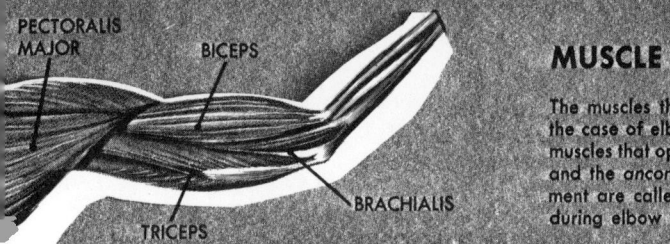

MUSCLE ACTION

The muscles that produce a given movement are called the *prime movers*. In the case of elbow flexion the prime movers are the *biceps* and *brachialis*. The muscles that oppose the movement are called the *antagonists*—here the *triceps* and the *anconaeus*. The muscles which stabilize the joint adjacent to the movement are called *fixation muscles*. The *pectoralis major* performs this function during elbow flexion, holding the upper arm fast against the shoulder.

PECTORALIS MAJOR
BICEPS
BRACHIALIS
TRICEPS

HOW MUSCLE OBTAINS ENERGY FOR CONTRACTION

Most of the energy for muscular contraction comes from the carbohydrates contained in bread, sugar, potatoes, and other sweet and starchy foods. In the small intestine carbohydrates are broken down into simple sugars which are absorbed into the blood.

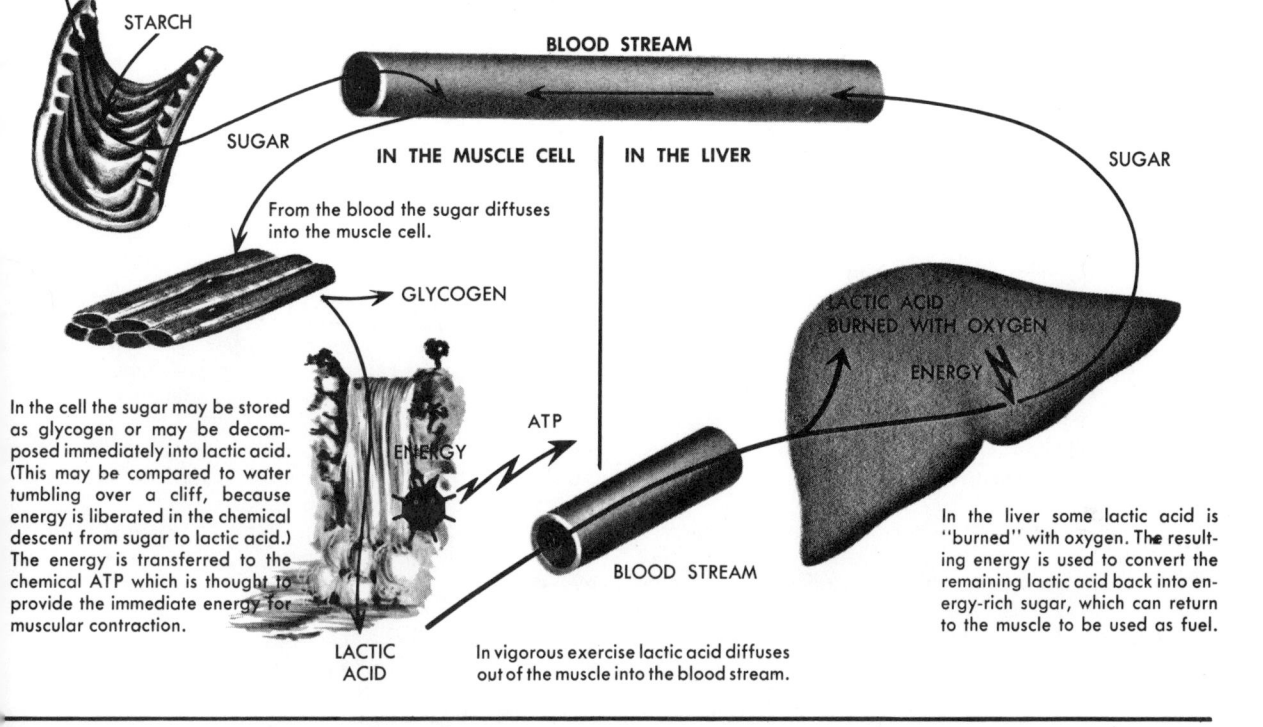

SMALL INTESTINE
STARCH
SUGAR

BLOOD STREAM

IN THE MUSCLE CELL

From the blood the sugar diffuses into the muscle cell.

GLYCOGEN

In the cell the sugar may be stored as glycogen or may be decomposed immediately into lactic acid. (This may be compared to water tumbling over a cliff, because energy is liberated in the chemical descent from sugar to lactic acid.) The energy is transferred to the chemical ATP which is thought to provide the immediate energy for muscular contraction.

ENERGY
ATP
LACTIC ACID

IN THE LIVER

SUGAR
LACTIC ACID BURNED WITH OXYGEN
ENERGY
BLOOD STREAM

In vigorous exercise lactic acid diffuses out of the muscle into the blood stream.

In the liver some lactic acid is "burned" with oxygen. The resulting energy is used to convert the remaining lactic acid back into energy-rich sugar, which can return to the muscle to be used as fuel.

ENERGY PRODUCTION WITH AND WITHOUT OXYGEN

In the two phases of energy production described above it can be seen that the reactions in the muscle cell do not require oxygen, whereas those in the liver do. This is illustrated in the activities of an underwater swimmer and a runner.

WITHOUT OXYGEN

While the swimmer is underwater his muscles generate quick energy by breaking down energy-rich glycogen into lactic acid. The same process provides muscle energy during a race.

GLYCOGEN
ENERGY
LACTIC ACID

WITH OXYGEN

When the swimmer surfaces, some lactic acid is burned with oxygen in the liver to convert the remaining lactic acid into energy-rich sugar that can be transported to the muscles to be used as fuel.

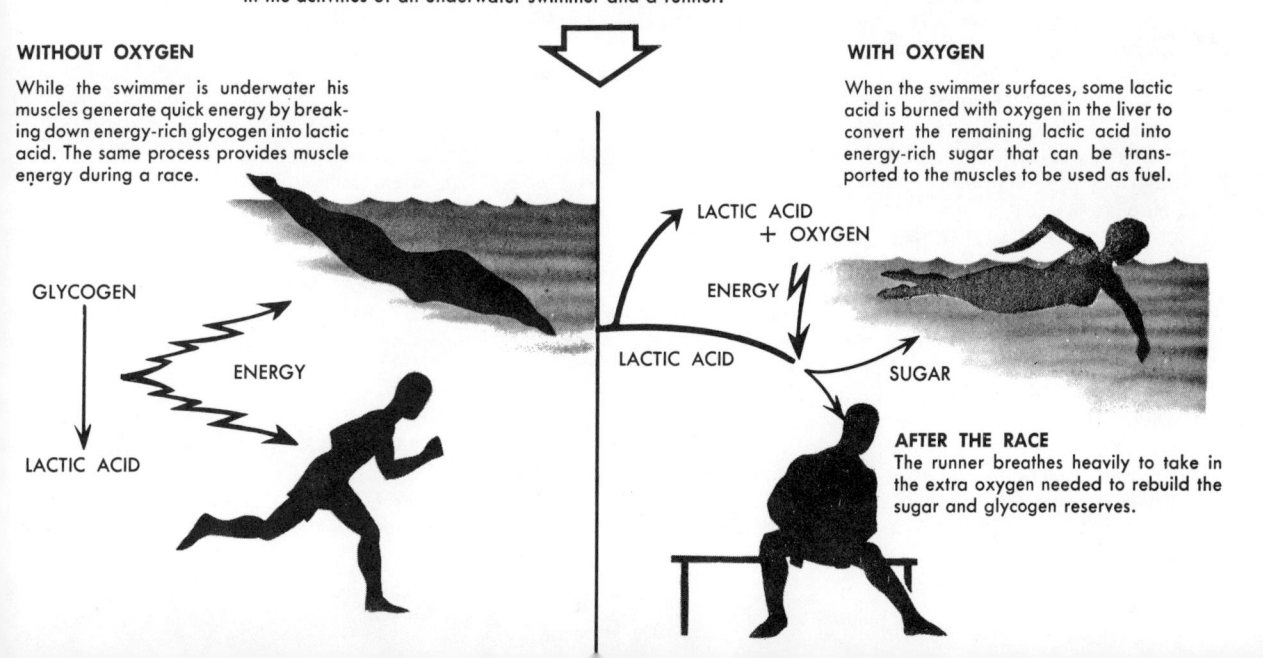

LACTIC ACID + OXYGEN
ENERGY
LACTIC ACID
SUGAR

AFTER THE RACE

The runner breathes heavily to take in the extra oxygen needed to rebuild the sugar and glycogen reserves.

Fatiguing exercise often leads to muscular stiffness and soreness. Pain is probably caused by the accumulation of acid waste products which irritate nerve endings. Although pain disappears rapidly when exercise is halted, soreness and stiffness usually persist. Stiffness is caused by collections of excess fluids in the muscle. Soreness seems to be associated with the direct effect of acid waste products on muscle cells and is relieved by light work and improved circulation.

The Nature of Muscular Contraction

An understanding of muscle contraction requires answers to three questions: (1) How is the muscle stimulated to contract? (2) Where is the energy for contraction obtained? (3) How is chemical energy converted into mechanical work?

Stimulating the Contraction. The membrane which encloses the muscle holds back certain electrically charged particles (ions) in the same way as a dam holds back water. The nerve ending secretes a chemical (acetylcholine) which causes the dam to burst by changing the membrane in such a way that ions flow through it. The process begins at the portion of the membrane near the nerve ending and spreads like a lit fuse along the surface of the muscle fiber.

The flow of ions in some, as yet unknown, way stimulates the muscular contraction, possibly associated with the entrance of calcium ions into the cell, or their liberation from a bound form within the cell. These ions may induce the liberation of energy from adenosine triphosphate (ATP), an energy-rich compound found within the muscle cell.

The Energy for Contraction. The principal source of muscle energy is glucose, obtained from sugars, starches, and other carbohydrate foods. Glucose enters the muscle from the blood and is stored in the muscle cell as the starch glycogen.

The Two Phases of Energy Production. Muscle can function without oxygen, for a while at least. This is made possible by breaking down glycogen into lactic acid, a fast energy-yielding process which does not require oxygen and produces a small amount of energy, stored as ATP. In the second phase of energy production, oxygen is used to convert lactic acid to carbon dioxide and water, and a larger quantity of ATP. The energy, stored as ATP (and phosphocreatine), is ready to be triggered by nerve stimulation to produce physical contraction.

How Chemical Energy Is Converted into Mechanical Work. The body has frequently been compared to a machine, and, continuing the metaphor, food has been described as a fuel. This raises the unanswered question "How do spaghetti, candy, and potatoes make possible running, jumping, and moving?" What exactly is involved in the crucial step, the conversion of chemical energy into the mechanical contraction of muscle?

The answer to this question is thought to lie in two protein fibers found in muscle tissue, actin and myosin.

According to one theory, the myosin molecules have bridges which link with the actin molecules. The bridges are believed capable of attaching to specific sites on the actin fibers. The bridges then pull the actin fiber a short distance, release it, and attach to a new site, ready for the next cycle. Each cycle of attaching to an active site, moving it a short distance, and then releasing the link, may require the decomposition of one molecule of ATP to ADP, yielding energy. In support of this view there is some evidence that myosin cannot link with actin in the presence of intact ATP. It is also speculated that in the absence of ATP the actin-myosin link would be fixed. This might explain the stiffness seen in *rigor mortis* following the consumption of the muscles' ATP supply.

This sliding-filament model of muscular contraction differs radically from earlier concepts which envisaged the physical basis of contraction as lying in the folding up of long protein molecules.

See also NERVOUS SYSTEM; REFLEX.

MUSCULAR DYSTROPHY [dĭs′trə-fē], an inherited disease involving progressive degeneration of the skeletal muscles. When first described, muscular dystrophy was confused with certain neurological disorders in which disease of the nerves resulted in muscle degeneration. It is now recognized that in these cases the nervous system is essentially intact and that the primary disturbance is an unexplained wasting-away of the muscles.

A false clue to the nature of the disease was obtained in 1928 when investigators discovered that muscle degeneration could be produced in rats by depriving them of vitamin E. It was immediately assumed that human muscular dystrophy might be caused by vitamin E deficiency and that it could therefore be cured by the administration of this vitamin. Further work has shown, however, that human muscular dystrophy is not caused by vitamin E deficiency, and that its course can in no way be altered by the administration of this vitamin.

Research into the cause of muscular dystrophy has tended to focus on the biochemical changes associated with the muscle degeneration. Significant increases in the concentrations of certain substances in the blood (transaminase and aldolase) and urine (creatine) have been observed. Although these findings probably only reflect an increased breakdown of muscle tissue, many investigators feel that the disorder is ultimately biochemical in nature, possibly involving the nucleic acids—the chemical transmitters of heredity.

Types of Muscular Dystrophy. Several types of muscular dystrophy are distinguished on the basis of the age of onset, the muscle groups affected, and the course of the illness. It is also possible that these clinical types correspond to differences in the basic biochemical defect underlying the disorder.

Childhood Dystrophy (Pseudohypertrophic-Duchenne—severe generalized) appears between the ages of 2 and 10 and is seen almost exclusively in males. The muscles of the buttocks are affected early, followed by involvement of the muscles of the abdomen, legs, and spine. A curious aspect of the disease is an increase in muscular size which lends a deceptive appearance of great power to severely weakened muscles. The outlook in cases of childhood dystrophy is poor: most patients do not survive beyond the age of 20.

Limb-Girdle Dystrophy appears between the ages of 10 and 40 and first affects the muscles of the pelvis, shoulder, and upper arm and leg. This form is less severe than childhood dystrophy.

Facioscapulohumeral Dystrophy (Landouzy-Déjerine—mild restrictive) is seen in the 10 to 18 age group. The muscles of the face, chest, shoulder, and back are affected early, followed by involvement of the spinal, abdominal, and leg muscles. The disease progresses slowly and some patients with this disability may have an almost normal life expectancy.

Myotonic Dystrophy (Dystrophia myotonica, distal dystrophy) may appear at any time after adolescence. The small hand muscles, the muscles of the forearms, and the muscles in the front of the legs are affected first. The muscles involved in chewing and swallowing are affected later. Associated defects include wasting-away of the gonads and reduced sexual drives. The outlook is poor in these cases.

The extent of disability in muscular dystrophy can be evaluated in terms of an eight-point scale progressing from mild to severe involvement.

(1) The patient can walk, but has a mild waddling gait and lordosis (forward curvature of the lower spine, giving a "pot-bellied" appearance). He can climb stairs without assistance.

(2) The patient can walk, but requires help in climbing stairs.

(3) The patient walks with severe waddling gait and lordosis, but cannot climb stairs. He can arise from a standard height chair.

(4) The patient walks, but cannot rise from a standard height chair.

(5) The patient cannot walk, but can perform all the activities of daily living from a wheelchair.

(6) The patient can roll the wheelchair, but needs help for some wheelchair activities.

(7) The patient requires back support to sit erect and can roll the chair only a short distance.

(8) Bed patient—requires help in all activities.

Treatment. Muscular dystrophy cannot be cured and the progression of the disease cannot be halted. The objective of treatment is to keep the patient at a maximum level of physical efficiency (through the use of braces and physical therapy) and to assist him and his family in making an optimum adjustment to the facts of his illness.

MUSTARD PLASTER, an irritant preparation consisting of powdered black mustard mixed with adhesive and spread on a sheet of paper, cotton cloth, or other material. The plaster is soaked in tepid water to free the volatile irritant oil from the mustard and is then applied to the skin. The irritation stimulates the flow of blood to the skin and deeper structures. The increased circulation helps relieve pain and congestion associated with chest and back inflammations and muscle soreness.

MUTATION [mū-tā'shən], change in a particular characteristic that suddenly appears in the offspring of plants and animals. These changes are caused by alteration of the gene, or carrier of genetic information, for the character involved. The new characteristic is therefore inheritable and can be passed on from generation to generation. Most mutations are harmful to the organisms involved, and the plant or animal usually dies before it has a chance to reproduce and pass its new characteristic on to the next generation. Rarely, however, the mutation is beneficial, and becomes a permanent characteristic of the organism.

Domestic animals and plants are often bred to take advantage of mutations favorable to man. Short-legged Ancon sheep and long-legged greyhounds both represent situations where man has put natural mutations to his own use. Mutations may also be artificially induced by certain chemicals and forms of radiation. X-rays beamed at various plants and animals may increase the mutation rate, in proportion to the dosage, by as much as 200 times. Mustard gas, a material used in chemical warfare, can also cause mutations.

In man, there are many examples of mutations that are detrimental. These include albinism, or total lack of pigmentation, and hemophilia, or "bleeding" disease.

MYASTHENIA GRAVIS [mī-əs-thē'nē-ə grăv'ĭs], a rare disease marked by muscle weakness and fatigue, particularly in the muscles of the eyes, face, neck, and chest. The cause is unknown, but evidence suggests that there is interference with the normal action of acetylcholine, a substance which is liberated from nerve endings to stimulate muscle contraction. Although abnormalities of the thymus gland in the upper part of the chest are frequently associated with myasthenia gravis, no direct connection has yet been made between the two. Drooping of the eyelids and double vision are common early symptoms. Other muscle groups may become involved, causing blankness of the facial expression, constantly open mouth, choking spells, and difficulty in speaking, eating, and breathing. The symptoms are usually slight, or completely absent in the morning, tending to increase in severity during the course of the day. The condition may improve or become worse during pregnancy. A number of drugs are available which augment the action of acetylcholine and relieve the muscle weakness. These compounds do not cure the disease and must be given regularly. Removal of the thymus has been attempted in treatment and is claimed to be of value in female patients under the age of 50.

See also ACETYLCHOLINE.

MYOPIA. *See* NEARSIGHTEDNESS.

MYXEDEMA [mĭk-sə-dē'mə], (Gr. "mucus" and "swelling"), an illness caused by severe deficiency of the thyroid hormone thyroxine. It affects women between 30 and 60 years most often. Thyroxine is the body's "efficiency expert," and its lack results in a slowing of virtually all bodily functions. Sluggishness, apathy, and irritability are frequent. The voice becomes hoarse and mentality is dulled as memory diminishes. Facial expression becomes dull, with puffy eyelids, thinned eyebrows, and dull, coarse hair. The heart rate slows, blood pressure falls, the bowels become sluggish and constipation is a frequent complaint. The body swells with edema, which may be mistaken for obesity or kidney disease. Because the metabolic rate drops, body-heat production diminishes and patients feel cold.

Some goiters, inflammations of the thyroid gland, overuse of antithyroid drugs, or thyroid surgery may cause diminished thyroxine production and myxedema. In skilled hands treatment is simple, consisting of careful administration of thyroxine.

See also THYROID GLAND.

N

NARCOLEPSY [när′kō-lĕp-sē], also known as Friedman's disease, is characterized by sudden short spells of overpowering sleepiness. The attacks are not related to fatigue or lack of sleep, and may occur at any time of the day, often causing the victim to appear lazy, inattentive, or impolite. Most cases are caused by abnormal brain function; however, some appear to result from psychological disturbances. The former can be adequately controlled with drugs. Patients with emotional difficulties are best treated by psychotherapy.

NARCOTICS [när-kŏt′ĭks], a group of drugs of varied chemical nature that relieve pain, produce drowsiness and sleep, and cause addiction. The term "narcotic" is also sometimes used more broadly to include the stupor- or sleep-producing properties of any drug, as in referring to the "narcosis" produced by ether. Narcotics are divided into two classes: the natural and the synthetic narcotics.

Natural Narcotics. The major source of the natural narcotics is the unripe seed capsule of the poppy, *Papaver somniferum*, a plant cultivated in the Middle and Far East. The milky juice which exudes when the poppy capsule is cut is dried to a brown powder known as opium. This substance has been used for thousands of years for its sleep-producing and pain-relieving (analgesic) action. Throughout the centuries when truly curative drugs and surgery were unknown, the analgesic action of opium was one of the few real services the physician could provide. In addition to its pain-relieving and sedative effects, opium and morphine (its major component) tend to produce a state of euphoria, or well-being.

In small doses morphine relieves pain, in large doses it induces deep sleep, and in still larger doses it produces coma and halts breathing. The principal toxic action of morphine is interference with breathing, caused by depression of the respiratory center of the brain. Morphine may also cause nausea, vomiting, and constipation.

Another well-known narcotic found in opium is codeine, which is chemically similar to morphine, but is less potent and not as dangerous. Codeine is widely used in medicine to relieve moderate pains and as a cough-suppressant.

Synthetic and "Semisynthetic" Narcotics. A group of narcotic analgesics can be prepared by chemically modifying the natural alkaloids, morphine or codeine. The most notorious member of this class of "semisynthetic" narcotics is heroin, prepared from morphine. This drug is not used in modern medicine. It is a major item in illegal narcotic traffic. Other derivatives of morphine are dihydromorphinone (Dilaudid), ethyl morphine, and nalorphine. The latter compound is of considerable interest because it acts as an antagonist of morphine and is an important antidote for acute morphine poisoning.

The strictly synthetic narcotic analgesics differ chemically from morphine. Most of these drugs, which include meperidine (Demerol), methadone, and levorphanol, were developed during or after World War II. They are similar to the natural narcotics, both in their analgesic effects and their tendency to produce addiction.

The Harrison Narcotic Act. Although the narcotic analgesics are the major drugs generally included under narcotics, this term is sometimes also used in a legal sense to include drugs which are listed and controlled by the Harrison Narcotic Act (1914). One such drug is cocaine, an alkaloid prepared from the coca leaf. This compound is not a sedative, but is, on the contrary, a stimulant which can produce marked restlessness and even convulsions.
See also DRUG ADDICTION.

NATIONAL FOUNDATION, THE, foundation established in 1938 by President Franklin Delano Roosevelt to conduct research toward the prevention of paralytic poliomyelitis and to give the best possible care to all polio sufferers. An annual March of Dimes conducted each January by volunteers has contributed more than $500,000,000 for research, patient care, and professional-public education. This effort was a large factor in the development of the Salk vaccine in 1955 and later of the Sabin vaccine, both to prevent paralytic polio. In 1958 the foundation expanded its program to include new efforts to prevent birth defects, arthritis, all types of virus diseases, and, in the future, any unmet health problems.

NATIONAL SAFETY COUNCIL, nonprofit co-operative organization, chartered by act of Congress, which furnishes leadership to the national safety movement. Founded in 1913, the council works for safety in all areas, including home, work, school, farm, and highway. It derives its support from members' dues, from sale of safety materials, and from contributions. It provides services to meet the safety needs of industrial concerns; insurance companies; various associations, traffic, home, farm, and community safety organizations; government departments; schools; and individuals.

NEARSIGHTEDNESS, also known as myopia, is a disturbance of vision in which distant objects appear blurred. In normal vision the image is focused on the retina, the light-sensitive layer in the rear of the eye. In myopia the image is focused in front of the retina.

Theoretically, any one of several mechanisms may cause myopia: the transparent portions of the eye, the lens and cornea, may be excessively curved, causing light to bend too strongly; the ciliary muscles, which adjust the curvature of the lens, may overcontract, producing the same effect; or the eye itself may be too large, so that the retina is too far back from the focusing structures. Which of these possible causes is actually responsible for nearsightedness is not known. It is suspected that mild degrees of myopia may be either caused by disturbances of the focusing mechanism or an oversized eye, or by a combination of the two, and that marked nearsightedness is primarily caused by an unusually large eye.

The condition is rarely seen in young children, but usually appears between the ages of 9 and 13. It tends to worsen during puberty and a few years thereafter, and then remains stationary.

Nearsightedness is effectively corrected by eyeglasses which focus objects farther back. Contact lenses are also effective. Eye exercises and calcium and other chemicals have been used in an attempt to treat nearsightedness by strengthening the eye or halting its growth; there is no clear proof that any of these help.
See also CONTACT LENSES; EYE; EYEGLASSES; FARSIGHTEDNESS.

NEMATODE [něm'ə-tōd], roundworm in the class Nematoda. *Nema* is the Greek word for "thread," and most of these worms are thin and threadlike. They are abundant nearly everywhere, in the earth, in the water, and as parasites within plants and animals, including man. There are over 10,000 known species. Great numbers of microscopic nematodes are free-living in moist soil, feeding on bacteria, all looking much alike. Many others are so small they can barely be seen without a lens. They are usually white or transparent and taper at both ends. Typically, they thrash about in an aimless fashion. Many species of nematodes found in the soil cause considerable damage to plants by attacking their roots and sucking the juices.

Some of the largest roundworms have been known for centuries as parasites of man, especially *Ascaris lumbricoides*, which reaches a length of more than one foot. The trichina worm, *Trichinella spiralis*, is a tiny parasite of hogs. At one stage it forms cysts in the muscles and may be present in raw pork, which, if eaten, causes illness in man. Hookworms, about one-half an inch long, are a common human parasite in warm countries throughout the world.
See also ELEPHANTIASIS OR ELEPHANT DISEASE; FILARIASIS; HOOKWORM; TRICHINOSIS.

NEPHROSIS [nĭ-frō'sĭs], a kidney condition marked by protein in the urine and abnormal accumulations of fluid in the face, abdomen, or other parts of the body. Nephrosis can occur at any age, but it is seen most commonly in children between the ages of one and four.

In children, nephrosis usually appears by itself. In adults it is more frequently seen in association with other diseases. Nephrosis may occur following the ingestion of certain drugs, a bee sting, or contact with poison oak. The cause of nephrosis is unknown; one popular theory considers it to result from an allergic-type reaction.

Signs and Symptoms. In the early stages, and in mild conditions, many individuals feel well enough to continue their normal daily activities. Usually the earliest sign is swelling (edema) about the eyes or ankles. In some cases the edema may involve the entire body. The retention of fluid in the tissues may lead to a weight gain of 5 to 20 lb. over a period of several weeks. In severe edema the skin appears puffy and pasty white. The abdomen may be distended with fluid and in rare cases fluid may collect in the space around the lungs (the pleural space), causing difficulty in breathing. When edema is present, the amount of urine passed is decreased. In children especially there is great susceptibility to mild and severe infections. Prior to the development of the newer antibiotics, many died of severe infection, such as pneumonia or bacterial invasion of the blood stream. In advanced cases, poor appetite, nausea, and diarrhea may be prominent, and when combined with marked loss of protein in the urine, malnutrition may result. Children may temporarily cease growing. The course of nephrosis is usually characterized by periods of edema alternating with edema-free intervals. The edema may vanish suddenly as the patient passes more urine, resulting in a rapid weight loss. In some cases, the increased urine flow is started by an infection or by specific drugs; in other cases the cause is unknown. This edema-free period may last weeks, months, or even permanently.

Urine and Blood Changes. At times so much protein may be lost that if the urine were boiled, it would coagulate into a solid white mass, much like the white of a hard-boiled egg, which is also a protein. Red blood cells may also be seen in the urine. Blood changes include a decreased quantity of proteins and an increase in the amount of blood fats.

In children, nephrosis has a relatively favorable outlook. More than half the cases may heal in about two to five years. In the remaining cases the edema may vanish, but the child ultimately dies of kidney failure. The prospect is less favorable for adults. The illness may persist for years or even decades. Death may result from kidney failure or associated diseases.

Treatment. There is no single specific effective treatment. An adequate diet to maintain nutrition is important, especially to sustain growth in children. High protein diets are desirable unless there is some degree of renal failure. Restoring the fluid-holding power of the blood by injections of whole blood or concentrated albumin (a blood protein) is sometimes of temporary value in reducing edema.

Adrenal hormones and ACTH (a pituitary hormone which stimulates secretion of adrenal hormones) have proven quite effective in increasing the urine flow and in restoring the urine and blood to normal. It may be necessary to administer these hormones repeatedly to maintain the improvement. These substances are most effective in children. The hormones must be used with caution since both children and adults may develop undesirable side effects, such as marked weight gain, increased hair growth on many parts of the body, or high blood pressure.
See also KIDNEY.

NERVOUS SYSTEM, a system of specialized tissue that controls the internal activities of the organism and regulates its interaction with the environment.

NERVOUS SYSTEM

The Evolution of the Nervous System

The evolution of the nervous system was shaped by the basic problems that confront all life forms: How can food be obtained, enemies avoided, and the species reproduced? Primitive nervous systems were geared to detect changes in the environment by analyzing chemical substances, largely through the sense of smell, and were eventually replaced by forms dominated by vision and hearing. These latter senses provided considerable advantage in that the organism could obtain more precise information from the environment over greater distances and in less time. With this, other nervous mechanisms evolved which enabled the organism to associate between past and present events, and thus to profit from past experience. These mechanisms enhanced the prospects for survival.

Rigid Versus Flexible Behavior

Some nervous systems developed complex sequences of behavior that insured the continuation of the species. Such behavior sequences included the elaborate nesting and social habits of insects, birds, and lower mammals. These rigid and inflexible patterns of activity are more or less built into the nervous system and, as methods of survival, suffer the serious disadvantage that they cannot be modified to accommodate even small changes in the environment. Thus, birds that instinctively flee predators of a particular shape and coloring might be easy victims of a new predator of a different species. Such animals, however, might adapt to difficult environmental problems over thousands, or millions, of generations by genetic mutation, combined with the competitive winnowing of the less fit animals that retained older and less adaptive behaviors. Evolution of this type can occur with the relatively rigid simpler nervous systems of lower forms remaining at their same level of complexity.

By contrast, the human nervous system is able to survive by virtue of its capacity for flexible behavior, its ability to explore and modify the environment and to change behavior to suit the needs of the moment. This demands a vastly more complex brain. The human nervous system not only discovers and selects alternative means of action but inquires into problems not directly concerned with survival. This higher inquiry becomes science, art, religion, politics, and many other fields of study. In the cases of some highly dedicated scientists, scholars, and artists the nervous system seems to survive in order to inquire and create. Survival may even be compromised by certain types of thinking, as when individuals sacrifice their lives or personal interests for the preservation of the lives of others, or for an abstract social ideal.

The Cortex, Old and New

What differences in nervous structure can account for the differences in flexibility of behavior described above? The significant developments can be traced in Fig. 1, which compares schematically the brains of the salamander (an amphibian), the tortoise (a reptile), the opossum (a lower mammal), and man.

The primitive brain of the salamander can be roughly divided into two functional units: one which regulates internal activity (visceral functions, for example, control of the heartbeat, regulation of digestive movements); and a second which guides the organism in its dealings with the environment (somatic functions). The activity of the internal organs is controlled by the cells of the hippocampal area located near the midline; these cells integrate the sense of smell with taste and the operation of the digestive and other internal organs of the body. Hippocampal integration is accomplished by the many connections of this structure with a central group of nuclei known as the *hypothalamus*.

In the outer portion of the salamander's brain is a group of cells (in the *piriform area*), which govern the connections between the sense of smell and the senses of touch, sight, and hearing. These cells also control the limb movements of the animal. These somatic functions are aided by a structure called the *thalamus*.

We see therefore that the inner nuclei of the salamander serve visceral control, while the outer nuclei govern somatic functions. These structures have come to be known as the *paleo-*, or "old," cortex. Between them appeared a highly significant evolutionary development, the *neo-*, or "new," cortex. This first appeared in reptiles. The paleocortex continued to regulate the sense of smell and internal body control, while the expanding neocortex permitted more complex integration of touch, hearing, and vision, with body movement. The significance of the enlarging neocortex becomes even clearer in the mammals, as shown in the opossum (Fig. 1). The increased versatility of behavior in the mammals as compared to the reptiles can be ascribed to the larger neocortex. The paleocortex is also larger in mammals, but the increase is relatively smaller.

In man the extraordinary importance of the neocortex becomes obvious. To be sure, the hippocampus of man is by itself larger than the entire brain of the opossum. Relatively, however, the hippocampus is dwarfed by the enormous increase in the neocortex, to which man owes his great skill with tools, his speech, and his culture and civilization.

From conception to adult life the neocortex expands to eventually dominate all other brain structures. Particularly important is the fact that the human nervous system is not complete at birth, but continues its development in early life under the influence of the environment. There is a great deal of evidence which suggests that the nervous system is "ripe" for particular types of learning early in life, which could not be absorbed later in life. This appears to be the case with language learning; young children acquire language with a facility and permanence which the adult cannot match. Because of the environmental stamp on the developing nervous system, it is often difficult to differentiate between the effects of early experience and a truly innate characteristic of the nervous system. In monkeys the mating behavior that superficially seems to be instinctual and innate, as is found in lower mammals, is really dependent on learning. Monkeys reared in isolation from other monkeys have great difficulty in mating. If a female reared in isolation does bear young, she does not perform any maternal functions. The early isolation blocks the necessary learning for such behavior. This development of the nervous system in early life after birth is called *maturation*, and is advantageous in enabling the organism to better adjust to its environment.

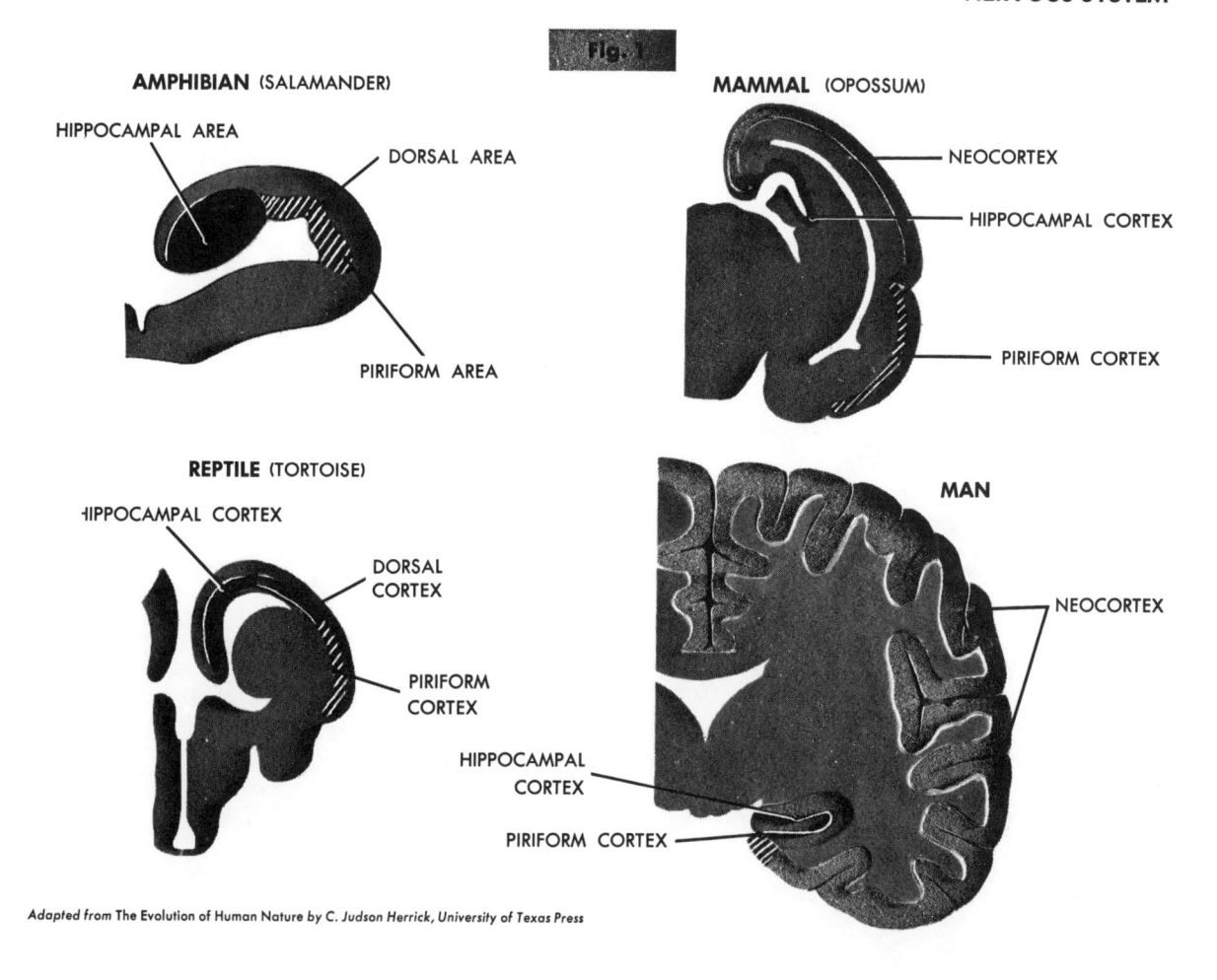

NERVOUS SYSTEM

Fig. 1

AMPHIBIAN (SALAMANDER) — HIPPOCAMPAL AREA, DORSAL AREA, PIRIFORM AREA

MAMMAL (OPOSSUM) — NEOCORTEX, HIPPOCAMPAL CORTEX, PIRIFORM CORTEX

REPTILE (TORTOISE) — HIPPOCAMPAL CORTEX, DORSAL CORTEX, PIRIFORM CORTEX

MAN — NEOCORTEX, HIPPOCAMPAL CORTEX, PIRIFORM CORTEX

Adapted from The Evolution of Human Nature by C. Judson Herrick, University of Texas Press

Brain Size as an Index of Intelligence

The evolutionary tendency toward increase in brain size did not always result in a proportionate increase in intelligence. The brains of the elephant (about 10 lb.) and the whale (about 14 lb.) far exceed in size that of man (about 3 lb.).

These larger animals require massive brains to control their enormous bulk. The ratio of brain weight to body weight, however, reveals the human advantage: for the whale, the ratio is 1:10,000; for the elephant, 1:500; for the gorilla, 1:250; and for man, 1:50. But such comparisons still do not accurately reflect brain capacity, since some monkeys have brain-body ratios of 1:50, like that of man. A more accurate ratio is the weight of the brain compared to the weight of the spinal cord. In the frog, the brain weighs less than the spinal cord; in the gorilla, it weighs 15 times more than the cord; in man, the ratio is 50:1.

Function and Structure of the Nervous System

As we have seen, the relations of the body with the environment are governed by the *somatic* nervous system, which notes the position of objects, listens for the sounds they emit, and moves the muscles that guide the body through space. The internal activities of the body are regulated by the *visceral*, or *autonomic*, nervous system that diverts the flow of blood, as needed, and sets the pace of activity of the digestive organs. These systems are complemented by higher structures that blend both autonomic and somatic functions into unified patterns of action. Such higher integrating structures are involved in emotion, thinking, and consciousness.

The Body and the Outside World—Somatic System. The world makes itself known to the mind by physical stimuli, such as light, sound, heat, and pressure on the skin, or by chemical stimuli which excite the senses of taste and smell. Nerve impulses carrying touch, temperature, and pain from the skin ascend to the brain via the spinal cord. Visual, sound, smell, and taste impulses enter the brain at levels above the spinal cord. All sense impulses pass to the neocortex by way of the thalamus, the sole exception being the sense of smell.

The centers of muscle control lie in the neocortex, not far from the cells which receive sense impulses.

Motor pathways from this area pass through the brain stem and spinal cord to the muscles of the arms, legs, head, and trunk. The movements of the body are controlled by these pathways, and are smoothed by groups of nerve cells (basal ganglia, striatum) in the lower brain and by the cerebellum. Much of this regulation of movement de-

NERVOUS SYSTEM

COMPARATIVE BRAIN DEVELOPMENT OF MAN AND LOWER ANIMALS

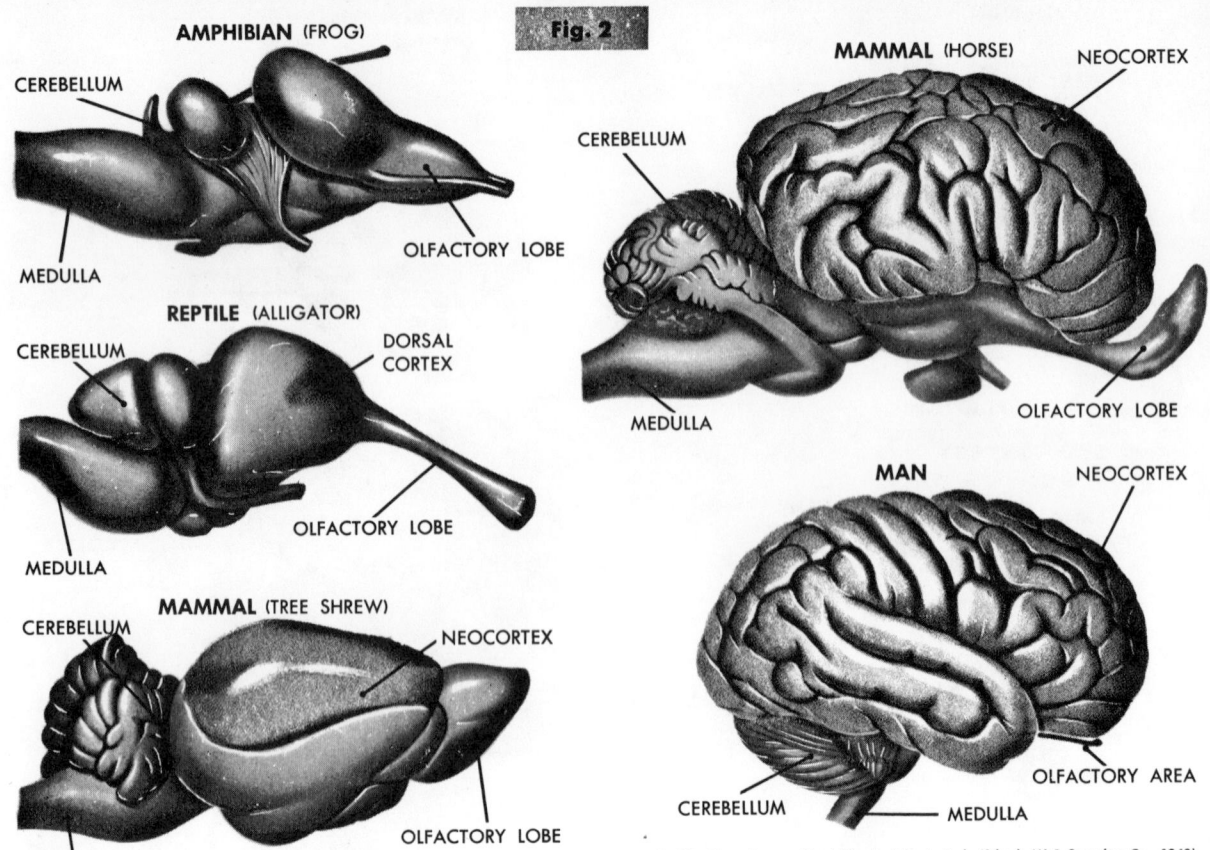

Fig. 2

Modified from Romer, Alfred, The Vertebrate Body (3d ed.), W. B. Saunders Co., 1962

pends on precise information about the position of all parts of the body before, during, and after movement. This information originates in the muscles and tendons and goes via the spinal cord back to the centers initiating the movement.

Control of the Internal Organs—Autonomic Nervous System. This part of the nervous system, closely associated with structures of the "old" cortex, has two subdivisions: The *parasympathetic system* tends to slow the heart, lower the blood pressure, increase the movements of the stomach, and promote digestion. The *sympathetic system* is associated with the emotional responses brought on by excitement and action. This system speeds the heartbeat, raises the blood pressure, retards stomach activity, and dilates the pupil of the eye. Important in the functioning of the sympathetic system are the adrenal glands, two small structures situated one astride each kidney. The glands are composed of distinct sections: an outer portion, or *cortex*, and an inner portion, or *medulla*. The relationship between the brain and the adrenal glands illustrates the two methods of long-distance communication in the body: one by electrochemical impulses along nerve fibers; the other by means of chemical messengers (hormones) traveling through the blood.

Sudden or acute emotional stresses may excite the inner portion, or medulla, of the gland by means of sympathetic nerve fibers. When stimulated in this way, the medulla secretes epinephrine and norepinephrine, two hormones which produce the sympathetic effects on the heart, blood vessels, and other structures.

The cortex, or outer layer, of the adrenal gland is responsive to chronic stresses and is activated more indirectly by a hormone (ACTH), secreted by the pituitary gland, which is located at the center of the skull. The adrenal cortical hormones help regulate the composition of the body fluids, and promote the conversion of protein to sugar in the liver.

The medullary hormones, epinephrine and norepinephrine, are also of interest in that they are probably involved in the transmission of impulses between some neurons. It might therefore be expected that epinephrine and norepinephrine in the bloodstream would throw many brain cells into chaotic activity. This is prevented by the *blood-brain barrier*, a filtering mechanism that prevents many chemical substances from easily reaching the brain cells.

Co-ordination of the Inner and Outer Worlds. Although we have considered separately the regulation of the internal and external environments (through visceral and somatic functions, respectively), in life these activities are blended together by higher brain structures. Thus, a frightened man running from danger is performing somatic functions (the contractions of the leg and body mus-

THE NERVOUS SYSTEM

The major component of the nervous system is the brain, which is the center of intelligence, memory, and personality. The spinal cord, the peripheral nerves, and other nerve structures link the brain with the outside world, and various parts of the body.

Artist: Leonard Dank

THE BRAIN

The cranial nerves connect the brain directly with the eye, ear, nose, and tongue and various internal organs.

SPINAL CORD IN CROSS SECTION

The peripheral nerves link the spinal cord to the organs and tissues of the body.

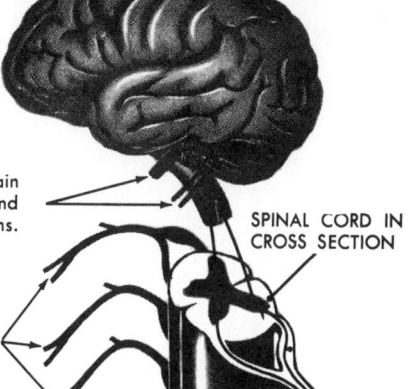

CONTACT WITH THE MUSCLES

The voluntary muscles are controlled by the motor area of the cerebral cortex — the convoluted "higher" brain. The nerve circuit shown here illustrates how the nerve fibers controlling the muscles of the arm pass through the brain and out of the spinal cord.

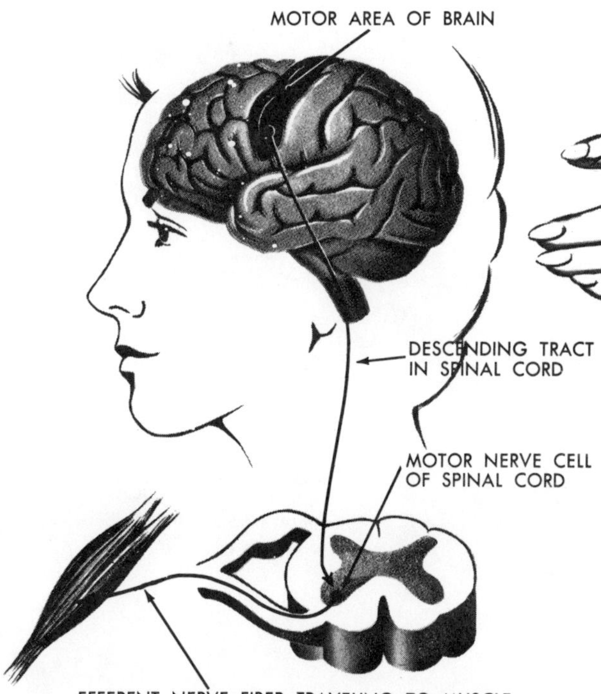

MOTOR AREA OF BRAIN

DESCENDING TRACT IN SPINAL CORD

MOTOR NERVE CELL OF SPINAL CORD

EFFERENT NERVE FIBER TRAVELING TO MUSCLE

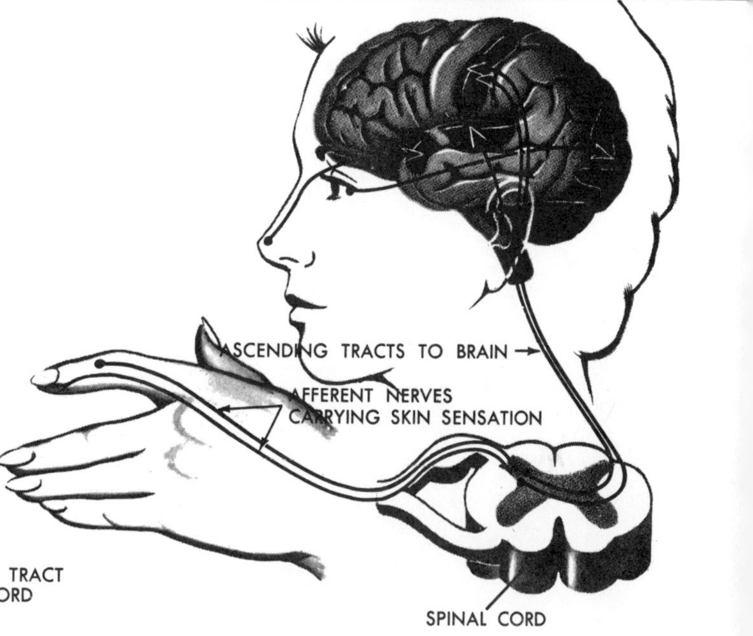

ASCENDING TRACTS TO BRAIN

AFFERENT NERVES CARRYING SKIN SENSATION

SPINAL CORD

CONTACT WITH THE OUTSIDE WORLD

The eye, ear, and nose receive information about distant objects in the outside world. The taste and skin receptors report to the brain the presence of objects in contact with the body. Impulses are carried to the brain by afferent fibers.

CONTACT WITH THE INTERNAL ORGANS

A special branch of the nervous system called the autonomic (or automatic) nervous system regulates the internal activities of the body. The nerve connections of this system to the heart and stomach are shown here. The dotted pathways belong to the *parasympathetic* branch of the system, which slows the heartbeat and stimulates the activity of the digestive organs. The solid pathways are *sympathetic* fibers, which speed the heartbeat and inhibit digestive activity.

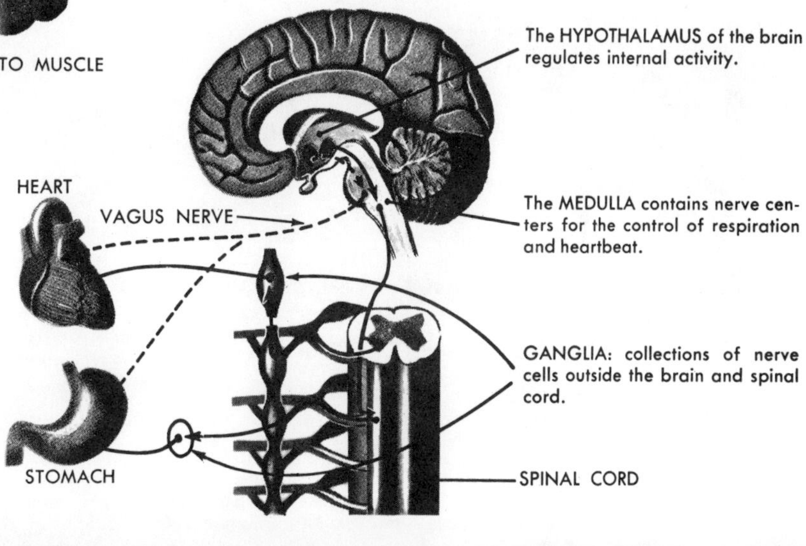

HEART

VAGUS NERVE

STOMACH

The HYPOTHALAMUS of the brain regulates internal activity.

The MEDULLA contains nerve centers for the control of respiration and heartbeat.

GANGLIA: collections of nerve cells outside the brain and spinal cord.

SPINAL CORD

THE NERVE CELL

THE NERVOUS SYSTEM

A CELL OF THE CENTRAL NERVOUS SYSTEM

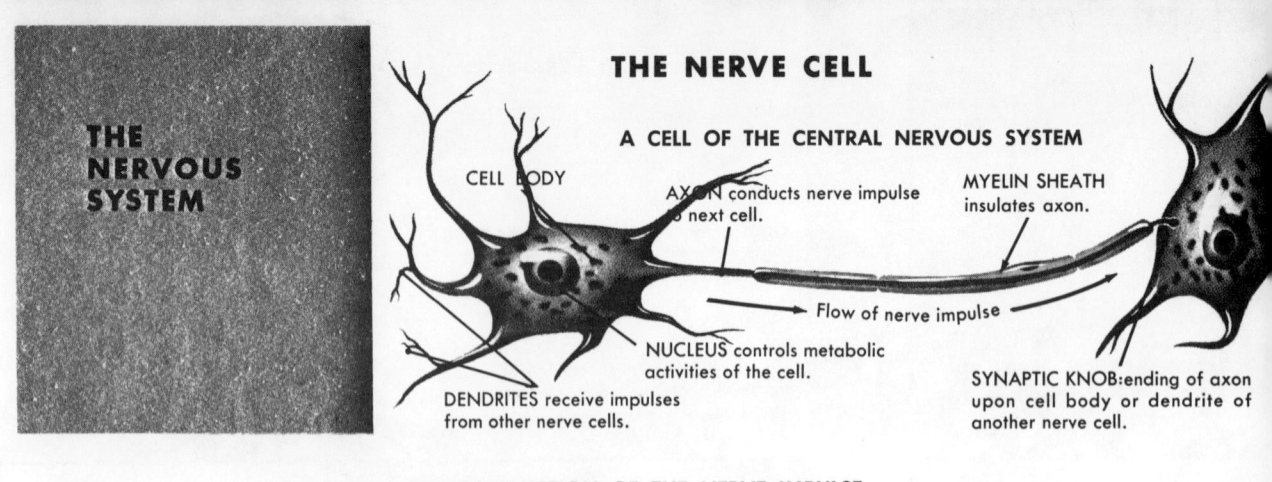

- **CELL BODY**
- **AXON** conducts nerve impulse to next cell.
- **MYELIN SHEATH** insulates axon.
- Flow of nerve impulse
- **NUCLEUS** controls metabolic activities of the cell.
- **DENDRITES** receive impulses from other nerve cells.
- **SYNAPTIC KNOB:** ending of axon upon cell body or dendrite of another nerve cell.

THE CONDUCTION OF THE NERVE IMPULSE

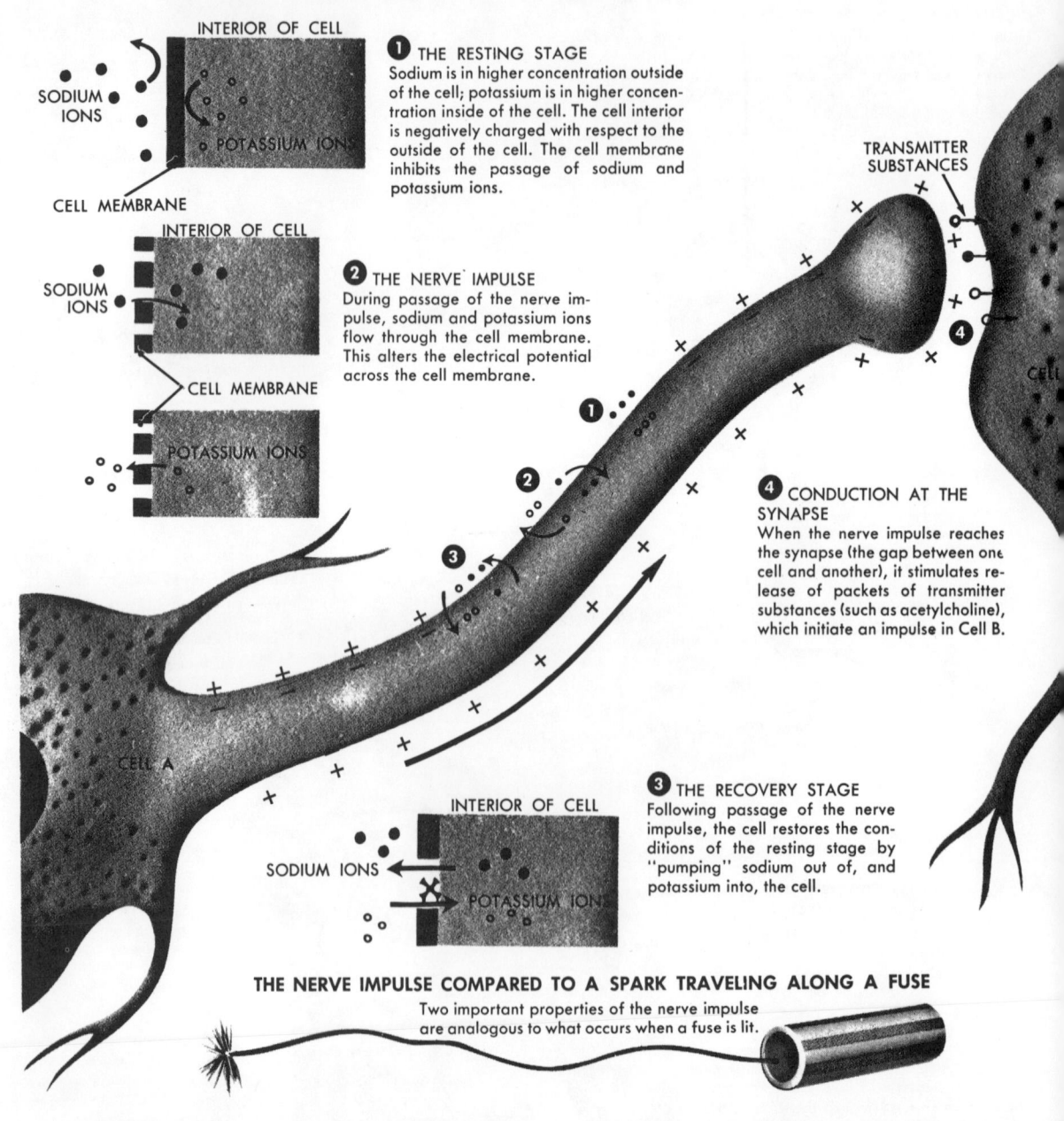

1. THE RESTING STAGE
Sodium is in higher concentration outside of the cell; potassium is in higher concentration inside of the cell. The cell interior is negatively charged with respect to the outside of the cell. The cell membrane inhibits the passage of sodium and potassium ions.

2. THE NERVE IMPULSE
During passage of the nerve impulse, sodium and potassium ions flow through the cell membrane. This alters the electrical potential across the cell membrane.

4. CONDUCTION AT THE SYNAPSE
When the nerve impulse reaches the synapse (the gap between one cell and another), it stimulates release of packets of transmitter substances (such as acetylcholine), which initiate an impulse in Cell B.

3. THE RECOVERY STAGE
Following passage of the nerve impulse, the cell restores the conditions of the resting stage by "pumping" sodium out of, and potassium into, the cell.

THE NERVE IMPULSE COMPARED TO A SPARK TRAVELING ALONG A FUSE

Two important properties of the nerve impulse are analogous to what occurs when a fuse is lit.

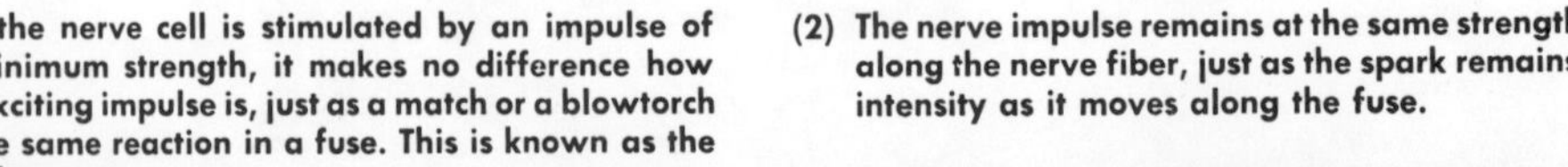

(1) As long as the nerve cell is stimulated by an impulse of a certain minimum strength, it makes no difference how strong the exciting impulse is, just as a match or a blowtorch produces the same reaction in a fuse. This is known as the *all-or-none-law*.

(2) The nerve impulse remains at the same strength as it travels along the nerve fiber, just as the spark remains at the same intensity as it moves along the fuse.

THE NERVOUS SYSTEM

SOME NERVE CIRCUITS
A CIRCUIT FOR THE EXECUTION OF A VOLUNTARY MOVEMENT

(1) Impulse originates in pyramidal cells of parietal lobe of the brain.
(2) Impulse passes along axons of pyramidal cells through pontine nuclei to the cerebellum, the muscle-coordinating center of the brain.
(3) Impulse reaches Purkinje cells of the cerebellum. Pattern of muscle action is selected.
(4) Action pattern passes to dentate nucleus of the cerebellum.
(5) Impulses ascend to red nucleus on way to the cerebrum.
(6) Impulses reach pyramidal cells of motor area of cerebral cortex.

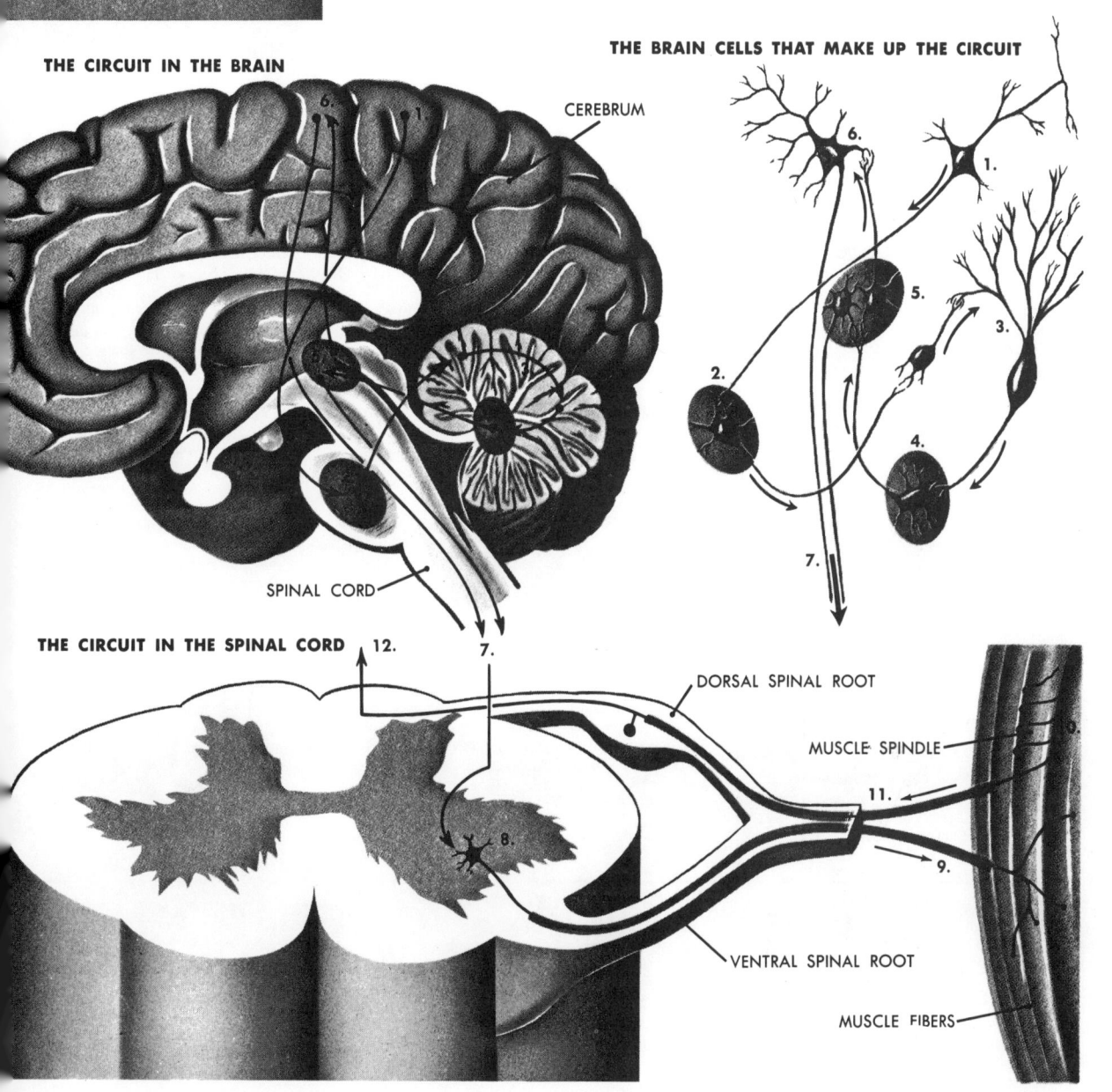

THE CIRCUIT IN THE BRAIN

THE BRAIN CELLS THAT MAKE UP THE CIRCUIT

CEREBRUM

SPINAL CORD

THE CIRCUIT IN THE SPINAL CORD

DORSAL SPINAL ROOT

MUSCLE SPINDLE

VENTRAL SPINAL ROOT

MUSCLE FIBERS

(7) Impulses from the cerebral cortex travel along descending tracts in the spinal cord to activate muscles.
(8) Motor nerve cell in spinal cord is activated.
(9) Impulses pass to muscle via spinal nerve.
(10) Muscle sensory receptor alters firing pattern as muscle contracts.
(11) Sensory impulses from the muscle travel to the spinal cord.
(12) Sensory impulses ascend spinal cord to brain. The information transmitted in this way apprises the brain of the state of muscular contraction, thus making possible coordinated movement.

THE NERVOUS SYSTEM

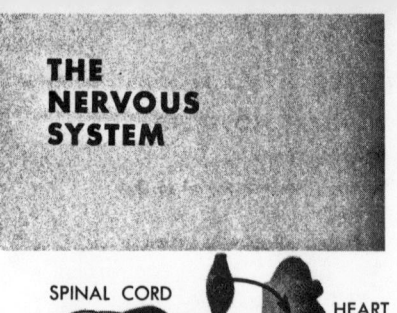

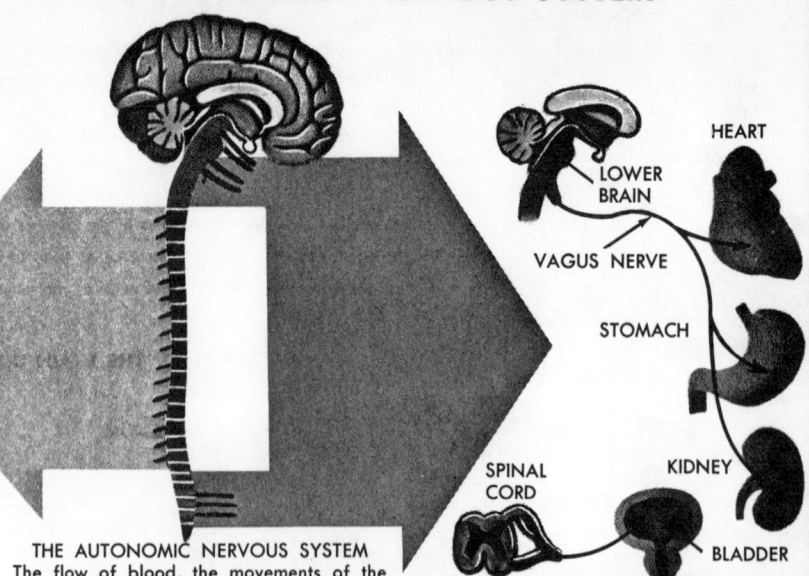

THE AUTONOMIC NERVOUS SYSTEM

THE SYMPATHETIC NERVOUS SYSTEM
During vigorous exercise, sympathetic nerves acting on the blood vessels direct blood from the digestive organs and skin to the muscles of the arms, legs, and trunk. This "emergency," or "alarm," system also increases the heartbeat and inhibits digestive activity.

THE AUTONOMIC NERVOUS SYSTEM
The flow of blood, the movements of the digestive tract, the secretions of the digestive and endocrine glands, and various other internal activities are under the unconscious, automatic control of the autonomic nervous system. The two major divisions of the system are the sympathetic system (left) and the parasympathetic system (right).

THE PARASYMPATHETIC NERVOUS SYSTEM
The fibers of the parasympathetic nervous system promote digestion by increasing the movements and secretions of the digestive organs. Parasympathetic stimulation also slows the heartbeat and stimulates the secretions of the glands lining the breathing passages.

THE CELL STRUCTURE AND CHEMISTRY OF THE AUTONOMIC SYSTEM

THE CHEMISTRY OF THE SYMPATHETIC SYSTEM
The impulse traveling via the sympathetic pathway to the heart or any other organ must cross two gaps: (1) between the preganglionic fiber (A) and the ganglion cell and (2) between fiber B and the heart tissue. Two different types of chemicals mediate this passage: (1) cholinergic substances at the first gap and (2) adrenergic substances at the second gap. Since most sympathetic endings are of type 2, sympathetic effects are generally associated with these adrenergic fibers.

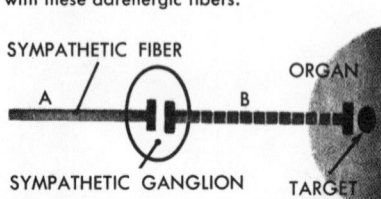

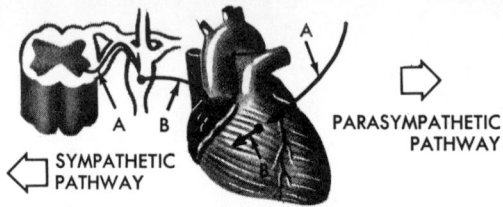

THE TWO CELLS OF THE AUTONOMIC SYSTEM
Both parts of the autonomic system have one cell in the brain or spinal cord and another contained in a ganglion outside of these structures. Above, the fibers "A" link the spinal cord and brain with the ganglion. The difference between the two systems can then be seen. The sympathetic cells are located in ganglia adjacent to the spinal cord. The parasympathetic cells are usually found close to, or within, the organ innervated.

THE CHEMISTRY OF THE PARASYMPATHETIC SYSTEM
The nerve impulses traveling along the parasympathetic pathway to the heart must cross: (1) the gap between fibers A and B and (2) the gap between fiber B and the heart tissue. A cholinergic substance mediates the passage of the impulse at both points.

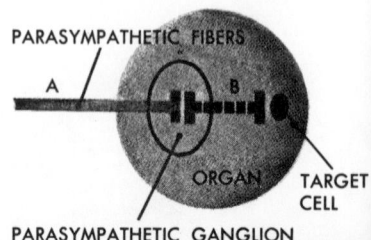

HOW DRUGS ACT UPON THE AUTONOMIC SYSTEM

LEVARTERENOL (NOREPINEPHRINE) acts upon the cells which are normally stimulated by sympathetic fibers.

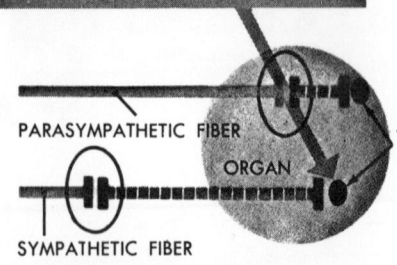

SOME IMPORTANT EFFECTS ARE:
(1) to constrict the small arteries
(2) to elevate the blood pressure.

ATROPINE blocks the action of cholinergic fibers on the target cells.

SOME IMPORTANT EFFECTS ARE:
(1) to dilate the pupils of the eyes and paralyze accommodation
(2) to inhibit secretions of the glands lining the mouth, nose, and upper respiratory passages
(3) to increase the heartbeat rate.

PILOCARPINE acts upon the cells which are normally stimulated by parasympathetic fibers.

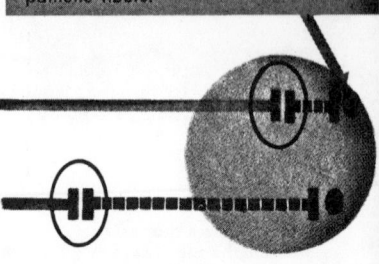

SOME IMPORTANT EFFECTS ARE:
(1) to induce sweating
(2) to induce salivation
(3) to contract the pupil of the eye.

cles to run), while, at the same time, sympathetic impulses raise his blood pressure and quicken his heartbeat. In contrast, the parasympathetic system dominates activity during the eating and digestion of food. At this time blood must be diverted from the skeletal muscles of the trunk and extremities to the stomach and intestines.

Higher Integration—Thinking and Consciousness

At one time certain schools of psychology described the brain schematically as a "black box." Impulses were fed into the box (input, or sensation); after a period impulses emerged (output, or muscle control) from the box. The task of psychology was to understand what happened in the box (the brain) between the input and the output. We have here described the input, or sensation; the output, or motor impulses; and the parts of the brain involved in sense activity and motor control. There remain the processes occurring between input and output; these involve the higher, integrating parts of the brain, structures which have no specific sensory or motor functions.

The frontal lobes of the brain are such higher structures. Consequently, it has been presumed that, along with many other parts of the brain, they are involved in higher mental processes, such as abstract thinking. In the operation frontal lobotomy, performed in certain types of mental disease, severance of the connections between these lobes and the thalamus produces certain subtle changes in personality and abstract thought.

A vital part of all co-ordination and integration is the *reticular formation*, a dense network of cells in the central core of the brain. This network extends from the upper reaches of the spinal cord through the brain stem and thalamus and fans out to all parts of the cerebral cortex. All sensory systems (touch, hearing, and so forth) feed into the reticular formation, and can lead it to activate or excite the rest of the nervous system. For this reason, it has become known as the *reticular activating system*.

The system has several distinctive properties which suggest that it is essential to consciousness and is fundamentally involved in the highest brain functions. It is *nonspecific*, as mentioned above; that is, it is alerted by any incoming sense impulses; it is rich in connections with other parts of the nervous system; it can excite or inhibit nervous activity; and it is connected with the hypothalamus and visceral control mechanisms, which suggest that it is one of the basic structures involved in emotion. Experimental evidence has confirmed the importance of the system in maintaining the waking state: electrical stimulation in this region arouses a sleeping animal; destruction of the region causes permanent sleep.

The Basic Nerve Unit—The Neuron

The neuron is the basic conducting unit of the nervous system. It contains, within the confines of a single cell, the basic properties of the nervous system as a whole. The input enters through a specialized signal-receiving region (dendrites and cell body), and integration between input and output occurs in a central region (the cell body). The output is discharged along the axon, a structure specifically designed for this purpose. The axon of one neuron ends on the dendrite or cell body of another neuron at a junction called a *synapse*.

Nerve impulses travel down the axon to the region of the synapse and there stimulate the release from small packets (vesicles) chemicals (called transmitter substances), which excite the dendritic membrane on the other side of the synapse. The electron microscope reveals some very small filaments crossing the synapse which keep the two sides of the synapse in precise association. This allows for the rapid and well-controlled release and destruction of the transmitter substance. Rapid destruction of the transmitting agent is extremely important, since otherwise the synapse could no longer transmit impulses. The substances most studied as probable transmitter agents are acetylcholine, epinephrine, and norepinephrine.

The Laws of Functioning. Like all physical systems, the nervous system is subject to certain laws of functioning which determine its properties. These can be studied in the region of the synapse. The incoming fiber, the axon, has two choices: it may "fire" (conduct a nerve impulse) or not fire; it cannot adjust the intensity of the nerve impulse. Across the synapse (that is, in the dendrite and cell body) the situation is quite different. It must be emphasized first of all that many axons impinge on a single dendrite.

Some axons may *inhibit* the dendrite; others may *excite* the dendrite. In effect, an incoming axon firing at a synapse may say to the dendrite "react" or "do not react." The dendrite and cell body usually do not fire in response to any single stimulation but average the effects of the activity of many incoming axons. A single quick tap on a hot iron, for example, may not produce the sensation of heat, but several consecutive taps may reveal what one tap fails to elicit. The consecutive taps produce consecutive reactions at the synapse which are added, or summated, over a time interval, to eventually fire the dendrite and cell body. This is known as *temporal summation*. The dendrite may also compute several impulses arriving at adjacent points, as when one compares weights of the same size and shape, one finds that the heavier weights cause more displacement of the skin, bones, and muscles of the hands, and generate a feeling of greater weight. In this case more impulses arrive at the dendrites and cell bodies simultaneously; this is termed *spatial summation*.

Types of Neurons. Many types of neurons are known; one of the bases for distinguishing among them is the speed at which they can conduct messages. Impulses in the fastest neurons move at the rate of 110 meters per second; in the slowest, at 0.5 meter per second. The speed of conduction is matched by the thickness of the myelin sheath, the insulating material around the axon. The more myelin, the faster the conduction. The slowest conducting fibers have no myelin at all, and are more primitive, since myelinated nerve fibers appeared and became progressively more prominent with the vertebrates as they evolved to higher forms. As brains enlarged, faster long-distance connections became necessary. This bears a striking analogy to the increasing prominence of freeways and turnpikes as cities enlarge, in order to keep the fast-moving, long-distance traffic from getting tangled up with slow-moving local traffic.

Neurons and Nerve Circuits. The complexity of the nervous system derives from the fact that billions of nerve cells are linked in a constantly changing variety of circuits.

NERVOUS SYSTEM

Despite this complexity, there are basically three types of neurons, again corresponding to the three basic types of function in the nervous system: (1) sensory neurons that conduct impulses to the nervous system (*afferent fibers*); (2) neurons that conduct impulses within the nervous system (association neurons); and (3) motor neurons that conduct impulses away from the nervous system (*efferent fibers*).

One of the simplest nerve circuits is that of the simple reflex. A painful stimulus applied to the skin (for example, touching a hot stove) excites a sensory neuron which conducts the impulse to an association neuron and directly to an effector, or motor cell, which stimulates the arm muscle to contract and draw the arm away from the stove. More than one set of neurons is actually involved in such a reaction. impulses are also transmitted up the spinal cord to alert the brain and generate the sensation of pain.

The Nervous System in Action

Like a polished athlete, the normally functioning nervous system makes the difficult look easy. The football player evading opponents to catch a pass and score a touchdown, moves so surely and naturally that it is difficult to appreciate the staggering complexity of nerve activity which underlies his movements. Literally billions of events are occurring every second: he is alerted through the activity of the reticular formation and has focused attention on tracking the football via the eye and optic nerve to thalamic visual relays and visual neocortex. The thalamus, the cortex, and the central reticular core are facilitating needed actions and perceptions, and inhibiting distracting stimuli, such as the roar of the crowd or pain from a bruised leg. Many other thalamic and neocortical areas are simultaneously co-ordinating running and positioning of the arms for the anticipated point of catch. Information (feedback) on the position of parts of the body comes from muscles, tendons, and the balance organs of the ear, and is correlated with vision and muscle control areas of the cortex to execute the over-all plan of the football player to catch, run, and score. The cerebellum, the basal ganglia, and other structures feed into the primary motor systems to enhance the smoothness of what would otherwise be a jerky and un-co-ordinated muscle action. We often take smoothness of function for granted and it is not until the jerky un-co-ordinated action of muscles appears, with disease of these systems, that we realize how much is necessary to attain smooth co-ordination.

In addition to all this, the nervous system is regulating body function through its control of hormone release: epinephrine and norepinephrine from the adrenal medulla speed the heartbeat; the antidiuretic hormone from the pituitary gland reduces loss of water in the urine to conserve water during the heavy losses from sweating, and so forth. This brief description is only a small sample of the processes underlying such an action.

Research on the Nervous System

Electricity and the Nervous System. Electricity has been a valuable tool in neurophysiology, both as a means of recording the normal electrical activity of nervous tissue and as a method of stimulating the brain.

The electrical activity from individual nerve cells reveals under what conditions neurons fire and how they can be kept from firing. The electrical activity of large numbers of brain cells produces the well-known "brain waves." These are measured in millionths of a volt, and can be recorded from the scalp. The waves are particularly informative in regard to states of arousal or consciousness.

The waves get broader and higher with drowsiness and sleep and become narrower and lower during arousal and periods of concentration, as when working on arithmetic problems. The reticular activating system is fundamental in the regulation of these brain-wave patterns. Abnormal brain-wave patterns are helpful in diagnosing conditions such as epilepsy and brain tumor.

The wave forms are often helpful in following pathways in the nervous system as they are actually functioning. Following a click, evoked responses can be detected as the impulse travels toward the brain: first in the auditory nerves, then the thalamus, and finally the auditory cortex. The activity of the visual and touch systems can be explored in similar fashion.

Changes in brain waves can also be observed in learning. Using the conditioning technique developed by the Russian physiologist Ivan Pavlov, some of the electrical patterns can be brought under experimental control. If a cat is exposed to a particular sound, brain-wave arousal patterns may appear. If the sound is repeated a number of times, it fails to evoke the arousal pattern. The arousal pattern may be induced once more if the animal is taught to expect some food with the sound. It is also known that an electrical pattern much like that accompanying light sleep can be generated in the brain of the cat by stimuli that the cat learns are unassociated with anything, in contrast to those which signal food. From this it has been learned that a mechanism exists in the brain for reducing responses to stimuli that are learned by the subject to be of no significance.

Electrical stimulation of the brain is a time-honored method for analyzing nervous system function. It received much attention following the discovery that a rat or a monkey can be made to work at a furious pace to receive as a reward an electrical impulse in certain parts of the brain. The animal can also be made to stop working by placing the current in certain other areas. When the electrode is placed in "pleasure," or "start," areas, the laboratory rats appear alert and excited. They will solve mazes and cross electrically charged grids to get to the controls for the brain stimulus. With stimulation in nonpleasurable "stop" areas, they appear to be in pain and will work to avoid repetition of the stimulus.

The presumed pleasurable or exciting effects described above may have been produced by electrical stimulation in a few human subjects, but ordinarily such effects are difficult to find. In some persons suffering from epilepsy it is possible to stimulate parts of the temporal cortex and elicit memories which seem to be activated and re-experienced as perceptions in the present, and which continue only so long as the current is applied. It has been postulated that the temporal lobe in some people is a storehouse for memories, but this cannot always be reliably demonstrated.

Chemical Investigations. Research into the chemistry of the nervous system has been stimulated by the discovery that certain drugs can produce profound effects on behavior, to the extent of inducing psychosislike reactions, or calming highly agitated mental patients. The effect of hormones on nervous function has been demonstrated by injecting hormones into areas of the brains of cats to put them into heat. Hormone injections into rats' brains have produced nesting behavior.

Surgical Investigations. Early investigations consisted largely of removing parts of the brain of experimental animals and observing the effects on behavior. A novel technique of surgically separating the two sides of the brain of animals without interfering with sensation and motor control on either side has revealed that it is possible to train each side of the brain independently of the other. The "split-brain" technique makes it possible to train a single animal in conflicting tasks simultaneously, each task being mastered by one-half of the brain.

Psychological Investigations. It is sometimes possible to make inferences about nervous structure and function by observing behavior, without physically acting upon the nervous system. This is illustrated by experiments which show that it is possible to interfere with memory by putting rats to sleep immediately after they have learned something new. On recovering from the immediate sleep they fail to remember the learning experience; when put to sleep 30 minutes after learning, memory is intact. It is evident that for some minutes after a learning experience the rat is consolidating what he has learned for permanent retention. It is this consolidation that can be experimentally manipulated. The experiment clearly suggests that nervous activity continues for an interval after the learning experience.

Understanding of the function of the nervous system is progressing rapidly because of the availability of many more precise, faster responding, and automatic tools. In addition, the large quantities of data obtained can now be computer-analyzed with great saving in time and effort. For these reasons, researchers in a variety of disciplines, including engineers, physicists, and biochemists, are collaborating with the neurophysiologists and psychologists in the ever-expanding effort of the human nervous system to understand itself.

See also BRAIN; REFLEX.

NEURALGIA [nyo͞o-răl′jə], excruciating pain along the course of one or more nerves. This may appear in various parts of the body, including the face (trigeminal neuralgia), the legs (sciatic neuralgia) and the chest (intercostal neuralgia). The cause of the pain is obscure; no abnormal changes can be detected in the nerve. The attacks usually occur at intervals ranging from seconds to years. Some forms of neuralgia have been treated by injecting alcohol into the nerve. Cutting the sensory fibers of the involved nerve is effective, but results in permanent numbness in the area the nerve supplies.

NEURITIS [nyo͞o-rī′tĭs], a general term for disturbances of the nerves lying outside the brain and spinal cord. Formerly the term "neuritis" designated only inflammations, but it has now been widened to include degeneration of nerves as well; for this reason many authorities prefer the newer, more inclusive expression "neuropathy."

Neuritis involving a few nerves, or only one, may be caused by infectious diseases (such as diphtheria or leprosy), by mechanical pressure on a nerve (such as crutch pressure), by irritation from injections directly into, or close to, nerves, or from unknown causes. A generalized neuritis, affecting many nerves, may be seen in diphtheria; in arsenic, lead, or mercury poisoning; in vitamin deficiencies such as beriberi and pellagra; in chronic alcoholism, pregnancy, diabetes, pernicious anemia, and gout; and in some forms of cancer.

The symptoms of neuritis result from interference either with impulses traveling toward the brain and spinal cord (sensations), or with impulses traveling in the reverse direction to muscles and glands (or with both). Pain is almost always present, and may be deep, pricking, or burning. There may be numbness or odd sensations such as "tingling" or "coldness." Complete paralysis is rare, but some degree of muscle weakness is common. The affected parts may atrophy and reflexes may be lost. Marked muscle tenderness is common. Excessive sweating or absence of sweating is frequently seen.

Specific treatment is directed at the underlying cause. In addition, aspirin or other pain-relieving drugs are given. Weakened muscles are massaged and stretched and the involved part may be splinted to avoid deformities.

NEUROSIS. While sensitive and irritable individuals are commonly described as "neurotic," in strict psychiatric usage this term is applied to individuals who adopt certain rigid, repetitious, and fruitless patterns of behavior in an attempt to reduce anxiety.

The central problem of neurosis is anxiety. According to Freud, a combination of constitutional and emotional factors are involved. He felt that neurosis was related to problems in early development, especially those occurring during the period of weaning, toilet-training, and the resolution of the Oedipus conflict. Other writers, such as Karen Horney and Harry Stack Sullivan, stress the role of society and difficulties between people in creating anxiety.

Whatever its origins, neurosis is generally agreed to result from efforts to control anxiety. The particular form a neurosis takes is felt to depend upon the way in which the individual deals with his anxiety.

See also ANXIETY; MENTAL ILLNESS; PSYCHIATRY; PSYCHOANALYSIS; PSYCHOTHERAPY.

NICOLLE [nē-kôl′], **CHARLES JEAN HENRI** (1866–1936), French physician who received the Nobel Prize in 1928 for his discovery of the body louse as the transmitting agent of typhus fever. He also made important investigations of numerous other infectious diseases, including trachoma and kala azar. In addition to his medical accomplishments, Nicolle enjoyed a reputation as a philosopher and writer and published several books.

NICOTINE [nĭk′ə-tēn], a liquid alkaloid obtained from the leaves of tobacco plants. Nicotine is one of the most physiologically active drugs known. It both stimulates and depresses the nervous system and may also act upon the smooth muscles of the intestines and the blood vessels. Nicotine has no important medical uses, but is of interest because of its action on the nervous system and its presence in tobacco smoke, where it is responsible for most of the observed effects of smoking (q.v.).

The most serious changes produced by smoking occur in the heart and blood vessels. Most smokers experience an increase in blood pressure and a constriction of the blood vessels in the skin with a lowering of the skin temperature. There may also be a rise in the pulse rate, and, in some heavy smokers, premature heartbeat and other irregularities. Smoking is known to abolish hunger contractions and to cause a laxative effect by stimulating muscular movements of the intestine. The regular after-breakfast cigarette to promote bowel activity, therefore, appears to have a sound scientific basis. Smoking also inhibits the secretion of urine, probably because of the action of nicotine in stimulating the secretions of a hormone from the pituitary gland, which in turn acts upon the kidney. Although many physicians prohibit smoking by patients with peptic ulcer, the adverse effects of smoking in this condition are not universally accepted.

NIGHT BLINDNESS, also known as nyctalopia, an impairment of vision under conditions of low illumination. Normal vision is a function of two sets of specialized cells in the retina, the light-sensitive layer of the eye: the cones, which are sensitive to daylight levels of illumination, and the rods, which make night vision possible. True night blindness occurs in some families as a result of an inherited absence of functioning rods. Vitamin A is essential for proper rod functioning and deficiencies of this vitamin, or liver diseases which interfere with its metabolism, may also cause night blindness. Epidemics of this disorder have been observed in populations subsisting on a vitamin A-deficient diet. A temporary night blindness may result from exposure to bright summer light or glare from snow. The high illumination interferes with the ability of the eye to adapt to darker conditions and it may take several days for normal dark adaption to return. Certain eye diseases, such as nearsightedness and glaucoma, may also cause night blindness. Poor night vision, without apparent physical cause, appears in some individuals, evidently as an expression of a psychological disorder.
See also Eye.

NITROGEN MUSTARD, also known as mustargen or mechlorethamine, an anticancer drug chemically related to the sulfur mustard gases which were used in World War I. Nitrogen mustard is valuable in cancer treatment because of its specific effect on primitive, rapidly reproducing cells, such as are found in malignant tumors. Apparently the drug interacts with the nucleic acids, the basic reproductive substances of the cell, causing the cancerous cells to disintegrate and inhibiting their reproduction. It also suppresses the activity of the blood cell-forming tissues in the bone marrow and lymph glands, and for this reason must be used with extreme caution. The actions of the drug have been compared to the effects of ionizing radiations in that they both act upon tumor tissues and cause similar changes in the blood. Nitrogen mustard is ordinarily given by injection into a vein, and may cause severe vomiting. It has been tried in many forms of cancer, but has been particularly useful in Hodgkin's disease, lymphosarcoma, and chronic leukemia. It has also been of value in relieving pain in various forms of advanced cancer. Unfortunately, the cancer usually resumes its growth after a period and successive doses are usually less effective than the first.

NOGUCHI [nō-gōō′chē], **HIDEYO** (1876–1928), Japanese bacteriologist, known for his studies of syphilis. Educated in Japan (M.D. degree, Tokyo, 1897), Noguchi went to the United States in 1898 and for many years worked with Simon Flexner at the Rockefeller Institute for Medical Research. He cultivated the organism responsible for syphilis, demonstrated the delayed effects of syphilis on the nervous system some 10 to 30 years after the original infection, and modified the Wassermann test for the detection of syphilis. He died of yellow fever while investigating that disease.

NOISE AND NOISE CONTROL. Noise is unwanted sound. A sonorous melody pouring forth from a radio may be pleasant to one family in a dwelling but a nuisance to neighbors attempting to sleep. If unwanted, it is noise.

Noise can affect man's ability to speak to his neighbors. If sufficiently intense, noise may also affect his behavior or permanently damage his hearing. Noise has become an annoying problem, since it is heard almost everywhere in modern cities. Jet aircraft, pneumatic drills, heavy trucks, and sirens all contribute to loud, unpleasant sounds. For these reasons and because it can make man's environment a more pleasant one, noise control has become a technology of considerable significance.

NOSE AND NASAL CAVITY. These structures, shaped from bone and cartilage, serve as breathing passages, as a site for the sense of smell, as an opening to balance pressure on the eardrum, and as a sounding board to form the sounds of speech.

Air passing through the nose is lightly filtered by the small hairs at the nasal opening and is warmed and moistened by the secretions of the mucous membranes lining the nasal cavity. Swelling of the mucosa, caused by irritants, allergies (hay fever), or infections (colds), may block the nasal passages and make breathing difficult. Deviation of the septum, the plate which divides the nasal cavity in two, may also impair breathing.

The sense of smell resides in specialized cells located at the rear of the nasal cavity. Odorous substances act on the sense endings after being dissolved in a fluid secretion which bathes the surface of the olfactory tissue.

The nasal cavity communicates with the middle ear via the eustachian tube. In this way air pressure is equalized on both sides of the eardrum.

Nasal vowels (as the "a" in "can't"—in some American dialects, for example, New Yorkese) are made by using the nasal cavity for resonance. Nasal consonants ("m" and "n") are made by closing the lips, thus diverting air through the nose. In the congenital condition of cleft palate the nose and mouth cavities communicate, interfering with the production of sounds.
See also SINUSITIS; SMELL, SENSE OF.

NOVOCAIN [nō′və-kān], trade name for the anesthetic procaine hydrochloride. It is most frequently injected into a specific area, such as the gums or a patch of skin, to produce a limited (local) anesthesia. Novocain is also the preferred drug for producing spinal anesthesia (*see* ANESTHESIA). The duration of anesthesia can be prolonged by mixing Novocain with adrenalin (epinephrine), a hormone which constricts the blood vessels of the skin and prevents the anesthetic from being carried away too rapidly by the blood. Although it is among the least toxic of anesthetics, it may cause a serious, and possibly fatal, reaction in rare sensitive individuals. Novocain achieved a short-lived fame when a Rumanian physician reported that regular injections of procaine rejuvenated senile patients. Later investigations, however, failed to substantiate these claims.

NUCLEIC ACIDS [nū-klē′ĭk], compounds found in all living organisms that play a fundamental role in the perpetuation and maintenance of life.

Research into the nature, structure, and function of nucleic acids has resulted in such a wealth of disclosures for the science of life that it is difficult to exaggerate the importance of these compounds. Life without nucleic acids is not possible. They transmit the coded instructions of heredity which ensure that each species shall reproduce its own kind, and they enable living cells to manufacture the materials necessary for life. It is possible that eventually detailed knowledge of the nucleic acids may enable man to effect changes more profound than those brought on by the discovery of atomic energy.

Occurrence. Two types of nucleic acids are known, one called ribonucleic acid (abbreviated RNA), the other called deoxyribonucleic acid (abbreviated DNA). Both are large molecules composed of repeating units of smaller molecules called nucleotides. At one time it was believed that DNA occurred only in animal cells and RNA only in plant cells. They were therefore referred to as animal nucleic acid and plant nucleic acid, respectively. DNA was mostly obtained from the thymus gland, and another name for it was thymus nucleic acid. The main source for RNA was yeast, and for a long time it was called yeast nucleic acid.

The microscope reveals that all higher animals and plants are built up of tiny units called cells. Simpler organisms, such as bacteria or amebae, consist of only one cell. The main constituents of a cell are the nucleus and the cytoplasm, which surrounds the nucleus. Early investigators erroneously believed that nucleic acids occurred only in the nuclei of cells. The term "nucleic acids" was coined at that time. Today this term is applied to a class of chemically defined compounds, regardless of their occurrence in nature.

RNA and DNA are present in all living plant, animal, and bacterial cells. Viruses are much smaller than cells, and can be detected only under powerful electron microscopes. Even these most primitive forms of life contain nucleic acid. Some contain only DNA, others only RNA, some contain both. DNA and RNA are found both in the nucleus and in the cytoplasm of the cell but a larger amount of DNA than RNA is present in the nucleus.

The amount of DNA remains constant in non-dividing cells. In dividing cells, however, before cell division the quantity doubles, and each one of the two daughter cells receives the same amount of DNA. The amount of RNA varies considerably from cell to cell. Even within one cell the amount of RNA varies with changes in the environmental conditions.

Biological Significance of DNA. The fact that there is no life without nucleic acids hints at some important roles of these compounds. Many observations have confirmed the idea that DNA structure contains the master plan of living organisms. The constancy of the amount of DNA and the doubling of this amount for cell division have pointed to a role of DNA in growth and reproduction. The finding that the composition of DNA is specific for each species has contributed to the belief that it is the DNA which ensures that a butterfly remains a butterfly and that an elephant's offspring will again be elephants. Chromosomes, the structures in the nucleus that have long been known to be the carriers of hereditary, or genetic, information, consist of DNA and protein. Convincing evidence for the role of DNA in heredity has been obtained in experiments on the transformation of bacteria. DNA extracted from certain bacteria can transfer some of the properties of this bacterial strain to a related strain. The bacteria thus transformed pass these newly acquired properties on to their progeny, which proves that their hereditary capacity has been permanently changed.

Changes in the hereditary characteristics of the cell are called mutations. Such changes can be artificially induced by exposing cells to certain chemicals or to certain types of radiation. It has been found that these mutagenic agents cause changes in the structure of DNA when solutions of pure DNA are treated with these agents. The basic event in a mutation is probably a change in the molecular structure of the chromosomal DNA.

Growth and reproduction are based on the cell's ability to divide and form two daughter cells. The mechanism of cell division is not fully understood; but it appears that during this process the DNA double molecules unwind, forming two single DNA strands, each of which goes to one of the daughter cells. The individual DNA strand serves as a "mold" for organizing nucleotides into the right sequence to make a new DNA chain, which is identical to the first one. The DNA molecule thus has the unique property of self-duplication.

Various hypotheses have been brought forth as to how specific arrangements of the four nucleotides along the DNA chains may represent the hereditary code. However, too little is as yet known about the actual sequence of nucleotides in the DNA molecules to permit more than speculation about this fundamental problem.

Biological Significance of RNA. Specific sections of the DNA are used in the non-dividing cell for the synthesis of still another kind of RNA—messenger RNA (mRNA)—in a process termed transcription. This mRNA combines with the ribosomes, complex cytoplasmic particles composed of RNA and protein which are active in protein synthesis. According to three specific nucleotides known as the anticodon, transfer RNA pairs with three of the mRNA nucleotides in the translation process. The specific triplet code or language of the cell has been deciphered (see chart *The Genetic Code*). The amino acids attached to the ends of the transfer RNA are combined at the ribosome site to form a row of amino acids known as a protein. Thus a specific sequence (gene) of the nucleotides of DNA is (a) transcribed into mRNA, which in turn is (b) translated by tRNA and (c) results in a specific array of amino acids producing a specific protein. In other words, the informational content of elm tree DNA produces specific enzymes and other proteins that ultimately form an elm tree cell and not some other kind of cell.

Proteins are, like the nucleic acids, polymers made up of hundreds of thousands of repeating units. Just as the nucleotides are the building units of the nucleic acids, the amino acids are the structural units of the proteins. Some 20 different amino acids have been found in the proteins. The amino acid composition and the sequence in which the amino acids are arranged give each protein its characteristic properties. Those proteins known as enzymes regulate almost all of the chemical reactions that occur within the individual cells and within the whole organism of higher plants and animals.

Nucleoproteins. In living organisms nucleic acids are found in combination with varying amounts of protein. Crude cell extracts contain these nucleoproteins, and procedures for the isolation of pure nucleic acids from natural sources always include measures designed to remove the protein portion. Proteins associated with DNA are rich in basic amino acids. They are called histones and protamines. Sperm cells are a rich source of DNA-proteins. The proteins associated with RNA usually have a more complex composition than the protamines and histones. The RNA-proteins of some viruses have been most thoroughly studied. Some plant viruses are known to consist of nothing but RNA-protein. It has been found that in these viruses the coiled RNA molecule forms a core that is surrounded by protein units. These protein units are also arranged in a spiral pattern.

Viruses can reproduce only by invading a living cell. When an animal or plant is infected with a virus disease, the virus particles penetrate into the host cells. Inside the host cell the virus nucleic acid takes over the control of production of nucleic acids and proteins. In other words, the host cell, following the wrong "blueprint," starts to produce virus nucleic acid and virus protein. This eventually results in the death of the host cell and in the release of many new virus particles, which can, in turn, attack new host cells. It has been shown for some viruses that their protein portion is not necessary to produce infection. It is the nucleic acid core of the virus which replaces the host cell's own hereditary code, directing the cell to make viruses instead of daughter cells. It must be assumed that in the case of plant viruses which contain only RNA-protein, the RNA can carry out the function usually performed by DNA, that of a carrier of hereditary information.

In 1967, a team of American biochemists headed by Arthur Kornberg replicated the infectious DNA core of a bacterial virus. In its bacterial host tissue, the synthetic DNA produced exact copies of itself, just as natural DNA does. The first isolation of a single gene, one from the common bacterium *E. coli*, was achieved in 1969, and in 1970 a team of scientists, headed by Nobel Prize winner H. Gobind Khorana, synthesized a gene which specifies the synthesis of alanine transfer RNA in yeast.

It is known that some forms of cancer in animals are initiated by viruses. Virus DNA appears to cause the host cell to "go wild," resulting in the uncontrolled growth of cells leading to a malignant tumor. The recognition that further progress in the fight against virus diseases, cancer, and hereditary diseases will to an extent depend on a better understanding of the structure and function of nucleic acids has greatly stimulated research in this field.

See also CELL; GENETICS; METABOLISM; PROTEINS.

NUCLEOPROTEINS [nū-klē-ō-prō′tēnz], large complex combinations of proteins and nucleic acids, found in all living cells. They apparently form part of the chromosomes, the cell structures involved in cell reproduction and in the transmission of inherited characteristics. Viruses are known to be composed of nucleoproteins.
See also NUCLEIC ACIDS.

NUTRITION [nū-trĭsh′ən], that branch of biology which deals with the relation of food substances to body function and health.

Concepts of nutrition have evolved from those of primitive man, who believed that the courage of the lion and the strength of the bull resided in their flesh and could be assimilated by eating their meat, to the sophisticated biochemistry of modern nutritionists, who recognize the relative energy values of foods and the role of vitamins in facilitating chemical reactions in the tissues.

Uses of Food

From the moment the egg is fertilized the organism must take in substances needed for energy, growth, and the chemical and physiological reactions which maintain life.

Energy. The body is in a sense a machine, and, like all machines, requires energy to function. The ultimate source of our energy is sunlight. Green plants capture the energy of sunlight and store it in carbohydrates (starches and sugars), the principal energy-yielding food.

Growth. In youth the body needs raw material to manufacture new tissue and in adult life it must continually repair its existing structures. The elements for growth and repair are supplied in protein.

Metabolism. This word describes the numerous complex reactions which underlie energy production, growth, and all the internal activities of the body; from the conduction of nerve impulses and the contraction of muscle to the transporting of oxygen through the blood and the secretions of hormones. These reactions are made possible by various vitamins and minerals, which, although required in comparatively small amounts, are nevertheless indispensable to life.

Essential Nutrients

The essential nutrients consist of those substances which the body needs and which it can obtain only from food.

Proteins are primarily tissue-building substances which

are found in meats, milk, eggs, and cereals. Proteins are composed of nitrogen-containing amino acids. The great variety of proteins found in all living things represent different combinations of about 22 amino acids, much in the same way as the different words of a language are constructed from varying arrangements of the letters of the alphabet. Many of these amino acids can be manufactured in the body if they are not available in the diet. Eight amino acids, which cannot be synthesized by the body, are called "essential." The proteins found in cereals lack one or more of these essential acids, and for this reason are called "incomplete."

Proteins are found in all body tissues, forming a large part of muscles, as well as bone, cartilage, and skin. Proteins also serve specialized functions: one group of protein molecules, called antibodies, circulate in the blood where they intercept bacterial invaders. Protein can also be used as a source of energy.

Carbohydrates are manufactured by green plants from carbon dioxide and water, using the energy of sunlight. The simpler carbohydrates are sugars, such as sucrose (cane or beet sugar) and lactose (milk sugar). The complex carbohydrates are starches, compounded of sugar units.

Carbohydrates are the principal energy-yielding substances in the diet, being found in cereals, vegetables, and fruits. We eat much processed sugar in the form of soft drinks, candy, ice cream, and similar foods. Carbohydrate-rich foods such as bread, cake, rice, spaghetti, and potatoes also form a major part of our diet.

Fats, or lipids, are a diverse group of compounds found in vegetables (olive oil, corn oil, wheat germ oil), dairy products (milk, cheese, eggs), fish, nuts, and meats. Fats yield over twice the energy of carbohydrates when processed by the body and form an important energy reserve when stored as fatty tissue. There is evidence that a number of fatty acids are essential and that their absence leads to skin abnormalities.

Fats, proteins, and carbohydrates taken in excess of the body's needs may be converted into fatty tissue and stored under the skin, in the abdomen, and around certain organs, such as the kidneys and ovaries.

Minerals

Calcium is the most abundant mineral in the body, comprising up to 2% of the adult's body weight, most of it found in the bones and teeth. Calcium is essential for blood clotting, for the action of certain enzymes, and for the normal contraction and relaxation of muscles.

Milk is the best source of calcium. Certain cheeses, such as Swiss or American, contain as much calcium per ounce as a cup of milk; others, such as cottage or cream cheese, contain much less.

Calcium absorption may be interfered with by spinach, chard, rhubarb, and by certain other foods which contain oxalic acid. This acid combines with calcium to form the insoluble calcium oxalate, which cannot be absorbed into the body.

In many areas where milk is in short supply, calcium deficiency is an important health problem. This may lead to osteomalacia, or softening of the bones.

Phosphorus and calcium are found in close association in the body. As with calcium, 80% to 90% of the phosphorus is contained in the bones and teeth. This element is essential to every cell as it forms part of compounds involved in energy-producing reactions.

Iodine forms an essential part of the thyroid hormone which controls the pace of body activity. The small amount of iodine required (0.2 to 0.3 mg.) is supplied by the ordinary diet. However, in certain areas of the world, such as Switzerland, the iodine content of the water, soil, and food is low, resulting in iodine deficiency and goiter (an enlargement of the thyroid gland). In such regions, children may suffer from cretinism, a condition of retarded growth and mental development resulting from a congenital undersupply of thyroid hormone.

Iron is necessary for the formation of hemoglobin, the red, oxygen-carrying pigment of the blood, which contains three-quarters of the body's iron. Iron is also stored in the liver, bone marrow, and spleen. The principal iron-containing foods of the diet are meat, poultry, fish, cereal products, and vegetables. Since only about 10% of the iron in food is absorbed into the body, the daily requirement of 1 to 2 mg. can be met by 10 to 20 mg. of food iron. Inadequate iron intake may lead to iron-deficiency anemia, such as is occasionally seen in young children and infants who subsist primarily on milk (which is low in iron).

Sodium, Potassium, and Chlorine. Sodium and chlorine are provided in common table salt (sodium chloride). Together with potassium they perform a number of vital functions which include regulation of the water balance between the cells and the body fluids and participation in muscle and nerve function, hormonal activity, and acid-base balance.

Salt is present in many foods and, because of taste preferences, is often consumed in excess. Fortunately, the body is able to excrete surplus salt in the urine.

Magnesium is important for the functioning of several enzymes. Low serum magnesium levels have been associated with muscle twitching and tremors.

Other substances which seem to play a role in human metabolism include manganese, sulfur, zinc, molybdenum, and cobalt. Little is known about the exact human requirement for these materials and the consequence of an inadequate supply.

Vitamins

The vitamins are a group of organic compounds which are needed in small quantities for the health of the organism. Although vitamins cannot be manufactured by the body and must be obtained in the diet, some, such as vitamin K, are synthesized by bacteria in the intestine. As a result, a vitamin K deficiency might arise, not from inadequate dietary intake but from interference with the normal bacterial population of the intestine. Such deficiencies have been reported following the use of antibiotics.

Vitamins act as chemical impresarios. They initiate and speed up essential chemical reactions in the tissues. Among other things vitamins are important for normal vision and bone growth (vitamin A), calcium absorption (vitamin D), blood clotting (vitamin K), and nerve function (vitamin B_1).

The vitamins are usually grouped into the fat-soluble (vitamins A, K, D, and E), and the water-soluble (B-com-

NUTRITION

plex, vitamin C). The distinction is important in terms of absorption and storage. The fat-soluble vitamins depend for absorption upon the special digestive mechanisms which exist for this purpose. In certain disorders fat absorption is impaired and deficiencies of the fat-soluble vitamins may be seen. The fat-soluble vitamins are also generally stored more effectively in the body than the water-soluble group, enabling the body to tide itself over periods of short supply.

Vitamins or Non-vitamins? A number of substances have been shown to be essential for the well-being of experimental animals, but their vital role in human nutrition remains questionable. One such compound is para-aminobenzoic acid, which is an essential growth factor for chicks and rats. The so-called "lipotropic" substances are apparently involved in fat metabolism: accumulations of fat in the livers of experimental animals have been observed in the absence of some of these materials, such as choline and methionine (an amino acid). It has not been proven, however, that these compounds are essential for the prevention of fatty liver in man.

Nutrition in Disease

The obvious relation between nutrition and disease is that of inadequate supply of a necessary element in the diet. In addition, there are disorders in which the diet is adequate, but the needed nutrient cannot be taken into the body. Finally, there are nutritional diseases caused by an oversupply of necessary food substances.

Vitamin Deficiencies. In certain parts of the world cereals are processed in such a way as to remove those portions of the grain which are rich in thiamine (vitamine B_1). Individuals who subsist largely on rice therefore develop beriberi, a deficiency disease marked by muscle weakness, disturbances of nerve function, accumulations of fluid in the tissues (edema), and heart involvement.

An ancient scourge of sailors was scurvy, caused by lack of vitamin C. The lack of fresh, vitamin-C-rich fruits on long sea voyages resulted in weakness, spongy gums and loose teeth, swollen tender joints, and hemorrhage into various joints. The English term "Limey" for sailor came into use following the British navy's introduction of limes into the sailor's diet for the purpose of preventing scurvy. Today scurvy, when found, is usually seen in the very young or among the elderly who live and cook alone and do not consume enough citrus fruit.

Absence of nicotinic acid, or niacin, in the diet causes pellagra, which affects the skin, digestive tract, and nervous system. This disease was formerly widespread in Europe, Egypt, and in the southeastern part of the United States. Niacin can be manufactured in the body from the amino acid tryptophan and deficiency can be avoided if enough tryptophan-containing proteins are included in the diet. Patients with pellagra often subsist on a diet based chiefly on corn and other incomplete proteins.

Children who receive insufficient amounts of vitamin D and little sunshine (which induces the formation of vitamin D in the skin) develop the characteristic bone deformities of rickets. In the absence of vitamin D, calcium absorption from the intestines declines and the bones do not receive their normal mineral support.

A few other vitamin deficiencies include night blindness, from lack of vitamin A. Skin and tongue disturbances in adults, and convulsive seizures and anemia in infants caused by pyridoxine deficiency; and underproduction of red blood cells from lack of folic acid.

Protein Deficiency. Kwashiorkor is an African word (meaning "red") which describes the reddish cast of the skin and hair of Negro infants suffering from a severe amino acid deficiency. This disease is a major health problem of young children among the poorer populations of Africa, India, South and Central America, and Asia. Characteristic symptoms include retarded growth, apathy, accumulation of fluids in the tissues (edema), and bleaching, loss of, and sparseness of the hair. The condition is often fatal unless substantial amounts of high-quality proteins are added to the diet.

Deficiency Disease from Inadequate Absorption. A unique form of vitamin deficiency occurs in pernicious anemia. Vitamin B_{12}, which is needed for red blood cell formation, is normally absorbed from the gastrointestinal tract with the aid of a substance called the "intrinsic factor." In pernicious anemia there is a deficiency of both intrinsic factor and hydrochloric acid in the stomach. Vitamin B_{12} is therefore not absorbed and red blood cell production declines. This vitamin also has a role in the metabolism of nerve and brain tissue and consequently neurological changes are seen in pernicious anemia. The condition is treated by giving the patient large amounts of vitamin B_{12} by mouth together with intrinsic factor preparations.

Disease from Excess Vitamin Intake—the Hypervitaminoses. Disorders resulting from overconsumption of vitamins have been observed in the cases of vitamins A and D. Prolonged intake of large amounts of vitamin A may produce enlargement of the liver, bone changes, and dryness and peeling of the skin. Oversupply of vitamin D causes vomiting, headache, diarrhea, and deposition of calcium in some tissues.

Diets

In many disorders physicians apply the principles of nutrition in the form of therapeutic diets, designed to produce a specific effect. In formulating such diets the physician applies the following criteria:

(1) The diet should provide all essential nutrients in adequate amounts.

(2) The diet should be patterned as much as possible after the patient's normal intake.

(3) The diet should consider the patient's activity, work, and exercise.

(4) The food should agree with the patient.

(5) The diet should consist of commonly used foods which are easily prepared and readily available.

(6) Feeding by mouth is preferable, but when the patient cannot, or will not, eat or drink enough, tube feeding may be used. In more serious cases, it may be necessary to introduce nutrients directly into the blood stream through a vein.

Diseases in Which Diet Therapy Is Important. In diabetes mellitus diets may be used to control the carbohydrate intake, and particularly the patient's weight, since it has been shown that obesity can aggravate diabetes.

Diets of bland foods, such as milk, cream, and soft-boiled eggs, are prescribed for peptic ulcer to avoid stimulating the secretion of gastric juice. In cirrhosis of the liver, a diet rich in protein foods is important.

There has been considerable discussion and controversy about the role of diets in the development and treatment of arteriosclerosis, or hardening of the arteries. Various studies have demonstrated that Western countries, which subsist on comparatively high-fat diets, have a significantly greater incidence of this disease than do parts of the Orient in which less fat is consumed. Although this relationship is still argued, many physicians recommend weight control and, particularly, low-fat diets, in controlling the disease. It is suggested that the intake of saturated fats (those with a higher hydrogen content) may be reduced, and that of polyunsaturated fats increased. This may be accomplished by eating less of the visible fats on meat, more lean meats, more fish and fowl, and by substituting skim milk for whole milk, and by using more corn oil, soybean oil, and cottonseed oil in cooking and baking. Reduction of the cholesterol intake, which was once popular, is now not believed to be of great importance in controlling the disease.

Low sodium diets have been used in treating high blood pressure and kidney diseases.

In gout, a form of arthritis, compounds called urates are deposited in and about certain joints. Since the urates are derived from uric acid, and ultimately from purines, many physicians limit the purine intake (although the body can produce urates from other sources) by omitting from the diet purine-rich foods, such as liver, kidney, sweetbreads, brains, heart, anchovies, sardines, gravies, and herring.

Diets rich in iron, proteins, and vitamins are prescribed for patients suffering from anemia to provide the raw materials needed for the manufacture of red blood cells. In allergic conditions the physician uses an elimination diet to isolate the allergy-producing food.

Diets and Weight Loss. Reducing diets are based on a simple and direct relationship between food and body weight. Food provides the body with energy. If more food is taken in than is burned as energy the excess is converted to fat and stored, chiefly under the skin. If less food is taken in than is burned as energy the stored fat is burned to make up the difference.

The energy requirement of the body varies with the person's age, occupation, body, size, and sex. Children require proportionately more food than adults in order to grow. The maximum food needs occur between the ages of 15 and 19. The more active the individual the more food energy is required. A typist needs about 2,500 calories per day to maintain body weight. A carpenter may require 3,500, and a laborer doing heavy manual work perhaps 5,500. The larger the person, the more food is necessary. Men tend to require slightly more food than women.

In dieting to lose weight the principal elements eliminated from the diet are starches, sugar, and fats. Protein-containing foods such as meats, eggs, and fish are stressed, since protein is the least fattening of foods.

Nutrition, Public Health, and Research

The once-prevalent classic deficiency diseases such as rickets, pellagra, and scurvy have all but disappeared in the United States. This decline can be attributed to the improvement in the standard of living of the population as a whole and to the improvement of the nutritive value of foods by artificially enriching them with vitamins. In the last few decades many states have passed laws requiring the addition of prescribed amounts of thiamine, riboflavin, niacin, and iron, to wheat, flour, macaroni, rice, corn meal, and other foods. Milk is fortified with vitamin D, and precooked infant cereals and infant foods are enriched with vitamins and minerals.

With these developments, obesity, rather than malnutrition, promises to become the major "nutritional" disease of the United States. The emphasis on nutritional research has shifted from the study of deficiency diseases to investigations of the role of diet in causing certain chronic and degenerative diseases.

See also METABOLISM; OBESITY; PROTEINS; VITAMINS.

NYSTAGMUS [nĭs-tăg′məs], involuntary, rhythmic, side-to-side, up-and-down, or rotating movements of the eyeballs. Congenital nystagmus is sometimes associated with poor vision resulting from birth defects. Nystagmus occurring later in life usually involves jerking movements which may become worse when the eye is turned in certain directions. It is frequently a sign of disease of the central nervous system, such as multiple sclerosis. There is no treatment for congenital nystagmus; the acquired form is treated by correcting the underlying nervous disease, whenever this is possible.

O

OBESITY [ō-bē′sə-tē] results from an imbalance between the food consumption and the energy requirements of the body. When more food is eaten than is needed for physical energy, the liver converts the excess into fat, most of which is stored beneath the skin. In extremely obese persons this fat layer may be several inches thick. The food-energy imbalance may be caused by increased appetite or by disturbances within the body which lower its energy requirements.

Increased appetite may result from disease or injury of

the appetite center of the brain (in the hypothalamus), or from a lowering of the blood sugar caused by excess secretion of the hormone insulin by the pancreas gland. A decreased secretion of thyroid hormone may cause obesity by lowering body activity. In certain glandular disorders there is a peculiar distribution of fat as in Cushing's syndrome, in which there is excessive secretion of hormones from the cortex, or outerlayer, of the adrenal gland. In this condition fat deposits are confined to the head, neck, and trunk, producing a typical "moon" face and "buffalo hump" back.

Physical disease as a cause of obesity is comparatively rare compared to eating habits and psychological stresses, which constitute the major factors leading to excess weight. Individuals, particularly in prosperous nations such as the United States, tend to carry the habits of food consumption developed in the active period of their youth into middle and old age when the energy output of the body declines. Others turn to eating as a satisfaction to compensate for social or economic frustration, or to relieve anxiety and frustration. Obesity that "runs in families" is more frequently caused by early training in a rich diet and access to a well-stocked pantry than by inherited organic disease.

Consequences of Obesity. The overweight person runs considerable medical hazards. He is susceptible to heart disease, liver ailments, gallstones, arthritis, cancer of the gall bladder, strokes, and diabetes. His activity is restricted and he is more likely to be involved in accidents than persons of normal weight. Every added pound increases his chances for early death.

Treatment. Thyroid extract may be used in cases of hypothyroidism. Severe obesity of psychological origin may require psychotherapy. Whatever the cause, restriction of food intake is essential. A planned diet and a medically supervised program of weight loss is advised to avoid malnutrition and other complications. A number of appetite-suppressing drugs, such as amphetamine, are available to aid the dieter.

See also NUTRITION.

OCCUPATIONAL THERAPY, a health service specialty which uses occupational activity to promote emotional and mental stability and to develop the use of weakened or injured limbs. For these purposes occupational therapists teach creative arts such as wood, metal, leather working and clay modeling; and job skills, such as typing and business machine operation. Most therapists work in hospitals, school clinics, sanitariums, or nursing homes. Training consists of a four-year college course leading to a bachelor's degree with a major in occupational therapy. After graduating and completing a period of clinical training, therapists may take the registration examination given by the American Occupational Therapy Association. Those who pass the examination are entitled to use the initials O.T.R. (Occupational Therapist, Registered) after their names.

OLD AGE, the period during which the human life cycle is drawing toward a conclusion. This phase of life, marked by declining vigor and health, is usually a time of social as well as physical transformation. The elderly person may find his social position changing as he is stripped of his right to make decisions and assume responsibilities and is gradually reduced to the status of a dependent. In modern societies, the onset of old age tends to be very sudden and is usually marked by compulsory retirement at the age of 55, 62, or 65. The social and economic repercussions of compulsory retirement aggravate the onset of old age for the wife as well as for the retired husband.

Societies differ widely in the way in which they define old age and in the age at which they think it begins. The attitude of a society toward old age is influenced in part by the proportion of the total population which older persons constitute. Societies with a small percentage of persons in the upper age levels and with low levels of technological development tend to prize the elderly for their wisdom and experience and to accord them respect and deference.

Societies in which older persons constitute a large proportion of the population and in which the economy is highly industrialized and dependent on the maintenance of a high level of productivity by working members of the group tend to regard the elderly as an economic burden. Under these circumstances there is much discussion of an "old age problem," of the "economic drain" which the elderly place upon the system, and of the slower progress which is made because of the conservatism of older citizens, who not only constitute an important group of voters, but who also control the major portion of the wealth available for investment and economic expansion.

In the United States and in most other Western nations the increase in the expectation of life resulting from medical advances, which have reduced death rates in all age groups from birth to 65, is increasing the number of elderly persons. Accompanied by lower birth rates, this also increases the proportion of the population which the aged make up. In the United States in 1960, 8.6% of a total population of 179,300,000, or nearly 16,000,000 persons, were 65 years of age or over. This figure was expected to increase to 10% or 12% of the total population of the United States by 1970.

Social and Economic Problems of Aging

Medical Care. The diseases of old age are chronic and require vast amounts of medical care and extensive hospital facilities and equipment. Various plans have been advanced to provide some type of protection against the financial disaster which often results from paying for medical care out of savings or retirement income. There is an increasing awareness that some provision must also be made for persons surviving into old age who lack the funds to pay for any medical care.

Pension Plans. Existing pension plans, including the federal old age pension system, often provide incomes which are not large enough to maintain retired persons. Other types of plans have been proposed whereby workers and their employers at all levels will be helped to save for retirement.

Housing. Elderly people, especially married couples, prefer to maintain separate households as long as they are physically and economically able to do so. The homes in which they raised their families are often too large, poorly located, too expensive to maintain, and not properly equipped for occupancy by elderly people. Living in homes for the aged or other institutions is unacceptable to many elderly persons. The problem of rehousing the retired portion of the population will require the construction of suitable accommodations at costs which persons on diminished incomes can afford.

Employment. To working men and women in good health, the sudden loss of employment by forced retirement is a situation to which it is difficult to adjust. There is a growing agitation for employment programs which would utilize the knowledge and skills of such workers on a part-time or consultant basis.

Social Activities. Many elderly persons find that the onset of old age means a sharp decline in the number and variety of their social contacts with the general population, a situation which causes acute unhappiness and maladjustment. Herding the senior citizens into "retirement villages" where they are isolated from the main stream of national and community life, and where they can socialize with each other mainly on the basis of their common medical problems and their boredom, does not appear to be a constructive solution to their problem.

Some sociologists believe that new programs are less important than a change in society's attitude toward older persons. They point out that part of the desire to isolate the elderly is due to the emphasis on youth in American society. The rejection of the aged is thus interpreted as an indication of society's dread of aging and death.

Geriatrics—The Medical Problems of the Aged

The medical specialty which deals with the problems of aging is called geriatrics.

The Phenomenon of Aging. Although knowledge of the basic mechanisms of aging is still lacking, theories are plentiful. Some theories attempt to explain aging as an evolutionary device which promotes the survival and welfare of the species. One such theory considers aging to be one of the means by which the survival of the species is insured, since the loss of reproductive power in old age guarantees that unfavorable changes in the tissues will not be passed on to future generations. Another evolutionary theory proposes that aging serves to restrict the growth and size of animals, thus improving efficiency. Another is that aging is simply an omission in the basic design of animals—nature provides a plan of growth and development for the organisms which enables them to reach the reproductive age, but beyond this point the animal is more or less on its own.

According to the "autointoxication" theory, aging results from the accumulation of certain materials within the cells. The "wear and tear" theory proposes that an organism, like a clock or motor, wears out because of the failure of its parts—such as the glands and the nervous system. The stress theory holds that aging develops as the limited energies of the organism are gradually reduced by repeated stressful experiences.

The Diseases of Old Age. It has been observed that elderly persons tolerate infections poorly. The skin becomes paper-thin and dry and susceptible to disease. Vision tends to fail as some of the structures of the eye lose their flexibility and become unable to make the adjustments which were possible earlier in life. Cataracts, an opacification of the transparent lens of the eye, is most commonly found in elderly people and may cause blindness. Some degree of arthritis, resulting from wear and tear and degenerative changes, is found in most people over 60.

Atherosclerosis, or hardening of the arteries, and heart disease are major forms of disability found in the aged. The arteries become plugged with deposits of fatlike substances which interfere with normal circulation. When the arteries which supply the heart muscle become clogged, heart disease results. Atherosclerosis of the arteries of the legs causes coldness, pins-and-needles sensations, and cramps of the leg muscles when walking.

Some of the changes seen in old age result from a decrease in the activity of the vital endocrine glands, which control the rate of bodily activity and the sexual functions. The menopause, or "change of life," results from a decline in the activity of the ovaries.

Rejuvenation. An ancient therapy for lost sexual vigor consisted of eating the reproductive organs of animals. In the 19th century a physician injected himself with extracts of dog testicles to produce the same effect. Many other attempts were made using male and female sex hormones. In the early part of this century various operations involving the male reproductive organs were designed to restore sexual potency. In one such operation the testes of a young chimpanzee were grafted into a human male.

More recently, some European physicians have attempted to revitalize tissues by injecting cells taken from the organs of young animals into the corresponding organs of human beings. A Rumanian physician claimed that she could reverse the changes associated with aging through the use of procaine injections.

Adapting to Advanced Age. Although in the opinion of most physicians the rejuvenation therapies cited above have failed to offer a specific antidote to aging, the individual by skillfully modifying his living habits can do a great deal to adapt his system for old age. Muscles tend to waste away if not used and should be given moderate exercise, such as walking, to maintain their tone. Mild exercise also helps the functioning of the circulatory system. Vigorous exercise, such as running and mountain climbing, should be avoided.

Diet is important, and it should be recognized that as energy expenditure declines with age, food requirements diminish correspondingly.

Learning capacity need not decline in old age. A noted professor at a large eastern university observed that students up to 70 years of age could learn Russian and shorthand as easily as students in their teens. Intellectual and creative activity can also flower in advanced years, as testified to by the examples of Titian, who painted his great "Battle of Lepanto" when he was 72 years old, and by Galileo, who made his most important astronomical discoveries and published his famous book *Dialogue on the New Sciences* in the eighth decade of his life.

ONCHOCERCIASIS [ŏng-kō-sûr-sī′ə-sĭs], an infection with the worm *Onchocerca volvulus*, which is sometimes called the "blinding filaria." The worm is transmitted by black flies which bite humans. Lumps, or nodules, con-

OPHTHALMIA

taining masses of adult worms develop under the skin, after which large numbers of microfilarias invade the superficial connective tissues of the skin. The eyes are also frequently attacked. In some parts of central Africa and Central and South America large percentages of the population are infected and many suffer from impaired vision or complete and irreversible blindness. Treatment consists of surgical removal of the nodules and the use of drugs to destroy the microfilarias (Hetrazan) and the adult worms (Suramin).
See also FILARIASIS.

OPHTHALMIA [ŏf-thăl′mē-ə], general medical term for inflammation of the eye. Causes include infection (gonorrheal ophthalmia), allergy (spring ophthalmia), and foreign bodies in the eye (caterpillar hair ophthalmia). In sympathetic ophthalmia inflammation develops in one eye some time after the other eye is injured. In such cases early treatment of the injured (or "exciting") eye may prevent further damage to both eyes.

OPHTHALMOSCOPE [ŏf-thăl′mə-skōp], an instrument used to examine the interior of the eye. Invented in 1851 by the German physicist Hermann von Helmholtz, it consists basically of a light source and a prism or mirror which projects the light rays into the eye. The examiner can see the reflected ray coming from the inside of the eye through a small opening in the mirror or prism. A revolving disc containing different lenses is located in front of this opening. By rotating different lenses into position the observer can neutralize the particular distortions of his own eye and that of the subject, enabling him to obtain a clear image of the retina.

OPIUM [ō′pē-əm], dried juice of the white poppy, *Papaver somniferum*. This plant, originally native to Asia Minor, was later cultivated in Egypt, India, Greece, and China as the use of opium spread. One of the oldest drugs known to man, opium has been used since prehistoric times, and for many centuries constituted the only effective means of relieving pain. In 1803 the German pharmacist Sertürner isolated morphine, the principal active ingredient of opium. Later codeine, papaverine, and other opium alkaloids were extracted. Morphine has now largely replaced opium in medical practice.
See also DRUG ADDICTION; HEROIN; MORPHINE.

OPTIC NERVE, bundle of nerve fibers which conduct visual impulses from the eye to the brain. The optic nerve carries nerve impulses from the retina, the light-sensitive structure at the rear of the eye, to the occipital region of the cerebrum at the back of the head. The individual fibers cross at the optic chiasma in such a way that impulses from the right halves of both eyes go to the right hemisphere of the brain, while impulses from the left halves go to the left hemisphere. See EYE.

OPTOMETRY [ŏp-tŏm′ə-trē], the measurement of the visual power of the eyes. The *optometrist* examines the eyes and prescribes eyeglasses, contact lenses, or eye exercises to correct visual defects. His work should be distinguished from that of the *ophthalmologist* (or oculist), who is a licensed physician and may use surgery or drugs to treat eye disorders, and the *optician*, who prepares eyeglasses according to the prescriptions of *ophthalmologists* or optometrists.

Most schools of optometry require two years of pre-optometry training at a recognized university, followed by three or four years of professional training in such subjects as anatomy, physiology, and optics. A doctorate or master's degree is required for teaching positions. The majority of optometrists are in private practice, either for themselves or as assistants to others. Some work in industry, in hospitals and clinics, or in the armed forces, where they hold officer's rank.
See also EYEGLASSES.

ORCHITIS [ôr-kī′tĭs], inflammation of the testis, which occurs most frequently as a complication of mumps in adult males. Approximately 20% of the male adults who contract mumps develop a high fever and painful, swollen, tense, and tender testicles about 5 to 7 days after the illness begins. In about 20% of the cases both testicles are involved. The inflammation usually subsides in from 7 to 10 days. Atrophy of the testicles is frequent, but sterility is uncommon. Cortisone and related drugs tend to relieve the inflammation, but their value in preventing testicular atrophy remains uncertain. A chronic painless orchitis may occur in syphilis, tuberculosis, leprosy, and in certain other infectious diseases.

ORGAN TRANSPLANTATION. In clinical medicine, transplantation of the body's organs and tissues may be attempted to replace or restore functions lost through disease, injury, or old age. Organ and tissue transplants are of three general types: (1) autotransplants, that is, operations in which tissues are taken from one location in a patient's body and implanted elsewhere in his body; (2) allotransplants, that is, procedures in which tissues taken from a donor are grafted into a different individual; and (3) heterotransplants, in which tissues are taken from an animal of one species and transferred to an individual belonging to another species.

All three types of organ transplantation are currently in use. Autografts of nerve, skin, cartilage, tendon, bone, veins, arteries, blood-forming tissues, and other organs are used to repair or replace damaged structures of the body. The body accepts, or has tolerance for, its own tissues. Provided that the graft receives adequate nourishment, it can be expected to function as long in its new as in its former location.

Rejection of Transplants. The body's response to the other types of transplants is usually not so benign, except under special conditions. The same defense mechanisms that the body employs to protect itself from foreign matter, including bacteria and viruses, are activated by an allotransplant or heterotransplant. White blood cells, antibodies, and other special cells attack the graft, ultimately destroying it. This reaction—the "rejection phenomenon"—is perhaps the major unsolved problem in transplantation medicine.

The rejection phenomenon is comparatively mild or even absent (1) if there is close genetic matching of donor and host tissue, as in blood transfusions, and (2) if the body's defense mechanisms are suppressed. To ensure careful matching of donor and host tissue, several methods for testing the compatibility of the two have been developed. The use of these methods enables the physician to estimate the likelihood that a graft will be accepted by the host. To suppress the body's defense mechanisms, steroid hormones and azathioprine, a drug which interferes with the rejection phenomenon, are given to the recipient of the transplant. These immuno-suppressive materials, as they are called, have been shown to prolong the lives of kidney, heart, and other types of transplants—but not with the degree of reliability that would ensure the utilization of transplantation as a routine clinical treatment.

Status of Transplantation. Research efforts, perhaps stimulated by recent experiences with heart and liver transplantation, are being conducted on numerous fronts, contributing not only to transplantation therapy but also to basic biological knowledge. In clinical practice, autografts are used extensively, as previously noted. Among homografts, carried out between individuals of the same species, cornea and cartilage transplants have been performed with reasonable success. Since both of these tissues have virtually no blood supply, their implantation does not excite the body's defense mechanisms, or does so only minimally. This fact may explain the longevity of these grafts. The routine use of blood transfusion is well known. Other homografts are less successful. By far the most experience, and the highest percentage of good results, have been accumulated with kidney transplantation. But here, as also in heart, lung, and liver transplantation, the physician must await further insights emerging from investigations of the rejection phenomenon before the full promise of these lifesaving operations can be achieved. See also KIDNEY TRANSPLANT.

ORTHODONTICS. See DENTISTRY.

ORTHOPEDICS [ôr-thə-pē′dĭks], the medical specialty that deals with the structures which support and move the body, including the bones, muscles, tendons, ligaments, bursae, fascia, and the nerves and blood vessels which supply them. The orthopedic surgeon treats fractures, dislocations, ruptures of ligaments or muscles, arthritis, poor posture, bone infections, and congenital deformities.

OSMOSIS [ŏz-mō′sĭs], the passage of a fluid through a semipermeable membrane. If a container is divided by such a membrane, and if colored water is poured into one compartment and a solution of sugar and water poured into the other compartment, then the colored water will soon pass through the membrane into the sugar-water solution. This is an example of osmosis. Some of the sugar water also passes into the colored water, but the flow is considerably less than the process just described.

In osmosis the more dilute solution passes into the less dilute solution, thus establishing a preferred direction of flow. The tendency for osmosis to occur is measured by the osmotic pressure of the solution. It increases as the concentration of the solution increases.

Osmosis is an important process in all living cells, the cell wall acting as the semipermeable membrane. In animals osmotic processes are continually in operation. These include the balance of moisture between tissues, blood, and lymph; the supply of nutrients from blood to cells; and the concentration of waste products in the kidneys.

OSTEOARTHRITIS. See ARTHRITIS.

OSTEOCHONDRITIS [ŏs-tē-ō-kŏn-drī′tĭs], a medical term describing a number of conditions in which there is destruction of a limited area of bone, frequently following injury. It is most commonly seen in growing children and may involve the head of the thigh bone (the femur), the knee, or the bones of the foot. Most of these conditions are satisfactorily treated with rest, casts, and Novocain injections. At times surgery is necessary to remove loose bony materials from joints where they interfere with motion.

OSTEOMALACIA [ŏs-tē-ō-mə-lā′shē-ə], abnormal condition of bone, characterized by an abundance of fibrous matrix and cartilage and a marked deficiency of the mineral portions (calcium phosphate) of the bone. This state leads to bone pain, deformity, defects called pseudofractures, and shortening of overall stature. The major defect is an inability of bone to calcify, or harden, which can arise from a variety of causes. Thus, osteomalacia is a sign of other diseases and not truly a disease itself. Some of the disorders which lead to osteomalacia are Vitamin D deficiency (rickets), an inherited resistance to Vitamin D in the usual amounts (Vitamin-D-resistant rickets), malnutrition in general, malabsorption of vitamins and nutrients due to intestinal disease, and defects of kidney function. Treatment varies with the cause of the bone disease and includes dietary supplements.

See also BONE; OSTEOPOROSIS; PARATHYROID GLANDS.

OSTEOMYELITIS [ŏs-tē-ō-mī-ə-lī′tĭs], infection of the bone by microorganisms. The two most common types are blood-borne, or hematogenous osteomyelitis, and tuberculous osteomyelitis.

The hematogenous type is most common in growing children, particularly boys, and usually affects the ends of the long bones, such as the femur of the thigh and the tibia of the leg. Less frequently the spine, pelvis, and other bones are attacked. Many cases begin with an injury or with a pustule or boil on the skin caused by staphylococcus bacteria. The bacteria travel through the blood and settle in the marrow of the bone, causing pain, redness, heat, and swelling in the area of the infection. Muscular spasms limit motion in adjacent joints, and the patient suffers from chills and fever. Treatment is with large doses of antibiotics which may cure the disease in its early phase. If the infection resists antibiotics or becomes firmly entrenched, surgery is necessary to remove the damaged bone and to drain the pus. Despite this, a chronic infection may develop and several operations may be needed.

Tuberculous osteomyelitis follows tubercular infection in other parts of the body, usually the lungs. The spine is affected most frequently, accounting for 40% to 50% of all cases. The disease develops more slowly than in the hematogenous type and the symptoms are less pronounced. Large amounts of pus and debris may accumuate, with surprisingly little disturbance of function.

OSTEOPATHY

Streptomycin, para-aminosalicylic acid, and isoniazid, given singly or in combination, may halt but not cure the disease. In some cases surgery to drain pus, to remove diseased tissue, or to permanently stiffen damaged joints may be necessary. Rest and good nutrition are important.

OSTEOPATHY [ŏs-tē-ŏp′ə-thē], a system of medicine which holds that body structure and function are unified and that health is derived from the body's natural capacity to resist harmful influences. Osteopathic doctors utilize the accepted basic medical tools of diagnosis and treatment, such as drugs, surgery, and X rays, but emphasize the body's natural capacity to resist disease when all of its systems are functioning normally.

The school of osteopathic medicine was founded in the 19th century by Andrew Taylor Still, a frontier medical doctor, who emphasized the attainment of total health rather than a search for a specific cure for each illness. Pursuing his ideas independently, Still opened the first osteopathic college at Kirksville, Mo., in 1892, and in 1894 the first class of 16 men and 3 women graduated.

In the United States doctors of osteopathy are licensed to practice in all states and have the same unlimited practice privileges as medical doctors in 39 states and the District of Columbia.

OSTEOPOROSIS [ŏs-tē-ō-pô-rō′sĭs], disorder of bone caused by decreased matrix and mineral portions. Many bones, but especially the spine, may develop osteoporosis. Bone pain and spontaneous fractures without obvious deformity lead to suspicion of osteoporosis. Old age combined with menopause usually produce osteoporosis. Excessive amounts of thyroid, adrenal, or pituitary hormones may also cause the disorder. Normal bone is continuously broken down and built up. Standing and the pull of muscles on bone are vital for this process of remodeling. Deprived of these stresses, bone dissolves rapidly. Complete bed rest, paralysis, or the prolonged periods without gravity which astronauts experience all cause bone to dissolve. The treatment of osteoporosis is not totally satisfactory. Hormones in low doses, calcium and protein in supplements in the diet, gradually increased exercise, and braces to aid in support are among the methods employed.

OTOSCLEROSIS [ō-tō-sklə-rō′sĭs], a disease of unknown cause in which deposits of bone in the ear cause progressive hearing loss and eventually deafness. Deposits of bone around the stapes, one of the three small bones of the middle ear, fix it in place and prevent it from transmitting sound to the inner ear. Otosclerosis usually begins in young adult life with a loss of sensitivity to deeper-pitched sounds, progressing later to sounds of all frequencies. Women are affected more frequently than men. Hearing aids are effective, and surgery frequently restores natural function. Two types of operation are used: in fenestration a tiny artificial window is made between the middle and inner ear, permitting sound vibrations to pass through; in stapes mobilization the stapes is cut free of the bony deposits.
See also DEAFNESS; EAR.

OVARIES [ō′və-rēz], the female sexual organs. At birth, the ovary contains several hundreds of thousands of primordial follicles, each of which is capable of maturing into a ripe ovum, or egg. The follicles develop under stimulation of a hormone (FSH) secreted by the pituitary gland in the skull. When mature, the ovum escapes from the follicle and the ovary; this is known as ovulation and occurs about midway between menstrual periods. Ordinarily, one ovum is discharged each month.

The ruptured follicle remains in the ovary to become the corpus luteum, or yellow body, and secretes the hormone progesterone, which prevents further eggs from ripening. The corpus luteum degenerates in about 10 days unless the egg is fertilized, in which case it continues to grow and maintains pregnancy through the secretion of progesterone. The ovaries also secrete estrogen, the female sex hormone which regulates the menstrual cycle and stimulates the development of the female sexual characteristics.
See also ENDOCRINE GLANDS; ESTROGENS; MENSTRUATION; PROGESTERONE; REPRODUCTION.

OXYTOCIN [ŏk-sĭ-tō′sĭn], a hormone secreted by the posterior portion of the pituitary gland in the skull. Oxytocin is important during nursing when it causes the smooth muscles of the breast to contract and eject milk. It is apparently released when the pituitary gland is stimulated by brain impulses which arise when the infant nurses at the breast.
See also PITUITARY GLAND.

P

PAGET'S DISEASE [păj′ĭts], also known as osteitis deformans, a chronic bone disease of unknown cause. It occurs principally in individuals over the age of 35. Men are affected more often than women. The bones of the pelvis, skull, spine, and thigh are most frequently affected, becoming thickened, enlarged, painful and deformed. A distinctive feature of the disease is increased blood flow through the diseased bones. The weakened bones may fracture easily under comparatively slight stress. Other complications are an increased susceptibility to bone cancer and heart failure. There is no specific treatment.

PAIN, sensation causing distress or suffering. Nerves carry messages of various sensations, including touch, pressure, position, temperature, and pain, to the spinal cord. They travel to the brain where they are sorted and interpreted and action decided upon.

How Pain Travels. Unlike the nerves, which carry other sensations, pain nerves are naked fibers which begin as loops. Each fiber joins with many others to form trunks. The spinal cord is the main trunk and carries thousands of these fibers. Each fiber carries its individual message from a particular region of the body. As the message travels to the upper spinal cord it enters a nerve network, called the reticular formation, where it begins to enter consciousness. An actual feeling of pain does not take place until the message travels to the great receiving area of the brain, called the thalamus. Here the source of pain is recognized and the message is switched to an appropriate part of the cerebral cortex for interpretation, processing, and reaction. Now the full message of pain is realized and the person is fully aware of his pain and its location. The reaction to an individual pain message varies as it is compared automatically with stored memories of other sensations and reactions, and as learned emotional responses are drawn forth. All the data are gathered to interpret the pain's intensity. Then reactions are decided upon. The stoic may decide to disregard his pain, the highly sensitive individual will scream in anguish.

Where Pain Arises. Caused by many types of stimuli, pain is the symptom which most often leads patients to the doctor, who searches for its source. Superficial pain, as on the skin, is easily pinpointed. Pain originating within the body in hollow organs or joints may be accurately localized, but such pain is often "referred" to other areas, because information about the pain's source is misinterpreted at the reticular formation or thalamic level. For example, the pain of early appendicitis may be referred to the middle of the upper abdomen, rather than felt in the right lower abdomen. A diseased upper molar may produce earache, as may some throat infections. A diseased hip is often felt as knee pain. And irritation or stimulation anywhere along the course of a pain fiber may be misinterpreted as arising at its end point. Phantom limb pain is an example of this phenomenon. After leg amputation, a patient may feel great pain apparently arising in the lost foot. Causalgia, a severe persistent pain, and the very sharp pain of neuritis, as in shingles, are other examples of pain due to injury and inflammation of the nerve fiber or trunk. Pressure on a nerve root from injury to a spinal disc causes the pain called sciatica.

Pain as Protector. Pain fibers—unlike other sensory fibers—are not selective. They respond to any type of stimulus intense enough to cause or threaten injury. The delicate ends of pain nerve loops lie by the myriad just under skin and mucosal surfaces, and in blood vessels and hollow organs, but only the capsule, or outer covering of solid organs, such as the liver and kidney, contain pain loops. If the body lacked these tiny sensitive "pain windows," we could be stabbed or burned without feeling pain at all, nor would physical ills, such as arthritis, appendicitis, or angina, cause pain. The distribution of pain fibers is not uniform. Pain loops are most numerous in body parts most sensitive to injury. The tip of the nose and palm of the hand have only 40–70 of these endings per square centimeter, but the groin has 200 per square centimeter. An identical blow to the sole of the foot, the groin, and the eye would be painless on the sole, painful in the groin, and very painful to the eye. The fragile eye is thus protected by possessing many more pain-sensitive nerve endings.

It is now obvious that no matter how unpleasant, pain is an extremely important sensation which the body uses to protect itself from injury and illness. The pain of angina tells the patient with heart disease he has exercised enough, or eaten or worried too much, and must stop for a rest. Pain is the symptom that often reveals underlying diseases which might otherwise remain concealed. The mechanism of the pain which arises inside our bodies is not clear. Cutting or piercing does not cause pain, but pressure, chemical irritation, stretching, and inflammation do cause pain.

Pain Threshold and Intensity. The reaction to a given pain stimulus, and how its intensity is interpreted, varies from individual to individual and, at different times, in the same individual.

Both the threshold and the intensity of pain may be altered in several ways. Soldiers in battle and athletes in intense competition may not feel severe or serious injuries until their attention is directed to them. Pain may be felt more acutely when one is anxious or depressed. When awareness is redirected, as in hypnosis, even surgery may be performed without anesthesia and without significant pain. Childbirth may also be made painless under hypnosis by a physician skilled in its use. Each individual's pain threshold tends to be fairly constant, but may be altered at times by awareness and anxiety. Prolonged severe pain lowers one's threshold of pain, as may excessive concern about one's state of health (hypochondriasis). Mental illness commonly raises the pain threshold by drilling perception or interpretation of pain.

How Pain Is Relieved. Relief of pain may be accomplished in a number of ways. The most important is to remove its cause, by medical or surgical means. The pain threshold can be raised by analgesics, such as aspirin, morphine, and codeine. One may temporarily block the nerve fiber's ability to carry messages with a local anesthetic, for instance, by local, temporary freezing, when suturing or in dental work. A spinal anesthetic temporarily "freezes" the whole spinal cord at the desired level. Attention may be redirected with the use of counterirritants, such as mustard plaster or oil of wintergreen, or by hypnosis. Considerable research has been done on effective types of distraction, such as music, and static noise, sounds called white sound, and visual stimuli, to reduce pain sensation. Pain conduction can also be reduced or stopped by surgical or chemical destruction of the main nerve trunk. Rarely, pain fibers are cut at the point where they enter the spinal cord in a very delicate operation called a rhizotomy. Of more academic interest than practical importance is leukotomy, surgical severing of nerve fibers leading to the cortex of the brain. After such sur-

THE NATURE OF PAIN

Pain is a warning signal that some part of the body is being injured, stretched, compressed, or in some other way being abnormally acted on. Despite the fact that pain is among the most common of human experiences, comparatively little is known about it. The nerve pathways which conduct pain impulses, the way in which pain is recognized as coming from specific tissues, and the factors affecting the experienced quality of pain, are still in doubt.

Artist: Leonard Dank

THE PERCEPTION OF PAIN

The experience of pain involves not only the recognition that a part of the body hurts, but also a feeling or emotional reaction that dominates consciousness.

The arrows indicate roughly the pain pathways in the brain. The gray arrows represent the passage of pain impulses to the higher regions of the brain (the cerebral cortex). The white arrows trace the radiation of pain to subcortical structures which may be involved in the feeling quality associated with pain

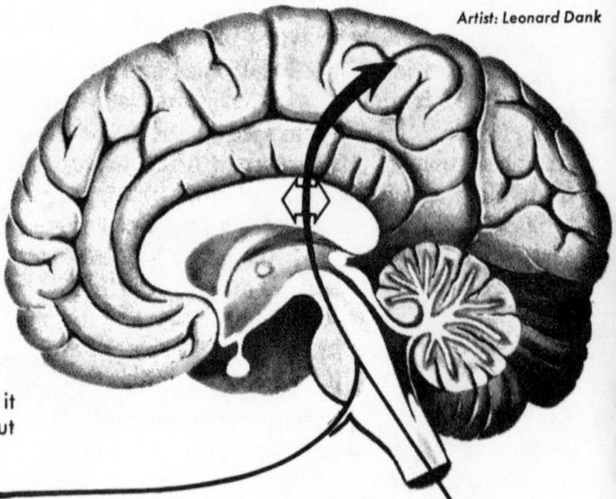

HOW PAIN IS PRODUCED

One of the differences between pain and other sensations is the way in which it is activated. The eye is stimulated only by light, and the ear only by sound, but pain impulses can be produced in several ways.

The pain of a toothache is caused by fluid swellings within the bony canal of the tooth. The throbbing pain develops as the nerve endings are compressed by each beat of the pulse which drives blood into the inflamed and swollen canal.

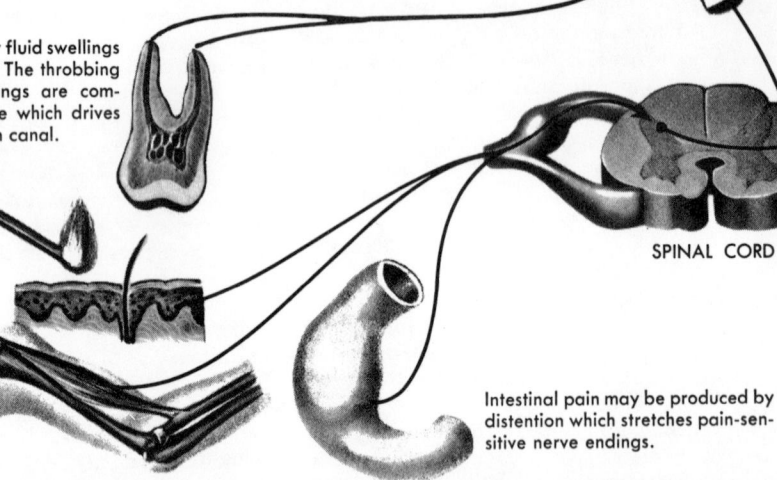

Skin pain may be caused by intense heat, cold, or mechanical injury to the skin.

SPINAL CORD

Muscle pain may be caused by the liberation of certain chemical substances into the tissues following vigorous exercise.

Intestinal pain may be produced by distention which stretches pain-sensitive nerve endings.

THE PROBLEM OF PAIN IN THE WRONG PLACES — "REFERRED" PAIN

In a number of disorders involving the deep tissues, pain appears some distance from the actual source of irritation. This phenomenon, known as "referred" pain, is important in medical diagnosis.

SOME EXAMPLES OF "REFERRED" PAIN

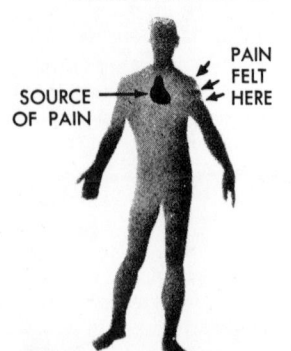

SOURCE OF PAIN
PAIN FELT HERE

In certain heart conditions pain is felt in the left arm.

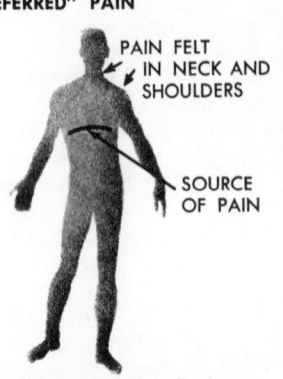

PAIN FELT IN NECK AND SHOULDERS
SOURCE OF PAIN

In disorders of the diaphragm pain may be experienced in the neck and shoulders.

SOME PROPOSED EXPLANATIONS

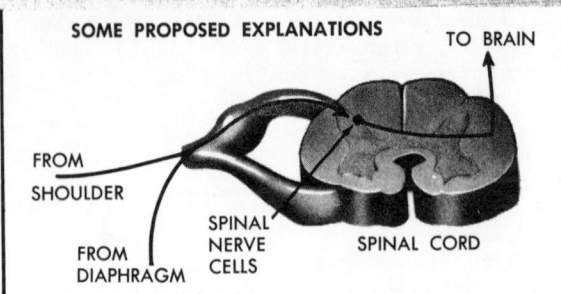

TO BRAIN
FROM SHOULDER
FROM DIAPHRAGM
SPINAL NERVE CELLS
SPINAL CORD

In the diagram above, it can be seen that nerve impulses from the shoulder and diaphragm enter the spinal cord at the same level. It is believed that impulses from the diaphragm may stimulate spinal nerve cells that normally relay nerve impulses from the shoulder. Messages from the spinal cells may then proceed to the brain along the pathways for shoulder pain. A second possibility is that the impulses from the diaphragm and shoulder share common nerve pathways in the brain and spinal cord. In this case the brain would interpret pain impulses from the diaphragm as coming from the shoulder, since pain from this region is more common.

PANCREAS

gery, pain is felt but no longer bothers the patient. Leukotomy severs association traits, so that past experiences, interpretations, responses, and emotional reactions no longer aid in the interpretation and reaction to pain. See also NERVOUS SYSTEM.

PALATE [păl'ĭt], the roof of the mouth, composed of the bony hard plate in front, which separates the mouth and nasal cavities, and the soft palate in the rear. The movable soft palate is raised during eating and swallowing to seal off the nose and mouth cavities. Movements of the soft palate are important in the production of speech. See also CLEFT PALATE.

PANCREAS [păn'krē-əs], a gland located in the abdominal cavity behind the stomach and liver. The pancreas may be described as a double gland: like the sweat and salivary glands, it is an exocrine gland which secretes through a duct; and like the thyroid and adrenal glands, it is an endocrine gland which pours secretions (hormones) directly into the blood stream.

The acinar cells of the pancreas secrete enzymes which are important in the digestion of fats, proteins, and carbohydrates. These secretions are increased by food substances and stomach acids which cause the small intestine to release hormones (secretin and pancreozymin) into the blood to stimulate the pancreas. Secretion may also be

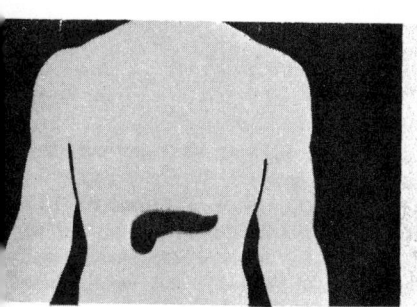

THE PANCREAS—A DOUBLE GLAND

The pancreas contains two types of glandular cells: the *acinar* cells are *exocrine* glands which pour their secretions into ducts; the islet cells are *endocrine* glands that empty their secretions directly into the blood stream.

Artist: Leonard Dank

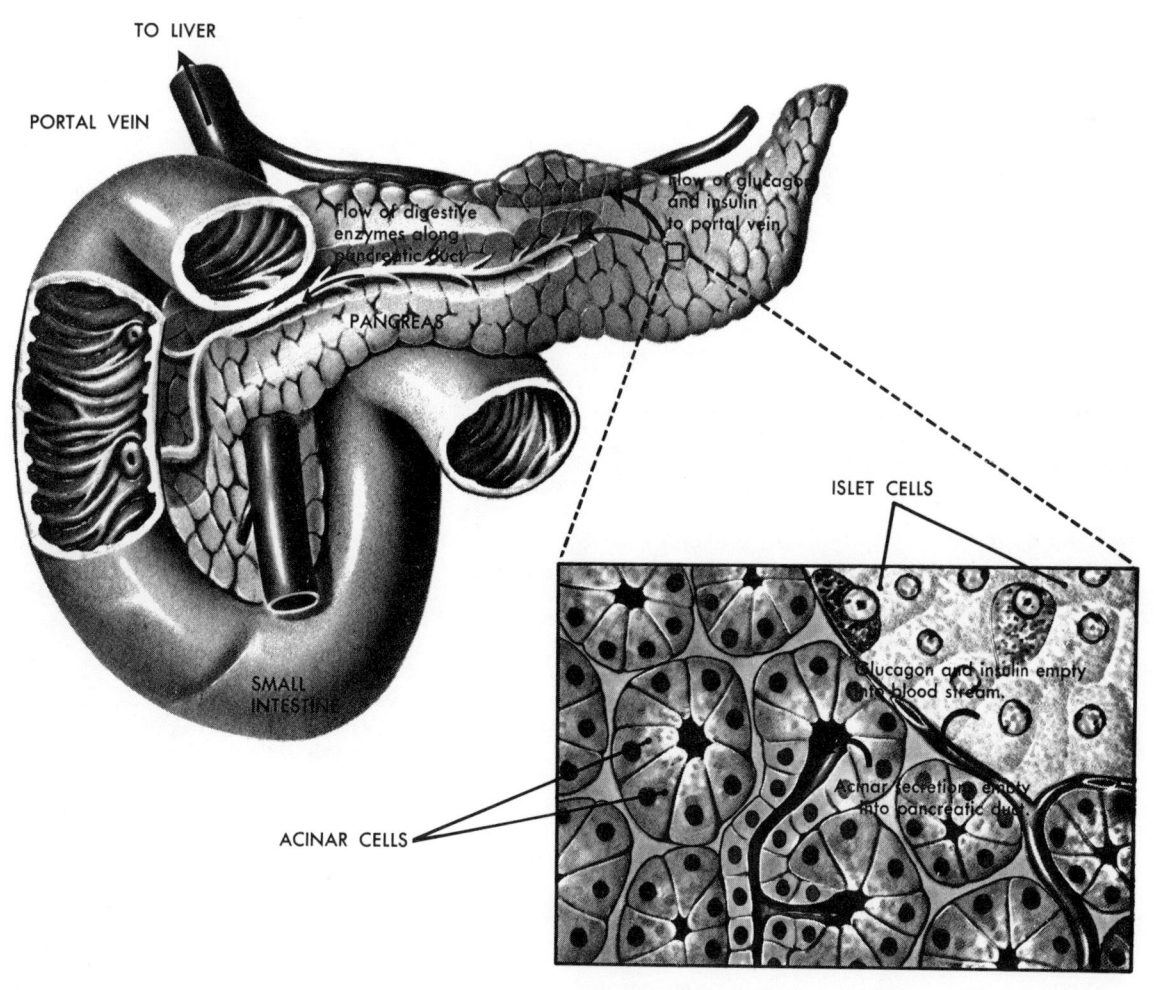

TO LIVER
PORTAL VEIN
Flow of digestive enzymes along pancreatic duct
Flow of glucagon and insulin to portal vein
PANCREAS
SMALL INTESTINE

ISLET CELLS
Glucagon and insulin empty into blood stream.
Acinar secretion empty into pancreatic duct
ACINAR CELLS

AN ENLARGED CROSS SECTION OF THE PANCREAS

THE ACINAR CELLS OF THE PANCREAS AND DIGESTION
The pancreas is a major source of digestive enzymes which break down carbohydrates, fats, and proteins into simpler substances that can be absorbed by the body. The enzymes empty into the small intestine. The flow of pancreatic enzymes is stimulated by the sight and smell of food which activate nerve pathways that lead from the brain to the pancreas. As the meal is digested further stimulation occurs when food substances reach the intestines and stimulate the flow of intestinal hormones that act on the pancreas.

THE ISLET CELLS OF THE PANCREAS AND THE UTILIZATION OF SUGAR
The pancreatic hormones *glucagon* and *insulin* regulate the utilization of sugar by the body. These substances are produced by the α and β cells respectively of the islet of Langerhans. Insulin lowers blood sugar concentration by promoting passage of sugar from the blood into the cells. Glucagon raises the blood sugar by stimulating release of sugar from the liver into the blood. A partial or complete inadequacy of insulin occurs in diabetes mellitus. In diabetes the body is unable to properly burn sugar (carbohydrates) as a fuel and uses proteins and fats instead. This causes derangements of body chemistry that produce the signs and symptoms of the disease.

increased by nervous stimulation, but this seems to be less important than hormonal regulation. The pancreatic juice flows through ducts into the small intestine. In some diseases in which pancreatic secretion is blocked or impaired, digestion is affected. This is particularly true of fat digestion, since the pancreas is the major source of a fat-splitting enzyme. In such conditions, undigested fat is passed in the feces, rendering them bulky and foul-smelling. Absorption of the fat-soluble vitamins A, D, E, and K may also be reduced, causing symptoms of vitamin deficiency.

The endocrine secretions of the pancreas are the hormones glucagon and insulin which are produced respectively by the α and β cells of the islet tissue. Glucagon increases the quantity of sugar in the blood while insulin lowers it. Insulin increases the utilization of sugar by the tissues and is also important for growth. Partial or complete inadequacy of insulin results in diabetes mellitus. *See also* DIABETES MELLITUS; DIGESTION; INSULIN.

PANCREATITIS [păng-krē-ə-tī′tĭs], inflammation of the pancreas. The cause of pancreatitis is not completely understood. However, it is known to be associated frequently with gallstones and it is believed that it may be caused by obstruction of the common channel through which bile and pancreatic juice empty into the intestine. It is more common in alcoholics. Acute pancreatitis may produce swelling of the pancreas, or hemorrhage and destruction of the pancreatic tissue. Severe abdominal pain is common, along with vomiting, fever, and distension of the abdomen. The symptoms apparently result from the destructive action of pancreatic enzymes which have escaped from their normal channels. The condition may be fatal. In some cases repeated attacks cause chronic pancreatitis and calcification, eventually leading to interruption of pancreatic function and diabetes. Treatment is directed at relieving pain and distension, inhibiting pancreatic secretion, replacing lost fluids, and preventing infection. Surgery in chronic cases is sometimes attempted to relieve obstructions to the flow of pancreatic juice. *See also* DIABETES MELLITUS; DIGESTION; PANCREAS.

PAPANICOLAOU'S [pa-pə-nĭk′ə-louz] **STAIN or PAP** [păp] **SMEAR**, a test for cancer of the womb named after its discoverer, George Nicholas Papanicolaou (1883–1962), a Greek-born American physician. The smear is obtained through a simple, painless procedure in which a wooden spatule is introduced into the vagina to remove fluid mixed with uterine cells. The material is then spread on a glass slide, dyed, and examined under the microscope. Through this procedure cancer may be detected and treated before it endangers the patient's life.

PARALYSIS [pə-răl′ə-sĭs], loss of the ability to move a part of the body at will. This "motor" paralysis may result from injury to, or disease of, the nerves which control muscle movement; from diseases of the muscles themselves; or from hysteria, a psychiatric disorder in which emotional conflicts are expressed in various physical disturbances. Interference with nerve function may also cause a "sensory" paralysis, an absence of normal sensation in a part of the body (*see* NEURITIS).

Motor paralysis caused by nerve disturbances may be "spastic," in which the muscles are tightly contracted, or "flaccid," in which the affected part is limp.

The type of paralysis depends upon which nerve fibers and cells are involved. Normally, the muscles are moved voluntarily by impulses which originate in the brain and travel through the spinal cord to the muscle. The brain also exerts a restraining influence on the nerve cells of the spinal cord which directly control the muscles (the motor cells). If the nerve pathway from the brain to the motor cells is interrupted, the brain loses control over the motor cells and the muscle goes into spasm (spastic paralysis). A flaccid paralysis develops when the motor nerve cell, or the fibers connecting this cell to the muscle, are affected.

Spastic paralysis may begin at birth from brain injury (as in cerebral palsy); or develop later from injury, infection, or tumor of the brain or spinal cord; or from a "stroke," a sudden disturbance of blood circulation in the brain or spinal cord.

Flaccid paralysis results from tumor, injury, or infection within the spinal column, or disease of the nerves leading from the spinal cord to the muscles. Muscle diseases such as muscular dystrophy or myasthenia gravis, may also cause paralysis of this type. A well-known form of flaccid paralysis occurs in poliomyelitis, in which the motor cells of the spinal cord are damaged.

Since the spinal cord contains fibers from both the brain and motor cells, spinal involvement can cause spastic paralysis in one part of the body, and flaccid paralysis in another.

If the paralysis is all on one side, the condition is called hemiplegia. If both legs are affected it is called paraplegia. Quadriplegia involves paralysis of both arms and both legs. Depending on the nerve affected, the muscles used in speaking, breathing, swallowing, and in bladder and bowel control may also be paralyzed.

The prospects for recovery depend upon the cause. Surgical removal of a tumor pressing on a nerve can produce complete return of movement. In infections, such as polio, recovery depends to a great extent on the amount of nerve tissue destroyed.

See also NERVOUS SYSTEM; POLIOMYELITIS.

PARANOIA [păr-ə-noi'ə], a mental disorder characterized by the gradual development of firm delusions which become the center of the individual's life. It develops in persons usually in their late forties who are sometimes described as "paranoid" personality types, being suspicious, rigid, resentful, and socially unhappy individuals who lack understanding of their own problems. Comparatively few paranoid personalities actually develop true paranoia. While pure paranoia is rare, paranoid symptoms may appear as aspects of other mental disorders, such as schizophrenia. The illness generally takes four forms:

Delusions of Persecution. The patient may feel that his life is in danger from organized plots against him. Such beliefs tend to isolate the individual from the community, causing him to lead a fear-ridden existence.

Delusions of Grandeur. This may be viewed as another aspect of ideas of persecution. The paranoiac reasons: "If I am persecuted then I must be someone of importance." He has an exalted idea of his abilities and may even identify himself with famous persons.

Litigious Type. The patient often reaches the psychiatrist via a long path of lawyers whom he has enlisted to argue his case against those he believes to have wronged him. In such cases, the paranoid person may consider himself to be persecuted by former employers, the local government, or various organizations.

Erotic Type. Such an individual believes that he or she is the object of someone's affections. Frequently a prominent member of the community or a movie star is chosen.

There is no known cure for paranoia. Most patients are permanently hospitalized.

PARAPLEGIA [păr-ə-plē'jē-ə], paralysis of both legs. This may be caused by infections, injuries, or tumors of the brain or spinal cord. A spastic, or cramplike, paralysis may be caused by disturbances of the nerve pathways from the upper brain to the nerve cells in the lower part of the spinal cord. A limp, or flaccid, paralysis results from damage to the nerve cells of the spine or of the nerves which lead from these cells directly to the leg muscles. Paraplegia may result from birth injury; in some nervous-system diseases paralysis and weakness develop slowly over a long period of time.

Paraplegia from spinal disturbances is frequently accompanied by loss of sensation in the lower part of the body. Normal sexual function and control of urination and defecation may also be lost. The skin of the buttocks and legs may be especially liable to injury and special care may be needed to prevent sores from excessive pressure.

See also PARALYSIS.

PARASITISM [păr'ə-sīt-īz-əm], a biological interrelation between two different organisms in which one species—the parasite—obtains its subsistence by living in or on the body of the other—the host. This living arrangement benefits the parasite, which could not survive otherwise, and is generally injurious to the host organism, which can live without the parasite. In some instances the host may actually die as a result of the relationship; in other instances the host may not be harmed but certainly is not benefited.

Parasitic relationships occur in both the plant and animal kingdoms. In either case the parasite is usually specially modified for its mode of existence so that a particular species is only capable of parasitizing a particular host. Further, the parasite may be restricted (because of structural modifications) to living on or in a particular site of the host's body. Outstanding among the modifications observed in animal parasites are reduction (simplification) or absence of the digestive tract (the parasite absorbs predigested, fluid food from its host); the addition of various organs—hooks or sucker discs, for example—with which the parasite attaches to its host; and elaboration of the reproductive system to produce enormous numbers of new parasites which must overcome great obstacles to reach new hosts.

Within the animal kingdom are found such ectoparasites as ticks, leeches, and lice that live on the host's skin; and such endoparasites as tapeworms and roundworms that live in the host's digestive tract. Other endoparasites live in the host's muscle tissue (the trichina worm) or in the host's blood (certain worms and one-celled organisms). Parasites themselves may act as hosts for still other parasites. An example is the bacterial organism, *Pasteurella pestis*, which causes bubonic plague. The bacterium lives parasitically within a flea, its host. The flea, in turn, is parasitic upon the skin of rats. In such a case the flea, which acts both as a host and a parasite, is termed an "intermediate" host. The rat is termed the "definitive" host.

Viruses constitute a final and very important group of parasites. They are, in a sense, living chemicals, and can be classified neither as plants nor as animals. All viruses, however, are parasites; they cannot live except in association with the organic molecules that are part of living protoplasm.

See also BACTERIA; FUNGUS; MALARIA; VIRUSES.

PARATHYROID [păr-ə-thī'roid] **GLANDS,** bean-shaped structures, which lie near the edge of the thyroid gland in the neck. There are usually four such glands, each less than ¼ in. long. Their secretions control bone development and maintain normal calcium and phosphate metabolism. These secretions are essential for life. Without the parathyroids one may quickly die of tetany.

Parathormone, secreted by the parathyroids, is one of the factors which regulate the amount of calcium and phosphate salts in the blood. These salts, essential to the structure of bone, are also required in exact concentrations for nerve and muscle function. The bulk of calcium

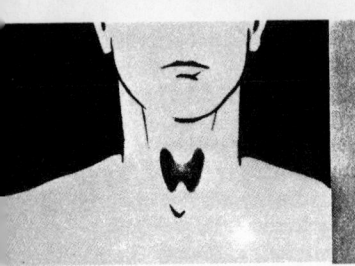

THE PARATHYROID GLANDS, VITAMIN D, AND CALCIUM METABOLISM

The parathyroid glands are small brownish-red structures which lie in contact with the thyroid gland of the throat. The actions of parathyroid hormone are in some respects similar to those of vitamin D, the "sunshine vitamin," that is produced in the skin by the ultraviolet rays of the sun. Together the hormone and the vitamin regulate the metabolism of calcium in the body.

THE REGULATION OF CALCIUM IN THE BODY

The secretion of parathyroid hormone is controlled by the concentration of calcium in the blood. As the latter decreases, parathyroid secretion increases. The hormone raises the blood calcium level by its action on bones and kidney. Vitamin D increases the absorption of calcium from the small intestine.

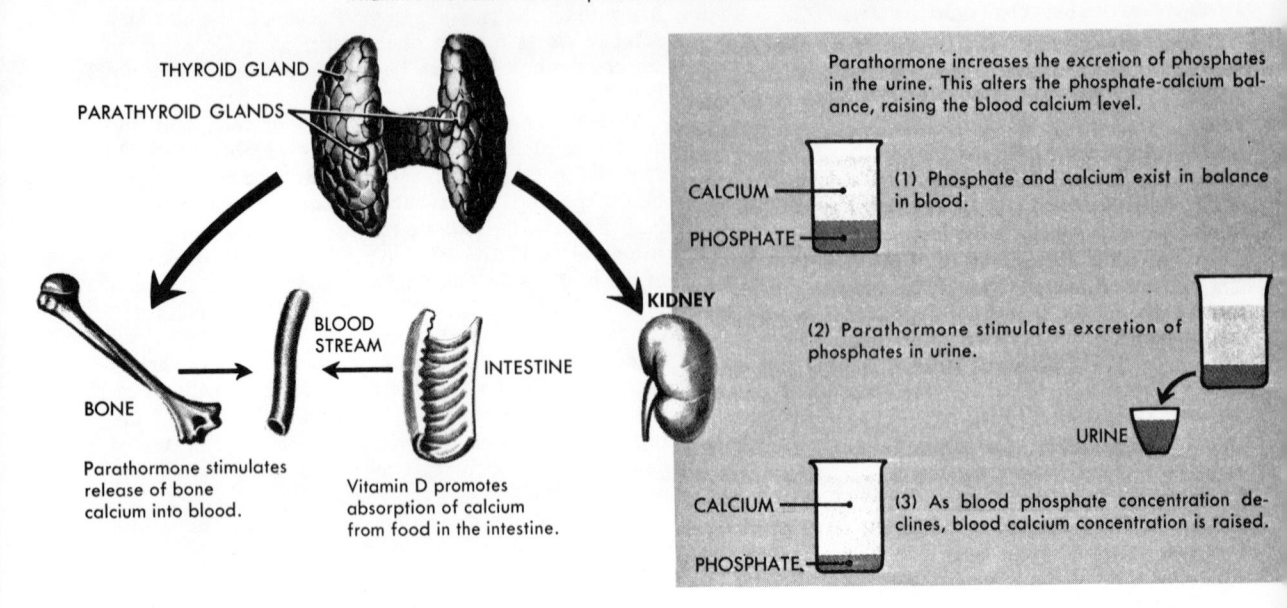

THYROID GLAND
PARATHYROID GLANDS
BLOOD STREAM
INTESTINE
KIDNEY
BONE

Parathormone stimulates release of bone calcium into blood.

Vitamin D promotes absorption of calcium from food in the intestine.

Parathormone increases the excretion of phosphates in the urine. This alters the phosphate-calcium balance, raising the blood calcium level.

CALCIUM
PHOSPHATE

(1) Phosphate and calcium exist in balance in blood.

(2) Parathormone stimulates excretion of phosphates in urine.

URINE

CALCIUM
PHOSPHATE

(3) As blood phosphate concentration declines, blood calcium concentration is raised.

---

and phosphate salts lie deposited in the bones and teeth. A smaller amount circulates in the bloodstream. When blood calcium falls below the normal level, parathormone is secreted. The hormone then acts on bone cells, which dissolve calcium into the blood. Parathormone causes the kidney to excrete phosphate and retain calcium, which also tends to increase blood calcium.

There are various causes of abnormalities of the parathyroid gland. Primary hyperparathyroidism (overfunction) or hypoparathyroidism (underfunction) result when the gland is at fault. It no longer responds appropriately to a change in blood-calcium concentration. Secondary hyper- or hypoparathyroidism result from malfunction in other areas, which affect the glands secondarily.

Removal of most of the parathyroid glands, often three out of four, is the treatment for primary hyperparathyroidism. It has also been used in some cases of secondary hyperparathyroidism. Hypoparathyroidism, on the other hand, is usually adequately corrected by feeding large quantities of calcium phosphate salts and by increasing their absorption in the intenstine by Vitamin D administration. The diagnosis and management of parathyroid abnormalities requires frequent determinations of calcium and phosphate in the blood and urine. These determinations are chemically somewhat difficult and require specialized facilities and techniques. Fortunately, disorders of parathyroid gland function are uncommon.
See also ENDOCRINE GLANDS.

PARATYPHOID FEVER. See TYPHOID FEVER.

PAREGORIC [păr-ə-gôr′ĭk], also called camphorated opium tincture, is a narcotic preparation containing comparatively small amounts of opium. For this reason it usually fails to induce sleep and relieve pain as do more potent morphine compounds. Paregoric has been traditionally used to treat colic, earache, and teething complaints in children, and is still popular as a remedy for diarrhea.

PARESIS [pə-rē′sĭs], **GENERAL,** a late phase of syphilis, appearing from 5 to 20 years or more after the original infection and characterized by destruction of brain tissue and mental deterioration. Patients are often flamboyant, giving money away or claiming to be famous persons. There is a loss of memory, and capacity for higher intellectual activity declines. Eventually the individual becomes severely retarded and bedridden. Early treatment of syphilis with penicillin has considerably reduced the incidence of general paresis. Once the disease has appeared, penicillin treatment can halt further deterioration, but cannot restore the tissue to its former state.
See also SYPHILIS.

PARKINSON'S [pär′kĭn-sənz] **DISEASE,** also known as paralysis agitans, a disease of the central nervous system seen primarily in middle-aged and elderly persons and marked by tremors, rigidity, and slowness of movement.

Parkinson's disease should not be confused with other disorders involving similar symptoms. These include postencephalitic Parkinsonism—a brain inflammation often caused by a virus infection—and forms of Parkinsonism arising as a side effect from the intensive use of some tranquilizing drugs.

Parkinson's disease affects certain centers of the brain (the basal ganglia and substantia nigra) involved in muscle control and automatic movements. Recent research indicates that the disease may be linked to a deficiency of a neural chemical, dopamine, in the basal ganglia. In many cases the first sign of disease is the so-called "pill-rolling" motion—a tremor in which the thumb and fingers of the hand beat against each other in a manner reminiscent of a pharmacist rolling a pill. At first this may appear after exercise or excitement, but later becomes constant. The tremors spread to the other muscles of the arm and may eventually involve all of the extremities and the eyelids, lips, tongue, and jaw as well. The tremors usually diminish when the patient uses the affected parts, and disappear entirely during sleep.

The patient's movements are slow and weak, resulting from muscle rigidity. The face acquires a frozen, expressionless stare, called a "Parkinsonian mask"; the speech may be slurred and drooling may be seen. The victim's body assumes a characteristic stooped posture with the elbows bent and the shoulders drawn together; he stands rigidly "like a statue" and moves forward with small mincing steps. The disease progresses slowly, leaving the mind clear, but eventually confines the patient to bed. A serious complication is bronchopneumonia.

Patients may survive for many years and are often able to continue working. Surgical procedures involving the destruction of tissue in the basal ganglia have produced improvement in some cases. Recently, dramatic improvements have been achieved in approximately two-thirds of the cases treated with L-dopa. This drug, an amino acid capable of crossing the blood-brain barrier, is converted by the body into dopamine, thus alleviating the characteristic deficiency of this chemical in the brain. Though it produces certain undesirable side effects, L-dopa was licensed for use as a prescription drug in 1970.

PASTEUR [päs-tûr'], **LOUIS** (1822–95), French chemist and bacteriologist, known for his many contributions to the study of infectious diseases. Pasteur received his bachelor of science degree at Besançon in 1842 and two years later was admitted to the École Normale in Paris.

Pasteurization. The now-familiar pasteurization process had its origins in Pasteur's investigation of the disease which was ruining the wine industry of Jura. Pasteur found that certain microorganisms were responsible, but it was impossible to destroy them at high temperatures without spoiling the taste of the wine. He discovered, however, that he could prevent their growth by heating the wine for a few moments to 50° C. to 60° C. (122° F. to 140° F.) The method has since been applied to other fields.

Silkworm Disease. In 1865 Pasteur undertook an investigation of pébrine, a disease of silkworms that threatened the silk industry of France. He identified the cause of the epidemic in the form of round parasites contained in the silkworm eggs and demonstrated that the disease could be eliminated by examining silkworm eggs microscopically, selecting for breeding only parasite-free eggs.

Shortly after completing this work, Pasteur suffered a stroke, which paralyzed his entire left side. He returned to work three months later, and although some effects of the stroke remained, he accomplished some of his finest work in the remaining years of his life.

Pasteur and the Prevention of Disease—Immunization. In 1877 Pasteur, successful advocate of the germ theory of disease and savior of the wine and silk industries of his native France, directed his energies to the investigation of splenic fever, or anthrax, a disease that was decimating the sheep of France. While working on anthrax, he was called away temporarily to fight an epidemic of chicken cholera. He isolated the responsible germ and found that the organisms could be grown in the laboratory and weakened in such a way that they lost their power to cause disease, but retained the ability to produce immunity against subsequent infections.

Returning to his studies on anthrax, Pasteur made similar weakened preparations of the anthrax bacillus, which had been discovered in 1849 in the blood of sheep that had died from the disease. On May 31, 1881, Pasteur tested the effectiveness of this preparation in protecting sheep against anthrax. He inoculated 48 sheep with live, vigorous anthrax bacilli; 24 of these animals had previously been treated with the weakened germs; the other 24 had not been treated. All of the treated sheep survived; the untreated died, and the anthrax problem was solved. Pasteur's work in the area of immunization made possible the subsequent development of live vaccines for many other diseases.

Pasteur's most spectacular success was undoubtedly his discovery of a means of preventing rabies. He began this work in 1880 and after numerous experiments found that weakened preparations of the rabies organism (which could not be seen under the microscope—we now know

Photograph of Louis Pasteur taken in the 1880's, when he was a professor at the Sorbonne, Paris. It was during these years that Pasteur discovered the rabies vaccine. (THE BETTMANN ARCHIVE)

it to be a virus) could be made from the spinal cords of rabid animals. The first patient was a nine-year-old Alsatian boy who had been bitten by a rabid dog. Pasteur's injections of the weakened virus succeeded in stimulating immunity in the boy before the disease could develop. This achievement brought Pasteur international fame and led to the establishment of the Pasteur Institute, supported by funds donated from many parts of the world.

Pasteur did not live to work in the new institute. He died in 1895, holding in one hand the hand of his wife and in the other a crucifix, a mark of Pasteur's devout religious faith, to which he had been loyal all his life.
See also RABIES; VACCINES.

PATCH TEST, a test used to detect skin sensitivity to contact with suspected irritants or allergic agents. A sample of the material to be evaluated is placed upon a piece of gauze, which is then covered with some nonporous material, such as oil, silk, or cellophane, and bound to the skin with an adhesive. If an inflammation develops under the patch, the test is positive.
See also ALLERGY.

PATERNITY [pə-tûr′nə-tē] **TESTS,** blood tests used to determine whether or not a man is the father of a particular child. In 1900 Karl Landsteiner demonstrated important differences in the blood of different individuals, leading to the discovery of blood types or blood grouping. Every person's blood belongs to group A, B, O, or AB. Subgroups in this system, as well as many new systems, were soon discovered. Inheritance of these factors is predictable, making it possible to determine whether a particular man could or could not be the father of a particular child. Knowledge of the man's blood grouping and that of the mother and child are required to determine possible paternity. Blood-group information is also obtained from other bodily secretions in some people. This secreting trait is also an inheritable characteristic, which may be of value in establishing paternity.

Applying the laws of genetic inheritance to specific blood groups has aided decisions in disputed paternity cases. In a given case, tests can exclude the possibility of paternity or establish the probability of paternity. Paternity tests can never establish paternity beyond doubt. If, however, a rare blood group combination or specific group is present, the probability may be extremely high. After the first month of life, an individual's blood group remains constant. It is impossible for children to acquire blood group characteristics that do not exist in one or both parents.

PAVLOV [päv′lôf], **IVAN PETROVICH** (1849–1936), Russian physiologist, famous for his studies of digestion and his subsequent discovery of conditioned reflexes. Pavlov received his medical degree in 1883 at St. Petersburg Military Medical Academy, where he continued as a tutor until 1888. After study in Germany he returned to the academy in 1890 to hold various positions, becoming professor of physiology in 1895. Following the Revolution of 1917, Pavlov held the distinguished post of director of the physiological laboratories of the Russian Academy of Medicine. His researches on the physiology of digestion, summarized in *The Work of the Digestive Glands* (trans., 1902), earned him the Nobel Prize of 1904.

While studying digestive responses, Pavlov found they were easily modified. Experimenting with salivation in dogs, he discovered that the animal could be trained or "conditioned" to salivate at the sound of a bell or the sight of a circle of light. These formerly neutral stimuli alone were capable of eliciting the response for food (salivation), even though no food was offered. These investigations led to a concept of the brain as a primary signal system, and the results were published in English in *Conditioned Reflexes* (1927).
See also DIGESTION.

PEDIATRICS [pē-dē-ăt′rĭks], that branch of medicine which deals with the diseases of children.

Children's Diseases

Many of the major ailments of children have yielded to the impact of steadily increasing medical knowledge. At one time diseases such as diphtheria, scarlet fever, and pneumonia claimed many young lives. As many as one out of every three newborn infants died in his first year of a digestive disease, whooping cough, or malnutrition. By 1890 the diphtheria and typhoid bacteria had been identified, and diphtheria antitoxin had been developed. In the early part of the 20th century vaccines for diphtheria, typhoid fever, and whooping cough were perfected and more recently vaccines for polio, measles, mumps, and German measles have been developed.

A greater understanding of the causes of nutritional diseases such as rickets and iron-deficiency anemia has led to methods of prevention by improving the diet of infants. Diabetes was brought under medical control and the treatment of other glandular disturbances improved. The ability of medicine to prevent many of the childhood infections was supplemented by the introduction of the antibiotic drugs, which rendered many previously lethal infections harmless.

Today the most frequent causes of death and disability among children are accidents. Burns, falls, and accidental poisonings are especially likely to involve younger children. Cancer has become the second major cause of death of children. Birth injuries, congenital malformations, and inherited defects of body chemistry remain as serious medical problems. Virus infections, which were little noticed while bacterial diseases were rampant, are now being identified as the cause of various ailments in children. Also to be considered are the mental disorders which sometimes impair the health of children.

The Pediatrician and His Responsibilities

Although early medical literature indicates an interest by physicians in diseases of infants and children, pediatrics did not emerge as a distinct specialty in medicine until the present century.

In many countries the pediatrician acts only as a consultant to other doctors who encounter problems in treating children. In the United States the pediatrician takes complete charge of the child's medical care.

Preparing for the Newborn Infant. The pediatrician may consult with the obstetrician before the birth of the child to prevent illnesses of the mother from affecting the health of the child. Diabetes, anemia, and malnutrition of the mother may be treated long before birth, to improve the infant's chances of a good start in life. Syphilis of the mother can be treated to prevent infection of the infant while it is in the womb. Tuberculosis in the mother may be passed on to the infant after birth, and for this reason the child must be removed from the tubercular mother until she has recovered. The pediatrician may also evaluate the possibility of blood incompatibilities between the mother and the child. This may require early treatment (see RH FACTOR).

Medical Problems at Birth. Many pediatricians choose to be present when the baby is born or to be called immediately after. This is especially true when the mother has an illness that may affect the infant's health, or when Caesarean operation, premature birth, or other conditions require immediate treatment.

Birth injuries may cause brain hemorrhages and breathing disturbances which may endanger the life of the infant during the first few weeks after birth. Most infections of the lungs, intestinal tract, or other tissues can now be controlled, but epidemics of certain resistant bacterial (staphylococci) or viral infections can still be dangerous. Premature infants are especially susceptible to all of these hazards.

Congenital defects may be mild and can often be corrected by surgery. On occasion the deformity involves the brain or some other vital organ, resulting in stillbirth or a permanent mental or physical handicap. Birth defects may be caused by German measles of the mother early in pregnancy or by exposure of the expectant mother to radiation. In the great majority of cases, however, no cause for congenital deformities can be found and mothers who feel that they were in some way responsible for the malformations of their children must be reassured that nothing could have been done to prevent the malformations.

The First Months of Life. The immediate problem confronting the mother of a newly born baby is its food. Water, first offered six to eight hours after birth, may be sufficient for a day, or even two, but some form of milk will be needed by the end of that time. Mother's milk is still the best food in respect to composition, cleanliness, and availability. In the United States and many other nations cow's milk supplies are so clean and techniques of preparing formulas are so improved that almost all infants thrive on them. For the first few months of life, cow's milk must be diluted with water and supplemented with some type of sugar. A frequently used formula consists of two-thirds milk, one-third water, and one tablespoonful of sugar for every 10 oz. of mixture. The baby usually requires from 12 to 32 oz. of this preparation over a 24-hour period. Formulas of various kinds have been prepared by commercial concerns and are available in cans in liquid or powdered forms, requiring only dilution and warming to make them ready for the baby. Vitamin preparations are given routinely throughout the first year of life.

What the Baby Eats. Although rigid schedules of feeding were once thought to be important, greater freedom is permitted today so that the baby may nurse when he is hungry and sleep between feedings as long as he chooses. By the age of two or three months the infant is usually ready for semisolid food such as cereal, followed in a few weeks by fruits and vegetables. Many varieties of these "baby foods," already cooked, strained, and sometimes fortified with vitamins and minerals, may be purchased at the grocery. Meats and desserts are available in similar form, and all of them are usually well tolerated by the baby. No other foods need be given during the first year of the infant's life, although some parents become anxious to bring the baby to their own table and let him share their food. The pediatrician can be helpful in planning such procedures and arranging suitable diets through the entire first year of the infant's life. By the end of the first year the baby is encouraged to adopt a schedule of eating and sleeping similar to that of the rest of the family.

Immunization. Routine visits to the pediatrician are made by the mother and child at intervals of about four weeks during the first six months of the infant's life and possibly less frequently in the last half of the first year. Not only is diet discussed, but the progress of growth and development is observed by the doctor and the important program of immunization is started. Vaccines for protection against diphtheria, tetanus, whooping cough, and polio are highly effective and may be given singly or in combinations at three or four consecutive visits. Another injection ("booster") is given a year later and again every two or three years to maintain the child's level of immunity. Smallpox vaccination is usually provided at the end of the first year and repeated at five-year intervals. Vaccines against such common viral diseases as mumps, measles, and German measles have been developed and have proven effective. In certain areas, vaccines for other diseases, such as typhoid fever, may be necessary.

Preschool Years

Pediatricians prefer to examine children of this age about three or four times a year to measure their rate of growth and observe their activities. Wide variations of the pattern of development can occur and yet be within normal limits. Parents are frequently concerned by minor delays in the appearance of walking or talking. Their fears are usually groundless. In some instances, however, when a definite retardation of growth or development can be detected by parent or doctor, detailed examinations must be made to determine the nature and severity of the disorder. Special training and altered programs of living may have to be planned.

The dietary problems at this age consist chiefly of maintenance of well-balanced meals at a time when the intake of food is diminished. For some children reducing the amount of milk taken throughout the day and restricting the amounts of cookies, candy, and soft drinks taken between meals will help maintain an adequate intake of vegetables, meats, and fruits at regular lunch and dinner times.

A daily nap is usually recommended throughout preschool years and from 10 to 12 hours of sleep at night are advisable throughout childhood. Parents should remember that individual requirements for rest may vary.

PEDICULOSIS

Every two or three years the child's immunization program should be reviewed to be certain that he is adequately protected against preventable diseases.

School Years

The first school years are not always pleasant for the child. The new environment, competition, and sometimes active strife with other pupils or with teachers undermine the feeling of safety he had at home. Exposure to new viruses may cause colds and minor infections.

The pediatrician can help at this time by encouraging the child, treating his complaints, and guiding the parents in their support of the troubled child. The school offers a fine opportunity for the physician and teacher to measure the physical growth and mental achievements of children and to compare them with the average of their age group. It is an opportunity to "screen" the children for defects, such as impairment of vision or hearing, dental disease, or other correctable deformities or infections. Behavior and intelligence can be observed over long periods of time by the teachers, who may detect deviations from the normal before either the parents or the physician are aware of them.

Adolescence. The teen-age patient is generally healthy and is not accustomed to seeking routine medical care and health supervision. Many of the medical problems of adolescence are minor, such as acne, obesity, or temporary abnormalities of development, and can be treated simply and successfully. Of outstanding importance are the adolescent's problems of adjusting to new responsibilities and a different position in the social life of his community. The transition is usually made successfully but occasionally rebellion against authority or frustration in achievements may lead to a disruption of the childhood habits and customary behavior. The pediatrician hopes that through the early detection of behavior deviations adolescent instability can be prevented.

PEDICULOSIS [pə-dĭk-yə-lō'sĭs], infestation by lice. There are three varieties of louse, each named according to the body area it prefers to infest. These are the head louse, the body louse, and the pubic, or crab, louse (so called because of its shape). These insects produce eggs called nits, which are cemented to the hairs or, in the case of body lice, to the clothing. The lice feed on the blood of the host.

Head lice occur most commonly in children. Body louse infestation is called "vagabonds' disease" and used to be characteristic of inhabitants of jails or flophouses. In World War I the "cootie" in the clothes of soldiers on both fronts was a considerable problem. Lice can be dangerous since they carry the organism which causes typhus fever. In all types of infestation, there is itching followed by scratching, which may result in infection.

Control of lice is not difficult. Modern chemicals are effective against both louse and nit in a matter of a day or two. Sterilization of clothing and laundering plus ironing the seams with a hot iron will prevent reinfestation.

See also TYPHUS FEVER.

PELLAGRA [pə-lā'grə, pə-lăg'rə], a nutritional disease characterized by disorders of the skin, digestive tract, and nervous system. The recorded history of pellagra dates back to 1735 when Gaspar Casal, physician to King Philip V, described *mal de la rosa*, a disease prevalent among the rural population of Spain. The name "pellagra" was derived from the Italian *pelle agra* ("rough skin"), a term used by the peasants of northern Italy to describe the disease. At one time or another pellagra has been prevalent in Egypt, Russia, Italy, Spain, and in the southern United States. Its incidence has declined in recent years owing to improvements in nutrition.

The American physician Joseph Goldberger, who first proved that pellagra was a nutritional disease, believed it to result from deficiency of a specific substance, vitamin B_2 (G). It has since been shown that Goldberger's vitamin B_2 includes a number of distinct substances, among them pantothenic acid, pyridoxine, riboflavin, and niacin, the latter being the specific antipellagric factor. The disorder may arise from improper diet, from inability to absorb foods normally from the intestine, or from increased need for antipellagric substances in amounts exceeding that provided by the normal diet. It is usually associated with other vitamin deficiencies and is frequently seen among chronic alcoholics.

Pellagra usually begins gradually with weakness, lack of appetite, and loss of weight. The skin eruptions ordinarily appear on exposed or irritated parts of the body, such as the hands, wrists, elbows, and neck, beginning as a reddening of the skin and later progressing to rough, scaly, deeply pigmented lesions. The skin disturbances frequently develop following exposure to sunlight. The tongue, gums, and palate frequently become swollen and reddened. The abdomen may become distended and painful, particularly after a large meal. In severe cases there is diarrhea, vomiting, anemia, and rapid pulse.

Nervous symptoms include headaches, dizziness, insomnia, numbness and burning of the extremities, and poor co-ordination. Characteristic mental changes are depression, hallucinations, and delirium. If the disease is allowed to progress the patient may become psychotic. Loss of the senses of taste and smell is common.

Treatment consists of niacin and a diet rich in proteins and vitamins, supplemented by nutrient substances such as dry, powdered brewer's yeast and liver extract. Severe cases require bed rest and medical and nursing care. Specific lesions on the skin and in the mouth are treated with local medications. The disorder can be prevented by an adequate diet.

PELVIS. See SKELETAL SYSTEM.

PEMPHIGUS VULGARIS [pĕm'fə-gəs vəl-gâr'ĭs], a serious skin disease of adult life. Of unknown cause, the disease appears suddenly, affecting any part of the body, including the membranes of the eye, mouth, throat, and vagina. Large blisters develop in the skin, surrounded by a reddened area. As the blisters rupture, the skin becomes denuded and raw in appearance. Internal changes also occur, and the victim becomes susceptible to infection.

Formerly a highly fatal disease, pemphigus can now be successfully treated with large doses of cortisone.

PENFIELD, WILDER GRAVES (1891–), Canadian neurosurgeon.

Penfield's major contributions to neurosurgery and functional neuroanatomy were made while he was a neurosurgeon at the Royal Victoria and Montreal General hospitals, and as director of the Montreal Neurological Institute (1934–60). Because the human brain is insensitive to direct trauma and touch, he was able to perform many brain operations under local anaesthetic, with awake patients. With their help, Penfield mapped out previously uncharted areas of function in the brain. He was also able to offer some patients permanent relief of epileptic seizures, radically changing medical and lay thinking about this previously dread condition. No longer were these patients "possessed of demons" but, rather, suffering from demonstrable lesions in their brains.
See also EPILEPSY.

PENICILLIN [pĕn-ə-sĭl'ĭn], the first, best known, and most widely used of the antibiotics. Penicillin was discovered in 1929 by Alexander Fleming, who noted that cultures of bacteria failed to grow when contaminated with the mold *Penicillium notatum*. Some years later a British group, led by H. W. Florey and B. Chain, followed Fleming's lead and extracted, purified, and mass-produced penicillin for large-scale medical use.

The natural penicillins (G, X, F, and K) differ slightly in chemical composition and in antibacterial action—penicillin G is the most commonly used. Although penicillin has been made synthetically, it is produced more economically from cultures of the mold.

There is still no complete explanation of penicillin's antibacterial action. The drug inhibits the growth of microorganisms and destroys them by interfering with their essential life-maintaining activities. Evidence suggests that penicillin prevents the organism from manufacturing proteins by reacting with substances in the cell wall.

Penicillin is generally effective against gram-positive bacteria (the bacteriologist's designation of bacteria which stain in a specific manner) and ineffective against gram-negative bacilli. In clinical practice it is used for gonorrhea, skin abscesses, "strep" throats, scarlet fever, tetanus, gas gangrene, syphilis, and in some types of pneumonia. Regular administration of penicillin by mouth helps to reduce recurrences of rheumatic fever in children and to prevent infection of the heart valves in individuals with congenital heart disease or in those who have recovered from bacterial endocarditis.

Among the penicillin-resistant organisms are those which cause leprosy, tuberculosis, cholera, typhoid fever, and several organisms which produce urinary tract infections. Penicillin is generally not effective against virus, yeast, and fungus infections (except actinomycosis).

A major advantage of penicillin is its safety. Undesirable reactions occur in only 1% to 8% of patients; these usually take the form of allergic reactions, such as skin eruptions and localized swellings. In rare cases severe reactions have been fatal. Sensitivity reactions are especially likely when penicillin is applied locally as an ointment. The drug can be given by intramuscular injection or by mouth. Oral administration is less likely to cause serious allergic reactions.

The Development of Penicillin-resistant Strains. In addition to those organisms which naturally resist penicillin action, it became evident early in the history of penicillin therapy that resistant strains could develop among bacteria that were ordinarily sensitive to penicillin. This has become a formidable problem, particularly in the case of the staphylococcus bacteria which commonly infect wounds and cause boils. Resistant strains are more likely to appear with increased use of penicillin and for this reason are prevalent in hospitals. To avoid developing penicillin-resistant bacteria, it is advised that penicillin not be used indiscriminately but only when absolutely necessary. A form of penicillin has been introduced which is useful against resistant staphylococci.

Since its introduction penicillin has been joined by a large number of other antibiotics, but because of its relatively low cost, high potency, ready solubility in body fluids, and low toxicity it remains one of the most important anti-infective agents.
See also ANTIBIOTICS.

PENTOTHAL SODIUM [pĕn'tə-thôl], also sodium pentothal, a fast-acting barbiturate used to produce anesthesia, and in psychiatry to produce a relaxed state in which the patient's problems can be more easily explored (narcosynthesis). The drug may dangerously depress breathing and must be used with caution.
See also BARBITURATES.

PERISTALSIS [pĕr-ə-stôl'sĭs], wavelike movements of the digestive tract. The peristaltic waves are generated by synchronized contractions of the smooth muscles in the walls of the digestive organs. Peristaltic movements of the esophagus, or gullet, aid in swallowing. Peristalsis of the stomach and intestine aids digestion and propels food and food wastes through the digestive tract.
See also DIGESTION; INTESTINE; STOMACH.

PERITONITIS [pĕr-ĭ-tə-nī'tĭs], inflammation of the peritoneum, the membrane which lines the abdominal cavity and covers the abdominal organs. It most frequently follows perforations of the intestinal tract or stomach, which permit bacteria to enter the abdominal cavity. This may occur in cases of ruptured appendix, stomach ulcers, or tumors of the bowel. Infection of the female reproductive organs (in gonorrhea and tuberculosis) may also cause peritonitis. In some cases, particularly in children, the infection travels to the abdomen via the blood stream from some other part of the body.

The symptoms vary with the location and extent of the infection and are combined with those of the condition leading to the peritonitis. Abdominal pain and tenderness, and nausea and vomiting are seen. The abdomen swells with fluid, the pulse rate increases, and the white blood cell count is elevated. A frequent complication is paralysis of the bowel (paralytic ileus). Prior to the introduction of antibiotics, peritonitis was a dreaded and often fatal complication following abdominal surgery. Treatment consists of surgery (in cases of perforated viscera), antibiotics, and intravenous administration of liquids to replace fluids and other substances which have escaped from the blood into the abdominal cavity.

PEPSIN, digestive enzyme found in gastric juices. Pepsin is produced in the inactive form pepsinogen by cells of the mucous lining of the stomach. The acid of the gastric juice transforms pepsinogen into pepsin, which breaks down proteins into the simpler substances peptones and peptides. See DIGESTION.

PEPTIDES [pĕp'tīdz], chemical relatives of the proteins, the principal structural element of animal tissues. Proteins contain hundreds or thousands of amino acids; peptides are composed of chains of two or more of the same acids. In the course of digestion proteins (in milk, meats, and so forth) are decomposed into peptides and amino acids, which are absorbed into the blood stream. Some of the antibiotic substances isolated from microorganisms are peptides.
See also AMINO ACIDS; PROTEIN.

PEPTONE [pĕp'tōn], one of a group of compounds obtained by the partial decomposition of proteins. Peptone is prepared commercially by the action of enzymes on meat and is added to some food supplements given to convalescent patients and others requiring added nutrition.

PERSONALITY. See PSYCHOLOGY.

PERSPIRATION [pûr-spə-rā'shən], secretion of the sudoriferous, or sweat, glands of the skin. The evaporation of sweat cools the body and is a principal means of temperature regulation. Salt (NaCl) is lost in perspiration, and excessive sweating with salt loss may produce muscle cramps resulting from a disturbance of the electrochemical balance of the body fluids. An unusually high concentration of salt in the perspiration is seen in cystic fibrosis and is used as a clue to the presence of the disease.

PERUTZ, MAX FERDINAND (1914–   ), English biochemist who used X-ray diffraction studies to determine the complicated spiral structure of hemoglobin, the globular protein that enables men and animals to breathe.

PETIT MAL [pə-tē' mȧl'], (Fr., "little malady), a form of epilepsy consisting of a momentary disturbance of consciousness from which the individual recovers rapidly and completely. Usually occurring in individuals under 20, it is popularly known as "faints" or "spells." The victim stops what he is doing and appears dazed but seldom falls. He generally resumes his activity in a few seconds, displaying no memory of the episode.
See also EPILEPSY.

PEYOTE or PEYOTL. See MESCAL.

PHAGOCYTOSIS, the ingestion of small particles by certain cells. Knowledge of this important phenomenon dates to Élie Metchnikoff's admirable studies in the 1890's. He concluded that the same process which serves nutritional needs in ameba had become a means of combating invading micro-organisms in higher animals. In man, the important phagocytic cells are the polymorphoneutrophils and the monocytes, leucocytes which reach the tissues from the blood. The liver, spleen, and lymph nodes also produce phagocytic cells which do not migrate through the body. When bacteria are encountered, the leucocyte's protoplasm flows out and incorporates them into the cell. Bacteria or foreign material ingested by leucocytes are stored in small saclike containers called vacuoles, to which other vacuoles called lysosomes attach themselves and discharge enzymes which destroy the bacteria. A number of factors influence the leucocyte's ability to phagocytose bacteria, including antibodies, which form after foreign material is introduced into the body, and which act by coating the bacteria's surface.

Phagocytosis is an important protective mechanism against bacterial invasion and, with antibody formation, is a mainstay of health.
See also ANTIBODIES AND ANTIGENS.

PHARMACOPEIA [fär-mə-kə-pē'ə], also spelled pharmacopoeia, a book containing a list of medicinal substances with descriptions, formulas, properties, identification tests, quantitative assays, safe dosages, and other standards to determine their strength and purity. They are compiled by recognized authorities usually under governmental auspices. Similar texts are known as formulary, codex, and dispensatory, the last generally being a commentary on one or more pharmacopeias.

Although descriptive lists of drugs are known from ancient China, Babylonia, and Egypt, the precursor of the pharmacopeia is generally considered to be a book entitled *Compositiones,* written by the Roman physician Scribonius Largus about 43 A.D. The *Nuovo receptario composito,* published by the Florentine guild of physicians and apothecaries in 1498, was made official and thus became the first pharmacopeia of the European world. The 16th-century *Dispensatorium* of. Valerius Cordus, printed by direct order of the senate of Nuremberg (hence also known as the Nuremburg pharmacopeia), is sometimes recognized as the first pharmacopeia. The first formulary to be entitled a pharmacopeia was published in 1548 by the French physician Jacques Dubois in Lyon. The first London pharmacopeia was published in 1618.

The first pharmacopeia in the United States was the Lititz (Pennsylvania) pharmacopeia, published in 1778 for use by the American Revolutionary army. The first national pharmacopeia in the United States was published in 1820 and was subsequently revised by a Pharmacopeial Commission every 10 years. The *National Formulary* was published by the American Pharmaceutical Association in 1888. When the Pure Food and Drugs Act was enacted in 1906, the *U.S. Pharmacopeia* (U.S.P.) and the *National Formulary* (N.F.) were established as the legal standards for all medicinal products in these books, whether manufactured in the United states or imported.

Today the necessity for legalized standards to define the character, establish the purity, and regulate the strength of medicines is recognized by all civilized nations. Even though all countries have not yet formally adopted national standards, in nearly every case where this has not been done the pharmacopeia of some other country is officially recognized.

Work on an *International Pharmacopeia* began in 1902, but it was not until 1950 that the first volume was completed and published in English, French, and Spanish.

PHARMACY [fär′mə-sē], branch of the healing arts which deals with the preparation, control, and distribution of medications. The term is also applied to the place where medicines are compounded, dispensed, and sold. Today all states require drugs to be handled by licensed pharmacists who have been trained in the techniques of compounding and dispensing drugs. American pharmacists may receive their training in any one of 76 accredited colleges of pharmacy. The college curriculum leading to a bachelor of science in pharmacy requires five years of study, and in California six years of study are required for a doctor of pharmacy degree. Many pharmacists pursue graduate study leading to a master of science and a doctor of philosophy degree.

In pharmacies, or drug stores, pharmacists compound and dispense prescriptions and assist the physician, dentist, and other members of the health professions by supplying them with professional information about pharmacy and pharmaceuticals. Pharmacists also practice their profession in hospitals, manufacturing laboratories, wholesale establishments, and in government service. Manufacturing pharmacy offers such varied positions as administration executive, professional service representative (who calls on physicians and community pharmacists), production manager, control chemist, and research scientist. The federal government employs pharmacists in the Army, Navy, Air Force, Public Health Service, Bureau of Narcotics, Food and Drug Administration, and the Veterans Administration. Pharmacists are also engaged as law enforcement officers for the state boards of pharmacy as well as other state and local regulatory agencies, such as the board of health.

PHARYNX [făr′ĭngks], portion of the digestive tube which lies behind the mouth, nose, and larynx. The pharynx is divided into a nasal portion, which lies above the nose, and an oral portion, which leads into the gullet, or esophagus. During swallowing, muscular action first expands and then contracts the pharynx, propelling the food mass into the esophagus.

PHENETHYLBIGUANIDE [fĕn-ĕth-əl-bī′gwə-nīd], also known as Phenformin, or DBI, a drug used in the treatment of diabetes. Although the manner in which the drug lowers the blood sugar is not completely understood, it evidently acts differently from insulin, the pancreatic hormone ordinarily used for this purpose. Phenethylbiguanide is given by mouth and is used principally in mild cases of diabetes which have developed in adult life. Side reactions affecting the gastrointestinal tract are common and the patient must be kept under close medical supervision.
See also DIABETES MELLITUS.

PHENOBARBITAL [fē-nō-bär′bə-tôl], drug used to induce sleep, to relieve apprehension, and to control epileptic convulsions. A slowly acting barbiturate, phenobarbital exerts its depressant action on the central nervous system for six hours or longer. Repeated use may lead to habituation and addiction.
See also BARBITURATES.

PHRENOLOGY [frĭ-nŏl′ə-jē], study of the relationship between skull contours and personality characteristics. Phrenology is rooted in the notion that the mind can be analyzed into a number of discrete faculties, such as cautiousness and spirituality, and that each faculty is located in a specific part of the brain. Bumps and depressions on the skull, according to this theory, represent the degree of development of various faculties. Using these signs, the phrenologist believes he can determine the subject's

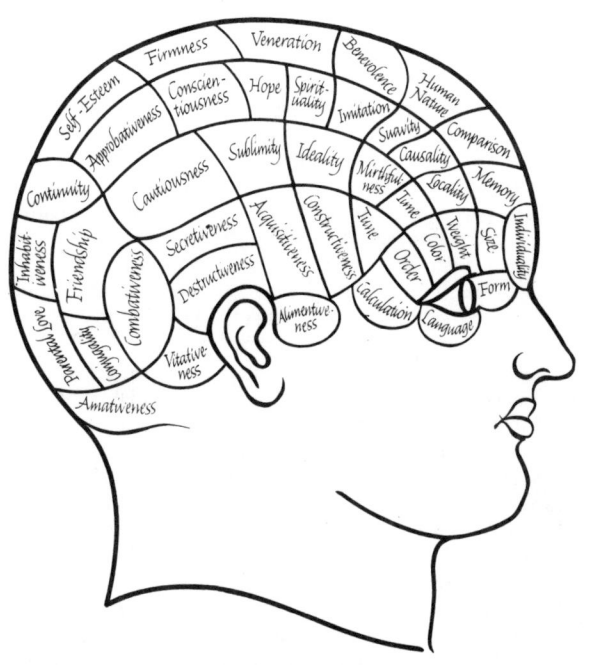

Chart indicating the seat of 42 human faculties, according to the theories of 18th- and 19th-century phrenologists. Modern studies of physiology and brain functioning show that such mapping of the brain is invalid.

personality and abilities. The practice of looking at the form of the skull to determine personal character was known in ancient cultures. It was brought to life again in the 19th century by two German scholars. F. J. Gall and J. G. Spurzheim. Their writings and teaching drew attention to specific areas of the brain associated with specific kinds of mental activities. Phrenology's principles have been largely refuted by modern anatomy and physiology, but they were important in provoking more intensive and detailed study of the brain. Such studies led to the discovery of specific brain areas for vision and hearing and to the development of neurophysiology.

PHYSICAL THERAPY, also called physiotherapy or physical medicine, consists of the application of electricity, heat, light, sound, and other forms of physical energy in the diagnosis and treatment of disease. A physician who specializes in physical medicine is called a physiatrist. A physical therapist (or physiotherapist) is not a physician, but is specially trained in the application of the techniques of physical medicine. He usually works under the direction of a physiatrist or orthopedic surgeon.

The most common form of physical therapy is the application of heat to the body. Heat stimulates the flow of blood to the tissues, thus speeding the natural healing process. The skin is heated through the use of hot packs, steam sprays, hot-water baths, paraffin baths, infrared lamps, and radiant-heat lamps.

Heating of deeper structures, such as muscle and tendon, is accomplished by diathermy and ultrasound. In diathermy treatment, the body is heated by a high-frequency electric current. Ultrasound consists of high-frequency sound waves that are beyond the range of human hearing. The sound waves beat rapidly against the tissues, thus heating them. Ultrasound is also used to soften hardened scar tissue, to treat bursitis, and to relieve the pain that frequently develops following amputation.

Exercise therapy is a basic technique of physical medicine that is important in speeding recovery from fractures and operations. In severe burn cases it is essential to exercise the part in order to prevent the soft tissues from hardening and stiffening. In virtually all situations where the patient is kept in a restricted position for any length of time, exercise is essential to maintain flexibility and strength. Weight lifting is a form of physical therapy used to develop power in weakened muscles.

Electricity is used in physical medicine to detect muscle and nerve diseases and to artificially stimulate muscles when the nerves are incapable of doing so. Normal muscles respond in a characteristic fashion to electric stimulation; failure to respond, or an abnormal response, indicates disease of the muscle or of the nerve supplying it. In such diseases, electric currents are often used as artificial nerves to exercise the muscle and to maintain it in good health until the nerve is able to function again.

Other techniques of physical medicine utilize massage, medicinal baths, and sun lamps. Massage cannot remove fat, as is commonly supposed. Its purpose is to loosen stiff tissues and to promote circulation. Medicinal baths are used in the treatment of skin diseases and burns. Sun lamps emit ultraviolet light, which tans the skin and is useful in the treatment of infections and skin diseases.

PHYSIOGNOMY [fĭz-ē-ŏg′nə-mē], study of facial characteristics as a means of judging personality characteristics. More broadly, it is the study of any external physical features as a means of determining psychological traits and attitudes. Aristotle wrote an early treatise on it. In the 19th century, police investigators tried to determine the physical characteristics of the "criminal type." They found, however, that the typical features appeared in many respectable citizens as well.

At the beginning of this century, physiognomy was modified and incorporated into physical anthropology and psychology. The anthropologists studied body dimensions to identify persons of certain cultures. The psychological study was emphasized first by Ernst Kretschmer, and later by William H. Sheldon, who associated personality features with body types, or "somatotypes." Other investigators, such as Harold Schlosberg, tried to identify those facial expressions which indicate specific emotions. However, physiognomy as the study of facial characteristics is now considered a pseudoscience.
See also PHRENOLOGY.

PHYSIOLOGY [fĭz-ē-ŏl′ə-jē], a branch of biology that studies the vital functions of living organisms. It is a companion science to anatomy, which studies the structures in which these functions occur. Physiology may be broadly divided into two fields—plant physiology and animal physiology. The basic studies in both areas are similar: how the plant or animal obtains its food; how the nutrients are transported throughout the body; how the organism reproduces; how the organism responds to its environment. Specific studies in plant physiology are the absorption of water and minerals, photosynthesis (the manufacture of food by green plants), and the function of plant hormones. Animal physiology includes studies in nutrition, digestion, respiration, excretion, circulation, nerve conduction, and muscular activity.

PHYSIOTHERAPY. See PHYSICAL THERAPY.

PIGMENT [pĭg′mənt]. In biological usage the term "pigment" refers to any one of a large variety of highly complex organic compounds—each having a particular color—that are found in the bodies of living organisms. Pigment granules are present in many different kinds of cells throughout the plant or animal body and are responsible for the characteristic colors of skin, hair, and eyes in animals, and of leaves, flower parts, and stems in plants.

Animal Pigments. The skin color of animals is due to the presence of pigment granules in the cells of the epidermis (the outer skin layer) or to special pigmented cells, called chromatophores, in the dermis (the inner skin layer). Epidermal pigmentation occurs chiefly in mammals; dermal pigmentation is characteristic of fishes, amphibians, and reptiles. The color of feathers and hair is due to pigment granules in these structures. The main pigments found in animal skin are melanin, a brownish-black coloring matter, and xanthin, a yellow-red pigment.

There are several pigments found in animal bodies which are not specifically associated with coloration. Among these are hemoglobin, a red pigment, found in red blood cells, which carries oxygen throughout the body; and rhodopsin, or visual purple, a purplish-red pigment, found in the retina of the eye, which plays an important role in vision.
See also EYE; HAIR.

PINEAL [pĭn′ē-əl] **BODY,** also known as epiphysis, a glandlike structure about 9 mm. long, located in the center of the brain. The French philosopher Descartes considered this structure to be the point of contact between mind and body; modern physiologists have been unable to ascribe a function to the pineal body.

PINEL [pē-nĕl′], **PHILIPPE** (1745–1826), French psychiatrist known for his reforms in the treatment of the mentally ill. As chief physician at two French hospitals he removed the chains from patients, some of whom had

PITUITARY GLAND

been bound for over 30 years. Pinel turned to psychiatry as a result of the tragic experience of a friend who became mentally ill. He heralded a new enlightenment in the attitude toward mental patients by stressing that the demented were ill. In his *Traité médico-philosophique sur l'aliénation mentale* (2d ed., 1809) he advanced the concept that mental disorders stemmed from diseased brain tissue.

PITUITARY [pĭ-tū′ə-tĕr-ē] **GLAND,** a pea-sized structure which rests in a bony depression below the brain. The pituitary has been described as the "master" endocrine gland and the "conductor" of the "endocrine orchestra" in recognition of its diverse effects on other endocrine glands. The gland is divided into anterior, intermediate, and posterior portions.

The *anterior pituitary* gland, or adenohypophysis, secretes hormones which travel through the blood to act upon the thyroid gland (TSH thyrotrophic hormone), the adrenal glands (ACTH), the gonads, and the breasts (in

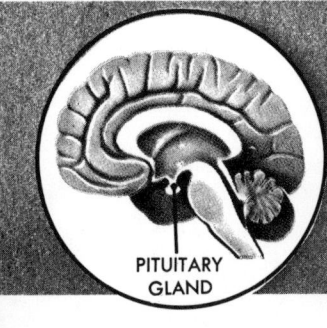

THE PITUITARY GLAND AND THE ENDOCRINE SYSTEM

The pituitary gland, or hypophysis, is a pea-sized organ situated below the brain. The gland is a major structure in the system of ductless (endocrine) glands, which regulate the internal activities of the body. The hormones of the pituitary control the secretions of several other endocrine glands, thus indirectly exerting far-reaching effects on many organs and tissues.

PITUITARY GLAND

THE PITUITARY CONSISTS OF ANTERIOR, INTERMEDIATE, AND POSTERIOR SECTIONS

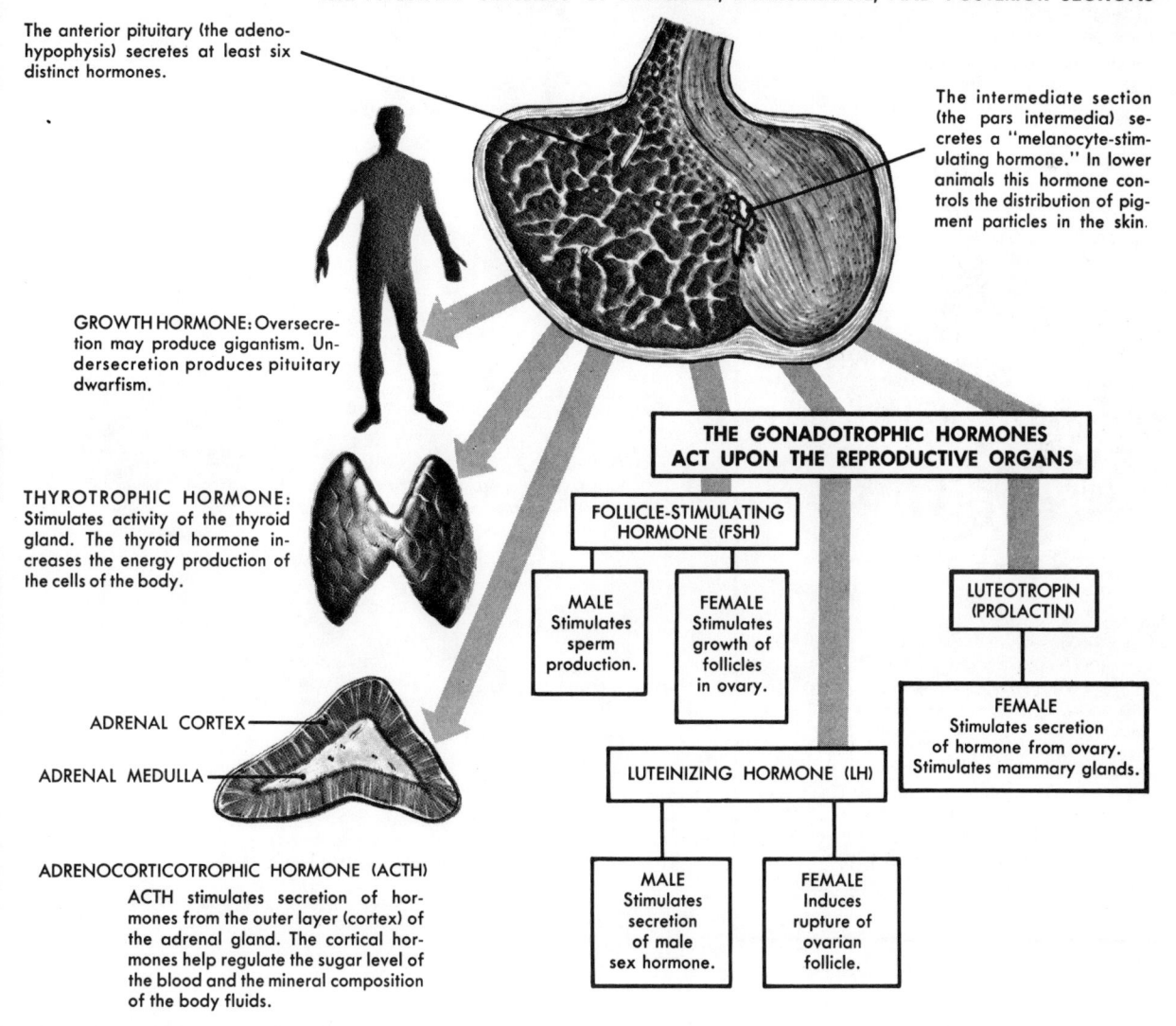

The anterior pituitary (the adenohypophysis) secretes at least six distinct hormones.

The intermediate section (the pars intermedia) secretes a "melanocyte-stimulating hormone." In lower animals this hormone controls the distribution of pigment particles in the skin.

GROWTH HORMONE: Oversecretion may produce gigantism. Undersecretion produces pituitary dwarfism.

THYROTROPHIC HORMONE: Stimulates activity of the thyroid gland. The thyroid hormone increases the energy production of the cells of the body.

ADRENAL CORTEX
ADRENAL MEDULLA

ADRENOCORTICOTROPHIC HORMONE (ACTH)
ACTH stimulates secretion of hormones from the outer layer (cortex) of the adrenal gland. The cortical hormones help regulate the sugar level of the blood and the mineral composition of the body fluids.

THE GONADOTROPHIC HORMONES ACT UPON THE REPRODUCTIVE ORGANS

FOLLICLE-STIMULATING HORMONE (FSH)

MALE	FEMALE
Stimulates sperm production.	Stimulates growth of follicles in ovary.

LUTEINIZING HORMONE (LH)

MALE	FEMALE
Stimulates secretion of male sex hormone.	Induces rupture of ovarian follicle.

LUTEOTROPIN (PROLACTIN)

FEMALE
Stimulates secretion of hormone from ovary. Stimulates mammary glands.

PITUITARY GONADOTROPHIC HORMONES REGULATE THE MENSTRUAL CYCLE

FIRST HALF OF MENSTRUAL CYCLE

PITUITARY

SECOND HALF OF MENSTRUAL CYCLE

FSH — LH LUTEOTROPIN

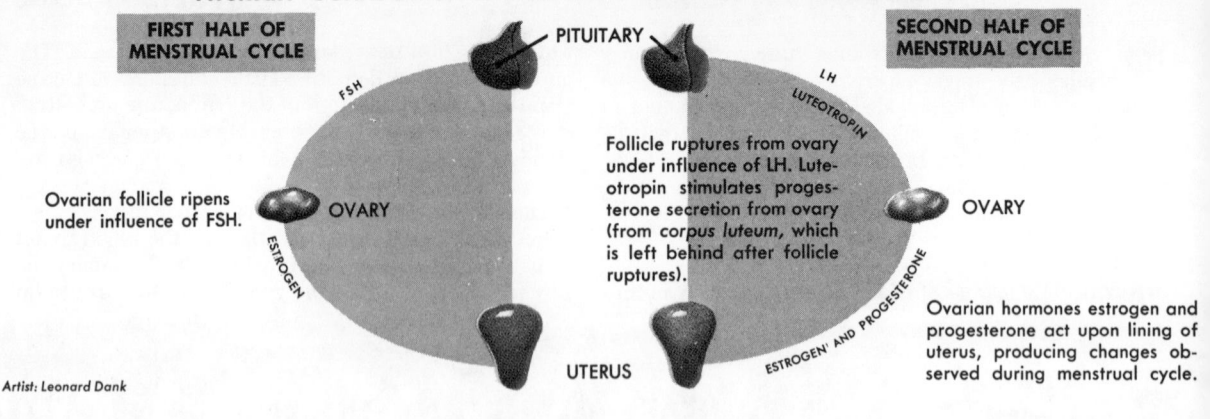

Ovarian follicle ripens under influence of FSH.

OVARY

Follicle ruptures from ovary under influence of LH. Luteotropin stimulates progesterone secretion from ovary (from *corpus luteum*, which is left behind after follicle ruptures).

OVARY

ESTROGEN

UTERUS

ESTROGEN AND PROGESTERONE

Ovarian hormones estrogen and progesterone act upon lining of uterus, producing changes observed during menstrual cycle.

Artist: Leonard Dank

THE POSTERIOR PITUITARY (NEUROHYPOPHYSIS)

The posterior pituitary is richly supplied with nerves from the hypothalamic region of the brain. Posterior pituitary hormones act upon the kidneys, circulatory system, uterus, and breasts.

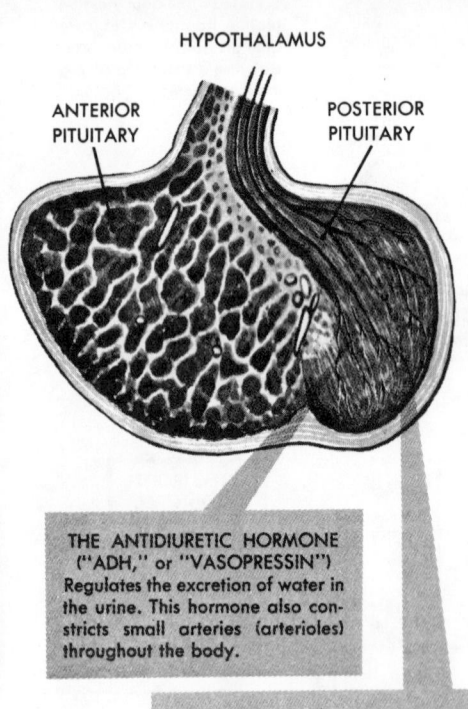

THE PITUITARY-BRAIN LINK

The pituitary sets the pace of endocrine activity and is itself controlled by stimulation from the nervous system. Thus both the chemical and nervous control of the internal activities of the body are brought under the direct regulation of the brain.

An example of the nature of these relationships is seen in the reactions which (on the basis of animal experimentation) are believed to follow a marked prolonged drop in the outside temperature.

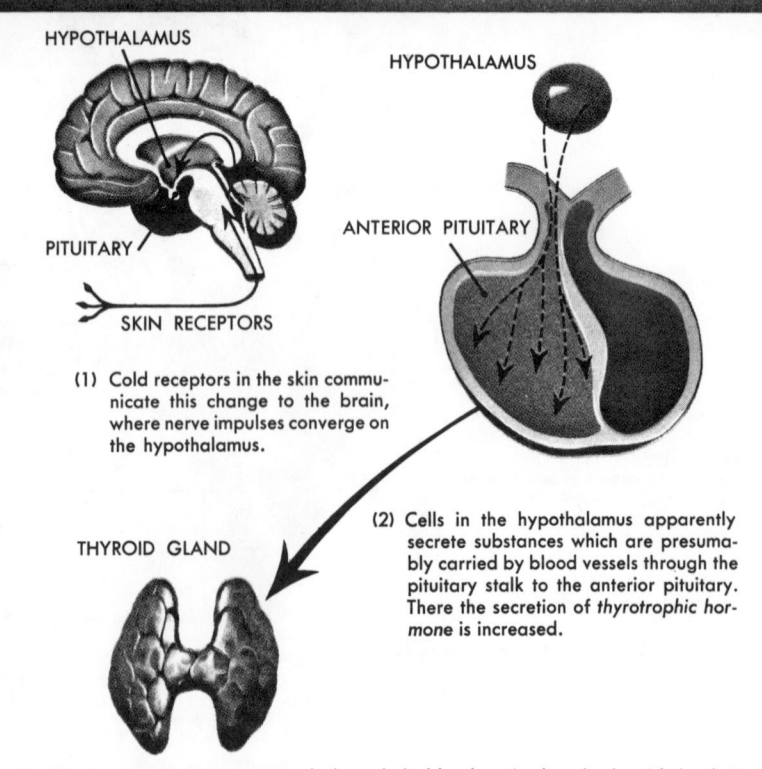

HYPOTHALAMUS
ANTERIOR PITUITARY
POSTERIOR PITUITARY

HYPOTHALAMUS
PITUITARY
SKIN RECEPTORS

HYPOTHALAMUS
ANTERIOR PITUITARY

(1) Cold receptors in the skin communicate this change to the brain, where nerve impulses converge on the hypothalamus.

THE ANTIDIURETIC HORMONE ("ADH," or "VASOPRESSIN")
Regulates the excretion of water in the urine. This hormone also constricts small arteries (arterioles) throughout the body.

OXYTOCIN
Stimulates contraction of uterus. Promotes ejection of milk from the breasts during lactation.

THYROID GLAND

(2) Cells in the hypothalamus apparently secrete substances which are presumably carried by blood vessels through the pituitary stalk to the anterior pituitary. There the secretion of *thyrotrophic hormone* is increased.

(3) The thyrotrophic hormone travels through the blood to stimulate the thyroid gland of the throat. The thyroid hormone acts upon the cells of the body to increase oxygen consumption and heat production.

THE "FEEDBACK" PHASE OF REGULATION

The thyroid hormone "feeds back" to the pituitary or hypothalamus to inhibit secretion of thyrotrophic hormone.

(A) Balance of thyroid-thyrotrophic hormone before events described above.

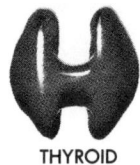

Thyrotrophic hormone stimulates thyroid.
Thyroid hormone inhibits pituitary.

THYROID — PITUITARY

(B) Secretion of thyrotrophic hormone by pituitary increases in response to cold.

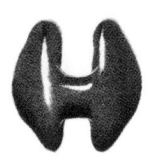

THYROTROPHIC HORMONE
THYROID HORMONE

(C) Secretion of thyroid hormone increases. Pituitary secretion is inhibited and new equilibrium is reached.

THYROTROPHIC HORMONE
THYROID HORMONE

women). This part of the pituitary also produces the growth hormone which promotes general growth and bone development in young animals.

The *intermediate zone* of the pituitary produces a hormone which controls the distribution of pigment particles in the skin. The function of this melanocyte-stimulating hormone (MSH) is not yet clear in humans.

The *posterior section*, or the neurohypophysis, produces hormones which regulate urine flow (ADH) and stimulate contractions of the uterus during childbirth and the flow of milk from the breasts.

Control of Anterior Pituitary Secretions. The secretions of the anterior pituitary are controlled by the level of hormones in the blood and by stimulation from the brain.

Feedback Control. This can be made clear by considering how the concentration of thyroid hormone is regulated. As the blood concentration of thyroid hormone falls, pituitary secretion of thyroid-stimulating hormone increases. This stimulates secretion and release of thyroid hormone by the thyroid gland. As thyroid-hormone level in the blood increases, pituitary secretion of thyroid-stimulating hormone declines. The exact manner in which thyroid hormone inhibits pituitary secretion is not yet clear.

Nervous Control. In states of stress pituitary secretion of ACTH (adrenal-stimulating hormone) increases. This increase apparently results from stimulation of the pituitary by the brain and is thought to be produced by substances secreted by particular cells of the brain (in the hypothalamus) and carried through the blood to the glands.

Control of Posterior Pituitary Secretions. The posterior pituitary hormones are regulated by nervous stimulation from the brain. An example of such stimulation is seen in the flow of milk from the breast of the nursing mother. Sensory impulses generated by the infant's sucking at the breast release nerve impulses in the brain which stimulate secretion of oxytocin by the posterior pituitary; this hormone, in turn, causes milk to flow from the mother's breast.

Disease of the Pituitary Gland. Over- or under-secretion of the pituitary hormones usually has far-reaching effects. An excess of growth hormone may cause gigantism and acromegaly (enlargement of certain bones). Excess secretion of ACTH causes Cushing's syndrome, characterized by abnormal deposits of fat, high blood pressure, a distinctive fullness of the face (moonface), and numerous abnormalities of body chemistry. A deficiency of the antidiuretic hormone results in diabetes insipidus, a disorder in which the patient passes enormous amounts of urine.

See also ENDOCRINE GLANDS.

PITYRIASIS ROSEA [pĭt-ĭ-rī′ə-sĭs rō′zē-ə], common skin disease of unknown origin. It begins with a "herald patch," a red, scaly area resembling ringworm. Within a few days similar patches appear between the neck and the knees. Itching may be mild or severe. Most cases disappear spontaneously in about six weeks. Ultraviolet light and soothing baths and lotions may relieve discomfort and shorten the course of the disease.

PLACENTA [plə-sĕn′tə], the disklike structure through which the developing embryo receives oxygen and nutrient substances from the mother's blood. The placenta is attached to the wall of the uterus and is connected to the embryo by the umbilical cord. Following the birth of the child, the placenta is expelled from the uterus along with the birth membranes as the afterbirth.

See also CHILDBIRTH.

PLAGUE [plāg], also known as Black Death, a highly fatal bacterial disease of rodents and man caused by the *Pasteurella pestis*. Historically, plague has been a formidable disease. The Black Death of the Middle Ages is estimated to have reduced the population of Europe by

PLANTS, POISONOUS

one quarter, or 25,000,000 people. The last major outbreak, in the late 19th century, originated in China and spread throughout the world. Plague still claims approximately 500,000 lives every year in Asia.

The principal carrier of plague is the rat, although plague is also found in squirrels, chipmunks, and other animals. An important link in the transmission of the disease to man is the rat flea, *Xenopsylla cheopis*. The bacteria enter the flea when it extracts a blood meal from an infected rodent. They multiply in the flea's digestive system, where they accumulate in such numbers that they are regurgitated into the body of healthy rodents when the flea seeks another meal. The fleas may transmit the disease to humans by bites or by depositing feces or vomitus on human skin or mucous membranes.

After an incubation period of 2 to 10 days, the lymph nodes in the groins or armpits become tender and enlarged—hence the term "bubonic plague" (from bubo, or enlarged lymph node). There are chills, fever, delirium, and rapid pulse and breathing. The patient may suffer from headache, dizziness, and thirst. Hemorrhages often appear in various parts of the body; hemorrhages into the skin produce the discolorations which give the disease its name (Black Death). A particularly dangerous form of plague occurs if the bacteria enter the lungs (pneumonic plague). In such cases the patient develops shortness of breath and coughs up bloody sputum. The sputum contains enormous numbers of plague bacilli and a single patient may contaminate his surroundings and all who approach him, triggering a violent epidemic of pneumonic plague which spreads through infected, airborne sputum.

Treatment consists of bed rest and anti-infective drugs. In cases of pneumonic plague, the patient must be strictly isolated in a screened room and attendants must wear coveralls, goggles, gloves, and hoods which must be sterilized or burned after use. Plague control requires elimination of the insects and rats involved in the cycle of infection. Immunity usually follows infection. Vaccines are available which provide temporary immunity against plague.

See also BLACK DEATH.

PLANTS, POISONOUS. Most plants are harmless, many are poisonous under certain conditions, and a few are nearly always poisonous. Many plants contain more than one type of poison. Notable for the number of poisonous species are the lily family, Liliaceae; the buttercup, or crowfoot, family, Ranunculaceae; the spurge family, Euphorbiaceae; the poppy family, Papaveraceae; the pulse, or pea, family, Leguminosae; and the nightshade family, Solanaceae.

There are five main groups of plant poisons. *Alkaloids* are most common in the lily, poppy, pea, and nightshade families. *Glucosides* yield toxic products under hydrolysis. Cyanogenetic glucosides are found in species of *Prunus* (the stone-fruits), *Sorghum*, and *Linum* (flax). The toxic principle is hydrocyanic, or prussic, acid, also called cyanide. Saponin glucosides are found in the common foxglove, *Digitalis purpurea*, and *Actinea solanines*. Oil glucosides are found in various plants in the mustard family, Cruciferae. Poisonous *resinoids* are found in the

PLANTS THAT ARE POISONOUS IF EATEN

COMMON NAME	BOTANICAL NAME	POISONOUS PARTS AND SPECIAL CHARACTERISTICS
Autumn crocus	Colchicum autumnale	Poisonous root
Belladonna	Atropa belladonna	All parts poisonous
Bittersweet	Solanum dulcamara	Berries, and juice of wilted leaves, are poisonous
Castor bean	Ricinus communis	Seeds fatal (used in medicine)
Chokecherry	Prunus virginiana	Wilted foilage very poisonous
Deadly nightshade	Solanum nigrum	Wilted foilage very poisonous
Dumbcane	Dieffenbachia seguine	Paralysis of mouth muscles from chewing the leaves
English ivy	Hedera helix	All parts are poisonous
Foxglove	Digitalis purpurea	Foilage dangerous (used in medicine)
Henbane	Hyoscyamus niger	Juice is very poisonous
Jequirity bean	Abrus precatorius	Bean poisonous (often used in jewelry)
Jerusalem cherry	Solanum pseudo capsicum	Orange-colored berries are highly poisonous
Jimsonweed	Datura stramonium	Seeds and other parts are poisonous
Johnson grass	Sorghum halepense	All parts are poisonous
Larkspur	Delphinium	Foilage poisonous
Mistletoe	Phoradendron flavescens	Berries are poisonous
Monkshood	Aconitum napelles	All parts poisonous
Narcissus	All forms (narcissus, jonquil, daffodil)	Bulbs poisonous
Oleander	Oleander nerium	All parts poisonous
Opium poppy	Papaver somniferum	Medicinal use
Poinsettia	Euphorbia pulcherrima	Juice poisonous
Paison hemlock	Conium maculatum	All parts very poisonous
Potato	Solanum tuberosum	Sprouts and green tubers should not be eaten
Rhododendron	Rhododendron	Foilage poisonous
Rhubarb, pie plant	Rheum rhaponticum	Cooked stem or small leaves are edible; large leaves are poisonous
Strychnine	Strychnos nux-vomica	Juice very poisonous
Water hemlock	Cicuta maculata	Roots poisonous
Wild black cherry	Prunus serotina	Wilted foilage very poisonous
Yew	Taxus	Leaves, bark and seeds are toxic; juice of the foilage is poisonous

PLANTS THAT ARE POISONOUS ON CONTACT

COMMON NAME	BOTANICAL NAME	PARTS
Autumn crocus	Colchicum autumnale	Leaves, corms
Box	Buxus sempervirens	Leaves
Buttercup	Ranunculus	Leaves
Gas plant	Dictamnus	Seed, pod, leaves
Hemp, marijuana	Cannabis sativa	Leaves, flowers
Iris	Iris	Rhizomes
Jack-in-the-pulpit	Arisaema triphyllum	Leaves, corms
Lady's slipper	Cypripedium	Leaves, stems
Maidenhair tree	Ginkgo biloba	Fruit pulp
Osage orange	Maclura pomifera	Milky juice
Poison ivy	Rhus toxicodendron	Leaves, fruit, bark
Poison oak	Rhus diversiloba	Leaves, fruit, bark
Poison sumac	Rhus vernix	Leaves, fruit, bark
Primula	Primula obconica	Leaves
Snow-on-the-mountain	Euphorbia	Milky juice
Tree of heaven	Ailanthus altissima	Flowers, leaves
Wild carrot	Daucus carota	Wet leaves
Wild parsnip	Pastinaca sativa	Leaves, stems

heaths and milkweed species. *Phytotoxins* are found in locusts and castor bean. A fifth potential poison is oxalic acid when it combines with calcium, but there is seldom enough oxalic acid in plants to cause such poisoning.

Most serious cases of plant poisoning in men and animals are due to eating part of a poisonous plant. Poisoning through contact with certain plants is usually less serious. Many well-known ornamental plants in homes and gardens can cause fatal illness if eaten, but many more animals than people are victims of plant poisoning, especially on the ranges when food is scarce. Several of the world's most poisonous plants have highly valuable medicinal properties, as well.

Poisoning by contact with plants is almost entirely limited to man. Such poisoning may produce a slight rash or a severe case of irritation and blisters. Plants that affect nearly everyone are poison ivy, poison oak, and poison sumac. Some people react with dermatitis to parsnip and lady's slipper. The white juice of spurges also causes dermatitis. *Primula obconica* is the worst offender of the primrose family.

PLASMA EXPANDERS, substances used as a temporary substitute for whole blood to prevent loss of fluids from the blood. Normally, large proteins maintain the osmotic pressure of the blood stream and prevent fluids from escaping into the tissues. Plasma expanders such as dextran, modified gelatin, and polyvinylpyrrolidone (PVP) are used as an emergency treatment for cases of acute shock caused by extensive burns or hemorrhages. In such cases proteins are lost, the osmotic pressure of the blood declines, and fluid escapes. The large molecules of the plasma expanders help restore the osmotic pressure of the blood and prevent further fluid loss.

PLASTIC SURGERY, a branch of medicine that specializes in the surgical alteration of the tissues of the body in order to correct deformity or to improve appearance.

The earliest accounts of plastic surgery are contained in the writings of the Hindu surgeon Sushruta, who lived in the 6th or 7th century B.C. In his works descriptions can be found of methods to transplant flaps of cheek skin to repair damaged noses. The basic teachings of early Hindu surgery eventually spread from India, by way of the southern Asian trade routes, to Persia and Arabia, finally reaching the Mediterranean civilizations, particularly those in Sicily and Italy. During the Renaissance in Europe, the art of transplanting skin was apparently revived from the archives, where it had lain dormant during the Dark Ages. Gasparo Tagliacozzi, a surgeon and anatomist of Bologna, who is generally considered the father of modern plastic surgery, popularized rhinoplasties (nose operations) in the 16th century.

Modern plastic surgery has two subdivisions: reconstructive plastic surgery and cosmetic surgery. Reconstructive plastic surgery attempts to restore a diseased, injured, or deformed part to normal. Surgery of this type seeks to restore function to burned hands, arms, feet, and legs. It also includes the removal of scars, the treatment of long-standing skin ulcers, and the correction of congenital deformities such as cleft palate, harelip, hairy moles, extra fingers (polydactylism), webbed fingers (syndactylism), and deformities of the genital organs.

Cosmetic plastic surgery attempts to improve the appearance of unsightly surface features. Among the cosmetic problems that can be successfully treated by plastic surgeons are oddly shaped noses, baggy eyelids, wrinkles, double chins, and underdeveloped or overdeveloped breasts.

The basic technique employed by plastic surgeons is grafting, a process in which healthy tissues are transplanted to replace or to repair imperfect structures. Tissues transplanted from one part of the body to another are known as autografts. A tissue transplanted from one individual to another is termed a "homograft." Such transplants can be successfully carried out using cartilage, bone, and corneal tissue (from the eye). In the case of skin and kidney tissue, successful transplants are ordinarily possible only between identical twins. The body treats the transplanted homografts as a foreign element and develops substances (antibodies) that react with and destroy the transplant. Thus the rejection of homografts results from the development of an immunity in the patient to the transplanted tissue, similar to the immunity that protects the body against invading bacteria.

When the skin or tissue to be transplanted is completely detached from its place and transferred to a new site, the transplant is termed a "free graft." The success of such a graft depends upon the blood supply and the thickness of the skin section. An extremely thin section may shrink and an overly thick section may not "take." Free-skin autografts are used to provide a new covering after injury, as for eyelids damaged by fire, and as a temporary dressing for raw or burned surfaces.

In cases involving deep, extensive tissue losses, thicker sections than can be used in free grafting are needed. For this purpose pedicles, or skin flaps, are used. To repair a wound on the cheek, a three-sided patch of skin may be rotated from adjacent cheek or neck tissue on a narrow skin pedicle. Elaborate reconstructions of badly damaged faces, hands, and feet are made through the use of pedicles.

In practice modern plastic surgery has benefited from the development of antibiotics, which reduce the incidence of infection during transplantation and greatly increase the percentage of favorable results. The refinement of surgical techniques, the availability of anesthetics and of drugs to control bleeding, and the vast gains in medical knowledge have also contributed to the success of this specialty. The next great advance is expected to be in the control of the mechanism by which the body rejects grafts of foreign tissue. This probably should make possible the permanent transplantation of kidneys, endocrine glands, lungs, and other major organs.

PLEURISY [plŏor'ə-sē], inflammation of the pleura, the membrane which envelops the lungs and lines the inner wall of the chest cavity. Pleurisy may be caused by bacterial, viral, or fungus infections of the lungs, by tumors, or by general bodily disorders such as rheumatic fever and rheumatoid arthritis. In many cases attacks of pleurisy occur in tuberculosis infections some time before the disease becomes clinically apparent in the lungs. The pleura becomes congested and thickened, and roughened patches may rub against each other. Extensive seepage of fluid between the pleural layers gives rise to "wet" pleurisy (or pleurisy with effusion). Large masses of fluid may compress the lungs and interfere with breathing.

The inner membrane (the visceral pleura) that covers the lungs is insensitive so that pain is not felt unless the inflammation extends to the parietal pleura, the layer adjacent to the chest wall. The pain is usually felt in the chest and may cause shortness of breath. Inflammations in the central region of the diaphragm may cause pain in the root of the neck or shoulder, the pain being "referred" along nerve pathways shared in common by these structures. Similarly irritation of the pleura of the lower chest or peripheral areas of the diaphragm may give rise to abdominal pain and be confused with appendicitis or other abdominal disorders.

Diagnosis of the cause of pleurisy is aided by examination of fluid withdrawn from the pleural space. The inflammation usually heals leaving adhesions—fibrous strands of scar tissue binding the inner and outer pleura. Extensive adhesions may impair expansion and contraction of the lungs. Treatment includes pain-relieving drugs (such as aspirin and codeine), removal of excessive fluid accumulations, and measures directed at the underlying condition.

PNEUMOCONIOSIS [nū-mō-kŏn-ē-ō'sĭs], any of a number of lung disorders caused by inhaling dust particles. The commonest form of pneumoconiosis is silicosis, resulting from inhalation of silica (SiO_2). This is seen in mining and stone-cutting industries and in occupations which use quartz, flint, and sand. Anthracosilicosis, which is caused by coal dust, occurs among miners. Other forms of pneumoconiosis result from the inhalation of asbestos fibers and beryllium and cotton dust. The principal symptoms seen in these disorders are shortness of breath and coughing. Tuberculosis is a frequent complication. A high incidence of lung cancer has been noted in asbestosis.
See also BERYLLIOSIS; SILICOSIS.

PNEUMONIA [nū-mōn'yə], inflammation of the lung, which may be caused by bacteria, viruses, fungi, or by irritant chemicals or gases. *Lobar pneumonia*, which often appears in acute bacterial pneumonia, involves the lobes, the primary subdivisions of the lungs, of which there are three in the right lung and two in the left. In *bronchopneumonia* the inflammation involves the smaller bronchopulmonary segments, each segment comprising the subdivisions of the lobes.

Pneumonia is one of the commonest infectious diseases of man. It occurs throughout the world and is most frequent during the winter months. Severe fatigue and exhaustion, exposure to extreme wet or cold, chronic alcoholism, malnutrition, and tuberculosis and other lung diseases may predispose to pneumonia. More than half the cases are preceded by a common cold, which may lead to pneumonia when plugs of infected mucus are sucked down the windpipe from the upper respiratory tract.

Causes. The pneumococcus bacteria are the most common cause of pneumonia, being found in over 80% of all cases. This organism may be a normal inhabitant of the mouth, nose, and pharynx and under predisposing conditions, such as those mentioned above, may cause pneumonia. Other pneumonia-causing bacteria are the staphylococcus, the cause of many hospital infections, and the Friedländer bacillus, which causes pneumonia in infants, aged persons, and alcoholics. Fungus pneumonias are in certain areas of the United States, such as the Mississippi Valley (histoplasmosis) and the San Joaquin Valley (coccidioidomycosis).

Epidemics of pneumonia are commonly associated with epidemics of influenza, such as occurred in World War I and in the 1957 epidemic of Asian influenza in the United States. In such epidemics death usually results, not from the influenza, but from the complicating pneumonia.

Pneumonia may occur following anesthesia for abdominal surgery. Presumably bacteria multiply in the lungs because of the accumulation of excessive secretions in the lung and the inability to cough out stagnant mucus effectively.

Lung Changes. In bacterial pneumonia the air sacs of the lung are packed with pus cells mixed with blood. During healing, the pus is absorbed into the blood stream or is removed from the air sacs by coughing. If recovery is delayed and the bacteria and pus cells remain, fibrous scar tissue may grow into the area, permanently closing the air spaces and destroying the function of that part of the lung. Occasionally the affected lung tissue is destroyed, forming a lung abscess, a collection of pus enclosed by a thick wall. In viral pneumonias the inflammation and pus are more commonly seen in the tissue which separates the air sacs. In all forms of pneumonia the covering of the lungs (the pleura) is frequently involved.

Symptoms. Typically the patient has aches and a mild fever associated with a common cold, lasting for several days to a week. Suddenly, as the cold is running its course, the patient develops a high "spiking" fever and suffers severe shaking chills. Within a matter of hours, or even minutes, he develops pleurisy: acute pain in the chest, which is aggravated by breathing. His cough worsens and he raises a rust-colored, or bloody and pus-laden, sputum. During the early stages of the disease, he may be slightly short of breath and suffer from headache, loss of appetite, and weakness. Later delirium may occur. Prior to the discovery of antibiotics, pneumonia was frequently fatal, especially in older persons. Today antibiotics are given early in the disease and usually cause the fever to subside within 24 to 36 hours.

Serious complications of pneumonia include extension of the infection to the pleural space (empyema), lung abscesses, heart or respiratory failure, and jaundice. Occasionally the infection may spread to the membrane which covers the heart (the pericardium), to the brain, heart valves, or to other parts of the body.

Treatment and Outlook. Treatment consists of complete bed rest, a large fluid intake, and the administration of antibiotics. Penicillin is the best treatment for the usual case of pneumonia, since it is highly effective against the pneumococcus bacteria. There is no antibiotic known to be effective in the treatment of viral pneumonia. The treatment of fungus-caused pneumonia is presently inadequate, although a new drug, Amphotericin B, has proved of some use in selected cases.

The outlook for the patient is generally excellent except in the case of aged and debilitated patients and in malnourished infants. Alcoholics may suffer dangerous complications, such as liver failure. Occasionally viral pneumonias may be rapidly fatal.

A grave problem results from pneumonia caused by drug-resistant staphylococcus bacteria. These organisms are often present in hospitals and can withstand usual antibiotic treatment. In such cases the physician must obtain a sample of the patient's sputum and grow the organisms in the laboratory to test the effectiveness of various antibiotics against them.

Occasionally lobar pneumonia in an older male patient indicates lung cancer. In such cases the prospects for recovery are lessened. Similarly, patients with chronic lung diseases may suffer respiratory failure upon developing pneumonia. This may be fatal unless treated vigorously and quickly.

PNEUMOTHORAX [nū-mō-thôr′ăks], a medical term denoting the presence of air in the pleural space which lies between the lung and the chest wall. Normally the pleural space contains no air, and permits the lung to expand during breathing. In pneumothorax the presence of air in the cavity may partially or completely collapse the lung. This may occur in cases of penetrating wounds of the chest, in lung diseases, or spontaneously without apparent cause.

Typically, the victim experiences sudden pain in the chest and shortness of breath. Occasionally no symptoms occur. In mild cases only bed rest may be necessary. In severe cases immediate withdrawal of air by means of a needle introduced into the pleural space is necessary to save a patient's life. Artificial pneumothorax, produced by introducing air into the pleural space, was formerly used in the treatment of tuberculosis. The method has fallen into disuse because of the danger of lung complications and the availability of antituberculous drugs.

PODIATRY [pō-dī′ə-trē] **or CHIROPODY** [kĭ-rŏp′ə-dē], allied medical specialties dealing with the diagnosis and treatment of disorders of the feet. Although state and national laws defining the scope of practice vary, the podiatrist generally deals with the common skin excrescences (corns and calluses) and with bunions, flat feet, fungus and bacterial infections of the feet, ingrown nails, circulatory disorders, warts, and gait problems. Two years of college are generally required for admission to a podiatry school. The course is four years in length and includes anatomy, physiology, biochemistry, and other basic medical sciences, as well as courses in specialized podiatric subjects.

POISONING. Although the number of deaths caused by infectious diseases has declined in the present century, fatalities caused by accidental poisoning have increased. In New York City, for example, more children die from poisoning than from measles, German measles, poliomyelitis, rheumatic fever, and scarlet fever combined. This increase is largely attributable to the introduction into the home of many new drugs, bleaching solutions, detergents, rat poisons, and cleaning and polishing products.

Nearly half of the poisonings occur in children under five years of age, especially in one- and two-year-old children who have the habit of mouthing objects. The "crawlers and creepers" frequently swallow solvents, insecticides, and cleaning products stored under the kitchen sink and on low shelves. In many cases poisoning occurs when harmful substances are transferred from their original containers into drinking glasses, soft-drink bottles, mayonnaise jars, saucers, cups, milk bottles, coffee cans, fruit cans, and other receptacles. These materials are then placed at low levels, such as on the floor, under the sink, in the washtub, and in other open places, such as on low tables and shelves, within easy reach of children.

Types of Poison

Internal Medicines. Aspirin is a major cause of poisoning in children. Because it is so widely used, parents apparently do not appreciate its danger to children, particularly when taken in large doses.

The most frequent victims of aspirin poisoning are children between two and three years of age. Flavored aspirin has caused an increase in the number of aspirin poisonings because of its attractiveness to children. Fortunately it is now manufactured in lower dosage than adult aspirin. In spite of many unwarranted claims there is as yet no safe closure device on bottles which children cannot remove.

Many poisonings occur from the accidental swallowing of oil of wintergreen (methylsalicylate). This substance is considerably more dangerous than aspirin.

Barbiturate poisoning in children results chiefly from adult negligence: when sleeping pills are carelessly put in pocketbooks or stored on low shelves and swallowed by unsuspecting children.

Iron tonics and vitamin preparations containing iron are often unrecognized hazards. Parents do not think of these preparations as poisonous and leave them in open places where they are easily discovered by children.

Poisonings caused by the tranquilizing drugs have risen along with the increasing popularity of these medications.

Household Preparations. Among the most dangerous of the household products are lye and lye-containing products, which are corrosive and often cause serious complications.

Bleaches are a common cause of poisoning in the one- and two-year-old age group. Fortunately, most patients are successfully treated with the stomach pump and by inducing vomiting. It should be kept in mind, however, that some highly concentrated chlorine compounds can cause serious corrosion, permanent injury, and death.

Lead Poisoning. This is more common in lower income groups living in substandard housing where the walls and ceilings contain multiple coatings of paint, some of which have a high lead content. Young children become poisoned when they swallow flakes of painted plaster and peelings from the ceiling and window sills. The possibility of lead poisoning has been lessened by the decision of toy and furniture manufacturers to cease using lead paint for toys or cribs. The use of indoor paint having a high lead content is also forbidden in most localities. The public at large is advised not to use lead-based paints for painting apartments.

Solvents. Turpentine and kerosene still cause many poisonings and deaths. Other frequent causes of poisoning in children are pine oil and furniture polish (especially from brands containing lemon oil).

Insecticides and Rat Poisons. These products cause

WHAT TO DO IN CASE OF POISONING

(1) Begin treatment while sending someone to call a physician.
(2) If alone, begin treatment first in cases of INHALED POISONS, SKIN CONTAMINATION, EYE CONTAMINATION, INJECTED POISONS, and CHEMICAL BURNS.
In cases of SWALLOWED POISONS call a physician before beginning treatment.

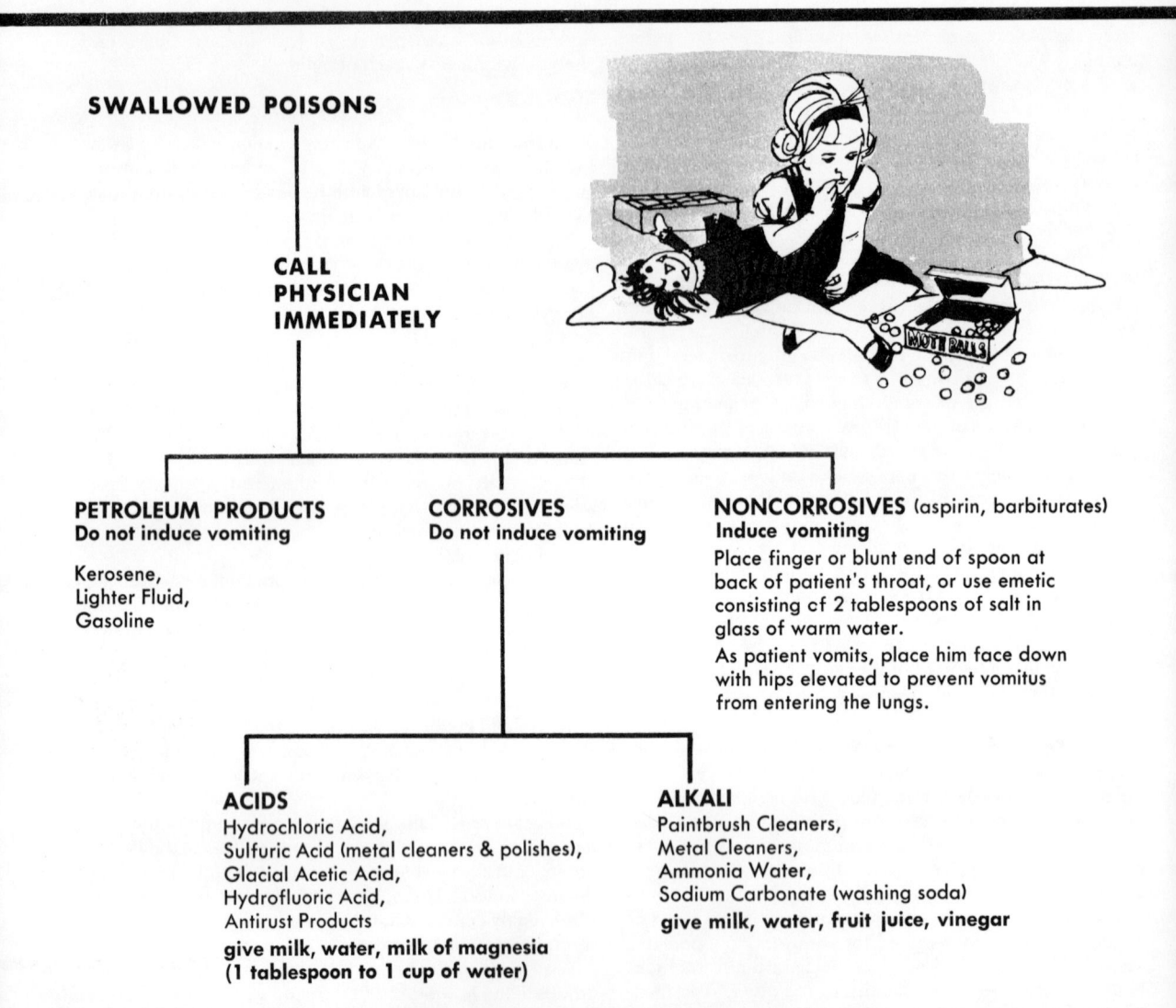

SWALLOWED POISONS

CALL PHYSICIAN IMMEDIATELY

PETROLEUM PRODUCTS
Do not induce vomiting

Kerosene,
Lighter Fluid,
Gasoline

CORROSIVES
Do not induce vomiting

NONCORROSIVES (aspirin, barbiturates)
Induce vomiting

Place finger or blunt end of spoon at back of patient's throat, or use emetic consisting of 2 tablespoons of salt in glass of warm water.

As patient vomits, place him face down with hips elevated to prevent vomitus from entering the lungs.

ACIDS
Hydrochloric Acid,
Sulfuric Acid (metal cleaners & polishes),
Glacial Acetic Acid,
Hydrofluoric Acid,
Antirust Products
give milk, water, milk of magnesia (1 tablespoon to 1 cup of water)

ALKALI
Paintbrush Cleaners,
Metal Cleaners,
Ammonia Water,
Sodium Carbonate (washing soda)
give milk, water, fruit juice, vinegar

INJECTED POISONS
Snake bite, scorpion bite
(1) Have patient lie down.
(2) Apply tourniquet above bite. Tourniquet should not be so tight as to cause throbbing, or to obliterate pulse.
(3) Apply ice-pack to bite.
(4) Carry patient to physician or hospital. He must not be allowed to walk.
(5) Avoid alcohol in any form.

INHALED POISONS
(Carbon monoxide in gas fumes; carbon tetrachloride in cleaning solutions, fire-extinguisher fluid, and solvents; ammonia)
(1) Carry patient immediately to fresh air.
(2) Loosen tight clothing.
(3) Apply artificial respiration if breathing has stopped or is irregular.
(4) Keep patient warm and quiet.
(5) Do not give alcohol in any form.

SKIN CONTAMINATION
(Insecticides, aniline dyes)
(1) Wash skin thoroughly with running water from shower, faucet, or hose.
(2) Continue washing while removing clothing.

EYE CONTAMINATION
(Ammonia, acids, alkalies)
Hold eyelids open and wash eyes with a gentle stream of running water. Continue until physician arrives.
Speed is important — immediate thorough washing may prevent much damage.
Do not apply chemicals to the eyes.

CHEMICAL BURNS
(Acids, alkalies)
(1) Wash thoroughly with running water.
(2) Cover lightly with clean cloth.
(3) Keep patient warm and in prone position.
(4) Do not give medications or apply any to burn.

POISONING HAZARDS FOR CHILDREN

KITCHEN
POLISHES AND WAXES (kerosene, oils, caustics, turpentine, oxalic acid),
DETERGENTS (strong alkaline solutions),
DRY-CLEANING FLUIDS (carbon tetrachloride, kerosene, petroleum distillates),
INSECTICIDES (DDT, chlordane, benzene hexachloride),
AMMONIA SOLUTIONS, MOTH BALLS, FLAKES (naphthalene),
RAT POISONS (phosphorus).

BATHROOM
IRON COMPOUNDS, MERCURIAL COMPOUNDS, ATROPINE EYE DROPS, IODINE, BELLADONNA PREPARATIONS,
HAIR DYES, TINTS (ammonium hydroxide, sodium hypochlorite solution, metallic dyes),
SHAMPOOS (denatured alcohol, sodium hexametaphosphate),
RUBBING ALCOHOL, DEPILATORIES (calcium thioglycolate, sulfides),
SUN TAN LOTIONS (denatured alcohol),
TRANQUILIZING DRUGS,
DIGITALIS (used for some types of heart disease,)
ASPIRIN,
BORIC ACID.

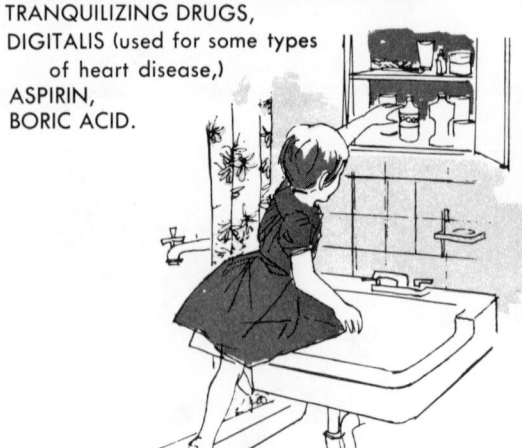

BEDROOM-PLAYROOM
CRAYONS, (aniline dyes),
PAINT ON CRIB, (lead),
LEAD TOYS,
NAIL PREPARATIONS (organic solvents),
CUTICLE REMOVERS (alkalies),
SLEEPING PILLS (barbiturates).

GARAGE AND WORKSHOP
PAINTS, PUTTY, VARNISHES (arsenic, cadmium, lead)
PAINT REMOVERS (benzene, kerosene, carbon tetrachloride),
PAINT BRUSH CLEANERS (acetone, turpentine, naphtha),
ANTIFREEZE (alcohols, ethylene glycol),
ANTIRUST PRODUCTS (sodium nitrite, hydrofluoric acid),
FIRE-EXTINGUISHING FLUIDS (carbon tetrachloride),
METAL CLEANERS (acids and alkalies),
DRAIN-PIPE CLEANER (lye),
FUMES FROM ENGINE (carbon monoxide).

many accidental poisonings because of careless handling and storage. A typical case occurred when a housewife purchased a chlordane concentrate in a soft drink bottle from an exterminator. Some months later her two-year-old child found the bottle under the sink and drank its contents. Although the product contained a lethal dosage of chlordane, prompt and vigorous treatment saved the child's life.

Poison Control Centers

Poison control centers were established following recognition of the fact that accidental poisonings in children constituted a major health problem. They were conceived as a means of co-ordinating data on the treatment of poisoning and making such information available to the physician. The first center was organized in Chicago in 1953 with the active support of the American Academy of Pediatrics. Shortly afterward centers were established in Boston and New York City and later the poison control center movement spread throughout the United States and Canada and to many European countries.

The centers collect information on every aspect of poisoning, including the toxic ingredients in chemicals and commercial products which may cause poisoning; the manner in which a poison acts; the number of poisonings attributable to a given substance; how, when, and where the poisoning occurred; and the side effects of drugs and toxicity of newly marketed drugs. Although some centers provide emergency treatment, their primary function is to furnish information to physicians. When a lay person calls, first aid instructions are given and the individual is advised to call a physician or to take the victim to the nearest hospital emergency clinic. Most poison control centers are located in hospitals.

The National Clearinghouse

To help the rapidly expanding poison control center movement, the U.S. Public Health Service established a national clearinghouse for poison control in Washington in 1957. The national clearinghouse receives reports from local centers, particularly on new toxic hazards, and makes the information promptly available to all existing centers. It receives information from chemical manufacturers on the ingredients of new products, their toxicity, and possible treatment. This data is prepared on a card index system which the clearinghouse disseminates to all centers. This serves as a chief source of information which the centers supply to all physicians who need it for the proper treatment of poisonings.

The clearinghouse also helps to establish new centers and to improve existing facilities. It publishes a monthly newsletter which is disseminated to all poison control centers, tabulates and analyzes reports received from local centers, and encourages research.

POISON IVY, POISON OAK, AND POISON SUMAC,

plants of the genus *Rhus*, in the sumac family, Anacardiaceae. Some sumacs are ornamental, and all have brilliant fall coloring.

Poison ivy, *R. radicans*, is a native of North America, including Mexico. It appears as a tall vine clinging to trees, walls, fences, or as a dense ground cover. Each leaf is composed of three leaflets. The tips are usually pointed, edges may be toothed. Poison ivy is a rampant pest and spreads rapidly. Upon contact, it produces a serious rash with big blisters in susceptible people. The rash can come from handling the plants and seemingly dead pieces of stems or roots. Some people are so sensitive to the poison that they develop a generalized illness with high fever. Poison ivy should not be burned. If the smoke comes in contact with the face, it may produce severe rash. Thorough washing with yellow laundry soap may prevent a rash if contact is suspected.

Poison oak, *R. diversiloba*, is a shrub or vine climbing to 8 ft., native from British Columbia to California. *R. toxicodendron*, also known as poison oak, is a low shrub native from New Jersey southward to Missouri, Mississippi, and Florida. The poisonous effect is exactly the same as that of poison ivy. There is no cure, although some people are helped by injections, others by lotions applied at once. A few people are completey immune.

Poison sumac, *R. vernix*, is a shrub or small tree that grows in swamps from Maine to Florida. The poison is at least as virulent as poison ivy, but owing to its habitat, people do not come into contact with it as often. Like all sumacs, poison sumac has pinnate leaves, with 7 to 13 leaflets. The berries are greenish-white on poison sumac, dull red on other, nonpoisonous sumacs. The treatment for poison sumac is the same as for poison ivy.

Weed killers, carefully used, are the best means of eradicating any poisonous plants. The plants are best avoided, unless clothing provides very good protection.

POLIOMYELITIS [pō-lē-ō-mī-ə-lī′tĭs], also known as infantile paralysis, is a contagious virus disease which may attack the nervous system, causing paralysis or death. Although it is likely that the disease has existed since early times, the first reports in the medical literature appeared in the 18th century. During the next hundred years the number of polio cases increased, culminating in the great epidemics of the 20th century, the first of which occurred in Norway and Sweden in 1905. Epidemics have since appeared in nearly all industrialized countries, particularly in those in the temperate zones.

In 1908 the Austrian physician Karl Landsteiner established that poliomyelitis was caused by a virus. There are three distinct types of polio virus. Individual strains of each type vary in their tendency to attack nerve tissues; some are rapidly destructive, whereas others cause no damage.

It is now generally believed that polio is acquired through the mouth, chiefly by fecal contamination of food, fingers, or other objects, or from carriers who harbor the virus in the intestinal tract. The apparent paradox that polio is often rampant in countries with high standards of living is explained by the pattern of exposure to the polio virus. In underdeveloped countries, where sanitary facilities are poor, fecal contamination of the food is common and infants are exposed to the polio virus at an age when they are still partly protected by immunity passed on from the mother. This results in a harmless infection and subsequent permanent immunity. In more advanced communities, fecal contamination of food is less likely, and exposure, when it does occur, is at a time when the child no longer enjoys partial immunity (which lasts about six months after birth) and suffers the full effects of the disease. The viruses spread rapidly under such conditions, as was observed in the United States in the period from 1943 to 1950. As with other communicable diseases, the spread follows a cyclic pattern. The viruses attack many individuals, leaving them with a permanent immunity—the number of immune persons steadily increases, eventually leading to a decline in the number of cases. This decline evidently occurred in the period from 1953 to 1960, and was undoubtedly accelerated by the Salk vaccine.

Symptoms. The incubation period is from 3 to 35 days, averaging 9 to 13 days for paralytic cases. Usually the infection produces no symptoms or only minor disturbances, such as fever and a feeling of illness. More pronounced symptoms include headache, sore throat, vomiting, and aches. Other cases begin in similar fashion and after a period of a few days develop paralysis ranging from mild, and sometimes temporary, weakness to full and permanent loss of function and atrophy of affected muscles. Paralysis reaches its height within a few days and then usually subsides to a varying degree. Whatever paralysis remains after one year is not likely to improve.

In general, the virus causes paralysis by attacking the nerve cells which supply the muscles. One form of polio attacks the cells in the spinal cord and usually involves the legs more often than the arms, but may also involve the neck and trunk. Bulbar poliomyelitis attacks the medulla, the part of the brain which lies directly above the spinal cord, and which includes centers that control swallowing, speaking, blood pressure, and breathing. Interference with breathing, a particularly dangerous complication of the disease, occurs more often when the cervical portion of the spinal cord, which controls the chest muscles or diaphragm, is affected.

Treatment. There is no specific drug for treating poliomyelitis. During the acute attack, rest and careful nursing are important. The skilled use of hot packs may help considerably. The iron lung, which breathes mechanically for the patient, is used when the breathing muscles are paralyzed. Tube feeding may be necessary if the swallowing muscles are affected. The permanent paralyses are treated by muscle-strengthening exercises, braces, and sometimes surgery to transplant tendons of healthy muscle to substitute for paralyzed muscles.

Prevention. Two safe and effective polio vaccines have been developed, both using viruses cultivated by the methods developed in 1949 by Dr. John F. Enders and his associates. An effective oral vaccine, developed by Dr. Albert B. Sabin of Cincinnati, has been given to some 80,000,000 persons in the U.S.S.R. and Eastern Europe, with a perfect record of safety. This vaccine uses doses of weakened live viruses and is usually given in syrup or candy. An immunity of nearly 100% is claimed for the oral vaccine, which is thought by its proponents to give a more durable and solid immunity than the killed-virus vaccine.

The other vaccine, developed by Dr. Jonas E. Salk of Pittsburgh, is injected and consists of a mixture of the three types of polio virus which have been killed by formaldehyde. The extensive field trials of 1954 proved that the vaccine was safe and that it afforded a protection of about 72% against paralytic poliomyelitis. Some difficulties were encountered when commercial production began in 1955: certain lots were found to be unsafe, and later great variations in potency were discovered. At present the Salk vaccine is safe and is becoming more dependable and effective; it is claimed to give 90% or better protection against paralysis. It is administered in a series of three injections separated by intervals of one to six months. Following this, booster injections are given once a year.

POLYCYTHEMIA [pŏl-ē-sī-thē'mē-ə], an increase in the number of circulating red cells in the blood. A secondary polycythemia may result from low oxygen content of the blood. This may occur in certain heart disorders in which blood bypasses the lungs and in lung ailments which impair diffusion of oxygen into the blood.

Primary polycythemia describes an increase of unknown cause in red blood cells. This occurs most frequently in individuals over 40, more often in men than women. Other blood elements, such as white cells and blood platelets, are also usually increased, and the blood volume is elevated. The condition may develop into leukemia (a massive overproduction of white blood cells). In primary polycythemia the blood becomes thick and flows sluggishly, leading to the formation of clots in the blood vessels and possibly causing a stroke or heart attack. The patient tends to bleed freely from minor cuts, owing to the increased congestion of the blood vessels and other factors. Spontaneous bleeding from the gums and nose is common. The skin is ruddy, and the victim may suffer from dizziness, headache, irritability, night sweats, fatigue, and weakness. The blood pressure is often elevated and the heart may be enlarged. Most patients develop a firm, enlarged spleen. Treatment consists of bleeding the patient to reduce blood volume and the use of radiation or drugs to inhibit the production of red blood cells in the bone marrow.

See also BLOOD.

POLYP [pŏl'ĭp], in medicine, a growth which is attached to adjacent tissues by a broad base or slender stalk. They are found especially on mucous membranes, such as those of the nose, stomach, urinary bladder, uterus, or intestines. Polyps in the intestines may cause bleeding, diarrhea, and intestinal pain; those in the stomach and colon tend to become cancerous. In cases of multiple intestinal polyps (polyposis) of the colon, which usually appears in family groups, it is necessary to remove the entire colon except the rectum to prevent the development of cancer.

POLYSACCHARIDES [pŏl-ĭ-săk'ə-rīdz], organic compounds composed of small carbohydrate units (monosaccharides). They are widely distributed in nature. Cellulose, the structural "backbone" of plants, and starch and glycogen, the energy-rich carbohydrate of plant and animal tissues respectively, are polysaccharides built of many units of the simple sugar, glucose. The polysaccharide chitin, found in insect shells, is composed of repeating units of the sugar derivative N-acetylglucosamine. Other polysaccharides, such as the chondroitin of cartilage and growing bone, are composed of more than one repeating unit.

PORPHYRIA [pôr-fîr'ē-ə], group of rare, inborn diseases, which block hemoglobin formation. There are two main forms, erythropoetic and hepatic. Erythropoetic porphyria, exceedingly rare, first appears in early infancy, showing up as a red stain on a diaper. Exposure to ultraviolet sunlight causes extensive skin damage, with slow-healing ulcers and severe scarring. Low hemoglobin produces anemia, and there may be abnormalities of the hair and teeth. A slightly different chemical derangement causes another, milder form of erythropoetic porphyria, which appears later in life and produces a similar but less severe skin disease.

In the more frequent hepatic form, symptoms are very variable, so that it is often confused with other diseases. The hepatic form may not appear until adulthood, then showing itself as severe abdominal pain or as a disease of the nervous system, with symptoms ranging from neuritis to mental illness. Because there is no cure for porphyria, treatment attempts to prevent or relieve symptoms. Patients must avoid sunshine and any medication which may harm the liver. Alcohol and barbiturates should also be avoided, as they may precipitate an attack.

POSTNASAL DRIP, the discharge of fluid secretions into the back part of the nose and throat from inflamed nasal and sinus tissues. This may occur in cases of "common cold," in sinusitis, and in allergic disorders affecting the nose. Chronic postnasal drip may cause coughing.

POSTPARTUM [pōst-pär′təm] **DEPRESSION,** a common condition occurring after childbirth, marked by weeping, sensitivity, and depression. The depression is thought to be a reaction to the new role of motherhood and the assumption of adult responsibilities. These changes in the status of the individual may produce unconscious hostility toward the husband, who is blamed for the new mother's situation, or toward the child. The unconscious hostility may in turn generate feelings of guilt and self-reproach, leading to depression. The condition may appear one to three days following birth and may persist as long as one or two weeks.
See also DEPRESSION

POSTURE [pŏs′chər]. In normal posture the head is held erect over the pelvis, the spine is arched slightly backward at the neck, the upper back is mildly rounded, and the lower back sways slightly forward. When viewed from the rear the normal spine is straight. These positions are maintained by muscular action so that when the position of the spine is momentarily changed by activity, it promptly returns to its normal balance.

These relationships are altered in poor posture; the head and neck are tilted forward, the upper back is more rounded, the lower back is markedly swayed, and the abdomen becomes flabby and pendulous, forming what is commonly known as a potbelly. The chest is flattened and the pelvis is tilted forward, causing the buttocks to protrude. Poor posture may result from habitual slouching or from a weakening of the muscles following long bouts of fever or disease. Young children who carry heavy loads on their back in work may develop poor posture. Bad sleeping conditions in a hammock or soft bed, or obesity may also be responsible. Extremely tall people commonly stoop. In addition to detracting from the general appearance, poor posture may cause deformity, arthritis of the spine, and abnormal pressures on the organs.

Treatment is most successful in young children. The spine gradually becomes fixed with age and only limited success can be obtained with adults. Muscle-strengthening exercises, corrective postural exercises, athletics, and dancing are helpful. Weight reduction is necessary in obese patients. Once correction is achieved it should be maintained by active exercises.

POTT, PERCIVAL (1714–88), English surgeon whose memory is preserved in two conditions which bear his name: Pott's fracture of the ankle and Pott's disease, or tuberculosis of the spine. Pott also wrote a classic treatise on hernia and in 1775 was the first to note the high frequency of cancer of the scrotum in chimney sweeps—an early association between a cancer-causing agent (in this case soot) and cancer.

PREGNANCY [prĕg′nən-sē]. The most reliable early sign of pregnancy is failure to menstruate. The problem of detecting early pregnancy has always been of great interest. The ancient Egyptians accomplished this by adding the woman's urine to a vessel of barley and earth. If the barley grew she was presumed pregnant. The good sense of this technique has since been verified by modern investigators who report that the urine of pregnant women contains high concentrations of estrogen, a hormone that stimulates plant growth.

The most widely used modern tests of pregnancy are the Aschheim-Zondek test and its modifications, which are based on the presence of hormones (chorionic gonadotrophins) in the woman's urine that are secreted by the tissues that envelop the embryo. The urine is injected into an immature rat, mouse, or rabbit: after a period of one to five days (depending on the animal) the animal's ovaries are inspected for characteristic changes. A more rapid technique, the so-called "frog test," consists of injecting the urine into a male frog; if the woman is pregnant the frog will expel spermatozoa within a few hours. These tests are not completely reliable within the first six to eight weeks: if the test is positive, the woman is pregnant; however, she may be pregnant even if the test is negative. A "hormonal" test is available which will induce menstruation if the woman is not pregnant. If the woman fails to menstruate on schedule she is given progesterone, a hormone normally involved in the regulation of the menstrual cycle. The progesterone is then abruptly withdrawn and menstruation should occur within one to five days if the subject is not pregnant.

Estimating the Date of Birth

If the date of conception is known the date of birth can be fixed at 266 days later (plus or minus 3). Since it is not usually possible to fix the time of conception, the date of birth is more often calculated as 280 days from the time of the last menstruation.

Boy, Girl, or Twins. There is no practical way of determining sex prior to birth. A technique has been devised of tapping the sac which surrounds the embryo (the amnion) and studying the cells of the amniotic fluid to determine sex, but this method is not suitable for general use.

The presence of twins can usually be determined after the sixth month by detecting two heartbeats—either

PREGNANCY

through the use of the stethoscope or electric recordings of the heartbeats (using the electrocardiograph). X-ray studies are also useful. Knowledge of the presence of twins is important to the obstetrician to anticipate problems which may occur during delivery.

The Course of Pregnancy

By the end of pregnancy the expectant mother should have gained an average of 17–18 lb. Ordinarily, increases in the mother's body weight do not affect the child (that is, fat mother does not mean fat child) unless the mother adds 30 or more pounds to her normal weight. Throughout pregnancy certain normal changes occur in the body. The breasts and parts of the abdominal area become pigmented, and the joints of the pelvis steadily relax. The breasts and the uterus and other reproductive organs become enlarged and congested. The body temperature is slightly raised and the blood volume is increased.

Physicians generally divide pregnancy into three periods called trimesters.

The First Trimester. During this time the well-known appetite changes appear: foods normally liked may be shunned and a craving for sweets and starches may develop. Whether this is whimsical behavior on the part of the prospective mother or is caused by physiological factors is still not known. Toward the end of the first month there may be some nausea in the morning ("morning sickness").

At the end of the third month the developing embryo is approximately 3 to 4 in. long. The external sexual features are noted, blood manufacture has begun, the kidney is developing, and the general outlines of the brain and spinal cord have been started.

The largest number of spontaneous abortions (commonly called "miscarriages") appear within the first trimester, resulting primarily from defects in the fertilized egg, or ovum ("blighted ovum").

The Second Trimester. The "morning sickness" disappears and is replaced by a feeling of well-being. By the 16th to the 20th week the mother feels a "snapping" sensation, or "butterflies," in the abdomen. This is caused by waves of fluid slapping against the womb produced by movements of the fetus. The abdomen is noticeably enlarged as the expanding uterus rises to a point midway between the umbilicus and the base of the breastbone.

At the end of the sixth month the fetus is approximately 14 in. long. Muscle development is complete, and the last layers have developed in the brain. Hairs appear and the nostrils open.

Spontaneous abortions during this period are infrequent and, when they do occur, result from disturbances in the mother rather than the fetus. A common cause is an "incompetent cervix," a weakness of the neck of the womb. This can be corrected by surgery, either before pregnancy or at the first signs of difficulty (usually about the 14th to 16th week). Other causes of late spontaneous abortion include kidney disease, syphilis, and premature separation of the placenta (the structure which links the circulatory systems of the mother and the fetus).

The Third Trimester. In the last few months of pregnancy the uterus expands to fill the abdomen, reaching the lower part of the breastbone. The womb bulges forward in smaller women for lack of sufficient abdominal room to expand. Pressure on the stomach, bladder, and other organs causes frequent urination, inability to consume large meals at a single sitting, and some difficulty in breathing. These symptoms are relieved in the last few weeks of pregnancy by a sinking of the womb ("lightening.").

Prematurity

Expulsion of the fetus from the womb in the early stages of pregnancy results in death of the fetus or spontaneous abortion. By the 32d week the fetus has developed sufficiently so that it may survive outside of the mother (it is now said to be viable). Delivery of the infant after this point and before the normal term is then referred to as premature birth. The popular belief that a premature birth will occur in the seventh but not the eighth month is not true. Definitions of prematurity vary. Public health organizations describe any infant under a specific weight as premature (the figure is usually set at 5 to 5½ lb.). Obstetricians generally prefer to define prematurity according to the time spent in the womb (the index to time spent *in utero* is the length of the infant rather than its weight). Premature infants require intensive nursing care in order to survive, and some large cities have established centers where entire rooms serve as incubators to maintain adequate temperatures and protect against infection. The frequency of abnormalities is higher in premature children owing to their lack of development and greater susceptibility to birth injury. The likelihood of survival increases with the time spent in the womb.

Health Hazards in Pregnancy

The Mother. Pregnancy normally imposes a strain on the heart, kidneys, and other organs of the mother. In women with heart and kidney disorders and certain diseases such as tuberculosis and diabetes special problems arise. These women require close medical supervision throughout pregnancy.

The Child. German measles of the mother early in pregnancy may cause a spontaneous abortion, stillbirth, or deformity of the newborn child. Syphilis may be transmitted from the mother to the fetus in the womb. This disease may also result in a late abortion or congenital deformity. For this reason many communities require blood examinations prior to marriage.

Another major danger to the unborn child is the Rh factor—a blood factor which is normally present in 85% of the population. The potentially dangerous combination is an Rh negative mother (who lacks the factor) and an Rh positive father (who has the factor). The Rh negative mother may develop anti-Rh substances (antibodies) in her blood if the child is Rh positive. In subsequent pregnancies with Rh positive children a reaction may occur between the blood of the mother and the child, and the infant may be stillborn or seriously ill at birth. To avoid this, the obstetrician tests the blood of both parents and closely follows the concentration of antibodies in the blood of the mother. He may deliver the child prematurely to prevent a serious reaction from occurring in the womb.

An increasingly serious problem in pregnancy is radiation. It has been established that high dosages of radiation may cause congenital abnormalities, and consequently it is generally considered advisable to limit X-ray exposures, particularly during pregnancy.

Ectopic and Tubal Pregnancy. An ectopic pregnancy occurs when the embryo develops outside of the womb. Normally the egg, or ovum, is fertilized in the Fallopian tube, the tunnel which leads from the ovary to the uterus. If the tube is abnormally shaped or scarred from previous infection, the fertilized ovum may be trapped, and the embryo develops in the tube instead of the uterus. This is known as a tubal pregnancy and accounts for the great majority of all ectopic pregnancies. In such cases immediate surgery may be needed to prevent rupturing of the tube.

Routine During Pregnancy. The pregnant woman should consume ample amounts of meat, eggs, and other high-protein foods. Dairy products are important to provide adequate amounts of calcium. Clothes should be loose-fitting and the shoes should be broad-based to avoid falling. Moderate exercise is beneficial, and ordinary housework need not be limited—except for activities which present the hazard of falling.

After Pregnancy. The reproductive organs return to normal size about six weeks after birth, but the pigmentation of the breasts and abdomen remains. Exercise is helpful in restoring tone to the stretched abdominal muscles.
See also CHILDBIRTH; EMBRYOLOGY; GYNECOLOGY; PEDIATRICS; REPRODUCTION.

PREVENTIVE MEDICINE, the medical specialty which deals with the prevention of disease. This branch of medicine was practiced long before the nature of disease was clearly understood. The Bible contains instructions for a kind of quarantine ("He that toucheth the dead body of any man shall be unclean seven days," Num. 19:11) and prohibits eating certain fish (which are now known to be capable of living in polluted waters), and pork (now known to harbor the organism which causes trichinosis). Instructions for washing and for disposing human wastes are found in Deuteronomy 23:10 and 12. In the 18th century the English physician Edward Jenner made one of the most significant advances in this field when he introduced vaccination for immunizing against smallpox. Another pioneer in preventive medicine, Ignaz Semmelweis, a 19th-century Hungarian physician, suffered considerable abuse from his colleagues in Vienna when he campaigned to have physicians wash their hands before delivering children, so as to prevent spreading the deadly childbirth (puerperal) fever.

It was not until Louis Pasteur firmly demonstrated the role of microorganisms in causing disease that the place of preventive measures could be fully understood and accepted. The English surgeon Joseph Lister applied this knowledge to surgery by using carbolic acid (phenol) to sterilize the operating field and the surgical instruments, thereby reducing the number of postoperative infections.

More recently, understanding of the physiology and biochemistry of noninfectious diseases has made possible new techniques in disease prevention, such as adding vitamins and nutrients to food to prevent deficiency diseases.

The Principles of Preventive Medicine. These principles can be illustrated by analyzing a simple disease such as poison ivy. In order to contract poison ivy the individual must be sensitive to the plant and must come in contact with it. A specialist in preventive medicine might attack this disease by attempting to destroy the plant, by roping off areas in which the plant grows, by teaching individuals to avoid the plant, or by finding a medication which when taken internally or rubbed on the skin would prevent the rash from developing. These possibilities fall into the general categories of disease prevention: (1) destruction of the disease-producing agent, (2) preventing the agent from reaching the individual, and (3) improving the ability of the individual to resist the effects of contact with the agent.

These techniques are regularly applied in modern communities and are so familiar that their actual role in disease prevention is seldom fully appreciated. Pork is thoroughly cooked to kill the organism which causes trichinosis. Water is chlorinated to destroy typhoid and cholera organisms. Milk is pasteurized to eliminate tuberculosis bacteria and other organisms. Food is refrigerated to prevent disease-producing germs from growing in it.

In insect-borne diseases, the disease-producing agent (pathogen) can be kept from reaching humans by destroying the insect carrier. The construction of the Panama Canal was made possible by destroying the breeding places of the mosquitoes which transmit yellow fever. Many diseases can be prevented by sanitary disposal of human wastes, to prevent flies and other insects from picking up and transmitting pathogens.

The third principle, improving the resistance of humans to disease, is best known in the form of immunization against such diseases as smallpox, tetanus, whooping cough, diphtheria, and polio. The principle also includes the use of drugs to prevent attacks of malaria and rheumatic fever and the fluoridation of water to prevent tooth decay.

Primary Versus Secondary Prevention. Primary prevention is possible when the cause of a disease is known and it can be prevented by the techniques described above. In other cases, although the disease cannot be prevented, serious damage can be avoided by early diagnosis and treatment. This is spoken of as secondary prevention.

The Individual, the Physician, and the Community. The individual can contribute to disease prevention by getting adequate rest and nutrition and by seeking professional help in the early stages of illness. The physician often practices preventive medicine, particularly in the case of the newborn baby. Certainly the most dramatic applications of the techniques discussed above are on the level of community effort, as practiced by public health agencies, which check food supplies and administer immunization programs. Perhaps the most ambitious public health program in preventive medicine is that of the World Health Organization, which is attempting to eliminate malaria from the face of the globe.
See also INDUSTRIAL MEDICINE; MALARIA; MEDICINE; TROPICAL MEDICINE.

PROGESTERONE [prō-jĕs′tə-rōn], a hormone which plays an important role in the normal menstrual cycle and in pregnancy. When the egg leaves its follicle in the ovary, the follicle is transformed into the corpus luteum. The corpus luteum manufactures progesterone, apparently

PROSTAGLANDINS

from cholesterol. Progesterone then acts upon the uterine lining, which has already been primed by the female sex hormone, estrogen, in preparation for the egg. If the egg is not fertilized, progesterone production ceases, menstruation occurs, and the corpus luteum degenerates; if the egg is fertilized, the corpus luteum continues to secrete progesterone. This maintains pregnancy, prevents eggs from maturing in the ovary, inhibits menstruation, and stimulates growth of the breasts. Later in pregnancy progesterone manufacture is taken over by the placenta, the structure through which the developing fetus receives nutrition.

Progesterone and progesteronelike compounds are used in medicine to maintain pregnancy in women who have had previous spontaneous abortions and in menstrual disorders. These drugs have also been tried as oral contraceptives on the basis of their ability to inhibit release of the egg from the ovary.

See also ENDOCRINE GLANDS; MENSTRUATION; PREGNANCY.

PROSTAGLANDINS, family of biologic compounds which act on smooth muscle of the vascular and reproductive systems. The name is derived from the prostate gland. The prostaglandins were first isolated in an effort to understand the observation that semen instilled into the uterus causes muscular contraction. The compounds, produced in the body from fatty acids, were found to exert localized effects on the function of highly specialized human tissue.

The prostaglandins can lower blood pressure and affect digestive function and nerve-cell activity. It is thought that they regulate the action of the more classic hormones at the cellular level by enhancing or blocking the hormone's effect on its target organ. The potential therapeutic value of the prostaglandins resides in their ability to terminate pregnancy at a very early stage, an effect that also signals their possible use as a single-dose contraceptive. Because of their effect on smooth muscles in parts of the body other than the uterus, prostaglandins may also prove useful in the therapy of hypertension, asthma, and kidney disease.

PROSTATE [prŏs'tāt] **GLAND,** a heart-shaped organ about 1½ in. long which surrounds the urinary passage (urethra) at the base of the bladder. It is found only in men and manufactures substances which enable the male sexual secretions to fertilize the egg in the female. The prostatic secretions, which contain minerals, lipids, and enzymes, are mixed with the seminal fluid during ejaculation and help maintain the viability of the sperm. Proper functioning of the prostate depends upon the presence of adequate amounts of male sex hormone in the blood.

The prostate may become infected, cancerous, or abnormally enlarged. These conditions may cause serious complications either by infecting the bladder and kidney or by obstructing urine flow through the urethra. If left untreated, this may result in impaired kidney function and death. Treatment consists of anti-infective medications for prostatitis and, in cases of cancerous or enlarged prostate, surgery and hormone therapy.

PROSTHETICS [prŏs-thĕt'ĭks], that branch of medicine which deals with the replacement of missing body parts. During the Middle Ages some amputees may have used a peg leg or forked stick strapped to the stump to provide support while standing and to permit a crude form of locomotion. Early artificial arms were used more to conceal the loss of a hand than to provide function, though there are a number of reports of knights who used these devices to hold a lance in battle. Prior to World War II little scientific effort was devoted to developing prosthetics; since then, however, fairly sophisticated devices capable of reproducing limb function have emerged.

Hand and Arm Prosthetics. It is possible to provide the arm amputee with only a few of the many complex functions performed by the normal hand. Substitutes for the hand may resemble a hand or may take the form of a hooklike tool if a delicate grasp is needed or if manual labor is to be performed. Mechanical hands, covered with flexible plastic gloves of an extremely lifelike appearance, are available. Hooks are made of aluminum or steel and are split and pivoted so that articles up to 3 in. thick may be grasped.

Power to operate the hand or hook may be generated by shrugging the shoulders to apply tension to a control cable connected between the hand or hook and a shoulder harness. The shoulder harness is also used to hold the artificial arm in place on the stump.

Artificial Legs. An artificial leg for below-the-knee amputations is usually suspended by a strap around the thigh just above the kneecap or by a corsetlike device about the thigh connected to the artificial leg. Legs for amputations through the thigh may be suspended by suction, created by a snug fit between socket and stump, or by a belt around the waist. A principal problem in such devices is the action of the knee joint during walking. The most common form of control is mechanical friction, but this is rapidly yielding to hydraulic devices which automatically compensate for changes in walking speed.

Training in the Use of Artificial Limbs. An artificial limb should be fitted as soon as the surgical wounds have healed: sometimes fitting can be made as early as six weeks after surgery. The amount of training required depends upon the site and extent of the amputation, the type of prosthesis, and the general physical condition of the patient. A young, healthy, below-the-knee amputee may require only one or two hours of training, while an elderly above-the-knee amputee may require 40 or 50 hours spread over several weeks.

Other Prosthetics. Artificial noses and ears are cast of soft plastics, such as polyvinyl chloride, and are tinted to match the complexion of the patient. When skillfully fashioned and colored, these facial prostheses are difficult to detect. Deep scars may be covered in the same manner. An artificial voice, in the form of a buzzer apparatus held to the throat, is available for patients who have lost normal use of the larynx. The patient moves his lips as he would normally, thus shaping the buzzer sounds into words.

PROTEINS [prō'tēnz, prō'tē-ĭnz], group of nitrogen-containing organic compounds found in skin, muscle, brain, and in all animal and vegetable cells. The term was originally used in 1839 by the Dutch biologist G. J. Mulder, who described protein as "unquestionably the most important of all known substances—without it no life appears possible—through its means the chief phenomena of life are produced."

The Chemical Nature of Proteins

Early investigations revealed that when muscle, wool, or gelatin were boiled with dilute acids, certain white crystalline substances were obtained. These substances came to be known as amino acids—the elementary building blocks from which proteins are made. The great variety of proteins derives from alternate combinations and arrangements of 20-odd basic amino acids, much as the words of a language are constructed from different combinations of the letters of the alphabet. The almost infinite variety of possible proteins can be readily grasped when one considers that some of the "words," or proteins, built from amino acids are composed of thousands of "letters." The properties of the different proteins are determined not only by the relative amounts of the constituent amino acids, but also by the specific spatial arrangement of the amino acid chains as well. Some proteins, such as those found in hair and muscle fibers, consist of a parallel grouping of zigzag chains, while in others the chains are not merely zigzag but exist in complicated loops and twists which are never quite the same in any two different types of protein.

The Types of Proteins

Proteins are often divided into three main classes: simple proteins, conjugated proteins, and derived proteins.

Simple proteins are composed only of amino acids. They include ovalbumin from egg white, lactalbumin from milk, albumin from blood, and myosin of muscle. The keratins are simple proteins found in hair, skin, nails, hooves, scales, horns, and feathers. The tough, fibrous protein collagen occurs in cartilage, ligaments, and tendons, where it provides support and protection.

Conjugated proteins are compounds of simple proteins with some nonprotein group. Hemoglobins, the red, oxygen-carrying chemicals of the blood, are conjugated proteins consisting of the protein globin in combination with heme, a red pigment chemically related to the green chlorophyll of plants. Other conjugated blood proteins include the globulins, which maintain the fluid-holding power of the blood. Different globulins are important in blood coagulation, immunity to infections, and allergic reactions.

Nucleoproteins are simple proteins conjugated with nucleic acids. They are present within plant and animal cells and are especially abundant in glandular tissues, such as liver, spleen, pancreas, and thymus. These proteins are believed to perform important functions in cell reproduction and in the transmission of inherited characteristics from parent to child. The viruses of smallpox and poliomyelitis appear to be nucleoprotein complexes.

Enzymes, which speed up reactions within living cells, may be simple or conjugated proteins. Other conjugated proteins include the lipoproteins, which are complexes of proteins and fatty substances found especially in brain and nerve tissue, and mucoproteins, combinations of proteins and carbohydrates.

Derived proteins are so called because they are obtained by the action of heat, acids, alkali, or enzymes on proteins of the other two classes. The proteins of cooked egg, meats, and fish fall into this class, as do those of skim milk, powder, and gelatin.

Proteins and Nutrition

While in some respects the proteins which form the structural tissue of the body can be compared to the bricks which make up a building, there is an important difference. Unlike the bricks, which remain in place, the proteins of the body are continuously destroyed and rebuilt. In normal growing children the rate of manufacture exceeds that of destruction; in healthy adults the rates of synthesis and destruction are closely balanced.

The body needs 21 amino acids for tissue proteins; it can manufacture 11 of these from carbohydrates and fats in amounts necessary for normal growth. The remaining 10 amino acids are called essential, since without them normal growth and health are not possible.

Because of these needs the nutritional value of food proteins is based upon its content of the 10 essential amino acids: arginine, histidine, isoleucine, leucine, lysine, methionine, phenylalanine, threonine, tryptophan, and valine.

Animal proteins, such as those found in meats, eggs, and milk, contain all of these essential acids, and are consequently nutritionally adequate. The proteins contained in corn, peanuts, cereals, and other vegetables, are of poor quality since they lack one or more essential amino acids.

Children who subsist largely on cereal foods may not grow properly and suffer from anemia. If the diet is not improved by feeding milk or otherwise supplying the deficient amino acids, a severe form of protein deficiency, called Kwashiorkor, results. This disease, which is marked by retarded growth, apathy, accumulation of fluids in the tissues (edema), and bleaching, loss, and sparseness of the hair, is often fatal. In adults, continued subsistence on proteins of poor quality often results in edema, anemia, and loss of protein in the urine. These symptoms are relieved by adding good-quality proteins to the diet.

Protein malnutrition may also develop in disease or following surgery. During prolonged illness the increased rate of tissue destruction and loss of appetite combine to produce loss of weight and a reduction in the quantity of blood proteins. These symptoms can be treated by encouraging the patient to eat a diet rich in high-quality proteins. In severe cases, amino acids have to be given by vein.

See also AMINO ACIDS; METABOLISM; NUTRITION.

PROTEINURIA [prō-tē-ĭ-nūr′ē-ə], protein in the urine, an abnormal finding which usually indicates kidney disease. Protein in the urine originates in the blood as plasma proteins. Normally, only trace quantities of protein are filtered from blood to urine, and these are completely reabsorbed by the kidney tubules. When the blood filter of the kidney, the glomerulus, is damaged, larger holes in it allow more protein molecules to pass through. The amount of protein exceeds the tubule's capacity to reabsorb, and protein appears in the urine. Because albumin is the smallest blood protein, it passes more easily through small kidney defects and is the predominant protein in the urine. Larger areas of kidney damage permit the larger proteins, globulins, to pass through.

Proteinuria is not always a sign of kidney damage. But most often, proteinuria suggests kidney disease and should be evaluated thoroughly whenever it is found.

PSORIASIS [sə-rī′ə-sĭs], chronic, recurring skin disease, which usually occurs in otherwise healthy individuals. It is uncommon in children or Negroes. Characteristically, red scaly patches appear on the front of the lower leg, outer side of the forearm, and scalp. The nails are sometimes affected, also, and some patients have lesions over the entire body. A form of arthritis is associated with psoriasis in some patients. Neither cause nor cure of psoriasis is known. A blow, or contact with chemical irritants, causes a new, typical lesion to appear in patients with the disease. Emotional upsets also precipitate a flare-up of the conditon in susceptible patients. Treatment is directed toward the symptoms and, while not curative, may be very effective. It must be related to the stage of the skin lesions. If they are acute, red, and inflamed, one salve or ointment may only irritate, but the same medication may be very effective when used on chronic scaling lesions. The eruptions often respond with dramatic improvement, when exposed to increasing doses of ultraviolet light (sunshine). Thus many patients may remain well during the summer.

PSYCHIATRY [sī-kī′ə-trē], that branch of medicine which deals with mental illness and emotional disorders.

History

Though psychological insights occurred throughout philosophy and literature, there was no formal practice of psychiatry until the 18th century, when medical personnel began to supervise the mentally ill. Prior to that time mental patients were maintained in monastic shelters or prisons.

The modern mental hospital may be said to have originated in revolutionary France under the guidance of Philippe Pinel (1745–1826), an enlightened and humane administrator who freed mental patients of their chains. Pinel abolished other coarse methods of treatment and introduced the practice of accurately recording case histories. Later Pinel's successor, Jean Esquirol, persuaded the French government to build a number of hospitals for the mentally ill. By the middle of the 19th century psychiatry was established as a discipline centered about the care of hospitalized patients. Disturbed individuals outside of institutions were usually treated by general practitioners, when they were treated at all.

The great classifier of mental disease was the German psychiatrist Emil Kraepelin (1856–1926). His textbook *Psychiatrie*, published in 1883, described and distinguished a number of disorders (dementia praecox, manic-depressive, psychosis, paranoia), introducing order into what had previously been a mass of unsystematized observations. Kraepelin's emphasis on the organic basis of disease was balanced by the approach of Adolf Meyer (1866–1950), a Swiss-born American psychiatrist, who believed that life experiences played a major role in causing mental illness.

Psychoanalysis and Psychiatry

Sigmund Freud (1856–1939) developed a systematic theoretical scheme for interpreting and treating emotional disorders. This system, called psychoanalysis, was revolutionary in a number of respects: (1) it offered an over-all explanation of normal as well as abnormal behavior; (2) it dealt with emotional disorders in individuals outside the mental hospital; (3) it conceived of the basis of mental illness as lying in childhood experiences; and (4) it offered a system of therapy based on an interpersonal relationship between patient and therapist.

Psychoanalysis spread from Vienna throughout Europe and to America and became a central technique in psychiatric practice. Splinter groups, differing in various points from the orthodox Freudian position, developed quickly, as Freud's early disciples, notably Carl Jung and Alfred Adler, set up schools of their own. Later, psychoanalysis became one of many techniques of psychotherapy, some of them based upon theories of human behavior greatly differing from Freud's original concept (see PSYCHOANALYSIS).

The Scope of Practice

Psychiatrists generally distinguish between two major groups of conditions: the organic diseases and the so-called functional disorders.

Organic Diseases. These involve physical changes in the tissues, such as might be caused by disease or injury to the brain and nervous system. In arteriosclerosis, or hardening of the arteries, narrowing of the arteries in the brain may diminish the blood supply to the brain, causing a decline in memory and mental alertness. Alcoholism may indirectly cause brain damage resulting from vitamin deficiencies. Many hereditary degenerative diseases of the nervous system cause psychiatric symptoms.

Functional Disorders. These include conditions in which there are disturbances in mental function without demonstrable tissue changes. Although these disorders are generally thought to originate from psychological stress, some authorities feel that they may really be caused by abnormalities in body chemistry. This point is still controversial.

This group of disorders may be subdivided into the psychoses, the neuroses, and the so-called character disorders. In the former, the individual suffers from distortions of reality in the form of hallucinations and delusions; extreme cases of psychosis usually require hospitalization. In the neuroses the individual is troubled by rigid, repetitive behavior which he is powerless to control. The aim of neurotic behavior is believed to be the control of anxiety. The neurosis may take the form of a phobia: an irrational dread of heights, closed places, or of any number of objects or situations. Neurosis may also appear as compulsive behavior (for example, repeated hand washing), or obsessive, nightmarish thoughts, such as the idea of burning one's house.

Persons with character disorders are essentially normal persons who are troubled by patterns of behavior which cause them difficulty in dealing with people. An example can be seen in the passive-aggressive personality who is unable to show open hostility, but may express his anger indirectly to those who do not deserve it. The passive-dependent person may become depressed when his slightest wish or need is not fulfilled.

Among the most difficult and perplexing patients seen by the psychiatrist are the psychopathic personalities, or sociopaths, who lie or cheat or abuse their friends and loved ones without apparent remorse or anxiety.

Diagnosing and Treating Disorders

The principal diagnostic procedure is the psychiatric interview, during which the patient's feelings and attitudes are explored by the psychiatrist and viewed in relation to his background and life history. The psychiatrist may call upon the psychologist to assess the patient's intelligence or to administer Rorschach (ink-blot) tests or other instruments for evaluating the central problems of the patient.

The psychiatrist makes use of two broad categories of treatment: the biological and the psychotherapeutic.

Biological Techniques. The biological approach makes use of drugs, surgery, and electrical stimulation.

Insulin coma therapy, introduced in Vienna by Manfred Sakel in 1932, was one of the earliest of these techniques. In this technique patients are given doses of insulin, a hormone which lowers the concentration of blood sugar. Since the brain depends upon sugar exclusively as an energy source, the individual lapses into a coma as the blood-sugar concentration falls. In some manner, as yet unknown, this "shock" to the nervous system produces improvement in some cases of early schizophrenia. Insulin shock treatment is no longer as popular as it once was.

Electroshock therapy is now widely used in mental hospitals. In this procedure an electric current is quickly passed through the brain, producing convulsions. The treatment is often effective in cases of depression and manias, and in some cases of schizophrenia. From 6 to 20 treatments are necessary to produce improvement.

Psychosurgery involves severing the fibers which link the frontal lobes with the rest of the brain. This is considered a drastic procedure and is used as a last resort when other forms of therapy fail. The operation apparently reduces anxiety and enables the patient to withstand frustration. In some cases, distressing personality changes, such as apathy, loss of drive, and a loss of a sense of social propriety, have resulted from the operation.

Psychopharmacology. A fairly recent and promising development in the treatment of the psychiatric disorders is the introduction of the tranquilizing drugs. Unlike the earlier barbiturates and other sedatives which calmed the patient by inducing drowsiness, the tranquilizers have the remarkable property of relieving depression and quieting excited patients without reducing mental alertness. Many of these compounds apparently affect the quality of the individual's emotional experience. Tranquilizers have quieted the wards of many mental hospitals and have significantly diminished the return rate in state hospitals.

Psychotherapy and Psychoanalysis. Psychoanalysis is the most intensive and prolonged form of psychotherapy, and is applied most often to the neuroses and character disorders. The analyst employs the technique of free association, in which the patient is expected to voice all thoughts which come to mind without attempting to censor those which he might feel to be embarrassing or irrelevant. The object of therapy is to give the patient an understanding of the history and nature of his disturbances so that he may act upon them. Treatment is given four or five times a week over a period of two to eight years, depending upon the individual case.

Other forms of psychotherapy are usually less intensive and ordinarily do not attempt to probe as deeply into the origins of the patient's problem. These shorter-term therapies may be applied to some psychotic patients as well as to neurotics and those suffering from character disorders.

Directive therapy differs from psychoanalysis and other types of psychotherapy in that the therapist attempts to suggest a course of action and attitude to be adopted by the patient. Directive therapy may make use of hypnosis or may rely solely on the strength and authority of the therapist.

Are Patients Cured? The word "cure" cannot be applied in its strictest sense to these modes of treatment. Although a single episode of depression may be interrupted or a patient freed of a delusion or an anxiety state relieved, these patterns of behavior tend to recur. If the recurrence is mild or temporary and does not disrupt adaptation or function, the patient may be said to be cured. Many patients, especially schizophrenics, may have to be treated continuously.

Biological Versus Nonbiological Psychiatrists. Psychiatrists tend to be divided into those who rely heavily on organic forms of treatment and those who are oriented to psychotherapy. The first group uses more electric shock, insulin shock, and drugs. They consider psychotherapy to be an adjunct to these forms of treatment. The second group relies heavily on psychoanalysis, seeking to understand the roots of the patient's disorder. The division is not, of course, hard and fast, as many psychiatrists use both approaches, modifying them to the case at hand.

Training. The psychiatrist's training consists of four years of medical school and one year of general internship, followed by a minimum of three years in residence in his specialty. During his residency the psychiatrist treats mentally ill patients under the supervision of trained practitioners. After his resident training, he must practice or work in a hospital for two or more years before he is eligible for certification by the specialty board. He may continue his training to specialize in a sub-field, such as child psychiatry, or enter a psychoanalytic institute to train as a psychoanalyst. Once he is fully trained, the psychiatrist may elect to remain in hospital work or he may enter research or private practice.

See also MENTAL ILLNESS; NEUROSIS; PSYCHOANALYSIS.

PSYCHOANALYSIS, also called "depth psychology," both a theory of human behavior and a method of treatment for some mental disorders. Psychoanalysis as a system was introduced by Sigmund Freud and later elaborated and modified by himself and others, including his daughter Anna Freud.

PSYCHOLOGY [sī-kŏl'ō jī]. As a science, psychology may be defined as the systematic study of the processes whereby the individual human being—or animal—interacts with the environment. As a profession, it may be defined as the attempt to apply the knowledge and methods of psychology to the solution of problems of human welfare.

Psychology as a Science

The definition of psychology as a science includes an emphasis on *systematic study of processes* in order to set scientific psychology apart from prescientific, or "common sense," psychology. This latter sort of psychology is likely to be casual and one-shot rather than systematic or cumulative and is likely to be more concerned with immediate prediction than with the formation of a complete picture of the processes involved as the organism lives its life. Many psychologists would prefer to substitute the term *behavior* for the term *processes* in the definition, for objectively observable behavior is the bedrock subject matter of the science. In fact, psychology is frequently described as a behavioral science. The general term *processes*, however, does not exclude *conscious* processes from the proper province of psychology. For purposes of definition it does not matter that the conscious processes of one individual can be studied by another individual only through observation of what that individual says and does.

The term *individual* is included in the definition to draw a distinction between psychology and those disciplines—such as sociology, cultural anthropology, and political science—that tend to focus their interest on groups, institutions, or cultures rather than on individuals. Actually, social psychology, a field on the border between psychology and sociology, often does concern itself with groups, but even in that borderline specialty there remains an emphasis on the individual as he behaves in a group or social setting. The definition also uses the general term *organism* rather than the more specific term *human organism* to indicate that psychologists, though primarily concerned with human beings, are interested in all organisms, or in the living organism in general, and seek the basic general laws of organismic interaction with the environment. Hence the frequent use of subhuman organisms in experimental research. The phrase *interacts with* is used instead of the frequently encountered *adjusts to* to emphasize the active and dynamic nature of behavior. Psychology does not regard living as a matter of relatively fixed and relatively passive responses to environmental events.

PSYCHOPATHIC PERSONALITY, a term describing one of the most perplexing disorders known to psychiatry. Superficially the psychopath appears charming and competent. His intelligence is often above average, and he is capable of mastering the most subtle occupational skills. This façade conceals a complete lack of morality and positive human feeling in all his personal relationships and an absence of normal occupational and social goals. Despite his excellent personal and intellectual equipment, the psychopath consistently fails in all endeavors. He repeatedly abandons his job and family in pursuit of the most casual impulse. His sexual life is shallow, impersonal, and promiscuous. He may cheat, steal, or even kill, showing no remorse. He is incapable of understanding his own behavior or profiting from his experience. It is important to distinguish psychopaths from psychotics and psychoneurotics. The psychopath neither has any bizarre notions concerning the world nor does he suffer from anxiety. An early writer, in describing this condition, marked the distinction between psychopaths and overtly deranged persons by designating the former as "morally insane."

Centuries of speculation have not clarified the nature of the disorder. Some have attributed it to a "constitutional inferiority," while others have cited family relationships and childhood experiences. Psychiatrists recognize in these persons the most difficult and fruitless subjects for treatment.

See also PSYCHIATRY.

PSYCHOPHARMACOLOGY [sī-kō-fär-mə-kŏl′ə-jē], the study of the effect of drugs on the mind. Drugs that produce mental effects have long been used in medical practice. These include opium, alcohol, cocaine, and more recently the barbiturates, which are widely used as sleeping pills. The subject has received special attention since the introduction of newer drugs, such as the tranquilizers, which calm excited psychotic patients, and the discovery of substances, such as lysergic acid diethylamide (LSD), which produce hallucinations and changes in mood. The psychopharmacological agents may be considered in three categories: the tranquilizers, the hallucinogens, and the stimulants.

PSYCHOSIS [sī-kō′sĭs], term given to a category of mental disorders in which the individual suffers from hallucinations, delusions, or other distortions of reality. This may take the form of a complete severance from the real world, as seen in certain trancelike states in schizophrenia, or a partial distortion of reality such as occurs in the paranoid, who is normal save for his belief that malevolent persons are "after him." Psychosis is a more serious disorder than neurosis; in the latter, the individual is aware of the real world but is the victim of persistent and troublesome patterns of behavior which he may be powerless to control.

See also MENTAL ILLNESS; NEUROSIS; PARANOIA; PSYCHIATRY; SCHIZOPHRENIA.

PSYCHOSOMATIC [sī-kō-sō-măt′ĭk] **MEDICINE,** branch of psychiatry which deals with physical illnesses that result in part from emotional conflicts. The basic principle of psychosomatic illness is the spilling over of anxiety, fear, resentment, and other forms of psychological tension into the nervous and hormonal channels which normally regulate the activities of the internal organs.

The focus of the conversion of psychological stress into physiological activity lies in certain portions of the brain involved in internal control. These areas control internal activity by means of the autonomic nervous system and through control of the endocrine glands. The autonomic, or visceral, nervous system is a vast network of fibers which co-ordinates the action of the heart, digestive system, and glands. The complex effects of emotions on the body are produced through the fibers of this system and by means of endocrine secretions (hormones) traveling in the blood stream. Fear, for example, may blanch the stomach lining, squeeze blood from the skin and intestines, quicken the heartbeat, and raise the blood pressure. Repeated or prolonged episodes of fear, tension, or anxiety may eventually cause permanent tissue damage. One concept of the mechanism of such tissue destruction was advanced by the physiologist Hans Selye, who stated that prolonged stress might produce body damage through the release of excessive amounts of certain hormones from the adrenal glands.

Disorders in which psychological factors are believed to be important include heart ailments, migraine headaches, peptic ulcers, asthma, skin eruptions, and hyperthyroidism. Menstrual difficulties and sexual problems often have a psychosomatic basis. Not all of the psychosomatic ailments involve actual tissue damage (for example, headaches may be caused by temporary constriction of the blood vessels of the head).

An intriguing question is why a specific organ should be affected in one individual but not another. Much of the theorizing in the field of psychosomatic medicine has been an attempt to answer this question. Some theorists have suggested that an inherited weakness of particular organs may be responsible: thus there would be "stomach types," "heart types," and so forth.

The psychiatrist Helen Flanders Dunbar proposed that particular personality types were susceptible to specific psychosomatic ailments. Franz Alexander stressed the nature of the emotional problem as a selecting factor: thus individuals with a strong desire to be dependent on others would develop peptic ulcer and asthma, whereas those with aggressive emotional patterns might develop migraine and high blood pressure. The bulk of the evidence to date favors a nonspecific theory, according to which sustained tension will "break through" at a point of least resistance. The psychosomatic ailments are treated both medically and psychiatrically.

PTOMAINES. *See* FOOD POISONING.

PTYALIN [*tī'ə-lĭn*], also salivary amylase, an enzyme found in saliva. While food is being chewed, ptyalin breaks down starch and other large carbohydrate molecules (polysaccharides) into simpler substances. This is the first stage of carbohydrate digestion, completed by enzymes in the small intestine which convert the products of ptyalin digestion into simple sugars (for example, glucose). *See also* DIGESTION; ENZYMES.

PUBLIC HEALTH, the organized efforts of the community to protect its members against disease. One of the earliest public health programs is detailed in the Biblical account of the Exodus of the Jews from Egypt. Moses introduced a strict hygienic code which included many principles observed in modern public health programs. The Jews were required to wash their hands before and after eating and to bathe before entering the synagogue. Individuals afflicted with *zob* (apparently a venereal disease) were banished from the camp, and all objects belonging to the infected person were cleansed or destroyed. Soldiers or others who had contact with a dead body were considered unclean and were excluded from camp for a week. Moses appointed health wardens, one for each 1,000 Jews, to enforce these and other stringent rules, and in this way preserved the health of the Jewish nation during its 40-year trial in the desert.

The Romans, a practical people who made few theoretical contributions to medicine, distinguished themselves in the field of public health and hygiene. Large-scale projects were undertaken to drain the malarial swamps around Rome. The great aqueducts supplied each citizen of Rome with over 100 gal. of water daily—a figure which compares favorably with the water supply of modern cities. The Romans also strictly supervised the sale of perishable foods.

In the 14th century the city of Venice instituted pioneering public health measures to deal with the plague, which was rampant at the time. A commission was appointed to supervise the disposal of the dead; it even specified the depth of graves. On the other side of the Adriatic, the republic of Ragusa required visiting ships to anchor at a point removed from the harbor. Persons suspected of having the plague were required to wait 30 days before entering the city. This period was eventually lengthened to 40 days, called a *quarantenaria*, and gave origin to the modern quarantine.

The importance of quarantine, the destruction of contaminated objects, and other health measures in the control of epidemics later became recognized in other cities. In Rome in 1656 the papal commissary of health installed sanitary guards at the gates of the city and required the sewers and aqueducts to be regularly inspected. The British Parliament created an office of public health in 1848 and brought water supplies, food distribution, and sewers under government inspection. Recognition of disease as a common problem of all nations was finally achieved in 1851, when an international conference convened in Paris to discuss measures to deal with plague, cholera, and yellow fever. This was the forerunner of other international public health activities such as the Pan American Sanitary Bureau (1902), the Health Organization of the League of Nations (1923), and the World Health Organization (1948).

Public Health and the Citizen

In the highly industrialized parts of the world each citizen is enveloped in a network of vital public health services which, although inconspicuous and often unappreciated, have helped to extend his average length of life some 20 years within the space of half a century. His water is purified of typhoid and cholera bacteria and other disease-producing microorganisms. His milk is pasteurized to destroy the germs of tuberculosis and undulant fever. His meat is inspected to prevent parasite-ridden products from reaching the market place. His dwelling is inspected to control the numbers of potentially disease-carrying insects and rats, and the law requires that his food be enriched with vitamins and minerals (iodine). The drugs he uses are regulated and inspected by government agencies, and his children's toys are kept free of lead-based paints and other dangerous substances. Early in life he is immunized against smallpox, diphtheria, and other diseases. The sewage-disposal systems of his community are supervised by public health agencies to prevent human wastes from becoming a source of infection. He may be regularly examined for tuberculosis and before marriage may be required to take blood tests to preclude the unknowing transmission of disease to his offspring. The concern of public health officials with man's surroundings now in-

PUBLIC HEALTH SERVICE

cludes purification of the air, control of noise, and protection against radioactive wastes.

While most of the above activities are performed by local public health authorities, health agencies on a higher level maintain a constant surveillance of disease patterns to locate epidemics in their early phase. In emergencies, public health officials can accomplish seemingly impossible measures to forestall epidemics: in this century authorities of both Moscow and New York administered millions of vaccinations within a short period of time to prevent the outbreak of smallpox epidemics. Other public health activities of a larger order include government hospitals, publication of health information, financing of research institutions and projects, the provision of school health services, and medical inspection of ship and plane arrivals and immigrants.

On a supranational level the World Health Organization and other groups seek to extend to all of mankind the considerable achievements of public health in the more highly developed countries. A highly successful campaign is being waged against yaws, a common and highly disfiguring disease of the tropics which can be cured by a single injection of penicillin. A world-wide campaign is also in progress against the greatest parasitic scourge of mankind—malaria.

See also HEALTH, EDUCATION, AND WELFARE, UNITED STATES DEPARTMENT OF; INDUSTRIAL MEDICINE; PREVENTIVE MEDICINE; RED CROSS; TROPICAL MEDICINE; WORLD HEALTH ORGANIZATION (WHO).

PUBLIC HEALTH SERVICE, agency of the U.S. government founded in 1798 to administer hospitals for U.S. merchant seamen. The activities of the service thereafter expanded greatly, and in 1939 it was transferred from the Department of the Treasury to the Federal Security Agency (FSA). When the FSA became the Department of Health, Education, and Welfare in 1953, the Public Health Service was included in that department.

The Public Health Service is the chief health agency of the government and co-operates closely with states, other federal agencies, foreign governments, and international agencies. In its work with states it helps control epidemics and supports a large program of research into epidemiology conducted in various colleges. The agency also sets and maintains standards of sanitation for milk and water, control of chronic and communicable diseases, and control of water and air pollution. It operates several hospitals and clinics in the United States, administers federal hospital construction programs, and assists states and communities in hospital planning. Hospitals for the care of specific beneficiaries designated by Congress include those for merchant seamen, members of the Coast Guard, and American Indians. In co-operation with the Bureau of Prisons it provides medical and health facilities for federal prisons.

By maintaining inspection and quarantine services at ports of entry, the Public Health Service attempts to prevent communicable diseases from entering the United States. It assists foreign governments of underdeveloped areas in raising their health standards through the World Health Organization.

The research facilities of the service and the skill of its experts are widely recognized and utilized. Its National Institutes of Health in Bethesda, Md., is the scene of major research activity in cancer, heart disease, arthritis, mental illness, and other major diseases. The service also provides grants to other research agencies throughout the nation.

PUERPERAL [pū-ûr′pər-əl] **FEVER,** also known as puerperal sepsis and childbirth fever, is an infection of the female genital tract occurring as a complication of childbirth or abortion. This infection may arise when organisms normally present in the genital tract enter the tissues through small bruises, abrasions, and lacerations developing from childbirth. Criminal abortions utilizing poor technique and improperly sterilized instruments are often responsible. Prior to knowledge of the role of microorganisms in causing disease, childbirth fever was a dreaded complication of birth. Bacteria were often introduced into the tissues by the unclean hands of attending physicians and midwives. (*See* SEMMELWEIS, IGNAZ PHILIPP.)

The symptoms vary with the nature of the infecting organism. Fever, chills, nausea, vomiting, and increased pulse and respiration are common. Extensive involvement of the reproductive organs may result in sterility. Infected fragments of tissue may travel through the blood stream to the lungs, causing serious complications. The infection may be fatal if it spreads to the blood, heart, or the peritoneum, the membrane which lines the abdominal cavity. Early treatment with antibiotics usually cures puerperal fever.

PULMONARY EMBOLISM [pŭl′mə-nĕr-ē ĕm′bə-līz-əm], obstruction of an artery in the lung by an embolus, a blood clot or foreign substance which has traveled from some other part of the body. Pulmonary embolism often follows the formation of blood clots in the veins, particularly the veins of the lower extremities. This may occur after surgery, in heart disease, after childbirth, or during prolonged bed rest. Sluggishness of the blood flow in the veins or irritation of the venous wall leads to the formation of a thrombus (blood clot) which may break loose and travel to the lungs to lodge in a pulmonary artery. Other types of emboli which may reach the lung include fat particles liberated from the marrow of broken bones, fragments of tumors, or nitrogen bubbles which may be released into the blood during rapid changes from high to low atmospheric pressures, as in deep-sea divers and caisson workers.

The emboli may obstruct the blood supply to a portion of the lungs, causing death (infarction) of the lung tissue. The most characteristic symptom of pulmonary embolism is sudden chest pain. There may be cyanosis (bluish tinting of the skin), shortness of breath, and rapid pulse. In severe cases there may be heart failure and shock. The average case clears within a few weeks. Anticoagulant drugs are given to prevent further blood clots from developing. Bed rest is important and the patient should avoid sudden straining movements which might dislodge new emboli from existing clots. Leg exercises in bedridden patients may help prevent pulmonary embolism.

See also DECOMPRESSION SICKNESS; EMBOLUS.

PURGATIVE. *See* LAXATIVES.

PURINES [pūr'ēnz], ring-structured compounds, building blocks of DNA and RNA, the body's nucleic acids. Adenine and guanine are the major purines. The breakdown products of purines are oxypurines, and the final compound in the metabolic pathway is uric acid. The pathways which lead to the formation and breakdown of nucleic acids are extremely complex, and many alternate pathways exist. Although purines are plentiful in the diet and found in high concentrations in anchovies, some other seafoods, liver, and sweetbreads, the body is also able to build up the purine ring from smaller building blocks.

An increased concentration of uric acid, caused by an abnormality of purine metabolism that is still incompletely understood, produces gout. This abnormality leads to increased uric acid in the blood, tissues, and often in the urine. The latter causes kidney stones. Because uric acid is very insoluble, it tends to form crystals and cause tissue damage. Classically, the joints are the site of uric acid deposition in gout, but other more vital areas, such as the heart and kidneys, may also be seriously affected. See also ARTHRITIS; NUCLEIC ACIDS.

PYELONEPHRITIS [pī-ə-lō-nĭ-frī'tĭs], infection of the kidney. It may be caused by intestinal bacteria which reach the kidney through the blood stream. In most cases the infecting organisms travel to the kidney from the lower parts of the urinary tract—the urethra and bladder. Sometimes catherization, the introduction of a tubular instrument into the urinary passages for diagnosis and treatment, may lead to pyelonephritis. Other predisposing factors include diabetes mellitus, bladder disturbances, and tumors, strictures, or stones obstructing the urinary passages.

Acute pyelonephritis may strike suddenly with chill, fever, headache, vomiting, and backache. The urine contains bacteria, proteins, and pus. The attack disappears rapidly but residual infection may remain.

Chronic pyelonephritis is more common in women, often beginning in childhood or pregnancy as an acute attack. Men may develop the condition from an enlarged prostate gland which blocks the flow of urine. In most cases there are no symptoms; in others the disease is marked by sporadic attacks of fever, headache, and back pain. The urine may contain bacteria, pus, and proteins. High blood pressure is seen in approximately 25% to 50% of the cases. The condition advances slowly, ultimately ending in kidney failure and death. Treatment consists of sulfa drugs and antibiotics and, if possible, removal of the predisposing factors.

PYLORUS. See STOMACH.

PYORRHEA [pī-ə-rē'ə], a disease of the gums and the underlying bone characterized by bleeding and infected gums and eventual loss of teeth. The principal causes of pyorrhea are (1) gum irritation from tartar deposits or ill-fitting tooth restorations; (2) poor mouth hygiene: mouth bacteria decompose food particles left in the spaces between the teeth liberating toxic chemicals (such as indole, skatole, ammonia) which irritate the gums; (3) poor "bite" or occlusion: failure of the upper and lower teeth to come into proper contact may cause gum irritation and trap food particles; (4) lack of proper gum stimulation resulting from a diet of soft modern-day foods. Less common causes of pyorrhea include diets deficient in vitamins, minerals, and proteins; and general bodily diseases such as diabetes and anemia. In a small number of cases the cause is unknown.

The early stage of pyorrhea is called gingivitis and is characterized by inflamed and bleeding gums. As the condition progresses, the gums and the underlying bone gradually recede. In this later stage (called periodontosis) spaces, or pockets, form between the roots of the teeth and the surrounding gum and bone. These spaces frequently become infected. Unless the condition is treated, the teeth loosen and may eventually fall out.

Dental treatment consists of removing tartar from the teeth, reconstructing old dental restorations, and correcting faulty occlusion through the use of dental appliances. In some cases surgery may be necessary to restore normal contours to swollen and distorted gums. The patient is taught how to use dental floss to remove food particles trapped between the teeth, how to use the toothbrush properly, and how to massage his gums. A well-balanced diet is an important part of treatment.
See also DENTISTRY.

PYRIDOXINE. See VITAMINS.

Q

QUARANTINE [kwôr'ən-tēn], enforced restriction of movement of people who have contracted a communicable disease or have been exposed to one. Members of a household, ship's crew, or an entire community may be quarantined in an effort to protect others from spread of the disease, and to prevent those infected from acquiring additional infections from the outside world. The word "quarantine" originally referred to the "forty days" (from Ital. *quaranta*) after arrival in port, during which the crew of a ship suspected of having an infectious illness aboard was denied contact with the shore. This measure was introduced in the 14th century when the port of Venice tried to protect itself from bubonic plague. Today the restriction period is usually estimated as the longest incubation period for the disease (the time between infection and development of symptoms), for example, 21 days for smallpox.

Since the actual value of quarantine in controlling the spread of infection is less than once thought, the trend has been toward less stringent quarantine laws throughout the world. Quarantine regulations vary widely from state to state and country to country. Smallpox, cholera, plague, and diphtheria are diseases whose spread is still especially combatted this way. For some diseases, like leprosy, which is practically noninfectious in many cases, there may be little scientific basis for quarantine, but it is enforced nevertheless, due to public fear of the illness. Other diseases still subject to quarantine in some areas are chicken pox, German measles, encephalitis, measles, whooping cough, poliomyelitis, scarlet fever, psittacosis, mumps, typhoid fever, and typhus fever.

QUININE [kwī′nīn], chief active component of the bark of the cinchona tree which is native to the Andes mountain region of South America. Formerly known as "Cardinal's bark" and "Jesuit bark," cinchona was introduced into Europe in the 17th century from Peru as an antimalarial drug. The cinchona and remijia trees, which yield the drug, were later cultivated by the Dutch in Java, and today this region produces most of the world's quinine. Quinine was largely superseded as a malarial drug by atabrine during World War II when loss of the quinine supply of the South Pacific stimulated the search for substitutes.

In addition to its action against malarial parasites, quinine also affects the heart and skeletal muscle, and is somewhat comparable to aspirin as an analgesic (pain-relieving) drug. Although little used for malaria today, it is employed to relieve the symptoms of myotonia congenita, a congenital disease in which voluntary effort causes severe muscular contractions. Quinine is also used to harden (sclerose) varicose veins and to relieve painful nocturnal muscle cramps. It was formerly used to stimulate contractions of the womb to bring on childbirth.

See also ATABRINE; CHLOROQUINE; MALARIA.

R

RABBIT FEVER. *See* TULAREMIA.

RABIES [rā′bēz], fatal virus disease of the central nervous system, caused by the bite of an infected dog, bat, or other animal. All warm-blooded animals are susceptible. Democritus and Aristotle described rabies several centuries before Christ. Celsus, in 100 A.D., recognized that rabies was caused by a dog bite and recommended cauterization of wounds produced by rabid dogs.

Before the 18th century rabies was a disease of wild animals only. The first epidemic caused by domestic dogs occurred in Italy in 1708. Today dogs, wolves, bats, coyotes, foxes, skunks, ground squirrels, and related animals carry the disease. In the past decade, most cases of rabies were caused by wild animals, rather than by dogs. The incubation period is usually 1–3 months, but varies from 10 days to 8 months. Mortality is nearly 100%.

Rabies in dogs is classified as "furious" or "dumb," but most dogs show both types. In furious rabies, the dog is highly excited, restless, and vicious. He attacks and bites. Partial paralysis of vocal muscles often makes the dog unable to bark. In dumb rabies, paralysis occurs so quickly that the animal does not attack others. Animals frequently die with no signs of the illness.

In man, two to four days of headache, low-grade fever, malaise, loss of appetite, nausea, and sore throat precede involvement of the nervous system. Usually there are abnormal sensations, such as burning of the skin at the site of the animal bite. The patient is bothered by drafts or the touch of his clothes on his skin. Facial twitching begins. Liquid touching the upper throat muscles sets off spasms, and any fluid is expelled. "Hydrophobia" was the Greek name for the disease, because the sight of water caused violent contractions of the throat muscles. Convulsions occur, agitation alternates with lucid periods, and most often, patients die in a convulsion or from progressive paralysis.

Diagnosis is simple if the person is known to have been bitten by a rabid animal, and develops classic symptoms. Today flourescent rabies antibody can be used to detect rabies in the blood. Animals which have bitten people should be blood-tested and kept under watch for 10 days for signs of rabies. All dogs should be routinely immunized against the disease.

Treatment. If an individual has been bitten, the area should be cleansed with soap. Benzalkonium chloride at the site markedly reduces infection, and injection of alcohol into the muscle near the bite is also helpful. Once the disease develops, the chances of survival are minimal, but in 1970 the first recorded survival of a rabies victim was achieved after a program of drug treatment directed at reversing the symptoms of the disease.

Louis Pasteur, in 1885, saved the life of a boy bitten by a rabid dog by injecting him with weakened rabies virus. Because this treatment often resulted in fatal reactions, new vaccines were developed. In the United States, an antirabies vaccine derived from duck embryos is used. A vaccine that stimulates the immune system to produce antibodies to the rabies virus is administered to those in contact with animals or those who will live in an area where rabies is endemic. An antirabies immune serum derived from horses may be administered in conjunction with the vaccine in treating the disease.

RACE. The term "race" is used in different ways by different persons. In spite of the fact that there are several ways in which the term may be serviceably and correctly used, it is more often than not employed in unsound ways. The term is essentially a biological or zoological one, and its reference is usually to physical traits, though sometimes physiological traits are included. In its correct usage the term never refers to behavioral or social traits.

The concept of race is primarily a classificatory device which provides a biological framework within which the various groups of mankind may be arranged in a systematic manner and within which their genetic relationships may be studied. From the genetic standpoint a race may be defined as a breeding population differing in the incidence of certain genes (hereditary particles) from other populations within the species. Such a population is actually or potentially capable of exchanging genes across whatever boundaries separate it from other populations. It is a *genogroup*, that is, a group that is distinguishable from other human groups on the basis of a differing frequency of genes. From the physical standpoint a race may be defined as a population characterized by a more or less distinct assemblage of physical traits, acquired through a common heredity, which distinguishes that population from other populations within the species.

From both genetic and physical standpoints the term

MAJOR GROUPS OF THE HUMAN RACE

Major Group: NEGROID

AFRICAN NEGROES

ETHNIC GROUP:
- A. **The True Negro:** West Africa and the Congo region.
- B. **The Half-Hamites:** East Africa and East Central Africa.
- C. **Forest Negro:** Equatorial and Tropical Africa.
- D. **Bantu-Speaking Negroids:** Central and Southern Africa.
- E. **Nilotic Negro:** Eastern Sudan and Upper Nile Valley.
- F. **Bushman:** Southwestern Africa.
- G. **Hottentot:** South Africa.

OCEANIC NEGROIDS

ETHNIC GROUP:
- A. **Papuans:** New Guinea.
- B. **Melanesians:** Melanesia.

AFRICAN PYGMIES, OR NEGRILLOS

ETHNIC GROUP:
- A. **African Pygmies, or Negrillos:** Equatorial Africa.

ASIATIC PYGMIES, OR NEGRITOS

ETHNIC GROUP:
- A. **Andamanese:** Andaman Islands.
- B. **Semang:** Central region of Malay Peninsula, and East Sumatra.
- C. **Philippine Negritos:** Philippine Islands.

OCEANIC PYGMIES, OR NEGRITOS

ETHNIC GROUP:
- A. **New Guinea Pygmies:** New Guinea.

Major Group: CAUCASOID

ETHNIC GROUP:
- A. **Basic Mediterranean:** Borderlands of the Mediterranean Basin.
- B. **Atlanto-Mediterranean:** Middle East, Eastern Balkans, East Africa, Portugal, Spain, British Isles.
- C. **Irano-Afghan Mediterranean:** Iran, Afghanistan, parts of India, Arabia, and North Africa.
- D. **Nordic:** Central Europe, Scandinavia and neighboring regions.
- E. **East Baltic:** East Baltic regions.
- F. **Lapps:** Northern Scandinavia, Kola Peninsula.
- G. **Alpine:** France along the Alps and into Russia.
- H. **Dinaric:** Eastern Alps from Switzerland to Albania, Asia Minor, and Syria.
- I. **Armenoids:** Asia Minor.
- J. **Hamites:** North and East Africa.
- K. **Indo-Dravidians:** India and Ceylon.
- L. **Polynesians:** Polynesia.

Subdivision: AUSTRALOID or ARCHAIC CAUCASOID

ETHNIC GROUP:
- A. **Australian:** Australia.
- B. **Veddah:** Ceylon.
- C. **Pre-Dravidian:** India.
- D. **Ainu:** Hokkaido (Yezo), Japan; and Sakhalin, U.S.S.R.

Major Group: MONGOLOID

CLASSICAL MONGOLOIDS

ETHNIC GROUP:
- A. An undetermined number of ethnic groups in the older populations of Tibet, Mongolia, China, Korea, Japan, and Siberia, including such tribes as the **Buryats** east and west of Lake Baikal, the

*Adapted from An Introduction to Physical Anthropology (3d ed., 1960).

Koryak of northern Siberia, the **Gilyak** of northernmost Sakhalin and the mainland north of the Amur estuary (who appear to have mixed with the Ainu), and the **Goldi** on the Lower Amur and Ussuri.

ARCTIC MONGOLOIDS

ETHNIC GROUP:
A. **Eskimo:** Extreme northeast of Asia, Arctic coast of North America, Greenland. The type includes the **Aleuts** of the Aleutian Islands, and the *Reindeer* and *Coastal* **Chukchi** of northeastern Siberia.

B. **Evenki** or **True Tungus** *(Americanoids):* Mongolia, Siberia, Asiatic highlands north of the Himalayas.

C. **Kamchadals:** Kamchatka.

D. **Samoyeds:** Kola Peninsula, White Sea and Yenisei regions.

The Mongoloids of the extreme northeast of the Asiatic continent are distinguished as the *Paleoasiatics*. These are considered to be the complex of ancient populations of Asia who early migrated to this extreme peripheral region. The populations believed to have migrated later into the northeast of the Asiatic continent are known as the *Neoasiatics*.

PALEOASIATICS: Chukchi, Koryak, Kamchadal, Gilyak, Eskimo, Aleut, Yukagir, Chuvantsy, Ostyak of Yenisei.

NEOASIATICS: Finnic tribes, Samoyedic tribes, Turkic including Yakut, Mongolic, Tungusic.

AMERICAN INDIANS

ETHNIC GROUP: A. An undetermined number of ethnic groups of North, Middle, Central, and South America.

INDO-MALAY

ETHNIC GROUP:
A. **Indonesian:** Southern China, Indochina, Burma, Thailand, interior of Malay Archipelago.

B. **Malay:** In addition to Indonesian distribution, Malay Peninsula, Philippines, Okinawa, and adjacent islands.

"race" should be applied only to groups of mankind that possess well-developed physical differences transmitted by heredity. Many populations are characterized by such heritable physical differences, and these may properly be distinguished as "races." Many populations, however, cannot be so distinguished but may be set off from the populations among which they live, or from other populations, by either linguistic, national, religious, or cultural differences. Such differences are not racial but social.

There is no such thing as a French, Jewish, Protestant, or Sicilian "race." The French people are made up of many different racial components, and they are properly spoken of as the French nation. The Jews may be characterized by either religious or cultural traits or both, and as in the case of the French many different racial components enter into their makeup. Protestants may be of any race, and they constitute a religious, not a racial, entity. Sicilians constitute a cultural-geographic entity, drawn from various racial sources and distinguishable from the mainland Italian national group by their cultural traits alone. Most of the unsound usages of the term "race" are due to its misapplication to such social or cultural groups.

Behavioral or mental traits are excluded from any definition of "race" or classification of "races." Such traits are the product of the interaction of innate and environmental factors. It is usually extremely difficult to disentangle the one from the other and discover what role each of these factors may have played in producing the end effect. When intelligence tests are administered to nonliterate peoples they invariably score lower than individuals brought up in the cultures in and for which the tests were originally designed. When individuals of different cultures are brought up in similar environments—as for example, some American Indians and Caucasoids—the Indians may score as high as the Caucasoids or higher.

It has been the universal experience that when opportunities have been improved for otherwise underprivileged groups, intelligence and achievement scores have improved. Achievement always implies opportunity. It is conceivable that some types of innate capacity for emotional and intellectual responses occur more frequently in some human groups than in others, though this has by no means been proved. What has been proved is that within any human population innate capacities vary as much as, if not more than, they do between different populations. There is no scientific evidence that genetic factors have played a major role in producing the cultural differences that exist between peoples. On the contrary, the evidence indicates beyond any shadow of doubt that the major factor in producing cultural differences between peoples has been the differences in the history of their cultural experience.

The abuse of the term "race," as well as the confusing and ambiguous manner in which the term is used by many, has led some authorities to suggest that the cause of clear thinking would be better served by the use of some such noncommittal term as "ethnic group." This term has the advantage of enabling the classifier to deal with groups that are clearly not racial but that possess a combination of physical and cultural traits rendering them distinguishable from other groups. For the purpose of further study it is desirable to recognize such groups but not to prejudge the issue by designating them as "races."

All living mankind comprises the single species *Homo sapiens*. Three large units of the human species are recognized. Each of these three large units is distinguished from the others by the possession of certain physical characters. Such large units are known as *major groups*. The three major groups are the *Caucasoid*, the *Mongoloid*, and the *Negroid*. Each of the major groups consists of a number of *ethnic groups*. An ethnic group is a population that maintains its differences, physical and cultural, from other populations of the species. The barriers that maintain these differences are either geographic or social.

There are many different classifications of the varieties of mankind. The one above is a fairly representative—and improvable—one.

RADIATION, BIOLOGICAL EFFECTS OF IONIZING. The two principal sources of ionizing radiations are *X rays* and *radioactive emissions* from unstable elements. X rays are generated in specially constructed vacuum tubes when fast-moving electrons (negatively charged subatomic particles) bombard a target. The energy of the electrons is converted into heat and a small quantity of deeply penetrating electromagnetic energy—the X rays.

Radioactive emissions are given off by atoms with unstable nuclei (the central portion of the atom consisting of positively charged protons and uncharged neutrons). Each element has a characteristic rate of emission and in losing energy via radiation becomes converted into a different substance.

The emissions take a number of forms and may consist of fragments of atomic nuclei (alpha particles, which are the nuclei of helium atoms), subatomic particles (such as electrons, or beta radiation), or high-energy electromagnetic radiation (gamma rays, which are similar to X rays). Combinations of these radiations occur frequently during the "decay" of many radioactive elements.

Effect of Radiation on Living Tissue. Radiation penetrating matter may act like subatomic "bullets" striking individual atoms in random fashion. Some of these "bullets" may knock an electron from the outer shell of the atom, thus disturbing the electron balance of the atom and leaving it charged. These charged atoms, called ions, may undergo abnormal chemical reactions within the cell. Since living tissues depend upon an orderly sequence of complex and balanced chemical reactions, the ionizing radiations interfere with normal processes and in sufficient doses are lethal.

Complex organisms are more vulnerable to radiation than simpler forms of life. For example, tiny, one-celled bacteria may withstand huge amounts of radiation which would be lethal to advanced animals, such as mammals.

Sensitivity of Tissues

Tissues differ widely in their susceptibility to radiation. Among the most sensitive are the tissues of the reproductive organs (the gonads), the blood-forming system (hematopoietic system), and the mucous membranes of the gastrointestinal tract. The skin is somewhat less sensitive. The nervous system, muscles, and bone are comparatively radiation resistant.

There are also important individual differences in radiation damage with respect to age. The fetus is much more radiosensitive than the infant after birth. Resistance increases with age so that the adult is less sensitive than the child. However, there is some indication that the very old and debilitated are more susceptible than adults in the prime of life.

The over-all effects on humans may be considered from two aspects: (1) the effect on future generations, or *genetic effects*, and (2) the effect on the individual receiving the radiation, or *somatic effects*.

Genetic Effects. Radiation influences future generations by its action upon the genes, the biochemical units of heredity which are passed from parents to their offspring. All physical characteristics of the individual are determined by genes. Thus there are genes that determine hair color; eye color; height; number of legs, arms, and feet; heart structure and so forth. Occasionally a gene changes spontaneously, causing the offspring to differ in appearance from the parents. These changes (called "mutations") are almost always harmful to the individual and the race, although in rare cases a beneficial change may occur. The most serious mutations are lethal, and the deformed offspring may be born dead or may die shortly after birth.

Spontaneous mutations ordinarily occur at a fairly constant rate for a given species. Radiation increases the normal mutation rate by its action on the genes of the reproductive cells. The radiation-induced mutations are believed to be no different than those occurring spontaneously. Results of animal experimentation indicate that the effects of radiation upon the germ cells are cumulative and persist over the life span of the individual, that is, they are not "threshold phenomena."

Somatic Effects. The somatic effects of radiation (the action upon tissues other than the reproductive cells) vary with the total dosage of radiation, the rate of exposure, and the amount of the body exposed. It is still uncertain as to whether there is a threshold effect on the somatic tissues, that is, a radiation dose below which no damage occurs. Available evidence indicates that at extremely low dosages no demonstrable effect occurs and that above a given radiation level damage becomes apparent and increases with higher dosages.

It is customary to divide radiation reaction into two categories: (1) *early*, from acute dosages delivered over a short time interval, and (2) *late*, occurring some time after an acute dose, or as a result of small doses distributed over a long period of time.

Early Effects of Acute Radiation

If only small areas of the body are exposed, the individual can tolerate and recover from comparatively huge amounts of radiation. This is part of the basis for the radiation therapy employed in the treatment of cancer. However, relatively small doses of acute total body irradiation, as from an atomic blast, cause profound reactions.

Total body doses cause complete halt of blood-cell formation, hemorrhages, and a decline in the body's resistance to disease. This leads to severe infections, particularly of the mouth and upper respiratory tract. The mucosa of the digestive tract is also destroyed, resulting in nausea, vomiting, diarrhea, and inability to digest or absorb food. Death occurs in from two to six weeks.

With smaller doses the effects are similar but less severe. Deaths are less frequent and occur after a longer period of time.

Aside from the vital organs described above, the parts of the body most commonly affected by radiation are:

Skin. The skin may show redness, blistering, and (with extremely high doses) ulceration and necrosis. Healing is usually complete, but late skin changes are not uncommon after large doses.

Lungs. Moderate doses may cause congestion. Extremely large doses may produce marked inflammation, fibrosis, and atrophy.

Gonads. In addition to damage to the genes, noted above, radiation may affect the tissues which manufacture the reproductive cells, thus causing sterility, as opposed to the mutations resulting from gene damage.

RADIATION SICKNESS

Late Effects of Radiation

Late effects of radiation may occur (1) months or years following apparent recovery from a significant amount of acute radiation or (2) after months to years of repeated exposures to small amounts of radiation, such as may occur among physicians (especially radiologists) and in miners in certain areas where the ores have a comparatively high level of radioactivity. Some late effects of radiation are as follows:

Damage to the blood-forming tissues, including the bone marrow. An increased incidence of aplastic anemia and leukemia was observed months to years after large-dose exposures associated with the atomic blasts at Hiroshima and Nagasaki. A higher-than-normal incidence of leukemia has also been found among physicians who are frequently exposed to radiation.

Eye Damage. The formation of cataracts months to years after exposure.

Bone Damage. A high frequency of bone cancer developed in workers engaged in applying radium paint to the luminous dials of watches. The workers moistened their paintbrushes with their lips, swallowing small amounts of radium-containing paint in the process. The paint was absorbed and concentrated in the bones, resulting in radiation cancers. In other cases large doses to children affected bone growth, causing skeletal deformities.

Cancer in Other Organs. Radiation cancers have also occurred in the skin, lungs, thyroid gland, and in other tissues.

Shortening of the life span, unrelated to any specific diseases. It has been observed in animals but has not yet been definitely confirmed in humans.

Human Exposure to Radiation

Natural sources of radiation include cosmic rays from outer space and gamma rays arising from small amounts of radioactive material normally occurring in the bricks and granite used in construction. In addition, small amounts of radioactive elements (principally potassium-40, carbon-14, and radon) are consumed and breathed by humans. Man and all other living organisms have always lived with this natural background radiation.

Among the man-made sources of radiation are those encountered by workers at radium and atomic plant installations and the radiation given in medical treatment and in taking X-ray photographs. Generally the radiation from these sources amounts to less than that received from the natural background.

Weapons testing has been of great concern with respect to the fallout of radioactive materials and the consequent harmful effects of radiation. Fallout occurs in three stages. (1) Local fallout is in the region of the blast. (2) Tropospheric fallout is in a belt around the earth at approximately the same latitude of the blast. (3) Stratospheric fallout is distributed over the entire planet.

Two elements of the fallout are of particular concern, strontium-90 and cesium-137. Both are strong sources of radiation and endure for many years. They may be deposited in soil and then become incorporated into plants and other foodstuffs (milk, meat) consumed by humans. Strontium-90 is chemically similar to calcium and tends to concentrate in bones (especially in children), where it may remain for some time. Cesium-137 is chemically similar to sodium and becomes widely distributed throughout the body, but it tends to be excreted over a period of several months. Because of its wider distribution cesium-137 causes irradiation of the highly susceptible reproductive tissues.

The final major source of radiation is from X rays used for diagnosis (X-ray photographs) and treatment (radiation therapy for cancer, and so forth).

How Much Radiation Is Acceptable?

The acceptable limits of radiation exposure have been the subject of considerable thought and debate. The "safe" level has been gradually, but constantly, lowered as knowledge of radiation effects has accumulated. Control of exposure is of course limited to safety precautions in occupations involving radioactive materials and to discreet use of radiation for medical purposes. The latter involves dosages almost as large as the natural background, and in some cases larger. The average exposure in Western industrialized nations is considerably larger than in underdeveloped nations where these important medical tools are lacking. Careful supervision of such medical radiation is important, and all personnel handling radiation should have special instruction in methods of protection and of minimizing unnecessary exposure. Such safety measures are employed by those specially educated in radiographic and radiotherapeutic techniques, namely radiologists and their trained technicians. Diagnostic X rays and radiotherapy are extremely valuable tools and in the proper hands may be safely utilized for great benefit.

RADIATION SICKNESS. See RADIATION, BIOLOGICAL EFFECTS OF IONIZING.

RADIATION THERAPY, the use of X-ray apparatus, radium, radioactive cobalt, and other sources of high-energy radiation in the treatment of human and animal diseases. Small doses of radiation stimulate healing and are used in treating inflammation. Larger doses destroy tissue and are used in the treatment of cancer. Special techniques have been devised to concentrate radiation in the tumor tissue, minimizing the effects on adjacent normal tissue.

Radiation is the preferred method of therapy for certain cancers of the skin and internal organs. In many cases X rays are combined with other forms of treatment to produce results which would be unobtainable by any single method. X-ray therapy may be used before surgery to reduce the size of a tumor, thus facilitating surgical removal. Preoperative radiation also helps to reduce chances of spread of the tumor cells during surgery. Following the operation, X rays are sometimes used to destroy any remaining cancer cells to prevent spread and regrowth.

The branch of medicine specializing in radiation therapy is known as radiology. To qualify as a radiologist, the medical school graduate receives three years of specialty training in the use of radiation in diagnosis and treatment. See also X RAYS, DIAGNOSTIC.

RAT-BITE FEVER, medical term designating two infectious diseases transmitted by rat bites.

Streptobacillary fever, also known as Haverhill fever, is

caused by the *Streptobacillus moniliformis*, a common inhabitant of the nose and throat of rats. The organism may be transmitted through bites or possibly contaminated milk. The disease develops with chills, fever, skin rash, headache, and joint and back pains from one to five days after the bite. One or more joints may become swollen, red, and painful. Penicillin is effective in treatment.

Spirillary rat-bite fever is caused by *Spirillum minus*. The wound heals at first, but from 5 to 28 days after exposure it becomes swollen and painful and may ulcerate. The lymph nodes in the area swell, and chills, fever, rash, and headache appear. The symptoms characteristically subside, only to reappear again within a few days. This pattern may continue for weeks unless treated. Penicillin and other antibiotics are used in treatment.

RAYNAUD'S [rā-nōz] **PHENOMENON,** group of three signs in the hands and feet caused by a sudden loss of circulating blood, after exposure to cold or emotional upset. The digits become white, blue, or purple, and painful. As the pallor subsides, pain usually increases, and the affected areas become flushed.

When Raynaud's phenomenon occurs without any other detectable disease, it is called Raynaud's disease. It may also be the herald of many other diseases, including scleroderma and systemic lupus, diseases of the blood vessels and connective tissue. Diseases characterized by increased nerve action on the blood vessels may also be preceded by Raynaud's phenomenon. When severe, there may be loss of tissue, gangrene, and total loss of fingers and toes. If there is no underlying disorder, the symptoms can be improved by protection from cold and by drugs which expand the blood vessels. Drugs or surgical severing of the nerve trunks at fault can release the nervous control. There is no complete cure. Raynaud's phenomenon occurs most often in women.

RED CROSS, volunteer societies organized to aid victims of suffering in time of war and peace. The idea from which the Red Cross developed came out of the experience of Henri Dunant, a young Swiss businessman. In 1859 he was traveling in Italy when the battle of Solferino occurred. This bloody conflict resulted in nearly 40,000 casualties. At the scene during the days immediately following, Dunant was shocked by so much suffering. He persuaded people of nearby villages to help him care for the wounded of both sides. The battle haunted Dunant. In 1862 he published *Un Souvenir de Solférino* (A Memory of Solferino), recounting the tragedy and suggesting that committees of volunteers be formed in all countries to care for war-wounded. He journeyed all over Europe to urge his idea.

Early Organization. Dunant's efforts caused the convocation of an international meeting in Geneva, Switzerland, in 1863. Delegates from 16 European nations met and recommended formation in every country of an organization now known as the Red Cross. The next year diplomats of 15 European states drafted the first treaty in international law designed to assure protection for the wounded of the armed forces in time of war and for those who attend and treat them. The treaty also called for the neutralization and protection of ambulances and military hospitals. A red cross on a white background, the design of the Swiss flag with the colors reversed, was chosen as the identifying emblem, to honor Dunant.

During the next century the Red Cross grew to be a world-wide voluntary organization noted for its work in behalf of the victims of war and disaster and for its health, safety, and welfare efforts in behalf of humanity. The first Geneva Convention has been amended, extended, and more clearly defined. Almost every government has now acceded to part or all of the Geneva Conventions.

The International Red Cross. The International Red Cross is composed of three bodies. With headquarters in Geneva, the International Committee of the Red Cross is composed of 25 Swiss citizens. It serves as the neutral intermediary in time of international or civil war, safeguards the principles of the Red Cross, and gives official recognition to national Red Cross societies. The League of Red Cross Societies, also in Geneva, is a federation of the officially recognized societies. It promotes Red Cross societies and helps develop their programs, co-ordinates disaster assistance among them, and provides technical aid to its members.

The International Red Cross Conference meets every four years. Representatives of governments signatory to

Left, Henri Dunant (*kneeling*) ministered to the wounded after the battle of Solferino in 1859. Shocked by the suffering he saw on the battlefield, Dunant determined to found an international organization to care for war-wounded. (Painting by E. A. Dumaresq). Right, Clara Barton, founder of the American National Red Cross.
(AMERICAN NATIONAL RED CROSS)

RED CROSS

the Geneva Conventions attend, to discuss Red Cross activities, the Geneva Conventions, and international humanitarian problems. Between meetings a standing commission co-ordinates the work of the International Red Cross.

The American National Red Cross. The Red Cross in the United States was organized in 1881 by Clara Barton, who was famous for her volunteer nursing of soldiers during the Civil War. In 1882 the U.S. government ratified the Geneva Convention. The Red Cross operates under a charter originally granted by Congress in 1900 and last amended in 1947. The organization is charged with assisting members of the armed forces and their families, providing for disaster preparedness and relief, devising and executing measures for the prevention of suffering, and, on request, aiding in meeting the terms of the Geneva Conventions. Some 3,600 chapters serve every county in the United States and its territories. They are supported by voluntary contributions from the public. Adult and youth membership totals about 44,000,000.

Within a year of its founding, the American Red Cross engaged in its first disaster relief activity—aiding forest fire victims. It has spent nearly $334,000,000 for disaster services, both in the U.S. and overseas. Victims of a disaster are given medical care, food, clothing, and shelter. As soon as possible, Red Cross workers and the affected families work together on a recovery plan. This may include continuation of the disaster relief, rebuilding or repairing of homes, and supplying occupational tools and equipment. All help given disaster victims is a gift. The first American Red Cross services to the military were provided during the Spanish-American War. During World War I the Red Cross inaugurated a broad welfare program for members of the armed forces wherever they were stationed. The program was subsequently expanded to include the servicemen's families and veterans. Approximately 35% of the organization's annual budget is allocated for these services.

In World War II and the Korean conflict blood and blood plasma obtained by the Red Cross from volunteer donors saved the lives of countless soldiers. The Red Cross blood program, inaugurated in 1948 and now the largest in the world, provides blood and blood products to about 4,100 civilian and military hospitals. More than 2,500,000 donations are contributed annually by the American public. Research in blood use, storage, and distribution is a significant part of the blood program.

Another important Red Cross program is its courses in first aid, water safety, and home nursing. About 3,000,000 completion certificates are issued each year. The Nursing Service also trains nurses for assignment in disaster areas and maintains reserves for Red Cross and community activities in the health field.

About 20,000,000 young people are enlisted for service to others through Red Cross enrollment in private, parochial, and public schools. Junior and high school Red Cross members also have opportunities to participate in international relief services and communications projects for youth. Some 2,000,000 volunteers serve in the Red Cross. Officers and committee members, nationally and in the

RED CROSS IN WAR AND PEACE

The goal of the Red Cross is to alleviate suffering. In time of war Red Cross workers administer to the sick and wounded. In peace the Red Cross provides food, clothing, shelter, and medical supplies to victims of such disasters as earthquakes, flood, and famine.

Eager hands reach for supplies of apples and dried milk, distributed by a Japanese Red Cross worker to victims of a severe typhoon.

American Red Cross field director (cross on helmet) with American forces during Italian campaign of World War II.

chapters, are volunteers, as well as most instructors of Red Cross courses. Volunteers, such as Gray Ladies, staff aides, and nurse's aides, are trained for their work in hospitals and institutions and in the chapter. Headquarters of the American National Red Cross is in Washington, D.C.

Canadian Red Cross. The Red Cross emblem was first raised in Canada during the Northwest Rebellion of 1885. Under the leadership of G. S. Ryerson, the Canadian Red Cross became a branch of the British Red Cross 11 years later. The organization aided the sick and wounded during the Boer War and World War I. In 1918 it decided to operate in peacetime as well as in wartime, and in 1927 the Canadian Red Cross was established as an independent national society by the International Committee for the Red Cross. Since then its activities have included programs for members of the armed forces, their families, veterans, refugees, and orphaned children overseas. The Canadian Red Cross instituted a blood donation program in 1947. Blood is given to any Canadian who is in need. Each province of Canada has a division of the Red Cross, and national co-ordinating headquarters is in Toronto. The 1952 conference of the International Red Cross was held in Toronto.

REED, WALTER (1851–1902), American physician known for his work as chairman of the U.S. Army Yellow Fever Commission. In Cuba, Reed and his associates James Carroll, Aristides Agramonte, and J. W. Lazear investigated the theory of the Cuban physician Carlos J. Finlay that yellow fever was transmitted by the stegomyia mosquito. Since at the time it was thought that animals could not be infected with yellow fever, it was necessary to use human volunteers to study the disease. In the course of the experiments Carroll was deliberately infected with yellow fever, but recovered. Lazear acquired the disease accidentally and died. The commission proved its case against stegomyia, and this knowledge was quickly applied by William Gorgas to rid Cuba of yellow fever. In recognition of his achievement, a U.S. Army general hospital is named after Walter Reed.

REGIONAL ENTERITIS, an inflammatory disease of the small intestine originally described by Dr. Burrill Crohn in 1932. The disease is worldwide, affects both sexes equally, and has a peak incidence between the ages of 15 and 35. A high proportion of patients are of Jewish origin and urban background. No specific cause of the disease has been identified. Earliest involvement occurs in the ileum, the lowest portion of the small intestine, which becomes swollen and red. Then the inner layer, or mucosa, develops many ulcers and bleeds. A few inches or many feet of intestine are affected. The illness may be active for a short period and then subside for long periods only to flare again.

Symptoms of the disease are varied, but diarrhea, colicky pain, and weight loss are the most common. Fever and pain in the lower right part of the abdomen may suggest appendicitis. Because food is absorbed from the small intestine patients often develop severe malnutrition. The bowel may erode into the abdominal skin and result in a fistula. Diagnosis is usually made from X-rays of the small intestine and at the time of operation.

About a third of the patients recover spontaneously; the rest have varying degrees of illness for the remainder of their lives. Steroid hormones and nonabsorbable sulfonamides are useful in controlling the illness. Surgery rarely removes all of the diseased bowel; its role is to eliminate complications of the disease. Many people have distinguished themselves in the arts, sciences, and business despite prolonged and progressive regional enteritis.

REICHSTEIN [rīkн'shtīn], **TADEUS** (1897–   ), Swiss organic chemist who shared the 1950 Nobel Prize with E. C. Kendall and P. S. Hench for work on cortisone and other adrenal hormones. Born in Poland, Reichstein was educated in Switzerland. He taught organic chemistry at the state technical college in Zurich and later directed the Pharmacological Institute and the organic chemistry laboratories at the University of Basel. In addition to his investigations of adrenal steroids, Reichstein is known for his synthesis of vitamin C (ascorbic acid).

REPRODUCTION [rē-prə-dŭk'shən], a term referring to the various means by which living organisms give rise to offspring. The ability to reproduce is one of the special qualities of living organisms and serves in part to distinguish them from nonliving matter. In both the plant and animal kingdoms two main types of reproduction are observed: asexual and sexual. Asexual reproduction, which is characteristic of most lower plants and animals, occurs when offspring arise from a single parent organism. The parent in such cases is neither male nor female; in fact, it usually lacks any special reproductive structures. In sexual reproduction the offspring arise from the joining of sex cells (typically, two cells of different kind) produced by the parents. Sexual reproduction is characteristic of higher plants and animals.

Human Reproduction

Because human beings are placental mammals, the biological processes of human reproduction do not differ greatly from those of other higher mammals. Egg cells from the female and sperm cells from the male unite, the egg is fertilized, and a child begins to develop. Egg and sperm are formed in organs called the gonads. Special organs in the male transport the sperm. Special organs in the female make fertilization possible and provide a suitable place for the fertilized egg to develop.

In the male, sperm cells are produced in the testes. These organs are located within the abdomen, near the kidney in the fetus. Before birth, the testes move down to the lower part of the abdomen and outside the body wall into a sac called the scrotum. Usually one testis is larger than the other. The slightly higher temperatures inside the body apparently inhibit the growth of human sperm. Sperm cells form within very small, highly coiled tubes called seminiferous or testicular, tubules. Sperm development begins at the time of puberty, usually about age 14. It continues throughout life, although it diminishes in old age. Between the tubules, there are specialized cells, which secrete male hormones, or androgens, which maintain male sex characteristics.

As sperm is produced, cells in the tubule wall secrete a fluid. This fluid forces the sperm out of the tubules and into a network which leads finally to the sperm duct, or vas deferens. Many sperm cells are temporarily stored in the coiled section of the sperm duct before it enters the abdominal cavity. Some sperm are also stored at the end of this duct, within the body, at the entrance to the seminal vesicle. The seminal vesicle provides secretions which enable the sperm to become very active. The prostate gland also secretes fluids before the sperm cells enter the final passageway, the urethra, which leads through the penis to the outside. The combination of these secretions and sperm is called semen. When semen passes through the urethra, the juncture from the bladder automatically closes so that no urine enters. When urine is expelled, the juncture from the sperm duct closes.

During sexual intercourse, sperm is deposited in the vagina of the female. It moves of its own accord into the oviduct, or fallopian tubes, where it may fertilize an egg cell. Hundreds of millions of sperm cells are produced by the body, whether or not there is sexual intercourse. They are periodically discharged, usually at night, during sleep. This discharge of sperm is known as ejaculation. This involves a sudden rush of blood into the labyrinth of arteries surrounding the urethra, which causes a swelling and stiffening of the penis. After the sperm is discharged, the blood gradually drains from the arteries, and they contract to normal size.

In the female, egg cells are produced in the ovaries. These two oval-shaped organs, each a little more than an inch long, are located deep in the abdomen. The eggs are formed in cellular structures, called follicles, within each ovary. The follicles also secrete female sex hormones. Estrogen, one of the female hormones, is secreted during the ripening of the egg. Another female hormone, progesterone, is produced in a modified part of the follicle called the corpus luteum, after the egg is expelled. Normally, one egg matures each month, with the ovaries alternating production. When mature, the egg breaks out of the follicle to start its journey down one of the fallopian tubes. If it encounters a male sperm here, fertilization takes place. The fertilized egg, called a zygote, continues to travel to the uterus and attaches itself to the soft, thickened tissues of the uterine wall.

Before the egg leaves the ovary, the wall of the uterus is quite thin. As soon as the egg is released, progesterone stimulates the uterus, which becomes enlarged. At the same time, the supply of blood to the uterus increases, and the walls of the uterus thicken. If the egg is not fertilized, it disintegrates, and the soft lining of the uterus breaks down and is passed out of the body through the vagina. This process is known as menstruation. The word comes from the Latin, *mensis,* meaning "month." Menstruation occurs each month, but stops when an egg has been fertilized. Then the uterine lining becomes a nursery for what is now the embryo. A series of membranes form around the embryo and the placenta begins to develop. At first, nutrients and oxygen from the mother's body filter through the membranes and waste products are carried out.

The innermost membrane, called the amnion, encloses a fluid which completely surrounds the embryo. Later, the edges of this membrane fuse and become the umbilical cord. This tube soon becomes the sole passageway for the exchange of materials between the growing embryo and the placenta. All materials to and from the mother's body are diffused through the placenta. There is no direct exchange. The embryo continues to grow until it takes on characteristic human form, when it is called a fetus. After four months, the fetus weighs about a quarter of a pound and is able to move independently. At the end of the pregnancy, about nine months or 280 days, what was once an embryo has become a human being, able to survive in the outside world. The baby will be about 20 in. long and weigh 7 or 8 lb.

Childbirth starts when the uterus begins a series of contractions to move the baby slowly toward the vagina, or birth canal. This muscular action is called labor. The bones of the pelvic girdle move apart to allow the baby to pass through. Early in this process, the fluid-filled amnion breaks and releases its contents. Later the contractions become very strong and the baby is pushed through the vagina into the outer world. The umbilical cord leading to the placenta is tied and cut by the doctor. In a few days the section attached to the baby dries up and falls away, only the navel remaining to show where it had been. The placenta is expelled by the body shortly after birth. It is called the afterbirth. Late in pregnancy, the mammary glands in the breasts enlarge and prepare to secrete milk. The first flow is a watery fluid with special properties, called colostrum. If the baby is not breast-fed, the mammary glands soon stop producing milk.

See also:
EMBRYOLOGY   GENETICS
FERTILIZATION

RESPIRATION [rĕs-pə-rā′shən], a process occurring in living organisms in which oxygen is taken into the body to burn foodstuffs and yield energy. Most living creatures obtain their life energy from respiration except certain bacteria and other simple organisms which can extract energy from food in the absence of oxygen.

How does the organism take in oxygen? Simple single-celled organisms, such as the ameba, do not possess lungs or other intricate structures to take in oxygen from the air. These creatures rely on diffusion. Oxygen passes into the cell as smoke spreads in the air throughout a room by the random motion of gas molecules. In more complex, many-celled organisms simple diffusion is unable to supply the amounts of oxygen needed. Consequently these creatures possess specialized organs of respiration, such as the gills of fish and the lungs of man. These structures bring oxygen to the circulatory system, which, in turn, carries it deep into the tissues of the organism. The insects are an interesting exception as they do not use their circulatory system for carrying oxygen. Instead they use a system of tubes (respiratory tracheae) that pipe fresh air directly to the tissues.

Breathing. The active work of breathing takes place during inspiration, when air is drawn into the lungs. To accomplish the intake, the arched horizontal sheet of muscle, called the diaphragm, is pulled downward like a huge piston, and the muscles attached to the ribs pull the chest cage outwards. The net effect is to expand the lungs, causing air to rush in to fill the increased volume. Expiration is usually a passive process resulting from the elastic recoil of

RESPIRATION 1.

THE RESPIRATORY TRACT

SECTION OF LUNG SHOWING BRONCHIAL TREE

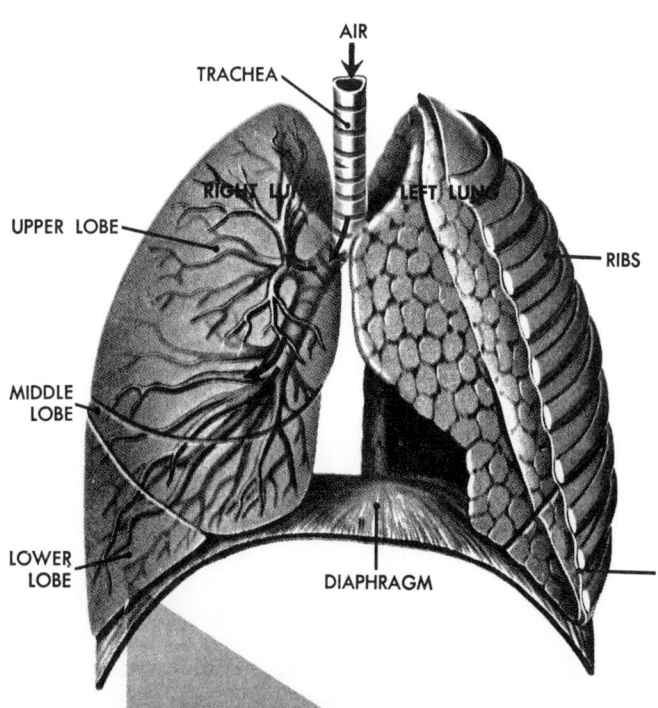

- AIR
- TRACHEA
- RIGHT LUNG
- LEFT LUNG
- UPPER LOBE
- RIBS
- MIDDLE LOBE
- LOWER LOBE
- DIAPHRAGM

CROSS SECTION OF TRACHEA

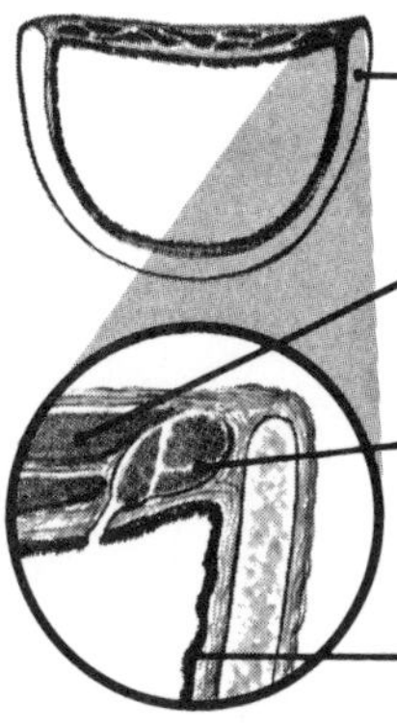

- Trachea is braced by open-ended cartilage rings.
- Layers of smooth muscle constrict or open the trachea in response to nervous stimulation.
- Glandular cells secrete mucous material that traps dust and foreign particles.
- Columnar cells: Movable hairlike projections (cilia) drive dust and foreign particles away from lungs.

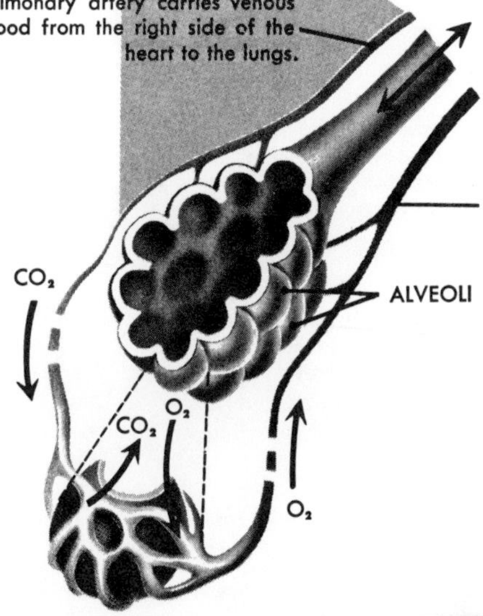

Cutaway view of the pleura. The pleura is seen here as a double-layered membrane that envelops the lungs and lines the chest cage. The pleural layers adhere to each other and are drawn out as the chest expands during inspiration.

Pulmonary artery carries venous blood from the right side of the heart to the lungs.

Air enters alveolus through respiratory bronchiole.

Pulmonary vein carries oxygenated blood from the lungs to the left side of the heart.

- CO_2
- O_2
- ALVEOLI

CAPILLARY NETWORK IN ALVEOLUS

THE EXCHANGE OF GASES IN THE LUNGS

The exchange of gases between the blood and the air of the lungs occurs in the alveoli. Here blood from the pulmonary artery passes through a network of fine blood vessels (capillaries), taking up oxygen and surrendering carbon dioxide. Oxygen-rich blood is carried from the lungs to the left side of the heart by the pulmonary vein.

THE ACTION OF THE DIAPHRAGM

As the diaphragm contracts the lungs expand, drawing in air. As the diaphragm relaxes the lungs contract, expelling air.

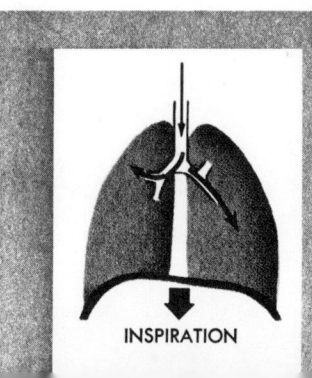

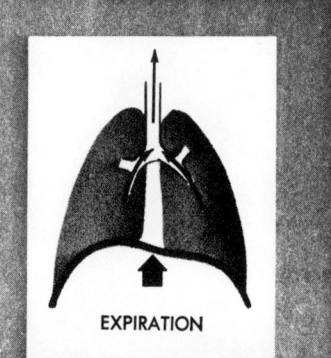

INSPIRATION EXPIRATION

RESPIRATION 2. THE CONTROL OF RESPIRATION

(A) HOW THE NORMAL RHYTHM OF RESPIRATION IS MAINTAINED

Without thought or awareness, we breathe rhythmically and automatically, a feat made possible by respiratory centers in the brain and by stretch-sensitive receptors in the lungs.

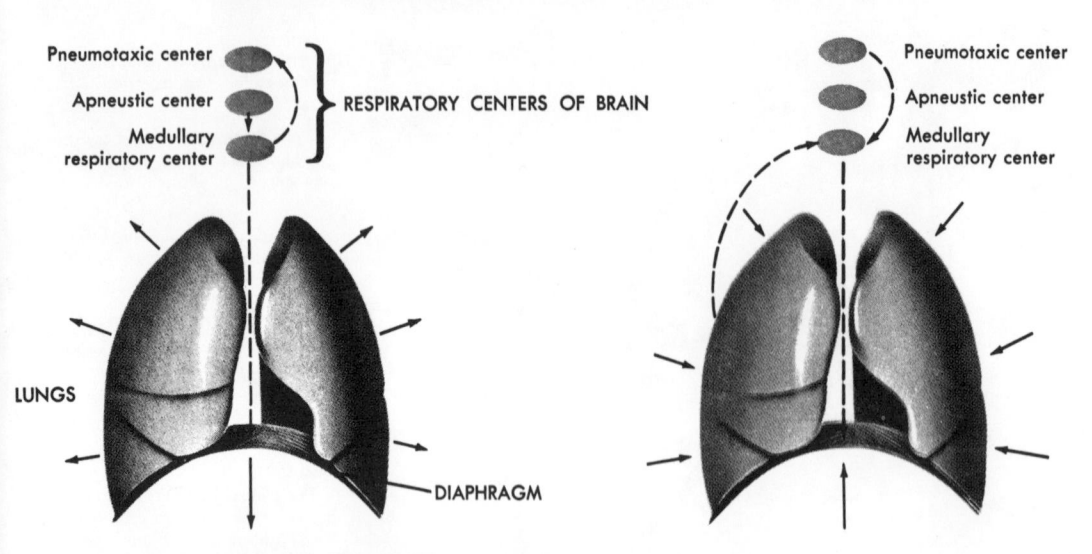

Pneumotaxic center
Apneustic center
Medullary respiratory center
RESPIRATORY CENTERS OF BRAIN

LUNGS

DIAPHRAGM

The apneustic center stimulates the medullary respiratory center, which stimulates the diaphragm to contract. This expands the lungs and draws in air. Impulses from the medullary respiratory center also reach the pneumotaxic center.

As the lungs expand, sensory receptors are stretched generating impulses that travel to the medullary center of the brain. Impulses from the pneumotaxic center also reach the medullary center. These actions on the medullary center inhibit inspiration, thus relaxing the diaphragm and permitting the lungs to recoil and expel air.

(B) HOW THE CHEMICAL COMPOSITION OF THE BLOOD AFFECTS RESPIRATION

Certain specialized cells in the great arteries (the aorta and carotid arteries) test the acidity of the blood and its concentration of oxygen and carbon dioxide. This information is referred to the respiratory centers, which adjust the depth of breathing accordingly. Of the three factors—acidity, oxygen concentration, and carbon dioxide concentration—the last seems to be most important for the normal regulation of breathing. This is emphasized by the fact that the cells of the respiratory center are themselves directly sensitive to the carbon dioxide content of the blood.

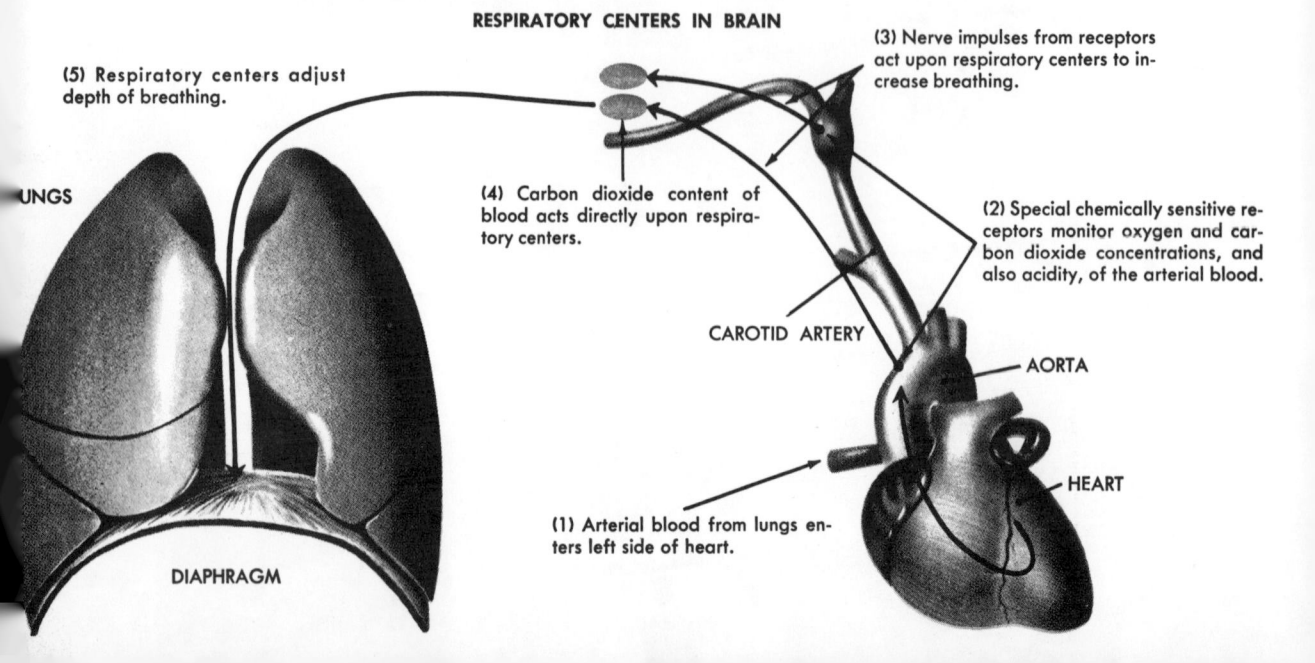

RESPIRATORY CENTERS IN BRAIN

(5) Respiratory centers adjust depth of breathing.

(4) Carbon dioxide content of blood acts directly upon respiratory centers.

(3) Nerve impulses from receptors act upon respiratory centers to increase breathing.

(2) Special chemically sensitive receptors monitor oxygen and carbon dioxide concentrations, and also acidity, of the arterial blood.

LUNGS

CAROTID ARTERY

AORTA

HEART

(1) Arterial blood from lungs enters left side of heart.

DIAPHRAGM

RESPIRATION 3. THE CHEMISTRY OF RESPIRATION

HOW OXYGEN AND CARBON DIOXIDE ARE TRANSPORTED IN THE BLOOD AND EXCHANGED IN THE LUNGS AND TISSUES

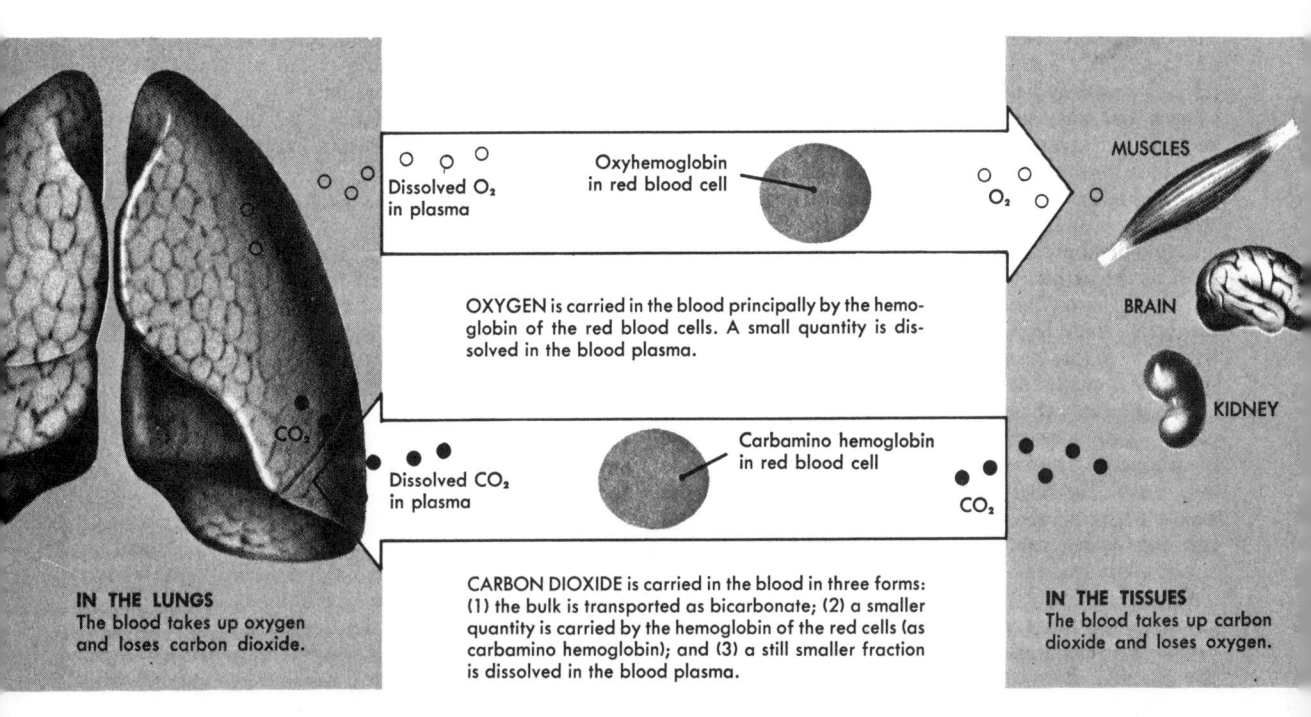

IN THE LUNGS
The blood takes up oxygen and loses carbon dioxide.

OXYGEN is carried in the blood principally by the hemoglobin of the red blood cells. A small quantity is dissolved in the blood plasma.

CARBON DIOXIDE is carried in the blood in three forms: (1) the bulk is transported as bicarbonate; (2) a smaller quantity is carried by the hemoglobin of the red cells (as carbamino hemoglobin); and (3) a still smaller fraction is dissolved in the blood plasma.

IN THE TISSUES
The blood takes up carbon dioxide and loses oxygen.

THE REACTIONS IN THE LUNGS

The red blood cell is the focal point of the reactions involved in gas exchange. In the diagram above oxygen and bicarbonate ions move into the cell and carbon dioxide moves out. Chloride ions also leave the cell to maintain the electrochemical balance, which is upset by the movement of the bicarbonate ions. Within the cell oxygen combines with hemoglobin to form oxyhemoglobin. Bicarbonate reacts with hydrogen ions to form H_2CO_3, which decomposes into carbon dioxide and water. Carbon dioxide is also liberated by carbamino hemoglobin (a compound of hemoglobin and CO_2).

THE REACTIONS IN THE TISSUES

In the tissues the reactions are the reverse of those that occur in the lungs. Carbon dioxide enters the red blood cell, where (1) some combines with water to form H_2CO_3, which then separates into H^+ and HCO_3^- — the latter escapes into the plasma; (2) some combines directly with hemoglobin to form carbamino hemoglobin; and (3) a small quantity dissolves in the cell fluids. Oxygen is released from oxyhemoglobin and enters the tissue fluids. Chloride ions enter the cell to compensate for the passage of HCO_3^- ions into the plasma.

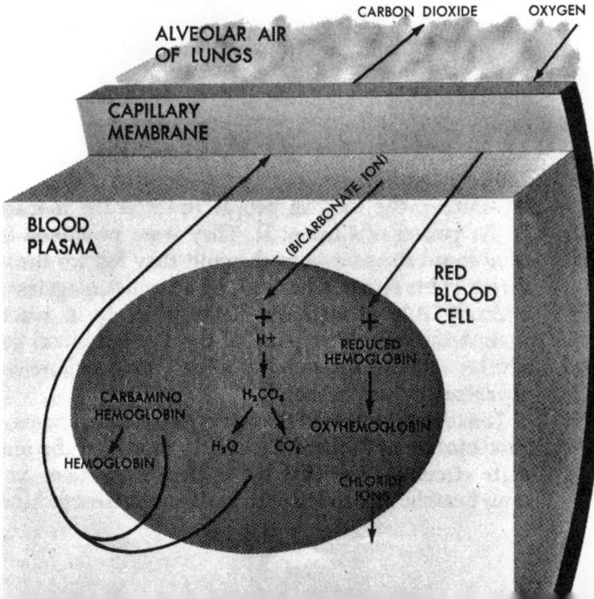

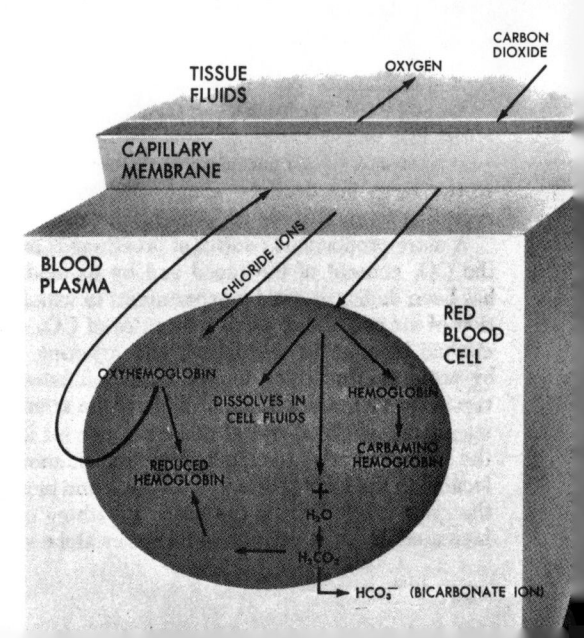

RESPIRATION

the lungs and rib cage as inspiration ceases. During vigorous exercise expiration is aided by contractions of the chest and abdominal muscles. Breathing requires physical work. During rest this work represents less than 1% of the total energy output of the body, but during vigorous exercise it may account for half or more of the entire output. In asthma, in which the air passages become narrowed, the work of breathing may be so great as to exhaust the patient.

Incoming air is led into the body by a system of branching pipes which end in the alveoli, the tiny air sacs of the lungs (of which there are approximately 500,000,000). The surface of each alveolus is covered with a branching network of thousands of minute blood vessels. This forms a virtual sheet of moving blood which is separated from the air by a layer of tissue one-hundred-thousandth of an inch thick across which oxygen diffuses into the blood and carbon dioxide out.

The diffusion of gases in the lungs results from gradients in partial pressure between the gases in the lungs and those dissolved in the blood. Venous blood entering the lungs has higher and lower partial pressures of carbon dioxide and oxygen, respectively, than the air contained in the alveoli of the lungs. After exchange of these gases, the blood leaving the lungs has partial pressures of oxygen and carbon dioxide close to those of the alveolar air.

In the blood, oxygen is carried in a loose chemical combination with hemoglobin, the red pigment of the blood cells. As the blood reaches distant tissues, the oxygen-hemoglobin combination breaks down, releasing oxygen which diffuses from the blood to the tissue fluids. Carbon dioxide enters the red blood cells and participates in a series of reactions known as the chloride shift, which might be described as a chemical game of musical chairs.

The Chloride Shift. In the red blood cells carbon dioxide combines with water to form carbonic acid (H_2CO_3). The rate of this combination would be too slow to absorb the necessary amounts of carbon dioxide were it not for the enzyme *carbonic anhydrase*, which speeds the reaction enormously. The carbonic acid splits into bicarbonate ions (HCO_3^-) and potentially harmful hydrogen ions (H^+). Fortunately hemoglobin is able to take up the hydrogen ions after surrendering its oxygen and thereby prevents a dangerous increase in the acidity of the blood. The bicarbonate ions pass out of the cell and in doing so would upset the balance of positive and negative electric charges of the blood were it not for the fact that an equal number of chloride ions enter the cell. Although most of the carbon dioxide is carried as bicarbonate in the blood plasma (the fluid portion of the blood excluding the cells), some (25%) is carried in direct combination with hemoglobin (as carbamino hemoglobin), and a small quantity is carried in solution in the plasma.

The reverse of these reactions occurs in the lungs. Here carbon dioxide leaves the blood and oxygen enters. Now bicarbonate ions enter the red blood cell, and chloride ions leave. The final stage of respiration occurs in the tissues where oxygen participates in a series of chemical reactions which culminate in the release of the energy contained in food and in the production of carbon dioxide.

Control of Breathing. The rhythmic inflation and deflation of the lungs is under the automatic guidance of several nerve centers located at the base of the brain in the medulla oblongata and pons. An important clue to the nature of this mechanism was obtained in 1868, when it was shown that inspiration could be halted by inflating the lungs of an animal under anesthesia. It is now known that this inflation causes stretch receptors in the lungs to send impulses to the brain (via the vagus nerves) to "turn off," or inhibit, the "gasping" (apneustic) center in the brain which stimulates inspiration. This phenomenon is believed by many to be the basis of normal rhythmic breathing.

Another puzzling aspect of respiration concerns the mechanism which controls the rate and depth of breathing. Since oxygen is so vital for the life and well-being of the organism, one might reasonably expect that breathing would increase when the oxygen content of the blood first declined. Actually oxygen lack does not appear to exert a significant effect until the oxygen pressure in the lungs has declined about 30% to a level corresponding to an altitude of 7,000 ft. above sea level.

A more pronounced control of breathing is exerted by the CO_2 content of the blood and by its acidity. This has been demonstrated by experiments in which inhalation of air containing small quantities of CO_2 caused a marked increase in ventilation, and lowering the CO_2 by rapid overbreathing tended to inhibit breathing. A rise in the CO_2, the acidity, or both, of the arterial blood stimulates special chemical receptors, one set located in the brain, and other so-called peripheral chemoreceptors located in the carotid artery in the neck and in the aorta, the great artery leaving the heart. Breathing is thereby increased. It is the peripheral receptors alone which, by relaying impulses to the breathing centers of the brain, stimulate breathing when the concentration of oxygen in the blood reaches dangerously low levels.

This type of regulation does not explain the increase in breathing during physical exercise. Even though much more oxygen is being used and more carbon dioxide being produced than at rest, the oxygen and carbon dioxide content of the arterial blood *does not change*. The factors accounting for the precise increase in breathing during exercise are still poorly understood.

See also LUNGS.

RESPIRATION, ARTIFICIAL. See ARTIFICIAL RESPIRATION.

RETICULOENDOTHELIAL [rĭ-tĭk′yə-lō-ĕn-dō-thē′lē-əl] **SYSTEM,** a vast, widely distributed network of specialized cells (macrophages) which constitute a major link in the body's defense against infection. The cells are often described as *fixed* and *wandering*. Fixed cells are found in the spleen, lymph glands, bone marrow, connective tissue, liver, and adrenal and pituitary glands. The wandering cells are so named because they may enter the blood stream and travel through the body. Certain fixed cells in the solid tissues of the lymph glands, spleen, and bone marrow may become wanderers under certain conditions.

These cells play an important role in inflammation, the body's response to invasion by bacteria or other foreign bodies. Wandering reticuloendothelial cells meet the invaders and engulf and destroy them (a process known as phagocytosis). In the same way reticuloendothelial cells

THE RETICULOENDOTHELIAL SYSTEM

The reticuloendothelial system comprises a group of specialized cells (macrophages) found in various organs and tissues of the body. These cells help protect the body against infection by their ability to consume and destroy (phagocytose) infectious microorganisms. There are two types of macrophages: those that are "fixed" and those that "wander" through the tissues.

PHAGOCYTOSIS—HOW MACROPHAGES ATTACK MICROORGANISMS AND OTHER FOREIGN PARTICLES

(1) In response to infection, wandering macrophages move toward the microorganisms. In some cases fixed macrophages may also become wanderers.

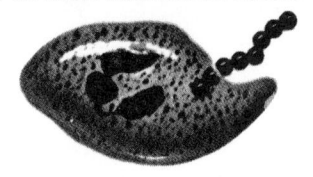

(2) Macrophage envelops microorganisms.

(3) Enzymes in the macrophage attack the microorganisms.

THE DISTRIBUTION OF MACROPHAGES IN THE BODY

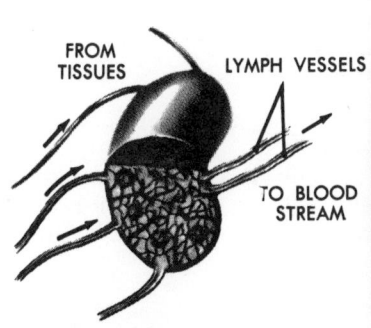

Lymph Nodes: Macrophages in the lymph nodes purify the lymphatic fluid before it drains into the blood stream.

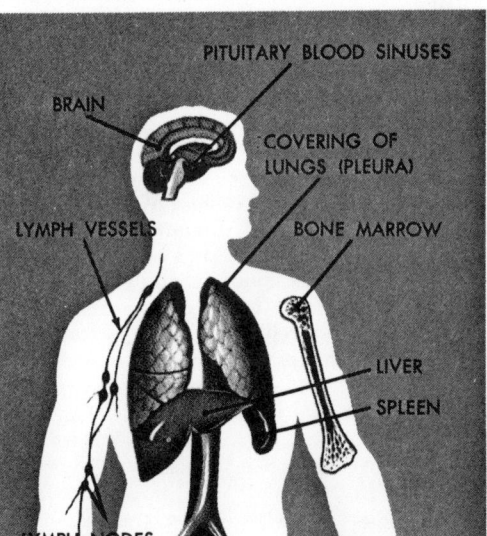

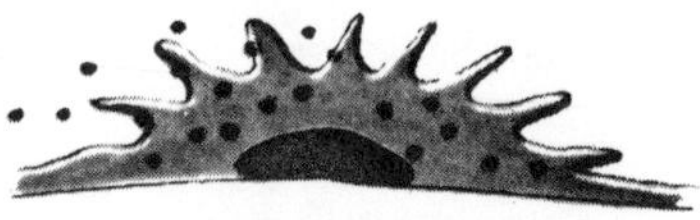

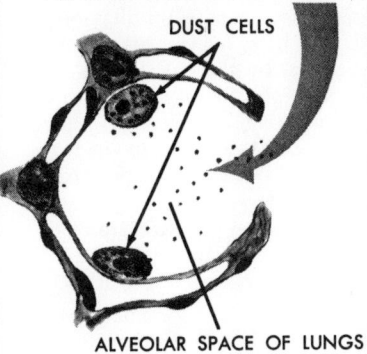

Lungs: Macrophages in lungs ("dust" cells) take up dust particles from inhaled air.

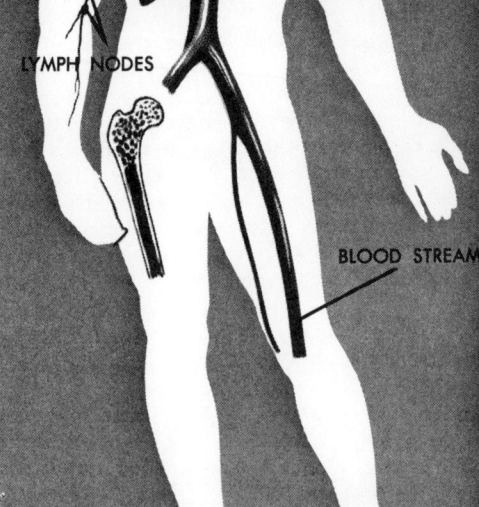

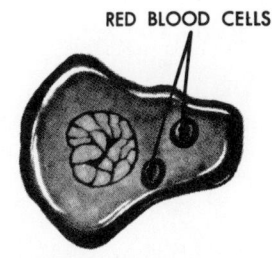

Kupffer cells lining the sinusoids of the liver phagocytose impurities from the blood and convert hemoglobin from broken-down red cells into bile pigment.

Macrophages of the spleen engulf and destroy old or fragile blood cells.

consume dust and other potentially harmful foreign particles entering the lungs. The cells of the system are also believed to participate in the production of antibodies, the specialized substances which the body manufactures to deal with infectious microorganisms. Reticuloendothelial cells in the spleen, liver, and bone marrow capture and destroy old blood cells, conserving the iron for the production of new cells. The cells of the system, particularly the Kupffer cells of the liver, convert the hemoglobin released from the destroyed blood cells into the bile pigments which are excreted in the bile fluid via the intestine.

A variety of highly fatal cancerlike diseases, including reticulum cell sarcoma and Hodgkin's disease, affect the reticuloendothelial system. These diseases are marked by progressive enlargement of the lymph glands and spleen. Other diseases of the system are characterized by accumulations of fatty substances within the RE cells.
See also LIVER; SPLEEN.

RETINA. See EYE.

RETINAL DETACHMENT, partial or complete separation of the retina, the light-sensitive layer in the rear of the eye, from its underlying attachment. This is more apt to occur in nearsighted persons and often follows severe injury to the eye or head. The patient experiences flashes of light, black spots, and the impression of a veil or curtain in the field of vision. The degree of visual loss depends upon the location and extent of the detachment. Treatment consists of surgical reattachment of the retina. The prospects of successful restoration of vision are good.

RETROLENTAL FIBROPLASIA [rĕt-rō-lĕn'təl fī-brō-plā'zhə], an eye disease which at one time caused blindness in premature infants. First described in 1941, the disease consisted of an abnormal formation of blood vessels in the retina, the light-sensitive layer of the eye. Researchers soon noted that the disorder was more common in premature infants who were kept in special incubators, and that it never developed in premature infants who were born in more primitive surroundings where incubators were not available. After considerable investigation it was discovered that excess oxygen supply in the incubators caused the unusual blood vessel growth. The disease was eliminated by correcting the oxygen supply.

RHEUMATIC [rōō-măt'ĭk] **FEVER,** disorder characterized by inflammations of the joints, heart, blood vessels, skin, and connective, or supporting, tissues throughout the body. The exact mechanism producing rheumatic fever is unclear. Although it usually occurs from one to three weeks after an attack of sore throat caused by Group A beta-hemolytic streptococci, the bacteria are apparently not present in the body when rheumatic fever develops. It has been suggested that the disease may be caused by an allergic-type reaction to substances given off by the streptococcus bacteria.

The disease is more frequent in children between the ages of 5 and 15, but adults may also be affected. Outbreaks closely parallel epidemics of streptococcal infections: approximately 3% to 5% of these infections result in rheumatic fever. Frequently, several members of the same family are affected.

In many cases the disease develops suddenly with the appearance of fever and a characteristic "migratory" arthritis, which passes from one joint to another in an unpredictable pattern. Other signs and symptoms include nosebleeds, abdominal pain, skin eruptions, and the appearance of subcutaneous nodules around bony prominences (such as over the elbows and spine). Involvement of the nervous system may cause chorea—purposeless, uncontrolled movements of the extremities. The most serious aspect of rheumatic fever is heart damage involving the linings of the heart and the heart muscle. The patient may experience chest pain and rapid and irregular heartbeat, and may develop enlargement of the heart. Heart failure and death may follow. Permanent damage to the heart valves is a common complication and recurrent attacks superimposed upon an already weakened heart may be fatal.

Treatment during the acute attack consists of complete bed rest and antibiotics to eliminate any streptococci present in the body. Salicylate drugs (such as aspirin) and cortisone and related drugs help relieve the inflammations. (The striking effectiveness of salicylates in rapidly controlling the symptoms of rheumatic fever is sometimes useful as a diagnostic test.) Following recovery antibiotics may be given indefinitely to prevent recurrences.
See also HEART DISEASES.

RHEUMATISM. See ARTHRITIS.

RHEUMATOID ARTHRITIS. See ARTHRITIS.

Rh FACTOR, blood group substance in the membrane of human red blood cells. In 1940, Karl Landsteiner injected red blood cells from a rhesus monkey (hence Rh) into rabbits. The antibodies produced were tested with human red blood cells. He found that 85% of the people tested had the factor, and thus are Rh positive. The 15% who did not are called Rh negative. Rh is now known to be three separate factors, separately inherited and called C, D, and E. The absent factors are termed c, d, e. With a separate maternal and paternal gene for each factor, a person's Rh type can vary from CDE/CDE to cde/cde.

The Rh discovery provided one reason for certain damaging transfusion reactions. It has also proved to be the explanation for most cases of a disease of the newborn, called erythroblastosis fetalis, which destroys red blood cells. When an Rh negative mother carries an Rh positive child, the baby's red cells may cross the placenta into the mother's circulation. Sensitized by the baby's cells, the mother produces antibodies to the Rh factor. The antibodies recross from mother to child, especially in later pregnancies. They coat the infant's red cells, producing a potentially fatal anemia. Many Rh negative mothers have several Rh positive children, without sufficient Rh antibody production to cause difficulty. The problem of Rh sensitization is now being reduced by preventing Rh antibody production in the mother after the delivery of each Rh positive baby.
See also BLOOD; PREGNANCY.

RHINITIS [rĭ-nī'tĭs], inflammation of the mucous membranes which line the nasal passages. A common cause of rhinitis is the common cold. Allergic rhinitis, better known

as hay fever, is caused by allergy-producing substances such as air-borne pollens and mold spores. The nasal tissues swell and may partially or completely obstruct breathing. Increased fluid secretions cause sneezing and nasal discharges. The sense of smell is impaired and bacterial infection may complicate the condition. Relief can often be obtained by nasal sprays and antihistamines which help reduce swelling and suppress the discharge.
See also COLD, COMMON; HAY FEVER.

RICHARDS, DICKINSON WOODRUFF (1895–   ), American physician who in 1956 shared the Nobel Prize in physiology and medicine with André F. Cournand and Werner Forssmann for research in heart catheterization. Forssmann first introduced a tube into his own heart through an arm vein. Cournand and Richards pushed tubes into the lung, as well as the heart, to measure blood pressure and blood composition. This technique proved important for diagnosis of heart disease and paved the way for advances in heart surgery.

RICHET [rē-shě'], **CHARLES ROBERT** (1850–1935), French physician who won the Nobel Prize for physiology and medicine in 1913 for his studies on anaphylaxis (hypersensitivity to injections of serum or other foreign substances). He studied and taught in Paris. He investigated many fields of physiology, but his most important work was in the field of serum therapy, in which he was a pioneer. His studies on anaphylaxis provided the foundation for all later studies of allergies.

RICKETS [rĭk'ĭts], disease of infancy and childhood caused by a deficiency of vitamin D. This vitamin regulates the absorption of calcium and the absorption and excretion of phosphorus—minerals important for the normal growth of bone. Deficiency of vitamin D results in decreased absorption of calcium and phosphorus from the intestine, and increased excretion of phosphorus in the urine. Rickets is essentially a disease of the temperate zones, being comparatively infrequent in the far north where vitamin D-rich fish foods are a dietary staple, and in the tropics, where abundant sunlight stimulates formation of the vitamin in the skin. Premature infants are especially susceptible to rickets.

Normal bone growth consists initially of construction of a soft framework of organic tissue, followed by the deposition of mineral salts which harden the bone. In rickets the absence of adequate amounts of calcium and phosphorus prevents proper mineralization. Consequently the bones remain soft and become easily deformed by the weight of the body and muscular tensions. The ribs develop characteristic beadlike enlargements known as the "rachitic rosary." The legs become bowed, the shins protrude convexly (saber shins), the spine develops curvatures, and malformations of the chest and pelvis appear. Other changes, such as irritability, sweating, and muscle weakness, may also appear. In a small number of cases severe muscular spasms may be seen (tetany).

Treatment consists of the administration of vitamin D. In some children suffering from an inherited resistance to vitamin D, especially heavy dosages of the vitamin are needed. In older children surgery may be necessary to correct the bone deformities. Since vitamin D occurs in comparatively few natural sources, artificial fortification of milk with the vitamin is one of the most effective means of prevention.
See also VITAMINS.

RICKETTSIALPOX [rĭ-kĕt'sē-əl-päks], infectious disease resembling chickenpox and caused by the microorganism *Rickettsia akari*. Transmitted by mites which normally infest mice and other small rodents, the disease develops one to two weeks after exposure with the appearance of a red pimple covered with a black scab at the location of the bite. Several days later a blisterlike eruption appears accompanied by fever, chills, headache, sweats, and muscle pains. The condition disappears within a few weeks, usually without complications. Antibiotics speed recovery.

RICKETTSIAS AND RICKETTSIAL DISEASES. Rickettsias are a group of microorganisms intermediate in size between the bacteria and viruses. They resemble bacteria in being visible under the optical microscope, but differ in their highly fastidious growth requirements. They may be cultivated only in the presence of living cells. Rickettsias normally live within the cells of ticks, lice, and other arthropods. In some cases the relationship is so ancient that the parasites do no harm, even invading the arthro-

THE TRANSMISSION OF RICKETTSIAL DISEASES

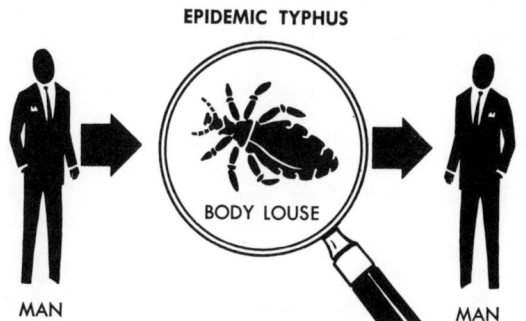

EPIDEMIC TYPHUS

MAN → BODY LOUSE → MAN

Epidemic typhus is carried from one human to another by the body louse. The louse tends to leave the bodies of fevered persons to seek hosts with normal temperatures.

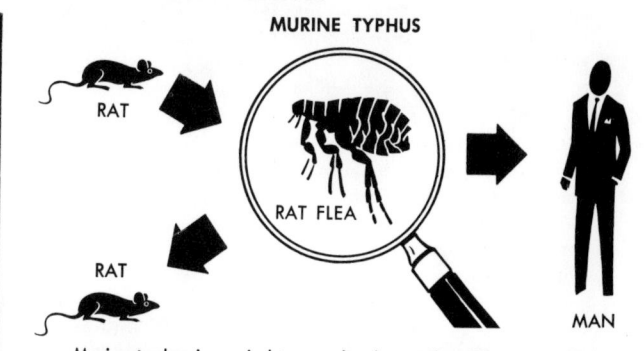

MURINE TYPHUS

RAT → RAT FLEA → MAN
RAT

Murine typhus is carried to man by the rat flea. The rat serves as a natural "reservoir" for the rickettsia. Apparently the rat and the rat flea serve as hosts to the rickettsia without suffering any ill effects.

ROCKY MOUNTAIN SPOTTED FEVER

Rocky Mountain spotted fever is transmitted to man by ticks. The rickettsia is maintained in nature through the cycle: domestic or wild animal ⇨ tick ⇨ domestic or wild animal. The ticks may also transmit the rickettsia directly to their own offspring.

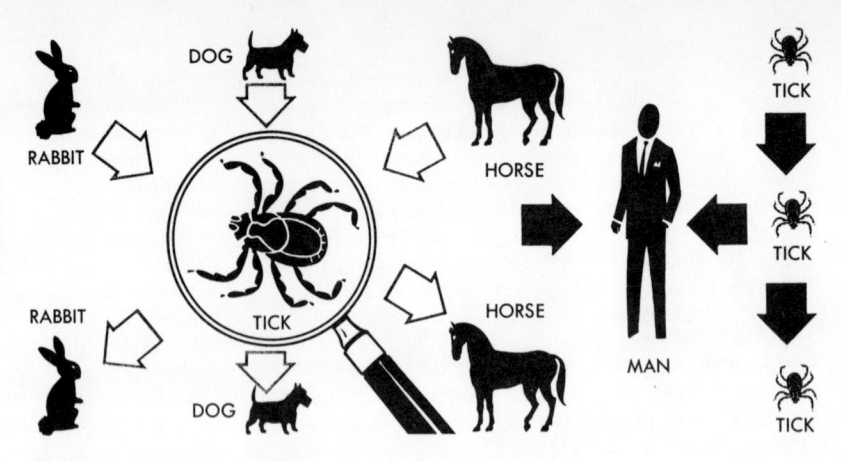

pod eggs without injuring them or affecting their development.

These organisms may transmit the rickettsia to men and other vertebrate animals, causing a number of similar diseases. These include typhus, scrub typhus, Rocky Mountain spotted fever, rickettsialpox, Q fever, and certain tick-borne diseases of Africa and the Mediterranean region. The rickettsial diseases are characterized by fever, rash (resulting from the tendency of these organisms to attack and weaken the walls of the blood vessels), and nervous and gastrointestinal symptoms. In some diseases (such as tsutsugamushi disease) sores develop at the site where the organisms have been introduced into the body.

Tetracycline antibiotics are used to treat these diseases. Preventive measures are directed against the ticks and body lice which transmit the infection. Some vaccines are also available. In addition to producing similar ailments, some rickettsias stimulate the body to produce defensive substances (antibodies) which cause certain bacteria of the genus *Proteus* to clump together, or agglutinate. This is called the Weil-Felix reaction and has been useful as a diagnostic test for the rickettsial diseases.

RIGOR MORTIS [rĭg′ər môr′tĭs], muscular rigidity which develops from four to ten hours after death and persists for from three to four days. Since certain conditions such as violent exercise or high fever occurring prior to death tend to hasten its onset, rigor mortis is not a reliable clue to the exact time of death.

RINGWORM, common, minor skin infection, caused by a variety of fungi. It is never caused by worms. Children are more susceptible than adults, and infections may clear spontaneously at puberty. The typical ringworm spot is red and itchy, with a slightly raised sharp border and paler center, simulating a ring. Although a minor infection, ringworm may be difficult to eradicate.

There are four common forms of ringworm. Best known is tineapedis, or athlete's foot. Tinea capitis is ringworm of the scalp. Tinea corporis is on the body, and Tinea cruris occurs in body creases, such as the groin. While each form is usually caused by a particular type of fungus, diagnosis must be confirmed and amplified by cultures taken from the ringworm lesion.

Treatment may be local, or medication may be given by mouth. Rarely, X-ray therapy is used. Ointments, creams, powders, and solutions are all useful. Medication by mouth is most often prescribed when the hair and nails are involved. It is important to realize that not all round, ringlike spots or rashes are fungus infections.

ROCKY MOUNTAIN SPOTTED FEVER, a severe disease caused by infection with a variety of rickettsias, microorganisms intermediate in size between viruses and bacteria. Originally reported in the Rocky Mountains in 1873, it has since been observed in all states except Maine and Vermont and in Canada, Mexico, and Central and South America. It occurs principally in the spring and summer when the ticks which transmit the infection (*Dermacentor variabilis* and *D. andersoni*) are most active.

After an incubation period of 3 to 12 days, the disease appears abruptly with headache, chills, fever, and muscle, bone, and joint pains. Mental confusion, tremors, deafness, muscle twitching, and coma may appear as the condition progresses. The spotted rash which gives the disease its name develops within a few days of the onset, appearing first on the ankles, wrists, palms, and soles and then extending to the rest of the body. In severe cases gangrene may develop in the skin and may possibly involve an entire limb. The fever lasts about two weeks. Prior to the availability of antibiotics, Rocky Mountain spotted fever was often fatal. Tetracyclines are effective in treatment. Prevention consists of tick control and vaccination.

Campers in tick-infested areas should inspect themselves and their clothing for ticks at least twice each day. The ticks should not be crushed but should be removed gently (to avoid leaving the mouth parts in the skin) using gloves or a piece of paper to cover the fingers. The wound should be cleansed with iodine or some other effective antiseptic.

See also RICKETTSIAS AND RICKETTSIAL DISEASES.

ROENTGEN [rĕnt′gən, rŭnt′gən] **or RÖNTGEN, WILHELM KONRAD** (1845–1923), German physicist whose discovery of X rays in 1895 inaugurated a new era in both physics and medicine.

Roentgen made his discovery by chance while he was studying the discharge of electricity through a high vacuum. To his surprise a fluorescent screen lying near the discharge tube, which was enclosed in black cardboard, glowed each time the tube was operated. The fluorescence still occurred, though weakened, when a solid body, such as a pack of cards, was placed between the tube and the screen. Roentgen concluded that the phenomenon was due to some unknown rays originating at the spot where the cathode rays struck the wall of the tube. He called them X rays. He was the first to obtain an X-ray photograph of the bones in a living hand.

ROSACEA [rō-zā'shə], skin disease in which the central portion of the face becomes red, scaly, and bumpy and is marked by pus pimples and swollen blood vessels. The patient may complain of itching or burning. It is seen principally in persons over 25. Glandular imbalance, improper diet (excessive amounts of caffeine and alcoholic beverages), and gastrointestinal disturbances are thought to be contributing factors. In some cases the nose may become enlarged and reddened (rhinophyma, or "potato nose"). Treatment consists of special diets (eliminating coffee, tea, chocolate, nuts, spices, and alcoholic beverages), vitamins, lotions, hormones, and ultraviolet and X-ray treatment.

ROSS, SIR RONALD (1857–1932), British physician who received the Nobel Prize in physiology and medicine in 1902 for his studies on malaria. Born in India, he studied medicine at St. Bartholomew's in London. He entered the Indian Medical Service in 1881, retiring in 1889 to live and work in England. He demonstrated the presence of the malaria plasmodium in the stomach wall of *Anopheles* mosquitoes that had bitten malarial patients. He thus proved the theory of Sir Patrick Manson, his friend and associate, that malaria is transmitted by mosquitoes.

S

SABIN, ALBERT BRUCE (1906–   ), U.S. medical researcher and doctor, noted for his development of a live-virus poliomyelitis vaccine. Born in Bialystok (then in Russia), he went to the United States in 1921, becoming a naturalized citizen in 1930. In 1939 he joined the faculty of the University of Cincinnati College of Medicine. His vaccine may be taken orally, provides immunity for a longer period of time than the killed-virus type, and protects against both infection and paralysis.

SACROILIAC [săk-rō-ĭl'e-ăk], the joint of the lower back between the sacrum, the fused lower portion of the spine, and the ilium, the large winged bone of the pelvis. Although the joint is bound by powerful ligaments, it is believed that sprains may occur and cause low back pain.

SAFETY. In its most general sense, safety is the condition of being free from harm. It may also be interpreted, however, as the active endeavor taken by the individual or group to promote precautionary measures against possible injury or accident. Accidents resulting in death tend to receive the most publicity, not only because of the seriousness and drama of such calamitous events, but because records for less severe cases are not as complete. Since death records are fairly comprehensive, the number of fatalities due to accidents is often used as an indication of the seriousness of the accident problem.

What Causes Accidents?

It was long thought that accidents were something that "just happened," and that while in some instances precautions might be taken there was no way to prevent them all. It is now recognized, however, that all accidents are caused by certain definable factors. And since they are caused, they can be prevented.

The cause of an accident cannot always be easily and quickly determined. Often many factors are involved. One of these is poor design. This includes such things as machinery with exposed gears, shafts, or drive belts, and narrow roads with sharp turns, blind corners, and narrow shoulders. These might be called engineering factors.

Another factor is the human element. Many authorities believe that carelessness or inattentiveness is a partial cause of nearly every accident. Lack of knowledge or lack of instruction in the proper handling of materials or operating equipment is included in this group.

It might be theoretically possible to eliminate nearly all accidents through better design, but unfortunately the completely foolproof machine has yet to be designed. In any case, engineering is only part of the solution of the accident problem. To be effective it must be combined with education and the establishment and enforcement of sensible rules of safety. These "three E's of safety"—engineering, education, and enforcement—have been combined to make vast reductions in accident rates.

Despite these reductions, accidents in the early 1960's took the lives of more than 90,000 persons annually in the United States. About 9,000,000 suffered disabling injuries each year. The annual cost to the national economy was about $15,000,000,000. This startling figure includes wage loss, medical expense, overhead cost of insurance, property damage, and lost production time. In Canada, in the early 1960's, motor vehicle traffic accidents alone totaled more than 250,000 each year, resulting in nearly 3,500 fatalities and nearly 100,000 persons injured.

Generally, accidents are broken down into four categories: home; motor vehicle; public places, excluding motor vehicle accidents; and work.

Home Safety

Home accidents claim more lives each year than any other category except that of motor vehicle. Falls are the most common type of home accident, followed by fires, suffocation, poisoning, firearms accidents, and the like.

SAFETY

Falls. Surprisingly enough, most falls occur while people are walking on a level surface. A partial list of the many conditions that can lead to falls includes clutter, such as toys strewn about the room or on stairways; broken, chipped, or badly worn floor coverings; water or grease spots; broken stairs and weak railings; slippery stairs and loose carpeting; insufficient lighting; poorly placed furniture; the practice of carrying too bulky or too large a load; and broken ladders or makeshift ladder substitutes. All these conditions can be remedied by more efficient housekeeping, careful maintenance of floors and equipment, having a proper place for everything and keeping things in their proper place, and getting help when it is needed.

Fires. Any building—no matter how "fireproof"—contains enough flammable material to become dangerous should a fire start.

Electrical wiring should be installed only by competent electricians. There should be voltage enough to carry the heavy loads imposed today by electric freezers, refrigerators, stoves, and automatic washers and dryers. Electrical cords should be checked frequently for dried, cracked, or frayed insulation and replaced as such faults are discovered.

Fire-retarding paint, available in all colors, should be used when redecorating. Curtains and drapes can be flameproofed by a commercial dry cleaner. Ash trays should be large and have grips for cigarette or cigar. Of course, one should never smoke while dozing or when in bed.

Flammable liquids such as kerosene should be stored in safety cans outside the house. Rubbish—old newspapers, oily rags, empty boxes and cartons, and the like—should not be permitted to accumulate.

Every member of the household should learn the proper escape routes from every room of the house in case of fire. If a fire starts, a door that feels hot should not be opened. If there is no other way out, a window may be used. Upper-floor bedrooms especially should be provided with some kind of fire escape device. Fire extinguishers strategically located throughout the house are excellent fire prevention measures.

Suffocation. Suffocation can result from the accidental inhaling of food particles or foreign objects or from smothering by bed clothes, thin plastic materials, cave-ins, and confinement in closed spaces such as old iceboxes. Thin plastic should never be used as covers for crib mattresses and should be kept away from small children. Plastic film used as wrapping by many laundries and dry cleaners should be destroyed as soon as the clothing is unpacked. Doors should be removed from unused refrigerators and iceboxes so that small children cannot be trapped inside.

Poisoning. Medicines and poisons such as those found in household cleansers and bug sprays should never be stored in places accessible to small children. Poisons and medicines should be clearly marked and stored separately in locked cabinets. Medicine prescribed for a given illness should be discarded, not saved for some possible future use.

Firearms. Many homes contain at least one gun, such as a shotgun used for hunting, or a war souvenir. More than half of all firearms accidents occur on home premises, many while cleaning or playing with guns. Guns should never be used by children as toys. They should be kept locked up, with ammunition stored in a locked cabinet separate from the gun rack. Gun safety rules should be learned and strictly adhered to.

Gas Poisoning. Most home accidents involving poison gases are caused by the inhalation of carbon monoxide, resulting from incomplete combustion of carbon in stoves, heating equipment, and motor vehicles. Heating and cooking equipment should be carefully maintained to assure proper combustion, and automobile engines should not be run in an enclosed area. Immediate and thorough ventilation is prescribed in the case of gas seepage.

Motor Vehicle Safety

Motor vehicle accidents form the largest of the four accident categories. Each year there is a larger number of vehicles on the road, with people driving greater distances than ever before. Safe driving requires that a driver respond quickly to changing road conditions. The techniques used for night driving differ from those used for driving in daylight.

A motorist cannot drive in the country in the same manner as he would in a city or town. And driving on a superhighway demands still another set of skills.

The safe driver must know how to handle his automobile under all the many conditions which exist. He must know his own limitations and avoid those conditions which he is not competent to meet. The safest and most efficient way for the novice to become a skilled driver is to enroll in a driver education course. Many secondary schools which offer such courses to their students also make them available to those beyond high school age.

Speeding, failing to yield the right of way, and driving left of center are factors in more than half of all motor vehicle fatalities. These three driver errors, combined with drunken driving, are involved in three-fourths of all fatal accidents and about half of all accident injuries.

Seat belts not only have saved many lives but have also reduced the seriousness and extent of injuries incurred in many motor vehicle accidents. The National Safety Council estimates that if every motorist used seat belts on every car trip, 5,000 lives could be saved each year and serious injuries reduced by one-third.

Public Safety

Public accidents include those occurring in public places, excluding private motor vehicles. Drownings not involving boats form the largest group of fatalities within this category, followed by falls and transportation accidents involving boats, aircraft, railroads, streetcars, bicycles, and animal-drawn vehicles.

Most drownings are the result of accidental submersion—falls from docks, bridges, shore installations, boats, and the like. Many of these fatalities could be avoided if the victims knew the basic rules of water safety, such as how to stay afloat when heavily clothed. Skill in swimming, with training in emergency water measures, could save many lives each year.

Three-fourths of the drownings associated with water transportation involve boats having a capacity of fewer than 10 persons. A boat owner should know his craft's capacity and the extent of his own abilities. He should never overload his boat, and he should not take on passengers until he has developed the skills necessary to be a safe operator.

Work Safety

Today, people are generally safer at work than anywhere else. Industry early took the lead in instituting practical safety measures and safety education programs. As new machinery was developed, hazards peculiar to it were determined and safeguards devised. The establishment and enforcing of work safety rules have also played an important part in the industrial work program.

The increasing use of safe work practices and the constant research in and development of safety equipment, clothing, and safeguarding devices for machinery have resulted in a reduction of on-the-job death rates by nearly 40% since 1933. For instance, of the 13,500 industrial fatalities in the United States in one year, approximately 3,300 occurred in farm work. This figure represents the highest group of fatalities among the U.S. labor force. However, the death rate per 100,000 workers was not as high as in the construction and extractive (mining, quarrying, and oil and gas drilling) industries.

National Safety Council members reported in a recent special survey that the average on-job disabling injury rate among member firms was 90% lower than the national rate, while off-job accidents ran some 25% below the national figure.

See also ARTIFICIAL RESPIRATION; FIRST AID.

SALIVARY [săl′ə-vĕr-ē] **GLANDS,** three pairs of glands situated below and in front of the ear (parotid glands), on the inside of the jaw (submaxillary glands), and under the floor of the mouth (sublingual glands). Mechanical reflex stimulation of the glands, caused by the presence of food in the mouth, stimulates the secretion of saliva. Secretion may also be stimulated by the sight or smell of foods which have come to be associated with the flow of saliva. This is the well-known conditioned reflex, first discovered by the Russian physiologist Pavlov, who found that after ringing a bell and presenting food to a dog a number of times, eventually the sound of the bell was sufficient to stimulate salivation.

Saliva is about 99.5% water mixed with organic substances. Particularly important among the latter are mucus and the enzymes salivary amylase and lysozyme. Salivary amylase helps digest starchy foods; lysozyme destroys a number of potentially dangerous bacteria. The composition of the saliva tends to vary with the factors stimulating its secretion. Foods tend to evoke secretion of a saliva rich in organic materials. Dried or powdered substances draw forth a watery saliva which efficiently cleanses the mouth. Saliva serves to moisten the food mass and thus is an aid in swallowing. It also keeps the soft parts of the mouth moist, clean, and lubricated.

The salivary glands serve as a channel of excretion for certain substances. Calcium salts excreted in the saliva may, in combination with organic materials, collect as tartar on the teeth. Certain viruses may be excreted in the saliva, for example, those of rabies and polio. The salivary glands also play a role in the regulation of the water balance of the body. A decrease in the fluid content of the body causes a decline in salivation, resulting in drying of the membranes of the mouth, which is experienced as a feeling of thirst.

SALK [sôk], **JONAS EDWARD** (1914–), American physician who developed the first successful antipoliomyelitis vaccine. Salk studied at the City College of New York and at the New York University College of Medicine. In 1953 he reported results of a preliminary investigation which suggested that a triple vaccine made from three types of polio virus inactivated with formaldehyde might effectively prevent the disease. The following year the vaccine was tested on several hundred thousand children, and in 1955 it was declared effective. Immediate widespread use of the vaccine drastically diminished the incidence of this crippling disease.
See also POLIOMYELITIS; VACCINES.

SALK VACCINE. *See* POLIOMYELITIS; VACCINES.

SALMONELLA [săl mŏ-něl′ə], genus of intestinal bacteria discovered by Daniel E. Salmon in 1885, which included the typhoid bacillus. The *Salmonella* were later separated into different bacteria on the basis of the antibody reactions they produced. More than 1,200 types are identified.

Most cases of salmonellosis in humans are caused by infected food. Although gastroenteritis is the most common manifestation of illness, Salmonella fever and bloodstream infections also occur. When *Salmonella* invades the bloodstream, it may produce osteomyelitis, inflammation of the lining of the heart, meningitis, and abscesses. Salmonella gastroenteritis has an incubation period of about eight hours. Upset stomach is followed by diarrhea and fever. It may last from three to seven days.

Identification of *Salmonella* still requires from six to ten days. These bacteria can infect any type of animal and may survive for months on fruits and vegetables in a refrigerator. Fowl are the most common carriers. Eggs and eggshells are a potent source of infection. Packaged foods, including dried milk and candies, have caused significant epidemics. The more serious Salmonella infections are treated with antibiotics, a treatment unnecessary for Salmonella gastroenteritis.

SANGER [săng′ər], **FREDERICK** (1918–), British biochemist who received the Nobel Prize in 1958 for his investigation of the structure of the insulin molecule. Educated at Cambridge, Sanger worked there on a Beit Memorial Fellowship (1944–51), and thereafter was associated with the medical research council. He was awarded the Corday-Morgan Medal of the Chemical Society in 1951. Sanger's research contributed much to the understanding of proteins, the most complex substances found in nature.

SANGER, MARGARET (1883–1966), American leader in the birth control movement and founder of the American Birth Control League. In 1915 Mrs. Sanger, a trained public health nurse, was indicted for sending birth control literature through the mails and in 1916 she was ar-

SARCOIDOSIS

rested for establishing a birth control clinic. Working alone at first, she gradually won a measure of public and legal support for her campaign. She organized the first American Birth Control Conference in 1921 and in 1922 traveled in Europe and Asia, lecturing and establishing clinics. She wrote many books and pamphlets on maternal welfare and birth control.

SARCOIDOSIS [sär-koi-dō′sĭs], disease characterized by the formation of nodules and scar tissue in the lungs lymph glands, skin, bones, eyes, and many other parts of the body. Although the cause is unknown, sarcoidosis has been at various times described as an unusual form of tuberculosis or as resulting from the body's reaction to beryllium or to pine pollen. It is most common between the ages of 20 and 40. American Negroes are especially susceptible.

The disease develops gradually, and the tissues may be extensively involved before any symptoms appear. Loss of weight, lack of energy, and mild fever may be seen in the early stages. Other symptoms are related to the specific organs attacked and include cough, shortness of breath, chest pain, disturbances in vision, nodules in the skin, and enlargement of the salivary and lymph glands, liver, and spleen. Heart failure may occur. Most cases recover after a period of some years. The lesions disappear completely or are replaced by scar tissue. No specific therapy is available, but cortisone and related drugs are often helpful in the early active reversible stages of the disease.

SCABIES [skā′bēz], infestation with the mite *Sarcoptes scabiei*. The mites, which are transmitted in soiled bed linen and infected towels or through personal contact, burrow under the skin, depositing eggs and an irritating excretum. The lesions consist of elevated red tracts of skin dotted with fluid swellings. The most common sites are the hands and wrists. About a month after infestation, the lesions itch intensely (particularly at night) as the patient develops a sensitivity to the mites and their excreta. Scratching may cause bacterial infection. Medications containing benzene hexachloride or benzyl benzoate effectively treat the condition.

SCAR, also called cicatrix, tough, inelastic tissue which replaces destroyed skin tissue. As scars develop, they may contract and cause deformity and loss of normal motion, particularly scarring following extensive burns. There are three main varieties of scars: atrophic, hypertrophic, and keloid.

The *atrophic scar* is flat, thin, and usually lacks pigmentation. It occurs commonly after inflammatory diseases, such as lichen planus, lupus erythematosus, syphilis, and scleroderma. The *hypertrophic scar* is a red, raised, firm growth with a fairly smooth border. It may follow injury or diseases such as shingles, syphilis, smallpox, and acne. The *keloid scar* is a reddish, raised, firm growth with a smooth, shiny surface and clawlike projections from the edge. More common in Negroes than whites, keloids may follow surgery, chemical or thermal burns, infections, or ulcerations. At first rubbery in consistency, they later become hard and brownish. Unsightly and deforming scars may at times be treated by surgery or dermal abrasion, a method which utilizes a stiff wire brush to remove the upper layers of the scar. Radiation and dry ice are sometimes used to treat keloids.

SCARLET FEVER, also called scarlatina, an infectious disease which occurs principally in children. Belonging to a group of bacteria (group A hemolytic streptococci) which commonly attack the upper breathing passages, the scarlet fever organisms produce a group of potent poisons (toxins) which cause the stippled red rash characteristic of the disease and possibly heart damage and other manifestations.

About two to five days after exposure the patient is suddenly prostrated with high fever, headache, vomiting, and sore throat. The lymph glands of the neck enlarge and the tongue assumes a strawberrylike appearance owing to enlargement of the projections (papillae) on its surface. The rash usually appears around the second or third day and varies greatly in intensity and extent. The groin and underarm area are frequently affected. The face is usually spared but becomes flushed except for the area around the mouth which remains pale. This is the characteristic "circumoral" pallor (literally, pallor "around the mouth"). The rash begins to fade in about two days, and eventually large areas of the skin peel, particularly on the hands and feet, where actual casts of fingers or of the sole may come off. After recovery the patient is usually immune to a second attack.

Scarlet fever is treated with penicillin. Prior to the availability of antibiotics, scarlet fever antitoxin was the only treatment, but this is rarely used today.

Formerly a major cause of death in children, scarlet fever is now a relatively mild disease. Antibiotics have virtually eliminated the once-common complication of extension of the infection to the inner ear. Rheumatic fever and kidney inflammation (glomerulonephritis) may still occur from two to three weeks after the acute phase of scarlet fever.

See also GLOMERULONEPHRITIS; HEMOLYTIC STREPTOCOCCI; RHEUMATIC FEVER.

SCHICK [shĭk], **BELA** (1877–1967), pediatrician, noted for the Schick test, which determines susceptibility to diphtheria. Born in Boglar, Hungary, he received his M.D. degree from Karl Franz University, Austria, in 1900. He taught pediatrics at the University of Vienna until 1923, then went to the United States, becoming a citizen in 1929. In succeeding years he became an outstanding consultant and teacher in many hospitals and universities of eastern United States. He helped found the American Academy of Pediatrics and wrote several works on child care, allergy, and children's diseases.

SCHICK TEST, test for susceptibility to diphtheria devised by the Hungarian physician Béla Schick. A small amount of diluted diphtheria toxin is injected into the skin. Several days later the area is observed for a reaction. If the injected skin becomes red and swollen, the individual is susceptible to diphtheria. If no reaction occurs, he is immune.

SCHISTOSOMIASIS [shĭs-tō-sō-mī′ə-sĭs], also known as

snail fever, or bilharziasis, disease caused by infestation with certain flatworms of the genus *Schistosoma*. Approximately 114,000,000 persons around the globe are estimated to have schistosomiasis which, next to malaria, is the most serious parasitic infestation of man.

The worm larvae infest snails, liberating immature forms, called cercariae, into fresh-water streams and rivers. These penetrate the skin of humans who come into contact with the water, or they enter the membranes of the mouth and throat if the water is consumed. The cercariae are carried through the heart and lungs via the blood stream, eventually settling in the liver. A few weeks later the adolescent worms migrate against the blood flow to take up permanent residence in veins in the intestines or pelvis. The adult worms may survive in the body for up to 25 years, each day liberating hundreds to thousands of eggs, some of which pass through the tissues to be excreted into the urine or feces. The disease exists in two major forms: intestinal and vesical schistosomiasis.

Intestinal schistosomiasis is caused by *S. mansoni* found in Egypt, Madagascar, Yemen, parts of South America, and the West Indies, and *S. japonicum* found in the Far East. In mild infections symptoms may not appear.

In other cases disturbances may arise in the three stages of the infection. (1) During the *incubation period* the patient may experience itching, skin rash, fever, hives, and asthmatic attacks as the organisms penetrate the skin and migrate through the tissues. (2) In the *acute phase* fever, weight loss, abdominal pains, and dysentery may result from the deposition of eggs in the tissues and their escape into the intestine and bladder. (3) A *chronic stage* may occur some one to five years after the initial infection, when inflammatory reactions caused by eggs lodged in the tissues produce cirrhosis of the liver, anemia, difficulty in breathing, headache, and irregular fever.

Vesical schistosomiasis is caused by *S. haematobium*, seen in Africa and the Middle East. The worms settle in the pelvic veins and most of the eggs are deposited in the bladder and urinary tract. Urination is painful and bloody urine is often seen, along with fever, weakness, dull pain in the pelvis, and anemia. Eggs are found in the urine. Ulcers of the urinary tract are common. Cancers of the bladder appear frequently in these patients.

Antimony compounds (tartar emetic, Fuadin) are available to destroy the adult worms, but they are highly toxic. Prevention of schistosomiasis requires sanitary disposal of human feces and urine and destruction of the snails which harbor the organism.

SCHIZOPHRENIA [skĭz-ō-frē′nē-ə], a major mental disease marked by a disorganization of the personality with bizarre behavior, hallucinations, incoherent speech, and detachment from the real world. It is the most common form of psychosis, accounting for approximately half of the chronic patients in state mental hospitals. The concept of schizophrenia as a single disease is questioned by some psychiatrists, and no single definition is acceptable.

Causes. Theories concerning the cause of schizophrenia are highly controversial. One group of theorists stresses the importance of psychological factors. The other searches for a physiological or biochemical cause. The first group traces the origins of the disease to an anxiety-laden early family life, beset with tension between the parents. Some even describe a "schizophrenogenic mother," an overprotective, cold, or distant person who produces the schizophrenic pattern by her inability to give herself to the child. The second group seeks an underlying organic disturbance. Several studies have attempted to demonstrate the influence of inheritance on schizophrenia. One such investigation found the greatest incidence of schizophrenia among children of schizophrenic parents.

Other investigators have examined the biochemistry of the schizophrenic in comparison with the normal and, in the words of one critic, such investigators have found the schizophrenic to be "a sorry physical specimen indeed: his liver, brain, kidney, and circulatory functions are impaired; he is deficient in practically every vitamin; his hormones are out of balance, and his enzymes are askew." This writer points out the great difficulty in determining whether such biochemical changes are the *cause* of the disease or the *result* of it. The biological school received encouragement from the fact that tranquilizing drugs were effective in calming agitated patients. It is felt that the action of these drugs may be related to the concentration of certain substances in the brain (serotonin or noradrenalin). Some investigators feel that imbalances of these substances may play a role in the disease.

Treatment. Treatment of schizophrenia falls into the same two groups as speculations concerning its cause: psychotherapy and physical or biological therapies. Psychotherapy is often used in conjunction with tranquilizing drugs which quiet the patient and make therapy possible. Other forms of treatment are insulin coma therapy, electroconvulsive therapy, and lobotomy. The tranquilizing drugs have been of great help with disturbed and agitated patients and have permitted the discharge of many who would otherwise be chronic hospital patients.

See also LOBOTOMY; MENTAL ILLNESS; PSYCHIATRY; SHOCK THERAPY.

SCIATICA [sī-ăt′ĭ-kə], a term describing pain radiating along the sciatic nerve, which runs from a point high in the buttock along the back of the thigh and then divides behind the knee into two branches which enter the leg and foot. The pain results from irritation which may be caused by spinal defects, inflammations, tumors, or injuries. Probably the commonest cause of sciatica is pressure exerted on the nerve by one of the cartilaginous discs of the spine which has slipped out of position. Treatment of sciatica is based upon the underlying cause. Cases of slipped discs may be treated by sedation, bed rest, braces, exercises, or, in difficult cases, by surgery to stiffen and strengthen the spine.

SCLERODERMA [sklĭr-ō-dûr′mə], a disease of the connective, or supporting, tissues of the body which may affect the skin, muscles, blood vessels, kidneys, heart, lungs, intestines, and other internal organs. Of unknown cause, scleroderma is most common in adult women. A mild form of scleroderma, called morphea, causes limited skin lesions anywhere on the body. Usually this does not involve internal changes. In the more severe chronic generalized form, the skin undergoes characteristic changes.

SCLEROSIS

The skin first becomes puffy, progresses to a waxy, leathery consistency, and ultimately becomes thin and tight, lending an expressionless, masklike appearance to the face. Internal changes may cause difficulty in breathing, talking, and swallowing, and also nausea, diarrhea, or constipation. Heart or kidney failure may occur. Muscle contractures are prominent and movement becomes extremely difficult. Although there is no specific treatment, a wide variety of drugs has been used. Cortisone-type medications have helped in some cases.
See also COLLAGEN DISEASES.

SCLEROSIS, MULTIPLE. *See* MULTIPLE SCLEROSIS.

SCOLIOSIS [skō-lē-ō'sĭs], lateral curvature of the spine, usually associated with other spinal deformities, such as round back. Scoliosis may be caused by paralysis, injury, tumors, or a shortened leg or may appear from unknown cause. The latter type is painless and is most common in females. Curvatures caused by injury or disease are usually painful. If the condition becomes progressively worse, surgery to fuse, or stiffen, the spine may be necessary. In other cases muscle-building exercises are prescribed. A shoe lift may correct scoliosis caused by a short leg.

SCOPOLAMINE [skə-pŏl'ə-mēn], drug obtained chiefly from the plants *Hyoscyamus niger* (henbane) and *Scopolia carniolica*, of the nightshade family, *Solanaceae*. Similar in many of its actions to atropine, scopolamine acts upon the central nervous system causing drowsiness, amnesia, fatigue, and sleep and stimulates breathing. It also interferes with the action of certain nerve fibers lying outside the spinal cord, thus inhibiting secretions of the salivary and sweat glands, dilating the pupils, and relaxing the smooth muscles of the stomach and intestines. It is used principally as a preanesthetic medication to produce sedation, maintain breathing, and dry the breathing passages. The trancelike state induced by scopolamine has been used to extract confessions from criminals.
See also ATROPINE.

SCROFULA [skrŏf'yə-lə], tuberculosis of the lymph glands of the neck, characterized by swelling of the neck and, in some cases, by open wounds which drain a thick greenish-yellow pus. Caused chiefly by the contaminated milk of tubercular cows, scrofula is much less common today than formerly, owing to the elimination of tuberculosis in cattle and the pasteurization of milk. Also called "king's evil," scrofula was once treated by the touch of kings. Modern therapy consists of rest, good diet, and antitubercular drugs.

SCRUB TYPHUS, an infectious disease caused by *Rickettsia tsutsugamushi*, widespread in Japan, India, Australia, and Southeast Asia. First described more than 100 years ago in Japan, it was of major military importance in World War II and remains a public health problem. Rickettsia are microorganisms which can grow only within living cells. Many animals from mites to rodents to man serve as host to the organisms. Scrub typhus is transmitted to man by mites. The organisms multiply at the site of a bite, then spread through the body. About 10 days later illness begins with high fever, chilliness, severe headache, and enlarged lymph nodes. The site of the original mite bite usually turns black and hard, and the individual develops a red rash over most of his body. Control is achieved by the antibiotics chloramphenicol or tetracycline. Insecticides to control the mites are the best means of avoiding the illness.
See also RICKETTSIAS AND RICKETTSIAL DISEASES.

SCURVY [skûr'vē], a nutritional disease caused by deficiency of vitamin C (ascorbic acid) in the diet. Called the "calamity of sailors" disease, scurvy was for centuries rampant among ships' crews during long voyages. In 1593 Sir Richard Hawkins, the English Admiral, wrote that within his own experience 10,000 sailors had died from the disease. The introduction of limes, oranges, and other ascorbic-acid-rich foods in sailors' diets is generally attributed to Capt. James Lind of the British navy (following his "Treatise on Scurvy" in 1753). As early as 1601, however, the ships of the East India Company carried such foods on the advice of an English privateer. The antiscurvy factor contained in these foods was independently identified in 1928 by Szent-Györgyi of Hungary, and King and Waugh of the United States.

Today most cases of scurvy are seen in recluses or food faddists who consume little fresh fruits or vegetables, the principal sources of vitamin C. Scurvy in infants (Barlow's disease) may occur when the child is placed on an inadequate artificial diet.

Vitamin C is essential for the proper formation of the cement substances found between the cells of bone and in connective tissue. It may also play a role in the manufacture of blood cells and possibly in the body's defense mechanisms against infection. In adults the early signs of deficiency are apathy, weakness, loss of appetite, mental depression, and pains in the extremities. Swellings caused by hemorrhages appear in the muscles and connective tissues of the legs. The most prominent advanced symptom is bleeding. The patient may hemorrhage into the skin, nose, viscera, or into almost any part of the body. The gums become spongy, swollen, and bloody, and the teeth may loosen and fall out.

Infants with scurvy suffer from irritability, lack of appetite, and in contrast to the adults, fever. The infant assumes a characteristic froglike position with the legs drawn up and the knees bent. The extremities are extremely tender, and large hemorrhages in the bone (between the bone and its covering membrane) may produce noticeable changes in the contours of the limbs. Anemia is almost always present. Scurvy is readily treated by the administration of vitamin C. The disease can be prevented by including citrus fruits, green vegetables, tomato juice, and other sources of the vitamin in the diet.
See also VITAMINS.

SEASICKNESS. *See* MOTION SICKNESS.

SEBACEOUS CYST. *See* CYST, SEBACEOUS.

SEBACEOUS GLAND. *See* SKIN.

SELYE [sĕl'yā], **HANS** (1907–), Canadian biochemist and histopathologist.

Selye performed the first experiment, clearly establishing the link between disease and the adrenal cortex. He had anticipated finding specific pathological changes in rats given a variety of drugs, poisons, and gland extracts. Instead, he noted similar responses to each substance. This led him to theorize that any life-threatening stress would elicit similar pathological findings, particularly in the adrenals. Selye named this common response the "alarm reaction." In the alarm reaction, he described a shock and countershock phase. In the latter phase, he found great enlargement and increased activity of the adrenal cortex. Lacking adrenals, the animals succumbed to shock.

Selye next studied the effects of milder but more prolonged stress, and suggested that diseases of adaptation resulted from prolonged stress. His theory gives credence to the concept that prolonged physical and emotional stress can cause specific illnesses. In man, such stress ills include arteriosclerosis, peptic ulcer, and rheumatoid arthritis. Although the relationship between stress and disease is accepted, the specific cause and effect remain imprecise.

SEMMELWEIS [zĕm'əl-vīs], **IGNAZ PHILIPP** (1818–65), Hungarian physician remembered for his discovery of the contagious nature of childbirth (puerperal) fever. While at the Vienna Krankenhaus, Semmelweis observed that the death rates from childbirth fever were highest among those women attended by students who had freshly come from autopsy rooms and pathology lectures. He then insisted that the students on his wards wash their hands carefully before delivering children. Although this resulted in an immediate decline in the death rate, his views were heatedly attacked by the great obstetricians of Vienna. Semmelweis was eventually forced to resign. He died in a mental hospital. Some years later his doctrine became generally accepted. A monument to his memory was erected in Budapest in 1894.

SENILITY [sĭ-nĭl'ə-tē], physical and mental state of old age characterized by personality changes resulting in part from the altered psychological and social situation of the elderly person and in part from actual damage to brain tissue. As his faculties begin to fail and as he finds himself increasingly alone, the aged individual may begin to feel that life has passed him by. He may become resentful of his declining influence on those around him and may feel that his experience qualifies him for a position of respect and importance in the family or even in public life. He is frequently dogmatic, inflexible, and conservative, and unable to accept or tolerate changes. Increased leisure may lead to introspection, and in reviewing his life the older person may be overcome by feelings of guilt or failure. This may culminate in a severe and sometimes pathological depression.

Whether or not such traits appear depends on the individual's earlier personality. The adverse character changes are often merely accentuations of features which were always present. For this reason it has been said that senility is a caricature of the previous personality. The social changes are less marked in smaller communities, where the aged person often retains responsibility as a respected elder, than in populous cities where the older individual becomes a neglected and anonymous citizen.

Although the exact nature of the brain changes in senility is not yet clear, they apparently involve a decrease in the blood supply to the brain and a lowered activity of brain tissue. Decline in brain function may result in memory impairment. At first the memory of recent events is vague and, later, events in the distant past are forgotten. The patient may attempt to compensate for his memory loss by fabrications. He may eventually become suspicious and feel that he is being persecuted because of the confusion resulting from his inability to recall where he has left his belongings or what he has been told. These changes may finally culminate in a psychosis (senile psychosis) characterized by confusion, agitation, depression, or exaggerated ideas of being persecuted. Hospitalization may be necessary.

One approach to the problems of senility is to keep the elderly person active and involved with people. He should be made to feel useful in a manner consistent with his physical and intellectual capacities. In cases of senile psychosis, medication and electroshock treatment for depression may be helpful.
See also OLD AGE.

SENSATION [sĕn-sā'shən]. All that we know of the world around us and about our own body comes from the messages started at sense receptors and carried by nerve fibers to the brain, where they are decoded and interpreted. Through this process we become aware of our environments, both external and internal. The messages are initiated by an appropriate sensory stimulus, which, by definition, is any change in energy that activates a sense organ.

SENSORY DEPRIVATION, also called perceptual isolation, experienced by people subjected to various kinds of isolation for extended periods of time. Different methods are used to reduce the amount and variation of sensory input. Subjects may be masked and immersed in water to exclude light, sound, and tactile impulses. Specially constructed environments are designed to control quantity and variability of sensory stimulation. In these experiments, scientists learn how much stimulation is needed for perception. They also learn how sensory experience may vary over time and observe unusual occurrences, such as hallucinations, thought disorders, disorientation in time and space, and increased irritability. These experiences resemble symptoms of mental illness, and are therefore called "artificial psychoses." Such studies are particularly important for future outer space exploration.

Physiological measurements indicate that there are also changes in the body which may underlie these changes in mental state. The connection between them is not clear, however. Studies of this type with mental patients have shown that schizophrenics are generally much less affected than normal people by sensory deprivation. This has caused some interest in the therapeutic use of decreased stimulation.

Future research with sensory deprivation will include the study of behavior under prolonged, that is, month-long, isolation of man in darkened rooms or in caves. Also, studies of isolation in groups of men are being conducted to determine the influence of diminished variability in sensory input on interactional behavior. It is clear that many social disruptions can be brought about by group isolation.

SEROTONIN [sĕr-ə-tō′nĭn], also called 5-hydroxytryptamine, a compound found in many venoms (such as wasp and toad venom) and in many tissues of the human body, particularly the brain, intestine, and blood platelets. Although the exact functions of serotonin are unknown, it apparently regulates nervous function, constricts blood vessels, stimulates the muscles of the intestinal wall, and inhibits the secretion of gastric juice. Evidence suggests that certain tranquilizing drugs, such as reserpine, act by liberating serotonin from a bound and inactive form. It has also been speculated that extreme variations in the serotonin concentrations of the tissues may play a role in mental illness.

See also CARCINOID SYNDROME; PSYCHOPHARMACOLOGY.

SERUM [sĭr′əm] **SICKNESS,** an allergic reaction to injected animal serums used to treat or to immunize against certain diseases. This may occur when the body manufactures substances (antibodies) which can react with the proteins of the serum. It usually develops from 6 to 12 days after the injection but may appear sooner in persons who have had previous injections. The most prominent symptoms are a red, itchy skin eruption; swollen lymph glands; and swellings of the face, hands, or feet. Fever and arthritis may also appear. Highly sensitized persons may experience a *serum accident* (anaphylactic shock), in which massive swellings on the body, lowered blood pressure, loss of consciousness, and convulsions develop shortly after the injection, possibly resulting in death within a few minutes.

Most cases of serum sickness are mild and clear spontaneously, but may require treatment with antihistamines and steroid drugs. Serum accidents must be quickly treated by an injection of epinephrine (adrenalin), plus administration of oxygen and steroids. To prevent reactions, persons who have previously received serum or who have a record of asthma, hay fever, or other allergic reactions should notify the physician of the fact before receiving a serum injection.

See also ALLERGY; ANTIBODIES AND ANTIGENS.

SEX DETERMINATION. See GENETICS; SEX.

SHIGA [shē-gä], **KIYOSHI** (1870–1957), Japanese bacteriologist known for his work on bacillary dysentery, an infectious intestinal disorder frequently seen in the tropics. The genus of dysentery bacilli is named *Shigella* in his honor. He also did important studies of leprosy, tuberculosis, and beriberi (a nutritional disease).

SHOCK, collapse of the circulatory system. Circulatory shock should be distinguished from insulin shock (caused by a drastic lowering of the sugar content of the blood), shell shock (an obsolete term for a condition better described as "combat fatigue"), electric shock, and various other usages of the term.

Causes. Shock occurs when the amount of blood in the body is insufficient to fill the space available in the arteries and veins or when blood cannot be moved properly through the vessels. This may be caused by (1) loss of blood or fluid from the circulatory system; (2) dilation, or expansion, of the blood vessels, causing blood to collect in various parts of the body; or (3) damage to the heart which interferes with its ability to pump blood through the circulatory system.

Loss of Blood or Fluid from the Circulatory System. A common cause of shock of this type is bleeding, or hemorrhage. The bleeding may occur within or outside the body. In both cases fluid is lost from the circulatory system, and shock results. A less obvious type of shock develops when the minute blood vessels in the tissues (the capillaries) are so altered that large amounts of blood fluid (plasma) leak out. This is often seen in cases of extensive burns. The blood, now depleted of much fluid, becomes thick and viscous, and shock ensues. Dehydration, fluid loss from excess vomiting and diarrhea, may also cause shock of this type.

Expansion of the Blood Vessels. Sudden, violent injury may generate a flood of nervous impulses, culminating in the sudden expansion of blood vessels in various parts of the body. The normal quantity of circulating blood is inadequate to fill this enlarged circulatory system, and shock results. This "neurogenic," or "primary," shock is the same mechanism which underlies fainting. Certain types of bacterial infection may also cause shock through expansion of the blood vessels.

In most cases of shock more than one factor may be operative. The adverse effect of infection is frequently added to the shock of hemorrhage in injured military personnel. Reflex dilation of blood vessels from pain often accompanies the shock from an acute heart attack.

Physiological Changes and Symptoms. In shock the pressure in the great veins which lead to the heart is lowered. As a consequence, the heart does not fill properly with blood and as a reflex reaction increases its rate of beating. The blood pressure falls, and the tissues of the body now fail to receive adequate amounts of blood—an effect which is particularly damaging to the extremely oxygen-sensitive tissues of the brain. A principal effect of shock is reduction in urine output, caused by diminished blood flow to the kidneys.

The patient in shock appears critically ill and may be confused. His vision may be clouded, and if in pain, he may be agitated and restless. The wrist pulse is rapid but feeble, and the skin is pale, cold, and clammy.

Treatment. General measures include lowering the head and elevating the legs to allow blood to flow to the brain where it is most needed. Oxygen may be given, and also medication to control pain. Fluid or whole blood as indicated is introduced into the veins to increase the blood volume. In cases of neurogenic shock, "pressor" medications may be given to contract the small blood vessels. Bacterially induced shock must be treated vigorously with antibiotics as well.

Prolonged or repeated shock may result in a condition of "irreversible" shock, involving the death of cells throughout the body. This type of shock resists measures which would normally be adequate. Although the blood volume may be restored, the contractibility of the vessels is lost and does not respond to pressor medications. Pa-

SHOCK

Shock is a circulatory disorder in which the normal flow of blood through the arteries and veins is disrupted. Potential causes include hemorrhage, nervous fright, burns, infection, and heart damage. These factors produce shock through combinations of several distinct basic mechanisms. Shock seldom results from a single cause.

MECHANISMS OF SHOCK

LOSS OF BLOOD VOLUME

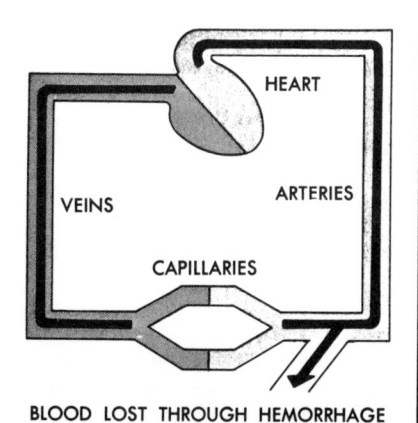

BLOOD LOST THROUGH HEMORRHAGE

In hemorrhage whole blood is lost. In burns, plasma escapes from the blood stream into the tissues. Shock develops when the diminished blood volume is insufficient to fill the available circulatory space.

SUDDEN EXPANSION OF BLOOD VESSELS

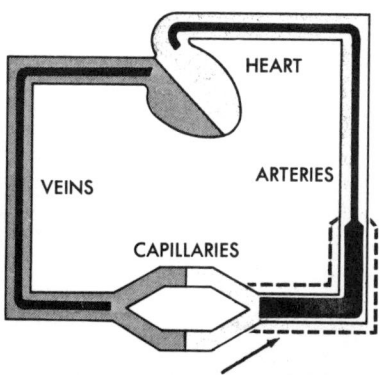

ARTERIAL CAPACITY INCREASES AS SMALL ARTERIES EXPAND

Severe injury, strong emotional reactions, and other stimuli which act strongly on the nervous system may contribute to shock by generating nerve impulses that result in the expansion of small arteries (arterioles). The normal blood volume is then unable to fill the suddenly increased circulatory space.

INTERFERENCE WITH THE MOVEMENT OF BLOOD

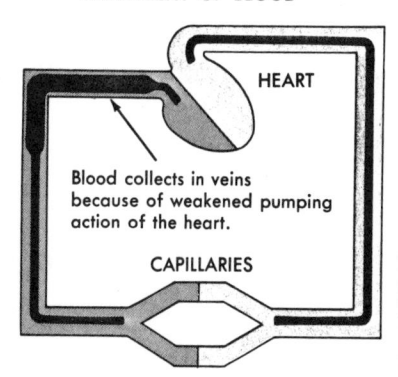

Blood collects in veins because of weakened pumping action of the heart.

In certain cases of heart disease the weakened heart may be unable to drive blood through the circulatory system with sufficient vigor to supply the tissues.

THE EFFECTS OF CIRCULATORY COLLAPSE

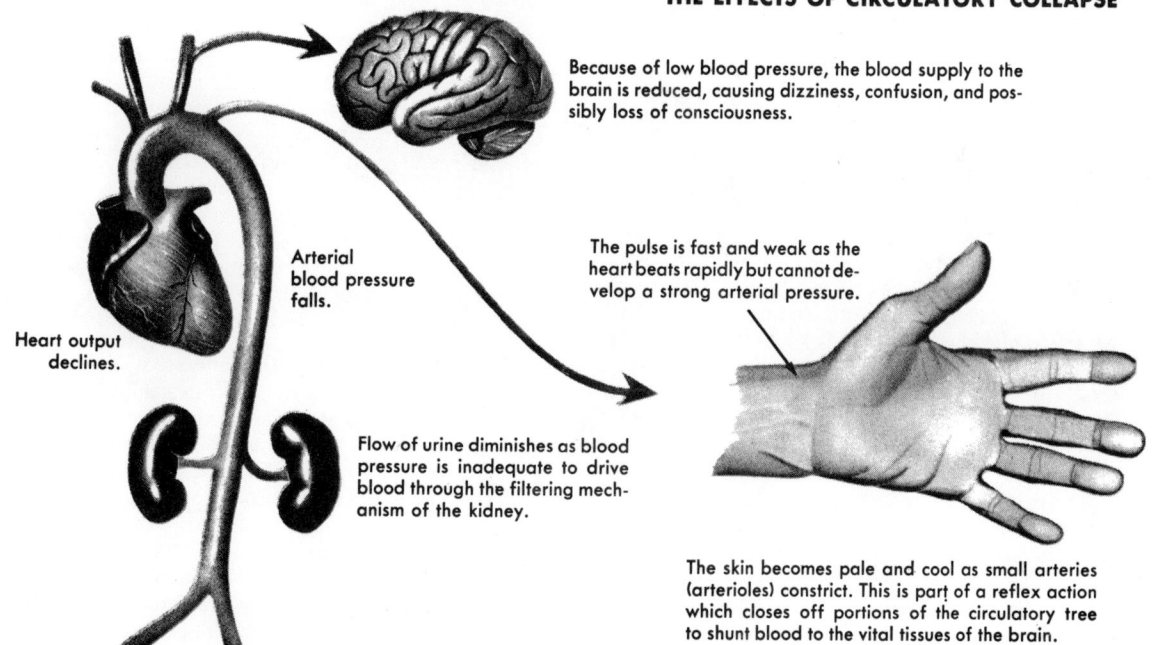

Heart output declines.

Arterial blood pressure falls.

Because of low blood pressure, the blood supply to the brain is reduced, causing dizziness, confusion, and possibly loss of consciousness.

The pulse is fast and weak as the heart beats rapidly but cannot develop a strong arterial pressure.

Flow of urine diminishes as blood pressure is inadequate to drive blood through the filtering mechanism of the kidney.

The skin becomes pale and cool as small arteries (arterioles) constrict. This is part of a reflex action which closes off portions of the circulatory tree to shunt blood to the vital tissues of the brain.

Body temperature drops and the physiological activity of cells throughout the body declines as they are deprived of their normal blood supply. If this continues for a long enough period the shock becomes "irreversible" and death follows.

SHOCK THERAPY

tients in this state may continue to live for hours or days but never recover.

See also SHOCK THERAPY.

SHOCK THERAPY, in psychiatry, a group of techniques in which comas or convulsions are induced to treat certain mental disorders.

Insulin shock therapy is based upon the injection of insulin, a pancreatic hormone that lowers the concentration of sugar in the blood. This results in the literal starvation of the cells of the brain which depend upon sugar for their energy. The parts of the brain are affected in a definite sequence. The higher brain ceases functioning before the more primitive structures succumb. The entire process takes several hours, culminating in a coma, the deepest stage of insulin shock. The patient is brought out of the coma by administering sugar (glucose) or glucagon, a pancreatic hormone which opposes the action of insulin. Treatments are usually given five or six days a week, and a series is completed after 40 to 50 treatments.

Insulin shock therapy produces considerable physical stress and is consequently not applicable to elderly patients or to those suffering from heart, liver, or kidney ailments or other chronic illnesses. Complications of treatment are seizures, respiratory difficulty, or heart failure. Usually these problems can be anticipated and can be prevented or minimized. In some cases the coma does not end in time, a condition known as "prolonged coma." This must be treated as a medical emergency.

Insulin therapy is less-frequently used today than formerly owing to the expense of its administration and the fact that similar results can be obtained more safely and economically through the use of tranquilizing drugs. Despite these drawbacks, insulin coma therapy is still valuable in the treatment of certain types of schizophrenia and is sometimes useful in the treatment of manic-depressive psychosis.

Convulsive shock therapies were introduced following observations that the symptoms of mental disease sometimes spontaneously disappeared after convulsions. In 1935 the Hungarian investigator Meduna produced convulsions by injections of camphor. Later a synthetic preparation, metrazol (in Europe "cardiazol"), came to be used in place of camphor.

The most widely used form of shock therapy is ECT, electroconvulsive therapy, which was introduced in Italy in 1937. This technique utilizes alternating current, applied through electrodes attached to the skull. The procedure is highly safe since only small amounts of current are used. Many physicians give a short-acting barbiturate to sedate the patient before the current is applied. In addition, a muscle-relaxing drug may be administered to prevent the strong muscular contractions of the convulsion from producing fractures or dislocations.

The principal side effects are temporary confusion and memory loss. ECT can be safely applied to elderly patients and pregnant women, but it is considered preferable not to treat patients who have had recent heart attacks, or those suffering from equally serious ailments.

The best success with electroconvulsive therapy has been obtained with depressed patients. A major use has been in quieting acutely agitated psychotic patients who are exhausting themselves by their activity. It is also helpful in certain types of schizophrenia. The treatment schedule varies. Most patients are treated two or three times a week, but in severely agitated cases, treatments may be given several times a day. At times maintenance treatment may be given every week, month, or at longer intervals.

See also PSYCHIATRY.

SICKLE CELL ANEMIA, blood disease characterized by crescent-shaped red blood cells which contain abnormal hemoglobin (the oxygen-carrying red pigment of the blood). An inherited disorder, sickle cell anemia is seen almost exclusively in Negroes. The peculiar shape of the blood cells causes them to be destroyed more rapidly than normal cells and makes them ill-suited for passage through small blood vessels.

Excessive red cell destruction results in anemia, with mild jaundice (a yellowish-green tinting of the eyes) and other symptoms characteristic of hemolytic (blood-destroying) anemias. Difficulty in passage of the cells through blood vessels causes frequent clotting (thrombosis) within the vessels. Attacks, or "crises," occur, which are marked by abdominal pains, fever, and a decrease of blood hemoglobin. Other signs and symptoms include bone and joint pains and leg ulcerations. An unusual feature of this disorder is the absence of enlargement of the spleen, which is frequently seen in adults suffering from other types of hemolytic anemia. Sickle cell anemia cannot be cured. Treatment consists principally of blood transfusions during periods of increased red cell destruction.

See also ANEMIA.

SILICOSIS [sĭl-ə-kō′sĭs], chronic lung disease caused by inhaling dust with a high concentration of silica (SiO_2). It is seen among workers engaged in the quarrying and mining of quartz, flint, or sand; in metal polishing and grinding industries; and in industries where sand and powdered flint are used. Silicosis develops as physical and chemical irritation by the silica particles causes the formation of nodules and fibrous tissue in the lungs. In the early stages breathing may not be impaired, but later coughing, wheezing, chest pain, and shortness of breath appear. Tuberculosis is a common complication. Once the disease has developed, little can be done beyond removing the individual from further exposure to the silica dust. Silicosis can best be prevented by engineering measures to reduce the amount of dust and by equipping workers with masks and respirators to reduce dust inhalation.

SINUSITIS [sī-nəs-ī′tĭs] usually refers to infection of the air cavities (sinuses) of the bones of the skull which communicate with the nasal passages. The most common cause of *acute* sinusitis is the common cold. Allergy is an important predisposing factor in *chronic* sinusitis.

Symptoms result from obstruction of the sinus pathways by pus, mucus, and swollen nasal tissues. Since the sinus secretions cannot drain properly when the patient is lying down, headaches are apt to be most severe in the morning and decrease during the day. Inflammation of the maxillary sinuses often causes aching of the upper teeth, which may lead the patient to consult a dentist mistakenly. The involved areas are tender, and nasal and postnasal discharges, sore throat, and interference with the sense of smell may occur. Complications involve extension of the infection to the bones of the skull or to the eye socket, the brain, and the linings of the brain (the meninges). Treatment consists of nasal sprays to reduce the swellings and to establish free drainage. Antibiotics are effective in treating acute sinusitis but are of less value in chronic sinusitis where suction, irrigation, or surgery may be necessary.

SKELETAL [skĕl'ə-təl] **SYSTEM,** the structure which houses, protects, and supports the soft tissues of the organism. In man the skeleton provides armor for vulnerable tissues (as the skull shields the brain) and is a principal element in locomotion. The body moves by means of muscular contractions which act upon the bones of the skeleton. Bone, the major constituent of the skeleton, is an ideal structural tissue, being light in weight, strong, and capable of changing its internal structure in response to external stress.

The long bones of the skeleton appear in the embryo as a cartilage model. Bone formation begins at centers of "ossification," which appear at specific points in the cartilage and gradually extend themselves. At birth this process of bone conversion is not yet complete, and growth continues in early life by the steady formation of cartilage and bone at the ends of long bones. When all of the cartilage has been replaced by bone, growth ceases. The various bones of the skeleton reach complete ossification at different times. Most of the long bones ossify between puberty and the 25th year. The entire skeleton consists of 206 bones (*see* BONE).

The skull contains 22 bones—8 bones in the cranium, which encases the brain, and 14 bones in the skeleton of the face. The thickness of the bones of the cranium is distributed to offer maximum protection for the underlying brain tissues. The thickness is greatest on the top of the skull and somewhat less on the sides where muscles add to the shielding. At birth the facial portion of the skull is only about one-eighth that of the cranium. This ratio changes with growth so that in the adult the facial and cranial portions of the skull are about equal. The "soft spots" (fontanels) seen in the infant's skull are gaps of unossified tissue which are completely filled in by about the middle of the second year.

Cranial Capacity. The dimensions of the skull, particularly as they relate to interior volume, or capacity, are of value to the physical anthropolgist and archeologist in estimating brain size and identifying skeletons. Studies have shown a steady increase in cranial capacity from prehistoric to modern man, with the exception of the large cranial capacity (1,660 cc.) of Cro-Magnon man, of about 25,000–8000 B.C., which exceeded in size that of modern man (1,450 cc.). The cranial capacity of the female is about 10% less than that of the male.

The spine is a flexible column composed of bony segments called vertebrae. Of the 33 vertebrae the 24 upper vertebrae are movable (true vertebrae), while the lower 9 are fused into the sacrum and coccyx and are fixed in place. The spine forms a protective bony enclosure around the spinal cord, the great nerve trunk that links the body and the brain. The movable vertebrae are separated by fibrocartilaginous discs—the same discs that occasionally slip and cause severe pain and various neurological disturbances. The discs are pulpy and elastic in consistency and are important as shock absorbers, flattening under the force of stresses applied to the spine, such as occurs when jumping and landing on the heels.

The Spinal Curves. The normal spine is curved from front to back, a backward curve in the chest area and a forward curve in the lower spine. Exaggerations of these curves may result in hunchback or lordosis (a potbellied appearance resulting from a marked lumbar curve). The spine may also curve to the right or left (scoliosis).

Chest Cage, or Thorax. This contains the heart and lungs and is composed of the spine in back, the breastbone in front, and the ribs joining the two. There are 12 pairs of ribs, occasionally one more or less. The upper seven pairs (the true ribs) join the breastbone. The remaining five pairs are called false ribs. Three of these are joined to the breastbone by cartilage, and the lower two are "floating" ribs, being unattached in the front. The ribs serve not only to protect the lungs but also function in breathing. Contractions of the rib muscles expand the chest cage, helping draw air into the lungs.

Shoulder Girdle. This is the bony structure by which the arms are attached to the body. The girdle is formed by the clavicle, or collarbone, in front, and the scapula, or shoulder blade, in back. The heavy muscles of the chest, shoulder, and back are attached to these two bones.

Arm and Hand. The bone of the upper arm is the humerus. The forearm consists of two bones, the radius and the ulna—so joined to make possible the movements of the forearm: pronation, in the "thumbs down" movement, and supination, in the "thumbs up" gesture. The hand consists of 27 bones—8 in the wrist, or carpus; 5 in the palm, or metacarpus; and 14 in the fingers.

Pelvis. The pelvis (Lat., "basin") is the bony enclosure formed by the hip bones and the lower part of the spine, or the sacrum and the coccyx. It contains the lower portion of the intestines, the bladder, and some of the reproductive organs. The female pelvis is shallower and wider than that of the male, and the bones are more delicate.

Leg and Foot. The skeleton of the lower extremity includes the femur, or thighbone, the longest and strongest bone of the body; the tibia, or shinbone; and the fibula. The foot contains 26 bones—7 tarsal bones in the ankle region; 5 metatarsals, corresponding to the bones of the palm; and 14 bones in the toes.

Skeleton as a Living Structure. Although solid and apparently as lifeless as brick, the skeleton is a living structure with an active physiological and biochemical life. Bone is constantly being destroyed and rebuilt, and its minerals are in chemical balance with those of the blood stream. This continuous destruction and rebuilding is important in the healing of fractures and in the adjustment of the bony structure to the weight it bears.

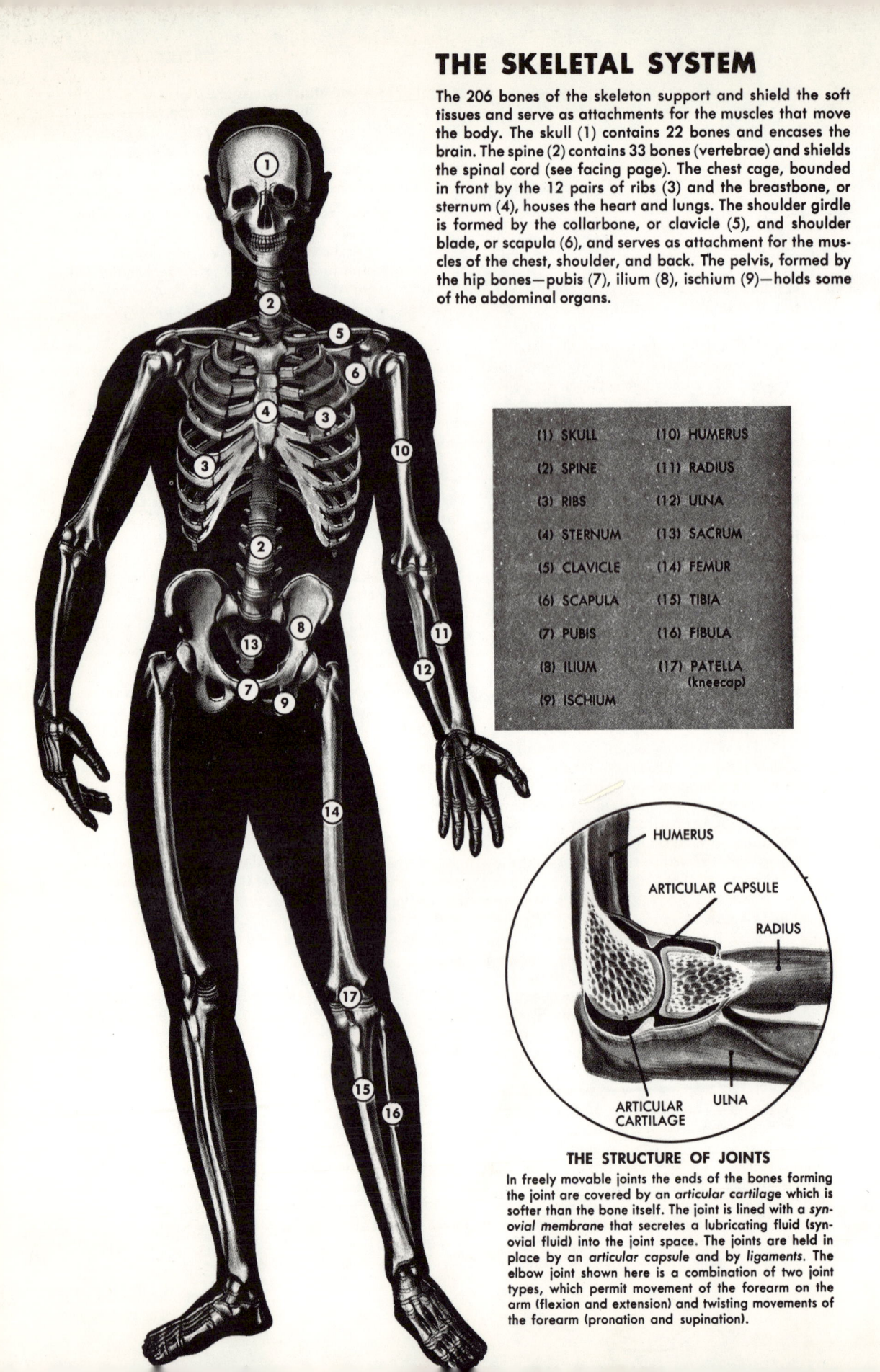

THE SKELETAL SYSTEM

The 206 bones of the skeleton support and shield the soft tissues and serve as attachments for the muscles that move the body. The skull (1) contains 22 bones and encases the brain. The spine (2) contains 33 bones (vertebrae) and shields the spinal cord (see facing page). The chest cage, bounded in front by the 12 pairs of ribs (3) and the breastbone, or sternum (4), houses the heart and lungs. The shoulder girdle is formed by the collarbone, or clavicle (5), and shoulder blade, or scapula (6), and serves as attachment for the muscles of the chest, shoulder, and back. The pelvis, formed by the hip bones—pubis (7), ilium (8), ischium (9)—holds some of the abdominal organs.

(1) SKULL	(10) HUMERUS
(2) SPINE	(11) RADIUS
(3) RIBS	(12) ULNA
(4) STERNUM	(13) SACRUM
(5) CLAVICLE	(14) FEMUR
(6) SCAPULA	(15) TIBIA
(7) PUBIS	(16) FIBULA
(8) ILIUM	(17) PATELLA (kneecap)
(9) ISCHIUM	

THE STRUCTURE OF JOINTS

In freely movable joints the ends of the bones forming the joint are covered by an *articular cartilage* which is softer than the bone itself. The joint is lined with a *synovial membrane* that secretes a lubricating fluid (synovial fluid) into the joint space. The joints are held in place by an *articular capsule* and by *ligaments*. The elbow joint shown here is a combination of two joint types, which permit movement of the forearm on the arm (flexion and extension) and twisting movements of the forearm (pronation and supination).

THE SPINAL COLUMN

The spinal column unites the major bony structures—the skull, the rib cage, and the shoulder and pelvic girdles—into the single unit called the skeleton. The principal functions of the skeletal system can be understood by examining in detail the structure of the vertebral column.

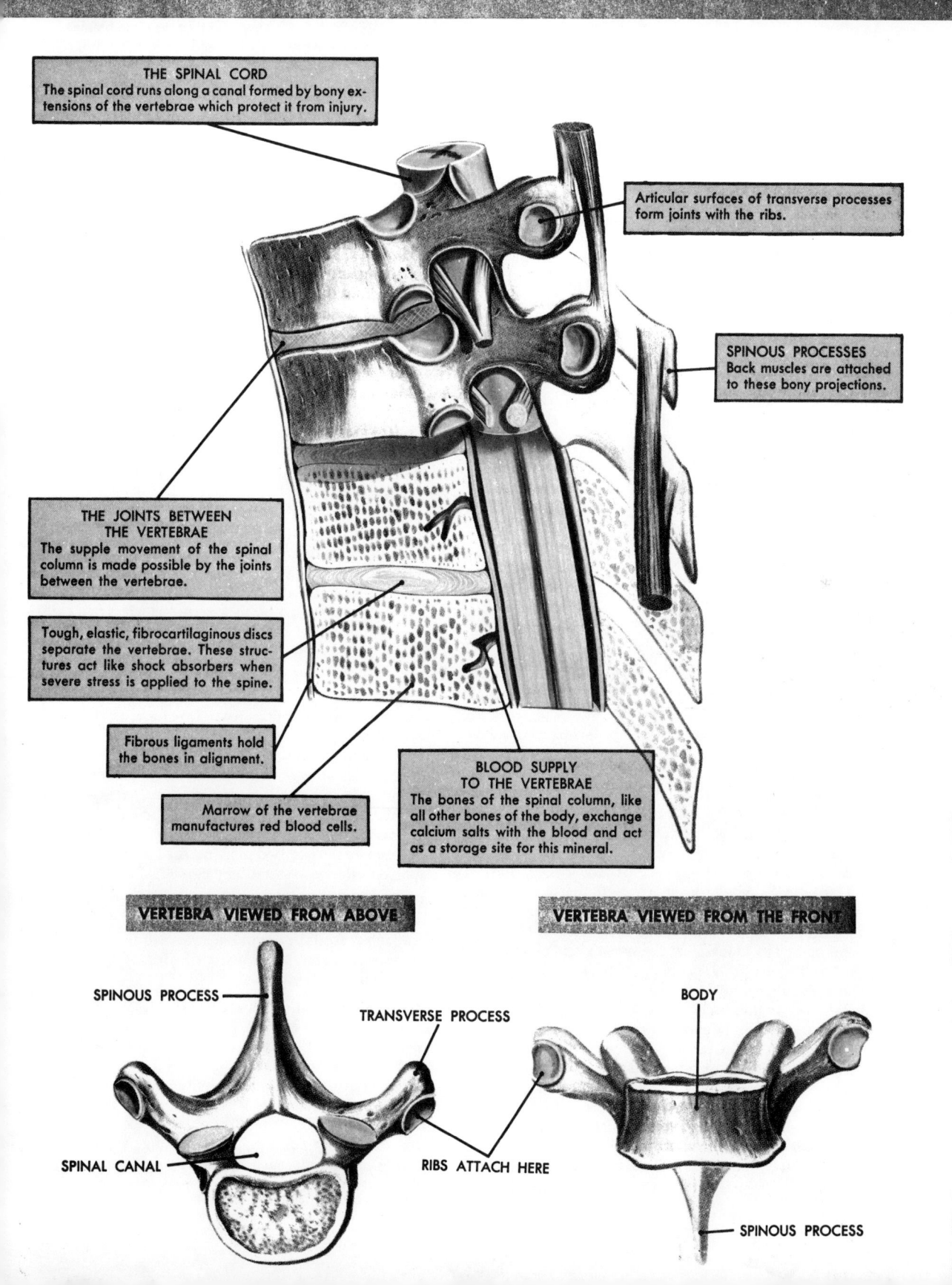

THE SPINAL CORD
The spinal cord runs along a canal formed by bony extensions of the vertebrae which protect it from injury.

Articular surfaces of transverse processes form joints with the ribs.

SPINOUS PROCESSES
Back muscles are attached to these bony projections.

THE JOINTS BETWEEN THE VERTEBRAE
The supple movement of the spinal column is made possible by the joints between the vertebrae.

Tough, elastic, fibrocartilaginous discs separate the vertebrae. These structures act like shock absorbers when severe stress is applied to the spine.

Fibrous ligaments hold the bones in alignment.

Marrow of the vertebrae manufactures red blood cells.

BLOOD SUPPLY TO THE VERTEBRAE
The bones of the spinal column, like all other bones of the body, exchange calcium salts with the blood and act as a storage site for this mineral.

VERTEBRA VIEWED FROM ABOVE

SPINOUS PROCESS
TRANSVERSE PROCESS
SPINAL CANAL
RIBS ATTACH HERE

VERTEBRA VIEWED FROM THE FRONT

BODY
SPINOUS PROCESS

SKIN

SKIN, the protective covering of the body. It is sensitive to heat, cold, pain, and touch, and is waterproof, flexible, and bacteria-resistant. The skin is divided into two layers: an upper *epidermis* beneath which is the *dermis*, or "true" skin.

Epidermis. This layer is thickest on the soles of the feet and the palms of the hands and is relatively thin on the rest of the body. It is marked by numerous elevated convolutions which correspond to ridges in the underlying true skin. The ridges of the epidermis serve to increase friction between the skin and contact surfaces when walking or grasping objects. The pattern of ridges on the fingertips is unique to each individual, a fact which makes fingerprints useful as a means of identification.

The epidermis is normally covered by a water-resistant, waxy secretion from the sebaceous glands and contains a water-insoluble protein (keratin). Corns and calluses are overgrowths of the epidermis, occurring in response to mechanical irritation of the skin. The coloring of the skin is in part dependent upon the pigment (melanin) contained in the epidermis. The color of the skin is intrinsically yellow; a reddish tint is contributed by the blood vessels of the dermis and a brownish cast is added by the pigment particles of the epidermis. The epidermis of darker skinned peoples contains greater quantities of melanin. Sunlight stimulates the formation of melanin in the skin, an effect which is recognized as tanning. Freckles are localized collections of pigment granules in the deeper parts of the epidermis.

Normal wear and tear constantly flakes off the upper cells of the epidermis. These cells are replaced by growth of the underlying basal layer of the epidermis. The epidermis has no blood supply of its own. Nutrient substances diffuse to the epidermal cells from the blood vessels of the dermis.

Dermis, or "True" Skin. This contains sweat glands, hair, sebaceous glands, nerves, and blood vessels suspended in a network of connective tissue fibers—tough, inelastic collagen fibers and elastic fibers. The upper *papillary* layer is ridged and gives the epidermis its convolutions. The lower *reticular* layer contains bundles of collagen fibers.

Sweating occurs through the simple coiled, tubular sweat glands. The evaporation of sweat from the skin cools the body and is a principal means of temperature regulation. At moderate temperatures the sweat evaporates immediately and is not felt. At higher temperatures, and particularly when the air is humid, the sweat collects on the skin, producing the discomfort experienced during hot, humid weather. The summer complaint of prickly heat is caused by blockage of the sweat glands. Salt (NaCl) is lost in the perspiration, and excessive sweating may upset the electrochemical balance of the body, causing muscle cramps. An unusually high concentration of salt in the perspiration is seen in cystic fibrosis and is used as a diagnostic clue to the disease.

The oil-secreting, or sebaceous, glands of the skin are usually found in association with hair and empty their secretion around the hair shaft. They are abundant in the face and on the scalp but are absent in the palms and soles. A common dermatological condition of adolescents (acne) occurs when dirt and sebum block the gland openings.

The skin contains special sensory structures for the sensations of light touch and cold and heat. Skin pain is detected by fine, naked nerve endings in the dermis and is of two varieties: quick, "bright" pain carried by rapidly conducting fibers and a slow, "burning" pain carried by more slowly conducting fibers. The distribution of touch receptors varies greatly. For example, the palmar surface of the fingertip can recognize two distinct points of pressure only 2.3 mm. apart, whereas on the subject's back the two points must be 67 mm. apart in order to be recognized as distinct.

Blood Supply and Temperature Regulation. The flow of blood to the skin serves two purposes: to nourish the skin and to regulate the temperature of the body. The flow is regulated by opening or closing the blood vessels, actions known respectively as vasodilation and vasoconstriction. This is made possible by nerves which end upon the smooth muscle in the walls of the small vessels of the skin. The nerves belong to the sympathetic nervous system, a division of the autonomic nervous system. This vast network of nerve tissue unconsciously co-ordinates the activity of the heart, glands, and other internal organs. These fibers work reflexively and in conjunction with emotional responses. Warming of the body causes reflex expansion of the blood vessels, bringing more blood to the skin to be cooled. Similarly, cooling the body constricts the blood vessels, thus reducing the flow of blood and heat loss through the skin.

It has also been demonstrated that during sweating, enzymes may be released into the skin which act upon certain proteins to produce a powerful vasodilating substance (bradykinin). The expansion and contraction of the blood vessels is also affected by emotional factors operating through the sympathetic system—as when fear causes one to turn "white" or when embarrassment produces blushing.

Hypodermis. This subcutaneous tissue, which lies immediately below the dermis, consists of loose connective tissue and is the principal site of fat storage in the body. In well-fed (obese) individuals this layer may be several inches thick. When not present in excess, the fat serves the useful purposes of heat conservation, energy storage, and protection. The nails consist of horny plates which are a modification of one of the layers of the epidermis. The nail emerges from the nail matrix at the root. As it grows, it glides over the nail bed pushing the free edge forward. Damage to the nail matrix may cause nail deformity.

Care of the Skin. The skin should be cleansed with a mild, nonirritating soap. Overexposure to sunlight and strong wind should be avoided. Diet is important in skin care, since the skin, as an organ of the body, rapidly reflects dietary deficiencies.

Aging of the Skin. With age the skin becomes thin and loses subcutaneous fat. The collagen and elastic fibers degenerate so that the skin loses its elasticity and ability to take up slack. Aging of the skin may be accelerated by overexposure to wind or sun. Other factors which contribute to aging are poor nutrition, glandular disturbances, and inheritance (some families appear to wear better than others). Cosmetic surgery, or face lifting, is a surgical attempt to combat the slack of aging by tightening the skin.

THE SKIN

The skin is a multipurpose organ which covers the body, protects it against bacteria and physical and chemical irritants, and helps to conserve or dissipate body heat. The skin also turns a large receptive surface to the outside world, being studded with nerve endings sensitive to pain, pressure, and temperature changes.

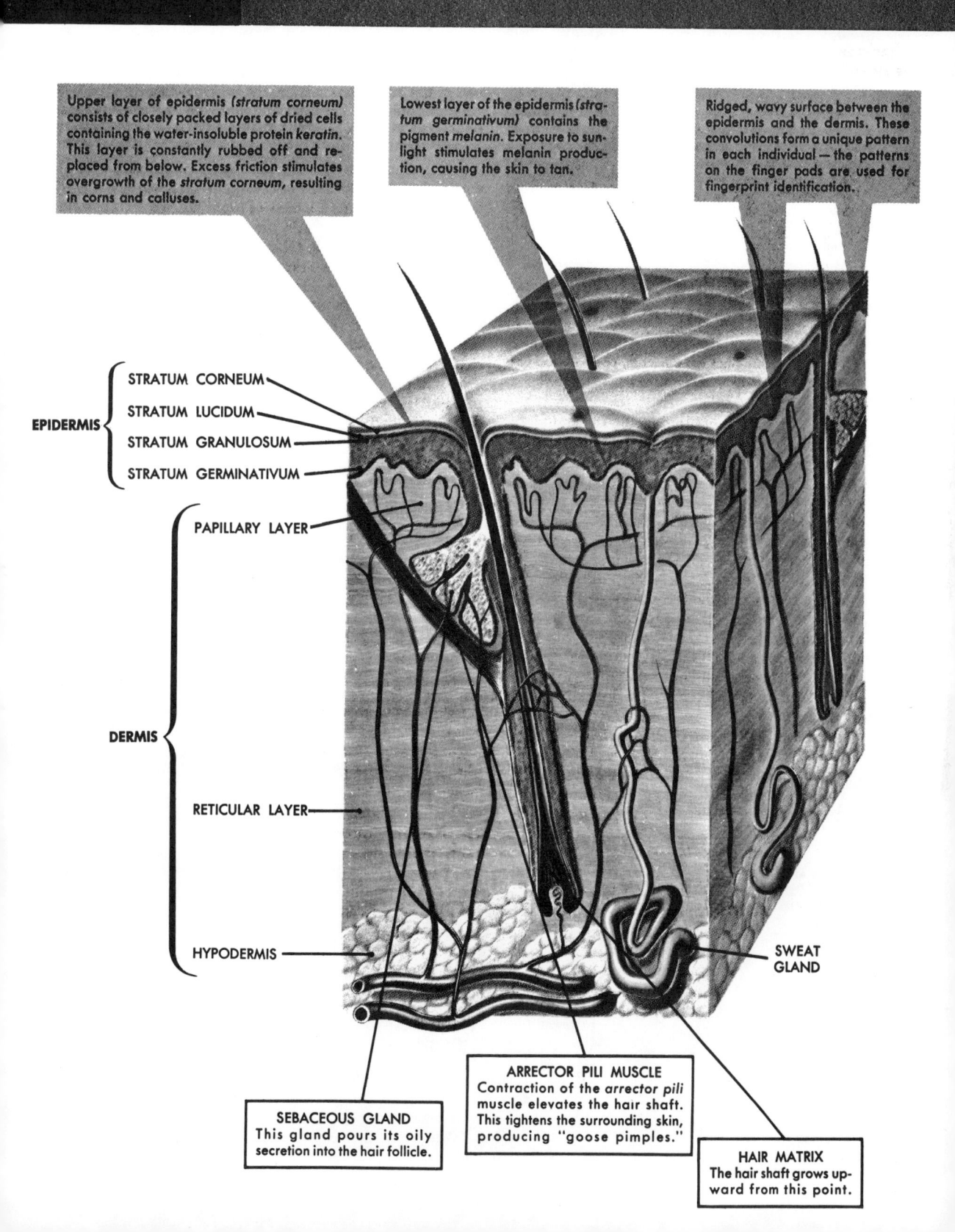

Upper layer of epidermis (*stratum corneum*) consists of closely packed layers of dried cells containing the water-insoluble protein *keratin*. This layer is constantly rubbed off and replaced from below. Excess friction stimulates overgrowth of the *stratum corneum*, resulting in corns and calluses.

Lowest layer of the epidermis (*stratum germinativum*) contains the pigment *melanin*. Exposure to sunlight stimulates melanin production, causing the skin to tan.

Ridged, wavy surface between the epidermis and the dermis. These convolutions form a unique pattern in each individual — the patterns on the finger pads are used for fingerprint identification.

EPIDERMIS
- STRATUM CORNEUM
- STRATUM LUCIDUM
- STRATUM GRANULOSUM
- STRATUM GERMINATIVUM

DERMIS
- PAPILLARY LAYER
- RETICULAR LAYER
- HYPODERMIS

SWEAT GLAND

SEBACEOUS GLAND
This gland pours its oily secretion into the hair follicle.

ARRECTOR PILI MUSCLE
Contraction of the *arrector pili* muscle elevates the hair shaft. This tightens the surrounding skin, producing "goose pimples."

HAIR MATRIX
The hair shaft grows upward from this point.

HOW THE SKIN HELPS TO REGULATE BODY TEMPERATURE

RESPONSES TO AN INCREASE IN BODY TEMPERATURE: Blood loses heat as it passes through the vessels of the skin. This is a major heat-regulating mechanism: as body temperature rises, the blood vessels of the skin expand. This is brought about in at least three ways: (1) through direct nerve stimulation that produces expansion; (2) through interruption of nerve impulses that normally keep the blood vessels contracted; (3) sweat gland activity — nerve stimulation induces the sweat glands to release an enzyme into the skin. This substance converts a skin protein into the vasodilating chemical *bradykinin*. The latter directly stimulates expansion of the blood vessels. Also the evaporation of sweat from the skin is an important cooling mechanism.

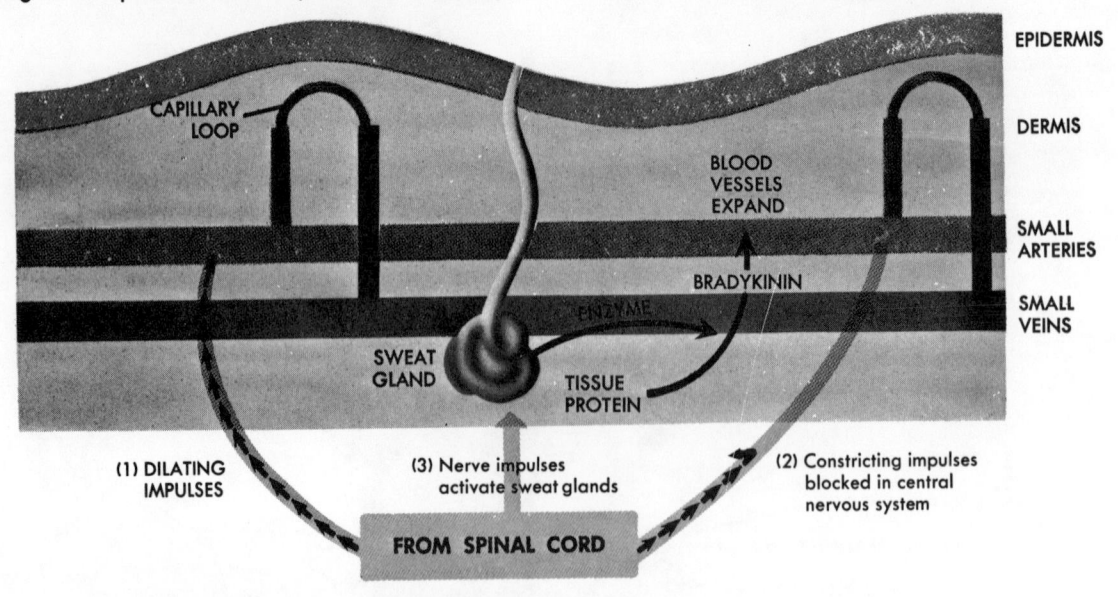

THE SKIN AS A SENSE ORGAN

Specialized nerve endings in the skin have been identified as serving the sensations of touch, pain, heat, cold, and deep pressure. The distribution of these receptors varies over the surface of the body. Touch receptors, for example, are more plentiful in the fingertips than in the back.

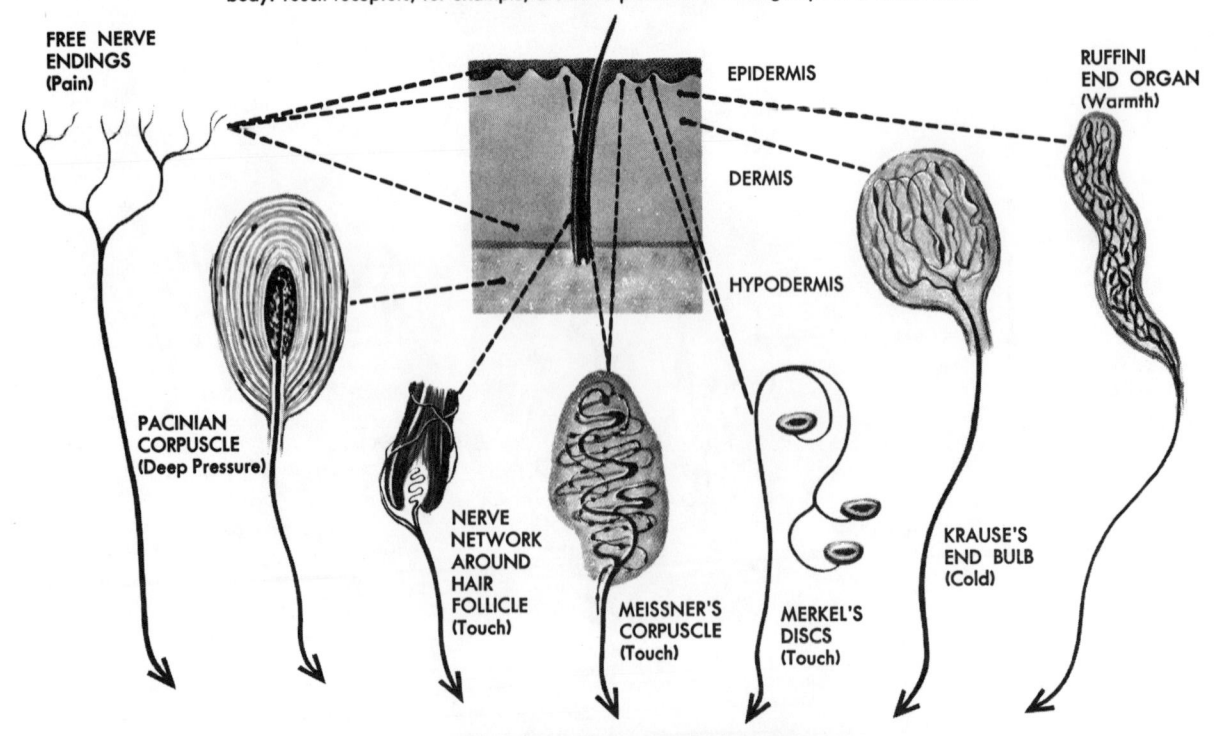

SKIN GRAFTING. See PLASTIC SURGERY.

SLEEP. The basic feature of sleep is a lowered level of awareness which differs from the unconsciousness of fainting or injury in that it is reversible, that is, the sleeping person can be awakened by strong stimulation such as the sound of an alarm clock. The depth of sleep is variable, being deepest during the first half of a sleep period and then becoming progressively but irregularly lighter. That sleep is not a complete loss of responsiveness is shown by the experience of dreaming and by the fairly frequent shifting of body position.

During sleep bodily processes are slowed significantly. The heartbeat becomes slower, respiration declines, the body temperature falls, urinary output lessens, glandular secretions diminish, and the muscles relax. The recuperative power of sleep can probably be attributed to this lowered general metabolism. Brain activity shares in this general decelerated pace. The pattern of rhythmic, spontaneous electrical activity becomes generally slower in frequency and higher in amplitude, indicating a lessening of spontaneous activity and an increase in synchronized "idling" of larger masses of brain cells.

Patterns of Sleep. There are two major patterns of sleep, the diphasic and the polyphasic. Man exhibits the diphasic pattern, consisting of one period of sleep in the 24-hour day. This varies somewhat in length from person to person, but averages about one-third of the total day. Other animals may have similar patterns, the duration and time of sleep varying with nocturnal or diurnal foraging habits. Infants and many animals show a polyphasic pattern, with many shorter periods of sleep and waking in any 24-hour period. The human infant gradually changes to fewer sleep periods, each of longer duration, until the adult pattern is achieved.

Theories of Sleep. Many hypotheses seeking to account for sleep have been advanced, but few have survived experimental test. It has been speculated that sleep is caused by the accumulation of toxic substances—probably waste products of metabolism—in the blood stream. However, Siamese twins with common blood circulation can have quite different sleep patterns. Sleep has also been ascribed to a decrease in the blood supply to the brain, but evidence shows that if anything, there is an increased blood supply to the brain during sleep.

Current concepts of the problem owe much to the efforts of Nathaniel Kleitman of the University of Chicago. He suggested that possibly the real problem is *wakefulness* rather than sleep, and that the question should be: What produces wakefulness? According to this view, sleep is the natural resting state of the living system, and wakefulness the to-be-explained departure from the "normal."

Pursuing this line of thought, Kleitman then distinguishes between "wakefulness of necessity" and "wakefulness of choice." The former is responsible for polyphasic sleep patterns of primitive animals and infants, and the latter for the diphasic pattern of higher animals in their adult phase. Wakefulness of necessity is stimulated by needs such as hunger, thirst, and the avoidance of pain and yields to sleep when these needs are satisfied. Wakefulness of choice represents the gradual control of the waking mechanism by external stimulation acting on individuals who have built up habits of responding to such stimulation and have learned to conform to social customs or other environmental demands in regulating their sleep cycle. As the experience of insomnia indicates, wakefulness of necessity may also be produced by worry, excitement, or pain.

Sleep, then, starts in the young as a reflection of satisfied needs when the infant is "at peace with the world," and wakefulness is a signal of a disturbance of the balance of body needs. Thus a cue is given to the part of the brain that may be critically involved in sleep and waking. Most of the centers regulating bodily needs are located in the hypothalamus of the brain. Carefully controlled destruction of some of the anterior regions of the hypothalamus in rats or cats produces a continuously insomniac animal, and conversely, destruction of some posterior regions leads to persistent somnolescence. Thus intimately associated with or a part of brain regions mediating regulation of bodily metabolic states are areas crucially involved with sleep and waking, a fact which strongly supports Kleitman's formulation.

The "sleep center" is probably able, by its activity, to inhibit the cerebral cortex of the brain, just as the "waking center" stimulates these higher regions. External stimulation is also capable of arousing brain activity, but in the infant this source is not yet fully developed and is of minor importance. As the infant matures, he becomes more susceptible to outside stimulation and thus acquires wakefulness of choice.

Much remains to be learned about sleep. The fundamental problem of why the life of the individual is dependent on sleep still eludes solution. There is also uncertainty about the mechanism that irresistibly induces sleep following long periods of sleep deprivation. The processes responsible for the action of sleep-producing drugs need more study. Increased understanding of these matters seems possible now that we know something about the general circumstances governing sleep and waking and about where in the nervous system these basic processes may lie.

See also NERVOUS SYSTEM.

SLEEPING PILLS. See BARBITURATES.

SLEEPING SICKNESS, also known as African trypanosomiasis, an infectious disease of humans and animals caused by the microorganisms *Trypanosoma gambiense* and *T. rhodesiense*, which are found in certain parts of tropical Africa. The parasites cause similar diseases, but *T. rhodesiense* is more lethal. The disease is transmitted to man by the bite of the tsetse fly. The organisms first multiply at the area of the bite, producing a raised, reddened circular area. Usually fever and headache develop within a few days, followed by weakness and possibly muscle tenderness and aching. An early sign is enlargement of the lymph nodes, first in the region of the bite and later in other parts of the body. A skin rash may be seen. The symptoms may disappear but recur over a period of months or years.

The most serious phase of the illness occurs when the trypanosomes attack the central nervous system, causing progressive physical and mental depression. At this time

SLEEPWALKING

the individual is overcome with a desire for sleep. Exertion becomes distasteful and is "not worth the effort." The victim is too sleepy even to eat and becomes weak and emaciated. Death may result from coma, convulsions, or complicating disease.

Whenever possible, treatment should be instituted before the organisms have attacked the central nervous system. Certain compounds are particularly effective in preventing the disease, and their use has reduced its incidence by over 90% in some areas.

See also TROPICAL MEDICINE.

SLEEPWALKING, or somnambulism, a condition in which the individual walks during sleep. It may be considered a form of dissociation (a separation of certain mental processes from consciousness). Sleepwalking may occur nightly or at irregular intervals and is most common during childhood. During episodes the sleepwalker generally avoids obstacles, although he may injure himself. He resembles a subject in hypnotic trance, responds to suggestions, but remembers none of the experience after awakening. If awakened while walking, he is surprised at finding himself out of bed. There is no evidence that it is dangerous to awaken a somnambulist, although it should be done as calmly as possible.

Recent studies of sleep and dreams show that many psychomotor activities may occur during deep sleep, especially in children, such as talking, bed-wetting, and screaming as in a nightmare. The meaning of such dissociated activities awaits further elucidation.

SLIPPED DISC, spinal injury of one of the spongy discs between each vertebra. The main weight-bearing portion of each vertebra is the body, a round cylinder as high as it is wide. Between each vertebral body is a tough fibrous disc with a soft, gelatinous center. The discs absorb shocks of normal movement, maintain the spaces between vertebrae so that nerves can travel unimpeded to and from the spinal cord, and allow some motion between vertebrae. A "slipped disc" is really a misnomer. The disc does not change position, but herniates, or protrudes. Herniation results from injury, especially from lifting heavy weights improperly. Pain starts suddenly and recurs when movement is attempted. The soft central jellylike portion of the disc is squeezed out through the fibrous periphery, leaving a narrowed intervertebral space. Nerves may be pinched, causing sciaticlike pain or changes in sensation and reflexes in the legs. Discs in the lower back, which bear more weight, are most often injured. Diagnosis may be evident by examination, but must be confirmed by X-ray. Myelogram—injection of radiopaque fluid into the spinal column—may be necessary to confirm the diagnosis. Healing may be spontaneous if the patient remains in bed. If conservative methods fail, surgery for spinal fusion, which allows bone to grow between vertebrae, is necessary. Manipulation of the spine, for instance, by a chiropractor, may cause permanent paralysis if a disc has been injured.

SMALLPOX or VARIOLA [və-rī′ō-lə], an acute and often highly fatal virus disease, which has occurred in epidemic form throughout the world since ancient times. One of the earliest known accounts is of an epidemic in China in 1122 B.C. Long prevalent in Africa and the East during the Middle Ages, smallpox was apparently widely spread by soldiers returning from the Crusades. The disease reached the Western Hemisphere during the 16th century, probably brought from central Africa by Negro slaves.

One of the striking features in the history of smallpox has been the marked variation in death rates in different epidemics. While it is true that factors such as nutrition, population immunity, and medical care may affect survival, many feel that differences in strains of the smallpox virus largely account for the varying mortality rates. A mild variant of the virus, called alastrim, or variola minor, is found in Africa south of the Sahara and in Central America and the West Indies.

The virus is quite resistant to drying and may be air borne or be carried on skin, clothing, and eating utensils. The organisms are believed to enter through the upper breathing passages. The incubation period ranges from 8 to 14 days. The disease begins with fever, vomiting, and headache and backache. A brief red rash may appear on the trunk before the characteristic raised rash of smallpox develops. The latter usually occurs about the third or fourth day, first on the inside of the mouth, the face, and forearms and later spreading widely over the body. Itching may be intense. The skin lesions fill with a clear fluid which changes within a few days into thick pus with crusting.

In severe cases death may occur within three to four days of the onset, even before the rash appears. In nonfatal cases recovery takes place within two to three weeks, usually with considerable scarring, but leaving the victim with an active immunity against a second infection. There is no specific treatment for smallpox. Antibiotics are not effective against the virus but are given to prevent bacterial infection of the lesions. The patients and whoever they have come in contact with must be strictly isolated.

Prevention and Control. In the 18th century the English physician Edward Jenner investigated the prevailing rural opinion that persons exposed to cowpox, a mild pock disease of cattle, became immune to smallpox. Jenner inoculated a young boy with cowpox virus. Six weeks later the child was exposed to smallpox and proved to be immune. Vaccination soon became widely accepted and eventually reduced smallpox from a major scourge to a rarity in those countries which practiced extensive vaccination.

World-wide control of smallpox remains to be achieved. Focal points of the disease still exist in parts of the world, and the public health danger has been increased by modern methods of transportation. A traveler exposed in India, for example, might be home in the United States for two weeks or longer before the onset of symptoms. Danger also arises in the case of vaccinated persons with waning immunity who may develop varioloid, a mild form of smallpox that may be improperly diagnosed, permitting the victim to spread the disease in the community. The World Health Organization and UNICEF have included vaccination in some of their field programs in an attempt to root out the remaining pockets of smallpox in the world.

SMELL, SENSE OF. Man's sensitivity to odor is greater by far than is usually recognized. It takes only 41 molecules of some substances to trigger his olfactory receptor. Such sensitivity is the more impressive since the smell receptor area is buried in the upper recesses of the nasal passages, squarely between the eyes. A sniff will draw the odorant to the proper site. To stop all smelling, one needs merely to hold his nose, thus quieting air currents in the nostrils. It is commonly thought that a head cold greatly diminishes the sense of taste. This is false. Instead, the reduced reaction to food flavor is due to the inability of the odor receptor area to function properly when choked with mucus.

Only very general statements can be made concerning the chemical and physical nature of normal odor stimuli. There is not yet a physical measure that will differentiate between odorous and odorless compounds, nor can qualities be assigned to a compound without resorting to the final test of actual sniffing.

Much more can be reliably stated about the smell organ, or receptor, although researchers have not yet agreed about its really crucial characteristics. Direct contact of molecules with the receptor cell itself seems to be essential. It takes only a tiny quantity of a given substance to produce reliable response. The compound's solubility in the fatty or proteinaceous parts of the cell surface may be important, as may also be the shape, size, and vibrational frequency of its molecule. Reaction of the receptor to a stimulus is rapid (a few milliseconds), and a long series of odorous materials can be identified, when streamed one after another into the nostrils at the rate of three per second. Finally, several component odor qualities may be perceived as a characteristic part of almost every odorous substance.

No acceptable system of logically grouping odors or odor qualities has yet been advanced, although systems including from 4 to 20 groups have been proposed. Fruity, sour, and burnt qualities are included in most, but sweet, minty, woody, fishy, and like terms are often excluded. Certain psychological approaches show promise for hastening the solution to the problem of determining the key dimensions of the sensation of smelling.

One method used for classifying types of odors employs the phenomenon of adaptation, or odor fatigue. It depends upon the qualitative similarities and differences between odors. For example, peppermint has a sharp, cool, minty odor. Spearmint, though similar, also has a "warm" component. Adaptation, or fatigue from constant exposure to one will diminish sensitivity to the other. The same process holds for various similar alcohols, aldehydes, esters, and other organic compounds. Some apparently related odorants, however, do not alter sensitivity for the other even after long exposure.

Sensitivity to odor, as well as taste, may be heightened as a consequence of certain diseases involving the endocrine organs. Distortion of the smell sense (parosmia) or total loss of it (anosmia) is fairly common, as the result of a hard blow to the head, measles, or drops in the eyes or nose. Of greater interest to the researchers in the field are the occasional instances of partial "odor blindness" to specific qualities, such as nutty, fruity, or burnt qualities, while reactions to sweet or sour may be normal.

See also SENSATION; TASTE, SENSE OF.

SMOKING AND HEALTH. Cigarette smoking is considered one of the most serious preventable health problems facing the United States today. It is not a new problem, however. As long as civilized man has used tobacco he has both praised its "medicinal" effects and condemned it as "loathesome" and injurious to the brain and lungs.

Present-day concern over possible ill effects of cigarette smoking began in the 1930's, when an alarming increase in lung-cancer deaths was noted in the United States. Public awareness of a correlation with cigarette smoking came in the early 1950's, with the publication of a number of epidemiological studies. In 1957 the U.S. Public Health Service took the public position that cigarette smoking was a factor in lung cancer.

During the next decade numerous health organizations throughout the world issued statements based on rapidly accumulating evidence. The consensus was that cigarette smoking is an important health hazard, especially in relation to lung cancer and cardiovascular diseases. In 1962 the Royal College of Physicians of London issued a report stating that "cigarette smoking is a cause of lung cancer and bronchitis and probably contributes to the development of coronary heart disease and various other less common diseases. It delays the healing of gastric and duodenal ulcers."

The Surgeon General of the U.S. Public Health Service, in 1962, appointed an expert advisory committee to study the situation and make recommendations. For more than a year the 10-man panel of experts evaluated some 5,000 research reports. The reports covered epidemiological studies, animal experimentation, and clinic and autopsy studies. The Surgeon General's Report on Smoking and Health of 1964 concludes that "cigarette smoking is a health hazard of sufficient importance in the United States to warrant appropriate remedial action."

In 1967 the Public Health Service published a review of 2,000 additional research studies, which not only confirmed the findings of the 1964 report but indicated that the extent of the hazard had been underestimated.

What the Reports Say. People who smoke have a substantially higher overall death rate than those who do not smoke. This means that smokers are more likely to die at an early age than nonsmokers. And their chances are great that this early death will result from lung cancer, coronary heart disease, bronchitis, or emphysema.

For men between the ages of 35 and 60, approximately one-third of all deaths that occur are excess deaths. This means they would not have died as early as they did if cigarette smokers had the same death rates as nonsmokers. Women smokers, too, have higher death rates than their nonsmoking counterparts. One out of 14 deaths among women at these ages is caused by a smoking-related disease.

A similar relationship has been discovered between smoking and illness. People who smoke have more illness, lose more time from work, spend more time sick in bed than those who have never smoked. Men and women in the U.S. labor force are losing an extra 77 million days from work each year. Those extra days lost are due to the higher rates of absenteeism among people who have ever smoked cigarettes, as compared to those who have never smoked. Americans spend 88 million extra days sick in bed and have more than 300 million extra days of

SNAKE BITE

restricted activity because of cigarette smoking.

The more a smoker smokes, the longer he smokes, and the earlier he starts, the greater his chance of disability and early death. Yet a substantial proportion of these early deaths and excess disability can be delayed or prevented if smokers give up cigarettes or reduce the amount they smoke.

SNAKE BITE. While there are a number of snakes having glands that secrete toxic substances, those dangerous to humans possess grooved or hollow fangs capable of injecting the venoms deep into the tissues. Poisonous snakes are widely distributed throughout the globe. They include the rattlesnake and copperhead of North America, the fer-de-lance and surucucú, or bushmaster, of South America, the African mamba, the European sand viper, the Indian cobras, and the Australian "death adders." The death rate from snake bites varies with the species of snake. In India an estimated 25,000 fatalities occur each year, while in Europe deaths from snake bite are extremely rare.

Snake venoms may cause death and illness by attacking the nervous system, destroying blood cells, coagulating the blood or preventing its coagulation, or by destroying tissue proteins and the cells of the body. Coral snake venoms attack the nervous system, causing salivation, tearing, depression, sleepiness, trembling, and convulsions. South American rattler venom attacks the nerve-muscle connections, causing visual disturbances and possibly complete blindness, as well as muscle paralysis, particularly about the neck. Spectacled cobra venom attacks the nervous system and the blood, resulting in salivation, vomiting, hemorrhage, blindness, and difficulty in breathing. The venom of the king cobra attacks the central nervous system and the phrenic nerve, which controls the breathing muscles. Its effects include breathing disturbances and extreme sweating. The venom of the North American rattler destroys tissue, producing pain, swelling, and discoloration around the bite, and nausea, vomiting, diarrhea, and collapse. The venom of the Indian daboia destroys tissue and inhibits blood clotting, resulting in pain and swelling in the region of the bite, hemorrhage, fall of blood pressure, bloody urine, and collapse. Some Latin American pit vipers also secrete venoms which attack blood and tissue, causing local pain and swelling, hemorrhages into the eyes, ears, mouth, and intestines, and thirst and diarrhea.

First-Aid Treatment of Snake Bites. The victim should lie perfectly still, and a tourniquet should be applied directly above the bite mark to prevent spread of the venom through the body. The tourniquet should be loosened for a few seconds at 10-minute intervals to permit circulation in the limb. The wound should not be incised except in cases of bites by North American rattlers and Indian daboia. In these cases, a poisonous substance is formed in the region of the bite by the action of the venom on the blood. Incisions should be made around these wounds and strong suction should be applied. A rubber bulb or pump can be used for this purpose. The patient should be hospitalized as quickly as possible. Medical treatment consists of antivenoms which neutralize the snake poison. The danger of snake bites can be minimized by wearing heavy boots, leather anklets, and gloves in snake-infested areas.

SNOW BLINDNESS, temporary blindness caused by overexposure to bright sunlight reflected from snow or sand. Normally the cornea, the outer covering of the eye, and the lens of the eye absorb the high-frequency waves (ultraviolet rays) of visible light, but under conditions of extreme exposure, adaptation fails and temporary blindness occurs. This is easily prevented through the use of sunglasses.

SOCIOPATHIC PERSONALITY, name of a group of personality disorders, formerly called psychopathic. The malfunction in conduct is expressed in inflexible and limited patterns of behavior, compatible at time with social success. It may be impossible to recognize the symptoms of personality disorder, especially when the particular features of the individual makeup are both accepted and rewarded by the culture.

According to psychoanalytic theory, neurosis and personality disorder may have the same background. A person with a character neurosis has conflicts which make it difficult for him to adapt to his own drives, his family, and job relationships. If such conflicts become incapacitating to others, rather than to himself, the person is said to have a personality disorder. Thus, neurosis and personality disorder differ only in their end product—the symptoms—but they have the same basic dynamics. Sociopathic behavior disorders are more common than psychoses but less crippling. The psychotic individual has lost contact with everyday reality and the neurotic suffers from his inappropriate attempts to reduce anxiety. The sociopathic personality, however, deals excellently with what *he* considers the world, and therefore he has no feelings of anxiety.

SOMNAMBULISM. *See* SLEEPWALKING.

SPEECH DISORDERS AND SPEECH THERAPY. It has been estimated that over 10% of children and roughly 5% of adults have speech deviations severe enough to warrant the attention of a speech therapist. Speech disorders are often divided into four categories: disorders of articulation, of voice, of language, and of fluency.

Speech Disorders

Disorders of articulation, consisting of the improper production of speech sounds, are by far the most common form of speech deviation, and are most frequently encountered in children. Articulatory errors usually take the form of omissions, substitutions, or distortions of sound. A child who omits a sound may say "at" for "hat" or "oo" for "you." Examples of the substitutions of one sound for another often heard in the speech of young children are "fumb" for "thumb," "yike" for "like," or "tate" for "cake." The distortion of a sound is heard in the "slurpy" *s* or *sh* of children or adults who have a so-called "lateral" lisp.

Although a variety of psychological and physical factors may play a part in the causation of articulatory disorders, the majority of children who have such difficulties are emotionally stable and constitutionally sound. They also tend to be of normal or even superior intelligence. Most articulatory problems fall into a category which may be referred to as "infantile" or "immature" articulation. In such cases the child has persisted in articulatory habits which are commonly found in younger children. It is important to note that while some children appear to speak like adults almost from the moment they begin to talk, it is entirely normal for a child to use some "baby talk" until the age of six or seven. Before that age the important question is not whether a child has articulatory errors but which sounds he is failing to say properly, since some sounds are easier and are therefore learned earlier than others.

A child of four and a half who has not yet learned to say *l, r, th, s,* and *sh* merely has some normal baby talk. If he also has difficulty with sounds such as *h, y, k,* and *g,* however, his articulation is decidedly immature. At age three, few consonants are demanded of a child beyond the relatively simple *m, p, b, w,* and *h.* A useful rule of thumb is that a child should be understood outside the home on most occasions by the age of four and a half years. The child with immature articulation is not necessarily immature in his language development (that is, in his vocabulary and sentence structure) or social behavior, but it is likely that he has been somewhat slow at beginning to talk. In some cases there appears to be a family tendency toward late development of speech and infantile errors of articulation. It is not true that immature articulation is generally caused by talking baby talk to a child.

Not all articulatory defects involve persistent infantile habits. Some are caused by imitation of a parent's speech errors. Others result from malocclusion of the teeth ("bad bite") and require the help of an orthodontist. However, only the more severe degrees of abnormal bite will interfere appreciably with articulation, and then only with the production of the "sibilant," or hissing, sounds: *s, z, sh, zh* (as in "pleasure"), *ch,* and *j.* "Tongue-tie" is a condition in which the lingual frenum (the connective tissue beneath the tongue) is unusually short and attached close to the tip of the tongue. It was once thought to be an important cause of articulatory difficulties, but it probably interferes with speech in very few cases.

There are three major organic disorders which may result in very severe articulatory problems: (1) hearing impairment, (2) cerebral palsy, and (3) cleft palate.

Hard-of-hearing persons often have their greatest difficulty in the perception of high-pitched sounds. These persons may fail to hear sounds such as *s, sh,* and *th* and will therefore distort or omit them in their own speech. A sentence such as "He stuck in his thumb" will typically sound like "He tuck in hid tumb." A person who has a more severe hearing loss involving the low pitches as well may have difficulty articulating all or most of his sounds, and his voice may be harsh, monotonous, and unnatural.

Cerebral palsy is a disturbance of motor co-ordination caused by brain injury, usually at or near the time of birth. When the speech muscles are affected, articulation tends to be slow, clumsy, labored, and exceedingly indistinct.

Cleft palate is a congenital abnormality in which the roof of the mouth fails to close in prenatal life. This leaves a gap, or cleft, in the roof of the mouth through which air escapes into the nasal cavity during speech. The result is a nasal voice with extreme distortion of all those consonants for which it is necessary to build up air pressure inside the mouth cavity, as with *p, t, k, f, th, s,* and many others. A sentence such as "Peter is a tall boy" becomes something like, "Hmeener in a hnall moy." The speech of a person with cleft palate is sometimes virtually impossible to understand.

Disorders of voice may be divided for the most part into disorders of pitch, of loudness, and of quality. One of the most common disorders of pitch is "persistent falsetto" in the male. This is caused by unconscious resistance to voice change on the part of a pubescent boy and results in an unusual, high-pitched, falsetto voice which may persist into adulthood if not treated. Inadequate loudness for normal conversation may result from a variety of causes, but is most likely to be a personality problem. "Harshness," "hoarseness," or "huskiness" are disorders of voice quality. These terms do not have exact scientific meanings, but refer in a general way to a feeling of "roughness" or strain which is imparted by certain voices.

Such disturbances of voice quality may be produced by abnormal vibration of the vocal cords resulting from an excessive tension of the vocal cords, which is in turn associated with emotional pressures. Abnormal vibration of the cords may also be caused by paralysis, growths, or ulcerations of the cords, by moist deposits on the cords (seen in sinusitis), or by inflammation of the cords caused by disease. An especially common cause of husky voice quality is abuse of the voice. This leads to the formation of small growths on the cords, called vocal "nodes" or "nodules" which are in actuality tiny calluses produced by excessive friction between the cords. Vocal nodes are seen most often in persons who use their voices professionally, such as teachers, singers, or public speakers. Usually, however, the voice can withstand a remarkable amount of use if it is produced efficiently.

Nasality is a voice quality disorder caused by improper use of the nasal passages, where the voice is modified and reinforced, as resonators. In normal speech the nasal passages are employed only for the production of the "nasal" consonants *m, n,* and *ng.* An unpleasant "twangy" voice quality occurs if the nasal passages are used in the formation of other sounds as well, especially the vowels and vowel-like consonants. In most cases nasality is caused by the habit of keeping the soft palate in a relaxed (lowered) position, thus leaving the posterior entrance to the nasal passages open. This habit may be an imitation of home or community vocal patterns, or may be caused by removal of enlarged adenoids, or by other speech habits such as articulating with inadequate vigor.

Nasality is often confused with a distinctly different pattern of speech known as "denasality," which results from failure to nasalize the consonants *m, n,* and *ng* properly. Thus "Mister Miller" becomes "Bister Biller"; the person sounds as though he has a cold in his nose. Denasality is almost always caused by an organic obstruction of the nasal passages, for example, enlarged adenoids, deviated nasal septum (an abnormal position of the bone separating the nasal passages), or swelling of the walls of the nasal cavities as seen in cases of allergy or infection.

There are two major conditions in which the voice may be lost outright. In "hysterical aphonia" the person usually can speak only in a whisper. This is a neurotic symptom, unconsciously employed as a makeshift solution for acute

SPEECH DISORDERS

emotional conflicts, and is similar to hysterical deafness or blindness. The other condition is the surgical removal of the larynx (laryngectomy) which is frequently performed in cases of laryngeal cancer. When the larynx, which houses the vocal cords, is removed the patient is in most cases unable even to whisper.

Disorders of language are disturbances in the use or interpretation of verbal symbols. They take two principal forms, the loss or impairment of language and the failure of language to develop.

Loss of language in whole or part is usually caused by brain damage: such cases are called "aphasia." The aphasic person may be unable to call forth familiar words (like the names for common objects) or may speak slowly, gropingly, and with errors in pronunciation and grammar. Some aphasics speak fluently, but in what may amount to an incomprehensible jargon. For example, in response to every question about his name, age, address, and so forth, a person with aphasia may consistently reply, "insofar as the girl is concerned," though he may be aware of the inappropriateness of his answer. On the receptive side, the aphasic may have difficulty understanding speech, though he may recognize that a familiar language is being spoken. Like the person who has not quite mastered a new language, he may feel that people are speaking too rapidly. In addition to having difficulties with spoken language, he may have similar problems in reading, writing, mathematics, and other activities involving symbols.

Delayed language development in children is one of the more common problems of speech therapy. The average child speaks his first word by about the age of one year and his first simple sentences by about age two. Children vary greatly in rate of speech development, however, and many normal children do not say their first words and sentences until considerably later. If a child does not speak any words at age two and a half years or sentences at three and a half years he should be examined carefully.

There are a number of factors which can seriously impede language development. One is mental deficiency. Many mentally deficient children never learn to speak at all. Another is deafness. The totally deaf child who is not carefully taught to speak by special techniques will not learn language. In such cases he is often referred to as a "deaf-mute." The deaf-mute ordinarily has perfectly normal speech organs. Still a third serious factor is cerebral palsy affecting the muscles of speech. In some cerebral palsied children these muscles are so severely paralyzed that no speech will ever be possible for them. A fourth factor is infantile psychosis, a very severe emotional disturbance in which contact with reality and normal relationships with others are impaired. Finally, some children with retarded speech probably have a congenital form of aphasia; that is, there has been injury or inadequate development in the "language areas" of the brain.

All of these factors are comparatively rare, and the ordinary child who is slow in learning to talk is not too likely to be suffering from any of them. There are many other reasons why children may be slow in talking. These probably include heredity, limited speech stimulation in the home, retarded physical development caused by illness or premature birth, and unwholesome parent-child relationships. Language development is never impeded by "something wrong with the child's throat."

Disorders of fluency are those in which the forward flow of speech is impeded—the chief example being stuttering, or stammering. The stutterer repeats sounds luh-luh-luh-luh-like this, or prolongs them lllllike this, or has complete stoppages like ------- this. These interruptions are usually accompanied by excessive tension in the muscles of speech and often by grimaces, gestures, bodily movements, breathing abnormalities, or extraneous words or sounds, as in the sentence, "John um Baker lives on well Tenth Street." The stutterer generally knows quite well what word he wants to say; he is simply unable for the moment to say it. He is likely to develop fears of inability to say particular words or sounds, to anticipate blocks on them beforehand, and to try to avoid them by such devices as saying, for example, "this evening" instead of "tonight," or "This is my mother's sister's son" instead of "This is my cousin."

Stuttering usually begins in early childhood and is more common in boys than girls by a ratio of about four to one. In many cases it disappears spontaneously during childhood. It appears chiefly in civilized societies and is not found at all among many "primitive" peoples. It frequently tends to "run" in families. It is a highly intermittent disorder; most stutterers are fluent when they sing, whisper, speak in unison with another person or talk to an infant or pet, when they are alone, and under many other conditions. They are most likely to have difficulty speaking when they expect to stutter and want very much not to. The stutterer exhibits no abnormality of bodily constitution or personality make-up which has been established to the satisfaction of most experts. He is not necessarily more "nervous" than anyone else or lacking in confidence, except about his speech. On the average, stutterers are as intelligent as other people.

Significance of Speech Impairment to the Individual

Impaired speech may gravely disable the individual in both his social and business life. A lisp may create a wholly unwarranted impression of immaturity on the listener. A person who distorts the *l* sound or has an unpleasant voice quality may feel chronically conspicuous and ill at ease in social situations. Children who stutter or have infantile speech are vulnerable to torment by their schoolmates. The sudden loss of speech in laryngectomy or aphasia is likely to be felt as a catastrophe and to be acutely demoralizing.

The lifelong communication problem of many persons with hearing loss, cleft palate, or cerebral palsy probably contributes considerably to the progressive attrition of personality sometimes associated with these disorders. The young child with severely delayed language development is frequently a behavior problem for want of adequate means of relating normally to others. Until he learns to speak he is also apt to appear intellectually retarded and for all practical purposes to be functioning on a retarded level in an environment in which intelligence consists so largely of verbal ability.

The outstanding example of the social and emotional consequences of speech impairment is afforded by severe stuttering. There are few deviations from the normal which are so harshly penalized by society. The stutterer generally learns to dread the listener's look of amusement or shocked surprise, or his impatient "Hurry up, young man—I don't have all day." He may also bitterly resent the listener's attempts to help him with words, his expressions of pity, his tendency to look away, and his confident advice to "Take it easy."

To escape such penalties, many stutterers do everything in their power to pass as normal speakers. They may continually substitute synonyms or circumlocutions in order to avoid difficult words. In the classroom the stutterer may talk as little as possible and may tell the teacher that he does not know the answer or declare that he is unprepared in order to avoid stuttering. At great inconvenience he may avoid making phone calls, asking for directions, or going into stores. He may avoid dances, parties, and dates, sometimes convincing himself that he does not enjoy "small talk" anyway. Stutterers have been known to leave school because of their stuttering, to choose a vocation chiefly on the basis of how much speaking it requires, to hide their speech problem successfully from wives or husbands for many years, or to live in virtual seclusion because of their stuttering.

Aims and Prospects of Therapy

Generally speaking, improvement is easiest in cases of defective articulation based on habit. Here the therapist is often concerned simply with hastening the process of speech maturation. With the assistance of speech therapy, the great majority of these children can be expected to acquire normal speech in a reasonably short time.

When defective articulation is due to severe organic disorders, as a hearing impairment, cerebral palsy, or cleft palate, it is usually necessary to carry on an intensive program of therapy over a period of years and to aim for relatively intelligible rather than normal speech. This is particularly true in cerebral palsy. In the case of hearing impairment there are a few individuals who will show rapid improvement through the use of hearing aids which may enable them to perceive sounds which they were unable to hear before. In cleft palate, speech therapy is of little value until the cleft has been closed by means of oral surgery or an artificial palate known as an "obturator." The outcome of speech therapy then depends in part on how well this closure has been made. Sometimes normal speech can be achieved if it is possible to perform a successful operation on the palate early in the child's life, before speech habits have been fully formed.

In disorders of voice the prospects for improvement are excellent when the problem is one of improper habits of voice production. On the other hand, the presence of organic or emotional problems may create stubborn obstacles in some cases.

In serious language retardation in children the outcome of therapy depends greatly on the cause of the problem. In cases of mental deficiency only limited improvement can be expected. The child may develop some language but will go no further than his restricted mental capacity will allow. In children diagnosed as having "congenital aphasia," on the other hand, the prospects for satisfactory language development through training aided by maturation may be very good. In loss of language in adulthood through a stroke or other brain injury (aphasia), there is nearly always a considerable amount of spontaneous recovery in the months immediately after the injury, but language is seldom restored to its former level, even with the aid of speech therapy.

Stuttering is often considered difficult to eliminate completely when it has been of long standing, but even in adulthood it can often be considerably reduced. It has been known to disappear with or without help at almost any age. In childhood the treatment of stuttering tends to be easier and is aided by a tendency toward spontaneous recovery. Brief episodes of stuttering are extremely common among young children, so that when it has been present for only a short time the outlook for spontaneous recovery is good.

Techniques of Therapy

Articulatory Disorders. When being treated for improper articulatory habits, the child is usually first taught the correct sound in isolation (as "ssss" rather than "soup" or "ess"). He must be trained to hear the sound accurately and vividly or, if necessary, instructed in the proper placement of his articulatory organs. He is then given practice in the use of the sound in progressively more complex contexts, as in syllables, words, sentences, and so on. Finally, he is taught to "carry over" his new articulatory habits to spontaneous speech.

The ordinary young child who has a few infantile errors can sometimes be helped by a parent or teacher. Usually it is not advisable to stop the child now and then in the midst of his conversation to demand that he repeat the word "soup" correctly. He should be taken aside regularly for a few minutes to work on the sound in isolation. The sound should be taught entirely by ear, that is, by imitation. The removal of tonsils and adenoids is of little benefit in cases of defective articulation unless the problem is chiefly one of "denasal" production of *m*, *n*, and *ng*.

When articulatory errors are complicated by organic abnormalities, the help of a trained speech therapist is always necessary. In the case of the child who is hard of hearing, therapy is usually made more effective by the use of hearing aids together with intensive training in the use of residual hearing. The cerebral palsied child usually requires intensive exercises in relaxation, control of speech rate, and accurate use of his speech organs. In cleft palate, special training needs to be given in directing the breath stream through the mouth instead of the nose.

Voice Disorders. The treatment of voice disorders makes use of such techniques as ear training, relaxation, and the habituation of more efficient pitch levels. In some voice cases psychotherapy or psychological guidance are necessary adjuncts to speech therapy. When the voice is lost through surgical removal of the larynx an effective substitute can usually be developed by teaching the patient to belch voluntarily while placing his speech organs in the usual positions for speech sounds. This is termed "esophageal speech."

Aphasia. Treatment of aphasia involves patient retraining in basic language skills which have been lost, as vocab-

SPERMATOZOON

ulary, grammar and pronunciation. With children who have failed to develop language the essential procedure is to contrive situations in which verbal responses are made useful and meaningful. For example, the therapist may play ball with the child, continually repeating the word "ball" in the expectation that the child will be stimulated to say the word. It is not wise to withhold a desired object from such a child "until he says it," but whenever possible the name of the object should be spoken when giving it to him.

SPERMATOZOON [spûr′mə-tō-zō-ŏn], the male reproductive cell, or gamete, which typically consists of a head, midpiece, and tail. The head of the spermatozoon is made up almost entirely of a nucleus which contains the chromosomes, or units of heredity. The midpiece contains the centriole and mitochondria, the organelles essential to cell division and cell respiration, respectively. The tail, which is used to propel the sperm as it swims toward the egg, remains outside the egg after fertilization. In some invertebrate animals, the sperm lacks a tail and reaches the egg by means of a creeping ameboid movement. Because they are highly motile and contain little stored food, sperm cells rarely live for more than a few hours after being expelled from the body. Many can exist for only a few minutes.
See also FERTILIZATION; REPRODUCTION.

SPHYGMOMANOMETER [sfĭg-mō-mə-nŏm′ə-tər], instrument for measuring blood pressure. A hollow rubber cuff wound around the patient's arm is connected by rubber tubing to a pressure gauge. The cuff is inflated with air so that it acts like a tourniquet, squeezing shut the arteries of the arm. A stethoscope (q.v.) is placed over a large artery in the arm, and the cuff is slowly deflated until a jet of blood is allowed through, producing a tapping sound. The pressure reading at this point represents the blood pressure during the contraction of the heart (systolic pressure). More air is released from the cuff until a smooth stream of blood passes through the artery. When this occurs, the sounds disappear, and the reading indicates the blood pressure during the phase of the expansion of the heart (diastolic pressure).
See also BLOOD.

SPINA BIFIDA [spī′nə bĭf′ĭ-də], a congenital cleft of the back of the spine caused by failure of the two parts of the spine to fuse during the course of development. The condition is seen most commonly in the lower back, and may be visible only under X ray (spina bifida occulta) or may be apparent as an actual bulging of the lower spinal membranes through the cleft. The skin overlying the defect may be dimpled, hairy, or pigmented. In severe cases interference with the nerve supply to the lower part of the body may cause wasting and weakness of the leg muscles, loss of skin sensation, and inability to control urinary flow. Surgical treatment may be helpful in some of these cases.

SPINAL ANESTHESIA. See ANESTHESIA.

SPINAL TAP, introduction of a needle into the space surrounding the spinal cord to inject anesthetics or other medications, to relieve fluid pressure, or to obtain a sample of the cerebrospinal fluid which bathes the central nervous system. The fluid may be examined for the presence of blood, proteins, sugar, and microorganisms. The spinal tap is used to aid in the diagnosis of brain injuries, syphilis, poliomyelitis, meningitis, and other conditions.
See also ANESTHESIA.

SPINE. See SKELETAL SYSTEM.

SPIROCHETES [spī′rō-kēts], spiral bacteria with flexible cell walls belonging to the order Spirochaetales. Spirochetes are found in mud and water, and as parasites in animals (Treponemataceae family). Among the latter are the organisms which produce syphilis, yaws, relapsing fever, and leptospirosis.
See also BACTERIA; SYPHILIS.

SPLEEN [splēn], a small organ about the size of a fist, located on the left side of the abdomen below the diaphragm. The spleen is a detour in the circulatory system. Within the organ, blood is diverted into a rich network of small channels and is thereby exposed to the action of the splenic cells. The spleen is intimately involved in blood physiology. Many of its functions derive from the membership of this organ in the reticuloendothelial system—a widely distributed network of cells which helps the body to resist invasion by microorganisms.

The Known Functions of the Spleen. *Red Blood Cell Production.* The spleen manufactures red blood cells in the embryo. This normally ceases at birth, when the bone marrow takes over the function.

The Spleen as a Blood Purifier. The cells of the spleen share with the other cells of the reticuloendothelial system the ability to engulf and destroy bacteria.

The Spleen and Infectious Diseases. The spleen manufactures special substances (antibodies) which can react with and destroy microorganisms.

White Blood Cell Production. The spleen manufactures lymphocytes, a type of white blood cell.

Red Cell Destruction. Large splenic cells take in and disintegrate red blood cells. Normally most red cells are not destroyed in this way, since the spleen attacks only older, fragmented, or oddly shaped red blood cells.

The Spleen as a Reservoir of Blood. In dogs, cats, and other mammals the spleen stores red blood cells and in periods of great activity or hemorrhage the spleen contracts, squeezing these cells into the general circulation. Although for some time it was believed that the spleen served the same function in man, this is now known to be not true.

The Spleen and the Blood Elements. In addition to the fact that the spleen destroys old or abnormal red cells and manufactures some white blood cells, the spleen in some obscure way apparently controls the number of red cells, white cells, and platelets (cell fragments) in the circulation. Some researchers have speculated that the spleen produces substances which inhibit the release of blood cells from the bone marrow. Another possibility is that the spleen produces antibodies which destroy blood cells. Precisely this is thought to happen in the disease called autoimmune acquired hemolytic anemia: antibodies produced in the spleen and other tissues destroy the patient's red blood cells.

The Spleen in Disease. An enlarged spleen is seen in a

THE SPLEEN

The spleen is located in the upper left section of the abdomen, lying between the stomach and the diaphragm, and in contact with the kidney, the large intestine, and the pancreas.

The spleen is part of the *reticuloendothelial system*—a system of specialized cells, widely distributed in various organs and tissues. In the spleen these cells purify the blood, destroy old blood cells, and manufacture disease-fighting antibodies. The spleen is also believed to regulate the blood concentration of red and white cells, and platelets (cell fragments, or "thrombocytes").

DIAPHRAGM — LIVER — STOMACH — SPLEEN — LARGE INTESTINE

EXTERNAL VIEW OF THE SPLEEN

VENUS BLOOD LEAVING SPLEEN GOES TO THE LIVER

TRABECULAE: The fibrous bands of the trabeculae support the soft tissue of the spleen.

AN ENLARGED CROSS-SECTION OF THE SPLEEN

CAPSULE — VEIN

WHITE PULP: Network of fibers and cells that sheathes the arteries of the spleen.

RED PULP: The red pulp consists of the same fibers and cells that make up the white pulp, and, in addition, blood. The red pulp is contained in the venous sinuses through which blood passes before entering the veins of the spleen. In the red pulp splenic cells engulf and destroy old or fragile red blood cells, and also purify the blood of bacteria and foreign particles.

VEIN — WHITE PULP — ARTERY

LYMPHOCYTES: White blood cells. These cells are manufactured by the spleen and are found in both the red and white pulp.

VENOUS SINUS
ARTERY

RED BLOOD CELL

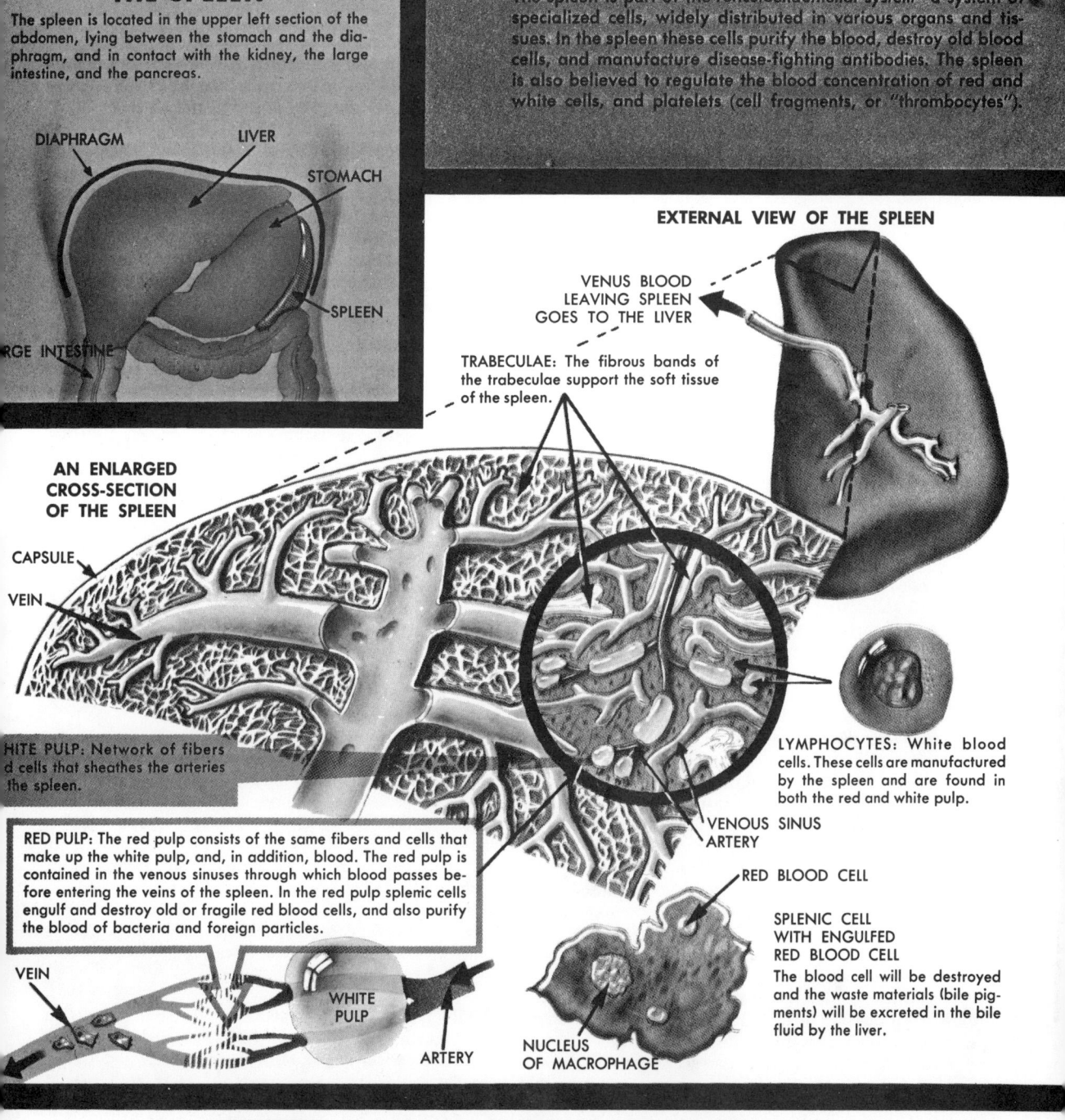

SPLENIC CELL WITH ENGULFED RED BLOOD CELL
The blood cell will be destroyed and the waste materials (bile pigments) will be excreted in the bile fluid by the liver.

NUCLEUS OF MACROPHAGE

THE SPLEEN IN DISEASE

In a number of disorders abnormal functioning of the spleen is associated with deficiencies of various blood elements.

ABNORMAL SPLENIC FUNCTIONING MAY BE ASSOCIATED WITH:

DEFICIENCY OF RED BLOOD CELLS — ANEMIA, which may cause pallor and yellowish tinting of eyes and skin (jaundice).

DEFICIENCY OF WHITE BLOOD CELLS — LEUKOPENIA, which may cause ulcerations and susceptibility to infection.

DEFICIENCY OF BLOOD PLATELETS — THROMBOCYTOPENIA, which may cause bleeding tendencies.

SPOTTED FEVER

great number of diseases, including blood disorders, obscure inherited and congenital diseases (such as Gaucher's disease), and infectious diseases such as malaria. Splenic enlargement is so characteristic of malaria that it is used as a quick means of estimating the incidence of malaria in a specific area. In some cases spleen enlargement is associated with blood abnormalities, such as a deficiency of red blood cells (anemia), deficiency of certain types of white blood cells (neutropenia), or deficiency of blood platelets (thrombocytopenia). At times all these elements may be reduced in concentration (pancytopenia). Splenectomy, or removal of the spleen, is occasionally effective in treating these conditions. The patient usually functions well without his spleen.

See also BLOOD; RETICULOENDOTHELIAL SYSTEM.

SPOTTED FEVER. See ROCKY MOUNTAIN SPOTTED FEVER.

SPRUE [sproo], a disease of the small intestine marked by impaired absorption of vitamins, proteins, fats, carbohydrates, minerals, and other nutrients into the body. Of unknown cause, the disease is seen most frequently in white persons who have settled in India, Ceylon, China, and other countries of the Far East. A distinction is sometimes made between tropical and nontropical sprue. It is not clear whether sprue is a single disease occurring in two forms or whether the tropical and nontropical forms are actually distinct ailments. Some investigators also consider celiac disease—an intestinal disorder of children—to be a precursor of some cases of nontropical sprue. It is known that tropical sprue usually improves when the patient returns to a temperate climate.

In sprue the normally convoluted lining of the small bowel becomes flattened and the absorbing surface is reduced. The patient suffers from multiple vitamin deficiencies, anemia, sore mouth and tongue, diarrhea, weakness, and loss of weight. These symptoms may develop gradually over a period of years or occur in brief explosive attacks. The abdomen may be noticeably distended. A principal sign of sprue is the characteristic greasy stool marked by a high fat content.

Improvement may occur on a diet free of gluten, a protein found in wheat and rye. This has led to speculation that sensitivity to gluten may play a role in causing the disease. Cortisone and related drugs may help those who do not respond to a gluten-free diet. Liver extract, vitamin B_{12}, and folic acid are given to correct the anemia. Multiple vitamin and mineral therapy is also important. Although these measures may substantially improve the patient's condition they do not cure the disease, and must be continued indefinitely.

STAPHYLOCOCCUS [stăf-ə-lō-kŏk'əs], spherical shaped bacterium, which usually grows in clusters resembling grapes (Greek *staphule*, "grape"). They absorb color from identifying Gram stain, and usually grow in white or yellow colonies in the test tube. Staphylococci are normally found on the skin and mucous membranes of man and many other animals. They are also a major cause of common infections, such as boils, abscesses, and pneumonia. Staphylococci which produce infection have the unique ability to clot blood by producing a coagulase.

Infections by staph, which may be fatal, are characterized by the destruction of tissue and the production of pus. When staph infections have proceeded to the point of large collections of pus, antibiotics are generally ineffective, because the blood supply carrying the antibiotic to these areas is insufficient. In such cases, surgical incision and drainage are necessary. The most common type of food poisoning, characterized by nausea, vomiting, and diarrhea, is caused by a staphylococcus. The staphylococcus produces a toxic substance, enterotoxin, as it multiplies in pastries or custards which are not adequately refrigerated.

It is interesting that while staph played a part in the discovery of penicillin—Sir Alexander Fleming observed its antibacterial effect on a staph culture in 1929—many strains are now penicillin-resistant. Widespread use of penicillin has contributed to the bacteria's resistance. The bacteria produce penicillinase, which renders penicillin ineffective. Although many hospital-acquired staph infections are resistant to regular penicillin, they are effectively combatted by the newer, semisynthetic penicillins.

See also BACTERIA; DRUGS; FOOD POISONING.

STARCH. See CARBOHYDRATES.

STEATOPYGIA [stē-ə-tō-pī'jē-ə, stē-ə-tō-pĭj'ē-ə], the condition of overdevelopment of the buttocks, especially in women, due to an excess accumulation of fatty tissue. It is a hereditary characteristic of certain racial groups, such as the Bushman-Hottentot peoples of South Africa.

STEATORRHEA [stē-ə-tō-rē'ə], excessive excretion of fat in the stool resulting from interference with the digestion and absorption of fat. Steatorrhea may be seen in diseases of the small intestines or in diseases of the pancreas, liver, or bile ducts, which result in deficiencies of fat-digesting enzymes and emulsifying agents. The presence of fat in the stools renders them pale, greasy, and foul-smelling. Because of the cause and effect relationship between gastrointestinal disorders and steatorrhea, examination of stools for their fat content is a useful diagnostic procedure in diseases of the gastrointestinal tract.

See also MALABSORPTION SYNDROMES.

STERILITY [stə-rĭl'ə-tē], in medicine, term used to describe a permanent inability to reproduce. There has been much confusion concerning the usage of this word, and many physicians now prefer the expression "infertility," describing individuals who have not reproduced. "Sterility" may then be defined as "permanent infertility."

The problem of infertility is more common than might be supposed, affecting approximately 1 out of 10 couples throughout the world. The frequency varies with the level of public health (prevalence of malaria, typhoid, and other diseases) and the cultural level of the community. Infertility is greater among professional and other highly educated groups, possibly reflecting the marked impact of the stress of modern life on these individuals. In discussing this point, infertility experts state that the professional man's ability to reproduce seems to decline in direct proportion to his involvement in his work—the more devoted are the less prolific.

Causes of Infertility. The human embryo is conceived in the Fallopian tubes (which connect the ovaries and the uterus) when the sperm and egg unite. Abnormalities or diseases of the body or reproductive structures may cause infertility by interfering with the production or movement of the egg and sperm, or with the subsequent implantation and development of the fertilized egg in the womb.

Infertility in the female may result from general bodily disease or from specific disturbances of the vagina, uterus, Fallopian tubes, or ovaries. In the first category are disturbances of the pituitary, thyroid, and other endocrine glands, which upset the hormonal balance of the body. In the second group are malformations of the vagina and infections or tumors of the cervix (the neck of the uterus), uterus, and Fallopian tubes that block the passage of sperm. Scar tissue around the openings of the Fallopian tubes may prevent the egg from entering the tubes. Cysts or infections of the ovary may interfere with ovulation—the ejection of the egg from the ovary.

The major cause of infertility in the male is underactivity of the sperm. The number and shape of the sperm may also affect reproductive potency. Among the other causes of male infertility are endocrine disturbances, undescended testicles, and syphilis, all of which interfere with sperm production; and gonorrhea, which blocks passage of the sperm from the testicles.

In many cases of infertility no physical cause can be found in either sex. In such instances emotional factors are apparently responsible.

Treatment. Fertility can be achieved in many cases by specific therapy directed at the underlying cause. This may require administration of hormones, treatment of infections, or surgical correction of scarring and abnormalities. Often in cases of infertility of psychogenic origin, changed emotional attitudes result in successful pregnancy. Physicians stress that successful treatment is always possible provided that all of the reproductive organs of the man and woman are present and intact.

STERILIZATION [stĕr-ə-lə-zā'shən], in microbiology, the destruction of every living organism present in a given environment. The microorganisms responsible for spoilage and disease multiply rapidly. Therefore they must be completely destroyed in order to preserve foods for human consumption and media for use in microbiological studies, as well as to render surgical instruments and materials safe for medical use.

Heat is the best agent for sterilizing various contaminated materials. As many bacteria are resistant to heat, it is necessary to expose them to high temperatures for long periods of time to ensure their complete destruction.

Other methods of sterilization utilize ultraviolet light, filters, high-frequency (ultrasonic) pulses, and chemicals. Ultraviolet lamps have been used in operating rooms to help maintain a germ-free field during operations. Solutions may be sterilized by passing them through "bacteriological" filters, the pores of which are too small to allow bacteria to pass through. While capable of removing bacteria and other large organisms, filtration does not remove viruses. Ultrasonic devices and various chemical agents, such as zephiran chloride, are used to sterilize surgical instruments.   *See also* BACTERIA; MICROBIOLOGY.

STERNBERG [stûrn'bûrg], **GEORGE MILLER** (1838–1915), American bacteriologist who was surgeon general of the United States Army from 1893 to 1902. He is best remembered for his isolation of the pneumococcus bacterium, a common cause of pneumonia, and for his *A Manual of Bacteriology* (1892), which was a standard textbook for many years.

STEROIDS [stĕr'oidz], group of naturally occurring substances which produce a great diversity of physiological effects in the human body. The steroids have in common a basic structure made up of 17 carbon atoms contained in four fused ring systems. In the different steroids different side chains are attached to this nucleus.

Normal Function. Steroid hormones are produced in the sex glands (gonads) and in the adrenal glands, two rounded organs situated one at the upper end of each kidney. A group of steroids with 18 carbon atoms, termed *estrogens*, or female sex hormones, induces sexual development in the female and controls the menstrual cycle. Estrone, estriol, and estradiol are some of the more important estrogens.

The *androgens*, or male sex hormones (steroids with 19 carbon atoms) are essential for sexual development in the male and for the sustained production of spermatozoa. Two important androgens are testosterone and androsterone.

The designation "male" and "female" sex hormones is not strictly correct, as androgenic and estrogenic substances are produced by both sexes. However, androgens predominate in the male, estrogens in the female.

Progesterone is a steroid hormone with 21 carbon atoms. It is essential for maintaining the normal course of pregnancy.

Adrenal corticoids are hormones with 21 carbon atoms produced by the adrenals. These steroids maintain the normal mineral composition of the blood and regulate the utilization of sugars and proteins in the body. Some 30 different steroids have been isolated from the adrenals, among them corticosterone, cortisone, and aldosterone.

Formation and Breakdown of Steroids in the Body. Cholesterol, a steroid with 27 carbon atoms, appears to be the main source for the formation of steroid hormones in the body. In addition to obtaining cholesterol from the diet (meat, egg yolk, among other foods), the human body can build up its own cholesterol from smaller molecules. Cholesterol is also involved in the formation of vitamin D_3. The final phase in the use of cholesterol and other steroids in the human body is their conversion to bile acids, which are secreted with bile into the intestines and then excreted with the feces.

Role of Steroids in Disease. Destruction or removal of the gonads (castration) results in striking physical and psychical changes: masculinization in the female and feminization in the male. Treatment of castrates with sex hormones will not restore fertility, but it will reverse the personality changes. A defect of the adrenals, with resulting failure to produce corticoid hormones, occurs in Addison's disease. This disease can be successfully controlled with corticoid hormone drugs.

Gallstones may contain up to 98% cholesterol, and it is believed by some that an abnormality in cholesterol utilization is responsible for gallstone formation. Patients suffering from gallstones often have a high concentration of cholesterol in the blood.

Atherosclerosis, a disease found mostly in older persons and characterized by hardening and thickening of the walls of the arteries, is also thought to be related to cholesterol production or utilization. Atherosclerosis is often associated with high blood cholesterol concentration. In man the blood cholesterol concentration bears little relation to the amount of cholesterol consumed with the diet.

Steroids as Drugs. Some steroids have important clinical applications. The leaves and seeds of foxglove (*Digitalis purpurea*) contain the highly toxic digitalis steroids which, in proper dosages, are useful in the treatment of certain types of heart disease. Cortisone and a number of closely related steroids are used in the treatment of rheumatic fever, arthritis, allergies, Addison's disease, and many other disorders.

STETHOSCOPE [stĕth'ə-skōp], device used to listen to sounds produced within the body. Prior to the invention of the stethoscope the physician placed his ear directly against the body of the patient in order to detect sounds. The first stethoscope, a sheet of paper rolled into a cylinder, was fashioned about 1817 by the French physician René Laënnec, in order to examine an obese young woman in whom direct listening was out of the question. The modern instrument consists of two earpieces connected by rubber tubing to a bell or diaphragm which is applied to the patient. Through the use of the stethoscope certain disorders of the heart, lungs, intestines, and blood vessels may be detected. In obstetrics the instrument is used to study the sounds of the fetal heart.

STILLBIRTH. See PREGNANCY.

STIMULANTS [stĭm'yə-lənts], a term applied in medicine principally to drugs which stimulate the central nervous system. These compounds have been used to increase mental alertness and efficiency, to counteract depression, and to stimulate breathing in certain cases of poisoning.

The amphetamines (Benzedrine and Dexedrine) have been widely used for some time to improve the mood of mildly depressed patients and those suffering from chronic illness. Newer drugs for this purpose, sometimes called "psychomotor stimulants," include piperidine derivatives (Pipradol and methylphenidate), the monamine oxidase inhibitors (Marsilid, Catron, Marplan, Niamid, and Nardil), and iminodibenzyl derivatives (Tofranil). While little is known about the nature of the action of these compounds, the monamine oxidase inhibitors are believed to prolong the action of certain hormones in the nervous system (serotinin, epinephrine, and norepinephrine). The psychomotor stimulants are also used to correct some behavior problems in children, to relieve despondency in the aged, and in chronically fatigued patients.

Stimulants used to counteract overdoses of barbiturates and similar depressant poisons are called "analeptics." These drugs, including Nikethamide, Picrotoxin, Metrazol, and Benzedrine are used in such cases to stimulate breathing and circulation and to combat drowsiness. At one time, Metrazol was also used in the treatment of schizophrenia and other mental disorders to produce convulsions.

STOMACH [stŭm'ək]. The stomach is a J-shaped organ which forms that part of the digestive tract between the esophagus and the small intestine. The walls of the stomach contain glandular cells that secrete gastric juice and three layers of smooth muscle that churn the stomach contents and propel it toward the intestines.

Stomach action in digestion begins with the sight or smell of food, which stimulates the flow of what the Russian physiologist Pavlov called appetite juice. If the food is pleasing to the eyes and nose, nervous impulses from the brain stimulate the glandular cells of the stomach to secrete gastric juice. This physiological effect confirms the judgment of the gourmet who believes that healthy digestion is aided by well-prepared food. This is termed the *cephalic*, or psychic, phase of gastric secretion.

Once in the stomach, the food stimulates further gastric secretion by way of the hormone gastrin. Gastrin is released from the cells lining the stomach and travels through the blood stream to act upon the gastric glands. The principal action of gastric juice is to split proteins (found in meat, eggs, milk, and other foods) into simpler compounds. This is accomplished by the enzyme pepsin. The hydrochloric acid contained in the stomach fluid provides the proper acid environment for pepsin action.

The production of hydrochloric acid, a powerful, corrosive, inorganic acid, quite different from the weak organic acids usually found in the body, is an interesting and as yet not completely understood process. The acid is prevented from corroding the stomach by a layer of mucus which covers the inside wall of the organ.

An important aspect of stomach digestion is the mechanical churning of the food accomplished by the waves of muscular contraction that sweep over the stomach at a regular rhythm of about three per minute. These peristaltic movements break up the food into smaller particles and thoroughly mix it with the gastric fluid. When the stomach contents become sufficiently fluid, small amounts pass through the pylorus into the small intestine. As more material accumulates in the intestine, chemical or mechanical stimulation of the intestinal wall inhibits stomach movement, thus reducing the rate of stomach emptying. These stimuli also inhibit the secretion of gastric juice. Fat is an especially powerful inhibitor of stomach action. The inhibition is apparently accomplished by a hormone, enterogastrone, which is released from the intestinal lining and travels through the blood to act upon the stomach.

Disturbance in Gastric Secretion. Anacidity, or absence of free hydrochloric acid in the stomach, is sometimes seen, especially in older persons, and may cause no observable disturbances in stomach function. It is also associated with pathological conditions, such as pernicious anemia and cancer of the stomach.

Hyperacidity, or excessive acid secretion, is often associated with duodenal ulcer. The cause of the excessive stomach secretions in the absence of food stimulation is still unknown. Some authorities cite the importance of psychological factors, since it has been observed that prolonged anger causes reddening and congestion of the gastric mucosa and increased flow of gastric juice.

Hunger Contractions. Muscular contractions of the empty stomach may produce the "pains" associated with hunger. The contractions can be relieved by the presence of any kind of bulk in the stomach. See also DIGESTION.

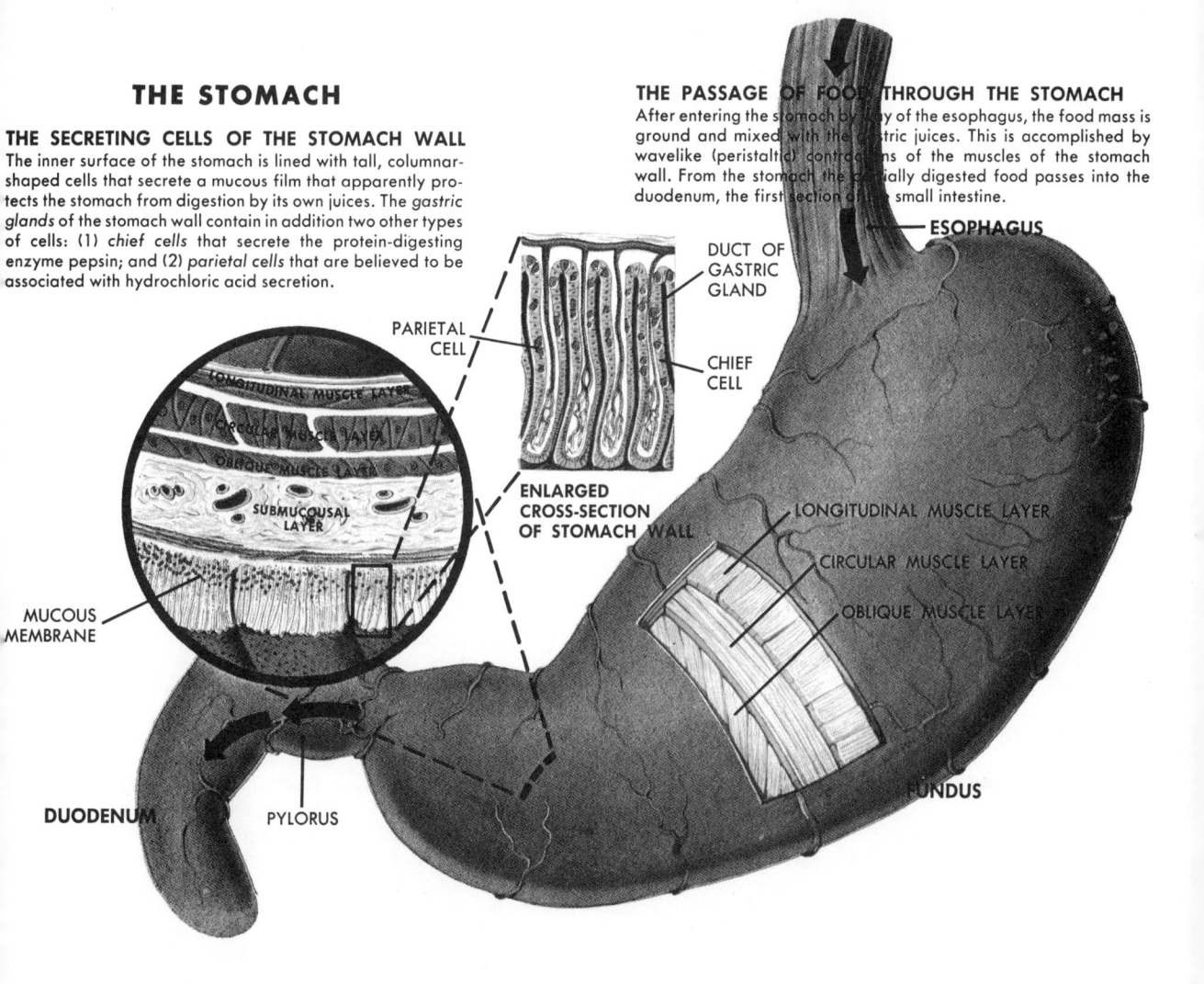

THE STOMACH

THE SECRETING CELLS OF THE STOMACH WALL
The inner surface of the stomach is lined with tall, columnar-shaped cells that secrete a mucous film that apparently protects the stomach from digestion by its own juices. The *gastric glands* of the stomach wall contain in addition two other types of cells: (1) *chief cells* that secrete the protein-digesting enzyme pepsin; and (2) *parietal cells* that are believed to be associated with hydrochloric acid secretion.

THE PASSAGE OF FOOD THROUGH THE STOMACH
After entering the stomach by way of the esophagus, the food mass is ground and mixed with the gastric juices. This is accomplished by wavelike (peristaltic) contractions of the muscles of the stomach wall. From the stomach the partially digested food passes into the duodenum, the first section of the small intestine.

STOMACH PUMP. See GASTROINTESTINAL INTUBATION.

STRABISMUS [strə-biz'məs], a muscular disorder of the eyes in which the eyes point in different directions. In cross-eyes one eye points inward, and in walleyes one eye points outward. In paralytic strabismus, caused by paralysis of one or more of the muscles which move the eyeball, two images are seen (diplopia, or double vision). In nonparalytic strabismus, seen most commonly in children, the eye muscles are normal and double vision is absent. Heredity plays an important role in childhood strabismus. Treatment consists of glasses, drops to relax the focusing muscles, exercises, and, in some cases, surgery to restore muscle balance.

STREPTOCOCCUS [strĕp-tə-kŏk'əs], genus of bacteria that produce lactic acid from the fermentation of sugars. Some members of the genus cause the lactic acid fermentation of the milk sugar, lactose, and are responsible for the souring of milk and cream. This fermentation is important in the production of cheese and butter. Other species of streptococci are normal inhabitants of the respiratory and digestive tracts of man and animals. A number of serious diseases, including scarlet fever, pneumonia, impetigo, erysipelas, and puerperal fever, are caused by streptococci. See also BACTERIA; MICROBIOLOGY.

STREPTOMYCIN [strĕp-tō-mī'sin], highly potent antibiotic, discovered by Dr. Selman A. Waksman and his colleagues in 1944. It is produced by a soil fungus, *Streptomyces griseus*. Streptomycin is used to treat tuberculosis and several other infections caused by bacteria, including tularemia, brucellosis, and plague. It is occasionally effective against streptococcal and staphylococcal infections, also, but is of no value against viruses. Given by injection only, it produces a number of serious side reactions, most of which are related to high doses rather than to allergy, such as may occur with penicillin. Streptomycin's most important toxic effect is damage to the vestibular apparatus in the inner ear, which controls equilibrium. Rarely, it causes deafness and damage to the nerves of the hands and feet.
See also ANTIBIOTICS; TUBERCULOSIS.

STRESS AND STRAIN. The stress at any point in a body is the internal force acting on a unit area at that point. It is convenient to define the normal stress as the force acting

STROKE

perpendicular to the unit area and the shear stress as the force acting parallel to the unit area.

Strain measures the deformation of the body due to the applied stress. Normal strain is defined as the fractional change in distance between two points. A lengthening is called tensile strain, and a reduction in length is called compressive strain. Shear strain is defined as the change in the angle between two straight lines drawn inside the body which were perpendicular before deformation. Hooke's law is a mathematical relationship which states that strain is proportional to the local stress, if the deformations are small.

STROKE, also known as apoplexy or cerebral vascular accident (CVA), is an injury to the brain caused by a temporary or permanent interruption in the flow of blood to the brain. This may be caused by rupture of a blood vessel, by formation of a blood clot within an artery (thrombosis), or by the obstruction of an artery by an embolus (a clot fragment or other substance which has traveled to the brain from another part of the body). Hemorrhages following ruptured blood vessels are often associated with high blood pressure and arteriosclerosis. Brain emboli are most often seen in cases of heart disease.

The disturbances caused by the stroke depend upon the particular blood vessel affected and the function of the brain tissue which it supplies. Since the left part of the brain largely controls the right part of the body, and vice versa, symptoms usually appear opposite to the side on which the damage occurs. Brain tissue receives its oxygen supply by means of the blood and is extremely sensitive to even brief periods of oxygen deprivation.

Symptoms. The symptoms usually appear suddenly. If the stroke occurs while the patient is walking, he may stumble and fall as his leg becomes paralyzed. If he is eating, the arm may suddenly feel heavy and fall limply to his side. If it occurs during sleep, the patient may not awaken then but may fall to the floor when he attempts to arise in the morning. While small strokes may produce only weakness of one arm or leg or one corner of the mouth, larger strokes may produce paralysis, loss of sensation, and difficulty in pronouncing words, forming sentences, and thinking properly. In some cases brain damage occurs without producing any apparent symptoms—in such instances "silent areas" of the brain are said to be involved —so called because their function is still unknown.

Coma, or loss of consciousness, and convulsions are not often seen in the course of a stroke and, if present, suggest extensive and severe damage. This may result from the severest type of vascular accident—actual bleeding into the brain tissue. Cerebral hemorrhage is often fatal.

Treatment. Treatment is directed first toward saving the patient's life and second to correcting the paralysis and weakness that persist after the crisis has passed. Immediately following the stroke, the patient may require skillful nursing care. It may be necessary to administer nutrition through the veins. In some cases the patient is unable to urinate, and a tubular instrument (a catheter) may have to be introduced into the urinary tract to maintain the flow of urine and prevent distension of the bladder. Sedatives are generally avoided as they tend to depress breathing.

The second stage of treatment consists of restoring function to the paralyzed area through a guided program of exercise (physical therapy). The prospects for recovery of lost function depend on the severity of the stroke. A person with minimal weakness of one arm may rapidly recover in a matter of days to weeks, whereas others with minimal symptoms may recover only slightly because the affected part of the brain has been irreparably damaged.

STRYCHNINE [strĭk'nĭn], alkaloid drug obtained from the seeds of *Nux vomica*, a tree native to India. Strychnine is a strong nervous system stimulant which, in sufficient doses, produces convulsions with powerful, sustained (tetanic) muscle contractions, and death through paralysis of the respiratory center of the brain. Once used as a tonic and intestinal stimulant, strychnine is now generally recognized to have no valid medical applications, except possibly as an antidote to barbiturate poisoning. It is still used in rat poisons.

STUTTERING, speech disorder marked by repetitious, labored, and hesitant speech. Affecting about 1% of the population, stuttering is a poorly understood disorder with a history extending to Biblical times. Moses is believed to have been a stutterer, as were Aesop, Aristotle, and Vergil, and in recent times Somerset Maugham and Sir Winston Churchill.

Abundant speculation as to the cause of stuttering has marked it as the "disorder of many theories." The ancient Greek physician Hippocrates attributed it to a "dryness of the tongue," and Aristotle considered it to be caused by a thick and hard tongue. The idea of a tongue abnormality as the basis of stuttering persisted into the 19th century, when European surgeons devoted great attention to devising surgical cures for stuttering, all of which failed.

A large variety of theories is currently held by workers in the field. These are divided into those ascribing stuttering to an organic abnormality of the nervous and muscle mechanisms employed in speech and those which hold that emotional and psychological disturbances are prominent. Supporting the first school are studies indicating that children who stutter are more awkward and are slow in learning how to walk and in performing other tasks requiring muscle co-ordination. Such children were also observed to be retarded in speech development. Evidence for a psychological theory of stuttering can be found in the many observations citing the tense family background of children who stutter.

Known Facts About Stuttering. The following facts can be offered: Stuttering is from four to eight times more frequent in males than females. Stuttering often appears in several members of the same family. Stuttering is more frequent in twins, left-handed persons, and in ambidextrous persons.

The stutterer has difficulty with about 10% of his words, repeating or prolonging the initial sound (for example, "l-l-like"). Associated with this is an exaggerated hesitancy before speaking and characteristic signs such as closing the eyes and dilating the nostrils. Stuttering is reduced when the individual reads or sings in chorus.

Stuttering in Children. Most cases of stuttering begin in childhood. As the youngster begins to talk he normally repeats 40 to 50 of every thousand words. In a family setting of warmth and relaxation speech fluency gradually develops. If, however, the parents are perfectionists, they may find this normal hesitancy alarming and diagnose the child as a stutterer. The parents' anxiety is communicated to the child, making him tense in speaking situations and eventually converting him into a stutterer.

Stuttering may begin more dramatically following a violent experience, such as being frightened by a dog, or being thrown into a lake. In such cases the incident may not be solely responsible for the stuttering, but simply acts as a precipitating factor on an already emotionally disturbed child.

The child is not immediately aware of his stuttering, but in time this is made painfully clear by the attitude of those around him, particularly his playmates. He then develops "secondary blocking"—speaking becomes forced and strained. Eventually he resorts to various devices and rituals designed to aid in speaking. These mechanisms include using synonyms in place of difficult words and making use of "starters" (acts such as stamping the feet or clenching the fist) which are designed to help the stutterer begin talking.

The Adult Stutterer. By the time the stutterer reaches adulthood, the act of speaking and all situations associated with it have assumed central importance in his life. He is constantly plagued by the fear of being unable to speak and dreads each moment when he must. He becomes obsessed with the pursuit of perfect speech and will, unrealistically, settle for nothing less. He enlists more and more devices to aid in speaking, resorting to coining new words when synonyms fail and becoming more and more attached to the starters, the neurotic aids to speech.

The net effect of his disability is to isolate the stutterer socially. He must go through life avoiding personal contacts demanding speech, thus handicapping him severely in his pursuit of employment. He may come to resent a world which places so much emphasis on speaking and he may feel that he is entitled to special consideration because of his handicap.

Treatment. There are two basic approaches to the treatment of stuttering: (1) psychotherapy and (2) speech therapy.

(1) The psychotherapeutic approach considers stuttering a manifestation of a deeper-lying personality disturbance. In childhood the aim of therapy is to reduce the anxiety and tension associated with speaking. This may be accomplished through the parents. The therapist attempts to make them aware of the importance of not making the child feel different from others, of encouraging the child to mix with others, and of avoiding concentrating on the child's speech problem. Above all they must envelop the child in an atmosphere of warmth and acceptance. In older stutterers the therapist seeks to uncover the neurotic conflicts of the stutterer and to help him resolve them.

(2) Speech therapists regard stuttering as a learned form of behavior which can be corrected by specific techniques. Among these are:

Voluntary Stuttering. The stutterer is encouraged to imitate himself, to stutter intentionally. Having some control over the act, he is then asked to alter consciously his pattern of stuttering. Finally he attempts to speak with greater fluency.

Differential Relaxation. The stutterer attempts to contract and relax consciously the muscles used in articulation. Thus he presses as hard or as lightly as possible in making specific sounds. In this way he develops greater control over the act of speech.

Adaptation. This employs successive readings of the same material. The stutterer usually improves in the later readings, thus demonstrating to himself that he can speak without stuttering.

See also SPEECH DISORDERS AND SPEECH THERAPY.

STY [stī], an infection of one or more of the glands which line the eyelid. Sties are frequently associated with poor health and inflammation of the eyelids. They are usually caused by the staphylococcus bacteria, the same organisms which produce boils and wound infections. *Internal sties* are found at the inside margin of the eyelid. *External sties* involve the glands located at the base of the lashes. The sty first appears as a red area. Eventually a yellow spot develops which ruptures and releases pus. The irritation causes the eye to tear and renders it sensitive to light. The symptoms are more pronounced in cases of internal sties. Treatment consists of hot wet compresses to bring the infection to a head, and local antibiotics. Recurrences are common.

See also STAPHYLOCOCCUS.

SUICIDE [sū′ə-sīd] (Lat. *sui*, "of oneself"; *cide*, "a killing"), the act of voluntarily taking one's own life. This includes failure to avoid death when possible to do so, and also self-initiated action which directly results in death, such as driving an automobile at very high speed on a crowded highway. However, it is sometimes difficult to determine whether the death was suicide or accidental. Furthermore, some attempts at suicide appear to be little more than dramatic gestures toward self-destruction. Under certain circumstances, such as taking a small number of sleeping pills and calling a physician, the probability of death may hardly exist. Under other circumstances, such as jumping from a high building, the probability is almost certain. Such factors must be weighed in determining suicide.

Theories as to Causes. In the vast literature of speculation and research on the subject of suicide the work of the 19th-century French sociologist Émile Durkheim (1858–1917) still holds a prominent place. Rejecting recorded reasons for suicide as unreliable evidence, Durkheim, in his study *Le suicide* (1897), drew upon population facts to show that high suicide rates were due to a loss of integration in society. He concluded that people commit suicide when the constraining influence of society's rules over the individual declines and cohesion in family, religious, and political life is lost. This condition of social disorganization, Durkheim maintained, produces various types of suicide: *egoistic*, resulting from an excessive sense of individuality; *anomic*, growing out of intensified competition for limitless goals; and *altruistic*, arising from an opposite condition, excessive domination of the individual by society which compels self-destruction for social ends. This is exemplified by the old custom (*suttee*), long since banned, in India which required a Hindu widow to sacrifice herself on the funeral pyre of her dead husband. Indian society had no place for widows and thus solved the problem of what to do with them. The Japanese practice of *hara-kiri* (ritualistic disemboweling) in the face of disgrace is another example of suicide demanded by social convention.

While social disorganization, which so impressed Durkheim, undoubtedly has an important bearing on suicide, largely through detaching the individual from society, nevertheless psychic processes must also be considered. Unfortunately the manner of their operation is far from clear. Suicide is sometimes held to be a symptom of mental disorder, but persons with a history or evidence of mental abnormality constitute only a small portion of the total number of suicides.

Explanations of suicide in terms of psychological motivation generally emphasize the turning inward of aggressive impulses generated by early childhood experiences of parental rejection or loss of parental love. The wish to be killed is held to be a blocked or disguised form of the wish to kill. Suicide satisfies both the aggressive impulses of the individual and his need for punishment arising from his sense of guilt because of the socially unacceptable desire to kill others.

The psychological love-deprivation-and-aggression theory and the social disorganization theory of suicide have been combined in the proposition that homicide and suicide are basically the same and differ only in the object toward which the underlying aggression is directed. According to this explanation, where social relationships are strong, homicide rates will be high and suicide rates will be low. Conversely, where social bonds are weak, suicide rates will exceed homicide rates. Some actuarial data support this theory, others do not. An additional difficulty in the theory arises from its treatment of suicide and homicide as similar acts. This ignores differences in associated values and reactions of society, particularly the criminal aspect of homicide, which is missing in suicide.

The psychological conflicts often found associated with suicide need to be traced to conflicting values in the individual's group relationships. Many of these conflicts revolve around the recurrent status problems of the aged, widowed, incapacitated, or those caught in insoluble dilemmas of politics or love. The study of the details of suicide actions in their social context is a way of revealing these dilemmas and the cultural significance of the means chosen as a solution.

Differences in the destructive probabilities of the means of suicide indicate that in many situations risk taking and chance, "gambling with death" rather than definitely seeking it, are the individual's solution to his dilemmas. Such risk taking dramatizes the social aspect of the conflict. It also communicates the individual's plight to others, and, depending on the degree of risk involved, invites them to do something about it.

Social control cannot be excluded from any analysis of suicide. Societies organize formally and informally to intervene in the suicide situation and prevent the act. Raymond Firth has shown that on the island of Tikopia, where many suicides take the form of swimming out to sea or undertaking a lone canoe voyage, the success of the attempt often hinges on the decision to embark a rescue fleet and on the composition and efficiency of the fleet in operation. In advanced, industrialized societies the policing of bridges, observation platforms of high buildings, or volcano craters, as in Japan, and the activities of suicide prevention organizations all reflect the kinds of social control which affect suicide rates. Indirect controls exist in regulations of insurance companies which specify waiting periods before payment of suicide death claims.

It seems clear that no one theory is sufficient to account for the complexities of the suicide act.

SULFA [sŭl'fə] **DRUGS or SULFONAMIDES,** group of drugs which constituted the major therapeutic tool in the treatment of infectious diseases prior to the development of the antibiotics. Although the first sulfa drug, sulfanilamide, was prepared in 1908, the antibacterial properties of these compounds were not fully tested until the early 1930's.

The sulfa compounds do not kill bacteria. The drugs apparently interfere with bacterial growth, injuring them in a manner which enables certain cells of the body to consume and destroy them. According to a widely accepted theory, the sulfa drugs act through their chemical resemblance to PABA (para-aminobenzoic acid), a substance needed for bacterial growth. Because of this resemblance the bacteria is "fooled" into consuming the sulfa drug instead of the vital PABA.

Bacteria originally susceptible to sulfa drugs may develop resistance after a period of exposure. This fact became generally appreciated in the early 1940's when the cure rate for gonorrhea treated with sulfa drugs dropped sharply. Outbreaks of sulfonamide-resistant respiratory infections (caused by hemolytic streptococci) appeared in U.S. military camps in 1944.

Although the introduction of antibiotics deprived the sulfonamide group of its unique status in the treatment of infectious diseases, the drugs are still of considerable importance. They are used in cases of urinary tract infections, meningococcal infections, cholera, bacillary dysentery, trachoma (a virus disease affecting the eyes), and other disorders. In many instances the drugs are given in conjunction with antibiotics, producing a total effect which might be unobtainable with either drug alone. Several nonabsorbable sulfonamides are used as "intestinal antiseptics," being given prior to abdominal surgery to reduce the number of bacteria in the intestine and to reduce the probability of postoperative abdominal infection.

The sulfonamides are potentially highly toxic drugs, and must be given under close medical supervision. A rare but serious complication of their use is the deposition of crystals in the kidney and the appearance of blood in the urine. Fever, anemia, skin eruptions, bone marrow depression, and liver involvement may also be seen. The use of mixtures of sulfa drugs instead of single preparations considerably reduces the frequency of kidney complications.

SULFONES [sŭl'fōnz], group of drugs used to treat leprosy. They are related chemically to sulfonamides. Before introduction of the sulfones in 1941, there were no drugs available to halt or cure leprosy. Because the bacillus, which causes leprosy is similar to the tuberculosis bacillus, the sulfones were also tested against tuberculosis, but without success.

Sulfones do not destroy but suppress the leprosy bacillus, so that the patient's own defenses slowly overcome the disease. They probably work by competing for paraminobenzoic acid, a chemical essential to the bacillus' growth. The drugs must be taken by mouth for many years before leprosy is controlled or cured. Unfortunately, they produce many severe side effects, including anemia due to destruction of red blood cells, nausea, vomiting, and skin rash. Although the sulfones act slowly, no better agents have been developed for control of leprosy.

SUNBURN is caused principally by the short ultraviolet waves in sunlight. These rays penetrate clouds and fog but are stopped by ordinary window glass. Reflected sunlight from water, snow, and sand can produce sunburn. Blondes are more susceptible than darker-complexioned persons. Within 24 hours after exposure the redness, blisters, and burning pains associated with sunburn reach maximum intensity. This is followed by peeling of the skin, with itching, and increase in pigmentation, or tanning. Treatment consists of soothing emulsions and wet compresses. Sunburn can be prevented by gradual, repeated exposures which build up protective pigmentation in the skin. Protective lotions and creams are also helpful.

SUPPOSITORY [sə-pŏz′ə-tôr-ē], a solid medicated mass shaped for introduction into the rectum, vagina, or urethra. Prepared from theobroma oil and glycerinated gelatin or other materials which melt at body temperature, suppositories are used to administer laxatives, anesthetics, sedatives, analgesics, and other medications. They are ordinarily given in cases of vomiting or in other instances when drugs cannot be administered by mouth. Lubricating suppositories are used for their laxative effect and to relieve irritation from painful hemorrhoids or fissures. Vaginal suppositories containing antiseptics and disinfectants are used as an aid to feminine hygiene.

SURGERY [sûr′jər-ē]. Three thousand years before the birth of Christ the Egyptians prepared the earliest known treatise on surgery. For the next 4,000 years surgery progressed slowly, impeded by beliefs in magic and devils as sources of disease and by an unwillingness to dissect the human body after death to discover the cause of disease and to obtain accurate anatomical knowledge.

During the Renaissance medicine made great strides, but surgery remained a questionable trade practiced mainly by itinerant barbers. These men went about cutting for bladder stones, draining blood from sick patients to release fevers and evil spirits, and generally causing more harm than good. Death and suffering were the expected results of surgery.

There were, nevertheless, some signs of an awakening. Following the invention of the printing press, books on anatomy by men such as Vesalius became available. In France, Ambroise Paré discarded the crude method of cauterizing wounds with boiling oil and devised techniques for ligating arteries to prevent hemorrhage.

Beginning of Modern Surgery. Modern abdominal surgery was inaugurated in 1809, when Ephraim McDowell, an unknown surgeon in the Kentucky wilderness, successfully removed an abdominal tumor. The fact that his patient survived undoubtedly saved McDowell from death at the hands of an angry mob which had gathered outside his home, outraged that anyone would attempt such a procedure.

Now two major problems held back the progress of surgery: the need for anesthesia and the ever-present danger of postoperative infection. In the 1840's surgery received the priceless gift of anesthesia from the independent efforts of doctors Crawford Long of Georgia, William Morton and Horace Wells of New England, and James Simpson of England. In the 1850's Louis Pasteur demonstrated the role of bacteria in infection. The English surgeon Joseph Lister soon applied this concept to surgery by using carbolic acid sprays to prevent postoperative infections—the beginning of modern aseptic technique.

These two discoveries, anesthesia and asepsis, have made possible the tremendous advances of modern surgery. In the 20th century still further important refinements were introduced. Surgeons discovered the nature and treatment of shock, the frequently fatal collapse of the circulation resulting from nervous reaction to the operation or from extensive loss of blood. Techniques were devised for processing and storing blood to be used in operations. The pathologist Karl Landsteiner made blood transfusions feasible by solving the mystery of blood groups. Surgeons mastered the technique of replacing diseased or damaged tissues with natural or artificial substitutes, leading to the use of bone grafts to heal fractures, eye parts (corneas taken from deceased persons) to restore sight, and skin grafts to repair damage from ulcers and burns.

Techniques of Modern Surgery

Aseptic Technique. The early use of a simple antiseptic by Lister has now mushroomed into an elaborate, almost ritualistic method of sterilizing and handling surgical instruments and preparing the surgical field. All objects that might carry bacterial contamination are banned from the operating room. Before the operation the drapes, towels, gauze, sponges, and surgical instruments are sterilized by steam under pressure in an autoclave. The surgeon, his assistants, and nurses wear cloth caps and masks over their noses and mouths. They scrub their hands and arms to above the elbows. The operating room dress consists of knee-length sterile gowns and sterile rubber gloves with long cuffs that fit tightly over the cuffs of the operating gowns. Before the drapes are applied to the patient, the area to be operated on is treated with soaps and chemicals to make it sterile. The patient is then ready for the operation.

Anesthesia. There are several kinds of anesthesia. In *general anesthesia* the patient is unconscious. In *spinal anesthesia* the patient may be conscious but loses sensation in the entire portion of the body which lies below the point in the spinal cord at which the anesthesia is injected. In *local anesthesia* sensation is lost in a limited part of the body, such as an arm, leg, or a small patch of skin.

General anesthesia is most commonly used. Usually a preanesthetic medication (a barbiturate) is injected into the patient's vein causing him to fall asleep quickly. Once the patient is completely unconscious, the anesthesia may be continued with anesthetic gases, such as ether or nitrous oxide, which are administered with a face mask. During the operation small quantities of gas are administered periodically to keep the patient anesthetized.

In spinal anesthesia the anesthetic is injected into the space around the spinal cord. The patient may remain awake throughout the operation but feels no pain, or he may be given light sedatives to let him sleep.

SURGERY

Local anesthesia is used for simple operations, such as removing a small skin growth. The anesthetic may be injected into the nerves which supply the area or directly into the area of the operation.

The Operating Room and the Surgical Team. Modern surgery is performed by a highly trained team consisting of the surgeon; his assistants, who may be surgeons in training; an anesthesiologist; and a "scrub" nurse. The surgeon's assistants keep the incision clear of blood with gauze sponges, ensure good exposure of the area being operated upon, and assist the surgeon in other ways. The scrub nurse passes instruments and supplies, counts sponges so that none may be left in the patient, and prepares suture materials. The anesthesiologist continuously checks the patient's heart and breathing rates and maintains the proper depth of anesthesia. During surgery there is no unnecessary word or gesture, and an observer is impressed with the quietness and speed of the experienced surgical team.

The different organs and organ systems of the body present the surgeon with special problems. With the advances in surgical technique, numerous surgical subspecialties have developed.

Abdominal Surgery

Abdominal surgery generally falls into two groups: operations which must be done immediately (emergency operations) and operations which can be delayed (elective operations).

Emergency Surgery. Probably the most common emergency procedure is that done for appendicitis, inflammation of the wormlike blind pouch in the intestine called the appendix. The classical symptoms of lower right abdominal pain associated with abdominal tenderness and frequently preceded by nausea and vomiting are widely known. Treatment consists of removing the appendix at its attachment to the upper portion of the large bowel. Delay in treatment may lead to serious complications, particularly perforation of the appendix, which permits the intestinal contents to spill into the abdominal cavity.

An important abdominal emergency arises when the intestine becomes obstructed. This may be caused by pinching of the intestine between strands of fibrous tissue (adhesions) which have developed following surgery, by loops of bowel bunched together in a hernia condition, or by a large cancer. Patients with obstructions usually have distended abdomens. These patients are given fluids and blood intravenously and are prepared for surgery as rapidly as possible, since the risk of surgery increases with every hour the obstruction persists.

Gastric and duodenal ulcers may require emergency surgery if perforations, or holes, develop through the base of the ulcers permitting digestive juices to pour into the intestinal cavity. This produces a characteristic sudden and severe abdominal pain and massive infection of the abdominal cavity. These patients usually seek prompt medical attention. Recovery is usually rapid after the perforated ulcer is closed and the abdominal cavity cleaned.

Some cases of acute inflammation of the gall bladder (acute cholecystitis) may also perforate and spread the contents of the bladder throughout the abdomen. In such cases the gall bladder is usually removed. In extremely severe cases the gall bladder may be drained by a tube leading out through the abdominal wall. The bladder is removed later when the patient's condition has improved.

Less commonly, emergency abdominal surgery is necessitated by disorders of the ovaries, the female reproductive organs which hang free on rather loose attachments to the abdominal wall. They may occasionally twist on themselves, obstructing their blood supply and causing gangrene. The condition requires surgical removal of the ovaries.

Abdominal organs most frequently involved in accidental injury are the spleen, liver, and kidneys, although any organ may be affected. Blood or intestinal contents may be spilled into the abdominal cavity, irritating the inner abdominal wall and causing severe pain. Immediate surgery is needed. A ruptured spleen must be removed. The liver, which is frequently lacerated in abdominal injuries, may be sewn up. Injured intestines are sutured to prevent further leakage of their contents.

Elective, or Nonemergency, Surgery. Elective surgery accounts for most abdominal operations. One of the most common is for chronic gall bladder disease (cholecystitis). Repeated attacks of mild inflammation frequently cause stones to form in the gall bladder. The stones may lead to infection or block the flow of bile fluid, causing the bile pigments to accumulate in the blood resulting in jaundice, a yellowish tinting of the eyes and skin. In such cases the gall bladder may be removed. Individuals without gall bladders lead normal lives and do not require a special diet.

Elective surgery is also called for in cases of gastric and duodenal ulcers which resist treatment by drugs and special diets. Most surgery for these conditions is directed at severing the vagus nerve connection to the stomach. This reduces the secretion of acid which caused the ulcer. In such cases surgery at the lower end of the stomach also permits it to empty faster and further reduces stomach acid production.

Removal of the spleen is done in certain forms of anemia in which this organ destroys blood elements faster than the bone marrow can produce them.

Another common elective operation is for repair of hernias. These are usually the result of congenital defects in the abdominal wall. Abdominal contents may protrude through the weakened area, and loops of bowel may become squeezed, or "strangulated," possibly resulting in gangrene. Hernias are repaired by tightening up the layers of the abdominal wall over the defect with silk sutures.

Surgery of the Heart and Blood Vessels

The Heart. The heart may be malformed at birth in such a way that blood flows in the wrong direction through abnormal openings. These can often be repaired by closing the hole with sutures or sewing a plasticlike patch in place. Such surgery is made possible by the heart-lung machine, a device which pumps and oxygenates blood while the heart is being repaired.

The large blood vessels arising from the heart may also be the site of congenital abnormalities which cause blood to be circulated in an abnormal fashion. Surgical correction in these cases is more difficult and less satisfactory than in heart surgery.

The Arteries. The commonest arterial disease is arteriosclerosis, or hardening of the arteries. In this condition deposits of cholesterol and calcium build up on the inside walls of the artery, narrowing its opening and reducing the flow of blood. At times the artery may be completely blocked by a blood clot. This is the most common cause of coronary heart attack. When arteriosclerosis occurs in large arteries, it may be possible to remove the clot, if one is present, or to clean out the core of deposited cholesterol and calcium on the inside of the vessel wall. The small coronary arteries supplying the heart muscle may also be treated in this way. If the affected vessel is badly diseased, part of it may be replaced by tubes of synthetic material.

Occasionally a weakened section of artery bulges out under the pressure of the blood. These local swellings, or aneurysms, should be removed lest they rupture or block other arteries. Synthetic patches may also be used to repair defects left after the removal of aneurysms.

The Veins. Varicose veins usually occur in the legs. The veins become elongated and dilated as the valves which normally prevent backflow fail. If a vein becomes large, painful, or inflamed, it may be removed by threading a long, heavy wire down the vein, tying it to one end of the vein wall, and pulling on the other end of the wire to strip the vein from the leg.

Surgery of the Chest, or Thoracic Surgery

Congenital defects of the chest most often involve the heart and the large vessels which arise from the heart (as described above). Other defects include failure of the esophagus to develop and abnormal connections between the esophagus and the trachea (the windpipe). A congenital defect of the diaphragm (the horizontal sheet of muscle between the abdomen and chest) may permit the abdominal organs to protrude into the chest cavity. These conditions require prompt surgical correction, frequently in the first day or two after birth.

Tuberculosis. Although tuberculosis is now principally treated with drugs, surgery may be necessary to remove parts of the lung where the infection has localized to form a small cavity.

Chest injuries involving the heart and lungs are often fatal if not immediately corrected. Tubes are placed into the chest to remove collections of blood and air compressing the lungs following puncture of the lung or a large blood vessel. If this does not result in prompt re-expansion of the lung, the chest must be opened and the leaks repaired with sutures. Occasionally the heart may be punctured so that blood leaks into the sac which surrounds the heart. The blood can be removed through a needle introduced into the chest but may reaccumulate and require opening the chest and direct repair of the injured heart.

Cancer of the lung is increasing and requires surgical removal of the tumor and surrounding tissue. At times an entire lung may be removed.

Orthopedic Surgery—Surgery of Muscle and Bone

Osteomyelitis, or bacterial infection of the bone, although less common than formerly, is still a serious problem which often requires surgical treatment to remove dead bone and to drain pus from the infected area.

Fractures are a principal concern of orthopedic surgeons. While most fractures can be treated by manipulating the bone and immobilizing it in a plaster cast, surgical treatment is needed if the broken bone protrudes through the skin. Surgery may also be required in some severe fractures to align the bone properly. In such cases a metal screw, plate, wire, or pin is used to hold the bone ends together. If fractures fail to heal normally, small pieces of healthy bone are taken from another bone in the patient's body and grafted to the fracture site, where they stimulate new bone growth.

Congenital defects of the muscles and bones may frequently be corrected by braces or other appliances. In severe cases surgery may help increase functioning of the affected part. Webbed fingers can be separated, and extra digits can be removed. Bones can be reshaped by removing segments, and tendons can be planted in new positions to enable muscles to function more efficiently. Tightened tissues can be cut and lengthened.

Surgery of the Eye and Ear

Emergency eye surgery may be performed to remove foreign particles from the eye. Most such particles are metallic and are removed by making an incision in the eye and drawing out the metal with a powerful magnet. Nonmagnetic foreign bodies can sometimes be grasped with forceps but are extremely difficult, and in some cases impossible, to remove. Injury to the eye may result in detachment of the retina, the light-sensitive layer in the rear of the eye. Special equipment has been designed to reattach the retina to the rear surface of the eye. The results are generally good.

Nonemergency operations account for the bulk of eye surgery. Removal of the lens of the eye, which focuses the image on the retina, restores sight to individuals suffering from cataract, a fairly common disorder seen in older persons in which the normally transparent lens is darkened. Cross-eye is corrected by lengthening or shortening the muscles which move the eyeballs so that the eyes move together. Another sight-restoring operation replaces diseased corneas (the transparent window in the front of the eye) with a normal cornea taken from the eye of a recently deceased person who has donated his cornea.

Ear surgery is directed primarily at restoring hearing. Perforated eardrums are replaced with artificial drums made of vein wall which are sutured in place of the nonfunctioning eardrum. Deafness from otosclerosis, in which one of the small bones of the middle ear is fixed in place, is treated by jarring the bone free or by making an artificial window between the middle and inner ears.

Surgery of the Nervous System

The Brain. Tumors of the brain pose a difficult problem for the neurosurgeon. Complete removal is frequently not possible, but partial removal sometimes temporarily relieves symptoms.

Skull injuries may lead to blood clots which compress brain tissue. In these cases surgery is often highly successful. A small opening is made in the skull overlying the clot, permitting evacuation of the blood.

Pressure on the brain may also be produced by abscesses, localized infections which are carried to the brain from other parts of the body. The infection may respond

SYMPATHECTOMY

to antibiotics, but usually surgery is necessary to drain the cavity.

In the congenital disease called hydrocephalus, normal drainage of the fluid (cerebrospinal fluid) surrounding the brain is blocked. If drainage is not established, fluid collects in the brain, steadily compressing the brain substance and interfering with function. Several ingenious operations have been devised to divert the cerebrospinal fluid into sites such as the ureter, abdominal cavity, or blood stream where it can be excreted or absorbed.

Spinal Cord. Spinal tumors are less common than brain tumors and can be more successfully treated. Most spinal tumors arise from tissues surrounding the spinal cord and produce symptoms by compressing the nerve tracts within the cord. Total removal of the tumor usually relieves the condition. In cases in which the tumor arises within the cord, surgery is of little value.

Surgery of the Urinary System and Male Reproductive Organs—Urology

Tumors—Cancerous and Noncancerous. Cancers of the kidney and the ureter, the tube leading from the kidney to the bladder, require removal of the organ, provided that the other kidney is functioning normally. Noncancerous tumors of the kidney and ureter may often be excised without disturbing normal function. Depending upon the type, bladder tumors may require simple excision or complete removal of the bladder. The tubes which carry urine from the kidney may then be implanted either in the skin or to a loop of bowel to allow drainage of urine.

Obstruction of urinary flow may be caused by stones in the kidney or ureter or by enlargement of the prostate gland, which envelops the urethra as it leaves the bladder. Most small stones are spontaneously passed in the urine, but large stones require surgical removal. In some cases the stone can be manipulated by a special instrument which is passed through the urethra and bladder and then into the ureter. If this fails, abdominal surgery is required. The ureter is opened, and the stone is removed.

Enlargement of the prostate gland is usually seen in men past 50. The enlarged gland may obstruct the flow of urine by constricting the urethra, the tube which conducts urine from the bladder. Frequently the prostate can be operated upon by introducing instruments through the penis. If the gland is too large, surgery through the bladder is required.

Infections. Although most infections of the genitourinary tract are treated with antibiotics, surgery is sometimes necessary to remove a kidney or to drain pus from an abscess.

See also FRACTURES; GYNECOLOGY; MEDICINE; PLASTIC SURGERY.

SYMPATHECTOMY [sĭm-pə-thĕk′tə-mē], an operation to sever certain fibers of the sympathetic part of the visceral, or autonomic, nervous system—branch of the nervous system that automatically controls the activity of the internal organs. Interruption of fibers controlling the smooth muscles in the walls of small arteries may allow these arteries to open wider, permitting passage of a greater volume of blood. This is of value in relieving the symptoms of arterial constriction in certain diseases of the blood vessels (for example, Buerger's disease and Raynaud's disease) and may also help to lower high blood pressure. Sympathectomy has also been performed to relieve severe pain in cases of pancreatitis and other pelvic disorders and to control excessive sweating (hyperhidrosis) in certain parts of the body.

See also NERVOUS SYSTEM.

SYPHILIS [sĭf-ə-lĭs], a serious venereal disease found throughout the world. Prior to the discovery of America by Columbus, syphilis was unknown in Europe. Many members of Columbus' crew returned with the disease, presumably having become infected through contact with the native women on the island of Haiti. The disease was rapidly spread through Spain and Portugal by the sailors and eventually caused a great epidemic during the late 15th and early 16th centuries. Spanish mercenaries brought the disease with them when they joined the army of Charles VIII of France in the campaign against Naples in 1495. Syphilis marched alongside the invading army through the Italian countryside. The French called it the "Neapolitan disease," and the Italians, with equal graciousness, called it *morbus Gallicus*, the "French disease." The following year the Neapolitans expelled the French army from Italy. In dispersing to their native lands, the soldiers carried syphilis to every corner of Europe. Later, infected Portuguese sailors spread the illness to Asia.

Syphilis, the "Great Imitator." Because of its ability to invade every tissue of the body and to produce symptoms resembling many other illnesses, syphilis has been called the "Great Imitator." It affects human beings exclusively and, unlike most diseases, can be transmitted by an infected mother to her unborn child, causing spontaneous abortion, stillbirth, or congenital syphilis.

The *Treponema pallidum*, the corkscrew-shaped microorganism which causes syphilis, can survive only in a liquid medium and is consequently ideally transmitted by sexual contact or kissing. The course of the disease is usually divided into several stages: primary, secondary, latent, and tertiary, or late, syphilis.

Primary syphilis appears as a sore, or chancre, on the genitals about three or four weeks after sexual contact with an infected person.

Secondary syphilis follows about four to six weeks later with the appearance of a widespread skin eruption, slight fever, headache, enlargement of the lymph glands, and sore throat. Lesions frequently occur in the mouth and about the genital and anal areas.

Latent syphilis is the stage during which the primary and secondary lesions heal and no visible signs of syphilis are present. However, the syphilitic organisms remain alive and active in the tissues, slowly damaging vital structures. Latent syphilis is frequently discovered through routine blood testing given to servicemen, pregnant women, or individuals about to be married.

Tertiary, or late, syphilis may appear up to 30 or more years after the original infection. The individual may undergo mental deterioration, becoming irritable, quarrelsome, and intemperate, and displaying other personality changes resulting from invasion of brain tissue by the treponema. The organisms may attack the spinal cord causing disorders of gait. An aneurysm, or "blowout," of the aorta (the large artery which leaves the heart) may result from weakening of the arterial wall by the syphilitic organisms. Other manifestations of late syphilis include heart disease, blindness (from involvement of the optic nerve), and liver disease.

Treatment. Penicillin is highly effective in treating syphilis. A course of injections is given, following which the patient is periodically examined for several years to be certain that no treponema remain. Although penicillin can halt further progression of tertiary syphilis, it cannot reverse the tissue damage which has already occurred.

Control. Despite the availability of an effective cure, the control of syphilis remains a difficult problem because of the social aspects of the disease. One method of control has been mentioned above—routine blood testing. Perhaps the most important aspect of control is locating and treating the contacts of the patient to halt further spread of the disease. This is obviously a tedious and difficult job, which requires considerable tact and skill.
See also VENEREAL DISEASES.

T

TABES DORSALIS [tā'bēz dôr-sā'lĭs], or locomotor ataxia, a late manifestation of syphilis involving the spinal cord. Occurring some 5 to 40 years after the original syphilitic infection, tabes may cause sharp stabbing pains in the lower limbs, sensations of numbness in the legs, and gastric crises, attacks of severe pain in the abdomen associated with vomiting. Men may become sexually impotent. The hip, knee, and ankle joints may become eroded into a "bag of bones." In addition, a characteristic drunken, staggering gait is often seen. Penicillin halts the progression of the disease and may relieve some symptoms, but it does not affect the sexual impotence and joint damage.

TAPEWORM, scientific name cestode, important group of parasites. The adult worms attach to the intestinal wall, where they may survive for many years. The larval forms of some species attack other organs, such as the liver, brain, lungs, and muscles.

Intestinal Tapeworms. The commonest and smallest tapeworm of man is the dwarf tapeworm, *Hymenolepis nana*, which is found throughout the world. Infectious eggs are passed in the stool, and humans acquire the infection by eating contaminated food or by putting soiled fingers in the mouth (this is apt to occur in children). The beef tapeworm, *Taenia saginata*, is also found throughout the world and is acquired by eating rare contaminated beef. The pork tapeworm, *T. solium*, is found in parts of Asia, Europe, and Latin America. Man becomes infected by eating undercooked pork. Cysticercosis, a dangerous form of self-infection, may also occur (see below). The fish tapeworm, *Dibothriocephalus latus*, is seen in the Soviet Union, Japan, Europe, and in the Great Lakes region of the United States and Canada. Human infection results from eating raw or improperly cooked fish.

With the exception of the dwarf tapeworm, these organisms must live for a period in the body of one or more animals before reaching maturity. An example is the fish tapeworm, which passes through two larval forms, first in water fleas and then in fish which consume the water fleas. The worms reach maturity in the human intestine.

Some tapeworms may reach a length of 30 ft. or more and may live for up to 25 years in the human body. The worms attach to the intestinal wall. The body is segmented. Each segment is a reproductive unit, and eggs are discharged as the terminal egg-laden segments break off and pass out in the feces.

Frequently no symptoms are present. Abdominal pains, digestive disturbances, and nausea occur in some cases. An anemia may occur in fish tapeworm infestations, resulting from the fact that the worm absorbs vitamin B_{12}, a vital blood-building factor. A number of drugs, including Atabrine, or quinacrine hydrochloride, are effective in treating intestinal tapeworm infestations. These conditions may be avoided by thoroughly cooking meat, such as fish and pork, and by the sanitary disposal of human feces.

Nonintestinal Infestations: *Hydatid Disease.* The larval form of the tapeworm *Eichinococcus granulosus* may attack the liver, lungs, muscles, bones, and other organs. The adult worms are found in dogs (in South America, Africa, Australia, and New Zealand). Man acquires the eggs from infected soil or by contact with the hair of infected dogs. Sheep and cattle may also become infected by grazing in contaminated areas. The cycle of infection continues when dogs are fed the organs of diseased sheep and cattle. The eggs hatch in the intestines, liberating the embryonic worms which are carried to the tissues via the blood stream. Large cysts develop in the affected organs and may reach considerable size.

Cysticercosis is caused by the eggs of the pork tapeworm. Individuals having the adult worm in their intestines pass the eggs in their stool and may then consume the eggs by contaminating their food with improperly washed hands. Cysts may appear in the muscles, eyes, brain, and heart. In severe infections several thousand may be present in the body.

Surgical removal of the cysts is the only treatment for hydatid disease and cysticercosis.

TASTE

TASTE, SENSE OF. Four fundamental component qualities of taste have been universally accepted: bitter, sweet, salty, and sour. Many different agents may be capable of producing any one of these taste reactions, although each is associated largely with one group of compounds. For example, the salty taste is produced by inorganic salts, but also by nitrates and sulfates.

Of great interest in the scientific study of taste are those agents which evoke two or more qualities. Monosodium glutamate, a well-known flavor additive, evokes at least the qualities of saltiness, sweetness, and bitterness, while the preservative sodium benzoate manifests all four basic qualities.

The receptors on the tongue responsible for the taste reaction are the taste buds, which can be stimulated only by a liquid solution that can penetrate a pore in the bud or the spaces among the taste cells. Although some respond to only one kind of stimulus, most react to two or three different qualities. In addition, the areas of the tongue are differentially sensitive. The tip, for example, is most receptive to sweet, the sides to sour. Smell-blindness (anosmia) is fairly common, but recorded instances of people suffering taste-blindness (ageusia) are very rare.

Sensitivity can be manipulated by either contrast or adaptation. In eating sweetened cereal before grapefruit, the sweet of the cereal sugar seems to increase the sourness of the fruit, which can be counteracted by "masking" with additional sweetener. But this is not true masking, since the measurement of the nerve impulses produced by the combination show that the sweet and sour intensities are at the same level, as if each had been introduced upon the tongue by itself. As with contrast, so, too, with stimulus adaptation. First, with continued exposure, the nerve impulses continue well after the sensation has disappeared. Secondly, the picture is further complicated by the finding that prolonged exposure to one salt will decrease sensitivity to another salt but will not affect sensitivity to a third salt.

See also SENSATION; SMELL, SENSE OF; TONGUE.

TEETH, specialized bonelike structures which are used as weapons (in lions, tigers, boars), as instruments for holding prey (in certain snakes and fishes), as a tool for cutting wood (beavers), or for uprooting trees and carrying weights (elephants). Man uses his teeth primarily to tear and grind food, preparing it for the action of the digestive juices of the stomach.

The Structure of the Teeth

The part of the tooth projecting above the gums (the crown) is capped by the enamel. Consisting of about 96% mineral salts, the enamel is the hardest substance in the body. It serves well as a grinding surface for the tooth and also resists bacterial penetration.

Underneath the enamel is the yellowish dentine, which forms the bulk of the tooth. Dentine is harder than bone but softer than enamel. It consists of about 70% mineral substances deposited in a framework of organic tissue. The dentine is constantly regenerated during the life of the tooth. Unlike the enamel, dentine is sensitive to touch, heat, and cold and is considerably more susceptible to decay.

At the heart of the tooth is the pulp cavity, which contains blood vessels and nerves. When this bone-enclosed chamber becomes engorged from infection or inflammation, each beat of the pulse becomes painful as it drives blood into the vessels of the pulp, further compressing the fluid within the chamber and thus squeezing nerve fibers.

The tooth is anchored in place by the periodontal membrane, which is attached to the cementum on the roots. The cementum is the outer layer of the roots and is a modified type of bone. The periodontal membrane is adjacent to the cementum and consists of tissue fibers which penetrate the cementum and attach the roots to the bone.

The Two Sets of Teeth

The teeth of many animals grow continuously throughout life. Man must make do with a set of permanent teeth which follow the "milk," or deciduous, teeth of infancy. The 20 deciduous teeth appear between the ages of 6 months and 24 months. The permanent teeth appear between the 6th and 25th years. As they mature the root of each overlying deciduous tooth is absorbed until it loosens and falls out.

There are 32 permanent teeth, their form and position in the mouth varying with their function. The eight incisors at the center have a sharp straight cutting edge and are used to cut into food. The adjacent canine teeth are sharp and pointed and serve to tear the food. The premolars, or bicuspids, and the molars grind and pulverize the food once it has been taken into the mouth. The third molars are the "wisdom" teeth, so called because they erupt some time after the 16th year, presumably when the individual has matured in wisdom.

Factors Affecting Tooth Growth and Health

Normal tooth growth requires an adequate supply of nutrients, particularly calcium and vitamins C and D. There is some evidence that the lack of mechanical stimulation of the gums from chewing the soft foods of modern civilization may contribute to susceptibility to decay. It has been observed that in primitive cultures in which the diet consists of rough foods, the incidence of decay is considerably less. In particular, among Eskimo women who chew leather to soften it, the teeth are noticeably resistant to decay. These women grind their teeth into stubs, but decay is not their problem. There is doubtless an important genetic, or inherited, element in resistance to dental disease. Dentists observe that some individuals develop decay and gum disease that cannot be solely attributed to poor dental hygiene. Some persons suffer from a congenital softness of the enamel and lose it rapidly through wear and tear.

The Positioning of the Teeth. Abnormal positioning, or malpositioning, of the teeth sometimes occurs without observable cause—the teeth erupt in the wrong position. An important known cause of improper positioning is the premature loss of the baby teeth, which ordinarily maintain the proper alignment of the emerging permanent teeth. This is particularly true of the deciduous molars.

The growing teeth may be easily malpositioned by habitual forces or pressures such as exerted by habits of thumb-sucking, "tongue thrusting," and "mouth breathing." Thumb-sucking causes protrusion of the front upper teeth ("buckteeth"). Tongue thrusting is an abnormality of

THE PERMANENT TEETH

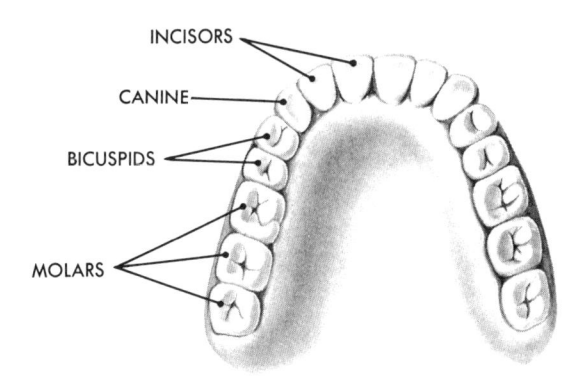

TEETH OF MAXILLARY (Upper) ARCH
- INCISORS
- CANINE
- BICUSPIDS
- MOLARS

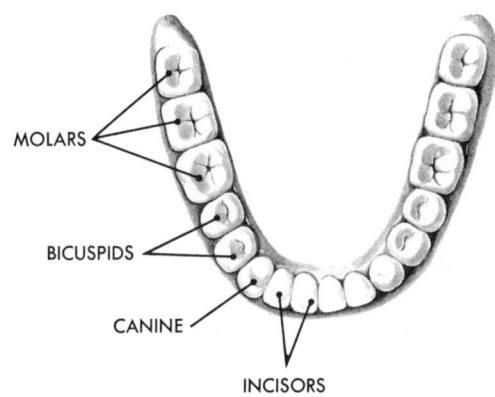

TEETH OF MANDIBULAR (Lower) ARCH
- MOLARS
- BICUSPIDS
- CANINE
- INCISORS

swallowing in which the tongue is thrust forward against the front teeth during the act of swallowing. This results in protrusion of both the upper and lower front teeth. Mouth breathing also produces protrusion of the front teeth. This occurs when the mouth is kept open while sleeping. The closed lips normally restrain the teeth, and when this containing action is lost the teeth "buck" out.

Care of the Teeth

Teeth care has three major objectives: (1) to remove food particles that contribute to decay; (2) to remove film and stains from the teeth; and (3) to stimulate the flow of the blood in the gums. Brushing accomplishes all three of these objectives. Ideally the teeth should be brushed after every meal to remove food particles. Although this is sometimes not practical, rinsing the mouth after meals can contribute substantially to cleansing of the mouth. Direct stimulation of inflamed areas is helpful in reducing the inflammation. Tartar and other gum irritants are most effectively removed by the dentist.
See also DENTISTRY; DENTITION.

TEETH, FALSE. See DENTISTRY.

TEETHING, the eruption of the "milk," or deciduous, teeth which occurs in infancy. The pressure of the emerging tooth against the overlying gum usually makes the process painful, causing the infant to be irritable and to reject food. Excess salivation may produce lip irritation and mouth sores. Although most infants pass through this period with no more than the usual irritability, some may develop mouth infections and fever. Occasionally the erupting tooth cannot penetrate the gum, making it necessary to lance the tissue.

TENDON [těn′dən], band of dense, white, tough tissue which connects muscle to bone. The shape, length, and thickness of the tendon vary with the muscle. Some long tendons, such as those around the wrist and ankle, help support the joints of the limbs. Particularly prominent is the Achilles' tendon, or heel cord, which connects the powerful gastrocnemius muscle of the calf to the heel bone (the calcaneus). Inflammation of the sheaths which envelop the tendons of the wrists and ankles is called tenosynovitis (which see).

TENNIS ELBOW, painful condition of the outer aspect of the elbow, possibly involving inflammation of a bursa (one of the fluid-filled sacs which are located at points of friction in the body). The condition is seen not only in tennis players, but also in fencers, golfers, butchers, and carpenters. The grip is weak, and the patient experiences pain upon attempting to pick up or turn objects. Treatment consists of rest and injections of cortisone and related drugs.

TENOSYNOVITIS [těn-ō-sĭn-ə-vī′tĭs], inflammation of the sheath which envelops certain tendons. Most commonly found in the tendon sheaths of the fingers and thumb, it may also occur in the tendons around the ankle joint. Tenosynovitis usually results from minor repeated injuries. It may also be caused by a single injury, with subsequent bacterial infection (acute suppurative tenosynovitis), or may appear without apparent cause. At times it occurs in association with rheumatoid arthritis or gout. In chronic cases symptoms consist of pain, redness, swelling, and limitation of motion. In some cases a snapping sensation (so-called "snapping finger") is felt upon movement. Treatment consists of rest, heat, and injection of cortisone and related drugs. Surgery is necessary in a small number of cases.

TESTOSTERONE [těs-tŏs′tə-rōn], male sex hormone. A male sex hormone was suspected in antiquity by observers who noted changes in castrated men. In 300 B.C. Aristotle compared the effect of castration in birds and men, but not until 1849 did Arnold A. Berthold discern the effect of transplanting testes into a castrate animal. In 1935 Adolf Butenandt synthesized a testosteronelike compound from cholesterol, the precursor of the steroids.

Testosterone is a steroid compound, which causes masculinization. It is produced primarily by the Leydig cells of the testes. It is probably also produced by action of the liver on another steroid precursor, made by the adrenal gland. Thus, there is some testosterone produced in women, just as the female hormone, estrogen, is produced in men. Testosterone production is regulated by another hormone, which is secreted by the pituitary gland. The effect of testosterone is most evident at puberty. Then its increased production produces typical male characteristics.

Certain malignant tumors are altered by changing the body's production of testosterone. Cancer of the prostrate may be treated for long periods by removing the testes and, thus, the major source of endogenous testosterone. Synthetic testosterone has several therapeutic uses, including treatment of breast cancer in women.

See also ENDOCRINE GLANDS; HYPOGONADISM.

TETANUS [tĕt′ə-nəs], also known as lockjaw, a serious bacterial disease marked by violent, uncontrolled muscle spasms. The *Clostridium tetani*, which causes the disease, is found in soil and in the intestinal tract of man and numerous animals. These bacteria are described as "spore-forming obligate anaerobes." This means that they cannot survive in the presence of oxygen, and that they form special structures, or spores, which can resist drying, heating, and antiseptic agents that would destroy the bacteria in their ordinary state. The hardiness of the tetanus spores poses special difficulties for sterilizing instruments and for cleansing wounds and accounts for the ability of these organisms to survive for months and years.

Tetanus most commonly follows injury, usually involving a deep penetrating wound where the bacteria can multiply free from the harmful effects of oxygen. Occasionally the wound may be as trivial as an insect bite, but in all cases the initiating factor is the deposition of spores into injured tissue where the special requirements for the growth of the tetanus organisms are present. The incubation period ranges from days to weeks but in some cases may extend to years after initial injury. Generally, the shorter the incubation period, the severer the disease.

Symptoms. The signs and symptoms of tetanus are caused by a toxin, or poison, secreted by the bacteria. The poison spreads from the site of infection up the motor nerves and spinal cord and produces an extreme excitability of muscle groups. Usually the initial symptom consists of a spasm of the jaw muscles which prevents movement (hence the expression "lockjaw"). Occasionally fever, headache, pain in the back and neck, and difficulty in swallowing may precede other symptoms. The muscle spasms spread. Involvement of the facial muscles may produce the hideous grin classically described as *risus sardonicus*.

At the height of the disease violent spasms may be set off by a noise, draft, or other inconsequential stimulus, causing the entire body to arch like a bow so that only the heels and back of the head contact the underlying surface. Death occurs in approximately 50% of the cases, resulting from interference with breathing or "exhaustion." If the patient recovers, there is usually no permanent loss of muscle function.

Treatment. Treatment is directed at cleaning the wound to prevent additional toxin production and to inactivate the existing toxin. Penicillin kills *Clostridia* and prevents secondary infections. Human tetanus antitoxin made from pooling and concentrating plasma from individuals immunized against tetanus is available to inactivate the tetanus toxin. It acts only on toxin not fixed to tissue and is administered immediately after the wound is received. Horse antitoxin is no longer used because of a potentially fatal allergic reaction. Muscular spasms can be controlled by sedatives and muscle-relaxing drugs—which diminish the reflex excitability of the spinal cord—as well as by maintaining darkness in the patient's room. A tracheotomy, that is, a small incision in the windpipe, may be performed if necessary. This allows a machine to breathe for the individual until muscle function returns.

Prevention. Immunization against tetanus can be achieved through the use of tetanus toxoid. This is a preparation of tetanus toxin which has lost its potency as a nerve poison, but which retains its ability to stimulate the body to manufacture immunizing substances (antibodies). A series of injections is given initially, and immunity can be maintained by "booster" doses given at intervals of several years. Tetanus immunization has been highly successful in preventing tetanus among personnel in the armed forces.

See also IMMUNITY; VACCINES.

TETRACYCLINES [tĕt-rə-sī′klīnz], a group of antibiotic drugs used in the treatment of a wide variety of infectious diseases, including those caused by bacteria (brucellosis, tularemia), rickettsia (Rocky Mountain spotted fever, typhus), and certain viruslike organisms (psittacosis). The best-known members of the group, aureomycin (chlortetracycline), terramycin (oxytetracycline), and achromycin (tetracycline) are similar in their effects. Organisms resistant to any member of the group are usually also resistant to the others. The drugs are usually administered by mouth, and, although ordinarily well tolerated, may cause certain side effects, such as mouth inflammation and diarrhea.

See also ANTIBIOTICS.

THORAZINE [thôr′ə-zēn], trade name for chlorpromazine, a major tranquilizing drug used to reduce anxiety and agitation in mental illness, in alcoholic delirium tremens, and in certain cases of neurosis. Thorazine, in common with other tranquilizing drugs, produces sedation without causing extreme drowsiness or unconsciousness. It is also valuable as a pain reliever in combination with narcotics, as an antiemetic (to prevent vomiting), and as a treatment for hiccups. Side effects such as headache, lowering blood pressure and body temperature, and dizziness, palpitations, and jaundice may be seen. Thorazine enhances the effects of alcohol and consequently should not be given to persons under its influence.

See also TRANQUILIZERS.

THROMBIN AND PROTHROMBIN, substances important in the clotting of the blood. Prothrombin is normally present in circulating blood. During the clotting reaction it is converted to thrombin, which, in turn, makes possible the production of the fibrin threads that form the matrix of the clot. Prothrombin is normally manufactured in the liver, and evidence indicates that vitamin K (which is manufactured by certain intestinal bacteria) is necessary for its production. In obstructive jaundice and certain other liver disorders bleeding tendencies may result from lowered prothrombin levels. A clinical test called the "prothrombin time" is used to measure the concentration of blood prothrombin and indirectly to test liver function.

THROMBOPHLEBITIS [thrŏm-bō-flĭ-bī′tĭs], formation of a blood clot (thrombus) in the wall of an inflamed vein. This may occur during convalescence from diseases, such as pneumonia and influenza, or from local infections of bone or other tissues which extend to the vein. Thrombosed veins lying close to the skin may be felt as tender cords. The surrounding tissues are usually red and swollen. In severe cases a reflex constriction of the blood vessels may reduce circulation in the affected limb. A serious complication of thrombophlebitis is pulmonary embolism, obstruction of a blood vessel in the lung by a dislodged clot fragment which has traveled from the limb to the lung via the blood stream. Treatment of thrombophlebitis includes bed rest with elevation of the limb to reduce swelling and anticoagulant drugs to prevent further clotting.
See also EMBOLUS; PULMONARY EMBOLISM; THROMBOSIS.

THROMBOPLASTINS [thrŏm-bō-plăs′tĭnz], group of substances important in blood clotting. Thromboplastins are found in many tissues of the body. A precursor of thromboplastin, called thromboplastinogen, is found in the small, colorless, disc-shaped platelets of the blood. When the platelets rupture, or when blood comes into contact with injured tissues, the thromboplastins, in conjunction with calcium and other substances, initiate a chain of reactions. This culminates in the formation of fibrin threads, the matrix of the blood clot.
See also BLOOD.

THROMBOSIS [thrŏm-bō′sĭs], the formation of a blood clot, or thrombus, within the circulatory system. It may be caused by diseases which damage the walls of the blood vessels (infections, arteriosclerosis), by mechanical injury to the vessel, by heart ailments which reduce the speed of blood flow, or by blood disorders which increase the sluggishness of the blood or enhance its tendency to clot.

The consequences of thrombosis depend upon whether the clot occurs in an artery or a vein and upon what part of the body is affected. Thrombosis of a vein leads to congestion of the local veins, tissue swelling, and a bluish discoloration of the tissues in the area. Venous thrombosis may occur in the veins of the legs following surgery or after prolonged confinement to bed. A dreaded complication of the latter condition is pulmonary embolism. A portion of the clot breaks off to become an embolus and travels through the blood to lodge in an artery of the lung. Massive pulmonary embolism may be fatal. The same effect may be produced by a pulmonary thrombosis—a blood clot arising directly in a lung artery. Blood clots in arteries of the brain (cerebral thrombosis) or of the heart (coronary thrombosis) may also cause rapid death of vital tissues and may be fatal.

Treatment of thrombosis is directed at preventing thrombus and embolus formation and re-establishing normal blood flow. Anticoagulant drugs are used to depress the coagulability of the blood (to prevent extension of the existing clot). Veins may be tied off to prevent emboli from breaking loose, and occluded segments of blood vessels may be surgically removed and replaced with artificial blood vessels made from synthetic fibers. Thrombosis may sometimes be prevented by regular administration of anticoagulants to patients who have had an attack of coronary thrombosis and by exercise and early ambulation of postoperative patients.
See also ANTICOAGULANTS.

THYMUS [thī′məs] **GLAND**, organ found in the upper part of the chest. The thymus has long been a mystery to physiologists and for some time its only generally accepted function was that of producing particular cells called thymocytes. Several lines of evidence suggested other activities for the thymus, including the fact that it enlarges steadily from infancy to puberty, after which it shrinks in size, and that it is enlarged in certain diseases, particularly in the muscle disorder myasthenia gravis. Research has indicated that the thymus is important in the mechanisms of immunity by which the body fights disease. Also, several growth-promoting and growth-inhibiting hormones have been isolated from the gland.

THYROID-BLOCKING DRUGS, or antithyroid drugs, are a group of diverse compounds which inhibit the manufacture or release of hormones from the thyroid gland. These drugs have been used principally in the treatment of toxic goiter (an enlargement of the thyroid gland involving overproduction of thyroid hormone), a condition which previously could be treated only by surgery. The thioamides (propylthiouracil, methylthiouracil) depress thyroid function but cause an increase in the size of the gland. Iodine depresses thyroid function only briefly but decreases the size of the gland. A more recent drug, Iothiouracil, is said to combine the advantages of both drugs.
See also GOITER; THYROID GLAND.

THYROID [thī′roid] **GLAND**, a gland in the front of the neck which straddles the windpipe, or trachea. The thyroid is one of the ductless, or endocrine, glands, which pour their secretions directly into the blood stream. The iodine-containing thyroid hormones, thyroxine and triiodothyronine, increase the energy production of the tissues and are essential for normal growth and development. Secretion of thyroid hormone is controlled by the pituitary gland of the skull which secretes a thyroid-stimulating hormone (TSH). Emotional stimuli and other forms of environmental stress increase or decrease the pituitary secretion of thyroid-stimulating hormone and thus indirectly stimulate or suppress thyroid activity. Other factors affecting thyroid activity are the availability of iodine in the diet and the intake of cabbage, Brussels sprouts, and other foods of the Brassica family which interfere with thyroid function.

Undersecretion of thyroid hormone in infancy produces *cretinism*, marked by stunted growth and mental impairment. In adults thyroid deficiency produces *myxedema*, characterized by lethargy, puffiness of the face, joint and muscle pains, and anemia. *Hyperthyroidism*, or thyroid overactivity, is often associated with emotional problems

and causes nervousness, muscle tremors, rapid pulse rate, and protrusion of the eyeballs. Visible enlargement of the thyroid gland, known as goiter, may accompany hypothyroid or hyperthyroid states or may appear without producing symptoms. Thyroid substance, an official preparation containing thyroxine, is effective in treating defective functioning of the thyroid gland and certain cases of goiter and menstrual disturbances.
See also CRETINISM; ENDOCRINE GLANDS; GOITER; HYPERTHYROIDISM; MYXEDEMA; PITUITARY GLAND.

THYROXINE. See THYROID GLAND.

TICK, small arachnid belonging to the same order, Acarina, as the mites. Ticks are better known than mites because of their large size (to 1 in.) and because many attack man and domestic animals. This arachnid may be distinguished by the presence of a pair of respiratory apertures near the bases of the fourth legs, pitlike olfactory organs on the first legs, and a piercing organ equipped with recurved teeth. The forward part of the back is usually covered by a leathery shield. The larvae have three pairs of legs, and adults have four. At all stages the tick is usually a bloodsucker. Mature females may be nearly ½ in. long. The castor-bean tick is a common parasite on dogs and domestic animals. Texas cattle fever and the dread Rocky Mountain spotted fever are transmitted by ticks.
See also ROCKY MOUNTAIN SPOTTED FEVER.

TINEA. See RINGWORM.

TINNITUS [tĭ-nī′təs], noises in the ear, usually described as "ringing," "buzzing," "hissing," or "roaring." Tinnitus often accompanies impaired hearing and may be caused by impacted wax in the ear, by diseases of the middle and inner ear, by brain tumors, or by large doses of certain drugs, such as quinine and aspirin.
See also DEAFNESS.

TISSUE, a layer or group of cells in the plant or animal body that have essentially similar form and function. The concept of tissue also includes the extracellular products of those cells. In multicellular animals, two basic types of cells are recognized: somatic, or body cells, which constitute the animal's body throughout its entire life; and germ cells, which are concerned only with reproduction. The somatic cells of the multicellular animal body are grouped into four main types of tissue which are classified on the basis of their function.

Epithelial tissue functions protectively (as a covering or lining for various organs), sensorially (as a receptor of specific external stimuli), or glandularly (secreting substances needed by the animal). The protective function is illustrated by the skin, which is composed of epithelial tissue. The sensory function is illustrated by the taste buds on the tongue or the olfactory receptors in the nasal passages—these are epithelial tissues. The secretory function of epithelium is illustrated by the salivary glands (whose secretion is saliva), which are composed of epithelial tissue.

Connective tissue acts to support the organism, helping it to retain a distinct form. The different kinds of connective tissues are composed primarily of intercellular products derived from the actual connective tissue cells. Bone is an example of a connective tissue, as are fat, or adipose, tissue, and cartilage.

Muscular tissue may be said to perform the function of enabling the animal to move. Muscular tissue has the unique ability to contract. It is this contractibility that makes locomotion possible.

Nervous tissue performs the specialized functions of receiving environmental stimuli and conducting impulses throughout the various parts of the body. In many animals a mass of specialized nerve cells, the brain, receives impulses from the body, interprets them, and then transmits responsive impulses ("instructions") back to various organs.

TONGUE, organ of taste and speech. The tongue also aids in digestion by helping to macerate food and propel it into the pharynx. The tongue consists of a central core of muscle fibers overlaid by connective tissue containing glands, nerves, blood vessels, and taste buds. Projections of connective tissue, covered by a thick superficial layer, form the papillae which give the surface of the tongue its rough appearance. The taste buds yield four qualities of taste sensation—sweet, salt, acid, and bitter—and are distributed in groups on the surface of the tongue.

The tongue movements are important in forming the sounds of speech and are produced by two groups of muscles: five outer muscles attached to bone at one end and the tongue at the other, and four intrinsic muscles which form the body of the tongue. The fine degree of tongue movement is made possible by a comparatively large number of motor cells in the brain devoted to muscle control. In contrast there is a smaller representation for other groups of muscles, such as those of the back and trunk, which do not require precise movement. Some anatomists feel that the musculature of the tongue varies among different racial groups owing to constant usage in forming the distinctive speech sounds of particular languages. This may be a factor in the difficulty experienced by adults in learning to speak foreign languages without an accent.

Characteristic tongue changes are sometimes seen in certain diseases and may be an aid in diagnosis. In some glandular disturbances the tongue becomes enlarged, as in cretinism and acromegaly. The tongue becomes red and inflamed in some cases of vitamin deficiency (pellagra caused by riboflavin deficiency). In scarlet fever the tongue papillae may enlarge or protrude, producing so-called raspberry or strawberry tongue. Specific disorders of the tongue include "black hairy tongue," in which the papillae are elongated and discolored. This may be caused by antibiotic lozenges and requires no specific treatment. Fissured tongue is a harmless congenital variation marked by deep clefts on the surface of the tongue.

TONSILLITIS [tŏn-səl-ī′tĭs], inflammation of the palatine tonsils, two masses of lymphatic tissue found in the rear of the mouth cavity. Tonsillitis is frequently caused by group A hemolytic streptococci—members of which also cause scarlet fever.

The inflammation appears suddenly. The earliest symptom is sore throat. The lymph nodes at the angle of the jaw become swollen and tender, and the patient may develop fever, chills, muscle aches, and headaches. The tonsils and adjacent tissues are red and swollen and covered with a thick exudate. In some cases the enlarged tonsils may make breathing and swallowing difficult. In untreated patients the fever disappears in about three days, and the throat soreness vanishes shortly afterward.

Penicillin and other antibiotics shorten the recovery time and are used to prevent serious complications, such as kidney inflammation (glomerulonephritis) and rheumatic fever, which sometimes follow hemolytic streptococcal infections. Other complications include tonsillar abscess formation and middle ear infections. Tonsillectomy, or surgical removal of the tonsils, is advisable for individuals who have had repeated bouts of tonsillitis or for those who have had rheumatic fever or glomerulonephritis.
See also HEMOLYTIC STREPTOCOCCI.

TORTICOLLIS [tôr-tĭ-kŏl'ĭs], condition in which the neck is twisted and the head tilted to one side. Torticollis is sometimes present at birth, or it may be caused by a variety of painful irritations about the neck; slipping of a joint; arthritis; muscle inflammations; or injury. Treatment consists of stretching the tightened muscles, collars, braces, or in some cases surgery.

TOXIN [tŏk'sĭn], in microbiology, a poisonous substance that is either excreted by, or contained within, a microorganism. Those toxins that have been well studied have been shown to be proteins or complexes containing protein. Toxins are generally divided into two groups: *exotoxins*, which are excreted by the microorganism; and *endotoxins*, which are contained within the body of the microorganism. The former can generally be completely neutralized by a specific antitoxin. The symptoms of diphtheria, tetanus, botulism, and gas gangrene are caused primarily by exotoxins. Cholera and some forms of dysentery are caused by bacteria that contain endotoxins.
See also ANTITOXIN; BACTERIA; TOXOID.

TOXOID [tŏk'soid], bacterial poison (toxin) that has been rendered harmless without removing its ability to stimulate the body to produce protective substances against it. Formaldehyde is generally used for converting toxin to toxoid. Heat and aging are also effective but are not so easily controlled. Toxoids are used to produce immunity against certain bacterial diseases, such as diphtheria and tetanus.
See also VACCINES.

TOXOPLASMOSIS [tŏk-sō-plăz-mō'sĭs], infectious disease which affects man, dogs, cats, chickens, cattle, and other animals. Found throughout the world, toxoplasmosis is caused by the microorganism *Toxoplasma gondii*. Although, for the most part, the manner in which the disease is transmitted is still not known, it has been recognized that the organisms can be passed from the mother to the child before birth. The resulting congenital toxoplasmosis is serious, and infants who survive may have impaired vision and be mentally deficient. Infection in adult life may go unnoticed in many cases or may cause rash, enlarged lymph nodes, cough, fever, headache, joint pain, and other symptoms. Sulfonamides are useful in treatment.

TRACHEOTOMY [trā-kē-ŏt'ə-mē], an operation in which an opening is made into the trachea (windpipe) to permit air to bypass the throat and enter the lungs directly. When the flow of air from the mouth to the lungs is blocked by a foreign body, infection, or throat injury, an emergency tracheotomy may be a lifesaving measure. The procedure consists of making an incision in the front of the throat, pulling the neck muscles aside, moving aside or dividing a portion of the thyroid gland, which sits astride the windpipe, and inserting a metal or plastic tube into the trachea. In extreme cases "stab," or "battlefield," tracheotomies have been performed: a knife or scalpel is plunged into the windpipe and a tube inserted. This procedure is dangerous because of the possibility of uncontrolled bleeding and of injury to important structures of the neck.

TRACHOMA [trə-kō'mə], highly contagious virus disease of the eyes which is a major cause of blindness throughout the world. An ancient disease which was accurately described in early Egyptian and Chinese writings, trachoma reached Europe via soldiers returning from the Crusades and the Napoleonic campaigns in Egypt. Today it is highly prevalent in the Near and Far East and is also found in central and southern Europe.

Trachoma is easily transmitted by direct contact, contaminated personal articles, and possibly by flies. The disease progresses in stages over a period of months or even years, beginning with tearing, sensitivity to light, and swelling of the eyelids. It progresses to invasion of the transparent outer covering of the eye (the cornea) by new blood vessels and to scarring and ulceration of the cornea and eyelids. Eventually blindness may result. The victim is not immune to second attacks. The disease is easily controlled and cured by antibiotics and sulfonamides. Surgery to remove disfiguring scars may be necessary in advanced cases. Trachoma can be prevented by isolation of infected cases and by proper hygiene. Serious complications can be avoided by early diagnosis and treatment.

TRACTION [trăk'shən], in medicine, force applied to produce tension on a part of the body. This force may be applied manually or by means of a halter, corset, or adhesive strips. Traction is used to treat fractures and dislocations of the neck and upper and lower extremities, and to stretch the neck, lower back, shoulders, and hips in the treatment of painful conditions of these structures. The tension must be maintained day and night in cases of fractures of the long bones. Intermittent traction may be applied in other conditions, such as slipped disc.

TRANSFUSION, BLOOD. See BLOOD.

TRENCH FOOT. See IMMERSION FOOT AND TRENCH FOOT.

TRENCH MOUTH. See VINCENT'S DISEASE.

TREPHINE [trĭ-fĭn′,trĭ-fēn′] **AND TREPHINING**, drill to bore a hole through the bony tables, or layers, of the skull, and the use of such a drill. The trephine is a small drill (bit)

TRICHINOSIS

with a central point, which acts as a pivot. The cutting teeth are placed at the periphery so that a small, button shaped piece of bone is removed.

Trephining is the oldest-known surgical procedure. Skulls of ancient peoples from thousands of years ago have been found with trephine holes. The procedure was probably used for supernatural reasons, but may also have been used to relieve increased intracranial pressure, as it is today.

Brain surgery (neurosurgery) is possible today because of refinements and extensions in the use of trephining. A flap of skull is raised by trephining three small round holes, then passing a cutting wire, called a Gigli saw, from one hole to another. By pulling back and forth on the wire, the holes are joined and a portion of skull removed. The brain, with its membranes intact, is thus exposed and amenable to surgery.

TRICHINOSIS [trĭk-ə-nō'sĭs], infestation by the roundworm *Trichinella spiralis*. Transmitted principally by eating contaminated pork, trichinosis is a major health problem in many parts of the world. The trichina worm differs from most worms in that (1) it is more commonly found in temperate rather than tropic zones; (2) females give birth to living embryos; and (3) critical symptoms are caused by the presence of the larvae in the tissues rather than by adult worms in the intestine. The live trichinosis larvae, enclosed in a protective wall, or cyst, are consumed with the food. The cyst wall is dissolved by the digestive juices, permitting the larvae to anchor on the lining of the small intestine where they mature and mate. The female discharges live larvae into the blood and lymph channels, through which they are carried to all parts of the body, particularly the diaphragm and the muscles of the back, shoulders, chest, and legs.

In mild infections no symptoms may appear. In other cases early symptoms develop from one to four days after swallowing the larvae. These symptoms are caused by larval invasion of the intestinal walls and include nausea, diarrhea, and vomiting. Later migration of the larvae through the body produces muscle pains and tenderness accompanied by weakness and fever. The eyelids often become puffy, and splinter hemorrhages may appear under the nails. There is a marked increase in the number of certain white blood cells (eosinophils). Severe cases may be fatal, but in most instances the symptoms subside as the body deposits a shell of hard tissue about the larvae. They remain indefinitely in this "encysted" state, occasionally causing persistent muscle aches.

Drugs such as piperazine may eliminate many or all of the worms early in the disease, but no treatment is effective once the larvae have become encysted. Adrenal cortical hormones, or ACTH, may help control some of the symptoms during the active phase of the illness. Prevention of trichinosis can be achieved by thoroughly cooking pork products: at least 30 minutes per lb. at 140° F.

TRICHOMONAS [trĭ-kŏm'ə-năs], genus of one-celled animals (protozoa), some members of which are parasites in plants and animals. *T. foetus* causes a serious reproductive disease in cattle. Transmitted by bulls, this organism causes temporary sterility and occasional abortion in cows. *T. vaginalis* commonly attacks the human reproductive tract, producing a greenish, frothy, vaginal discharge in women and inflammation of the urethra in men. Although many locally applied medications have been used to treat *T. vaginalis*, the condition often resists treatment.

TRIGEMINAL [trī-jĕm'-ə-nəl] **NEURALGIA**, or *tic douloureux*, a nerve disorder marked by attacks of severe stabbing pains of the face. The pains occur along the course of the branches of the trigeminal nerve, the fifth of the 12 cranial nerves which connect directly with the brain without traveling through the spinal cord. The exact cause is unknown. The condition appears in middle-aged persons, beginning with short attacks followed by pain-free intervals lasting weeks, months, or even years.

During attacks the painful paroxysms may occur only a few times a day or several times a minute. The attacks gradually increase in frequency and extent. Movement, pressure, or even drafts about "trigger" points around the nose and mouth may precipitate an attack. This sensitivity may cause great difficulty in shaving, eating, and talking. Treatment is generally unsatisfactory. Sedatives and other drugs may provide temporary relief, and alcohol injections into the nerve trunks have reduced pain for up to 18 months. Surgical interruption of part or all of the nerve fibers of the trigeminal nerve is used in cases which resist other forms of therapy.

TRIPHOSPHOPYRIDINE NUCLEOTIDE [trī-fŏs-fôr-pĭr'ə-dēn nū'klē-ə-tīd] (TPN), a chemical widely distributed in the tissues of the body, where it participates in energy-producing reactions. TPN is a coenzyme, that is, when combined with specific enzymes, it forms a complex which is capable of accepting or donating electrons (negatively charged particles). Thus it forms part of the chain of reactions which begins with food substances and culminates in the production of energy, carbon dioxide, and water. *See also* METABOLISM.

TROPICAL MEDICINE, branch of medicine which deals with diseases of the tropics and subtropics. This includes diseases which occur principally in the tropics but also in colder climates (such as bacillary and amebic dysentery, typhoid fever, cholera, and malaria), as well as diseases which occur only in the tropics.

The Tropical Diseases. Many of the tropical diseases are geographically restricted because they are transmitted by strictly tropical insects. Filariasis, caused by a microscopic worm, is transmitted by certain tropical mosquitoes and flies. Yellow fever is a viral disease transmitted by tropical mosquitoes. At times human intervention has permitted this disease to spread beyond the tropics, as when trading vessels carried infected mosquitoes as far north as Halifax, Portland, Maine, and northern European ports.

Some diseases are strikingly confined to particular localities of the tropics. Tropical ulcer—also known as oriental sore, or Bagdad boil—is a parasitic, ulcerative skin disease. It has a spotty distribution along the Mediterranean coast of Europe, Asia Minor, and North Africa, as well as in small areas on the Black Sea, two limited areas in northeast Brazil, and one in the center of the South American continent. This pattern apparently results from the fact that the parasites which cause the disease (Leishmania) are harbored by certain dogs and rodents (Turkish gerbils) and are transmitted to man by certain sandflies (Phlebotomus) which are erratically distributed. Other diseases with sharply defined distributions are African sleeping sickness, a parasitic disease transmitted by tsetse flies and found only in a belt across central Africa, between the equator and 30° S. lat., and Chagas' disease, also parasitic, transmitted by bugs of the genus *Panstrongylus*, and found in specific areas of South and Central America.

Some diseases are confined to the tropics by circumstances unrelated to their mode of transmission. Hookworm occurs in these regions because the immature worms require a period of development in warm, moist soil and because the worms enter the body by penetrating the skin of the feet—it is mainly in warm climates that persons regularly go about without shoes. Limitations in diet of tropical areas result in kwashiorkor, a wasting disease seen mostly in children and caused by a protein-deficient diet. Beriberi and pellagra are vitamin-deficiency diseases long associated with the tropics because of the deficient diets of many tropical peoples. A complex and poorly understood disease of the tropics is tropical sprue—a disorder in which foods are not properly absorbed from the digestive tract. Although at one time the disease was thought to occur principally in Europeans residing in the tropics, it has been diagnosed in non-Europeans and in residents of northern climates. (See SPRUE.)

Research and Prevention. Tropical medicine emerged as a medical specialty during the 19th century, when explorers, traders, armies, missionaries, and settlers penetrated the tropics and brought the tropical diseases to the attention of medical investigators. During this era the organisms which cause filariasis, dysentery, leprosy, and hookworm infestation were isolated and the insect transmission of yellow fever and malaria were recognized. Dramatic circumstances attended many of these discoveries: Sir Patrick Manson is said to have demonstrated the transmission of malaria by producing it in his own son through the bite of a mosquito. American soldiers in Cuba who aided in yellow fever experiments risked death by exposing themselves to mosquitoes laden with yellow-fever virus.

Today the American Society of Tropical Medicine and Hygiene, the International Congress for Microbiology, the American Foundation for Tropical Hygiene, and numerous other institutes, organizations, and foundations are engaged in the study of tropical diseases. These diseases are a fertile field for the practice of preventive medicine—as demonstrated by the achievements of William Gorgas, who successfully controlled yellow fever in Havana and Panama by eliminating the breeding place of the mosquitoes.

More recently, several large-scale public health campaigns have been undertaken against tropical ailments. The United Nations Children's Fund has waged a widespread campaign against yaws, a highly destructive infectious disease. The World Health Organization of the United Nations is conducting the most ambitious program of its kind—a world-wide campaign against malaria, designed to banish this scourge completely from the planet.

TRUTH SERUM is not a serum, nor does it make people tell the truth. The term refers to drugs which depress the brain for the purpose of removing inhibitions and inducing talkativeness in the patient (or prisoner, or suspect). Barbiturates, ethyl alcohol, and combinations of the two have been used for these purposes. In psychiatry the terms "narcoanalysis" and "narcosynthesis" refer to the use of such drugs in producing a semiconscious state. The patient in this state is more communicative and a clearer picture of his emotional state and its origins can be obtained. The material volunteered by the subject under the influence of the drugs may be true, wildly fantastic, or a mixture of both.

TRYPANOSOMA [trĭp-ə-nō-sō′mə], genus of protozoa of the order Protomonadida. Trypanosomes are blood parasites of vertebrates. They are characterized by a single flagellum, attached, through most of its length, by a delicate undulating membrane to the spindle-shaped cell body. The best-known species are *T. gambiense* and *T. rhodesiense*, both responsible for varieties of African sleeping sickness. This dread disease is transmitted by the bite of the tsetse fly. *T. cruzi* is responsible for Chagas' disease in Central and South America. Related protozoans cause a variety of diseases in man and domestic animals throughout the tropics. Many species of *Trypanosoma*, however, are not pathogenic.

TRYPANOSOMIASIS, AFRICAN. See SLEEPING SICKNESS.

TRYPSIN. See ENZYMES.

TSETSE [tsĕt′sē] **FLY,** one of some 20 species of biting flies belonging to the genus *Glossina*, of the order Diptera. They are brownish insects, mottled with darker color, somewhat larger than the common housefly. Blood is their sole food, and, unlike mosquitoes, both the male and female bite and suck blood from the victim. The female gives birth to living young. These larvae are deposited on the ground in a hidden spot, where they become transformed into pupae and adults. Tsetse flies dominate most of Africa and are a serious threat to horses, cattle, and other domesticated mammals, as well as man. The flies act as hosts and vectors of protozoa known as trypanosomes. These cause African trypanosomiasis in cattle and sleeping sickness in man. Eradication is difficult, since insecticides are ineffective in killing the concealed pupae. The best method is clearing away the vegetation from around villages.

TUBERCULOSIS [tū-bûr-kyə-lō′sĭs], disease caused by the bacteria *Mycobacterium tuberculosis*. A major cause of death among infectious diseases, tuberculosis is found throughout the world. Although the disease has a long history (early medical documents described it as phthisis, or consumption), modern medical knowledge of the disorder was not acquired until the 19th century. It was then that lung tuberculosis, skin tuberculosis (lupus vulgaris), and tuberculosis of the lymph glands of the neck (scrofula) were established as different manifestations of the same disease, the tubercle bacillus was isolated, and tuberculosis of birds and cattle was recognized.

Tuberculosis is usually spread by infected, air-borne droplets, coughed up by individuals with the active disease and inhaled by susceptible persons. The bacilli lodge in the lungs, where conditions favor their multiplication. The body may successfully combat the infection at this point.

If, however, body resistance is impaired by poor health, or if another onslaught of germs reaches the lung, the bacteria multiply and destroy lung tissue. In rare cases the tubercle bacilli are consumed with contaminated food or milk which has not been pasteurized, and the primary focus of infection is in the digestive tract.

The disease progresses slowly. Months may elapse before the early symptoms are apparent—these include fatigue, afternoon temperature, hoarseness, and persistent cough. The bacteria may eventually spread to other parts of the body. Two of the most serious complications are *meningeal* and *miliary* tuberculosis. In the former the bacteria attack the meninges, the tissues which envelop the brain and spinal cord. In the latter the organisms enter the blood stream and spread rapidly throughout the body.

Treatment

The outlook for tuberculosis patients has improved considerably since the introduction of streptomycin, PAS (para-aminosalicylic acid), and isoniazid. Before these drugs were available tuberculosis treatment consisted of rest, adequate diet, and possibly surgery. Today drug therapy using usually at least two of the compounds mentioned forms the basis of treatment. Surgery may still be necessary, and in these cases all or part of the lung may be removed. Less frequently a part of the lung is permanently or temporarily collapsed.

With the emphasis on drug therapy there has been a tendency to shift the place of treatment from remote sanatoriums to general hospitals. After an initial period of hospitalization treatment is continued at home.

It must be borne in mind that tuberculosis is a chronic disease, and it is debatable as to whether an absolute cure can be achieved. Some tubercle bacilli appear to remain in the lung in a quiescent state even after the progress of the disease has been satisfactorily halted. Relapses may occur if poor general health or stress permit the dormant germs to become reactivated.

Detection, Prevention, and Control

Because of the absence of well-defined symptoms early in the course of the disease, tuberculosis may go undetected for some time. It steadily undermines the health of the victim and permits him to transmit the infection to his family and fellow workers. For these reasons early detection is important and is facilitated by the use of special tests and X rays. In considering these methods the distinction between tuberculosis *infection* and tuberculosis *disease* should be made clear. In infection, the tuberculosis bacteria are present in the body. In tuberculosis disease the bacteria are multiplying and causing inflammation and tissue destruction. Tuberculosis infection may lead to tuberculosis disease if, as noted above, the body's defenses against the bacteria prove inadequate.

The Tuberculin Test. This is the principal means of detecting tuberculosis *infection*. A substance known as tuberculin is prepared from tubercle bacilli and introduced between the layers of the skin. There are several ways of administering the test. The most accurate is the Mantoux method: a measured amount of a dilute solution of tuberculin is introduced between the layers of the skin of the forearm. The arm is examined between 48 and 72 hours later. If a hard, raised, red spot of a specific circumference is visible at the site of the injection, the test is positive—that is, the individual has been infected with tubercle bacilli. The inflamed spot results from an allergic-type reaction between the tuberculin and special antituberculous substances (antibodies) which the body had developed in response to the tuberculosis infection. Individuals who test positive with tuberculin should be further examined with X ray and other tests to determine if the infection has progressed into disease.

Immunity Against Tuberculosis. The best-known and most widely used vaccine against tuberculosis is BCG (Bacillus Calmette-Guérin—named for the French scientists who developed it), which is prepared from live, weakened bacilli. The greatest drawback of the vaccine is that it cannot be given to those who need it most—individuals who have tuberculosis infection but have not yet developed the disease. (It is estimated that approximately a fifth of the population of the United States is currently *infected* and that 2,000,000 of these will eventually develop tuberculosis.) It is felt that the introduction of the live bacilli into individuals who already have the infection may overwhelm the body's defenses and lead to the disease. For this reason a tuberculin test is always given first and positive reactors are not immunized. Several authorities thus do not recommend the vaccine on a mass basis but suggest its use for nontuberculin reactors who have been exposed to tuberculosis.

It is evident then that despite the great advances in drug therapy and the availability of vaccines several crucial problems in tuberculosis treatment and prevention remain. Further research is needed to determine the best way of preventing infections and of preventing the infected from developing disease. Better drugs are needed, drugs that the patient can tolerate and that would actually eliminate all of the bacilli from the body and that would not need to be taken for extended periods.

See also MEDICINE; PREVENTIVE MEDICINE; PUBLIC HEALTH.

TULAREMIA [tōō-lə-rē′mē-ə], also called rabbit fever, disease caused by the *Pasteurella tularensis*, a bacterium which infects rabbits, rodents, and other wild animals, and transmitted by blood-sucking flies and ticks. Probably no other disease can compare to tularemia in the versatility of its transmission. At least 20 routes of infection have been described, including contact with infected animals, consumption of infected meats or water, and insect bites. Found in many parts of the world, including North America, Europe, and northern Asia, tularemia is seen principally among hunters, farmers, campers, butchers, and laboratory workers.

The bacteria usually produce a lesion at the point of entry into the body. This may involve skin ulcers or swelling and inflammation of the eye, with itching, tearing, sensitivity to light, and pain. If the organisms are consumed in food, mouth ulcers may appear. The local lymph glands enlarge as the bacteria travel through the lymph system. General symptoms, such as headache, vomiting, chills, and fever, appear suddenly. Fever may persist for a month. Lung involvement is a serious complication. An attack of tularemia usually confers immunity. Streptomycin and tetracycline are highly effective in treating tularemia. Since the disease cannot be eradicated in the wild rodent population, sportsmen in infected areas should avoid using streams for drinking water. Rabbit meat should be thoroughly cooked, and rubber gloves should be worn while preparing the game. Some prophylactic vaccines are available against tularemia.

TUMOR [tū′mər], in medicine, a term used to indicate any swelling, but more specifically a group of cells which multiply independently of the growth of the host. Tumors are divided into two major categories, benign and malignant. Either type may arise in any tissue or in any location in the body. Benign tumors may grow to large size and cause considerable trouble by pressing on adjacent structures, but they remain in one location and do not invade the tissues of the host. Malignant tumors, or cancers, may be extremely small but are capable of invading adjacent tissues and of causing considerable destruction. Individual cells or groups of cells may break off from a malignant tumor and can be carried by the blood stream or lymphatic system to a distant part of the body, where the tumor cells may become implanted and grow a new tumor, called a "metastasis." Benign tumors do not metastasize. Both benign and malignant tumors of glandular tissue may upset normal body function by secreting excessive amounts of hormones (for example, tumors of the adrenal and pituitary glands).

The distinction between benign and malignant tumors is obviously crucial. A malignant tumor requires extensive surgery and treatment, whereas a benign tumor may not require treatment unless it involves glandular tissue, becomes excessive in size, or is located in areas subject to repeated irritation. A frequently used method of distinguishing between the two is the biopsy, in which a portion of the tumor is removed and examined under the microscope.
See also CANCER.

TWINS, two individuals delivered during the same birth. The term is normally applied only to those species in which multiple births are the exception rather than the rule. Twins occur approximately once in every 85 human births in the United States. Triplets occur once in every 85^2 births, and quadruplets once in every 85^3. The likelihood of bearing twins increases with a woman's age. The percentage of twins born to women over 40 is three to four times that of women over 20, with a peak around age 37. The prenatal and infant mortality rate for twins is about five times that of single births, and more than half of all twin births are premature. In recent years the incidence of multiple births greater than triplets has increased. The increase is associated with certain substances used in fertility control. The reason for this increase, as well as for the geometric pattern of decreasing incidence of twins, triplets and so on, is unknown. There are two types of twins: one-egg, or identical, and two-egg, or fraternal.

Identical twins occur when a single egg is fertilized, divides into a cell mass, then cleaves. Cleavages may form into two or more separate embryos from the usual one. The cause of this division of the initial cell mass is unknown, but it has been established that it occurs after fertilization. The two embryos, each with its own umbilical cord, share a common placenta during gestation. Since the single egg is fertilized by a single sperm, the identical embryos must be of the same sex, have the same hair, eye and skin color, fingerprints, and blood type. Studies of identical twins have shown that they also share other physical traits and tend to live about the same length of time. There is also a tendency for identical twins to be susceptible to the same diseases. Since identical twins have such a great number of biological similarities, they offer a unique set of conditions for psychological studies and eugenic investigations, and are widely sought for such studies.

Fraternal twins occur when eggs are discharged into the uterus, or when one is discharged and splits before being fertilized, and each egg is then fertilized by a sperm. Unlike identical twins, fraternal twins each have their own placenta, although these fuse, so that at birth the placenta may appear to have come from identical twins. Since there are two separate fertilizations, the fraternal twins do not have to be of the same sex, nor share any of the other traits common to identical twins. Fraternal twins are biologically no more alike than if they had been born from separate pregnancies. Birth records show that about 37% of all twins born are of opposite sexes, and that there is an approximately equal chance of any baby being male or female. From these facts it is deduced that 75% of all twins are fraternal and the balance are identical. If three, four, or more babies are born at the same time, they may be identical, fraternal, or any combination of the two.

Conjoined twins, called diplopagus, are born united to each other. Although the cause of these diplopagii is not known for sure, it is probable that they result from the fusion of identical twins (one egg, common placenta) at a very early stage of growth. If both twins are joined but complete at birth, they are known as Siamese twins, after Eng and Chang, born in Siam in 1811. If such twins do not share a common vital organ, they can usually be separated surgically after birth.

TYPHOID [tī′foid] **FEVER,** an acute infectious disease caused by the bacterium *Salmonella typhosa*. Long a major public health problem, typhoid is transmitted by food or water which has been contaminated with the feces of typhoid victims or carriers. The bacteria, which infect only man, enter the lymph stream through the intestine and pass into the blood, from where they penetrate various organs.

The course of the illness varies. Following an incubation period of 10 to 12 days some individuals may remain free of symptoms. Others become mildly ill for a week or two or develop a serious illness lasting four to six weeks. In a few cases death occurs within a few days. Typically there is a gradual development of headache, remittent fever, cough, and constipation. The patient may bleed from the nose, the spleen enlarges, and groups of characteristic "rose spots" appear on the trunk. The fever is usually high (102° to 105° F.) and unremitting in the third week, and during this time there may be sweats, slow pulse beat and delirium. Following this, the fever usually subsides gradually. Relapses may occur, possibly caused by pockets of bacteria in the gall bladder (a favorite target of the organisms), bone marrow, or spleen. Serious and often fatal complications of the disease are hemorrhage or perforation of the small intestine. Chloramphenicol is effective in treating typhoid fever and has greatly reduced the death rate. An attack of typhoid usually confers immunity against future attacks.

Control and Prevention of Typhoid. Typhoid infection is spread principally via the feces or urine of patients or carriers—individuals who have recovered from the disease but continue to harbor the organisms in their gall bladders, whence they reach the stools. An important aspect of control and prevention is the isolation of patients, the safe removal of their excrement, and the identification and treatment of carriers. Adequate sanitation, including proper sewage disposal and purification of drinking water, has been responsible for much of the dramatic decline in the frequency of typhoid fever. A vaccine of killed typhoid bacilli is available and has been used extensively by the military to reduce the incidence of the disease under conditions in which strict sanitary control is not possible.

Other Salmonella Infections. In addition to the organism responsible for typhoid fever, the salmonella group of bacteria includes several other disease-producing organisms. A number of these organisms infect domestic animals and may be spread by infected meat or dairy products.

Enteric Fevers. These are caused by *S. paratyphi* (paratyphoid), *S. schottmuelleri*, or *S. hirschfeldii*. They are similar to but milder than typhoid. The course of the illness is shorter (1 to 3 weeks) and complications are less frequent than in typhoid fever.

Gastroenteritis (usually epidemic). This follows the consumption of food which is heavily contaminated with salmonella organisms. From 6 to 48 hours after eating, headache, chills, and abdominal pain develop suddenly, accompanied by fever, vomiting, and diarrhea. The disease lasts two to five days, and the mortality rate is low.

Septicemic Infection. In these cases the organisms (usually *S. choleraesuis*) invade the blood stream. The principal symptom is fever, but headache, delirium, vomiting, constipation, and diarrhea may also occur. The bacteria may settle in any tissue of the body, causing complications such as pneumonia, kidney infection, and arthritis.

TYPHUS [tī′fəs] **FEVER.** The two major forms of typhus are epidemic, or louse-borne, typhus, and endemic, or murine, or flea-borne, typhus. The microorganisms responsible for these disorders are *Rickettsia* (*R. prowazeki* in the case of louse-borne typhus and *R. mooseri* in the case of flea-borne typhus). These organisms share some of the properties of bacteria and viruses, but are distinct from both (see RICKETTSIAS AND RICKETTSIAL DISEASES).

Epidemic Typhus. This is a major epidemic disease and, with the possible exception of malaria, has been the cause of more human misery than any other disorder. Although the earliest accurate description of louse-borne typhus was given by Fracastorius in 1546, some believe that typhus was also the cause of the great epidemic in Athens in 430 B.C., described by Thucydides. The disease has had considerable political impact by way of its affinity for campaigning armies. At the siege of Granada in 1489, 17,000 Spanish soldiers died from typhus. In 1528 the French army attacking Naples was crippled by typhus. The Europeans rallying to fight the Turks in the 16th century were decimated by typhus even before they reached the battlefield. In modern times outbreaks of typhus appeared in the Yugoslavian army in 1944 and in Italy and North Africa, where it threatened to spread to the invading Allied forces.

The typhus organisms are spread by human body lice, which dwell in the seams of clothing and prosper under conditions in which the same clothes are worn for weeks or months. The louse itself dies from the infection but may pass the organism to a human when it bites the skin to take a blood meal. It defecates at the same time and the individual may rub the germ-laden excrement into the itchy wound. The spread of typhus in communities results largely from the fact that infected lice tend to leave the bodies of persons with high fever and also tend to evacuate the corpses of those who have died from the disease.

From about 10 to 14 days after exposure the disease usually begins suddenly with chills, severe headache, weakness, widely distributed aches and pains, and rapidly mounting fever. The principal symptoms during the first week are a persistent headache, coughing, pains in the back and legs, and constipation. Between the fourth and seventh days pink spots appear on the trunk, later spreading to include all parts of the body except the face, palms, and soles and eventually becoming hemorrhagic. The critical period of the illness appears between the second and third weeks. The patient passes into a delirium and stupor and loses awareness of his surroundings. The pulse becomes quick, blood pressure falls, kidney activity declines, and gangrene of the toes, ear lobes, tip of the nose, and fingers may appear. The patient may develop pneumonia. Death from typhus is more likely in older persons. The fatality rate is approximately 10% in children, rising to 50% to 60% in middle-aged persons. Certain antibiotics (such as chloramphenicol and tetracyclines) are effective in treating epidemic typhus. A vaccine is available which, although it does not always prevent contraction of the disease, reduces the fatality rate to almost zero. Prevention and control of typhus can be achieved with delousing procedures (DDT powder).

Brill-Zinsser Disease, or Recrudescent Typhus. This is a recurrent, usually milder, form of typhus appearing in persons (usually emigrants from the Soviet Union and Poland) who have previously had the disease. Many of the symptoms seen in epidemic typhus appear in these cases. Transmission by the louse or flea is not involved.

Murine, or Flea-borne, Typhus. This is a milder form of typhus which occurs as a natural infection of rats and mice and which is transmitted to man by bites of the rat flea. Unlike epidemic typhus, it is not transmitted from person to person. Although murine typhus is probably an ancient disease, its sporadic nature and similarity to epidemic typhus have obscured its identification as a distinct condition. The symptoms and course of the disease are similar to, but much milder than, those of epidemic typhus. Treatment and control measures involve use of DDT in rat-infested areas to destroy the fleas and elimination of the rats. A vaccine is available.

U

ULCERATIVE COLITIS. See COLITIS.

ULCERS [ŭl′sərz] are patches of destroyed tissue which may appear anywhere on the skin or mucous membranes.

Ulcers of the Skin. Skin ulcers may be caused by infection, by physical or chemical injury to the skin, or by disturbances of the nerve or blood supply of the skin. Ulcers caused by infection appear at the site where the organisms enter the skin or occur in conjunction with a generalized infection. Vascular ulcers, caused by disturbances in the circulation, generally appear on the lower extremities. The most important are the arteriosclerotic ulcers which result from a narrowing, or "hardening," of the arteries of the legs with a subsequent reduction in the blood supply and devitalization of the tissues. Such ulcers, also seen frequently in diabetics (who are especially susceptible to arteriosclerosis), may be brought on by slight injuries normally tolerated by those with healthy circulation.

Vascular ulcers of the lower extremities are also seen in severe cases of varicose veins, appearing typically in the inside region of the ankle joint. Neurogenic ulcers, caused by loss of skin sensation and other disturbances of nervous control, are seen in certain nervous disorders (leprosy, late syphilis) and also in diabetes. In diabetic neuropathy a deep, penetrating ulcer may occur on the sole of the foot. Chronic ulcers of the legs are also seen in certain types of anemia. Bedsores (decubitus ulcers) appear on the buttocks, heels, and other pressure points in patients confined to bed for long periods—the constant pressure on the skin interferes with local circulation, causing tissue death.

Treatment of skin ulcers depends upon the underlying cause. Infectious ulcers often heal when the invading organisms are removed. Vascular ulcers are treated by a variety of methods directed at improving circulation. These include drugs to expand the blood vessels and surgery to replace occluded segments of arteries with synthetic tubing. Extensive ulcers often require skin grafts.

Ulcers of the Digestive System. The great majority of such ulcers ("peptic" ulcers) appear in the stomach and the duodenum, the portion of the small intestine immediately adjacent to the stomach. An estimated 5% to 10% of the population suffer from peptic ulcers at some time during their life. The ulcers usually first appear in persons 30 to 40 years old, affecting men four times as often as women. The exact cause is unknown. Some evidence suggests that an inherited predisposition and psychological stress may play a role. It is also not clear as to whether ulcers of the duodenum and ulcers of the stomach (gastric ulcers) have a common underlying cause. In gastric ulcer patients, stomach secretions are normal, but in cases of duodenal ulcers the patients tend to produce larger volumes of gastric juice with a higher acid concentration. This may result from overactivity of the nerves which stimulate stomach secretion or from a larger population of acid cells in the stomach. Changes in the mucous lining of the stomach, which normally prevents the stomach from being digested by its own juices, may also be responsible. The condition may be made worse by the administration of certain drugs.

The major symptom of ulcer is abdominal pain, occurring several hours after eating (frequently in the middle of the night). The pain is often relieved by eating and occurs periodically, especially in the spring and fall. The patient may remain pain-free for varying lengths of time. Important complications are bleeding, perforation of the ulcer through the stomach or duodenal wall, and obstruction of the stomach exit by scar tissue. Bleeding may be marked by the passage of black or tarry stools.

Treatment is directed at reducing the secretion of gastric juice and neutralizing the stomach acid (with nonabsorbable antacids). A diet of bland foods (including milk) helps avoid stimulation of stomach secretion. Frequent eating is recommended to buffer the stomach acid. Rest and avoidance of smoking may also contribute to healing. Although these measures are effective in healing any one episode of ulcer, recurrences are common. Attention may be given to psychological stresses, and in some cases the patient may be hospitalized to remove him from the pressures of his domestic life. Psychotherapy may also be helpful. Surgery may be necessary in cases of complications or to treat ulcers which resist other forms of therapy.

UREA [yōō-rē′ə], also called carbamide, H_2NCONH_2, a colorless or whitish crystalline powder. It is a product of animal, including human, metabolism. The human body excretes 25 to 30 g. in the urine each day.

UREMIA, literally, urine in the blood. Excessive toxins accumulate in the blood when the kidney is unable to remove them from the bloodstream. During the course of each day, 300 gallons of blood flow through the kidneys for purification. About 150 quarts are filtered, then further altered by the action of the kidney tubules producing 1½ qts. of urine daily in the normal adult. If the kidneys are diseased and fail to form sufficient filtrate, or if they are unable to purify the filtrate adequately, uremia may occur. Untreated uremia is always fatal. Uremia symptoms are myriad. The early signs, which may go on for quite a long time, include pallor, puffiness caused by fluid retention, lethargy, and fatigue. The blood pressure rises, convulsions may occur. Coma and death follow.

Any severe form of kidney disease may cause uremia.

URIC ACID

Enlargement of the prostate gland may obstruct the flow or urine enough to damage the kidneys by back pressure. When treated early enough, this and other forms of kidney disease that cause uremia are reversible. People who suffer from permanent kidney failure may now be treated by dialysis artificial kidneys, and, in rare instances, by kidney transplant.
See also KIDNEY, ARTIFICIAL.

URIC [yŏŏr'ĭk] **ACID,** a compound manufactured in the tissues from proteins (found in meats and eggs) and purines (found in liver, kidney, and other organ tissues) and excreted by man, birds, and some reptiles and lower animals. In birds, and in some reptiles, uric acid is the final product of protein metabolism.

In man, uric acid is manufactured from purine-containing foods and from body purines—especially from the breakdown of cell nuclei, in which purines are found in the nucleic acids (the reproductive elements of the cell). The acid is transported through the blood and excreted in the urine. Of considerable medical significance is the fact that uric acid is only slightly soluble in water. As a result, increased excretion of uric acid may lead to precipitation of the acid in the urinary tract and the formation of calculi, or kidney stones. In gout, the blood uric acid is elevated, and uric acid salts may be deposited about various joints and in the ear lobes. For this reason persons suffering from gout are often advised to restrict their intake of purine-rich foods. High concentrations of blood uric acid are also seen in leukemia, polycythemia, and other blood disorders, and in certain kidney ailments.
See also ARTHRITIS; METABOLISM.

URINARY BLADDER. See BLADDER, URINARY.

URINE [yŏŏr'ĭn] is manufactured in the kidneys from blood. It contains urea, uric acid, and other waste products of body activity, minerals such as potassium and sodium chloride, and some vitamins, hormones, and enzymes filtered from the blood. The examination of urine is one of the oldest, and still one of the most valuable, diagnostic tools of the physician. The ancient Egyptians recognized the presence of blood in the urine as a possible indication of parasitic infestation. They also added a woman's urine to barley as a test for pregnancy and if the plant grew the test was considered positive. This procedure evidently had some merit since it is now known that pregnant urine contains increased amounts of hormones that can stimulate plant growth.

Examination of urine is used to detect diseases of the kidney or disorders of body chemistry which cause specific changes in urine composition. Urine examination is also the most commonly used test of pregnancy (see PREGNANCY).

Urine Examination as a Clue to Kidney Disease. Microscopic examination of the urine may reveal the presence of pus cells, red blood cells, and various formed bodies (cellular casts), which may indicate infection, tumors, or injury of the kidney or the urinary passages. The presence of excessive proteins in the urine may indicate damage to the filtering mechanism of the kidneys, which normally hold back large protein molecules. The density, or specific gravity, of the urine is a clue to the fluid-concentrating power of the kidney. A measure of the efficiency of kidney function is obtained by administering a specific chemical (Phenolsulfonphthalein) and observing the rate at which it is excreted in the urine.

Urine Testing for Nonkidney Ailments. Perhaps the best-known urine test is that done for sugar, to detect diabetes mellitus, a disease in which the body cannot normally utilize sugar and consequently excretes large amounts in the urine. In the arthritic disease, gout, large amounts of uric acid (the breakdown product of purines found in organ foods such as liver and pancreas) are excreted periodically in the urine. In some muscle-wasting diseases excessive amounts of certain nitrogen compounds are excreted. Abnormal excretion of specific enzymes and hormones may be caused by tumors or inflammation of the endocrine glands, or by ulcers. The quantity of calcium and phosphorus in the urine may be a clue to the presence of certain bone and kidney diseases.
See also KIDNEY.

UTERUS [ū'tər-əs] **or WOMB,** thick-walled muscular organ in which the embryo develops during pregnancy. The lining of the uterus undergoes periodic changes during the menstrual cycle, first enlarging and then sloughing off (as the menstrual flow) in response to changes in the secretion of female hormones. In childbearing the uterus enlarges several times its size. The muscular walls of the organ contract during labor, aiding in the expulsion of the child from the womb.
See also MENSTRUATION; PREGNANCY.

V

VACCINATION [văk-sə-nā'shən], introduction of specially treated microorganisms into the body for the purpose of immunization. Usually the disease-producing organism is modified by being grown under conditions that differ in some way from its normal environment. The strain of yellow fever virus used for immunization was grown in tissue culture until it had lost its ability to produce disease. In smallpox vaccination, introduced by Edward Jenner in

1796, the closely related virus of cowpox, vaccinia, is used in unmodified form. Though this virus can cause a disease in calves, it produces only a mild local reaction in man. The immunity produced by cowpox vaccination is not permanent. Revaccination every 5–7 years is necessary to maintain an adequate level of resistance to smallpox.

See also IMMUNITY; SMALLPOX OR VARIOLA; VACCINES.

VACCINES [văk′sēnz], suspensions of living or dead microorganisms or their products, used to produce immunity against disease. The earliest known form of immunization was practiced by the ancient Chinese, who scratched the pus from a sore of a patient with mild smallpox into the skin of a previously uninfected person. This usually produced a mild case of smallpox and subsequent immunity. The practice, known as variolation, was introduced into Europe during the 18th century but encountered opposition when fatal cases of smallpox resulted.

A far better method of smallpox prevention was developed toward the end of the 18th century by the English physician Edward Jenner. Jenner observed that milkmaids and other farm workers who had contracted cowpox, a disease of cattle that superficially resembled human smallpox, appeared thereafter to be immune from smallpox. To test his observation, Jenner introduced the pus from the pocks of infected cattle into humans and later proved that the vaccinated persons were immune to material taken from human smallpox victims. Jenner used a live virus preparation (although he did not recognize it as such at the time) which differed from the smallpox virus in its ability to produce disease but retained its ability to stimulate immunity. The French bacteriologist Louis Pasteur developed a method of vaccination based upon weakening (attenuating) the disease-producing microorganism. Pasteur inoculated chickens with chicken cholera bacteria that had been weakened by cultivation in the laboratory, and showed that the animals were immune to further infection. Later Pasteur applied a similar technique to develop a vaccine to protect cattle, sheep, horses, and other animals against anthrax.

Today a considerable number of vaccines are available which offer protection against viral and bacterial diseases. Some of these preparations contain living microorganisms (like those used by Pasteur and Jenner); others consist of killed bacteria or viruses or of material extracted from the microorganisms or produced by them.

How Vaccines Work. Harmful microorganisms generally produce two effects in the body: (1) they produce disease by destroying tissue or interfering with body function, and (2) they stimulate certain cells of the body to produce specific substances (antibodies) that can neutralize the invaders. The *natural* immunity that follows disease is largely based upon the presence of these antibodies in the body or the ability of the body to produce them rapidly when needed. Vaccines are designed to stimulate the body to produce antibodies without causing disease.

Types of Vaccines

Live Preparations. As described above, these consist of living, weakened microorganisms which do not cause disease but retain their antibody-stimulating power. An attenuated bacterial vaccine against tuberculosis (BCG) has been widely used in certain European countries. The vaccine is not used on a mass basis in the United States but is reserved for previously noninfected persons who live or work with tuberculous patients, for example, doctors, nurses, and employees of tuberculosis sanatoria (*see* TUBERCULOSIS). Live virus preparations are used in yellow fever and poliomyelitis. Many authorities believe that the live virus vaccines induce active immunity more effectively than inactivated or killed virus preparations.

The Sabin vaccine is a mixture of attenuated strains of the three poliomyelitis viruses. After several years of preliminary testing, it was released in 1960 for use in the United States. The vaccine is given by mouth, and the viruses multiply in the intestine, thereby simulating natural infection with virulent virus. Some authorities have objected to the vaccine, feeling that the virus may spontaneously change (mutate) to a more virulent form and be passed on to contacts of the vaccinated individual, producing serious disease. For this reason it has been recommended that the vaccine be given in mass doses to stimulate immunity simultaneously in many members of the community.

Killed Preparations. Suspensions of killed microorganisms are generally safe but may be less effective than live preparations. Pertussis (whooping cough) vaccine is today the most widely used killed bacterial preparation in the United States. Typhoid vaccine is used in countries where typhoid fever is prevalent, but in industrialized countries it is used principally for laboratory and military personnel and for travelers. The Salk poliomyelitis vaccine is a killed or inactivated suspension of three polio viruses.

Autogenous Preparations. Autogenous (self-produced) vaccines are killed suspensions of bacteria that have been isolated from chronic infections in the individual's own body. Such a vaccine, say of killed *Staphylococcus aureus* bacteria, may be obtained from the pus fluid of boils of an individual suffering from recurrent boils. This preparation is then used to immunize the patient in the hope that anti-*S. aureus* antibodies will be produced. The treatment is sometimes but not always effective.

Preparations from Parts or Products of Bacteria. Certain vaccines contain bacterial toxins (poisonous substances secreted by the bacteria). Diphtheria toxin neutralized by antidiphtheria antibodies ("toxin-antitoxin") was formerly used to immunize against diphtheria. Now, however, diphtheria toxoid is used. A toxoid is prepared by treating toxin with formaldehyde to render it harmless. Toxoids are also used to immunize against tetanus and a few other diseases.

Complex chemicals (polysaccharides) extracted from the capsule or surface of certain bacteria are capable of producing immunity against typhoid and certain related bacteria. These materials immunize against infection with the whole organisms, and yet the injected material is so nontoxic that it causes little or no unpleasant reaction.

Serums. The term "serum" refers to the fluid part of the blood left after the cells and clotting substances have been removed. This part of the blood contains antibodies capable of attacking specific microorganisms: serum from an individual who has recovered from, and is immune to, German measles contains anti-German measles antibodies. Horses and other animals are exposed to certain organisms (anthrax and plague bacteria) to stimulate production of antibodies so that their serum (now containing the necessary antibodies) can be used to treat human victims of the disease.

Convalescent serum, obtained from persons recovering from a disease, can be injected into other persons to provide temporary passive immunity. It is called passive because the body does not actively manufacture antibodies and temporary because the immunity vanishes when the limited number of antibodies disappear from the blood. An allergic-type reaction, called serum sickness, may result from the use of serums.

See also ALLERGY; ANTIBODIES AND ANTIGENS; IMMUNITY.

VACUOLE. See CELL.

VARICOSE [văr′ə-kōs] **VEINS,** dilation of veins, most commonly seen in the legs but also occurring elsewhere in the body, such as in the scrotum and in the region of the anus. Blood returns to the heart by means of the veins. This return flow is aided by contractions of the leg muscles (during walking), which pump blood against gravity through the veins toward the heart. Delicate valves within the veins normally prevent the blood from flowing in the reverse direction. In varicose veins the valves are "incompetent," permitting the backflow of blood and causing the veins to become engorged and distended.

The condition begins primarily in young adults. The fact that varicose veins are frequently seen in several members of the same family suggests the presence of a basic inherited tissue weakness that causes the condition to appear when stress is applied to the venous system. This stress may take the form of occupations which require standing for long periods of time (thus prolonging the action of gravity but minimizing muscle action) or of repeated pregnancies, in which the pressure of the fetus on the veins may obstruct the flow of blood. Periods of brief intense activity, such as heavy lifting, may also strain the valves.

Ordinarily the symptoms are slight, consisting of a feeling of heaviness or fatigue in the legs or a burning sensation of the skin. The ankles may become swollen and the skin around the joint may become thickened and discolored. In some cases clotting of the blood within the vein (thrombophlebitis) may occur. Another complication is ulceration of the skin of the inside region of the ankle and lower leg.

Treatment. Some cases with small, localized varices can be treated by injecting the veins with a sclerosing solution, an irritant that induces blood clotting and subsequent scarring of the vein. In other instances the vein is tied high up in the thigh to prevent backflow of blood and then is removed entirely (stripped). Frequently combinations of these methods are used. Despite treatment the condition may recur. Some patients must wear elastic stockings, even after surgical correction, and reinjection or reoperation may be necessary.

VASECTOMY [văs-ĕk′-tō-mē], a method of producing sterility in the male without causing any other sexual changes. It is a quick and safe surgical procedure which closes each of the two small ducts (vas deferens) that carry the male sperm cells (spermatozoa) from one of the testes to the urethra and penis. The procedure can be performed in a doctor's office under local anesthesia, requiring no hospitalization and little, if any, loss of working time. The operation creates a mechanical obstruction which causes sterility without producing any change in sexual desire, potency, or function.

The chief utility of vasectomy is as a reliable, voluntary method of preventing further births in families who do not want any additional children. However, vasectomy may also be indicated for medical reasons. It may for example, be performed to prevent infection of the testes after a prostate operation, to preclude the transmission of an undesirable hereditary condition, or to avoid the impregnation of a woman whose health would be endangered by child-bearing.

In the United States the procedure has become increasingly popular as a safe, convenient, and almost totally effective method of birth control. It has also been widely promoted by the family-planning programs of such nations as India, Pakistan, and Korea that desire to reduce their rapid rates of population growth.

Though fertility can be restored after vasectomy in a considerable number of cases, and research is underway on methods of making the operation more regularly reversible, it is generally regarded as a permanent method of birth prevention and is recommended primarily for those couples who already have their desired number of children.

See also BIRTH CONTROL; STERILITY.

VASOCONSTRICTORS [văs-ō-kən-strĭk′tərz], drugs which constrict the blood vessels. The principal vasoconstrictor used in medicine is levarterenol (norepinephrine), a substance normally secreted by the adrenal gland and by certain nerve fibers of the sympathetic nervous system. This autonomic branch of the nervous system raises the blood pressure, increases the heart beat, expands the breathing passages, and otherwise prepares the body for vigorous exertion. Levarterenol is especially effective in cases of circulatory failure (shock) caused by overwhelming infection, burns, hemorrhage, or surgery. In these cases it raises the dangerously lowered blood pressure by constricting small arteries throughout the body.

Other drugs, such as epinephrine and ephedrine, also facilitate the action of the sympathetic nervous system, but are less effective as vasoconstrictors than levarterenol. Ergotamine is another vasoconstrictor which acts directly on the muscles of the blood vessel walls. It is used primarily in certain cases of migraine headaches to provide relief by constricting the dilated arteries of the head.

VASODILATORS [văs-ō-dī-lā′tərz], drugs that expand blood vessels. Vasodilators accomplish the expansion (1) by acting upon the autonomic nervous system, which adjusts the size of the blood vessels in response to body needs, or (2) by directly relaxing the smooth muscle in the vessel wall. The specific effect on the body varies with the drug employed. Nitrites (such as nitroglycerin) promote blood flow to the heart, hydralazine hydrochloride (Apresoline) lowers the blood pressure, and

phenoxybenzamine (Dibenzyline) increases circulation to the extremities. Depending upon their actions, various drugs of the group are therefore used in cases of heart disease, high blood pressure, and hardening of the arteries (arteriosclerosis).
See also VASOCONSTRICTORS.

VASOPRESSIN, also called Pitressin, a hormone released from the pituitary gland of the skull. Also called the antidiuretic hormone (ADH), vasopressin helps control the volume of urine production and is used specifically for this purpose in treatment of diabetes insipidus.
See also DIABETES INSIPIDUS; ENDOCRINE GLANDS; KIDNEY; PITUITARY GLAND.

VECTOR [vĕk′tər], **DISEASE,** an insect or other animal that carries infectious organisms from an infected to a noninfected individual. The vector may carry infected materials, such as feces, to food or may harbor the disease germs within its own body. In the latter case the vector may transmit the germs to the human host by excreting them upon his skin or, as in the case of the mosquito, by injecting them into his body while partaking of blood. Malaria, yellow fever, plague, and Rocky Mountain spotted fever are among the many diseases transmitted by vectors.
See also BACTERIA; VIRUSES.

VEINS, vessels which conduct blood from the tissues to the heart. The smallest veins are found in the tissues and increase in size as they approach the heart, terminating in the superior *vena cava* and inferior *vena cava*, which empty into the heart. The walls of the smaller veins are thin, consisting of a single layer of lining cells and some connective tissue and smooth muscle fibers. In the larger veins three layers are discernible, including a layer of smooth muscle fibers which aids in regulating the size of the venous channel. In the medium-sized veins of the extremities, valves prevent the backflow of blood away from the heart.
See also ARTERY; BLOOD.

VENEREAL [və-nēr′ē-əl] **DISEASES,** group of infectious diseases which are usually transmitted by sexual contact. Found throughout the world, they are among the commonest of the infectious diseases, being outranked in frequency only by the common cold and measles.

Gonorrhea, the most prevalent venereal disease, was clearly referred to in early Chinese writings and in the Bible. The name, meaning "flow of seed," was first used by Galen (c.150–200 A.D.) to describe the typical profuse urethral discharge. The gonorrhea bacteria (*Neisseria gonorrhoeae*) may spread from the urinary tract to the reproductive organs, possibly resulting in sterility in both men and women.

The history of syphilis, the most serious of the venereal diseases, is somewhat obscure. One school of thought maintains that the disease was carried from the New to the Old World by Columbus' sailors. Others have argued that syphilis was present in Europe before that time. Whatever its origins, the disease did not become widespread in Europe until the 16th century. Because of the ability of the syphilitic organism, the *Treponema pallidum*, to attack any tissue of the body and produce a vast range of symptoms, syphilis has often been confused with other diseases and has been called the "great imitator." Among the more serious complications of syphilis are involvement of the heart, great blood vessels, and nervous system.

The *Trichomonas vaginalis*, a protozoan parasite, causes venereal disease which, although extremely common, is fortunately usually not dangerous. The organism produces a greenish-white vaginal discharge in women and slight inflammation of the urethra in men. Other so-called minor venereal diseases include the chancroid (or soft chancre), *granuloma inguinale*, and *lymphogranuloma venereum*. Chancroid and *granuloma inguinale* are bacterial diseases which produce genital ulcerations similar to those of syphilis. *Granuloma inguinale* is comparatively difficult to transmit, and infection of both sexual partners is unusual. *Lymphogranuloma venereum* is caused by a large virus and causes inflammation of the lymph glands of the groin. Arthritis, fever, headache, skin eruptions, and nervous system involvement may also be seen.

Frequently, acute inflammations of the reproductive tracts are seen which cannot be ascribed to any of the above diseases. The incidence of such cases, labeled "nonspecific" or "nongonococcal" urethritis (N.G.U.), is increasing and in some clinics outnumbers gonorrhea.

The Venereal Diseases and Public Health. With the development of quick, accurate diagnostic techniques and effective, rapid treatment (antibiotics), it was hoped, and expected, that venereal disease would cease to be a public health problem. Paradoxically, however, the incidence of the diseases seems to remain the same from year to year and even increases. Syphilis, for example, has been increasing in the United States for several years. This failure in large part results from the social problems associated with the diseases, particularly the difficulty in interviewing infected patients and tracing and treating their contacts.
See also GONORRHEA; LYMPHOGRANULOMA VENEREUM; SYPHILIS.

VERRUCA. See WART.

VERTIGO [vûr′tə-gō], sensation of dizziness in which the surroundings appear to whirl about, and the individual may lose his balance and stagger and fall. Vertigo may be caused by disturbances of the balancing mechanisms of the ear and brain. This may result from tumors or infections of the ear, from circulatory disturbances (high blood pressure, arteriosclerosis) affecting the ear, or from brain tumors, generalized body infections, or drug reactions involving the vestibular apparatus (semicircular canals) or the vestibular nerve. Visual impulses are also important in maintaining balance, and vertigo consequently commonly occurs when the normal horizontal and vertical lines of the environment are altered, as in the various types of motion sickness (seasickness, airsickness). The clinical pattern of vertigo varies with the underlying disorder: sudden attacks lasting for a few hours are characteristic of certain inner ear disturbances (Ménière's syndrome), while a persistent vertigo may be caused by disease of the brain. Treatment depends on the cause.

VESALIUS [vĭ-sā'lē-əs], ANDREAS (1514–64), Flemish anatomist and founding father of modern medicine. Born in Belgium, Vesalius studied in Louvain and Paris. He was appointed professor of anatomy and surgery at the University of Padua, Italy, when he was 24 years old. For centuries anatomy had been taught by reading aloud the anatomy texts of the Greek physician Galen, whose authority was virtually undisputed for 1,300 years before Vesalius. A limited amount of dissection was permitted in Padua of the 16th century, and Vesalius took full advantage of the new freedom. He dissected animal and human corpses, and taught the anatomy he saw, rather than Galen's gospel. His precise, thorough, and largely accurate observations of the human body became the science of modern anatomy.

In 1543, when he was 29 years old, Vesalius published the results of his anatomical research in *De human corporis fabrica* (*The Fabric of the Human Body*). Its magnificent engravings were made by Stephan Calcar, who is thought to have learned as much anatomy as Vesalius. The book went through innumerable editions, roused a storm of protest from the Galenists, and opened Vesalius to charges of vivisection. He left Padua and became a court physician, his career in research at an end. He was shipwrecked and died on the way home from a visit to Jerusalem. His work remains the cornerstone of modern medicine.

VIGNEAUD [vē-nyō'], VINCENT DU (1901–), American biochemist who received the 1955 Nobel Prize for synthesizing oxytocin, a hormone which stimulates contractions of the womb at birth. His other contributions include studies on hormones, amino acids, proteins, vitamins, and synthesis of penicillin.

VINCENT'S DISEASE or VINCENT'S ANGINA, also called trench mouth. In this ulcerative condition of the mouth, throat, and gums, a thick, membranelike coating forms, and the illness may be confused with diphtheria. Infection is most often associated with a *Bacteroides fusiformis* and *Borrelia vincentii*. Poor oral hygiene, contaminated food utensils, debilitating chronic disease, and malnutrition are common predisposing factors in Vincent's disease.

Symptoms are usually confined to the mouth, with painful, bleeding gums and foul-smelling breath. Swallowing may be painful, and there may be fever and general malaise. Sometimes the oral lesions are prominent on the tonsils. Lymph glands under the chin are likely to be inflamed, tender, and enlarged. Vincent's disease can occur in any mucous membrane, such as the bronchi, rectum, or vagina. Treatment is simple, with local irrigations and appropriate antibiotic therapy, once the infectious organisms are identified. Response is prompt, and there is usually complete healing.

VIRUSES [vī'rə-sĭz], the smallest and most elementary forms of lifelike organic structures. Viruses are "obligate" parasites—an expression used by microbiologists to designate organisms which cannot exist independently of other living things. Viruses can survive in an extracellular environment but can reproduce only by invading the living cells of plants and animals.

Cells, Nucleic Acids, and Viruses. Bacteria, protozoa, and other microorganisms consist of single cells. More complicated life forms, such as ants, snakes, and elephants, consist of millions and billions of cells living in complex interaction, each cell contributing to the total functioning of the organism. The cells of all living creatures share the ability to obtain energy from food and to employ this energy to manufacture chemical substances essential for existence. The cells differ in the specific substances manufactured (depending on the specific function). Each species produces its unique array of proteins—thus turtle proteins differ from human proteins. The cell "knows" what enzymes and proteins to produce by virtue of "instructions" contained in the nucleic acids—complex molecules found in the nucleus and cytoplasm of the cell. The instructions are in the form of a code, which is determined by the specific order in which the component parts of the nucleic acid molecule are linked together. The nucleic acids reproduce themselves during cell division and are transmitted from generation to generation, ensuring that each species reproduces its own kind.

The heart of the virus is a nucleic acid. The smallest viruses consist of nothing more than a core of nucleic acid wrapped in a protein jacket. More complex viruses contain nucleic acids, proteins, carbohydrates, and fatty substances. The virus is thus essentially a complex molecule containing biochemical "know-how." The cell contains both the information for protein manufacture and the means for carrying it out. The virus contains merely the information. The obligate parasitic nature of the virus is then clear: the virus is in effect a chemical engineer lacking a chemical factory. To survive, it must make use of the chemical machinery of whole cells which it invades.

The Virus in the Cell. A particularly well-studied group of viruses are the bacteriophages, viruses which attack bacteria. Many bacteriophages consist of a tadpole-shaped outer protein jacket, which transports the active nucleic acid portion of the virus from cell to cell by means of a tail. The virus attaches to the bacteria by its tail and by means of the enzyme lysozyme eats a hole in the bacterial cell wall. It then injects its nucleic acid into the cell. The viral nucleic acid then takes command of the manufacturing resources of the cell, forcing it to manufacture virus materials instead of its normal complement of proteins and enzymes. New viruses are evidently produced in an assembly-line fashion. Viral nucleic acid and viral proteins are manufactured separately and are then assembled into whole viruses. Eventually the cell becomes laden with new virus particles, and the wall bursts, releasing the viruses, which are then able to infect other bacteria.

Lysogeny—Coexistence Between Virus and Bacteria. In some instances the virus does not destroy the bacterial cell, but merges with the nucleic acids of the cell and is reproduced, being transmitted from bacterial generation to generation. It is, however, potentially lethal. If the bacterium is exposed to changes in its environment, such as ultraviolet light or temperature variation, the virus may become active, multiply, and cause the bacterium to burst.

Animal and Plant Viruses. Although less is known about the details of virus-cell interaction among animal and plant viruses than among bacteria, the general features described above apparently apply: penetration of the virus into the cell, multiplication of the virus, and finally de-

VIRUSES 1

VIRUSES, CELLS, NUCLEIC ACIDS, AND PROTEINS
Elephants, sponges, whales, flowers, and all other living things are composed of microscopic cells. Viruses are an exception to this rule and this in part accounts for their unique and ambiguous position between the living and the nonliving.

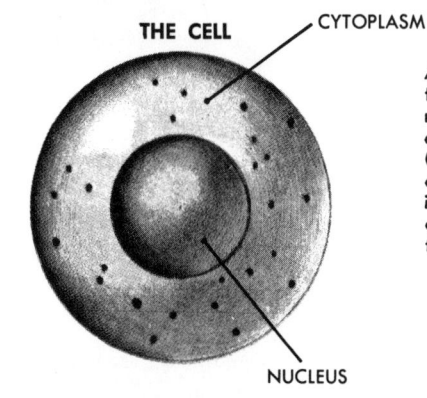

THE CELL — CYTOPLASM

All cells are able to produce energy, either from sunlight (plant cells) or from food substances (animal cells), and are able to use this energy to manufacture tissue materials. The chemical reactions underlying these activities are guided by "information" contained in certain chemicals (deoxyribose nucleic acids — "DNA") in the *nucleus* of the cell. Chemical copies of these instructions (ribonucleic acids — "RNA") are manufactured in the nucleus and travel to the *ribosomes* where they direct the synthesis of *proteins*. These three materials, DNA, RNA, and proteins, are basic to the life of the cell and to all living things, including viruses.

NUCLEUS

DNA, RNA, AND PROTEINS IN THE CELL

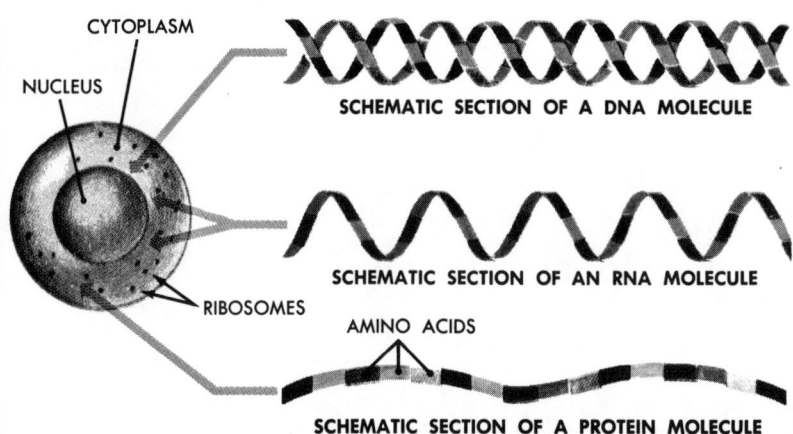

CYTOPLASM
NUCLEUS
RIBOSOMES

SCHEMATIC SECTION OF A DNA MOLECULE

DNA — the "master" chemical — lies in the nucleus of the cell. The information contained in DNA is written into the order of its constituent chemicals and is transmitted from generation to generation.

SCHEMATIC SECTION OF AN RNA MOLECULE

RNA is shaped in the nucleus on the DNA mold. The inherited information is thus stamped into the RNA and is carried by it from the nucleus to the ribosomes to guide the synthesis of proteins.

AMINO ACIDS

SCHEMATIC SECTION OF A PROTEIN MOLECULE

PROTEINS, the basic building materials of the cell, are manufactured on the RNA mold from subunits called amino acids. Many of these proteins are enzymes — agents which promote specific chemical reactions.

DNA, RNA, AND PROTEINS IN VIRUSES

Viruses consist of nucleic acids (either DNA or RNA) wrapped in a protein jacket. The significance of this structure lies in the fact that while cells contain inherited chemical instructions and the energy-producing apparatus to carry them out, viruses contain only the former. They are in effect wandering nucleic acid blueprints — chemical engineers without a factory.

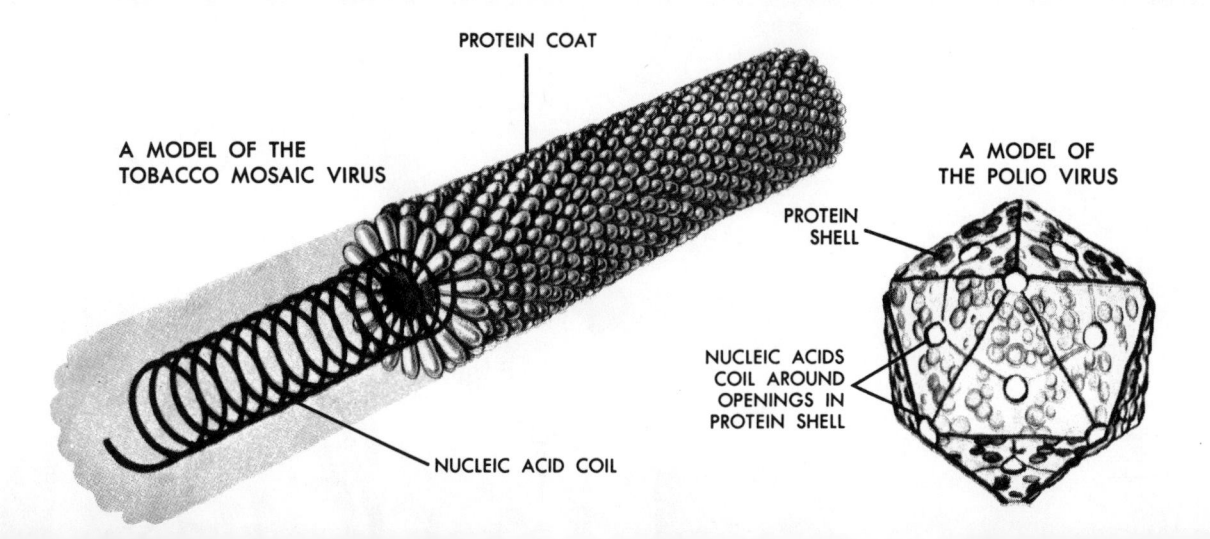

PROTEIN COAT

A MODEL OF THE TOBACCO MOSAIC VIRUS

NUCLEIC ACID COIL

A MODEL OF THE POLIO VIRUS

PROTEIN SHELL

NUCLEIC ACIDS COIL AROUND OPENINGS IN PROTEIN SHELL

VIRUSES II

HOW VIRUSES ATTACK CELLS

Normally, the activities of the cell are controlled by its own nucleic acids. In virus infections control of cell chemistry is pirated by the nucleic acids of the virus—the machinery of the cell is taken over by a new nucleic acid "master." Under the direction of the viral nucleic acids new virus particles are synthesized.

The sequence described below occurs when a bacterial virus—a bacteriophage—attacks a bacterium. The over-all pattern of events is believed to be similar in many respects to what occurs in other types of virus-cell interactions.

(1) ATTACHING TO AND ENTERING THE CELL

A tadpole-shaped bacteriophage attaches by its tail to the wall of a bacterial cell. Chemicals in the bacteriophage tail drill a hole in the cell wall: the tail contracts, and the infectious heart of the virus — the nucleic acid (in this case DNA) — is injected into the cell. The protein jacket remains outside.

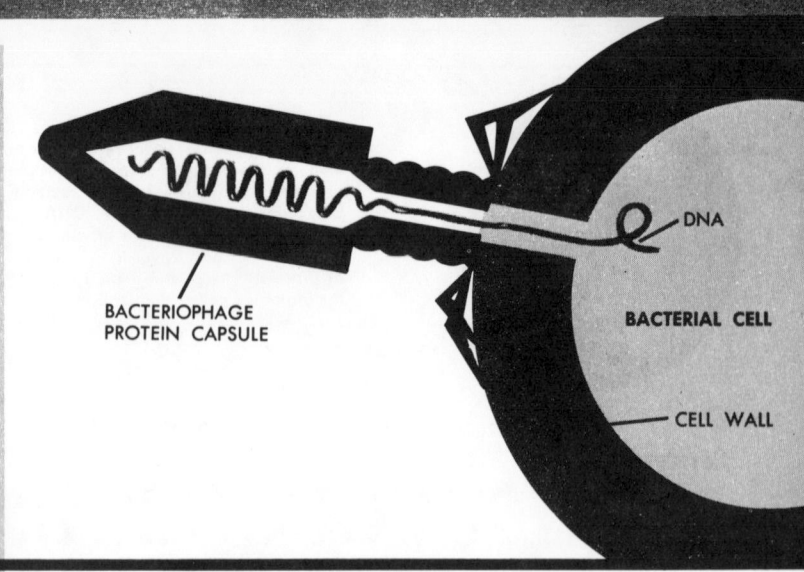

(2) SYNTHESIS OF VIRUS PARTS

Once in the cell, the viral nucleic acid inhibits the activity of the cell nucleic acids and turns the chemistry of the cell to its own purposes. New virus particles are made in assembly-line fashion. Virus nucleic acids and virus proteins are produced independently, just as engines and car bodies are manufactured on separate production lines in an automobile factory, to be assembled at a later stage.

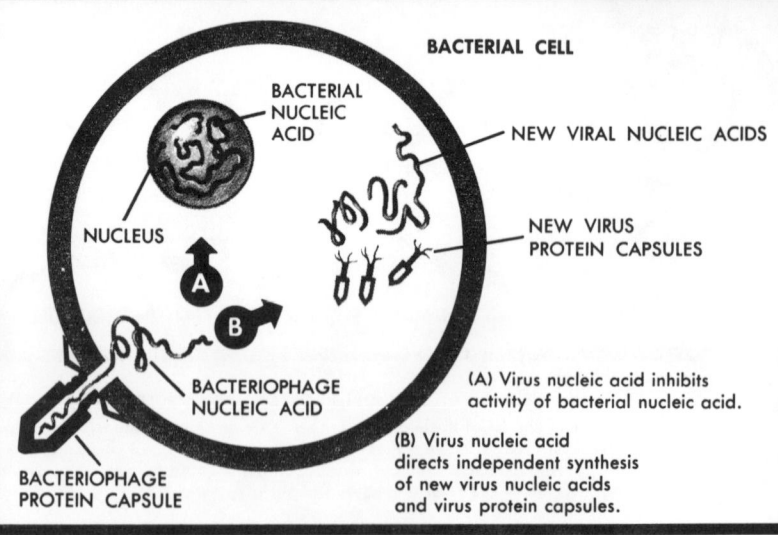

(A) Virus nucleic acid inhibits activity of bacterial nucleic acid.

(B) Virus nucleic acid directs independent synthesis of new virus nucleic acids and virus protein capsules.

(3) ASSEMBLY AND RELEASE

The viral nucleic acids are packed in the protein capsules. Finished viruses accumulate and eventually burst through the cell wall, now ready to infect other bacteria.

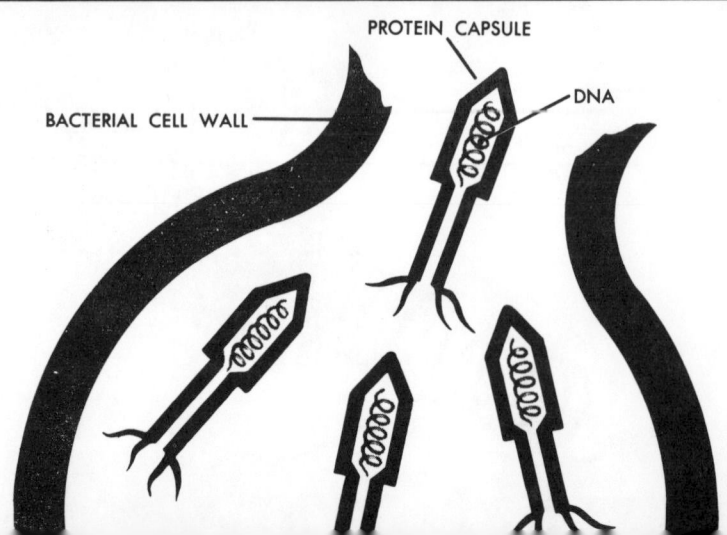

VIRUSES III

HOW VIRUSES MAY BE INHERITED—LYSOGENY

Bacteriophages do not always destroy the bacteria they invade. In some cases the viral nucleic acid merges with the bacterial nucleic acids and becomes part of the inheritance which the bacteria transmits to succeeding generations. This is called *lysogeny*.

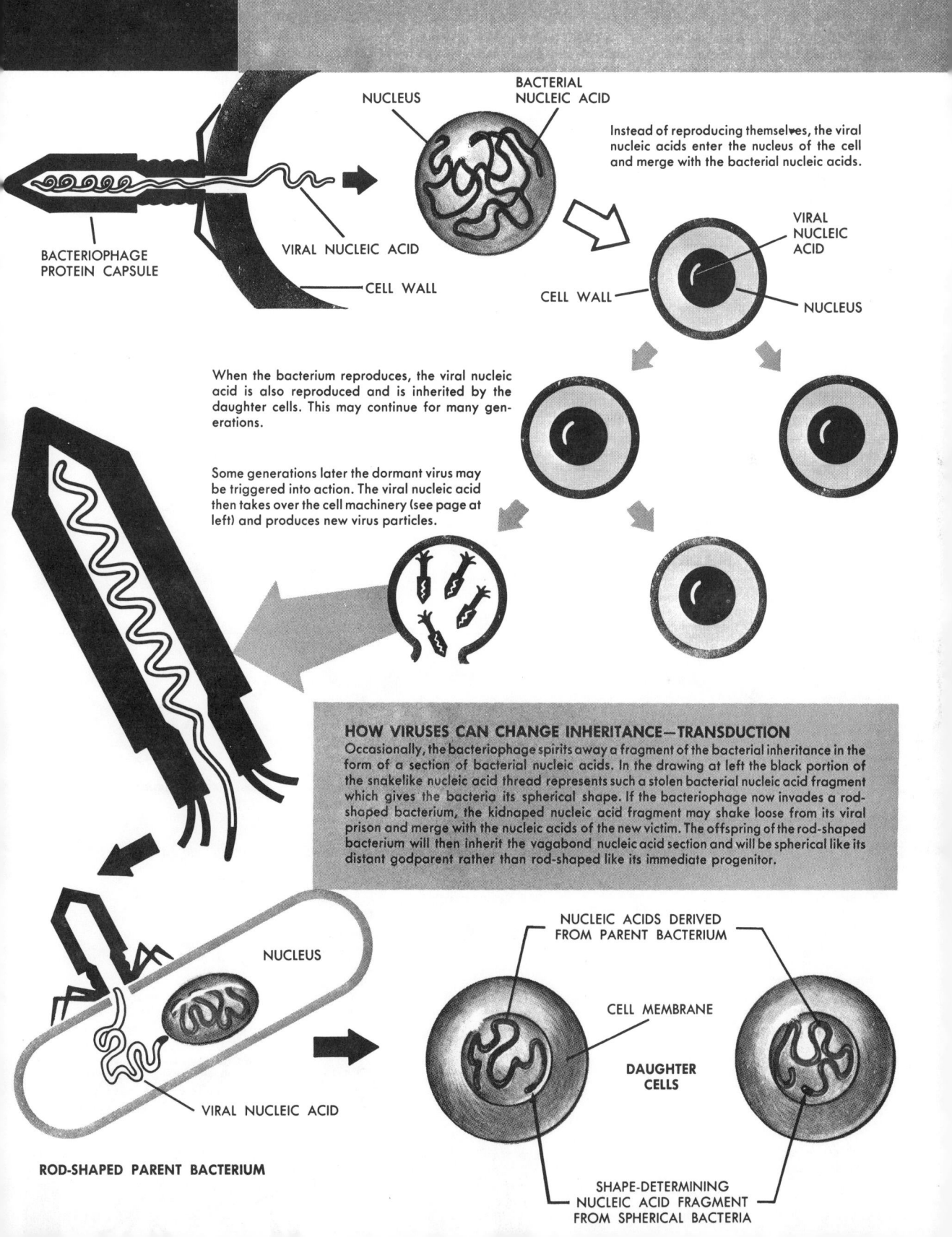

Instead of reproducing themselves, the viral nucleic acids enter the nucleus of the cell and merge with the bacterial nucleic acids.

When the bacterium reproduces, the viral nucleic acid is also reproduced and is inherited by the daughter cells. This may continue for many generations.

Some generations later the dormant virus may be triggered into action. The viral nucleic acid then takes over the cell machinery (see page at left) and produces new virus particles.

HOW VIRUSES CAN CHANGE INHERITANCE—TRANSDUCTION

Occasionally, the bacteriophage spirits away a fragment of the bacterial inheritance in the form of a section of bacterial nucleic acids. In the drawing at left the black portion of the snakelike nucleic acid thread represents such a stolen bacterial nucleic acid fragment which gives the bacteria its spherical shape. If the bacteriophage now invades a rod-shaped bacterium, the kidnaped nucleic acid fragment may shake loose from its viral prison and merge with the nucleic acids of the new victim. The offspring of the rod-shaped bacterium will then inherit the vagabond nucleic acid section and will be spherical like its distant godparent rather than rod-shaped like its immediate progenitor.

VIRUSES IV — VIRUSES AND HUMAN DISEASE

HOW VIRUSES SPREAD

ENTEROVIRUSES, such as polio and the "ECHO" viruses, infect the digestive tract and are spread by infected excrement.

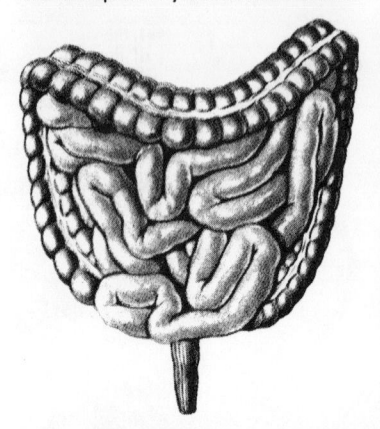

"ARBOR" (arthropod-borne) viruses infect vertebrate animals and are spread by bloodsucking mosquitoes, ticks, and other arthropods.

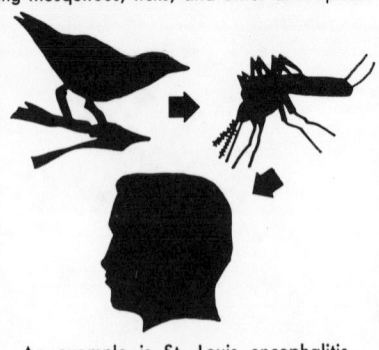

An example is St. Louis encephalitis, which is carried to man by mosquitoes from wild and domestic birds.

RESPIRATORY VIRUSES, such as those which cause influenza and the common cold, are spread by infected air-borne secretions from the nose and throat.

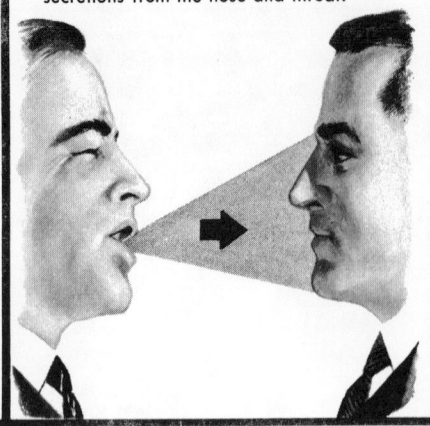

THE ACTION OF VIRUSES IN THE BODY

Viruses differ in their tendency to invade various tissues. In the tissues the viruses may (1) destroy cells or (2) stimulate abnormal reproduction of cells, leading to *tumors*. The latter effect is presumably associated with the role of viruses in *cancer*.

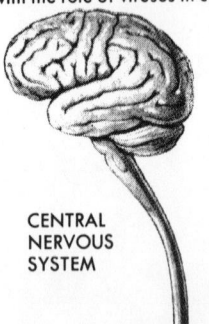

⇐ POLIO
⇐ RABIES
⇐ ENCEPHALITIS

CENTRAL NERVOUS SYSTEM

HEART

YELLOW FEVER
VIRAL HEPATITIS

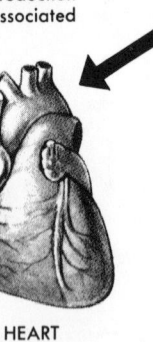

LIVER

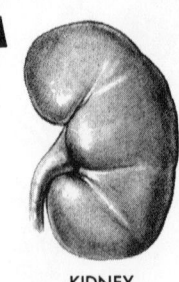

KIDNEY

HOW THE BODY DEFENDS ITSELF AGAINST VIRUSES

The body throws up two defenses against viruses: one in the blood stream, the other in the individual cell.

SPECIFIC ANTIBODIES ATTACK SPECIFIC VIRUSES

ANTIBODIES — BLOOD — VIRUS — INTERFERON — NUCLEUS — VIRAL NUCLEIC ACID — CELL

(1) ANTIBODIES IN THE BLOOD

In response to virus infection the body produces substances (antibodies) which can attack the specific infecting virus. In many cases the antibody build-up is not sufficiently rapid or massive to prevent the initial onslaught of disease, but often provides long-lasting immunity against subsequent infections by *the same virus*. Vaccines produce immunity by introducing dead or weakened viruses into the tissues to stimulate antibody production. The antibodies thus developed are usually effective only against the specific virus contained in the vaccine.

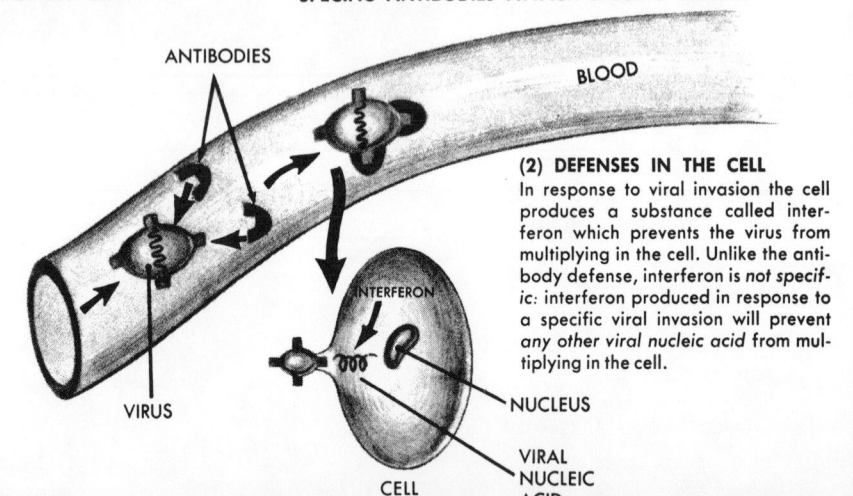

(2) DEFENSES IN THE CELL

In response to viral invasion the cell produces a substance called interferon which prevents the virus from multiplying in the cell. Unlike the antibody defense, interferon is *not specific*: interferon produced in response to a specific viral invasion will prevent *any other viral nucleic acid* from multiplying in the cell.

struction of the cell and release of the virus particles. The existence of lysogeny in plant and animal viruses is still uncertain, but it is known that some types of viruses may be present in a latent form in tissues, sporadically giving rise to disease. A familiar example of such a virus is *herpes simplex*, the organism responsible for cold sores. Recurrent attacks of cold sores are common, and the virus is thought to be present in the tissues at all times.

Mixed Infections. Two viruses may attack the same cell, resulting in independent multiplication of both viruses within the cell. In some instances the viruses may combine in the cell, producing progeny which differ from either of the parent viruses. A final possibility is that a small protein, interferon, produced by cells in response to the introduction of foreign nucleic acids (such as viruses) and other material, alters the cells so that virus multiplication is halted.

The last situation is called *interference* and was clinically observed in 1937, when investigators noted that monkeys infected with a particular virus (lymphocytic choriomeningitis) resisted infection with polio virus. The phenomenon differs from ordinary immunity in two important respects: (1) the resistance to infection with a second virus persists only as long as the first infection remains, and (2) the resistance occurs within the cell, whereas immunity is usually based upon the presence of antiviral substances in the blood. The role of interferon in human virus infections is not yet clear, but it has been speculated that some chronic latent virus infections may protect the individual against disease caused by certain other virus infections or aid in his recovery from infection.

Mutation. Viruses, as all other forms of life, may undergo spontaneous changes, or mutations, possibly altering their disease-producing potential. Such mutations are particularly significant in disease prevention, since a vaccine prepared against the virus may be ineffective against the mutant. A classic example is the influenza group of viruses, which appear to mutate frequently, making it difficult to prepare an effective vaccine. In some cases where mutation results in a loss of the ability to produce disease, the virus may be used as a "live virus vaccine" (for example, Sabin polio vaccines).

Diseases

Virus Diseases of Man. Viruses which cause human disease may be transmitted by person-to-person contact by infected droplets from the mouth and nose or by contamination with infected excrement. Some human virus infections are considered "accidental" in that the virus is normally passed in a cycle between animals and carriers, such as mosquitoes, flies, and ticks. Human infection occurs when man is bitten by the carriers of the virus.

Infection of the human host having occurred, the viruses are usually selective in their choice of tissue targets; this preference is designated as *virus tropism*. The viruses may selectively invade organ systems, such as the respiratory tract (pneumotropism), the nervous system (neurotropism), the viscera (viscerotropism), or the skin (dermotropism). In the tissues the viruses may produce one or two basic types of change: excessive growth (hyperplasia) or cellular death (necrosis). The effects on the body as a whole range from an imperceptible infection to a rapidly fatal disease. The outcome of the infection depends mainly upon the location of the infected site and the resistance which the body can bring to bear in preventing the spread of the virus.

The latter falls into two categories, *natural* and *acquired* resistance. Natural resistance refers to the resistance against infection demonstrated by the organism which has not been exposed previously to the disease. This is as yet poorly understood but is apparently related to age, sex, nutrition, and inherited factors. An example of the effect of age on natural resistance can be cited among mice. Newborn mice are considerably more susceptible to fatal infection with viruses of the Coxsackie group than are adult mice. Acquired resistance, or active immunity, describes the resistance of the organism following infection. This depends upon the ability of the body to manufacture specific antiviral substances. Several virus infections may produce a lifelong immunity, including measles, mumps, smallpox, and yellow fever. In others the state of immunity is of short duration and reinfection occurs readily.

Arthropod-borne (Arbor) Virus Infections. These viruses are maintained in nature by bloodsucking arthropods, such as mosquitoes and ticks which supply the link in transmission from infected to susceptible birds. The pattern of these diseases is complicated by bird migrations and by transmission to wild and domestic animals. Human infections may appear as only mild fevers or go totally unnoticed. However, the total impact of arthropod-borne virus diseases is considerable, involving large-scale epidemics and occasionally causing death or permanent physical and mental damage.

Enterovirus Diseases. These organisms primarily infect the human digestive tract and are transmitted by infected human excrement. Included in the group are the viruses responsible for poliomyelitis and the Coxsackie and ECHO viruses, which may cause a number of disorders involving fever, diarrhea, and inflammation of the central nervous system (aseptic meningitis). By far the greater majority of enterovirus infections are limited and do not produce observable symptoms of disease. This fact has led to the comparison of an infected population to an iceberg: a relatively small fraction of the infections produce overt disease, while the majority of infections lie below the surface of clinical detection. This pattern of distribution limits the recurrence and spread of disease, since the inapparent infections produce effective immunity.

Respiratory viruses include, among others, the common cold and influenza viruses. The latter have been responsible for numerous epidemics, including the devastating world-wide epidemic of 1918. The viruses are spread by air-borne droplets from nose and throat secretions.

Other Diseases. Many important viruses do not fall into any of the above groups. The rabies virus produces a highly lethal disease of the human nervous system and is transmitted by the bite of infected animals. Louis Pasteur prepared the first vaccine of living, weakened virus to immunize against rabies before the existence of viruses as a distinct group of disease-producing agents was recognized. The miscellaneous group also includes the viruses which cause smallpox, measles, mumps, and other diseases.

Viruses and Tumors. It has been definitely proved that

many types of animal cancers are caused by viruses. The earlier speculations that virus-induced tumors were different from "classical" tumors have not been confirmed. Investigations suggest that the tumor-producing viruses may be transmitted like other viruses, through contact with infected materials; and also that the viruses may exist for some time in a latent form in the tissues before tumors develop, and they may even be transmitted from generation to generation. These properties suggest some reasons why the cause of cancer has evaded detection.
See also CANCER; MICROBIOLOGY; VACCINES.

VISION. *See* EYE.

VITAMINS [vī′tə-mĭnz], organic substances which must be supplied in small quantities in the diets of animals and men for normal growth and development. Diseases caused by vitamin deficiencies were successfully treated and prevented long before the vitamin concept was developed. Early Greek, Roman, and Arabic physicians prescribed goat's liver (rich in vitamin A) for night blindness. The British physician James Lind in 1757 demonstrated that small amounts of fresh fruits, particularly lemon juice, prevent scurvy, a serious disorder caused by lack of vitamin C. As a result of Lind's work, lemon juice or lime juice was eventually included as a regular part of the British sailor's diet (hence the expression "limey").

Knowledge of the importance of vitamins in animal diets came in two phases: (1) recognition of the role of vitamins in disease, and (2) recognition of the importance of vitamins for normal growth.

Vitamins in Disease. The first phase began in 1885, when the Japanese physician Kanehiro Takaki introduced barley into the diet of Japanese sailors. At that time it was estimated that 40% of the navy, which subsisted largely on polished rice, suffered from beriberi. Takaki's innovation practically eliminated beriberi from the Japanese fleet, but he improperly attributed his success to the additional protein contained in the barley. In 1897 Christiaan Eijkman, a Dutch physician working in Java, moved closer to the problem of beriberi by demonstrating that a similar disease could be produced in hens by feeding them a diet of polished rice. He further observed that the symptoms vanished if the hens were fed unpolished rice. Eijkman also drew the wrong conclusions, reasoning that the rice polishings contained a substance which counteracted poisons or microbes present in the rice itself.

In 1911 Casimir Funk originated the "vitamine" theory of food substances essential to prevent certain diseases. He believed that he had isolated the pure antiberiberi material and labeled it a "vitamine," thinking that it was an amine and vital to life. The logic does not apply, since many of the vitamins are not amines, but the name has persisted, minus the final *e*.

Evidence was soon obtained that there existed more than one vitamin. In 1912 guinea pigs fed a diet designed to produce experimental beriberi developed scurvy instead, the same disease that had earlier been rampant among British sailors. The concept of multiple vitamins and their role in deficiency was further extended in 1913, when it was found that rats fed on fat-deficient diets (lacking fat-soluble vitamin A) developed an eye condition.

Vitamins for Normal Growth. The essential role of vitamins in normal growth was demonstrated by the Nobel Prize-winning English investigator F. G. Hopkins, who found that rats would not grow when given adequate amounts of proteins, fats, carbohydrates, and minerals unless small amounts of milk or other foods were added to the diet. The growth-promoting effects of these foods were caused by the presence of unknown constituents (vitamins) in low concentrations. In 1905 microorganisms were introduced as an experimental tool in vitamin studies. By observing the effects of different media on bacterial growth, researchers discovered several vitamins essential for bacteria. Some of these vitamins were later shown to be necessary for animals as well.

Naming the Vitamins. The alphabetic naming of vitamins was introduced in the early 20th century in order to avoid the cumbersome use of such terms as "beriberi preventive factor." The fat-soluble material which prevented an eye disorder from developing in rats was labeled vitamin A. The substance which prevented experimental beriberi was named vitamin B and the antiscurvy substance was called vitamin C. Vitamin B was later found to be a mixture of several vitamins, which were designated by subscripts—vitamin B_1, vitamin B_2, and so forth.

Functions. All normal activities of living things are made possible by chemical reactions which produce energy or synthesize tissue or vital substances. These reactions are initiated and expedited by enzymes; a specific enzyme facilitates a specific reaction. The vitamins function as components of enzyme systems. The fact that vitamins are needed in only small amounts is a consequence of the fact that enzymes are not consumed in the reactions which they promote. When the diet contains adequate amounts of the required vitamins, there is no advantage in giving extra amounts.

In addition to the obvious source of vitamin supply in the diet, several other avenues of vitamin supply are known. Certain intestinal bacteria synthesize vitamins, which are absorbed into the body through the intestinal wall. Some vitamins are synthesized in the tissues. The capacity for vitamin synthesis varies among different species. Rats can synthesize vitamin C and do not require it in the diet. In contrast, man, guinea pigs, and monkeys must be given the vitamin in the diet. Man does not ordinarily require vitamin K because it is synthesized by intestinal microorganisms.

Fat-Soluble and Water-Soluble Vitamins. The fat-soluble vitamins include vitamins A, D, E, and K. Among the water-soluble vitamins are the B-complex group and vitamin C. The distinction between these groups is important in that in certain disorders of fat digestion (for example, steatorrhea) deficiencies of fat-soluble vitamins may occur while the water-soluble vitamins are normally absorbed. Also, fat-soluble vitamins are stored in the liver, but the storage of water-soluble vitamins in the body is insignificant. Consequently the latter group must be supplied more regularly in the diet.

Fat-Soluble Vitamins

Vitamin A is present in high concentration in fish-liver oils; cod-liver oil is the commonest source. Yellow-orange pigments, or carotenes, known as provitamins, are found in leafy green vegetables and yellow vegetables, such as carrots, sweet potatoes, and spinach. The body can convert these substances into active vitamin A.

The vitamin is important in vision. Retinene, a vitamin A derivative, is converted into the light-sensitive pigment rhodopsin, which enables the eye to function at night under conditions of low illumination. The vitamin is also necessary to maintain the normal structure of the skin and the tissues lining the glands and intestinal tract.

Vitamin A deficiency results in damage to the eye, causing night blindness and eye inflammation. Other symptoms include eruptions and dryness of the skin and atrophy of the oil and sweat glands of the skin. There also appears to be an increased susceptibility to colds and to various types of infection.

The recommended daily intake of vitamin A is 1,500 United States Pharmacopoeia (U.S.P.) units for infants, 3,000 U.S.P. units for children up to 6 years, and 4,000 U.S.P. units for children over 6 and for adults. Excessive intake of vitamin A may produce toxic symptoms such as excessive bone fragility and enlargement of the liver and spleen. The amount of vitamin A necessary to produce these effects is many times the usual daily intake.

Vitamin D exists in two forms. Vitamin D_3, the naturally occurring form, is produced by the action of sunlight on 7-dehydrocholesterol in the skin. Vitamin D_2, or calciferol, is produced commercially by the ultraviolet irradiation of the plant steroid ergosterol. The best source of the vitamin is fish-liver oils.

Vitamin D regulates absorption of calcium and phosphorus from the intestines and is essential for normal bone growth. Deficiency in children causes rickets, a disorder marked by weak and improperly formed bones. The disease is more common in underprivileged children in cloudy, northern regions, and is rare in the tropics, where abundant sunlight stimulates production of the vitamin in the skin. Vitamin D deficiency in adults causes osteomalacia, or softening of the bones.

The recommended daily intake is 400 U.S.P. units. Overdoses may cause loss of appetite, diarrhea, demineralization of bone, and deposition of calcium in the soft tissues, particularly the kidneys. The amount of vitamin D required to produce these effects is more than 100 times the daily requirement.

Vitamin E is widely distributed in human tissues; no specific symptoms of deficiency are known. The vitamin has a sparing effect on vitamin A, increasing the storage of this vitamin in the liver.

Vitamin K is synthesized by intestinal bacteria and is therefore not ordinarily required in the human diet. The vitamin is essential for the production of prothrombin, a substance important in blood clotting. Vitamin K deficiency may occur in disorders affecting fat absorption (such as obstruction of the bile ducts and sprue). The deficiency is marked by decreased clotting power of the blood, and a tendency to bleed profusely from minor wounds. Vitamin K deficiency sometimes occurs in infants before the usual intestinal bacteria have established themselves, causing "hemorrhagic diseases of the newborn."

Water-Soluble Vitamins

Vitamin B_1, or thiamine, is found in high concentrations in the outside bran coats of grains, in yeasts, and, to a lesser extent, in meats. The vitamin forms a part of enzyme systems that enable the body to convert carbohydrates to energy. It is particularly important for the normal functioning of the nervous system. Deficiency of the vitamin results in beriberi. The body's requirement of thiamine depends upon the amount of carbohydrates consumed in the diet. The recommended daily intake ranges from 0.25 mg. for infants to 1 mg. for adults.

Vitamin B_2, or riboflavin, also called vitamin G, is a bright-yellow pigment found in yeast and liver and other animal tissues. Deficiency in man causes cheilosis, involving inflammation of the tongue and fissures at the corners of the mouth. Riboflavin deficiency is not usually encountered by itself in man, but more often it accompanies other deficiency diseases, such as pellagra and beriberi. The recommended daily intake ranges from 0.6 mg. for infants up to 1.2 mg. for adults.

Nicotinic acid, or niacin, is found in yeasts and various meats. It is converted in the body into coenzymes, which makes possible numerous chemical reactions. Niacin deficiency results in pellagra (literally "rough skin"), a serious disease marked by skin eruptions, digestive disturbances, and mental changes. It is likely that other dietary factors are also involved. Niacin can be manufactured in the body from tryptophan, one of the amino acids found in protein foods (for example, milk and milk products). The dietary requirement is consequently related to the intake of this amino acid; the recommended daily intake is approximately 20 mg.

Folic acid is widely distributed in plant and animal tissues and is essential for the manufacture of important structural components of body cells. Experimental deficiencies produced in animals cause anemia. Deficiencies in man are encountered in sprue, a disorder in which absorption of nutrients through the intestinal wall is impaired. Folic acid corrects the anemia in this condition and is also effective in treating certain types of anemia in infants and pregnant women. Because folic acid is so liberally distributed in nature and, in addition, is synthesized by intestinal bacteria, it is not considered likely that dietary deficiencies could occur.

Pantothenic acid is another widely distributed vitamin, found in liver, kidney, egg yolk, yeast, vegetables, milk, and grains. The vitamin is important for the production of energy and for the synthesis of several hormones. Various experimental deficiencies in animals have caused graying of the hair, hemorrhages, and skin inflammation in rats and poor feathering and disturbances of growth in chickens. Deficiencies in man are unlikely, and no minimum requirement has been set.

Biotin. The best food source of biotin is liver, but it is also found in egg yolk and yeast. The vitamin functions in various enzyme systems involved in the manufacture of tissue. Experimental deficiencies of biotin (causing skin and nerve lesions and death in animals) have been produced by feeding large quantities of raw egg white. The egg white contains a protein, called avidin, which combines with biotin and prevents its absorption. Avidin is destroyed by cooking and thus does not ordinarily interfere with biotin absorption. Biotin is synthesized by intestinal bacteria, and deficiencies in man are usually not seen.

Vitamin B₆, or pyridoxine, is found in yeast, liver, and numerous plants. The vitamin takes part in reactions involving certain amino acids (the building blocks of proteins) and fatty acids. Pyridoxine deficiency in man is extremely rare; no minimum requirement can be given.

Vitamin B₁₂, or cyanocobalamin, is found in high concentrations in liver and is necessary for the production of deoxyribonucleic acid (DNA), an essential component of cell nuclei. Vitamin B₁₂ deficiency causes pernicious anemia, a disorder characterized by anemia and degeneration of nervous tissue. In pernicious anemia the patient lacks the essential "intrinsic factor," which is normally produced by the stomach and is essential for the absorption of vitamin B₁₂. Administration of vitamin B₁₂ is effective in treating the disease.

Inositol is found in high concentration in certain plant products, particularly wheat germ, and in certain fatty compounds of the body. Inositol deficiency has not been observed in man, and no minimum requirement can be given.

Para-aminobenzoic acid is widely distributed in plants and animals and is found in high concentration in liver and yeast. It appears to be a precursor of folic acid.

Vitamin C, or ascorbic acid, is present in high concentration in citrus fruits. It protects certain other vitamins from destruction in the tissues, particularly folic acid coenzymes. Vitamin C deficiency causes scurvy, a disorder marked by loosening of the teeth, small hemorrhages throughout the body, anemia, edema, and joint pain. The recommended daily intake of ascorbic acid is 10 mg. for infants, 20 mg. for children, and 30 mg. for adults.

See also:
BERIBERI PELLAGRA
DIGESTION RICKETS
METABOLISM SCURVY
NUTRITION SPRUE

VOCAL CORDS. See LARYNX.

W

WAKSMAN [wăks'mən], **SELMAN ABRAHAM** (1888–1973), American microbiologist who was awarded the Nobel Prize in physiology and medicine in 1952 for the discovery of streptomycin. Born in the Ukraine, Waksman went to the United States in 1910 and was naturalized in 1916. He was educated at Rutgers University and the University of California and joined the teaching staff at Rutgers in 1918. In 1915 he began studies of soil bacteria, which led to the discovery of streptomycin. The Nobel citation specified the importance of streptomycin as the first antibiotic effective against tuberculosis. Among his books are *Soil Microbiology* (1952) and *My Life with the Microbes* (1954).
See also ANTIBIOTICS.

WART [wôrt], also known as verruca, growth of the upper layer of the skin presumably caused by a virus. Warts are most common in adolescence, and may occur on any part of the body, usually on the hands, fingers, face, scalp, knees, and the soles of the feet. If untreated, warts may spread, remain unchanged for weeks to years, or disappear spontaneously. It has been experimentally demonstrated that some warts can be passed from person to person. There are four principal types of warts. (1) Flat, or juvenile, warts are flat-topped, slightly raised, tan-colored spots usually seen on the face and hands. These are most common in children, and may occur in linear arrangement along the course of scratch marks. (2) Common warts are raised, irregular, thick growths occurring anywhere on the body. (3) Plantar warts are painful, callous-covered warts seen on the sole of the foot. (4) Moist, or "venereal," warts are cauliflower-shaped growths found in areas where skin and mucous membrane join (such as the anus and genital region). Warts can be removed by surgery, electric cautery, dry ice, acids, or X rays, but they tend to recur.

WASSERMANN [väs'ər-män], **AUGUST VON** (1866–1925), German physician who devised a laboratory test for the diagnosis of syphilis. He studied in Erlangen, Munich, Strasbourg, and Vienna. In 1906 he became director of the department of experimental therapy and serum research at the Robert Koch Institute for Infectious Diseases in Berlin and in 1913 director of the Kaiser Wilhelm Institute for Experimental Therapy at Berlin-Dahlem. In 1906 he devised the complement fixation test (the "Wassermann test") for the diagnosis of syphilis.

WASSERMANN [wŏs'ər-mən] **TEST,** also known as the cardiolipin test, diagnostic procedure used to detect syphilis. The test is based on the presence of special substances (antibodies) contained in the blood of individuals who have syphilis. In the original test, fetal liver containing *Treponema pallidum* (the organism which causes syphilis) was mixed with a sample of blood. If the blood contained syphilis antibodies a reaction would occur in which *complement* (a substance normally present in blood) was consumed. The present method utilizes a purified extract of beef heart to which fatty substances have been added (hence the designation "cardiolipin"). A positive Wassermann test is not always an indication of syphilis, since false

positive reactions may occur following certain illnesses or after certain vaccination procedures.
See also SYPHILIS.

WATER POLLUTION. Water is polluted when its natural character and its ability to support plant or animal life are altered to an appreciable degree by the introduction of any alien substance. Generally, one thinks of water pollution as a byproduct of the disposal of municipal sewage or industrial wastewater. In the larger perspective, however, the introduction of anything, even sea water, into a body of fresh water is a form of pollution, and pollution can result from natural processes not normally under man's control.

Sources of Pollution. Pollution may be introduced from a point source or from a diffuse source, or may result from a combination of the two. In the case of point-source pollution, the contaminants are discharged into the body of water at one location or at individual points not widely separated. Among the sources of such pollution are municipal or industrial sewers, the outlet pipes of wastewater treatment plants, and abandoned mines. Diffuse-source pollution results from the runoff of rain from farms, woodlands, and uninhabited land areas. Polluting substances washed from farms may include livestock manure, insecticides, weed killers, fertilizers, organic matter from decaying vegetation, and soil from both cultivated and uncultivated land.

Effects of Pollution. Pollution may be classified as to the effects it exerts on the receiving waterway, stream, lake, or estuary. These effects may be visual, chemical or biochemical, biological, sedimentary, thermal, or ecological, or a combination of two or more.

Visual effects are most pronounced near the discharge point of a wastewater outlet. They generally appear as a "plume," usually composed mostly of small particles and dissolved substances that impart a color to the water. Color is more noticeable in many industrial wastes than in municipal wastes.

Chemical effects often occur where industrial wastes are discharged. Generally the most noticeable effect is on the water's acid-alkalinity relationship, as measured by the pH of the water. Municipal wastes generally have a pH that is approximately normal and therefore exert little influence on the pH of receiving waters. Other chemical effects depend on the particular wastes discharged. For example, wastes from some industries contain metals, certain of which may be toxic, for example, mercury, chromium, or lead. Wastes from pesticide production may contain exotic organic chemicals harmful to aquatic life.

Biochemical effects of wastewaters are most important. These effects result from the degradation of organic matter by microbiological organisms, principally bacteria and protozoa. Organic matter is essential to the life and growth of microorganisms, which utilize the organic matter in the presence of oxygen to produce energy and cell growth. In the course of this action, the oxygen, normally dissolved in water, may be used up. Biochemical oxidation of the organic matter eventually results in the production of carbon dioxide and water and a stable residual matter. However, if the amount of oxygen in the water is not sufficient to satisfy the needs of the microorganisms as they consume the organic matter, the water will become devoid of oxygen and a septic condition will result. The water may become black and foul-smelling and fish and other aquatic life will die.

Biological or bacteriological effects are of particular importance when the supply may be used as a source of drinking water for a municipality. All domestic sewage contains bacteria and other microorganisms, and some of these organisms are pathogenic, or harmful to humans. Fortunately, most of these harmful organisms die off in a relatively short time when discharged into natural streams. But when the pollution load is great, a flowing stream cannot purify itself quickly and poses a health hazard to a municipality's water supply.

Sedimentary effects occur when the wastes contain suspended matter in any appreciable quantity. When discharged into a slow-flowing or quiet body of water, these suspended solids settle out. If the material is organic in character it will undergo decomposition in the absence of oxygen and will produce soluble products, methane and carbon dioxide gases, and sometimes the odorous hydrogen sulfide. It will also produce a residue of sludge which covers the bottom and interferes with the food supply of bottom-feeding fishes. Inorganic sediments also may cover the bottom and prevent growth of the bottom organisms on which higher life forms depend for food.

Thermal effects obviously are most evident where hot water, with or without pollutants, is discharged into a body of water. When the volume and temperature of the wastes are high, the receiving waters may be warmed to a degree that adversely affects the normal chain-of-life growth of aquatic forms.

The ecological effect is the total effect of pollution on the environment. As indicated above, bottom sediment may interfere with the life cycle of worms, which serve as food for higher life forms and thus such sediment may cause the eventual disappearance of fish life. Chemicals and oxygen-demanding substances likewise may interfere with the life cycle of some organisms in the chain of plant and animal feeding, growth, and reproduction.

Certain chemicals may serve to "fertilize" the growth of algae or other free-floating bottom and attached plants. The result may be an overgrowth, or bloom, followed by death, decay, and oxygen-depletion, with all the undesirable effects indicated previously. The residue from such growths, along with sludge and other solid residues from municipal and industrial wastes, contribute to the aging or eutrophication of lakes. Under natural conditions, the complete eutrophication, or "filling up," of a lake with organic and inorganic debris might take 10,000 years or more. On the other hand, under the influence of the wastewaters from modern civilization some lakes may disappear or fill up in much less than 1,000 years.

Extent of Pollution. In 1970 the total domestic sewage of the United States, for example, amounted to about 21,-000,000,000 gal. of sewage a day containing 32,000,000 lb. of solid matter and requiring some 27,000,000 lb. of oxygen. Added to these wastes are the wastes from thousands of industrial plants. About half of the industrial wastes produced are discharged into municipal sewers. The rest is treated or discharged directly into receiving waters. The total load of wastes produced by U.S. industry is about equal to that from humans. Obviously, if there were no waste treatment facilities, there would be few streams or lakes that would not be grossly polluted.

The establishment of the municipal waste-treatment or pollution-abatement facilities that existed by 1970 involved the expenditure of some $10,000,000,000. Some estimates indicate than an equal sum is needed for treatment of municipal wastes plus some $50,000,000,000 for the separation and handling of storm waters. From a technological viewpoint, both municipal and industrial wastes can be treated satisfactorily to prevent water pollution. The cost of building the needed facilities is great and the most important question today is how to finance the needed construction.

See also AIR POLLUTION.

WEIGHT CONTROL. *See* NUTRITION.

WHIPPLE, GEORGE HOYT (1878–), American pathologist, who in 1934 shared the Nobel Prize in physiology and medicine with William P. Murphy and George R. Minot for his studies on the effectiveness of liver in the treatment of anemia in dogs. Whipple was educated at Yale and Johns Hopkins. He held positions at Johns Hopkins, the University of California, and the University of Rochester. Whipple's studies on pernicious anemia were carried out independently of the joint work of Murphy and Minot.

WHIPWORM INFECTION, also known as trichuriasis, infestation with the parasitic intestinal roundworm *Trichurus trichiura*. Found throughout the world in regions with warm moist soil, the infection is contracted by consuming contaminated food or water. The eggs hatch in the small intestine and a few days later the larvae migrate to establish permanent residence in the cecum, the first part of the large intestine, where they may remain for months or years. In the intestines adult worms excrete thousands of eggs per day in the feces. The eggs require a few weeks of development in warm moist soil before they are suitable for infecting a new victim to continue the cycle.

Mild infections may go unnoticed, but in severer cases abdominal pain and tenderness, nausea, vomiting, flatulence, and headache develop. In extremely heavy infections (most frequently seen in children) the stools may be loose and bloody and the victim may suffer from severe anemia and weight loss. Treatment with dithiazinine usually eliminates the worms. Infestation can be prevented by sanitary disposal of human feces and by proper personal hygiene. Whipworm infection is commonly associated with hookworm and roundworm in the same person.

WHOOPING COUGH, also known as pertussis, an acute infectious disease of the breathing passages caused by the bacteria *Hemophilus pertussis* (more recently called *Bordetella pertussis*). Epidemics of whooping cough occur in large cities throughout the world, usually at intervals of two to four years. While the disease may occur at any age, it is more frequent and more serious in early childhood. Females are more often affected than males—an unusual feature of incidence for an infectious disease.

Three Stages. The bacteria are transmitted by infected air-borne droplets. Whooping cough is often described as occurring in three stages: *catarrhal, paroxysmal,* and *convalescent.* Following an incubation period of seven to fourteen days, the *catarrhal* stage, resembling a common cold, begins with a mild cough, sneezing, and nasal discharge. This phase persists for about two weeks to be followed by a *paroxysmal,* or *spasmodic,* stage, which is marked by explosive coughing. Several complications may occur at this time. These include bronchopneumonia and collapse of small portions of the lung (Atelectasis); the latter may result from plugs of mucus lodged in the air passages of the lungs. Convulsions are also seen. In the *convalescent* stage the coughing attacks gradually decrease and the patient improves, but secondary infections may bring a recurrence of the paroxysms for many months. Following recovery the patient is immune to further attacks.

Treatment and Prevention. Therapy against the whooping cough organisms consists of specially prepared blood serum and Chloramphenicol and tetracycline antibiotics. These are generally used in severe cases. In milder attacks treatment is directed at the symptoms and consists of oxygen, if necessary, and bed rest. Vaccination against whooping cough is usually given in infancy, followed by several "booster" doses at 2-year intervals. Control of epidemics emphasizes isolation of patients, particularly during the highly contagious catarrhal stage.

WINDAUS [vĭn'dous], **ADOLF** (1876–1959), German organic chemist who clarified the structure of cholesterol and a number of other steroids and showed their relation to vitamin D, the chemistry of which he worked out. In addition to working on vitamin D, for which he received the Nobel Prize in 1928, he studied the cardiac glycosides of digitalis, vitamin B_1, and a number of important natural products.

WISDOM TOOTH. *See* TEETH.

WORLD FEDERATION FOR MENTAL HEALTH, organization which originated in 1920 as the International Committee for Mental Hygiene. The founders were Clifford Whittingham Beers, a leader in U.S. mental health programs, and Clarence Meredith Mincks, pioneer in Canadian programs. The present name was adopted in 1948. The federation co-operates with the World Health Organization on problems of mental health. Headquarters are in London.

WORLD HEALTH ORGANIZATION (WHO), U.N. specialized agency, established to perform a variety of functions in achieving its objective: "the attainment by all peoples of the highest possible level of health." The idea for WHO originated with a proposal for the creation of a specialized health institution made in 1945 at the San Francisco Conference on International Organization. The constitution of the World Health Organization was drafted and signed in July, 1946, in New York by representatives from 61 countries. The constitution came into force on Apr. 7, 1948. Thus, World Health Day is celebrated on Apr. 7 each year. WHO began functioning officially as a permanent organization on Sept. 1, 1948.

The World Health Organization may help governments, upon request, to strengthen their health services and may furnish technical assistance to such governments. It may stimulate work to eradicate epidemic or endemic diseases and promote the improvement of nutrition, sanitation, or working conditions and other aspects of environmental hygiene. Campaigns to control and eradicate diseases such as malaria, tuberculosis, syphilis, yaws, influenza, cholera, rabies, alcoholism, and mental disease have been undertaken by WHO.

X

X RAYS, DIAGNOSTIC. Toward the end of the 19th century the German physicist Wilhelm Konrad Roentgen produced a photograph showing the bones of his wife's hand. Roentgen accomplished this by allowing radiation (the "X" rays which he had recently discovered) to pass through the hand and register upon a sensitive plate behind it. Since that early photograph the invisible X rays have become an indispensable tool of medicine, enabling physicians to diagnose fractures and diseases of the bones, lungs, and viscera.

ROTATING-ANODE X-RAY TUBE
The modern X-ray tube operates on the principle discovered by Roentgen in 1895. A high-power, high-vacuum device, it produces intense heat that would have melted Roentgen's tubes. Most of this heat is dissipated by a rapid rotation of the anode.

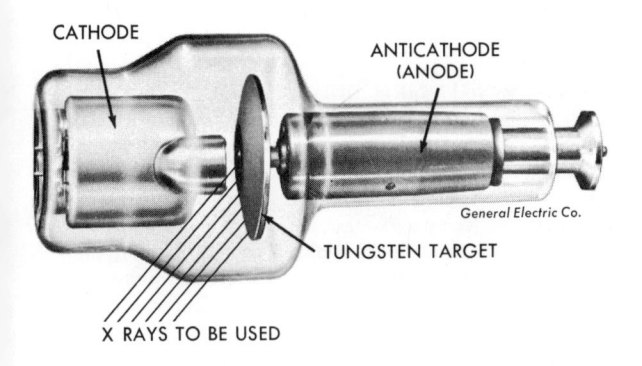

CATHODE
ANTICATHODE (ANODE)
General Electric Co.
TUNGSTEN TARGET
X RAYS TO BE USED

The basic principle of X-ray diagnosis is that the various tissues of the body differ in their density and the resistance which they offer to the passage of radiation. The denser the tissue, the whiter it appears on the X-ray film. Air spaces and extremely loose tissues appear as black, and structures of intermediate density are seen as varying shades of gray. Reading and accurately interpreting X-ray plates is a highly skilled undertaking which requires great familiarity with the normal appearance of structures on X-ray films. If one lacks such experience, an error of diagnosis is inevitable. For example, growth lines in the long bones of children can be mistaken for fractures, and normal blood vessels in the lungs can be (and have been) mistaken for streaks of diseased tissue.

Bones, with their high calcium content, are denser, heavier, and harder than other tissues and appear white on X-ray plates. Fractures may be seen as darker lines or areas within the bone. Diseases of bone may also alter the density of the bone and produce changes in the X-ray film. For example, spread of cancer from the prostate gland to bone produces areas of increased density, and spread of cancer from the breast to bone may cause areas of decreased density.

Diseased tissue in the lungs may appear as abnormal areas of white or light gray against the background of normally dark gray or black lung fields. Solid white patches in the lung may be caused by pneumonia or by areas of dead tissue which have been deprived of their blood supply. Other variations from the normal pattern may indicate tuberculosis, cancer, or other diseases. Through the expert use of X rays the heart and the soft tissues of the upper abdomen can be visualized and made to appear white against the blackness of air in the lungs. Air in the stomach or gas in the colon appears black on the film.

Special Techniques. X-ray studies of the digestive tract are made by administering barium sulfate suspensions in the form of enemas to examine the large intestine or by mouth to visualize the esophagus, stomach, and small intestine. The barium produces a strong contrast with surrounding soft tissues and enables the physician to inspect the size, shape, and position of the gastrointestinal organs.

Iodine is another dense material which is administered in the form of organic compounds to study the blood vessels, the air passages (bronchi) of the lungs, and many other parts of the body. Certain iodine compounds are excreted by the liver or kidneys, making possible X-ray examination of the gall bladder and bile ducts (which carry the liver secretions) and the kidneys, ureter, and bladder.

For some purposes less dense contrast materials are employed. Helium or oxygen may be injected into joint cavities, the spinal canal, or the cavities of the brain (the ventricles).

See also RADIATION THERAPY.

Y

YAWS [yôz], also known as frambesia or pian, is an infectious disease caused by the *Treponema pertenue*, a microorganism identical in appearance to *T. pallidum*, which causes syphilis. Seen in tropical areas of high rainfall and dense vegetation, yaws may affect up to 75% of the population under the age of 14 in some localities. The organism enters through abraded skin following direct contact with an infected person, and it is believed that insects may also play a role in transmission. Three to four weeks after exposure the primary lesion, or "mother yaw," appears—a painless, raised, ulcerated growth, seen usually on the leg. Several weeks later similar growths appear. "Crab yaws"—painful lesions on the sole of the foot—may be extremely disabling. The yaws tend to heal, although relapses may occur from time to time. After several years, destructive "late-lesions" similar to those seen in syphilis may appear on the skin and in the bones. Yaws is rarely fatal and an immunity develops over a period of time.

YELLOW FEVER, also known as yellow jack, an acute infectious disease caused by a virus and transmitted by certain mosquitoes. The earliest recorded epidemic of yellow fever occurred in the Yucatán Peninsula of Central America in 1648. Throughout the 17th, 18th, and 19th centuries the disease was prevalent in the Caribbean and occasionally epidemics flared in warm weather in Baltimore, New York, and other coastal cities of the United States. There were an estimated 500,000 cases in the United States between 1793 and 1900. A great epidemic in Spain in the 19th century caused 60,000 deaths.

Knowledge of the cause and transmission of the disease was an outgrowth of the Spanish-American War at the end of the 19th century. Numerous cases of yellow fever among soldiers of the U.S. Army in Cuba led to the establishment of a yellow fever commission, headed by Maj. Walter Reed. This group demonstrated that the organism which caused the disease was considerably smaller than bacteria (we now know it to be a virus), and that it could be transmitted by the mosquito *Aëdes aegypti*. On the basis of these findings the Army physician William Gorgas was able to eliminate yellow fever from Havana by destroying the breeding sites of the mosquito. Later Gorgas supervised similar sanitary measures in Panama, facilitating construction of the Panama Canal.

This success led to the expectation that the disease could be brought under control by attacking the *A. aegypti*, thus destroying the man-mosquito cycle which perpetuated the infection in a given region. Despite these campaigns, however, yellow fever persisted and epidemics reappeared. Eventually it was recognized that other, forest-dwelling mosquitoes (*Haemagogus*, and *A. simpsoni* and *A. africanus*) could maintain and transmit the infection among primates and marsupials (wombat, opossum). These mosquitoes could also transmit the infection to man in jungle areas. Thus, today two forms of yellow fever are recognized: the *urban form*, spread by the *A. aegypti* and occurring in highly populated regions, and the *jungle* (or sylvan) *form*, spread by the mosquitoes cited above.

In both types the illness varies markedly from a mild, fleeting fever to a rapidly fatal disease. Following an incubation period of three to six days, fever, headache, and backaches appear suddenly. In the ensuing three to four days the face is flushed, the eyes are congested, the pulse is slow, and nausea and vomiting occur. At the end of this time the fever diminishes, the flushing and congestion fade, and a tendency to bleed appears. Hemorrhages may occur from the gums or nose or into the skin, intestines, and stomach. Bleeding into the stomach may result in the classic "black vomit," an ominous sign. The organs most severely attacked are the kidneys, the heart, and the liver (involvement of which may cause jaundice, a yellowish tinting of the skin and eyes). Albumin appears in the urine, and in severe cases kidney failure may develop. The death rate has been estimated at 10%. A permanent immunity follows recovery. No specific treatment is available for yellow fever. Bed rest and analgesics are helpful. Fluid is administered to replace that which has been lost through vomiting.

Prevention and Control. Urban yellow fever can usually be controlled by measures against the *A. aegypti*, which usually breed in stagnant water in and around human dwellings. This has been highly successful in the Americas, but less so in Africa, where the *A. aegypti* is apparently able to survive in the forests. The difficulty in eradicating forest mosquitoes places the emphasis in jungle yellow fever prevention upon vaccination with two strains of weakened yellow fever virus (known as the "French neurotropic" and "17D" strains). Mass vaccinations have been used in South America (Colombia) and in Africa.

A curious aspect of the geographic distribution of yellow fever is its absence from certain parts of the world (for example, Asia) although suitable mosquito carriers are present. A possible explanation of this fact may lie in the pattern of overlapping immunity: research has indicated that exposure to certain virus diseases, such as dengue, results in the production of blood substances (antibodies) capable of neutralizing the yellow fever virus.

INDEX

Bold type indicates pages with illustrations.

Abdominal pain, 24, 125, 295, 382, 397
Abdominal surgery, 382
Abducens nerve, 104
Abortion, 1, 49, 50, 330; spontaneous (miscarriage), 1, 86, 119, 322, 324, 384
Abscess, 1–2, 221, 305
Accessory nerve, 104
Accidents, 349–351; poisoning, 315–319
Acclimatization, 2
Acetanilide, 18
Acetic acid, 40, 158
Acetylcholine, 2, 97, 107, 241, 267, 268, 270, 271, 278, 281
Achilles' tendon, 177, 387
Achlorhydria, 2
Achondroplasia, 132
Acidosis, 2–3, 119, 227
Acne, 3, 5–6, 34, 352, 362
Acoustic nerve, 31, 104, 108, **135**
Acromegaly, 3, 147, 191, 194, 215, 248, 311, **390**
Acrosome, 141
Actidione, 19, 20
Actin, 49, 268, 270
Actinomycetes, 3–4, 19
Actinomycosis, 4, 126, 305
Acupuncture, 4, 96, 251
Adam's apple, 4, 233
Adams-Stokes attack, 250
Adaptation, evolutionary, 2, 46, 187
Addison's disease, 3, 4–5, 7, 36, 58, 103, 147, 227, 255, 375
Adenine, 41, 85, 189, 331
Adenohypophysis, 144, 309
Adenoids, 5, 108, 369
Adenomyosis, 195
Adenosine triphosphate (ATP), 30–31, 84, 104, 231, 261, 269, 270
Adhesions, 5
Adipose tissue, 390
Adolescence, 5–6, 194, 304
Adrenal cortex, 3, 4, 6–7, 41, 105, 144, 145, **146**, 147, 227, 276, 290, **309**, 355
Adrenal crisis, 5
Adrenal gland, 3, 6–7, 10, 59, 74, 102, 144, **145–146**, 211, 215, 276, 309, 329, 344; Addison's disease, 3, 4–5, 7, 103, 147, 227, 375; alarm reaction, 355; Cushing's disease, 7, 105, 147, 290
Adrenal hormones, 6–7, 41, 144–146, 240, 273, 294, 329; aldosterone, 6, 7, 375; androgens, 6–7, 77, 145; corticosteroids, 102–103, 146, 227, 375; corticosterone, 375; cortisone, 3, 5, 7, 12, 26, 27, 30, 102–103, 131, 375; glucocorticoids, 6, 145; hydrocortisone, 3, 5, 6, 131; mineralocorticoids, 6, 145, 146
Adrenalin (epinephrine), 2, 6–7, 14, 30, 41, 59, 130, 144–146, 148, 150, 212, 262, 276, 281, 282, 285, 376, 400
Adrenal medulla, 6, 7, 144, 145, **146**, 150, 276, **309**
Adrenergic fiber, 2, 125, 280
Adrenocorticosteroids, 227
Adrenocorticotrophic hormone (ACTH), 3, 7, 145, 146, 273, 276, 309, 311
Aëdes mosquito, 111, 265, 414
Aesculapius, 251
Afferent nerve fiber, **277**, 282
Afibrinogenemia, 159
Agammaglobulinemia, 7, 181–182, 191
Ageusia, 386
Agglutination, 21, **56**, 62–63
Aging, 291; of skin, 291, 362
Agranulocytosis, 7, 61
Air pollution, 7–9
Albinism, 9, 183, 255
Albumins, **56**, 127, 325; in urine, 325–326

Alcohol, 10, 79, 128, 170, 172, 328; as antiseptic, 23; and barbiturates, 130
Alcoholism, alcoholics, 9–10, 38, 98, 226, 258, 283, 298, 304, 315, 326; acute (drunkenness), 10, 14; Antabuse therapy, 10, 18; coma, 100; delirium tremens, 9, 111, **196**, 388
Aldolase, 270
Aldosterone, 6, 7, 375
Aldosteronism, cause of alkalosis, 10
Alkaloids, 312
Alkalosis, 10–11, 19
Alkaptonuria, 183, 262
Alkylating agents, 77
Allergic shock, 15, 211, 356
Allergies, 3, 11–12, 18, 20, 21, 100–101, 126, 211; drug, 11, 15, 20, 30, 126, 131, 211, 305; food, 11, 289; insect bites, 11, 22, 30, 222; patch test, 302; skin, 11, 12, 118, 126, 137, 211, 212; treatment, 12, 22, 103, 199
Allotransplants, 292
Alpha globulins, **56**, 191
Altitude, acclimatization to, 2, 12
Alveolar sacs (alveoli), 70, 143, 242, **341**, 344, **345**
Ameba, 12–13, 81, 340
Amenorrhea, 257
Amentia, 258
Amethopterin, 77
Amino acids, 14, 41, 46, 47, 84, 121, 122, 238, 239, 240, 260–262, 286, 287, 288, 325, 403; essential, 14, 260, 287, 325; incomplete, 287
Aminobenzene, 18
Aminophylline, 30
Aminopterin, 77
Aminopyrine, 7, 15
Amnesia, 14, 100
Amnestic confabulatory syndrome, 231
Amniocentesis, 189–190
Amniotic fluid, 88, 189, 340
Amphetamines, 38, 128, 129–130, 290, 376
Amputation, 14; phantom limb pain, 295
Amylase: pancreatic, 122; Salivary, 121, 122, 329, 351
Amyloidosis, 14–15
Anabolism, 260
Anacidity, stomach, 376
Analeptics, 376
Analgesics, 15, 27, 28, 36, 111, 129, 130, 200, 272, 295, 332
Anaphase, cellular, 264, **264**
Anaphylactic shock, 15, 211, 356
Anaphylaxis, 15, 347
Anatomy, 43, 45, 46, 308, 381, 402
Androgens, 6–7, 77, 145, 146, 339, 375
Androsterone, 72, 375
Anemia, 11, 15–16, 18, 26, 61, 63, 103, 206, 208, 213, 353, 373, 374; aplastic, 336; in children, 302, 303, 409; deficiency, 15–16, 61, 126, 208, 287, 288, 289, 325; hemolytic, 15, 61, 208, 226, 358, 372; hypochromic, 15; pernicious, 2, 16, 61, 63, 126, 192, 263, 283, 288, 410; sickle-cell, 15, 358
Anesthesia, 16–18, 36, 96, 106, 130, 151, 253, 265, 285, 295, 381–382; in childbirth, 88, 295; electrical induction, 249; epinephrine and, 150, 285; hypnosis as, 216, 295
Aneurysm, 18, 25, 208, 383, 384–385
Angina pectoris, 203, 204, 295
Angioneurotic edema, 18
Aniline, 18, 75
Ankylosing spondylitis, 24
Anopheles mosquito, 245, **246**, 247, 265, 349
Anorexia nervosa, 18, 125
Anosmia, 367, 386

Anoxia, 18, 29, 86
Antabuse, 10, 18
Antacids, gastric, 18–19
Anthracosilicosis, 314
Anthrax, 19, 31, 126, 190, 220, 263, 301, 399–400
Antibiotics, 19–21, 31, 34, 88, 130, 192, 221, 254, 287, 302, 305, 346, 380; achromycin, 2, 31, 388; actinomycin, 4, 19, 77; allergic reactions to, 11, 15, 20, 211, 305; aureomycin, 2, 31, 388; and cancer, 77; chloramphenicol, 19, 21, 131, 255, 396, 412; enzyme inhibitors, 148; erythromycin, 21, 131; resistance to, 20, 131, 305, 315, 374, 388; streptomycin, 4, 11, 19, 20, 131, 225, 238, 243, 294, 377, 394–395, 410; terramycin, 31, 388; tetracycline, 2, 4, 19, 20, 96, 131, 193, 348, 388, 395, 396, 412
Antibodies, 7, 11, 12, 21–22, 23, 158, 181, 191, 218–219, 221, 222, 287, 346, 372, 399–400, **406**; agglutination, 21, **56**, 62; immunological response to transplants, 21, 230–231, 292, 313
Anticoagulants, 22, 26, 131, 204, 208, 389
Anticodon, 285
Anticonvulsants, 130
Antidiuretic hormone (ADH), 145, 146, 227, 230, 282, 310, 311, 401
Antigens, 21–22, 62–63
Antihemophilic factor (AHF), 61
Antihistamines, 12, 22, 67, 128, 199, 211, 212, 221, 347
Antimetabolites, 77, 236
Antipyretics, 15, 130
Antireticular cytotoxic serum (ACS), 64
Antiseptics, 22–23, 102, 127, 221, 238, 381
Antitoxin, 23, 218–219, 391
Aorta, 23–24, 26, 57–58, 201, 202, 342, 344; aneurysms, 18, 24, 384–385
Aortic valve, 206
Aphasia, 24, 199, 370, 371–372
Aphonia, hysterical, 369–370
Apomorphine, 143, 265
Appendicitis, 24, 125, 193, 295, 382
"Arbor" (arthropod-borne) viruses, 406, 407
Arcus senilis, 24
Areola, 70
Arm: bones, 268, 359, **360**; muscles, 268–269
Aromatic amines, 75
Arrhythmia, 206
Arsenic, 24–25, 35; poisoning, 255, 283
Arsphenamine, 138
Arteries, 26, 57–58, 99, 177, 201; first aid in bleeding, **160**, **161**; grafts, 18, 25, 26, 292; surgery, 383
Arterioles, 57–58, 59, 216
Arteriosclerosis, 25–26, 52, 119, 178, 258, 289, 383, 397; aneurysms, 18, 25, 208; and blood pressure, 25, 26, 58; cerebral, 14, 25, 86, 326, 378; coronary, 203, **204**, 205; death rate, 238; and leg amputation, 14, 178; and memory loss, 14, 326; obliterans, 182; stress and, 26, 355
Arthritis, 26–28, 36, 242, 262, 290, 291; drugs, 15, 26, 27, 28, 29, 225; gout, 3, 27, 178, 289, 331, 387, 398; in hemophiliacs, 208; infectious, 27, 178; "migratory," 26, 346; osteoarthritis, 26–27, 29; rheumatoid, 3, 15, 26, 29, 99, 103, 127, **178**, 221, 355, 387; of the spine, 24, 26, 27, 242, 321
Artificial organs, 47, 230, 250, 254
Artificial respiration, 28–29, 161
Ascaris (roundworm), 28–29, 126, 273

INDEX

Asepsis, 22, 213, 238, 253, 381
Asian flu, 221, 314
Asparaginase, 236
Aspergillosis, 29
Asphyxiation, 29, 161
Aspirin, 11, 15, 26, 28, 29–30, 72, 130, 131, 295; poisoning, 315, 316, 318
Association neuron, 282
Asthma, 11, 12, 22, 30, 70, 79, 102, 103, 126, 127, 143, 148, 150, 199, 211, 242, 329, 344
Atabrine, 30, 385
Ataxia, 30, 385; Marie's, 248
Atelectasis, 242, 412
Atherosclerosis, 25, 97, 127, 258, 262, 291, 376
Athetoid palsy, 86
Atomic radiation, 220
Atrioventricular (AV) node, 201
Atrium, 57, 201, 202, **205**; congenital defect, **204**
Atropine, 31, 38, 111, 280, 354
Audiometry, 136
Auditory nerve, 31, 104, 108, **135**
Auricle, 57
Autism, 31
Autoclave, 263
Autografts, 292, 293, 313
Autointoxication theory, 291
Autonomic drugs, 130–131
Autonomic (automatic) nervous system, 68, 125, 130, 275, 276, **277**, 280, 328, 362, 384
Autopsy, 31
Autosensitization, 12
Autosomes, 184
Autotrophism, 237
Axon, 67, **268, 278**, 281
Azathioprine, 293

Bacillus, 31
Bacitracin, 31
Backache, 196, 241–242, 349
Bacteria, 3–4, 31–32, **33**, 34, 41, 81, 126, 176, 182, 243, 262, 263, 299, 347, 372, 396, 411; aerobic vs. anaerobic, 32; agglutination, **56**; antibiotic-producing, 19, 34; antiseptics, 22, 23; cocci, 98; enteric, 131, 396; enzymes and, 148; gram-positive vs. gram-neagtive, 32, 305; intestinal, 32, 131, 224, 287, 351, 408, 409; phagocytosis, **56**, 306, 344, **345**; resistance to drugs, 20, 31, 305, 315, 374, 377; toxins of, 34, 42, 126, 176, 391; viral attack on, 35, 402, **404–405**
Bacterial diseases, 34, 126, 253, 263, 314; immunity, 218–219
Bacterial infection, 7, 34, 64, 221, 243; abscesses, 1–2; and arthritis, 27, 178
Bacteriological warfare, 42
Bacteriology, 43, 46, 213
Bacteriophage, 35, 402, **404–405**
Baghdad boil, 234, 392
Balance, body, 31, 136–137, 401
Ballistocardiograph, 35
Barbiturates, 11, 35–36, 128, 129, 130, 131, 327, 328, 381; and alcohol, 130; overdose, 100, 130, 161, 376; poisoning, 100, 315, 316, 378
Barium enema, 147, 182, 413
Barlow's disease, 354
Barton, Clara, 36, **337**, 338
Basal ganglia, 275, 282, 301
Basal metabolic rate (BMR), 36, 224, 260
Baths, medicinal, 36–37, 308
BCG vaccine, 37, 394, 399
Beadle, George Wells, 37, 46, 183, 188
Bedsores, 37, 397
Bed-wetting, 37
Behavior, 283, 326–327, 328; animal studies, 151, 282–283; child development, 89–95; compensatory, 100; compulsive, 326; conditioned response, 90, 282; learned, 255–256; rigid vs. flexible, 274
Belladonna, 31, 38
Bell's Palsy, 38
Bends, the, 110–111, 220

Benzedrine, 38, 376
Beriberi, 38, 126, 175, 180, 288, 393, 408
Bertillon measurements, 39
Berylliosis, 39
Beta globulins, **56**, 191
Beta hemolytic infections, 208
Bibliotherapy, 39
Biceps, 39, **269**
Bicuspids (premolars), 117, 386, **387**
Bile, 39, 41, 97, 125, 181, 207–208, 225, 239, 240, 244, 346; acids, 97, 240, 375; pigments, 207–208, 225–226, 239, 240, 346, 373, 382; salts, 39, 121, 240
Bile ducts, 96, 98, 181, 225, **239**, 240, 413
Binet-Simon Test of Intelligence, 39
Biochemistry, 39–42, 45, 46, 85, 188
Bioengineering, 47–48
Bioinstrumentation, 47–48
Biological clocks, 42
Biological warfare, 42
Biology, 42–46; molecular, 46–47
Bionics, 48
Biophysics, 45, 48–49
Biopsy, 49
Biotin, 409
Birth control, 49–50, 175, 351–352, 400
Birth defects, 86, 303
Birth injuries, 302, 303
Birthmarks, 50–51
Bis-phenols, 22, 23
Black Death, 34, 51, 148, 251, 311–312
Blackwater fever, 245
Black widow spider, 51, 222
Bladder, urinary, 52, 92, 152, 227, 384; cancer of, 74, 75, 353; infection, 34, 106; stones, 73; x-rays, 413
Blastodisc, 139–140, 141
Blastomycosis, 52, 126, 263
Blastula, 141, 142
Blindness, 52–55, 191, 197, 385, 391; in diabetics, 52, 119; hysteric, 127, 370; premature infants, 346
Blind spot, 55
Blister beetle, 222
Blood, 55–63; acidity-alkalinity balance of, 2–3, 19, 127, 207, 227, 262, 342, 344; arterial vs. venous, and color, 207; calcium concentration, 144, 145–146, 299–300; carbon-dioxide concentration, 29, 342, 344; cholesterol level, 25, 376; circulation, 57–60, 198, 242; composition, 55; disorders, 61, 373, 374; fat level of, 25, 26; functions, 55–57, **122**, 207, 340, **342–343**; groups and typing, 62–63, 302, 346; oxygen content, 12, 15, 18, 105, 320, 342, 344; protein, 56, 57, 137, 240, 325
Blood bank, 63
Blood-brain barrier, 276
Blood cells, red, 55, **56**, 63, 207, 225–226, 240, 343, 344, 345–346, 372, 373; deficiency, see Anemia; excess: polycythemia, 61, 64, 143, 320; sickle-cell, 358
Blood cells, white, 1–2, 16, 21, 55, **56**, 57, 63, 77, 158, 221, 235–236, 244, 292, 320, 372; deficiency: see Leukopenia and Neutropenia; excess: leukocytosis, 24, 61, 63, 236; granulocytes, 7, 61, 235, 236; leukocytes, **56**, 236, 306; lymphocytes, 236, 372, **373**; phagocytes, 218, 306
Blood clots, clotting, 22, 25–26, **56**, 60–61, 159, 209, 224, 240, 287, 388, 389; disorders, 61, 159, 208, 240
Blood count, 63
Bloodletting, 64, 252
Blood plasma, 55, **56**, 63, 227, 343, 344; expanders, 313
Blood platelets, 16, 55, **56**, 60, 63, 320, 372; deficiencies, 11, 61, 63, 235, 373, 374
Blood poisoning, 34, 64, 221, 255
Blood pressure, 58, 202; and arteriosclerosis, 25, 26, 58; dialostic vs. systolic, 58, 216, 372; drug effects on, 2, 6, 131, 400–401; effect of smoking on, 284; high, 127, 137, 164, 206, 215–
216, 227, 289, 328, 329, 378, 384; measurement, 58, 372; regulation of, 2, 59, 212, 227, 276, **280**, 281
Blood serum, 62
Blood sugar, 118–119, 145, 147, 150, 192, 212, 215, 217, 222–223, 238, 240, 254, 262, 290, 298
Blood transfusions, 61–63, 292, 293, 346, 381; and hemolytic anemia, 15
Blood vessels, 57–60, 362, **364**; surgery, 383, 389
Blue baby, 64, 206
BMR (basal metabolic rate), 36
Body fluids, 243, 287; excess, **see** Edema; osmosis, 293; regulation, **56**, 57, 59, 145–146, 212, 227, **230**, 309, 351; salt content, 206, 207, 306
Body temperature, 158–159, 163; regulation, 57, 158, 362, **364**
Body types, 64, 308
Boil, 34, 65
Bone(s), 65, **66**, 320, 359, **360–361**, 390; calcium content, 73, 287, 293, 347; diseases of, 179, 293–294, 409; fracture, 162, 179, 359; grafts, 65, 179, 292, 313; growth, 194, 347, 359; mineralization, 347; ossification, 359; x-rays of, 413
Bone cancer, 336; amputation, 14
Bone infection. See Osteomyelitis
Bone marrow, 15, 16, 61, 65, 77, 236, 336, **361**, 372; grafts, 236, 292; RE cells, 238, 344–346
Bornholm disease, 103
Botany, 43, 45, 46
Botulism, 23, 34, 67, 176, 219, 391
Bradycardia, 67, 206
Bradykinin, 362, 364
Braille system, 53–54, **197**
Brain, 67–69, 181, 199, 258, 274, **275–277**, 281, 305; aneurysm, 18; auditory center, **135**; biochemistry, 40, 41; blood supply, 202, 258; concussion, 100, 258; damage from stroke, 378; electrical stimulation of, 282; embolism, 61, 139, 378; encephalitis, 143, 258; fetal damage, 86, 258; hemorrhage, 25, 86, 100, 378; hydrocephaly, 215; meningitis, 34, 64, 103, 108, 126, 256–257; microcephaly, 258, 263; motor area, 277, **279**; occipital (visual) center, 153, 155, 292; olfactory area, **276**; pain perception, 295, **296**; research, 282–283; respiratory center, 129, **277**, 342, 344; senility, 355; size, 103, 200, 275, 359; during sleep, 365; subdural hematoma, 207; surgery, 240, 280, 283, 383–384, 392; syphilitic damage, 258, 300, 384; tumors, 30, 282, 383, 401
Brain waves, 45, 136, 139, 249; research, 282
Breakbone fever, 111
Breast, 69–70; cancer, 74, 76, 77, 78, 248, 388, 413; hormone action on, 70, 145, 309, 310, 311, 324; mastitis, 248; in pregnancy, 70, 322, 323, 324, 340; pre-menstrual, 257; surgery, 248, 313
Breastbone (sternum), 359, **360**
Breast feeding, 70, 248, 294, 303
Breathing, 119, 340, **341–343**, 344
Breech birth, 89
Brill-Zinsser disease, 396
Brittle bone disease, 179
Brocken specter, 70
Bromides, 70
Bronchi, 70, **71**, 106, 150, 242
Bronchial arteries and veins, 242
Bronchial asthma, 11, 30, 70, 102
Bronchial tree, **71**, 76, **341**
Bronchiectasis, 70, 240
Bronchioles, 70, 143, 242, 341
Bronchitis, 70–71, 102, 143, 367
Brucellosis, 20, 34, 71, 159, 219, 263, 377, 388
Bubonic plague, 312
Buerger's disease, 71–72, 384
Bumps, the (coccidioidomycosis), 98
Bunion, **72**, **177**, 178
Burns, 72, 163, 308; chemical, first aid, 317

INDEX

Bursitis, 15, 27; achilles, **177**
Butazolidin, 26, 27

Caesarean section, 89
Caisson disease, 110, 220
Calcaneus, 177, 387
Calciferol, 409
Calcium, 72–73, 232, 287, 293, 299–300, 347, 361, 386, 409; absorption, 287, 288; blood level, 144, 145–146, 299–300; regulation of, **300**
Calculi (stones), 73, 181, 398
Callus, 73, 178, 179, 362
Calorimeter, 45
Camphor, 73, 225, 358
Canaliculi, 66; bile, **239**
Cancer, 73–78, 127, 283, 395; cause of, 73; cell growth, 73, **75**; in children, 302; danger signals, 78, 208; death rates, 73, 238, 302; detection methods, 77–78, 413; drug therapy, 4, 77, 151, 207, 284; immunity, 76; incidence and distribution, map 74; kinds of, 73; metastasis, 73, 76, 395; radiation as cause of, 73, 75–76, 336; radiation therapy, 78, 335, 336; viral, 73–74, 286, 406, 407–408
Candicidin, 19, 20
Capillaries, 57, 58, 59, 78, 232
Carbohydrates, 40, 78–79, 192, 222, 238, 240, 260, 262, 286, 287; digestion, 121, **122**, 260, **261**, 329; metabolic disorders, 262
Carbolic acid, 22, 213, 238, 253
Carbon cycle, 32, 79
Carbon dioxide, 40; excess in body, 29, 267, 344; exchange for oxygen, **56**, 207, 242, 341–343, 344; in photosynthesis, 41, 79
Carbon disulfide poisoning, 258
Carbon monoxide, 79; poisoning, 18, 79, 100, 161, 208, 220, 258, 317, 350
Carcinogens, 73, 74–75
Carcinoid syndrome, 79
Carcinoma, 73
Cardiac muscle, 267
Cardiac reserve, 203
Cardiazol, 358
Cardiolipin test, 410
Cardiology, 253, 254
Caries, 112, 167
Carotenoids, 48
Carotic sinus reflex, 202
Carotid artery, **58**, 202, 342, 344
Carpus, 196, 359
Cartilage, 40, 65, 80, 194, 320, 359; grafts, 292, 293, 313; in joints, 80, **360**
Cascara, 233
Castor oil, 79, 157, 233
Castration, 151, 375, 387
Catabolism, 260
Catalepsy, 80
Cataplexy, 80
Catatonia, 80
Cathartics, 233
Catheter, 80, 347
Causalgia, 295
Cauterization, 80, 381
Cavernous hemangiomata, 51
Cavity, dental, 80–81, 111, 112, **113–114**
Celiac disease, 81, 244, 374
Celiac ganglion, **280**
Cell, 81–86, 237, 285, 402; basic types, 390; cancerous *vs.* normal, 73, **75**; chemical synthesis in, 41, 82, 84, 260, **403**; cleavage, 141, 142; differentiation, 142–143, 237; division, 82, 85, 237, 325; energy production in, 40–41, 46, 82, 84, 192, 231, 237–238, **261**; growth, 194–195; meiotic division, 137–138, 141, 254–255; mitotic division, 141, 255, 263–264; osmosis, 293; specialization, 81, 142; structure, 82, 83–84; theory, 46, 81; viral attack on, 402, **404–406**, 407
Cellulose, 40, 78–79, 82, 192, 320
Cereals, 170, 175, 287, 288, 289, 325
Cerebellum, 30, 275, **276**, 279, 282

Cerebral arteriosclerosis, 25, 86; amnesia, 14, 326
Cerebral cortex, 135, 240, 281, 282, 295–296, 365; evolution, paleo- to neocortex, 274, **275**
Cerebral embolism, 61, 139, 378
Cerebral hemorrhage, 25, 86, 100, 378
Cerebral malaria, 245
Cerebral palsy, 86–87, 258, 298; speech problem, 369, 370, 371
Cerebral thrombosis, 61, 378, 389
Cerebrotonia, 64
Cerebrum, 240, 267, **279**, 292
Cervix, 195, 217, 375; cancer of, 74, 77, 195; "incompetent," 322
Chagas' disease, 87, 393
Chalazion, 87
Chancroid (chancre), 401
Character disorders, 259, 326–327, 328, 368
Charcot-Marie-Tooth disease, 248
Charcot's joint, 87
Chemical warfare, 87–88
Chemotaxis, 56
Chemotherapy, 76–77, 78, 88
Chickenpox, 88, 126, 143, 181, 219, 332, 347
Chiggers, 88, 198, 222
Childbed fever. *See* Puerperal fever
Childbirth, 88–89, 196, 252, 253, 295, 303, 311, 340; date estimate, 321; multiple birth, 321–322, 395; premature, 303, 322, 346
Child development, 89–95, 194, 303–304; speech, 368–369, 370, 371, 378–379
Childhood diseases, 238, 302, 303
Chinese traditional medicine, 4, 95–96, 251
Chiropody, 315
Chiropractic, 96, 366
Chitin, 40, 320
Chlamydozoaceae, 20
Chloral hydrate, 96
Chlorambucil, 77
Chlorine, 287; as poison gas, 87
Chlorine bleach poisoning, 315
Chloroform, 17, 96, 225
Chlorophyll, 40, 48–49, 82, 325
Chloroplast, 82, 148, 237
Chloroquine, 30, 96, 245
Chlorpromazine, 388
Chlorpropamide, 96, 119
Cholanzitis, 96
Cholecystectomy, 181, 382
Cholera, 34, 96–97, 149, 219, 263, 305, 329, 332, 380, 391; bacteria, 33, 96, 231, 323; vaccine, 219, 399
Cholesterol, 25, 97, 151, 181, 205–206, 234, 262, 289, 324, 375–376, 387
Choline, 97, 238, 262, 288
Cholinergic fiber, 2, 125, 280
Chordotomy, 97
Chorea, 97, 346
Choriocarcinoma, 77
Choroid, **152**, 153, **154**
Choroiditis, 97
Chromatid, 264
Chromatin, 264; filaments, **84**, 85
Chromatophores, 308
Chromosomes, 47, 82, 85, 97–98, 182–184, **185**, 285, 286; maps, 186; in meiosis, 137–138, 141, 188, 254–255; in mitosis, 141, 255, 263–264; nondisjunction and trisomics, 188; sex, 183–184
Chyme, 121
Ciliary muscle, **152**, 153, **154–155**, 157, 273
Circulatory system, 55, 57–60, 201, 310, 340, 372; collapse, 356, **357**; development of, 142
Cirrhosis, 127; of the liver, 10, 98, 137, 209, 289, 353
Citric acid cycle, 231, **261**
Clavacin, 19
Clavicle, 359, **360**
Cleft palate, 98, 126, 187–188, 198, 284, 313; and speech, 369, 370, 371
Clonal reproduction, 190

Clostridium botulinum, 34, 67, 176
Clostridium tetani, **33**, 388
Clubfoot, 98, 126
Cobalt therapy, 336
Cocaine, 98, 130, 272, 328
Coccidioidomycosis (coccidioidae granuloma), 98, 263, 314
Coccyx, 359
Cochlea, 108, 134–135, 136
Codeine, 98, 200, 265, 272, 292, 295
Cod-liver oil, 98–99, 175, 240
Colchicine, 27
Cold, common, 99, 126, 284, 407
Cold sores, 99, 407
Colic, 99; biliary, 181
Colitis, 99; ulcerative, 99, 103, 125
Collagen, 65, **66**, 325, 362; diseases, 26–27, 99, 221
Collarbone (clavicle), 359, **360**
Collateral circulation, 203
Colon, 99, **123**, 131, 132, 224; cancer of, 74, 78
Color vision, 99–100, 156
Colostrum, 340
Coma (optical aberration), 1
Coma (unconscious state), 100, 258; diabetic, 119, 227; insulin, 223, 358; treatment, 38
Combat fatigue, 100, 356
Compensatory behavior, 100
Complement fixation, 21, 67
Concussion, 14, 100, 258
Conduction deafness, 108
Congenital defects, 126, 132, 302, 303, 322–323, 383; heart disease, 34, 126, 204–205, 206, 305, 382
Conjunctiva, **152**, 154, 159
Conjunctivitis, 100–101, 193
Connective tissue, 344, 390; development of, 142; diseases, 26–27, 99, 221
Constipation, 101, 125
Contact dermatitis, 11, 12, 22, 118, 126
Contact lenses, 30, 101–102, 273
Contraception, 49–50, 324
Cornea, 102, **152**, 153, **155**, 227, 273, 391; transplants, 52, 102, 293, 313, 383
Corns (heloma), 102, **177**, 178, 362
Coronary (artery) disease, 203–204, 205, 262, 383
Coronary thrombosis, 164, 203, **204**, 383, 389
Corpulmonale, 102
Corpus luteum, 145, **146**, 257, 294, 310, 323–324, 340
Corticosteroids, 102–103, 146, 221, 227, 236
Corticosterone, 375
Cortisone, 3, 7, 102–103, 375; as a drug, 5, 12, 26, 27, 30, 103, 131, 199, 212, 215, 221, 305, 376
Cosmetic surgery, 313, 362
Cowpox, 103, 252–253, 366, 399
Coxsackie virus, 103, 256, 407
Cranial capacity, 103, 200, 275, 359
Cranial nerves, 103–104, **277**
Cranium, 359
Creatine, 104, 270
Creeping eruption, 232
Cretinism, 104, 132, 147, 192, 258, 287, 389, 390
Cross-eyedness, 156, 377, 383
Cross-fertilization, 210
Croup, 104, 143, 232
Cryptococcosis, 104
Culex mosquito, 265
Curare, 2, 17, 105, 148
Curettage, 105
Cushing's disease, 7, 105, 147, 290
Cushing's syndrome, 105, 311
Cyanide, 105, 312; poisoning, 18, 105, 148
Cyanosis, 29, 79, 105, 330
Cybernetics, 106
Cyclopropane, 17, 106
Cyclothymic personality type, 259
Cysticercosis, 385
Cystic fibrosis, 106, 125, 189, 244, 306, 362

INDEX

Cystinuria, 183
Cystitis, 34, 106
Cystocele, 106, 196
Cytochromes, 107
Cytogenetics, 188
Cytology, 43, 85–86
Cytoplasm, 82, 83, 189, 237, 264, 285
Cytosine, 41, 85 189
Cytoxan, 77

D & C (dilatation and curettage), 1
Darwin, Charles, 45, 46, 107, 183
Deafness, 107–109, 294, 383; lip reading, 109; occupational, 220; sign language, 109
Death, 109–110, 348
Death rates, 110, 238, 351; from accidents, 349, 351; arteriosclerosis, 238; cancer, 73, 238, 302; infectious diseases, 238, 302, 315, 396, 414; from poisoning, 315; smoking and, 367
Decompression sickness, 110–111, 139, 220
Decubitus ulcers, 37, 397
Deficiency diseases, 15–16, 126, 175, 244, 287, 288, 289, 293, 302, 304, 323, 325, 347, 354, 374, 393, 408
Dehydration, 111
Delirium, 111
Delirium tremens, 9, 111, 130, 196, 388
Deltoid muscle, 111
Delusions, 326, 328
Dementia, 111; praecox, 326
Demerol, 111, 200, 272
Denasality, 369
Dendrite, 278, 281
Dendrons, 67
Dengue fever, 111, 222, 414
Dental decay, 80–81, 111, 113, 167, 323, 386
Dentistry, 111–117, 167, 252, 387; specializations, 112, 117
Dentition, 117
Dentures, 112, 115, 117
Deoxyribonucleic acid. See DNA
Deoxyribosephosphate, 4, 189
Depressants, 129, 130
Depression, 117–118, 200, 247, 255, 326, 327, 358, 376
Dermal abrasion, 352
Dermatitis, 118; contact, 11, 12, 22, 118, 126, 313
Dermatology, 213
Dermatomyositis, 118
Dermatophytosis, 30
Dermis, 308, 362, 363–364
Dexedrine, 38, 376
Dextran, 112, 118, 313
Dextrose, 192
Diabetes insipidus, 118, 227, 311, 401
Diabetes mellitus, 2, 3, 52, 63, 87, 118–119, 147, 178, 181, 192, 215, 217, 222–223, 240, 262, 283, 290, 298, 322, 397; in children, 302, 303; coma, 119, 227; diagnosis, 398; diet, 288; drugs, 96, 119, 223, 254, 307; and heart disease, 119, 205; hereditary tendency, 118, 126; ketosis, 227
Diabinase, 223
Diagnosis, computer aid, 249
Dialysis, 398
Diaphragm, 119–120, 210–11, 296, 340, 341–342, 383; pain, 296
Diaphragmatic hernia, 210
Diarrhea, 120, 132
Diastole, 58, 202
Diastolic pressure, 58, 216, 372
Diathermy, 120–121, 213, 225, 249, 308
Dicumarol, 22, 121, 240
Diet, 121, 291, 362; and heart disease, 204–205, 289; infants', 303; reducing, 289, 290; therapeutic, 288–289
Differentiation, 237; embryonic, 140, 142–143
Digestion, 121–125, 224, 238, 239, 260, 261, 376–377; hormone control of, 124, 125, 145, 224, 297–298, 376; nervous control of, 124, 125, 276, 277, 280, 281, 298

Digestive system, 123, 168, 224; development of, 142; peristalsis, 123, 305; smooth muscle, 267, 305; viral infections, 182, 406, 407; x-rays, 147, 182, 413
Digitalis, 125, 131, 253, 376
Dihydromorphinone, 272
Dihydrostreptomycin, 19, 20–21, 108
Dilantin, 150
Dilaudid, 272
Dimethylaniline, 18
Diphosphopyridine nucleotide (DPN), 125
Diphtheria, 23, 29, 34, 38, 104, 125, 126, 206, 219, 231, 252, 263, 283, 302, 332, 391; immunization, 125, 219, 302, 303, 391, 399; Schick test, 352
Diplococcus, 98, 125–126
Diploid nuclei, 141, 158, 254
Diplopagus, 395
Diplopia, 377
Directive therapy, 327
Disease, types of, 126–127
Dislocations, first aid, 162
Dissociation, mental, 127
Distal distrophy, 271
Diuretics, 127, 131
Diver's paralysis, 110, 220
Diverticulosis, 127
DNA (deoxyribonucleic acid), 41, 46–47, 84, 85, 131, 140, 148, 183, 189, 237, 260, 285–286, 331, 403; viral, 403–405; Watson-Crick helix, 85, 189
Dopamine, 301
Dramamine, 127–128, 266
Dressings, 163
Drive theory of psychoanalysis, 151
Dropsy. See Edema
Drosophila, 183–184, 186, 188, 189
Drowning, 128, 161
Drug addiction, 128–130, 272; alcohol, 10, 128, 130; amphetamines, 38, 128, 129–130; opiates, 128, 129, 130
Drugs, 130–132, 252, 254, 306; action on nervous system, 129–130, 280, 283, 376, 378; allergic reactions to, 11, 15, 20, 30, 126, 131, 211, 305; anesthetic, 16, 17, 130; anticancer, 4, 77, 151, 207, 284; and congenital defects, 126; enzyme-inhibiting, 148; irritants, 225; resistance to, 20, 131, 305, 374, 380; steroids as, 376; tolerance, 128, 129, 130; toxicity, 77, 131
Dual personality, 127
Duodenal ulcer, 63, 215, 376, 382, 397
Dwarfism, 131–132; congenital, 126, 131; pituitary, 132, 147, 193, 217, 309
Dysentery, 34, 132–133, 393; amebic, 13, 99, 126, 132, 133, 263, 392; bacillary, 99, 131, 132–133, 263, 380, 391, 392
Dysmenorrhea, 258

Ear, 133–137, 256, 294; and balance, 31, 136–137, 401; cartilage, 80; infections, 5, 108, 256; structure of, 108, 133–135; surgery, 294, 383
Eardrum, 108, 133–134, 284, 383
Ebers Papyrus, 251
ECHO viruses, 137, 256, 406
Eclampsia, 137
Ectoderm, 140, 141–142
Ectomorph, 64
Ectoparasites, 299
Ectopic pregnancy, 323
Eczema, 11, 12, 137
Edema, 38, 57, 59, 127, 137, 191, 253, 271, 273, 288, 325; angioneurotic, 18; premenstrual, 127
Efferent nerve fiber, 277, 282
Egg, 137–138, 139–141, 146, 185, 257, 294, 339, 340; fertilization, 141, 158, 255, 339, 340; meiosis, 137–138, 141, 158, 188, 254–255
Ehrlich, Paul, 88, 138
Elbow joint, 360; tennis elbow, 27, 387
Electric shock, 138–139, 161, 162, 356; therapy, 223, 327, 353, 358
Electric stimulation therapy, 308
Electrocardiogram (ECG), 45, 139, 203, 249, 250

Electroencephalogram (EEG), 45, 136, 139, 150, 249
Electronics, medical, 249–250
Electron microscope, 45, 49, 82, 263
Elephantiasis, 139, 159, 160, 265
Embolism (embolus), 58, 61, 139, 182, 330, 378; cerebral, 61, 139, 378; pulmonary, 139, 330, 389
Embryo, 138, 141–143, 158, 322, 340, 372
Embryology, 45, 46, 81, 139–143, 212
Emetic, 143
Emotion, 143, 281, 328–329
Emphysema, 102, 106, 143, 367
Empyema, 221, 314
Encephalitis, 143, 258, 332, 406
Encephalopathy, lead, 234
Endemic diseases, 149–150
Endocarditis, bacterial, 34–35, 305
Endocrine diseases, 147, 258
Endocrine system, 74, 144–148, 291, 297, 309, 328, 375
Endocrinology, 45, 46, 213, 254
Endoderm, 140, 141–142
Endodontia, 112, 117
Endometriosis, 195
Endomitosis, 186
Endomorph, 64
Endoparasites, 299
Endoplasmic reticulum, 82, 83–84
Endotoxins, 34, 391
Enema, 101, 147
Energy production, 260, 261, 269, 286, 340; cellular, 40–41, 46, 82, 84, 192, 231, 237–238, 261; in liver, 260, 261, 269; muscle, 269, 270
Enteric fevers, 396
Enteritis, regional, 339
Enterobacteriaceae, 131
Enterogastrone, 124, 376
Enterotoxin, 374
Enteroviruses, 182, 406, 407
Entomology, 43
Enuresis, 37
Environmental medicine, 213
Enzymes, 14, 40, 41, 82, 147–148, 286, 325, 403, 408, 409; digestive, 121, 122, 224, 261, 297, 298, 376; genetic control of, 41, 46, 82, 84, 140, 148, 182, 183, 188; respiratory, 261
Enzymology, 40
Ephedrine, 95, 148, 400
Epidemics, 148–150, 329, 330, 407
Epidermis, 308, 362, 363–364
Epigenesis, 140, 142
Epiglottis, 150
Epilepsy, 100, 130, 150, 258, 282, 305; first aid, 164; petit mal, 150, 306
Epinephrine, 150, 376
Epiphysis, 194, 308
Episiotomy, 89
Episome, 131
Epithelial tissue, 390
Erasistratus, 150–151
Ergotamine (tartrate), 200, 400
Erysipelas, 377
Erythroblastosis, 189; fetalis, 63, 346
Escherichia coli, 131, 188, 189, 286
Esophageal speech, 371
Esophagus, 121, 123, 203, 307, 377, 383; cancer of, 74
Essential oils, 157–158; as antiseptics, 22, 23
Estradiol, 375
Estriol, 375
Estrogens, 50, 77, 145, 146, 151, 257, 294, 310, 321, 324, 340, 375, 388
Estrone, 72, 375
Ether, 16, 17, 130, 131, 151, 241, 253, 265, 381
Ethology, 151
Ethyl morphine, 272
Eugenics, 183, 188, 189–190
Eunuchoidism, 151–152, 217
European relapsing fever, 241
Eustachian tube, 5, 108, 134, 284
Evolution, 46, 68, 107, 140, 152, 221, 274, 291; genetics and, 183, 187, 189
Excretion, 55–57, 121, 152

INDEX

Excretory system, 142, 152
Exercise: breathing, 344; energy production, 269; heartbeat, 203; and muscularity, 267
Exercise therapy, 308
Exfoliate dermatitis, 118
Exocrine glands, 106, 297
Exophthalmos, 152, 216
Exotoxins, 34, 391
Expectorant, 152
Extrasystole, 206
Eye, 152–156, 291, 295, 346; antiseptics for, 23; astigmatism, 1, 30, 102, 156; cancer of (retinoblastoma), 52, 76; cataracts, 52, 80, 119, 291, 336, 383; color, 153, 255; first aid, 164–166, 317; glaucoma, 52, 191, 284; gonorrhea of, 23, 34, 52, 193, 292; inflammations, 12, 52, 97, 100–101, 292, 409; muscles, **155**; structure of, **152**, 153, **154–155**; surgery, 48, 383
Eyeglasses, 156, 157, 273, 292

Fabricius, Hieronymus, 139–140
Facial bones, 359
Facial nerves, 104
Facioscapulohumeral dystrophy, 270–271
Fainting, 157, 164, 356; Adams-Stokes attack, 250
Faith healing, 157
Fallopian tubes, 195, 217, 257, 323, 340, 375; inflammation of, 125, 193, 195
Farcy, 191
Farsightedness, 157
Fat(s), 79, 157–158, 205, 227, 238, 239, 240, 260, 262, 287, 289, 376; digestion, 39, 121, **122**, 240, 260, **261**, 298; metabolic disorders, 262, 298, 374, 408; saturated vs. unsaturated, 26, 158, 289; storage, 262, 287, 362; tissue, 287, 362, 390
Fatty acids, 121, 122, 158, 238, 260, 261, 262, 287
Feces, 152, 225–226, 240, 298, 374, 407
Feedback, 69, 106; heart action, 202; hormonal, 144, **311**
Femoral artery, **58**; first aid in bleeding, **160**
Femur, 359, **360**
Fermentation, 79, 110, 170, 174, 253, 377
Fertilization, 141, 158, 255, 323, 339, 340
Fetus, 322, 340; radiation effects on, 322–323, 335
Fever, 36, 158–159, 221; drugs, 15, 18, 130
Fever therapy, 159
Fibrillation, heart, 206
Fibrin, 56, 60–61, 159, 208, 388, 389
Fibrinogen, 56, 60–61, 159, 208, 240
Fibroid tumors, 195
Fibroma, 73, 159
Fibrositis, 27, 159
Fibrous tissue, 80, 159
Fibula, 359, **360**
Filariasis, 159–160, 243, 247, 265, 392, 393
Fingers, 196, 383; bones, 359, **360**; joint disorders, 26, 387
First aid, 160–166, 316–318
Fleas, 166; as disease carriers, 126, 251, 299, 312, 347, 396
Fleming, Sir Alexander, 19, 166, 305, 374
Florey, Howard W., 19, 166, 305
Fluke, 166–167; liver, 209
Fluoridation, 167, 323
Fly, 222, 232; as disease carrier, 167, 214, 234
Folic acid, 16, 77, 288, 409
Follicle-stimulating hormone (FSH), 145, 146, 257, 294, 309, 310
Follicular cyst, 195
Fontanelles, 65, 359
Food, 167–176; deficiencies, 126, 175, 287, 288; dietetic, 121, 288–289; infants', 303; spoilage, 34, 174; storage, 171, 174; synthetic, 176
Food allergies, 11, 289

Food metabolism, 238–240, 260, **261**, 262
Food poisoning, 125, 126, 176–177, 182, 263, 351; staph, 34, 176, 182, 374
Foot, 177; bones of, 359, **360**; disorders, **177–178**, 397
Forceps, 178
Formaldehyde, 391
Fovea, **154**, 156
Fractures, 179, 383; first aid, 162, 179; x-rays, 413
Freckles, 50–51, 255, 362
Freud, Sigmund, 128, 180, 256, 283, 326, 327
Friedländer bacillus, 314
Friedman's disease. See Narcolepsy
Fröhlich's syndrome, 180
Frostbite, 163, 182, 220
Fugue state, 127
Fungal diseases, 20, 126, 263, 305, 314, 348
Fungi, 126, 238, 244, 263; antibiotic-producing, 19; antiseptics, 23

Galactose, 232
Galen, 45, 180–181, 251, 252, 401, 402
Gall bladder, 39, 181, **239**, 290; removal, 181, 382; x-rays, 413
Gallstones, 39, 73, 97, 125, 181, 290, 298, 375–376, 382
Gametes, 137, 141, 185, 372
Gamma globulin, 7, 56, 181–182, 191, 219, 266
Ganglia, 2, 275, **277**, 280, 282, 301
Gangrene, 14, 182, 337
Gas gangrene, 20, 64, 148, 182, 219, 305, 391
Gas poisoning, 87–88, 350
Gastrectomy, 182
Gastric glands, 211, 215, 376, **377**
Gastric juice, 122, 124, 182, 306, 376, 377, 397
Gastric (stomach) ulcers, 63, 182, 208, 376, 382, 397
Gastrin, 124, 376
Gastritis, 10, 125
Gastrocnemius-soleus muscles, 177, 387
Gastroenteritis, 182, 351, 396
Gastroenterology, 253, 254
Gastrointestinal tract, 41, **123**, 182, 213, 335, 374; x-ray examination, 147, 182, 413
Gastrulation, 141–142
Gaucher's disease, 374
Genes, 41, 82, 98, 140, 141, 182–184, **185**, 186–189, 286; dominant vs. recessive, 185, 186; and enzymes, 46, 140, 182, 188; mutations, 47, 85, 148, 183, 184, 187, 188–189, 335; nature of, 188–189; sex-linked, 184; synthesis of, 189, 286
Genetic code, 47, 85, 189
Genetic crossing over, 85, 184, 186
Genetic defects, 132, 183, 187–188, 189
Genetics, 45, 46, 81, 183–190, 209, 212; biochemical, 188; fruit fly experiments, 183–184; Mendelian experiments, 183, 186, 256; principles of, 184–186, 256
Genetic surgery, 190
Genotype, 187, 189
Geriatrics, 291
Germ, terminology, 190
German measles, 181, 190, 219, 249, 332; during pregnancy, 64, 108, 126, 190, 303, 322; vaccine, 190, 302, 303, 399
Germ cells, 190, 390
Germicide, 190
Germ layers, 140, 141–142
Germ theory, 22, 126, 190, 262–263, 301
Germ warfare, 42
Gestation, 190–191, 321
Gigantism, 147, 191, 194, 309, 311
Gingivitis, 331
Glands: endocrine, 74, 144–148, 291, 297; exocrine, 106, 297
Glaucoma, 52, 191, 284
Globin, 207, 208, 325
Globulins, **56**, 191, 325, 326
Glomerulonephritis, 191–192, 208, 352, 391

Glomerulus, 227, **228–229**, 325
Glossitis, 192
Glossopharyngeal nerve, 104
Glottis, 103, 210, 233
Glucagon, 147, 297, 298
Glucocorticoid hormones, 6, 145
Glucose, 67, 79, 118, 119, 192, 222, 232, 262, 270, 320; tolerance test, 192
Glucosides, 312
Glycerin, 158
Glycerol, 121, 122, 260, 261
Glycine, 262
Glycogen, 79, 192, 222, 238, 239, 240, 261, 262, 269, 270, 320
Goiter, 147, 192, 224, 287, 389, 390
Golgi bodies, 82
Gonadotropins, 193, 217, 309, 310, 321
Gonads, 144, 145, 193, 217, 309, 335, 339, 375; radiation effects, 335
Gonococcus, 193
Gonorrhea, 27, 34, 178, 193, 195, 263, 380, 401; bacteria, **33**, 126, 193, 401; of the eye (g. neonatorum), 23, 34, 52; and infertility, 193, 195, 375, 401
Goose pimples, 363
Gorgas, William, 245, 339, 393, 414
Gout, 3, 27, 178, 283, 289, 331, 387, 398
Grafting, 292–293, 313, 381
Gramicidin, 19, 31
Granulocytes, 7, 61, 235, 236
Granuloma, 193; coccidioidal, 263; inguinale, 401
Griseofulvin, 21, 30
Growth, 142, 193–195, 237, 285, 286; adolescent, 5–6, 194; cellular, 194–195; hormonal control of, **146**, 193; need of vitamins, 408
Growth hormone (STH), 3, 132, 144–145, 147, 193, 217, 309, 311
Guanine, 41, 85, 189, 331
Guinea worm, 195
Gums, disorders of, 112, 116, 117, 331, 386
Gynecology, 195–196, 253, 254

Habituation, 128; marihuana, 248
Hair, 196, 362, **363**; color, 308; excessive, in women, 211
Hallucinations, 196, 326, 328
Hallucinogens, 128, 130, 241, 248, 259, 328
Hallux valgus, 72, **177**, 178
Hand, 26, 196; artificial, 324; bones, 359, **360**
Handicapped, rehabilitation of, 197–198
Hansen's disease, 234–235
Hardening of the arteries, 25–26, 97, 127
Harelip, 126, 187–188, 198, 313
Harvey, William, 46, 57, 61, 139, 198, 252
Hashish, 248
Haverhill fever, 199, 336–337
Haversian canals, 65, **66**
Hay fever, 11, 21, 22, 126, 148, 199, 211, 284, 347
Headache, 199–200; histamine and, 211; migraine, 199–200, 329, 400
Head deformation, 200
Hearing, sense of, 31, 133, **134–135**; tests, 136; theories of, 135–136
Hearing aids, 108, 201
Hearing loss, 107–109, 284, 294, 390; and speech, 109, 369, 370, 371
Heart, 57, 201–203, **205**, 406; artificial, 47, 250; enlargement, 206; fibrillation, 206; flutter, 206; muscle, 267; sounds, 202; surgery, 205, 206, 382–383; systole and diastole, 57–58, 202; transplants, 293; x-rays, 413
Heart attack, 59, 125, 203–204; 383; emergency aid, 164, 203
Heartbeat, 202, 206–207; arrhythmia, 206; bradycardia, 67, 206; effect of smoking on, 284; regulation of, 2, 202–203, 276, **277**, 280, 281
Heartburn, 125, 203
Heart disease, 203–207, 291, 329, 378,

385; arteriosclerosis, 25, 203; congenital, 34, 126, **204-205**, 206, 305, 382; coronary disease, 203-204, 205, 262, 383; and diabetes, 119, 205; diagnostic aids, 250; diet and, 204-205, 289; and ECG, 139, 203, 250; obesity and, 290; pain, 295, **296**; rheumatic fever, 26, 29, 34, **205**, 206, 238, 305, 346; and shock, 357
Heart failure, 36, 59, 100, 137, 203, 206, 216, 238, 253, 346; aortic insufficiency, 24; congestive, 64, 70, 127, 164, 206
Heart-lung machine, 206, 207, 382
Heart murmur, 205, 206
Heart valves, **205**, 206, 346
Heat cramps, 207, 220
Heat exhaustion, 163, 207, 220
Heat therapy, 308; lamps, 213, 225, 308
Heel spur, 207
Hematology, 213, 253, 254
Hematoma, 207
Hematopoietic system, 335
Heme, 207, 208, 325
Hemiplegia, 299
Hemodialysis, 230
Hemoglobin, 15, 18, 56, 61, 63, 105, 207-208, 225, 226, 240, 262, 287, 308, 320-321, 325, 343, 344, 346; A vs. F, 208
Hemolytic streptococci, 208, 346, 352, 380, 390-391
Hemophilia, 61, 126, 189, 208
Hemophilus influenza, 104
Hemorrhage, 22, 208-209, 240, 354, 372; and anemia, 15; aneurysm rupture, 18, 208; cerebral, 25, 86, 100, 378; diseases, 61, 208-209; first aid, 160, 161; shock, 208, 356, **357**
Hemorrhoids, 209
Heparin, 22, 209
Hepatic veins, 60, **239**
Hepatitis, 98, 181, 209; infectious, 129, 149, 209, 406; toxic, 209
Hepatogenous jaundice, 225, 226
Hereditary diseases, 126-127
Heredity, 182-183, **184-185**, 189, 209, 256; biochemistry of, 40, 41; and cancer, 73, 76
Hermaphrodite, 209-210
Hernia, 210; surgery, 382
Heroin, 128, 129, 210, 265, 272
Herpangina, 103
Herpetology, 43, 45
Heterotransplants, 292
Heterotrophism, 237-238
Hetrazan, 139, 160, 292
Hexachlorophene, 22, 23
Hexylamine, 18
Hiccups, 120, 210-211, 388
Hip, 27; girdle, 359, **360**, 361
Hippocampal cortex, 274, **275**
Hippocrates, 45, 117, 126, 211, 217, 244, 251, 266, 378
Hirsutism, 211, 257
Histamine, 11, 14, 22, 126, 211, 212, 221, 262
Histidine, 14, 262, 325
Histology, 43
Histones, 286
Histoplasmosis, 126, 211, 314
Hives, 11, 22, 137, 150, 212
Hodgkin's disease, 159, 212, 284, 346
Homeopathy, 196, 212, 252
Homeostasis, 68, 212, 237
Homografts, 293, 313
Hong Kong flu, 221
Hooke, Robert, 46, 81
Hookworm, 126, 212, 273, 393
Hormones, 14, 41, 46, 57, 130, 131, 144-147, 276, 283, 309, 375; body fluid control, 57, 145, 146, 227, **230**, 309; and cancer, 73, 74; in cancer therapy, 77; in digestive control, **124**, 125, 145, 224, 297-298, 376; feedback mechanism, 144, **311**; gastric, 124, 376; pancreatic, 145, 147
Horse serum, 15, 211, 399-400
Hospitals, 213-214
Humerus, 111, **268**, 359, **360**
Humors, four (ancient medicine), 126, 251

Hunchback, 214, 359
Hunger pains, 376
Hyaline cartilage, 80
Hyaline membrane disease, 242
Hyaluronidase, 214-215
Hydrocephalus, 215, 384
Hydrochloric acid in stomach, 18-19, 121, 182, 288, 376, 377
Hydrocortisone, 3, 5, 6, 131
Hydronephrosis, 215
Hyperacidity, 215, 376
Hyperchlorhydria, 19
Hyperemesis gravidarum, 264
Hyperglycemia, 215, 222
Hyperhidnosis, 384
Hyperinsulinism, 215
Hypermetropia, 157
Hyperparathyroidism, 179, 300
Hyperplasia, 407
Hypertension (high blood pressure), 127, 215-216, 227, 289, 329, 378, 384
Hyperthyroidism, 36, 147, 152, 215, 216, 224, 260, 329, 389-390
Hyperventilation syndrome, 216
Hypervitaminosis, 288
Hypnosis, 216, 295, 327
Hypnotics, 129, 130, 216
Hypochondriasis, 216, 295
Hypodermis, 362, **363-364**
Hypoglossal nerve, 104
Hypoglycemia, 216-217, 223
Hypogonadism, 217
Hypoparathyroidism, 300
Hypopharynx, cancer of, 74
Hypothalamus, 144, 158, 180, 274, **277**, 281, 290, 310, 311, 365
Hypothyroidism, 224, 260, 290, 390
Hysterectomy, 217; vaginal, 196
Hysteria, 127, 217; paralysis, 127, 298; psychogenic amnesia, 14
Hysterical aphonia, 369-370
Hysterical blindness, 127, 370
Hysterical conversion, 200
Hytadid disease, 385

Ichthyology, 43, 45
Ichthyosis, 217
Icterus, 225; neonatorum, 226
Idiopathic mental deficiency, 258
Ileocecal valve, 121, 224
Ileum, **123**, 339
Ileus, 223-224; paralytic, 305
Ilium, 349, **360**
Immersion foot, 217-218
Immortality, 218
Immunity, 21, 34, 212, 218-219; bacterial diseases, 218-219; to cancer, 76; defects: agammaglobulinemia, 7; kinds of, 218; rickettsial diseases, 126; and transplants, 21, 230-231, 292-293, 313; viral diseases, 126, 406, 407, 414
Immunization, 21, 34, 218-219, 251, 301, 323, 329-330, 399-400; of children, 303, 304
Immunological response, 21-22
Immunosuppression, 293
Impetigo, 219, 377
Incisors, 117, 386, **387**
Incus (anvil), 133, **134**
Independent assortment, genetic principle of, 184-186, 256
Industrial medicine, 219-220
Infant mortality rate, 238
Infarction, 59, 330; myocardial, 59, 203
Infection(s), 253, 344; allergic aspect of, 12; bacterial, 1-2, 7, 34, 64, 221, 243, 380; and blood diseases, 236; body defense against; fever response, 158; and heart disease, 206; postoperative, 22, 238, 381; viral, 302, 303, 404
Infectious diseases, 126, 263, 302, 372, 401; bacterial, 34, 126, 218-219, 263; as cause of blindness, 52; death rate decline, 238, 302; drugs, 19-21; epidemics, 148-149, 329, 330, 407; fungal, 126, 263, 305, 348; immunity, 126, 218-219; protozoan, 126, 182, 263; rickettsial, 126, 347-348; viral, 126, 302, 303, 404, 406, 407-408
Infiltration anesthesia, 17

Inflammation, 56, 221, 225, 344; connective-tissue diseases, 26-27; drugs, 28, 103, 221
Influenza, 221, 238, 252, 406; epidemics, 148, 221, 314, 407; hemophilus, 104; viruses and vaccines, 221, 407
Infrared lamps, 308
Inguinal canal and hernia, 210
Inoculation, 222
Inositol, 222, 238, 410
Insect bites, 222; allergic reaction, 11, 22, 30, 222
Insecticide poisoning, 315, 317, 319
Insomnia, 222, 365
Instinct, 101, 151
Insulin, 39, 41, 118, 119, 131, 145, 146, 147, 192, 215, 217, 222-223, 240, 254, 262, 290, 297, 298; allergic reaction to, 11; types of, 223
Insulin shock, 211, 223, 356; therapy, 223, 327, 353, 358
Intelligence, 6, 223, 275
Intelligence quotient (I.Q.), 6, 190, 223; retarded, 258, 259
Intelligence tests, 6, 39, 69, 223
Interferon, **406**, 407
Internal medicine, 253, 254
Interphase cellular, 264
Intertrigo, 223
Intestinal cancer, 208
Intestinal glands, 224
Intestines, 101, 296, 339; bacteria of, 32, 131, 224, 287, 351, 408, 409; colitis, 99, 103, 125; large (colon), 99, 121, **123**, 131, 132, 224; obstructions (ileus), 223-224, 382; small, digestion, 121, **122-124**, 224, 244, 260, **261**, 297, 298, 376; strangulation, 382; worm infections, 28-29, 126, 166-167, 212-213, 299, 353, 385, 412, 413; x-rays, 182, 413
Intoxication: acute, 10, 14; pathological, 9, 258
Intra-uterine device (IUD), 50
Intravenous feeding, 224
"Intrinsic factor," 16, 288, 410
Intussusception, 224
Involuntary nervous system, 68
Iodine, 175, 224, 389, 413; as antiseptic, 22, 23, 224; thyroid need for, 104, 147, 192, 224, 258, 287
Iothiouracil, 389
Ipecac, 143, 152
Iris, **152**, 153, **154**
Iron, 287, 289; hemoglobin component, 207; poisoning, 315
Iron-deficiency anemia, 15, 208, 287, 289
Iron lung, 225
Irritants, 225
Islets of Langerhans, 145, 147, **297**, 298
Isoniazid, 20, 225, 238, 243, 294, 394

Jaundice, 39, 96, 125, 181, 209, 225-226, 240, 373, 382; in hemolytic anemia, 61, 208, 225, 226
Jejunum, **123**
Jenner, Edward, 103, 148, 226, 253, 323, 366, 398, 399
Joint(s), **360-361**, 387; arthritic diseases, 26-27, 99, **178**, 262, 289; cartilage, 80; Charcot's, 87; sprains, 162, 177

Kala-azar, 234, 263
Kanamycin, 21
Kappa particles, 189
Karolymph, 85
Keloids, 352
Kenny, Elizabeth, 226-227
Keratin, 325, 362, 363
Keratitis, 227
Ketone bodies, 119, 227, 240, 262
Kidney, 41, 127, 152, 227-230, 310, 382, 397, 406; arteriosclerosis, 25, 238; artificial, 47, 230, 398; transplants, 230-231, 293, 313, 398; x-rays, 413
Kidney disease, 12, 27, 80, 178; and acidosis, 2; cancer, 208, 384; diagnosis, 398; and edema, 137, 273; glomerulonephritis, 191-192, 208, 352, 391; hydronephrosis, 215; nephrosis, 127,

INDEX

227, 273; proteinuria and, 325–326; pyelonephritis, 34, 331; stones, 73, 331, 384, 398; surgery, 384; and uremia, 397–398
Kinesthetic sense, 231
Knee, arthritic diseases, 26, 27
Knock-knees, 231
Koch, Robert, 19, 22, 126, 190, 231, 263
Korsakoff's psychosis, 9, 231, 258
Krause's end bulb, 364
Krebs cycle, 231–232, **261**
Kupffer cells, liver, 238, **239**, 240, **345**, 346
Kwashiorkor, 175, 232, 288, 325, 393
Kyphosis, 214

Labia, 195, 196
Laboratory facilities, 213
Lachrymators, 88
Lactation, 70, 145, 310, 311
Lactic acid, 40, 192, 232, 267, 269, 270
Lactose, 232, 287
Laënnec's cirrhosis, 98
Lamarck, Jean Baptiste de, 43, 46, 221
Landouzy-Déjerine dystrophy, 270–271
Landsteiner, Karl, 62, 63, 302, 319, 346, 381
Language, 101, 369–371; foreign accent, 390; learning, 274, 291
Language disorders, 370; aphasia, 24, 370, 371–372
Laparotomy, 232
Larva migrans, 232
Laryngectomy, 370; and speech, 371
Larynx, 29, 104, 150, 232–233, 324; cancer of, 370; cartilage, 80, 233; diphtheria, 29, 125
Laser, medical applications, 48
Laughing gas, 17, 233, 265
Laxatives, 101, 233
L-dopa, 301
Lead, 411; poisoning, 15, 233–234, 258, 283, 315
Learning, 68, 90–95, 274, 291; animal studies, 151, 282, 283; conditioned response, 90, 282; and memory, 255, 283
Lecithin, 67, 234, 238, 262
Leech, 234, 299
Leeuwenhoek, Anton van, 46, 81, 234, 252, 262
Leg(s): arteriosclerosis, 14, 178, 182; artificial, 324; bone growth, 194; bones, 359, **360**
Leishmaniasis, 234, 263, 392
Lens, 153, **154–155**, 157, 272–273; aberration, 1; cataracts, 52, 80
Leprosy, 157, 234–235, 305, 332, 380–381, 393, 397
Leptospiroses, 235
Leucotomy, 240
Leukemia, 16, 36, 61, 73, 74, 75, 103, 235–236, 320, 336; kinds of, 235; treatment, 77, 235–236, 284
Leukocytes, **56**, 236, 306
Leukocytosis, 24, 61, 63, 236
Leukopenia, 11, 61, 236, 373
Leukorrhea, 196, 236
Leukotomy, 295, 297
Levarterenol, 280, 400
Levorphanol, 272
Leydig cells, 387
Lice, 241, 299, 304; as disease carriers, 126, 241, 304, 347–348, 396
Lichen planus, 236, 352
Life, 236–238, 285; spontaneous origin disproven, 46, 262
Ligaments, 360, **361**; arthritis, 26
Limnology, 43
Linear order, genetic principle of, 186, 188–189
Linkage, genetic principle of, 186
Lipase, 121, 122
Lipids, 39, 40, 287
Lipoidoses, 16
Lipoma, 238
Lipotropic factors, 238, 262, 288
Lister, Joseph, 22, 213, 238, 253, 323, 381
Lithotomy, 238
Liver, 125, 238, **239**, 240, 263, 382, 406;

bile production, 39, 41, 181, 207, 239, 240; cancer, 74, 77; "fatty," 238, 262, 288; functions and products of, 41, 79, 192, 238–240, 260, **261**, 262, 269, 388–389; protein conversion to sugar, 6, 7, 14, **146**, 240; RE cells, 238, 240, 344–346; transplants, 293
Liver disorders, 97, 225–226, 244, 290, 385; cirrhosis, 10, 98, 137, 209, 289, 353; hepatitis, 98, 129, 149, 181, 209; yellow atrophy, 209
Lobectomy, 240
Lobotomy, 179, 240–241, 281, 327, 353
Lordosis, 241, 271, 359
LSD (lysergic acid diethylamide), 128, 130, 241, 248, 259, 328
Lumbago, 241–242
Lung, 57, 59, 70, **71**, 242, 340, **341**; carbon dioxide-oxygen exchange in, **56**, 207, 242, 341–343, 344; collapse of, 242, 315; embolism, 139, 330, 389; macrophage action in, 345, 346; radiation effects, 335, 336; surgery, 240, 383; transplants, 293; x-rays, 413
Lung diseases, 213, 242, 313–315; cancer, 74, 76, 78, 208, 314, 315, 336, 367, 383, 413; pleurisy, 313–314; pneumoconiosis, 314; silicosis, 120, 314, 358
Lupus erythematosus, 99, 242–243, 352; disseminatus, 26
Lupus vulgaris, 160, 243, 393
Luteinizing hormone (LH), 145, 146, 257, 309, 310
Luteotrophic hormone (LTH), 145, 309, 310
Lymphadenitis, 243
Lymphangitis, 208, 243
Lymphatic system, 121, **122**
Lymph glands (nodes), 75, 243, 248, **345**; RE cells, 344–346; tuberculosis (scrofula), 354, 393
Lymphocytes, 236, 372, **373**
Lymphocytic leukemia, 235
Lymphogranuloma venereum, 243, 401
Lymphoma, 73
Lymphosarcoma, 75, 77, 244, 284
Lymph vessels, **345**
Lysergic acid, 41, 241
Lysins, 158
Lysogeny, 35, 402, **405**, 407
Lysosomes, 82, 306
Lysozyme, 166, 351, 402

Macroglobulins, 191
Macrophages, 344, **345**, **373**
Maduromycosis (madura foot), 244
Malabsorption, 16, 126, 244, 287, 288, 293, 298, 374; syndromes, 244
Malaria, 15, 126, 149, 159, 222, 231, 244–247, 263, 265, 323, 329, 330, 349, 374, 392, 393, 401; cycle, 245, **246**; drugs, 30, 96, 245, 332
Malleus (hammer), 133, **134**
Malnutrition, 175, 288, 289, 293, 302, 303, 325
Malta fever. See Brucellosis
Maltase, 122
Maltose, 122
Mammary gland, 309, 340
Mange, 247
Mania, 118, 327
Manic-depressive psychosis, 117–118, 247, 255, 259, 326, 358
Marie's syndrome, 248
Marihuana, 130, 248
Marsh test, 25
Masculinization, adrenal imbalance, 7, 211
Mastectomy, 248
Mastitis, 248
Mastoidectomy, 248
Mastoiditis, 248
Measles, 97, 143, 181, 218–219, 249, 332, 407; gamma globulin, 181, 219; vaccine, 249, 302, 303
Meat, 168, 169, 173, 175, 204, 287, 289
Mechlorethamine, 284
Medical training, 214, 251, 252, 253–254
Meiosis, 85, 137–138, 141, 158, 188, 254–255
Melancholia, 255

Melanin, 14, 255, 308, 362
Melanocyte-stimulating hormone, 309, 311
Melanoma, malignant, 255; retinal, 52
Melioidosis, 191, 255
Memory, 68, 94, 255–256, 282, 283
Memory loss, 14, 86, 111, 258; fugue, 127; senility, 355
Menarche, 257
Mendel, Gregor Johann, 32, 46, 182, 183, 256
Mendelian principles of genetics, 186, 187, 256
Ménière's disease, 108, 256, 401
Meninges, 215, 256; tuberculosis, 394
Meningioma, 256
Meningitis, 108, 256–257; bacterial, 34, 64, 126, 256, 257, 263, 351; epidemic, 126; viral, 103, 256, 257
Meningococcus, 34, 88, 126, 256, 380
Menopause, 255, 257, 291, 294; hormone treatment, 151, 257
Menorrhagia, 257
Menstruation, **146**, 257–258, 324, 340; after childbirth, 89; cycle, 145, 151, 193, 212, 257, 294, **310**, 323; heavy flow, 195, 257
Mental disorders, 127, 254, 258–259, 302, 309, 326, 356; delirium, 111; dementia, 111, 326; depression, 117–118, 255, 326, 327; functional (psychogenic), 258–259, 326; hydrocephalus, 215; melancholia, 255; organic, 258, 259, 326; paranoia, 299, 326, 328; and suicide, 380; treatment, 259, 327, 358
Mental retardation, 258, 259, 370
Meperidine, 111, 272
Mercuric chloride, 102
Mercurochrome (merbromin), 22, 23, 259
Mercury, 411; poisoning, 258, 283
Merthiolate, 22, 23, 190
Mescaline, 130, 259
Mesoderm, 140, 141–142
Mesomorph, 64
Metabolic diseases, 127, 213, 262
Metabolism, 237, 238–240, 260–262, 286; basal rate (BMR), 36, 224, 260; cellular, 82, 84, 260, **261**; food, 238, 260, **261**; and genes, 46; genetic abnormalities, 183; liver, 238–240, 260, **261**, 262, 269; muscle, 267, **269**, 270; normal vs. diabetic, 119
Metacarpus, 196, 359
Metals: in human body, 148, 240; toxic, 411
Metaphase, cellular, 264, **264**
Metaphen, 23
Metastasis, 73, 76, 395
Metatarsal bones and arch, 177, 359
Methacholine, 131
Methadone, 129, 272
Methamphetamine, 38
Methemoglobin, 208
Methionine, 238, 288, 325
Methotrexate, 77
Metrazol, 358, 376
Microbiology, 43, 46, 262–263; Koch's postulates, 190, 231, 263
Microcephaly, 258, 263
Microorganisms, 262–263; cultures, 104–105
Micropyle, 158
Microscopes, 45, 46, 49, 82, 263
Microtome, 45
Migraine headache, 199–200, 329, 400
Milk, 169, 170, 171, 287, 289, 303, 323, 394
Milk of magnesia, 19, 233, 263
Mineralocorticoid hormones, 6, 145, 146
Mineral oil, 233
Minerals, 260, 287; body need for, 148, 286; deficiency diseases, 175
Minot, George Richards, 263, 267, 412
Miotic drugs, 191
Miracle drugs, 254
Mites, 222, 247, 352, 390; as disease carriers, 126, 354
Mitochondria, 82, 83–84, 148, 231
Mitosis, 141, 255, 263–264
Mitral valve, **204–205**, 206
Molars, 117, 386, **387**

Molecular biology, 46-47
Moles, 50-51, 73, 313
Monamine oxidase inhibitors, 376
Mongolism, 188, 258
Monilia, 195
Monocytes, 306
Mononucleosis, infectious, 220
Monosaccharides, 222
Morgan, Thomas Hunt, 32, 46, 183, 186
Morphea, 353
Morphine, 98, 111, 129, 130, 210, 264-265, 272, 292, 295
Morphogenesis, 142
Morton, William T. G., 16, 241, 265, 381
Mosquitoes, 222, 231, 245, 247, 265, 392, 393, 406, 407, 414
Motion sickness, 265-266, 401
Motor neuron, 268, 275, 277, 282, 298
Mouth: cancer, 74; digestive action, 121
Mouth breathing, 386-387
Moxibustion, 4, 96, 251
Mucoproteins, 325
Mucous membranes, antiseptics for, 23
Multiphasic screening, 48
Multiple personality, 266
Multiple sclerosis, 30, 258, 266, 289
Mumps, 108, 126, 143, 181, 219, 266, 292, 332, 407; vaccine, 266, 302, 303
Murine typhus, 347, 396
Muscle, 41, 267-270, 283, 390; arm, 268-269; and arthritis, 26; childhood development of, 90, 92, 94, 95; embryonic development of, 142; fatigue and pain, 267, 270, 296; fixation, *vs.* prime mover, 269; paralysis, 298; soreness, 267, 270; stiffness, 267, 270; strains, 163; types of, 267
Muscle action, 49, 67, 68, 267-268, 269, 270; energy for, 79, 104, 192, 269, 270; isometric, 267; isotonic, 267; nerve control of, 267, 268, 275-276, 277, 279
Muscle coordination, 282; ataxia, 30
Muscle cramps, 178, 291, 362; contracture, 267; nocturnal, 332
Muscle-nerve junction. See Myoneural junction
Muscle relaxants, 67, 105
Muscular dystrophy, 270-271, 298
Mustard gas, 77, 87, 284; and mutation, 271
Mustard plaster, 225, 271, 295
Mustargen, 284
Mutation, 47, 85, 148, 183, 184, 187, 188-189, 271, 285, 407; causes of, 189; radiation-induced, 85, 188, 189, 271, 335
Mutation theory, 46, 243
Myasthenia gravis, 271, 298, 389
Mycobacteria, 32, 393
Mycology, 43, 45
Myelin sheath, 266, 278, 281
Myelogram, 366
Myocardial infarction, 59, 203, 204
Myocarditis, 103, 206
Myofibril, 268
Myoglobin, 226
Myoneural junction, 2, 267, 268, 270
Myosin, 49, 268, 270, 325
Myositis, 27
Myotonia congenita, 332
Myotonic dystrophy, 271
Myxedema, 36, 147, 271, 389

Nails, 362
Nalorphine, 272
Narcoanalysis, 36
Narcolepsy, 38, 80, 272
Narcotics, 15, 128, 129, 130, 210, 272
Nasality, 369
Natural selection, 46, 68, 107, 187
Nearsightedness, 156, 272-273, 284, 346
Necrosis, 407
Neisseria bacteria, 126, 193, 401
Nematode, 265, 273
Neocortex, 274, 275-276, 282
Neomycin, 21
Neoplastic disease, 127
Nephron, 227, 228-229, 230
Nephrosis, 127, 227, 273
Nerve block, 17

Nerve cells, 67, 195, 278, 281; sympathetic *vs.* parasympathetic, 2, 280; types of, 281-282
Nerve deafness, 108
Nerve fibers, 267, 276, 277, 280, 281; pain fibers, 295; types of, 282
Nerve gas, 88
Nerve grafts, 292
Nerve impulses, 67, 278-280, 282; transmitter substances, 2, 278, 280, 281
Nerve-muscle junction, 2, 267, 268, 270
Nervous disorders, 247-248, 298-299; multiple sclerosis, 30, 258, 266, 289; neuralgia, 225, 283; neuritis, 283, 295; Parkinsonism, 300-301
Nervous system, 273-283, 311, 390; autonomic, 68, 125, 130, 275, 276, 277, 280, 328, 362, 384; central, 129-130, 376, 406; central, cell, 278; childhood development of, 274; control of digestion, 124, 125, 276, 277, 280, 281, 298; drug action on, 129-130, 280, 283, 376, 378; electrical activity, 150, 282; embryonic development of, 142; motor control, 267, 268, 275-276, 277, 279; pain perception, 295, 296; voluntary, 277, 279
Neuralgia, 225, 283
Neuritis, 283, 295
Neurogenic shock, 162, 356
Neurogenic ulcers, 397
Neurohypophysis, 144, 310, 311
Neurology, 213, 253
Neuropathy, 283
Neurosis, 23, 127, 259, 283, 326, 327, 328, 368; anorexia nervosa, 18, 125; combat, 100; treatment, 259
Neurospora, 183, 188
Neurosurgery, 253, 254, 283, 305, 383-384, 392
Neurotic depression, 255
Neutropenia, 374
Neutrophilia, 236
Nevi (birthmarks), 50-51
Niacin, 126, 258, 288, 289, 304, 409
Nicotine, 283-284
Nicotinic acid, 288, 409
Night blindness, 99, 156, 284, 288, 408, 409
Nitrogen mustard, 77, 284
Nitroglycerin, 203, 400
Nitrous oxide, 17, 265, 381
Noise, 284; and hearing loss, 108
Noradrenalin (norepinephrine), 6-7, 145-146, 262, 276, 280, 281, 282, 353, 376, 400
Nose, 284, 313; cartilage, 80; deviated septum, 118, 284; diphtheria of, 125; olfactory receptors, 367, 390
Notochord, 142
Novocain, 285, 293
Nucleic acids, 40, 47, 84, 85, 140, 260, 285-286, 325, 331, 398, 402, 403; viral, 402, 403-405
Nucleoli, 83-84, 85, 264
Nucleoproteins, 286, 325
Nucleotides, 85, 189, 285, 286
Nucleus, cellular, 82, 83-84, 264, 285, 403-405
Nursing service, 214
Nutrients, essential, 286-288; malabsorption, 16, 126, 244, 287, 288, 293, 298, 374
Nutrition, 55, 174, 286-289, 325
Nycalopia, 284
Nystagmus, 289
Nystatin, 20, 21

Obesity, 288, 289-290; Fröhlich's syndrome, 180
Obstetrics, 213, 254
Occupational diseases, 220, 226
Occupational medicine, 219-220
Occupational therapy, 213, 290
Ochronosis, 27
Ocular muscles, 153
Oculist, 292
Oculomotor, 104
Oil of wintergreen, 295, 315

Oils, 157-158; edible, 157, 171, 287, 289; essential, 22, 23, 157-158
Old age, 290-291, 294, 355
Olfactory nerve, 104
Olfactory receptors, 367, 390
Oligomenorrhea, 257
Onchocerciasis, 160, 291-292
Oocytes, 137
Oogenesis, 141
Oogonia, 137
Open-heart surgery, 206, 207
Ophthalmia, 292
Ophthalmologist, 292
Opium, 129, 130, 264, 272, 292, 300, 328; derivatives, 98, 128, 129, 130, 265, 272, 292
Optical aberration, 1
Optic chiasma, 153, 155
Optician, 292
Optic nerve, 52, 104, 152-155, 292, 385
Optometry, 292
Orchitis, 266, 292
Organ of corti, 134, 135
Organogenesis, 142
Organs, 81, 86; differentiation, 139, 140, 142-143
Oriental sore, 234, 392
Orinase, 223
Orthodontics, 116, 117
Orthopedics, 253, 254, 293; surgery, 383
Osmoreceptors, 230
Osmosis, 293
Ossicles, 108, 133
Ossification, 359
Osteitis deformans, 294
Osteoarthritis, 26-27, 29
Osteoblast, 65, 194
Osteochondritis, 293
Osteoclast, 194
Osteogenesis imperfecta, 179
Osteoma, 73
Osteomalacia, 99, 287, 293, 409
Osteomyelitis, 15, 235, 293-294, 351, 383
Osteopathy, 294
Osteoporosis, 179, 294
Otosclerosis, 108, 294, 383
Ovarian follicle, 145, 146, 257, 294, 309, 310, 323, 340
Ovarian hormones, 145, 146, 151, 340
Ovaries, 70, 74, 137, 141, 144, 145-146, 217, 257, 294, 310, 340, 382; cysts and tumors, 195, 375
Overeating, 64, 290
Ovulation, 257, 294, 375; hormone control of, 145, 257
Oxalic acid, 287, 313
Oxygen: deficiency, 15, 18, 29, 61, 86, 105, 208, 344; in energy production, 261, 269, 270, 340; exchange for carbon dioxide, 56, 207, 242, 341-343, 344; supply in incubators, 346
Oxyhemoglobin, 207, 343
Oxytetracycline, 20, 132, 388
Oxytocin, 145, 294, 310, 311

Pacemaker, 201, 202; electronic, 47, 249, 250
Paget's disease, 294-295
Pain, 105, 295, 296, 297
Pain relievers. See Analgesics; Narcotics
Palate, 297
Paleobotany, 45
Paleocortex, 274, 276
Paleontology, 45
Palsy: athetoid, 86; Bell's, 38; pseudo-bulbar, 233
Pancreas, 41, 131, 144, 145, 147, 222, 290, 297-298; acinar cells, 297, 298; cystic fibrosis, 106, 125; digestive role, 121, 122, 124, 125, 224, 244, 297-298; islet cells, 145, 147, 297, 298; tumors, 215, 217
Pancreatic hormones, 145, 147, 297, 298
Pancreatitis, 244, 298, 384
Pancreozymin, 124, 297
Pancytopenia, 374
Panhysterectomy, 217
Pantothenic acid, 304, 409
Papaverine, 292
"Pap" smear, 77, 78, 195, 298

INDEX

Para-aminobenzoic acid (PABA), 288, 380, 410
Para-aminosalicylic acid (PAS), 294, 394
Paraffin baths, 36, 308
Paralysis, 298–299; agitans, 300; hysteric, 127, 298
Paranoia, 299, 326, 328; alcoholic, 9
Parasites, 12, 130, 263, 299, 353
Parasitology, 43
Parasympathetic system, 276, **277**, **280**, 281; fiber, 2, **280**
Parathormone, 145, 299–300
Parathyroid gland, 144, **145–146**, 147, 179, 299–300
Paratyphoid fever, 396
Paregoric, 300
Parenchymal cells (liver), 238, **239**
Paresis, general, 300
Parkinson's disease, 300–301
Parosmia, 366
Parotid glands, 121, **122**, 266, 351
Parotitis, epidemic, 266
Pars intermedia, 309
Parthenogenesis, 141
Pasteur, Louis, 22, 32, 46, 174, 238, 253, 262, 301, 323, 332, 381, 399, 407
Pasteurella pestis, 251, 299, 311
Pasteurization, 253, 301, 323
Patch test, 302
Paternity tests, 63, 302
Pathology, 45, 213, 253, 254
Pavlov, Ivan, 216, 282, 302, 351, 376
Pediatrics, 253, 254, 302–304
Pedicles, 313
Pediculosis, 304
Pellagra, 10, 126, 175, 193, 288, 289, 304, 390, 393, 409
Pelvis, 359, **360**, 361
Pemphigus vulgaris, 304–305
Penicillin, 19, 20, 88, 166, 189, 305, 374; allergic reaction to, 11, 15, 20, 21, 131, 211, 305; uses, 20, 193, 305, 314, 385
Penis, 340
Pentobarbital, 36
Pentosuria, 183
Pentothal, sodium, 17, 305
Pepsin, 121, 122, 182, 306, 376, 377
Peptic ulcers, 19, 125, 127, 284, 289, 329, 355, 397
Peptidase, 122
Peptides, 306
Peptone, 121, 122, 306
Perceptual isolation, 355–356
Percussion, 253
Periarteritis nodosa, 221
Periodontal membrane, **113**, 386
Periodontia, 117
Periodontosis, 331
Periosteum, 65, **66**
Peristalsis, 305; bronchial tube, 70; colon, 99, **123**; esophagus, **123**; stomach, **123**, 376, 377
Peritoneum, 305, 330
Peritonitis, 24, 99, 305–306
Pernio, 88
Personality: body types and, 64; changes, 240, 258, 281; disorders, 259, 326–327; multiple, 266; psychopathic (sociopathic), 327, 328, 368
Perspiration, 152, 158, 306, 362, 384
Phages, 243
Phagocytes, 218, 306
Phagocytosis, **56**, 306, 344, **345**
Phantom pain, 14, 295
Pharmacopeia, 306–307
Pharynx, 307
Phenacetin, 15
Phenethylbiguanide (DBI), 119, 307
Phenobarbital, 36, 150, 307
Phenol, 22, 190, 213, 253
Phenolphthalein, 233
Phenylalanine, 14, 189, 258, 262, 325
Phenylamine, 15
Phenylketonuria, 127, 189
Phenylpyruvic oligophrenia, 14, 258, 262
Phlebotomy, 64
Phobias, 23, 259, 326
Phosphates, 73, 293, 299–300
Phosphatidye choline, 234

Phospholipids, 234
Phosphoramides, 77
Phosphorus, 287, 347
Photobiology, 48
Photosynthesis, 41, 48–49, 79, 82, 237, 308
Phrenology, 181, 307
Physiatrist, 308
Physical therapy (physical medicine, physiotherapy), 307–308, 378
Physiognomy, 308
Physiology, 45, 46, 308
Phytotoxins, 313
Pigment, 308, 309
Pilocarpine, 280
Pineal body (epiphysis), **194**, 308
Pinel, Philippe, 254, 308–309, 326
Pink eye, 100
Pinocytic vesicle, **83**
Piriform cortex, 274, **275**
Pituitary disorders, 36, 105, 118, 147, 180, 211, 311; acromegaly, 3, 147, 191, 194, 215, 311; Cushing's syndrome, 105, 311; diabetes insipidus, 118, 227, 311; dwarfism, 132, 147, 193, 217, 309; gigantism, 147, 191, 194, 309, 311; hypogonadism, 217
Pituitary gland, 3, 7, 41, 70, 74, 144, **145–146**, 257, 309–311, 344, 345
Pituitary hormones, 144–146, 294, 309–311; adrenocorticotrophic (ACTH), 3, 7, 145, 146, 273, 276, 309, 311; antidiuretic (ADH), 145, 146, 227, 230, 282, 310, 311, 401; follicle-stimulating (FSH), 145, 146, 257, 294, 309, 310; gonadotropins, 193, 217, 309, 310; growth (STH), 3, 132, 144, 145, 147, 193, 217, 309, 311; luteinizing (LH), 145, 146, 257, 309, 310; luteotrophic (LTH), 145, 309, 310; oxytocin, 145, 294, 310, 311; polypeptides, 19, 41; thyroid-stimulating (TSH), 144, 145, 309–311, 389; vasopressin, 118, 310
Pityriasis rosea, 311
Placenta, 70, 88, 138, 311, 340; as "master gland of pregnancy," 144, **145**, 193, 324; previa, 89
Plague, bubonic (Black Death), 34, 51, 148, 166, 231, 251, 263, 299, 311–312, 329, 332, 377, 401; vaccine, 312, 399–400
Plantar callus (wart), **177**, 410
Plant poisons, 312–313, 319
Plaque, 112
Plasmids, 131
Plasmodium, 244–245, **246**, 265
Plastic surgery, 313
Plastids, 82, 189
Platelet factor, 56, 60–61
Pleura, 313–314, **341**, 345
Pleural space, 242, 273, 314, 315
Pleurodynia, 103
Pneumococcus, 34, 126, 257, 314, 375
Pneumoconiosis, 314
Pneumonia, 20, 29, 34, 64, 70, 71, 97, 125, 221, 255, 256, 257, 302, 305, 314–315, 413; bacterial, 126, 263, 314–315, 377; broncho-, 314, 412; fungal, 314; lobar, 159, 314, 315; viral, 314–315
Pneumothorax, 242, 315
Podiatry, 315
Poison(ing), 148, 315–319, 350; and coma, 100; first aid, 160, 161–162, 316–318; heavy metals, 258, 283; mental damage, 258; plants, 312–313, 319
Poison gas, 87–88, 350
Poison ivy, oak, and sumac, 11, 22, 313, 319
Poliomyelitis, 29, 126, 150, 181, 226–227, 319–320, 332, 351; paralysis, 298, 299, 320; vaccines, 218, 219, 238, 272, 302, 303, 320, 349, 351, 399, 407; virus, 325, 406
Polyarteritis nodosa, 99
Polycyclic hydrocarbons, 73, 74
Polycythemia, 61, 64, 143, 320
Polydactylism, 313
Polymixins, 31
Polymorphoneutrophils, 306

Polyp, 320
Polypeptides, 19, 41
Polyploidy, 187
Polyposis, 320
Polysaccharides, 79, 320, 329, 399
Population control, 50, 175, 176, 400
Porphyria, 320–321
Porphyrin pigments, 40
Portal circulation, 60
Portal cirrhosis, 98
Portal vein, 60, **239**, 297
Port-wine stains, 50–51
Postencephalitic Parkinsonism, 301
Postnasal drip, 321
Post-necrotic cirrhosis, 98
Postpartum depression, 321
Posture, 321
Potassium, 287
Pott's disease, 321
Pregnancy, 208, 209, 303, 321–323, 400; breast development, 70, 322; diabetic mother, 119, 322; early signs of, 257, 321; fallopian (tubal), 195, 323; and gallstones, 181; German measles, 64, 108, 126, 190, 303, 322; gestation period, 190–191, 321, 340; hormone control of, 144, 323–324; "master gland" of, see Placenta; miscarriage, 1, 86, 119, 322, 328, 384; morning sickness, 264, 322; neuritis, 283; prematurity, 303, 322; syphilitic mother, 303, 322; termination, 1, 49, 50, 324; tests, 321, 398; toxemias of, 137
Presbycusis, 108
Preventive medicine, 323
Prickly heat, 362
Prodroma, migraine, 199, 200
Progesterone, 72, 145, 146, 257, 294, 310, 321, 323–324, 340
Progestin, 50
Prolactin, 145, 309
Prolapse, 196
Pronation, 359, 360
Pronuclei, 158
Prophase, cellular, 264
Prostaglandins, 324
Prostate gland, 324, 340, 384, 398; cancer, 74, 76, 77, 324, 388, 413; stones, 73, 384
Prostatitis, 324
Prosthetic group (of enzymes), 148
Prosthetics, 48, 324
Prosthodontia, 117
Protamines, 286
Protein-bound iodine (PBI), 224
Proteins, 40, 47, 79, 140, 238, 239, 260, 324–325; basic types of, 325; blood, 56, 57, 137, 240, 325; deficiency diseases, 175, 232, 288, 325; digestion, 121, **122**, 260, 306, 376; incomplete, 287, 288; metabolic conversion to sugar, 6, 7, 14, **146**, 240; metabolic disorders, 262; in nutrition, 286–287, 288, 289, 325; putrefaction, 110, 716; synthesis, 41, 82, **84**, 85, 260, 285, 325, **403**
Proteinuria, 325–326
Proteose, 121, 122
Prothrombin, 22, 56, 60–61, 240, 388–389, 409
Protoplasm, 82, 236, 237
Protozoans, 12–13, 81, 126, 182, 262, 263, 411
Protozoology, 43, 46
Pseudohermaphrodites, 211
Pseudohypertrophic-Duchenne dystrophy, 270
Psittacosis, 332, 388
Psoriasis, 326
Psychedelics, 128, 129, 130
Psychiatry, 213, 254, 326–327, 358
Psychoanalysis, 254, 326, 327
Psychogenic headache, 199, 200
Psychology, 45, 46, 327–328; animal studies, 151, 282–283
Psychomotor epilepsy, 150
Psychomotor stimulants, 376
Psychoneurosis, 259, 328
Psychopaths, 327, 328, 368
Psychopharmacology, 327, 328

INDEX

Psychosis, 127, 259, 326, 327, 328, 353, 368; alcoholic, 9, 231; involuntional, 200, 255; Korsakoff's, 9, 258; LSD and, 241; manic-depressive, 117-118, 247, 255, 259, 326, 358; senile, 355; toxic, 200
Psychosomatic illness, 127, 259, 328-329
Psychosomatic medicine, 157, 328-329
Psychosurgery, 240-241, 259, 327
Psychotherapy, 259, 326, 327, 353, 358, 379
Psychotic reaction, 259
Ptomaine poisoning, 176
Ptyalin, 122, 329
Public health, 323, 329-330, 401
Puerperal fever, 22, 208, 253, 323, 330, 355, 377
Pulmonary artery, 57, 201, 202, 242, 330, **341**; congenital defects, **205**, 206
Pulmonary circulation, 57, 59, 242
Pulmonary embolism, 139, 330, 389
Pulmonary thrombosis, 389
Pulmonary vein, 57, 242, **341**
Pulse, 58
Pupil, **152**, 153, 276, 280
Purines, 27, 41, 289, 331, 398
Purkinje cell, **279**
Purkinje shift, 156
Pus, 1-2, 3, 23, 221, 374
Putrefaction, 32, 110, 176, 238
Pyelonephritis, 34, 331
Pyloric sphincter, 121, **123**
Pylorus, 376, **377**
Pyorrhea, 112, 331
Pyrimidines, 41
Pyruvate, 261

Q fever, 126, 348
Quarantine, 329, 331-332
Quinine, 15, 30, 35, 96, 245, 332

Rabbit fever. *See* Tularemia
Rabies, 332-333, 351, 406; vaccination, 143, 301-302, 332-333, 407
Race classifications, 64, *table* 333-334
Rachitic rosary, 347
Radiant-heat lamps, 308
Radiation, 220, 335-336; as cause of cancer, 73, 75-76, 336; as cause of mutation, 85, 188, 189, 271, 335; genetic *vs.* somatic effects, 335; during pregnancy, 322-323
Radiation dermatitis, 118
Radiation therapy, 78, 213, 335, 336
Radiography, 213, 336
Radiology, 254, 336
Radius (bone), **268**, 359, **360**
Rapid Eye Movement (REM), 128
Rat-bite fever, 336-337
Rat flea, 166, 312, 347, 396
Raymond's phenomenon and disease, 337, 384
Rectocele, 196
Red Cross, 337-339
Reed, Walter, 160, 339, 414
Reflex, 68, 101; conditioned, 282, 302, 351; of newborn, 89
Reflexology, 38
Rehabilitation. *See* Handicapped
Rejuvenation, 291
Relaxin, 145
Renin (kidney secretion), 227
Rennin (enzyme), 121
Reproduction, 237, 285, 339-340, 375; asexual *vs.* sexual, 339; bacterial, 32; clonal, 190; gametogenesis, 137, 140-141; parthenogenesis, 141; of viruses, 286, 402, **404-405**
Reserpine, 41, 356
Resinoids, 312
Respiration, 79, 152, 238, 242, 340-344, 359; artificial, 28-29, 161; diaphragm in, 119, 120, 340, **341**; mechanical (iron lung), 225; role of blood in, 55, 340, 342-343, 344
Respiratory center, **277**, 342, 344; depression, 129, 272
Respiratory system, 232-233, **341-343**; embryonic developments of, 142; viral infections, 406, 407

Reticular activating system, 281
Reticular formation, 281, 282, 295
Reticulocytes, 15
Reticuloendothelial system, 225, 238, 240, 344-346, 372, 373
Reticulum cell sarcoma, 346
Retina, 153, **154**, 155, 156, 292, 308; blind spot, 55; detachment, 52, 346, 383; rods and cones, 99-100, 153, **154**, 156, 284; tumors, 52
Retinene, 409
Retrolental fibroplasia, 346
Rheumatic diseases, 15, 26-28, 225; baths, 36, 37
Rheumatic fever, 26, 29, 34, 97, 103, **205**, 206, 208, 238, 305, 346, 352, 391
Rheumatoid arthritis, 3, 15, 26, 29, 99, 103, 127, **178**, 221, 355, 387
Rheumatoid spondylitis, 26
Rh factor, 15, 21, 63, 108, 346
Rh-immune globulin, 189
Rhinitis, 346-347; allergic, 11, 199, 346-347
Rhizotomy, 295
Rhodopsin, 156, 308, 409
Rib cage and ribs, 359, **360**, 361
Ribonuclease, 148
Ribonucleic acid. *See* RNA
Ribose, 260
Ribosomes, 82, **83-84**, 285, 403
Rickets, 99, 104, 126, 132, 175, 240, 288, 289, 293, 347, 409
Rickettsias, 20, 126, 347-348, 396
Rigor mortis, 270, 348
Ringworm, 263, 348
RNA (ribonucleic acid), 47, 84, 85, 140, 148, 237, 260, 285-286, 331, **403**; messenger (mRNA), 285-286; transfer (tRNA), 260, 285-286
Rocky Mountain spotted fever, 126, 256, 348, 388, 401
Roentgen, Wilhelm Konrad, 254, 348-349, 413
Root canal therapy, 112, 113, **114**
Rosacea, 349
Rubefacients, 225

Sabin vaccine, 238, 272, 320, 349, 399, 407
Sacroiliac, 349
Sacrum, 349, 359, **360**
Safety, 349-351
St. Louis encephalitis, 143, 406
St. Vitus' dance, 97
Salicylate poisoning, 30
Salicylates, 26, 28, 346
Salivary glands, 106, 121, **122**, 124, 351, 390; stones, 73
Salk vaccine, 238, 272, 320, 351, 399
Salmonella, 131, 176, 351, 395-396; gastroenteritis, 182, 351; *typhi*, 34, 131
Salpingitis, 193
Salt, 287, 289; in body fluid, 206, 207, 306, 362; in diet, 206
Salvarsan, 25, 138
Sanger, Margaret, 49, 351-352
San Joaquin fever, 98, 263, 314
Saphenous vein, **60**
Sarcoidosis, 352
Sarcoma, 73
Scabies, 222, 247, 352
Scapula, 359, **360**
Scarlet fever, 34, 97, 159, 208, 219, 252, 263, 302, 305, 332, 352, 377, 390
Scar tissue, 352; adhesions, 5
Schick test, 352
Schistosomiasis, 352-353
Schizophrenia, 6, 31, 196, 200, 233, 241, 258, 259, 299, 328, 353, 355; catatonic, 80; treatment, 327, 353, 358
Sciatica, 295, 353, 366
Scissors gait, 86
Sclera, 102, **152**, 153, **154**
Scleroderma, 337, 352, 353-354
Scoliosis, 354, 359
Scopolamine, 31, 354
Scorpion bites, 222, 316
Scrofula, 354, 393
Scrotum, 339, 400; cancer of, 74

Scrub typhus, 348, 354
Scurvy, 126, 175, 179, 252, 288, 289, 354, 408, 410
Sea sickness, 265-266, 401
Sebaceous glands, 3, 5, 106, 362, **363**
Secretin, 124, 297
Sedatives, 35, 70, 96, 129, 130, 200, 272, 327, 354
Segregation, genetic principle of, 184, 256
Self-allergies, 12, 15, 242
Semen, 340
Semicircular canals, 136-137, 401
Seminiferous tubules, 339
Senility, 25, 355
Senior citizen population, 290-291
Sense impulses, neural transmission, 275, 277, 279, 281, 282
Sense organs, 355; development of, 142
Sensory deprivation, 355-356
Sensory neurons, 277, 282, 295
Sensory paralysis, 283, 298
Septicemia, 64, 396
Septum, 284; deviated, 118, 284, 369
Serotonin, 79, 353, 356, 376
Serum, 399-400
Serum accident, 356
Serum hepatitis, 129, 209
Serum sickness, 11, 22, 150, 356, 400
Sewage, 411; treatment, 412
Sex characteristics, hormonal control of, 7, 144, 145, 151, 294, 339, 375, 387-388
Sex chromosomes, 183-184
Sex glands, 3, 144, 147, 180, 193, 309, 375
Sex hormones, 25, 41, 97, 144, 191, 239, 375, 387-388; adrenal, 6-7, 147, 375; androgens, 145, 339, 375; in cancer therapy, 77; estrogens, 50, 77, 145, 146, 151, 257, 294, 310, 340, 375, 388; progesterone, 72, 145, 146, 257, 294, 310, 340, 375
Shellfish poisoning, 177
Shell shock, 356
Shigella, 131, 132, 356
Shinbone (tibia), 347, 359, **360**
Shingles, 88, 295, 352
Shock, 160, 227, 356-358, 400; first aid, 162; hemorrhagic, 208, 356; neurogenic, 162, 356; symptoms, 160, 357
Shock therapy, 223, 259, 327, 353, 358
Short-wave diathermy, 120
Shoulder: girdle, 359, **360**, 361; muscle, 111
Siamese twins, 395
Silicosis, 220, 314, 358
Silkworm disease, 301
Silver nitrate, 23, 193
Sinoauricular (SA) node, 201, 250
Sinusitis, 358-359
Sitz bath, 37
"606" (Salvarsan), 25, 138
Skeletal muscle, 267, **268**, 270
Skeleton, 65, 73, 359, **360-361**; embryonic development of, 142, 359; growth, 191
Skin, 362, **363-364**, 390, 409; aging, 291, 362; care, 362; color, 255, 308, 362; contamination, first aid, 317; development of, 142; grafts, 12, 292, 313; pain, 105, 296, 362, 364; radiation effects, 75, 335, 336; as sense organ, 105, 362, 364; tanning, 362, 363, 381
Skin diseases, 3, 139, 232, 308; abscesses, 1-2, 305; allergies, 11, 12, 118, 126, 137, 211, 212; cancer, 74, 75, 77, 255, 336; eczema, 11, 12, 137, 329; fungal, 126, 263; infections, 23, 34, 263; mange group, 247; morphea, 353; psoriasis, 326; scabies, 222, 247; scleroderma, 337, 352, 353-354; tuberculosis, 160, 243, 393; ulcers, 397
Skull, 359, **360**, 361; deformation, 200; of newborn, 65, 359; trephine, 391-392
Sleep, 281, 303, 365
Sleeping pills, 216, 222
Sleeping sickness, 71, 222, 231, 263, 365-366, 393
Slipped disc, 353, 359, 366, 391
Smallpox, 103, 126, 143, 148, 149, 219,

INDEX

332, 352, 366; vaccination, 103, 143, 218, 219, 226, 251, 252–253, 303, 330, 366, 398–399; virus, 325, 366, 407
Smell, sense of, 284, 366–367
Smoking, 284, 367–368, 397; and lung cancer, 76, 367
Smooth muscle, 267; stomach, 376, **377**
Snail fever, 353
Snake bite, 368; first aid, 316, 368
Snow blindness, 368
Sociopaths, 327, 328, 368
Sodium, 287, 289
Sodium chloride, 206, 287
Sodium pentothal, 17, 305
Somatic cells, 390
Somatic functions and system, 274, 275–276
Somatotypes, 64, 308
Somnambulism, 366
Spanish fly, 222
Spasticity, 298, 299; in palsy, 86, 298
Speciation, 187
Speech, 390; deafness and, 109, 370; disorders, 368–372, 378–379; esophageal, 371; role of nasal structure in, 284, 369
"Speed," "speedball," 130
Sperm, 137–138, 158, 185, 324, 339–340, 372, 375; hormone control of production, 145, 193, 309, 375; meiosis, 141, 158, 188, 254–255
Spermatogenesis, 141
Spermatozoon, 81, 141, 372
Sphincters, 121, **123**
Sphygmomanometer, 58, 372
Spider bites, 51, 222
Spina bifida, 372
Spinal anesthesia, 17–18, 285, 295, 381
Spinal cord, 30, 275, 276, 277, **279–280**, 281, 295–296, 298, 299, 359, **361**, 385; tumors, 384
Spinal discs, 359, **361**; slipped disc, 353, 359, 366, 391
Spine, 359, **360–361**; arthritic conditions, 24, 26, 27, 214, 321; cartilage, 80, **361**; deformities, 214, 241, 347, 354, 359, 372; diseases, 214, 293, 294
Spinous process, 361
Spirillary rat-bite fever, 337
Spirochetes, 372
Spleen, 225, 372–374, 382; malarial involvement, 245, 374; RE cells, 238, 344–346
Splenectomy, 374, 382
Spondylitis: ankylosing, 24; rheumatoid, 26
Spondylolisthesis, 242
Spotted fever, 126, 256, 348, 388
Sprains: ankle, **177**; first aid, 162
Sprue, 16, 126, 244, 374, 393, 409
Stapes (stirrup), 108, 133–135; mobilization, 294
Staphylococcal infections, 27, 34, 88, 104, 219, 221, 293, 303, 374, 377
Staphylococcus, 19, 20, **33**, 34, 64, 98, 131, 305, 314, 315, 374; food poisoning, 34, 176, 182, 374
Starch(es), 40, 78–79, 192, 222, 261, 287, 289, 320; indigestion, 121, 122, 260; photosynthesis, 41
Starvation, 2, 36, 175, 227, 262
Steatopygia, 374
Steatorrhea, 374, 408
Sterility, 193, 195, 217, 335, 374–375, 401
Sterilization (for microorganisms), 375, 381
Sterilization (sexual), 50, 400
Sternum (breastbone), 359, **360**
Sternutators, 88
Steroids, 40, 41, 293, 375–376, 387
Stethoscope, 253, 376
Stillbirth, 86, 119, 303, 322, 384
Stimulants, 129–130, 328, 376, 378
Stomach, 224, 376, **377**; achlorhydria, 2; acid, 18–19, 121, 182, 211, 288, 376, 382, 397; cancer, 63, 74, 77–78, 182, 208, 376; digestion, 121, **122–124**, 125, 376; nervous control of, 124, 125, 276, **277**, 281; pains, 125, 382; removal of, 182, 382; ulcers, 63, 182, 208, 376, 382, 397; x-rays, 182, 413
Stomach glands, 211, 215, 376, **377**
Strabismus, 377
Strawberry marks, 51
Streptobacillary fever, 199, 336–337
Streptococcal infections, 26, 27, 34, 104, 191, 206, 208, 219, 243, 305, 346, 377
Streptococcus, **33**, 34, 64, 98, 126, 377; hemolytic, 208, 346, 352, 380, 390–391
Streptomyces, 4; *griseus*, 19, 377
Stress and strain, 329, 355, 377–378; adrenal response to, 3, 7, 145, 146, 276, 329; and arteriosclerosis, 26, 355
Stroke, 164, 290, 378; amnesia, 14; aphasia, 371; arteriosclerosis, 25, 86, 238, 378; embolism, 61, 139, 378; first aid, 164; hemorrhage, 25, 86, 100, 378; paralysis, 298, 378; ruptured aneurysm, 18; thrombosis, 61, 378
Strontium-90 fallout, 336
Strychnine, 378
Stuttering, 370, 371, 378–379
Sty, 379
Subdural hematoma, 207
Sublingual glands, 121, **122**, 351
Submaxillary glands, 121, **122**, 351
Substrate, 40, 147–148
Subtilin, 31
Succinylcholine, 105
Sugar(s), 40, 78–79, 173, 192, 222, 238, 239, 262, 269, 287, 289, 320; conversion from protein, 6, 7, 14, 146, 240; role in diabetes, 118–119; in digestion, 121, 122, 260, 261
Suicide, 379–380
Sulfa drugs (sulfonamides), 7, 18, 20, 67, 88, 131; sensitivity to, 7, 11
Sulfanilamide, 18, 380
Sulfones, 235, 380–381
"Summer grippe," 137
Sunburn, 163, 381
Sunlight: overexposure, 163, 362; sensitivity to, 242, 321; and vitamin-D formation, 288, 300, 409
Supination, 359, 360
Suppositories, 101, 381
Surgery, 213, 252, 253, 254, 381–384, 392; abdominal, 382; aseptic, 22, 213, 238, 253, 323, 381; ear, 294, 383; eye, 48, 383; heart, 205, 206, 293, 382–383; laser use, 48; lung, 240, 383; oral, 112; orthopedic, 383; plastic, 313; specialties, 253, 382–384; thoracic, 254, 383; urological, 384
Sweat glands, 106, 152, 207, 306, 362, **363–364**
Sydenham's chorea, 97
Sympathectomy, 384
Sympathetic system, 276, **277, 280**, 281, 362, 400; fiber, 2, **280**
Synapse (nerve gap), 2, **278**, 281
Syncope, 157
Syndactylism, 313
Synovial membrane, 360; arthritis, 26
Syphilis, 24, 27, 52, 87, 178, 192, 206, 208, 263, 284, 352, 375, 384–385, 397, 401; ataxia, 30, 385; bacteria, **33**, 34, 384, 401; diagnosis, 21, 67, 410; mental effects, 258, 300, 384; paresis (late) stage, 300, 384; and pregnancy, 303, 322, 384; treatment, 20, 25, 159, 305, 385
Systemic circulation, 57
Systemic lupus, 337
Systole, 57, 202
Systolic pressure, 58, 216, 372

Tabes dorsalis, 385
Tachycardia (heart flutter), 206
Talus, 177
Tanning, 362, 363, 381
Tapeworm, 126, 299, 385
Tarsal bones, 359
Tartar (calculus), **116,** 351, 387
Taste, sense of, 386, 390
Teeth, 111–117, 168, 386–387; bridges, 112, **115**; calcium in, 287, 293, 386; cavities, 80–81, 111, 112, **113–114**; crowns, 112, **114;** decay, 80–81, 111, 113, 167, 323, 386; extraction, 112, 113, 115; fillings, **114;** impaction, 112, **113;** malocclusion, 111, 112, **116**, 117, 369, 386–387; normal, **113;** root canal therapy, 112, 113, **114**, 117; tartar, **116**, 351, 387
Telophase, cellular, 264
Temperature: acclimatization to, 2; cold, body reaction, **310–311;** inversion, 8
Temporal lobe, 282
Tendons, 80, **268,** 387; bursitis, 27; grafts, 292
Tennis elbow, 27, 387
Tenosynovitis, 387
Testes (testicles), 74, 141, 144, 151, 217, 339, 387–388; orchitis, in mumps, 266, 292; undescended, 193, 217, 375
Testicular hormones, 145, 339
Testosterone, 7, 144, 375, 387–388
Tetanus, 23, 34, 38, 126, 218–219, 231, 305, 388, 391; bacteria, **33**, 388; vaccine, 219, 303, 388, 391, 399
Tetany, 299, 347
Thalamus, 240, 274, 275, 281, 282, 295
Thighbone (femur), 359, **360**
Thinking, thought, 92–93, 94, 281
Thioamides, 389
Thoracic duct, 121
Thoracic surgery, 254, 383
Thorax, 359
Thorazine, 388
Throat infection, streptococcal, 26, 126, 206, 208, 305, 346
Throat obstruction, clearing, 28, **166**
Thrombin, 56, 60–61, 388–389
Thromboangiitis obliterans, 71
Thrombocytopenia, 11, 63, 373, 374
Thrombophlebitis, 137, 389, 400
Thrombosis, 25, 58, 61, 358, 389; cerebral, 61, 378, 389; coronary, 164, 203, **204,** 383, 389; pulmonary, 389
Thrombus, 22, 61, 139, 203, 330, 389
Thymine, 41, 85, 189
Thymus gland, 271, 389
Thyroid cartilege, 233
Thyroid disorders, 131, 147, 206; cretinism, 104, 132, 147, 192, 258, 287, 389; diagnosis, 36, 224; goiter, 147, 192, 224, 287, 389, 390; hyperthyroidism, 36, 147, 152, 215, 216, 224, 329, 389–390; hypothyroidism, 224, 260, 290, 390; myxedema, 36, 147, 271, 389; self-allergy, 12
Thyroid gland, 3, 64, 74, 104, 144, **145,** 192, 224, **300,** 309, 310–311, 389–390; cancer of, 76, 336
Thyroid hormones, 41, 104, 132, 144–146, 147, 192, 224, 287, 290, 294, 311, 389
Thyroid-stimulating hormone (TSH), 144, 145, 309–311, 389
Thyroxine, 14, 131, 144, 224, 262, 271, 389, 390
Tibia, 359, **360**
Ticks, 299, 390; as disease carriers, 126, 222, 347–348, 390, 406, 407
Tinea pedis, 30, 348
Tinnitus, 390
Tissue(s), 81, 86, 390; basic kinds, 390; cultures, 105; destruction (catabolism), 260; differentiation, 142; susceptibility to radiation, 335, 336; synthesis (anabolism), 260, 262; transplants, 12, 21, 292–293, 381
Toes, **177–178;** bones, 359
Tolbutamide, 119
Tolerance, drug, 128, 129, 130
Tongue, 386, 390; inflammation of (glossitis), 192; taste buds, 386, 390; thrusting, 112, 386–387
Tonsils, 208, 390; diphtheria of, 125
Tophi, 27
Torticollis, 391
Torulosis, 104
Touch, sense of, 105, 362, **364**
Tourniquet, **160,** 161, 368
Toxic chemicals, 226, 411
Toxic diseases, 127
Toxic hepatitis, 209

INDEX

Toxins, bacterial, 34, 42, 126, 176, 391, 399
Trachea, 70, 71, 232–233, 242, 341, 383, 391; diphtheria, 125
Tracheo-bronchial tree, **71**, 76, **341**
Tracheotomy, 104, 125, 391
Trachoma, 52, 380, 391
Tranquilizers, 130, 200, 259, 301, 327, 328, 353, 356, 358, 388; poisoning, 315, 318
Transaminase, 270
Transamination, 260
Transplants, 79–80, 254, 292–293, 313, 381; corneal, 52, 102, 293, 313, 383; kidney, 230–231, 293, 313; rejection of, 12, 21, 230–231, 292–293, 313
Tremadota, 166–167
Trench fever, 241
Trench foot, 217–218
Trench mouth, 402
Trephining, 250–251, 391–392
Treponema pallidum, 33, 384, 401, 410
Trichinella spiralis (trichina worm), 273, 299, 392
Trichinosis, 323, 392
Trichomonas, 195, 392; *vaginalis*, 392, 401
Trichuriasis, 412
Tridione, 150
Trigeminal nerve, 104, 392
Trigeminal neuralgia, 392
Tri-iodothyronine, 224, 389
Triphosphopyridine nucleotide (TPN), 392
Trisomics, 188
Trochlear nerve, 104
Tropical diseases, 247, 392–393
Tropism: behavior, 101; viral, 407
Trypanosoma, 87, 365, 393
Trypanosomiasis: African, 365; South American, 87
Trypsin, 122
Tryptophan, 188, 288, 325, 409
Tsetse fly, 71, 231, 365, 393
Tsutsugamushi disease, 126, 348, 354
Tubal pregnancy, 195, 323
Tuberculin test, 37, 394
Tuberculosis, 12, 15, 20, 27, 32, 34, 70, 126, 178, 192, 219, 220, 231, 256, 257, 263, 303, 305, 313, 323, 358, 377, 383, 393–394; drugs, 20, 225, 238, 254, 377, 394; fever pattern, 159; immunization, 37, 394, 399; of the lymph glands (scrofula), 354, 393; and osteomyelitis, 293; of the skin (lupus vulgaris), 160, 243, 393; of the spine, 321; x-rays, 394, 413
Tularemia, 219, 263, 377, 388, 394–395
Tumors, 395, 406, 407–408; benign *vs.* malignant, 73, 395; fibroid, 195
Typhoid fever, 34, 64, 131, 149, 159, 176, 263, 302, 305, 323, 332, 392, 395–396; vaccine, 219, 302, 303, 396, 399
Typhus, 20, 126, 159, 166, 219, 241, 304, 332, 348, 354, 388, 396; epidemic, 347, 396; murine (endemic), 347, 396; vaccine, 219, 396
Tyrocidine, 19
Tyrosine, 14, 262
Tyrothricin, 19

Ulcerative colitis, 99, 103, 125
Ulcers, 397; corneal, 102; decubitus (bedsores), 37, 397; foot sole, 178, 397; peptic, 19, 125, 127, 284, 289, 329, 355, 397; perforated, 382, 397; skin, 397; tropical (oriental sore), 234, 392; vascular, 397
Ulna, 359, 360
Ultrasound therapy, 308
Ultraviolet lamp, 249, 308
Ultraviolet radiation, 381; and cancer, 75
Umbilical cord, 88, 89, 311, 340
Umbilical hernia, 210
Unconsciousness, 164; fainting, 157, 164; shock, 162
Undulant fever, 34, 71, 159, 219
Urates, 289
Urea, 228–229, 239, 240, 397, 398
Uremia, 397–398
Ureter, 52, 152, 227, 384, 413

Urethra, 52, 152, 227, 324, 340, 384; trichomonas inflammation, 392, 401
Urethritis, nongonococcal (N.G.U.), 401
Uric acid, 331, 398; and gout, 27, 289, 331, 398
Urinalysis, 398
Urinary infections, 20, 34, 106, 305, 380, 384
Urine, 227, 397, 398; hormonal regulation, 145, 146, 227, 230, 310, 311, 401; in nephrosis, 273; production and path of, 227; **228–229**, 401; proteins in, 325–326, 398
Urology, 253, 254; surgery, 384
Uterus, 89, 195, 322, 398; cancer, 74, 77, 195, 217; contraction in childbirth, 311, 340, 398; disorders of, 195–196, 375; hysterectomy, 196, 217; implantation of ovum, 138, 340; menstruation, 146, 195, 257, 310, 340; retroversion (tipping), 196
Uveitis, 52

Vaccination, 148, 150, 212, 222, 226, 238, 252–253, 303, 304, 329–330, 398–399
Vaccines, 21, 218–219, 348, 399–401, 406; BCG (tuberculosis), 37, 394, 399; cholera, 219, 399; diphtheria, 125, 219, 302, 303, 391, 399; German measles, 190, 302, 303, 399; influenza, 221, 407; live, 301, 349, 399, 407; measles, 249, 302, 303; mumps, 266, 302, 303; plague, 312, 399–400; polio, 218, 219, 238, 272, 302, 303, 320, 349, 351, 399, 407; rabies, 143, 301–302, 332–333, 407; smallpox, 103, 143, 218, 219, 226, 251, 252–253, 303, 366, 398–399; tetanus, 219, 303, 388, 391, 399; toxoids, 391, 399; typhoid fever, 219, 302, 303, 396, 399; typhus, 219, 396; whooping cough, 302, 303, 399, 412; yellow fever, 218, 219, 398, 399, 414
Vacuoles, 82, **83**, 306
Vagina, 196, 340, 375, 381
Vaginal discharge, 196, 236, 392, 401
Vagus nerve, 104, 143, **277**, **280**, 382
Varicella, 88
Varicose veins, 137, 332, 383, 397, 400
Variolation, 399
Vascular ulcers, 397
Vas deferens, 340, 400
Vasectomy, 50, 400
Vasoconstrictors, 400
Vasodilation, 59, 362, **364**
Vasodilators, 400–401
Vasopressin, 118, 310, 401
Vegetable foods, 168, 170, 173, 287
Veins, 57, 59–60, 201, 389, 401; grafts, 292; varicose, 137, 332, 383, 397, 400
Vena cava, **57**, **60**, 201, 401
Venereal diseases, 243, 401
Venous circulation, 59–60; blood color, 207
Venous thrombosis, 389
Ventricle, 57, 201–202, **205**
Vernal conjunctivitis, 101
Verruca (wart), 73, 410
Vertebrae, 359, **360–361**, 366
Vertigo, 256, 401
Vesalius, Andreas, 46, 251, 252, 381, 402
Vesicants, 87, 225
Vibrio comma, 33, 96
Villi, 224
Vincent's disease (angina), 402
Viral diseases, 126, 286, 302, 305, 404, 407–408; immunity, 126, 406, 407, 414; and myocarditis, 206; research, 272; transmission, 406, 407; vaccination, 303, 398–399, 406, 407
Viral encephalitis, 143, 406
Viral gastroenteritis, 182
Viral hepatitis, 209, 406
Viral pneumonia, 314–315
Virology, 43
Viruses, 83, 126, 262, 263, 285, 286, 299, 347, 351, 402–408; and antibiotics, 20; "arbor," 406, 407; bacteriophages, 35, 402, **404–405**; and

cancer, 73–74, 286, 406, 407–408; Coxsackie, 103, 256, 407; ECHO, 137, 256, 406; entero, 182, 406, 407; interference phenomenon, **406**, 407; lysogeny, 35, 402, **405**, 407; mutation, 407; reproduction of, 286, 402, **404–405**; structure of, 402, **403**; and transduction, 35, **405**; tropism, 407
Visceral functions and system, 274, 275, 276, 281
Vision, 48, 153–156, 291; binocular, 156; color, 99–100, 156; dark adaptation, 153, 156; double, 377; and vitamin A, 156, 408, 409
Visual cortex, 153, **155**
Vitamin A, 99, 156, 193, 240, 287, 298, 408–409; daily dose, 409; deficiencies, 99, 284, 288, 409; overdoses, 288, 409; sources, 408–409
Vitamin B₁ (thiamine), 38, 180, 231, 258, 287, 288, 289, 408, 409
Vitamin B₂ (riboflavin), 289, 304, 408, 409
Vitamin B₆ (pyridoxine), 225, 288, 304, 410
Vitamin B₁₂, 16, 126, 240, 263, 374, 410; deficiencies, 16, 288, 410
Vitamin C, 287, 386, 408, 410; deficiencies, 126, 175, 252, 288, 354, 408
Vitamin D, 97, 99, 193, 240, 287, 289, 298, 300, 375, 386, 408, 409; daily dose, 409; deficiencies, 99, 175, 288, 293, 347, 409; overdoses, 288, 409; sources, 409
Vitamin E, 270, 287, 298, 408, 409
Vitamin K, 224, 240, 287, 298, 388, 408, 409
Vitamins, 148, 174, 239, 240, 260, 286, 408–410; B group, 40, 287–288, 408; fat- *vs.* water-soluble, 287–288, 408; malabsorption, 293, 298, 374; overdoses, 127, 288, 315, 409; synthesis, 408
Vocal cords, 233, 369–370
Voice: artificial, 324; disorders of, 369, 371
Volvulus, 182
Vomiting, 143

Warts, 73, 410
Wassermann test, 284, 410–411
Water: chlorination, 323; fluoridation, 167, 323; pollution, 411–412
Weight control, 288–289; amphetamine in, 38, 290; diet and, 289, 290
Weil-Felix reaction, 348
Weil's disease, 235
Wen (sebaceous cyst), 106
Whipworm infection, 412
Whirlpool baths, 36
Whooping cough, 126, 219, 238, 252, 412; vaccine, 302, 303, 399, 412
Wiener, Norbert, 69, 106
Woolsorters' disease, 19, 220
Worms, parasitic, 28–29, 126, 159–160, 166–167, 195, 212–213, 232, 247, 265, 273, 291–292, 299, 353, 385, 392, 393, 412

Xanthin, 308
Xanthine, 127
X chromosomes, 183–184
X-rays, 213, 220, 249, 254, 335, 336, 394, 413; and congenital defects, 126, 323; in dentistry, 112, **113**; discovery, 348–349; fluoroscope, 167; gastrointestinal ("GI") series, 182, 413; and mutation, 188, 189, 271, 335; during pregnancy, 322, 323

Yaws, 330, 393, 414
Y chromosomes, 183–184
Yeast, 409, 410; infections, 305
Yellow fever, 149, 222, 252, 265, 323, 329, 339, 392, 393, 401, 406, 407, 414; vaccine, 218, 219, 398, 399, 414

Zephiran, 22; chloride, 375
Zona pellucida, **138**
Zygote, 137–138, 141, 158, 255, 340